MIRRORS

FOR

MAN

26 Plays of the World Drama

Leonard R. N. Ashley
Brooklyn College of The City University of New York

Winthrop Publishers, Inc.
Cambridge, Massachusetts

Library of Congress Cataloging in Publication Data

Ashley, Leonard R N   Comp.
   Mirrors for man: 26 plays of the world drama.

   Includes bibiliographical references.
   1. Drama — Collections.   I. Title.
PN6112.A88   808.82   73-23085
ISBN 0-87626-558-1

For Anne Constance Nelligan Ashley

Copyright © 1974 by Winthrop Publishers, Inc.
   17 Dunster Street, Cambridge, Massachusetts 02138

iv

The process of reading is not a half-sleep, but, in the highest sense, a gymnast's struggle . . . the reader must do something for himself . . . the text furnishing the hints, the clue, the start or framework. Not the book needs so much to be the complete thing, but the reader of the book does. — Walt Whitman

Contents

Acknowledgments

Bertolt Brecht, *The Threepenny Opera*, from Series One of FROM THE MODERN REPERTOIRE, edited by Eric Bentley. Reprinted by permission of Indiana University Press.

Namiki Gohei III, *The Subscription Scroll*, translated by A. C. Scott. From KANJINCHO, A JAPANESE KABUKI PLAY. Reprinted by permission of A. C. Scott.

Lorraine Hansberry, "Me Tink Me Hear Sounds in De Night." Reprinted by permission of William Morris Agency, Inc. Copyright © 1960 by Robert Nemiroff and Robert Nemiroff as Executor for the Estate of Lorraine Hansberry.

Henrik Ibsen, *The Wild Duck*. From THE OXFORD IBSEN, Volume VI, translated and edited by James Walter McFarlane. Copyright © 1960 by Oxford University Press, Inc. Reprinted by permission.

Adrienne Kennedy, *The Owl Answers*. Reprinted by permission of William Morris Agency, Inc. Copyright © 1969 by Adrienne Kennedy.

Molière, *The Miser*, from THE MISER AND OTHER PLAYS, translated by John Wood (Penguin Classics 1953). Copyright © John Wood, 1953. Reprinted with permission of Penguin Books, Ltd.

Eugene O'Neill, *The Long Voyage Home*. Copyright 1919 and renewed 1947 by Eugene O'Neill. Reprinted from THE LONG VOYAGE HOME: SEVEN PLAYS OF THE SEA by Eugene O'Neill, by permission of Random House, Inc. No performances—whether amateur or professional—may be permitted without written consent. Public readings, radio and television broadcasts are likewise forbidden. All inquiries concerning these rights should be addressed to Random House, Inc.

Luigi Pirandello, *Six Characters in Search of An Author*. From the book NAKED MASKS: FIVE PLAYS by Luigi Pirandello. Edited by Eric Bentley. Copyright for *Six Characters in Search of An Author* 1922 by E. P. Dutton & Co., Inc. Renewal, 1950 in the names of Stefano, Fausto and Lietta Pirandello. Published by E. P. Dutton & Co., Inc. and used with their permission.

Heinz Politzer, "How Epic is Bertolt Brecht's Epic Theatre?" Reprinted from *Modern Language Quarterly*, 23 (1962), by permission of the publisher.

Carolee Schneemann, *Meat Joy*. Reprinted by permission of the author and Ronald Hobbs Literary Agency.

George Bernard Shaw, *Mrs. Warren's Profession*. Reprinted by permission of The Society of Authors on behalf of the George Bernard Shaw Estate.

August Strindberg, *Miss Julie*. Reprinted by permission of Collins-Knowlton-Wing, Inc. Copyright © 1955 by Elizabeth Sprigge.

Prolegomenon

Don't panic. The title of this preface is just a trick to get you to turn to this page to find out what it might contain. The first rule of theatre: catch the attention. For what? Here a chat before the curtain goes up, something about this book and the drama it contains and how to read it. George Borrow says prefaces are seldom read. I hope this one will be an exception.

Mirrors for Man is another anthology of plays. Since 1900 there have been about 800 collections of plays published, many of them (like this one) designed for introductory courses and surveys. Why another? Frankly, because I think no other book attempts to do what needs to be done. Some other collections are limited to the plays of one nation or to a single type of drama, such as comedy or tragedy. Such books are for those who wish to specialize; they come later. Some other books are confined to modern plays or even to Western plays. This one is not, nor is it composed of plays chosen principally in the light of available criticism or extant documents which state in other than dramatic terms the playwrights' intentions. It is not crammed with interpretive apparatus: the job of teachers and students is to interpret for themselves. The instructor is not stuck with my way of organizing a course, for all teachers have developed methods of their own and every class has its own capabilities. I have arranged readable and teachable plays chronologically and have provided the raw materials for many kinds of courses. A general introduction and separate introductions to individual plays will sketch in the backgrounds I think necessary and save classroom time by talking privately with the student in this way. I have tried to make the introductions all add up to something but I do not present, for instance, this play as a study in character, that one for plot, still another for "meaning." Every play since Aristotle has been thought to contain six basic elements (plot, character, thought, diction, music, spectacle), albeit in varying proportions, and each of the plays here simultaneously uses and demonstrates all the elements of drama.

At the same time I have not abdicated my responsibility of doing something more than sending my publisher a list of play titles. In fact, I have substituted for the standard, impersonal, perfunctory introduction extensive material here and at the end of the book for a study of the nature of drama from which students may learn to read, or even write, plays with enjoyment and profit. I have tried not to fill up the pages with too much undigested material such as biographical notes, bibliographical information, and definitions taken bodily from easily available reference books. Students can find such information for themselves in the library, or if they operate in a pre-Gutenberg situation, they can ask their lecturer to provide it for them. This introduction is personal, for it seemed to me to be an opportunity to speak directly to you.

I have resisted the temptation to be this original in my choice of plays. I am trying to help you learn, and so I chose nothing merely for its novelty. Too many other textbooks forget that though instructors choose them, students must use them. Beginning students have to be considered. They will not be bored with the standard pieces they should read before going on to Maeterlinck and Čapek, Goll or Galsworthy, Harold Pinter or Edward Albee. If students go no further than an introductory course, they should at least have read the masterpieces. It is foolish for the beginning student to "avoid the much-travelled roads" and to struggle with outré collections designed for the teacher — and the bored teacher at that — not the student. On one's first trip to Paris it is snobbish and silly not to see the Eiffel Tower. The unusual and the things less accessible must come later. One goes to the Louvre before other museums, even if one is especially interested in modern art. So you will find Shakespeare here and not Abse or Arbuzov (which do occur in some introductory anthologies that are otherwise quite good). Perhaps the instructors "did" Macbeth last year; they should not substitute Timon of Athens or Troilus and Cressida because they are tired of Macbeth. If they want you to read Hamlet they may let you tackle Macbeth on your own — I have provided careful notes of the sort which occupy a couple of weeks in classrooms presided over by teachers who fill their time doing your work — and cover Hamlet in class. Teachers who won't give you first things first are not keeping your interests at heart, and those that "can't face" masterpieces of drama any more do not need a fresh anthology; they need a fresh approach, or perhaps a sabbatical leave.

The conscientious instructors can pick and choose from this collection confident that everything is suitable for an introductory course (or even an advanced course where the introductory courses have not done their job). They may omit and supplement as they please. Each play here has won its way into a collection constructed after many hours of soul-searching about what could be left out to make the size feasible, not what could be put in. (Anthologies with Christopher Fry and Saul Bellow result from asking the latter questions and following fads.) The selection must be arbitrary, being based on taste, and less than ideal, because of copyright limitations as well as price and size considerations. Still, this collection is not only teachable, but worth teaching at the college level and since it is bigger than most such collections, it gives both the teacher and the student greater freedom than is permitted by six, or nine, or eleven plays. Few courses will be given in which all these plays will be taken up in equal detail, though I have forced no play into the ghetto at the back of the book which some anthologists favor. Instructors will place the emphasis where they wish, reading this play closely with the class, discussing that one in general, assigning another to be read (perhaps written about in a term paper or report) by the student, skimming or omitting others. So many plays can be used in so many ways.

This introduction is a preface in the tradition of Charles Lamb, "a talk with the reader." Read it like a play: right through once to begin. Later the students and instructors may return to it in whole or in part to re-examine certain points in connection with certain plays. The students will find the practical advice in the introduction's concluding pages useful in reading each play assigned. This introduction must be more useful than snippets of criticism which present interpretations to close the readers' minds or deliberately chosen contradictions intended to "make them think" but which too often make them despise critics and leave them baffled and frustrated. I, too, want you to think.

So much for introduction to the introduction, which perhaps has been in its chatty way longer than it needs to be. Now the curtain is up and the rustling candy boxes are open. Indeed, you are ready for something significant to occur.

Start by sitting down in a comfortable place and putting yourself in a mood to be pleased. Start to read each play that way too. For the moment you will not be bothered by learned commentators on the animal imagery in Shakespeare, a character study of Amanda in *The Glass Menagerie* ending with the assertion that she "embodies all those sad and poignant women who live on illusion, hope and yesterday's magnolias," or dogmatic theories such as Eric Bentley's on the play as "an intellectual thing": "Great drama has been a 'drama of ideas' from the first." The difficult terms are carefully defined in the glossary, a major feature of this book. Because the Greeks and Romans got there first, many of the commonest terms are strange-looking enough. But first remember that drama is play. I hope you will read this essay and the others in the book, imaginatively participate in them, play with their ideas, as you will with the plays themselves. Read them with the conviction that Goethe was right when he said that all literary art not only instructs and exalts but delights. The drama when it is good always gives pleasure. It ought to be fun. This introduction is discursive. The plays that follow are dramatic. They should grip you, like the Ancient Mariner, emotionally and intellectually. You must read them with enthusiasm.

Drama began in enthusiasm (a Greek term denoting the high achieved when the god possesses the person). In all cultures drama arose out of magic and ritual. In ancient Greece, before the complex structures of tragedy and comedy were invented, before drama had character or diction or "thought" in Professor Bentley's sense at all, the Dionysiac revelers lost themselves in imagining that they were the god of fertility and wine himself and came up with "productions," if we may call them that, as exciting and as mindless as some of those we see presented today by rock-intoxicated off-off-Broadway ensembles. Thespis on a cart in Icaria grooving on Dionysus. *Pretending* to be someone else, *mimesis*, impersonation and Aristotle's "imitation of an action" came later. But first came improvisation and only later the ritual chants of dithyrambs; first enthusiasts and later actors. In modern improvisational theatre, in street theatre, in Happenings, in music and dance and getting "carried away" we have the origins of drama, which comes from a Greek verb meaning to do, to act. We have come very far from that to plays which are intellectually profound — and many, as critic John Simon says, are "mock-profound" — and designed for blind men. Edward Albee, for instance, says the theatre is something to hear (though the word *theatre* comes from the Greek for "a place to see"):

> But a play, though it does exist physically on the stage and can be read, is enormously aural. And the structure of a play is apprehended, in the mind, by the ear, very much the way a musical composition is.

If this encourages you to read plays aloud, fine. They were meant to be heard, those words, and all good plays are musicals, with a magical mystery trip in the words; they are not meant to be experienced without the "music" any more than a libretto is designed to exist without the score. But plays must have spectators as well as auditors. We speak of going to *see* a play. And a play these days may have "no lack of void" as far as something to look at is concerned or it may consist of a lot of people scrambling up a cargo net carrying heavy burdens. LeRoi Jones' *Slave Ship* went on, thrillingly, for half an hour, as I remember, before I heard the first word of dialogue (and that was in Yoruba). Modern stage characters are ever more inarticulate in words and prone to lapse into significant silences, which must be heard too. But there is always something to look at that is working on the emotions if not the brain, even if it is only a space or the rest of the audience. Plays that got, as playwright and actor Harley Granville Barker complained, "so austerely intellectual that . . . performance seemed a profanation" did not last long, or should not. There was action before there were words and the orchestra was a dancing place before it acquired the most expensive seats and was given over to passive rather than active playgoers.

Theatre is play and participation. I like the word "playhouse" better than "auditorium" and I expect to get involved when I am face to face with actors in the theatre and not seeing their photographs flicker on a screen or captured safe behind glass in my familiar television room. I expect the marriage of all the arts of the theatre and the teamwork of the author and all his collaborators (from the director and actors to the designers of lighting, costumes, and scenery) to draw the magic circle and work the magic that will draw me into it. "Astonish me!" is the rule of the theatre.

The trick is done with mirrors. To make observers into participants one creates with more or less verisimilitude — and there are all sorts of reality, not merely "the banality of surfaces" and the world of the camera and the tape-recorder — what Coleridge called "the willing suspension of disbelief." You can show contractors putting up a tent for a party or football players in their dressing room and make the audience cry, as David Storey contrives to do, "That's really what it's like." Arnold Wesker can give you an idea of what it is like to work in a hotel kitchen or "backstage" in a big restaurant. Of course you could always just seek out the same experiences in "real life." But is there no magic in making people who have never been in a football players' locker room with Storey or in the Khitrov market ("the lower depths") with Gorki say, "That's really what it's like"? "Not to go to the theatre," wrote Schopenhauer, "is like making one's toilet without a mirror," stressing the theatre's educational aspect. Shakespeare wrote of "playing, whose end, both at the first and now, was and is to hold the mirror up to Nature — to show virtue her own feature, scorn her own image, and the very age and body of the time his form and pressure." So we have so-called "realistic" theatre, reflecting life, and "expressionistic" and other types of theatre which reflect what is really there too, though the "slice of life" is seen in a fun-house mirror and dazzles us with its distortion.

One distorting mirror was the Greek tragedy in which the poet (maker) imposed upon the *mythos* a pattern that was to bring significance out of chaos, purge pity and fear, and inspire and instruct mankind in connection with his relationship to other men and to the gods. Greek tragedies, with their carefully-wrought exposition of the story (fable), their protagonists and antagonists locked in the central conflict which sparked the plot and exposed the character of the agents, their complications, suspense, crises, climaxes, startling peripeties, terrible recognitions, and awe-inspiring catastrophes, offered mirrors which made everything sharper and clearer. Plato thought tragedy dangerously irrational and unsuited to the best and happiest way of life, but for thousands of years, always redefining tragedy to suit the context of their times, men have welcomed the magic mirror and consulted it for the truth. It may sometimes have given them messages they did not want to hear but never anything they did not need to know about the pride and the peril of being human.

"The drama's laws the drama's patrons give," said Dr. Johnson, and through the centuries changing times have wrought many different kinds of mirrors of reality for the theatre and even encouraged some critics to talk about "the escape from realism" and "unrealistic" devices in plays. But all theatre must be realistic, whether it be a Japanese nō play or a melodrama, a comedy or a farce, a frankly obscene Roman extravaganza or an austere and didactic Morality play, in that it has its starting point in reality and in the end must do something significant to alter our view of reality, of ourselves and the world in which we live. Of course the theatre has escapism and divertissements, but even then the thoughtful person will ask what is being evaded and why people flee into fantasy. In fact, the Theatre of the Absurd may be the most realistic of all, and no serious student will imagine for a moment that a play like *America Hurrah* exists without reference to the real world. Fashions in mirrors change and some people like them to be tinted to present a flattering reflection, while others wish them to be lighted so that every pimple will be clearly seen. The mirror of a play can draw the whole room into a little round glass or cover the walls so as to extend our horizons. In a wilderness of mirrors (such as in the plays of Jean Genet and some other modern masters) there is an infinity of reflections, and things to reflect upon.

The mirror of the drama captures images for us. "The greatest mystery," wrote critic André Malraux, "is not that we have been flung at random between the profusion of the earth and the galaxy of the stars, but that in this prison we can fashion images of ourselves sufficiently powerful to deny our nothingness." Even modern dramas that shriek our "nothingness" can do so in the theatre, for the audience at a play enters into conventions with the dramatist and (as Felix Krull in Thomas Mann's novel found that it did with the actor Müller-Rosé) willingly co-operates in its own deception, knowing that out of lies about the truth wisdom may come and that order lacking in life can be found in art, where the aesthetic, the cultural, and the intellectual are combined. The cinema giant François Truffaut spoke of the sense of community that mass art in drama and film used to create when "everyone in the audience used the same means to follow the action and understand it." These plays will show you how the mass communication of theatre in the past was accomplished, sent by the author and his collaborators in the audience who knew how to play the game and what the various signals meant. They will also show you how and why we arrived at the present state of communication (and non-communication) in the theatre. The art of the drama is the slowest of all the literary arts to change; ancient Greek plays and modern Happenings and street theatre can be meaningfully put side by side in an anthology to the greater understanding of both "where it came from" and "where it's at." It is a history of change and yet (as the French say) the more things change the more they are the same. The great masterpieces of ancient Greece can be represented by *Antigone* and the myth can be shown as reshaped in our own time by Anouilh. Plautus' *Pot of Gold* will be echoed in Molière's *Miser*, both plays dedicated to what the French genius called "making honest men laugh"; both plays present real challenges to the reader in that they are quintessentially theatre pieces, fast-paced farces with most of the emphasis on the visual aspects and not on the words (unlike certain other plays by Plautus and most of the plays of Terence, who was accused of borrowing "style" from other writers, conscious of the need for literary elegance in his work; unlike Molière's *Misanthrope* and *Tartuffe*, both highly-regarded but probably so praised because so literary). The embodied abstractions of *Everyman* and its unabashed didacticism will be found adopted and adapted in a number of surprisingly different and modern plays. The theme of ambition we can see treated in two Elizabethan masterpieces, Marlowe's *Faustus* and Shakespeare's *Macbeth*, while *Macbeth* is parodied in *Ubu the King*, grandfather of the Theatre of the Absurd, just as *Woyzeck* is the parent of modern experiments in expressionism and other so-called "non-realistic" theatre. *The Beggar's Opera*, a favorite of mine, has been squeezed out by implacable editors, but Brecht's redaction, *The Threepenny Opera*, is included and students can easily find a copy of John Gay's masterpiece in the library. *The Country Wife* was thought more suitable for the beginning student than the complexity of *The Way of the World*, but it has a vigor and a charm that may cause many to look deeper into Restoration drama and the comedy of manners in general, and may bring them at last to experience Congreve and modern successors such as Wilde, Maugham, Berman, and others. *The London Merchant,* a great hit in its time and important in the development of bourgeois tragedy, has had to be omitted but *The School for Scandal* represents the laughing comedy of the eighteenth century and *The Lady of the Camellias* (where prostitution is treated in a very different way from the Shavian argument of *Mrs. Warren's Profession*) shows what France in the nineteenth century made of the sentimental drama of the previous age. *The Subscription Scroll* has to stand as representative of the riches of Asian drama, and I would like to include more non-Western plays. I must admit that Indian plays such as *Shakuntula* bore me horribly, but *The Little Clay Cart's* courtesan might have been an amusing contrast with Camille and Mrs. Warren. Another pair might have been the *Hoei lan kia* (anonymous, thirteenth or fourteenth century) and Brecht's *Caucasian Chalk Circle*, but there was no room for Chinese drama (not even *Lady Precious Stream*), any more than for Hugo von Hoffmannsthal's *Jedermann* (useful to read in connection with the English version of the story) or for radio drama (I would have liked *Under Milk Wood* or Orson Welles' old-hat invasion from Mars broadcast) or television plays (there are more good ones than most college professors will admit and their impact is immense). Of course we had to have an Ibsen (I was torn between *Hedda Gabler* and *The Wild Duck* and chose the latter because my students always find it exciting) and a Strindberg. Strindberg's brief play *The Stronger* would have made some important points about economy and essence in drama and I have found that even beginners are capable of much more with the dream-like, complex, so-called "chamber plays" than most teachers would give them credit for. However, I chose *Miss Julie* because of interesting parallels with *The Cherry Orchard*'s story of the failure of the aristocracy and the rise of the peasantry. There was no room for a favorite short poetic play by Yeats but Synge's tragic masterpiece, *Riders to the Sea*, could not be omitted and it was possible to use a brief O'Neill, *The Long Voyage Home* (without getting arty and putting in *Hughie*), to represent his tragic powers at their height. Pirandello must stand for all the plays about the nature of illusion and reality which seek inventive theatrical means of expression and contain thought not inferior to technique. Among casualties in the modern list count Yvan Goll's *Methusalem, or The Eternal Bourgeois, Beshenye dengi* (*Easy Money*) by Aleksandr Nikolaevich Ostrovski, a Genet, a Nkosi, a folk play of the simplest sort, and the high perfection of a Garcia Lorca, *Paradise Now* from the Living Theatre, or a "ridiculous" Roland Tavel play or something from the marvelous Ellen Stewart's (La Mama's) unpredictable but never unproductive theatre, and — well, all the plays one couldn't get (example: Grove Press captives) or couldn't fit in come marching at one like the robots out of Čapek's play

Rossum's Universal Robots). But we do have *The Glass Menagerie* and can ask: What more recent American play that you miss here do you think is better than that one? And instead of *Purlie Victorious* or *Raisin in the Sun* we offer *The Owl Answers*, though there is no revolutionary play by LeRoi Jones nor a "dynamite" one by Ed Bullins nor one I wish I could give greater currency by its inclusion — say, *The River Niger* or some other interesting new achievement, in the vein of Chekhov, by Douglas Turner Ward. There is Jean-Claude van Itallie to represent the off-Broadway play that made it big (as Tom Eyen and Lanford Wilson and many deserving others never quite did) and *Meat Joy* (with notes) to explain the vogue of the Happening. We end with a brief piece of guerrilla theatre, Guadalupe de Saavedra's *Justice*, a powerfully simple statement that may at once indicate that the oldest traditions of the theatre are by no means dead and that the newest uses of it are just coming to birth.

Of course many people still believe that the theatre (like the novel) is dead. The Fabulous Invalid struggles on, but it must be admitted that in some important centers the theatre indeed is sick. As I write, half the theatres on Broadway are dark and most of the rest are full of dull plays and partially-revived musicals. The Broadway theatre is still just about as "empty and lousy" as television's David Susskind found it a few years back. The Twentieth Century Fund estimates that in the whole country a mere two or three percent of the public constitutes the whole audience for culture — unless one wishes to redefine "culture," which might be a good idea at this juncture — and even those are staying away from the legitimate theatre in droves and would not leave their TV sets if you gave them freebees. Acting on Broadway (as the articulate actor William Redford testifies) cannot be a profession and can hardly be a living. In America the live theatre does not cross-pollinate with film and television as it tends to do in London and Paris and the excitement is not with nameless instant Broadway stars briefly featured in raucous musicals or with mediocre talents that deserve nothing more than good-conduct medals for long service as — shall we say? — "the worst lady of the American theatre." Broadway does not draw our upper class, only the ugly "beautiful people." It does not appeal to coteries (not enough money in that) and cannot appeal to everyone (as *The Lady of the Camellias* did in its day). Its audience is the Scarsdale Crowd, the Jersey Girls, and cloak-and-suiters on expense accounts, plus some teenagers who heard the record and want to see it brilliantly and expensively mounted. (It has to be killed before it can be mounted, some claim, but I must admit that frenetic directors often appear to give life to material that was stillborn when it left the writers.) The expense (unions, greed, and other evils to which the flesh is heir) is a problem. One cannot afford to stage a play, only a hit. And only one production in more than a dozen even gets its "nut" paid off, let alone makes a profit. Every year millions are lost on Broadway (and thousands bored and disappointed). When *Via Galactica* fails or *Dude* turns out to be a dud, hundreds of thousands of dollars go up in smoke, the instant the reviews are out. ("I lost my job through the *New York Times*.")

Never was cheapness so expensive. Too often off-Broadway is just not quite Broadway at not quite off-off-Broadway prices. Off-off is exciting and consistently more worthwhile than Lincoln Center. Shakespeare-in-the-Park producer Joseph Papp may work another miracle with Lincoln Center. So far it has always been a failure. Robert Brustein, head of Yale Drama School, damned it before it opened, and was right. It is one of those similar unfortunate attempts at "culture" for business or political reasons. Everywhere there is pretension and vanity of vanities. Even college theatre (which until half a dozen years ago got along on *The Glass Menagerie, Our Town, The Crucible,* Anouilh's *Antigone,* and Shakespeare) is not quite as good as it used to be — it has become more adventurous but has less style than ever and is often wrecked on the shoals of modern plays like *The Zoo Story* which it has not the maturity to bring off. What we used to think of as college level production is being done professionally (I should say, as a business) in the Shakespeare festivals (San Diego, Portland, Yellow Springs, two Stratfords, etc.) and in struggling civic and community theatre groups. Little Theatres bravely carry on, occasionally with heart-warming success, and now we have bigger and better "little theatres," as in Minneapolis and elsewhere, which suggests that if and when Broadway finally succumbs, drama will live "on the road." (Road shows are already bringing in more money than Broadway productions of the same.) If we are to believe Marshall McLuhan, radio ("the medium of frenzy") is "hotting up the tribal blood of Africa, India, and China," television ("cool") is anesthetizing America, and the live theatre is dying, Egypt, dying.

But it was ever thus. In 1835 Alexis de Tocqueville (who wrote the best single book to date on the United States) observed what Puritanism, business ethics, and confused class lines in America meant for the theatre here: "The population indulges in this kind of amusement only with the greatest reserve." Still the drama struggles on and if we have not (as yet) achieved in the theatre what American artists have achieved in the cinema or the novel, there is more to American theatre than "dull plays, bad plays, and hits you can't get tickets for." Collections of the most recent plays show immense variety and verve and a healthy desire to experiment. Some such book might be used to supplement this text if students are ready for the more difficult products of their own time after they have mastered the seminal plays of the past. In Athens (with 42 theatres to Broadway's 36), where Westerners tend to assume the drama was born, things are terrible too: apathy, censorship, dark theatres, the whole bit. After all, New York theatre is not so badly off and, more encouragingly, there is more to theatre in the United States than what's happening on a few islands off the east coast in Manhattan and Brooklyn. Excellent theatre schools (such as Yale, and many others) are turning out sound technicians and if there is any writing talent around it will likely get a hearing. There are even some college courses in drama that are building the audiences the new drama will need. I hope some of them will use this book and that it will help dedicated teachers to communicate the most precious thing they can communicate to their students: their love of drama. To that all the rest can be added. Then their students will find drama, in the lofts, in the bars, in the streets, in the best theatres too, or they will go out and make it themselves as an aesthetic, cultural, intellectual, emotional way of expressing themselves and speaking to and about their generation.

It is to make drama live today, both the old worth saving and the new worth creating, that we study the stately, operatic Greek drama and the lively comedy of Plautus (who, though his name means "Flatfoot," was light on his poetic feet), the early didactic drama and the recent Absurdist plays, the theatre of spectacle at one extreme (jugglers, acrobats, extravaganzas, pantomime up to Marcel Marceau, *Marat/Sade*, "more a production than a play," and its successors) and declamation at the other (closet drama, radio drama), images for the eye and for the mind, circuses and Shakespeare. And the theatre of today is not so different from the past, for theatrical ideas ("the orchestration of platitudes," says Thornton Wilder, who ought to know) and theatrical conditions are not so different from what they have always been. Novelty in the theatre generally means the revival of something not seen for a long while since it was shelved as worn out and old-fashioned. Look at the new theatre, the movies: *Tom Jones*, Tony Richardson's fairly recent film of (of course) a classic eighteenth-century novel. What's new? Some scenes reminiscent of the Keystone Cops of 50 years ago, some closeups supposedly invented by D. W. Griffith about the same time, and a couple of startling moments when characters on the screen take notice of the audience and break the illusion by addressing them. That was not original when Molière's Harpagon did it in *The Miser*, and it is not unrelated to the Elizabethan soliloquy or the modern plays where actors "interreact" with the audience. What was the origin of the fad of "theatre in the round"? Not the pioneering director Margot Jones in Dallas, surely, but Thespis on the cart. The thrust stage? Shakespeare's *Globe*, the temporary platforms in innyards? Musicals? Back through melodrama to ballad opera to poetic tragedy with masterful music working always in the iambic pentameter cadences to the Greeks with their chanting choruses and singing actors. Alienation? Epic theatre? Old hat. Theatre of cruelty? *Ubu the King*, Grand Guignol, *Titus Andronicus*, Seneca. In fact, Artaud is trying to take us back to the real wellsprings of drama in *The Theatre and Its Double*, to burn masterpieces only if they have got in the way of our capturing the fire which kindled them. Improvisation? *Commedia dell'arte*. New staging techniques? Re-read *The Subscription Scroll*. Happenings? Street theatre? Inspiration and free creation by actors? Right back to the mysteries of Isis and Osiris and prancing around in animal skins and spontaneous revels around the carcass of a fallen mastodon. No wonder the oldest dramas that survive do not appear hopelessly antique, that the medieval *Quem quæritis?* trope, a little masterpiece of religious drama, would still make a good television opera, that we can construct anthologies of old plays and defend their relevance and new plays and point out their similarities to their predecessors.

Great art has permanent influence, permanent freshness; it belongs not only to its own age (which makes background and context important) but to all time (which makes it up-to-date and universal). Always at the heart of drama is the *agon* or conflict. Shaw wrote: "The end may be reconciliation or destruction; or, as in life itself, there may be no end; but the conflict is indispensible; no conflict, no drama." If the dramatist can touch on some conflict truly basic to the human condition, his play can survive centuries and resist all enemies, even translators. If the work speaks to the heart and the head and what it says is moving and true, it can last forever and be recreated in each generation by loving and talented hands.

The plays in this volume are about as permanent as anything human beings can make. They are classics. If there are other plays that would be easier for you to read, or for a season or so be more "contemporary" and "with it," you can always read them on your own. Here, I contend, there is no reason why you ought to get anything but the best and the best for your purpose, which is to learn to understand and appreciate drama through reading and discussion.

There's the rub: reading. Plays ought not to be read. I'd like to give a course some time where my students learned what the theatre and the drama are all about by going to repeated productions of great plays presented live and in whatever order the course we had decided upon demanded. Not just whatever plays happened to be available in town but the ones that were needed for our purposes. A course without textbooks.

The next best thing is a course with a workable textbook and a method for handling it. At last we come to some practical advice. First, "the play's the thing." Stay with the "primary material" — what a description of "monuments of unaging intellect" — and don't read the critics until after you have formed your own opinion of the work of art. Then, if you wish, is the time to test your ideas against those of someone else, to read the "secondary material." My short introductions to each play will not, I think, be able to do much more than to say a few words to direct your attention when the curtain goes up and if I do express my views, consider them not as pearls before swine but as sand in the oyster: with irritation you can make your own pearls. Don't be looking for *the* interpretation. A play is not a crossword puzzle to be filled in but a symphony to be played.

Play it in your head. Go to plays whenever possible and learn whatever you can about the physical theatre, acting, and other things connected with the production of drama. When you read, stage the play in your head. Visualize the action. Speak the speeches aloud. Imagine how actors would say the lines and how other actors would receive them. See it all, with scenery, costumes, lights, even music if necessary. Read the play in the time it would take to present it in the theatre, for you must get the overall shape of it, the feel of all the parts working together. If the dramatist has provided intermissions for any good reason, take them. Get up and walk around. Smoke. Have a cup of coffee. And think about what you have been seeing in the theatre of your head. Some playwrights are just giving you time to stretch, to go to the toilet or buy an orange drink. Others are making more profound use of your temporary return to the "world of reality." If there are no intervals indicated, read the play through at a single sitting, after you have done whatever research is necessary to enable you to see in your mind's eye the set and the action.

After your "first performance" of a play, ask yourself not only what the plot is — beginning students often tend to struggle more to get the story straight than anything else — but what the structure of the play is. What is the main plot and what are the principal events in the series of crises that lead to the climax? Are there subplots or parallel actions? Is there comic relief? Where? Why? Is the action probable, improbable, inevitable, impossible? Is it intended to be believed? In what way? Identify the elements of the structure. Are they the classic exposition, complication, climax, peripety, *dénouement*, conclusion? If not, why not? What are they? How are they handled, arranged, unified, emphasized?

Look at the list of characters again. Are the names significant? Run down the list, characterizing each in a sentence or two of your own or in phrases from the play (if the dramatist has been that helpful). Perhaps you should draw a plan of the relationships of the characters. (A Restoration drama design looks like a formal garden.) Are the characters abstractions? Intended to appear real or representative? Individuals or types? Stock characters, humor characters, stereotypes? Are there any obvious contrasts, parallels, foils? Who are the major and who are the minor characters? Are there people in the play who are not characters at all (that is, neither acting themselves nor acted upon) and, if so, what are they doing there? If you were staging the play, could you cut the cast? How? Has the plot been imposed upon the characters or does it appear to arise out of their natures and circumstances? Do you find any inconsistencies in characterization? Does anyone ever act "out of character"? Where did you get the concept of that "character" and how and why is it violated (or sustained)? Which character changes the most? Discuss the basis of the psychology of the characters in the play.

Is the setting accidental (The Present) or deliberate? Why? Are the time and place indicated? Are they important? Indispensable? If you could set the play in another time and place (including Now) would you do so? Why or why not? With what alterations? Describe the set(s) and explain why each is essential to the play. Were any scenes of the play dictated by scenic considerations? Omitted because of staging problems? Was there any symbolism connected with the setting? What details of setting were dictated by the nature of the physical theatre? How closely is the play tied to the physical theatre of its origin? If the play was not originally conceived for the modern theatre, could it be adapted to modern staging? What kind of a setting would it require today? Think of various ways of staging it.

Ask yourself similar questions about makeup, costume, and lighting, paying special attention to the possibilities offered by these arts to create mood and set tone. What can these arts contribute to an overall style for the play?

What use of symbolism might be made? How are designers' decisions in these areas connected with setting and acting style? If it is a "costume play," what would it lose (or gain) in modern dress? For classic plays, look at photographs or drawings of a number of productions and decide what elements recur in design and why.

Turning to the words themselves, is the diction noteworthy for its passion, power, or poetry? Do you detect a desire to be literary? Are the descriptive passages made dramatic? Should anything be cut? Are there any passages you would excise if you were putting on the play? (For example, *The Lady of the Camellias* and even *Hamlet* are longer than modern audiences like. How do you balance the demands of the audience against the demands of the play?) Are there any words or passages that are still unclear to you? (Make a note to discuss them in class.) Are there any allusions you need to look up? Is the play written in some definable style or dialect or obviously translated from a foreign tongue? Would some historical information assist you in understanding anything said in the play? Are there any songs? What effect do they have? Distinguish between what is integral to the play and what is merely decorative.

Now — what was the purpose of this play? Let's say its *major* purpose, for a dramatist often does several things at once. (The best symbol might be the juggler of Our Lady, the man who gave pleasure by his skill while he offered up his prowess and his prayers at the same time.) Is the dramatist trying chiefly to show (tell) a story? To reveal a character? To present a problem (with or without solution) and if so, a real problem or one devised to be stated and solved only in the theatre? To reform manners? To satirize? To mock? To fantasize? To shock? To discuss ideas? To display something or someone (scenery, machinery, actors)? To teach? To thrill? To inform or confuse? And while you're at it, what kind of a play is this: tragedy? comedy? tragicomedy? melodrama? farce? history? propaganda? — "pastoral, pastoral-comical, historical-pastoral-comical, tragical-historical, tragical-comical-historical-pastoral, scene individable or poem unlimited"? Could the communication have been couched as well (better) in any other form? What circumstances of the playwright's life and character or times and situation dictated, suggested or compelled this form? How is the form related to the content? How is the content the form?

What imagery and symbolism (if any) does the dramatist use to give significance to speeches, situations, persons, places or things? Is the title of the play a clue? (Why is *Hedda Gabler* not called *Hedda Tesman*? Or in the plays you will read: Exactly who or what is "the wild duck"? Did you catch the naughty pun in *The Country Wife* and what does this warn you is coming? What *does* "the owl" answer? And so on.) Basically, what is the theme of the play? (Try to respond more in terms of the questions the play asks than in terms of the answers it gives, if any.) What is the unifying symbol, if there is one? (This is easy in *The Glass Menagerie*, for instance, but don't miss the significance also of the fire escape and the movies, the names of the Paradise Dancehall and Blue Mountain, the unicorn that loses its horn to become more normal, and the many references to light: lightning, candles, light reflected in glass, and the rest.) Clues may be found in such obvious places as the title (*The Cherry Orchard*) or such unusual places as the comic scenes in *Faustus*. Try not to miss anything that you are supposed to notice and at the same time try not to read in meaning where none is intended. This is not to say that a play cannot mean something to you that its author never intended nor that your "production" cannot draw hidden meanings from the play of which the author may well have been unconscious, but at least as a start try to receive the play as he foresaw and intended it should be received and give it the performance he might have seen in *his* head first. The words of a dead man are indeed modified in the guts of the living, but hear him first before you interpret him for your own time and yourself.

Re-read any passages that require further study but always remember that you were not intended to see the play from backstage but rather from up front and a technique that might be pulled off in performance may be ruined by unwise poring over the text. There is a famous critical discussion as to how many children Lady Macbeth had; this and other interesting but futile critical games arise from considering the blueprint as if it were the building, the score as if it were what you hear at a concert. Remember that the text of a play may tell you, if you study it that carefully, more about how it was all done than what it all means when it is fleshed out in performance (which is fine if you want to learn the tricks of the trade but may be inimical to full participation in the magic of live theatre. Keep things in proportion and remind yourself that the playwright is only one member of the team, in some ages more important than in others, and that we have from time to time an actor (or actor-manager)'s theatre, a director's theatre, etc. The dramatist, if he is fully aware of the fact that he must triple-space his work and leave room for all the other artists to interpret what he gives them, can never write a whole play. In a way, he may be said to create the materials of a play, or to do all the painting except laying in the colors. (A misleading image. Find your own.) The dramatist asks that his interpreters be true to his original intentions — but they are not always so and there is nothing that can prevent a Bert Lahr from mugging in *Waiting for Godot* or some idiot from staging *Troilus and Cressida* in Civil War costume or playing a melodrama for laughs or a comedy like *The Cherry Orchard* for tears. The dramatist asks for what Molière called "*personnes qui ont des yeux pour découvrir dans la lecture tout le jeu du théâtre,*" so try to be that person who can see in what he reads the play of the theatre, the kind of reader who finds all that a playing of the play can offer. Of course you may conceive, in the end, a production quite beyond the imaginings of the dramatist. I recall the Urban Arts Corps doing Irwin Shaw's *Bury the Dead* with nude dancers and a dozen musical numbers, including a gospel shout, not to mention Katharine Hepburn in a cowboy suit in a Shakespearian comedy, or — and this worked, to my vast surprise — a production of *King*

Lear with bright lights and acrobats. Diarist Samuel Pepys saw *Macbeth* in the seventeenth century with witches on trapezes and loved it.

If you want your own production of the play, imagine two: the one the dramatist seems to have conceived and your own conception, or reinterpretation. Then consider how each is tailored to its time.

Once you have taken the play apart to understand it, put it back together to appreciate it. Do not murder to dissect; see all the parts functioning as a whole. Put it all back together by reading it through at playing speed, running your production as a movie of the mind. (Staging in the head can at best give you a kind of movie: the thrill of live actors actually present can never be captured outside the real theatre.) During the breaks, if any, write down any questions or comments that remain. Perhaps the motivation of characters is clear now, that *deus ex machina* conclusion a little more acceptable now. This time through you may notice many things you missed the first time. The second time through your command of pace will be better and you will sense the balance of speeches and scenes or, perhaps, note the prolepsis (foreshadowing) you missed before.

Read the plays as often as you like. After some performances in your head, the study of individual scenes is not likely to make you lose your sense of the whole but strive always to keep a sense of proportion: *"il faut voir les choses en place,"* says Voltaire, *"pour en bien juger."* ("One must see things in place in order to judge them well.") Remembering that a play is to be played, that it comes to life on the stage before an audience, that it is a form of mass communication and deals in mass psychology in a way that a poem or a novel does not, helps to keep everything in the proper perspective. With that fact firmly before you, you will realize the importance of playing it in your head and not just reading it as you would a narrative poem. You will understand how and why dramatic poetry is different from lyric poetry, why what you can face calmly on a page if you read it can be convulsively funny in performance. You will learn that the stage directions must be fully imagined and that silences can be as eloquent as words. You will see that a play is an experience, a happening, existing in continuing time (which can be magisterially manipulated by the masters, as for instance a whole night passing in a page or two of *Faustus* or eternity in an instant being felt in a pregnant pause).

The plays in this book are so rich that a lifetime could not exhaust their capacity to move and modify. But do not be overawed by them: they are masterpieces, after all, of mass communication and they ought to be able to communicate to you as one of the masses, right? They are classics and timeless; therefore, they are relevant to you and your situation here and now and even the most old-fashioned of them is not out of date. Read them with enthusiasm. Read with a pencil and write all over them. Surely you can make notes on the blueprints about the structures you are erecting in your mind. Fill the margins. A clean textbook has never been properly used.

There is some useful material at the back of the book that you ought to read carefully. Here I would like to thank my students and the others who have taught me about drama, especially Professor Elmer Hall and Professor George Ian Duthie (who introduced me to the theatre and the drama at McGill University), Professor Gerald Eades Bentley and the late Professor Alan S. Downer (who taught me at Princeton University), and my colleagues at the University of Utah, the University of Rochester, The New School for Social Research, and Brooklyn College of The City University of New York, many of whom have made useful comments over the years, though I must accept responsibility for most of the ideas and all of the errors you may find here. I am especially grateful to Paul O'Connell of Winthrop Publishers for his confidence that another drama anthology might do well in the world as well as do good, and his unflagging support of my endeavors which here at last have achieved print. Finally, wherever first-rate translations of foreign works were available, they were especially made for *Mirrors for Man*. Every reader will be grateful for the excellent work of these translators and I wish personally to thank Professors Alex Szogyi and Yvette Louria for the kind advice they gave me with the translations I prepared myself. Walter Sorell's translation of *Woyzeck* and mine of *The Lady of the Camellias* are the only complete and accurate versions of these texts in translation, the *Ubu the King* I did with Professor Margaret Ganz captures the spirit as well as conveys the meaning of the original, and Professor Alex Szogyi's rendering of *Antigone* has already been tailored for the English-speaking stage after having been translated by an eminent scholar with an unusually deep interest in, and gift for, the theatre. Finally, the major contribution to the success of *Mirrors for Man* will come from the instructors who adopt it and the students who use it well, for a mirror reflects those who look into it. To these students of drama I dedicate my anthology and say with Shakespeare:

Still be kind
and eche out our performance with your mind.

Antigone

Drama, as we have said, develops out of ritual, and Greek drama derived from the worship of Dionysus, a Thracian deity imported into Greece almost 800 years before Christ. Despite its origins in rowdy dithyrambs to the god of wine and revelry, Greek drama now has, among many people, the reputation of being majestic but cold, full of *sophia* (wisdom) but lacking in life, more likely to improve than to move. In *Antigone* we present a Greek play that is even more exciting than it is dignified, even more disturbing than it is impressive.

The most perfect example of Greek tragedy, Aristotle suggested, was Sophocles' *Oedipus the King*, and it is true that that is somewhat better constructed (it does not rely so much on narrative, for example) and even better known than *Antigone* (Who has not heard of the "Oedipus complex" and the myth which underlies it?). But for modern readers, and those of college age particularly, the Antigone situation will probably appear more relevant and more engrossing. That's what the play ought to be called, in fact: *The Antigone Situation*. Antigone is not so much a heroine as a catalyst that precipitates the problem, a problem in which Creon, King of Thebes, is central. In working out — or working through — the dilemma, Sophocles seems more subtle than in *Oedipus the King*, for Antigone and Creon are locked in an *agon* (struggle) in which nothing is simple or sure but the fact that human life is essentially tragic and that high virtues such as resolution and determination, conscientiousness and courage avail only to lend dignity to disaster when the proud will not adapt nor the rigid bend. The Chinese say that the pliant bamboo survives; men are brittle.

The great geniuses of the theatre that miraculously flourished in the fifth century B.C. were Aeschylus (525–426 B.C.), Sophocles (c. 496–c. 406 B.C.), Euripides (c. 486–c. 406 B.C.) and the master of comedy, Aristophanes (c. 448–c. 385 B.C.). Each believed that the "imitation of an action" presented in the theatre had to be, in one sense or another, "serious," important and didactic. In *Antigone*, there is plenty of seriousness and no lack of message, but the play may appeal to moderns in a relativistic age because it deals in moral ambiguities, because its heroes and villains are not clear-cut, and at least part of its message is as complex and confusing as life itself. *Antigone* tells us that Authority will always try to set up immutable laws and that Individual Conscience will defy them. There will always be an Establishment determined to exercise its power and ready to crush

1

Anarchy, which is born of exceptions to the rules. The motives of the people involved will be as involved as people are, compounded of pride and fear and other elements with names as different as the ancient *hubris* and the modern "ego-tripping." There will always be conflicts and politics and authoritarians and individualists; often it will be difficult to tell which is which. There will always be reasonable new codes and age-old tribal feelings, intellect and instinct, reason and emotion at loggerheads. Always something has to give, and that which does not give ends in catastrophe, for change is as inescapable in life as cause and effect, and in everything the old is always dying and the new coming to birth.

Sophocles wrote some 123 plays (only seven and some fragments remain). He made many innovations in the drama, such as expanding the chorus (from 12 to 15) and adding a third actor. But few people are profoundly intrigued today by the theatrical conditions of his vast theatres, or by the fact that actors had to wear masks and padded costumes and high-platformed shoes and to chant their lines loudly — Sophocles led the dancing chorus as a teenager but had a voice not powerful enough for an adult actor — to communicate. The Greek tragedy was more like an oratorio than a modern play. Like an opera, it was stylized and tended to strive for bold effects and simple grandeur. Its parades and *parabasis* (choral ode), its *episodes* of action and *exodus* of explanation were formal, its conventions increasingly stiff from the time that Thespis of Icaria (a little village near Marathon) won the first prize in the drama contest at the theatre of Dionysus Eleuthereus in Athens in 534 B.C. It is fundamentally what Sophocles can do for us and not what he did for the drama of his time that grips us; not that *Oedipus the King* impressed Aristotle but that it has profoundly affected men ever since (even if it did not win the first prize — which went that year to Philocles, Aeschylus' nephew); not that *Antigone* has all the magnitude of Greek tragedy but that it has dazzling sublety and enduring pertinence, confronting man-made laws with natural piety and daring to leave the outcome unresolved.

Imagine a production of *Antigone* in a vast, sun-drenched theatre focused on an *orchestra* (a round dancing place) backed by a permanent *skene* (scene building) with a raised platform, three massive doors, and two wings (*paraskena*). A reference book can give you pictures and diagrams of the theatre, but it is harder to visualize the effect of the chorus, moving and chanting in unison, and the actors, stalking in stately fashion and seeming (like the characters they portray) somehow larger than life. Consider the religious origins of this drama, the altar to Dionysus in the center of the orchestra, the restraints against violence and impropriety enjoined upon the author and the sense in the audience of the dignity of the civic occasion, financed by some civic-minded patron (*choregos*) but in a way the business of the whole community, an audience gathered in a festive but at the same time pious mood to see the ancient myths translated into poetry, movement, and music.

To understand *Antigone* it helps for the modern student to know the

Theban myth — for the Greeks, part poetry, part history, part theology —
which underlies the play. Cadmus, brother of Europa, was the son of
Agenor, King of Phoenicia. Cadmus settled in Thrace and, as a result of
instructions given him by an oracle, set up a citadel which later became the
city of Thebes. A line of kings followed; one of these was Laius. A homo-
sexual, he stole away a son of Pelops, King of Pisa in Elis, and upon Laius
and his family Pelops called down the curse of the gods. It was foretold that
the son of Laius and his wife Jocasta (sister of Creon; daughter of Pentheus,
second king of Thebes) would murder his father and marry his mother. To
prevent this, Laius had the baby's feet pierced and tied together and
abandoned the infant on a hillside of Mount Cithaeron (where the rites
of Dionysus were celebrated). The baby was found by a shepherd, was
named Oedipus ("swollen feet"), and was given to Polybus, King of
Corinth, who raised him as his own child. When Oedipus grew up and
learned of the prophecy, he fled from Corinth to evade the curse, thinking
Polybus his father, but on the road between Delphi (where the oracle was)
and Daulis (in Phocia) he encountered Laius and, not recognizing him as
his father, got into an argument with him and slew him. The first part of
the prophecy had been fulfilled, though Oedipus did not know it. Meanwhile, outside the city of Thebes other events were taking shape that were
to complete the fate of Oedipus, for a female monster, The Sphinx ("stran-
gler"), appeared, perched on a rock, and challenged each passerby to solve
her riddle: "What goes on four feet in the morning, on two feet at noon,
and on three feet in the evening?" The Sphinx killed those who could not
answer the riddle. Oedipus came along and solved the puzzle: the answer
was Man, who crawls as an infant, walks erect as an adult, and walks with
a cane when elderly. The Sphinx threw herself down from the rock and
was destroyed. The citizens of Thebes rejoiced and rewarded Oedipus by
making him king, marrying him to the widow of Laius. This was, of course,
Jocasta, Oedipus' own mother. The second part of the prophecy was fulfilled. By Jocasta, Oedipus had two sons (Eteocles and Polyneices) and two
daughters (Antigone and Ismene). Oedipus flourished until Thebes had a
plague, the oracle was consulted, and the people were told to expel the
murderer of Laius. Teiresias, the blind soothsayer, revealed that this was
none other than Oedipus himself, whereupon Jocasta hanged herself and
Oedipus, horrified, tore out his own eyes. Fleeing Thebes, the blind Oedipus
(accompanied by his daughter Antigone) found refuge at Colonus (very
near Athens, and the birthplace of Sophocles). Here the Eumenides ("kindly
ones") took him from the earth.

   Antigone returned to Thebes and at this point we become directly concerned with the matter of the play under discussion. (Other plays deal
with other aspects of this legend.) Oedipus' flight had left the kingdom of
Thebes to his two sons as joint rulers, but they argued and finally decided
that they should rule in alternate years. Eteocles ruled the first year and
Polyneices withdrew from Thebes. At the end of the first year, Polyneices
attempted to take his turn on the throne, but Eteocles would not permit

him to return. Thereupon Polyneices appealed to Adrastus, King of Argos, for help. Adrastus organized an expedition (the "Seven Against Thebes"). Adrastus' brother-in-law, Amphiaraüs, foretold that the expedition would be disastrous; Teiresias foretold that the Thebans would win if Menoceus (son of Creon, nephew of Jocasta) would commit suicide as a sacrifice. He did so and in a decisive battle all major participants except Adrastus were killed: Eteocles and Polyneices slew one another in single combat. So Creon became king of Thebes. His first act was to forbid the burial of Polyneices, thereby giving the dead man's soul no rest. Antigone undertook to disobey this order and to make a symbolic gesture toward the burial of her brother, in defiance of Creon. Thus the conflict arose, and *Antigone* tells us of its outcome. The story of Thebes ends ten years after the events of the play when Adrastus persuaded the descendants of the Seven Against Thebes to try again. In the War of The Epigoni ("descendants"), Thebes was captured and razed to the ground. Adrastus' son Aegialeus was killed, Adrastus died of grief, and the tale of Thebes was over.

The Greek drama began in choruses telling the myths of Dionysus. It developed into dialogue, first between parts of the chorus (*strophe* and *antistrophe*) and later between actors and chorus, which presented other myths, such as the one we have summarized here. The myths served as sources for ideas, ideas as sources for plays. "Ideas are to drama what counterpoint is to music," said Freidrich Hebbel; "nothing in themselves but the *sine qua non* for everything." The ideas in *Antigone* are interesting in themselves and, more important for the dramatist, not only can the play be analogous to life and significant in its statement of these ideas but also ideas can generate the conflict which makes the plot run. Because the details of the story were known to his audience, Sophocles could jump right into it at an exciting point (*in medias res*) and move ahead swiftly without excessive exposition, concentrating on *why* things happen. At the expense of suspense he has gained speed and the opportunity for that philosophical profundity and psychological insight that characterize great Greek tragedies and give them their power to rivet the attention, fascinate the intellect, and purge (or purify — the meaning of Aristotle's *catharthis* has been debated for millennia) the emotions of pity and awe, presenting in a vivid way the ironies and the essential tragedy of the human condition.

ANTIGONE

Sophocles

*Translated from the Greek
by R. C. Jebb*

CHARACTERS IN THE PLAY

ANTIGONE ⎫ *daughters of Oedipus*
ISMENE ⎭
CREON, *King of Thebes*
EURYDICE, *his wife*
HAEMON, *his son*
TEIRESIAS, *the blind prophet*
GUARD, *set to watch the corpse of Polyneices*
FIRST MESSENGER
SECOND MESSENGER, *from the house*
CHORUS OF THEBAN ELDERS

SCENE: — *The same as in the Oedipus the King, an open space before the royal palace, once that of Oedipus, at Thebes. The back-scene represents the front of the palace, with three doors, of which the central and largest is the principal entrance into the house. The time is at daybreak on the morning after the fall of the two brothers, Eteocles and Polyneices, and the flight of the defeated Argives.* ANTIGONE *calls* ISMENE *forth from the palace, in order to speak to her alone.*

ANTIGONE: Ismene, sister, mine own dear sister, knowest thou what ill there is, of all bequeathed by Oedipus, that Zeus fulfils not for us twain while we live? Nothing painful is there, nothing fraught with ruin, no shame, no dishonour, that I have not seen in thy woes and mine.

And now what new edict is this of which they tell, that our Captain hath just published to all Thebes? Knowest thou aught? Hast thou heard? Or is it hidden from thee that our friends are threatened with the doom of our foes?

ISMENE: No word of friends, Antigone, gladsome or painful, hath come to me, since we two sisters were bereft of brothers twain, killed in one day by a twofold blow; and since in this last night the Argive host hath fled, I know no more, whether my fortune be brighter, or more grievous.

ANTIGONE: I knew it well, and therefore sought to bring thee beyond the gates of the court, that thou mightest hear alone.

ISMENE: What is it? 'Tis plain that thou art brooding on some dark tidings.

ANTIGONE: What, hath not Creon destined our brothers, the one to honoured burial, the other to unburied shame? Eteocles, they say, with due observance of right and custom, he hath laid in the earth, for his honour among the dead below. But the hapless corpse of Polyneices — as rumour saith, it hath been published to the town that none shall entomb him or mourn, but leave unwept, unsepulchred, a welcome store for the birds, as they espy him, to feast on at will.

Such, 'tis said, is the edict that the good Creon hath set forth for thee and for me, — yes, for *me*, — and is coming hither to proclaim it clearly to those who know it not; nor counts the matter light, but, whoso disobeys in aught, his doom is death by stoning before all the folk. Thou knowest it now; and thou wilt soon show whether thou art nobly bred, or the base daughter of a noble line.

ISMENE: Poor sister, — and if things stand thus, what could I help to do or undo?

ANTIGONE: Consider if thou wilt share the toil and the deed.

ISMENE: In what venture? What can be thy meaning?

ANTIGONE: Wilt thou aid this hand to lift the dead?

ISMENE: Thou wouldst bury him, — when 'tis forbidden to Thebes?

ANTIGONE: I will do my part, — and thine, if thou wilt not, — to a brother. False to him will I never be found.

ISMENE: Ah, over-bold! when Creon hath forbidden?

ANTIGONE: Nay, he hath no right to keep me from mine own.

ISMENE: Ah me! think, sister, how our father perished, amid hate and scorn, when sins bared by his own search had moved him to strike both eyes with self-blinding hand; then the mother wife, two names in one, with twisted noose did despite unto her life; and last, our two brothers in one day, — each shedding, hapless one, a kinsman's blood, — wrought out with mutual hands their common doom. And now *we* in turn — we two left all alone — think how we shall perish, more miserably than all the rest, if, in defiance of the law, we brave a king's decree or his powers. Nay, we must remember, first, that we were born women, as who should not strive with men; next, that we are ruled of the stronger, so that we must obey in these things, and in things yet sorer. I, therefore, asking the Spirits Infernal to pardon, seeing that force is put on me herein, will hearken to our rulers; for 'tis witless to be over busy.

ANTIGONE: I will not urge thee, — no, nor, if thou yet shouldst have the mind, wouldst thou be welcome as a worker with *me*. Nay, be what thou wilt; but I will bury him: well for me to die in doing that. I shall rest, a loved one with him whom I have loved, sinless in my crime; for I owe a longer allegiance to the dead than to the living: in that world I shall abide for ever. But if *thou* wilt, be guilty of dishonouring laws which the gods have stablished in honour.

ISMENE: I do them no dishonour; but to defy the State, — I have no strength for that.

ANTIGONE: Such be thy plea: — I, then, will go to heap the earth above the brother whom I love.

ISMENE: Alas, unhappy one! How I fear for thee!

ANTIGONE: Fear not for me: guide thine own fate aright.

ISMENE: At least, then, disclose this plan to none, but hide it closely, — and so, too, will I.

ANTIGONE: Oh, denounce it! Thou wilt be far more hateful for thy silence, if thou proclaim not these things to all.

ISMENE: Thou hast a hot heart for chilling deeds.

ANTIGONE: I know that I please where I am most bound to please.

ISMENE: Aye, if thou canst; but thou wouldst what thou canst not.

ANTIGONE: Why, then, when my strength fails, I shall have done.

ISMENE: A hopeless quest should not be made at all.

ANTIGONE: If thus thou speakest, thou wilt have hatred from me, and will justly be subject to the lasting hatred of the dead. But leave me, and the folly that is mine alone, to suffer this dread thing; for I shall not suffer aught so dreadful as an ignoble death.

ISMENE: Go, then, if thou must; and of this be sure, — that, though thine errand is foolish, to thy dear ones thou art truly dear.

(*Exit* ANTIGONE *on the spectators' left.* ISMENE *retires into the palace by one of the two sidedoors. When they have departed, the* CHORUS OF THEBAN ELDERS *enters.*)

strophe 1

CHORUS (*singing*): Beam of the sun, fairest light that ever dawned on Thebe of the seven gates, thou hast shone forth at last, eye of golden day, arisen above Dirce's streams! The warrior of the white shield, who came from Argos in his panoply, hath been stirred by thee to headlong flight, in swifter career;

systema 1

LEADER OF THE CHORUS: who set forth against our land by reason of the vexed claims of Polyneices; and, like shrill-screaming eagle, he flew over into our land, in snow-white pinion sheathed, with an armed throng, and with plumage of helms.

antistrophe 1

CHORUS: He paused above our dwellings; he ravened around our sevenfold portals with spears athirst for blood; but he went hence, or ever his jaws were glutted with our gore, or the Fire-god's pine-fed flame had seized our crown of towers. So fierce was the noise of battle raised behind him, a thing too hard for him to conquer, as he wrestled with his dragon foe.

systema 2

LEADER: For Zeus utterly abhors the boasts of a proud tongue; and when he beheld them coming on in a great stream, in the haughty pride of clanging gold, he smote with brandished fire one who was now hasting to shout victory at his goal upon our ramparts.

strophe 2

CHORUS: Swung down, he fell on the earth with a crash, torch in hand, he who so lately, in the frenzy of the mad onset, was raging against us with the blasts of his tempestuous hate. But those threats fared not as he hoped; and to other foes the mighty War-god dispensed their several dooms, dealing havoc around, a mighty helper at our need.

systema 3

LEADER: For seven captains at seven gates, matched against seven, left the tribute of their panoplies to Zeus who turns the battle; save those two of cruel fate, who, born of one sire and one mother, set against each other their twain conquering spears, and are sharers in a common death.

antistrophe 2

CHORUS: But since Victory of glorious name hath come to us, with joy responsive to the joy of Thebe whose chariots are many, let us enjoy forgetfulness after the late wars, and visit all the temples of the gods with night-long dance and song; and may Bacchus be our leader, whose dancing shakes the land of Thebe.

systema 4

LEADER: But lo, the king of the land comes yonder, Creon, son of Menoeceus, our new ruler by the new fortunes that the gods have given; what counsel is he pondering, that he hath proposed this special conference of elders, summoned by his general mandate?

(*Enter* CREON, *from the central doors of the palace, in the garb of king, with two attendants.*)

CREON: Sirs, the vessel of our State, after being tossed on wild waves, hath once more been safely steadied by the gods: and ye, out of all the folk, have been called apart by my summons, because I knew, first of all, how true and constant was your reverence for the royal power of Laius; how, again, when Oedipus was ruler of our land, and when he had perished, your steadfast loyalty still upheld their children. Since, then, his sons have fallen in one day by a twofold doom, — each smitten by the other, each stained with a brother's blood, — I now possess the throne and all its powers, by nearness of kinship to the dead.

No man can be fully known, in soul and spirit and mind, until he hath been seen versed in rule and law-giving. For if any, being supreme guide of the State, cleaves not to the best counsels, but, through some fear, keeps his lips locked, I hold, and have ever held, him most base; and if any makes a friend of more account than his fatherland, that man hath no place in my regard. For I — be Zeus my witness, who sees all things always — would not be silent if I saw ruin, instead of safety, coming to the citizens; nor would I ever deem the country's foe a friend to myself; remembering this, that our country is the ship that bears us safe, and that only while she prospers in our voyage can we make true friends.

Such are the rules by which I guard this city's greatness. And in accord with them is the edict which I have now published to the folk touching the sons of Oedipus; — that Eteocles, who hath fallen fighting for our city, in all renown of arms, shall be entombed, and crowned with every rite that follows the noblest dead to their rest. But for his brother, Polyneices, — who came back from exile, and sought to consume utterly with fire the city of his fathers and the shrines of his fathers' gods, — sought to taste of kindred blood, and to lead the remnant into slavery; — touching this man, it hath been proclaimed to our people that none shall grace him with sepulture or lament, but leave him unburied, a corpse for birds and dogs to eat, a ghastly sight of shame.

Such the spirit of my dealing; and never, by deed of mine, shall the wicked stand in honour before the just; but whoso hath good will to Thebes, he shall be honoured of me, in his life and in his death.

LEADER OF THE CHORUS: Such is thy pleasure, Creon, son of Menoeceus, touching this city's foe, and its friend; and thou hast power, I ween, to take what order thou wilt, both for the dead, and for all us who live.

CREON: See, then, that ye be guardians of the mandate.

LEADER: Lay the burden of this task on some younger man.

CREON: Nay, watchers of the corpse have been found.

LEADER: What, then, is this further charge that thou wouldst give?

CREON: That ye side not with the breakers of these commands.

LEADER: No man is so foolish that he is enamoured of death.

CREON: In sooth, that is the meed; yet lucre hath oft ruined men through their hopes.

(*A* GUARD *enters from the spectators' left.*)

GUARD: My liege, I will not say that I come breathless from speed, or that I have plied a nimble foot; for often did my thoughts make me pause, and wheel round in my path, to return. My mind was holding large discourse with me; 'Fool, why goest thou to thy certain doom?' 'Wretch, tarrying again? And if Creon hears this from another, must not thou smart for it?' So debating, I went on my way with lagging steps, and thus a short road was made long. At last, however, it carried the day that I should come hither — to thee; and, though my tale be nought, yet will I tell it; for I come with a good grip on one hope, — that I can suffer nothing but what is my fate.

CREON: And what is it that disquiets thee thus?

GUARD: I wish to tell thee first about myself — I did not do the deed — I did not see the doer — it were not right that I should come to any harm.

CREON: Thou hast a shrewd eye for thy mark; well dost thou fence thyself round against the blame; clearly thou hast some strange thing to tell.

GUARD: Aye, truly; dread news makes one pause long.

CREON: Then tell it, wilt thou, and so get thee gone?

GUARD: Well, this is it — The corpse — some one hath just given it burial, and gone away, — after sprinkling thirsty dust on the flesh, with such other rites as piety enjoins.

CREON: What sayest thou? What living man hath dared this deed?

GUARD: I know not; no stroke of pickaxe was seen there, no earth thrown up by mattock; the ground was hard and dry, unbroken, without track of wheels; the doer was one who had left no trace. And when the first day-watchman showed it to us, sore wonder fell on all. The dead man was veiled from us; not shut within a tomb, but lightly strewn with dust, as by the hand of one who shunned a curse. And no sign met the eye as though any beast of prey or any dog had come nigh to him, or torn him.

Then evil words flew fast and loud among us, guard accusing guard; and it would e'en have come to blows at last, nor was there any to hinder. Every man was the culprit, and no one was convicted, but all disclaimed knowledge of the deed. And we were ready to take red-hot iron in our hands; — to walk through fire; — to make oath by the gods that we had not done the deed, — that we were not privy to the planning or the doing.

At last, when all our searching was fruitless, one spake, who made us all bend our faces on the earth in fear; for we saw not how we could gainsay him, or escape mischance if we obeyed. His counsel was that this deed must be reported to thee, and not hidden. And this seemed best; and the lot doomed my hapless self to win this prize. So here I stand, — as unwelcome as unwilling, well I wot; for no man delights in the bearer of bad news.

LEADER: O king, my thoughts have long been whispering, can this deed, perchance, be e'en the work of gods?

CREON: Cease, ere thy words fill me utterly with wrath, lest thou be found at once an old man and foolish. For thou sayest what is not to be borne, in saying that the gods have care for this corpse. Was it for high reward of trusty service that they sought to hide his nakedness, who came to burn their pillared shrines and sacred treasures, to burn their land, and scatter its laws to the winds? Or dost thou behold the gods honouring the wicked? It cannot be. No! From the first there were certain in the town that muttered against me, chafing at this edict, wagging their heads in secret; and kept not their necks duly under the yoke, like men contented with my sway.

'Tis by them, well I know, that these have been beguiled and bribed to do this deed. Nothing so evil as money ever grew to be current among men. This lays cities low, this drives men from their homes, this trains and warps honest souls till they set themselves to works of shame; this still teaches folk to practise villainies, and to know every godless deed.

But all the men who wrought this thing for hire have made it sure that, soon or late, they shall pay the price. Now, as Zeus still hath my reverence, know this — I tell it thee on my oath: — If ye find not the very author of this burial, and produce him before mine eyes, death alone shall not be enough for you, till first, hung up alive, ye have revealed this outrage, — that henceforth ye may thieve with better knowledge whence lucre should be won, and learn that it is not well to love gain from every source. For thou wilt

find that ill-gotten pelf brings more men to ruin than to weal.

GUARD: May I speak? Or shall I just turn and go?

CREON: Knowest thou not that even now thy voice offends?

GUARD: Is thy smart in the ears, or in the soul?

CREON: And why wouldst thou define the seat of my pain?

GUARD: The doer vexes thy mind, but I, thine ears.

CREON: Ah, thou art a born babbler, 'tis well seen.

GUARD: May be, but never the doer of this deed.

CREON: Yea, and more, — the seller of thy life for silver.

GUARD: Alas! 'Tis sad, truly, that he who judges should misjudge.

CREON: Let thy fancy play with 'judgment' as it will; — but, if ye show me not the doers of these things, ye shall avow that dastardly gains work sorrows.

(CREON goes into the palace.)

GUARD: Well, may he be found! so 'twere best. But, be he caught or be he not — fortune must settle that — truly thou wilt not see me here again. Saved, even now, beyond hope and thought, I owe the gods great thanks.

(The GUARD goes out on the spectators' left.)

strophe 1
CHORUS (singing): Wonders are many, and none is more wonderful than man; the power that crosses the white sea, driven by the stormy south-wind, making a path under surges that threaten to engulf him; and Earth, the eldest of the gods, the immortal, the unwearied, doth he wear, turning the soil with the offspring of horses, as the ploughs go to and fro from year to year.

antistrophe 1
And the light-hearted race of birds, and the tribes of savage beasts, and the sea-brood

of the deep, he snares in the meshes of his woven toils, he leads captive, man excellent in wit. And he masters by his arts the beast whose lair is in the wilds, who roams the hills; he tames the horse of shaggy mane, he puts the yoke upon its neck, he tames the tireless mountain bull.

strophe 2

And speech, and wind-swift thought, and all the moods that mould a state, hath he taught himself; and how to flee the arrows of the frost, when 'tis hard lodging under the clear sky, and the arrows of the rushing rain; yea, he hath resource for all; without resource he meets nothing that must come: only against Death shall he call for aid in vain; but from baffling maladies he hath devised escapes.

antistrophe 2

Cunning beyond fancy's dream is the fertile skill which brings him, now to evil, now to good. When he honours the laws of the land, and that justice which he hath sworn by the gods to uphold, proudly stands his city: no city hath he who, for his rashness, dwells with sin. Never may he share my hearth, never think my thoughts, who doth these things!

(*Enter the* GUARD *on the spectators' left, leading in* ANTIGONE.)

LEADER OF THE CHORUS: What portent from the gods is this? — my soul is amazed. I know her — how can I deny that yon maiden is Antigone?

O hapless, and child of hapless sire, — of Oedipus! What means this? Thou, brought a prisoner? — thou, disloyal to the king's laws, and taken in folly?

GUARD: Here she is, the doer of the deed: — we caught this girl burying him: — but where is Creon?

(CREON *enters hurriedly from the palace.*)

LEADER: Lo, he comes forth again from the house, at our need.

CREON: What is it? What hath chanced, that makes my coming timely?

GUARD: O king, against nothing should men pledge their word; for the afterthought belies the first intent. I could have vowed that I should not soon be here again, — scared by thy threats, with which I had just been lashed: but, — since the joy that surprises and transcends our hopes is like in fulness to no other pleasure, — I have come, though 'tis in breach of my sworn oath, bringing this maid; who was taken showing grace to the dead. This time there was no casting of lots; no, this luck hath fallen to me, and to none else. And now, sire, take her thyself, question her, examine her, as thou wilt; but I have a right to free and final quittance of this trouble.

CREON: And thy prisoner here — how and whence hast thou taken her?

GUARD: She was burying the man; thou knowest all.

CREON: Dost thou mean what thou sayest? Dost thou speak aright?

GUARD: I saw her burying the corpse that thou hadst forbidden to bury. Is that plain and clear?

CREON: And how was she seen? how taken in the act?

GUARD: It befell on this wise. When we had come to the place, — with those dread menaces of thine upon us, — we swept away all the dust that covered the corpse, and bared the dank body well; and then sat us down on the brow of the hill, to windward, heedful that the smell from him should not strike us; every man was wide awake, and kept his neighbour alert with torrents of threats, if anyone should be careless of this task.

So went it, until the sun's bright orb stood in mid heaven, and the heat began to burn: and then suddenly a whirlwind lifted from the earth a storm of dust, a trouble in the sky, and filled the plain, marring all the leafage of its woods; and the wide air was choked therewith: we closed our eyes, and bore the plague from the gods.

And when, after a long while, this storm

had passed, the maid was seen; and she cried aloud with the sharp cry of a bird in its bitterness, — even as when, within the empty nest, it sees the bed stripped of its nestlings. So she also, when she saw the corpse bare, lifted up a voice of wailing, and called down curses on the doers of that deed. And straightway she brought thirsty dust in her hands; and from a shapely ewer of bronze, held high, with thrice-poured drink-offering she crowned the dead.

We rushed forward when we saw it, and at once closed upon our quarry, who was in no wise dismayed. Then we taxed her with her past and present doings; and she stood not on denial of aught, — at once to my joy and to my pain. To have escaped from ills one's self is a great joy; but 'tis painful to bring friends to ill. Howbeit, all such things are of less account to me than mine own safety.

CREON: Thou — thou whose face is bent to earth — dost thou avow, or disavow, this deed?

ANTIGONE: I avow it; I make no denial.

CREON (*to* GUARD): Thou canst betake thee whither thou wilt, free and clear of a grave charge.

(*Exit* GUARD.)

(*to* ANTIGONE) Now, tell me thou — not in many words, but briefly — knewest thou that an edict had forbidden this?

ANTIGONE: I knew it: could I help it? It was public.

CREON: And thou didst indeed dare to transgress that law?

ANTIGONE: Yes; for it was not Zeus that had published me that edict; not such are the laws set among men by the Justice who dwells with the gods below; nor deemed I that thy decrees were of such force, that a mortal could override the unwritten and unfailing statutes of heaven. For their life is not of to-day or yesterday, but from all time, and no man knows when they were first put forth.

Not through dread of any human pride could I answer to the gods for breaking *these*. Die I must, — I knew that well (how should I not?) — even without thy edicts. But if I am to die before my time, I count that a gain: for when any one lives, as I do, compassed about with evils, can such an one find aught but gain in death?

So for me to meet this doom is trifling grief; but if I had suffered my mother's son to lie in death an unburied corpse, that would have grieved me; for this, I am not grieved. And if my present deeds are foolish in thy sight, it may be that a foolish judge arraigns my folly.

LEADER OF THE CHORUS: The maid shows herself passionate child of passionate sire, and knows not how to bend before troubles.

CREON: Yet I would have thee know that o'erstubborn spirits are most often humbled; 'tis the stiffest iron, baked to hardness in the fire, that thou shalt oftenest see snapped and shivered; and I have known horses that show temper brought to order by a little curb; there is no room for pride, when thou art thy neighbour's slave. — This girl was already versed in insolence when she transgressed the laws that had been set forth; and, that done, lo, a second insult, — to vaunt of this, and exult in her deed.

Now verily I am no man, she is the man, if this victory shall rest with her, and bring no penalty. No! be she sister's child, or nearer to me in blood than any that worships Zeus at the altar of our house, — she and her kinsfolk shall not avoid a doom most dire; for indeed I charge that other with a like share in the plotting of this burial.

And summon her — for I saw her e'en now within, — raving, and not mistress of her wits. So oft, before the deed, the mind stands self-convicted in its treason, when folks are plotting mischief in the dark. But verily this, too, is hateful, — when one who hath been caught in wickedness then seeks to make the crime a glory.

ANTIGONE: Wouldst thou do more than take and slay me?

CREON: No more, indeed; having that, I have all.

ANTIGONE: Why then dost thou delay? In thy discourse there is nought that pleases me, — never may there be! — and so my words must needs be unpleasing to thee. And yet, for glory — whence could I have won a nobler, than by giving burial to mine own brother? All here would own that they thought it well, were not their lips sealed by fear. But royalty, blest in so much besides, hath the power to do and say what it will.

CREON: Thou differest from all these Thebans in that view.

ANTIGONE: These also share it; but they curb their tongues for thee.

CREON: And art thou not ashamed to act apart from them?

ANTIGONE: No; there is nothing shameful in piety to a brother.

CREON: Was it not a brother, too, that died in the opposite cause?

ANTIGONE: Brother by the same mother and the same sire.

CREON: Why, then, dost thou render a grace that is impious in his sight?

ANTIGONE: The dead man will not say that he so deems it.

CREON: Yea, if thou makest him but equal in honour with the wicked.

ANTIGONE: It was his brother, not his slave, that perished.

CREON: Wasting this land; while *he* fell as its champion.

ANTIGONE: Nevertheless, Hades desires these rites.

CREON: But the good desires not a like portion with the evil.

ANTIGONE: Who knows but this seems blameless in the world below?

CREON: A foe is never a friend — not even in death.

ANTIGONE: 'Tis not my nature to join in hating, but in loving.

CREON: Pass, then, to the world of the dead, and, if thou must needs love, love them. While I live, no woman shall rule me.

(*Enter* ISMENE *from the house, led in by two attendants.*)

CHORUS (*chanting*): Lo, yonder Ismene comes forth, shedding such tears as fond sisters weep; a cloud upon her brow casts its shadow over her darkly-flushing face, and breaks in rain on her fair cheek.

CREON: And thou, who, lurking like a viper in my house, wast secretly draining my life-blood, while I knew not that I was nurturing two pests, to rise against my throne — come, tell me now, wilt thou also confess thy part in this burial, or wilt thou forswear all knowledge of it?

ISMENE: I have done the deed, — if she allows my claim, — and share the burden of the charge.

ANTIGONE: Nay, justice will not suffer thee to do that: thou didst not consent to the deed, nor did I give thee part in it.

ISMENE: But, now that ills beset thee, I am not ashamed to sail the sea of trouble at thy side.

ANTIGONE: Whose was the deed, Hades and the dead are witnesses: a friend in words is not the friend that I love.

ISMENE: Nay, sister, reject me not, but let me die with thee, and duly honour the dead.

ANTIGONE: Share not thou my death, nor claim deeds to which thou hast not put thy hand: my death will suffice.

ISMENE: And what life is dear to me, bereft of thee?

ANTIGONE: Ask Creon; all thy care is for him.

ISMENE: Why vex me thus, when it avails thee nought?

ANTIGONE: Indeed, if I mock, 'tis with pain that I mock thee.

ISMENE: Tell me, — how can I serve thee, even now?

ANTIGONE: Save thyself: I grudge not thy escape.

ISMENE: Ah, woe is me! And shall I have no share in thy fate?

ANTIGONE: Thy choice was to live; mine, to die.

ISMENE: At least thy choice was not made without my protest.

ANTIGONE: One world approved thy wisdom; another, mine.

ISMENE: Howbeit, the offence is the same for both of us.

ANTIGONE: Be of good cheer; thou livest; but my life hath long been given to death, that so I might serve the dead.

CREON: Lo, one of these maidens hath newly shown herself foolish, as the other hath been since her life began.

ISMENE: Yea, O king, such reason as nature may have given abides not with the unfortunate, but goes astray.

CREON: Thine did, when thou chosest vile deeds with the vile.

ISMENE: What life could I endure, without her presence?

CREON: Nay, speak not of her 'presence'; she lives no more.

ISMENE: But wilt thou slay the betrothed of thine own son?

CREON: Nay, there are other fields for him to plough.

ISMENE: But there can never be such love as bound him to her.

CREON: I like not an evil wife for my son.

ANTIGONE: Haemon, beloved! How thy father wrongs thee!

CREON: Enough, enough of thee and of thy marriage!

LEADER OF THE CHORUS: Wilt thou indeed rob thy son of this maiden?

CREON: 'Tis Death that shall stay these bridals for me.

LEADER: 'Tis determined, it seems, that she shall die.

CREON: Determined, yes, for thee and for me. — (*to the two attendants*) No more delay — servants, take them within! Henceforth they must be women, and not range at large; for verily even the bold seek to fly, when they see Death now closing on their life.

(*Exeunt attendants, guarding* ANTIGONE *and* ISMENE. — CREON *remains.*)

strophe 1

CHORUS (*singing*): Blest are they whose days have not tasted of evil. For when a house hath once been shaken from heaven, there the curse fails nevermore, passing from life to life of the race; even as, when the surge is driven over the darkness of the deep by the fierce breath of Thracian sea-winds, it rolls up the black sand from the depths, and there is a sullen roar from wind-vexed headlands that front the blows of the storm.

antistrophe 1

I see that from olden time the sorrows in the house of the Labdacidae are heaped upon the sorrows of the dead; and generation is not freed by generation, but some god strikes them down, and the race hath no deliverance.

For now that hope of which the light had been spread above the last root of the house of Oedipus — that hope, in turn, is brought low — by the blood-stained dust due to the gods infernal, and by folly in speech, and frenzy at the heart.

strophe 2

Thy power, O Zeus, what human trespass can limit? That power which neither Sleep, the all-ensnaring, nor the untiring months of the gods can master; but thou, a ruler to whom time brings not old age, dwellest in the dazzling splendour of Olympus.

And through the future, near and far, as through the past, shall this law hold good: Nothing that is vast enters into the life of mortals without a curse.

antistrophe 2

For that hope whose wanderings are so wide is to many men a comfort, but to many a false lure of giddy desires, and the disappointment comes on one who knoweth nought till he burn his foot against the hot fire.

For with wisdom hath some one given forth the famous saying, that evil seems good, soon or late, to him whose mind the god draws to mischief; and but for the briefest space doth he fare free of woe.

LEADER OF THE CHORUS: But lo, Haemon, the last of thy sons; — comes he grieving for the doom of his promised bride, Antigone, and bitter for the baffled hope of his marriage?

(*Enter* HAEMON.)

CREON: We shall know soon, better than seers could tell us. — My son, hearing the fixed doom of thy betrothed, art thou come in rage against thy father? Or have I thy good will, act how I may?

HAEMON: Father, I am thine; and thou, in thy wisdom, tracest for me rules which I shall follow. No marriage shall be deemed by me a greater gain than thy good guidance.

CREON: Yea, this, my son, should be thy heart's fixed law, — in all things to obey thy father's will. 'Tis for this that men pray to see dutiful children grow up around them in their homes, — that such may requite their father's foe with evil, and honour, as their father doth, his friend. But he who begets unprofitable children — what shall we say that he hath sown, but troubles for himself, and much triumph for his foes? Then do not thou, my son, at pleasure's beck, dethrone thy reason for a woman's sake; knowing that this is a joy that soon grows cold in clasping arms, — an evil woman to share thy bed and thy home. For what wound could strike deeper than a false friend? Nay, with loathing, and as if she were thine enemy, let this girl go to find a husband in the house of Hades. For since I have taken her, alone of all the city, in open disobedience, I will not make myself a liar to my people — I will slay her.

So let her appeal as she will to the majesty of kindred blood: If I am to nurture mine own kindred in naughtiness, needs must I bear with it in aliens. He who does his duty in his own household will be found righteous in the State also. But if any one transgresses, and does violence to the laws, or thinks to dictate to his rulers, such an one can win no praise from me. No, whomsoever the city may appoint, that man must be obeyed, in little things and great, in just things and unjust; and I should feel sure that one who thus obeys would be a good ruler no less than a good subject, and in the storm of spears would stand his ground where he was set, loyal and dauntless at his comrade's side.

But disobedience is the worst of evils. This it is that ruins cities; this makes homes desolate; by this, the ranks of allies are broken into headlong rout; but, of the lives whose course is fair, the greater part owes safety to obedience. Therefore we must support the cause of order, and in no wise suffer a woman to worst us. Better to fall from power, if we must, by a man's hand; then we should not be called weaker than a woman.

LEADER: To us, unless our years have stolen our wit, thou seemest to say wisely what thou sayest.

HAEMON: Father, the gods implant reason in men, the highest of all things that we call our own. Not mine the skill — far from me be the quest! — to say wherein thou speakest not aright; and yet another man, too, might have some useful thought. At least, it is my natural office to watch, on thy behalf, all that men say, or do, or find to blame. For the dread of thy frown forbids the citizen to speak such words as would offend thine ear; but I can hear these murmurs in the dark, these moanings of the city for this maiden; 'no woman,' they say, 'ever merited her doom less, — none ever was to die so shamefully for deeds so glorious as hers; who, when her own brother had fallen in bloody strife, would not leave him unburied, to be

devoured by carrion dogs, or by any bird:
— deserves not *she* the meed of golden
honour?'

Such is the darkling rumour that spreads
in secret. For me, my father, no treasure is
so precious as thy welfare. What, indeed, is
a nobler ornament for children than a pros-
pering sire's fair fame, or for sire than son's?
Wear not, then, one mood only in thyself;
think not that thy word, and thine alone,
must be right. For if any man thinks that
he alone is wise, — that in speech, or in
mind, he hath no peer, — such a soul, when
laid open, is ever found empty.

No, though a man be wise, 'tis no shame
for him to learn many things, and to bend
in season. Seest thou, beside the wintry torrent's course, how the trees that yield to it
save every twig, while the stiff-necked perish
root and branch? And even thus he who
keeps the sheet of his sail taut, and never
slackens it, upsets his boat, and finishes his
voyage with keel uppermost.

Nay, forego thy wrath; permit thyself to
change. For if I, a younger man, may offer
my thought, it were far best, I ween, that
men should be all-wise by nature; but, otherwise — and oft the scale inclines not so —
'tis good also to learn from those who speak
aright.

LEADER: Sire, 'tis meet that thou shouldest
profit by his words, if he speaks aught in
season, and thou, Haemon, by thy father's;
for on both parts there hath been wise
speech.

CREON: Men of my age — are we indeed to be
schooled, then, by men of his?

HAEMON: In nothing that is not right; but if I
am young, thou shouldest look to my merits,
not to my years.

CREON: Is it a merit to honour the unruly?

HAEMON: I could wish no one to show respect
for evil-doers.

CREON: Then is not she tainted with that
malady?

HAEMON: Our Theban folk, with one voice,
denies it.

CREON: Shall Thebes prescribe to me how I
must rule?

HAEMON: See, there thou hast spoken like a
youth indeed.

CREON: Am I to rule this land by other judgment than mine own?

HAEMON: That is no city which belongs to one
man.

CREON: Is not the city held to be the ruler's?

HAEMON: Thou wouldst make a good monarch
of a desert.

CREON: This boy, it seems, is the woman's
champion.

HAEMON: If thou art a woman; indeed, my
care is for thee.

CREON: Shameless, at open feud with thy
father!

HAEMON: Nay, I see thee offending against
justice.

CREON: Do I offend, when I respect mine own
prerogatives?

HAEMON: Thou dost not respect them, when
thou tramplest on the gods' honours.

CREON: O dastard nature, yielding place to
woman!

HAEMON: Thou wilt never find me yield to
baseness.

CREON: All thy words, at least, plead for that
girl.

HAEMON: And for thee, and for me, and for
the gods below.

CREON: Thou canst never marry her, on this
side the grave.

HAEMON: Then she must die, and in death
destroy another.

CREON: How! doth thy boldness run to open
threats?

HAEMON: What threat is it, to combat vain resolves?

CREON: Thou shalt rue thy witless teaching of wisdom.

HAEMON: Wert thou not my father, I would have called thee unwise.

CREON: Thou woman's slave, use not wheedling speech with me.

HAEMON: Thou wouldest speak, and then hear no reply?

CREON: Sayest thou so? Now, by the heaven above us — be sure of it — thou shalt smart for taunting me in this opprobrious strain. Bring forth that hated thing, that she may die forthwith in his presence — before his eyes — at her bridegroom's side!

HAEMON: No, not at my side — never think it — shall she perish; nor shalt thou ever set eyes more upon my face: — rave, then, with such friends as can endure thee.

(*Exit* HAEMON)

LEADER: The man is gone, O king, in angry haste; a youthful mind, when stung, is fierce.

CREON: Let him do, or dream, more than man — good speed to him! — But he shall not save these two girls from their doom.

LEADER: Dost thou indeed purpose to slay both?

CREON: Not her whose hands are pure: thou sayest well.

LEADER: And by what doom mean'st thou to slay the other?

CREON: I will take her where the path is loneliest, and hide her, living, in a rocky vault, with so much food set forth as piety prescribes, that the city may avoid a public stain. And there, praying to Hades, the only god whom she worships, perchance she will obtain release from death; or else will learn, at last, though late, that it is lost labour to revere the dead.

(CREON *goes into the palace.*)

strophe

CHORUS (*singing*): Love, unconquered in the fight, Love, who makest havoc of wealth, who keepest thy vigil on the soft cheek of a maiden; thou roamest over the sea, and among the homes of dwellers in the wilds; no immortal can escape thee, nor any among men whose life is for a day; and he to whom thou hast come is mad.

antistrophe

The just themselves have their minds warped by thee to wrong, for their ruin: 'tis thou that hast stirred up this present strife of kinsmen; victorious is the love-kindling light from the eyes of the fair bride; it is a power enthroned in sway beside the eternal laws; for there the goddess Aphrodite is working her unconquerable will.

(ANTIGONE *is led out of the palace by two of* CREON's *attendants who are about to conduct her to her doom.*)

But now I also am carried beyond the bounds of loyalty, and can no more keep back the streaming tears, when I see Antigone thus passing to the bridal chamber where all are laid to rest.

(*The following lines between* ANTIGONE *and the* CHORUS *are chanted responsively.*)

strophe 1

ANTIGONE: See me, citizens of my fatherland, setting forth on my last way, looking my last on the sunlight that is for me no more; no, Hades who gives sleep to all leads me living to Acheron's shore; who have had no portion in the chant that brings the bride, nor hath any song been mine for the crowning of bridals; whom the lord of the Dark Lake shall wed.

systema 1

CHORUS: Glorious, therefore, and with praise, thou departest to that deep place of the dead: wasting sickness hath not smitten thee; thou hast not found the wages of the sword; no, mistress of thine own fate, and still alive thou shalt pass to Hades, as no other of mortal kind hath passed.

antistrophe 1

ANTIGONE: I have heard in other days how dread a doom befell our Phrygian guest, the daughter of Tantalus, on the Sipylian heights; how, like clinging ivy, the growth of stone subdued her; and the rains fail not, as men tell, from her wasting form, nor fails the snow, while beneath her weeping lids the tears bedew her bosom; and most like to hers is the fate that brings me to my rest.

systema 2

CHORUS: Yet she was a goddess, thou knowest, and born of gods; we are mortals, and of mortal race. But 'tis great renown for a woman who hath perished that she should have shared the doom of the godlike, in her life, and afterward in death.

strophe 2

ANTIGONE: Ah, I am mocked! In the name of our fathers' gods, can ye not wait till I am gone, — must ye taunt me to my face, O my city, and ye, her wealthy sons? Ah, fount of Dirce, and thou holy ground of Thebe whose chariots are many; ye, at least, will bear me witness, in what sort, unwept of friends, and by what laws I pass to the rock-closed prison of my strange tomb, ah me unhappy! who have no home on the earth or in the shades, no home with the living or with the dead.

strophe 3

CHORUS: Thou hast rushed forward to the utmost verge of daring; and against that throne where Justice sits on high thou hast fallen, my daughter, with a grievous fall. But in this ordeal thou art paying, haply, for thy father's sin.

antistrophe 2

ANTIGONE: Thou hast touched on my bitterest thought, — awaking the ever-new lament for my sire and for all the doom given to us, the famed house of Labdacus. Alas for the horrors of the mother's bed! alas for the wretched mother's slumber at the side of her own son, — and my sire! From what manner of parents did I take my miserable being! And to them I go thus, accursed, unwed, to share their home. Alas, my brother, ill-starred in thy marriage, in thy death thou hast undone my life!

antistrophe 3

CHORUS: Reverent action claims a certain praise for reverence; but an offence against power cannot be brooked by him who hath power in his keeping. Thy self-willed temper hath wrought thy ruin.

epode

ANTIGONE: Unwept, unfriended, without marriage-song, I am led forth in my sorrow on this journey that can be delayed no more. No longer, hapless one, may I behold yon day-star's sacred eye; but for my fate no tear is shed, no friend makes moan.

(CREON *enters from the palace.*)

CREON: Know ye not that songs and wailings before death would never cease, if it profited to utter them? Away with her — away! And when ye have enclosed her, according to my word, in her vaulted grave, leave her alone, forlorn — whether she wishes to die, or to live a buried life in such a home. Our hands are clean as touching this maiden. But this is certain — she shall be deprived of her sojourn in the light.

ANTIGONE: Tomb, bridal-chamber, eternal prison in the caverned rock, whither I go to find mine own, those many who have perished, and whom Persephone hath received among the dead! Last of all shall I pass thither, and far most miserably of all, before the term of my life is spent. But I cherish good hope that my coming will be welcome to my father, and pleasant to thee, my mother, and welcome, brother, to thee; for, when ye died, with mine own hands I washed and dressed you, and poured drink-offerings at your graves; and now, Polyneices, 'tis for tending thy corpse that I win such recompense as this.

And yet I honoured thee, as the wise will deem, rightly. Never, had I been a mother of children, or if a husband had been mouldering in death, would I have taken this task upon me in the city's despite. What law, ye ask, is my warrant for that word? The husband lost, another might have been found, and child from another, to replace the first-born; but, father and mother hidden with Hades, no brother's life could ever bloom for me again. Such was the law whereby I held thee first in honour; but Creon deemed me guilty of error therein, and of outrage, ah brother mine! And now he leads me thus, a captive in his hands; no bridal bed, no bridal song hath been mine, no joy of marriage, no portion in the nurture of children; but thus, forlorn of friends, unhappy one, I go living to the vaults of death.

And what law of heaven have I transgressed? Why, hapless one, should I look to the gods any more, — what ally should I invoke, — when by piety I have earned the name of impious? Nay, then, if these things are pleasing to the gods, when I have suffered my doom, I shall come to know my sin; but if the sin is with my judges, I could wish them no fuller measure of evil than they, on their part, mete wrongfully to me.

CHORUS: Still the same tempest of the soul vexes this maiden with the same fierce gusts.

CREON: Then for this shall her guards have cause to rue their slowness.

ANTIGONE: Ah me! that word hath come very near to death.

CREON: I can cheer thee with no hope that this doom is not thus to be fulfilled.

ANTIGONE: O city of my fathers in the land of Thebe! O ye gods, eldest of our race! — they lead me hence — now, now — they tarry not! Behold me, princes of Thebes, the last daughter of the house of your kings, — see what I suffer, and from whom, because I feared to cast away the fear of Heaven!

(ANTIGONE is led away by the guards.)

strophe 1

CHORUS: (singing): Even thus endured Danae in her beauty to change the light of day for brass-bound walls; and in that chamber, secret as the grave, she was held close prisoner; yet was she of a proud lineage, O my daughter, and charged with the keeping of the seed of Zeus, that fell in the golden rain.

But dreadful is the mysterious power of fate; there is no deliverance from it by wealth or by war, by fenced city, or dark, sea-beaten ships.

antistrophe 1

And bonds tamed the son of Dryas, swift to wrath, that king of the Edonians; so paid he for his frenzied taunts, when, by the will of Dionysus, he was pent in a rocky prison. There the fierce exuberance of his madness slowly passed away. That man learned to know the god, whom in his frenzy he had provoked with mockeries; for he had sought to quell the god-possessed women, and the Bacchanalian fire; and he angered the Muses that love the flute.

strophe 2

And by the waters of the Dark Rocks, the waters of the twofold sea, are the shores of Bosporus, and Thracian Salmydessus; where Ares, neighbour to the city, saw the accurst, blinding wound dealt to the two sons of Phineus by his fierce wife, — the wound that brought darkness to those vengeance-craving orbs, smitten with her bloody hands, smitten with her shuttle for a dagger.

antistrophe 2

Pining in their misery, they bewailed their cruel doom, those sons of a mother hapless in her marriage; but she traced her descent from the ancient line of the Erechtheidae; and in far-distant caves she was nursed amid her father's storms, that child of Boreas, swift as a steed over the steep hills, a daughter of gods; yet upon her also the gray Fates bore hard, my daughter.

(*Enter* TEIRESIAS, *led by a Boy, on the spectators' right.*)

TEIRESIAS: Princes of Thebes, we have come with linked steps, both served by the eyes of one; for thus, by a guide's help, the blind must walk.

CREON: And what, aged Teiresias, are thy tidings?

TEIRESIAS: I will tell thee; and do thou hearken to the seer.

CREON: Indeed, it has not been my wont to slight thy counsel.

TEIRESIAS: Therefore didst thou steer our city's course aright.

CREON: I have felt, and can attest, thy benefits.

TEIRESIAS: Mark that now, once more, thou standest on fate's fine edge.

CREON: What means this? How I shudder at thy message!

TEIRESIAS: Thou wilt learn, when thou hearest the warnings of mine art. As I took my place on mine old seat of augury, where all birds have been wont to gather within my ken, I heard a strange voice among them; they were screaming with dire, feverish rage, that drowned their language in a jargon; and I knew that they were rending each other with their talons, murderously; the whirr of wings told no doubtful tale.

Forthwith, in fear, I essayed burnt-sacrifice on a duly kindled altar; but from my offerings the Fire-god showed no flame; a dank moisture, oozing from the thigh-flesh, trickled forth upon the embers, and smoked, and sputtered; the gall was scattered to the air; and the streaming thighs lay bared of the fat that had been wrapped round them.

Such was the failure of the rites by which I vainly asked a sign, as from this boy I learned; for he is my guide, as I am guide to others. And 'tis thy counsel that hath brought this sickness on our State. For the altars of our city and of our hearths have been tainted, one and all, by birds and dogs, with carrion from the hapless corpse, the son of Oedipus; and therefore the gods no more accept prayer and sacrifice at our hands, or the flame of meat-offering; nor doth any bird give a clear sign by its shrill cry, for they have tasted the fatness of a slain man's blood.

Think, then, on these things, my son. All men are liable to err; but when an error hath been made, that man is no longer witless or unblest who heals the ill into which he hath fallen, and remains not stubborn.

Self-will, we know, incurs the charge of folly. Nay, allow the claim of the dead; stab not the fallen; what prowess is it to slay the slain anew? I have sought thy good, and for thy good I speak: and never is it sweeter to learn from a good counsellor than when he counsels for thine own gain.

CREON: Old man, ye all shoot your shafts at me, as archers at the butts; — ye must needs practise on me with seer-craft also; — aye, the seer-tribe hath long trafficked in me, and made me their merchandise. Gain your gains, drive your trade, if ye list, in the silver-gold of Sardis and the gold of India; but ye shall not hide that man in the grave, — no, though the eagles of Zeus should bear the carrion morsels to their Master's throne — no, not for dread of that defilement will I suffer his burial: — for well I know that no mortal can defile the gods. — But, aged Teiresias, the wisest fall with a shameful fall, when they clothe shameful thoughts in fair words, for lucre's sake.

TEIRESIAS: Alas! Doth any man know, doth any consider . . .

CREON: Whereof? What general truth dost thou announce?

TEIRESIAS: How precious, above all wealth, is good counsel.

CREON: As folly, I think, is the worst mischief.

TEIRESIAS: Yet thou art tainted with that distemper.

CREON: I would not answer the seer with a taunt.

TEIRESIAS: But thou dost, in saying that I prophesy falsely.

CREON: Well, the prophet-tribe was ever fond of money.

TEIRESIAS: And the race bred of tyrants loves base gain.

CREON: Knowest thou that thy speech is spoken of thy king?

TEIRESIAS: I know it; for through me thou hast saved Thebes.

CREON: Thou art a wise seer; but thou lovest evil deeds.

TEIRESIAS: Thou wilt rouse me to utter the dread secret in my soul.

CREON: Out with it! — Only speak it not for gain.

TEIRESIAS: Indeed, methinks, I shall not, — as touching thee.

CREON: Know that thou shalt not trade on my resolve.

TEIRESIAS: Then know thou — aye, know it well — that thou shalt not live through many more courses of the sun's swift chariot, ere one begotten of thine own loins shall have been given by thee, a corpse for corpses; because thou hast thrust children of the sunlight to the shades, and ruthlessly lodged a living soul in the grave; but keepest in this world one who belongs to the gods infernal, a corpse unburied, unhonoured, all unhallowed. In such thou hast no part, nor have the gods above, but this is a violence done to them by thee. Therefore the avenging destroyers lie in wait for thee, the Furies of Hades and of the gods, thou mayest be taken in these same ills.

And mark well if I speak these things as a hireling. A time not long to be delayed shall awaken the wailing of men and of women in thy house. And a tumult of hatred against thee stirs all the cities whose mangled sons had the burial-rite from dogs, or from wild beasts, or from some winged bird that bore a polluting breath to each city that contains the hearths of the dead.

Such arrows for thy heart — since thou provokest me — have I launched at thee, archer-like, in my anger, — sure arrows, of which thou shalt not escape the smart. — Boy, lead me home, that he may spend his rage on younger men, and learn to keep a tongue more temperate, and to bear within his breast a better mind than now he bears.

(*The Boy leads* TEIRESIAS *out.*)

LEADER OF THE CHORUS: The man hath gone, O king, with dread prophecies. And, since the hair on this head, once dark, hath been white, I know that he hath never been a false prophet to our city.

CREON: I, too, know it well, and am troubled in soul. 'Tis dire to yield; but, by resistance, to smite my pride with ruin — this, too, is a dire choice.

LEADER: Son of Menoeceus, it behoves thee to take wise counsel.

CREON: What should I do, then? Speak, and I will obey.

LEADER: Go thou, and free the maiden from her rocky chamber, and make a tomb for the unburied dead.

CREON: And this is thy counsel? Thou wouldst have me yield?

LEADER: Yea, King, and with all speed; for swift harms from the gods cut short the folly of men.

CREON: Ah me, 'tis hard, but I resign my cherished resolve, — I obey. We must not wage a vain war with destiny.

LEADER: Go, thou, and do these things; leave them not to others.

CREON: Even as I am I'll go: — on, on, my servants, each and all of you, — take axes in your hands, and hasten to the ground that ye see yonder! Since our judgment hath taken this turn, I will be present to unloose her, as I myself bound her. My heart misgives me, 'tis best to keep the established laws, even to life's end.

(CREON *and his servants hasten out on the spectators' left.*)

strophe 1

CHORUS (*singing*): O thou of many names, glory of the Cadmeian bride, offspring of loud-thundering Zeus! thou who watchest over famed Italia, and reignest, where all guests are welcomed, in the sheltered plain of Eleusinian Deo! O Bacchus, dweller in Thebe, mother-city of Bacchants, by the softly-gliding stream of Ismenus, on the soil where the fierce dragon's teeth were sown!

antistrophe 1

Thou hast been seen where torch-flames glare through smoke, above the crests of the twin peaks, where move the Corycian nymphs, the votaries, hard by Castalia's stream.

Thou comest from the ivy-mantled slopes of Nysa's hills, and from the shore green with many-clustered vines, while thy name is lifted up on strains of more than mortal power, as thou visitest the ways of Thebe:

strophe 2

Thebe, of all cities, thou holdest first in honour, thou, and thy mother whom the lightning smote; and now, when all our people is captive to a violent plague, come thou with healing feet over the Parnassian height, or over the moaning strait!

antistrophe 2

O thou with whom the stars rejoice as they move, the stars whose breath is fire; O master of the voices of the night; son begotten of Zeus; appear, O king, with thine attendant Thyiads, who in night-long frenzy dance before thee, the giver of good gifts, Iacchus!

(*Enter* MESSENGER, *on the spectators' left.*)

MESSENGER: Dwellers by the house of Cadmus and of Amphion, there is no estate of mortal life that I would ever praise or blame as settled. Fortune raises and Fortune humbles the lucky or unlucky from day to day, and no one can prophesy to men concerning those things which are established. For Creon was blest once, as I count bliss; he had saved this land of Cadmus from its foes; he was clothed with sole dominion in the land; he reigned, the glorious sire of princely children. And now all hath been lost. For when a man hath forfeited his pleasures, I count him not as living, — I hold him but a breathing corpse. Heap up riches in thy house, if thou wilt; live in kingly state; yet, if there be no gladness therewith, I would not give the shadow of a vapour for all the rest, compared with joy.

LEADER OF THE CHORUS: And what is this new grief that thou hast to tell for our princes?

MESSENGER: Death; and the living are guilty for the dead.

LEADER: And who is the slayer? Who the stricken? Speak.

MESSENGER: Haemon hath perished; his blood hath been shed by no stranger.

LEADER: By his father's hand, or by his own?

MESSENGER: By his own, in wrath with his sire for the murder.

LEADER: O prophet, how true, then, hast thou proved thy word!

MESSENGER: These things stand thus; ye must consider of the rest.

LEADER: Lo, I see the hapless Eurydice, Creon's wife, approaching; she comes from the house by chance, haply, — or because she knows the tidings of her son.

(*Enter* EURYDICE *from the palace.*)

EURYDICE: People of Thebes, I heard your words as I was going forth, to salute the goddess Pallas with my prayers. Even as I was loosing the fastenings of the gate, to open it, the message of a household woe smote on mine ear: I sank back, terror-stricken, into the arms of my handmaids, and my senses fled. But say again what the tidings were; I shall hear them as one who is no stranger to sorrow.

MESSENGER: Dear lady, I will witness of what I saw, and will leave no word of the truth untold. Why, indeed, should I soothe thee with words in which I must presently be found false? Truth is ever best. — I attended thy lord as his guide to the furthest part of the plain, where the body of Polyneices, torn by dogs, still lay unpitied. We prayed the goddess of the roads, and Pluto, in mercy to restrain their wrath; we washed the dead with holy washing; and with freshly-plucked boughs we solemnly burned such relics as there were. We raised a high mound of his native earth; and then we turned away to enter the maiden's nuptial chamber with rocky couch, the caverned mansion of the bride of Death. And, from afar off, one of us heard a voice of loud wailing at that bride's unhallowed bower; and came to tell our master Creon.

And as the king drew nearer, doubtful sounds of a bitter cry floated around him! he groaned, and said in accents of anguish, 'Wretched that I am, can my foreboding be true? Am I going on the wofullest way that

ever I went? My son's voice greets me. —
Go, my servants, — haste ye nearer, and
when ye have reached the tomb, pass
through the gap, where the stones have been
wrenched away, to the cell's very mouth, —
and look, and see if 'tis Haemon's voice that
I know, or if mine ear is cheated by the
gods.'

This search, at our despairing master's
word, we went to make; and in the furthest
part of the tomb we descried *her* hanging by
the neck, slung by a thread-wrought halter
of fine linen: while *he* was embracing her
with arms thrown around her waist, — be-
wailing the loss of his bride who is with the
dead, and his father's deeds, and his own ill-
starred love.

But his father, when he saw him, cried
aloud with a dread cry and went in, and
called to him with a voice of wailing: —
'Unhappy, what a deed hast thou done!
What thought hath come to thee? What
manner of mischance hath marred thy
reason? Come forth, my child! I pray thee —
I implore!' But the boy glared at him with
fierce eyes, spat in his face, and, without a
word of answer, drew his cross-hilted sword:
— as his father rushed forth in flight, he
missed his aim; — then, hapless one, wroth
with himself, he straightway leaned with all
his weight against his sword, and drove it,
half its length, into his side; and, while sense
lingered, he clasped the maiden to his faint
embrace, and, as he gasped, sent forth on
her pale cheek the swift stream of the oozing
blood.

Corpse enfolding corpse he lies; he hath
won his nuptial rites, poor youth, not here,
yet in the halls of Death; and he hath witnessed to mankind that, of all curses which
cleave to man, ill counsel is the sovereign
curse.

(EURYDICE *retires into the house.*)

LEADER: What wouldst thou augur from this?
The lady hath turned back, and is gone,
without a word, good or evil.

MESSENGER: I, too, am startled; yet I nourish
the hope that, at these sore tidings of her
son, she cannot deign to give her sorrow

public vent, but in the privacy of the house
will set her hand-maids to mourn the household grief. For she is not untaught of discretion, that she should err.

LEADER: I know not; but to me, at least, a
strained silence seems to portend peril, no
less than vain abundance of lament.

MESSENGER: Well, I will enter the house, and
learn whether indeed she is not hiding some
repressed purpose in the depths of a passionate heart. Yea, thou sayest well: excess
of silence, too, may have a perilous meaning.

(*The* MESSENGER *goes into the palace. Enter*
CREON, *on the spectators' left, with attendants,
carrying the shrouded body of* HAEMON *on a
bier. The following lines between* CREON *and
the* CHORUS *are chanted responsively.*)

CHORUS: Lo, yonder the king himself draws
near, bearing that which tells too clear a tale,
— the work of no stranger's madness, — if
we may say it, — but of his own misdeeds.

strophe 1
CREON: Woe for the sins of a darkened soul,
stubborn sins, fraught with death! Ah, ye
behold us, the sire who hath slain, the son
who hath perished! Woe is me, for the
wretched blindness of my counsels! Alas,
my son, thou hast died in thy youth, by a
timeless doom, woe is me! — thy spirit hath
fled, — not by thy folly, but by mine own!

strophe 2
CHORUS: Ah me, how all too late thou seemest
to see the right!

CREON: Ah me, I have learned the bitter lesson!
But then, methinks, oh then, some god
smote me from above with crushing weight,
and hurled me into ways of cruelty, woe is
me, — overthrowing and trampling on my
joy! Woe, woe, for the troublous toils of
men!

(*Enter* MESSENGER *from the house.*)

MESSENGER: Sire, thou hast come, methinks, as
one whose hands are not empty, but who
hath store laid up besides; thou bearest
yonder burden with thee; and thou art soon
to look upon the woes within thy house.

CREON: And what worse ill is yet to follow upon ills?

MESSENGER: Thy queen hath died, true mother of yon corpse — ah, hapless lady! — by blows newly dealt.

antistrophe 1
CREON: Oh Hades, all-receiving, whom no sacrifice can appease! Hast thou, then, no mercy for me? O thou herald of evil, bitter tidings, what word dost thou utter? Alas, I was already as dead, and thou hast smitten me anew! What sayest thou, my son? What is this new message that thou bringest — woe, woe is me! — of a wife's doom, — of slaughter heaped on slaughter?

CHORUS: Thou canst behold: 'tis no longer hidden within.

(*The doors of the palace are opened, and the corpse of* EURYDICE *is disclosed.*)

antistrophe 2
CREON: Ah me, — yonder I behold a new, a second woe! What destiny, ah what, can yet await me? I have but now raised my son in my arms, — and there, again, I see a corpse before me! Alas, alas, unhappy mother! Alas, my child!

MESSENGER: There, at the altar, self-stabbed with a keen knife, she suffered her darkening eyes to close, when she had wailed for the noble fate of Megareus who died before, and then for his fate who lies there, — and when, with her last breath, she had invoked evil fortunes upon thee, the slayer of thy sons.

strophe 3
CREON: Woe, woe! I thrill with dread. Is there none to strike me to the heart with two-edged sword? — O miserable that I am, and steeped in miserable anguish!

MESSENGER: Yea, both this son's doom, and that other's, were laid to thy charge by her whose corpse thou seest.

CREON: And what was the manner of the violent deed by which she passed away?

MESSENGER: Her own hand struck her to the heart, when she had learned her son's sorely lamented fate.

strophe 4
CREON: Ah me, this guilt can never be fixed on any other of mortal kind, for my acquittal! I, even I, was thy slayer, wretched that I am — I own the truth. Lead me away, O my servants, lead me hence with all speed, whose life is but as death!

CHORUS: Thy counsels are good, if there can be good with ills; briefest is best, when trouble is in our path.

antistrophe 3
CREON: Oh, let it come, let it appear, that fairest of fates for me, that brings my last day, — aye, best fate of all! Oh, let it come, that I may never look upon to-morrow's light.

CHORUS: These things are in the future; present tasks claim our care: the ordering of the future rests where it should rest.

CREON: All my desires, at least, were summed in that prayer.

CHORUS: Pray thou no more; for mortals have no escape from destined woe.

antistrophe 4
CREON: Lead me away, I pray you; a rash, foolish man; who have slain thee, ah my son, unwittingly, and thee, too, my wife — unhappy that I am! I know not which way I should bend my gaze, or where I should seek support; for all is amiss with that which is in my hands, — and yonder, again, a crushing fate hath leapt upon my head.

(*As* CREON *is being conducted into the palace, the* LEADER OF THE CHORUS *speaks the closing verses.*)

LEADER: Wisdom is the supreme part of happiness; and reverence towards the gods must be inviolate. Great words of prideful men are ever punished with great blows, and, in old age, teach the chastened to be wise.

The Pot of Gold

When the grandeur that was Rome began, it was very much overshadowed by the glory that had been Greece. Greek art was reverenced and Roman drama followed in its footsteps. The religious aspects of Greek drama vanished, but the Greek myths remained. The open-air Greek theatre gave way to an enclosed auditorium, but the Greek *skene* with its three doors and raised platform became a row of three houses with a street in front of it. The Attic dignity and philosophical speculation gave way to boisterousness and in the end obscenity, but the spirit of Greek writers of "New Comedy," such as Menander, remained in the Roman theatre.

Using Greek meters and plots and characters from Greek "New Comedy," Plautus became a master of a very popular broad Roman comedy, for he had the true knack — Julius Cæsar praised it as *vis comica* — for eliciting laughter. His epitaph praises his versifying ("all his measures beyond measure wept for him" at his death) but his works have survived, surely, because of his clever manipulation of stock characters, his ingenuity in plotting, and his jokes, some of which you may have heard as recently as in *A Funny Thing Happened on the Way to the Forum* or last night's situation comedy on television. Horace grumpily said Plautus wore the dress of comedy in a slovenly way, but Plautus survives on vitality and verve.

Julius Cæsar's librarian, Marcus Terentius Varro (who wrote 620 books himself), made up a list of 21 plays which he considered Plautus had written, narrowing it down from the 130 plays that had been attributed to Plautus. In contrast, all the works of the other Roman comic genius, Terence (born in Carthage *c.* 195 B.C.), have survived. Terence, born in Africa as a slave, became more deft, perhaps, with parallel plots and other devices and in his half dozen comedies outshone Plautus in literary polish. It was Terence who coined phrases like "a word to the wise is sufficient" and "I am a man; nothing human is alien to me." It was Plautus, however, who has kept them laughing.

The record of Plautus' life has been put together mostly from hints in his plays themselves. Titus Maccius Plautus (*c.* 255–184 B.C.) was born at Sarsina in Umbria, northern Italy. In Rome he was a stagehand or stage carpenter, which enabled him to save money and eventually to leave Rome and start in foreign trade. His business failed and he found himself turning a flourmill for a baker. He wrote three plays, beginning about 224 B.C., which launched him on a literary career in a time when people liked knockabout comedy and pantomime, *palliatæ* and other ancestors of the *commedia dell'arte* (such as the *atellanæ*, with its rude jokes), imitation Greek tragedy and extravagant spectacle in the *Circus Maximus* or the Flavian Amphitheatre. In 240 B.C. a Greek, Livius Andronicus, adapted a Greek "New Comedy" for the Roman stage. Then Gnæus Nævius (*c.* 264–194 B.C.) from Campania began to write original plays in Latin.

Plautus, it might be said, created the musical comedy, borrowing from Greek "properties" and tailoring them for the audiences of his time, packing them with songs and jokes and topical references. So vital were his works that five centuries later (says Arnobius the Elder) they were still "running" in the reign of the emperor Diocletian and nearly two thousand years later they were strongly influencing another master of comedy, Molière: *The Pot of Gold (Aulularia)* was the basis of *The Miser (L'Avare)* as Terence's *Phormio* served for *Les Fourberies de Scapin*. Shakespeare rewrote Plautus' story of the Menæchmi twins as *The Comedy of Errors*, Ben Jonson borrowed several of Plautus' devices and characters (including the *miles gloriosus* or boasting soldier), and in modern times Plautus' work is echoed in things as different as the "boffo" comedy of burlesque "top bananas," the light-hearted foolery of the musical *The Boys from Syracuse* and the sophisticated wit of Jean Giraudoux's *Amphytrion 38*. Try to see how many of Plautus' comic elements (mistaken identity, the clever servant, etc.) you can identify in modern plays, films, television series, and comic strips.

Plautine comedies have come down to us in various stages of disrepair: lines are missing from some plays, even whole scenes. *The Pot of Gold* breaks off abruptly: the rest is lost. You might wish to try your hand at completing it in the style of Plautus, striving as he does for liveliness onstage and belly-laughs in the audience. Ancient plot summaries give us an outline of what needs to be supplied: Lyconides gets his servant Strobilus to return the money and obtains from Euclio not only the hand of Phædria in marriage but the pot of gold itself, as a dowry. Don't worry about probability in the plot (see the *Menæchmi*) or harmony of the elements (see *Miles Gloriosus*) if that deprives you of opportunities to enhance the already well-developed character of Euclio or devise new twists for the servant (for ingenuity see Tranio in *Mostellaria*). Wrap it up quickly (see *Captivi*, which the German critic Lessing went so far as to call the best play ever presented on the stage) and miss no chances for a sight gag or a funny line.

If you think writing in the style of Plautus is beyond you — don't decide that until you give it a good try — compare and contrast *The Pot of Gold* with Molière's *Miser*. What do you think appealed to Plautus' imagination in the play and what does he do with his materials?

THE POT OF GOLD

Plautus

*Translated from the Latin
by Paul Nixon*

ARGUMENT OF THE PLAY (I)

A miserly old man named Euclio, a man who would hardly trust his very self, on finding a pot full of treasure buried within his house, hides it away again deep in the ground, and, beside himself with terror, keeps watch over it. His daughter had been wronged by Lyconides. Meanwhile an old gentleman, one Megadorus, is persuaded by his sister to marry, and asks the miser for his daughter's hand. The dour old fellow at length consents, and, fearing for his pot, takes it from the house and hides it in one place after another. The servant of this Lyconides, the man who had wronged the girl, plots against the miser; and Lyconides himself entreats his uncle, Megadorus, to give up the girl, and let him, the man that loves her, marry her. After a time Euclio, who had been tricked out of his pot, recovers it unexpectedly and joyfully bestows his daughter upon Lyconides.

ARGUMENT OF THE PLAY (II)*

Euclio, on finding a pot full of gold, is dreadfully worried, and watches over it with the greatest vigilance. Lyconides wrongs his daughter. This girl, undowered though she is, Megadorus wishes to marry, and he cheerfully supplies cooks and provisions for the wedding feast. Anxious about his gold, Euclio hides it outside the house. Everything he does having been witnessed, a rascally servant of the girls' assailant steals it. His master informs Euclio of it, and receives from him gold, wife, and son.

DRAMATIS PERSONÆ

The Household God of Euclio, *the Prologue*
Euclio, *an old gentleman of Athens*
Staphyla, *his old slave*
Eunomia, *a lady of Athens*
Megadorus, *an old gentleman of Athens,
    Eunomia's brother*
Pythodicus, *his slave*
Congrio ⎫
Anthrax ⎬ *cooks*
Strobilus, *slave of Lyconides*
Lyconides, *a young gentleman of Athens,
    Eunomia's son*
Phaedria, *Euclio's daughter*
Music Girls

Scene: — *Athens. A street on which are the houses of Euclio and Megadorus, a narrow lane between them; in front, an altar.*

PROLOGUE

Spoken by Euclio's Household God
    That no one may wonder who I am, I shall inform you briefly. I am the Household God of that family from whose house you saw me come. For many years now I have possessed this dwelling, and preserved it for the sire and grandsire of its present occupant. Now this man's grandsire as a suppliant entrusted to me, in utter secrecy, a hoard of gold: he buried it in the centre of the hearth, entreating me to guard it for him. When he died he could not bear — so covetous was he — to reveal its existence to his own son, and he chose to leave him penniless rather than apprise him of this treasure. Some land,

---

Plautus, 5 volumes in the Loeb Classical Library, edited by T. E. Page et al.

* ARGUMENT (II): In Latin the nine lines of verse form an acrostic of *AULULARIA* (*The Pot of Gold*). The play itself in Latin verse is a mixture of meters.

a little only, he did leave him, whereon to toil and moil for a miserable livelihood.

After the death of him who had committed the gold to my keeping, I began to observe whether the son would hold me in greater honour than his father had. As a matter of fact, his neglect grew and grew apace, and he showed me less honour. I did the same by him: so he also died. He left a son who occupies this house at present, a man of the same mould as his sire and grandsire. He has one daughter. She prays to me constantly, with daily gifts of incense, or wine, or something: she gives me garlands. Out of regard for her I caused Euclio to discover the treasure here in order that he might the more easily find her a husband, if he wished. For she has been ravished by a young gentleman of very high rank. He knows who it is that he has wronged; who he is she does not know, and as for her father, he is ignorant of the whole affair.

I shall make the old gentleman who lives next door here (*pointing*) ask for her hand to-day. My reason for so doing is that the man who wronged her may marry her the more easily. And the old gentleman who is to ask for her hand is the uncle of the young gentleman who violated her by night at the festival of Ceres. (*an uproar in Euclio's house*) But there is old Euclio clamouring within as usual, and turning his ancient servant out of doors lest she learn his secret. I suppose he wishes to look at his gold and see that it is not stolen.

(*Exit.*)

ACT ONE

EUCLIO (*within*): Out with you, I say! Come now, out with you! By the Lord, you've got to get out of here, you snook-around, you, with your prying and spying.

(*Enter* STAPHYLA *from* EUCLIO'S *house, followed by* EUCLIO *who is pushing and beating her.*)

STAPHYLA (*groaning*): Oh, what makes you go a-hitting a poor wretch like me, sir?

EUCLIO (*savagely*): To make sure you are a poor wretch, so as to give a bad lot the bad time she deserves.

STAPHYLA: Why, what did you push me out of the house for now?

EUCLIO: I give my reasons to you, you, — you patch of beats, you? Over there with you, (*pointing*) away from the door! (STAPHYLA *hobbles to place indicated.*) Just look at her, will you, — how she creeps along! See here, do you know what'll happen to you? Now by heaven, only let me lay my hand on a club or a stick and I'll accelerate that tortoise crawl for you!

STAPHYLA (*aside*): Oh, I wish Heaven would make me hang myself, I do! Better that than slaving it for you at this rate, I'm sure.

EUCLIO (*aside*): Hear the old criminal mumbling away to herself, though! (*aloud*) Ah! those eyes of yours, you old sinner! By heaven, I'll dig 'em out for you, I will, so that you can't keep watching me whatever I do. Get farther off still! still farther! still — Whoa! Stand there! You budge a finger's breadth a nail's breadth, from that spot; you so much as turn your head till I say the word, and by the Almighty, the next minute I'll send you to the gallows for a lesson, so I will. (*aside*) A worse reprobate than this old crone I never did see, no, never. Oh, but how horribly scared I am she'll come some sly dodge on me when I'm not expecting it, and smell out the place where the gold is hidden. She has eyes in the very back of her head, the hellcat. Now I'll just go see if the gold is where I hid it. Dear, dear, it worries the life out of me!

(*Exit* EUCLIO *into house.*)

STAPHYLA: Mercy me! What's come over master, what crazy streak he's got, I can't imagine, — driving a poor woman out of the house this way ten times a day, often. Goodness gracious, what whim-whams the man's got into his head I don't see. Never shuts his eyes all night: yes, and then in the daytime he's sitting around the house the whole livelong day, for all the world like a lame cobbler. How I'm going to hide the young mistress's disgrace now is beyond me, and she with her time so near. There's nothing better for me to do, as I see, than tie a rope round my neck and dangle myself out into one long capital I.

SCENE TWO

(*Re-enter* EUCLIO *from house.*)

EUCLIO (*aside*): At last I can feel easy about leaving the house, now I have made certain everything is all right inside. (*to* STAPHYLA) Go back in there this instant, you, and keep watch inside.

STAPHYLA (*tartly*): I suppose so! So I'm to keep watch inside, am I? You aren't afraid anyone'll walk away with the house, are you? I vow we've got nothing else there for thieves to take — all full of emptiness as it is, and cobwebs.

EUCLIO: It is surprising Providence wouldn't make a King Philip or Darius of me for your benefit, you viper, you! (*threateningly*) I want those cobwebs watched! I'm poor, poor; I admit it, I put up with it; I take what the gods give me. In with you, bolt the door. I shall be back soon. No outsider is to be let in, mind you. And in case anyone should be looking for a light, see you put the fire out so that no one will have any reason to come to you for it. Mark my words, if that fire stays alive, I'll extinguish you instantly. And then water — if anyone asks for water, tell him it's all run out. As for a knife, or an axe, or a pestle, or a mortar, — things the neighbours are all the time wanting to borrow — tell 'em burglars got in and stole the whole lot. I won't have a living soul let into my house while I'm gone — there! Yes, and what's more, listen here, if Dame Fortune herself comes along, don't you let her in.

STAPHYLA: Goodness me, she won't get in: she'll see to that herself, I fancy. Why, she never comes to our house at all, no matter how near she is.

EUCLIO: Keep still and go inside. (*advances on her*).

STAPHYLA (*hurrying out of reach*): I'm still, sir, I'm going!

EUCLIO: Mind you lock the door, both bolts. I'll soon be back.

(*Exit* STAPHYLA *into house.*)

It's agony having to leave the house, downright agony. Oh my God, how I do hate to go! But I have my reasons. The director of our ward gave notice he was going to make us a present of two shillings a man; and the minute I let it pass without putting in my claim, they'd all be suspecting I had gold at home, I'm sure they would. No, it doesn't look natural for a poor man to think so little of even a tiny bit of money as not to go ask for his two shillings. Why, even now, hard as I try to keep every one from finding out, it seems as if every one knew: it seems as if every one has a heartier way of saying good day than they used to. Up they come, and stop, and shake hands, and keep asking me how I'm feeling, and how I'm getting on, and what I'm doing. Well, I must get along to where I'm bound; and then I'll come back home just as fast as I possibly can.

(*Exit* EUCLIO.)

ACT TWO

(*Enter* EUNOMIA *and* MEGADORUS *from latter's house.*)

EUNOMIA: Brother, I do hope you'll believe I say this out of my loyalty to you and for your welfare, as a true sister should. Of course I'm well enough aware you men think us women are a bother; yes, awful chatterboxes — that's the name we all have, and (*ruefully*) it fits. And then that common saying: "Never now, nor through the ages, never any woman dumb." But just the same, do remember this one thing, brother, — that I am closer to you and you to me than anyone else in the whole world. So both of us ought to advise and counsel each other as to what we feel is to either's advantage, not keep such things back or be afraid to speak out openly; we ought to confide in one another fully, you and I. This is why I've taken you aside out here now — so that we can have a quiet talk on a matter that concerns you intimately.

MEGADORUS (*warmly*): Let's have your hand, you best of women!

EUNOMIA (*pretending to look about*): Where is she? Who on earth is that best of women?

MEGADORUS: Yourself.

EUNOMIA: You say that — you?

MEGADORUS (*banteringly*): Oh well, if you deny it —

EUNOMIA: Really now, you ought to be truthful. There's no such thing, you know, as picking out the best woman: it's only a question of comparative badness, brother.

MEGADORUS: My own opinion precisely: I'll never differ with you there, sister, you may count on that.

EUNOMIA: Now do give me your attention, there's a dear.

MEGADORUS: It is all your own: use me, command me — anything you wish.

EUNOMIA: I'm going to advise you to do something that I think will be the very best thing in the world for you.

MEGADORUS: Quite like you, sister.

EUNOMIA: I certainly hope so.

MEGADORUS: And what is this something, my dear?

EUNOMIA: Something that will make for your everlasting welfare. You should have children — God grant you may! — and I want you to marry.

MEGADORUS: Oh-h-h, murder!

EUNOMIA: How so?

MEGADORUS: Well, you're knocking my poor brains out with such a proposition, my dear girl: you're talking cobble-stones.

EUNOMIA: Now, now, do what your sister tells you.

MEGADORUS: I would, if it appealed to me.

EUNOMIA: It would be a good thing for you.

MEGADORUS: Yes — to die before marrying. (*pause*) All right, I'll marry anyone you please, on this condition, though: her wedding to-morrow, and her wake the day after. Still wish it, on this condition? Produce her! Arrange for the festivities!

EUNOMIA: I can get you one with ever so big a dowry, dear. To be sure, she's not a young girl — middle-aged, as a matter of fact. I'll see about it for you, brother, if you want.

MEGADORUS: You don't mind my asking you a question, I dare say?

EUNOMIA: Why, of course not; anything you like.

MEGADORUS: Now supposing a man pretty well on in life marries a lady of maturity and this aged female should happen to show intentions of making the old fellow a father — can you doubt but that the name in store for that youngster is Postumus? [1] See here, sister, I'll relieve you of all this and save you trouble. I'm rich enough, thanks be to heaven and our forbears. And I have no fancy at all for those ladies of high station and hauteur and fat dowries, with their shouting and their ordering and their ivory trimmed carriages and their purple and fine linen that cost a husband his liberty.

EUNOMIA: For mercy's sake tell me who you do want to marry, then!

MEGADORUS: I'm going to. You know the old gentleman — rather hard up, poor fellow, — that lives next door, Euclio?

EUNOMIA: Yes indeed. Why, he seems quite nice.

MEGADORUS. It's his daughter — there's the engagement I'm eager for. Now don't make

---

1 The last born, or born after the father's death.

a fuss, sister. I know what you're about to say — that she's poor. But this particular poor girl suits me.

EUNOMIA: God's blessing on your choice, dear!

MEGADORUS: I trust so.

EUNOMIA (*about to leave*): Well, there's nothing I can do?

MEGADORUS: Yes — take good care of yourself.

EUNOMIA: You too, brother.

(*Exit* EUNOMIA.)

MEGADORUS: Now for an interview with Euclio, if he's at home. (*looking down street*) Hullo, though! here he is! Just getting back from somewhere or other.

SCENE TWO

(*Enter* EUCLIO.)

EUCLIO (*without seeing* MEGADORUS): I knew it! Something told me I was going on a fool's errand when I left the house; that's why I hated to go. Why, there wasn't a single man of our ward there, or the director either, who ought to have distributed the money. Now I'll hurry up and hurry home: I'm here in the body, but that's where my mind is.

MEGADORUS (*advancing with outstretched hand*): Good day to you, Euclio, yes, and the best of everything to you always!

EUCLIO (*taking hand gingerly*): God bless you, Megadorus.

MEGADORUS: How goes it? All right, are you? Feeling as well as you could wish?

EUCLIO (*aside*): There's something behind it when a rich man puts on that smooth air with a poor one. Now that fellow knows I've got gold: that's why he's so uncommon smooth with his salutations.

MEGADORUS: You say you are well?

EUCLIO: Heavens, no: I feel low, very low — in funds.

MEGADORUS (*cheerily*): Well, well, man, if you have a contented mind, you've got enough to enjoy life with.

EUCLIO (*aside, frightened*): Oh, good Lord! The old woman has let on to him about the gold! It's discovered, clear as can be! I'll cut her tongue out, I'll tear her eyes out, the minute I get at her in the house!

MEGADORUS: What is that you're saying to yourself?

EUCLIO (*startled*): Just . . . how awful it is to be poor. And I with a grown-up girl, without a penny of dowry, that I can't get off my hands or find a husband for.

MEGADORUS (*clapping him on the back*): There, there, Euclio! Cheer up. She shall be married: I'll help you out. Come now, call on me, if you need anything.

EUCLIO (*aside*): When he agrees to give he wants to grab! Mouth wide open to gobble down my gold! Holds up a bit of bread in one hand and has a stone in the other! I don't trust one of these rich fellows when he's so monstrous civil to a poor man. They give you a cordial handshake, and squeeze something out of you at the same time. I know all about those octopuses that touch a thing and then — stick.

MEGADORUS: I should be glad to have a moment of your time, Euclio. I want to have a brief talk with you on a matter that concerns us both.

EUCLIO (*aside*): Oh, God save us! My gold's been hooked, and now he wants to make a deal with me! I see it all! But I'll go in and look. (*hurries toward house*)

MEGADORUS: Where are you off to?

EUCLIO: Just a moment! . . . I'll be back . . . the fact is . . . I must see to something at home.

(*Exit into house.*)

MEGADORUS: By Jove! I suppose he'll think I'm making fun of him when I speak about his giving me his daughter; poverty never made a fellow closer-fisted.

(*Re-enter* EUCLIO.)

EUCLIO (*aside*): Thank the Lord, I'm saved! It's safe — that is, if it's all there. Ah, but that was a dreadful moment! I nearly expired before I got in the house. (*to* MEGADORUS) Here I am, Megadorus, if you want anything of me.

MEGADORUS: Thanks. Now I trust you won't mind answering the questions I'm going to ask.

EUCLIO (*cautiously*): No-no — that is, if you don't ask any I don't like to answer.

MEGADORUS: Frankly now, what do you think of my family connections?

EUCLIO (*grudgingly*): Good.

MEGADORUS: And my sense of honour?

EUCLIO: Good.

MEGADORUS: And my general conduct?

EUCLIO: Not bad, not disreputable.

MEGADORUS: You know my age?

EUCLIO: Getting on, getting on, I know that — (*aside*) financially, too.

MEGADORUS: Now Euclio, I've always considered you a citizen of the true, trusty type, by Jove, I certainly have, and I do still.

EUCLIO (*aside*): He's got a whiff of my gold. (*aloud*) Well, what do you want?

MEGADORUS: Now that we appreciate each other, I'm going to ask you — and may it turn out happily for you and your girl and me — to give me your daughter in marriage. Promise you will.

EUCLIO (*whining*): Now, now, Megadorus! This is unlike you, unworthy of you, making fun of a poor man like me that never harmed you or yours. Why, I never said or did a thing to you to deserve being treated so.

MEGADORUS: Good Lord, man! I didn't come here to make fun of you, and I'm not making fun of you: I couldn't think of such a thing.

EUCLIO: Then why are you asking for my daughter?

MEGADORUS: Why? So that we may all of us make life pleasanter for one another.

EUCLIO: Now here's the way it strikes me, Megadorus, — you're a rich man, a man of position: but as for me, I'm poor, awfully poor, dreadfully poor. Now if I was to marry off my daughter to you, it strikes me you'd be the ox and I'd be the donkey. When I was hitched up with you and couldn't pull my share of the load, down I'd drop, I, the donkey, in the mud; and you, the ox, wouldn't pay any more attention to me than if I'd never been born at all. You would be too much for me: and my own kind would haw-haw at me: and if there should be a falling out, neither party would let me have stable quarters: the donkeys would chew me up and the oxen would run me through. It is a very hazardous business for donkeys to climb into the ox set.

MEGADORUS: But honourable human beings — the more closely connected you are with them, the better. Come, come, accept my offer: listen to what I say and promise her to me.

EUCLIO: But not one penny of dowry can I give.

MEGADORUS: Don't. Only let me have a girl that's good, and she has dowry enough.

EUCLIO (*forcing a laugh*): I mention this just so that you mayn't think I've found some treasure.

MEGADORUS: Yes, yes, I understand. Promise.

EUCLIO: So be it. (*aside, starting at noise*) Oh, my God! Can it be I'm ruined, ruined?

MEGADORUS: What's the matter?

EUCLIO: That noise? What was it — a sort of clinking sound?

(*Exit into house hurriedly.*)

MEGADORUS (*not noticing his departure*): I told them to do some digging in my garden here. (*looking around*) But where is the man? Gone away and left me — without a word! Scorns me, now he sees I desire his friendship! Quite the usual thing, that. Yes, let a wealthy man try to get the regard of a poorer one, and the poor one is afraid to meet him half-way: his timidity makes him injure his own interests. Then when it's too late and the opportunity is gone he longs to have it again.

(*Re-enter* Euclio.)

Euclio (*to* Staphyla *within*): By heaven, if I don't have your tongue torn out by the very roots, I give you orders, give you full authority, to hand me over to anyone you please to be skinned alive. (*approaches* Megadorus)

Megadorus: Upon my word, Euclio! So you think I am the proper sort of man to make a fool of, at my time of life, and without the slightest reason.

Euclio: Bless my soul! I'm not making a fool of you, Megadorus: I couldn't if I would.

Megadorus (*doubtfully*): Well now, do you mean I am to have your daughter?

Euclio: On the understanding she goes with the dowry I mentioned.

Megadorus: You consent, then?

Euclio: I consent.

Megadorus: And may God prosper us!

Euclio: Yes, yes, — and mind you remember our agreement about the dowry: she doesn't bring you a single penny.

Megadorus: I remember.

Euclio: But I know the way you folks have of juggling things: now it's on and now it's off, now it's off and now it's on, just as you like.

Megadorus: You shall have no occasion to quarrel with me. But about the marriage — there's no reason for not having it to-day, is there?

Euclio: Dear, dear, no! The very thing, the very thing!

Megadorus: I'll go and make arrangements, then. (*turning to leave*) Anything else I can do?

Euclio: Only that. Go along. Good-bye.

Megadorus (*calling at the door of his house*): Hey, Pythodicus! quick! (*Enter* Pythodicus)

Down to the market with me — come, look alive! (*Exeunt.*)

Euclio (*looking after them*): He's gone! Ah, ye immortal gods, doesn't money count! That is what he's gaping after. That is why he's so set on being my son-in-law. (*goes to the door and calls*) Where are you, you blabber, telling the whole neighbourhood I'm going to give my daughter a dowry! Hi-i! Staphyla! It's you I'm calling. Can't you hear!

SCENE THREE

(*Enter* Staphyla) Hurry up with the dishes inside there and give them a good scouring. I have betrothed my daughter: she marries Megadorus here to-day.

Staphyla: God bless them! (*hastily*) Goodness, though! It can't be done. This is too sudden.

Euclio: Silence! Off with you! Have things ready by the time I get back from the forum. And lock the door, mind; I shall be here soon. (*Exit* Euclio.)

Staphyla: What shall I do now? Now we're all but ruined, the young mistress and me: now it's all but public property about her being disgraced and brought to bed. We can't conceal it, we can't keep it dark any longer now. But I must go in and do what master ordered me before he gets back. Oh deary me! I'm afraid I've got to take a drink of trouble and tribulation mixed.

(*Exit* Staphyla *into house.*)

SCENE FOUR   *An hour has elapsed.*

(*Enter* Pythodicus *bringing cooks,* Anthrax *and* Congrio, *music girls,* Phrygia *and* Eleusium, *and attendants, with provisions from the market and two lambs.*)

Pythodicus (*importantly*): After master did the marketing and hired the cooks and these music girls at the forum, he told me to take and divide all he'd got into two parts.

Anthrax: By Jupiter, you shan't make two parts of me, let me tell you that plainly! If you'd like to have the whole of me anywhere, why, I'll accommodate you.

CONGRIO (*to* ANTHRAX): You pretty boy, yes, you nice little everybody's darling, you! Why, if anyone wanted to make two parts of a real man out of you, you oughtn't to be cut up about it.

PYTHODICUS: Now, now, Anthrax, I mean that otherwise from what you make out. Look here, my master's marrying to-day.

ANTHRAX: Who's the lady?

PYTHODICUS: Daughter of old Euclio that lives next door here. Yes sir, and what's more, he's to have half this stuff here, and one cook and one music girl, too, so master said.

ANTHRAX: You mean to say half goes to him and half to you folks?

PYTHODICUS: Just what I do mean.

ANTHRAX: I say, couldn't the old boy pay for the catering for his daughter's wedding his own self?

PYTHODICUS (*scornfully*): Pooh!

ANTHRAX: What's the matter?

PYTHODICUS: The matter, eh? You couldn't squeeze as much out of that old chap as you could out of a pumice stone.

ANTHRAX (*incredulously*): Oh, really now!

PYTHODICUS: That's a fact. Judge for yourself. Why, I tell you he begins bawling for heaven and earth to witness that he's bankrupt, gone to everlasting smash, the moment a puff of smoke from his beggarly fire manages to get out of his house. Why, when he goes to bed he strings a bag over his jaws.

ANTHRAX: What for?

PYTHODICUS: So as not to chance losing any breath when he's asleep.

ANTHRAX: Oh yes! And he puts a stopper on his lower windpipe, doesn't he, so as not to chance losing any breath while he's asleep?

PYTHODICUS (*ingenuously*): You should believe me, I believe, just as I should believe you.

ANTHRAX (*hurriedly*): Oh, no, no! I do believe, of course!

PYTHODICUS: But listen to this, will you? Upon my word, after he takes a bath it just breaks him all up to throw away the water.

ANTHRAX: D'ye think the old buck could be induced to make us a present of a couple of hundred pounds to buy ourselves off with?

PYTHODICUS: Lord! He wouldn't make you a loan of his hunger, no sir, not if you begged him for it. Why, the other day when a barber cut his nails for him he collected all the clippings and took 'em home.

ANTHRAX: My goodness, he's quite a tight one, from what you say.

PYTHODICUS: Honest now, would you believe a man could be so tight and live so wretched? Once a kite flew off with a bit of food of his: down goes the fellow to the magistrate's, blubbering all the way, and there he begins, howling and yowling, demanding to have the kite bound over for trial. Oh, I could tell hundreds of stories about him if I had time. (*to both cooks*) But which of you is the quicker? Tell me that.

ANTHRAX: I am, and a whole lot better, too.

PYTHODICUS: At cooking I mean, not thieving.

ANTHRAX: Well, I mean cooking.

PYTHODICUS (*to* CONGRIO): And how about you?

CONGRIO (*with a meaning glance at* ANTHRAX): I'm what I look.

ANTHRAX: He's nothing but a market-day cook, that chap: he only gets a job once a week.

CONGRIO: You running me down, you? You five letter man, you! You T-H-I-E-F!

ANTHRAX: Five letter man yourself! Yes, and five times — penned!

SCENE FIVE

PYTHODICUS (*to* ANTHRAX): Come, come, shut up, you: and this fattest lamb here, (*pointing*) take it and go over to our house.

ANTHRAX (*grinning triumphantly at* CONGRIO): Aye, aye, sir.

(*Exit* ANTHRAX *into house of* MEGADORUS *leading lamb.*)

PYTHODICUS: Congrio, you take this one he's left (*pointing*) and go into that house there, (*pointing to* EUCLIO's) and as for you, (*indicating some of the attendants*) you follow him. The rest of you come over to our house.

CONGRIO: Hang it! That's no way to divide: they've got the fattest lamb.

PYTHODICUS: Oh well, I'll give you the fattest music girl. (*turning to girls*) That means you, Phrygia: you go with him. As for you, Eleusium, you step over to our place. (*Exeunt* ELEUSIUM *and others into house of* MEGADORUS.)

CONGRIO: Oh, you're a wily one, Pythodicus! Shoving me off on this old screw, eh? If I ask for anything there, I can ask myself hoarse before I get a thing.

PYTHODICUS: An ungrateful blockhead is what you are. The idea of doing you a favour, when it's only thrown away!

CONGRIO: Eh? How so?

PYTHODICUS: How so? Well, in the first place there won't be an uproarious gang in that house to get in your way: if you need anything, just you fetch it from home so as not to waste time asking for it. Here at our establishment, though, we do have a great big uproarious gang of servants, and knick-knackery and jewellery and clothes and silver plate lying about. Now if anything was missing, — of course it's easy for you to keep your hands off, provided there's nothing in reach, — they'd say: "The cooks got away with it! Collar 'em! Tie 'em up! Thrash 'em! Throw 'em in the dungeon!" Now over there (*pointing to* EUCLIO's) nothing like this will happen to you — as there's nothing at all about for you to filch. (*going toward* EUCLIO's *house*) Come along.

CONGRIO (*sulkily*): Coming. (*he and the rest follow*)

SCENE SIX

PYTHODICUS (*knocking at door*): Hey! Staphyla! Come here and open the door.

STAPHYLA (*within*): Who is it?

PYTHODICUS: Pythodicus.

STAPHYLA (*sticking her head out*): What do you want?

PYTHODICUS: Take these cooks and the music girl and the supplies for the wedding festival. Megadorus told us to take 'em over to Euclio's.

STAPHYLA (*examining the provisions disappointedly*): Whose festival are they going to celebrate, Pythodicus? Ceres'?

PYTHODICUS: Why hers?

STAPHYLA: Well, no tipple's[2] been brought, as I notice.

PYTHODICUS: But there'll be some all right when the old gent gets back from the forum.

STAPHYLA: We haven't got any firewood in the house.

CONGRIO: Any rafters in it?

STAPHYLA: Mercy, yes.

CONGRIO: There's firewood in it, then: never mind going for any.

STAPHYLA: Hey? You godless thing! even though you are a devotee of Vulcan, do you want us to burn our house down, all for your dinner or your pay? (*advances on him*)

CONGRIO (*shrinking back*): I don't, I don't!

PYTHODICUS: Take 'em inside.

STAPHYLA (*brusquely*): This way with you.

(*Exeunt* CONGRIO *and others into* EUCLIO's *house.*)

SCENE SEVEN

PYTHODICUS (*as they leave*): Look out for things. (*starting for* MEGADORUS's *house*) I'll go see what the cooks are at. By gad, it's the devil's own job keeping an eye on those chaps. The only way is to make 'em cook dinner in the dungeon and then haul it up

---

2 The use of wine was forbidden at the festival called the *Cereris nuptiæ*.

in baskets when it's done. Even so, though, if they're down there gobbling up all they cook, it's a case of starve in heaven and stuff in hell. But here I am gabbling away just as if there wasn't anything to do, and the house all full of those young Grabbits. (*Exit* PYTHODICUS.)

SCENE EIGHT

(*Enter* EUCLIO *from forum carrying a small package and a few forlorn flowers.*)

EUCLIO: Now I did want to be hearty to-day, and do the handsome thing for daughter's wedding, yes I did. Off I go to the market — ask for fish! Very dear! And lamb dear . . . and beef dear . . . and veal and tunny and pork . . . everything dear, everything! Yes, and all the dearer for my not having any money! It just made me furious, and seeing I couldn't buy anything, I up and left. That's how I circumvented 'em, the whole dirty pack of 'em. Then I began to reason things out with myself as I walked along. "Holiday feasting makes everyday fasting," says I to myself, "unless you economize." After I'd put the case this way to my stomach and heart, my mind supported my motion to cut down daughter's wedding expenses just as much as possible. Now I've bought a little frankincense here and some wreaths of flowers: we'll put 'em on the hearth in honour of our Household God, so that he may bless daughter's marriage. (*looking toward house*) Eh! What's my door open for? A clattering inside, too! Oh, mercy on us! It can't be burglars, can it?

CONGRIO (*within, to an attendant*): See if you can't get a bigger pot from one of the neighbours: this here's a little one: it won't hold it all.

EUCLIO: Oh, my God! my God! I'm ruined! They're taking my gold! They're after my pot! Oh, oh, Apollo, help me, save me! Shoot your arrows through them, the treasure thieves, if you've ever helped a man in such a pinch before! But I must rush in before they ruin me entirely!

(*Exit* EUCLIO.)

SCENE NINE

(*Enter* ANTHRAX *from house of* MEGADORUS.)

ANTHRAX (*to servants inside*): Dromo, scale the fish. As for you, Machaerio, you bone the conger and lamprey as fast as you know how. I'm going over next door to ask Congrio for the loan of a bread-pan. And you there! if you know what's good for you, you won't hand me back that rooster till it's plucked cleaner than a ballet dancer. (*sound of scuffle in* EUCLIO's *house*) Hullo, though! What's the row in the house next door? Hm! the cooks settling down to business, I reckon! I'll hustle back, or we'll be having a rumpus at our place, too.

(*Exit.*)

ACT THREE

(*Enter* CONGRIO *and his associates tumbling out of* EUCLIO's *house, slamming door behind them.*)

CONGRIO (*in burlesque panic*): Hi — i — i! Citizens, natives, inhabitants, neighbours, foreigners, every one — give me room to run! Open up! Clear the street! (*stopping at some distance from the house*) This is the first time I ever came to cook for Bacchantes at a Bacchante den. Oh dear, what an awful clubbing I and my disciples did get! I'm one big ache! I'm dead and gone! The way that old codger took me for a gymnasium! (EUCLIO's *door opens and he appears, cudgel in hand*) Oh — ow — ow! Good Lord be merciful! I'm done for! He's opening the den: he's at the door: he's after me! I know what I'll do: (*retires*) he's taught me my lesson, my master has. I never in all my life saw a place where they were freer-handed with their wood: (*rubbing his shoulders*) why, when he drove the lot of us out he let us have big sticks of it, all we could stagger under.

SCENE TWO

EUCLIO (*going into street*): Come back. Where are you running to now? Stop him, stop him!

CONGRIO: What are you yelling for, stupid?

EUCLIO: Because I am going to report your name to the police this instant.

CONGRIO: Why?

EUCLIO: Well, you carry a knife.

CONGRIO: And so a cook should.

EUCLIO: And how about your threatening me?

CONGRIO: It's a pity I didn't jab it through you, I'm thinking.

EUCLIO: There isn't a more abandoned villain than you on the face of the earth, or one I'd be gladder to go out of my way to punish more, either.

CONGRIO: Good Lord! That's evident enough, even if you didn't say so: the facts speak for themselves. I've been clubbed till I'm looser than any fancy dancer. Now what did you mean by laying hands on me, you beggar?

EUCLIO: What's that? You dare ask me? Didn't I do my duty by you — is that it? (*lifts cudgel*)

CONGRIO (*backing away*): All right: but by gad, you'll pay heavy for it, or I'm a numskull.

EUCLIO: Hm! I don't know anything about the future of your skull, but (*chuckling and tapping his cudgel*) it must be numb now. (*savagely*) See here, what the devil were you doing in my house without my orders while I was gone? That's what I want to know.

CONGRIO: Well then, shut up. We came to cook for the wedding, that's all.

EUCLIO: And how does it concern you, curse you, whether I eat my food cooked or take it raw — unless you are my guardian?

CONGRIO: Are you going to let us cook dinner here or not? That's what I want to know.

EUCLIO: Yes, and I want to know whether my things at home will be safe?

CONGRIO: All I hope is I can get safe away with my own things that I brought there. That'll do for me: don't worry about my hankering for anything you own.

EUCLIO (*incredulous*): I know. You needn't go on. I quite understand.

CONGRIO: Why won't you let us cook dinner here now? What have we done? What have we said that you didn't like?

EUCLIO: A pretty question, you villainous rascal, with your making a public highway of every nook and cranny in my whole house! If you had stayed by the oven where your business lay, you wouldn't be carrying that cloven pate: it serves you right. (*with forced composure*) Now further, just to acquaint you with my sentiments in the matter, — you come any nearer this door without my permission, and I will make you the most forlorn creature in God's world. Now you know my sentiments. (*Exit into house.*)

CONGRIO (*calling after him*): Where are you off to? Come back! So help me holy Mother of Thieves, but I'll soon make it warm for you, the way I'll rip up your reputation in front of the house here, if you don't have my dishes brought back! (*as* EUCLIO *closes the door*) Now what? Oh, hell! It certainly was an unlucky day when I came here! Two shillings for the job, and now it'll take more than that to pay the doctor's bill.

SCENE THREE

(*Re-enter* EUCLIO *from house with object under his cloak.*)

EUCLIO (*aside*): By heaven, wherever I go this goes (*peering under cloak*) too: I won't leave it there to run such risks, never. (*to* CONGRIO *and others*) Very well, come now, in with you, cooks, music girls, every one! (*to* CONGRIO) Go on, take your understrappers inside if you like, the whole hireling herd of 'em. Cook away, work away, scurry around to your hearts' content now.

CONGRIO: A nice time for it, after you've clubbed my head till it's all cracks!

EUCLIO: In with you. You were engaged to get up a dinner here, not a declamation.

CONGRIO: I say, old boy, I'll come to you with my bill for that basting, by the Lord I will.

I was hired a while ago to be cook, not to be thumped.

EUCLIO: Well, go to law about it. Don't bother me. Away with you: get dinner, or else get to the devil out of here.

CONGRIO: You just get to — (*mildly, as he pushes in past him*) one side, then.

(*Exeunt* CONGRIO *and his associates into house.*)

SCENE FOUR

EUCLIO (*looking after them*): He's disappeared. My Lord, my Lord! It's an awful chance a poor man takes when he begins to have dealings or business with a wealthy man. Here's Megadorus now, trying to catch me — oh, dear, dear! — in all sorts of ways. Sending cooks over here and pretending it's because of regard for me! Sent 'em to steal this (*looking under cloak*) from a poor old man — that's what his sending 'em was because of! And then of course that dunghill cock of mine in there, that used to belong to the old woman, had to come within an inch of ruining me, beginning to scratch and claw around where this (*looking under cloak*) was buried. Enough said. It just got me so worked up I took a club and annihilated that cock, the thief, the redhanded thief! By heaven, I do believe the cooks offered that cock a reward to show them where this (*looking under cloak*) was. I took the handle (*looking under cloak*) out of their hands! (*looking down street*) Ah, but there is son-in-law Megadorus swaggering back from the forum. I suppose it would hardly do for me to pass him without stopping for a word or two, now.

SCENE FIVE

(*Enter* MEGADORUS.)

MEGADORUS (*not seeing* EUCLIO): Well, I've told a number of friends of my intentions regarding this match. They were full of praise for Euclio's daughter. Say it's the sensible thing to do, a fine idea. Yes, for my part I'm convinced that if the rest of our well-to-do citizens would follow my example and marry poor men's daughters and let the dowries go, there would be a great deal more unity in our city, and people would be less bitter against us men of means than they are, and our wives would stand in greater awe of marital authority than they do, and the cost of living would be lower for us than it is. It's just the thing for the vast majority of the people; the fight comes with a handful of greedy fellows so stingy and grasping that neither law nor cobbler can take their measure. And now supposing some one should ask: "Who are the rich girls with dowries going to marry, if you make this rule for the poor ones?" Why, anyone they please, let 'em marry, provided their dowry doesn't go along with 'em. In that case, instead of bringing their husbands money, they'd bring them better behaved wives than they do at present. Those mules of theirs that cost more than horses do now — they'd be cheaper than Gallic geldings by the time I got through.

EUCLIO (*aside*): God bless my soul, how I do love to hear him talk! Those thoughts of his about economizing — beautiful, beautiful!

MEGADORUS: Then you wouldn't hear them saying: "Well, sir, you never had anything like the money I brought you, and you know it. Fine clothes and jewellery, indeed! And maids and mules and coachmen and footmen and pages and private carriages — well, if I haven't a right to them!"

EUCLIO (*aside*): Ah, he knows 'em, knows 'em through and through, these society dames! Oh, if he could only be appointed supervisor of public morals — the women's!

MEGADORUS: Wherever you go nowadays you see more wagons in front of a city mansion than you can find around a farmyard. That's a perfectly glorious sight, though, compared with the time when the tradesmen come for their money. The cleanser, the ladies' tailor, the jeweller, the woollen worker — they're all hanging round. And there are the dealers in flounces and underclothes and bridal veils, in violet dyes and yellow dyes, or muffs, or balsam scented foot-gear; and then the lingerie people drop in on you, along with shoemakers and squatting cobblers and slipper and sandal merchants and dealers in mallow dyes; and the belt makers flock around, and the girdle makers along with 'em. And now you may think you've got them all paid off. Then up come weavers and lace men and cabinet-makers — hundreds of 'em — who plant themselves like jailers in your halls and want you to settle up. You bring 'em in and square accounts. "All paid off now, anyway," you may be thinking, when in march the fellows who do the saffron dyeing — some damned pest or other, anyhow, eternally after something.

EUCLIO (aside): I'd hail him, only I'm afraid he'd stop talking about how the women go on. No, no, I'll let him be.

MEGADORUS: When you've got all these fellows of fluff and ruffles satisfied, along comes a military man, bringing up the rear, and wants to collect the army tax. You go and have a reckoning with your banker, your military gentleman standing by and missing his lunch in the expectation of getting some cash. After you and the banker have done figuring, you find you owe him money too, and the military man has his hopes postponed till another day. These are some of the nuisances and intolerable expenses that big dowries let you in for, and there are plenty more. Now a wife that doesn't bring you a penny — a husband has some control over her: it's the dowered ones that pester the life out of their husbands with the way they cut up and squander. (seeing EUCLIO) But there's my new relative in front of the house! How are you, Euclio?

SCENE SIX

EUCLIO: Gratified, highly gratified with your discourse — I devoured it.

MEGADORUS: Eh? you heard?

EUCLIO: Every word of it.

MEGADORUS (looking him over): But I say, though, I do think it would be a little more in keeping, if you were to spruce up a bit for your daughter's wedding.

EUCLIO (whining): Folks with the wherewithal and means to let 'em spruce up and look smart remember who they are. My goodness, Megadorus! I haven't got a fortune piled up at home (peers slyly under cloak) any more than people think, and no other poor man has, either.

MEGADORUS (genially): Ah well, you've got enough, and heaven make it more and more, and bless you in what you have now.

EUCLIO (turning away with a start): "What you have now!" I don't like that phrase! He knows I have this money just as well as I do! The old hag's been blabbing!

MEGADORUS (pleasantly): Why that secret session over there?

EUCLIO (taken aback): I was — damme sir, — I was framing the complaint against you that you deserve.

MEGADORUS: What for?

EUCLIO: What for, eh? When you've filled every corner of my house with thieves, confound it! When you've sent cooks into my house by the hundred and every one of 'em a Geryonian[3] with six hands apiece! Why, Argus, who had eyes all over him and was set to guarding Io once by Juno, couldn't ever keep watch on those fellows, not if he tried. And that music girl besides! She could take the fountain of Pirene at Corinth and drink it dry, all by herself, she could, — if it ran wine. Then as for the provisions ——

MEGADORUS: Bless my soul! Why, there's enough for a regiment. I sent you a lamb, too.

EUCLIO: Yes, and a more shearable beast than that same lamb doesn't exist, I know that.

MEGADORUS: I wish you would tell me how the lamb is shearable.

---

3 Geryon was a giant with three heads and bodies.

EUCLIO: Because it's mere skin and bones, wasted away till it's perfectly — (*tittering*) sheer. Why, why, you put that lamb in the sun and you can watch its inwards work: it's as transparent as a Punic[4] lantern.

MEGADORUS (*protestingly*): I got that lamb in myself to be slaughtered.

EUCLIO (*dryly*): Then you'd best put it out yourself to be buried, for I do believe it's dead already.

MEGADORUS (*laughing and clapping him on the shoulder*): Euclio, we must have a little carouse to-day, you and I.

EUCLIO (*frightened*): None for me, sir, none for me! Carouse! Oh my Lord!

MEGADORUS: But see here, I'll just have a cask of good old wine brought over from my cellars.

EUCLIO: No, no! I don't care for any! The fact is, I am resolved to drink nothing but water.

MEGADORUS (*digging him in the ribs*): I'll get you properly soaked to-day, on my life I will, you with your "resolved to drink nothing but water."

EUCLIO (*aside*): I see his game! Trying to fuddle me with his wine, that's it, and then give this (*looking under cloak*) a new domicile! (*pauses*) I'll take measures against that: yes, I'll secrete it somewhere outside the house. I'll make him throw away his time and wine together.

MEGADORUS (*turning to go*): Well, unless I can do something for you, I'll go take a bath and get ready to offer sacrifice. (*Exit into house.*)

EUCLIO (*paternally to object under cloak*): God bless us both, pot, you do have enemies, ah yes, many enemies, you and the gold entrusted to you! As matters stand, pot, the best thing I can do for you is to carry you off to the shrine of Faith: I'll hide you away there, just as cosy! You know me, Faith, and I know you: don't change your name, mind, if I trust this to you. Yes, I'll go to you, Faith, relying on your faithfulness. (*Exit EUCLIO.*)

ACT FOUR

(*Enter STROBILUS.*)

STROBILUS (*self-complacently*): This is the way for a good servant to act, the way I do: no thinking master's orders are a botheration and nuisance. I tell you what, if a servant wants to give satisfaction, he'd just better make it a case of master first and man second.[5] Even if he should fall asleep, he ought to do it with an eye on the fact that he's a servant. He's got to know his master's inclinations like a book, so that he can read his wishes in his face. And as for orders, he must push 'em through faster than a fast four-in-hand. If a chap minds all this, he won't be paying taxes on rawhide, or ever spend his time polishing a ball and chain with his ankles. Now the fact is, master's in love with the daughter of poor old Euclio here; and he's just got word she's going to be married to Megadorus there. So he's sent me over to keep my eyes peeled and report on operations. I'll just settle down alongside this sacred altar (*does so*) and no one'll suspect me. I can inspect proceedings at both houses from here.

SCENE TWO

(*Enter EUCLIO without seeing STROBILUS.*)

EUCLIO (*plaintively*): Only be sure you don't let anyone know my gold is there, Faith: no fear of anyone finding it, not after the lovely way I tucked it in that dark nook. (*pauses*) Oh my God, what a beautiful haul he would

---

4 Perhaps of glass, of which the Phœnicians were reputedly the inventors.　5 For when a slave's slaving it like I am for a master who is in love, if he sees his master's heart is running away with him, it's the slave's duty, in my opinion, to hold him in and save him and not hurry him on the way he's headed. It's like boys learning to swim: they lie on a rush float so as not to have to work so hard and so as to swim more easily and use their arms. In the same way I hold that a slave ought to be his master's float, if his master's in love, so as to support him and not let him go to the bottom like —

get, if anyone should find it — a pot just crammed with gold! For mercy's sake, though, Faith, don't let him! (*walks slowly toward house*) Now I'll have a bath, so that I may sacrifice and not hinder my prospective son-in-law from marrying my girl the moment he claims her. (*looking down street toward temple*) Take care now, Faith, do, do, do take care I get my pot back from you safe. I've trusted my gold to your good faith, laid it away in your grove and shrine.

(*Exit* EUCLIO *into house.*)

STROBILUS (*jumping up*): Ye immortal gods! What's all this I heard the fellow tell of! A pot just crammed with gold hidden in the shrine of Faith here! For the love of heaven, Faith, don't be more faithful to him than to me. Yes, and he's the father of the girl that is master's sweetheart, or I'm mistaken. I'm going in there: I'll search that shrine from top to bottom and see if I can't find the gold somewhere while he's busy here. But if I come across it — oh, Faith, I'll pour you out a five pint pot of wine and honey! There now! that's what I'll do for you; and when I've done that for you, why, I'll drink it up for myself. (*Exit to temple at a run.*)

SCENE THREE

(*Re-enter* EUCLIO *from house.*)

EUCLIO (*excitedly*): It means something — that raven cawing on my left just now! And all the time a-clawing the ground, croaking away, croaking away! The minute I heard him my heart began to dance a jig and jumped up into my throat. But I must run, run! (*Exit to temple.*)

SCENE FOUR

(*A few moments elapse. Then the sound of a scuffle down the street. Re-enter* EUCLIO *dragging* STROBILUS.)

EUCLIO: Come! out, you worm! crawling up from underground just now! A minute ago you weren't to be found anywhere, and (*grimly*) now you're found you're finished! Oh-h-h-h, you felon! I'm going to give it to you, this very instant! (*beats him*)

STROBILUS: What the devil's got into you? What business have you got with me, old fellow? What are you pounding me for? What are you jerking me along for? What do you mean by battering me?

EUCLIO (*still pummelling him*): Mean, eh? You batterissimo. You're not a thief: you're three thieves.

STROBILUS: What did I steal from you?

EUCLIO (*threateningly*): You kindly give it back.

STROBILUS: Back? What back?

EUCLIO: A nice question!

STROBILUS: I didn't take a thing from you, honestly.

EUCLIO: Well, what you took dishonestly, then! Hand it over! Come, come, will you!

STROBILUS: Come, come, what?

EUCLIO: You shan't get away with it.

STROBILUS: What is it you want?

EUCLIO: Down with it!

STROBILUS: Down with it, eh! Looks as if you'd downed too much of it yourself already, old boy.

EUCLIO: Down with it, I tell you! None of your repartee! I'm not in the humour for trifling now.

STROBILUS: Down with what? Come along, speak out and give it its name, whatever it is. Hang it all, I never took a thing nor touched a thing, and that's flat.

EUCLIO: Show me your hands.

STROBILUS (*stretching them out*): All right — there they are: have a look.

EUCLIO (*dryly*): I see. Come now, the third one: out with it.

STROBILUS (*aside*): He's got 'em! The old chap's mad, stark, staring mad! (*to* EUCLIO, *virtuously*) Now aren't you doing me an injury?

EUCLIO: I am, a hideous injury — in not hanging you. And I'll soon do that, too, if you don't confess.

STROBILUS: Confess what?

EUCLIO: What did you carry off from here? (*pointing toward temple*)

STROBILUS (*solemnly*): May I be damned, if I carried off a thing of yours. (*aside*) Likewise if I didn't want to.

EUCLIO: Come on, shake out your cloak.

STROBILUS (*doing so*): Anything you say.

EUCLIO: Um! probably under your tunic.

STROBILUS (*cheerfully*): Feel anywhere you please.

EUCLIO: Ugh! you rascal! How obliging you are! That I may think you didn't take it! I'm up to your dodges. (*searches him*) Once more now — out with your hand, the right one.

STROBILUS (*obeying*): There you are.

EUCLIO: Now the left one.

STROBILUS (*obeying*): Why, certainly: here's the both of 'em.

EUCLIO: Enough of this searching. Now give it here.

STROBILUS: What?

EUCLIO: Oh-h! Bosh! You must have it!

STROBILUS: I have it? Have what?

EUCLIO: I won't say: you're too anxious to know. Anything of mine you've got, hand it over.

STROBILUS: Crazy! You went all through me as much as you liked without finding a solitary thing of yours on me.

EUCLIO (*excitedly*): Wait, wait! (*turns toward temple and listens*) Who's in there? Who was that other fellow in there along with you? (*aside*) My Lord! this is awful, awful! There's another one at work in there all this time. And if I let go of this one, he'll skip off. (*pauses*) But then I've searched him already: he hasn't anything. (*aloud*) Off with you, anywhere! (*releases him with a final cuff*)

STROBILUS (*from a safe distance*): You be everlastingly damned!

EUCLIO (*aside, dryly*): Nice way he has of showing his gratitude. (*aloud, sternly*) I'll go in there, and that accomplice of yours — I'll strangle him on the spot. Are you going to vanish? Are you going to get out, or not? (*advances*)

STROBILUS (*retreating*): I am, I am!

EUCLIO: And kindly see I don't set eyes on you again.

(*Exit* EUCLIO *toward temple.*)

SCENE FIVE

STROBILUS: I'd sooner be tortured to death than not give that old fellow a surprise to-day. (*reflecting*) Well, after this he won't dare hide his gold here. What he'll most likely do is bring it out with him and put it somewhere else. (*listening*) Hm-m-m! There goes the door! Aha! the old boy's coming out with it. I'll just back up by the doorway for a while. (*hides by* MEGADORUS's *house*)

SCENE SIX

(*Re-enter* EUCLIO *with pot.*)

EUCLIO: I used to fancy Faith, of all deities, was absolutely faithful, and here she's just missed making a downright ass of me. If that raven hadn't stood by me, I'd be a poor, poor ruined man. By heavens, I'd just like that raven to come and see me, the one that warned me, I certainly should, so that I might pay him a handsome — compliment. As for tossing him a bite to eat, why, that would amount to throwing it away. (*meditating*) Let me think now; where is some lonely spot to hide this in? (*after a moment*) There's that grove of Silvanus outside the wall, solitary, willow thickets all around. There's where I'll pick my place. I'd sooner trust Silvanus than Faith, and that's settled. (*Exit* EUCLIO.)

STROBILUS: Good! Good! The gods are with me: I'm a made man! Now I'll run on ahead and climb some tree there so as to sight the place where the old fellow hides it. What if master did tell me to wait here! I'd sooner look for a thrashing along with the cash, and that's settled. (*Exit* STROBILUS.)

SCENE SEVEN

(*Enter* LYCONIDES *and* EUNOMIA.)

LYCONIDES: That's the whole story, mother: you see how it is with me and Euclio's daughter as well as I do. And now, mother, I beg you, beg you again and again, as I did before: do tell my uncle about it, mother dear.

EUNOMIA: Your wishes are mine, dear; you know that yourself: and I feel sure your uncle will not refuse me. It's a perfectly reasonable request, too, if it's all as you say and you actually did get intoxicated and treat the poor girl so.

LYCONIDES: Is it like me to look you in the face and lie, my dear mother?

PHAEDRIA (*within Euclio's house*): Oh — oh! Nurse! Nurse dear! Oh, God help me! The pain!

LYCONIDES: There, mother! There's better proof than words gives. Her cries! The child!

EUNOMIA (*agitated*): Come, darling, come in to your uncle with me, so that I may persuade him to let it be as you urge.

LYCONIDES: You go, mother: I'll follow you in a moment.

(*Exit* EUNOMIA *into* MEGADORUS's *house.*)
I wonder (*looking around*) where that fellow Strobilus of mine is that I told to wait for me here. (*pauses*) Well, on thinking it over, if he's doing something for me, it's all wrong my finding fault with him. (*turning toward* MEGADORUS's *door*) Now for the session that decides my fate. (*Exit.*)

SCENE EIGHT

(*Enter* STROBILUS *with pot.*)

STROBILUS (*elated*): Woodpeckers that haunt the Hills of Gold, eh! I can buy 'em up my own single self. As for the rest of your big kings — not worth mentioning, poor beggarlets! I am the great King Philip. Oh, this is a grand day! Why, after I left here a while ago I got there long before him and was up in a tree long before he came: and from there I spotted where the old chap hid the stuff. After he'd gone I scrabbled down, dug up the pot full of gold! Then I saw him coming back from the place; he didn't see me, though. I slipped off a bit to one side of the road. (*looking down street*) Aha! there he comes! I'll home and tuck this out of sight. (*Exit* STROBILUS.)

SCENE NINE

(*Enter* EUCLIO *frantic.*)

EUCLIO (*running wildly back and forth*): I'm ruined, I'm killed, I'm murdered! Where shall I run? Where shan't I run? Stop thief! Stop thief! What thief? Who? I don't know! I can't see! I'm all in the dark! Yes, yes, and where I'm going, or where I am, or who I am — oh, I can't tell, I can't think! (*to audience*) Help, help, for heaven's sake, I beg you, I implore you! Show the man that took it. Eh, what's that? What are you grinning for? I know you, the whole lot of you! I know there are thieves here, plenty of 'em, that cover themselves up in dapper clothes and sit still as if they were honest men. (*to a spectator*) You, sir, what do you say? I'll trust you, I will, I will. Yes, you're a worthy gentleman; I can tell it from your face. Ha! none of them has it? Oh, you've killed me! Tell me, who has got it, then? You don't know? Oh dear, oh dear, oh dear! I'm a ruined man! I'm lost, lost! Oh, what a plight! Oh, such a cruel, disastrous, dismal day — it's made a starveling of me, a pauper! I'm the forlornest wretch on earth! Ah, what is there in life for me when I've lost all that gold I guarded, oh, so carefully! I've denied myself, denied my own self comforts and pleasures; yes, and now others are making merry over my misery and loss! Oh, it's unendurable!

(*Enter* LYCONIDES *from house of* MEGADORUS.)

LYCONIDES: Who in the world is raising all this howling, groaning hullabaloo before our house here? (*looking round*) Upon my word, it's Euclio, I do believe. (*drawing back*) My time has certainly come: it's all out. He's just learned about his daughter's child, I suppose. Now I can't decide whether to leave or stay, advance or retreat. By Jove, I don't know what to do!

SCENE TEN

EUCLIO (*hearing sound of voice only*): Who's that talking here?

LYCONIDES (*stepping forward*): I'm the poor wretch, sir.

EUCLIO: No, no, I'm the poor wretch, a poor ruined wretch, with all this trouble and tribulation.

LYCONIDES: Keep your courage up, sir.

EUCLIO: For heaven's sake how can I?

LYCONIDES: Well, sir, that outrage that distresses you — (*hesitantly*) I'm to blame, and I confess it, sir.

EUCLIO: Hey? What's that?

LYCONIDES: The truth.

EUCLIO: How have I ever harmed you, young man, for you to act like this and try to ruin me and my children?

LYCONIDES: It was some demon got hold of me, sir, and led me on.

EUCLIO: How is this?

LYCONIDES: I admit I've done wrong sir; I deserve your reproaches, and I know it; more than that, I've come to beg you to be patient and forgive me.

EUCLIO: How did you dare do it, dare touch what didn't belong to you?

LYCONIDES (*penitently*): Well, well, sir, — it's done, and it can't be undone. I think it must have been fated; otherwise it wouldn't have happened, I'm sure of that.

EUCLIO: Yes, and I think it must have been fated that I'm to shackle you at my house and murder you!

LYCONIDES: Don't say that, sir.

EUCLIO: Then why did you lay hands on what was mine, without my permission?

LYCONIDES: It was all because of drink . . . and . . . love, sir.

EUCLIO: The colossal impudence of it! To dare to come to me with a tale like that, you shameless rascal! Why, if it's legal to clear yourself that way, we should be stripping ladies of their jewellery on the public highways in broad daylight! And then when we were caught we'd excuse ourselves on the score that we were drunk and did it out of love. Drink and love are altogether too cheap, if your drunken lover can do what he likes and not suffer for it.

LYCONIDES: Yes, but I've come of my own accord, sir, to entreat you to pardon my madness.

EUCLIO: I have no patience with men who do wrong and then try to explain it away. You knew you had no right to act so: you should have kept hands off.

LYCONIDES: Well, now that I did venture to act so, I have no objection to holding to it, sir, — I ask nothing better.

EUCLIO (*more angry*): Hold to it? Against my will?

LYCONIDES: I won't insist on it against your will, sir; but I do think my claim is just. Why, you'll soon come to realize the justice of it yourself, sir, I assure you.

EUCLIO: I'll march you off to court and sue you, by heaven I will, this minute, unless you bring it back.

LYCONIDES: I? Bring what back?

EUCLIO: What you stole from me.

LYCONIDES: I stole something of yours? Where from? What?

EUCLIO (*ironically*): God bless your innocence — you don't know!

LYCONIDES: Not unless you say what you're looking for.

EUCLIO: The pot of gold, I tell you; I want back the pot of gold you owned up to taking.

LYCONIDES: Great heavens, man! I never said that or did it, either.

EUCLIO: You deny it?

LYCONIDES: Deny it? Absolutely. Why, I don't know, haven't any idea, about your gold, or what that pot is.

EUCLIO: The one you took from the grove of Silvanus — give it me. Go, bring it back. (pleadingly) You can have half of it, yes, yes, I'll divide. Even though you are such a thief, I won't make any trouble for you. Do, do go and bring it back, oh do!

LYCONIDES: Man alive, you're out of your senses, calling me a thief. I supposed you had found out about something else that does concern me, Euclio. There's an important matter I'm anxious to talk over quietly with you, sir, if you're at leisure.

EUCLIO: Give me your word of honour: you didn't steal that gold?

LYCONIDES (shaking his head): On my honour.

EUCLIO: And you don't know the man that did take it?

LYCONIDES: Nor that, either, on my honour.

EUCLIO: And if you learn who took it, you'll inform me?

LYCONIDES: I will.

EUCLIO: And you won't go shares with the man that has it, or shield the thief?

LYCONIDES: No.

EUCLIO: What if you deceive me?

LYCONIDES: Then, sir, may I be dealt with as great God sees fit.

EUCLIO: That will suffice. All right now, say what you want.

LYCONIDES: In case you're not acquainted with my family connections, sir, — Megadorus here is my uncle: my father was Antimachus, and my own name is Lyconides: Eunomia is my mother.

EUCLIO: I know who you are. Now what do you want? That's what I wish to know.

LYCONIDES: You have a daughter.

EUCLIO: Yes, yes, at home there!

LYCONIDES: You have betrothed her to my uncle, I understand.

EUCLIO: Precisely, precisely.

LYCONIDES: He has asked me to inform you now that he breaks the engagement.

EUCLIO (furious): Breaks the engagement, with everything ready, the wedding prepared for? May all the everlasting powers above consume that villain that's to blame for my losing my gold, all that gold, poor God-forsaken creature that I am!

LYCONIDES: Brace up, sir: don't curse. And now for something that I pray will turn out well and happily for yourself and your daughter — "God grant it may!" Say that.

EUCLIO (doubtfully): God grant it may!

LYCONIDES: And God grant it may for me, too! Now listen, sir. There isn't a man alive so worthless but what he wants to clear himself when he's done wrong and is ashamed. Now, sir, if I've injured you or your daughter without realizing what I was doing, I implore you to forgive me and let me marry her as I'm legally bound to. (nervously) It was the night of Ceres' festival . . . and what with wine and . . . a young fellow's natural impulses together . . . I wronged her, I confess it.

EUCLIO: Oh, oh, my God! What villainy am I hearing of?

LYCONIDES (patting his shoulder): Lamenting, sir, lamenting, when you're a grandfather, and this your daughter's wedding day? You see it's the tenth month since the festival — reckon it up — and we have a child, sir. This explains my uncle's breaking the engagement: he did it for my sake. Go in and inquire if it isn't just as I tell you.

EUCLIO: Oh, my life is wrecked, wrecked! The way calamities swarm down and settle on me one after another! Go in I will, and have the truth of it!

(*Exit into his house.*)

LYCONIDES (*as he disappears*): I'll soon be with you, sir. (*after a pause, contentedly*) It does look as if we were pretty nearly safe in the shallows now. (*looking around*) Where in the world my fellow Strobilus is I can't imagine. Well, the only thing to do is to wait here a bit longer; then I'll join father-in-law inside. Meanwhile I'll let him have an opportunity to inquire into the case from the old nurse that's been his daughter's maid: she knows about it all. (*waits in doorway*)

ACT FIVE

(*Enter* STROBILUS.)

STROBILUS: Ye immortal gods, what joy, what bliss, ye bless me with! I have a four pound pot of gold, chock full of gold! Show me a man that's richer! Who's the chap in all Athens now that Heaven's kinder to than me?

LYCONIDES: Why, it surely seemed as if I heard some one's voice just then. (*catches a glimpse of* STROBILUS'*s face, the latter wheeling around as he sees* LYCONIDES)

STROBILUS (*aside*): Hm! Is that master there?

LYCONIDES (*aside*): My servant, is it?

STROBILUS (*aside, after a quick glance*): It's the governor.

LYCONIDES (*aside*): Himself.

STROBILUS (*aside*): Here goes. (*moves toward* LYCONIDES)

LYCONIDES (*aside*): I'll go meet him. No doubt he's followed instructions and been to see that old woman I mentioned, my girl's nurse.

STROBILUS (*aside*): Why not tell him I've found this prize? Then I'll beg him to set me free. I'll up and let him have the whole story. (*to* LYCONIDES, *as they meet*) I've found ——

LYCONIDES (*scoffingly*): Found what?

STROBILUS: No such trifle as youngsters hurrah over finding in a bean.[6]

LYCONIDES: At your old tricks? You're chaffing. (*pretends to be about to leave*).

STROBILUS: Hold on, sir: I'll tell you all about it this minute. Listen.

LYCONIDES: Well, well, then, tell away.

STROBILUS: Sir, to-day I've found — boundless riches!

LYCONIDES (*interested*): You have? Where?

STROBILUS: A four pound pot, sir, I tell you, a four pound pot just full of gold!

LYCONIDES: What's all this you've done? He's the man that robbed old Euclio. Where is this gold?

STROBILUS: In a box at home. Now I want you to set me free.

LYCONIDES (*angrily*): I set you free, you, you great lump of iniquity?

STROBILUS (*crestfallen, then laughing heartily*): Go along with you, sir! I know what you're after. Gad! that was clever of me, testing you in that way! And you were just getting ready to drop on it! Now what would you be doing, if I really had found it?

LYCONIDES: No, no, that won't pass. Off with you: hand over the gold.

STROBILUS: Hand over the gold? I?

LYCONIDES: Yes, hand it over, so that it may be handed over to Euclio.

STROBILUS: Gold? Where from?

LYCONIDES: The gold you just admitted was in the box.

STROBILUS: Bless your heart, sir, my tongue's all the time running on foolish-like.

LYCONIDES: [line missing]

---

6 It is uncertain what they did find.

STROBILUS: That's what I say.

LYCONIDES (*seizing him*): See here, do you know what you'll get?

STROBILUS: By heaven, sir, you can even kill me, but you won't have it from me, never ——

The rest of the play is lost, save for a few fragments. Apparently Lyconides, on returning the pot of gold, was given permission to marry Euclio's daughter; and Euclio, having a change of heart, or influenced by his Household God, gave it to the young couple as a wedding present.

Everyman

Tertullian (*c.* 160–230 A.D.) was one of the Fathers of the Church who reacted against the frank obscenity of the later Roman drama, thundering about theatres as the sinks of sin and pronouncing an anathema on actors. The Church destroyed the drama, root and branch, and yet it was from the rituals of the Roman Catholic Church that drama was revived in the West; in one of the tropes of the Easter Mass emerged in the tenth century a liturgical drama that was to be the foundation of a new histrionic art.

In the ninth century the Mass was sung with embellishments, vowels being strung out as in the *Gloria* of the modern chorus of the Christmas hymn *Angels We Have Heard On High*. To these musical tropes, words were added based on Mark 16:1–7 to tell the story of the three Marys arriving at the tomb of Christ on Easter morning to receive the joyful news of the Resurrection:

Quem quæritis in sepulchro, o Christicolæ?	Whom do you seek in the sepulchre, O followers of Christ?
[Marys.] *Jesum Nazarenum crucifixum, o Coelicolæ.*	Jesus of Nazareth, Who was crucified, O celestial ones.
[Angel of the Resurrection.] *Non est hic; surrexit, sicut prædixerat. Ite, nuntiate quia surrexit de sepulchro.*	He is not here; He is risen, as He foretold. Go, announce that He is risen from the sepulchre.

After this, all sang a *Te Deum* of praise to God as the Easter bells rang out in joy. With the tenth-century instructions written in Latin by Ethelwold, Bishop of Winchester, we have a description of the first play known in England, though the rituals of the Old Religion (of the Druids) in very ancient times produced ceremonies that still survive, in much altered form, not only in Morris dances and sword dances but also in folk plays of the Summer King, Robin Hood, etc. With the tenth-century *Quem quæritis* trope we have a true play: there is dialogue, action, impersonation (three priests in copes as the three Marys) and dramatic convention, scenery (a side altar serves as the tomb) and music, symbolism in the costumes, a moral message as well as an artistic effort.

From this little Easter play in time developed whole cycles of Miracle plays (based on the lives of saints) and Mystery plays (based on the mysteries of religion, and the Bible), which were presented at first in the church by the clergy and later in the streets, on pageant wagons, by the Guilds, the trade unions of the Middle Ages. These craft plays in time included such masterpieces of comedy and tragedy as *The Second Shepherd's Play* from the Wakefield cycle of 32 plays and *Abraham and Isaac*, not part of a cycle that now exists. They flourished in the fourteenth and early fifteenth centuries and led directly to the popular Morality plays of the fifteenth and sixteenth centuries. These plays taught religion, as did the stained glass windows, the Stations of the Cross, the vestments, music, and much else in the church, through the medium of art, indoctrinating a largely illiterate public through demonstration and spectacle and conveying ideas through sermon and symbolism.

Sermon and symbolism are wedded in the concept of allegory; one of the earliest and best examples in the English drama is the Morality play of *Everyman*, a play which in its simplicity and power served as a model and a measure of much of the subsequent drama, even when the theatre ceased to be a pulpit for Christianity. Though the subject was serious and the characters abstract, the anonymous author of *Everyman* contrived to introduce a touch of humor (in the character of Cousin, for example) and to individuate the persons of the play to a certain extent, taking them methodically but not dully through a plot that, while it lacked some suspense, was rich in climax and irony. To an audience not as accustomed to entertainment as modern people and yet, of course, delighted by jugglers and mimes at fairs, fools in the court and folk plays among the commonality, *Everyman* brought what was considered a vital message on "holy dying" and a lively theatrical experience. It is a much better play than others of its period: more unified in tone than *Mankind*, less verbose than *The Castle of Perseverence*, more timeless than *Wisdom*. *Everyman* is a masterpiece, its author often as human and as haunting as John Bunyan of *Pilgrim's Progress*. In an age in which drama was often crude and artless, *Everyman* was (said T. S. Eliot) "within the limitations of art." "It is essential," asserted Eliot, "that a work of art should be self-consistent, that an artist should consciously or unconsciously draw a circle beyond which he does not trespass: on the one hand actual life is always the material, and on the other hand an abstraction from actual life is a necessary condition. . . ."

The view of actual life enshrined in this play is that of the Roman Catholic Church, a view so international in the fifteenth century that the nationality of the anonymous author of *Everyman* is difficult to establish. A Dutch play *Elckerlijk* was printed before 1500 and there are four editions in English (two from John Skot and two fragmentary ones from Reginald Pynson) of the early sixteenth century (*c.* 1508–1537). The Dutch play, says Professor Zandvoort, is better than the English one, so the Dutch one therefore must have come first. Professor de Vocht makes similar claims for the English version. Other critics argue that the better play (whichever it is) must be an improvement upon the original version, therefore a translation of the original. So far the arguments have tended to suggest to most people that Piet Dorland of Diest wrote the original, *Elckerlijk*, in Dutch and that the English *Everyman* was a translation in which Roman Catholic stress on the priesthood and Protestant emphasis on salvation by action (Good Deeds) were mingled.

Bishop Percy who, as the collector of *Reliques of English Poetry*, was interested in old plays called this one another of the medieval "rude attempts to excite terror and pity," but his Protestantism may have blinded him to some of its merits. When *Everyman* was revived in this century by William Poel it enjoyed great success and Ben Greet played it regularly in repertory. A German version, *Jedermann* (1912), by Hugo von Hofmannstahl (1874–1929, also the author of the Morality play *Das Salzburger grosse Welttheater*), has been performed annually at Salzburg,* while the Dutch *Elckerlijk* has been presented each year since 1950 at Delft. It is *Everyman*'s intrinsic merit that will probably capture the interest of the modern reader or theatregoer rather than its original connection with an emerging semi-professional theatre in the early sixteenth century, its influence on other Moralities (such as John Skelton's *Magnyfycence* and Sir David Lindsay's *Ane Pleasant Satyre of the Thrie Estatis*) and Interludes (as in the work of Henry Medwall and John Heywood in the Tudor times), and its connection with great plays of a later period (such as Marlowe's *Doctor Faustus* and the tragedies of Shakespeare). The basic techniques of *Everyman* are still evident in our modern "allegories" in which psychology or politics replace theology (such as the political plays of Clifford Odets and Bertolt Brecht, the *J.B.* of Archibald Macleish, and the *avant-garde* plays of off-Broadway's experimental theatre, of black theatre, of the *Teatro Campesino*, etc.). A play like *Everyman* has so much in it that is fundamental to drama that it is always viable and, indeed, always "modern."

---

* There were no performances from 1937 to 1945, when it was banned by the Nazis. Originally produced by Max Reinhardt.

EVERYMAN

Anonymous (Fifteenth Century)

A modern version
by L. R. N. Ashley

CHARACTERS

GOD

MESSENGER	KNOWLEDGE
DEATH	CONFESSION
EVERYMAN	BEAUTY
FELLOWSHIP	STRENGTH
KINDRED	DISCRETION
COUSIN	FIVE SENSES
GOODS	ANGEL
GOOD DEEDS	DOCTOR

*Here begins a Treatise on how the High Father
of Heaven sends Death to Summon Every
Creature to Come and Give Account of his
Life in this World, in the Form of a Moral Play.*

MESSENGER (*as Prologue*): I pray you all give
    audience
And hear this matter with reverence,
In form a moral play.
The Summoning of Everyman it is called,
That of our lives and ending shows
How transitory is our day.
The matter is wondrous precious,
But the meaning is more precious.

And sweet to take away.
The story says: Man, in the beginning
Look well, and take warning of the ending,
Be you never so gay!
You think sin the beginning full sweet,
Which in the end causes the soul to weep,
When the body lies in clay.
Here you shall see how Fellowship and
    Jollity,
With Strength, Pleasure, and Beauty,
Will fade from you as flowers in May;
For you shall hear how our Heavenly King
Calls Everyman to a general reckoning.
Give audience, and hear what He will say.
    (*Exit.*)

(GOD *speaks.*)

GOD: I perceive, here in My majesty,
    That all creatures are to Me unkind,
    Living without fear in worldly prosperity.
    Of spiritual things the people are so blind,
    Drowned in sin, they know Me not for
        their God.
    On worldly riches is all their mind;
    They fear not My righteousness, the sharp
        rod.
    My law that I showed, when for them I
        died,
    They clean forget, and shedding of My
        blood red;
    I hung between two thieves, it's not denied,
    To get them life I suffered until dead.
    I healed their feet, with thorns they hurt
        my head.
    I could do no more than I did, truly;
    And now I see the people do clean
        forsake Me.
    They live the Seven Deadly Sins damnable,
    As Pride, Covetousness, Wrath, and Lechery
    Now in the world are made commendable;
    And thus they leave the angels, the heavenly
        company.
    Every man lives so for his own pleasure,
    And yet of life men never can be sure.
    I see the more that I forbear
    The worse they are from year to year.
    All that lives declines so fast;
    Therefore I will, in all My haste,
    Have a reckoning of every man's person;
    For, if I have the people thus alone

In their life and wicked tempests,
Truly they will become much worse than
    beasts;
For now one would by envy another eat;
Charity they all do clean forget.
I hoped well that every man
In My glory would make his mansion,
And to that I had them all elect.
But now I see, like traitors abject,
They thank me not for the pleasure to
    them meant,
Nor yet for their being, that I to them have
    lent.
I proferred the people great quantities of
    mercy,
And few there be that ask it heartily.
They are encumbered with worldly riches
So that I must to them do justice,
On every man living, without fear.
Where are you, Death, you mighty
    messenger?

(*Enter* DEATH.)

DEATH: Almighty God, I am here at Your will,
    Your commandment to fulfill.

GOD: Go you to Everyman,
    And show him, in My name,
    A pilgrimage to undertake,
    Which he in no way may escape;
    Ask that he bring with him a sure
        reckoning
    Without delay or any tarrying. (GOD *with-
        draws.*)

DEATH: Lord, I will in the world go run over all,
    And cruelly search out both great and small.
    Every man I will beset who lives beastly
    Out of God's laws, and dreads not folly.
    He that loves riches I will strike with my
        dart,
    To blind his sight, from Heaven him to
        part —
    Except that alms be his good friend —
    In Hell to dwell, world without end.
    Look, there I see Everyman walking.
    Little he thinks about my coming;
    His mind is on fleshly lusts and his treasure,
    And great pain it shall cause him to appear
    Before the Lord, Heavenly King.

(*Enter* EVERYMAN.)

Everyman, stand still! Where are you
    going
So gaily? Have you your Maker quite forgot?

EVERYMAN: Why ask you?
    Why would you know?

DEATH: Yes, sir; I will show you:
    In great haste I am sent you see
    From God out of His majesty.

EVERYMAN: What, sent to me?

DEATH: Yes, certainly.
    Though you have forgotten Him here,
    He thinks of you in the heavenly sphere,
    As, before we go, you shall know.

EVERYMAN: What wishes God of me?

DEATH: That shown shall be:
    A reckoning He must needs have
    Without any longer respite.

EVERYMAN: To give a reckoning longer leisure
        I crave;
    This obscure matter troubles my wit.

DEATH: You must take on yourself a long
        journey;
    Therefore your account book with you bring,
    For to return there is not any way.
    And see you be sure of your reckoning,
    For before God you shall answer, and show
    Your many evil deeds, and good (a few);
    How you have spent your life, and in what
        way,
    Before the Lord of Paradise today.
    Get ready that we may be on the way,
    For know you cannot send any attorney.

EVERYMAN: All unprepared am I such
        reckoning to give.
    I know you not. What messenger are you?

DEATH: I am Death, that fears no man,
    Each man arrests and spares no man;
    For it is God's commandment
    That all to me shall be obedient.

EVERYMAN: O Death, you come when I had
        you least in mind!
    But in your power it lies me to save;
    Yet of my goods will I give you, if you'll
        be kind;

Yes, a thousand pounds shall you have,
If you defer this matter till another day.

DEATH: Everyman, it may not be. There is
no way.
I covet no gold, silver, or riches,
Nor heed pope, emperor, king, duke, nor
princes;
For, if I would receive gifts great,
All the world I might get;
But my custom is clean contrary.
I give you no respite. Come on, and not
tarry.

EVERYMAN: Alas, shall I have no longer respite?
I may say Death gives no warning!
To think of you, it makes my heart sick,
For all unready is my book of reckoning.
But if twelve years I might have abiding,
My counting-book I would make so clear
That my reckoning I should not need to fear.
Therefore, Death, I pray you, for God's
mercy.
Spare me till I am provided with remedy.

DEATH: It avails not to cry, weep, and pray;
But haste you quickly that you haste on
that journey,
And test your friends, if you can;
For, know you well, time waits for no man,
And in the world each living creature
For Adam's sin must die by nature.

EVERYMAN: Death, if I should this pilgrimage
take,
And my reckoning surely make,
Show me, for the sake of charity,
Should I not come again shortly?

DEATH: No, Everyman; once you are there,
You may never more come here,
Trust me verily.

EVERYMAN: O gracious God in the high seat
celestial,
Have mercy on me in this dire need!
Shall I have no company from this vale
terrestrial
Of my acquaintance, that way me to lead?

DEATH: Yes, if any be so hardy
That would go with you and bear you
company.
Hurry to be gone to God's magnificence,

Your reckoning to give before His
presence.
What, think you that your life is given free
And your worldly goods also?

EVERYMAN: I had thought so, verily.

DEATH: No, no; it was but lent; see
That as soon as you go,
Another shall a while have it, and then
go also,
Even as you have done.
Everyman, you are mad! You have your
senses five,
And here on earth will not amend your life;
For suddenly do I come.

EVERYMAN: O wretched person, whither shall
I flee?
That I might escape this endless sorrow?
Now, gentle Death, spare me until tomorrow,
That I may amend me
With good advisement.

DEATH: No, to that I will not consent,
Nor no man will I respite;
But to the heart suddenly I shall smite
Without any advisement.
And now out of your sight I will fly
See that you make ready shortly,
For you may say this is the day
That no man living may escape away. (*Exit*
DEATH.)

EVERYMAN: Alas, I well may weep with sighs
deep!
Now I have no kind of company
To help me in my journey, and me to keep;
And also my accounting is all unready.
What shall I do now to excuse me?
I wish to God I'd not been born at all;
For to my soul great profit that would be
For now huge and great pains do me appall.
The time passes. Lord, help, Who all
wrought!
For though I mourn it avails nought.
The day passes and is almost done.
I know not what to do or where to run.
To whom were I best my appeal to make?
Suppose to Fellowship I were to break
The news and told him of this chance?
For in him is my trust, a happy chance,
We have in the world on many a day

Been good friends in sport and play.
I see him over there certainly.
I trust that he will bear me company;
Therefore to him I'll speak to ease my
  sorrow.
Well met, good Fellowship, and good
  morrow!

(FELLOWSHIP *speaks.*)

FELLOWSHIP: Everyman, good morrow, by this
    day!
  Sir, why do you look so piteously?
  If anything's amiss, I pray you say,
  That I may help to remedy.

EVERYMAN: Yes, good Fellowship, I say
  I am in great jeopardy.

FELLOWSHIP: My true friend, speak to me your
    mind;
  I will not forsake you to my life's end
  In the way of good company.

EVERYMAN: That was well spoken, and
    lovingly.

FELLOWSHIP: Sir, to me your sorrow all confess;
  I pity you to see you in distress.
  If any's wronged you, I'll make right again
  Though for you on the ground I shall lie
    slain.
  To know that ere I die would be no pain.

EVERYMAN: For that, Fellowship, my thanks
    must be.

FELLOWSHIP: Oh by your thanks I set not a
    straw.
  Show me your grief, and say no more.

EVERYMAN: If I my secret should to you break,
  And then you turned your mind from
    me,
  And would not comfort when you hear me
    speak,
  Then I should ten times sorrier be.

FELLOWSHIP: Sir, as I say I will do, indeed.

EVERYMAN: Then you are a good friend in need!
  I have found you true here before.

FELLOWSHIP: And so you shall ever more;
  For, in faith, if you went to Hell,
  I would not forsake you on the way.

EVERYMAN: You speak like a good friend; I
    believe you well.
  I shall deserve it, if I may.

FELLOWSHIP: I speak of no deserving, by this day!
  For he that will say but nothing do
  Is not worthy with good company to go;
  Therefore show me the grief in your mind,
  As to your friend most loving and kind.

EVERYMAN: I shall show you how it is:
  Commanded am I to make a journey —
  A long way, hard and dangerous —
  And give a full account, without delay,
  Before the high judge, Adonai.[1]
  Therefore, I pray you, bear me company,
  As you have promised, on this journey.

FELLOWSHIP: That is matter indeed. Promise is
    duty;
  But, if I should take such a voyage on me,
  I know it well, it would cause me pain.
  Also it frightens me, that's certain.
  But let us take counsel here as well as we can,
  For your words would scare a strong man.

EVERYMAN: Why, you said if I had need
  You would not ever forsake me, alive
    or dead,
  Though it were to Hell, truly.

FELLOWSHIP: So I said, certainly,
  But such pleasures be set aside, the truth
    to say.
  And also, if we took such a journey,
  When should we come back again?

EVERYMAN: Well, never again, till the day of
    doom.

FELLOWSHIP: In faith, then I will not go there!
  Who has these tidings brought?

EVERYMAN: Indeed, Death was with me here.

FELLOWSHIP: Now, by God, Who has
    redemption brought,
  If Death were the messenger,
  For no man who is alive today

---

1 A Hebrew name for God, literally "My Lord," used
in the synagogue whenever the ineffable name of God
(Yahweh) appeared in the text to be read.

Will I go on that hated journey —
Not for the father that begot me!

EVERYMAN: By God, you promised otherwise to me.

FELLOWSHIP: I knew not what I said, truly,
But if you will eat, and drink, and make
good cheer,
Or hang around in women's company,
I would not forsake you while the day is
clear,
Trust me verily.

EVERYMAN: Yes, for that you would be ready!
To go to mirth, solace, and play,
Your mind will sooner apply,
Than to bear me company in my long
journey.

FELLOWSHIP: Now, in faith, I will not go that
way,
But if you wished to murder, or any
man kill,
In that will I help you with a good will.

EVERYMAN: O, that is simple advice, indeed.
Gentle fellow, help me in my necessity!
We've long been friends, now I'm in need;
And now, gentle Fellowship, remember
me.

FELLOWSHIP: Whether we have been friends
or no,
By Saint John, with you I will not go.

EVERYMAN: Yet, I pray you, take the trouble,
do so much for me
As to accompany in charity,
And comfort me until I reach the town.

FELLOWSHIP: No, if you gave me a new gown,
I would not a foot with you go;
But, if you had tarried, I would not have
left you so.
And with the same speed God grant you in
your journey
From you I will depart as fast as I may.

EVERYMAN: Where are you going, Fellowship?
Will you leave me alone?

FELLOWSHIP: Yes, by my faith, and God make
you His own.

EVERYMAN: Farewell, good Fellowship; for you
my heart is sore.
Adieu for ever! I shall see you no more.

FELLOWSHIP: In faith, Everyman, farewell
now at the end,
For you I will remember that parting is
mourning. (*Exit* FELLOWSHIP.)

EVERYMAN: Alas, shall we thus separate
indeed —
Ah, Lady, help! — without any more
comfort?
See, Fellowship forsakes me in my greatest
need.
For help in this world where can I
resort?
Fellowship here before with me would
merry make
And now little sorrow for me does he take.
It is said, "In prosperity men friends may
find,
Who in adversity are all unkind."
Now where for help now shall I flee?
Seeing that Fellowship's forsaken me?
To my relatives I will, truly,
Praying them to help me in my necessity.
I believe that they will do so,
For "kind will creep where it may not
go."[2]
I will go see, for there I see them go.
Where are you now, my friends and
kinsmen?

(*Enter* KINDRED *and* COUSIN.)

KINDRED: Here are we now at your command-
ment.
Cousin, I pray you show us your intent
In any way, and do not spare.

COUSIN: Yes, Everyman, and to us declare
Whatever it is that you're disposed to do,
For, know you well, we'll live and die with
you.

KINDRED: In wealth and woe we will with you
hold.
Commanding his kin a man may be bold.

---

2 Kinship will find a way; "Blood is thicker than
water."

EVERYMAN: My thanks, my friends and kinsmen
kind.
Now shall I show you the grief in my mind:
I was commanded by a messenger,
That is a high king's chief officer;
He bade me take a pilgrimage, to my
pain,
From which I know I'll not return again;
Also I must give a reckoning straight,
For the Devil, my enemy, for me does wait,
And intends my happiness to hinder.

KINDRED: What account is that which you
must render?
That I would know.

EVERYMAN: Of all my works I must show
How I have lived and my days spent;
Also with ill deeds how I have abused
The time of life that to me was lent;
And of all virtues that I have refused.
Therefore, I pray you, go there with me
To help make my account, in charity.

COUSIN: What, to go there? Is that the matter?
No, Everyman, I'd rather fast on bread
and water
For the next five years in scorn.

EVERYMAN: Alas, that I was ever born!
For now I never shall be merry,
If you forsake me.

KINDRED: Ah, sir, what, you are a merry
man!
Take heart, cheer up and make no moan.
But one thing I warn you, by Saint Anne —
As for me, you shall go alone.

EVERYMAN: My cousin, can I prevail on you
to go?

COUSIN: No, by our Lady! I have a cramp
in my toe.
Trust not to me, for, God give me speed,
I will deceive you in your direst need.

KINDRED: It will not help us to entice.
You shall have my maid with all my heart;
She loves to go to feasts, that wanton
nice,
And to dance, and abroad to start.
I will give her leave to help you in that
journey,
If you and she can agree.

EVERYMAN: Now tell me exactly what is on
your mind:
Will you go with me, or stay behind?

KINDRED: Stay behind? Yes, that will I do,
and may!
Therefore farewell till another day. (*Exit*
KINDRED.)

EVERYMAN: How should I be merry or glad?
For fair promises men to me make,
But when I have most need they me
forsake.
I am deceived; that makes me sad.

COUSIN: Cousin Everyman, farewell now,
For truly I will not go with you.
Also of my own an unready reckoning
I have to account; therefore I am
tarrying.
Now God keep you, for now I go. (*Exit*
COUSIN.)

EVERYMAN: Ah, Jesus, is this what it has come
to?
Lo, fair words make fools glad again;
They promise, and nothing will do certain.
My kinsmen promised me faithfully
To abide with me steadfastly;
And now fast away they flee.
Even so Fellowship promised me.
With what friend can I myself provide?
I waste my time longer here to abide.
Yet in my mind a thing there is:
All my life I have loved riches;
If now my Goods would help me right
He would make my heart very light.
I will speak to him in this distress.
Where are you Goods, my riches?

GOODS (*within*): Who calls me? Everyman?
What, are you in haste?
I lie here in corners, gathered, piled so high,
And in chests I am locked so fast,
Also sacked in bags. You may see with
your eye
I cannot stir; in packages I lie.
What do you want? Quickly do say.

EVERYMAN: Come here, Goods, in all the haste
you may,
For advice I must require for me.

(*Enter* GOODS.)

GOODS: Sir, if you have in the world any
  sorrow or adversity,
  That I can help you to remedy shortly.

EVERYMAN: It is another disease that troubles
  me;
  Not of this world, and I must tell you so.
  I am sent for another way to go,
  To give a straight account in general
  Before the highest Jupiter of all;
  You've given joy and pleasure in my life
  to me,
  Therefore, I pray you, go with me;
  For, it may be, you may before God
  Almighty
  My reckoning help to clean and purify;
  For it is said every now and then
  That "money makes wrong all right again."

GOODS: No, Everyman, I sing another song to
  men.
  I follow no man in such voyages;
  For, if I went your fate to see,
  You should fare much the worse for me;
  For because on me you set your mind,
  Your reckoning I have blotted and made
  blind,
  That your account you cannot make truly —
  And all because of your great love of
  me.

EVERYMAN: That would grieve me all the more
  When I should come to that fearful answer.
  Up, let us go together.

GOODS: Oh, no! I am too brittle, I may not
  endure.
  I will follow no man one foot, you may
  be sure.

EVERYMAN: Alas, I have loved you, and had
  great pleasure
  Each day of my life in goods and treasure.

GOODS: That's your damnation, it's no lie to
  say it,
  But everlasting's not the way I play it.
  If you had loved me moderately during
  Life, and to the poor gave part of me,
  Then you should now not in this dolor be,
  Nor in this great sorrow and care.

EVERYMAN: Lo, I was much deceived when
  unaware,

And now may blame the wasting of
  my time.

GOODS: What, did you think I was a friend
  so fine?

EVERYMAN: I had thought so.

GOODS: No, Everyman, I say no.
  Just for a while was I yours, you see;
  A season you had me in prosperity.
  My nature it is man's soul to kill;
  If I save one, a thousand lives I spill.
  And do you think that I'll your follower be?
  No, not from this world, verily.

EVERYMAN: I had thought otherwise.

GOODS: Therefore to your soul Goods is a thief;
  For when you're dead my practice lies
  In then deceiving someone else likewise,
  As I have you, who in me puts belief.

EVERYMAN: O false Goods, cursed may you
  be,
  You traitor to God, that has deceived me
  And caught me in your snare!

GOODS: By Mary! You brought yourself to
  care,
  For that I'm very glad;
  I must laugh, for I cannot be sad.

EVERYMAN: Ah, Goods, you long have had my
  heartfelt love;
  I gave you that which should be God's
  above.
  But will you not go with me indeed?
  I ask you truth to say.

GOODS: No, may God be my speed!
  Therefore farewell, and so good day. (*Exit*
  GOODS.)

EVERYMAN: O, to whom shall I make my moan
  And beg to go with me my heavy journey?
  First Fellowship said he would be my own —
  His words were very pleasant and gay,
  But afterwards he left me alone.
  Then I spoke to my kinsmen in despair
  And they also gave me words fair —
  They lacked no fair speaking,
  But all forsook me in the ending.
  Then I went to my Goods I loved the best
  In hope to have comfort, but there I had
  least;

For my Goods sharply did me tell
That he brings many to Hell.
Then of myself I was ashamed.
And so I am worthy to be blamed.
Thus may I justly myself hate.
Of whom shall I now counsel take?
I think I never shall succeed
Until I go to my Good Deed.
But, alas, she is so weak,
That she can neither walk nor speak.
Yet I will venture on her now.
My Good Deeds, where are you?

(GOOD DEEDS *speaks from the ground.*)

GOOD DEEDS: Here I lie, cold in the
    ground,
Your sins have me sorely bound,
So I cannot stir.

EVERYMAN: O Good Deeds, I stand in fear!
I must beg counsel of you,
For help would be very welcome now.

GOOD DEEDS: Everyman, I have understanding
That you are summoned an account to make
Before Messias, the Jerusalem King;
If you take my advice, that journey with
    you will I take.

EVERYMAN: Therefore I come to you my
    moan to make.
I pray you, will go with me?

GOOD DEEDS: I'm willing but too weak to stand,
    verily.

EVERYMAN: Why, did something on you fall?

GOOD DEEDS: Yes, sir, I may thank you for all;
If you had perfectly cheered me,
Your account book all ready would be.
Look how the records of your works and
    deeds speak!
Behold how they lie under the feet
To your soul's heaviness.

EVERYMAN: Our Lord Jesus, help me!
For one letter here I cannot see.

GOOD DEEDS: There is a blind reckoning in
    time of distress.

EVERYMAN: Good Deeds, I pray you help me
in this need,

Or else I am for ever damned indeed;
Therefore help me to make a reckoning
Before the Redeemer of everything,
That King is, and was, and ever shall.[3]

GOOD DEEDS: Everyman, I am sorry for your
    fall.
And gladly would I help you, were I able.

EVERYMAN: Good Deeds, your counsel I
    pray give to me.

GOOD DEEDS: That shall I do verily;
Even though on my feet I cannot go,
I have a sister to accompany you also,
Called Knowledge, which shall with you
    abide,
To help you make that dreadful
    reckoning.

(*Enter* KNOWLEDGE.)

KNOWLEDGE: Everyman, I will go with you,
    and be your guide,
In your greatest need be at your side.

EVERYMAN: In good condition now am I in
    everything,
And am wholly content with this good thing,
Thanked be God, my creator.

GOOD DEEDS: And when she has brought you
    there
Where you shall heal the pain of your heart,
Then go with your reckoning and your
    Good Deeds together,
To make you joyful at heart
Before the blessed Trinity.

EVERYMAN: My Good Deeds, thanks from me!
I am well content, certainly,
With your words sweet.

KNOWLEDGE: Now let us go together lovingly
To Confession, that cleansing river.

EVERYMAN: I weep for joy; I wish we now
    were there!
But, I pray you, give me information:
Where dwells that holy man, Confession?

---

3 A prayer concludes: " . . . Who was in the beginning,
art now, and ever shall be, world without end," referring to the timelessness of God.

KNOWLEDGE: In church, the house of salvation:
We shall find him in that place,
That shall comfort us, by God's grace.

(KNOWLEDGE *leads* EVERYMAN *to* CONFESSION.)

Lo, this is Confession. Kneel down and ask
mercy,
For he is in high esteem with God Almighty.

EVERYMAN: O glorious fountain, that all un-
cleanliness can clarify,
Wash from me the spots of vice unclean,
So that on me no sin may be seen.
I come with knowledge, for my redemption,
Contrite of heart, full of contrition;
For I am commanded a pilgrimage to take
And great accounting before God to
make.
Confession, mother of salvation,
Pray help Good Deeds for my exclamation.

CONFESSION: I know your sorrow well, Every-
man.
Because with Knowledge you have come
to me,
I will comfort you as well as I can,
And a precious jewel you shall have from me
Called penance, voider of adversity;
With it your body shall chastisement see,
With abstinence and perseverance in God's
service.
Here shall you receive that scourge of
me
Which is penance strong, that you must
endure,
Remembering the Savior Who was sharply
Scourged for your sins and suffered
patiently.
So must you, before that painful pilgrimage.
Knowledge, keep him on that painful
voyage,
And by that time Good Deeds will make
you three.
In any case, be confident of mercy,
Your time draws near, but you will saved be.
Ask God for mercy and He will grant truly.
When with the penance scourge a man
himself does bind,
The balm of forgiveness then ever shall he
find.

EVERYMAN: Thanked be God for His gracious
work!
For now I will my penance begin;
This has rejoiced and lightened my heart,
Though the knots be painful and hard
within.

KNOWLEDGE: Look to it that your penance you
fulfill
However painful it to you may be;
And Knowledge shall give you counsel
at will
How to make your accounting clearly.

EVERYMAN: O eternal God, O heavenly
figure,
O way of righteousness, O goodly vision,
Who descended to be born of virgin pure
Because He wanted each man to redeem,
Which Adam forfeited by his disobedience,
O blessed Godhead, elect and high
divine,
Forgive my grievous offense;
Here I cry for mercy in these people's
presence.
O spiritual treasure, O ransomer and
redeemer,
Of all the world the hope and conductor,
Mirror of joy and founder of mercy,
Who illuminates Heaven and Earth thereby,
Hear my complaint, however late it be;
Receive my prayers, unworthy of Thy
benignity.
Though I am a sinner most abominable
Let my penance be written in Moses'
table.
O Mary, pray to the Maker of each thing,
To grant me help at my ending.
And save me from the Devil, my enemy,
For Death assails me strongly.
And, blessed Lady, by means of thy
prayer,
Of your Son's glory make me partner,
By means of His Passion, this I crave.
I beseech you, help my soul to save.
Knowledge, give me the scourge of penance;
My flesh with that shall give acquittance.
Now I'll begin, if God will grant me grace.

KNOWLEDGE: Everyman, God grant you time
and space!

Thus I commend you to the hands of our
Savior.
Now you may make your reckoning sure.

EVERYMAN: In the name of the Holy Trinity,
My body sore punished shall be.
Take this, body, for the sin of the flesh!
(*Scourges himself.*)
Also, you delight to go gay and fresh
And in the way of damnation did me bring;
Therefore suffer now strokes of punish-
ing.
Now of penance I will wade the water clear,
To save me from Purgatory, that sharp fire.

(GOOD DEEDS *rises from the floor.*)

GOOD DEEDS: I thank God now that I can go
And am delivered from sickness and woe.
Therefore, with Everyman I'll go, myself
not spare;
His good works I will help him to declare.

KNOWLEDGE: Now, Everyman, be merry and
glad!
Your Good Deeds come now; you need not
be sad.
Now is your Good Deeds whole and sound,
Walking upright upon the ground.

EVERYMAN: My heart is light, and shall be
evermore;
Now I will smite faster than I did before.
(*Scourges himself.*)

GOOD DEEDS: Everyman, pilgrim, my special
friend,
Blessed be you without end;
For you is prepared eternal glory.
You have made me whole and sound,
In any attack on you I'll stand my ground.

EVERYMAN: Welcome, Good Deeds. Now I
hear your voice,
I weep for the very sweetness of love.

KNOWLEDGE: Be sad no more but evermore
rejoice;
God sees your action from His throne above.
Put on this garment for His love, (*Gives him
a garment symbolic of penance.*)
A benefit wet with your tears,
Or else before God you may miss

It when your journey's end comes after
all.

EVERYMAN: Gentle Knowledge, what do you
it call?

KNOWLEDGE: It is a garment of sorrow;
From pain redemption borrow;
Contrition it is,
That yields forgiveness;
It pleases God very well.

GOOD DEEDS: Everyman, wear it now your
soul to heal.

EVERYMAN (*putting on the garment*): Now
blessed be Jesus, Mary's Son,
For now I don true contrition.
And let us go now without tarrying.
Good Deeds, have we clear our reckoning?

GOOD DEEDS: Yes, indeed, I have it here.

EVERYMAN: Then I trust we need not fear.
Now, friends, let us not part again.

KNOWLEDGE: No, Everyman, we will not,
for certain.

GOOD DEEDS: Still you must bring men three,
Three persons of great force.

EVERYMAN: Who should they be?

GOOD DEEDS: Discretion and Strength, of
course.
And your Beauty may not stay behind.

KNOWLEDGE: Also, you must call to mind
Your Five Senses for your counselors.

GOOD DEEDS: You must have them ready at
all hours.

EVERYMAN: How shall I get them unto me?

KNOWLEDGE: You must call them all
together,
And they will hear immediately.

EVERYMAN: My friends, come here and be
present,
Discretion, Strength, my Five Senses,
Beauty.

(*Enter* BEAUTY, STRENGTH, DISCRETION, *and* FIVE
SENSES.)

BEAUTY: Here at your call we all are ready.
What do you wish us all to do?

GOOD DEEDS: That you will with Everyman go,
And help him on his pilgrimage.
Say yes or no: will you go on that voyage?

STRENGTH: We will not fail nor wither
In giving help and comfort, believe me.

DISCRETION: So with him all will go together.

EVERYMAN: Almighty God, loved may you be!
I give You praise that I together brought
Strength, Discretion, Beauty, Five Senses,
lacking nought.
And my Good Deeds, with Knowledge
clear,
Are also in my company right here.
I have what I need for my business.

STRENGTH: And I, Strength, will stand by in
distress,
Though you would in battle fight on the
ground.

FIVE SENSES: And though it were through
the world round,
We will not depart for sweet nor sour.

BEAUTY: No more will I, until death's hour,
Whatsoever comes of all.

DISCRETION: Everyman, consider first of all;
Go with a good advisement and
deliberation.
We give you virtuous admonition.
All shall be well.

EVERYMAN: My friends, listen to what I will
tell:
I pray God reward you in His heavenly
sphere.
Now listen, all that are here,
I will make my last testament
Here before all you present:
In alms half my goods I give with my two
hands
By way of charity, with good intent,
And the other half my alms still stands
Bequeathed, to be returned where it ought
to be.
This I do to spite the fiend of Hell,
To escape completely his peril
Ever after this day.

KNOWLEDGE: Everyman, listen to what I
say:
Go to Priesthood, I advise,
And receive in any wise
The Holy Sacrament and unction together.
Then quickly see you return hither;
We will all await you here.

FIVE SENSES: Yes, Everyman, hurry and pre-
pare, for here
There is no emperor, king, duke, nor baron,
That from God has commission
As large as has the least priest being;
For of the blessed sacraments, pure and
benign,
He holds the keys, with remedy sure
For man's redemption — it is ever sure —
Which God, for our soul's medicine,
Gave us out of His heart with great pain
Here in this transitory life, for you and
me.
The blessed sacraments just seven be:
Baptism, confirmation, the priesthood good,
And the sacrament of God's precious flesh
and blood,
Marriage, the holy extreme unction, and
penance.
These seven are good to have in
remembrance,
Gracious sacraments of high divinity.

EVERYMAN: Gladly would I receive that holy
body,
And meekly to my spiritual father go.

FIVE SENSES: Everyman, that is the best that
you can do.
God will you to salvation bring,
For priesthood excels each other thing:
To us the priests the Scripture teach,
Converting man from sin, Heaven to reach;
God has to priests more power given
Than to any angel that's in Heaven.
With five words[4] he can consecrate,
God's body, flesh and blood, to make,

---

4 At the Consecration of the Mass the priest says:
"Hoc est enim corpus meum" ("For this is My body")
and those who believe in Transubstantiation hold that
thereupon the bread and wine become the body and
blood of Christ.

And holds his Maker between his hands.
The priest binds and unbinds all bands,
Both on Earth and in Heaven.
You, priesthood, administer sacraments
   seven;
Though we kissed your feet, you were
   worthy;
You are the surgeon that makes sin not
   deadly;
No remedy we find under God
But only the priesthood.
Everyman, God gave priests that dignity.
And put them in His place among us to be.
They rank above the angels in degree.[5]

(*Exit* EVERYMAN *to receive the last sacraments from the priest.*)

KNOWLEDGE: If priests be good, that's their rank
   surely.
But when Jesus hung on His cross with
   pain all apart
There He gave out of His blessed heart
The same sacrament in great torment.
He sold them not us to us, that Lord omni-
   potent.
Therefore Saint Peter, the apostle, can say
That Jesus' curse have all they
Who God, their Savior, do buy and sell,
Or they for money absolution tell.
Sinful priests give sinners example bad;
Their bastards sit by other men's fires, I've
   heard;
And some haunt women's company
In unclean lives, with lusts and lechery:
These men with sin are blind.

FIVE SENSES: I trust to God none such we'll find.
Therefore let us our priesthood honor,
And follow their doctrine for our souls'
   succor.
We are their sheep, they our shepherds be,
By whom we all are kept in surety.
Peace, for there I see Everyman come,
Who has made true satisfaction.

GOOD DEEDS: I think it is he indeed.

(*Enter* EVERYMAN.)

EVERYMAN: Now Jesus give you prosperous
   speed!
I have received the sacrament for my
   redemption,

And then my extreme unction.
Blessed be they who counseled me to take it!
And now, friends, let us go without
   longer respite:
I thank God that you have waited so long.
Now put each of you in this cross your hand,
And quickly follow me.
I go before where I would be; God be our
   guide!

STRENGTH: Everyman, we will not from
   you go
Till you've completed this voyage long.

DISCRETION: I, Discretion, will stay with you
   also.

KNOWLEDGE: And though this pilgrimage be
   difficult and long,
From you I will never go.

STRENGTH: Everyman, I will as reliable be
As ever I was to Judas Maccabee.[6]

(*They go together to the grave.*)

EVERYMAN: Alas, I am so faint I cannot stand;
My limbs under me do fold.
Friends, let us not return to this land,
Not for all the world's gold;
For into this cave must I creep
And turn to earth, there to sleep.

BEAUTY: What, into this grave? Alas!

EVERYMAN: Yes all men shall decay, both great
   and less.

BEAUTY: And what, should I smother here?

EVERYMAN: Yes, by my faith, and never more
   appear.
In this world we shall live no more at all,
But in Heaven, before the highest Lord of all.

----

5 This pro-clerical propaganda reminds us that *Everyman* (whether originally Dutch or English) is pre-Reformation and imbued with the theology of the Roman Catholic Church. Though its ultimate source was a Buddhist work (transmitted through the eighth-century *Barlaam and Josaphat*, attributed to St. John Damascene) it is steeped in the doctrines of medieval Christianity. 6 Judas was the ancient leader of the Maccabee sect. See the *Apocrypha*, I Maccabees 3:19.

BEAUTY: I cross out all this! *Adieu,* by Saint
John!
I take my cap in my lap, and am gone.

EVERYMAN: What, Beauty, where will you be?

BEAUTY: Peace, I am deaf; I look not behind me.
Not if you gave me all the gold in your
chest. (*Exit* BEAUTY.)

EVERYMAN: Alas, on what may I trust?
Beauty goes fast away from me;
She promised with me to live and die.

STRENGTH: Everyman, I also will forsake you
and deny;
Your game pleases me not at all.

EVERYMAN: Why, then, will you forsake me all?
Sweet Strength, tarry a little space.

STRENGTH: No, sir, by the cross of grace!
I will hurry from you fast,
Though you weep and be downcast.

EVERYMAN: You would always stay by me,
you said.

STRENGTH: Yes, I have you far enough
conveyed.
You are old enough, I understand,
Your pilgrimage to take in hand;
I repent this far I came.

EVERYMAN: Strength, for your displeasure I'm
to blame;
But promise is debt and cannot be
forgot.

STRENGTH: In faith, I care not.
You are just a fool to complain;
You spend your speech and waste your
brain.
Go, thrust yourself into the ground! (*Exit*
STRENGTH.)

EVERYMAN: I had thought you reliable
would be found.
He that trusts in his Strength
Will find himself deceived at length.
Both Strength and Beauty forsake me,
Though they promised fair and lovingly.

DISCRETION: Everyman, I will after Strength
be gone;
As for me, I will leave you alone.

EVERYMAN: Why, Discretion, will you forsake
me?

DISCRETION: Yes, in faith, away I must be.
For when Strength goes before
I follow evermore.

EVERYMAN: Yet, I pray you, for the love of the
Trinity,
Look in my grave once piteously.

DISCRETION: No, so close I will not come;
Farewell, everyone! (*Exit* DISCRETION.)

EVERYMAN: O everything fails, save God
alone —
Beauty, Strength, and Discretion;
For when Death blows his blast
They all run and flee me fast.

FIVE SENSES: Everyman, my leave now of
you I take;
I will follow the others, for here you
I forsake.

EVERYMAN: Alas, then may I wail and weep,
For I took you for my best friend.

FIVE SENSES: I will no longer with you keep;
Now farewell, and that's the end. (*Exit*
FIVE SENSES.)

EVERYMAN: O Jesus, help! All have forsaken me.

GOOD DEEDS: No, Everyman, I will stay. You'll
see
I will not forsake you indeed;
You will find me a good friend in need.

EVERYMAN: My thanks, Good Deeds! Now
may I true friends see.
They have forsaken me, every one;
I have loved them better than Good Deeds
alone.
Knowledge, will you forsake me also?

KNOWLEDGE: Yes, Everyman, when you to
Death shall go;
But not yet, for no kind of danger.

EVERYMAN: Thank you, Knowledge, with
all my heart.

KNOWLEDGE: No, still I will not from here
depart
Till I see what for you's to come.

EVERYMAN: I think, alas, that I must be gone
  To make my reckoning and my debts pay,
  For I see my time is almost gone away.
  Take example, all you that this do hear
    or see,
  How they that I loved best do forsake me,
  Except my Good Deeds that stays on truly.

GOOD DEEDS: All earthly things are only
    vanity:
  Beauty, Strength, and Discretion dis-
    solve in air,
  Foolish friends and kinsmen that spoke
    fair —
  All flee except Good Deeds, and that am I.

EVERYMAN: Have mercy on me, God most
    mighty;
  And stand by me, you mother and maid,
    Holy Mary.

GOOD DEEDS: Fear not; I'll your speaker
    be.

EVERYMAN: Here I cry God mercy.

GOOD DEEDS: Shorten our end, diminish our
    pain;
  Let us go and never come again.

EVERYMAN: Into Your hands, Lord, my soul
    I commend;
  Receive it, Lord, that it be not lost.
  As You redeemed me, so me defend,
  And save me from the fiend's boast,
  That I may appear with that blessed host
  That shall be saved at the day of doom.
  In manas tuas, of might's most
  For ever, *commendo spiritum meum.*[7]

(EVERYMAN *and* GOOD DEEDS *descend into the grave.*)

KNOWLEDGE: Now has he suffered what we all
    shall endure;
  His Good Deeds shall make all secure.
  Now has he made ending.
  I think I hear the angels sing
  And make great joy and melody
  Where Everyman's soul received shall be.

ANGEL: Come to Jesus, you excellent elect, you!
  Here above you shall go
  Because of your special virtue.
  Now the soul from the body has to go,
  Your reckoning is crystal clear.
  Now come you into the heavenly sphere,
  Unto which all you shall come
  That live well before the day of doom.
    (*Exit* KNOWLEDGE.)

(*Enter* DOCTOR.)

DOCTOR (*as a final Chorus*): This moral men
    should keep in mind.
  You hearers, value it, both old and young,
  And forsake Pride, for he deceives you in
    the end;
  And remember Beauty, Five Senses,
    Strength, and Discretion,
  Each one at the last every man forsakes,
  Only his Good Deeds to the grave he takes.
  But be careful, if they be few
  Before God they'll be small use to you.
  Then no excuse may be there for every man,
  Alas, what shall he do then?
  For after death amends may no man make,
  For then Mercy and Pity do him forsake.
  If man's reckoning is not clear when he
    does come,
  God will say: "*Ite, maledicti, in ignem
    eternum.*"[8]
  And he that has his account whole and
    sound
  High up in Heaven he shall be crowned;
  Unto which place God brings us in fair
    weather
  That we may live body and soul together.
  In that, help the Trinity!
  Amen, say you, in charity.

Thus Ends this Moral Play of EVERYMAN.

---

7 "Into Thy hands I commend my spirit"—words of Christ on the cross. Luke 23:46.   8 "Depart from Me, ye cursed, into everlasting fire." Matthew 25:41.

The Tragical History of Doctor Faustus

Everyman, though it deals with man facing death, is not a tragedy, for Everyman ends happily, going to the common fate of all men of necessity and not perishing due to some fault or failure of his own. It remained for two lawyers, Thomas Norton and Thomas Sackville (later Earl of Dorset), to produce in *Gorboduc, or Ferrex and Porrex* (acted before Queen Elizabeth, Sackville's cousin, in 1561–1562) "the first regular English tragedy" and for Christopher Marlowe to write the first masterpiece of the *genre* in English.

Using a German legend also adapted by Calderón and Goethe, Marlowe wedded myth to Morality play and transformed an inaccurate translation of Johann Spies' *Historia von D. Johann Fausten, dem weitbeschreuyen Zauberer und Schwartzkunstler* (1587) into a thoroughly English play which combines the episodic structure of the chronicle history plays then popular with an astounding power and poetry only to be equalled by Shakespeare in the succeeding decades. Though we do not know precisely when it was written, or how much of the quarto edition of 1604 and the longer one of 1616 are by Marlowe, it is clearly a milestone in the development of drama and probably the greatest achievement of the author of *The Jew of Malta* and *Edward II*, the two parts of *Tamburlaine*, and other plays.

It is difficult to harmonize this play with what we know of Marlowe as a person. Christopher Marlowe (1564–1593) was, according to the testimony of his roommate Thomas Kyd (author of *The Spanish Tragedy*), not only "intemperate and of a cruel heart" but an out-and-out atheist. From a man who had himself been arrested for posting "lewd and mutinous libels" on a churchyard wall, this was a strong charge. Moreover, one Richard Baines stirred up the Privy Council by testifying to them that Marlowe had uttered "the most horrible blasphemes and damnable opinions" and Marlowe was being sought for arrest, on a warrant from the Privy Council, when his adventurous life was suddenly ended in Eleanor Bull's tavern at Deptford. In a fight, Ingram Friser stabbed Marlowe in the eye with Marlowe's own dagger. This gory end was more likely to have been somehow connected with Marlowe's life as a spy — he infiltrated the Jesuits at Douai to report on plots to assassinate Elizabeth and performed other missions under the direction of Sir Francis Walsingham, head of the "CIA" of that day — than with atheism and Sir Walter Raleigh's "School of Night." Yet Marlowe seems a strange man, with what we should call today "sick jokes" on religion and blasphemous dinner-table conversation, to have written *Doctor Faustus*, a play imbued not just with profound religious feeling and a stern warning against the godless speculations of daring Renaissance scholars but with old-fashioned Roman Catholicism at that, as Sister Mary Genevieve in *The Catholic Educational Review* (1934) and other critics have noted. Paul H. Kocher says:

> Faustus is in some sense Marlowe. The truth may be that for all his overt and ostentatious gibing at Christianity Marlowe sometimes experienced a dark hour when he was overwhelmed by fear of his own apostasy and by need for the love of God. Or perhaps it is best to say that these feelings were latent in him but available at the call of his poetic inspiration.

Whatever the wellspring of his inspiration, Marlowe hit upon a subject perfectly suited to his own interest in supermen ("overreachers" presented in "high, astounding terms") and the fascination of his age with the sensuous in blank verse (Marlowe's incantatory "mighty line") and the sensational (particularly the supernatural) in plot. In *Doctor Faustus* we have (says Una Ellis-Fermor) "the greatest conflict that the drama has ever undertaken to present," the struggle of man in the spiritual sphere for his very soul, his yearning for knowledge (which, as Bacon said, is power) and his need for grace. In presenting this story of universal significance, Marlowe draws on dramatic devices as antiquated in his time as a parade of The Seven Deadly Sins and as fresh in ours as expressionistic devices for delving beneath what O'Neill called "the banality of surfaces" to the inner truth, devices to make tangible and visible upon the stage inner states of mind and spiritual realities. The Old Man is what Faustus might have become. Faustus himself is each of us, Everyman Extraordinaire. The Good and Bad Angels, whom Marlowe made characters and whom the modern director might present as Faustus' own voice recorded and arguing back to him, are essentially ideas in the protagonist's mind. Even the unforgettable character of Mephistophilis is not so much an agent of the Devil as a dark side of the nature of man, a devious and destructive masochist and *molochiste* urge, the reverse of the coin of creativity and ambition to succeed. In *Doctor Faustus* we have a tension between the medieval and the Renaissance worlds and between the Morality and the heroic play; we have also a conflict, whether we care to interpret it in terms of old religion or new psychology, which makes the impact of the tragedy stunning and the implications complex.

In his study of the play J. P. Brockbank quotes a passage from the first complete English edition of de la Primaudaye's *French Academy* (1618), apt in Marlowe's age of moral and intellectual ferment and in ours as well:

> The ill success of our age affordeth us too many miserable testimonies, wherein at this day we see nothing but contrarieties of opinions and un-

certainties, through their subtleties and bold curiosities, who have sought to pluck (as a man would say) out of heaven the secrets hid from the Angels; yea, which is worse, have boasted that they have attained to the knowledge of them, filling our times with trouble and confusion under that false pretence.

What "trouble and confusion" has our science brought us, what monsters have we created with our marvels, and what sense of security and sustenance of hope have we lost for every raid upon the "secret" and advance into the unknown! We may not be willing to accept the warning that *Doctor Faustus* gives "only to wonder at unlawful things" and not to venture where Heaven forbids, but neither can we escape the suspicion that the vast power we have bought with our innocence may be wasted in foolish pranks and irresponsible applications — and the farcical scenes of *Doctor Faustus* are no less a part and, in the end no less horrifying than the tragic — and in the end destroy us, just when (too late) we are ready to burn our books. The frightening thing about *Doctor Faustus* is not that it is an anti-intellectual play but that, at heart, it is an appeal to reason: it is not to say that we should not strive for knowledge but only that there is at last one essential fact that the ambitious mind tends to ignore and which in the end will undo all. "Theirs was the giant race before the flood," wrote Dryden of the dramatists of this period. Surely there was never a theme as worthy of their abilities as that of *Doctor Faustus*. In Marlowe it found a brave spokesman.

It has been thought best to select for the text here the 1604 version of *Doctor Faustus*. Sir Walter Greg and others have argued that the 1616 text is better, but I tend to agree with C. L. Barber and M. M. Mahoud that students ought to be given the "A-text" (1604) and, of course, as a term paper project students might always compare and evaluate the "A" and "B" texts (1604 and 1616) and the criticism on their validity. It is an exercise in logic and sensitivity as well as bibliography, and very illuminating. For the text I have provided rather elaborate notes which will indicate the sort of scholarship and annotation required to read plays of this period and, with this example, students can then go on to read Shakespeare with the assistance of their instructor (or with more readily accessible reference books) but without my interference.

THE TRAGICAL HISTORY OF DOCTOR FAUSTUS

Christopher Marlowe

*A modernized text
of the quarto of 1604
with notes by L. R. N. Ashley*

DRAMATIS PERSONÆ

THE POPE
CARDINAL OF LORRAIN
THE EMPEROR OF GERMANY
THE DUKE OF VANHOLT
FAUSTUS
VALDES ⎫
CORNELIUS ⎭ *friends to* FAUSTUS
WAGNER, *servant to* FAUSTUS
A CLOWN
ROBIN
RALPH
A VINTNER
A HORSE-COURSER
A KNIGHT
AN OLD MAN
SCHOLARS, FRIARS, *and* ATTENDANTS
THE DUCHESS OF VANHOLT
LUCIFER
BELZEBUB
MEPHISTOPHILIS
A GOOD ANGEL
AN EVIL ANGEL
THE SEVEN DEADLY SINS
DEVILS
SPIRITS *in the shapes of* ALEXANDER THE GREAT,
   of his PARAMOUR *and of* HELEN.
CHORUS

PROLOGUE

(*Enter* CHORUS.)

CHORUS: Not marching now in fields of
      Thrasymene,
   Where Mars did mate the Carthaginians;[1]
   Nor sporting in the dalliance of love,

In courts of kings where state[2] is overturn'd;
Nor in the pomp of proud audacious
      deeds,
Intends our Muse to vaunt her heavenly
      verse:
Only this, gentlemen, — we must perform
The form[3] of Faustus' fortunes, good or bad:
To patient judgments we appeal our plaud,[4]
And speak for Faustus in his infancy.
Now is he born, his parents base of stock,
In Germany, within a town call'd Rhodes:[5]
Of riper years, to Wertenberg[6] he went,
Whereas his kinsmen chiefly brought him
      up.
So soon he profits in divinity,[7]
The fruitful plot of scholarism grac'd,[8]
That shortly he was grac'd with doctor's
      name,
Excelling all whose sweet delight disputes[9]
In heavenly matters of theology;
Till swoln with cunning, of a self-
      conceit,[10]
His waxen wings[11] did mount above his
      reach,

---

1 *Thrasymene . . . Carthaginians:* Not presenting now a play about Hannibal (perhaps an allusion to a lost play given by this company), the Carthaginian who won at Lake Trasimene, 217 B.C. *Mars:* Roman god of War. *Mate:* join with or rival. **2** *state:* government or order (perhaps an allusion to another sort of play). **3** *perform/The form:* wordplay was a popular device of Elizabethan drama, especially after the Euphuism (excessively elegant and mannered language) of *Euphues, or The Anatomy of Wit* (1578) and *Euphues and his England* (1580), novels by playwright John Lyly (c. 1533–1606). **4** *appeal our plaud:* make our appeal for applause. **5** *Rhodes:* Roda, a town in the German duchy of Saxe-Altenberg. The "real" Dr. Faustus (fl. 1507–1540) was born at Knittlingen in Swabia. **6** *Wertenberg:* Wittenberg, site of a famous university. (Shakespeare's Hamlet was supposed to be a student there.) **7** *divinity:* the study of theology. **8** *grac'd:* He adorned the university and they granted him a doctor's degree. A pun on the Grace Book of English universities where degree candidates were listed. **9** *whose sweet delight disputes:* whose pleasure it was to debate. **10** *cunning, of a self-conceit:* knowledge made him egotistical. **11** *waxen wings:* an allusion to Icarus, whose waxen wings fell off when he flew too near the sun.

And, melting, heavens conspir'd his over-
throw;
For, falling to a devilish exercise,
And glutted now with learning's golden gifts,
He surfeits upon cursed necromancy;[12]
Nothing so sweet as magic is to him,
Which he prefers before his chiefest bliss:
And this the man that in his study sits.[13]
(*Exit.*)

SCENE ONE

(FAUSTUS *discovered in his study.*)

FAUSTUS: Settle thy studies, Faustus, and begin
To sound the depth of that thou wilt
profess:[1]
Having commenc'd,[2] be a divine in show,
Yet level[3] at the end of every art,
And live and die in Aristotle's works.
Sweet Analytics,[4] 'tis thou hast ravish'd me!
Bene disserere est finis logices.[5]
Is, to dispute well, logic's chiefest end?
Affords this art no greater miracle?
Then read no more; thou hast attain'd
that end:
A greater subject fitteth Faustus' wit:
Bid Economy farewell, and Galen[6] come,
Seeing, *Ubi desinit philosophus, ibi incipit
medicus:*[7]
Be a physician, Faustus; heap up gold,
And be eternis'd for some wondrous cure:
Summum bonum medicinæ sanitas,[8]
The end of physic is our body's health.
Why, Faustus, hast thou not attain'd that
end?
Is not thy common talk found aphorisms?[9]
Are not thy bills[10] hung up as monu-
ments,
Whereby whole cities have escap'd the
plague,
And thousand desperate maladies been
eas'd?
Yet art thou still but Faustus, and a man.
Couldst thou make men to live eternally,
Or, being dead, raise them to life again,
Then this profession were to be esteem'd.
Physic, farewell! Where is Justinian?[11]
(*Reads.*)
*Si una eademque res legatur duobus, alter
rem, alter valorem, rei, etc.*[12]

A pretty case of paltry legacies! (*Reads.*)
*Exhœreditare filium non potest pater,
nisi, etc.*[13]
Such is the subject of the institute,
And universal body of the law:
This study fits a mercenary drudge,
Who aims at nothing but external trash;
Too servile and illiberal for me.
When all is done,[14] divinity is best:
Jerome's Bible,[15] Faustus; view it well.
(*Reads.*)
Stipendium peccati mors est. Ha! *Stipendium,
etc.*[16]

---

12 *necromancy:* magic concerned with communicating with the dead. 13 *in his study sits:* the Chorus here probably drew the arras (curtain) of the inner stage, discovering Faustus in his study at Wittenberg. As the next scene followed immediately, as the Chorus (who is, of course, a single person) left the stage by a side door, Faustus would advance onto the open platform stage.

1 *profess:* teach publicly. 2 *commenc'd:* another pun on academic language. 3 *level:* aim. 4 *Analytics:* Aristotle's work on Logic. 5 *Bene . . . :* "To argue well is the aim of Logic." 6 *Galen:* Claudius Galenus (c. 130–201 A.D.), most famous Greek physician after Hippocrates. 7 *Ubi . . . :* "Where the philosopher stops, the physician begins." 8 *Summum . . . :* this quotation from Galen (Faustus is looking through his books, turning pages and commenting on what he sees) is translated in the next line. Note the use of Latin, the language of the educated, even in popular works such as *Everyman* and *Doctor Faustus*. Note also, however, that when familiar tags are not the material quoted, the sense is often given also in English. 9 *aphorisms:* medical precepts concisely put. 10 *bills:* medical prescriptions. 11 *Justinian:* a book of laws codified by the Byzantine emperor Justinian (483–556 A.D.). 12 *Si una . . . :* "If the same thing is bequeathed to two persons, one shall have the thing itself and the other shall have the monetary value of the thing." 13 *Exhœreditare . . . :* "A father is not able to disinherit his son unless. . . ." Note the irony of the son (man) who throws away salvation, the gift of the Father, as Faustus will do. Faustus is full of pride and finds professions like medicine and law tedious, beneath him. In attempting to overreach, he will fall below the level of man. 14 *when all is done:* could mean also "when life is at an end." 15 *Jerome's Bible:* The Vulgate, the Bible translated into Latin by St. Jerome, fifth century. 16 *Stipendium . . . :* "The wages of sin is death." Romans 6:23.

The reward of sin is death: that's hard.
(*Reads.*)
*Si peccasse negamus, fallimur, et nulla
est in nobis veritas;*[17]
If we say that we have no sin, we deceive
ourselves, and there's no truth in us.
Why, then, belike we must sin, and so
consequently die:
Ay, we must die an everlasting death.
What doctrine call you this, *Che será,
será,*[18]
What will be, shall be? Divinity, adieu!
These metaphysics of magicians,
And necromantic books are heavenly;[19]
Lines, circles, scenes, letters and characters;[20]
Ay, these are those that Faustus most
desires.
O, what a world of profit and delight,
Of power, of honour, of omnipotence,
Is promis'd to the studious artisan![21]
All things that move between the quiet poles
Shall be at my command: emperors and
kings
Are but obeyed in their several provinces,
Nor can they raise the wind, or rend the
clouds;
But his dominion that exceeds in this,[22]
Stretcheth as far as doth the mind of man;
A sound magician is a mighty god:
Here, Faustus, tire[23] thy brains to gain a
deity.

(*Enter* WAGNER.)

Wagner, commend me to my dearest friends,
The German Valdes and Cornelius;
Request them earnestly to visit me.

WAGNER: I will, sir. (*Exit.*)

FAUSTUS: Their conference will be a greater
help to me
Than all my labours, plod I ne'er so fast.

(*Enter* GOOD ANGEL *and* EVIL ANGEL.)

GOOD ANGEL: O, Faustus, lay thy damned book
aside,
And gaze not on it, lest it tempt thy soul,
And heap God's heavy wrath upon thy
head!

Read, read the Scriptures: — that is
blasphemy.

EVIL ANGEL: Go forward, Faustus, in that
famous art
Wherein all Nature's treasure is contain'd:
Be thou on earth as Jove[24] is in the sky,
Lord and commander of these elements.

(*Exeunt* ANGELS.)

FAUSTUS: How am I glutted with conceit of
this![25]
Shall I make spirits fetch me what I please,
Resolve me of all ambiguities,
Perform what desperate enterprise I will?
I'll have them fly to India for gold,
Ransack the ocean[26] for orient pearl,
And search all corners of the new-found
world

---

17 *Si peccasse . . .* : translated in next lines. John 1:8.
18 *Che será . . .* : "What will be, will be." Faustus'
logic is not so good. The missing factor in his syllogism
is that Christ died to save us and we need not die but can
be redeemed by His sacrifice. If Faustus remembered
Christ, he would not turn to magic—and, having turned
to it, his sins could be forgiven if he would call on
Christ. **19** *heavenly:* actually hellish. Faustus is completely confused. **20** *lines,* etc.: in magic arts diagrams
were drawn on the ground, on paper, etc. **21** *artisan:*
workman, adept. **22** *But his dominion . . .* : But he
whose power excels in magic. **23** *tire:* another version
has "try." Elizabethan texts, partly because they were
never printed until the dramatic company had worn
them out playing them, partly because they were cheaply
and carelessly printed by typesetters who spelled words
as they pleased to fill out a line, etc., are unreliable, to
say the least. In the best texts there are numerous obvious errors (and very likely some unnoticed ones),
while in the worst there are completely unreadable passages. Quartos of *Doctor Faustus* appeared 1604, 1609,
1616, 1619, 1620, 1624, 1631, 1663, overseen by no
"editor" at all in the modern sense. Bibliographers have
attempted to approximate what Marlowe wrote in the
first place, with varying degrees of credibility. **24** *Jove:*
God. **25** *conceit of this:* the idea of attaining this.
26 *ocean:* in Elizabethan English, three syllables. There
is some variation, but iambic pentameter blank verse
ought to have ten syllables to the line. [Read lines
aloud.]

For pleasant fruits and princely delicates;
I'll have them read me strange philosophy,
And tell the secrets of all foreign kings;
I'll have them wall all Germany with brass,
And make swift Rhine circle fair Werten-
berg;
I'll have them fill the public schools with
silk,[27]
Wherewith the students shall be bravely
clad;
I'll levy soldiers with the coin they bring,
And chase the Prince of Parma[28] from our
land,
And reign sole king of all the provinces;
Yea, stranger engines for the brunt of war,
Than was the fiery keel[29] at Antwerp's
bridge,
I'll make my servile spirits to invent.

(*Enter* VALDES *and* CORNELIUS.)

Come, German Valdes and Cornelius,
And make me blest with your sage
conference.
Valdes, sweet Valdes, and Cornelius,
Know that your words have won me at the
last[30]
To practise magic and concealed arts:
Yet not your words only, but mine own
fantasy,
That will receive no object;[31] for my head
But ruminates on necromantic skill.
Philosophy is odious and obscure;
Both law and physic are for petty wits;
Divinity is basest of the three,
Unpleasant, harsh, contemptible, and vile:
'Tis magic, that hath ravish'd me.
Then, gentle friends, aid me in this attempt;
And I, that have with concise syllogisms
Gravell'd the pastors[32] of the German
church,
And made the flowering pride of Wertenberg
Swarm to my problems, as the infernal spirits
On sweet Musæus[33] when he came to hell,
Will be as cunning as Agrippa[34] was,
Whose shadow[35] made all Europe honour
him.

VALDES: Faustus, these books, thy wit, and our
experience,
Shall make all nations to canonise us.[36]
As Indian Moors obey their Spanish lords,

So shall the spirits of every element
Be always serviceable to us three;
Like lions shall they guard us when we
please;
Like Almain rutters[37] with their horsemen's
staves.
Or Lapland giants, trotting by our sides;
Sometimes like women, or unwedded
maids,
Shadowing more beauty in their airy brows
Than have the white breasts of the queen
of love:[38]
From Venice shall they drag huge argosies,[39]
And from America the golden fleece[40]

---

27 *silk:* only those with higher degrees wore silk gowns. **28** *Prince of Parma:* Alessandro Farnese, Duke of Parma, was governor of The Netherlands (*provinces*) under Philip II of Spain. Notice the mixed desires of Faustus and what he says he will do with magic power. [Contrast what he does accomplish once he attains magic power.] **29** *fiery keel:* The Dutch, in April, 1584, sailed a burning ship under a bridge over the river Scheldt built by Parma in his attempt to blockade Antwerp. The bridge was destroyed. In what sense in the story of Faustus is a "bridge" destroyed and how is the agent responsible itself destroyed in the business? **30** *at the last:* apparently these two German magicians have been trying to win Faustus over to the practice of magic. Have their "words" done it, or something in Faustus himself? Why is it important where the responsibility lies? **31** *no object:* a summary of how Faustus has been determined to overlook all objections and to cast aside all other occupations in favor of being a magician. **32** *gravell'd the pastors:* perplexed the clergy with logical argument. **33** *Musæus:* a mythical poet, often confused with the legendary Orpheus. Note the mention of Hell. **34** *Agrippa:* Henry Cornelius Agrippa von Nettesheim (1486–1535) wrote on alchemy and the occult and was reputed to be a magician. **35** *shadow:* apparition. **36** ff. *these books,* etc.: compare the promise by Valdes of what magic will do for them with what it actually does accomplish for Faustus. If magic is so powerful, why do Cornelius and Valdes need Faustus to join them? **37** *Almain rutters:* German horsemen. **38** *queen of love:* the goddess Venus. Magic seems to promise sexual opportunities. **39** *argosies:* fleets. **40** *fleece:* an allusion to the classical Jason and the Golden Fleece combined with a typically Elizabethan anti-Spanish sentiment referring to Philip II of Spain (who was among the members of the Order of the Golden Fleece, a high decoration).

That yearly stuffs old Philip's treasury;
If learned Faustus will be resolute.

FAUSTUS: Valdes, as resolute am I in this
As thou to live: therefore object it not.[41]

CORNELIUS: The miracles that magic will
perform
Will make thee vow to study nothing
else.
He that is grounded in astrology,
Enrich'd with tongues, well seen in minerals,
Hath all the principles magic doth require:
Then doubt not, Faustus, but to be renown'd,
And more frequented for this mystery
Than heretofore the Delphian oracle.[42]
The spirits tell me they can dry the sea,
And fetch the treasure of all foreign wrecks,
Ay, all the wealth that our forefathers hid
Within the massy entrails of the earth:
Then tell me, Faustus, what shall we three
want?[43]

FAUSTUS: Nothing, Cornelius. O, this cheers
my soul!
Come, show me some demonstrations
magical,
That I may conjure in some lusty[44] grove,
And have these joys in full possession.

VALDES: Then haste thee to some solitary
grove,
And bear wise Bacon's and Albertus'
works,[45]
The Hebrew Psalter, and New Testament;
And whatsoever else is requisite
We will inform thee ere our conference
cease.

CORNELIUS: Valdes, first let him know the
words of art;[46]
And then, all other ceremonies learn'd,
Faustus may try his cunning by himself.

VALDES: First I'll instruct thee in the rudiments,
And then wilt thou be perfecter than I.

FAUSTUS: Then come and dine with me, and,
after meat,
We'll canvass every quiddity[47] thereof;
For, ere I sleep, I'll try[48] what I can do:
This night I'll conjure, though I die therefore. (*Exeunt.*)

SCENE TWO

(*Enter two* SCHOLARS.)

FIRST SCHOLAR: I wonder what's become of
Faustus, that was wont to make our schools
ring with *sic probo*.[1]

SECOND SCHOLAR: That shall we know, for see,
here comes his boy.[2]

(*Enter* WAGNER.)

FIRST SCHOLAR: How now, sirrah![3] where's thy
master?

WAGNER: God in heaven knows.

SECOND SCHOLAR: Why, dost not thou know?

WAGNER: Yes, I know; but that follows not.[4]

FIRST SCHOLAR: Go to, sirrah! leave your jesting, and tell us where he is.

---

41 *object it not:* Faustus seems unaware that Valdes is selling the idea, not objecting to it. Perhaps he is not listening, enchanted by his own fancies. What might he notice if he paid more attention to Valdes and Cornelius? What are they up to? 42 *frequented . . . Delphian oracle:* in the ancient world the oracle of Apollo at Delphi was consulted for advice, though it always spoke in ambiguities. 43 *want:* lack. But what do Valdes and Cornelius *want* of Faustus? 44 *lusty:* pleasant. 45 *Bacon's and Albertus' works:* magical books of Roger Bacon (1214–1294) and Albert, Count von Bollstädt (1206?–1280). The Psalms in Hebrew and The New Testament in Latin were also required. A magic did have to be "enriched in tongues." 46 *words of art:* magical formulæ. 47 *quiddity:* essential element (a term of the logic of the Scholastics). 48 *I'll try:* what Faustus proposes to try before he sleeps (dies) is fatal to his soul. He seems not fully aware of what "though I die therefore" implies.

1 *sic probo:* "thus I prove," a triumphant wind-up of a scholarly argument. What *has* become of Faustus the logician? Where has his celebrated logic failed him already? Why? 2 *boy:* servant, not necessarily young, as bellhops and porters, etc., are called "boy." The widespread American use of the word "man" is a direct reaction to former use of "boy." 3 *sirrah:* an impolite form of address. 4 *that follows not:* note Wagner's use of logic. How does it compare with his master's?

WAGNER: That follows not necessary by force of argument, that you, being licentiates,[5] should stand upon: therefore acknowledge your error, and be attentive.

SECOND SCHOLAR: Why, didst thou not say thou knewest?

WAGNER: Have you any witness on't?[6]

FIRST SCHOLAR: Yes, sirrah, I heard you.

WAGNER: Ask my fellow[7] if I be a thief.

SECOND SCHOLAR: Well, you will not tell us?

WAGNER: Yes, sir, I will tell you;[8] yet, if you were not dunces, you would never ask me such a question, for is not he *corpus naturale?* and is not that *mobile?* then wherefore should you ask me such a question? But that I am by nature phlegmatic, slow to wrath, and prone to lechery (to love, I would say), it were not for you to come within forty foot of the place of execution, although I do not doubt to see you both hanged the next sessions. Thus having triumphed over you, I will set my countenance like a precisian, and begin to speak thus: — Truly, my dear brethren, my master is within at dinner, with Valdes and Cornelius, as this wine, if it could speak, would inform your worships: and so, the Lord bless you, preserve you, and keep you, my dear brethren, my dear brethren! (*Exit.*)

FIRST SCHOLAR: Nay, then, I fear he has fallen into that damned art for which they two are infamous through the world.

SECOND SCHOLAR: Were he a stranger, and not allied to me, yet should I grieve for him. But, come, let us go and inform the Rector,[9] and see if he by his grave counsel can reclaim him.

FIRST SCHOLAR: O, but I fear me nothing can reclaim him!

SECOND SCHOLAR: Yet let us try what we can do.[10] (*Exeunt.*)

SCENE THREE

(*Enter* FAUSTUS *to conjure.*)

FAUSTUS: Now that the gloomy shadow of the earth,[1]
Longing to view Orion's drizzling look,
Leaps from th' antarctic world unto the sky,
And dims the welkin with her pitchy breath,
Faustus, begin thine incantations,
And try if devils will obey thy hest,
Seeing thou hast pray'd and sacrific'd[2] to them.
Within this circle is Jehovah's name,[3]
Forward and backward anagrammatis'd,
Th' abbreviated names of holy saints,
Figures of every adjunct to the heavens,
And characters of signs and erring stars,
By which the spirits are enforc'd to rise:
Then fear not, Faustus, but be resolute,
And try the uttermost magic can perform. —

---

5 *licentiates:* holders of a degree or license. Because you hold degrees, that gives you no license to hold me in contempt, is what Wagner is saying. The humor of the Gravediggers in *Hamlet* is of this same word-manipulating, nit-picking kind and such word play was the stock in trade of Elizabethan comedians, who would improvise this sort of thing if it were not written into the script for them, as Shakespeare complained. 6 *on't:* to it. 7 *ask my fellow:* a reference to an old joke involving two thieves who vouch for each other. 8 ff. *I will tell you:* Wagner does a parody of scholastic argument and follows it up with his Puritan imitation of a *precision,* a stock figure of fun in the Elizabethan theatre (cf. Malvolio in Shakespeare's *Twelfth Night*). 9 *Rector:* nominal head of the university, the Rector Magnificus would be the one to correct errors and apply discipline. 10 *try what we can do:* as the logic of Wagner's foolery parallels Faustus' arguments, so the end of Scene 2 parallels Faustus' words at the end of Scene 1.

1 *gloomy shadow,* etc.: the heavens seem wet and unpropitious. Orion is a constellation associated with rain. The *welkin* (heaven) is black, which is ominous. 2 *sacrific'd:* apparently not only were the magicians' detailed instructions but also Faustus' previous activities omitted. 3 *Jehovah's name:* the conjuration involves taking the tetragrammaton (four letters) symbolizing the name of God and rearranging them in the form of a cross, along with abbreviated saints' names, signs of the Zodiac, symbols for the wandering planets, etc. A *grimoire* or book of magic gives all the details.

Sint mihi dei Acherontis propitii! Valeat numen triplex Jehovæ! Ignei, aërii, aquatani spiritus, salvete! Orientis princeps Belzebub, inferni ardentis monarcha, et Demogorgon, propitiamus vos, ut appareat et surgat Mephistophilis, quod tumeraris: per Jehovam, Gehennam, et consecratam aquam quam nunc spargo, signumque crucis quod nunc facio, et per vota nostra, ipse nunc surgat nobis dicatus Mephistophilis![4]

(*Enter* MEPHISTOPHILIS.)

I charge thee to return, and change thy
   shape;
Thou art too ugly to attend on me:
Go, and return an old Franciscan friar;[5]
That holy shape becomes a devil best.

(*Exit* MEPHISTOPILIS.)

I see there's virtue in my heavenly words:
Who would not be proficient in this art?
How pliant is this Mephistophilis,
Full of obedience and humility!
Such is the force of magic and my spells:[6]
No, Faustus, thou art conjuror laureat,
That canst command great Mephistophilis:
Quin regis Mephistophilis fratris imagine.[7]

(*Re-enter* MEPHISTOPHILIS [*like a Franciscan friar*].)

MEPHISTOPHILIS: Now, Faustus, what wouldst
   thou have me do?

FAUSTUS: I charge thee wait upon me whilst
   I live,
To do whatever Faustus shall command,
Be it to make the moon drop from her sphere,
Or the ocean to overwhelm the world.

MEPHISTOPHILIS: I am a servant to great Lucifer,
And may not follow thee without his leave:
No more than he commands must we per-
   form.

FAUSTUS: Did not he charge thee to appear to
   me?

MEPHISTOPHILIS: No, I came hither of mine
   own accord.

FAUSTUS: Did not my conjuring speeches raise
   thee? speak.

MEPHISTOPHILIS: That was the cause, but yet
   per accidens;[8]
For, when we hear one rack the name of
   God,
Abjure the Scriptures and his Saviour Christ,
We fly, in hope, to get his glorious soul;
Nor will we come, unless he use such means
Whereby he is in danger to be damn'd.
Therefore the shortest cut for conjuring
Is stoutly to abjure the Trinity,
And pray devoutly to the prince of hell.

FAUSTUS: So Faustus hath
Already done; and holds this principle,
There is no chief but only Belzebub;
To whom Faustus doth dedicate himself.
This word "damnation"[9] terrifies not him,

---

4 *Sint mihi . . . :* "Grant me your favor, gods of Acheron! Let the triple name of Jehovah prevail! Spirits of fire, air, and water, hail! Belzebub, Prince of the East, monarch of the fires of Hell, and Demogorgon, we propitiate you, that Mephistophilis may rise up and appear, as we petition. Why do you wait? By Jehovah, Gehenna, and the holy water which I now sprinkle, and the sign of the cross which I now make, and by our vows, now let Mephistophilis rise up himself to serve us." In the 1616 text the word *Dragon* comes in before *quod tumeraris*, which F. S. Boas says was a stage direction for a dragon to appear. In any case, read before an audience in Elizabethan England, many of whom completely believed in the efficacy of such charms, the effect of the speech must have been terrifying, even without a stage dragon. 5 *Franciscan*, etc.: Note the anti-Catholicism. Anti-Catholicism sentiment, rampant after the reign of Bloody Mary, Elizabeth's older sister, had an upsurge after the defeat of the Spanish Armada (1588) and is common in English plays of the period. Marlowe was an anti-Catholic spy, though (oddly enough) the theology of the play shows a close acquaintance with Roman Catholic books. 6 *my spells:* even when Faustus' misconception is later cleared up he will not abandon it. 7 *Quin regis . . . :* "Indeed you rule, Mephistophilis, in the image of a friar." 8 *per accidens:* the term from Scholastic logic has a touch of humor in it and also a point which Faustus chooses to ignore: Mephistophilis did not come as a result of Faustus' command but only in connection with it, of his own free will, which is to say Faustus is not in command of Mephistophilis, who only serves Lucifer. 9 *damnation:* Faustus says he is not afraid to put his soul in peril, that damnation does not worry him.

For he confounds hell in Elysium:[10]
His ghost be with the old philosophers!
But, leaving these vain trifles[11] of men's
    souls,
Tell me what is that Lucifer thy lord?

MEPHISTOPHILIS: Arch-regent and commander
    of all spirits.

FAUSTUS: Was not that Lucifer an angel once?

MEPHISTOPHILIS: Yes, Faustus, and most dearly
    lov'd of God.

FAUSTUS: How comes it, then, that he is prince
    of devils?

MEPHISTOPHILIS: O, by aspiring pride and
    insolence;[12]
For which God threw him from the face of
    heaven.

FAUSTUS: And what are you that live with
    Lucifer?[13]

MEPHISTOPHILIS: Unhappy spirits that fell with
    Lucifer.
Conspir'd against our God with Lucifer,
And are for ever damn'd with Lucifer.

FAUSTUS: Where are you damn'd?

MEPHISTOPHILIS: In hell.

FAUSTUS: How comes it, then, that thou are
    out of hell?

MEPHISTOPHILIS: Why, this is hell,[14] nor am
    I out of it.
Think'st thou that I, who saw the face of
    God,
And tasted the eternal joys of heaven,
Am not tormented with ten thousand hells,
In being depriv'd of everlasting bliss?
O, Faustus, leave these frivolous demands,
Which strike a terror to my fainting soul!

FAUSTUS: What, is great Mephistophilis so
    passionate[15]
For being deprived of the joys of heaven?
Learn thou of Faustus manly fortitude,
And scorn those joys thou never shalt
    possess.
Go bear these tidings to great Lucifer:
Seeing Faustus hath incurr'd eternal death[16]
By desperate thoughts against Jove's deity,

Say, he surrenders up to him his soul,
So he will spare him four-and-twenty years,
Letting him live in all voluptuousness;
Having thee ever to attend on me,
To give me whatsoever I shall ask,
To tell me whatsoever I demand,
To slay mine enemies, and aid my friends,
And always be obedient to my will.
Go and return to mighty Lucifer,
And meet me in my study at midnight,
And then resolve me of thy master's mind.

MEPHISTOPHILIS: I will, Faustus. (*Exit.*)

FAUSTUS: Had I as many souls as there be stars,
I'd give them all for Mephistophilis.
By him I'll be great emperor[17] of the world,
And make a bridge through the moving air,
To pass the ocean with a band of men;
I'll join the hills that bind the Afric shore,
And make that country continent to Spain,
And both contributory to my crown:
The Emperor shall not live but by my leave,
For any potentate of Germany.[18]

---

10 *confounds hell in Elysium:* he does not believe in Hell any more than he does in the Elysium (paradise) of the ancients. But, of course, Mephistophilis has just come from Hell at his command, Faustus believes.   11 *vain trifles:* Faustus believes souls and salvation are "vain trifles"; meanwhile he quizzes Mephistophilis on details known to everyone. [Note how the quick exchange of single lines affects the pace and impact of the scene at this point.]   12 *aspiring pride and insolence:* compare Faustus himself. How can Mephistophilis afford to be so frank with Faustus?   13 *Lucifer:* what effect is achieved through the repetition of this word?   14 *Why, this is hell:* a most "modern" idea, the existential conception of Hell as a state of mind, of apartness, alienation. [How sincere is Mephistophilis? How do you know?]   15 *passionate:* regretful.   16 *incurr'd eternal death:* has Faustus actually done so at this point? Why does he say this?   17 *I'll be great emperor:* how have Faustus' plans for the use of his magical powers changed since you first heard them? What is the explanation of this?   18 *potentate of Germany:* Thomas Nashe accused Marlowe of a "drumming decasyllabon" in his iambic pentameter, while others have praised what Ben Jonson called his "mighty line." What use does Marlowe make of polysyllables? What are some other favorite devices that create the music of his lines?

Now that I have obtained what I desir'd,
I'll live in speculation of this art,
Till Mephistophilis return again. (*Exit.*)

SCENE FOUR

(*Enter* WAGNER *and* CLOWN.)

WAGNER: Sirrah boy, come hither.

CLOWN: How, boy! swowns,[1] boy! I hope you have seen many boys with such pickade-vaunts[2] as I have: boy, quotha![3]

WAGNER: Tell me, sirrah, hast thou any comings in?[4]

CLOWN: Ay, and goings out too; you may see else.

WAGNER: Alas, poor slave! see how poverty jesteth in his nakedness! the villain is bare and out of service,[5] and so hungry, that I know he would give his soul[6] to the devil for a shoulder of mutton, though it were blood-raw.

CLOWN: How! my soul to the devil for a shoulder of mutton, though 'twere blood-raw! not so, good friend: by'r lady, I had need have it well roasted, and good sauce to it, if I pay so dear.

WAGNER: Well, wilt thou serve me, and I'll make thee go like *Qui mihi discipulus?*[7]

CLOWN: How, in verse?

WAGNER: No, sirrah; in beaten silk and staves-acre.[8]

CLOWN: How, how, knaves-acre![9] ay, I thought that was all the land his father left him. Do you hear? I would be sorry to rob you of your living.

WAGNER: Sirrah, I say in staves-acre.

CLOWN: Oho, oho, staves-acre! why, then, be-like, if I were your man, I should be full of vermin.

WAGNER: So thou shalt, whether thou beest with me or no. But, sirrah, leave your jesting, and bind yourself presently unto me for seven years, or I'll turn all the lice about

thee into familiars,[10] and they shall tear thee in pieces.

CLOWN: Do you hear, sir? you may save that labour; they are too familiar with me already: swowns, they are as bold with my flesh as if they had paid for their meat and drink.

WAGNER: Well, do your hear, sirrah? hold, take these guilders.[11] (*Gives money.*)

CLOWN: Gridirons! what be they?

WAGNER: Why, French crowns.[12]

CLOWN: Mass,[13] but for the name of French crowns, a man were as good have as many English counters.[14] And what should I do with these?

WAGNER: Why, now, sirrah, thou art at an hour's warning, whensoever and wheresoever the devil shall fetch thee.

---

1 *swowns:* God's wounds! 2 *pickadevaunts:* pointed beards. 3 *quotha:* says he. 4 *comings in:* income. 5 *out of service:* lacking a job. 6 *give his soul:* what comparison to Faustus? How would the Clown make a better bargain than Faustus? 7 *go like Qui mihi . . . :* appear as my servant. Compare Faustus toward Mephistophilis. 8 *beaten silk:* embroidered silk. *Stavesacre:* larkspur seed used to kill lice. 9 *knave's-acre:* a slum in London (now Poulteney Street in Soho). 10 *familiars:* familiar spirits were supposed to accompany a witch in animal form (one of the witches in *Macbeth*, for instance, has a cat named Greymalkin). The Clown puns on "familiar" in his speech. 11 *guilders:* Dutch florins. The Clown misunderstands the word as "gridirons," perhaps a pun involving British coins bearing the symbol of the portcullis, a grid-like structure used to guard a gate. 12 *crowns:* pun involving coins (bearing the symbol of the crown) and bald heads (from the "French disease," syphilis). Note that these jokes, though obscure now, were readily understandable to the common people of the pit, for whom they were written. When they have to be explained—indeed that is not always possible—their little humor evaporates. It is perhaps enough to notice that the author wanted to be amusing at this point and to consider his motives, not his success with us. 13 *Mass:* By the Mass (an oath). 14 *counters:* tokens used by merchants.

CLOWN: No, no; here, take your gridirons again.[15]

WAGNER: Truly, I'll none of them.

CLOWN: Truly, but you shall.

WAGNER: Bear witness I gave them him.

CLOWN: Bear witness I gave them you again.

WAGNER: Well, I will cause two devils presently to fetch thee away. — Baliol[16] and Belcher!

CLOWN: Let your Baliol and your Belcher come here, and I'll knock them, they were never so knocked since they were devils: say I should kill one of them, what would folks say? "Do ye see yonder tall fellow in the round slop?"[17] he has killed the devil." So I should be called Kill-devil all the parish over.

(*Enter two* DEVILS; *and the* CLOWN *runs up and down crying.*)

WAGNER: Baliol and Belcher, — spirits, away!

(*Exeunt* DEVILS.)

CLOWN: What, are they gone? a vengeance on them! they have vile long nails. There was a he-devil and a she-devil: I'll tell you how you shall know them; all he-devils has horns, and all she-devils has clifts[18] and cloven feet.

WAGNER: Well, sirrah, follow me.

CLOWN: But, do you hear? if I should serve you, would you teach me to raise up Banios and Belcheos?[19]

WAGNER: I will teach thee to turn thyself to anything, to a dog, or a cat, or a mouse, or a rat, or anything.

CLOWN: How! a Christian fellow to a dog, or a cat, a mouse, or a rat! no, no sir; if you turn me into anything, let it be in the likeness of a little pretty frisking flea, that I may be here and there and everywhere: O, I'll tickle the pretty wenches' plackets![20] I'll be amongst them, i'faith.

WAGNER: Well, sirrah, come.

CLOWN: But, do you hear, Wagner?

WAGNER: How! — Baliol and Belcher![21]

CLOWN: O Lord! I pray, sir, let Banio and Belcher go sleep.

WAGNER: Villain, call me Master Wagner, and let thy left eye be diametarily[22] fixed upon my right heel, with *quasi vestigiis nostris insistere.*[23] (*Exit.*)

CLOWN: God forgive me, he speaks Dutch fustian.[24]
Well, I'll follow him; I'll serve him, that's flat.[25] (*Exit.*)

SCENE FIVE

(FAUSTUS *discovered in his study.*)

FAUSTUS: Now, Faustus, must
Thou needs be damn'd, and canst thou not be sav'd:[1]
What boots[2] it, then, to think of God or heaven?

---

15 ff. *take your gridirons again:* the Clown realizes that by returning what he has taken he can call the bargain off. Compare Faustus' inability to break his bargain. One major factor with Faustus is his fear, but see the Clown's attitude: he is willing to be famous as a Kill-devil. **16** *Baliol:* Belial. A pun on the name of the Oxford college is very unlikely to be intended, even from Marlowe, a Cambridge man. **17** *round slop:* full, round-cut trousers. **18** *clifts:* clefts. **19** *Banios and Belcheos:* the Clown has the names wrong and Banios sounds like *bagnios* (brothels). **20** *plackets:* opening in petticoats. As a flea he could get into private parts. **21** *Wagner:* Wagner takes offense, wanting to be called Master Wagner. **22** *diametarily:* in a straight line. **23** *Quasi . . . :* as if treading in my tracks. The idea basically is that the Clown should heel like a dog. **24** *fustian:* nonsense. The Clown does not know Latin from Dutch. **25** *that's flat:* that's sure. Here and elsewhere, consider how the comic scenes are not, as some critics think, interpolations by another hand but part of Marlowe's overall design for the play. To what extent can they be called "comic relief"? To what extent do they reinforce the meaning of the more serious scenes? How is each comic scene related to the important points made in the rest of the play?

1 *canst thou not be sav'd:* is Faustus really now irrevocably damned? **2** *boots:* avails.

Away with such vain fancies, and despair;
Despair in God,[3] and trust in Belzebub:
Now go not backward; no Faustus, be
  resolute:
Why waver'st thou? O, something soundeth
  in mine ears,
"Abjure this magic, turn to God again!"
Ay, and Faustus will turn to God again.
To God? he loves thee not;
The god thou serv'st is thine own appetite,
Wherein is fix'd the love of Belzebub:
To him I'll build an altar and a church,
And offer lukewarm blood of new-born
  babes.

(*Enter* GOOD ANGEL *and* EVIL ANGEL.)

GOOD ANGEL: Sweet Faustus,[4] leave that
  execrable art.

FAUSTUS: Contrition, prayer, repentance —
  what of them?

GOOD ANGEL: O, they are means to bring thee
  unto heaven!

EVIL ANGEL: Rather illusions, fruits of lunacy,
  That make men foolish that do trust them
  most.

GOOD ANGEL: Sweet Faustus, think of
  heaven and heavenly things.

EVIL ANGEL: No, Faustus; think of honour and
  wealth.

(*Exeunt* ANGELS.)

FAUST: Of wealth!
  Why, the signiory of Embden[5] shall be mine.
  When Mephistophilis shall stand by me,
  What god can hurt thee, Faustus? thou
  art safe:
  Cast no more doubts. — Come, Mephisto-
  philis,
  And bring glad tidings from great
  Lucifer; —
  Is't not midnight? — come, Mephistophilis,
  Veni, veni Mephistophile![6]

(*Enter* MEPHISTOPHILIS.)

Now tell me what says Lucifer, thy lord?

MEPHISTOPHILIS: That I shall wait on Faustus
  whilst he lives,
  So[7] he will buy my service with his soul.

FAUSTUS: Already Faustus hath hazarded that
  for thee.

MEPHISTOPHILIS: But, Faustus, thou must
  bequeath it solemnly,
  And write a deed of gift with thine own
  blood;
  For that security[8] craves great Lucifer.
  If thou deny it, I will back to hell.

FAUSTUS: Stay, Mephistophilis, and tell me,
  what good will my soul do thy lord?

MEPHISTOPHILIS: Enlarge his kingdom.

FAUSTUS: Is that the reason why he tempts
  us thus?

MEPHISTOPHILIS: *Solamen miseris socios
  habuisse doloris.*[9]

FAUSTUS: Why, have you any pain that torture
  others!

MEPHISTOPHILIS: As great as have the human
  souls of men.
  But, tell me, Faustus, shall I have thy soul?
  And I will be thy slave, and wait on thee,

---

3 *Despair in God:* Faustus should be saying "Trust in
God, and denounce Belzebub." He has things all reversed, as in magic conjurations the name of God is
spelled backwards, in Black Masses everything is reversed, etc. How do you explain his attitude at this
point? 4 *Sweet Faustus:* the Good and Evil Angels are
really warring attitudes within the mind of Faustus, here
represented like characters from the Morality plays.
[What examples can you find in other Elizabethan
plays you may know—say Shakespeare's *Macbeth* or
Lear—of external evidences of mental states, expressionistic dramatic devices to present the inner reality?]
5 *Embden:* Emden, the chief city of East Friesland, was
a rich port with trade relations with Elizabethan England. 6 *Veni, veni . . . :* Come, come, Mephistophilis.
7 *so:* if. 8 *that security:* this deed in blood was firmly
believed in and a number of them were actually signed
by demented (or demoniacal) individuals. 9 *Solamen
. . . :* "It is consolation in misery to have a fellow
sufferer." Misery loves company.

And give thee more[10] than thou hast wit
to ask.

FAUSTUS: Ay, Mephistophilis, I give it thee.

MEPHISTOPHILIS: Then, Faustus, stab thy arm
courageously,
And bind thy soul, that at some certain day
Great Lucifer may claim it as his own;
And then be thou as great as Lucifer.

FAUSTUS (*stabbing his arm*): Lo, Mephistophilis,
for love of thee,
I cut mine arm, and with my proper[11] blood
Assure my soul to be great Lucifer's,
Chief lord and regent of perpetual night!
View here the blood that trickles from mine
arm,
And let it be propitious for my wish.

MEPHISTOPHILIS: But, Faustus, thou must
Write it in manner of a deed of gift.

FAUSTUS: Ay, so I will (*Writes*). But,
Mephistophilis,
My blood congeals,[12] and I can write no
more.

MEPHISTOPHILIS: I'll fetch thee fire[13] to dissolve
it straight. (*Exit.*)

FAUSTUS: Why might the staying of my blood
portend?
Is it unwilling I should write this bill?
Why streams it not,[14] that I may write
afresh?
Faustus gives to thee his soul: ah, there it
stay'd!
Why shouldst thou not? is not thy soul
thine own?[15]
Then write again, *Faustus gives to thee his
soul.*

(*Re-enter* MEPHISTOPHILIS *with a chafer of
coals.*)

MEPHISTOPHILIS: Here's fire; come Faustus, set
it on.

FAUSTUS: So, now the blood begins to clear
again;
Now will I make an end[16] immediately.
(*Writes.*)

MEPHISTOPHILIS: O, what will not I do to
obtain his soul! (*Aside.*)[17]

---

10 *give thee more:* Mephistophilis promises even more than Faustus can ask for. In what sense does Faustus get more than he asked for? In what sense is he denied what he does ask for? What is the bargain exactly? Does Faustus keep it? Does the Devil keep it? 11 *proper:* own. This is the French influence on the language (*propre*). What other examples of French influence do you see in the vocabulary of the play? Of Latin? Of other languages? Discuss Marlowe's vocabulary. How much is the word choice influenced by his subject? By his own college education? (He was one of the "University Wits," masters of arts down from the universities earning a living by their pens in London.) 12 *my blood congeals:* what can this signify? Using Biblical references ("for the blood is the life") and other received ideas, discuss the symbolism of blood in the play. 13 *fire:* the Elizabethans thought of fire as symbolic of physical passion. How could this idea apply here? 14 *Why streams it not:* why is Faustus so dense about the meaning of the incident? 15 *is not thy soul thy own:* what is the orthodox religious answer to this question? 16 *make an end:* what double meaning do you see here? Discuss the irony in Faustus' remarks throughout the play. What does the presence of irony add to the overall effect? 17 *Aside:* the presence of members of the audience around the edges of the platform stage, in fact seated on the stage itself, made asides, soliloquies, and other such conventions of the Elizabethan theatre much more acceptable than on the modern proscenium stage. Here and throughout the play consider the effect of the physical theatre on the play presented in it. How, for instance, does lack of scenery and lighting effects—Elizabethan plays were done under an open sky, in the afternoon—encourage poetry? How does lack of scenery affect the structure and the speed of playing? What is the effect of actors in clothes indistinguishable from those of members of the audience with the exception of certain conventions (a cloak for the Prologue, a crown for a king, etc.)? What is gained (or lost) by *Doctor Faustus*, divided here into scenes for convenience in discussion and into acts and scenes in some versions (because of custom) being played as a single uninterrupted action, as it was on the Elizabethan stage? (Shakespeare's plays were speedy "one-acters" in their original productions too.) Consider *Doctor Faustus'* potential as a radio play, as a teleplay, as a film. Which medium, in your opinion, would suit it best, and why? What changes would you make in it, for example, to adapt it for television production?

FAUSTUS: *Consummatum est;*[18] this bill is
   ended,
And Faustus hath bequeathed his soul to
   Lucifer.
But what is this inscription on mine arm?
Homo, fuge:[19] whither should I fly?
If unto God, he'll throw me down to hell.
My senses are deceiv'd; here's nothing
   writ: —
I see it plain; here in this place is writ,
Homo, fuge: yet shall not Faustus fly.

MEPHISTOPHILIS: I'll fetch him somewhat to
   delight his mind.[20]

(*Aside, and then exit.*)

(*Re-enter* MEPHISTOPHILIS *with* DEVILS, *who
give crowns and rich apparel to* FAUSTUS, *dance,
and then depart.*)

FAUSTUS: Speak, Mephistophilis, what means
   this show?

MEPHISTOPHILIS: Nothing, Faustus, but to
   delight thy mind withal,
And to show thee what magic can perform.

FAUSTUS: But may I raise up spirits when I
   please?

MEPHISTOPHILIS: Ay, Faustus, and do greater
   things than these.

FAUSTUS: Then there's enough for a thousand
   souls.
Here, Mephistophilis, receive this scroll,
A deed of gift of body and of soul:
But yet conditionally[21] that thou perform
All articles prescrib'd between us both.

MEPHISTOPHILIS: Faustus, I swear by hell and
   Lucifer
To effect all promises between us made!

FAUSTUS: Then hear me read them. (*Reads*) *On
these conditions following. First that Faustus
may be a spirit in form and substance. Se-
condly, that Mephistophilis shall be his servant, and at his command. Thirdly, that
Mephistophilis shall do for him, and bring
him whatsoever he desires. Fourthly, that he
shall be in his chamber or house invisible.
Lastly, that he shall appear to the said John
Faustus, at all times, in what form or shape*

*soever he please. I, John Faustus, of Werten-
berg, Doctor, by these presents, do give both
body and soul to Lucifer prince of the east,
and his minister Mephistophilis; and furthermore grant unto them, that, twenty-four
years being expired, the articles abovewrit-
ten inviolate, full power to fetch or carry the
said John Faustus, body and soul, flesh,
blood, or goods, into their habitation wheresoever. By me, John Faustus.*

MEPHISTOPHILIS: Speak, Faustus, do you deliver
   this as your deed?

FAUSTUS: Ay, take it, and the devil give thee
   good[22] on't!

MEPHISTOPHILIS: Now, Faustus, ask what thou
   wilt.

FAUSTUS: First will I question with thee about
   hell.
Tell me, where is the place that men call hell?

MEPHISTOPHILIS: Under the heavens.

FAUSTUS: Ay, but whereabout?

MEPHISTOPHILIS: Within the bowels of these
   elements,
Where we are tortur'd and remain for ever:
Hell hath no limits,[23] nor is circumscrib'd
In one self place; for where we are is hell,
And where hell is, there must we ever be:
And, to conclude, when all the world dis-
   solves,

---

18 *Consummatum est:* the last words of Christ on the
cross. "It is finished." What is the irony here? To what
extent is it all over for Doctor Faustus? **19** *Homo, fuge:*
"Man, flee." Faustus' human nature, which rebelled
at signing in blood, is still trying to tell him something. What psychological reality is here expressed in
symbolic terms? **20** *delight his mind:* why does Mephistophilis move so quickly at this point? As Faustus
asks, "What means this show?" **21** *conditionally:*
what conditions is Faustus making? Are they kept?
22 *the devil give thee good:* is the introduction of
humor at this point useful or unfortunate? Explain.
23 *Hell hath no limits:* in an age when Hell was
preached as a place of physical torture, of fire and
brimstone, this is a most advanced and unorthodox
view: hell as a state of mind.

And every creature shall be purified,
All places shall be hell that are not heaven.

FAUSTUS: Come, I think hell's a fable.[24]

MEPHISTOPHILIS: Ay, think so still, till
experience change thy mind.

FAUSTUS: Why, think'st thou, then, that
Faustus shall be damn'd?

MEPHISTOPHILIS: Ay, of necessity, for here's
the scroll
Wherein thou hast given thy soul to Lucifer.

FAUSTUS: Ay, and body too: but what of that?
Think'st thou that Faustus is so fond[25] to
imagine
That, after this life, there is any pain?
Tush, these are trifles and mere old wives'
tales.

MEPHISTOPHILIS: But, Faustus, I am an instance
to prove the contrary,
For I am damn'd, and am now in hell.

FAUSTUS: How! now in hell!
Nay, an this be hell, I'll willingly be damn'd
here:
What! walking, disputing, etc.
But, leaving off this, let me have a wife,
The fairest maid in Germany;
For I am wanton and lascivious,
And cannot live without a wife.

MEPHISTOPHILIS: How! a wife!
I prithee, Faustus, talk not of a wife.[26]

FAUSTUS: Nay, sweet Mephistophilis, fetch me
one, for I will have one.

MEPHISTOPHILIS: Well, thou wilt have one? Sit
there till I come: I'll fetch thee a wife in
the devil's name. (*Exit.*)

(*Re-enter* MEPHISTOPHILIS *with a* DEVIL *drest
like a* WOMAN, *with fireworks.*)

MEPHISTOPHILIS: Tell me, Faustus, how dost
thou like thy wife?

FAUSTUS: A plague on her for a hot whore!

MEPHISTOPHILIS: Tut, Faustus,
Marriage is but a ceremonial toy;
If thou lovest me, think no more of it.
I'll cull thee out the fairest courtesans,

And bring them every morning to thy bed:
She whom thine eye shall like, thy heart
shall have,
Be she as chaste as was Penelope,[27]
As wise as Saba,[28] or as beautiful
As was bright Lucifer before his fall.
Hold, take this book,[29] peruse it thoroughly:
(*Gives book.*)
The iterating of these lines brings gold;
The framing of this circle on the ground
Brings whirlwinds, tempests, thunder, and
lightning;
Pronounce this thrice devoutly to thyself,
And men in armour shall appear to thee,
Ready to execute what thou desir'st.

FAUSTUS: Thanks, Mephistophilis: yet fain
would I have a book wherein I might
behold all spells and incantations, that
I might raise up spirits when I please.

MEPHISTOPHILIS: Here they are in this book.
(*Turns to them.*)

FAUSTUS: Now would I have a book where I
might see all characters and planets of
the heavens, that I might know their
motions and dispositions.

MEPHISTOPHILIS: Here they are too. (*Turns to
them.*)

FAUSTUS: Nay, let me have one book more, —
and then I have done, — wherein I might
see all plants, herbs, and trees, that grow
upon the earth.

MEPHISTOPHILIS: Here they be.

FAUSTUS: O, thou art deceived.

---

24 *hell's a fable:* how can Faustus hold this view,
knowing what he knows? In what tone should Mephistophilis respond? Indeed, how would you play Mephistophilis in this play? **25** *fond:* foolish. **26** *talk not of
a wife:* what does Faustus' asking for a wife (instead of,
for instance, a concubine) tell you of his background?
What is Mephistophilis' objection to a wife? Why would
he object to marriage as an institution? **27** *Penelope:*
the wife of Ulysses, faithful while he was on his odyssey.
28 *Saba:* the Queen of Sheba. **29** *take this book:* what
other examples can you find of Mephistophilis changing
the subject abruptly? What are his motives?

MEPHISTOPHILIS: Tut, I warrant thee. (*Turns to them.*)

FAUSTUS: When I behold the heavens,[30] then I repent,
And curse thee, wicked Mephistophilis,
Because thou hast depriv'd me[31] of those joys.

MEPHISTOPHILIS: Why, Faustus,
Thinkest thou heaven is such a glorious thing?
I tell thee, 'tis not half so fair as thou,
Or any man that breathes on earth.

FAUSTUS: How prov'st thou that?

MEPHISTOPHILIS: 'Twas made for man, therefore is man more excellent.

FAUSTUS: If it were made for man, 'twas made for me:
I will renounce this magic and repent.[32]

(*Enter* GOOD ANGEL *and* EVIL ANGEL.)

GOOD ANGEL: Faustus, repent; yet God will pity thee.

EVIL ANGEL: Thou art a spirit;[33] God cannot pity thee.

FAUSTUS: Who buzzeth in mine ears I am a spirit?
Be I a devil, yet God may pity me;
Ay, God will pity me, if I repent.

EVIL ANGEL: Ay, but Faustus never shall repent.

(*Exeunt* ANGELS.)

FAUSTUS: My heart's so harden'd, I cannot repent:
Scarce can I name salvation, faith, or heaven,
But fearful echoes thunder in mine ears,
"Faustus, thou art damn'd!" then swords, and knives,
Poison, guns, halters, and envenom'd[34] steel
Are laid before me to despatch myself;
And long ere this I should have slain myself,
Had not sweet pleasure conquer'd deep despair.
Have not I made blind Homer[35] sing to me
Of Alexander's love[36] and Œnon's death?
And hath not he, that built the walls of Thebes

With ravishing sound of his melodious harp[37]
Made music with my Mephistophilis?
Why should I die, then, or basely despair!
I am resolv'd; Faustus shall ne'er repent. —
Come, Mephistophilis, let us dispute again,
And argue of divine astrology.[38]
Tell me, are there many heavens above the moon?
Are all celestial bodies but one globe,
As is the substance of this centric earth?

MEPHISTOPHILIS: As are the elements, such the spheres,
Mutually folded in each other's orb,
And Faustus,
All jointly move upon one axletree,[39]
Whose terminus is term'd the world's wide pole;
Nor are the names of Saturn, Mars, or Jupiter
Feign'd but are erring stars.

FAUSTUS: But, tell me, have they all one motion, both *situ et tempore?*[40]

---

30 *behold the heavens:* the heavens (according to the Bible) declare the glory of God. In "Lucifer in Starlight," George Meredith's sonnet, their order causes the Devil to go back to Hell, impressed by the "unalterable law" of the universe. What effect have the heavens, here and elsewhere in the play, on Faustus? 31 *thou hast depriv'd me:* how guilty is Mephistophilis? Faustus himself? 32 *I will renounce this magic and repent:* why is this statement of itself insufficient to constitute a full repentance? What more need Faustus do? Why does he fail to do it now? 33 *spirit:* devil (already damned). 34 *envenom'd:* poisoned. 35 *blind Homer:* it was a tradition that Homer, author of *The Iliad* and *The Odyssey*, was blind. Faustus appears to have been conjuring up his ghost, not merely reading his books. 36 *Alexander's love:* Paris (Alexander) when he lived as a shepherd on Mount Ida fell in love with the nymph Œnone. When he deserted her, she died of a broken heart. Cf. George Peele's play *The Arraignment of Paris* (written in the 1580's and presented at court). 37 *he . . . harp:* Amphion, son of Zeus and Antiope, put up the walls of Thebes simply by playing the harp (lyre) that the god Hermes gave him. 38 *astrology:* astronomy. 39 *axletree:* axis. 40 *situ et tempore:* in place and time.

MEPHISTOPHILIS: All jointly move from east to west in twenty-four hours upon the poles of the world; but differ in their motion upon the poles of the zodiac.

FAUSTUS: Tush,
These slender trifles Wagner can decide:
Hath Mephistophilis no greater skill?
Who knows not the double motion of the planets?
The first is finish'd in a natural day;
The second thus; as Saturn in thirty years;
Jupiter in twelve; Mars in four; the Sun, Venus, and Mercury in a year; the Moon in twenty-eight days. Tush, these are freshmen's suppositions. But, tell me, hath every sphere a dominion or *intelligentia*?[41]

MEPHISTOPHILIS: Ay.

FAUSTUS: How many heavens or spheres are there?

MEPHISTOPHILIS: Nine; the seven planets, the firmament, and the empyreal heaven.

FAUSTUS: Well resolve me in this question; why have we not conjunctions, oppositions, aspects eclipses, all at one time, but in some years we have more, in some less?

MEPHISTOPHILIS: *Per inæqualem motum respectu totius.*[42]

FAUSTUS: Well, I am answered. Tell me who made the world?

MEPHISTOPHILIS: I will not.[43]

FAUSTUS: Sweet Mephistophilis, tell me.

MEPHISTOPHILIS: Move me not, for I will not tell thee.

FAUSTUS: Villain, have I not bound thee to tell me anything?

MEPHISTOPHILIS: Ay, that is not against our kingdom,[44] but this is.
Think thou on hell, Faustus, for thou art damned.

FAUSTUS: Think, Faustus, upon God that made the world.

MEPHISTOPHILIS: Remember this.[45] (*Exit.*)

FAUSTUS: Ay, go, accursed spirit, to ugly hell!
'Tis thou hast damn'd distressed Faustus' soul
Is't not too late?

(*Re-enter* GOOD ANGEL *and* EVIL ANGEL.)

EVIL ANGEL: Too late.

GOOD ANGEL: Never too late, if Faustus can repent.

EVIL ANGEL: If thou repent, devils shall tear thee in pieces.

GOOD ANGEL: Repent, and they shall never raze thy skin.[46]

(*Exeunt* ANGELS.)

FAUSTUS: Ah, Christ, my Saviour,[47]
Seek to save distressed Faustus' soul!

(*Enter* LUCIFER, BELZEBUB, *and* MEPHISTOPHILIS.)

LUCIFER: Christ cannot save thy soul, for he is just:
There's none but I have interest in the same.

FAUSTUS: O, who art thou that look'st so terrible?

LUCIFER: I am Lucifer,
And this is my companion-prince in hell.

---

41 *dominion or intelligentia:* ruling spirit. **42** *Per inæqualem.* . . . : "By their unequal movements in respect to the whole." That is, the various planets move at different speeds within the total cosmos. Discuss whether the Elizabethan audience could have been expected to follow this sort of thing. If not, what would the effect be? What about a modern audience? How would you play it? **43** *I will not:* why will Mephistophilis not respond? **44** *not against our kingdom:* was this condition in the agreement? Should Faustus have expected it to be urged? **45** *remember this:* what sort of a threat is this? **46** *they shall never raze thy skin:* clearly physical fear overcomes Faustus' desire to avoid spiritual death. To what extent should this arouse our pity? Our contempt? **47** *Christ, my Saviour:* why does this prayer not suffice for salvation? What should the fact that the devils do not tear him "in pieces" for uttering it tell Faustus? Why does Lucifer, who hitherto sent underlings, appear in person at this time? Why does Lucifer bring a "pastime"?

FAUSTUS: O, Faustus, they are come to fetch away thy soul!

LUCIFER: We come to tell thee thou dost injure us;
Thou talk'st of Christ, contrary to thy promise:
Thou shouldst not think of God: think of the devil,
And of his dam too.

FAUSTUS: Nor will I henceforth: pardon me in this,
And Faustus vows never to look to heaven,
Never to name God,[48] or to pray to Him,
To burn his Scriptures, slay his ministers,
And make my spirits pull his churches down.

LUCIFER: Do so, and we will highly gratify thee.
Faustus, we are come from hell to show thee some pastime: sit down, and thou shalt see all the Seven Deadly Sins appear in their proper shapes.

FAUSTUS: That sight will be as pleasing unto me,
As Paradise was to Adam, the first day
Of his creation.

LUCIFER: Talk not of Paradise nor creation; but mark this show: talk of the devil, and nothing else. — Come away!

(*Enter the* SEVEN DEADLY SINS.)

Now, Faustus, examine them of their several names and dispositions.

FAUSTUS: What art thou, the first?

PRIDE: I am Pride.[49] I disdain to have any parents. I am like to Ovid's flea;[50] I can creep into every corner of a wench; sometimes, like a perriwig, I sit upon her brow; or, like a fan of feathers, I kiss her lips; indeed, I do — what do I not? But, fie, what a scent is here! I'll not speak another word, except the ground were perfumed, and covered with cloth of arras.[51]

FAUSTUS: What art thou, the second?

COVETOUSNESS: I am Covetousness, begotten of an old churl,[52] in an old leathern bag:[53] and,

might I have my wish, I would desire that this house and all the people in it were turned to gold, that I might lock you up in my good chest: O, my sweet gold!

FAUSTUS: What art thou, the third?

WRATH: I am Wrath. I had neither father nor mother: I leapt out of a lion's mouth when I was scarce half an hour old; and ever since I have run up and down the world with this case of rapiers,[54] wounding myself when I had nobody to fight withal. I was born in hell; and look to it, for some of you shall be my father.[55]

FAUSTUS: What art thou, the fourth?

ENVY: I am Envy,[56] begotten of a chimney-sweeper and an oyster-wife. I cannot read, and therefore wish all books were burnt. I am lean with seeing others eat. O, that there would come a famine through all the world, that all might die, and I live alone! then thou shouldst see how fat I would be. But must thou sit, and I stand? come down, with a vengeance!

FAUSTUS: Away, envious rascal! — What art thou, the fifth?

GLUTTONY: Who I, sir? I am Gluttony. My parents are all dead, and the devil a penny they have left me, but a bare pension, and that is thirty meals a day, and ten bevers,[57] — a small trifle to suffice nature. O, I come of a royal parentage! my grandfather was a Gammon[58] of Bacon, my grandmother a

---

48 *Never to name God*, etc.: this passage seems to have been censored in the 1616 text. 49 *I am Pride*: how would you costume each of the Seven Deadly Sins? 50 *Ovid's flea*: the medieval *Carmine de pulice* ("Song of the Flea") was falsely attributed to the Latin poet Ovid (43 B.C.–17 A.D.). 51 *arras*: Flemish tapestry. 52 *churl*: miser. 53 *leathern bag*: a purse. 54 *case of rapiers*: pair of swords. 55 *some of you shall be my father*: some of you shall give birth to wrath. 56 *I am Envy*: using this speech as a sample, explain how Marlowe makes these abstractions interesting and individual. 57 *bevers*: snacks between meals. 58 *gammon*: side.

Hogshead of Claret-wine; my godfathers were these, Peter Pickle-herring and Martin Martlemas-beef,[59] O, but my godmother, she was a jolly gentlewoman, and well-beloved in every good town and city; her name was Mistress Margery March-beer[60] Now, Faustus, thou hast heard all my progeny;[61] wilt thou bid me to supper?

FAUSTUS: No, I'll see thee hanged: thou wilt eat up all my victuals.

GLUTTONY: Then the devil choke thee!

FAUSTUS: Choke thyself, glutton! — What art thou, the sixth?

SLOTH: I am Sloth. I was begotten on a sunny bank, where I have lain ever since; and you have done me great injury to bring me from thence: let me be carried thither again by Gluttony and Lechery. I'll not speak another word for a king's ransom.

FAUSTUS: What are you, Mistress Minx, the seventh and last?

LECHERY: Who I, sir? I am one that loves an inch of raw mutton[62] better than an ell of fried stock-fish; and the first letter of my name begins with L.

FAUSTUS: Away, to hell, to hell! (*Exeunt the Sins.*)

LUCIFER: Now, Faustus, how dost thou like this?

FAUSTUS: O, this feeds my soul!

LUCIFER: Tut, Faustus, in hell is all manner of delight.

FAUSTUS: O, might I see hell, and return again, How happy were I then!

LUCIFER: Thou shalt; I will send for thee at midnight. In meantime take this book; peruse it thoroughly, And thou shalt turn thyself into what shape thou wilt.

FAUSTUS: Great thanks, mighty Lucifer! This will I keep as chary[63] as my life.

LUCIFER: Farewell, Faustus, and think on the devil.

FAUSTUS: Farewell, great Lucifer.

(*Exeunt* LUCIFER *and* BELZEBUB.)

Come, Mephistophilis.

(*Exeunt.*)

SCENE SIX

(*Enter* CHORUS.)

CHORUS: Learned Faustus,
    To know the secrets of astronomy
    Graven in the book of Jove's high firmament,
    Did mount himself to scale Olympus' top,
    Being seated in a chariot burning bright,   5
    Drawn by the strength of yoky dragons' necks.
    He now is gone to prove cosmography,[1]
    And, as I guess, will first arrive in Rome,
    To see the Pope and manner of his court,
    And take some part of holy Peter's feast,   10
    That to this day is highly solemnis'd. (*Exit.*)

SCENE SEVEN

(*Enter* FAUSTUS *and* MEPHISTOPHILIS.)

FAUSTUS: Having now, my good Mephistophilis,
    Pass'd with delight the stately town of Trier,[1]
    Environ'd round with airy mountain-tops,

---

59 *Martlemas-beef:* salted beef hung up at Martinmas (the Feast of St. Martin, 11 November), for the winter. **60** *March-beer:* fine ale, made in Spring and aged two years. **61** *progeny:* ancestors. **62** *mutton:* prostitute. **63** *L:* for Lechery. There are puns on *ell*, L, and *'ell.* **64** *chary:* carefully. Actually, Faustus has not been very careful of his life, but the humor in this line is not intended by him but rather apprehended by the audience. Discuss the extent to which Faustus' folly makes him a figure of fun or an object of pity. What is achieved by creating a mixed reaction to a dramatic character and how does *Doctor Faustus*, in avoiding black and white motives and messages, represent an advance over the Morality play? In what way is all crime ridiculous, all evil ludicrous?

1 *prove cosmography:* explore the universe.

1 *Trier:* a city in Germany, on the Moselle river.

With walls of flint, and deep-entrenched
  lakes,
Not to be won by any conquering prince;
From Paris next, coasting the realm of
  France,
We saw the river Maine fall into Rhine,
Whose banks are set with groves of fruitful
  vines;
Then up to Naples, rich Campania,
Whose buildings fair and gorgeous to
  the eye,
The streets straight forth, and pav'd with
  finest brick,
Quarter the town in four equivalents:
There saw we learned Maro's[2] golden tomb,
The way he cut, an English mile in length,
Through a rock of stone, in one night's
  space;
From thence to Venice, Padua, and the rest,
In one of which a sumptuous temple stands,
That threats the stars with her aspiring top.
Thus hitherto hath Faustus spent his time:
But tell me now what resting-place is
  this?
Hast thou, as erst I did command,
Conducted me within the walls of Rome?

MEPHISTOPHILIS: Faustus, I have; and, because
  we will not be unprovided, I have taken up
  his Holiness' privy-chamber for our use.

FAUSTUS: I hope his Holiness[3] will bid us
  welcome.

MEPHISTOPHILIS: Tut, 'tis no matter, man; we'll
  be bold with his good cheer.
  And now, my Faustus, that thou mayst
    perceive
  What Rome containeth to delight thee with,
  Know that this city stands upon seven hills
  That underprop the groundwork of the
    same:
  Just through the midst runs flowing Tiber's
    stream
  With winding banks that cut it in two parts;
  Over the which four stately bridges lean,
  That make safe passage to each part of
    Rome:
  Upon the bridge call'd Ponte Angelo
  Erected is a castle passing strong,[4]
  Within whose walls such store of ordnance
    are,

And double cannons fram'd of carved brass,
As match the days within one complete year;
Besides the gates, and high pyramides,[5]
Which Julius Cæsar brought from Africa.

FAUSTUS: Now, by the kingdoms of infernal
  rule,
  Of Styx, of Acheron, and the fiery lake
  Of ever-burning Phlegethon, I swear
  That I do long to see the monuments
  And situation of bright-splendent Rome:
  Come, therefore, let's away.

MEPHISTOPHILIS: Nay, Faustus, stay: I know
  you'd fain see the Pope,
  And take some part of holy Peter's feast,
  Where thou shalt see a troop of bald-
    pate friars,[6]
  Whose *summum bonum*[7] is in belly-cheer.

FAUSTUS: Well, I'm content to compass[8] then
  some sport,
  And by their folly make us merriment.
  Then charm me, that I
  May be invisible,[9] to do what I please,
  Unseen of any whilst I stay in Rome.

(MEPHISTOPHILIS *charms him.*)

MEPHISTOPHILIS: So, Faustus, now
  Do what thou wilt, thou shalt not be
    discern'd.

---

2 *Maro:* Publius Vergilius Maor (70–19 B.C.), known as
Virgil, author of *The Aeneid.* In the Middle Ages he
had some reputation (unfounded) as a magician, hence
the fabulous tunnel mentioned, through Mount Posilipo
from the Bay of Naples to the Baiæ Bay.   3 *his Holiness:*
the Pope.   4 *a castle passing strong:* Hadrian's tomb,
with an angel put on top, became the Castel Sant'-
Angelo.   5 *pyramides:* (four syllables) this could be the
obelisk brought to Rome from Heliopolis in the first
century by Caligula (which stands before St. Peter's
now) or that brought from Egypt by Constantius in the
fourth century; it is probably the former.   6 *bald-pate
friars:* these religious men had their hair cut in a ton-
sure.   7 *summum bonum:* "chief good." With vows of
chastity, eating was their sole physical indulgence.
8 *compass:* obtain.   9 *invisible:* a stage convention
allowed a man to wear a "cloak of invisibility" and be
accepted by the audience as not visible, as carrying a lit
lantern on stage indicated darkness or (in the Chinese
theatre) stagehands dressed in black were not seen.

(*Sound a Sonnet.*[10] *Enter the* POPE *and the* CARDINAL OF LORRAIN *to the banquet, with* FRIARS *attending.*)

POPE: My lord of Lorrain, will't please you draw near?

FAUSTUS: Fall to, and the devil choke you, an you spare!

POPE: How now! who's that which spake? — Friars, look about.

FIRST FRIAR: Here's nobody, if it like your Holiness.

POPE: My lord, here is a dainty dish was sent me from the Bishop of Milan.

FAUSTUS: I thank you, sir. (*Snatches the dish.*)

POPE: How now! who's that which snatched the meat from me? will no man look? — My lord, this dish was sent me from the Cardinal of Florence.

FAUSTUS: You say true; I'll ha't.[12] (*Snatches the dish.*)

POPE: What, again! — My lord, I'll drink to your grace.

FAUSTUS: I'll pledge your grace. (*Snatches the cup.*)

CARDINAL OF LORRAIN: My lord, it may be some ghost, newly crept out of Purgatory, come to beg a pardon of your Holiness.

POPE: It may be so. — Friars, prepare a dirge to lay the fury of this ghost. — Once again, my lord, fall to. (*The* POPE *crosses himself.*)

FAUSTUS: What, are you crossing of yourself? Well, use that trick no more,[13] I would advise you. (*The* POPE *crosses himself again.*) Well, there's the second time. Aware the third; I give you fair warning.

(*The* POPE *crosses himself again, and* FAUSTUS *hits him a box of the ear; and they all run away.*)

Come on, Mephistophilis; what shall we do?

MEPHISTOPHILIS: Nay, I know not: we shall be cursed with bell, book, and candle.[14]

FAUSTUS: How! bell, book, and candle, — candle, book, and bell, —
Forward and backward, to curse Faustus to hell!
Anon[15] you shall hear a hog grunt, a calf bleat, and an ass bray,
Because it is Saint Peter's holiday.

(*Re-enter all the* FRIARS *to sing the Dirge.*)

FIRST FRIAR: Come, brethren, let's about our business with good devotion.

(*They sing.*)

Cursed be he that stole away his Holiness' meat from the table!
        maledicat Dominus![16]

Cursed be he that struck his Holiness a blow on the face!
        maledicat Dominus!

Cursed be he that took Friar Sandelo a blow on the pate!
        maledicat Dominus!

Cursed be he that disturbeth our holy dirge! maledicat Dominus!
Cursed be he that took away his Holiness' wine! maledicat Dominus!
        Et omnes Sancti![17] *Amen!*

(MEPHISTOPHILIS *and* FAUSTUS *beat the Friars, and fling fireworks*[18] *among them; and so exeunt.*)

---

10 *Sound a Sonnet:* give a trumpet fanfare. Note that this is a direction, a music cue, not a description of an action. What does that tell you about the text? 11 *like:* please. 12 *I'll ha't:* I'll have it. 13 *use that trick no more:* why is Faustus angered by the making of the sign of the cross? 14 *bell, book, and candle:* used in the rite of excommunication. 15 *anon:* soon. 16 ff. *maledicat Dominus:* "May God curse him." 17 *Et omnes Sancti!:* "And all the saints!" 18 *fireworks:* squibs were often used for stage confusion as cannons were fired for battle effects. It was the firing of a cannon, charged with wadding, that set fire to the thatched roof and burned down Shakespeare's theatre, The Globe, during a performance of his *Henry VIII.* "Thunder and lightning" was a common stage direction, especially in tragedy (where a disturbance on the human plane was, according to a Theory of Correspondences, supposed to be reflected in the natural world).

SCENE EIGHT

(*Enter* CHORUS.)

CHORUS: When Faustus had with pleasure ta'en
    the view
  Of rarest things, and royal courts of kings,
  He stay'd his course, and so returned home;
  Where such as bear his absence but with
    grief,
  I mean his friends and near'st com-
    panions,
  Did gratulate his safety with kind words,
  And in their conference of what befell,
  Touching[1] his journey through the world
    and air,
  They put forth questions of astrology,
  Which Faustus answer'd with such
    learned skill
  As they admir'd and wonder'd at his wit.
  Now is his fame spread forth in every land:
  Amongst the rest the Emperor is one,
  Carolus the Fifth, at whose palace now
  Faustus is feasted 'mongst his noblemen.
  What there he did, in trial of his art,
  I leave untold; your eyes shall see['t]
    perform'd.[2] (*Exit.*)

SCENE NINE

(*Enter* ROBIN *the Ostler, with a book in his
hand.*)

ROBIN: O, this is admirable! here I ha' stolen
one of Doctor Faustus' conjuring books, and,
i'faith, I mean to search some circles for my
own use. Now will I make all the maidens in
our parish dance at my pleasure, stark naked,
before me; and so by that means I shall see
more than e'er I felt or saw yet.

(*Enter* RALPH, *calling* ROBIN.)

RALPH: Robin, prithee,[1] come away; there's a
gentleman tarries to have his horse, and he
would have his things rubbed and made
clean: he keeps such a chafing[2] with my
mistress about it; and she has set me to
look thee out; prithee, come away.

ROBIN: Keep out, keep out, or else you are
blown up, you are dismembered, Ralph: keep
out, for I am about a roaring piece of work.

RALPH: Come, what doest thou with that same
book? thou canst not read?

ROBIN: Yes, my master and mistress shall find
that I can read, he for his forehead,[3] she for
her private study; she's born to bear with
me, or else my art fails.

RALPH: Why, Robin, what book is that?

ROBIN: What book! why, the most intolerable[4]
book for conjuring that e'er was invented by
any brimstone devil.

RALPH: Canst thou conjure with it?

ROBIN: I can do all these things easily with it;
first, I can make thee drunk with ippocras[5]
at any tavern in Europe for nothing; that's
one of my conjuring works.

RALPH: Our Master Parson says that's nothing.

ROBIN: True, Ralph: and more, Ralph, if thou
hast any mind to Nan Spit, our kitchen-
maid, then turn her and wind her to thy
own use, as often as thou wilt, and at midnight.

RALPH: O, brave, Robin! shall I have Nan Spit,
and to mine own use? On that condition I'll
feed thy devil with horse-bread as long as
he lives, of free cost.

ROBIN: No more, sweet Ralph: let's go and
make clean our boots, which lie foul upon
our hands,[6] and then to our conjuring in the
devil's name. (*Exeunt.*)

SCENE TEN

(*Enter* ROBIN *and* RALPH *with a silver goblet.*)

---

1 *touching:* concerning. 2 *perform'd:* why is this
scene, once announced, not immediately seen?

1 *prithee:* pray you (please). 2 *chafing:* argument.
3 *forehead:* a suggestion that the master will sprout
horns on his forehead, being cuckolded. 4 *intolerable:*
Robin has made an amusingly illiterate word choice.
5 *ippocras:* hippocras (a spiced sweet wine). 6 *boots
. . . upon our hands:* another awkward expression, in
the tradition of Shakespeare's Dogberry, Sheridan's
Mrs. Malaprop, characters in Dickens and elsewhere
—a common device of comedy.

ROBIN: Come, Ralph: did not I tell thee, we were for ever made by this Doctor Faustus' book? *ecce, signum!*[1] here's a simple purchase for horse-keepers: our horses shall eat no hay as long as this lasts.

RALPH: But, Robin, here comes the Vintner.[2]

ROBIN: Hush! I'll gull[3] him supernaturally.

(*Enter* VINTNER.)

Drawer, I hope all is paid; God be with you! — Come, Ralph.

VINTNER: Soft, sir; a word with you. I must yet have a goblet paid from you, ere you go.

ROBIN: I a goblet, Ralph, I a goblet! — I scorn you; and you are but a, etc.[4] I a goblet! search me.

VINTNER: I mean so, sir, with your favour.[5] (*Searches* ROBIN.)

ROBIN: How say you now?

VINTNER: I must say somewhat to your fellow. — You, sir!

ROBIN: Me, sir! me, sir! search your fill. (VINTNER *searches him.*) Now, sir, you may be ashamed to burden honest men[6] with a matter of truth.

VINTNER: Well, one of you hath this goblet about you.

ROBIN: You lie, drawer, 'tis afore me (*aside*). — Sirrah you, I'll teach you to impeach honest men; — stand by; — I'll scour you for a goblet; — stand aside you had best, I charge you in the name of Belzebub. — Look to the goblet, Ralph (*aside to* RALPH).

VINTNER: What mean you, sirrah?

ROBIN: I'll tell you what I mean. (*Reads from a book*) *Sanctobulorum Periphrasticon*[7] — nay, I'll tickle you, Vintner. — Look to the goblet, Ralph (*aside to* RALPH). — (*Reads*) *Polypragmos Belseborams framanto pacostiphos tostu, Mephistophilis, etc.*

(*Enter* MEPHISTOPHILIS, *sets squibs at their backs, and then exit. They run about.*)

VINTNER: O, *nomine Domini!*[8] what meanest thou, Robin? thou hast no goblet.

RALPH: *Peccatum peccatorum!*[9] — Here's thy goblet, good Vintner. (*Gives the goblet to* VINTNER, *who exits.*)

ROBIN: *Misericordia pro nobis!*[10] what shall I do? Good devil, forgive me now, and I'll never rob thy library more.

(*Re-enter* MEPHISTOPHILIS.)

MEPHISTOPHILIS: Monarch of hell, under whose black survey
Great potentates do kneel with awful fear,
Upon whose altars thousand souls do lie,
How am I vexed with these villains' charms?
From Constantinople[11] am I hither come,
Only for pleasure of these damned slaves.

ROBIN: How, from Constantinople! you have had a great journey: will you take sixpence in your purse to pay for your supper, and be gone?

----

1 *ecce, signum!:* "behold, the sign!"   2 *Vintner:* wine-seller, a drawer of wine.   3 *gull:* trick. The tricking of the unwary, especially country bumpkins in London, produced a whole popular literature of "gulling" and "conny-catching" toward the end of the sixteenth century, to which the playwright Robert Greene (*ca.* 1558–1592) and other "University Wits" contributed pamphlets, etc. Thomas Dekker (*ca.* 1570–*ca.* 1641) contributed an anatomy of London gulls in *The Guls Hornebooke* (1609).   4 *you are but a, etc.:* the "etc." suggests that the clown here *ad lib*, which (to judge from Shakespeare's remarks in *Hamlet*) it was hard to keep such merry wags as Will Kempe and other Elizabethan stage "fools" from doing anyway.   5 *favour:* permission.   6 *burden honest men:* challenge the veracity of honest men.   7 *Sanctobulorum Periphrasticon:* nonsense syllables (based on *periphrasis*) parodying magical abracadabra. *Polypragmos*, etc., is more such nonsense.   8 *O, nomine Domini!:* "Oh, in the name of God!"   9 *Peccatum peccatorum!:* "Sin of sins!"   10 *Misericordia pro nobis!:* "Mercy on us!"   11 *from Constantinople:* what does this wild-goose chase for Mephistophilis do to the character that has been established for him?

MEPHISTOPHILIS: Well, villains, for your presumption, I transform thee into an ape, and thee into a dog; and so be gone!

(*Exit.*)

ROBIN: How, into an ape! that's brave: I'll have fine sport with the boys; I'll get nuts and apples enow.[12]

RALPH: And I must be a dog.

ROBIN: I'faith,[13] thy head will never be out of the pottage-pot.

(*Exeunt.*)[14]

SCENE ELEVEN

(*Enter* EMPEROR,[1] FAUSTUS, *and a* KNIGHT, *with* ATTENDANTS.)

EMPEROR: Master Doctor Faustus, I have heard strange report of thy knowledge in the black art, how that none in my empire nor in the whole world can compare with thee for the rare effects of magic: they say thou hast a familiar spirit, by whom thou canst accomplish what thou list. This, therefore, is my request, that thou let me see some proof of thy skill, that mine eyes may be witnesses to confirm what mine ears have heard reported: and here I swear to thee, by the honour of mine imperial crown, that, whatever thou doest, thou shalt be no ways prejudiced or endamaged.

KNIGHT: I'faith, he looks much like a conjurer. (*aside.*)

FAUSTUS: My gracious sovereign, though I must confess myself far inferior to the report men have published, and nothing answerable to the honour of your imperial majesty, yet, for that love and duty binds me thereunto, I am content to do whatsoever your majesty shall command me.[2]

EMPEROR: Then, Doctor Faustus, mark what I shall say.
As I was sometime solitary set
Within my closet,[3] sundry thoughts arose
About the honour of mine ancestors,
How they had won by prowess such exploits,
Got such riches, subdu'd so many kingdoms,
As we that do succeed, or they that shall
Hereafter possess our throne, shall
(I fear me) ne'er attain to that degree
Of high renown and great authority:
Amongst which kings is Alexander the
Great,
Chief spectacle[4] of the world's pre-eminence,
The bright shining of whose glorious acts
Lightens the world with his reflecting beams,
As when I hear but motion made of him,
It grieves my soul I never saw the man:
If, therefore, thou, by cunning of thine art,
Canst raise this man from hollow vaults
below,
Where lies entomb'd this famous conqueror,
And bring with him his beauteous paramour,[5]
Both in their right shapes, gesture, and attire
They us'd to wear during their time of life,
Thou shalt both satisfy my just desire,
And give me cause to praise thee whilst I
live.

FAUSTUS: My gracious lord, I am ready to accomplish your request, so far forth as by art and power of my spirit I am able to perform.

KNIGHT: I'faith, that's just nothing at all. (*aside.*)

FAUSTUS: But, if it like your grace, it is not in my ability to present before your eyes the true substantial bodies of those two deceased princes, which long since are consumed to dust.

---

12 *enow:* enough. 13 *I'faith:* in faith (truly). 14 *Exeunt:* note that the transformation threatened by Mephistophilis cannot be effected on the Elizabethan stage and the clowns go off as they came on. In a teleplay or film would you have them changed into animals? If so, at what point?

1 Stage Direction: the Emperor is Charles V, Emperor of the Holy Roman Empire. 2 *I must confess myself . . . :* such modesty doesn't sound like Faustus as we know him. How would you deliver the lines? 3 *closet:* private room. 4 *chief spectacle,* etc.: most to be noticed in the world's history. 5 *paramour:* lover.

KNIGHT: Ay, marry Master Doctor, now there's a sign of grace in you, when you will confess the truth. (*aside*.)

FAUSTUS: But such spirits as can lively resemble Alexander and his paramour shall appear before your grace, in that manner that they both lived in, in their most flourishing estate; which I doubt not shall sufficiently content your imperial majesty.

EMPEROR: Go to, Master Doctor; let me see them presently.[6]

KNIGHT: Do you hear, Master Doctor? you bring Alexander and his paramour before the Emperor!

FAUSTUS: How then, sir?

KNIGHT: I'faith, that's as true as Diana turned me to a stag.[7]

FAUSTUS: No, sir; but, when Actæon died, he left the horns[8] for you. — Mephistophilis, be gone. (*Exit* MEPHISTOPHILIS.)

KNIGHT: Nay, an you go to conjuring, I'll be gone. (*Exit*.)

FAUSTUS: I'll meet with you anon for interrupting me so. — Here they are, my gracious lord.

(*Re-enter* MEPHISTOPHILIS *with* SPIRITS *in the shapes of* ALEXANDER *and his* PARAMOUR.)

EMPEROR: Master Doctor, I heard this lady, while she lived, had a wart or mole in her neck: how shall I know whether it be so or no?

FAUSTUS: Your highness may boldly go and see.

EMPEROR: Sure, these are no spirits, but the true substantial bodies of those two deceased princes. (*Exeunt* SPIRITS.)

FAUSTUS: Wilt please your highness now to send for the knight that was so pleasant with me here of late?

EMPEROR: One of you call him forth. (*Exit* ATTENDANT.)

(*Re-enter the* KNIGHT *with a pair of horns on his head*.)[9]

How now, sir knight! why, I had thought thou hadst been a bachelor, but now I see thou hast a wife, that not only gives thee horns, but makes thee wear them. Feel on thy head.

KNIGHT: Thou damned wretch and execrable dog,
Bred in the concave of some monstrous rock,
How dar'st thou thus abuse a gentleman?
Villain, I say, undo what thou hast done!

FAUSTUS: O, not so fast, sir! there's no haste: but, good, are you remembered how you crossed me in my conference with the Emperor? I think I have met with you for it.

EMPEROR: Good Master Doctor, at my entreaty release him:[10] he hath done penance sufficient.

---

6 *presently:* immediately. 7 *turned me to a stag:* that's as true as I am Actæon, whom Diana transformed into a stag (when he chanced upon her bathing in the woods — his own hounds then hunted him down). 7 *horns:* another reference to cuckolding, the cheated husband being a standard butt of Elizabethan humor. (The French still think this funny.) 9 Stage Direction: it was impossible to get the horns on the Knight's head on stage, so he had to go off and come on again. Faustus, however, "meets" (gets even) with the taunting Knight. But the Knight (who did not believe in Faustus' power) made nowhere near as much of a mockery of it as Faustus did himself by playing silly tricks with it. There is a profound pessimism behind this slapstick as Marlowe suggests that great powers are achieved by human beings who waste them (to put golf-players on the moon, etc.). 10 *release him:* the mighty (the emperor, or God) are quick to forgive and forget, but Faustus, himself vengeful and petty, assumes in the long run that God will be the same and dares not appeal to Him. Without that sincere appeal, God cannot grant grace. Faustus commits the Sin against the Holy Ghost: lack of faith in God's goodness, mercy, and power to forgive. That is the one unpardonable sin, so Faustus is lost. In this trivial matter of the horns on the Knight that end is forecast. God could redeem Faustus even faster than Faustus can remove his curse on the Knight, but Faustus cannot bring himself to ask and so cannot receive.

FAUSTUS: My gracious lord, not so much for the injury he offered me here in your presence, as to delight you with some mirth, hath Faustus worthily requited this injurious knight; which being all I desire, I am content to release him of his horns: — and, sir knight, hereafter speak well of scholars. — Mephistophilis, transform him straight. (MEPHISTOPHILIS *removes the horns*.)[11] — Now, my good lord, having done my duty, I humbly take my leave.

EMPEROR: Farewell, Master Doctor: yet, ere you go,
Expect from me a bounteous reward.

(*Exeunt* EMPEROR, KNIGHT, *and* ATTENDANTS.)

FAUSTUS: Now, Mephistophilis, the restless course
That time doth run with calm and silent foot,
Shortening my days and thread of vital life,
Calls for the payment of my latest years:
Therefore, sweet Mephistophilis, let us
Make haste to Wertenberg.

MEPHISTOPHILIS: What, will you go on horseback or on foot?

FAUSTUS: Nay, till I'm past this fair and pleasant green, I'll walk on foot.

(*Enter a* HORSE-COURSER.)[12]

HORSE-COURSER: I have been all this day seeking one Master Fustian: mass, see where he is! — God save you Master Doctor!

FAUSTUS: What, horse-courser! you are well met.

HORSE-COURSER: Do you hear, sir? I have brought you forty dollars for your horse.

FAUSTUS: I cannot sell him so: if thou likest him for fifty, take him.

HORSE-COURSER: Alas, sir, I have no more! — I pray you, speak for me.

MEPHISTOPHILIS: I pray you, let him have him: he is an honest fellow, and he has a great charge,[13] neither wife nor child.

FAUSTUS: Well, come, give me your money. (HORSE-COURSER *gives* FAUSTUS *money*): my

boy will deliver him to you. But I must tell you one thing before you have him; ride him not into the water, at any hand.[14]

HORSE-COURSER: Why, sir, will he not drink of all waters?

FAUSTUS: O, yes, he will drink of all waters; but ride him not into the water; ride him over hedge or ditch, or where thou wilt, but not into the water.

HORSE-COURSER: Well, sir. — Now am I made man for ever: I'll not leave my horse for forty: if he had but the quality of hey-ding-ding, hey-ding-ding,[15] I'd make a brave living on him: he has a buttock as slick as an eel (*aside*). — Well, God b'wi'ye,[16] sir: your boy will deliver him me: but, hark you, sir; if my horse be sick or ill at ease if I bring his water[17] to you, you'll tell me what it is?

FAUSTUS: Away, you villain! what, dost think I am a horse-doctor? (*Exit* HORSE-COURSER.)

What art thou,[18] Faustus, but a man condemn'd to die?
Thy fatal time doth draw to final end;
Despair doth drive distrust into my thoughts:
Confound these passions with a quiet sleep:
Tush, Christ did call the thief upon the Cross;
Then rest thee, Faustus, quiet in conceit.

(*Sleeps in his chair*.)

(*Re-enter* HORSE-COURSER, *all wet, crying*.)

---

11 *removes the horns*: since the horns cannot be made to vanish, they have to be removed in sight of the audience. 12 *horse-courser*: a dealer in horses. 13 *charge*: responsibility. What is the "great charge" of an unmarried man? 14 *not into the water, at any hand*: under no conditions must the magical horse go into running water, which reverses charms. 15 *hey-ding-ding*: high spirits. 16 *b'wi'ye*: be with you. 17 *his water*: a sample of urine for analysis. 18 *What art thou . . .* : a very swift change of tone for Faustus. What is the basis for Faustus' quiet attitude "in conceit" (in imagination)?

HORSE-COURSER: Alas, alas! Doctor Fustian, quotha? mass, Doctor Lopus[19] was never such a doctor: has given me a purgation, has purged me of forty dollars; I shall never see them more. But yet, like an ass as I was, I would not be ruled by him, for he bade me I should ride him into no water; now I, thinking my horse had had some rare quality that he would not have had me know of, I, like a venturous youth,[20] rid him into the deep pond at the town's end. I was no sooner in the middle of the pond, but my horse vanished away, and I sat upon a bottle of hay, never so near drowning in my life. But I'll seek out my doctor, and have my forty dollars again, or I'll make it the dearest horse! — O, yonder is his snipper-snapper. Do you hear? you, hey-pass,[21] where's your master?

MEPHISTOPHILIS: Why, sir, what would you? you cannot speak with him.

HORSE-COURSER: But I will speak with him.

MEPHISTOPHILIS: Why, he's fast asleep: come some other time.

HORSE-COURSER: I'll speak with him now, or I'll break his glass-windows[22] about his ears.

MEPHISTOPHILIS: I tell thee, he has not slept[23] this eight nights.

HORSE-COURSER: An he have not slept this eight weeks, I'll speak with him.

MEPHISTOPHILIS: See, where he is, fast asleep.

HORSE-COURSER: Ay, this is he. — God save you, Master Doctor, Master Doctor, Master Doctor Fustian! forty dollars, forty dollars for a bottle[24] of hay!

MEPHISTOPHILIS: Why, thou seest he hears thee not.

HORSE-COURSER: So-ho, ho! so-ho, ho![25] (Hollows[26] in his ear.) No, will you not wake? I'll make you wake ere I go. (Pulls FAUSTUS by the leg, and pulls it away.)[27] Alas, I am undone! what shall I do?

FAUSTUS: O, my leg, my leg! — Help, Mephistophilis! call the officers. — My leg, my leg!

MEPHISTOPHILIS: Come, villain, to the constable.

HORSE-COURSER: O Lord, sir, let me go, and I'll give you forty dollars more!

MEPHISTOPHILIS: Where be they?

HORSE-COURSER: I have none about me: come to my ostry,[28] and I'll give them you.

MEPHISTOPHILIS: Be gone quickly. (HORSE-COURSER runs away.)

FAUSTUS: What, is he gone? farewell he! Faustus has his leg again, and the Horse-courser, I take it, a bottle of hay for his labour: well, this trick shall cost him forty dollars more.

(Enter WAGNER.)

How now, Wagner! what's the news with thee?

WAGNER: Sir, the Duke of Vanholt doth earnestly entreat your company.

FAUSTUS: The Duke of Vanholt! an honourable gentleman, to whom I must be no niggard of my cunning.[29] — Come, Mephistophilis, let's away to him. (Exeunt.)

---

19 Lopus: Doctor Roderigo Lopez was a Spanish Jew, physician to Elizabeth, who was convicted and executed for a plot to poison the queen. That was in 1594. When did Marlowe write Doctor Faustus? When did Marlowe die? What does this tell you about this part of the text? **20** like a venturous youth: what human failing is alluded to here? How is the horse-courser's misfortune with the magic horse related to Faustus' flaw and fate? **21** snipper-snapper . . . hey-pass: servant . . . trickster. **22** glass-windows: eyeglasses. **23** not slept: why has Faustus been unable to sleep? Or is Mephistophilis lying to put off the horse-courser? How would you read the line? **24** Bottle: bundle. **25** So-ho: a hunting cry. (There is a district of London with this name.) **26** hollows: hollers. **27** pulls it away: a spectacular effect attempted on stage. How would you arrange it? **28** ostry: hostelry. **29** cunning: skill.

SCENE TWELVE[1]

(*Enter the* DUKE OF VANHOLT, *the* DUCHESS, *and* FAUSTUS.)

DUKE: Believe me, Master Doctor, this merriment hath much pleased me.

FAUSTUS: My gracious lord, I am glad it contents you so well. — But it may be, madam, you take no delight in this. I have heard that great-bellied[2] women do long for some dainties or other: what is it, madam? tell me, and you shall have it.

DUCHESS: Thanks, good Master Doctor: and, for I see your courteous intent to pleasure me, I will not hide from you the thing my heart desires; and, were it now summer, as it is January and the dead time of the winter, I would desire no better meat[3] than a dish of ripe grapes.

FAUSTUS: Alas, madam, that's nothing! — Mephistophilis, be gone. (*Exit* MEPHISTOPHILIS.) Were it a greater thing than this, so it would content you, you should have it.

(*Re-enter* MEPHISTOPHILIS *with grapes.*)

Here they be, madam: wilt please you taste on them?

DUKE: Believe me, Master Doctor, this makes me wonder above the rest, that being in the dead time of winter and in the month of January, how you should come by these grapes.

FAUSTUS: If it like your grace, the year is divided into two circles over the whole world, that, when it is here winter with us, in the contrary circle it is summer with them, as in India, Saba, and farther countries in the east; and by means of a swift spirit that I have, I had them brought hither, as you see. — How do you like them, madam? be they good?

DUCHESS: Believe me, Master Doctor, they be the best grapes that e'er I tasted in my life before.

FAUSTUS: I am glad they content you so, madam.

DUKE: Come, madam, let us in, where you must well reward this learned man for the great kindness he hath showed to you.

DUCHESS: And so I will, my lord; and, whilst I live, rest beholding for this courtesy.

FAUSTUS: I humbly thank your grace.

DUKE: Come, Master Doctor, follow us, and receive your reward.[4] (*Exeunt.*)

---

1 As the scene opens it is clear Faustus and Mephistophilis have already made the trip announced in the closing lines of Scene II and, moreover, that Faustus has been at the court of Vanholt for some time. What do you think of the handling of time here? In a modern play there could be a curtain to indicate a lapse of time. Besides the arrangements necessary to get corpses offstage (see the end of *Hamlet*, for example) and such, was the Elizabethan stage, in your opinion much inconvenienced by the lack of an act curtain? Discuss the handling and telescoping of time in this and other Elizabethan plays you may know—in *Macbeth*, for instance, 11 years elapse—remembering that the story of Faustus involves a pact with the Devil for 24 years and that the classical unities of time and place cannot be adhered to in the light of the nature of the plot. Discuss the pros and cons of concentrating the play on the last day of Faustus' life, with flashbacks if necessary, comparing advantages and disadvantages with Marlowe's approach. 2 *great-bellied:* pregnant. 3 *meat:* food. 4 *receive your reward:* if Faustus represents science (knowledge) or even technology, it is interesting to speculate how men in power (Duke of Vanholt) share in the responsibility for the misapplication of abilities and discoveries. The scientist is often interested in doing a thing just because it can be done, or in attempting it just because people say it cannot be done: for him it is an intellectual problem. To what extent are scientists to be harnessed to society's needs, or to the planned progress of humanity, and who ought to make long-range decisions to see that great minds are not frittered away (to choose one of Swift's examples from *Gulliver's Travels*) extracting sunbeams from cucumbers? There is not space in notes such as these to indicate all the areas that class discussions may probe as a result of stimulating ideas found in this play, but a note such as this may serve to indicate that students will find more interest and profit in a work if it is connected with other things they know, especially modern problems they think relevant. A good instructor can produce lively discussion (always better than dull lectures) and keep it from straying too far from *Doctor Faustus* while still relating literature to life, what the students do not yet know with what they do. The rule is always: "Only connect."

SCENE THIRTEEN

(*Enter* WAGNER.)

WAGNER: I think my master means to die
  shortly,
For he hath given to me all his goods:
And yet, methinks, if that death were near,
He would not banquet, and carouse, and
  swill
Amongst the students, as even now he doth,
Who are at supper with such belly-cheer[1]
As Wagner ne'er beheld in all his life.
See, where they come! belike[2] the feast is
  ended. (*Exit.*)

SCENE FOURTEEN

(*Enter* FAUSTUS *with two or three* SCHOLARS, *and*
MEPHISTOPHILIS.)

FIRST SCHOLAR: Master Doctor Faustus, since
our conference about fair ladies, which was
the beautifulest in all the world, we have
determined with ourselves that Helen of
Greece was the admirablest lady that ever
lived: therefore, Master Doctor, if you will
do us that favour, as to let us see that peerless dame of Greece, whom all the world
admires for majesty, we should think ourselves much beholding unto you.

FAUSTUS: Gentlemen,
For that I know your friendship is unfeign'd,
And Faustus' custom is not to deny
The just requests of those that wish him well,
You shall behold that peerless dame of
  Greece,
No otherways[1] for pomp and majesty
Than when Sir Paris cross'd the seas with
  her,
And brought the spoils to rich Dardania.[2]
Be silent, then, for danger is in words.

(*Music sounds, and* HELEN *passeth over the
stage.*[3])

SECOND SCHOLAR: Too simple is my wit to tell
  her praise,
Whom all the world admires for majesty.

THIRD SCHOLAR: No marvel though the angry
  Greeks pursu'd

With ten years' war the rape[4] of such a
  queen,
Whose heavenly beauty passeth all compare.

FIRST SCHOLAR: Since we have seen the pride
  of Nature's works,
And only paragon of excellence,
Let us depart; and for this glorious deed
Happy and blest be Faustus evermore!

FAUSTUS: Gentlemen, farewell: the same I wish
  to you.

(*Exeunt* SCHOLARS.)

(*Enter an* OLD MAN.)

OLD MAN: Ah, Doctor Faustus, that I might
  prevail
To guide thy steps unto the way of life,
By which sweet path thou mayst attain
  the goal
That shall conduct thee to celestial rest!
Break heart, drop blood, and mingle it with
  tears,
Tears falling from repentant heaviness[5]
Of thy most vile and loathsome filthiness,
The stench whereof corrupts the inward soul
With such flagitious[6] crimes of heinous sin

---

1 *belly-cheer:* gluttony. By now, how many of the
Seven Deadly Sins has Faustus committed? What is
Faustus' principal sin?   2 *belike:* it seems.

1 *no otherways:* just as. 2 *Dardania:* Troy. 3
passeth over the stage: look at a picture of some
scholar's idea of the Elizabethan stage (our knowledge
of actual stages is sketchy) and determine where it
would be best to stage the apparition of Helen. What
is gained by having her distant and mute? In *The
Iliad,* Homer refrains from physical description of
Helen, leaving each person to imagine her in his own
terms of perfect beauty. Would you consider having
the characters on stage viewing a Helen not seen by
the audience? Defend your answer. 4 *rape:* abduction. Paris stole Helen from her husband Menelaus,
King of Lacedæmon. 5 *heaviness:* heaviness of heart,
sorrow. 6 *flagitious:* profoundly wicked. Make a list of
the most unusual words in the text. Shakespeare often
made up words when he needed them. Does Marlowe
do this? Investigate the state of the language at the time
these men came to use it: what was the attitude of the
Elizabethans, for instance, to neologisms?

As no commiseration may expel,
But mercy, Faustus, of thy Saviour sweet,
Whose blood alone must wash away thy
   guilt.

FAUSTUS: Where art thou, Faustus? wretch,
   what hast thou done?[7]
Damn'd art thou, Faustus, damn'd; despair
   and die![8]
Hell calls for right,[9] and with a roaring voice
Says, "Faustus, come; thine hour is almost
   come;"
And Faustus now will come to do thee right.

(MEPHISTOPHILIS *gives him a dagger.*)

OLD MAN: Ah, stay, good Faustus, stay thy
   desperate steps!
I see an angel hovers o'er thy head,
And, with a vial full of precious grace,
Offers to pour the same into thy soul:
Then call for mercy, and avoid despair.

FAUSTUS: Ah my sweet friend, I feel
Thy words to comfort my distressed soul!
Leave me a while to ponder on my sins.

OLD MAN: I go, sweet Faustus; but with heavy
   cheer,[10]
Fearing the ruin[11] of thy hopeless soul. (*Exit.*)

FAUSTUS: Accursed Faustus, where is mercy
   now?
I do repent; and yet I do despair:
Hell strives with grace for conquest in my
   breast:[12]
What shall I do to shun the snares of death?

MEPHISTOPHILIS: Thou traitor, Faustus, I arrest
   thy soul
For disobedience to my sovereign lord:
Revolt, or I'll in piece-meal tear thy flesh.[13]

FAUSTUS: Sweet Mephistophilis, entreat thy
   lord
To pardon my unjust presumption,
And with my blood again I will confirm
My former vow I made to Lucifer.

MEPHISTOPHILIS: Do it, then, quickly, with
   unfeigned heart,
Lest greater danger do attend thy drift.

FAUSTUS: Torment, sweet friend, that base and
   crooked age,

That durst dissuade me from thy Lucifer,
With greatest torments that our hell affords.

MEPHISTOPHILIS: His faith is great; I cannot
   touch his soul;
But what I may afflict his body with
I will attempt, which is but little worth.

FAUSTUS: One thing, good servant, let me crave
   of thee,
To glut the longing of my heart's desire, —
That I might have unto my paramour
That heavenly Helen which I saw of late,
Whose sweet embracings may extinguish
   clean
Those thoughts that do dissuade me from
   my vow,
And keep mine oath I made to Lucifer.

MEPHISTOPHILIS: Faustus this, or what else
   thou shalt desire,
Shall be perform'd in twinkling of an eye.[14]

(*Re-enter* HELEN.)

----

7 *what hast thou done:* why does the Old Man's speech
have such a great and immediate effect upon Faustus?
8 *damn'd; despair and die:* alliteration was a favorite
ornament of early English poetry, even before rhyme.
What are its advantages and pitfalls? How would
Doctor Faustus be different with much greater use of
"apt alliteration's artful aid"? If written entirely in
rhyming couplets, like many earlier plays? If written
entirely in blank verse? If written entirely in prose?
9 *right:* its due (according to the bargain). 10 *heavy
cheer:* sadness. 11 *fearing the ruin:* at this point are
you still in doubt about the outcome of the play? Explain. What is the function of the Old Man's pessi-
mistic statement here? 12 *strives . . . in my breast:*
discuss this conflict in terms of the overall theme of
the tragedy. What is the essential conflict that serves
as the spring of the plot? If (as Aristotle said) a plot
is a climactic series of events with a beginning, a
middle, and an end—where is the "middle" of the
Faustus story? (The beginning and end are clear and
forcefully presented.) Does something happen to the
nature of the bargain between its signing and its due
date? To Faustus' character because of the bargain?
13 *tear thy flesh:* evil constantly threatens Faustus
with physical suffering. What is worse than this? 14
twinkling of an eye: what is the source of this
familiar expression? How does its origin add effect
to its use by Mephistophilis?

FAUSTUS: Was this the face that launch'd a
     thousand ships,
And burnt the topless towers of Ilium? —
Sweet Helen, make me immortal with a
     kiss.[15] —

(*Kisses her.*)

Her lips suck forth my soul: see, where it
     flies! —
Come, Helen, come, give me my soul again.
Here will I dwell, for heaven is in these lips,
And all is dross that is not Helena.
I will be Paris, and for love of thee,
Instead of Troy, shall Wertenberg be sack'd;
And I will combat with weak Menelaus,
And wear thy colours on my plumed crest;[16]
Yes, I will wound Achilles in the heel,[17]
And then return to Helen for a kiss.
O, thou art fairer than the evening air
Clad in the beauty of a thousand stars;
Brighter art thou than flaming Jupiter
When he appear'd to hapless Semele;[18]
More lovely than the monarch of the sky
In wanton Arethusa's[19] azur'd arms;
And none but thou shalt be my paramour!
     (*Exeunt.*)

SCENE FIFTEEN

(*Enter the* OLD MAN.)

OLD MAN: Accursed Faustus, miserable man,
     That from thy soul exclud'st the grace of
          heaven,
     And fly'st the throne of his tribunal-seat!

(*Enter* DEVILS.)

Satan begins to sift[1] me with his pride:
As in this furnace God shall try my faith,
My faith, vile hell, shall triumph over thee,
Ambitious fiends, see how the heavens smile
At your repulse, and laugh your state[2] to
     scorn!
Hence, hell! for hence I fly unto my God.[3]

(*Exeunt — on one side,* DEVILS, *on the other,*
OLD MAN.)

SCENE SIXTEEN

(*Enter* FAUSTUS, *with* SCHOLARS.)

FAUSTUS: Ah, gentlemen!

FIRST SCHOLAR: What ails Faustus?

FAUSTUS: Ah, my sweet chamber-fellow, had I
     lived with thee, then had I lived still! but
     now I die eternally.[1] Look, comes he not?
     comes he not?

SECOND SCHOLAR: What means Faustus?

THIRD SCHOLAR: Belike he is grown into some
     sickness by being over solitary.[2]

---

15 *Was this the face*, etc.: this passage is even more
famous than Marlowe's line "Who ever loved who loved
not at first sight," which Shakespeare did not disdain to
quote. What do you think are the reasons for its force
and fame? Relate the image to the destruction of Faustus
himself. How will Helen's kiss bring death rather than
immortality?   **16** *plumed crest:* this is a reference to the
wearing of a mistress' ribbons on a knight's helmet in
the Age of Chivalry, not a custom of ancient Greece.
How might the anachronism be explained by the illustrations in the books in which Faustus got his ideas of
the Trojan War?   **17** *in the heel:* Achilles, hero at the
siege of Troy, was dipped by his mother into the river
Styx as a baby. This was designed to make him immortal, but a small place (on his heel, where his
mother held him) remained vulnerable because un-
immersed. It proved his downfall. What is Faustus'
"Achilles heel"?   **18** *Semele:* Jove (Jupiter) was in love
with this maiden but he appeared to her in his form
as god of thunder and lightning and she was consumed. In what way will Faustus be destroyed in
connection with Helen?   **19** *Arethusa:* Arethusa was a
nymph loved by Alpheus, a river god. When he pursued her, Arethusa was turned into a fountain by the
goddess Diana; she then was "wanton" with the sky.
"The monarch of the sky" is ambiguous and could
mean either Phoebus, who drove the chariot of the
sun, or Semele, the moon goddess, reflected in the
waters of Arethusa. This second Semele was the
daughter of Cadmus and Harmonia. Her child (by
Zeus) was Dionysus. Why is there so much Greek
mythology in this play?

1 *sift:* test. **2** *state:* power. **3** *fly unto my God:*
watch for an echo of this in Faustus' last speech.

1 *die eternally:* why is this not redundant? What
important point is being made here? **2** *over solitary:*
the Scholar means reclusive rather than alienated, but
discuss both concepts. How has Faustus cut himself off
from mankind? In what way is he in Hell already?

FIRST SCHOLAR: If it be so, we'll have physicians to cure him. —
'Tis but a surfeit;[3] never fear, man.

FAUSTUS: A surfeit of deadly sin, that hath damned both body and soul.

SECOND SCHOLAR: Yet, Faustus, look up to heaven; remember God's mercies are infinite.

FAUSTUS: But Faustus' offence can ne'er be pardoned: the serpent that tempted Eve may be saved, but not Faustus. Ah, gentlemen, hear me with patience, and tremble not at my speeches! Though my heart pants and quivers to remember that I have been a student here these thirty years, O, would I had never seen Wertenberg, never read a book! and what wonders I have done, all Germany can witness, yea, all the world; for which Faustus hath lost both Germany and the world, yea, heaven itself, heaven, the seat of God, the throne of the blessed, the kingdom of joy; and must remain in hell for ever, hell, ah, hell, for ever! Sweet friends, what shall become of Faustus, being in hell for ever?[4]

THIRD SCHOLAR: Yet, Faustus, call on God.

FAUSTUS: On God, whom Faustus hath abjured! on God, whom Faustus hath blasphemed! Ah, my God, I would weep! but the devil draws in my tears. Gush forth blood,[5] instead of tears! yea, life and soul! O, he stays my tongue! I would lift up my hands; but see, they hold them, they hold them!

ALL: Who, Faustus?

FAUSTUS: Lucifer and Mephistophilis. Ah gentlemen, I gave them my soul for my cunning!

ALL: God forbid!

FAUSTUS: God forbade it, indeed, but Faustus hath done it: for vain pleasure of twenty-four years hath Faustus lost eternal joy and felicity. I writ them a bill with mine own blood: the date is expired; the time will come, and he will fetch me.

FIRST SCHOLAR: Why did not Faustus tell us of this before, that divines might have prayed for thee?

FAUSTUS: Oft have I thought to have done so; but the devil threatened to tear me in pieces, if I named God, to fetch both body and soul, if I once gave ear to divinity: and now 'tis too late. Gentlemen, away, lest you perish with me.

SECOND SCHOLAR: O, what shall we do to save Faustus?

FAUSTUS: Talk not of me, but save yourselves, and depart.

THIRD SCHOLAR: God will strengthen me; I will stay with Faustus.

FIRST SCHOLAR: Tempt not God,[6] sweet friend; but let us into the next room, and there pray for him.

FAUSTUS: Ay, pray for me, pray for me; and what noise soever ye hear, come not unto me, for nothing can rescue me.

SECOND SCHOLAR: Pray thou, and we will pray that God may have mercy upon thee.

FAUSTUS: Gentlemen, farewell: if I live till morning, I'll visit you; if not, Faustus is gone to hell.[7]

---

3 *surfeit:* overabundance. Elizabethan psychology was based on the concept of Galen's four elements (fire, water, earth, air) and concomitant liquids ("humours") in the body. The concept of what we should call the "well-adjusted personality" or "well-balanced mind" depended upon the proper relationship of these elements, not too little or too much, a sort of psychosomatic "golden mean." In *Hamlet*, for example, Horatio is "not passion's slave" because all his humours are well-balanced; Hamlet has too much water in his system and is melancholy.   4 *Faustus' offence,* etc.: discuss the rhetoric of this passage, especially the use of repetition. 5 *blood:* compare the scene in which Faustus signed the bond in blood. Why are we reminded of the bond at this point through Faustus' confession to the Scholars? 6 *tempt not God:* consider this idea in terms of Faustus' life. How is it that the Scholars are wiser than Faustus? What blinded him? 7 *hell . . . farewell:* ending a scene with a rhymed couplet was sometimes used to give it a final fillip, a sense of completeness. Couplets were often used, once plays came to be written chiefly in blank verse, to stress important ideas: "The play's the thing/Wherein I'll catch the conscience of the king." What use do you see made of them in *Doctor Faustus?*

ALL: Faustus, farewell.

(*Exeunt* SCHOLARS. — *The clock strikes eleven.*)

SCENE SEVENTEEN[1]

FAUSTUS: Ah, Faustus.
Now hast thou but one bare hour to live,
And then thou must be damn'd perpetually!
Stand still, you ever-moving spheres of
    heaven,
That time may cease, and midnight never
    come;
Fair Nature's eye,[2] rise, rise again, and
    make
Perpetual day; or let this hour be but
A year, a month, a week, a natural day,
That Faustus may repent and save his soul!
O lente, lente currite, noctis equi![3]
The stars move still, time runs, the clock
    will strike,
The devil will come, and Faustus must be
    damn'd.[4]
O, I'll leap up to my God! — Who pulls me
    down? —
See, see, where Christ's blood streams in the
    firmament![5]
One drop would save my soul, half a drop:
    ah, my Christ! —
Ah, rend not my heart for naming of my
    Christ!
Yet will I call on him: O, spare me,
    Lucifer![6] —
Where is it now? tis gone: and see, where
    God
Stretcheth out his arm, and bends his ireful
    brows!
Mountains and hills, come, come, and fall
    on me,
And hide me from the heavy wrath of
    God!
No, no!
Then will I headlong run into the earth:
Earth, gape![7] O, no, it will not harbour me!
You stars that reign'd at my nativity,
Whose influence hath allotted death and
    hell,
Now draw up Faustus, like a foggy mist,
Into the entrails of yon labouring clouds,
That, when you vomit forth into the air,
My limbs may issue from your smoky
    mouths,

So that my soul may but ascend to
    heaven!

(*The clock strikes the half-hour.*)

Ah, half the hour is past! 'twill all be past
    anon.
O God,
If thou wilt not have mercy on my soul,
Yet for Christ's sake, whose blood hath
    ransom'd me,
Impose some end to my incessant pain;
Let Faustus live in hell a thousand years,
A hundred thousand, and at last be sav'd!
O, no end is limited to damned souls!
Why wert thou not a creature wanting[8] soul?
Or why is this immortal that thou hast?   40
Ah, Pythagoras' metempsychosis,[9] were that
    true,
This soul should fly from me, and I be
    chang'd
Unto some brutish beast! all beasts are
    happy,
For, when they die,
Their souls are soon dissolv'd in
    elements;
But mine must live still to be plagu'd in hell.
Curs'd be the parents that engender'd me!
No, Faustus, curse thyself,[10] curse Lucifer
That hath depriv'd thee of the joys of
    heaven.

---

1 Various editors have divided the play in different
ways. Argue for or against beginning a new scene at
this point. 2 *Nature's eye:* the sun. 3 *O lente . . . :*
"Run slowly, slowly, horses of the night," adapted
from Ovid's *Amores,* I.13. In its original context, the
idea is expressed by a lover in his mistress' arms. What
additional coloration does the line take on in the light
of that knowledge? 4 *The stars . . . :* how is the
inevitability of Faustus' fate suggested here by the
movement of the verse? 5 *See, see . . . :* discuss the
effectiveness of this famous image. 6 *Lucifer:* at the
last moment, the name of Lucifer is substituted for
that of Christ. 7 *Earth, gape!:* how is it that the grave
itself offers no rest for Faustus? 8 *wanting:* lacking.
9 *Pythagoras' metempsychosis:* Pythagoras of Samos (fl.
6th Cent. B.C.) had a doctrine of the transmigration of
souls after death which he may have picked up from his
contacts with the Egyptians. 10 *curse thyself:* to what
extent has Faustus cursed himself already?

(The clock strikes twelve.)

O, it strikes, it strikes! Now, body, turn
 to air,
Or Lucifer will bear thee quick[11] to hell!

(Thunder and lightning.)

O soul, be chang'd into little water-drops,
And fall into the ocean, ne'er be found!

(Enter DEVILS.*)*

My God, my God, look not so fierce on me!
Adders and serpents, let me breathe a
 while!
Ugly hell, gape not! come not, Lucifer!
I'll burn my books![12] — Ah, Mephistophilis!

(Exeunt DEVILS *with* FAUSTUS.*)*

SCENE EIGHTEEN[1]

(Enter CHORUS.*)*

CHORUS: Cut is the branch that might have
 grown full straight,
And burned is Apollo's laurel-bough,[2]
That sometime[3] grew within this learned
 man.
Faustus is gone: regard his hellish fall,
Whose fiendful fortune may exhort the
 wise,
Only to wonder at unlawful things,
Whose deepness doth entice such forward
 wits[4]
To practise more than heavenly power
 permits.

(Exit.)

Terminat hora diem, terminat auctor opus.[5]

11 *quick:* alive (not speedily), as in the Bible's "the quick and the dead." 12 *I'll burn my books:* Faustus' last cry is against the knowledge that damned him. What knowledge would have saved him? Discuss the play as a positive recommendation to get true knowledge, not an anti-intellectual or reactionary diatribe against the burgeoning knowledge of the Renaissance.

1 Modern dramatists seem to have a horror of "the moral writ large" at the end of their plays. What would be lost or gained if you cut the Chorus' last speech in production? Is it anti-climactic? Unnecessary? 2 *Apollo's laurel-bough:* symbol of learning. Faustus knew, among other things, the advanced ideas of Agostino Ricci, who amended Aristotle's cosmology (1513). 4 *forward wits:* discuss Faustus as the Renaissance man, the "overreacher," the iconoclast. 5 *Terminat . . . . :* "The hour ends the day, the author ends his work." What does the presence of this colophon tell you about the manuscript from which the play was printed. Would this sentence be of any use in the playhouse working copy?

Finally, there are many overreaching questions about the play that could not be handled in this line-by-line commentary that the editor offers you here. Your instructor should raise these matters with you. Some of you may wish to undertake background studies into witchcraft and other subjects connected with the play or to compare and contrast Faustus with other Marlovian "overreachers" in "one-man" plays like *The Jew of Malta* and the two parts of *Tamburlaine*, which are also studies of the villain-as-hero. Some may wish to attempt to bring the comic scenes up to what they consider to be the higher level of the tragic scenes, to provide a tighter construction or more interesting development in the middle of the play, to add or subtract characters or scenes, or even to recast the play in modern terms with a Faustus resident in the America of today and confronted with similar problems in very different contexts. This commentary is intended only as a guide and as a model for the close reading of other plays, stressing the importance of detail and language comprehension.

The Tragedy of Macbeth

Related to *Everyman* in that it is a play in which the materialistic things of the world are shown to be of no use to a man in the long run and to *Doctor Faustus* in many ways, including the metaphor of what Caroline Spurgeon in *Shakespeare's Imagery and What It Tells Us* (1935) calls "a notably small man enveloped in a coat far too big for him," Shakespeare's noble tragedy of *Macbeth* ties in with other plays in this collection, including, as you will see, Jarry's *Ubu the King*.

Now Jarry's play might also have been paired with *Hamlet*, or *Hamlet* with Tom Stoppard's *Rosencrantz and Guildenstern are Dead*, but there are a number of reasons why the greatest dramatist in English should be represented here not by *Hamlet*, or *Lear*, but by *Macbeth*, for (as poet and critic Lascelles Abercrombie writes) it wholly illustrates the process of evil in tragedy:

> No other play sweeps our imaginations at once into the full strength and current like this. From the very first word of it, we know, or at least feel, that the powers of evil are to have their will with the life of man. Their temptation is the most devilish possible: what Macbeth dare not even desire is suddenly and awfully made to *appear* as the thing fated for him: all he has to do is to act accordingly. — Of course! Once induce him to act, and the thing *is* thereby fated: it has been done! — All falls out as the witches prophesied. Macbeth acts, and has his ambition: but the witches did not tell him what he now finds out — that this is to descend alive into hell. Egged on by his wife, his first atrocious treachery, the murder of the king, gives him the vulgar aggrandizement he desires; but a whole series of crimes must maintain it, each more futile than the last, each more patently ignoble in its motive. And when at last his own destruction stares at him, his life is not merely drenched in wickedness; it has ceased to have any meaning; it has become a phantasmagoria of horrible nonsense; a tale told by an idiot.

That, a passage from *The Idea of Great Poetry* (1925), gives some hint of the significance of *Macbeth* and the theme which served Shakespeare as the inspiration of great poetry, which provided him with the "imperial theme" of his monumental tragedy.

Today students may be less gripped by the supernatural than was the superstitious King James, whom the play was designed to flatter, and less interested in the metaphysical aspects of *Macbeth* than the psychological complexities of *Hamlet*, but the play is distinctly modern in its "radical pessimism" (O. J. Campbell) and its hero who thinks the world absurd, "a tale/Told by an idiot, full of sound and fury,/Signifying nothing." Here is Macbeth, one of Shakespeare's rationalist villains (as Robert Penn Warren points out), with his essential humanity cloaked in borrowed robes of greatness or blindly wandering in a world of darkness and confusion, where "Fair is foul and foul is fair." Macbeth has a disturbing message for modern man.

Moreover, for the beginning student, there is not simply a gripping and fascinating story in the play but a structure that is quite easy to grasp. Except for the "awful parenthesis" of the Porter's Scene, there is a straightforward and unrelenting concentration in *Macbeth* upon his career in crime and its inevitable outcome in a catastrophe which destroys the protagonist of the drama and replaces the disorder he has created with a new order and peace for a nation wracked by violence. The plot could not be easier to understand nor the principal characters — and there are only two, Macbeth and his queen — more clearly or more compellingly delineated. Then, also, the structure of the imagery is easy to follow in *Macbeth*: imagery of medicine and disease, of light and color, of music and disharmony, and (especially) of clothes. The imagery creates the mood and meaning of the play and tells its story of murderous ambition even more forcefully than in, for example, that other tale of criminal overreaching, *Richard III* (or *Doctor Faustus*). The images of nature (violated by Macbeth's inhuman acts) show a storm in the heavens as well as tumult in the body politic, bloody babes and blasted seeds, the earth feverous and the woods themselves moving, infected air and open graves, hewn boughs and uprooted trees, violence and disorder on the human plane reflected in the cosmos, nature disturbed by unnatural deeds. And just as in nature humans, having the extra gift of reason, should be above the beasts, the images tell us that when humans lose their sense of place and proportion and rush on to crimes without letting reason give them pause, they will sink to the level of ravening wolves and tigers, evil serpents and toads, birds of prey. The play is full of the birds and beasts of night, the familiars of the witches, rooks, owls, bats, and so on; for the hell-hound Macbeth has brought moral darkness upon all and blinded the world to the glory of God's sun. In this world of disorder and disintegration, creatures of doubtful origin move in fog, the stars are hidden, the powers of darkness are abroad, night thickens, the sun is strangled, blackness sews up the eyelids, torches are extinguished, the moon is in eclipse, murky hell prevails. Then in the end the Sacred Wood, nature itself, moves to blast tyranny and plant justice and new life. The mastery of imagery that Shakespeare shows incomparably in plays such as *Lear* can well be studied by the beginner in *Macbeth* where, though it may be less complex, it is no less rewarding.

All of which is not to say that any play by a dramatist of the stature of Shakespeare is going to be without complexity. A glance at the critics will show that Dolora C. Cunningham (for instance) sees *Macbeth* as the tragedy of the hardened heart, Francis Fergusson dissects it as a *locus classicus* of tragedy as the imitation of an action, Robert G. Collmer and Karl Jaspers discuss it as an existentialist tragedy, Lily B. Campbell, dissects it as a trenchant study in fear, Elmer Edgar Stoll examines its psychology as a "steep tragic contrast" and J. I. M. Stewart sees in it something "which beckons us toward an actual mystery in things." It is true that critics prefer to argue about *Hamlet* and some other plays, but that fact the students may welcome, for the body of criticism on *Macbeth* is not yet too huge for the comprehension of people with a reasonable amount of time at their disposal.

In the theatre, *Macbeth* is seldom attempted and even more seldom successful. Among British actors, for instance, it is considered bad luck to quote from the play and (presumably) disaster to appear in it, though Sir John Gielgud and Garrick, Sir Donald Wolfit and Lord Olivier, among others, have triumphed in it. It is argued that students, with a few notes which have been provided by the editor, can produce *Macbeth* in the theatre of their mind whatever their lack of experience and can thereby gain the confidence needed to approach other masterpieces by William Shakespeare (1564–1616), our great playwright who was "not for an age but for all time."

Our emphasis in this play, a product of the Elizabethan era in which audiences were intoxicated and made imaginative by the poet's words, has been upon the language; but the reader should not ignore the spectacle and the *silences* of *Macbeth*. As Harold Pinter said (quoted in Ronald Hayman's study of him, 1968):

> There are two silences. One when no word is spoken. The other when perhaps a torrent of language is employed. The speech is speaking a language locked beneath it. That is its continual reference. The speech we hear is an indication of that we don't hear. It is a necessary avoidance, a violent, shy, anguished or mocking smoke screen which keeps the other in its place. When true silence falls we are still left with echo but are nearer nakedness. One way of looking at speech is to say it is a constant stratagem to cover nakedness.

In *Macbeth* there is far more than the torrent of language by our greatest master of words, and in analyzing just what that is we grasp not merely Shakespeare the poet but the essential genius of Shakespeare the dramatist.

THE TRAGEDY OF MACBETH

William Shakespeare

DRAMATIS PERSONÆ

DUNCAN, *King of Scotland*
MALCOLM, ⎱ *his sons*
DONALBAIN, ⎰
MACBETH, ⎱ *Generals of the Scottish Army*
BANQUO, ⎰
MACDUFF, ⎫
LENNOX, ⎪
ROSS, ⎪
MENTEITH, ⎬ *Noblemen of Scotland*
ANGUS, ⎪
CAITHNESS, ⎭
FLEANCE, *Son to* BANQUO
SIWARD, *Earl of Northumberland, General of
    the English forces*
YOUNG SIWARD, *his son*
SEYTON, *an Officer attending on* MACBETH
Boy, *son to* MACDUFF
A Sergeant
A Porter
An Old Man
An English Doctor
A Scottish Doctor
LADY MACBETH
LADY MACDUFF
A Gentlewoman, attending on LADY MACBETH
Three Witches
HECATE
The Ghost of BANQUO
Apparitions
*Lords, Gentlemen, Officers, Soldiers, Mur-
    derers, Messengers, Attendants*

SCENE—SCOTLAND; ENGLAND
[TIME—THE ELEVENTH CENTURY]

ACT ONE

SCENE ONE   Scotland. An open place.

Thunder and lightning.[1] *Enter three* WITCHES.

1. WITCH: When shall we three meet again
    In thunder, lightning, or in rain?

2. WITCH: When the hurlyburly's[2] done,
    When the battle's lost and won.

3. WITCH: That will be ere the set of sun.

1. WITCH: Where the place

2. WITCH: Upon the heath.

3. WITCH: There to meet with Macbeth.

1. WITCH: I come, Graymalkin!

2. WITCH: Paddock calls.[3]

3. WITCH: Anon![4]

ALL: Fair is foul, and foul is fair.
    Hover through the fog and filthy air.
    (*Exeunt.*)

SCENE TWO   A camp near Forres.

Alarum within.[1] *Enter* KING DUNCAN, MALCOLM,
DONALBAIN, LENNOX, *with* ATTENDANTS, *meeting
a bleeding* SERGEANT.[2]

KING: What bloody man is that? He can
    report,
    As seemeth by his plight, of the revolt
    The newest state.

---

1 *Thunder and lightning:* The Elizabethans had a Theory of Correspondence which said that disruption on one level of creation produced parallel disruptions on other levels. Thus thunder and other natural effects accompanied evil, comets were portents, a star appeared in the east to herald the birth of Christ, the night before Caesar is murdered in *Julius Caesar* a lion (symbolic of ruler) walks in the streets and the weather is bad. 2 *hurlyburly:* uproar. 3 *Paddock calls:* Paddock (a toad) summons me. In the previous line Graymalkin (a grey cat) is answered. These creatures were familiars, evil spirits who attended witches in the form of animals. Cf. superstitions about black cats, etc. James I, for whom this play was written, was a firm believer in — and author in defense of the reality of — witchcraft. 4 *Anon:* At once. Addressed to another familiar.

1 *Alarum within:* trumpet call. 2 *Sergeant* (three syllables): an officer, also called "Captain" in some texts.

MALCOLM: This is the sergeant
Who like a good and hardy soldier fought
'Gainst my captivity. Hail, brave friend!
Say to the King the knowledge of the broil[3]
As thou didst leave it.

SERGEANT: Doubtful it stood,
As two spent swimmers that do cling
    together
And choke their art. The merciless
    Macdonwald
(Worthy to be a rebel, for to that
The multiplying villanies of nature
Do swarm upon him) from the Western
    Isles[4]
Of kerns and gallowglasses[5] is supplied;
And Fortune, on his damned quarrel smiling,
Show'd like a rebel's whore.[6] But all's too
    weak,
For brave Macbeth (well he deserves that
    name),
Disdaining Fortune, with his brandish'd
    steel,
Which smok'd with bloody execution
(Like valor's minion),[7] carv'd out his passage
Till he fac'd the slave;
Which[8] ne'er shook hands nor bade farewell
    to him
Till he unseam'd him from the nave to th'
    chaps[9]
And fix'd his head upon our battlements.

KING: O valiant cousin! worthy gentleman!

SERGEANT: As whence the sun 'gins his
    reflection
Shipwracking storms and direful thunders
    break,
So from that spring whence comfort seem'd
    to come
Discomfort swells. Mark, King of Scotland,
    mark.
No sooner justice had, with valor arm'd,
Compell'd these skipping kerns to trust their
    heels
But the Norweyan lord, surveying vantage,
With furbish'd arms and new supplies of
    men,
Began a fresh assault.[10]

KING: Dismay'd not this
Our captains, Macbeth and Banquo?

SERGEANT: Yes,
As sparrows eagles, or the hare the lion.[11]
If I say sooth, I must report they were
As cannons overcharg'd with double cracks,
    so they
Doubly redoubled strokes upon the foe.
Except[12] they meant to bathe in reeking
    wounds,
Or memorize another Golgotha,[13]
I cannot tell —
But I am faint: my gashes cry for help.

KING: So well thy words become thee as thy
    wounds;
They smack of honor both. Go get him sur-
    geons.

(*Exit* SERGEANT, *attended.*)

(*Enter* ROSS.)

Who comes here?

MALCOLM: The worthy Thane of Ross.

LENNOX: What a haste looks through his eyes!
    So should he look
That seems to speak things strange.

ROSS: God save the King!

KING: Whence cam'st thou, worthy thane?

ROSS: From Fife, great King,
Where the Norweyan banners flout the sky

---

3 *broil:* battle. **4** *Western Isles:* the Hebrides. **5** *kerns and gallowglasses:* light and heavy Irish picked infantrymen, respectively. **6** *Show'd like a rebel's whore:* falsely appeared to favor the rebel. **7** *minion:* favorite. **8** *which:* Macbeth. **9** *unseam'd him . . . . :* cut him in half, from the navel to the chops. **10** *Norweyan lord:* Sweno, King of Norway, according to Holinshed's Chronicle (Shakespeare's source) distinguishes between the Norwegian raid and Macdonwald's rebellion. Shakespeare combines them for economy's sake, as he makes other changes in the story (the young king of the chronicle becomes old Duncan, etc.). **11** *As sparrows eagles . . . . :* as sparrows dismay eagles (a reversal of natural order, as shall be the killing of a falcon by a mousing owl in Act II, sc. iv and the murder of a king by a subject, which it echoes). **12** *except:* unless. **13** *memorize another Golgotha:* make the place memorable like Golgotha ("Place of the Skulls"), where Christ was crucified.

And fan our people cold. Norway himself,[14]
With terrible numbers,
Assisted by that most disloyal traitor
The Thane of Cawdor, began a dismal
conflict,
Till that Bellona's bridegroom, lapp'd in
proof,[15]
Confronted him with self-comparisons,[16]
Point against point, rebellious arm 'gainst
arm,
Curbing his lavish spirit; and to conclude,
The victory fell on us.

KING: Great happiness!

ROSS: That now
Sweno, the Norways' king, craves composition;[17]
Nor would we deign him burial of his
men
Till he disbursed, at Saint Colme's Inch,[18]
Ten thousand dollars to our general use.

KING: No more that Thane of Cawdor shall
deceive
Our bosom interest. Go pronounce his present death
And with his former title greet Macbeth.

ROSS: I'll see it done.

DUNCAN: What he hath lost noble Macbeth
hath won.

(Exeunt.)

SCENE THREE   A blasted heath.

Thunder. Enter the three WITCHES.

1. WITCH: Where hast thou been, sister?

2. WITCH: Killing swine.

3. WITCH: Sister, where thou?

1. WITCH: A sailor's wife had chestnuts in her
lap
And munch'd and munch'd and munch'd.
'Give me,' quoth I.
'Aroint[1] thee, witch!' the rump-fed ronyon[2]
cries.
Her husband's to Aleppo gone, master o'
th' Tiger;[3]
But in a sieve I'll thither sail[4]

And, like a rat without a tail,[5]
I'll do, I'll do, and I'll do.

2. WITCH: I'll give thee a wind.

1. WITCH: Th' art kind.

3. WITCH: And I another.

1. WITCH: I myself have all the other,
And the very ports they blow,
All the quarters that they know
I' th' shipman's card.
I will drain him dry as hay.
Sleep shall neither night nor day
Hang upon his penthouse lid.
He shall live a man forbid.
Weary sev'nights, nine times nine,
Shall he dwindle, peak, and pine.[6]
Though his bark cannot be lost,
Yet it shall be tempest-tost.
Look what I have.

2. WITCH: Show me! show me!

1. WITCH: Here I have a pilot's thumb,
Wrack'd as homeward he did come.[7]

(Drum within.)

3. WITCH: A drum, a drum!
Macbeth doth come.

---

14 *Norway himself:* the Norwegian King in person. 15
Bellona's bridegroom, lapp'd in proof: the bridegroom of
the goddess of war, in armour (Macbeth). 16 *self-comparisons:* stroke for stroke, with equal skill and courage. 17 *composition:* peace terms. 18 *Saint Colme's
Inch:* Inchcolm, an island in the Firth of Forth.

1 *"Aroint":* "Be off!" 2 *ronyon:* scab (the whole
expression is a vulgar "fat-rumped mangy person").
3 *Tiger:* name of the ship. 4 *in a sieve . . . :* witches
were supposed to be able to do such impossible things.
5 *rat without a tail:* witches were supposed to be able
to take any animal shape desired but always with
some defect, only God being able to make perfect
creatures. 6 *dwindle, peak, and pine:* by melting a
waxen image, witches were supposed to be able to
cause these effects. 7 *pilot's thumb:* hands, fingers,
and other parts of corpses were used in black magic
and were preferably taken from those who had been
hanged or otherwise died violently.

ALL: The Weird Sisters[8], hand in hand,
Posters[9] of the sea and land,
Thus do go about, about,
Thrice to thine, and thrice to mine,
And thrice again, to make up nine.
Peace! The charm's wound up.

(*Enter* MACBETH *and* BANQUO.)

MACBETH: So foul and fair a day I have not
seen.[10]

BANQUO: How far is't call'd to Forres? What
are these,
So wither'd, and so wild in their attire,
That look not like th' inhabitants o' th'
earth,
And yet are on't? Live you? or are you
aught
That man may question? You seem to
understand me,
By each at once her choppy[11] finger laying
Upon her skinny lips. You should be women.
And yet your beards forbid me to interpret
That you are so.

MACBETH: Speak, if you can. What are you?

1. WITCH: All hail, Macbeth! Hail to thee,
Thane of Glamis!

2. WITCH: All hail, Macbeth! Hail to thee,
Thane of Cawdor!

3. WITCH: All hail, Macbeth, that shalt be King
hereafter![12]

BANQUO: Good sir, why do you start and seem
to fear
Things that do sound so fair? I' th' name of
truth,
Are ye fantastical,[13] or that indeed
Which outwardly ye show? My noble
partner
You greet with present grace and great pre-
diction
Of noble having and of royal hope,
That he seems rapt withal.[14] To me you
speak not.
If you can look into the seeds of time
And say which grain will grow and which
will not,

Speak then to me, who neither beg nor fear
Your favors nor your hate.

1. WITCH: Hail!

2. WITCH: Hail!

3. WITCH: Hail!

1. WITCH: Lesser than Macbeth, and greater.

2. WITCH: Not so happy, yet much happier.

3. WITCH: Thou shalt get[15] kings, though thou
be none.
So all hail, Macbeth and Banquo!

1. WITCH: Banquo and Macbeth, all hail!

MACBETH: Stay, you imperfect[16] speakers, tell
me more!
By Sinel's[17] death I know I am Thane of
Glamis;
But how of Cawdor? The Thane of Cawdor
lives,
A prosperous gentleman; and to be King
Stands not within the prospect of belief,
No more than to be Cawdor. Say from
whence
You owe this strange intelligence, or why
Upon this blasted heath you stop our way
With such prophetic greeting. Speak, I
charge you.

(WITCHES *vanish.*)

---

8 *Weird Sisters:* Norse goddesses of destiny who were
(unlike the witches here) supernatural. The Folio text
has "wayward sisters," which at least makes no super-
human claims for them. 9 *posters:* travelers who move
swiftly. 10 *So foul and fair . . . :* the weather is bad
but the battle is won. Cf. the chant of the witches in
Act I, sc. i. 11 *choppy:* chapped. 12 Cf. Matthew
Gwinne's pageant for King James at Oxford, August
1605, in which three sybils greet the king: *First Sybil:*
Hail, thou who rulest Scotland! *Second Sybil:* Hail,
thou who rulest England! *Third Sybil:* Hail, thou who
rulest Ireland! 13 *fantastical:* imaginary. 14 *rapt
withal:* entranced, lost in contemplation of it. 15 *get:*
beget. 16 *imperfect:* incomplete. 17 *Sinel:* the previous
Thane of Glamis, Macbeth's father.

BANQUO: The earth hath bubbles, as the water has,
  And these are of them. Whither are they vanish'd?

MACBETH: Into the air, and what seem'd corporal melted
  As breath into the wind. Would they had stay'd!

BANQUO: Were such things here as we do speak about?
  Or have we eaten on the insane root[18]
  That takes the reason prisoner?

MACBETH: Your children shall be kings.

BANQUO: You shall be King.

MACBETH: And Thane of Cawdor too. Went it not so?

BANQUO: To th' selfsame tune and words. Who's here?

(*Enter* Ross *and* ANGUS.)

ROSS: The King hath happily receiv'd, Macbeth,
  The news of thy success; and when he reads
  Thy personal venture in the rebels' fight,
  His wonders and his praises do contend
  Which should be thine or his. Silenc'd with that,
  In viewing o'er the rest o' th' self-same day,
  He finds thee in the stout Norweyan ranks,
  Nothing afeard of what thyself didst make,
  Strange images of death. As thick as hail
  Came post with post,[19] and every one did bear
  Thy praises in his kingdom's great defense
  And pour'd them down before him.

ANGUS: We are sent
  To give thee from our royal master thanks;
  Only to herald thee into his sight,
  Not pay thee.

ROSS: And for an earnest[20] of a greater honor,
  He bade me, from him, call thee Thane of Cawdor;
  In which addition,[21] hail, most worthy Thane!
  For it is thine.

BANQUO: What, can the devil speak true?

MACBETH: The Thane of Cawdor lives. Why do you dress me
  In borrowed robes?

ANGUS: Who was the Thane lives yet,
  But under heavy judgment[22] bears that life
  Which he deserves to lose. Whether he was combin'd
  With those of Norway, or did line[23] the rebel
  With hidden help and vantage, or that with both
  He labor'd in his country's wrack, I know not,
  But treasons capital, confess'd and prov'd,
  Have overthrown him.

MACBETH (*aside*): Glamis, and Thane of Cawdor!
  The greatest is behind.[24] — (*to* Ross *and* ANGUS) Thanks for your pains.
  (*aside to* BANQUO) Do you not hope your children shall be kings,
  When those that gave the Thane of Cawdor to me
  Promis'd no less to them?

BANQUO: (*aside to* MACBETH): That, trusted home,[25]
  Might yet enkindle you unto the crown,
  Besides the Thane of Cawdor. But 'tis strange!
  And oftentimes, to win us to our harm,
  The instruments of darkness tell us truths,
  Win us with honest trifles, to betray 's
  In deepest consequence. —
  Cousins, a word, I pray you.

MACBETH (*aside*):   Two truths are told,
  As happy prologues to the swelling[26] act

---

18 *insane root:* insanity-producing root. **19** *post with post:* messenger after messenger. **20** *earnest:* token, pledge. **21** *addition:* title. **22** *judgment:* sentence. **23** *line:* support. **24** *behind:* yet to come. **25** *trusted home:* wholly believed. **26** *swelling:* stately.

Of the imperial theme. — I thank you,
gentlemen. —
(*aside*) This supernatural soliciting
Cannot be ill; cannot be good. If ill,
Why hath it given me earnest of success,
Commencing in a truth? I am Thane of Caw-
dor.
If good, why do I yield to that suggestion
Whose horrid image doth unfix my hair
And make my seated[27] heart knock at my
ribs
Against the use of nature? Present fears
Are less than horrible imaginings.
My thought, whose murder yet is but fan-
tastical,
Shakes so my single state of man that func-
tion
Is smother'd in surmise and nothing is
But what is not.

BANQUO: Look how our partner's rapt.

MACBETH (*aside*): If chance will have me King,
why, chance may crown me,
Without my stir.[28]

BANQUO: New honors come upon him,
Like our strange garments, cleave not to
their mold[29]
But with the aid of use.

MACBETH (*aside*):   Come what come may,
Time and the hour runs through the
roughest day.

BANQUO: Worthy Macbeth, we stay upon your
leisure.

MACBETH: Give me your favor.[30] My dull brain
was wrought
With things forgotten. Kind gentlemen, your
pains
Are regist'red where every day I turn
The leaf to read them. Let us toward the
King.
(*aside to* BANQUO) Think upon what hath
chanc'd; and, at more time,
The interim having weigh'd it,[31] let us speak
Our free hearts each to other.

BANQUO (*aside to* MACBETH): Very gladly.

MACBETH (*aside to* BANQUO): Till then, enough.
— Come, friends.

(*Exeunt.*)

SCENE FOUR   Forres.   The palace.

Flourish[1]. *Enter* KING DUNCAN, LENNOX, MAL-
COLM, DONALBAIN, *and* ATTENDANTS.

KING: Is execution done on Cawdor? Are not
Those in commission yet return'd?

MALCOLM: My liege,
They are not yet come back. But I have
spoke
With one that saw him die; who did report
That very frankly he confess'd his treasons,
Implor'd your Highness' pardon, and set
forth
A deep repentance. Nothing in his life
Became him like the leaving it. He died
As one that had been studied[2] in his death
To throw away the dearest thing he ow'd
As 'twere a careless trifle.

KING: There's no art
To find the mind's construction in the face.[3]
He was a gentleman on whom I built
An absolute trust.

(*Enter* MACBETH, BANQUO, *and* ANGUS.)

                         O worthiest cousin,
The sin of my ingratitude even now
Was heavy on me! Thou art so far before
That swiftest wing of recompense is slow
To overtake thee. Would thou hadst less
deserv'd,
That the proportion both of thanks and pay-
ment
Might have been mine! Only I have left to
say,
More is thy due than more than all can pay.

MACBETH: The service and the loyalty I owe,
In doing it pays itself. Your Highness' part

---

27 *seated:* fixed. 28 *Stir:* stirring. 29 *strange . . . mold:*
new clothes do not fit us. 30 *Give me your favor:* "Pardon me." 31 *interim having weigh'd it:* having had
time to consider it.

1 *Flourish:* fanfare. 2 *studied:* rehearsed. 3 *There's
no art . . . :* "You cannot read a man's character in
his face."

Is to receive our duties; and our duties
Are to your throne and state, children and
    servants,
Which do but what they should by doing
    everything
Safe toward⁴ your love and honor.

KING: Welcome hither.
I have begun to plant thee and will labor
To make thee full of growing. Noble Ban-
    quo,
That hast no less deserv'd nor must be
    known
No less to have done so, let me infold thee
And hold thee to my heart.

BANQUO: There if I grow,
The harvest is your own.

KING: My plenteous joys,
Wanton in fulness, seek to hide themselves
In drops of sorrow. Sons, kinsmen, thanes,
And you whose places are the nearest, know
We will establish our estate upon
Our eldest, Malcolm, whom we name here-
    after
The Prince of Cumberland;⁵ which honor
    must
Not unaccompanied invest him only,
But signs of nobleness, like stars,⁶ shall
    shine
On all deservers. From hence to Inverness,
And bind us further to you.

MACBETH: The rest is labor, which is not us'd
    for you!
I'll be myself the harbinger,⁷ and make joy-
    ful
The hearing of my wife with your approach;
So, humbly take my leave.

KING: My worthy Cawdor!

MACBETH (aside): The Prince of Cumberland!
    That is a step
On which I must fall down, or else o'erleap,
For in my way it lies. Stars, hide your fires!
Let not light see my black and deep desires.
The eye wink at the hand;⁸ yet let that be,
Which the eye fears, when it is done, to see.

(Exit.)

KING: True, worthy Banquo: he is full so
    valiant,⁹
And in his commendations I am fed;
It is a banquet to me. Let's after him,
Whose care is gone before to bid us wel-
    come.
It is a peerless kinsman.

(Flourish. Exeunt.)

SCENE FIVE   Inverness. Macbeth's castle.

Enter MACBETH'S WIFE, alone, with a letter.

LADY (reads): 'They met me in the day of success; and I have learn'd by the perfect'st report they have more in them than mortal
knowledge. When I burn'd in desire to question them further, they made themselves air,
into which they vanish'd. Whiles I stood
rapt in the wonder of it, came missives¹ from
the King, who all-hail'd me Thane of Cawdor, by which title, before, these Weird Sisters saluted me, and referr'd me to the coming on of time with "Hail, King that shalt
be!" This have I thought good to deliver
thee, my dearest partner of greatness, that
thou mightst not lose the dues of rejoicing
by being ignorant of what greatness is
promis'd thee. Lay it to thy heart, and farewell.'

---

4 *Safe toward:* to safeguard, safeguarding (?). The
language here, from formality or insincerity, is
"language of effort," awkward and a little obscure.
5 *establish our estate . . . Prince of Cumberland:* Duncan nominates his son Malcolm as heir apparent to the
throne, though Scotland is an elective monarchy. By
doing so, he deprives the ambitious Macbeth of his
hope of succeeding on the old king's death, a mature
cousin not being able to compete with a son (even a
young one) thus designated. 6 *stars:* a sunburst or
star worn on the left side was a symbol of British
orders of Knighthood (such as The Garter), so the
image is especially apt. 7 *harbinger:* messenger,
herald. 8 *eye wink at the hand:* eye not see what the
hand does. 9 *full so valiant:* fully as valiant (as you
say he is).

1 *missives:* apparently messengers, not letters.

Glamis thou art, and Cawdor, and shalt be —
What thou art promis'd. Yet do I fear thy
   nature.
It is too full o' th' milk of human kindness
To catch the nearest way. Thou wouldst be
   great;
Art not without ambition, but without
The illness[2] should attend it. What thou
   wouldst highly,
That wouldst thou holily; wouldst not play
   false,
And yet wouldst wrongly win. Thou'ldst
   have, great Glamis,
That which cries 'Thus thou must do,' if thou
   have it;
And that which rather thou dost fear to do
Than wishest should be undone. Hie thee
   hither,
That I may pour my spirits in thine ear
And chastise with the valor of my tongue
All that impedes thee from the golden
   round[3]
Which fate and metaphysical[4] aid doth seem
To have thee crown'd withal.

(*Enter* MESSENGER.)

                    What is your tidings?

MESSENGER: The King comes here to-night.

LADY: Thou'rt mad to say it!
Is not thy master with him? who, were't so,
Would have inform'd for preparation.

MESSENGER: So please you, it is true. Our
   Thane is coming.
One of my fellows had the speed of him,[5]
Who, almost dead for breath, had scarcely
   more
Than would make up his message.

LADY: Give him tending;
He brings great news.

(*Exit* MESSENGER.)

                    The raven himself is hoarse
That croaks the fatal entrance of Duncan
Under my battlements. Come, you spirits
That tend on mortal thoughts, unsex me
   here,

And fill me, from the crown to the toe, top-
   full
Of direst cruelty! Make thick my blood;
Stop up th' access and passage to remorse,
That no compunctious visitings of nature[6]
Shake my fell purpose nor keep peace be-
   tween
Th' effect and it! Come to my woman's
   breasts
And take my milk for gall, you murd'ring
   ministers,
Wherever in your sightless[7] substances
You wait on nature's mischief![8] Come, thick
   night,
And pall[9] thee in the dunnest[10] smoke of
   hell,
That my keen knife see not the wound it
   makes,
Nor heaven peep through the blanket of
   the dark
To cry 'Hold, hold!'

(*Enter* MACBETH.)

                    Great Glamis! worthy Cawdor!
Greater than both, by the all-hail hereafter!
Thy letters have transported me beyond
This ignorant present, and I feel now
The future in the instant.

MACBETH: My dearest love,
Duncan comes here to-night.

LADY: And when goes hence?

MACBETH: To-morrow, as he purposes.

LADY: O, never
Shall sun that morrow see!
Your face, my Thane, is as a book where
   men
May read strange matters. To beguile the
   time,

---

2 *illness:* evil. 3 *golden round:* crown. 4 *meta-*
physical: more than human. 5 *had the speed of him:*
passed him on the way. 6 *compunctious visitings of*
nature: natural compunctions to pity. 7 *sightless:*
invisible. 8 *mischief:* evil. Some old words have lost
their force, as has *naughty* as used in *Lear*, etc. 9
pall: drape. 10 *dunnest:* blackest.

Look like the time,[11] bear welcome in your eye,
Your hand, your tongue; look like the innocent flower,
But be the serpent under't. He that's coming
Must be provided for; and you shall put
This night's great business into my dispatch,
Which shall to all our nights and days to come
Give solely sovereign sway and masterdom.

MACBETH: We will speak further.

LADY: Only look up clear.
To alter favor ever is to fear.[12]
Leave all the rest to me.

(*Exeunt.*)

SCENE SIX Inverness. Before Macbeth's castle.

Hautboys[1] *and torches. Enter* KING DUNCAN, MALCOLM, DONALBAIN, BANQUO, LENNOX, MACDUFF, ROSS, ANGUS, *and* ATTENDANTS.

KING: This castle hath a pleasant seat. The air
Nimbly and sweetly recommends itself
Unto our gentle senses.

BANQUO: This guest of summer,
The temple-haunting martlet,[2] does approve
By his lov'd mansionry[3] that the heaven's breath
Smells wooingly here. No jutty, frieze,
Buttress, nor coign of vantage, but this bird
Hath made his pendent bed and procreant cradle.
Where they most breed and haunt, I have observ'd
The air is delicate.

(*Enter* LADY MACBETH.)

KING: See, see, our honor'd hostess!
The love that follows us sometime is our trouble,
Which still we thank as love. Herein I teach you
How you shall bid God 'ild[4] us for your pains
And thank us for your trouble.

LADY: All our service
In every point twice done, and then done double,
Were poor and single[5] business to contend
Against those honors deep and broad wherewith
Your Majesty loads our house. For those of old,[6]
And the late[7] dignities heap'd up to them, 19
We rest your hermits.[8]

KING: Where's the Thane of Cawdor?
We cours'd him at the heels and had a purpose
To be his purveyor;[9] but he rides well.
And his great love, sharp as his spur, hath holp[10] him
To his home before us. Fair and noble hostess,
We are your guest to-night.

LADY: Your servants ever
Have theirs, themselves, and what is theirs, in compt,[11]
To make their audit at your Highness' pleasure,
Still to return your own.

KING: Give me your hand;
Conduct me to mine host. We love him highly
And shall continue our graces towards him.
By your leave, hostess.

(*Exeunt.*)

---

11 *to beguile the time* . . . : "To deceive people, assume the expression the occasion demands." **12** *To alter favor* . . . : "To change your expression [to betray anxiety] is to arouse suspicion."

1 *Hautboys:* woodwind music (*haut bois,* French), oboes. **2** *martlet:* a small bird whose use in heraldry (as a symbol of a son who will inherit little or nothing and has "no foot to stand on") connects it with Macbeth. **3** *mansionry:* nesting. **4** *'ild:* reward. **5** *single:* small. **6** *those of old:* former honors. **7** *late:* recent (as Macbeth's new title). **8** *hermits:* those who pray for you. **9** *purveyor:* forerunner. **10** *holp:* old past tense of "help." **11** *in compt:* on deposit, ready for withdrawal.

SCENE SEVEN   Inverness. Macbeth's castle.

Hautboys. Torches. Enter a SEWER,[1] *and divers* SERVANTS *with dishes and service, and cross the stage. Then enter* MACBETH.

MACBETH: If it were done when 'tis done, then 'twere well
It were done quickly. If th' assassination
Could trammel up the consequence, and catch,
With his surcease, success; that but this blow
Might be the be-all and the end-all here,
But here, upon this bank and shoal of time,
We'ld jump[2] the life to come. But in these cases
We still have judgment here, that we but teach
Bloody instructions, which, being taught, return
To plague th' inventor. This even-handed justice
Commends th' ingredients of our poison'd chalice
To our own lips. He's here in double trust:
First, as I am his kinsman and his subject—
Strong both against the deed; then, as his host,
Who should against his murderer shut the door,
Not bear the knife myself. Besides, this Duncan
Hath borne his faculties[3] so meek, hath been
So clear in his great office, that his virtues
Will plead like angels, trumpet-tongu'd, against
The deep damnation of his taking-off;
And pity, like a naked new-born babe,
Striding the blast, or heaven's cherubin, hors'd
Upon the sightless couriers of the air,
Shall blow the horrid deed in every eye,
That tears shall drown the wind. I have no spur
To prick the sides of my intent, but only
Vaulting ambition, which o'erleaps itself
And falls on th' other side.[4]

(*Enter* LADY MACBETH.)

How now? What news?

LADY: He has almost supp'd. Why have you left the chamber?

MACBETH: Hath he ask'd for me?

LADY: Know you not he has?

MACBETH: We will proceed no further in this business.
He hath honor'd me of late, and I have bought
Golden opinions from all sorts of people,
Which would be worn now in their newest gloss,
Not cast aside so soon.

LADY: Was the hope drunk
Wherein you dress'd yourself? Hath it slept since?
And wakes it now to look so green and pale
At what it did so freely? From this time
Such I account thy love. Art thou afeard
To be the same in thine own act and valor
As thou art in desire? Wouldst thou have that
Which thou esteem'st the ornament of life,
And live a coward in thine own esteem,
Letting 'I dare not' wait upon 'I would,'
Like the poor cat i' th' adage?[5]

MACBETH: Prithee peace!
I dare do all that may become a man.
Who dares do more is none.

LADY: What beast was't then
That made you break this enterprise to me?
When you durst do it, then you were a man;
And to be more than what you were, you would

---

1 *Sewer:* steward, butler. 2 *jump:* risk. 3 *faculties:* powers. 4 . . . *other side:* The critics are divided on the value of this soliloquy, some calling it bombast (a word derived from the stuffing crammed into Elizabethan clothes to create a shape). The student must decide, in the light of its meaning and its function in the play, whether it is empty rhetoric or significant revelation of character. 5 *cat i' th' adage:* the cat wanted to eat fish but not to wet her feet.

Be so much more the man. Nor time nor place
Did then adhere,[6] and yet you would make both.
They have made themselves, and that their[7] fitness now
Does unmake you. I have given suck, and I know
How tender 'tis to love the babe that milks me.
I would, while it was smiling in my face,
Have pluck'd my nipple from his boneless gums
And dash'd the brains out, had I so sworn as you
Have done to this.

MACBETH: If we should fail?

LADY: We fail?
But screw your courage to the sticking place,[8]
And we'll not fail. When Duncan is asleep
(Whereto the rather shall his day's hard journey
Soundly invite him), his two chamberlains
Will I with wine and wassail[9] so convince
That memory, the warder of the brain,
Shall be a fume, and the receipt of reason
A limbeck only.[10] When in swinish sleep
Their drenched natures lie as in a death,
What cannot you and I perform upon
Th' unguarded Duncan? what not put up-on
His spongy[11] officers, who shall bear the guilt.
Of our great quell?[12]

MACBETH: Bring forth men-children only;
For thy undaunted mettle should compose
Nothing but males.[13] Will it not be receiv'd,
When we have mark'd with blood those sleepy two
Of his own chamber and us'd their very daggers,
That they have done't?

LADY: Who dares receive it other,[14]
As we shall make our griefs and clamor roar
Upon his death?

MACBETH: I am settled and bend up

Each corporal agent[15] to this terrible feat,
Away, and mock the time[16] with fairest show;
False face must hide what the false heart doth know.[17]

(*Exeunt.*)

ACT TWO

SCENE ONE   Inverness. Court of Macbeth's castle.

Enter BANQUO, *and* FLEANCE *with a torch before him.*

BANQUO: How goes the night, boy?

FLEANCE: The moon is down; I have not heard the clock.

BANQUO: And she goes down at twelve.

FLEANCE: I take't, 'tis later, sir.

BANQUO: Hold, take my sword. There's husbandry[1] in heaven;
Their candles are all out. Take thee that too.
A heavy summons lies like lead upon me,
And yet I would not sleep. Merciful powers,

---

6 *adhere:* suit.   7 *that their:* their very.   8 *But . . . sticking place:* "Just screw up your courage to the notch that holds the bowstring of a crossbow."   9 *wassail:* carousing.   10 *. . . a limbeck only:* "the receptacle which should distill thought [reason] will become merely a vessel of undistilled liquids."   11 *spongy:* drink-sodden.   12 *quell:* killing.   13 *mettle . . . males:* there is a pun here based on mettle (substance) and males (boys), metal and mails (suits of chain-mail).   14 *who dares receive it other:* "Who dares to interpret it otherwise?"   15 *corporal agent:* bodily faculty.   16 *mock the time:* deceive people.   17 *Show . . . know:* here and elsewhere, note how rhymed couplets are used to "underline" important ideas and to provide flourish for exits, etc.

1 *husbandry:* frugality (as if heaven were saving its lights).

Restrain in me the cursed thoughts that nature
Gives way to in repose!

(*Enter* MACBETH, *and a* SERVANT *with a torch.*)

MACBETH: Give me my sword.
Who's there?

MACBETH: A friend.

BANQUO: What, sir, not yet at rest? The King's abed.
He hath been in unusual pleasure and
Sent forth great largess to your offices.[2]
This diamond he greets your wife withal
By the name of most kind hostess, and shut up
In measureless content.

MACBETH: Being unprepar'd,
Our will became the servant to defect,[3]
Which else should free have wrought.

BANQUO: All's well.
I dreamt last night of the three Weird Sisters.
To you they have show'd some truth.

MACBETH: I think not of them.
Yet when we can entreat an hour to serve,
We would spend it in some words upon that business,
If you would grant the time.

BANQUO: At your kind'st leisure.

MACBETH: If you shall cleave to my consent, when 'tis,[4]
It shall make honor for you.

BANQUO: So I lose none
In seeking to augment it but still keep
My bosom franchis'd and allegiance clear,
I shall be counsell'd[5]

MACBETH: Good repose the while!

BANQUO: Thanks sir. The like to you!

(*Exeunt* BANQUO *and* FLEANCE.)

MACBETH: Go bid thy mistress, when my drink is ready,
She strike upon the bell. Get thee to bed.

(*Exit* SERVANT.)

Is this a dagger which I see before me,
The handle toward my hand? Come, let me clutch thee!
I have thee not, and yet I see thee still.
Art thou not, fatal vision, sensible[6]
To feeling as to sight? or art thou but
A dagger of the mind, a false creation,
Proceeding from the heat-oppressed brain?
I see thee yet, in form as palpable
As this which now I draw.
Thou marshall'st me the way that I was going,
And such an instrument I was to use.
Mine eyes are made the fools o' th' other senses,
Or else worth all the rest. I see thee still;
And on thy blade and dudgeon gouts of blood,[7]
Which was not so before. There's no such thing.
It is the bloody business which informs
Thus to mine eyes. Now o'er the one half-world
Nature seems dead, and wicked dreams abuse
The curtain'd sleep. Now witchcraft celebrates
Pale Hecate's[8] offerings; and wither'd murder,
Alarum'd by his sentinel, the wolf,
Whose howl's his watch, thus with his stealthy pace,
With Tarquin's[9] ravishing strides, towards his design
Moves like a ghost. Thou sure and firm-set earth,

---

2 *Sent . . . offices:* "Sent large gifts to your servants' quarters." 3 *Being unprepar'd . . . defect:* "Lacking time for adequate preparation, our good will was hampered by deficiencies." 4 *If you shall cleave . . . :* "If you will join my cause when the time comes." 5 *So I lose none . . . :* "So long as I lose no honor in seeking to add to it but retain my heart free [from guilt] and my duty unblemished, I shall take your advice." 6 *sensible:* perceptible. 7 *And on thy blade . . . :* "And on your blade and hilt big drops of blood." 8 *Hecate:* goddess of sorcery. 9 *Tarquin:* Roman tyrant who ravished Lucrece. Shakespeare published a long poem called *The Rape of Lucrece.*

Hear not my steps which way they walk, for fear
Thy very stones prate of my whereabout
And take the present horror from the time,
Which now suits with it. Whiles I threat he lives;
Words to the heat of deeds too cold breath gives.

(*A bell rings.*)

I go, and it is done. The bell invites me.
Hear it not, Duncan, for it is a knell
That summons thee to heaven, or to hell.

(*Exit.*)

SCENE TWO[1] Inverness. Macbeth's castle.

Enter LADY MACBETH.

LADY: That which hath made them drunk hath made me bold;
What hath quench'd them hath given me fire. Hark! Peace!
It was the owl that shriek'd, the fatal bellman
Which gives the stern'st good-night. He is about it.
The doors are open, and the surfeited grooms
Do mock their charge with snores. I have drugg'd their possets,[2]
That death and nature do contend about them
Whether they live or die.

MACBETH (*within.*): Who's there? What, ho?

LADY: Alack, I am afraid they have awak'd,
And 'tis not done! Th' attempt, and not the deed,
Confounds[3] us. Hark! I laid their daggers ready;
He could not miss 'em. Had he not resembled
My father as he slept, I had done't.

(*Enter* MACBETH.)

My husband!

MACBETH: I have done the deed. Didst thou not hear a noise?

LADY: I heard the owl scream and the crickets cry.
Did you not speak?

MACBETH: When?

LADY: Now.

MACBETH: As I descended?

LADY: Ay.

MACBETH: Hark!
Who lies i' th' second chamber?

LADY: Donalbain.

MACBETH: This is a sorry sight.[4]

(*Looks on his hands.*)

LADY: A foolish thought, to say a sorry sight.

MACBETH: There's one did laugh in's sleep, and one cried 'Murder!'
That they did wake each other. I stood and heard them.
But they did say their prayers and address'd them
Again to sleep.

LADY: There are two lodg'd together.

MACBETH: One cried 'God bless us!' and 'Amen!' the other,
As[5] they had seen me with these hangman's[6] hands.
List'ning their fear, I could not say 'Amen!'
When they did say 'God bless us!'

LADY: Consider it not so deeply.

MACBETH: But wherefore could not I pronounce 'Amen'?
I had most need of blessing, and 'Amen'
Stuck in my throat.

_____

1 Scene II: The first three scenes of this act follow each other in continuity. Overall the action of the play, however, covers some 11 years. 2 *possets:* bedtime milk punch. 3 *confounds:* ruins. 4 *This is a sorry sight:* "This [blood] is a miserable sight." 5 *as:* as if. 6 *hangman's:* executioner's. The hangman, who sometimes had to draw and quarter the partly-hanged victim, might have blood on his hands.

LADY: These deeds must not be thought
After these ways. So, it will make us mad.

MACBETH: Methought I heard a voice cry 'Sleep
no more!
Macbeth does murder sleep'—the innocent
sleep,
Sleep that knits up the ravell'd sleave[7] of
care,
The death of each day's life, sore labor's
bath,
Balm of hurt minds, great nature's second
course,
Chief nourisher in life's feast.

LADY: What do you mean?

MACBETH: Still it cried 'Sleep no more!' to all
the house;
'Glamis hath murder'd sleep, and therefore
Cawdor
Shall sleep no more! Macbeth shall sleep no
more!'

LADY: Who was it that thus cried? Why,
worthy Thane,
You do unbend your noble strength to
think
So brainsickly of things. Go get some water
And wash this filthy witness from your
hand.
Why did you bring these daggers from the
place?
They must lie there. Go carry them and
smear
The sleepy grooms with blood.

MACBETH: I'll go no more.
I am afraid to think what I have done;
Look on't again I dare not.

LADY: Infirm of purpose!
Give me the daggers. The sleeping and the
dead
Are but as pictures. 'Tis the eye of child-
hood
That fears a painted[8] devil. If he do bleed,
I'll gild[9] the faces of the grooms withal,
For it must seem their guilt.

(*Exit. Knocking within.*)

MACBETH: Whence is that knocking?

How is't with me when every noise appals
me?
What hands are here? Ha! they pluck out
mine eyes!
Will all great Neptune's ocean wash this
blood
Clean from my hand?[10] No. This my hand
will rather
The multitudinous seas incarnadine,
Making the green one red.[11]

(*Enter* LADY MACBETH.)

LADY: My hands are of your color, but I
shame
To wear a heart so white. (*Knock.*) I hear a
knocking
At the south entry. Retire we to our cham-
ber.
A little water clears us of this deed.
How easy is it then! Your constancy
Hath left you unattended.[12] (*Knock.*) Hark
more knocking.
Get on your nightgown, lest occasion call
us
And show us to be watchers. Be not lost
So poorly in your thoughts.

MACBETH: To know my deed, 'twere best not
know myself.

(*Knock.*)

Wake Duncan with thy knocking! I would
thou couldst!

(*Exeunt.*)

SCENE THREE   Inverness. Macbeth's castle.

(*Enter a* PORTER. *Knocking within.*)

---

7 *knits up the ravell'd sleave:* "straightens out the
tangled skein." 8 *painted:* depicted. 9 *gild:* paint.
Note the pun on gilt and guilt. 10 *Clean from my hand:*
note that this line is echoed later in the play when Lady
Macbeth's unwitting prophecy comes to pass. 11
Making the green one red: an example of a line that
editors have debated. Should it be "Making the green
one, red" or "Making the green .. one red"? 12 *Your
constancy hath left you unattended:* "Your firmness has
deserted you."

PORTER: Here's a knocking indeed! If a man were porter of hell gate, he should have old[1] turning the key. (*Knock.*) Knock, knock, knock! Who's there, i' th' name of Belzebub? Here's a farmer that hang'd himself on th' expectation of plenty.[2] Come in time! Have napkins enow[3] about you; here you'll sweat for't. (*Knock.*) Knock, knock! Who's there, in th' other devil's name? Faith, here's an equivocator,[4] that could swear in both the scales against either scale; who committed treason enough for God's sake, yet could not equivocate to heaven. O, come in, equivocator! (*Knock.*) Knock, knock, knock! Who's there? Faith, here's an English tailor come hither for stealing out of a French hose.[5] Come in, tailor. Here you may roast your goose.[6] (*Knock.*) Knock, knock! Never at quiet! What are you? But this place is too cold for hell. I'll devil-porter it no further. I had thought to have let in some of all professions that go the primrose way to th' everlasting bonfire. (*Knock.*) Anon, anon! (*Opens the gate.*) I pray you remember the porter.[7]

(*Enter* MACDUFF *and* LENNOX.)

MACDUFF: Was it so late, friend, ere you went to bed,
That you do lie so late?

PORTER: Faith, sir, we were carousing till the second cock[8]; and drink, sir, is a great provoker of three things.

MACDUFF: What three things does drink especially provoke?

PORTER: Marry, sir, nose-painting, sleep, and urine. Lechery, sir, it provokes, and unprovokes: it provokes the desire, but it takes away the performance. Therefore much drink may be said to be an equivocator with lechery: it makes him, and it mars him; it sets him on, and it takes him off; it persuades him, and disheartens him; makes him stand to, and not stand to; in conclusion, equivocates him in a sleep, and, giving him the lie, leaves him.

MACDUFF: I believe drink gave thee the lie last night.[9]

PORTER: That it did, sir, i' the very throat on me; but I requited him for his lie; and, I think, being too strong for him, though he took up my legs sometime, yet I made a shift to cast[10] him.

MACDUFF: Is thy master stirring?

(*Enter* MACBETH.)

Our knocking has awak'd him; here he comes.

LENNOX: Good morrow, noble sir.

MACBETH: Good morrow, both.

MACDUFF: Is the King stirring, worthy Thane?

MACBETH: Not yet.

MACDUFF: He did command me to call timely on him;
I have almost slipp'd the hour.

MACBETH: I'll bring you to him.

MACDUFF: I know this is a joyful trouble to you;
But yet 'tis one.

MACBETH: The labor we delight in physics[11] pain.
This is the door.

MACBETH: I'll make so bold to call,
For 'tis my limited service.[12]

---

1 *Should have old:* would have plenty of. **2** *hang'd himself:* who committed suicide when he discovered that his hoarded produce did not sell for what he expected, because of a crop surplus. The low price of wheat in 1606 has caused some critics to date the play by this line. **3** *enow:* enough. **4** *equivocator:* liar, devious arguer. Some critics think this a reference to a Father Garnet, a Jesuit executed for complicity in Guy Fawkes' Gunpowder Plot (5 November, 1605). At his trial Father Garnet argued that misleading arguments were justified if the end were just, thus his perjury ought to be allowed. **5** *English tailor . . . French hose:* because French tights were cut very tight, only a very clever tailor could steal cloth in making them. **6** *goose:* pressing iron. **7** *remember the porter:* a request for a tip. **8** *second cock:* middle of the night. **9** *gave thee the lie:* "made a liar of you" (also, stretched you out). **10** *cast:* vomit up. **11** *physics:* cures. **12** *limited service:* appointed task.

(*Exit.*)

LENNOX: Goes the King hence to-day?

MACBETH: He does; he did appoint so.

LENNOX: The night has been unruly. Where we lay,
  Our chimneys were blown down; and, as they say,
  Lamentings heard i' th' air, strange screams of death,
  And prophesying, with accents terrible,
  Of dire combustion[13] and confus'd events
  New hatch'd to th' woeful time. The obscure bird[14]
  Clamor'd the livelong night. Some say the earth
  Was feverous and did shake.

MACBETH: 'Twas a rough night.

LENNOX: My young remembrance cannot parallel
  A fellow to it.

(*Enter* MACDUFF.)

MACDUFF: O horror, horror, horror! Tongue nor heart
  Cannot conceive nor name thee!

MACDUFF *and* LENNOX: What's the matter?

MACDUFF: Confusion now hath made his masterpiece!
  Most sacrilegious murder hath broke ope
  The Lord's anointed temple[15] and stole thence
  The life o' th' building!

MACBETH: What is't you say? the life?

LENNOX: Mean you his Majesty?

MACDUFF: Approach the chamber, and destroy your sight
  With a new Gorgon.[16] Do not bid me speak
  See, and then speak yourselves.

(*Exeunt* MACBETH *and* LENNOX.)

              Awake, awake!
  Ring the alarum bell. Murder and treason!
  Banquo and Donalbain! Malcolm! awake!

Shake off this downy sleep, death's counterfeit,[17]
  And look on death itself! Up, up, and see
  The great doom's image![18] Malcolm! Banquo!
  As from your graves rise up and walk like sprites
  To countenance this horror! Ring the bell!

(*Bell rings.*)

(*Enter* LADY MACBETH.)

LADY: What's the business,
  That such a hideous trumpet calls to parley
  The sleepers of the house? Speak, speak!

MACDUFF: O gentle lady,
  'Tis not for you to hear what I can speak!
  The repetition[19] in a woman's ear
  Would murder as it fell.

(*Enter* BANQUO.)

              O Banquo, Banquo,
  Our royal master's murder'd!

LADY: Woe, alas!
  What, in our house?

BANQUO: Too cruel anywhere.
  Dear Duff, I prithee contradict thyself
  And say it is not so.

(*Enter* MACBETH, LENNOX, *and* ROSS.)

MACBETH: Had I but died an hour before this chance,
  I had liv'd a blessed time; for from this instant
  There's nothing serious in mortality;[20]
  All is but toys,[21] renown and grace is dead;

---

13 *combustion:* tumult. 14 *obscure bird:* bird of darkness (the owl). 15 *Lord's anointed temple:* a reference to the sacredness of Kings, conceived (as *Richard II* and other plays emphasize) as ruling by divine right. 16 *Gorgon:* a creature in mythology the sight of which turned men to stone. 17 *counterfeit:* imitation. 18 *great doom's image:* the likeness of Judgment Day. 19 *repetition:* report. 20 *serious in mortality:* worthwhile in life. 21 *toys:* trifles.

The wine of life is drawn, and the mere lees
Is left this vault to brag of.

(*Enter* MALCOLM *and* DONALBAIN.)

DONALBAIN: What is amiss?

MACBETH: You are, and do not know't.
The spring, the head, the fountain of your
blood
Is stopp'd, the very source of it is stopp'd.

MACDUFF: Your royal father's murder'd.

MALCOLM: O, by whom?

LENNOX: Those of his chamber, as it seem'd,
had done't.
Their hands and faces were all badg'd with
blood;
So were their daggers, which unwip'd we
found
Upon their pillows.
They star'd and were distracted. No man's
life
Was to be trusted with them.

MACBETH: O, yet I do repent me of my
fury
That I did kill them.

MACDUFF: Wherefore did you so?

MACBETH: Who can be wise, amazed,[22] tem-
perate, and furious,
Loyal and neutral, in a moment? No man.
The expedition[23] of my violent love
Outrun the pauser, reason. Here lay Dun-
can,
His silver skin laced with his golden blood,
And his gash'd stabs look'd like a breach in
nature
For ruin's wasteful entrance; there, the mur-
derers,
Steep'd in the colors of their trade, their
daggers
Unmannerly breech'd[24] with gore. Who could
refrain
That had a heart to love and in that heart
Courage to make 's love known?

LADY: Help me hence, ho!

MACDUFF: Look to[25] the lady.

MALCOLM (*aside to* DONALBAIN): Why do we
hold our tongues,
That most may claim this argument for
ours?[26]

DONALBAIN (*aside to* MALCOLM): What should
be spoken here, where our fate,
Hid in an auger hole,[27] may rush and seize
us?
Let's away.
Our tears are not yet brew'd.[28]

MALCOLM (*aside to* DONALBAIN): Nor our strong
sorrow
Upon the foot of motion.[29]

BANQUO: Look to the lady.

(LADY MACBETH *is carried out.*)

And when we have our naked frailties hid,[30]
That suffer in exposure, let us meet
And question this most bloody piece of
work,
To know it further. Fears and scruples shake
us.
In the great hand of God I stand, and thence
Against the undivulg'd pretense I fight
Of treasonous malice.

MACDUFF: And so do I.

ALL: So all.

MACBETH: Let's briefly put on manly readiness[31]
And meet i' th' hall together.

ALL: Well contented.

(*Exeunt all but* MALCOLM *and* DONALBAIN.)

---

22 *amazed:* bewildered. **23** *expedition:* haste. **24** *Unmannerly breech'd:* covered in an unseemly fashion.
25 *Look to:* look after. Why does Lady Macbeth faint
(or pretend to do so) at this point? **26** *That most may
claim this argument for ours:* who are chiefly concerned in this matter. **27** *auger hole:* secret place. **28**
Our tears are not yet brewed: "We have not yet had
time to appreciate fully the need for tears." **29** *Nor
our strong sorrow . . . . :* "Nor our profound sorrow
opportunity to express itself in any action." **30** *naked
frailties hid:* our poor bodies dressed. **31** *briefly put
on manly readiness:* quickly arm(?).

MALCOLM: What will you do? Let's not consort with them.
To show an unfelt sorrow is an office
Which the false man does easy. I'll to England.

DONALBAIN: To Ireland I. Our separated fortune
Shall keep us both the safer. Where we are,
There's daggers in men's smiles; the near in blood,
The nearer bloody.[32]

MALCOLM: This murderous shaft that's shot
Hath not yet lighted, and our safest way
Is to avoid the aim. Therefore to horse!
And let us not be dainty of[33] leave-taking
But shift[34] away. There's warrant in that theft
Which steals itself when there's no mercy left.

(*Exeunt.*)[35]

SCENE FOUR Inverness. Outside Macbeth's castle.

(*Enter* ROSS *with an* OLD MAN.)

OLD MAN: Threescore and ten I can remember well;
Within the volume of which time I have seen
Hours dreadful and things strange; but this sore night
Hath trifled former knowings.

ROSS: Ah, good father,
Thou seest the heavens, as troubled with man's act,
Threaten his bloody stage.[1] By th' clock 'tis day,
And yet dark night strangles the traveling lamp.[2]
Is't night's predominance, or the day's shame,
That darkness does the face of earth entomb
When living light should kiss it?

OLD MAN: 'Tis unnatural,
Even like the deed that's done. On Tuesday last
A falcon, tow'ring in her pride of place,
Was by a mousing owl hawk'd at and kill'd.[3]

ROSS: And Duncan's horses (a thing most strange and certain),
Beauteous and swift, the minions of their race,
Turn'd wild in nature, broke their stalls, flung out,
Contending 'gainst obedience, as they would make
War with mankind.

OLD MAN: 'Tis said they eat each other.

ROSS: They did so, to th' amazement of mine eyes
That look'd upon't.

(*Enter* MACDUFF.)

Here comes the good Macduff.
How goes the world, sir, now?

MACDUFF: Why, see you not?

---

32 *the near in blood/The nearer bloody:* "The more closely related to the king, the more greatly threatened. 33 *dainty of:* meticulous about. 34 *shift:* steal. 35 *Exeunt:* The scene ends with the flight of the king's sons to escape the fate of their father, but it began with the drunken Porter who joked of being porter of Hell's gate. Some critics find the scene "a tasteless intrusion of low and bawdy comedy into the tragedy at a supremely tense moment" and claim Shakespeare could not have written it (as those who misunderstood the function of the comic scenes in Doctor Faustus attribute them to some other author than Marlowe). Others find the scene a magnificent example of comic relief. Cf. Thomas De Quincey's famous essay on "The Knocking at the Gate in MACBETH" (1851). What purpose — other than covering the time between Macbeth's exit in the last scene and his reappearance in this one — do you think the Porter's scene serves? Do you agree with De Quincy that it is an "awful parenthesis"?

1 *bloody stage:* the earth. 2 *traveling lamp:* the sun. 3 *'Tis unnatural . . . kill'd:* the Theory of Correspondences at work, as in Ross' speech which follows.

Ross: Is't known who did this more than bloody deed?

Macduff: Those that Macbeth hath slain.

Ross: Alas, the day!
What good could they pretend?

Macduff: They were suborn'd.[4]
Malcolm and Donalbain, the King's two sons,
Are stol'n away and fled, which puts upon them
Suspicion of the deed.

Ross: 'Gainst nature still!
Thriftless ambition, that wilt ravin up[5]
Thine own live's means! Then 'tis most like
The sovereignty will fall upon Macbeth.

Macduff: He is already named, and gone to Scone[6]
To be invested.

Ross: Where is Duncan's body?

Macduff: Carried to Colmekill,[7]
The sacred storehouse of his predecessors
And guardian of their bones.

Ross: Will you to Scone?

Macduff: No, cousin, I'll to Fife.

Ross: Well, I will thither.

Macduff: Well, may you see things well done there. Adieu!
Lest our old robes sit easier than our new!

Ross: Farewell, father.

Old Man: God's benison[8] go with you, and with those
That would make good of bad, and friends of foes!

(*Exeunt omnes.*)

ACT THREE

Scene One   Forres. The palace.

(*Enter* Banquo.)

Banquo: Thou hast it now — King, Cawdor, Glamis, all,

As the weird women promis'd; and I fear
Thou play'dst most foully for't. Yet it was said
It should not stand in thy posterity,
But that myself should be the root and father
Of many kings. If there come truth from them
(As upon thee, Macbeth, their speeches shine),
Why, by the verities on thee made good,
May they not be my oracles as well
And set me up in hope? But, hush, no more!

(*Sennet*[1] *sounded. Enter* Macbeth, *as King;* Lady Macbeth, *as Queen;* Lennox, Ross, Lords, *and* Attendants.)

Macbeth: Here's our chief guest.

Lady: If he had been forgotten,
It had been as a gap in our great feast,
And all-thing[2] unbecoming.

Macbeth: To-night we hold a solemn supper, sir,
And I'll request your presence.

Banquo: Let your Highness
Command upon me, to the which my duties
Are with a most indissoluble tie
For ever knit.

Macbeth: Ride you this afternoon?

Banquo: Ay, my good lord.

Macbeth: We should have else desir'd your good advice
(Which still hath been both grave and prosperous)

---

4 *They were suborn'd:* "They (Malcolm and Donalbain) bribed them (the grooms of the King's chamber)." 5 *ravin up:* devour. 6 *Scone:* the ancient royal city where Scottish kings were crowned (cf. the last line of the play). 7 *Colmekill:* the ancient burial place of Scottish kings on the island of Iona. 8 *benison:* blessing.

1 *Sennet:* trumpet call. 2 *all-thing:* altogether.

In this day's council; but we'll take tomorrow.
Is't far you ride?

BANQUO: As far, my lord, as will fill up the
time
'Twixt this and supper. Go not my horse
the better,
I must become a borrower of the night
For a dark hour or twain.

MACBETH: Fail not our feast.

BANQUO: My lord, I will not.

MACBETH: We hear our bloody cousins are
bestow'd
In England and in Ireland, not confessing
Their cruel parricide, filling their hearers
With strange invention. But of that to-
morrow,
When therewithal we shall have cause of
state
Craving us jointly.[3] Hie you to horse.
Adieu,
Till you return at night. Goes Fleance with
you?

BANQUO: Ay, my good lord. Our time does call
upon 's.

MACBETH: I wish your horses swift and sure
of foot,
And so I do commend you to their backs.
Farewell.

(*Exit* BANQUO.)

Let every man be master of his time
Till seven at night. To make society
The sweeter welcome, we will keep ourself
Till supper time alone. While then[4], God be
with you!

(*Exeunt all but* MACBETH *and a* SERVANT.)

Sirrah, a word with you. Attend those
men
Our pleasure?

SERVANT: They are, my lord, without the palace
gate.

MACBETH: Bring them before us.

(*Exit* SERVANT.)

To be thus[5] is nothing,
But to be safely thus. Our fears in Banquo
Stick deep; and in his royalty of nature
Reigns that which would be fear'd. 'Tis
much he dares,
And to that dauntless temper[6] of his mind
He hath a wisdom that doth guide his valor
To act in safety. There is none but he
Whose being I do fear; and under him
My Genius is rebuk'd,[7] as it is said
Mark Antony's was by Caesar. He chid the
sisters
When first they put the name of King upon
me,
And bade them speak to him. Then, pro-
phet-like,
They hail'd him father to a line of kings.
Upon my head they placed a fruitless crown
And put a barren sceptre in my gripe,[8]
Thence to be wrench'd with an unlineal
hand,
No son of mine succeeding. If't be so,
For Banquo's issue have I filed[9] my mind;
For them the gracious Duncan have I mur-
der'd;
Put rancors in the vessel of my peace
Only for them, and mine eternal jewel[10]
Given to the common enemy of man[11]
To make them kings, the seed of Banquo
kings!
Rather than so, come, Fate, into the list,
And champion me to th' utterance![12] Who's
there?

(*Enter* SERVANT *and two* MURDERERS.)

Now go to the door and stay there till we
call.

(*Exit* SERVANT.)

Was it not yesterday we spoke together?

MURDERERS: It was, so please your Highness.

---

3 *Craving us jointly:* demanding attention from both of
us. 4 *While then:* until then. 5 *To be thus:* to be what
I am (King). 6 *temper:* quality. 7 *Genius is rebuk'd:*
my spirit is cowed. 8 *gripe:* grip. 9 *filed:* defiled. 10
eternal jewel: soul. 11 *common enemy of man:* the
Devil. 12 *to th' utterance:* to the death (*à l'outrance,*
French).

MACBETH: Well then, now
Have you consider'd of my speeches? Know
That it was he, in the times past, which held
  you
So under fortune,[13] which you thought had
  been
Our innocent self. This I made good to you
In our last conference, pass'd in probation
  with you
How you were borne in hand, how cross'd;
  the instruments;
Who wrought with them; and all things else
  that might
To half a soul[14] and to a notion[15] craz'd
Say 'Thus did Banquo.'

1. MURDERER: You made it known to us.

MACBETH: I did so; and went further, which
  is now
Our point of second meeting. Do you find
Your patience so predominant in your
  nature
That you can let this go? Are you so gos-
  pell'd[16]
To pray for this good man and for his
  issue,
Whose heavy hand hath bow'd you to the
  grave
And beggar'd yours for ever?

1. MURDERER: We are men, my liege.

MACBETH: Ay, in the catalogue ye go for men,
As hounds and greyhounds, mongrels,
  spaniels, curs,
Shoughs, water-rugs, and demiwolves[17] are
  clept
All by the name of dogs. The valued file[18]
Distinguishes the swift, the slow, the subtle,
The housekeeper,[19] the hunter, every one
According to the gift which bounteous
  nature
Hath in him closed; whereby he does re-
  ceive
Particular addition, from the bill[20]
That writes them all alike; and so of men.
Now, if you have a station in the file,
Not i' th' worst rank of manhood, say't;
And I will put that business in your bosoms
Whose execution takes your enemy off,
Grapples you to the heart and love of us,

Who wear our health but sickly in his life,
Which in his death were perfect.

2. MURDERER: I am one, my liege,
Whom the vile blows and buffets of the
  world
Have so incensed that I am reckless what
I do to spite the world.

1. MURDERER: And I another,
So weary with disasters, tugg'd with for-
  tune,
That I would set my life on any chance,
To mend it or be rid on't.

MACBETH: Both of you
Know Banquo was your enemy.

MURDERERS: True, my lord.

MACBETH: So is he mine; and in such bloody
  distance
That every minute of his being thrusts
Against my near'st of life; and though I
  could
With barefaced power sweep him from my
  sight
And bid my will avouch[21] it, yet I must
  not,
For certain friends that are both his and
  mine,
Whose loves I may not drop, but wail his
  fall
Who I myself struck down. And thence it is
That I to your assistance do make love,
Masking the business from the common
  eye
For sundry weighty reasons.

2. MURDERER: We shall, my lord,
Perform what you command us.

---

13 *held you so under fortune:* prevented your good
fortune. 14 *half a soul:* a half-wit. 15 *notion:* mind.
16 *Gospell'd:* taught by the gospel. 17 *Shoughs,
water-rugs and demi-wolves:* shaggy dogs, long-haired
water dogs, half-wolves. 18 *valued file:* classification
by valuable traits. 19 *housekeeper:* watchdog. 20
Particular addition, from the bill: special additional
qualities in opposition to the list. 21 *avouch:* justify.

1. Murderer: Though our lives —

Macbeth: Your spirits shine through you.
Within this hour at most
I will advise you where to plant yourselves,
Acquaint you with the perfect spy[22] o' th'
time,
The moment on't; for't must be done to-
night,
And something[23] from the palace; always
thought
That I require a clearness,[24] and with him,
To leave no rubs nor botches[25] in the work,
Fleance his son, that keeps him company,
Whose absence is no less material to me
Than is his father's, must embrace the fate
Of that dark hour. Resolve yourselves
apart;[26]
I'll come to you anon.

Murderers: We are resolv'd, my lord.

Macbeth: I'll call upon you straight.[27] Abide
within.

(Exeunt Murderers.)

It is concluded. Banquo, thy soul's flight,
If it find heaven, must find it out tonight.

(Exit.)

Scene Two   Forres. The palace.

(Enter Lady Macbeth and a Servant.)

Lady: Is Banquo gone from court?

Servant: Ay, madam, but returns again tonight.

Lady: Say to the King I would attend his leisure
For a few words.

Servant: Madam, I will.

(Exit.)

Lady: Naught's had, all's spent,
Where our desire is got without content.
'Tis safer to be that which we destroy
Than by destruction dwell in doubtful joy.

(Enter Macbeth.)

How now, my lord? Why do you keep
alone,
Of sorriest fancies your companions making,[1]
Using those thoughts which should indeed
have died
With them they think on? Things without
all remedy
Should be without regard. What's done is
done.

Macbeth: We have scotch'd the snake, not
kill'd it.
She'll close,[2] and be herself, whilst our poor
malice
Remains in danger of her former tooth.
But let the frame of things disjoint, both the
worlds suffer,[3]
Ere we will eat our meal in fear and sleep
In the affliction of these terrible dreams
That shake us nightly. Better be with the
dead,
Whom we, to gain our peace, have sent to
peace,
Than on the torture[4] of the mind to lie
In restless ecstasy.[5] Duncan is in his grave;
After life's fitful fever he sleeps well.
Treason has done his worst. Nor steel nor
poison,
Malice domestic,[6] foreign levy, nothing,
Can touch him further.

Lady: Come on.
Gentle my lord, sleek o'er[7] your rugged
looks;

---

22 *perfect spy:* exact observation. 23 *something:* some
distance. 24 *always thought that I require a clearness:*
"remember that I must not fall under suspicion." 25
rubs nor botches: flaws or mistakes. 26 *Resolve yourselves apart:* "Decide among yourselves." 27 *straight:*
right away.

1 *Of sorriest fancies your companions making:* "Entertaining the most miserable imaginings." 2 *We have
scotch'd . . . she'll close:* "We have only wounded the
snake, not killed it, and it will heal itself." 3 *But let
the frame . . . worlds suffer:* "But let the universe
collapse, both Heaven and Earth suffer." 4 *torture:*
rack. 5 *ecstasy:* frenzy. 6 *Malice domestic:* civil
strife. 7 *sleek o'er:* compose, smooth.

Be bright and jovial among your guests to-night.

MACBETH: So shall I, love; and so, I pray, be you.

Let your remembrance apply to[8] Banquo;
Present him eminence both with eye and tongue[9] —
Unsafe the while, that we
Must lave[10] our honors in these flattering streams
And make our faces vizards[11] to our hearts,
Disguising what they are.

LADY: You must leave this.

MACBETH: O, full of scorpions is my mind, dear wife!
Thou know'st that Banquo, and his Fleance, lives.

LADY: But in them Nature's copy's not eterne.[12]

MACBETH: There's comfort yet! They are assailable.
Then be thou jocund. Ere the bat hath flown
His cloister'd flight, ere to black Hecate's summons
The shard-borne[13] beetle with his drowsy hums
Hath rung night's yawning peal, there shall be done
A deed of dreadful note.

LADY: What's to be done?

MACBETH: Be innocent of the knowledge, dearest chuck,[14]
Till thou applaud the deed. Come, seeling[15] night,
Scarf up the tender eye of pitiful day,
And with thy bloody and invisible hand
Cancel and tear to pieces that great bond[16]
Which keeps me pale! Light thickens, and the crow
Makes wing to th' rooky[17] wood.
Good things of day begin to droop and drowse,
Whiles night's black agents to their preys do rouse.
Thou marvel'st at my words; but hold thee still:

Things bad begun make strong themselves by ill.
So prithee go with me.

(*Exeunt.*)

SCENE THREE   Forres. A park near the palace.

Enter three MURDERERS.[1]

1. MURDERER: But who did bid thee join with us?

3. MURDERER: Macbeth.

2. MURDERER: He needs not our mistrust, since he delivers
Our offices, and what we have to do,
To the direction just.

1. MURDERER: Then stand with us.
The west yet glimmers with some streaks of day.
Now spurs the lated traveller apace
To gain the timely inn, and near approaches
The subject of our watch.

3. MURDERER: Hark: I hear horses.

BANQUO (*within*): Give us a light there, ho!

---

8 *remembrance apply to:* thoughts focus on. 9 *Present him eminence . . . :* "In attention and speech honor him." 10 *lave:* wash. 11 *vizards:* masks. 12 *eterne:* eternal. 13 *shard-borne:* an example of a word on which critics disagree — "born of a dunghill" or "borne aloft on scaly wings"? 14 *chuck:* a term of endearment. 15 *seeling:* blinding, as the eyelids of a falcon were sewn shut with thread. 16 *that great bond:* Banquo's lease on life, Macbeth's link with humanity, the prophecy. 17 *rooky:* full of rooks. Descriptive verse serves in place of lighting effects and scenery on the bare, daylit platform of the Elizabethan theatre. A play like *Macbeth*, often shrouded in darkness or requiring battle scenes, makes great demands on the power of the poet and the imagination of the auditors.

1 *Enter . . . :* note that the conversation of the three has been in progress for some time. As with the earlier scene with the murderers (full of exposition about an earlier conversation with them), Shakespeare seems to be economizing. Some critics have suggested that Macbeth (in disguise) is the third murderer. But see his reaction later to news of the escape of Fleance.

2. MURDERER: Then 'tis he! The rest
That are within the note of expectation[2]
Already are i' th' court.

1. MURDERER: His horses go about.

3. MURDERER: Almost a mile; but he does
    usually,
So all men do, from hence to th' palace gate
Make it their walk.[3]

(*Enter* BANQUO, *and* FLEANCE *with a torch.*)

2. MURDERER: A light, a light!

3. MURDERER: 'Tis he.

1. MURDERER: Stand to't.

BANQUO: It will be rain to-night.

1. MURDERER: Let it come down!

(*They fall upon* BANQUO.)

BANQUO: O, treachery! Fly, good Fleance, fly,
    fly, fly!
Thou mayst revenge. O slave!

(*Dies.* FLEANCE *escapes.*)

3. MURDERER: Who did strike out the light?

1. MURDERER: Was't not the way?[4]

3. MURDERER: There's but one down; the son
    is fled.

2. MURDERER: We have lost
Best half of our affair.

1. MURDERER: Well, let's away, and say how
    much is done.

(*Exeunt.*)

SCENE FOUR   Forres. Hall in the palace.

Banquet prepared. Enter MACBETH, LADY MAC-
BETH, ROSS, LENNOX, LORDS, *and* ATTENDANTS.

MACBETH: You know your own degrees,[1] sit
    down. At first
And last the hearty welcome.

LORDS: Thanks to your Majesty.

MACBETH: Ourself will mingle with society
And play the humble host.

Our hostess keeps her state,[2] but in best
    time
We will require her welcome.

LADY: Pronounce it for me, sir, to all our
    friends,
For my heart speaks they are welcome.

(FIRST MURDERER *appears at the door.*)

MACBETH: See, they encounter[3] thee with their
    hearts' thanks.
Both sides are even. Here I'll sit i' th' midst.
Be large in mirth anon we'll drink a mea-
    sure[4]
The table round. (*Goes to the door.*)
There's blood upon thy face.

MURDERER: 'Tis Banquo's then.

MACBETH: 'Tis better thee without than he
    within.[5]
Is he dispatch'd?

MURDERER: My lord, his throat is cut. That I
    did for him.

MACBETH: Thou art the best o' th' cut-throats!
    Yet he's good
That did the like for Fleance. If thou didst
    it,
Thou art the nonpareil.[6]

MURDERER: Most royal sir,
Fleance is scap'd.

MACBETH (*aside*): Then comes my fit again. I
    had else been perfect;
Whole as the marble, founded as the rock,[7]

---

2 *within the note of expectation:* on the guest list and
expected.   3 *their walk:* Shakespeare could not bring the
horses on stage.   4 *Was't not the way:* "Wasn't it the
right thing to do?"

1 *degrees:* rank (reflected in seating arrangements, below the salt, etc.).   2 *keeps her state:* remains seated
in her chair.   3 *encounter:* meet.   4 *measure:* goblet.
5 *'Tis better . . . :* "Better it should be on you than in
him."   6 *nonpareil:* one without parallel (French).   7
founded as the rock: firm as a rock.

As broad and general as the casing[8] air.
But now I am cabin'd, cribb'd, confin'd,
    bound in
To saucy[9] doubts and fears. — But Banquo's
    safe?

MURDERER: Ay, my good lord. Safe in a ditch
    he bides,
With twenty trenched gashes on his head,
The least a death to nature.

MACBETH: Thanks for that!
There the grown serpent lies; the worm
    that's fled
Hath nature that in time will venom
    breed,
No teeth for th' present. Get thee gone.
    To-morrow
We'll hear ourselves[10] again.

(*Exit* MURDERER.)

LADY: My royal lord,
You do not give the cheer. The feast is sold
That is not often vouch'd,[11] while 'tis a-
    making,
'Tis given with welcome. To feed were best
    at home.[12]
From thence, the sauce to meat is ceremony;
Meeting were bare without it.

(*Enter the* GHOST OF BANQUO, *and sits in* MAC-
BETH's *place.*)

MACBETH: Sweet remembrancer!
Now good digestion wait on appetite,
And health on both!

LENNOX: May't please your Highness sit.

MACBETH: Here had we now our country's
    honor, roof'd,[13]
Were the graced person of our Banquo
    present;
Who may I rather challenge for unkindness
Than pity for mischance!

ROSS: His absence, sir,
Lays blame upon his promise. Please't your
    Highness
To grace us with your royal company.

MACBETH: The table's full.

LENNOX: Here is a place reserved, sir.

MACBETH: Where?

LENNOX: Here, my good lord. What is't that
    moves your Highness?

MACBETH: Which of you have done this?

LORDS: What, my good lord?

MACBETH: Thou canst not say I did it. Never
    shake
Thy gory locks at me.

ROSS: Gentlemen, rise. His Highness is not
    well.

LADY: Sit, worthy friends. My lord is often
    thus,
And hath been from his youth. Pray you
    keep seat.
The fit is momentary; upon a thought
He will again be well. If much you note
    him,
You shall offend him and extend his pas-
    sion.
Feed, and regard him not. — Are you a
    man?

MACBETH: Ay, and a bold one, that dare look
    on that
Which might appal the devil.

LADY: O proper stuff!
This is the very painting of your fear.
This is the air-drawn dagger which you said
Led you to Duncan. O, these flaws[14] and
    starts
(Impostors to true fear) would well
    become
A woman's story at a winter's fire,
Authorized by her grandam.[15] Shame itself!
Why do you make such faces? When all's
    done,
You look but on a stool.[16]

---

8 *casing:* surrounding. **9** *saucy:* insolent. **10** *hear ourselves:* confer. **11** *The feast is sold* . . . : "The feast
seems sold [not given] that does not see the host often
welcoming the guests." **12** *To feed were best at home:*
"Eating [as opposed to dining] is to be done at home."
13 *Our country's honor, roof'd:* all the nobility of the
country under one roof. **14** *flaws:* outbursts. **15** *Authorized by her grandam:* vouched for by her grandmother. **16** *You look but on a stool:* "The chair you
stare at is empty."

MACBETH: Prithee see there! behold! look! lo!
    How say you?
  Why, what care I? If thou canst nod, speak
    too.
  If charnel houses[17] and our graves must
    send
  Those that we bury back, our monuments
  Shall be the maws of kites.[18]

(GHOST *vanishes*.)

LADY: What, quite unmann'd in folly?

MACBETH: If I stand here, I saw him.

LADY: Fie, for shame!

MACBETH: Blood hath been shed ere now, i'
    th' olden time,
  Ere humane statute purg'd the gentle weal,[19]
  Ay, and since too, murders have been per-
    form'd
  Too terrible for the ear. The time has been
  That, when the brains were out, the man
    would die,
  And there an end! But now they rise
    again,
  With twenty mortal murders on their
    crowns,[20]
  And push us from our stools. This is more
    strange
  Than such a murder is.

LADY: My worthy lord,
  Your noble friends do lack you.

MACBETH: I do forget.
  Do not muse at me, my most worthy
    friends.
  I have a strange infirmity, which is nothing
  To those that know me. Come, love and
    health to all!
  Then I'll sit down. Give me some wine, fill
    full.
  I drink to th' general joy o' th' whole table,
  And to our dear friend Banquo, whom we
    miss.
  Would he were here! To all, and him, we
    thirst,
  And all to all.[21]

LORDS: Our duties, and the pledge.

(*Re-enter* GHOST.)

MACBETH: Avaunt, and quit my sight! Let the
    earth hide thee!
  Thy bones are marrowless, thy blood is
    cold;
  Thou hast no speculation[22] in those eyes
  Which thou dost glare with!

LADY: Think of this, good peers,
  But as a thing of custom. 'Tis no other.
  Only it spoils the pleasure of the time.

MACBETH: What man dare, I dare.
  Approach thou like the rugged Russian
    bear,
  The arm'd rhinoceros, or th' Hyrcan[23] tiger;
  Take any shape but that, and my firm nerves
  Shall never tremble. Or be alive again
  And dare me to the desert with thy sword.
  If trembling I inhabit then, protest me
  The baby of a girl.[24] Hence, horrible
    shadow!
  Unreal mock'ry, hence!

(GHOST *vanishes*.)[25]

                          Why, so! Being gone,
  I am a man again. Pray you sit still.

LADY: You have displaced the mirth, broke
    the good meeting
  With most admired[26] disorder.

MACBETH: Can such things be,
  And overcome[27] us like a summer's cloud

---

17 *charnel houses:* vaults for bones dug up in making
new graves. **18** *our monuments . . . kites:* our tombs
shall be the bellies of rapacious birds. **19** *purg'd the
gentle weal:* cleansed the society and made it civilized.
20 *mortal murders on their crowns:* deadly wounds
on their heads. **21** *all to all:* all [good wishes] to
everyone. **22** *speculation:* sight. **23** *Hyrcan:* from
Hyrcania near the Caspian Sea. **24** *protest me . . .
girl:* call me a baby girl. **25** *Ghost:* in Roman Catholic
theology the ghosts of the dead might come from Purgatory (where the dead expiated sins), but for Protes-
tants who did not believe in Purgatory, ghosts could
only come from Hell as emissaries of the Devil. In the
tradition of Senecan tragedy, which underlies *The
Spanish Tragedy* and *Hamlet*, ghosts come for revenge, appearing only to those they choose. **26** *admired:* amazing (not admirable). **27** *overcome:* come
over.

Without our special wonder? You make me
strange
Even to the disposition that I owe,[28]
When now I think you can behold such
sights
And keep the natural ruby of your cheeks
When mine is blanch'd with fear.

Ross: What sights, my lord?

LADY: I pray you speak not. He grows worse
and worse;
Question enrages him. At once, good night.
Stand not upon the order of your going,[29]
But go at once.

LENNOX: Good night, and better health
Attend his Majesty!

LADY: A kind good night to all!

(*Exeunt all but* MACBETH *and* LADY MACBETH.)

MACBETH: It will have blood, they say; blood
will have blood.
Stones have been known to move and trees
to speak;
Augurs and understood relations have
By maggot-pies and choughs and rooks[30]
brought forth
The secret'st man of blood.[31] What is the
night?[32]

LADY: Almost at odds with morning, which is
which.

MACBETH: How say'st thou that Macduff
denies his person
At our great bidding?

LADY: Did you send to him, sir?

MACBETH: I hear it by the way; but I will
send.
There's not a one of them but in his house
I keep a servant fee'd.[33] I will to-morrow
(And betimes[34] I will) unto the Weird
Sisters.
More shall they speak; for now I am bent
to know[35]
By the worst means the worst. For mine
own good
All causes shall give way. I am in blood
Stepp'd in so far that, should I wade no
more,
Returning were as tedious as go o'er.

Strange things I have in head, that will to
hand,
Which must be acted ere they may be
scann'd.[36]

LADY: You lack the season of all natures,[37]
sleep.

MACBETH: Come, we'll to sleep. My strange
and self-abuse[38]
Is the initiate fear that wants hard use.[39]
We are yet but young in deed.[40]

(*Exeunt.*)

SCENE FIVE[1]   A heath.

Thunder. Enter the three WITCHES, *meeting*
HECATE.

1. WITCH: Why, how now, Hecate? You look
angerly.

---

28 *strange even to the disposition that I owe:* a stranger
to the nature of my own disposition.   **29** *Stand not upon
the order of your going:* "Do not trouble to go in order
of rank."   **30** *maggot-pies . . . choughs . . . rooks:* magpies, jackdaws, rooks (tell-tale birds).   **31** *secret'st man
of blood:* least suspected murderer.   **32** *What is the
night:* "What time of night is it?"   **33** *servant fee'd:*
a servant paid to spy.   **34** *betimes:* speedily.   **35** *bent
to know:* bent on knowing.   **36** *scann'd:* examined.
37 *season of all natures:* preservative of all creatures.
38 *strange and self-abuse:* strange delusion.   **39**
initiate's fear that wants hard use: the fear of the beginner who lacks practice.   **40** *young in deed:* novices
at this work.

1 SCENE V: This scene is interpolated in the (probably) cut version of Shakespeare's play we have and
introduces Hecate, completely at variance with Shakespeare's view of the nature of the hags we see elsewhere in *Macbeth*. In the Folio text (1623) stage directions also require two songs from *The Witch*, a play
by Thomas Middleton (*c.* 1570–1627) which also includes a Hecate. Middleton collaborated with other
dramatists (with Dekker on *The Honest Whore*; with
Rowley on *A Fair Quarrel* and others; with Webster,
Drayton and Munday on *Caesar's Fall*, etc.) but the
Hecate scenes appear to indicate revision of, rather
than collaboration on, *Macbeth*, in its present state
the shortest text of a Shakespeare play.

HECATE: Have I not reason, beldams as you
 are,
 Saucy and overbold? How did you dare
 To trade and traffic with Macbeth
 In riddles and affairs of death;
 And I, the mistress of your charms,
 The close contriver of all harms,
 Was never call'd to bear my part
 Or show the glory of our art?
 And, which is worse, all you have done
 Hath been but for a wayward son,
 Spiteful and wrathful, who, as others do,
 Loves for his own ends, not for you.
 But make amends now. Get you gone
 And at the pit of Acheron[2]
 Meet me i' th' morning. Thither he
 Will come to know his destiny.
 Your vessels and your spells provide,
 Your charms and everything beside.
 I am for th' air. This night I'll spend
 Unto a dismal and a fatal end.
 Great business must be wrought ere noon.
 Upon the corner of the moon
 There hangs a vaporous drop profound.
 I'll catch it ere it come to ground;
 And that, distill'd by magic sleights,
 Shall raise such artificial sprites
 As by the strength of their illusion
 Shall draw him on to his confusion.
 He shall spurn fate, scorn death, and
  bear
 His hopes 'bove wisdom, grace, and fear;
 And you all know security[3]
 Is mortals' chiefest enemy.

(*Music and a song within.* 'Come away, come
away,' &c.)

Hark! I am call'd. My little spirit, see,
Sits in a foggy cloud and stays for me.

(*Exit.*)[4]

1. WITCH: Come, let's make haste. She'll soon
 be back again.

(*Exeunt.*)

SCENE SIX   Forres. The palace.

Enter LENNOX *and another* LORD.

LENNOX: My former speeches have but hit
 your thoughts,[1]
 Which can interpret farther. Only I say
 Things have been strangely borne.[2] The
  gracious Duncan
 Was pitied of Macbeth. Marry, he was dead!
 And the right valiant Banquo walk'd too
  late;
 Whom, you may say (if't please you)
  Fleance kill'd,
 For Fleance fled. Men must not walk too
  late.
 Who cannot want the thought how mon-
  strous
 It was for Malcolm and for Donalbain
 To kill their gracious father? Damned
  fact!
 How it did grieve Macbeth! Did he not
  straight,
 In pious rage, the two delinquents tear,
 That were the slaves of drink and thralls of
  sleep?
 Was not that nobly done? Ay, and wisely
  too!
 For 'twould have anger'd any heart alive
 To hear the men deny't. So that I say
 He has borne all things well; and I do think
 That, had he Duncan's sons under his key
 (As, an't please heaven, he shall not), they
  should find
 What 'twere to kill a father. So should
  Fleance.
 But peace! for from broad words, and 'cause
  he fail'd
 His presence at the tyrant's feasts, I hear
 Macduff lives in disgrace. Sir, can you tell
 Where he bestows himself?

LORD: The son of Duncan,
 From whom this tyrant holds the due of
  birth,
 Lives in the English court, and is received

---

2 *Acheron:* river in Hades.   3 *security:* overconfidence.
4 *Exit:* some texts have Hecate exiting before the song,
but her speech is clearly a response to "Come away"—
"I am call'd."

1 *hit your thoughts:* coincided with your ideas.   2
borne: managed.

Of the most pious Edward[3] with such grace
That the malevolence of fortune nothing
Takes from his high respect.[4] Thither Mac-
duff
Is gone to pray the holy King[5] upon his
aid
To wake Northumberland[6] and warlike Si-
ward;
That by the help of these (with Him above
To ratify the work) we may again
Give to our tables meat, sleep to our nights,
Free from our feasts and banquets bloody
knives,
Do faithful homage and receive free hon-
ors —
All which we pine for now. And this report
Hath so exasperate the King that he
Prepares for some attempt of war.

LENNOX: Sent he to Macduff?

LORD: He did; and with an absolute 'Sir, not
I!'
The cloudy[7] messenger turns me his back
And hums, as who should say, 'You'll rue
the time
That clogs[8] me with this answer.'

LENNOX: And that well might
Advise him to a caution t' hold what dis-
tance
His wisdom can provide. Some holy angel
Fly to the court of England and unfold
His message ere he come, that a swift bless-
ing
May soon return to this our suffering
country
Under a hand accursed!

LORD: I'll send my prayers with him.

(*Exeunt.*)

ACT FOUR

SCENE ONE   A cavern. In the middle, a cauldron boiling.

Thunder. Enter the three WITCHES.

1. WITCH: Thrice the brinded[1] cat hath
mew'd.

2. WITCH: Thrice and once the hedgepig[2]
whin'd.

3. WITCH: Harpier[3] cries: 'tis time, 'tis time.

1. WITCH: Round about the cauldron go;
In the poison'd entrails throw.
Toad, that under cold stone
Days and nights has thirty-one
Swelt'red venom sleeping got,[4]
Boil thou first i' th' charmed pot.

ALL: Double, double, toil and trouble;
Fire burn, and cauldron bubble.

2. WITCH: Fillet of a fenny snake,[5]
In the cauldron boil and bake;
Eye of newt, and toe of frog,
Wool of bat, and tongue of dog,
Adder's fork, and blindworm's[6] sting,
Lizard's leg, and howlet's[7] wing;
For a charm of powerful trouble
Like a hell-broth boil and bubble.

ALL: Double, double, toil and trouble;
Fire burn, and cauldron bubble.

3. WITCH: Scale of dragon, tooth of wolf,
Witch's mummy, maw and gulf[8]
Of the ravin'd[9] salt-sea shark,
Root of hemlock, digg'd i' th' dark;
Liver of blaspheming Jew,
Gall of goat, and slips of yew
Sliver'd in the moon's eclipse;
Nose of Turk and Tartar's lips;
Finger of birth-strangled babe
Ditch-deliver'd by a drab.[10]

---

3 *Edward:* Edward the Confessor, King of England 1042–1066. 4 *nothing takes from his high respect:* does not diminish the respect in which he (Malcolm) is held. 5 *King:* Malcolm, considered as rightful king of Scotland. 6 *Northumberland:* either the English county or the earl (Siward). 7 *cloudy:* agitated. 8 *clogs:* burdens.

1 *brinded:* brindled. 2 *hedge-pig:* hedgehog. 3 *Harpier:* a familiar of some sort. 4 *Swelt'red venom sleeping got:* sweated out venom while dormant. 5 *Fillet of a fenny snake:* slice of a snake from a fen. 6 *blindworm:* legless lizard. 7 *howlet:* owlet. 8 *maw and gulf:* stomach and gullet. 9 *ravin'd:* ravenous. 10 *Ditch-deliver'd by a drab:* born in a ditch of a harlot.

Make the gruel thick and slab.[11]
Add thereto a tiger's chaudron[12]
For th' ingredients of our cauldron.

ALL: Double, double, toil and trouble;
Fire burn, and cauldron bubble.

2. WITCH: Cool it with a baboon's blood,
Then the charm is firm and good.

(*Enter* HECATE.)[13]

HECATE: O, well done! I commend your pains,
And every one shall share i' th' gains.
And now about the cauldron sing
Like elves and fairies in a ring,
Enchanting all that you put in.

(*Music and a song,* 'Black spirits,' &c. *Exit* HECATE.)

2. WITCH: By the pricking of my thumbs,
Something wicked this way comes.
                    Open locks,
                    Whoever knocks!

(*Enter* MACBETH.)

MACBETH: How now, you secret, black, and
    midnight hags?
What is't you do?

ALL: A deed without a name.

MACBETH: I conjure you by that which you
    profess
(Howe'er you come to know it), answer me.
Though you untie the winds and let them
    fight
Against the churches; though the yesty[14]
    waves
Confound and swallow navigation up;
Though bladed corn be lodged[15] and trees
    blown down;
Though castles topple on their warders'
    heads;
Though palaces and pyramids do slope[16]
Their heads to their foundations; though the
    treasure
Of nature's germens[17] tumble all together,
Even till destruction sicken—answer me
To what I ask you.

1. WITCH: Speak.

2. WITCH: Demand.

3. WITCH: We'll answer.

1. WITCH: Say, if th' hadst rather hear it from
    our mouths
Or from our masters.

MACBETH: Call 'em! Let me see 'em.

1. WITCH: Pour in sow's blood, that hath eaten
Her nine farrow;[18] grease that's sweaten
From the murderer's gibbet throw
Into the flame.

ALL: Come, high or low;
Thyself and office[19] deftly show!

(*Thunder.* FIRST APPARITION, *an Armed Head.*)

MACBETH: Tell me, thou unknown power—

1. WITCH: He knows thy thought.
Hear his speech, but say thou naught.

1. APPARITION: Macbeth! Macbeth! Macbeth!
    Beware Macduff;
Beware the Thane of Fife. Dismiss me.
    Enough.

(*He descends.*)

MACBETH: Whate'er thou art, for thy good
    caution thanks!
Thou hast harp'd[20] my fear aright. But one
    word more—

1. WITCH: He will not be commanded. Here's
    another,
More potent than the first.

(*Thunder.* SECOND APPARITION, *a Bloody Child.*)

2. APPARITION: Macbeth! Macbeth! Macbeth!

MACBETH: Had I three ears, I'ld hear thee.

2. APPARITION: Be bloody, bold, and resolute;
    laugh to scorn

---

11 *slab:* thick. 12 *chaudron:* entrails. 13 *Enter:* some texts add *"and Three Other Witches."* They exit with Hecate after line 43. 14 *yesty:* yeasty, foaming. 15 *lodged:* destroyed. 16 *slope:* bend. 17 *germens:* seeds. 18 *farrow:* piglets. 19 *office:* function. 20 *harp'd:* hit upon.

The power of man for none of woman
born
Shall harm Macbeth.

(*Descends.*)

MACBETH: Then live, Macduff. What need I
fear of thee?
But yet I'll make assurance double sure
And take a bond of fate.[21] Thou shalt not
live!
That I may tell pale-hearted fear it lies
And sleep in spite of thunder.

(*Thunder.* THIRD APPARITION, *a Child
Crowned, with a tree in his hand.*)

What is this
That rises like the issue[22] of a king
And wears upon his baby-brow the round
And top of sovereignty?[23]

ALL: Listen, but speak not to't.

3. APPARITION: Be lion-mettled, proud, and
take no care
Who chafes, who frets, or where conspirers
are.
Macbeth shall never vanquish'd be until
Great Birnam Wood to high Dunsinane Hill
Shall come against him.

(*Descends.*)

MACBETH: That will never be.
Who can impress[24] the forest, bid the tree
Unfix his earth-bound root? Sweet bode-
ments,[25] good!
Rebellion's head[26] rise never till the Wood
Of Birnam rise, and our high placed Mac-
beth
Shall live the lease of nature,[27] pay his
breath
To time and mortal custom.[28] Yet my
heart
Throbs to know one thing. Tell me, if your
art
Can tell so much—shall Banquo's issue ever
Reign in this kingdom?

ALL: Seek to know no more.

MACBETH: I will be satisfied. Deny me this,
And an eternal curse fall on you! Let me
know.

Why sinks that cauldron? and what noise[29]
is this?

(*Hautboys.*)

1. WITCH: Show!

2. WITCH: Show!

3. WITCH: Show!

ALL: Show his eyes, and grieve his heart!
Come like shadows, so depart!

(*A show of eight Kings, the last with a glass*[30]
in his hand; and BANQUO's GHOST *following.*)

MACBETH: Thou art too like the spirit of Ban-
quo. Down!
Thy crown does sear mine eyeballs. And
thy hair,
Thou other gold-bound brow, is like the
first.
A third is like the former. Filthy hags!
Why do you show me this? A fourth? Start,
eyes!
What, will the line stretch out to th' crack
of doom?
Another yet? A seventh? I'll see no more.
And yet the eighth appears, who bears a
glass
Which shows me many more; and some
I see
That twofold balls and treble sceptres carry.
Horrible sight! Now I see 'tis true;
For the blood-bolter'd Banquo smiles upon
me

---

21 *take a bond of fate:* get a guarantee from fate (by killing Macduff). **22** *issue:* offspring. **23** *round and top of sovereignty:* crown. **24** *impress:* conscript. **25** *bodements:* prophecies. **26** *Rebellion's head:* some texts have "rebellious dead" (i.e., Banquo). **27** *live the lease of nature:* live out his natural life. **28** *mortal custom:* the custom of mortals to die, natural death. **29** *noise:* the music has begun. **30** *glass:* mirror. The line of kings, Banquo's posterity through Fleance, was supposed to be that from which King James VI of Scotland (and I of England) was descended. The "twofold balls [orbs] and treble sceptres [one for Scotland, two for England —which has a rod with a dove surmounting it as well as the standard sceptre]" are coronation regalia foretelling the uniting of the two kingdoms under James I.

And points at them for his. (*Apparitions vanish.*) What? Is this so?

1. WITCH: Ay, sir, all this is so. But why
Stands Macbeth thus amazedly?
Come, sisters, cheer we up his sprites
And show the best of our delights.
I'll charm the air to give a sound
While you perform your antic round,[31]
That this great king may kindly say
Our duties did his welcome pay.

(*Music. The* WITCHES *dance, and vanish.*)[32]

MACBETH: Where are they? Gone? Let this pernicious hour
Stand aye accursed in the calendar!
Come in, without there!

(*Enter* LENNOX.)

LENNOX: What's your Grace's will?

MACBETH: Saw you the Weird Sisters?

LENNOX: No, my lord.

MACBETH: Came they not by you?

LENNOX: No, indeed, my lord.

MACBETH: Infected be the air whereon they ride,
And damn'd all those that trust them! I did hear
The galloping of horse. Who was't came by?

LENNOX: 'Tis two or three, my lord, that bring you word
Macduff is fled to England.

MACBETH: Fled to England?

LENNOX: Ay, my good lord.

MACBETH (*aside*): Time, thou anticipat'st[33] my dread exploits.
The flighty purpose never is o'ertook[34]
Unless the deed go with it. From this moment
The very firstlings of my heart[35] shall be
The firstlings of my hand. And even now,
To crown my thoughts with acts, be it thought and done!
The castle of Macduff I will surprise,[36]

Seize upon Fife, give to the edge o' th' sword
His wife, his babes, and all unfortunate souls
That trace him in his line.[37] No boasting like a fool!
This deed I'll do before this purpose cool.
But no more sights! — where are these gentlemen?
Come, bring me where they are.

(*Exeunt.*)[38]

---

31 *antic round:* grotesque dance. **32** *vanish:* even the traps in the platform would not have made this easy on the Elizabethan stage, for plays were presented in broad daylight and some of the audience even sat on the stage. In the seventeenth century, staging of Shakespeare was elaborate: Samuel Pepys liked the witches on trapezes better than the rest of the play. In the eighteenth century, Shakespeare was tailored to contemporary taste: see Hazelton Spencer's *Shakespeare Improved.* In the nineteenth century, Shakespeare was overwhelmed with scenery, the new limelight, and historical accuracy in costuming, etc. Charles Kean at the Princess' Theatre (1853) produced *Macbeth* with great care as to the mounting but used the botched text prepared in the seventeenth century by Sir William D'Avenant (1606–1668), who thought of it more in terms of opera and spectacle than of drama. Modern productions have interpreted the witches in many ways and in Theodore Komisarjevsky's production at Stratford (1933) they became nightmares and Banquo's ghost only Macbeth's own shadow, while in a 1971 "off-off-Broadway" production the whole play appears to have been a dream of Macbeth. Other productions have been essayed on bleak platforms in dazzling light or (as in the case of Orson Welles' film) shrouded in dry-ice fog. Probably the *Macbeth* starring Maurice Evans and Dame Judith Anderson (1941 on stage, 1961 on television) was the best American production and the worst perhaps of recent years those directed by Ray Boyle, Jack Landau, and Gladys Vaughan. **33** *anticipat'st:* foretold. **34** *o'ertook:* realized, accomplished. **35** *firstlings of my heart:* impulses. **36** *surprise:* suddenly attack. **37** *souls that trace him in his line:* relatives. **38** *Exeunt:* The apparitions in this scene seem to prove that the witches are not merely the deluded old hags Reginald Scot speaks of in his *Discoverie of Witchcraft* (1584), an attack on superstition, but really in league with evil spirits, as James himself argued of witches in his *Dæmonologie* (1597). In Holinshed's *Chronicles of*

SCENE TWO   Fife. Macduff's castle.

Enter MACDUFF'S WIFE, *her* SON, *and* ROSS.

WIFE: What had he done to make him fly the land?

ROSS: You must have patience, madam.

WIFE: He had none.
His flight was madness. When our actions do not,
Our fears do make us traitors.

ROSS: You know not
Whether it was his wisdom or his fear.

WIFE: Wisdom? To leave his wife, to leave his babes,
His mansion, and his titles,[1] in a place
From whence himself does fly? He loves us not,
He wants the natural touch. For the poor wren,
(The most diminutive of birds) will fight,
Her young ones in her nest, against the owl.
All is the fear, and nothing is the love,
As little is the wisdom, where the flight
So runs against all reason.

ROSS: My dearest coz,
I pray you school[2] yourself. But for your husband,
He is noble, wise, judicious, and best knows
The fits o' th' season.[3] I dare not speak much further;
But cruel are the times, when we are traitors
And do not know ourselves; when we hold rumor
From what we fear,[4] yet know not what we fear,
But float upon a wild and violent sea
Each way and none. I take my leave of you.
Shall not be long but I'll be here again.
Things at the worst will cease,[5] or else climb upward
To what they were before. — My pretty cousin,
Blessing upon you!

WIFE: Father'd he is, and yet he's fatherless.

ROSS: I am so much a fool, should I stay longer,
It would be my disgrace and your discomfort.[6]
I take my leave at once.

(*Exit.*)

WIFE: Sirrah,[7] your father's dead;
And what will you do now? How will you live?

SON: As birds do, mother.

WIFE: What, with worms and flies?

SON: With what I get, I mean; and so do they.

WIFE: Poor bird! thou'dst never fear the net nor lime,[8]
The pitfall nor the gin.[9]

SON: Why should I, mother? Poor birds they are not set for.
My father is not dead, for all your saying.

WIFE: Yes, he is dead. How wilt thou do for a father?

England, Scotlande and Irelande (1577), Shakespeare's principal source for details of *Macbeth*, the witches are "three women in strange and wild apparel resembling the creatures of an elder world" but he is not sure whether they are supernaturally-gifted or not. "Afterwards the common opinion was that these women were either the Weird Sisters, that is (as you would say) the goddesses of destiny, or else some nymphs or fairies, imbued with knowledge of prophecy by their necromantical science, because everything came to pass as they had spoken." Note that in the play the witches only seem to urge Macbeth the way that he was going anyway and that they neither compel him to act nor actually foretell any of his villainies.

1 *titles:* possessions. 2 *school:* restrain. 3 *fits o' th' season:* disorders of the time. 4 *hold rumor from what we fear:* believe rumors because of fear. 5 *cease:* stop (getting worse once they reach the worst). 6 *my disgrace and your discomfort:* i.e., "I should weep." 7 *Sirrah:* ordinarily used to address inferiors (as hitherto in the play), *sirrah* here is used as a term of affection. 8 *lime:* smeared on branches to catch birds. 9 *gin:* engine trap.

SON: Nay, how will you do for a husband?

WIFE: Why, I can buy me twenty at any market.

SON: Then you'll buy 'em to sell[10] again.

WIFE: Thou speak'st with all thy wit; and yet, i' faith,
With wit enough for thee.

SON: Was my father a traitor, mother?

WIFE: Ay, that he was!

SON: What is a traitor?

WIFE: Why, one that swears, and lies.[11]

SON: And be all traitors that do so?

WIFE: Every one that does so is a traitor and must be hanged.

SON: And must they all be hanged that swear and lie?

WIFE: Every one.

SON: Who must hang them?

WIFE: Why, the honest men.

SON: Then the liars and swearers are fools; for there are liars and swearers enow to beat the honest men and hang up them.

WIFE: Now God help thee, poor monkey! But how wilt thou do for a father?

SON: If he were dead, you'ld weep for him. If you would not, it were a good sign that I should quickly have a new father.

WIFE: Poor prattler, how thou talk'st!

(*Enter a* MESSENGER.)

MESSENGER: Bless you, fair dame! I am not to you known,
Though in your state of honor I am perfect.[12]
I doubt some danger does approach you nearly.
If you will take a homely[13] man's advice,
Be not found here. Hence with your little ones!
To fright you thus methinks I am too savage;

To do worse to you were fell cruelty,
Which is too nigh your person. Heaven preserve you!
I dare abide no longer.

(*Exit.*)

WIFE: Whither should I fly?
I have done no harm. But I remember now
I am in this earthly world, where to do harm
Is often laudable, to do good sometime
Accounted dangerous folly. Why then, alas,
Do I put up that womanly defense
To say I have done no harm?—What are these faces?

(*Enter* MURDERERS.)

MURDERERS: Where is your husband?

WIFE: I hope, in no place so unsanctified
Where such as thou mayst find him.

MURDERERS: He's a traitor.

SON: Thou liest, thou shag-hair'd villain!

MURDERERS: What, you egg![14]

(*Stabs him.*)

    Young fry[15] of treachery!

SON: He has kill'd me, mother.
Run away, I pray you!

(*Dies.*)

(*Exit* LADY MACDUFF, *crying 'Murder!' and pursued by the* MURDERERS.)

SCENE THREE   England. Before King Edward's palace.

Enter MALCOLM *and* MACDUFF.

MALCOLM: Let us seek out some desolate shade, and there

---

10 *sell:* betray. It was traditional for noble childen to speak wisely or wittily, whatever their ages. **11** *swears, and lies:* takes an oath and breaks it. **12** *perfect:* informed. **13** *homely:* plain. **14** *egg:* from such Macduffs could be hatched in time. **15** *fry:* spawn, as in "small fry."

Weep our sad bosoms empty.

MACDUFF: Let us rather
Hold fast the mortal[1] sword and, like good
  men,
Bestride our downfall'n birthdom.[2] Each new
  morn
New widows howl, new orphans cry, new
  sorrows
Strike heaven on the face, that it resounds
As if it felt with Scotland and yell'd out
Like syllable of dolor.[3]

MALCOLM: What I believe, I'll wail;
What know, believe; and what I can re-
  dress,
As I shall find the time to friend, I will.
What you have spoke, it may be so per-
  chance.
This tyrant, whose sole name blisters our
  tongues,
Was once thought honest; you have loved
  him well;
He hath not touched you yet. I am young;
  but something
You may deserve of him through me,[4] and
  wisdom[5]
To offer up a weak, poor, innocent lamb
T' appease an angry god.

MACDUFF: I am not treacherous.

MALCOLM: But Macbeth is.
A good and virtuous nature may recoil
In[6] an imperial charge. But I shall crave your
  pardon.
That which you are, my thoughts cannot
  transpose.
Angels are bright still, though the brightest
  fell.
Though all things foul would wear[7] the
  brows of grace,
Yet grace must still look so.[8]

MACDUFF: I have lost my hopes.

MALCOLM: Perchance even there where I did
  find my doubts.
Why in that rawness[9] left you wife and
  child,
Those precious motives, those strong knots
  of love,
Without leave-taking? I pray you,

Let not my jealousies[10] be your dishonors,
But mine own safeties. You may be rightly
  just,
Whatever I shall think.

MACDUFF: Bleed, bleed, poor country!
Great tyranny, lay thou thy basis sure,
For goodness dare not check thee! Wear
  thou thy wrongs;
The title is affeer'd![11] Fare thee well, lord.
I would not be the villain that thou
  think'st
For the whole space that's in the tyrant's
  grasp
And the rich East to boot.

MALCOLM: Be not offended.
I speak not as in absolute fear of you.
I think our country sinks beneath the yoke,
It weeps, it bleeds, and each new day a
  gash
Is added to her wounds. I think withal[12]
There would be hands uplifted in my right;
And here from gracious England have I
  offer
Of goodly thousands. But, for[13] all this,
When I shall tread upon the tyrant's head
Or wear it on my sword, yet my poor
  country
Shall have more vices than it had before,
More suffer and more sundry ways than
  ever.
By him that shall succeed.

MACDUFF: What should he be?

MALCOLM: It is myself I mean; in whom I
  know
All the particulars of vice so grafted

---

1 *mortal:* deadly. 2 *Bestride our downfall'n birthdom:* protect our unhappy native kingdom. 3 *Like
syllable of dolor:* similar sound of suffering. 4 *something you may deserve of him through me:* "You may
stand to gain something from him by betraying me."
5 *wisdom:* it may be wise. 6 *recoil in:* give way
under. 7 *would wear:* would desire to wear. 8 *so:*
like itself. 9 *rawness:* unprotected state. 10 *jealousies:*
suspicions. 11 *affeer'd:* legally confirmed. 12 *withal:*
moreover. 13 *for:* despite.

That, when they shall be open'd,[14] black
   Macbeth
Will seem as pure as snow, and the poor
   state
Esteem him as a lamb, being compar'd
With my confineless harms.

MACDUFF: Not in the legions
   Of horrid hell can come a devil more
   damn'd
   In evils to top Macbeth.

MALCOLM: I grant him bloody,
   Luxurious,[15] avaricious, false, deceitful,
   Sudden,[16] malicious, smacking of every sin
   That has a name. But there's no bottom,
   none,
   In my voluptuousness. Your wives, your
   daughters,
   Your matrons, and your maids could not
   fill up
   The cistern of my lust; and my desire
   All continent impediments would o'erbear
   That did oppose my will. Better Macbeth
   Than such an one to reign.

MACDUFF: Boundless intemperance
   In nature[17] is a tyranny. It hath been
   Th' untimely emptying of the happy throne
   And fall of many kings. But fear not yet
   To take upon you what is yours. You
   may
   Convey[18] your pleasures in a spacious
   plenty,
   And yet seem cold—the time you may so
   hoodwink.
   We have willing dames enough. There can-
   not be
   That vulture in you to devour so many
   As will to greatness dedicate themselves
   Finding it so inclin'd.

MALCOLM: With this there grows
   In my most ill-composed affection[19] such
   A stanchless[20] avarice that, were I King,
   I should cut off the nobles for their lands,
   Desire his jewels, and this other's house,
   And my more-having would be as a sauce
   To make me hunger more, that I should
   forge
   Quarrels unjust against the good and loyal,
   Destroying them for wealth.

MACDUFF: This avarice
   Sticks deeper, grows with more pernicious
   root
   Than summer-seeming[21] lust; and it hath
   been
   The sword[22] of our slain kings. Yet do not
   fear.
   Scotland hath foisons to fill up your will
   Of your mere own.[23] All these are port-
   able,[24]
   With other graces weigh'd.

MALCOLM: But I have none. The king-becom-
   ing graces,
   As justice, verity, temperance, stableness,
   Bounty, perseverance, mercy, lowliness,
   Devotion, patience, courage, fortitude,
   I have no relish[25] of them, but abound
   In the division[26] of each several crime,
   Acting it many ways. Nay, had I power, I
   should
   Pour the sweet milk of concord into hell,
   Uproar the universal peace, confound
   All unity on earth.

MACDUFF: O Scotland, Scotland!

MALCOLM: If such a one be fit to govern,
   speak.
   I am as I have spoken.

MACDUFF: Fit to govern?
   No, not to live. O nation miserable,
   With an untitled tyrant bloody-scepter'd,
   When shalt thou see thy wholesome days
   again,
   Since that the truest issue of thy throne
   By his own interdiction[27] stands accurs'd
   And does blaspheme his breed? Thy royal
   father

---

14 *open'd:* in blossom. Like *grafted,* above, the image is drawn from flowers. 15 *Luxurious:* lecherous. 16 *Sudden:* violent. 17 *nature:* man's nature. 18 *Convey:* secretly manage. 19 *ill-composed affection:* evilly constituted character. 20 *stanchless:* unending. 21 *summer-seeming:* seemly for summer (i.e., youth?) 22 *sword:* cause of death. 23 *foisons to fill up your will of your mere own:* abundance enough of your own to satisfy your greed. 24 *portable:* supportable. 25 *relish of:* taste for. 26 *division:* variation. 27 *interdiction:* curse.

Was a most sainted king; the queen that bore thee,
Oftener upon her knees than on her feet,
Died[28] every day she lived. Fare thee well!
These evils thou repeat'st upon thyself
Have banish'd me from Scotland. O my breast,
Thy hope ends here!

MALCOLM: Macduff, this noble passion,
Child of integrity, hath from my soul
Wiped the black scruples[29] reconciled my thoughts
To thy good truth and honor. Devilish Macbeth
By many of these trains[30] hath sought to win me
Into his power; and modest wisdom plucks me
From over-credulous haste; but God above
Deal between thee and me! for even now
I put myself to[31] thy direction and
Unspeak mine own detraction, here abjure
The taints and blames I laid upon myself
For[32] strangers to my nature. I am yet
Unknown to woman, never was forsworn,
Scarcely have coveted what was mine own,
At no time broke my faith, would not betray
The devil to his fellow, and delight
No less in truth than life. My first false speaking
Was this upon myself. What I am truly,
Is thine and my poor country's to command;
Whither indeed, before thy here-approach,
Old Siward with ten thousand war-like men
Already at a point[33] was setting forth.
Now we'll together; and the chance of goodness
Be like our warranted quarrel![34] Why are you silent?

MACDUFF: Such welcome and unwelcome things at once
'Tis hard to reconcile.

(*Enter a* DOCTOR.)

MALCOLM: Well, more anon. Comes the King forth, I pray you?

DOCTOR: Ay, sir. There are a crew of wretched souls
That stay[35] his cure. Their malady convinces
The great assay of art;[36] but at his touch,
Such sanctity hath heaven given his hand,
They presently amend.

MALCOLM: I thank you, doctor.

(*Exit* DOCTOR.)

MACDUFF: What's the disease he means?

MALCOLM: 'Tis call'd the evil.[37]
A most miraculous work in this good king,
Which often since my here-remain in England
I have seen him do. How he solicits heaven
Himself best knows; but strangely-visited[38] people,
All swol'n and ulcerous, pitiful to the eye,
The mere[39] despair of surgery, he cures,
Hanging a golden stamp[40] about their necks,
Put on with holy prayers; and 'tis spoken,
To the succeeding royalty he leaves
The healing benediction. With this strange virtue,[41]
He hath a heavenly gift of prophecy,
And sundry blessings hang about his throne
That speak[42] him full of grace.

(*Enter* ROSS.)

MACDUFF: See who comes here.

MALCOLM: My countryman; but yet I know him not.[43]

---

28 *Died:* i.e., prepared for Heaven. 29 *scruples:* suspicions. 30 *trains:* plots. 31 *to:* in. 32 *For:* as. 33 *at a point:* ready. 34 *"chance . . . quarrel":* "May our chance of success be equal to the justice of our cause." 35 *stay:* await. 36 *Their malady . . . art:* "Their sickness defies all efforts of medical science." 37 *the evil:* scrofula, which English kings (including James) used to touch people to cure. 38 *strangely-visited:* oddly afflicted. If the skin eruption was psychosomatic, the King's Touch might well cure it. 39 *mere:* utter. 40 *stamp:* medal or coin. 41 *virtue:* power. 42 *speak:* proclaim. 43 *know him not:* he is recognized by his costume as a Scot.

MACDUFF: My ever gentle cousin, welcome
hither.

MALCOLM: I know him now. Good God betimes
remove
The means[44] that makes us strangers!

ROSS: Sir, amen.

MACDUFF: Stands Scotland where it did?

ROSS: Alas, poor country,
Almost afraid to know itself! It cannot
Be call'd our mother, but our grave; where
nothing,[45]
But who knows nothing, is once seen to
smile;
Where sighs and groans, and shrieks that
rent the air,
Are made, not mark'd;[46] where violent
sorrow seems
A modern ecstasy.[47] The dead man's knell
Is there scarce ask'd for who; and good
men's lives
Expire before the flowers in their caps,
Dying or ere they sicken.

MACDUFF: O, relation
Too nice,[48] and yet too true!

MALCOLM: What's the newest grief?

ROSS: That of an hour's age doth hiss the
speaker;[49]
Each minute teems a new one.

MACDUFF: How does my wife?

ROSS: Why, well.

MACDUFF: And all my children?

ROSS: Well too.

MACDUFF: The tyrant has not batter'd at their
peace?

ROSS: No; they were well at peace when I did
leave 'em.

MACDUFF: Be not a niggard of your speech.
How goes't?

ROSS: When I came hither to transport the
tidings
Which I have heavily[50] borne, there ran a
rumor

Of many worthy fellows that were out;[51]
Which was to my belief witness'd the rather
For that I saw the tyrant's power[52] afoot.
Now is the time of help. Your eye[53] in Scot-
land
Would create soldiers, make our women
fight
To doff their dire distresses.

MALCOLM: Be't their comfort
We are coming thither. Gracious England
hath
Lent us good Siward and ten thousand
men.
An older and a better soldier none
That Christendom gives out.

ROSS: Would I could answer
This comfort with the like! But I have
words
That would be howl'd out in the desert air,
Where hearing should not latch[54] them.

MACDUFF: What concern they?
The general cause? or is it a fee-grief[55]
Due to some single breast?

ROSS: No mind that's honest
But in it shares some woe, though the main
part
Pertains to you alone.

MACDUFF: If it be mine,
Keep it not from me, quickly let me have
it.

ROSS: Let not your ears despise my tongue for
ever,
Which shall possess them with the heaviest
sound
That ever yet they heard.

MACDUFF: Humh! I guess at it.

---

44 *means:* Macbeth's rule. 45 *nothing:* no one. 46
mark'd: noticed. 47 *modern ecstasy:* ordinary emotion. 48 *Too nice:* too accurate. 49 *That of an hour's
age doth hiss the speaker:* "The newest grief when
an hour old is hissed [as stale news]." 50 *heavily:*
sadly. 51 *out:* up in arms. 52 *tyrant's power:* Macbeth's army. 53 *eye:* presence (or, sight of you?).
54 *latch:* catch. 55 *fee-grief:* personal sorrow.

Ross: Your castle is surprised; your wife and
  babes
  Savagely slaughter'd. To relate the manner,
  Were, on the quarry of these murder'd
  deer,
  To add the death of you.

Malcolm: Merciful heaven!
  What, man! Ne'er pull your hat upon your
  brows.
  Give sorrow words. The grief that does not
  speak
  Whispers the o'erfraught heart and bids
  it break.

Macduff: My children too?

Ross: Wife, children, servants, all
  That could be found.

Macduff: And I must be from thence?
  My wife kill'd too?

Ross: I have said.

Malcolm: Be comforted.
  Let's make us medicines of our great
  revenge
  To cure this deadly grief.

Macduff: He has no children.[56] All my pretty
  ones?
  Did you say all? O hell-kite![57] All?
  What, all my pretty chickens and their dam
  At one fell swoop?

Malcolm: Dispute[58] it like a man.

Macduff: I shall do so;
  But I must also feel it as a man.
  I cannot but remember such things were
  That were most precious to me. Did heaven
  look on
  And would not take their part? Sinful Mac-
  duff,
  They were all struck for thee! Naught[59] that
  I am,
  Not for their own demerits, but for mine,
  Fell slaughter on their souls. Heaven rest
  them now!

Malcolm: Be this the whetstone of your
  sword. Let grief
  Convert to anger; blunt not the heart, enrage it.

Macduff: O, I could play the woman with mine
  eyes
  And braggart with my tongue! But, gentle
  heavens,
  Cut short all intermission. Front to front[60]
  Bring thou this fiend of Scotland and my-
  self.
  Within my sword's length set him. If he
  scape,
  Heaven forgive him too!

Malcolm: This tune goes manly.
  Come, go we to the King. Our power is
  ready;
  Our lack is nothing but our leave.[61] Mac-
  beth
  Is ripe for shaking, and the powers above
  Put on their instruments.[62] Receive what
  cheer you may.
  The night is long that never finds the day.

(*Exeunt.*)

ACT FIVE[1]

Scene One   Dunsinane. Macbeth's castle.

Enter a Doctor of Physic *and a* Waiting-
Gentlewoman.

---

56 *He has no children:* Cf. I, viii, 54. There is a famous
essay by L. C. Knights on "How Many Children Had
Lady Macbeth" (1933) and much critical confusion
about this apparent contradiction in the play, though
the problem is solved simply by imagining that Macbeth's children died in infancy or, at any rate, before
this point in time.   57 *hell-kite:* hellish bird of prey.
58 *Dispute:* answer.   59 *Naught:* wicked.   60 *Front to
front:* face to face.   61 *Our lack is nothing but our
leave:* "Nothing remains for us to do but to take our
leave."   62 *Put on their instruments:* arm themselves.

1 ACT V. The text of *Macbeth* is based on the Folio
text (1623), which seems to have been based on a playhouse prompt-book (or a transcript), in turn adapted
from Shakespeare's holograph manuscript. The state
of the meter and rhyme in Act V suggests that Shakespeare finished the play in a great hurry or else that
this inferior material was from a collaborator or (as in
the case of the Hecate scenes earlier) a revisor.

DOCTOR: I have two nights watched with you, but can perceive no truth in your report. When was it she last walked?

GENTLEWOMAN: Since his Majesty went into the field I have seen her rise from her bed, throw her nightgown upon her, unlock her closet,[2] take forth paper, fold it, write upon't, read it, afterwards seal it, and again return to bed; yet all this while in a most fast sleep.

DOCTOR: A great perturbation in nature, to receive at once the benefit of sleep and do the effects of watching![3] In this slumb'ry agitation, besides her walking and other actual performances, what, at any time, have you heard her say?

GENTLEWOMAN: That, sir, which I will not report after her.

DOCTOR: You may to me, and 'tis most meet you should.

GENTLEWOMAN: Neither to you nor any one, having no witness to confirm my speech.

(*Enter* LADY MACBETH, *with a taper.*)

Lo you, here she comes! This is her very guise,[4] and, upon my life, fast asleep! Observe her; stand close.

DOCTOR: How come she by that light?

GENTLEWOMAN: Why, it stood by her. She has light by her continually.
'Tis her command.

DOCTOR: You see her eyes are open.

GENTLEWOMAN: Ay; but their sense[5] is shut.

DOCTOR: What is it she does now? Look how she rubs her hands.

GENTLEWOMAN: It is an accustomed action with her, to seem thus washing her hands. I have known her continue in this a quarter of an hour.

LADY: Yet here's a spot.

DOCTOR: Hark, she speaks! I will set down what comes from her, to satisfy[6] my remembrance the more strongly.

LADY: Out, damned spot! out, I say! One; two. Why then 'tis time to do 't. Hell is murky. Fie, my lord, fie! a soldier, and afeard? What need we fear who knows it, when none can call our power to account? Yet who would have thought the old man to have had so much blood in him?[7]

DOCTOR: Do you mark that?

LADY: The Thane of Fife had a wife. Where is she now? What, will these hands ne'er be clean? No more o' that, my lord, no more o' that! You mar all with this starting.

DOCTOR: Go to, go to! You have known what you should not.

GENTLEWOMAN: She has spoke what she should not, I am sure of that. Heaven knows what she has known.

LADY: Here's the smell of the blood still. All the perfumes of Arabia will not sweeten this little hand. Oh, oh, oh!

DOCTOR: What a sigh is there! The heart is sorely charged.[8]

GENTLEWOMAN: I would not have such a heart in my bosom for the dignity of the whole body.

DOCTOR: Well, well, well.

GENTLEWOMAN: Pray God it be, sir.

DOCTOR: This disease is beyond my practice.[9] Yet I have known those which have walked in their sleep who have died holily in their beds.

LADY: Wash your hands, put on your nightgown, look not so pale! I tell you yet again,

---

2 *closet:* ordinarily a small room, here perhaps a chest. 3 *effects of watching:* acts of a person awake. 4 *guise:* custom. 5 *sense:* sight. 6 *satisfy:* confirm. 7 *Out . . . blood in him:* Here, and elsewhere in her sleepwalking speeches, note how Lady Macbeth, recalling phrases and scenes that have caused her guilt, summarizes earlier action of the play. For example, "one, two" refers to the bell struck to summon Macbeth to the murder. 8 *sorely charged:* heavily laden. 9 *practice:* professional experience (or skill).

Banquo's buried. He cannot come out on 's[10] grave.

DOCTOR: Even so?

LADY: To bed, to bed! There's knocking at the gate. Come, come, come, come, give me your hand! What's done cannot be undone. To bed, to bed, to bed!

(*Exit.*)

DOCTOR: Will she go now to bed?

GENTLEWOMAN: Directly.

DOCTOR: Foul whisperings are abroad. Unnatural deeds
Do breed unnatural troubles. Infected minds
To their deaf pillows will discharge their secrets.
More needs she the divine than the physician.
God, God forgive us all! Look after her;
Remove from her the means of all annoyance,[11]
And still keep eyes upon her. So good night.
My mind she has mated,[12] and amazed my sight.
I think, but dare not speak.

GENTLEWOMAN: Good night, good doctor.

(*Exeunt.*)

SCENE TWO   The country near Dunsinane.

Drum and Colors. Enter MENTEITH, CAITHNESS, ANGUS, LENNOX, SOLDIERS.

MENTEITH: The English power is near, led on by Malcolm,
His uncle Siward, and the good Macduff.
Revenges burn in them; for their dear causes
Would to the bleeding and the grim alarm
Excite the mortified[1] man.

ANGUS: Near Birnam Wood
Shall we well meet them; that way are they coming.

CAITHNESS: Who knows if Donalbain be with his brother?

LENNOX: For certain, sir, he is not. I have a file[2]
Of all the gentry. There is Siward's son
And many unrough[3] youths that even now
Protest[4] their first of manhood.

MENTEITH: What does the tyrant?

CAITHNESS: Great Dunsinane he strongly fortifies.
Some say he's mad; others, that lesser hate him,
Do call it valiant fury; but for certain
He cannot buckle his distemper'd[5] cause
Within the belt of rule.[6]

ANGUS: Now does he feel
His secret murders sticking on his hands.
Now minutely revolts upbraid his faith-breach.[7]
Those he commands move only in command,
Nothing in love. Now does he feel his title
Hang loose about him, like a giant's robe
Upon a dwarfish thief.

MENTEITH: Who then shall blame
His pester'd[8] senses to recoil and start,
When all that is within him does condemn
Itself for being there?

CAITHNESS: Well, march we on
To give obedience where 'tis truly owed.
Meet we the medicine of the sickly weal;[9]
And with him pour we in our country's purge
Each drop of us.[10]

---

10 *out on's:* out of his. **11** *annoyance:* injury. **12** *mated:* baffled.

1 *mortified:* dead. **2** *file:* list. **3** *unrough:* beardless. **4** *Protest:* assert. **5** *distemper'd:* swollen. **6** *rule:* control. **7** *Now . . . faith-breach:* "Now every minute rebellions rebuke his breach of faith." **8** *pester'd:* tormented. **9** *Meet we the medicine of the sickly weal:* "Let us meet up with (Malcolm) the cure of the sickness of our state." **10** *Each drop of us:* "Every drop of our blood."

LENNOX: Or so much as it needs
  To dew the sovereign[11] flower and drown
    the weeds.
  Make we our march towards Birnam.

(*Exeunt, marching.*)

SCENE THREE Dunsinane. A room in the
castle.

Enter MACBETH, DOCTOR, *and* ATTENDANTS.

MACBETH: Bring me no more reports. Let them[1]
  fly all!
  Till Birnam Wood remove to Dunsinane,
  I cannot taint with fear. What's the boy
    Malcolm?
  Was he not born of woman? The spirits
    that know
  All mortal consequences have pronounced
    me thus:
  'Fear not, Macbeth. No man that's born of
    woman
  Shall e'er have power upon thee.' Then fly,
    false thanes,
  And mingle with the English epicures.
  The mind I sway[2] by and the heart I bear
  Shall never sag with doubt nor shake with
    fear.

(*Enter* SERVANT.)

  The devil damn thee black, thou cream-
    faced loon![3]
  Where got'st thou that goose look?

SERVANT: There is ten thousand —

MACBETH: Geese, villain?

SERVANT: Soldiers, sir.

MACBETH: Go prick thy face and over-red[4] thy
  fear,
  Thou lily-liver'd boy. What soldiers,
    patch?[5]
  Death of thy soul! Those linen[6] cheeks of
    thine
  Are counsellors to fear. What soldiers,
    whey-face?

SERVANT: The English force, so please you.

MACBETH: Take thy face hence.

(*Exit* SERVANT.)

                Seyton! — I am sick at heart,
  When I behold — Seyton, I say! — This
    push[7]
  Will cheer me ever, or disseat me now.[8]
  I have lived long enough. My way of life
  Is fallen into the sere,[9] the yellow leaf;
  And that which should accompany old age,
  As honor, love, obedience, troops of
    friends,
  I must not look to have; but, in their stead,
  Curses not loud but deep, mouth-honor[10]
    breath,
  Which the poor heart would fain deny, and
    dare not.
  Seyton!

(*Enter* SEYTON.)

SEYTON: What's your gracious pleasure?

MACBETH: What news more?

SEYTON: All is confirmed, my lord, which was
  reported.

MACBETH: I'll fight, till from my bones my
  flesh be hacked.
  Give me my armor.

SEYTON: 'Tis not needed yet.

MACBETH: I'll put it on.
  Send out moe horses,[11] skirr[12] the country
    round;
  Hang those that talk of fear. Give me mine
    armor.
  How does your patient, doctor?

---

11 *dew the sovereign:* make grow the royal (or
remedial).

1 *them:* Macbeth's nobles. 2 *sway:* hold sway. 3
loon: fool. 4 *over-red:* cover with red. 5 *patch:*
fool. 6 *linen:* i.e., white. 7 *push:* effort. 8 *Will
cheer me ever, or disseat me now:* "Will cheer [then
pronounced *chair*] me ever, or unthrone me evermore."
Elizabethan pronunciation made puns possible (for
instance on *room* and *Rome,* pronounced alike in
Julius Caesar) and rhymes obvious which the modern
reader or audience cannot notice. 9 *sere:* withered.
10 *mouth-honor:* empty flattery, lip service. 11 *moe
horses:* more horsemen. 12 *skirr:* scour.

DOCTOR: Not so sick, my lord,
  As she is troubled with thick-coming fan-
    cies
  That keep her from her rest.

MACBETH: Cure her of that!
  Canst thou not minister to a mind dis-
    eased,
  Pluck from the memory a rooted sorrow,
  Raze out[13] the written troubles of the brain
  And with some sweet oblivious[14] antidote
  Cleanse the stuff'd bosom of that perilous
    stuff
  Which weighs upon the heart?

DOCTOR: Therein the patient
  Must minister to himself.

MACBETH: Throw physic to the dogs, I'll none
    of it! —
  Come, put mine armor on. Give me my
    staff. —
  Seyton, send out. — Doctor, the thanes fly
    from me. —
  Come, sir, dispatch.[15] — If thou couldst,
    doctor, cast
  The water[16] of my land, find her disease,
  And purge it to a sound and pristine health,
  I would applaud thee to the very echo,
  That should applaud again. — Pull't off, I
    say.[17] —
  What rhubarb, senna, or what purgative
    drug,
  Would scour these English hence? Hear'st
    thou of them?

DOCTOR: Ay, my good lord. Your royal pre-
    paration
  Makes us hear something.

MACBETH: Bring it after me![18]
  I will not be afraid of death and bane
  Till Birnam Forest come to Dunsinane.

(Exeunt all but the DOCTOR.)

DOCTOR: Were I from Dunsinane away and
    clear,
  Profit again should hardly draw me here.

(Exit.)

SCENE FOUR   Country near Birnam Wood.

Drum and colors. Enter MALCOLM, SIWARD,
MACDUFF, SIWARD'S SON, MENTEITH, CAITH-
NESS, ANGUS, LENNOX, ROSS, and SOLDIERS,
marching.

MALCOLM: Cousins, I hope the days are near
    at hand
  That chambers[1] will be safe.

MENTEITH: We doubt it nothing.[2]

SIWARD: What wood is this before us?

MENTEITH: The Wood of Birnam.

MALCOLM: Let every soldier hew him down a
    bough
  And bear't before him. Thereby shall we
    shadow[3]
  The numbers of our host and make dis-
    covery[4]
  Err in report of us.

SOLDIERS: It shall be done.

SIWARD: We learn no other but the confident
    tyrant
  Keeps still in Dunsinane and will endure
  Our setting down before't.[5]

MALCOLM: 'Tis his main hope;
  For where there is advantage to be given,
  Both more and less[6] have given him the
    revolt;
  And none serve with him but constrained
    things,
  Whose hearts are absent too.

MACDUFF: Let our just censures
  Attend the true event,[7] and put we on
  Industrious soldiership.
SIWARD: The time approaches

---

13 *Raze out:* erase. **14** *oblivious:* causing oblivion.
15 *dispatch:* hurry. **16** *cast the water:* analyze the
urine. **17** *off, I say:* Macbeth is speaking of some
armor he has been putting on. **18** *Bring it:* the piece
of armor.

1 *chambers:* a man's home. **2** *We doubt it nothing:*
"We don't doubt it." **3** *shadow:* conceal. **4** *discovery:* reconnaissance. **5** *endure . . . before't:* will
permit it to be beseiged. **6** *more and less:* men both
high and low. **7** *Let our just censures attend the true
event:* "Let our justifiable criticism await the outcome
of our action."

That will with due decision make us know
What we shall say we have, and what we
    owe.[8]
Thoughts speculative their unsure hopes
    relate,
But certain issue strokes must arbitrate;
Towards which advance the war.

(*Exeunt, marching.*)

SCENE FIVE   Dunsinane. Within the castle.

Enter MACBETH, SEYTON, *and* SOLDIERS, *with
drum and colors.*

MACBETH: Hang out our banners on the out-
    ward walls.
    The cry is still, 'They come!' Our castle's
        strength
    Will laugh a siege to scorn. Here let them
        lie
    Till famine and the ague[1] eat them up.
    Were they not forced[2] with those that should
        be ours,
    We might have met them dareful,[3] beard to
        beard,
    And beat them backward home.

(*A cry within of women.*)

                        What is that noise?

SEYTON: It is the cry of women, my good lord.

(*Exit.*)

MACBETH: I have almost forgot the taste of
    fears.
    The time has been, my senses would have
        cool'd
    To hear a night-shriek, and my fell[4] of hair
    Would at a dismal treatise rouse and stir
    As life were in't. I have supp'd full with
        horrors.
    Direness, familiar to my slaughterous
        thoughts,
    Cannot once start[5] me.

(*Enter* SEYTON.)

                        Wherefore was that cry?

SEYTON: The Queen, my lord, is dead.

MACBETH: She should[6] have died hereafter;

There would have been a time for such a
    word.[7]
To-morrow, and to-morrow, and to-morrow
Creeps in this petty pace from day to day
To the last syllable of recorded time;
And all our yesterdays have lighted fools
The way to dusty death. Out, out, brief
    candle!
Life's but a walking shadow, a poor player,
That struts and frets his hour upon the
    stage
And then is heard no more. It is a tale
Told by an idiot, full of sound and fury,
Signifying nothing.[8]

(*Enter a* MESSENGER.)

Thou com'st to use thy tongue. Thy story
    quickly!
MESSENGER: Gracious my lord,
    I should report that which I say I saw,
    But know not how to do't.

MACBETH: Well, say, sir!

MESSENGER: As I did stand my watch upon the
    hill,
    I look'd toward Birnam, and anon methought
    The wood began to move.

MACBETH: Liar and slave!

MESSENGER: Let me endure your wrath if 't be
    not so.
    Within this three mile may you see it com-
        ing;

---

8 *owe:* own.

1 *ague:* fever. 2 *forced:* reinforced. 3 *dareful:* dar-
ingly. 4 *fell:* pelt. 5 *start:* startle. 6 *should:* either
"should preferably" or "should inevitably." 7 *word:*
message. "Finally, his sensibility has grown so dull
that even the intelligence of his wife's death . . .
hardly touches him, and seems little more than one
additional incident in the weary, meaningless tale of
human life" — Edward Dowden (1875). 8 *To-morrow
. . . nothing:* "My opinion is that Macbeth's soliloquies
are not poetry but rhetoric. They are tirades. That is,
they do not trace any pensive motion of the soul or
heart but are a volley of words discharged. Macbeth
is neither thinking nor feeling aloud; he is declaiming" — Mary McCarthy (1962).

I say, a moving grove.

MACBETH: If thou speak'st false,
Upon the next tree shalt thou hang alive,
Till famine cling[9] thee. If thy speech be
    sooth,[10]
I care not if thou dost for me as much.
I pull in resolution,[11] and begin
To doubt th' equivocation of the fiend,
That lies like truth. 'Fear not, till Birnam
    Wood
Do come to Dunsinane!' and now a
    wood
Comes toward Dunsinane. Arm, arm, and
    out!
If this which he avouches[12] does appear,
There is nor flying hence nor tarrying here.
I 'gin to be aweary of the sun,[13]
And wish th' estate[14] o' th' world were now
    undone.
Ring the alarum bell! Blow wind, come
    wrack,[15]
At least we'll die with harness on our
    back![16]

(*Exeunt.*)

SCENE SIX   Dunsinane. Before the castle.

Drum and colors.[1] *Enter* MALCOLM, SIWARD,
MACDUFF, *and their* ARMY, *with boughs.*

MALCOLM: Now near enough. Your leavy
    screens throw down
    And show like those you are. You, worthy
        uncle,
    Shall with my cousin, your right noble son,
    Lead our first battle. Worthy Macduff and
        we
    Shall take upon 's what else remains to
        do,
    According to our order.

SIWARD: Fare you well.
    Do we[2] but find the tyrant's power to-night,
    Let us be beaten if we cannot fight.

MACDUFF: Make all our trumpets speak, give
    them all breath,
    Those clamorous harbingers of blood and
        death.

(*Exeunt. Alarums continued.*)

SCENE SEVEN   Another part of the field.

Enter MACBETH.

MACBETH: They have tied me to a stake. I
    cannot fly,
    But bear-like I must fight the course.[1] What's
        he
    That was not born of woman? Such a one
    Am I to fear, or none.

(*Enter* YOUNG SIWARD.)

YOUNG SIWARD: What is thy name?

MACBETH: Thou'lt be afraid to hear it.

YOUNG SIWARD: No; though thou call'st thy-
    self a hotter name
    Than any is in hell.

MACBETH: My name's Macbeth.

YOUNG SIWARD: The devil himself could not
    pronounce a title
    More hateful to mine ear.

MACBETH: No, nor more fearful.

YOUNG SIWARD: Thou liest, abhorred tyrant!
    With my sword
    I'll prove the lie thou speak'st.

---

9 *cling:* wither. 10 *sooth:* truth. 11 *pull in resolution:* put reins on confidence. 12 *avouches:* vouches
to. 13 *sun:* life. But, in a Theory of Order in which
each thing or person is in a hierarchy and each hierarchy parallels the others, the sun = the King (as it
also equals the oak, gold, the lion, the best of each
list), so Macbeth may also be saying he is weary of
kingship. 14 *estate:* order. 15 *wrack:* ruin. 16 *harness on our back:* Macbeth's courage in facing ruin
when even hopes desert him endears to us a man who
has throughout the play waded in blood and adds
another dimension to a man more complex than a
simple villain who "acts in the end as the Macbeth
whose praises we have heard in the second scene of
the play" — R. S. Crane (1953). Crane suggests that in
the end we want Macbeth to die as much for his own
peace as for justice.

1 *colors:* flags.   2 *Do we:* if we.

1 *fight the course:* a reference to the popular Elizabethan sport of bear-baiting.

(*Fight, and* YOUNG SIWARD *slain.*)

MACBETH: Thou wast born of woman.
  But swords I smile at, weapons laugh to
    scorn,
  Brandish'd by man that's of a woman born.

(*Exit.*)

(*Alarums. Enter* MACDUFF.)

MACDUFF: That way the noise is. Tyrant, show
    thy face!
  If thou be'st slain and with no stroke of
    mine,
  My wife and children's ghosts will haunt
    me still.
  I cannot strike at wretched kerns, whose
    arms
  Are hired to bear their staves.[2] Either thou,
    Macbeth,
  Or else my sword with an unbattered edge
  I sheathe again undeeded.[3] There thou
    shouldst be.
  By this great clatter one of greatest note
  Seems bruited.[4] Let me find him, Fortune!
  And more I beg not.

(*Exit. Alarums.*)

(*Enter* MALCOLM *and* SIWARD.)

SIWARD: This way, my lord. The castle's
    gently render'd.[5]
  The tyrant's people on both sides do
    fight;
  The noble thanes do bravely in the war;
  The day almost itself professes[6] yours,
  And little is to do.

MALCOLM: We have met with foes
  That strike beside us.[7]

SIWARD: Enter, sir, the castle.

(*Exeunt. Alarum.*)

SCENE EIGHT   Another part of the field.

Enter MACBETH.

MACBETH: Why should I play the Roman fool
    and die
  On mine own sword?[1] Whiles I see lives,
    the gashes

Do better upon them.[2]

(*Enter* MACDUFF.)

MACDUFF: Turn, hellhound, turn!

MACBETH: Of all men else I have avoided
    thee.
  But get thee back! My soul is too much
    charged
  With blood of thine already.

MACDUFF: I have no words;
  My voice is in my sword, thou bloodier
    villain
  Than terms can give thee out![3]

(*Fight. Alarum.*)

MACBETH: Thou losest labor.
  As easy mayst thou the intrenchant[4] air
  With thy keen sword impress as make me
    bleed.
  Let fall thy blade on vulnerable crests.
  I bear a charmed life, which must not yield
  To one of woman born.

MACDUFF: Despair thy charm!
  And let the angel[5] whom thou still hast
    served
  Tell thee, Macduff was from his mother's
    womb
  Untimely ripp'd.[6]

MACBETH: Accursed be that tongue that tells
    me so,

---

2 *staves:* spears. 3 *undeeded:* having done nothing.
4 *bruited:* announced. 5 *gently render'd:* given up
without a struggle. 6 *professes:* declares itself. 7
strike beside us: fight along with us (or deliberately
miss striking us).

1 *On my own sword:* Brutus (*Julius Caesar*) and other
Stoic Romans committed suicide by running on their
own swords. 2 *Whiles I see lives, the gashes do
better upon them:* "As long as I see other men living
it is better to inflict the wounds upon them [than on
myself]." 3 *give thee out:* describe. 4 *intrenchant:*
uncuttable. 5 *angel:* Devil [fallen angel Lucifer]. 6
Untimely ripp'd: prematurely born [by Caesarian section?], excluding him from the "man of woman born"
category on a technicality.

For it hath cow'd my better part of man![7]
And be these juggling fiends no more be-
lieved,
That palter[8] with us in a double sense,
That keep the word of promise to our ear
And break it to our hope! I'll not fight with
thee!

MACDUFF: Then yield thee, coward,
And live to be the show and gaze o' th'
time!
We'll have thee, as our rarer monsters
are,
Painted upon a pole, and underwrit
'Here may you see the tyrant.'[9]

MACBETH: I will not yield,
To kiss the ground before young Malcolm's
feet
And to be baited with the rabble's curse.
Though Birnam Wood be come to Dun-
sinane,
And thou opposed, being of no woman
born,
Yet I will try the last. Before my body
I throw my warlike shield. Lay on, Macduff,
And damn'd be him that first cries 'Hold,
enough!'

(*Exeunt fighting.*[10] *Alarums.*)

(*Retreat and flourish. Enter, with drum and
colors,* MALCOLM, SIWARD, ROSS, THANES, *and*
SOLDIERS.)

MALCOLM: I would the friends we miss were
safe arrived.

SIWARD: Some must go off;[11] and yet, by these
I see,
So great a day as this is cheaply bought.

MALCOLM: Macduff is missing, and your noble
son.

ROSS: Your son, my lord, has paid a soldier's
debt.
He only lived but till he was a man,
The which no sooner had his prowess con-
firm'd
In the unshrinking station[12] where he fought
But like a man he died.

SIWARD: Then he is dead?

ROSS: Ay, and brought off the field. Your
cause of sorrow
Must not be measured by his worth, for
then
It hath no end.

SIWARD: Had he his hurts before?

ROSS: Ay, on the front.

SIWARD: Why then, God's soldier be he!
Had I as many sons as I have hairs,
I would not wish them to a fairer death.
And so his knell is knoll'd.

MALCOLM: He's worth more sorrow,
And that I'll spend for him.

SIWARD: He's worth no more.
They say he parted well and paid his score,
And so, God be with him! Here comes
newer comfort.

(*Enter* MACDUFF, *with* MACBETH's *head.*)

MACDUFF: Hail, King! for so thou art. Behold
where stands
Th' usurper's cursed head. The time is free.[13]
I see thee compass'd with thy kingdom's
pearl,[14]
That speak my salutation in their minds;
Whose voices I desire aloud with mine —
Hail, King of Scotland!

ALL: Hail, King of Scotland!

(*Flourish.*)

MALCOLM: We shall not spend a large expense
of time

---

7 *better part of man:* spirit. **8** *palter:* play false. **9**
the tyrant: Macduff threatens to exhibit a captive Macbeth as a side-show freak. **10** *Exeunt fighting:* We
cannot see the death of Macbeth because if he is
killed on stage the lack of a curtain will make it awkward to carry off the corpse (as in *Hamlet*). Moreover, the plot calls for Macbeth's head to be severed
and carried on a spear, a trick unstageable on the
Elizabethan platform (and often played down or
omitted entirely in our less blood-thirsty modern
times). **11** *go off:* die. Note the theatrical language.
12 *unshrinking station:* he held his ground. **13** *The
time is free:* "The people are liberated." **14** *kingdom's pearl:* wise nobility.

Before we reckon with your several loves[15]
And make us even with you. My thanes and kinsmen,
Henceforth be earls, the first that ever Scotland
In such an honor named. What's more to do
Which would be planted newly with the time —
As calling home our exiled friends abroad
That fled the snares of watchful tyranny,
Producing forth the cruel ministers[16]
Of this dead butcher and his fiend-like queen,
Who, as 'tis thought, by self and violent hands[17]
Took off her life — this, and what needful else
That calls upon us,[18] by the grace of Grace
We will perform in measure,[19] time, and place.
So thanks to all at once and to each one,

Whom we invite to see us crown'd at Scone.[20]

(*Flourish. Exeunt omnes.*)

---

15 *reckon with your several loves:* reward your individual services. **16** *ministers:* agents. **17** *self and violent hands:* suicide. There is some suggestion that this charge might be true in the doctor's attempt to take precaution against it (V, i, 84) and that she lacked the hardness of heart to live with her evil, that the unsexing and resolve she sought failed to dehumanize her. **18** *calls upon us:* demands our [the royal plural] attention. **19** *in measure:* fittingly. **20** *crown'd at Scone:* If Malcolm is so determined to do things "in measure, time, and place," he might well have staged a legal election of himself as king before announcing his formal coronation on the Stone of Scone. But the play ends with order restored and violence, cancelled by more violence, has given way to peace.

The Country Wife

The *Interregnum* of the Puritans
Contriv'd to put a Pax on Song and Dance,
Suppress'd the Theatre; and the Law held sway
Until our good King CHARLES's golden Day.
But with the Restoration, Theatres two
(In Drury Lane and The Haymarket too)
Were once again set up for publick View.
Soon others follow'd, legally and not,
And Restoration Drama was begot.
The Drama flourish'd for the Cavaliers,
Their Ladies (masked, as if to hide their Fears);
Some worthy Burghers and some Citizens
Also with Pit and Boxes soon made friends.
One of the most sophisticated Men
Who fed this hungry Publick by their Pen
Was "Manly" WILLIAM WYCHERLEY, who wrote
The Country Wife, our Comedy of note.
Now, CONGREVE's masterpiece *Way of the World*
Is most ingeniously knit and purl'd
But the Design's so intricate that here
The Country Wife much better doth appear.
It pictures *mores* as licentious
With equal Smut but without so much fuss.
Moreover, in his Language, WYCHERLEY
Has little Rhet'ric, more Reality
And, if his meaty Matter have a Fault,
'Tis only 'tis preserv'd with too much Salt.
No less than CONGREVE he'll catch on his Page
Th' bewigged, beribboned, and benighted Age,
With Satire and with Sense, with Force and Fun,
Restore to us the Restoration.
  WYCHERLEY only four Plays ever writ
But each of them was a comedick Hit.
In Sixteen Seventy-One *Love in a Wood*
Began his Favor, and it did him Good
Both in his Bedroom and upon the Stage,

As sometime happen'd in that bawdy Age,
For through it he met *Lady* CLEVELAND,
A duchess King CHARLES once had had in hand.
Later our Author did obtain a Post
With BUCKINGHAM, a duke who wrote the most
Droll Play call'd *The Rehearsal*. Later on
Our Author was the tutor to the Son
Of CHARLES himself (the Son being natural).
Then from high Patronage our man did fall
For marrying a Countess shunned by all.
She died, and he inherited her Debt.
For four Years went to Jail. He'd be there yet
Except in Sixteen Hundred Eighty-Five
King JAMES II being then alive
Pried him from Prison and a Pension Paid
Because of *The Plain Dealer* that he made.
(Earlier on, despite his busy life
The Dancing Master and *The Country Wife*
He'd manag'd to indite. They did arrive
In Sixteen Seventy-Two and Seventy-Five.)
A country Hermit, City Friend of POPE,
He lived and died. The latter dash'd the Hope
Of an obnoxious Nephew, would-be Heir,
Whom WYCHERLEY quite wittily could tell:
"My Deathbed is my Marriage-bed as well."
Eleven days before he died, he wed.
He cut the Nephew live; *she* cut him dead.
    Our Author who termed Love "London Disease"
Could not succeeding Sentimentals please.
Nor could Victorians approve a Chap
Who us'd Expressions like "Horn" and "the Clap."
But he's outlived MACAULAY's old reproach
("Filthy to handle, noisome to approach")
And in the Modern Theatre's still a hit—
A Master of The Comedy of Wit!
    The Country Wife he based upon a plot
Of *Eunuchus* which Roman TERENCE got
From some old Tale of a comick Philander
Invented by the Attic bard MENANDER.
And so the first Ingredient: *Something old*.
And then on SHADWELL he improv'd (so bold)
And then from JONSON he took Humours plain
And gave a Twist. That's *Something new* again.
And then from MOLIÈRE Suggestions few:
That's *Something borrowed*. And for *Something blue*
His bawdy wit and Smut from London's Street.

Put it together, and the Play's complete.
   Now as ye read it see the grand Design:
For read for Structure and not Line-by-Line.
See at the Centre Margery PINCHWIFE
Wed to a Gentleman who all his Life
With Fraud, Hypocrisy, and Hope of Gain
Th' Establishment still struggles to maintain.
See all around, corrupt, with Affectation
Swirl all the "civilized" of this, our Nation.
Enter to them one Horner, horny Rake
Willing to take a Wife. (*Whose* Wife to take?)
See him plead impotent. He thus contrives
To cuckold Gentry with their willing Wives.
What will the Outcome be, I hear you ask,
Intrigue and then the Falling of the Mask?
With Mr. PINCHWIFE's sister and her Beau
The Sub-Plot may go as ye wish, y' know,
But in the World of Fidgets, Quacks, and Sparks,
Of Gulls and Parrots and young Horner's Larks,
Both Common Sense and Cynicism say
The *Status Quo* of Surfaces must stay:
The World of Screen, and Fan, Mask and Façade
Remains—and underneath the evil and the flaw'd.
They're Restoration born so let 'em rest.
If *we* learn and reform that's for the Best.
   So look into this highly-polish'd Play
   And see your Face, and mend it while ye may.

L.R.N.A.

THE COUNTRY WIFE

A Comedy,
Acted at the Theatre-Royal

William Wycherley

THE PERSONS

Mr. HORNER*
Mr. HARCOURT
Mr. DORILANT
Mr. PINCHWIFE
Mr. SPARKISH**
Sir JASPER FIDGET
Mrs. MARGERY PINCHWIFE
Mrs. ALITHEA PINCHWIFE
Lady FIDGET
Mrs. DAINTY FIDGET
Mrs. SQUEAMISH
Old Lady SQUEAMISH
A QUACK
LUCY, ALITHEA's *Maid*
A BOY
WAITERS, SERVANTS, *and* ATTENDANTS

THE SCENE: LONDON, 1675

[*Mr. is pronounced "Master" and Mrs. ("Mistress") is used both for married and unmarried women.*]

Note: The text is based on the quarto printed for Thomas Dring, London, 1675, but has been modernized in spelling, capitalization, and punctuation, and incorporates certain emendations in the speeches and stage directions.
* *Horner* suggested to the Restoration audience the "horning" (cuckolding) of husbands.
** *Sparkish* meant having gallant airs. Always examine the names a dramatist gives for clues to personality or significance, even though modern practice has tended away from obvious names such as are used in Restoration and eighteenth-century plays, the novels of Dickens, etc.

PROLOGUE

Spoken by MR. HART[1]

Poets, like cudgelled bullies, never do
At first or second blow submit to you;
But will provoke you still, and ne'er have
   done,
Till you are weary first with laying on.
The late so baffled scribbler of this day,[2]
Though he stands trembling, bids me boldly
   say,
What we before most plays are used to do,
For poets out of fear first draw on you;
In a fierce prologue the still pit defy,
And ere you speak, like Castril give the lie.[3]
But though our Bayes's[4] battles oft I've
   fought,
And with bruised knuckles their dear
   conquests bought;
Nay, never yet feared odds upon the stage,
In prologue dare not hector with the age;
But would take quarter from your saving
   hands,
Though Bayes within all yielding counter-
   mands,
Says, you confederate wits no quarter give,
Therefore his play shan't ask your leave to
   live.
Well, let the vain rash fop, by huffing so,
Think to obtain the better terms of you;
But we, the actors, humbly will submit,
Now, and at any time, to a full pit;
Nay, often we anticipate your rage,
And murder poets for you on our stage:[5]
We set no guards upon our tiring-room,
But when with flying colours there you come,

---

1 The actor who played Mr. Horner in the original production, probably that by the King's Men at The Theatre-Royal in Drury Lane in January, 1675. 2 *baffled scribbler:* the author's *The Gentleman Dancing Master* "lasted but 6 days, being like't but indifferently" (John Downes). 3 *Castril:* the "angry boy" in Ben Jonson's *The Alchemist.* Cf. Act II, sc. ii. 4 *Bayes:* poet, dramatist after Dryden (poet laureate, crowned with bay leaves) in *The Rehearsal* (1672). 5 *murder poets:* by acting their works badly.

We patiently, you see, give up to you
Our poets, virgins, nay, our matrons too.[6]

ACT ONE

Scene One   Horner's Lodging.

Enter Horner, *and* Quack *following him at a distance.*

Horner (*aside*): A quack is as fit for a pimp as a midwife for a bawd; they are still but in their way, both helpers of nature. (*aloud*) Well, my dear doctor, hast thou done what I desired?

Quack: I have undone you for ever with the women, and reported you throughout the whole town as bad as a eunuch, with as much trouble as if I had made you one in earnest.

Horner: But have you told all the midwives you know, the orange wenches at the playhouses,[1] the city husbands, and old fumbling keepers of this end of the town, for they'll be the readiest to report it?

Quack: I have told all the chambermaids, waiting-women, tire-women,[2] and old women of my acquaintance; nay, and whispered it as a secret to 'em, and to the whisperers of Whitehall; so that you need not doubt 'twill spread, and you will be as odious to the handsome young women as —

Horner: As the smallpox. Well —

Quack: And to the married women of this end of the town, as —

Horner: As the great ones;[3] nay, as their own husbands.

Quack: And to the city dames, as aniseed Robin,[4] of filthy and contemptible memory; and they will frighten their children with your name, especially their females.

Horner: And cry, "Horner's coming to carry you away." I am only afraid 'twill not be believed. You told 'em 'twas by an English-French disaster, and an English-French chirurgeon, who has given me at once not only a cure, but an antidote for the future against that damned malady, and that worse distemper, love, and all other women's evils?

Quack: Your late journey into France has made it the more credible, and your being here a fortnight before you appeared in public, looks as if you apprehended the shame, which I wonder you do not. Well, I have been hired by young gallants to belie 'em t'other way; but you are the first would be thought a man unfit for women.

Horner: Dear Mr. Doctor, let vain rogues be contented only to be thought abler men than they are, generally 'tis all the pleasure they have; but mine lies another way.

Quack: You take, methinks, a very preposterous way to it, and as ridiculous as if we operators in physics should put forth bills to disparage our medicaments, with hopes to gain customers.

Horner: Doctor, there are quacks in love as well as physic, who get but the fewer and worse patients for their boasting; a good name is seldom got by giving it one's self; and women, no more than honour, are compassed by bragging. Come, come, Doctor, the wisest lawyer never discovers the merits of his cause till the trial; the wealthiest man conceals his riches, and the cunning gamester his play. Shy husbands and keepers, like old rooks, are not to be cheated but by a new unpractised trick; false friendship will pass now no more than false dice upon 'em; no, not in the city.

(*Enter* Boy.)

---

6 *virgins . . . matrons:* those who had "the liberty of the scenes" backstage often took liberties with the actresses who were not overchaste.

1 *orange wenches:* the girls who sold oranges at the theatre were notorious for prostitution. Nell Gwynn (Charles II's mistress) began as one. 2 *tire-women:* ladies' maids, wardrobe mistresses. 3 *great ones:* great poxes, i.e., syphilis. 4 *aniseed Robin:* an hermaphrodite. See Charles Cotton's poem on him in *Poems on Several Occasions* (1687), pp. 457–458.

Boy: There are two ladies and a gentleman coming up.

(*Exit* Boy.)

Horner: A pox! Some unbelieving sisters of my former acquaintance, who, I am afraid, expect their sense should be satisfied of the falsity of the report. No — this formal fool and women!

(*Enter* Sir Jasper Fidget, Lady Fidget *and* Mrs. Dainty Fidget.)

Quack: His wife and sister.

Sir Jasper: My coach breaking just now before your door, sir, I look upon as an occasional reprimand to me, sir, for not kissing your hands,[5] sir, since your coming out of France, sir; and so my disaster, sir, has been my good fortune, sir; and this is my wife and sister, sir.

Horner: What then, sir?

Sir Jasper: My lady, and sister, sir. — Wife, this is Master Horner.

Lady Fidget: Master Horner, husband!

Sir Jasper: My lady, my Lady Fidget, sir.

Horner: So, sir.

Sir Jasper: Won't you be acquainted with her, sir? (*aside*) So, the report is true, I find, by his coldness or aversion to the sex; but I'll play the wag with him. (*aloud*) Pray salute my wife, my lady, sir.

Horner: I will kiss no man's wife, sir, for him, sir; I have taken my eternal leave, sir, of the sex already, sir.

Sir Jasper (*aside*)[6]: Ha ha ha! I'll plague him yet. (*aloud*) Not know my wife, sir?

Horner: I do know your wife, sir; she's a woman, sir, and consequently a monster, sir, a greater monster than a husband, sir.

Sir Jasper: A husband! How, sir?

Horner: So, sir; but I make no more cuckolds, sir. (*makes horns*)

Sir Jasper: Ha ha ha! Mercury! Mercury![7]

Lady Fidget: Pray, Sir Jasper, let us be gone from this rude fellow.

Mrs. Dainty: Who, by his breeding, would think he had ever been in France?

Lady Fidget: Foh! He's but too much a French fellow, such as hate women of quality and virtue for their love to their husbands, Sir Jasper; a woman is hated by 'em as much for loving her husband as for loving their money. But pray let's be gone.

Horner: You do well, madam, for I have nothing that you came for. I have brought over not so much as a bawdy picture, no new postures, nor the second part of the *Ecole des Filles*;[8] nor —

Quack: Hold, for shame, sir! (*aside to* Horner) What d'ye mean? You'll ruin yourself for ever with the sex —

Sir Jasper: Ha ha ha! He hates women perfectly, I find.

Mrs. Dainty: What pity 'tis he should.

Lady Fidget: Ay, he's a base rude fellow for't. But affectation makes not a woman more odious to them than virtue.

Horner: Because your virtue is your greatest affectation, madam.

Lady Fidget: How, you saucy fellow! Would you wrong my honour?

Horner: If I could.

Lady Fidget: How d'ye mean, sir?

Sir Jasper: Ha ha ha! No, he can't wrong your ladyship's honour, upon my honour. He, poor man — hark you in your ear — a mere eunuch.

---

5 *kissing your hands:* saying hello. 6 *aside:* the proximity of the audience to the actors, who played in front of the set rather than in it in this period, made asides practical on stage. 7 *mercury:* a drastic cure for venereal disease. 8 *Ecole des Filles:* a pornographic book published in Paris (1655) and soon after condemned to be burnt.

LADY FIDGET: Oh, filthy French beast! Foh foh! Why do we stay? Let's be gone: I can't endure the sight of him.

SIR JASPER: Stay but till the chairs[9] come; they'll be here presently.

LADY FIDGET: No, no.

SIR JASPER: Nor can I stay longer. 'Tis, let me see, a quarter and half quarter of a minute past eleven. The council will be sat; I must away. Business must be preferred always before love and ceremony with the wise, Mr. Horner.

HORNER: And the impotent, Sir Jasper.

SIR JASPER: Ay, ay, the impotent, Master Horner; ha ha ha!

LADY FIDGET: What, leave us with a filthy man alone in his lodgings?

SIR JASPER: He's an innocent man now, you know. Pray stay, I'll hasten the chairs to you. — Mr. Horner, your servant; I should be glad to see you at my house. Pray come and dine with me, and play at cards with my wife after dinner; you are fit for women at that game yet, ha ha! (aside) 'Tis as much a husband's prudence to provide innocent diversion for a wife as to hinder her unlawful pleasures; and he had better employ her than let her employ herself. (aloud) Farewell.

HORNER: Your servant, Sir Jasper.

(Exit SIR JASPER.)

LADY FIDGET: I will not stay with him, foh!

HORNER: Nay, madam, I beseech you stay, if it be but to see I can be as civil to ladies yet as they would desire.

LADY FIDGET: No, no, foh! You cannot be civil to ladies.

MRS. DAINTY: You as civil as ladies would desire?

LADY FIDGET: No no no! Foh foh foh!

(Exeunt LADY FIDGET and MRS. DAINTY FIDGET.)

QUACK: Now, I think, I, or you yourself, rather, have done your business with the women.

HORNER: Thou art an ass. Don't you see, already upon the report, and my carriage, this grave man of business leaves his wife in my lodgings, invites me to his house and wife, who before would not be acquainted with me out of jealousy?

QUACK: Nay, by this means you may be the more acquainted with the husbands, but the less with the wives.

HORNER: Let me alone; if I can but abuse the husbands, I'll soon disabuse the wives. Stay — I'll reckon you up the advantages I am like to have by my stratagem. First, I shall be rid of all my old acquaintances, the most insatiable sort of duns,[10] that invade our lodgings in a morning; and next to the pleasure of making a new mistress is that of being rid of an old one,[11] and of all old debts. Love, when it comes to be so, is paid the most unwillingly.

QUACK: Well, you may be so rid of your old acquaintances; but how will you get any new ones?

HORNER: Doctor, thou wilt never make a good chemist, thou art so incredulous and impatient. Ask but all the young fellows of the town if they do not lose more time, like huntsmen, in starting the game, than in running it down. One knows not where to find 'em, who will or will not. Women of quality are so civil, you can hardly distinguish love from good breeding, and a man is often mistaken: but now I can be sure she that shows an aversion to me loves the sport, as those women that are gone, whom I warrant to be right. And then the next thing is, your women of honour, as you call 'em, are only chary of their reputations, not their persons; and 'tis scandal they would avoid, not men. Now may I have, by the reputation of a eunuch, the privileges of one, and be seen in a lady's chamber in a morning as early as her husband; kiss virgins before their

---

9 *chairs:* sedan chairs. **10** *duns:* bill collectors. **11** *next to . . . old one:* this is one of the most famous of Restoration epigrams.

parents or lovers; and may be, in short, the *passe-partout*[12] of the town. Now, doctor.

QUACK: Nay, now you shall be the doctor; and your process is so new that we do not know but it may succeed.

HORNER: Not so new either; *probatum est,*[13] doctor.

QUACK: Well, I wish you luck, and many patients, whilst I go to mine.

(*Exit* QUACK.)

(*Enter* HARCOURT *and* DORILANT.)

HARCOURT: Come, your appearance at the play yesterday has, I hope, hardened you for the future against the women's contempt, and the men's raillery; and now you'll abroad as you were wont.

HORNER: Did I not bear it bravely?

DORILANT: With a most theatrical impudence, nay, more than the orange-wenches show there, or a drunken vizard-mask,[14] or a great-bellied actress; nay, or the most impudent of creatures, an ill poet; or what is yet more impudent, a second-hand critic.

HORNER: But what say the ladies? Have they no pity?

HARCOURT: What ladies? The vizard-masks, you know, never pity a man when all's gone, though in their service.

DORILANT: And for the women in the boxes, you'd never pity them when 'twas in your power.

HARCOURT: They say 'tis pity but all that deal with common women should be served so.

DORILANT: Nay, I dare swear they won't admit you to play at cards with them, go to plays with 'em, or do the little duties which other shadows of men are wont to do for 'em.

HORNER: What do you call shadows of men?

DORILANT: Half-men.

HORNER: What, boys?

DORILANT: Ay, your old boys, old *beaux gar-*

çons,[15] who, like superannuated stallions, are suffered to run, feed, and whinny with the mares as long as they live, though they can do nothing else.

HORNER: Well, a pox on love and wenching! Women serve but to keep a man from better company. Though I can't enjoy them, I shall you the more. Good fellowship and friendship are lasting, rational, and manly pleasures.

HARCOURT: For all that, give me some of those pleasures you call effeminate too; they help to relish one another.

HORNER: They disturb one another.

HARCOURT: No, mistresses are like books. If you pore upon them too much, they doze you, and make you unfit for company; but if used discreetly, you are the fitter for conversation by 'em.

DORILANT: A mistress should be like a little country retreat near the town; not to dwell in constantly, but only for a night and away, to taste the town the better when a man returns.

HORNER: I tell you, 'tis as hard to be a good fellow, a good friend, and a lover of women, as 'tis to be a good fellow, a good friend, and a lover of money. You cannot follow both, then choose your side. Wine gives you liberty, love takes it away.

DORILANT: Gad, he's in the right on't.

HORNER: Wine gives you joy; love, grief and tortures, besides the chirurgeons. Wine makes us witty; love, only sots. Wine makes us sleep; love breaks it.

DORILANT: By the world he has reason, Harcourt.

HORNER: Wine makes —

---

12 *passe-partout:* French, "goes everywhere." 13 *probatum est:* Latin, "it is proved." Q.E.D. 14 *vizard-mask:* prostitute (from the masks they wore). 15 *beaux garçons:* French, gallants, fops too old to be active.

DORILANT: Ay, wine makes us — makes us princes; love makes us beggars, poor rogues, egad — and wine —

HORNER: So, there's one converted. No, no, love and wine, oil and vinegar.[16]

HARCOURT: I grant it; love will still be uppermost.

HORNER: Come, for my part, I will have only those glorious manly pleasures of being very drunk and very slovenly.

(*Enter* BOY.)

BOY: Mr. Sparkish is below, sir.

(*Exit* BOY.)

HARCOURT: What, my dear friend! A rogue that is fond of me only, I think, for abusing him.

DORILANT: No, he can no more think the men laugh at him than that women jilt him; his opinion of himself is so good.

HORNER: Well, there's another pleasure by drinking I thought not of, — I shall lose his acquaintance, because he cannot drink: and you know 'tis a very hard thing to be rid of him; for he's one of those nauseous offerers at wit, who, like the worst fiddlers, run themselves into all companies.

HARCOURT: One that, by being in the company of men of sense, would pass for one.

HORNER: And may so to the short-sighted world; as a false jewel amongst true ones is not discerned at a distance. His company is as troublesome to us as a cuckold's when you have a mind to his wife's.

HARCOURT: No, the rogue will not let us enjoy one another, but ravishes our conversation; though he signifies no more to't than Sir Martin Mar-all's gaping and awkward thrumming upon the lute does to his man's voice and music.[17]

DORILANT: And to pass for a wit in town shows himself a fool every night to us, that are guilty of the plot.

HORNER: Such wits as he, are, to a company of reasonable men, like rooks to the game-sters, who only fill a room at the table, but are so far from contributing to the play that they only serve to spoil the fancy of those that do.

DORILANT: Nay, they are used like rooks too, snubbed, checked, and abused; yet the rogues will hang on.

HORNER: A pox on 'em, and all that force nature, and would be still what she forbids 'em! Affectation is her greatest monster.

HARCOURT: Most men are the contraries to that they would seem. Your bully, you see, is a coward with a long sword; the little humbly-fawning physician, with his ebony cane, is he that destroys men.

DORILANT: The usurer, a poor rogue, possessed of mouldy bonds and mortgages; and we they call spendthrifts, are only wealthy, who lay out his money upon daily new purchases of pleasure.

HORNER: Ay, your arrantest[18] cheat is your trustee or executor; your jealous man, the greatest cuckold; your churchman the greatest atheist; and your noisy pert rogue of a wit, the greatest fop, dullest ass, and worst company, as you shall see; for here he comes.

(*Enter* SPARKISH.)

SPARKISH: How is't, sparks, how is't? Well, faith, Harry, I must rally thee a little, ha ha ha, upon the report in town of thee, ha ha ha! I can't hold i'faith; shall I speak?

HORNER: Yes; but you'll be so bitter then.

SPARKISH: Honest Dick and Frank here shall answer for me; I will not be extreme bitter, by the universe.

HARCOURT: We will be bound in a ten thousand pound bond, he shall not be bitter at all.

DORILANT: Nor sharp, nor sweet.

---

16 *oil and vinegar:* they don't mix.   **17** *Sir Martin . . . :* The hero of Dryden's *Sir Martin Mar-all* pantomimes a serenade while his servant, concealed, sings and plays. **18** *arrantest:* most arrant, boldest.

HORNER: What, not downright insipid?

SPARKISH: Nay then, since you are so brisk, and provoke me, take what follows. You must know, I was discoursing and rallying with some ladies yesterday, and they happened to talk of the fine new signs in town —

HORNER: Very fine ladies, I believe.

SPARKISH: Said I, "I know where the best new sign is." "Where?" says one of the ladies. "In Covent Garden," I replied. Said another, "In what street?" "In Russel Street," answered I. "Lord," says another, "I'm sure there was never a fine new sign there yesterday." "Yes, but there was," said I again, "and it came out of France, and has been there a fortnight."

DORILANT: A pox! I can hear no more, prithee.

HORNER: No, hear him out; let him tune his crowd[19] a while.

HARCOURT: The worst music, the greatest preparation.

SPARKISH: Nay, faith, I'll make you laugh. "It cannot be," says a third lady. "Yes, yes," quoth I again. Says a fourth lady —

HORNER: Look to't, we'll have no more ladies.

SPARKISH: No — then mark, mark, now. Said I to the fourth, "Did you never see Mr. Horner? He lodges in Russel Street, and he's a sign of a man, you know, since he came out of France." Ha ha ha!

HORNER: But the devil take me if thine be the sign of a jest.

SPARKISH: With that they all fell a-laughing, till they bepissed themselves. What, but it does not move you, methinks? Well, I see one had as good go to law without a witness, as break a jest without a laughter on one's side. Come, come, sparks, but where do we dine? I have left at Whitehall an earl, to dine with you.

DORILANT: Why, I thought thou hadst loved a man with a title, better than a suit with a French trimming to't.

HARCOURT: Go to him again.

SPARKISH: No, sir, a wit to me is the greatest title in the world.

HORNER: But go dine with your earl, sir; he may be exceptious.[20] We are your friends, and will not take it ill to be left, I do assure you.

HARCOURT: Nay, faith, he shall go to him.

SPARKISH: Nay, pray, gentlemen.

DORILANT: We'll thrust you out, if you won't; what, disappoint anybody for us?

SPARKISH: Nay, dear gentlemen, hear me.

HORNER: No, no, sir, by no means; pray go, sir.

SPARKISH: Why, dear rogues —

DORILANT: No, no.

(*They all thrust him out of the room.*)

ALL: Ha ha ha!

(*Enter* SPARKISH.)

SPARKISH: But, sparks, pray hear me. What, d'ye think I'll eat then with gay shallow fops and silent coxcombs? I think wit as necessary at dinner as a glass of good wine; and that's the reason I never have any stomach when I eat alone. Come, but where do we dine?

HORNER: Even where you will.

SPARKISH: At Chateline's?

DORILANT: Yes, if you will.

SPARKISH: Or at the Cock?

DORILANT: Yes, if you please.

SPARKISH: Or at the Dog and Partridge?

HORNER: Ay, if you have a mind to't; for we shall dine at neither.

SPARKISH: Pshaw! With your fooling we shall lose the new play; and I would no more miss seeing a new play the first day, than I would

---

19 *crowd:* fiddle. 20 *exceptious:* peevish.

miss sitting in the wit's row.[21] Therefore I'll go fetch my mistress, and away.

(*Exit* SPARKISH.)

(*Enter* PINCHWIFE.)

HORNER: Who have we here? Pinchwife?

PINCHWIFE: Gentlemen, your humble servant.

HORNER: Well, Jack, by thy long absence from the town, the grumness[22] of thy countenance, and the slovenliness of thy habit, I should give thee joy, should I not, of marriage?

PINCHWIFE (*aside*): Death! Does he know I'm married too? I thought to have concealed it from him at least. (*aloud*) My long stay in the country will excuse my dress; and I have a suit of law that brings me up to town, that puts me out of humour. Besides, I must give Sparkish tomorrow five thousand pounds to lie with my sister.

HORNER: Nay, you country gentlemen, rather than not purchase, will buy anything; and he is a cracked title,[23] if we may quibble. Well, but am I to give thee joy? I heard thou wert married.

PINCHWIFE: What then?

HORNER: Why, the next thing that is to be heard, is thou'rt a cuckold.

PINCHWIFE (*aside*): Insupportable name!

HORNER: But I did not expect marriage from such a whoremaster as you; one that knew the town so much, and women so well.

PINCHWIFE: Why, I have married no London wife.

HORNER: Pshaw! That's all one. That grave circumspection in marrying a country wife, is like refusing a deceitful pampered Smithfield jade,[24] to go and be cheated by a friend in the country.

PINCHWIFE (*aside*): A pox on him and his simile! (*aloud*) At least we are a little surer of the breed there, know what her keeping has been, whether foiled or unsound.

HORNER: Come, come, I have known a clap

gotten in Wales,[25] and there are cousins, justices' clerks, and chaplains in the country; I won't say coachmen. But she's handsome and young?

PINCHWIFE (*aside*): I'll answer as I should do. (*aloud*) No, no, she has no beauty but her youth, no attraction but her modesty; wholesome, homely, and housewifely, that's all.

DORILANT: He talks as like a grazier[26] as he looks.

PINCHWIFE: She's too awkward, ill-favoured, and silly to bring to town.

HARCOURT: Then methinks you should bring her to be taught breeding.

PINCHWIFE: To be taught! No, sir, I thank you. Good wives and private soldiers should be ignorant. (*aside*) I'll keep her from your instructions, I warrant you.

HARCOURT (*aside*): The rogue is as jealous as if his wife were not ignorant.

HORNER: Why, if she be ill-favoured, there will be less danger here for you than by leaving her in the country. We have such variety of dainties that we are seldom hungry.

DORILANT: But they have always coarse, constant, swingeing stomachs in the country.

HARCOURT: Foul feeders indeed.

DORILANT: And your hospitality is great there.

HARCOURT: Open house; every man's welcome.

PINCHWIFE: So, so, gentlemen.

HORNER: But prithee, why shouldst thou marry

---

21 *wit's row:* beaux at the play often sat where they could make cracks to the actors. Once the Duke of Buckingham, hearing a particularly silly line in a play, jumped up and made a couplet of it *extempore* (in iambic pentameter), breaking up the play. 22 *grumness:* sorrowfulness. 23 *cracked title:* an invalid title to property. 24 *Smithfield jade:* a horse from a notoriously unreliable market. "Jade" can mean both worn-out horse and whore. 25 *Wales:* used here as an unlikely, bucolic place. 26 *grazier:* one who fattens cattle for market.

her? If she be ugly, ill-bred, and silly, she must be rich then.

PINCHWIFE: As rich as if she brought me twenty thousand pound out of this town; for she'll be as sure not to spend her moderate portion, as a London baggage would be to spend hers, let it be what it would — so 'tis all one. Then, because she's ugly, she's the likelier to be my own; and being ill-bred, she'll hate conversation; and since silly and innocent, will not know the difference betwixt a man of one-and-twenty and one of forty.

HORNER: Nine — to my knowledge. But if she be silly, she'll expect as much from a man of forty-nine, as from him of one-and-twenty. But methinks wit is more necessary than beauty; and I think no young woman ugly that has it, and no handsome woman agreeable without it.

PINCHWIFE: 'Tis my maxim, he's a fool that marries; but he's a greater that does not marry a fool. What is wit in a wife good for, but to make a man a cuckold?

HORNER: Yes, to keep it from his knowledge.

PINCHWIFE: A fool cannot contrive to make her husband a cuckold.

HORNER: No, but she'll club with a man that can; and what is worse, if she cannot make her husband a cuckold, she'll make him jealous, and pass for one; and then 'tis all one.

PINCHWIFE: Well, well, I'll take care for one. My wife shall make me no cuckold, though she had your help, Mr. Horner. I understand the town, sir.

DORILANT (*aside*): His help!

HARCOURT (*aside*): He's come newly to town, it seems, and has not heard how things are with him.

HORNER: But tell me, has marriage cured thee of whoring, which it seldom does?

HARCOURT: 'Tis more than age can do.

HORNER: No, the word is, I'll marry and live honest; but a marriage vow is like a penitent gamester's oath, and entering into bonds and penalties to stint himself to such a particular small sum at play for the future, which makes him but the more eager; and not being able to hold out, loses his money again, and his forfeit to boot.

DORILANT: Ay, ay, a gamester will be a gamester whilst his money lasts, and a whoremaster, whilst his vigour.

HARCOURT: Nay, I have known 'em, when they are broke, and can lose no more, keep a fumbling with the box in their hands to fool with only, and hinder other gamesters.

DORILANT: That had wherewithal to make lusty stakes.

PINCHWIFE: Well, gentlemen, you may laugh at me, but you shall never lie with my wife; I know the town.

HORNER: But prithee, was not the way you were in better? Is not keeping better than marriage?

PINCHWIFE: A pox on't! The jades would jilt me; I could never keep a whore to myself.

HORNER: So, then you only married to keep a whore to yourself. Well, but let me tell you, women, as you say, are soldiers, made constant and loyal by good pay, rather than by oaths and covenants. Therefore I'd advise my friends to keep rather than marry, since too I find, by your example, it does not serve one's turn; for I saw you yesterday in the eighteen-penny place[27] with a pretty country-wench.

PINCHWIFE (*aside*): How the devil! Did he see my wife then? I sat there that she might not be seen. But she shall never go to a play again.

HORNER: What! Dost thou blush, at nine-and-forty, for having been seen with a wench?

---

27 *eighteen-penny place:* for a shilling and a half at the theatre one could get a seat in the middle gallery, frequented by whores. Pinchwife sat there to keep his wife away from the beaux in the more expensive pit (orchestra) and boxes.

DORILANT: No; faith, I warrant 'twas his wife, which he seated there out of sight; for he's a cunning rogue, and understands the town.

HARCOURT: He blushes. Then 'twas his wife; for men are now more ashamed to be seen with them in public than with a wench.

PINCHWIFE (aside): Hell and damnation! I'm undone, since Horner has seen her, and they know 'twas she.

HORNER: But prithee, was it thy wife? She was exceeding pretty: I was in love with her at that distance.

PINCHWIFE: You are like never to be nearer to her. (Offers to go.) Your servant, gentlemen.

HORNER: Nay, prithee stay.

PINCHWIFE: I cannot; I will not.

HORNER: Come, you shall dine with us.

PINCHWIFE: I have dined already.

HORNER: Come, I know thou hast not. I'll treat thee, dear rogue; thou sha't spend none of thy Hampshire[28] money to-day.

PINCHWIFE (aside): Treat me! So, he uses me already like his cuckold.

HORNER: Nay, you shall not go.

PINCHWIFE: I must; I have business at home.

(Exit PINCHWIFE.)

HARCOURT: To beat his wife. He's as jealous of her as a Cheapside husband of a Covent Garden wife.[29]

HORNER: Why, 'tis as hard to find an old whoremaster without jealousy and the gout, as a young one without fear or the pox.
As gout in age from pox in youth proceeds;
So wenching past, then jealousy succeeds;
The worst disease that love and wenching breeds.

(Exeunt HARCOURT, DORILANT, HORNER.)

ACT TWO

SCENE ONE   Pinchwife's House.

MRS. MARGERY PINCHWIFE and ALITHEA. PINCHWIFE peeping behind at the door.

MRS. PINCHWIFE: Pray, sister, where are the best fields and woods to walk in, in London?

ALITHEA: A pretty question! Why, sister, Mulberry Garden and St. James's Park; and for close walks, the New Exchange.[1]

MRS. PINCHWIFE: Pray, sister, tell me why my husband looks so grum here in town, and keeps me up so close, and will not let me go a-walking, nor let me wear my best gown yesterday.

ALITHEA: Oh, he's jealous, sister.

MRS. PINCHWIFE: Jealous! What's that?

ALITHEA: He's afraid you should love another man.

MRS. PINCHWIFE: How should he be afraid of my loving another man, when he will not let me see any but himself?

ALITHEA: Did he not carry you yesterday to a play?

MRS. PINCHWIFE: Ay, but we sat amongst ugly people. He would not let me come near the gentry, who sat under us, so that I could not see 'em. He told me none but naughty women sat there, whom they toused and moused;[2] but I would have ventured, for all that.

ALITHEA: But how did you like the play?

MRS. PINCHWIFE: Indeed I was weary of the play, but I liked hugeously the actors. They are the goodliest, properest men, sister!

ALITHEA: Oh, but you must not like the actors, sister.

---

28 *Hampshire:* a county "in the country." 29 *Cheapside husband . . . Covent Garden wife:* Cheapside was full of rich silk merchants and linen drapers. Meaning "a rich merchant with a would-be fashionable wife."

1 *Mulberry Garden*, etc.: Mulberry Garden stood where Buckingham Palace now is. The New Exchange offered "close" (i.e., indoor) walks: it is the scene of Act III, sc. ii. 2 *toused and moused:* teased, groped, etc.

MRS. PINCHWIFE: Ay, how should I help it, sister? Pray, sister, when my husband comes in, will you ask leave for me to go a-walking?

ALITHEA (*aside*): A-walking! Ha ha! Lord, a country-gentlewoman's leisure is the drudgery of a footpost; and she requires as much airing as her husband's horses. (*aloud*) But here comes your husband; I'll ask, though I'm sure he'll not grant it.

MRS. PINCHWIFE: He says he won't let me go abroad for fear of catching the pox.

ALITHEA: Fy! The smallpox, you should say.

(*Enter* PINCHWIFE.)

MRS. PINCHWIFE: O my dear, dear bud, welcome home; why dost thou look so fropish?[3] Who has nangered thee?

PINCHWIFE: You're a fool.

(MRS. PINCHWIFE *goes aside, and cries.*)

ALITHEA: Faith, so she is, for crying for no fault, poor tender creature!

PINCHWIFE: What, you would have her as impudent as yourself, as arrant a jilflirt, a gadder, a magpie; and to say all, a mere notorious town-woman?

ALITHEA: Brother, you are my only censurer; and the honour of your family will sooner suffer in your wife there than in me, though I take the innocent liberty of the town.

PINCHWIFE: Hark you, mistress, do not talk so before my wife. The innocent liberty of the town!

ALITHEA: Why, pray, who boasts of any intrigue with me? What lampoon has made my name notorious? What ill women frequent my lodgings? I keep no company with any women of scandalous reputations.

PINCHWIFE: No, you keep the men of scandalous reputations company.

ALITHEA: Where? Would you not have me civil? Answer 'em in a box at the plays? In the drawing-room at Whitehall? In St. James's Park? Mulberry Garden? Or —

PINCHWIFE: Hold, hold! Do not teach my wife where the men are to be found; I believe she's the worse for your town documents already. I bid you keep her in ignorance, as I do.

MRS. PINCHWIFE: Indeed, be not angry with her, bud, she will tell me nothing of the town, though I ask her a thousand times a day.

PINCHWIFE: Then you are very inquisitive to know, I find?

MRS. PINCHWIFE: Not I indeed, dear; I hate London. Our place-house[4] in the country is worth a thousand of't; would I were there again.

PINCHWIFE: So you shall, I warrant. But were you not talking of plays and players when I came in? (*to* ALITHEA) You are her encourager in such discourses.

MRS. PINCHWIFE: No, indeed, dear; she chid me just now for liking the playermen.

PINCHWIFE (*aside*): Nay, if she be so innocent as to own to me her liking them, there is no hurt in't. (*aloud*) Come, my poor rogue, but thou likest none better than me?

MRS. PINCHWIFE: Yes, indeed, but I do. The playermen are finer folks.

PINCHWIFE: But you love none better than me?

MRS. PINCHWIFE: You are my own dear bud, and I know you. I hate a stranger.

PINCHWIFE: Ay, my dear, you must love me only; and not be like the naughty town-women, who only hate their husbands, and love every man else; love plays, visits, fine coaches, fine clothes, fiddles, balls, treats, and so lead a wicked town-life.

MRS. PINCHWIFE: Nay, if to enjoy all these things be a town-life, London is not so bad a place, dear.

PINCHWIFE: How! If you love me, you must hate London.

---

3 *fropish:* peevish.   4 *place-house:* manor house.

ALITHEA (*aside*): The fool has forbid me discovering to her the pleasures of the town, and he is now setting her agog upon them himself.

MRS. PINCHWIFE: But, husband, do the townwomen love the playermen too?

PINCHWIFE: Yes, I warrant you.

MRS. PINCHWIFE: Ay, I warrant you.

PINCHWIFE: Why, you do not, I hope?

MRS. PINCHWIFE: No, no, bud. But why have we no playermen in the country?

PINCHWIFE: Ha! — Mrs. Minx, ask me no more to go to a play.

MRS. PINCHWIFE: Nay, why, love? I did not care for going; but when you forbid me, you make me, as 'twere, desire it.

ALITHEA (*aside*): So 'twill be in other things, I warrant.

MRS. PINCHWIFE: Pray let me go to a play, dear.

PINCHWIFE: Hold your peace, I wo' not.

MRS. PINCHWIFE: Why, love?

PINCHWIFE: Why, I'll tell you.

ALITHEA (*aside*): Nay, if he tell her, she'll give him more cause to forbid her that place.

MRS. PINCHWIFE: Pray why, dear?

PINCHWIFE: First, you like the actors; and the gallants may like you.

MRS. PINCHWIFE: What, a homely country girl? No, bud, nobody will like me.

PINCHWIFE: I tell you yes, they may.

MRS. PINCHWIFE: No, no, you jest — I won't believe you; I will go.

PINCHWIFE: I tell you then, that one of the lewdest fellows in town, who saw you there, told me he was in love with you.

MRS. PINCHWIFE: Indeed! Who, who, pray who was't?

PINCHWIFE (*aside*): I've gone too far, and slipped before I was aware; how overjoyed she is!

MRS. PINCHWIFE: Was it any Hampshire gallant, any of our neighbors? I promise you, I am beholden to him.

PINCHWIFE: I promise you, you lie; for he would but ruin you, as he has done hundreds. He has no other love for women but that; such as he look upon women like basilisks,[5] but to destroy 'em.

MRS. PINCHWIFE: Ay, but if he loves me, why should he ruin me? Answer me to that. Methinks he should not; I would do him no harm.

ALITHEA: Ha ha ha!

PINCHWIFE: 'Tis very well; but I'll keep him from doing you any harm, or me either. But here comes company; get you in, get you in.

MRS. PINCHWIFE: But, pray, husband, is he a pretty gentleman that loves me?

PINCHWIFE: In, baggage, in. (*Thrusts her in, and shuts the door.*)

(*Enter* SPARKISH *and* HARCOURT.)

What, all the lewd libertines of the town brought to my lodging by this easy coxcomb! 'Sdeath, I'll not suffer it.

SPARKISH: Here, Harcourt, do you approve my choice? (*to* ALITHEA) Dear little rogue, I told you I'd bring you acquainted with all my friends, the wits and —

(HARCOURT *salutes her.*)

PINCHWIFE (*aside*): Ay, they shall know her, as well as you yourself will, I warrant you.

SPARKISH: This is one of those, my pretty rogue, that are to dance at your wedding tomorrow; and him you must bid welcome ever, to what you and I have.

PINCHWIFE (*aside*): Monstrous!

SPARKISH: Harcourt, how dost thou like her, faith? Nay, dear, do not look down; I should hate to have a wife of mine out of countenance at anything.

---

5 *basilisks:* the glance of these legendary creatures was fatal.

PINCHWIFE (*aside*): Wonderful!

SPARKISH: Tell me, I say, Harcourt, how dost thou like her? Thou hast stared upon her enough, to resolve me.

HARCOURT: So infinitely well, that I could wish I had a mistress too, that might differ from her in nothing but her love and engagement to you.

ALITHEA: Sir, Master Sparkish has often told me that his acquaintance were all wits and raillieurs,[6] and now I find it.

SPARKISH: No, by the universe, madam, he does not rally now; you may believe him. I do assure you, he is the honestest, worthiest, true-hearted gentleman — a man of such perfect honour, he would say nothing to a lady he does not mean.

PINCHWIFE (*aside*): Praising another man to his mistress!

HARCOURT: Sir, you are so beyond expectation obliging, that —

SPARKISH: Nay, egad, I am sure you do admire her extremely; I see't in your eyes. He does admire you, madam. By the world, don't you?

HARCOURT: Yes, above the world, or the most glorious part of it, her whole sex: and till now I never thought I should have envied you, or any man about to marry, but you have the best excuse for marriage I ever knew.

ALITHEA: Nay, now, sir, I'm satisfied you are of the society of the wits and raillieurs, since you cannot spare your friend, even when he is but too civil to you; but the surest sign is, since you are an enemy to marriage, for that I hear you hate as much as business or bad wine.

HARCOURT: Truly, madam, I was never an enemy to marriage till now, because marriage was never an enemy to me before.

ALITHEA: But why, sir, is marriage an enemy to you now? Because it robs you of your friend here; for you look upon a friend married, as one gone into a monastery; that is, dead to the world.

HARCOURT: 'Tis indeed, because you marry him; I see, madam, you can guess my meaning. I do confess heartily and openly, I wish it were in my power to break the match; by Heavens I would.

SPARKISH: Poor Frank!

ALITHEA: Would you be so unkind to me?

HARCOURT: No, no, 'tis not because I would be unkind to you.

SPARKISH: Poor Frank! No, gad, 'tis only his kindness to me.

PINCHWIFE (*aside*): Great kindness to you indeed! Insensible fop, let a man make love to his wife to his face!

SPARKISH: Come, dear Frank, for all my wife there, that shall be, thou shalt enjoy me sometimes, dear rogue. By my honour, we men of wit condole for our deceased brother in marriage, as much as for one dead in earnest. I think that was prettily said of me, ha, Harcourt? But come, Frank, be not melancholy for me.

HARCOURT: No, I assure you, I am not melancholy for you.

SPARKISH: Prithee, Frank, dost think my wife that shall be there, a fine person?

HARCOURT: I could gaze upon her till I became as blind as you are.

SPARKISH: How, as I am? How?

HARCOURT: Because you are a lover, and true lovers are blind, stock blind.

SPARKISH: True, true; but by the world she has wit too, as well as beauty. Go, go with her into a corner, and try if she has wit; talk to her anything, she's bashful before me.

HARCOURT: Indeed, if a woman wants wit in a corner, she has it nowhere.

---

6 *raillieurs*: those who rail, mockers. Wycherley makes the verb "to rally."

ALITHEA (*aside to* SPARKISH): Sir, you dispose of me a little before your time —

SPARKISH: Nay, nay, madam, let me have an earnest of your obedience, or — go, go, madam —

(HARCOURT *courts* ALITHEA *aside*.)

PINCHWIFE: How, sir! If you are not concerned for the honour of a wife, I am for that of a sister; he shall not debauch her. Be a pander to your own wife, bring men to her, let 'em make love before your face, thrust 'em into a corner together, then leave 'em in private! Is this your town wit and conduct?

SPARKISH: Ha ha ha! A silly wise rogue would make one laugh more than a stark fool, ha ha! I shall burst. Nay, you shall not disturb 'em; I'll vex thee, by the world. (*Struggles with* PINCHWIFE *to keep him from* HARCOURT *and* ALITHEA.)

ALITHEA: The writings are drawn, sir, settlements made; 'tis too late, sir, and past all revocation.

HARCOURT: Then so is my death.

ALITHEA: I would not be unjust to him.

HARCOURT: Then why to me so?

ALITHEA: I have no obligation to you.

HARCOURT: My love.

ALITHEA: I had his before.

HARCOURT: You never had it; he wants, you see, jealousy, the only infallible sign of it.

ALITHEA: Love proceeds from esteem; he cannot distrust my virtue. Besides, he loves me, or he would not marry me.

HARCOURT: Marrying you is no more sign of his love than bribing your woman, that he may marry you, is a sign of his generosity. Marriage is rather a sign of interest than love; and he that marries a fortune covets a mistress, not loves her. But if you take marriage for a sign of love, take it from me immediately.

ALITHEA: No, now you have put a scruple in my head; but in short, sir, to end our dispute, I must marry him. My reputation would suffer in the world, else.

HARCOURT: No; if you do marry him, with your pardon, madam, your reputation suffers in the world, and you would be thought in necessity for a cloak.

ALITHEA: Nay, now you are rude, sir. Mr. Sparkish, pray come hither; your friend here is very troublesome, and very loving.

HARCOURT (*aside to* ALITHEA): Hold! Hold! —

PINCHWIFE: D'ye hear that?

SPARKISH: Why, d'ye think I'll seem to be jealous, like a country bumpkin?

PINCHWIFE: No, rather be a cuckold, like a credulous cit[izen].

HARCOURT: Madam, you would not have been so little generous as to have told him.

ALITHEA: Yes, since you could be so little generous as to wrong him.

HARCOURT: Wrong him! No man can do't, he's beneath an injury: a bubble, a coward, a senseless idiot, a wretch so contemptible to all the world but you, that —

ALITHEA: Hold, do not rail at him, for since he is like to be my husband, I am resolved to like him. Nay, I think I am obliged to tell him you are not his friend. Master Sparkish, Master Sparkish!

SPARKISH: What, what? Now, dear rogue, has not she wit?

HARCOURT (*speaks surlily*): Not so much as I thought, and hoped she had.

ALITHEA: Mr. Sparkish, do you bring people to rail at you?

HARCOURT: Madam —

SPARKISH: How! No; but if he does rail at me, 'tis but in jest, I warrant; what we wits do for one another, and never take any notice of it.

ALITHEA: He spoke so scurrilously of you, I

had no patience to hear him; besides, he has been making love to me.

HARCOURT (*aside*): True, damned tell-tale woman!

SPARKISH: Pshaw! To show his parts[7] — we wits rail and make love often, but to show our parts: as we have no affections, so we have no malice, we —

ALITHEA: He said you were a wretch, below an injury.

SPARKISH: Pshaw!

HARCOURT (*aside*): Damned, senseless, impudent, virtuous jade! Well, since she won't let me have her, she'll do as good, she'll make me hate her.

ALITHEA: A common bubble.

SPARKISH: Pshaw!

ALITHEA: A coward.

SPARKISH: Pshaw, pshaw!

ALITHEA: A senseless, drivelling idiot.

SPARKISH: How! Did he disparage my parts? Nay, then, my honour's concerned; I can't put up that, sir, by the world — brother, help me to kill him — (*aside*) I may draw now, since we have the odds of him: 'tis a good occasion, too, before my mistress. (*Offers to draw.*)

ALITHEA: Hold, hold!

SPARKISH: What, what?

ALITHEA (*aside*): I must not let 'em kill the gentleman neither, for his kindness to me; I am so far from hating him, that I wish my gallant had his person and understanding. Nay, if my honour —

SPARKISH: I'll be thy death.

ALITHEA: Hold, hold! Indeed, to tell the truth, the gentleman said after all, that what he spoke was but out of friendship to you.

SPARKISH: How! Say, I am, I am a fool, that is, no wit, out of friendship to me?

ALITHEA: Yes, to try whether I was concerned enough for you; and made love to me only to be satisfied of my virtue, for your sake.

HARCOURT (*aside*): Kind, however.

SPARKISH: Nay, if it were so, my dear rogue, I ask thee pardon; but why would not you tell me so, faith?

HARCOURT: Because I did not think on't, faith.

SPARKISH: Come, Horner does not come; Harcourt, let's be gone to the new play. Come, madam.

ALITHEA: I will not go, if you intend to leave me alone in the box, and run into the pit, as you use to do.

SPARKISH: Pshaw! I'll leave Harcourt with you in the box to entertain you, and that's as good; if I sat in the box, I should be thought no judge but of trimmings. Come away, Harcourt, lead her down.

(*Exeunt* SPARKISH, HARCOURT, *and* ALITHEA.)

PINCHWIFE: Well, go thy ways, for the flower of the true town fops, such as spend their estates before they come to 'em, and are cuckolds before they're married. But let me go look to my own freehold. How!

(*Enter* LADY FIDGET, MRS. DAINTY FIDGET, *and* MRS. SQUEAMISH.)

LADY FIDGET: Your servant, sir; where is your lady? We are come to wait upon her to the new play.

PINCHWIFE: New play!

LADY FIDGET: And my husband will wait upon you presently.

PINCHWIFE (*aside*): Damn your civility. (*aloud*) Madam, by no means; I will not see Sir Jasper here, till I have waited upon him at home; nor shall my wife see you till she has waited upon your ladyship at your lodgings.

LADY FIDGET: Now we are here, sir —

PINCHWIFE: No, Madam.

---

7 *parts:* abilities.

MRS. DAINTY: Pray, let us see her.

MRS. SQUEAMISH: We will not stir till we see her.

PINCHWIFE (*aside*): A pox on you all! (*Goes to the door, and returns.*) She has locked the door, and is gone abroad.

LADY FIDGET: No, you have locked the door, and she's within.

MRS. DAINTY: They told us below she was here.

PINCHWIFE (*aside*): Will nothing do? (*aloud*) Well, it must out then. To tell you the truth, ladies, which I was afraid to let you know before, lest it might endanger your lives, my wife has just now the smallpox come out upon her; do not be frightened; but pray be gone, ladies; you shall not stay here in danger of your lives; pray get you gone, ladies.

LADY FIDGET: No, no, we have all had 'em.

MRS. SQUEAMISH: Alack, alack.

MRS. DAINTY: Come, come, we must see how it goes with her; I understand the disease.

LADY FIDGET: Come!

PINCHWIFE (*aside*): Well, there is no being too hard for women at their own weapon, lying, therefore I'll quit the field.[8]

(*Exit* PINCHWIFE.)

MRS. SQUEAMISH: Here's an example of jealousy.

LADY FIDGET: Indeed, as the world goes, I wonder there are no more jealous, since wives are so neglected.

MRS. DAINTY: Pshaw! As the world goes, to what end should they be jealous?

LADY FIDGET: Foh! 'Tis a nasty world.

MRS. SQUEAMISH: That men of parts, great acquaintance, and quality, should take up with and spend themselves and fortunes in keeping little playhouse creatures, foh!

LADY FIDGET: Nay, that women of understanding, great acquaintance, and good quality, should fall a-keeping too of little creatures, foh!

MRS. SQUEAMISH: Why, 'tis the men of quality's fault; they never visit women of honour and reputation as they used to do; and have not so much as common civility for ladies of our rank, but use us with the same indifferency and ill-breeding as if we were all married to 'em.

LADY FIDGET: She says true; 'tis an arrant shame women of quality should be so slighted; methinks birth, birth should go for something; I have known men admired, courted, and followed for their titles only.

MRS. SQUEAMISH: Ay, one would think men of honour should not love, no more than marry, out of their own rank.

MRS. DAINTY: Fy, fy upon 'em! They are come to think cross breeding for themselves best, as well as for their dogs and horses.

LADY FIDGET: They are dogs and horses for't.

MRS. SQUEAMISH: One would think, if not for love, for vanity a little.

MRS. DAINTY: Nay, they do satisfy their vanity upon us sometimes; and are kind to us in their report, tell all the world they lie with us.

LADY FIDGET: Damned rascals, that we should be only wronged by 'em! To report a man has had a person, when he has not had a person, is the greatest wrong in the whole world that can be done to a person.

MRS. SQUEAMISH: Well, 'tis an arrant shame noble persons should be so wronged and neglected.

LADY FIDGET: But still 'tis an arranter shame for a noble person to neglect her own honour, and defame her own noble person with little inconsiderable fellows, foh!

MRS. DAINTY: I suppose the crime against our honour is the same with a man of quality as with another.

---

8 *quit the field:* give up.

LADY FIDGET: How! No sure, the man of quality is likest one's husband, and therefore the fault should be the less.

MRS. DAINTY: But then the pleasure should be the less.

LADY FIDGET: Fy fy fy, for shame, sister! Whither shall we ramble? Be continent in your discourse, or I shall hate you.

MRS. DAINTY: Besides, an intrigue is so much the more notorious for the man's quality.

MRS. SQUEAMISH: 'Tis true that nobody takes notice of a private man, and therefore with him 'tis more secret; and the crime's the less when 'tis not known.

LADY FIDGET: You say true; i'faith, I think you are in the right on't. 'Tis not an injury to a husband, till it be an injury to our honours; so that a woman of honour loses no honour with a private person; and to say truth —

MRS. DAINTY (aside to MRS. SQUEAMISH): So, the little fellow is grown a private person — with her —

LADY FIDGET: But still my dear, dear honour —

(Enter SIR JASPER FIDGET, HORNER, and DORILANT)

SIR JASPER: Ay, my dear, dear of honour, thou hast still so much honour in thy mouth —

HORNER (aside): That she has none elsewhere.

LADY FIDGET: Oh, what d'ye mean to bring in these upon us?

MRS. DAINTY: Foh! These are as bad as wits.

MRS. SQUEAMISH: Foh!

LADY FIDGET: Let us leave the room.

SIR JASPER: Stay, stay; faith, to tell you the naked truth —

LADY FIDGET: Fy, Sir Jasper! Do not use that word "naked."

SIR JASPER: Well, well, in short I have business at Whitehall, and cannot go to the play with you, therefore would have you go —

LADY FIDGET: With those two to a play?

SIR JASPER: No, not with t'other, but with Mr. Horner; there can be no more scandal to go with him than with Mr. Tattle, or Master Limberham.

LADY FIDGET: With that nasty fellow! No — no.

SIR JASPER: Nay, prithee, dear, hear me (Whispers to LADY FIDGET.)

HORNER: Ladies. . . .

(HORNER and DORILANT draw near MRS. SQUEAMISH and MRS. DAINTY FIDGET.)

MRS. DAINTY: Stand off.

MRS. SQUEAMISH: Do not approach us.

MRS. DAINTY: You herd with the wits, you are obscenity all over.

MRS. SQUEAMISH: And I would as soon look upon a picture of Adam and Eve without fig leaves, as any of you, if I could help it; therefore keep off, and do not make us sick.

DORILANT: What a devil are these?

HORNER: Why, these are pretenders to honour, as critics to wit, only by censuring others; and as every raw, peevish, out-of-humoured, affected, dull, tea-drinking, arithmetical fop, sets up for a wit by railing at men of sense, so these for honour, by railing at the court, and ladies of as great honour as quality.

SIR JASPER: Come, Mr. Horner, I must desire you to go with these ladies to the play, sir.

HORNER: I, sir?

SIR JASPER: Ay, ay, come, sir.

HORNER: I must beg your pardon, sir, and theirs; I will not be seen in women's company in public again for the world.

SIR JASPER: Ha ha, strange aversion!

MRS. SQUEAMISH: No, he's for women's company in private.

SIR JASPER: He — poor man — he — ha ha ha!

MRS. DAINTY: 'Tis a greater shame amongst lewd fellows to be seen in virtuous women's company, than for the women to be seen with them.

HORNER: Indeed, madam, the time was I only hated virtuous women, but now I hate the other too; I beg your pardon, ladies.

LADY FIDGET: You are very obliging, sir, because we would not be troubled with you.

SIR JASPER: In sober sadness, he shall go.

DORILANT: Nay, if he wo' not, I am ready to call upon the ladies, and I think I am the fitter man.

SIR JASPER: You, sir! No, I thank you for that. Master Horner is a privileged man amongst the virtuous ladies; 'twill be a great while before you are so. He he he! He's my wife's gallant; he he he! No, pray withdraw, sir, for as I take it, the virtuous ladies have no business with you.

DORILANT: And I am sure he can have none with them. 'Tis strange a man can't come amongst virtuous women now, but upon the same terms as men are admitted into the Great Turk's seraglio.[9] But heavens keep me from being an ombre player[10] with 'em! But where is Pinchwife?

(*Exit* DORILANT.)

SIR JASPER: Come, come, man; what, avoid the sweet society of womankind? That sweet, soft, gentle, tame, noble creature, woman, made for man's companion —

HORNER: So is that soft, gentle, tame, and more noble creature a spaniel,[11] and has all their tricks; can fawn, lie down, suffer beating, and fawn the more; barks at your friends when they come to see you, makes your bed hard, gives you fleas, and the mange sometimes. And all the difference is, the spaniel's the more faithful animal, and fawns but upon one master.

SIR JASPER: He he he!

MRS. SQUEAMISH: Oh, the rude beast!

MRS. DAINTY: Insolent brute!

LADY FIDGET: Brute! Stinking, mortified, rotten French wether,[12] to dare —

SIR JASPER: Hold, an't please your ladyship. For shame, Master Horner! Your mother was a woman. (*aside*) Now shall I never reconcile 'em. (*aside to* LADY FIDGET) Hark you, madam, take my advice in your anger. You know you often want one to make up your drolling[13] pack of ombre players, and you may cheat him easily; for he's an ill gamester, and consequently loves play. Besides, you know you have but two old civil gentlemen (with stinking breaths too) to wait upon you abroad; take in the third into your service. The other are but crazy;[14] and a lady should have a supernumerary gentleman-usher as a supernumerary coach-horse, lest sometimes you should be forced to stay at home.

LADY FIDGET: But are you sure he loves play, and has money?

SIR JASPER: He loves play as much as you, and has money as much as I.

LADY FIDGET: Then I am contented to make him pay for his scurrility. Money makes up in a measure all other wants in men. (*aside*) Those whom we cannot make hold for gallants, we make fine.[15]

SIR JASPER (*aside*): So, so; now to mollify, wheedle him. (*aside to* HORNER) Master Horner, will you never keep civil company? Methinks 'tis time now, since you are only fit for them. Come, come, man, you must e'en fall to visiting our wives, eating at our tables, drinking tea with our virtuous relations after dinner, dealing cards to 'em, reading plays and gazettes to 'em, picking fleas out of their shocks for 'em, collecting receipts, new songs, women, pages, and footmen for 'em.

HORNER: I hope they'll afford me better employment, sir.

SIR JASPER: He he he! 'Tis fit you know your work before you come into your place. And

---

9 *seraglio:* that is, as eunuchs. 10 *ombre:* a card game. Perhaps there is a pun on the Spanish *hombre,* concerning playing the man. 11 *spaniel:* Charles II made this dog popular as a pet. 12 *wether:* castrated ram. 13 *drolling:* clownish. 14 *crazy:* broken down. 15 *make fine:* make pay a penalty.

since you are unprovided of a lady to flatter, and a good house to eat at, pray frequent mine, and call my wife mistress, and she shall call you gallant, according to the custom.

HORNER: Who, I?

SIR JASPER: Faith, thou sha't for my sake; come, for my sake only.

HORNER: For your sake —

SIR JASPER: Come, come, here's a gamester for you; let him be a little familiar sometimes; nay, what if a little rude? Gamesters may be rude with ladies, you know.

LADY FIDGET: Yes; losing gamesters have a privilege with women.

HORNER: I always thought the contrary, that the winning gamester had most privilege with women; for when you have lost your money to a man, you'll lose anything you have, all you have, they say, and he may use you as he pleases.

SIR JASPER: He he he! Well, win or lose, you shall have your liberty with her.

LADY FIDGET: As he behaves himself; and for your sake I'll give him admittance and freedom.

HORNER: All sorts of freedom, madam?

SIR JASPER: Ay, ay, ay, all sorts of freedom thou canst take. And so go to her, begin thy new employment; wheedle her, jest with her, and be better acquainted one with another.

HORNER (aside): I think I know her already; therefore may venture with her my secret for hers.

(HORNER and LADY FIDGET whisper.)

SIR JASPER: Sister cuz,[16] I have provided an innocent playfellow for you there.

MRS. DAINTY. Who, he?

MRS. SQUEAMISH: There's a playfellow, indeed!

SIR JASPER: Yes sure. What, he is good enough to play at cards, blindman's buff, or the fool with, sometimes!

MRS. SQUEAMISH: Foh! We'll have no such playfellows.

MRS. DAINTY: No, sir; you shan't choose playfellows for us, we thank you.

SIR JASPER: Nay, pray hear me. (whispering to them)

LADY FIDGET: But, poor gentleman, could you be so generous, so truly a man of honour, as for the sakes of us women of honour, to cause yourself to be reported no man? No man! And to suffer yourself the greatest shame that could fall upon a man, that none might fall upon us women by your conversation? But, indeed, sir, as perfectly, perfectly the same man as before your going into France, sir? As perfectly, perfectly, sir?

HORNER: As perfectly, perfectly, madam. Nay, I scorn you should take my word; I desire to be tried only, madam.

LADY FIDGET: Well, that's spoken again like a man of honour; all men of honour desire to come to the test. But, indeed, generally you men report such things of yourselves, one does not know how or whom to believe; and it is come to that pass, we dare not take your words no more than your tailor's, without some staid servant of yours be bound with you. But I have so strong a faith in your honour, dear, dear, noble sir, that I'd forfeit mine for yours, at any time, dear sir.

HORNER: No, madam, you should not need to forfeit it for me; I have given you security already to save you harmless, my late reputation being so well known in the world, madam.

LADY FIDGET: But if upon any future falling-out, or upon a suspicion of my taking the trust out of your hands to employ some other, you yourself should betray your trust, dear sir? I mean, if you'll give me leave to speak obscenely,[17] you might tell, dear sir.

---

16 *cuz:* cousin, any relative but a sibling or parent.   17 *obscenely:* perhaps a pun on *proscenium*, downstage or directly.

HORNER: If I did, nobody would believe me. The reputation of impotency is as hardly recovered again in the world as that of cowardice, dear madam.

LADY FIDGET: Nay, then, as one may say, you may do your worst, dear, dear sir.

SIR JASPER: Come, is your ladyship reconciled to him yet? Have you agreed on matters? For I must be gone to Whitehall.

LADY FIDGET: Why, indeed, Sir Jasper, Master Horner is a thousand, thousand times a better man than I thought him. Cousin Squeamish, sister Dainty, I can name him now. Truly, not long ago, you know, I thought his very name obscenity; and I would as soon have lain with him as have named him.

SIR JASPER: Very likely, poor madam.

MRS. DAINTY: I believe it.

MRS. SQUEAMISH: No doubt on't.

SIR JASPER: Well, well — that your ladyship is as virtuous as any she, I know; and him all the town knows, he he he! Therefore, now you like him, get you gone to your business together, go, go to your business, I say, pleasure, whilst I go to my pleasure, business.

LADY FIDGET: Come, then, dear gallant.

HORNER: Come away, my dearest mistress.

SIR JASPER: So, so; why, 'tis as I'd have it.

(*Exit* SIR JASPER.)

HORNER: And as I'd have it.

LADY FIDGET: Who for his business from his wife will run,
Takes the best care to have her business done.

(*Exeunt* LADY FIDGET, MRS. SQUEAMISH, MRS. DAINTY FIDGET, HORNER.)

ACT THREE

SCENE ONE   Pinchwife's House.

Enter ALITHEA *and* MRS. PINCHWIFE.

ALITHEA: Sister, what ails you? You are grown melancholy.

MRS. PINCHWIFE: Would it not make any one melancholy to see you go every day fluttering about abroad, whilst I must stay at home like a poor lonely sullen bird in a cage?

ALITHEA: Ay, sister; but you came young, and just from the nest to your cage, so that I thought you liked it, and could be as cheerful in't as others that took their flight themselves early, and are hopping abroad in the open air.

MRS. PINCHWIFE: Nay, I confess I was quiet enough till my husband told me what pure lives the London ladies live abroad, with their dancing, meetings, and junketings, and dressed every day in their best gowns; and I warrant you, play at nine-pins every day of the week, so they do.

(*Enter* PINCHWIFE.)

PINCHWIFE: Come, what's here to do? You are putting the town-pleasures in her head, and setting her a-longing.

ALITHEA: Yes, after nine-pins. You suffer none to give her those longings, you mean, but yourself.

PINCHWIFE: I tell her of the vanities of the town like a confessor.

ALITHEA: A confessor! Just such a confessor as he that, by forbidding a silly hostler to grease the horse's teeth, taught him to do't.

PINCHWIFE: Come, Mrs. Flippant, good precepts are lost when bad examples are still before us. The liberty you take abroad makes her hanker after it, and out of humour at home, poor wretch. She desired not to come to London; I would bring her.

ALITHEA: Very well.

PINCHWIFE: She has been this week in town, and never desired till this afternoon to go abroad.

ALITHEA: Was she not at a play yesterday?

PINCHWIFE: Yes; but she ne'er asked me; I was myself the cause of her going.

ALITHEA: Then if she ask you again, you are the cause of her asking, and not my example.

PINCHWIFE: Well, tomorrow night I shall be rid of you; and the next day, before 'tis light, she and I'll be rid of the town, and my dreadful apprehensions. Come, be not melancholy; for thou sha't go into the country after tomorrow, dearest.

ALITHEA: Great comfort.

MRS. PINCHWIFE: Pish! What d'ye tell me of the country for?

PINCHWIFE: How's this! What, pish at the country?

MRS. PINCHWIFE: Let me alone; I am not well.

PINCHWIFE: Oh, if that be all — what ails my dearest?

MRS. PINCHWIFE: Truly, I don't know; but I have not been well since you told me there was a gallant at the play in love with me.

PINCHWIFE: Ha!

ALITHEA: That's by my example too!

PINCHWIFE: Nay, if you are not well, but are so concerned, because a lewd fellow chanced to lie, and say he liked you, you'll make me sick too.

MRS. PINCHWIFE: Of what sickness?

PINCHWIFE: Oh, of that which is worse than the plague: jealousy.

MRS. PINCHWIFE: Pish, you jeer! I'm sure there's no such disease in our receipt-book[1] at home.

PINCHWIFE: No, thou never met'st with it, poor innocent. (aside) Well, if thou cuckold me, 'twill be my own fault — for cuckolds and bastards are generally makers of their own fortune.

MRS. PINCHWIFE: Well, but pray, bud, let's go to a play tonight.

PINCHWIFE: 'Tis just done, she comes from it. But why are you so eager to see a play?

MRS. PINCHWIFE: Faith, dear, not that I care one pin for their talk there; but I like to look upon the playermen, and would see, if I could, the gallant you say loves me. That's all dear bud.

PINCHWIFE: Is that all, dear bud?

ALITHEA: This proceeds from my example!

MRS. PINCHWIFE: But if the play be done, let's go abroad, however, dear bud.

PINCHWIFE: Come, have a little patience and thou shalt go into the country on Friday.

MRS. PINCHWIFE: Therefore I would see first some sights to tell my neighbours of. Nay, I will go abroad, that's once.

ALITHEA: I'm the cause of this desire too!

PINCHWIFE: But now I think on't, who, who was the cause of Horner's coming to my lodgings today? That was you.

ALITHEA: No, you, because you would not let him see your handsome wife out of your lodging.

MRS. PINCHWIFE: Why, O Lord! Did the gentleman come hither to see me indeed?

PINCHWIFE: No, no. You are not the cause of that damned question too, Mistress Alithea? (aside) Well, she's in the right of it. He is in love with my wife — and comes after her — 'tis so — but I'll nip his love in the bud, lest he should follow us into the country, and break his chariot-wheel near our house, on purpose for an excuse to come to't. But I think I know the town.

MRS. PINCHWIFE: Come, pray, bud, let's go abroad before 'tis late; for I will go, that's flat[2] and plain.

PINCHWIFE (aside): So! The obstinacy already of the town-wife; and I must, whilst she's here, humour her like one. (aloud) Sister, how shall we do, that she may not be seen or known?

ALITHEA: Let her put on her mask.

PINCHWIFE: Pshaw! A mask makes people but the more inquisitive, and is as ridiculous a

---

1 *receipt-book:* book of home remedies. 2 *flat:* certain.

disguise as a stage-beard; her shape, stature, habit will be known. And if we should meet with Horner, he would be sure to take acquaintance with us, must wish her joy, kiss her, talk to her, leer upon her, and the devil and all. No, I'll not use her to a mask, 'tis dangerous; for masks have made more cuckolds than the best faces that ever were known.

ALITHEA: How will you do then?

MRS. PINCHWIFE: Nay, shall we go? The Exchange will be shut, and I have a mind to see that.

PINCHWIFE: So — I have it — I'll dress her up in the suit we are to carry down to her brother, little Sir James; nay, I understand the town-tricks. Come, let's go dress her. A mask! No — a woman masked, like a covered dish, gives a man curiosity and appetite; when, it may be, uncovered, 'twould turn his stomach. No, no.

ALITHEA: Indeed your comparison is something a greasy one; but I had a gentle gallant used to say, "A beauty masked, like the sun in eclipse, gathers together more gazers than if it shined out."

(*Exeunt* ALITHEA, MRS. PINCHWIFE, PINCHWIFE.)

SCENE TWO   The New Exchange.

Enter HORNER, HARCOURT, *and* DORILANT.

DORILANT: Engaged to women, and not sup with us!

HORNER: Ay, a pox on 'em all.

HARCOURT: You were much a more reasonable man in the morning, and had as noble resolutions against 'em as a widower of a week's liberty.

DORILANT: Did I ever think to see you keep company with women in vain?

HORNER: In vain! No — 'tis since I can't love 'em, to be revenged on 'em.

HARCOURT: Now your sting is gone, you looked in the box amongst all those women like a

drone in the hive; all upon you, shoved and ill-used by 'em all, and thrust from one side to t'other.

DORILANT: Yet he must be buzzing amongst 'em still, like other old beetle-headed[1] liquorish drones. Avoid 'em, and hate 'em, as they hate you.

HORNER: Because I do hate 'em, and would hate 'em yet more, I'll frequent 'em. You may see by marriage, nothing makes a man hate a woman more than her constant conversation. In short, I converse with 'em, as you do with rich fools, to laugh at 'em and use 'em ill.

DORILANT: But I would no more sup with women, unless I could lie with 'em, than sup with a rich coxcomb, unless I could cheat him.

HORNER: Yes, I have known thee sup with a fool for his drinking; if he could set out your hand that way only, you were satisfied, and if he were a wine-swallowing mouth, 'twas enough.

HARCOURT: Yes, a man drinks often with a fool, as he tosses with a marker, only to keep his hand in use. But do the ladies drink?

HORNER: Yes, sir; and I shall have the pleasure at least of laying 'em flat with a bottle, and bring as much scandal that way upon 'em as formerly t'other.

HARCOURT: Perhaps you may prove as weak a brother among 'em that way as t'other.

DORILANT: Foh! Drinking with women is as unnatural as scolding with 'em. But 'tis a pleasure of decayed fornicators, and the basest way of quenching love.

HARCOURT: Nay, 'tis drowning love, instead of quenching it. But leave us for civil women too!

DORILANT: Ay, when he can't be the better for 'em. We hardly pardon a man that leaves his friend for a wench, and that's a pretty lawful call.

---

1 *beetle-headed:* block-headed.

HORNER: Faith, I would not leave you for 'em, if they would not drink.

DORILANT: Who would disappoint his company at Lewis's[2] for a gossiping?

HARCOURT: Foh! Wine and women, good apart, together are as nauseous as sack and sugar.[3] But hark you, sir, before you go, a little of your advice; an old maimed general, when unfit for action, is fittest for counsel. I have other designs upon women than eating and drinking with them; I am in love with Sparkish's mistress, whom he is to marry tomorrow. Now how shall I get her?

(*Enter* SPARKISH, *looking about.*)

HORNER: Why, here comes one will help you to her.

HARCOURT: He! He, I tell you, is my rival, and will hinder my love.

HORNER: No; a foolish rival and a jealous husband assist their rival's designs; for they are sure to make their women hate them, which is the first step to their love for another man.

HARCOURT: But I cannot come near his mistress but in his company.

HORNER: Still the better for you, for fools are most easily cheated when they themselves are accessaries; and he is to be bubbled[4] of his mistress as of his money, the common mistress, by keeping him company.

SPARKISH: Who is that that is to be bubbled? Faith, let me snack; I han't met with a bubble since Christmas. Gad, I think bubbles are like their brother woodcocks,[5] go out with the cold weather.

HARCOURT (*aside to* HORNER): A pox! He did not hear all, I hope.

SPARKISH: Come, you bubbling rogues you, where do we sup? — Oh, Harcourt, my mistress tells me you have been making fierce love to her all the play long, ha ha! — But I —

HARCOURT: I make love to her?

SPARKISH: Nay, I forgive thee, for I think I know thee, and I know her; but I am sure I know myself.

HARCOURT: Did she tell you so? I see all women are like these of the Exchange, who, to enhance the prize of their commodities, report to their fond customers offers which were never made 'em.

HORNER: Ay, women are apt to tell before the intrigue, as men after it, and so show themselves the vainer sex. But hast thou a mistress, Sparkish? 'Tis as hard for me to believe it, as that thou ever hadst a bubble, as you bragged just now.

SPARKISH: Oh, your servant, sir; are you at your raillery, sir? But we were some of us beforehand with you today at the play. The wits were something bold with you, sir; did you not hear us laugh?

HORNER: Yes; but I thought you had gone to plays to laugh at the poet's wit, not at your own.

SPARKISH: Your servant, sir; no, I thank you. Gad, I go to a play as to a country treat; I carry my own wine to one, and my own wit to t'other, or else I'm sure I should not be merry at either. And the reason why we are often louder than the players, is, because we think we speak more wit, and so become the poet's rivals in his audience. For to tell you the truth, we hate the silly rogues; nay, so much, that we find fault even with their bawdy upon the stage, whilst we talk nothing else in the pit as loud.[6]

HORNER: But why shouldst thou hate the silly poets? Thou hast too much wit to be one; and they, like whores, are only hated by each other. And thou dost scorn writing, I'm sure.

SPARKISH: Yes; I'd have you to know I scorn writing; but women, women, that make men

---

2 *Lewis's:* a tavern.   3 *sack and sugar:* sherry and sugar—sherry is best dry.   4 *bubbled:* duped.   5 *woodcocks:* birds easily ensnared.   6 *loud:* Restoration audiences were often vocal and unruly. As late as the eighteenth century, actors like Colley Cibber were hissed off the stage and performances aborted.

do all foolish things, make 'em write songs too. Everybody does it. 'Tis even as common with lovers, as playing with fans; and you can no more help rhyming to your Phillis, than drinking to your Phillis.

HARCOURT: Nay, poetry in love is no more to be avoided than jealousy.

DORILANT: But the poets damned your songs, did they?

SPARKISH: Damn the poets! They turned 'em into burlesque, as they call it. That burlesque is a hocus-pocus trick they have got, which, by the virtue of *Hictius doctius topsy turvy*,[7] they make a wise and witty man in the world, a fool upon the stage, you know not how; and 'tis therefore I hate 'em too, for I know not but it may be my own case; for they'll put a man into a play for looking asquint. Their predecessors were contented to make serving-men only their stage-fools; but these rogues must have gentlemen, with a pox to 'em, nay, knights; and, indeed, you shall hardly see a fool upon the stage but he's a knight. And to tell you the truth, they have kept me these six years from being a knight in earnest, for fear of being knighted in a play, and dubbed a fool.

DORILANT: Blame 'em not, they must follow their copy, the age.

HARCOURT: But why shouldst thou be afraid of being in a play, who expose yourself every day in the play-houses, and at public places?

HORNER: 'Tis but being on the stage, instead of standing on a bench in the pit.

DORILANT: Don't you give money to painters to draw you like? And are you afraid of your pictures at length in a playhouse, where all your mistresses may see you?

SPARKISH: A pox! Painters don't draw the smallpox or pimples in one's face. Come, damn all your silly authors whatever, all books and booksellers, by the world; and all readers, courteous or uncourteous!

HARCOURT: But who comes here, Sparkish?

(*Enter* PINCHWIFE *and* MRS. PINCHWIFE *in man's clothes*, ALITHEA *and* LUCY.)

SPARKISH: Oh, hide me! There's my mistress too. (SPARKISH *hides himself behind* HARCOURT.)

HARCOURT: She sees you.

SPARKISH: But I will not see her. 'Tis time to go to Whitehall, and I must not fail[8] the drawing-room.

HARCOURT: Pray, first carry me, and reconcile me to her.

SPARKISH: Another time. Faith, the king will have supped.

HARCOURT: Not with the worse stomach for thy absence. Thou art one of those fools that think their attendance at the king's meals as necessary as his physicians, when you are more troublesome to him than his doctors or his dogs.

SPARKISH: Pshaw! I know my interest, sir. Prithee hide me.

HORNER: Your servant, Pinchwife. What, he knows us not!

PINCHWIFE (*aside, to his wife*): Come along.

MRS. PINCHWIFE: Pray, have you any ballads? Give me sixpenny worth.

BOOKSELLER: We have no ballads.

MRS. PINCHWIFE: Then give me *Covent Garden Drollery*, and a play or two — Oh, here's *Tarugo's Wiles*, and *The Slighted Maiden*.[9] I'll have them.

PINCHWIFE (*aside to her*): No; plays are not for your reading. Come along; will you discover yourself?

---

7 *Hictius, etc.*: nonsense words. 8 *fail*: miss. 9 *Covent Garden*, etc.: *Covent Garden Drollery* (songs, 1672), *Tarugo's Wiles* (play by the very minor Thomas St. Serfe, 1668), *The Slighted Wife* (play by Sir Robert Staplyton, 1663). Samuel Pepys called *Tarugo's Wiles* "the most ridiculous, insipid play that I ever saw in my life" and *The Slighted Wife* he found had "little good in it." Wycherley had used a song from *Covent Garden Drollery* in the second act of his *The Gentleman Dancing Master*.

HORNER: Who is that pretty youth with him, Sparkish?

SPARKISH: I believe his wife's brother, because he's something like her; but I never saw her but once.

HORNER: Extremely handsome; I have seen a face like it too. Let us follow 'em.

(*Exeunt* PINCHWIFE, MRS. PINCHWIFE, ALITHEA, *and* LUCY; HORNER *and* DORILANT *following them.*)

HARCOURT: Come, Sparkish, your mistress saw you, and will be angry you go not to her. Besides, I would fain be reconciled to her, which none but you can do, dear friend.

SPARKISH: Well, that's a better reason, dear friend. I would not go near her now for hers or my own sake, but I can deny you nothing; for though I have known thee a great while, never go, if I do not love thee as well as a new acquaintance.

HARCOURT: I am obliged to you indeed, dear friend. I would be well with her, only to be well with thee still; for these ties to wives usually dissolve all ties to friends. I would be contented she should enjoy you a-nights, but I would have you to myself a-days as I have had, dear friend.

SPARKISH: And thou shalt enjoy me a-days, dear, dear friend, never stir; and I'll be divorced from her, sooner than from thee. Come along.

HARCOURT (*aside*): So, we are hard put to't, when we make our rival our procurer; but neither she nor her brother would let me come near her now. When all's done, a rival is the best cloak to steal to a mistress under, without suspicion; and when we have once got to her as we desire, we throw him off like other cloaks.

(*Exit* SPARKISH, HARCOURT *following him. Enter* PINCHWIFE *and* MRS. PINCHWIFE.)

PINCHWIFE (*to* ALITHEA): Sister, if you will not go, we must leave you. (*aside*) The fool her gallant and she will muster up all the young saunterers of this place, and they will leave

their dear seamstresses to follow us. What a swarm of cuckolds and cuckold-makers are here! (*to his wife*) Come, let's be gone, Mistress Margery.

MRS. PINCHWIFE: Don't you believe that; I han't half my bellyful of sights yet.

PINCHWIFE: Then walk this way.

MRS. PINCHWIFE: Lord, what a power of brave signs are here! Stay — the Bull's-Head, the Ram's-Head, and the Stag's-Head, dear —

PINCHWIFE: Nay, if every husband's proper sign here were visible, they would be all alike.[10]

MRS. PINCHWIFE: What d'ye mean by that, bud?

PINCHWIFE: 'Tis no matter — no matter, bud.

MRS. PINCHWIFE: Pray tell me: nay, I will know.

PINCHWIFE: They would be all Bulls, Stags, and Rams-heads.

(*Exeunt* PINCHWIFE *and* MRS. PINCHWIFE. *Enter* SPARKISH, HARCOURT, ALITHEA, *and* LUCY, *at the other side.*)

SPARKISH: Come, dear madam, for my sake you shall be reconciled to him.

ALITHEA: For your sake I hate him.

HARCOURT: That's something too cruel, madam, to hate me for his sake.

SPARKISH: Ay indeed, madam, too, too cruel to me, to hate my friend for my sake.

ALITHEA: I hate him because he is your enemy; and you ought to hate him too, for making love to me, if you love me.

SPARKISH: That's a good one! I hate a man for loving you! If he did love you, 'tis but what he can't help; and 'tis your fault, not his, if he admires you. I hate a man for being of my opinion? I'll n'er do't, by the world.

ALITHEA: Is it for your honour, or mine, to suffer a man to make love to me, who am to marry you tomorrow?

---

10 *all alike:* that is, the Horned Head, for cuckolds.

SPARKISH: Is it for your honour, or mine, to have me jealous? That he makes love to you, is a sign you are handsome; and that I am not jealous, is a sign you are virtuous. That I think is for your honour.

ALITHEA: But 'tis your honour too I am concerned for.

HARCOURT: But why, dearest madam, will you be more concerned for his honour than he is himself? Let his honour alone, for my sake and his. He! He has no honour —

SPARKISH: How's that?

HARCOURT: But what my dear friend can guard himself.

SPARKISH: Oh ho — that's right again.

HARCOURT: Your care of his honour argues his neglect of it, which is no honour to my dear friend here. Therefore once more, let his honour go which way it will, dear madam.

SPARKISH: Ay, ay; were it for my honour to marry a woman whose virtue I suspected, and could not trust her in a friend's hands?

ALITHEA: Are you not afraid to lose me?

HARCOURT: He afraid to lose you, madam! No, no — you may see how the most estimable and most glorious creature in the world is valued by him. Will you not see it?

SPARKISH: Right, honest Frank, I have that noble value for her that I cannot be jealous of her.

ALITHEA: You mistake him. He means, you care not for me, nor who has me.

SPARKISH: Lord, madam, I see you are jealous! Will you wrest a poor man's meaning from his words?

ALITHEA: You astonish me, sir, with your want of jealousy.

SPARKISH: And you make me giddy, madam, with your jealousy and fears, and virtue and honour. Gad, I see virtue makes a woman as troublesome as a little reading or learning.

ALITHEA: Monstrous!

LUCY (aside): Well, to see what easy husbands these women of quality can meet with! A poor chambermaid can never have such lady-like luck. Besides, he's thrown away upon her. She'll make no use of her fortune, her blessing, none to a gentleman, for a pure cuckold; for it requires good breeding to be a cuckold.

ALITHEA: I tell you then plainly, he pursues me to marry me.

SPARKISH: Pshaw!

HARCOURT: Come, madam, you see you strive in vain to make him jealous of me. My dear friend is the kindest creature in the world to me.

SPARKISH: Poor fellow!

HARCOURT: But his kindness only is not enough for me, without your favour; your good opinion, dear madam, 'tis that must perfect my happiness. Good gentleman, he believes all I say; would you would do so! Jealous of me! I would not wrong him nor you for the world.

SPARKISH: Look you there. Hear him, hear him, and do not walk away so.

(ALITHEA walks carelessly to and fro.)

HARCOURT: I love you, madam, so —

SPARKISH: How's that? Nay, now you begin to go too far indeed.

HARCOURT: So much, I confess, I say, I love you, that I would not have you miserable, and cast yourself away upon so unworthy and inconsiderable a thing as what you see here. (Clapping his hand on his breast, points at SPARKISH.)

SPARKISH: No, faith, I believe thou wouldst not. (Now his meaning is plain.) But I knew before thou wouldst not wrong me, nor her.

HARCOURT: No, no, Heavens forbid the glory of her sex should fall so low, as into the embraces of such a contemptible wretch, the least of mankind — my dear friend here — I injure him!

(Embracing SPARKISH.)

ALITHEA: Very well.

SPARKISH: No, no, dear friend, I knew it. Madam, you see he will rather wrong himself than me, in giving himself such names.

ALITHEA: Do not you understand him yet?

SPARKISH: Yes; modestly he speaks of himself, poor fellow!

ALITHEA: Methinks he speaks impudently of yourself, since — before yourself too; insomuch that I can no longer suffer his scurrilous abusiveness to you, no more than his love to me. (*Offers to go.*)

SPARKISH: Nay, nay, madam, pray stay — his love to you! Lord, madam, has he not spoke yet plain enough?

ALITHEA: Yes, indeed, I should think so.

SPARKISH: Well then, by the world, a man can't speak civilly to a woman now, but presently she says he makes love to her. Nay, madam, you shall stay, with your pardon, since you have not yet understood him, till he has made an *eclaircissement*[11] of his love to you, that is, what kind of love it is. Answer to thy catechism, friend; do you love my mistress here?

HARCOURT: Yes, I wish she would not doubt it.

SPARKISH: But how do you love her?

HARCOURT: With all my soul.

ALITHEA: I thank him; methinks he speaks plain enough now.

SPARKISH (*to* ALITHEA): You are out still. But with what kind of love, Harcourt?

HARCOURT: With the best and the truest love in the world.

SPARKISH: Look you there then, that is with no matrimonial love, I'm sure.

ALITHEA: How's that? Do you say matrimonial love is not best?

SPARKISH: Gad, I went too far ere I was aware. But speak for thyself, Harcourt; you said you would not wrong me nor her.

HARCOURT: No, no, madam, e'en take him for Heaven's sake.

SPARKISH: Look you there, madam.

HARCOURT: Who should in all justice be yours, (*Claps his hand on his breast.*), he that loves you most.

ALITHEA: Look you there, Mr. Sparkish, who's that?

SPARKISH: Who should it be? Go on, Harcourt.

HARCOURT: Who loves you more than women titles, or fortune fools. (*Points at* SPARKISH.)

SPARKISH: Look you there, he means me still, for he points at me.

ALITHEA: Ridiculous!

HARCOURT: Who can only match your faith and constancy in love.

SPARKISH: Ay.

HARCOURT: Who knows, if it be possible, how to value so much beauty and virtue.

SPARKISH: Ay.

HARCOURT: Whose love can no more be equalled in the world, than that heavenly form of yours.

SPARKISH: No.

HARCOURT: Who could no more suffer a rival, than your absence, and yet could no more suspect your virtue, than his own constancy in his love to you.

SPARKISH: No.

HARCOURT: Who, in fine, loves you better than his eyes, that first made him love you.

SPARKISH: Ay — nay, madam, faith, you shan't go till —

ALITHEA: Have a care, lest you make me stay too long.

SPARKISH: But till he has saluted you; that I may be assured you are friends, after his

---

11 *eclaircissement:* French, open declaration.

honest advice and declaration. Come, pray, madam, be friends with him.

(*Enter* PINCHWIFE *and* MRS. PINCHWIFE.)

ALITHEA: You must pardon me, sir, that I am not yet so obedient to you.

PINCHWIFE: What, invite your wife to kiss men? Monstrous! Are you not ashamed? I will never forgive you.

SPARKISH: Are you not ashamed, that I should have more confidence in the chastity of your family than you have? You must not teach me, I am a man of honour, sir, though I am frank[12] and free; I am frank, sir —

PINCHWIFE: Very frank, sir, to share your wife with your friends.

SPARKISH: He is a humble, menial friend, such as reconciles the differences of the marriage bed; you know man and wife do not always agree. I design him for that use, therefore would have him well with my wife.

PINCHWIFE: A menial friend! You will get a great many menial friends, by showing your wife as you do.

SPARKISH: What then? It may be I have a pleasure in't, as I have to show fine clothes at a play-house the first day, and count money before poor rogues.

PINCHWIFE: He that shows his wife or money, will be in danger of having them borrowed sometimes.

SPARKISH: I love to be envied, and would not marry a wife that I alone could love; loving alone is as dull as eating alone. Is it not a frank age? And I am a frank person; and to tell you the truth, it may be I love to have rivals in a wife, they make her seem to a man still but as a kept mistress; and so good night, for I must to Whitehall. Madam, I hope you are now reconciled to my friend; and so I wish you a good night, madam, and sleep if you can; for tomorrow you know I must visit you early with a canonical gentleman. Good night, dear Harcourt.

(*Exit* SPARKISH.)

HARCOURT: Madam, I hope you will not refuse my visit tomorrow, if it should be earlier with a canonical gentleman than Mr. Sparkish's.

PINCHWIFE: This gentlewoman is yet under my care, therefore you must yet forbear your freedom with her, sir. (*coming between* ALITHEA *and* HARCOURT).

HARCOURT: Must, sir?

PINCHWIFE: Yes, sir, she is my sister.

HARCOURT: 'Tis well she is, sir — for I must be her servant, sir. Madam —

PINCHWIFE: Come away, sister; we had been gone, if it had not been for you, and so avoided these lewd rakehells, who seem to haunt us.

(*Enter* HORNER *and* DORILANT.)

HORNER: How now, Pinchwife!

PINCHWIFE: Your servant.

HORNER: What! I see a little time in the country makes a man turn wild and unsociable, and only fit to converse with his horses, dogs, and his herds.

PINCHWIFE: I have business, sir, and must mind it; your business is pleasure, therefore you and I must go different ways.

HORNER: Well, you may go on, but this pretty young gentleman — (*takes hold of* MRS. PINCHWIFE).

HARCOURT: The lady —

DORILANT: And the maid —

HORNER: Shall stay with us; for I suppose their business is the same with ours, pleasure.

PINCHWIFE (*aside*): 'Sdeath, he knows her, she carries it so sillily! Yet if he does not, I should be more silly to discover it first.

ALITHEA: Pray, let us go, sir.

_____

12 *frank:* the word is used in this passage in two senses, "liberal" and "open," as the word "jealousy" was played with earlier.

PINCHWIFE: Come, come —

HORNER (*to* MRS. PINCHWIFE): Had you not rather stay with us? — Prithee, Pinchwife, who is this pretty young gentleman?

PINCHWIFE: One to whom I'm a guardian. (*aside*) I wish I could keep her out of your hands.

HORNER: Who is he? I never saw anything so pretty in all my life.

PINCHWIFE: Pshaw! Do not look upon him so much, he's a poor bashful youth, you'll put him out of countenance. Come away, brother. (*offers to take her away*).

HORNER: Oh, your brother!

PINCHWIFE: Yes, my wife's brother. Come, come, she'll stay supper for us.

HORNER: I thought so, for he is very like her I saw you at the play with, whom I told you I was in love with.

MRS. PINCHWIFE (*aside*): O jeminy! Is that he that was in love with me? I am glad on't, I vow, for he's a curious fine gentleman, and I love him already, too. (*to* PINCHWIFE) Is this he, bud?

PINCHWIFE (*to his wife*): Come away, come away.

HORNER: Why, what haste are you in? Why won't you let me talk with him?

PINCHWIFE: Because you'll debauch him; he's yet young and innocent, and I would not have him debauched for anything in the world. (*aside*) How she gazes on him! The devil!

HORNER: Harcourt, Dorilant, look you here, this is the likeness of that dowdy he told us of, his wife; did you ever see a lovelier creature? The rogue has reason to be jealous of his wife, since she is like him, for she would make all that see her in love with her.

HARCOURT: And, as I remember now, she is as like him here as can be.

DORILANT: She is indeed pretty, if she be like him.

HORNER: Very pretty? A very pretty commendation! She is a glorious creature, beautiful beyond all things I ever beheld.

PINCHWIFE: So, so.

HARCOURT: More beautiful than a poet's first mistress of imagination.

HORNER: Or another man's last mistress of flesh and blood.

MRS. PINCHWIFE: Nay, now you jeer, sir; pray don't jeer me.

PINCHWIFE: Come, come. (*aside*) By Heavens, she'll discover herself!

HORNER: I speak of your sister, sir.

PINCHWIFE: Ay, but saying she was handsome, if like him, made him blush. (*aside*) I am upon a rack![13]

HORNER: Methinks he is so handsome he should not be a man.

PINCHWIFE (*aside*): Oh, there 'tis out! He has discovered her! I am not able to suffer any longer. (*to his wife*) Come, come away, I say.

HORNER: Nay, by your leave, sir, he shall not go yet. (*aside to them*) Harcourt, Dorilant, let us torment this jealous rogue a little.

HARCOURT: } How?
DORILANT: }

HORNER: I'll show you.

PINCHWIFE: Come, pray let him go, I cannot stay fooling any longer; I tell you his sister stays supper for us.

HORNER: Does she? Come then, we'll all go to sup with he and thee.

PINCHWIFE: No, now I think on't, having stayed so long for us, I warrant she's gone to bed. (*aside*) I wish she and I were well out of their hands. (*to* MRS. PINCHWIFE) Come, I must rise early tomorrow; come.

HORNER: Well then, if she be gone to bed, I wish her and you a good night. But pray,

---

13 *upon a rack:* tortured.

young gentleman, present my humble service to her.

MRS. PINCHWIFE: Thank you heartily, sir.

PINCHWIFE (*aside*): 'Sdeath, she will discover herself yet in spite of me. (*aloud*) He is something more civil to you, for your kindness to his sister, than I am, it seems.

HORNER: Tell her, dear sweet little gentleman, for all your brother there, that you have revived the love I had for her at first sight in the playhouse.

MRS. PINCHWIFE: But did you love her indeed, and indeed?

PINCHWIFE (*aside*): So, so. (*aloud*) Away, I say.

HORNER: Nay, stay. Yes, indeed, and indeed, pray do you tell her so, and give her this kiss from me. (*kisses her*)

PINCHWIFE (*aside*): O Heavens! What do I suffer? Now 'tis too plain he knows her, and yet —

HORNER: And this, and this — (*kisses her again*)

MRS. PINCHWIFE: What do you kiss me for? I am no woman.

PINCHWIFE (*aside*): So, there, 'tis out. (*aloud*) Come, I cannot, nor will stay any longer.

HORNER: Nay, they shall send your lady a kiss too. Here, Harcourt, Dorilant, will you not? (*they kiss her*)

PINCHWIFE (*aside*): How! Do I suffer this? Was I not accusing another just now for this rascally patience, in permitting his wife to be kissed before his face? Ten thousand ulcers gnaw away their lips. (*aloud*) Come, come.

HORNER: Good night, dear little gentleman; madam, good night; farewell, Pinchwife. (*aside to* HARCOURT *and* DORILANT) Did not I tell you I would raise his jealous gall?

(*Exeunt* HORNER, HARCOURT, *and* DORILANT.)

PINCHWIFE: So, they are gone at last; stay, let me see first if the coach be at this door.

(*Exit* PINCHWIFE.)

(*Enter* HORNER, HARCOURT, *and* DORILANT.)

HORNER: What, not gone yet? Will you be sure to do as I desired you, sweet sir?

MRS. PINCHWIFE: Sweet sir, but what will you give me then?

HORNER: Anything. Come away into the next walk.

(*Exit, dragging away* MRS. PINCHWIFE.)

ALITHEA: Hold! Hold! What d'ye do?

LUCY: Stay, stay, hold —

HARCOURT: Hold, madam, hold, let him present him;[14] he'll come presently. Nay, I will never let you go till you answer my question.

LUCY: For God's sake, sir, I must follow 'em.

(ALITHEA *and* LUCY *struggle with* HARCOURT *and* DORILANT.)

DORILANT: No, I have something to present you with too, you shan't follow them.

(*Enter* PINCHWIFE.)

PINCHWIFE: Where? — How? — What's become of? — Gone — Whither?

LUCY: He's only gone with the gentleman, who will give him something, an't please your worship.

PINCHWIFE: Something! Give him something, with a pox! Where are they?

ALITHEA: In the next walk only, brother.

PINCHWIFE: Only, only! Where, where?

(*Exits and returns presently, then goes out again.*)

HARCOURT: What's the matter with him? Why so much concerned? But, dearest madam —

ALITHEA: Pray let me go, sir; I have said and suffered enough already.

HARCOURT: Then you will not look upon, nor pity, my sufferings?

---

14 *present him:* give him something.

ALITHEA: To look upon 'em, when I cannot help 'em, were cruelty, not pity; therefore, I will never see you more.

HARCOURT: Let me then, madam, have my privilege of a banished lover, complaining or railing, and giving you but a farewell reason why, if you cannot condescend to marry me, you should not take that wretch, my rival.

ALITHEA: He only, not you, since my honour is engaged so far to him, can give me a reason why I should not marry him; but if he be true, and what I think him to me, I must be so to him. Your servant, sir.

HARCOURT: Have women only constancy when 'tis a vice, and are, like Fortune, only true to fools?

DORILANT (to LUCY, *who struggles to get away from him*): Thou sha't not stir, thou robust creature; you see I can deal with you, therefore you should stay the rather, and be kind.

(*Enter* PINCHWIFE.)

PINCHWIFE: Gone, gone, not to be found! Quite gone! Ten thousand plagues go with 'em! Which way went they?

ALITHEA: But into t'other walk, brother.

LUCY: Their business will be done presently sure, an't please your worship; it can't be long in doing, I'm sure on't.

ALITHEA: Are they not there?

PINCHWIFE: No, you know where they are, you infamous wretch, eternal shame of your family, which you do not dishonour enough yourself you think, but you must help her to do it too, thou legion of bawds!

ALITHEA: Good brother —

PINCHWIFE: Damned, damned sister!

ALITHEA: Look you here, she's coming.

(*Enter* MRS. PINCHWIFE, *running, with her hat full of oranges and dried fruit under her arm, and* HORNER *following.*)

MRS. PINCHWIFE: O dear bud, look you here what I have got, see!

PINCHWIFE (*aside, rubbing his forehead*): And what I have got here too, which you can't see.

MRS. PINCHWIFE: The fine gentleman has given me better things yet.

PINCHWIFE: Has he so? (*aside*) Out of breath and coloured![15] I must hold yet.

HORNER: I have only given your little brother an orange, sir.

PINCHWIFE (*to* HORNER): Thank you, sir. (*aside*) You have only squeezed my orange, I suppose, and given it me again; yet I must have a city patience.[16] (*to his wife*) Come, come away.

MRS. PINCHWIFE: Stay, till I have put up my fine things, bud.

(*Enter* SIR JASPER FIDGET.)

SIR JASPER: Oh, Master Horner, come, come; the ladies stay for you. Your mistress, my wife wonders you make not more haste to her.

HORNER: I have stayed this half hour for you here, and 'tis your fault I am not now with your wife.

SIR JASPER: But, pray, don't let her know so much; the truth on't is, I was advancing a certain project to his majesty about — I'll tell you.

HORNER: No, let's go, and hear it at your house. Good night, sweet little gentleman; one kiss more. You'll remember me now, I hope. (*kisses her*)

DORILANT: What, Sir Jasper, will you separate friends? He promised to sup with us, and if

---

15 *coloured:* flushed. 16 *city patience:* either the patience expected of a sophisticated city-dweller or, more likely, of a city husband who does not want to make an open admission that he thinks himself cuckolded.

you take him to your house, you'll be in danger of our company too.

SIR JASPER: Alas, gentlemen, my house is not fit for you; there are none but civil women there, which are not for your turn. He, you know, can bear with the society of civil women now, ha ha ha! Besides, he's one of my family — he's — he he he!

DORILANT: What is he?

SIR JASPER: Faith, my eunuch, since you'll have it;[17] he he he!

(*Exeunt* SIR JASPER FIDGET *and* HORNER.)

DORILANT: I rather wish thou wert his or my cuckold. Harcourt, what a good cuckold is lost there for want of a man to make him one! Thee and I cannot have Horner's privilege, who can make use of it.

HARCOURT: Ay, to poor Horner 'tis like coming to an estate at three-score, when a man can't be the better for't.

PINCHWIFE: Come.

MRS. PINCHWIFE: Presently, bud.

DORILANT: Come, let us go too. (*to* ALITHEA) Madam, your servant. (*to* LUCY) Good night, strapper.

HARCOURT: Madam, though you will not let me have a good day, or night, I wish you one; but dare not name the other half of my wish.

ALITHEA: Good night, sir, for ever.

(*Exeunt* DORILANT *and* HARCOURT.)

MRS. PINCHWIFE: I don't know where to put this here, dear bud; you shall eat it. Nay, you shall have part of the fine gentleman's good things, or treat, as you call it, when we come home.

PINCHWIFE: Indeed, I deserve it, since I furnished the best part of it. (*strikes away the orange*)

The gallant treats, presents, and gives the ball;
But 'tis the absent cuckold pays for all.

(*Exeunt* PINCHWIFE *and* MRS. PINCHWIFE.)

ACT FOUR

SCENE ONE   Pinchwife's House in the Morning.

Enter ALITHEA *dressed in new clothes, and* LUCY.

LUCY: Well — madam, now have I dressed you, and set you out with so many ornaments, and spent upon you ounces of essence and pulvillio[1]; and all this for no other purpose but as people adorn and perfume a corpse for a stinking second-hand grave: such, or as bad, I think Master Sparkish's bed.

ALITHEA: Hold your peace.

LUCY: Nay, madam, I will ask you the reason why you would banish poor Master Harcourt for ever from your sight; how could you be so hard-hearted?

ALITHEA: 'Twas because I was not hard-hearted.

LUCY: No, no; 'twas stark love and kindness, I warrant.

ALITHEA: It was so; I would see him no more because I love him.

LUCY: Hey day, a very pretty reason!

ALITHEA: You do not understand me.

LUCY: I wish you may [understand] yourself.

ALITHEA: I was engaged to marry, you see, another man, whom my justice will not suffer me to deceive or injure.

LUCY: Can there be a greater cheat or wrong done to a man than to give him your person without your heart? I should make a conscience of it.

ALITHEA: I'll retrieve it for him after I am married a while.

LUCY: The woman that marries to love better, will be as much mistaken as the wencher that marries to live better. No, madam, mar-

---

17 *you'll have it:* you insist on knowing.

1 *essence and pulvillio:* perfume and scented wig-powder.

rying to increase love is like gaming to become rich; alas, you only lose what little stock you had before.

ALITHEA: I find by your rhetoric you have been bribed to betray me.

LUCY: Only by his merit, that has bribed your heart, you see, against your word and rigid honour. But what a devil is this honour! 'Tis sure a disease in the head, like the megrim or falling-sickness,[2] that always hurries people away to do themselves mischief. Men lose their lives by it; women, what's dearer to 'em, their love, the life of life.

ALITHEA: Come, pray talk you no more of honour, nor Master Harcourt; I wish the other would come to secure my fidelity to him and his right in me.

LUCY: You will marry him then?

ALITHEA: Certainly, I have given him already my word, and will my hand too, to make it good, when he comes.

LUCY: Well, I wish I may never stick pin more, if he be not an arrant natural,[3] to t'other fine gentleman.

ALITHEA: I own he wants[4] the wit of Harcourt, which I will dispense withal for another want he has, which is want of jealousy — which men of wit seldom want.

LUCY: Lord, madam, what should you do with a fool to your husband? You intend to be honest, don't you? Then that husbandly virtue, credulity, is thrown away upon you.

ALITHEA: He only that could suspect my virtue should have cause to do it; 'tis Sparkish's confidence in my truth that obliges me to be so faithful to him.

LUCY: You are not sure his opinion may last.

ALITHEA: I am satisfied, 'tis impossible for him to be jealous after the proofs I have had of him. Jealousy in a husband — Heaven defend me from it! It begets a thousand plagues to a poor woman, the loss of her honour, her quiet, and her —

LUCY: And her pleasure.

ALITHEA: What d'ye mean, impertinent?

LUCY: Liberty is a great pleasure, madam.

ALITHEA: I say, loss of her honour, her quiet, nay, her life sometimes; and what's as bad almost, the loss of this town; that is, she is sent into the country, which is the last ill-usage of a husband to a wife, I think.

LUCY (aside): Oh, does the wind lie there? (aloud) Then of necessity, madam, you think a man must carry his wife into the country, if he be wise.[5] The country is as terrible, I find, to our young English ladies, as a monastery to those abroad; and on my virginity, I think they would rather marry a London jailer, than a high sheriff of a county, since neither can stir from his employment. Formerly women of wit married fools for a great estate, a fine seat, or the like; but now 'tis for a pretty seat only in Lincoln's Inn Fields, St. James's Fields, or the Pall Mall.[6]

(Enter SPARKISH, and HARCOURT, dressed like a Parson.)

SPARKISH: Madam, your humble servant, a happy day to you, and to us all.

HARCOURT: Amen.

ALITHEA: Who have we here?

SPARKISH: My chaplain, faith — O madam, poor Harcourt remembers his humble service to you; and, in obedience to your last commands, refrains coming into your sight.

ALITHEA: Is not that he?

SPARKISH: No, fy, no; but to show that he ne'er intended to hinder our match, has sent his brother here to join our hands. When I get me a wife, I must get her a chaplain, according to the custom; that is his brother, and my chaplain.

ALITHEA: His brother!

---

2 megrim or falling-sickness: migraine or epilepsy. 3 natural: fool. 4 wants: lacks. 5 the country: Wilde mocks this assumption in The Importance of Being Earnest. 6 Lincoln's Inn Fields, etc.: fashionable parts of London.

Lucy (*aside*): And your chaplain, to preach in your pulpit then —

Alithea: His brother!

Sparkish: Nay, I knew you would not believe it. I told you, sir, she would take you for your brother, Frank.

Alithea: Believe it!

Lucy (*aside*): His brother! Ha ha he! He has a trick left still, it seems.

Sparkish: Come, my dearest, pray let us go to church before the canonical hour[7] is past.

Alithea: For shame, you are abused still.

Sparkish: By the world, 'tis strange now you are so incredulous.

Alithea: 'Tis strange you are so credulous.

Sparkish: Dearest of my life, hear me. I tell you this is Ned Harcourt of Cambridge, by the world; you see he has a sneaking college look. 'Tis true he's something like his brother Frank; and they differ each other no more than in their age, for they were twins.

Lucy: Ha ha ha!

Alithea: Your servant, sir; I cannot be so deceived, though you are. But come, let's hear, how do you know what you affirm so confidently?

Sparkish: Why, I'll tell you all. Frank Harcourt coming to me this morning to wish me joy, and present his service to you, I asked him if he could help me to a parson. Whereupon he told me he had a brother in town who was in orders;[8] and he went straight away, and sent him, you see there, to me.

Alithea: Yes, Frank goes and puts on a black coat, then tells you he is Ned; that's all you have for't.

Sparkish: Pshaw! Pshaw! I tell you, by the same token, the midwife put her garter about Frank's neck, to know 'em asunder, they were so like.

Alithea: Frank tells you this too?

Sparkish: Ay, and Ned there too. Nay, they are both in a story.

Alithea: So, so; very foolish.

Sparkish: Lord, if you won't believe one, you had best try him by your chambermaid there; for chambermaids must needs know chaplains from other men, they are so used to 'em.

Lucy: Let's see. Nay, I'll be sworn he has the canonical smirk, and the filthy, clammy palm of a chaplain.

Alithea: Well, most reverend doctor, pray let us make an end of this fooling.

Harcourt: With all my soul, divine heavenly creature, when you please.

Alithea: He speaks like a chaplain indeed.

Sparkish: Why, was there not "soul," "divine," "heavenly," in what he said?

Alithea: Once more, most impertinent black-coat, cease your persecution, and let us have a conclusion to this ridiculous love.

Harcourt (*aside*): I had forgot, I must suit my style to my coat, or I wear it in vain.

Alithea: I have no more patience left; let us make once an end of this troublesome love, I say.

Harcourt: So be it, seraphic lady, when your honour shall think it meet and convenient so to do.

Sparkish: Gad, I'm sure none but a chaplain could speak so, I think.

Alithea: Let me tell you, sir, this dull trick will not serve your turn; though you delay our marriage, you shall not hinder it.

Harcourt: Far be it from me, munificent patroness, to delay your marriage; I desire nothing more than to marry you presently, which I might do, if you yourself would; for my noble, good-natured, and thrice-generous patron here would not hinder it.

---

7 *canonical hour*: according to ecclesiastical (canon) law, marriages had to be performed in the morning, before noon. 8 *orders*: holy orders.

SPARKISH: No, poor man, not I, faith.

HARCOURT: And now, madam, let me tell you plainly nobody else shall marry you; by Heavens! I'll die first, for I'm sure I should die after it.

LUCY: How his love has made him forget his function, as I have seen it in real parsons!

ALITHEA: That was spoken like a chaplain too? Now you understand him, I hope.

SPARKISH: Poor man, he takes it heinously to be refused; I can't blame him, 'tis putting an indignity upon him, not to be suffered. But you'll pardon me, madam, it shan't be; he shall marry us. Come away, pray, madam.

LUCY: Ha ha he! More ado! 'Tis late.

ALITHEA: Invincible stupidity! I tell you, he would marry me as your rival, not as your chaplain.

SPARKISH: Come, come, madam. (*pulling her away*)

LUCY: I pray, madam, do not refuse this reverend divine the honour and satisfaction of marrying you; for I dare say, he has set his heart upon't, good doctor.

ALITHEA: What can you hope or design by this?

HARCOURT (*aside*): I could answer her, a reprieve for a day only, often revokes a hasty doom. At worst, if she will not take mercy on me, and let me marry her, I have at least the lover's second pleasure, hindering my rival's enjoyment, though but for a time.

SPARKISH: Come, madam, 'tis e'en twelve o'clock, and my mother charged me never to be married out of the canonical hours. Come, come; Lord, here's such a deal of modesty, I warrant, the first day.

LUCY: Yes, an't please your worship, married women show all their modesty the first day, because married men show all their love the first day.

(*Exeunt* ALITHEA, SPARKISH, HARCOURT, LUCY.)

SCENE TWO   A bedchamber in Pinchwife's House.

PINCHWIFE *and* MRS. PINCHWIFE.

PINCHWIFE: Come, tell me, I say.

MRS. PINCHWIFE: Lord! Han't I told it a hundred times over?

PINCHWIFE (*aside*): I would try, if in the repetition of the ungrateful tale, I could find her altering it in the least circumstance; for if her story be false, she is so too. (*aloud*) Come, how was't, baggage?

MRS. PINCHWIFE: Lord, what pleasure you take to hear it, sure!

PINCHWIFE: No, you take more in telling it, I find; but speak, how was't?

MRS. PINCHWIFE: He carried[1] me up into the house next to the Exchange.

PINCHWIFE: So, and you two were only in the room!

MRS. PINCHWIFE: Yes, for he sent away a youth that was there, for some dried fruit, and China oranges.

PINCHWIFE: Did he so? Damn him for it — and for —

MRS. PINCHWIFE: But presently came up the gentlewoman of the house.

PINCHWIFE: Oh, 'twas well she did; but what did he do whilst the fruit came?

MRS. PINCHWIFE: He kissed me a hundred times, and told me he fancied he kissed my fine sister, meaning me, you know, whom he said he loved with all his soul, and bid me to be sure to tell her so, and to desire her to be at her window by eleven of the clock this morning, and he would walk under it at that time.

PINCHWIFE (*aside*): And he was as good as his word, very punctual; a pox reward him for't.

MRS. PINCHWIFE: Well, and he said if you were not within, he would come up to her, meaning me, you know, bud, still.

---

1 *carried:* took.

PINCHWIFE (aside): So — he knew her certainly; but for this confession, I am obliged to her simplicity. (aloud) But what, you stood very still when he kissed you?

MRS. PINCHWIFE: Yes, I warrant you; would you have had me discover myself?

PINCHWIFE: But you told me he did some beastliness to you, as you call it; what was't?

MRS. PINCHWIFE: Why, he put —

PINCHWIFE: What?

MRS. PINCHWIFE: Why, he put the tip of his tongue between my lips, and so mousled me — and I said, I'd bite it.

PINCHWIFE: An eternal canker seize it, for a dog!

MRS. PINCHWIFE: Nay, you need not be so angry with him neither, for to say truth, he has the sweetest breath I ever knew.

PINCHWIFE: The devil! You were satisfied with it then, and would do it again?

MRS. PINCHWIFE: Not unless he should force me.

PINCHWIFE: Force you, changeling! I tell you, no woman can be forced.

MRS. PINCHWIFE: Yes, but she may sure, by such a one as he, for he's a proper, goodly, strong man; 'tis hard, let me tell you, to resist him.

PINCHWIFE (aside): So, 'tis plain she loves him, yet she has not love enough to make her conceal it from me; but the sight of him will increase her aversion for me and love for him; and that love instruct her how to deceive me and satisfy him, all idiot as she is. Love! 'Twas he gave women first their craft, their art of deluding. Out of Nature's hands they came plain, open, silly, and fit for slaves, as she and Heaven intended 'em; but damned Love — well — I must strangle that little monster whilst I can deal with him. (aloud) Go fetch pen, ink, and paper out of the next room.

MRS. PINCHWIFE: Yes, bud.

(Exit MRS. PINCHWIFE.)

PINCHWIFE: Why should women have more invention in love than men? It can only be, because they have more desires, more soliciting passions, more lust, and more of the devil.

(Enter MRS. PINCHWIFE.)

Come, minx, sit down and write.

MRS. PINCHWIFE: Ay, dear bud, but I can't do't very well.

PINCHWIFE: I wish you could not at all.

MRS. PINCHWIFE: But what should I write for?

PINCHWIFE: I'll have you write a letter to your lover.

MRS. PINCHWIFE: O Lord, to the fine gentleman a letter!

PINCHWIFE: Yes, to the fine gentleman.

MRS. PINCHWIFE: Lord, you do but jeer; sure you jest.

PINCHWIFE: I am not so merry; come, write as I bid you.

MRS. PINCHWIFE: What, do you think I am a fool?

PINCHWIFE (aside): She's afraid I would not dictate any love to him, therefore she's unwilling. (aloud) But you had best begin.

MRS. PINCHWIFE: Indeed, and indeed, but I won't, so I won't.

PINCHWIFE: Why?

MRS. PINCHWIFE: Because he's in town; you may send for him if you will.

PINCHWIFE: Very well, you would have him brought to you; is it come to this? I say take the pen and write, or you'll provoke me.

MRS. PINCHWIFE: Lord, what d'ye make a fool of me for? Don't I know that letters are never writ but from the country to London, and from London into the country? Now he's in town, and I am in town too; therefore I can't write to him, you know.

PINCHWIFE (aside): So, I am glad it is no worse; she is innocent enough yet. (aloud) Yes, you may, when your husband bids you, write letters to people that are in town.

Mrs. Pinchwife: Oh, may I so? Then I'm satisfied.

Pinchwife: Come, begin: — "Sir" — (Dictates.)

Mrs. Pinchwife: Shan't I say, "Dear Sir?" — You know one says always something more than bare "Sir."

Pinchwife: Write as I bid you, or I will write "whore" with this penknife in your face.

Mrs. Pinchwife: Nay, good bud — "Sir" — (She writes.)

Pinchwife: "Though I suffered last night your nauseous, loathed kisses and embraces" — Write!

Mrs. Pinchwife: Nay, why should I say so? You know I told you he had a sweet breath.

Pinchwife: Write!

Mrs. Pinchwife: Let me but put out "loathed."

Pinchwife: Write, I say!

Mrs. Pinchwife: Well then. (She writes.)

Pinchwife: Let's see, what have you writ? (Takes the paper and reads.) "Though I suffered last night your kisses and embraces" — Thou impudent creature! Where is "nauseous" and "loathed"?

Mrs. Pinchwife: I can't abide to write such filthy words.

Pinchwife: Once more write as I'd have you, and question it not, or I will spoil thy writing with this. I will stab out those eyes that cause my mischief. (Holds up the penknife.)

Mrs. Pinchwife: O Lord! I will.

Pinchwife: So — so — let's see now. (reads) "Though I suffered last night your nauseous, loathed kisses and embraces" — go on — "yet I would not have you presume that you shall ever repeat them" — so —

Mrs. Pinchwife (She writes): I have writ it.

Pinchwife: On, then — "I then concealed myself from your knowledge, to avoid your insolencies." —

Mrs. Pinchwife (She writes): So —

Pinchwife: "The same reason, now I am out of your hands" —

Mrs. Pinchwife (She writes): So —

Pinchwife: "Makes me own to you my unfortunate, though innocent frolic, of being in man's clothes" —

Mrs. Pinchwife (She writes): So —

Pinchwife: "That you may for evermore cease to pursue her, who hates and detests you" —

Mrs. Pinchwife (She writes on): So — (sighs)

Pinchwife: What, do you sigh? — "detests you — as much as she loves her husband and her honour."

Mrs. Pinchwife: I vow, husband, he'll ne'er believe I should write such a letter.

Pinchwife: What, he'd expect a kinder from you? Come, now your name only.

Mrs. Pinchwife: What, shan't I say, "Your most faithful humble servant till death"?

Pinchwife: No, tormenting fiend! (aside) Her style, I find, would be very soft. (aloud) Come, wrap it up now, whilst I go fetch wax and a candle; and write on the back side, "For Mr. Horner."

(Exit Pinchwife.)

Mrs. Pinchwife: "For Mr. Horner." — So, I am glad he has told me his name. Dear Mr. Horner! But why should I send thee such a letter that will vex thee, and make thee angry with me? Well, I will not send it. Ay, but then my husband will kill me — for I see plainly he won't let me love Mr. Horner — but what care I for my husband? I won't, so I won't, send poor Mr. Horner such a letter — . But then my husband — but oh, what if I writ at bottom my husband made me write it? Ay, but then my husband would see't — Can one have no shift?[2] Ah, a London woman would have had a hundred pre-

---

2 *shift:* device.

sently. Stay — what if I should write a letter, and wrap it up like this, and write upon't too? Ay, but then my husband would see't — I don't know what to do. But yet evads[3] I'll try, so I will — for I will not send this letter to poor Mr. Horner, come what will on't. "Dear, sweet Mr. Horner — " (*Writes and repeats what she writes.*) — so — "my husband would have me send you a base, rude, unmannerly letter; but I won't" — so — "and would have me forbid you loving me; but I won't" — so — "and would have me say to you, 'I hate you,' poor Mr. Horner; but I won't tell a lie for him" — there — "for I'm sure if you and I were in the country at cards together" — so — "I could not help treading on your toe under the table" — so — "or rubbing knees with you, and staring in your face, till you saw me" — very well — "and then looking down, and blushing for an hour together" — so — "but I must make haste before my husband comes. And now he has taught me to write letters, you shall have longer ones from me, who am, dear, dear, poor, dear Mr. Horner, your most humble friend, and servant to command till death, — Margery Pinchwife." Stay, I must give him a hint at bottom — so — now wrap it up just like t'other — so — now write "For Mr. Horner" — But oh now, what shall I do with it? For here comes my husband.

(*Enter* PINCHWIFE.)

PINCHWIFE (*aside*): I have been detained by a sparkish coxcomb,[4] who pretended a visit to me; but I fear 'twas to my wife. (*aloud*) What, have you done?

MRS. PINCHWIFE: Ay, ay, bud, just now.

PINCHWIFE: Let's see't; what d'ye tremble for? What, you would not have it go?

MRS. PINCHWIFE: Here — . (*aside*) No, I must not give him that; so I had been served if I had given him this.

(*He opens and reads the first letter.*)

PINCHWIFE: Come, where's the wax and seal?

MRS. PINCHWIFE (*aside*): Lord, what shall I do now? Nay, then, I have it — . (*aloud*) Pray

let me see't. Lord, you will think me so arrant a fool, I cannot seal a letter; I will do't, so I will. (*Snatches the letter from him, changes it for the other, seals it, and delivers it to him.*)

PINCHWIFE: Nay, I believe you will learn that, and other things too, which I would not have you.

MRS. PINCHWIFE: So, han't I done it curiously[5]? (*aside*) I think I have; there's my letter going to Mr. Horner, since he'll needs have me send letters to folks.

PINCHWIFE: 'Tis very well; but I warrant, you would not have it go now?

MRS. PINCHWIFE: Yes, indeed, but I would, bud, now.

PINCHWIFE: Well, you are a good girl then. Come, let me lock you up in your chamber, till I come back; and be sure you come not within three strides of the window when I am gone, for I have a spy in the street.

(*Exit* MRS. PINCHWIFE, PINCHWIFE *locks the door.*)

At least, 'tis fit she think so. If we do not cheat women, they'll cheat us, and fraud may be justly used with secret enemies, of which a wife is the most dangerous; and he that has a handsome one to keep, and a frontier town, must provide against treachery, rather than open force. Now I have secured all within, I'll deal with the foe without, with false intelligence.

(*Holds up the letter. Exit* PINCHWIFE.)

SCENE THREE   Horner's Lodging.

HORNER *and* QUACK.

QUACK: Well, sir, how fadges[1] the new design? Have you not the luck of all your brother projectors, to deceive only yourself at last?

---

3 *evads:* in faith (originally "y vads"). 4 *coxcomb:* foolish fop. 5 *curiously:* skillfully, with art.

1 *fadges:* fares.

HORNER: No, good domine[2] doctor, I deceive you, it seems, and others too; for the grave matrons, and old, rigid husbands think me as unfit for love, as they are; but their wives, sisters, and daughters know, some of 'em, better things already.

QUACK: Already!

HORNER: Already, I say. Last night I was drunk with half a dozen of your civil persons, as you call 'em, and people of honour, and so was made free of their society and dressing-rooms for ever hereafter; and am already come to the privileges of sleeping upon their pallets, warming smocks, tying shoes and garters, and the like, doctor, already, already, doctor.

QUACK: You have made good use of your time, sir.

HORNER: I tell thee, I am now no more interruption to 'em, when they sing, or talk bawdy, than a little squab French page who speaks no English.

QUACK: But do civil persons and women of honour drink, and sing bawdy songs?

HORNER: Oh, amongst friends, amongst friends. For your bigots in honour are just like those in religion; they fear the eye of the world more than the eye of Heaven, and think there is no virtue but railing at vice, and no sin but giving scandal. They rail at a poor, little, kept player, and keep themselves some young, modest pulpit comedian to be privy to their sins in their closets, not to tell 'em of them in their chapels.

QUACK: Nay, the truth on't is, priests, amongst the women now, have quite got the better of us lay-confessors, physicians.

HORNER: And they are rather their patients; but —

(*Enter* LADY FIDGET, *looking about her.*)

Now we talk of women of honour, here comes one. Step behind the screen there,[3] and but observe if I have not particular privileges with the women of reputation already, doctor, already.

(QUACK *retires.*)

LADY FIDGET: Well, Horner, am not I a woman of honour? You see, I'm as good as my word.

HORNER: And you shall see, madam, I'll not be behind-hand with you in honour; and I'll be as good as my word too, if you please but to withdraw into the next room.

LADY FIDGET: But first, my dear sir, you must promise to have a care of my dear honour.

HORNER: If you talk a word more of your honour, you'll make me incapable to wrong it. To talk of honour in the mysteries of love, is like talking of Heaven or the Deity in an operation of witchcraft, just when you are employing the devil. It makes the charm impotent.

LADY FIDGET: Nay, fy! Let us not be smutty. But you talk of mysteries and bewitching to me; I don't understand you.

HORNER: I tell you, madam, the word "money" in a mistress's mouth, at such a nick of time, is not a more disheartening sound to a younger brother, than that of "honour" to an eager lover like myself.

LADY FIDGET: But you can't blame a lady of my reputation to be chary.

HORNER: Chary! I have been chary of it already, by the report I have caused of myself.

LADY FIDGET: Ay, but if you should ever let other women know that dear secret, it would come out. Nay, you must have a great care of your conduct; for my acquaintance are so censorious (oh, 'tis a wicked, censorious world, Mr. Horner!), I say, are so censorious, and detracting, that perhaps they'll talk to the prejudice of my honour, though you should not let them know the dear secret.

HORNER: Nay, madam, rather than they shall prejudice your honour, I'll prejudice theirs;

---

2 *domine:* from Latin *dominus,* "lord," a term used for schoolmasters and other professionals. **3** *screen there:* compare the use of the screen here with that in *The School for Scandal.*

and, to serve you, I'll lie with 'em all, make the secret their own, and then they'll keep it. I am a Machiavel[4] in love, madam.

LADY FIDGET: Oh, no, sir, not that way.

HORNER: Nay, the devil take me, if censorious women are to be silenced any other way.

LADY FIDGET: A secret is better kept, I hope, by a single person than a multitude; therefore pray do not trust anybody else with it, dear, dear Mr. Horner. (*embracing him*)

(*Enter* SIR JASPER FIDGET.)

SIR JASPER: How now!

LADY FIDGET (*aside*): Oh, my husband — ! Prevented — and what's almost as bad, found with my arms about another man — that will appear too much — what shall I say? (*aloud*) Sir Jasper, come hither. I am trying if Mr. Horner were ticklish, and he's as ticklish as can be. I love to torment the confounded toad; let you and I tickle him.

SIR JASPER: No, your ladyship will tickle him better without me, I suppose. But is this your buying china? I thought you had been at the china-house.

HORNER (*aside*): China-house! That's my cue, I must take it. (*aloud*) A pox! Can't you keep your impertinent wives at home? Some men are troubled with the husbands, but I with the wives; but I'd have you to know, since I cannot be your journeyman by night, I will not be your drudge by day, to squire your wife about, and be your man of straw, or scarecrow only to pies[5] and jays, that would be nibbling at your forbidden fruit; I shall be shortly the hackney gentleman-usher[6] of the town.

SIR JASPER (*aside*): He he he! Poor fellow, he's in the right on't, faith. To squire women about for other folks is as ungrateful an employment, as to tell[7] money for other folks. (*aloud*) He he he, be'n't angry, Horner.

LADY FIDGET: No, 'tis I have more reason to be angry, who am left by you, to go abroad indecently alone; or, what is more indecent, to pin myself upon such ill-bred people of your acquaintance as this is.

SIR JASPER: Nay, prithee, what has he done?

LADY FIDGET: Nay, he has done nothing.

SIR JASPER: But what d'ye take ill, if he has done nothing?

LADY FIDGET: Ha ha ha! Faith, I can't but laugh, however; why, d'ye think the unmannerly toad would come down to me to the coach? I was fain to come up to fetch him, or go without him, which I was resolved not to do; for he knows china very well, and has himself very good, but will not let me see it, lest I should beg some; but I will find it out, and have what I came for yet.

HORNER (*aside to* LADY FIDGET, *as he follows her to the door*): Lock the door, madam.

(*Exit* LADY FIDGET, *and locks the door.*)

(*aloud*) So, she has got into my chamber and locked me out. Oh, the impertinency of woman-kind! Well, Sir Jasper, plain-dealing is a jewel; if ever you suffer your wife to trouble me again here, she shall carry you home a pair of horns. By my lord mayor she shall; though I cannot furnish you myself, you are sure, yet I'll find a way.

SIR JASPER (*aside*): Ha ha he! At first coming in, and finding her arms about him, tickling him it seems, I was half jealous, but now I see my folly. (*aloud*) He he he! Poor Horner!

HORNER: Nay, though you laugh now, 'twill be my turn ere long. Oh, women, more impertinent, more cunning, and more mischievous than their monkeys, and to me almost as ugly! — Now is she throwing my things about and rifling all I have; but I'll get in to her the back way, and so rifle her for it.

SIR JASPER: Ha ha ha! Poor angry Horner!

HORNER: Stay here a little, I'll ferret her out to you presently, I warrant.

---

4 *Machiavel:* Machiavelli, thought a master of deceit because of the perversion of the ideas in his *The Prince* by his translator, Innocent Gentillet. 5 *pies:* magpies. 6 *hackney gentleman-usher:* ladies' companion for hire. 7 *tell:* count (as in "bank teller").

(*Exit* HORNER *at the other door.*)

(SIR JASPER *calls through the door to his Wife, she answers from within.*)

SIR JASPER: Wife; My Lady Fidget! Wife! He is coming into you the back way.[8]

LADY FIDGET: Let him come, and welcome, which way he will.

SIR JASPER: He'll catch you, and use you roughly, and be too strong for you.

LADY FIDGET: Don't you trouble yourself, let him if he can.

QUACK (*behind*): This indeed I could not have believed from him, nor any but my own eyes.

(*Enter* MRS. SQUEAMISH.)

MRS. SQUEAMISH: Where's this woman-hater, this toad, this ugly, greasy, dirty sloven?

SIR JASPER (*aside*): So, the women all will have him ugly; methinks he is a comely person. But his wants make his form contemptible to 'em; and 'tis e'en as my wife said yesterday, talking of him, that a proper handsome eunuch was as ridiculous a thing as a gigantic coward.

MRS. SQUEAMISH: Sir Jasper, your servant; where is the odious beast?

SIR JASPER: He's within his chamber, with my wife; she's playing the wag with him.

MRS. SQUEAMISH: Is she so? And he's a clownish beast, he'll give her no quarter, he'll play the wag with her again, let me tell you. Come, let's go help her. What, the door's locked?

SIR JASPER: Ay, my wife locked it.

MRS. SQUEAMISH: Did she so? Let us break it open then.

SIR JASPER: No, no, he'll do her no hurt.

MRS. SQUEAMISH: No — (*aside*) But is there no other way to get in to 'em? Whither goes this? I will disturb 'em.

(*Exit* MRS. SQUEAMISH *at another door.*)

(*Enter* OLD LADY SQUEAMISH.)

LADY SQUEAMISH: Where is this harlotry, this impudent baggage, this rambling tomrigg?[9] Oh, Sir Jasper, I'm glad to see you here; did you see my vil'd[10] grandchild come in hither just now?

SIR JASPER: Yes.

LADY SQUEAMISH: Ay, but where is she then? Where is she? Lord, Sir Jasper, I have e'en rattled myself to pieces in pursuit of her; but can you tell what she makes here? They say below, no woman lodges here.

SIR JASPER: No.

LADY SQUEAMISH: No! What does she here then? Say, if it be not a woman's lodging, what makes her here? But are you sure no woman lodges here?

SIR JASPER: No, nor no man neither; this is Mr. Horner's lodging.

LADY SQUEAMISH: Is it so? Are you sure?

SIR JASPER: Yes, yes.

LADY SQUEAMISH: So; then there's no hurt in't, I hope. But where is he?

SIR JASPER: He's in the next room with my wife.

LADY SQUEAMISH: Nay, if you trust him with your wife, I may with my Biddy. They say he's a merry harmless man how, e'en as harmless a man as ever came out of Italy with a good voice,[11] and as pretty, harmless company for a lady, as a snake without his teeth.

SIR JASPER: Ay, ay, poor man.

(*Enter* MRS. SQUEAMISH.)

MRS. SQUEAMISH: I can't find 'em. Oh, are you here, grandmother? I followed, you must know, my Lady Fidget hither; 'tis the prettiest lodging, and I have been staring on the prettiest pictures —

---

8 *back way:* but, as Lady Fidget says, "Let us not be smutty." 9 *baggage . . . tomrigg:* slut . . . tomboy (or strumpet). 10 *vil'd:* defiled. 11 *good voice:* castrati sang soprano.

(*Enter* LADY FIDGET *with a piece of china in her hand, and* HORNER *following.*)

LADY FIDGET: And I have been toiling and moiling for the prettiest piece of china, my dear.

HORNER: Nay, she has been too hard for me, do what I could.

MRS. SQUEAMISH: O Lord, I'll have some china too. Good Mr. Horner, don't think to give other people china, and me none; come in with me too.

HORNER: Upon my honour, I have none left now.

MRS. SQUEAMISH: Nay, nay, I have known you deny your china before now, but you shan't put me off so. Come.

HORNER: This lady had the last there.

LADY FIDGET: Yes indeed, madam, to my certain knowledge, he has no more left.

MRS. SQUEAMISH: Oh, but it may be he may have some you could not find.

LADY FIDGET: What, d'ye think if he had had any left, I would not have had it too? For we women of quality never think we have china enough.

HORNER: Do not take it ill; I cannot make china for you all, but I will have a roll-waggon[12] for you too, another time.

MRS. SQUEAMISH: Thank you, dear toad.

LADY FIDGET (*aside to* HORNER): What do you mean by that promise?

HORNER (*aside to* LADY FIDGET): Alas, she has an innocent, literal understanding.

LADY SQUEAMISH: Poor Mr. Horner! He has enough to do to please you all, I see.

HORNER: Ay, madam, you see how they use me.

LADY SQUEAMISH: Poor gentleman, I pity you.

HORNER: I thank you, madam: I could never find pity, but from such reverend ladies as you are; the young ones will never spare a man.[13]

MRS. SQUEAMISH: Come, come, beast, and go dine with us; for we shall want a man at ombre after dinner.

HORNER: That's all their use of me, madam, you see.

MRS. SQUEAMISH: Come, sloven, I'll lead you, (*pulls him by the cravat*) to be sure of you.

LADY SQUEAMISH: Alas, poor man, how she tugs him! Kiss, kiss her; that's the way to make such nice women quiet.

HORNER: No, madam, that remedy is worse than the torment; they know I dare suffer anything rather than do it.

LADY SQUEAMISH: Prithee kiss her, and I'll give you her picture in little,[14] that you admired so last night; prithee do.

HORNER: Well, nothing but that could bribe me; I love a woman only in effigy, and good painting as much as I hate them. I'll do't, for I could adore the devil well painted. (*kisses* MRS. SQUEAMISH)

MRS. SQUEAMISH: Foh, you filthy toad! Nay, now I've done jesting.

LADY SQUEAMISH: Ha ha ha! I told you so.

MRS. SQUEAMISH: Foh! A kiss of his —

SIR JASPER: Has no more hurt in't than one of my spaniel's.

MRS. SQUEAMISH: Nor no more good neither.

QUACK (*behind the screen*): I will now believe anything he tells me.

(*Enter* PINCHWIFE.)

LADY FIDGET: O Lord, here's a man! Sir Jasper, my mask, my mask! I would not be seen here for the world.

SIR JASPER: What, not when I am with you?

---

12 *roll-waggon:* a cylindrical vase. Horner makes it a phallic symbol, for (of course) they are not really talking about his china. **13** *spare a man:* younger women are more demanding. **14** *picture in little:* miniature.

LADY FIDGET: No, no, my honour — let's be gone.

MRS. SQUEAMISH: O grandmother, let's be gone; make haste, make haste, I know not how he may censure us.

LADY FIDGET: Be found in the lodging of anything like a man! Away!

(*Exeunt* SIR JASPER FIDGET, LADY FIDGET, OLD LADY SQUEAMISH, *and* MRS. SQUEAMISH.)

QUACK (*behind the screen*): What's here? Another cuckold? He looks like one, and none else sure have any business with him.

HORNER: Well, what brings my dear friend hither?

PINCHWIFE: Your impertinency.

HORNER: My impertinency! Why, you gentlemen that have got handsome wives, think you have a privilege of saying anything to your friends, and are as brutish as if you were our creditors.

PINCHWIFE: Nor, sir, I'll ne'er trust you any way.

HORNER: But why not, dear Jack? Why diffide in me[15] thou know'st so well?

PINCHWIFE: Because I do know you so well.

HORNER: Han't I been always thy friend, honest Jack, always ready to serve thee, in love or battle, before thou wert married, and am so still?

PINCHWIFE: I believe so; you would be my second now, indeed.

HORNER: Well then, dear Jack, why so unkind, so grum, so strange to me? Come, prithee kiss me, dear rogue. Gad, I was always, I say, and am still as much thy servant as —

PINCHWIFE: As I am yours, sir. What, you would send a kiss to my wife, is that it?

HORNER: So, there 'tis — a man can't show his friendship to a married man, but presently he talks of his wife to you. Prithee, let thy wife alone, and let thee and I be all one, as we were wont. What, thou art as shy of my

kindness as a Lombard Street alderman of a courtier's civility at Locket's![16]

PINCHWIFE: But you are over-kind to me, as kind as if I were your cuckold already, yet I must confess you ought to be kind and civil to me, since I am so kind, so civil to you, as to bring you this. Look you there, sir. (*Delivers him a letter.*)

HORNER: What is't?

PINCHWIFE: Only a love letter, sir.

HORNER: From whom? — How! This is from your wife — hum — and hum — (*reads*)

PINCHWIFE: Even from my wife, sir; am I not wondrous kind and civil to you now too? (*aside*) But you'll not think her so.

HORNER (*aside*): Ha! Is this a trick of his or hers?

PINCHWIFE: The gentleman's surprised I find. What, you expected a kinder letter?

HORNER: No faith, not I, how could I?

PINCHWIFE: Yes, yes, I'm sure you did. A man so well made as you are, must needs be disappointed, if the women declare not their passion at first sight or opportunity.

HORNER (*aside*): But what should this mean? Stay, the postscript. (*reads aside*) "Be sure you love me, whatsoever my husband says to the contrary, and let him not see this, lest he should come home and pinch me, or kill my squirrel." [17] It seems he knows not what the letter contains.

PINCHWIFE: Come, ne'er wonder at it so much.

HORNER: Faith, I can't help it.

---

15 *diffide in me:* distrust me. 16 *Lombard Street alderman, etc.:* Locket's was an expensive restaurant (frequented by Lord Foppington in Sir John Vanbrugh's *The Relapse* as late as 1697). A courtier there might ask a moneylender from Lombard Street, the financial centre, for a loan—or spend so much he might welsh on one already received. 17 *squirrel:* she is afraid Pinchwife's anger might be vented on her pet.

PINCHWIFE: Now, I think I have deserved your infinite friendship and kindness, and have showed myself sufficiently an obliging kind friend and husband; am I not so, to bring a letter from my wife to her gallant?

HORNER: Ay, the devil take me, art thou, the most obliging, kind friend and husband in the world, ha ha!

PINCHWIFE: Well, you may be merry, sir; but in short I must tell you, sir, my honour will suffer no jesting.

HORNER: What dost thou mean?

PINCHWIFE: Does the letter want a comment? Then know, sir, though I have been so civil a husband as to bring you a letter from my wife, to let you kiss and court her to my face, I will not be a cuckold, sir; I will not.

HORNER: Thou art mad with jealousy. I never saw thy wife in my life but at the play yesterday, and I know not if it were she or no. *I* court her, kiss her!

PINCHWIFE: I will not be a cuckold, I say; there will be danger in making me a cuckold.

HORNER: Why, wert thou not well cured of thy last clap?

PINCHWIFE: I wear a sword.[18]

HORNER: It should be taken from thee, lest thou shouldst do thyself a mischief with it; thou art mad, man.

PINCHWIFE: As mad as I am, and as merry as you are, I must have more reason from you ere we part. I say again, though you kissed and courted last night my wife in man's clothes, as she confesses in her letter —

HORNER (*aside*): Ha!

PINCHWIFE: Both she and I say you must not design it again, for you have mistaken your woman, as you have done your man.

HORNER (*aside*): Oh — I understand something now. (*aloud*) Was that thy wife? Why wouldst thou not tell me 'twas she? Faith, my freedom with her was your fault, not mine.

PINCHWIFE (*aside*): Faith, so 'twas.

HORNER: Fy! I'd never do't to a woman before her husband's face, sure.

PINCHWIFE: But I had rather you should do't to my wife before my face, than behind my back; and that you shall never do.

HORNER: No — you will hinder me.

PINCHWIFE: If I would not hinder you, you see by her letter she would.

HORNER: Well, I must e'en acquiesce then, and be contented with what she writes.

PINCHWIFE: I'll assure you 'twas voluntarily writ; I had no hand in't, you may believe me.

HORNER: I do believe thee, faith.

PINCHWIFE: And believe her too, for she's an innocent creature, has no dissembling in her; and so fare you well, sir.

HORNER: Pray, however, present my humble service to her, and tell her I will obey her letter to a tittle,[19] and fulfill her desires, be what they will, or with what difficulty soever I do't; and you shall be no more jealous of me, I warrant her, and you.

PINCHWIFE: Well then, fare you well; and play with any man's honour but mine, kiss any man's wife but mine, and welcome.

(*Exit* PINCHWIFE.)

HORNER: Ha ha ha, doctor!

QUACK (*reappears from behind the screen*): It seems he has not heard the report of you, or does not believe it.

HORNER: Ha ha! Now, doctor, what think you?

QUACK: Pray let's see the letter — hum — "for — dear — love you — " (*reads the letter*)

HORNER: I wonder how she could contrive it! What say'st thou to't? 'Tis an original.

QUACK: So are your cuckolds too, originals; for they are like no other common cuckolds, and I will henceforth believe it not impos-

---

18 . . . *sword:* "Be careful how you speak." 19 *to a tittle:* in every particular.

sible for you to cuckold the Grand Signior[20] amidst his guards of eunuchs, that I say —

HORNER: And I say for the letter, 'tis the first love letter that ever was without flames, darts, fates, destinies, lying and dissembling in't.

(*Enter* SPARKISH *pulling in* PINCHWIFE.)

SPARKISH: Come back, you are a pretty brother-in-law, neither go to church nor to dinner with your sister bride!

PINCHWIFE: My sister denies her marriage, and you see is gone away from you dissatisfied.

SPARKISH: Pshaw! Upon a foolish scruple, that our parson was not in lawful orders, and did not say all the common-prayer; but 'tis her modesty only, I believe. But let women be never so modest the first day, they'll be sure to come to themselves by night, and I shall have enough of her then. In the meantime, Harry Horner, you must dine with me; I keep my wedding at my aunt's in the Piazza.[21]

HORNER: Thy wedding! What stale maid has lived to despair of a husband, or what young one of a gallant?

SPARKISH: Oh, your servant, sir — this gentleman's sister then — no stale maid.

HORNER: I'm sorry for't.

PINCHWIFE (*aside*): How comes he so concerned for her?

SPARKISH: You sorry for't? Why, do you know any ill by her?

HORNER: No, I know none but by thee; 'tis for her sake, not yours, and another man's sake that might have hoped, I thought.

SPARKISH: Another man! Another man! What is his name?

HORNER: Nay, since 'tis past, he shall be nameless. (*aside*) Poor Harcourt! I am sorry thou hast missed her.

PINCHWIFE (*aside*): He seems to be much troubled at the match.

SPARKISH: Prithee, tell me — Nay, you shan't go, brother.

PINCHWIFE: I must of necessity, but I'll come to you to dinner.

(*Exit* PINCHWIFE.)

SPARKISH: But, Harry, what, have I a rival in my wife already? But with all my heart, for he may be of use to me hereafter; for though my hunger is now my sauce, and I can fall on heartily without, the time will come when a rival will be as good sauce for a married man to a wife, as an orange to veal.[22]

HORNER: O thou damned rogue! Thou hast set my teeth on edge with thy orange.

SPARKISH: Then let's to dinner — there I was with you again. Come.

HORNER: But who dines with thee?

SPARKISH: My friends and relations, my brother Pinchwife, you see, of your acquaintance.

HORNER: And his wife?

SPARKISH: No, gad, he'll ne'er let her come amongst us good fellows; your stingy country coxcomb keeps his wife from his friends, as he does his little firkin[23] of ale, for his own drinking, and a gentleman can't get a smack on't. But his servants, when his back is turned, broach it at their pleasures, and dust it away,[24] ha ha ha! Gad, I am witty, I think, considering I was married today, by the world; but come —

HORNER: No, I will not dine with you, unless you can fetch her too.

SPARKISH: Pshaw! What pleasure canst thou have with women now, Harry?

HORNER: My eyes are not gone; I love a good prospect yet, and will not dine with you unless she does too; go fetch her therefore, but do not tell her husband 'tis for my sake.

SPARKISH: Well, I'll go try what I can do; in the

---

20 *Grand Signior:* the Sultan of Turkey. 21 *Piazza:* a fashionable arcade in Covent Garden. 22 *orange to veal:* a sauce rather like that now used on duck was then used on veal, spiced with cinnamon and cloves. 23 *firkin:* barrel. 24 *dust it away:* down it.

meantime, come away to my aunt's lodging, 'tis in the way to Pinchwife's.

HORNER (*aside to* QUACK): The poor woman has called for aid, and stretched forth her hand, doctor; I cannot but help her over the pale out of the briars.

(*Exeunt* SPARKISH, HORNER, QUACK.)

SCENE FOUR   Pinchwife's House.

MRS. PINCHWIFE *alone, leaning on her elbow. A table, pen, ink, and paper.*

MRS. PINCHWIFE: Well, 'tis e'en so, I have got the London disease they call love; I am sick of my husband, and for my gallant. I have heard this distemper called a fever, but methinks 'tis like an ague; for when I think of my husband, I tremble, and am in a cold sweat, and have inclinations to vomit; but when I think of my gallant, dear Mr. Horner, my hot fit comes, and I am all in a fever indeed; and, as in other fevers, my own chamber is tedious to me, and I would fain be removed to his, and then methinks I should be well. Ah, poor Mr. Horner! Well, I cannot, will not stay here; therefore I'll make an end of my letter to him, which shall be a finer letter than my last, because I have studied it like anything. Oh sick, sick! (*Takes the pen and writes.*)

(*Enter* PINCHWIFE. *Seeing her writing, he steals softly behind her and looking over her shoulder, snatches the paper from her.*)

PINCHWIFE: What, writing more letters?

MRS. PINCHWIFE: O Lord, bud, why d'ye fright me so?

(*She offers to run out; he stops her, and reads.*)

PINCHWIFE: How's this? Nay, you shall not stir, madam. "Dear, dear, dear Mr. Horner" — very well — I have taught you to write letters to good purpose — but let us see't. "First, I am to beg your pardon for my boldness in writing to you, which I'd have you to know I would not have done, had not you said first you loved me so extremely, which if you do, you will never suffer me to lie in the arms of another man whom I loathe, nauseate, and detest." — Now you can write these filthy words! But what follows? "Therefore, I hope you will speedily find some way to free me from this unfortunate match, which was never, I assure you, of my choice; but I'm afraid 'tis already too far gone. However, if you love me, as I do you, you will try what you can do; but you must help me away before tomorrow, or else, alas, I shall be for ever out of your reach, for I can defer no longer our — our — " What is to follow "our"? — speak, what — "our journey into the country," I suppose — Oh woman, damned woman! And Love, damned Love, their old tempter! For this is one of his miracles; in a moment he can make those blind that could see, and those see that were blind, those dumb that could speak, and those prattle who were dumb before; nay, what is more than all, make these dough-baked,[1] senseless, indocile[2] animals, women, too hard for us their politic lords and rulers, in a moment. But make an end of your letter, and then I'll make an end of you thus, and all my plagues together.

(*Draws his sword.*)

MRS. PINCHWIFE: O Lord, O Lord, you are such a passionate man, bud!

(*Enter* SPARKISH.)

SPARKISH: How now, what's here to do?

PINCHWIFE: This fool here now!

SPARKISH: What! Drawn upon your wife? You should never do that, but at night in the dark, when you can't hurt her. This is my sister-in-law, is it not? Ay, faith, e'en our country Margery; (*pulls aside her handkerchief*) one may know her. Come, she and you must go dine with me; dinner's ready, come. But where's my wife? Is she not come home yet? Where is she?

PINCHWIFE: Making you a cuckold; 'tis that they all do, as soon as they can.

---

1 *dough-baked:* half-baked.   2 *indocile:* unteachable.

SPARKISH: What, the wedding day? No, a wife that designs to make a cully of her husband will be sure to let him win the first stake of love, by the world.[3] But come, they stay dinner for us; come, I'll lead down our Margery.

PINCHWIFE:[4] No — sir, go, we'll follow you.

SPARKISH: I will not wag without you.

PINCHWIFE (aside): This coxcomb is a sensible torment to me amidst the greatest in the world.

SPARKISH: Come, come, Madam Margery.

PINCHWIFE: No; I'll lead her my way. What, would you treat your friends with mine, for want of your own wife?

(Leads her to the other door, and locks her in and returns.)
　　(aside) I am contented my rage should take breath —

SPARKISH: I told Horner this.

PINCHWIFE: Come now.

SPARKISH: Lord, how shy you are of your wife! But let me tell you, brother, we men of wit have amongst us a saying, that cuckolding, like the smallpox, comes with a fear; and you may keep your wife as much as you will out of danger of infection, but if her constitution incline her to't, she'll have it sooner or later, by the world, say they.

PINCHWIFE (aside): What a thing is a cuckold, that every fool can make him ridiculous! (aloud) Well, sir; but let me advise you, now you are come to be concerned, because you suspect the danger, not to neglect the means to prevent it, especially when the greatest share of the malady will light upon your own head, for
　　Hows'e'er the kind wife's belly comes to
　　　　swell,
　　The husband breeds for her, and first is
　　　　ill.[5]

(Exeunt PINCHWIFE, SPARKISH.)

ACT FIVE

SCENE ONE   Pinchwife's House.

Enter PINCHWIFE and MRS. PINCHWIFE. A table and candle.

PINCHWIFE: Come, take the pen and make an end of the letter, just as you intended; if you are false in a tittle, I shall soon perceive it, and punish you as you with this deserve. (Lays his hand on his sword.) Write what was to follow — let's see — "You must make haste, and help me away before tomorrow, or else I shall be for ever out of your reach, for I can defer no longer our" — What follows "our"?

MRS. PINCHWIFE: Must all out, then, bud? (MRS. PINCHWIFE takes the pen and writes.) Look you there, then.

PINCHWIFE: Let's see — "For I can defer no longer our — wedding — Your slighted Alithea." — What's the meaning of this? My sister's name to't? Speak, unriddle.

MRS. PINCHWIFE: Yes, indeed, bud.

PINCHWIFE: But why her name to't? Speak — speak, I say.

MRS. PINCHWIFE: Ay, but you'll tell her then again. If you would not tell her again —

PINCHWIFE: I will not. I am stunned, my head turns round — speak.

MRS. PINCHWIFE: Won't you tell her, indeed, and indeed?

PINCHWIFE: No; speak, I say.

MRS. PINCHWIFE: She'll be angry with me; but I had rather she should be angry with me than you, bud; and, to tell you the truth, 'twas she made me write the letter, and taught me what I should write.

PINCHWIFE (aside): Ha! I thought the style was somewhat better than her own. (aloud) But how could she come to you to teach you, since I had locked you up alone?

---

3 *first stake of love*, etc.: in case she gets pregnant. 4 *Pinchwife*: the 1675 quarto assigns the speech to Mrs. Pinchwife, but this seems to be an error. 5 *husband breeds*, etc.: the husband's head grows a cuckold's horns before the wife's belly begins to swell.

Mrs. Pinchwife: Oh, through the keyhole, bud.

Pinchwife: But why should she make you write a letter for her to him, since she can write herself?

Mrs. Pinchwife: Why, she said because — for I was unwilling to do it —

Pinchwife: Because what — because . . . ?

Mrs. Pinchwife: Because, lest Mr. Horner should be cruel, and refuse her; or be vain afterwards, and show the letter, she might disown it, the hand not being hers.

Pinchwife (aside): How's this? Ha! Then I think I shall come to myself again. This changeling could not invent this lie; but if she could, why should she? She might think I should soon discover it. Stay — now I think on't too, Horner said he was sorry she had married Sparkish; and her disowning her marriage to me makes me think she has evaded it for Horner's sake; yet why should she take this course? But men in love are fools; women may well be so. (aloud) But hark you, madam, your sister went out in the morning, and I have not seen her within since.

Mrs. Pinchwife: Alack-a-day, she has been crying all day above, it seems, in a corner.

Pinchwife: Where is she? Let me speak with her.

Mrs. Pinchwife (aside): O Lord, then he'll discover all! (aloud) Pray hold, bud; what, d'ye mean to discover me? She'll know I have told you then. Pray, bud, let me talk with her first.

Pinchwife: I must speak with her, to know whether Horner ever made her any promise, and whether she be married to Sparkish or no.

Mrs. Pinchwife: Pray, dear bud, don't, till I have spoken with her, and told her that I have told you all; for she'll kill me else.

Pinchwife: Go then, and bid her come out to me.

Mrs. Pinchwife: Yes, yes, bud.

Pinchwife: Let me see —

Mrs. Pinchwife (aside): I'll go, but she is not within to come to him. I have just got time to know of Lucy her maid, who first set me on work, what lie I shall tell next; for I am e'en at my wit's end.

(Exit Mrs. Pinchwife.)

Pinchwife: Well, I resolve it; Horner shall have her. I'd rather give him my sister than lend him my wife; and such an alliance will prevent his pretensions to my wife, sure. I'll make him of kin to her, and then he won't care for her.

(Enter Mrs. Pinchwife.)

Mrs. Pinchwife: O Lord, bud! I told you what anger you would make me with my sister.

Pinchwife: Won't she come hither?

Mrs. Pinchwife: No, no. Alack-a-day, she's ashamed to look you in the face; and she says, if you go in to her, she'll run away downstairs, and shamefully go herself to Mr. Horner, who has promised her marriage, she says: and she will have no other, so she won't.

Pinchwife: Did he so? — Promise her marriage! — Then she shall have no other. Go tell her so; and if she will come and discourse with me a little concerning the means, I will about it immediately. Go.

(Exit Mrs. Pinchwife.)

His estate is equal to Sparkish's, and his extraction as much better than his, as his parts are; but my chief reason is I'd rather be akin to him by the name of brother-in-law than that of cuckold.

(Enter Mrs. Pinchwife.)

Well, what says she now?

Mrs. Pinchwife: Why, she says she would only have you lead her to Horner's lodging, with whom she first will discourse the matter before she talks with you, which yet she cannot do; for alack, poor creature, she says she can't so much as look you in the face, therefore she'll come to you in a mask. And you must excuse her, if she make you no answer to any question of yours, till you have brought her to Mr. Horner; and if you will not chide her, nor question her, she'll come out to you immediately.

PINCHWIFE: Let her come; I will not speak a word to her, nor require a word from her.

MRS. PINCHWIFE: Oh, I forgot; besides, she says she cannot look you in the face, though through a mask; therefore would desire you to put out the candle.

PINCHWIFE: I agree to all. Let her make haste. (*Puts out the candle.*) There, 'tis out.

(*Exit* MRS. PINCHWIFE.)

My case is something better. I'd rather fight with Horner for not lying with my sister, than for lying with my wife; and of the two, I had rather find my sister too forward than my wife. I expected no other from her free education, as she calls it, and her passion for the town. Well, wife and sister are names which make us expect love and duty, pleasure and comfort; but we find 'em plagues and torments, and are equally, though differently, troublesome to their keeper; for we have as much ado to get people to lie with our sisters as to keep 'em from lying with our wives.

(*Enter* MRS. PINCHWIFE *masked, and in hoods and scarfs and a night-gown and petticoat of* ALITHEA's, *in the dark.*)

What are you come, sister? Let us go then. But first, let me lock up my wife. Mrs. Margery, where are you?

MRS. PINCHWIFE: Here, bud.

PINCHWIFE: Come hither, that I may lock you up; get you in. (*Locks the door.*) Come, sister, where are you now?

(MRS. PINCHWIFE *gives him her hand; but when he lets her go, she steals softly to the other side of him, and is led away by him mistaken for his sister,* ALITHEA.)

SCENE TWO   Horner's Lodging.

HORNER and QUACK.

QUACK: What, all alone? Not so much as one of your cuckolds here, nor one of their wives! They use to take their turns with you, as if they were to watch you.

HORNER: Yes, it often happens that a cuckold is but his wife's spy, and is more upon family duty when he is with her gallant abroad, hindering his pleasure, than when he is at home with her playing the gallant. But the hardest duty a married woman imposes upon a lover is keeping her husband company always.

QUACK: And his fondness wearies you almost as soon as hers.

HORNER: A pox! Keeping a cuckold company, after you have had his wife, is as tiresome as the company of a country squire to a witty fellow of the town, when[1] he has got all his money.

QUACK: And as at first a man makes a friend of the husband to get the wife, so at last you are fain to fall out with the wife to be rid of the husband.

HORNER: Ay, most cuckold-makers are true courtiers; when once a poor man has cracked his credit for 'em, they can't abide to come near him.

QUACK: But at first, to draw him in, are so sweet, so kind, so dear! Just as you are to Pinchwife. But what becomes of that intrigue with his wife?

HORNER: A pox! He's as surly as an alderman that has been bit; and since he's so coy, his wife's kindness is in vain, for she's a silly innocent.

QUACK: Did she not send you a letter by him?

HORNER: Yes; but that's a riddle I have not yet solved. Allow the poor creature to be willing, she is silly too, and he keeps her up so close —

QUACK: Yes, so close, that he makes her but the more willing, and adds but revenge to

---

1 *when:* after.

her love; which two, when met, seldom fail of satisfying each other one way or other.

HORNER: What! Here's the man we are talking of, I think.

(*Enter* PINCHWIFE, *leading in his wife masked, muffled, and in her sister's gown.*)

Pshaw!

QUACK: Bringing his wife to you is the next thing to bringing a love letter from her.

HORNER: What means this?

PINCHWIFE: The last time, you know, sir, I brought you a love letter; now, you see, a mistress; I think you'll say I am a civil man to you.

HORNER: Ay, the devil take me, will I say thou art the civilest man I ever met with; and I have known some. I fancy I understand thee now better than I did the letter. But, hark thee, in thy ear —

PINCHWIFE: What?

HORNER: Nothing but the usual question, man: is she sound, on thy word?

PINCHWIFE: What, you take her for a wench, and me for a pimp?

HORNER: Pshaw! "Wench" and "pimp," paw[2] words; I know thou art an honest fellow, and hast a great acquaintance among the ladies, and perhaps hast made love for me, rather than let me make love to thy wife.

PINCHWIFE: Come, sir, in short, I am for no fooling.

HORNER: Nor I neither; therefore prithee, let's see her face presently. Make her show, man; art thou sure I don't know her?

PINCHWIFE: I am sure you do know her.

HORNER: A pox! Why dost thou bring her to me then?

PINCHWIFE: Because she's a relation of mine —

HORNER: Is she, faith, man? Then thou art still more civil and obliging, dear rogue.

PINCHWIFE: Who desired me to bring her to you.

HORNER: Then she is obliging, dear rogue.

PINCHWIFE: You'll make her welcome for my sake, I hope.

HORNER: I hope she is handsome enough to make herself welcome. Prithee, let her unmask.

PINCHWIFE: Do you speak to her; she would never be ruled by me.

HORNER: Madam — (MRS. PINCHWIFE *whispers to* HORNER.)   She says she must speak with me in private. Withdraw, prithee.

PINCHWIFE (*aside*): She's unwilling, it seems, I should know all her indecent conduct in this business. (*aloud*) Well then, I'll leave you together, and hope when I am gone, you'll agree; if not, you and I shan't agree, sir.

HORNER: What means the fool? If she and I agree 'tis no matter what you and I do. (*Whispers to* MRS. PINCHWIFE, *who makes signs with her hand for him to be gone.*)

PINCHWIFE: In the meantime I'll fetch a parson, and find out Sparkish, and disabuse him. You would have me fetch a parson, would you not? Well then — now I think I am rid of her, and shall have no more trouble with her. Our sisters and daughters, like usurers' money, are safest when put out; but our wives, like their writings, never safe, but in our closets under lock and key.

(*Exit* PINCHWIFE.)

(*Enter* BOY.)

BOY: Sir Jasper Fidget, sir, is coming up.

(*Exit* BOY.)

HORNER: Here's the trouble of a cuckold now we are talking of. A pox on him! Has he not enough to do to hinder his wife's sport, but he must other women's too? Step in here, madam.

(*Exit* MRS. PINCHWIFE. *Enter* SIR JASPER FIDGET.)

SIR JASPER: My best and dearest friend.

---

2 *paw:* naughty.

HORNER (*aside to* QUACK): The old style, doctor. (*aloud*) Well, be short, for I am busy. What would your impertinent wife have now?

SIR JASPER: Well guessed, i'faith; for I do come from her.

HORNER: To invite me to supper! Tell her, I can't come; go.

SIR JASPER: Nay, now you are out, faith; for my lady, and the whole knot of the virtuous gang, as they call themselves, are resolved upon a frolic of coming to you tonight in a masquerade, and are all dressed already.

HORNER: I shan't be at home.

SIR JASPER (*aside*): Lord, how churlish he is to women! (*aloud*) Nay, prithee don't disappoint 'em; they'll think 'tis my fault. Prithee, don't. I'll send in the banquet and the fiddles. But make no noise on't; for the poor virtuous rogues would not have it known, for the world, that they go a-masquerading; and they would come to no man's ball but yours.

HORNER: Well, well — get you gone; and tell 'em, if they come, 'twill be at the peril of their honour and yours.

SIR JASPER: He he he! We'll trust you for that; farewell.

(*Exit* SIR JASPER.)

HORNER: Doctor, anon you too shall be my guest
But now I'm going to a private feast.

(*Exeunt* HORNER *and* QUACK.)

SCENE THREE   The Piazza of Covent Garden.

SPARKISH *and* PINCHWIFE.

SPARKISH (*with the letter in his hand*): But who would have thought a woman could have been false to me? By the world, I could not have thought it.

PINCHWIFE: You were for giving and taking liberty; she has taken it only, sir, now you find in that letter. You are a frank person, and so is she, you see there.

SPARKISH: Nay, if this be her hand — for I never saw it.

PINCHWIFE: 'Tis no matter whether that be her hand or no; I am sure this hand, at her desire, led her to Mr. Horner, with whom I left her just now, to go fetch a parson to 'em at their desire too, to deprive you of her for ever; for it seems yours was but a mock marriage.

SPARKISH: Indeed, she would needs have it that 'twas Harcourt himself, in a parson's habit, that married us; but I'm sure he told me 'twas his brother Ned.

PINCHWIFE: Oh, there 'tis out; and you were deceived, not she; for you are such a frank person. But I must be gone. You'll find her at Mr. Horner's. Go, and believe your eyes.

(*Exit* PINCHWIFE.)

SPARKISH: Nay, I'll to her, and call her as many crocodiles, sirens, harpies, and other heathenish names as a poet would do a mistress who had refused to hear his suit, nay more, his verses on her. But stay, is not that she following a torch[1] at t'other end of the Piazza? And from Horner's certainly — 'tis so.

(*Enter* ALITHEA *following a torch, and* LUCY *behind*.)

You are well met, madam, though you don't think so. What, you have made a short visit to Mr. Horner? But I suppose you'll return to him presently, by that time the parson can be with him.

ALITHEA: Mr. Horner and the parson, sir!

SPARKISH: Come, madam, no more dissembling, no more jilting; for I am no more a frank person.

ALITHEA: How's this?

LUCY (*aside*): So, 'twill work, I see.

SPARKISH: Could you find out no easy country

---

1 *torch*: torchbearer, to light her way, for there was no street-lighting at this time.

fool to abuse? None but me, a gentleman of wit and pleasure about the town? But it was your pride to be too hard for a man of parts, unworthy false woman! False as a friend that lends a man money to lose; false as dice, who undo those that trust all they have to 'em.

LUCY (*aside*): He has been a great bubble, by his similes, as they say.

ALITHEA: You have been too merry, sir, at your wedding dinner, sure.

SPARKISH: What, d'ye mock me too?

ALITHEA: Or you have been deluded.

SPARKISH: By you.

ALITHEA: Let me understand you.

SPARKISH: Have you the confidence (I should call it something else, since you know your guilt) to stand my just reproaches? You did not write an impudent letter to Mr. Horner, who I find now has clubbed with you in deluding me with his aversion for women, that I might not, forsooth, suspect him for my rival?

LUCY (*aside*): D'ye think the gentleman can be jealous now, madam?

ALITHEA: I write a letter to Mr. *Horner!*

SPARKISH: Nay, madam, do not deny it. Your brother showed it me just now; and told me likewise, he left you at Horner's lodging to fetch a parson to marry you to him, and I wish you joy, madam, joy, joy; and to him too, much joy; and to myself more joy, for not marrying you.

ALITHEA (*aside*): So, I find, my brother would break off the match; and I can consent to't, since I see this gentleman can be made jealous. (*aloud*) Oh, Lucy, by his rude usage and jealousy, he makes me almost afraid I am married to him. Art thou sure 'twas Harcourt himself, and no parson, that married us?

SPARKISH: No, madam, I thank you. I suppose that was a contrivance too of Mr. Horner's and yours, to make Harcourt play the par-

son; but I would as little as you have him one now, no, not for the world. For, shall I tell you another truth? I never had any passion for you till now, for now I hate you. 'Tis true, I might have married your portion,[2] as other men of parts of the town do sometimes; and so, your servant.[3] And to show my unconcernedness, I'll come to your wedding, and resign you with as much joy, as I would a stale wench to a new cully; nay, with as much joy as I would after the first night, if I had been married to you. There's for you; and so your servant, servant.

(*Exit* SPARKISH.)

ALITHEA: How was I deceived in a man!

LUCY: You'll believe then a fool may be made jealous now? For that easiness in him that suffers him to be led by a wife, will likewise permit him to be persuaded against her by others.

ALITHEA: But marry Mr. Horner! My brother does not intend it, sure; if I thought he did, I would take thy advice, and Mr. Harcourt for my husband. And now I wish that if there be any overwise woman of the town, who, like me, would marry a fool for fortune, liberty, or title, first, that her husband may love play, and be a cully to all the town but her, and suffer none but Fortune to be mistress of his purse; then, if for liberty, that he may send her into the country, under the conduct of some housewifely mother-in-law; and if for title, may the world give 'em none but that of Cuckold.

LUCY: And for her greater curse, madam, may he not deserve it.

ALITHEA: Away, impertinent! Is not this my old Lady Lanterlu's?[4]

LUCY: Yes, madam. (*aside*) And here I hope we shall find Mr. Harcourt.

(*Exeunt* LUCY, ALITHEA.)

---

2 *portion:* inheritance, dowry, money. 3 *your servant:* goodbye. 4 *Lanterlu's:* lanterloo was a card game.

SCENE FOUR   Horner's Lodging.

Enter HORNER, LADY FIDGET, MRS. DAINTY FID-
GET, *and* MRS. SQUEAMISH. *A table, banquet, and
bottles.*

HORNER (*aside*): A pox! They are come too
soon — before I have sent back my new
mistress. All I have now to do is to lock her
in, that they may not see her.

LADY FIDGET: That we may be sure of our welcome, we have brought our entertainment
with us, and are resolved to treat thee, dear
toad.

MRS. DAINTY: And that we may be merry to
purpose, have left Sir Jasper and my old
Lady Squeamish quarrelling at home at backgammon.

MRS. SQUEAMISH: Therefore let us make use
of our time, lest they should chance to interrupt us.

LADY FIDGET: Let us sit then.

HORNER: First, that you may be private, let me
lock this door and that, and I'll wait upon
you presently.

LADY FIDGET: No, sir, shut 'em only, and your
lips for ever; for we must trust you as much
as our women.

HORNER: You know all vanity's killed in me;
I have no occasion for talking.

LADY FIDGET: Now, ladies, supposing we had
drank each of us two bottles, let us speak
the truth of our hearts.

MRS. DAINTY: ⎫
MRS. SQUEAMISH: ⎬ Agreed.

LADY FIDGET: By this brimmer,[5] for truth is
nowhere else to be found. (*aside to* HORNER)
Not in thy heart, false man!

HORNER (*aside to* LADY FIDGET): You have
found me a true man, I'm sure.

LADY FIDGET (*aside to* HORNER): Not every way.
(*aloud*) But let us sit and be merry. (LADY
FIDGET *sings.*)

Why should our damned tyrants oblige us
to live
On the pittance of pleasure which they only
give?
We must not rejoice
With wine and with noise;
In vain we must wake in a dull bed alone,
Whilst to our warm rival the bottle, they're
gone.
Then lay aside charms,
And take up these arms.
'Tis wine only gives 'em their courage and
wit;
Because we live sober, to men we submit.
If for beauties you'd pass,
Take a lick of the glass,
'Twill mend your complexions, and when
they are gone,
The best red we have is the red of the
grape.
Then, sisters, lay't on,
And damn a good shape.

MRS. DAINTY: Dear brimmer! Well, in token of
our openness and plain-dealing, let us throw
our masks over our heads.

HORNER (*aside*): So, 'twill come to the glasses
anon.

MRS. SQUEAMISH: Lovely brimmer! Let me
enjoy him first.

LADY FIDGET: No, I never part with a gallant
till I've tried him. Dear brimmer, that makest
our husbands short-sighted!

MRS. DAINTY: And our bashful gallants bold.

MRS. SQUEAMISH: And, for want of a gallant,
the butler lovely in our eyes. Drink, eunuch.

LADY FIDGET: Drink, thou representative of a
husband. Damn a husband!

MRS. DAINTY: And, as it were a husband, an
old keeper.

MRS. SQUEAMISH: And, an old grandmother.

HORNER: And an English bawd, and a French
chirurgeon.

---

5 *brimmer:* glass.

LADY FIDGET: Ay, we have all reason to curse 'em.

HORNER: For my sake, ladies?

LADY FIDGET: No, for our own; for the first spoils all young gallants' industry.

MRS. DAINTY: And the other's art makes 'em bold only with common women.

MRS. SQUEAMISH: And rather run the hazard of the vile distemper amongst them, than of a denial amongst us.

MRS. DAINTY: The filthy toads choose mistresses now as they do stuffs, for having been fancied and worn by others.

MRS. SQUEAMISH: For being common and cheap.

LADY FIDGET: Whilst women of quality, like the richest stuffs, lie untumbled, and unasked for.

HORNER: Ay, neat, and cheap, and new, often they think best.

MRS. DAINTY: No, sir, the beasts will be known by a mistress longer than by a suit.

MRS. SQUEAMISH: And 'tis not for cheapness neither.

LADY FIDGET: No; for the vain fops will tape up druggets[6] and embroider 'em. But I wonder at the depraved appetites of witty men; they used to be out of the common road, and hate imitation. Pray tell me, beast, when you were a man, why you rather chose to club with a multitude in a common house for an entertainment, than to be the only guest at a good table.

HORNER: Why, faith, ceremony and expectation are insufferable to those that are sharp bent. People always eat with the best stomach at an ordinary, where every man is snatching for the best bit.

LADY FIDGET: Though he get a cut over the fingers. But I have heard people eat most heartily of another man's meat, that is, what they do not pay for.

HORNER: When they are sure of their welcome and freedom; for ceremony in love and eat-ing is as ridiculous as in fighting: falling on briskly is all should be done on those occasions.

LADY FIDGET: Well then, let me tell you, sir, there is nowhere more freedom than in our houses; and we take freedom from a young person as a sign of good breeding; and a person may be as free as he pleases with us, as frolic, as gamesome, as wild as he will.

HORNER: Han't I heard you all declaim against wild men?

LADY FIDGET: Yes, but for all that, we think wildness in a man as desirable a quality as in a duck or rabbit. A tame man! Foh!

HORNER: I know not, but your reputations frightened me as much as your faces invited me.

LADY FIDGET: Our reputation! Lord, why should you not think that we women make use of our reputation, as you men of yours, only to deceive the world with less suspicion? Our virtue is like the statesman's religion, the Quaker's word, the gamester's oath, and the great man's honour — but to cheat those that trust us.

MRS. SQUEAMISH: And that demureness, coyness, and modesty, that you see in our faces in the boxes at plays, is as much a sign of a kind woman, as a vizard-mask in the pit.

MRS. DAINTY: For, I assure you, women are least masked when they have the velvet vizard on.

LADY FIDGET: You would have found us modest women in our denials only.

MRS. SQUEAMISH: Our bashfulness is only the reflection of the men's.

MRS. DAINTY: We blush when they are shamefaced.

HORNER: I beg your pardon, ladies; I was deceived in you devilishly. But why that mighty pretence to honour?

---

6 *druggets:* cheap cloths.

LADY FIDGET: We have told you; but sometimes 'twas for the same reason you men pretend business often, to avoid ill company, to enjoy the better and more privately those you love.

HORNER: But why would you ne'er give a friend a wink then?

LADY FIDGET: Faith, your reputation frightened us as much as ours did you, you were so notoriously lewd.

HORNER: And you so seemingly honest.

LADY FIDGET: Was that all that deterred you?

HORNER: And so expensive — you allow freedom, you say.

LADY FIDGET: Ay, ay.

HORNER: That I was afraid of losing my little money, as well as my little time, both which my other pleasures required.

LADY FIDGET: Money! Foh! You talk like a little fellow now; do such as we expect money?

HORNER: I beg your pardon, madam; I must confess, I have heard that great ladies, like great merchants, set but the higher prices upon what they have, because are not in necessity of taking the first offer.

MRS. DAINTY: Such as we make sale of our hearts?

MRS. SQUEAMISH: We bribed for our love? Foh!

HORNER: With your pardon, ladies; I know, like great men in offices, you seem to exact flattery and attendance only from your followers; but you have receivers about you, and such fees to pay, a man is afraid to pass your grants.[7] Besides, we must let you win at cards, or we lose your hearts; and if you make an assignation, 'tis at a goldsmith's, jeweller's, or china-house, where for your honour you deposit to him, he must pawn his to the punctual cit,[8] and so paying for what you take up, pays for what he takes up.

MRS. DAINTY: Would you not have us assured of our gallants' love?

MRS. SQUEAMISH: For love is better known by liberality than by jealousy.

LADY FIDGET: For one may be dissembled, the other not. (aside) But my jealousy can be no longer dissembled, and they are telling ripe. (aloud) Come, here's to our gallants in waiting, whom we must name, and I'll begin. This is my false rogue. (claps him on the back)

MRS. SQUEAMISH: How!

HORNER (aside): So, all will out now.

MRS. SQUEAMISH (aside to HORNER): Did you not tell me, 'twas for my sake only you reported yourself no man?

MRS. DAINTY (aside to HORNER): Oh, wretch! Did you not swear to me, 'twas for my love and honour you passed for that thing you do?

HORNER: So, so.

LADY FIDGET: Come, speak, ladies; this is my false villain.

MRS. SQUEAMISH: And mine too.

MRS. DAINTY: And mine.

HORNER: Well then, you are all three my false rogues too, and there's an end on't.

LADY FIDGET: Well then, there's no remedy; sister sharers, let us not fall out, but have a care of our honour. Though we get no presents, no jewels of him, we are savers of our honour, the jewel of most value and use, which shines yet to the world unsuspected, though it be counterfeit.

HORNER: Nay, and is e'en as good as if it were true, provided the world think so; for honour, like beauty now, only depends on the opinion of others.

LADY FIDGET: Well, Harry Common, I hope you can be true to three. Swear; but 'tis to no purpose to require your oath, for you are as often forsworn as you swear to new women.

HORNER: Come, faith, madam, let us e'en pardon one another; for all the difference I find

---

7 *pass your grants:* accept your gifts. 8 *cit:* citizen, as indicated earlier.

betwixt we men and you women, we foreswear ourselves at the beginning of an amour, you as long as it lasts.

(*Enter* SIR JASPER FIDGET *and* OLD LADY SQUEAMISH.)

SIR JASPER: Oh, my Lady Fidget, was this your cunning, to come to Mr. Horner without me? But you have been nowhere else, I hope.

LADY FIDGET: No, Sir Jasper.

LADY SQUEAMISH: And you came straight hither, Biddy?

MRS. SQUEAMISH: Yes, indeed, lady grandmother.

SIR JASPER: 'Tis well, 'tis well; I knew when once they were thoroughly acquainted with poor Horner, they'd ne'er be from him. You may let her masquerade it with my wife and Horner, and I warrant her reputation safe.

(*Enter* BOY.)

BOY: O sir, here's the gentleman come, whom you bid me not suffer to come up without giving you notice, with a lady too, and other gentlemen.

HORNER: Do you all go in there, whilst I send 'em away; and, boy, do you desire 'em to stay below till I come, which shall be immediately.

(*Exeunt* SIR JASPER FIDGET, LADY FIDGET, LADY SQUEAMISH, MRS. SQUEAMISH, *and* MRS. DAINTY FIDGET.)

BOY: Yes, sir.

(*Exit* BOY *and* HORNER *at the other door*; HORNER *returns with* MRS. PINCHWIFE.)

HORNER: You would not take my advice, to be gone home before your husband came back; he'll now discover all. Yet pray, my dearest, be persuaded to go home, and leave the rest to my management; I'll let you down the back way.

MRS. PINCHWIFE: I don't know the way home, so I don't.

HORNER: My man shall wait upon you.

MRS. PINCHWIFE: No, don't you believe that I'll go at all; what, are you weary of me already?

HORNER: No, my life, 'tis that I may love you long, 'tis to secure my love, and your reputation with your husband; he'll never receive you again else.

MRS. PINCHWIFE: What care I? D'ye think to frighten me with that? I don't intend to go to him again; you shall be my husband now.

HORNER: I cannot be your husband, dearest, since you are married to him.

MRS. PINCHWIFE: Oh, would you make me believe that? Don't I see every day at London here, women leave their first husbands, and go and live with other men as their wives? Pish, pshaw! You'd make me angry, but that I love you so mainly.

HORNER: So, they are coming up — in again, in, I hear 'em.

(*Exit* MRS. PINCHWIFE.)

Well, a silly mistress is like a weak place, soon got, soon lost. A man has scarce time for plunder; she betrays her husband first to her gallant, and then her gallant to her husband.

(*Enter* PINCHWIFE, ALITHEA, HARCOURT, SPARKISH, LUCY, *and a* PARSON.)

PINCHWIFE: Come, madam, 'tis not the sudden change of your dress, the confidence of your asseverations, and your false witness there, shall persuade me I did not bring you hither just now; here's my witness, who cannot deny it, since you must be confronted. Mr. Horner, did not I bring this lady to you just now?

HORNER (*aside*): Now must I wrong one woman for another's sake; but that's no new thing with me, for in these cases I am still on the criminal's side against the innocent.

ALITHEA: Pray speak, sir.

HORNER (*aside*): It must be so. I must be impudent, and try my luck; impudence uses to be too hard for truth.

PINCHWIFE: What, you are studying an evasion or excuse for her! Speak, sir.

HORNER: No, faith, I am something backward only to speak in women's affairs or disputes.

PINCHWIFE: She bids you speak.

ALITHEA: Ah, pray, sir, do; pray satisfy him.

HORNER: Then truly, you did bring that lady to me just now.

PINCHWIFE: Oh ho!

ALITHEA: How, sir?

HARCOURT: How, Horner?

ALITHEA: What mean you, sir? I always took you for a man of honour.

HORNER (aside): Ay, so much a man of honour that I must save my mistress, I thank you, come what will on't.

SPARKISH: So, if I had had her, she'd have made me believe the moon had been made of a Christmas pie.

LUCY (aside): Now could I speak, if I durst, and solve the riddle, who am the author of it.

ALITHEA: O unfortunate woman! A combination against my honour! Which most concerns me now, because you share in my disgrace, sir, and it is your censure, which I must now suffer, that troubles me, not theirs.

HARCOURT: Madam, then have no trouble, you shall now see 'tis possible for me to love too, without being jealous; I will not only believe your innocence myself, but make all the world believe it. (aside to HORNER) Horner, I must now be concerned for this lady's honour.

HORNER: And I must be concerned for a lady's honour too.

HARCOURT: This lady has her honour, and I will protect it.

HORNER: My lady has not her honour, but has given it to me to keep, and I will preserve it.

HARCOURT: I understand you not.

HORNER: I would not have you.

MRS. PINCHWIFE (peeping in behind): What's the matter with 'em all?

PINCHWIFE: Come, come, Mr. Horner, no more disputing; here's the parson. I brought him not in vain.

HARCOURT: No, sir, I'll employ him, if this lady please.

PINCHWIFE: How! What d'ye mean?

SPARKISH: Ay, what does he mean?

HORNER: Why, I have resigned your sister to him; he has my consent.

PINCHWIFE: But he has not mine, sir; a woman's injured honour, no more than a man's, can be repaired or satisfied by any but him that first wronged it; and you shall marry her presently, or — (Lays his hand on his sword.)

(Enter MRS. PINCHWIFE.)

MRS. PINCHWIFE: O Lord, they'll kill poor Mr. Horner! Besides, he shan't marry her whilst I stand by, and look on; I'll not lose my second husband so.

PINCHWIFE: What do I see?

ALITHEA: My sister in my clothes!

SPARKISH: Ha!

MRS. PINCHWIFE: Nay, pray now don't quarrel about finding work for the parson; he shall marry me to Mr. Horner. (to PINCHWIFE) For now, I believe, you have enough of me.

HORNER (aside): Damned, damned loving changeling!

MRS. PINCHWIFE: Pray, sister, pardon me for telling so many lies of you.

HORNER: I suppose the riddle is plain now.

LUCY: No, that must be my work. Good sir, hear me. (Kneels to PINCHWIFE, who stands doggedly with his hat over his eyes.[9])

PINCHWIFE: I will never hear woman again, but make 'em all silent thus — (Offers to draw upon his wife.)

---

9 hat over his eyes: a sign of displeasure.

HORNER: No, that must not be.

PINCHWIFE: You then shall go first, 'tis one to me. (*Offers to draw on* HORNER, *stopped by* HARCOURT.)

HARCOURT: Hold!

(*Enter* SIR JASPER FIDGET, LADY FIDGET, LADY SQUEAMISH, MRS. DAINTY FIDGET, *and* MRS. SQUEAMISH.)

SIR JASPER: What's the matter? What's the matter? Pray, what's the matter, sir? I beseech you communicate, sir.

PINCHWIFE: Why, my wife has communicated, sir, as your wife may have done too, sir, if she knows him, sir.

SIR JASPER: Pshaw, with him! Ha ha he!

PINCHWIFE: D'ye mock me, sir? A cuckold is a kind of a wild beast; have a care, sir —

SIR JASPER: No, sure, you mock me, sir. He cuckold you! It can't be, ha ha he! Why, I'll tell you, sir — (*offers to whisper*)

PINCHWIFE: I tell you again, he has whored my wife, and yours too, if he knows her, and all the women he comes near; 'tis not his dissembling, his hypocrisy, can wheedle me.

SIR JASPER: How! Does he dissemble? Is he a hypocrite? Nay, then — how — wife — sister, is he a hypocrite?

LADY SQUEAMISH: A hypocrite! A dissembler! Speak, young harlotry, speak, how?

SIR JASPER: Nay, then — oh, my head too! — O thou libidinous lady!

LADY SQUEAMISH: O thou harloting harlotry! Hast thou done't then?

SIR JASPER: Speak, good Horner, art thou a dissembler, a rogue? Hast thou —

HORNER: So!

LUCY (*aside to* HORNER): I'll fetch you off, and her too, if she will but hold her tongue.

HORNER (*apart to* LUCY): Canst thou? I'll give thee —

LUCY (*to* PINCHWIFE): Pray have but patience to hear me, sir, who am the unfortunate cause of all this confusion. Your wife is innocent, I only culpable; for I put her upon telling you all these lies concerning my mistress, in order to the breaking off the match between Mr. Sparkish and her, to make way for Mr. Harcourt.

SPARKISH: Did you so, eternal rotten tooth? Then, it seems, my mistress was not false to me; I was only deceived by you. Brother, that should have been, now man of conduct, who is a frank person now, to bring your wife to her lover, ha?

LUCY: I assure you, sir, she came not to Mr. Horner out of love, for she loves him no more —

MRS. PINCHWIFE: Hold, I told lies for you, but you shall tell none for me; for I do love Mr. Horner with all my soul, and nobody shall say me nay; pray, don't you go to make poor Mr. Horner believe to the contrary; 'tis spitefully done of you, I'm sure.

HORNER (*aside to* MRS. PINCHWIFE): Peace, dear idiot.

MRS. PINCHWIFE: Nay, I will not peace.

PINCHWIFE: Not till I make you!

(*Enter* DORILANT *and* QUACK.)

DORILANT: Horner, your servant; I am the doctor's guest, he must excuse our intrusion.

QUACK: But what's the matter, gentlemen? For Heaven's sake, what's the matter?

HORNER: Oh, 'tis well you are come. 'Tis a censorious world we live in; you may have brought me a reprieve, or else I had died for a crime I never committed, and these innocent ladies had suffered with me. Therefore, pray satisfy these worthy, honourable, jealous gentlemen — that — (*whispers*)

QUACK: Oh, I understand you; is that all? Sir Jasper, by Heavens, and upon the word of a physician, sir — (*whispers to* SIR JASPER)

SIR JASPER: Nay, I do believe you truly. Pardon me, my virtuous lady, and dear of honour.

LADY SQUEAMISH: What, then all's right again?

SIR JASPER: Ay, ay, and now let us satisfy him too.

(*They whisper with* PINCHWIFE.)

PINCHWIFE: A eunuch! Pray, no fooling with me.

QUACK: I'll bring half the chirurgeons in town to swear it.

PINCHWIFE: They! They'll swear[10] a man that bled to death through his wounds died of an apoplexy.

QUACK: Pray, hear me, sir. Why, all the town has heard the report of him.

PINCHWIFE: But does all the town believe it?

QUACK: Pray, inquire a little, and first of all these.

PINCHWIFE: I'm sure when I left the town, he was the lewdest fellow in't.

QUACK: I tell you, sir he has been in France since; pray, ask but these ladies and gentlemen, your friend Mr. Dorilant. Gentlemen and ladies, han't you all heard the late sad report of poor Mr. Horner?

ALL THE LADIES: Ay, ay, ay.

DORILANT: Why, thou jealous fool, dost thou doubt it? He's an arrant French capon.

MRS. PINCHWIFE: 'Tis false, sir, you shall not disparage poor Mr. Horner, for to my certain knowledge —

LUCY: Oh, hold!

MRS. SQUEAMISH (*aside to* LUCY): Stop her mouth!

LADY FIDGET (*to* PINCHWIFE): Upon my honour, sir, 'tis as true.

MRS. DAINTY: D'ye think we would have been seen in his company?

MRS. SQUEAMISH: Trust our unspotted reputations with him?

LADY FIDGET (*aside to* HORNER): This you get, and we too, by trusting your secret to a fool.

HORNER: Peace, madam. (*aside to* QUACK) Well,

doctor, is not this a good design, that carries a man on unsuspected, and brings him off safe?

PINCHWIFE (*aside*): Well, if this were true — but my wife —

(DORILANT *whispers with* MRS. PINCHWIFE.)

ALITHEA: Come, brother, your wife is yet innocent, you see; but have a care of too strong an imagination, lest, like an over-concerned timorous gamester, by fancying an unlucky cast, it should come. Women and fortune are truest still to those that trust 'em.

LUCY: And any wild thing grows but the more fierce and hungry for being kept up, and more dangerous to the keeper.

ALITHEA: There's doctrine for all husbands, Mr. Harcourt.

HARCOURT: I edify,[11] madam, so much, that I am impatient till I am one.

DORILANT: And I edify so much by example, I will never be one.

SPARKISH: And because I will not disparage my parts, I'll ne'er be one.

HORNER: And I, alas, can't be one!

PINCHWIFE: But I must be one — against my will to a country wife, with a country murrain to me!

MRS. PINCHWIFE (*aside*): And I must be a country wife still too, I find; for I can't, like a city one, be rid of my musty husband, and do what I list.

HORNER: Now, sir, I must pronounce your wife innocent, though I blush whilst I do it; and I am the only man by her now exposed to shame, which I will straight drown in wine, as you shall your suspicion; and the ladies' troubles we'll divert with a ballet. Doctor, where are your maskers?

---

10 *swear:* to hide an illegal duel. (Charles II issued a proclamation against dueling, 13 August, 1660, though the practice continued.)   11 *edify:* am learning.

LUCY: Indeed, she's innocent, sir, I am her witness; and her end of coming out was but to see her sister's wedding; and what she has said to your face of her love to Mr. Horner, was but the usual innocent revenge on a husband's jealousy — was it not, madam? Speak.

MRS. PINCHWIFE (*aside to* LUCY *and* HORNER): Since you'll have me tell more lies — (*aloud*) Yes, indeed, bud.

PINCHWIFE:

For my own sake fain I would all believe;
Cuckolds, like lovers, should themselves
    deceive
But — (*sighs*)
His honour is least safe (too late I find)
Who trusts it with a foolish wife or friend.

A DANCE OF CUCKOLDS[12]

HORNER:

Vain fops but court and dress, and keep a
    pother,
To pass for women's men with one another;
But he who aims by women to be prized,
First by the men, you see, must be despised.

(*Exeunt omnes.*)

EPILOGUE

Spoken by MRS. KNEP[1]

Now you the vigorous, who daily here
O'er vizard-mask in public domineer,
And what you'd do to her, if in place where;
Nay, have the confidence to cry, "Come out!"
Yet when she says, "Lead on!" you are not
    stout;
But to your well-dressed brother straight turn
    around,

And cry, "Pox on her, Ned, she can't be sound!"
Then slink away, a fresh one to engage,
With so much seeming heat and loving rage,
You'd frighten listening actress on the stage;
Till she at last has seen you huffing come,
And talk of keeping in the tiring-room,
Yet cannot be provoked to lead her home.
Next, you Falstaffs[2] of fifty, who beset
Your buckram maidenheads, which your
    friends get;
And whilst to them you of achievements boast,
They share the booty, and laugh at your cost.
In fine, you essenced boys, both old and young,
Who would be thought so eager, brisk, and
    strong,
Yet do the ladies, not their husbands wrong;
Whose purses for your manhood make excuse,
And keep your Flanders mares for show, not
    use;
Encouraged by our woman's man today,
A Horner's part may vainly think to play;
And may intrigues so bashfully disown,
That they may doubted be by few or none;
May kiss the cards at picquet, ombre, loo,
And so be thought to kiss the lady too;
But, gallants, have a care, faith, what you do.
The world, which to no man his due will give,
You by experience know you can deceive,
And men may still believe you vigorous,
But then we women — there's no cozening us.

FINIS

---

12 *Dance of Cuckolds:* a suitable tune would have been "Cuckolds All [in] a Row," from John Playford's *The Dancing Master*, a popular book of songs and dances. See W. Chappell, *The Ballad Literature and Popular Music of the Olden Time* (1859), I: 341. It was the custom of plays in this period, as with masques earlier in the seventeenth century, to end in a dance.

1 The first quarto assigns the Epilogue to Mr. Hart, as Horner, but it was spoken by the actress who played Lady Fidget in the original production. 2 *Falstaffs:* See Shakespeare's I *Henry VI*, II, iv.

The Miser

Jean-Baptiste Poquelin (1622–1673), who took the stage name of "Molière," was very likely the greatest of the French dramatists of "the Golden Age." When we consider that this group included the marvelous poet-dramatist Pierre Corneille (who began with *Mélite* in 1630 in a converted tennis court and followed with important contributions to intrigue comedy and the classic "cloak and sword" drama, of which *Le Cid* is the epitome) and Jean Racine (author of fine tragedies like *Andromaque* and *Phèdre* which well fulfilled Racine's aim in tragedy: "We should like our work to be as solid and as full of useful instruction as were those of antiquity"), that is high praise indeed.

Molière started as an amateur actor, failed, had to be bailed out of debt by his father, and did not learn his lesson; he immediately launched on a tour of the provinces which was to last 13 years. His little troupe played French tragedy, Italian *commedia dell'arte* and farce, and Spanish melodrama and intrigue comedy. In 1658 they played before the king in Corneille's *Nicomède* and were a disaster — until they offered Molière's *Le Docteur amoureux* as a face-saving encore. That play was a huge success; the trifle that had gone so well in the country struck the sophisticated court as fresh and delightful. The next year Molière presented his *Les Précieuses Ridicules* (*The Precious Damsels*) and by 1661 he and his company were installed in the best theatre, the Théâtre du Palais Royal. From then until 1673 he triumphed in satirical comedy — he tried writing one tragedy, *Don Garcia*, which was a failure, though it did lead to him writing an interesting *L'Impromptu de Versailles** attacking the classic tragedians of the Hôtel de Bourgogne theatre–and created such masterpieces as *Tartuffe* (1664, revised 1669), *Le Misanthrope* (1666), *Le Médecin malgré lui* (*The Physician in Spite of Himself*, 1666), *L'Avare* (*The Miser*, 1668), *Le Bourgeois*

---

* Molière, who lifted farce to the level of genius, expresses his comic theory in this play: "the business of comedy is to represent in general all the defects of mankind." With devices from Plautus, characters from the *commedia dell'arte*, burlesque techniques from Paul Scarron (1610–1660), and unflagging inventiveness of his own, Molière created modern comedy, writing his plays first in prose and then (when time permitted) versifying them in twelve-syllable Alexandrines (six iambic feet), rhymed in couplets and so named because they had been employed for old French poems about Alexander the Great.

Gentilhomme (The Would-Be Gentleman, 1670) and *Le Malade imaginaire (The Imaginary Invalid,* 1673).

Like Shakespeare, Molière also produced and acted in his own plays, working as a fully professional man of the theatre, drawing on the heritage of the past and setting new standards of perfection. Molière was like Shakespeare in other respects as well, and the rest of this introductory note to *The Miser* (which is Molière's version of Plautus' *Pot of Gold*) consists of a lecture which used to be given by Benoît Constant (1841–1909), who was a great comic star, using the name of Coquelin.* Other analysis and praise of Molière might be found (in George Meredith's famous *Essay on Comedy,* for instance, or in the journals of Goethe, who told Eckermann: "Molière is so great that one is astonished anew every time one reads him. He is a man by himself; his pieces border on tragedy; they are apprehensive; and no one has the courage to imitate them. . . . I read some pieces by Molière every year. . . ."). But here let us consider the opinions of a theatre-man, one who played for a generation the parts which had been handed down from Molière through Samson and Régnier and who loved the playwright because he "knew how to take care of his actors," like Shakespeare, giving them great roles with which to reach the hearts and minds of men. *Mesdames et messieurs*—Coquelin:

---

* One of the most famous theatre stories concerns the overtired man who consulted a Parisian doctor about his health. "You are overworked, under a strain, depressed. You don't need medicine. Just relax—go and see Coquelin!" "But doctor," was the reply, "I *am* Coquelin."

Molière and Shakespeare
BENOÎT CONSTANT

Everything has been said about Molière, and in France he has been the object of the most extravagant theories. There is only one suggestion that no one has ventured: this is to deny that he is the author of his works. In England there is a school which declares that Shakespeare was but a man of straw, and that the true poet of *Hamlet* and of *The Tempest* was the lord chancellor Bacon. We have not yet a school like this. Is an hypothesis of this sort impossible? Could we not, with equal likelihood, attribute the paternity of *The School for Wives* and *Don Juan* to the great Condé, for instance, to whom tradition already imputes at least one line of *Tartuffe* —

Il est de faux dévots ainsi que de faux braves, —

and who was the avowed protector of Molière? He prided himself, as we know, on his wit and on his freedom of thought, and he was fond of the stage. Why may he not have had a hand in these plays? That would explain why this same *Tartuffe* was acted at his house in full long before it was revised; why it was at his house again that the revised version was first seen; and also why Molière left no manuscripts behind him.

It would not be difficult, I think, if some imaginative scholar would but undertake it, to establish this hypothesis as solidly as the famous Baconian theory; and it could be proved that Molière and Shakespeare are but masks, just as it has been proved that Napoleon and Mr. Gladstone have never existed and that the first of these is a sun myth and the second an old Breton deity — no doubt, the deity of eloquence!

But I have no intention of fighting the Baconian revelation, or of building up any theory of that kind; I wish only to throw on paper a few notes inspired by the study and the comparison of the two masters of the stage.

If Molière seems like a belated twin of Shakespeare, it is not only because of an admirable equality of genius, it is also because of the many likenesses shown in their lives and in their habits. First actors, then authors, then managers, they entered the profession very young and pretty poor; and both made money by the theatre and died rich, one at fifty-two and the other at fifty-one; leaving almost the same number of works, as to which they seem to have been negligent, since these were printed in full only after their deaths, and by the care of their comrades. Born in the burgher class, they had princes for friends and knew the royal favor; and Louis XIV asked Molière for *The Magnificent Lovers*, as Queen Elizabeth had asked Shakespeare for *The Merry Wives of Windsor*. Thus one and the other, turn by turn, amused the court and the city, the people of quality and the rabble. Their free genius brought them out safely.

Wherefore the classic Ben Jonson cried out against his comrade Shakespeare; wherefore also the rigorous Boileau condemned judicially the author of *The Misanthrope*, thrust into the sack of Scapin. Nevertheless, they went on, taking their property where they found it, borrowing everywhere the matter which their alchemic genius turned to gold, bearing in mind no rules but to be true and to please; pleasing indeed, and always pleasing, the foolish as well as the wise, the ignorant as well as the refined.

Not only did they skirmish with pedants, but they also quarreled with the envious, a viler tribe: Shakespeare had Greene, Molière had Visé; they were hunted even into their private life, and infamous vices were imputed to them. They were, however, excellent comrades, liking a large life, good fare, and frank friendships; they gladly had wit-combats at the Syren or at the Cross of Lorraine; and they kept open house. If we believe the legend, it was because Shakespeare entertained too liberally his old friend Ben Jonson and his compatriot Drayton that he took to his bed and died. It is thus that our Regnard died; but it is not thus that Molière died. His heart-rending death is familiar; and God, who does not disdain an antithesis, crowned these careers so alike with the most opposite ends, making a comedy of the death of the great tragedian and of the death of the great comedian a tragedy.

In yet another point the end of Shakespeare differed from that of Molière. He had retired. He was living in his dear Stratford as a rich country gentleman, taking very good care of his property; even careless of his glory, and not having written, when he died, perhaps one verse in four years. His will does not mention his works, nor do the four lines inscribed over his tomb. Aeschylus also, in the epitaph he wrote for himself, forgot his hundred tragedies, but he had fought at Marathon, and this he recalled proudly; and it is conceivable that he should claim this glory in preference to the other. But the tomb of Shakespeare makes no similar claim: it begs that it be left alone, and this is not for the sake of *Hamlet* or of *Lear* or of so many masterpieces, but for Jesus' sake.

Molière never retired; scarcely even did he take a vacation: he worked while ill and he worked when dying; and he died almost on the stage. One of the reasons for this difference — not enough noticed, I think — is that Molière was a much better actor than Shakespeare.

Shakespeare the actor has left no trace. It is vaguely known that he played the old Adam in *As You Like It* and the Ghost in *Hamlet*. But it was not he, but Burbage, who "created" his great parts. It seems probable that, becoming an actor by accident, he was such without passion, and that he ceased to play as soon as possible.

Not so Molière. There is no doubt that his vocation as an actor was his master passion. He did not leave the paternal roof for the purpose of writing plays — but for the purpose of acting them. And we know that these were not comedies — the Illustrious Theatre had in stock at first nothing but tragedies. When he wrote *L'Étourdi,* his first work, Molière had been an actor for nine years, and for fifteen when he wrote the *Précieuses Ridicules*. Never could his great success as an author tempt him to leave the boards. He not only continued to act in his own plays, but he acted in the plays of others and did not consider this as lost time. He acted, as we have said, although coughing and spitting blood; and to Boileau, who advised him to leave the stage, he replied, "It is for my honor that I remain" — so much did he love his profession, which was killing him. But then he excelled in it. His contemporaries are unanimous on this point. He was extraordinary — "Better actor even than author," one of them goes so far as to say. We can imagine what joy it must have been to see him in his great parts — Sganarelle, Orgon, Alceste, Harpagon.

He had come to this degree of excellence only by dint of hard work, for his appearance was not pleasing and his voice difficult to manage. It was his voice, above all, that gave him trouble; but, notwithstanding the hiccough that remained, he made it so rich in varied inflections that it seemed as though he had many voices. He was particular about the articulation: it is to him that we owe the right way of pronouncing certain words; for example, the infinitives in *er*. He left nothing to chance, and insisted that an actor should have counted all his steps and decided upon every glance before he stepped upon the stage. We have in the *Impromptu* a theatrical criticism of his that we can compare to the theatrical criticism of Shakespeare in *Hamlet*. At bottom they agree: they have the same passion for nature, the same aversion from overemphasis — but Molière had the advantage in that he practiced what he preached.

It will be objected that he was not good in tragic characters. That is possible; it is so human to err! But perhaps we have been too quick to believe his enemies on this point. The manner of acting tragedy in those days was very different from his theories. He may have disconcerted the public by abstaining from bombastic delivery and by bringing down the heroes to a more natural level. Notice, however, that he played Corneille up to the very last. It seems likely that if the pit had disapproved of him so strongly in these parts, he would not have been so insistent; then it would have affected the receipts — and Molière was a manager. Finally, it was he who trained Baron; and Baron in tragedy, as in comedy, was incomparable. This passion of Molière's for his profession as actor was eminently advantageous. It increased his power of observation. The gaze he fixed on man was in some sort a double mirror; he studied first to know, and afterwards to reproduce. What might have escaped him had he only written the play came to him when he acted it. Then — forgive me the metaphor — the ink became blood. Therefore it is, I think, because Molière was a greater actor than Shakespeare that he was a more sure and more complete observer, although in a narrower sphere.

And to this quality of actor, which was accompanied in both by the gift of stage management, they each owed the dramatic force that today animates their works. We feel that these were not written coldly in the silence of the closet, but thrown alive upon the stage. And it is this too — I think the remark is Sainte-Beuve's — that explains the indifference of Shakespeare and Molière to the printing of their works. They did not recognize these on paper. *Tartuffe* and *Hamlet* existed for them only before the footlights. It was only there that they felt their plays bone of their bone and flesh of their flesh.

It has been possible, after much erudition, to establish the chronological sequence of the works of Shakespeare; and through this study has been evolved the history of his thought. It is at first a period of experiment; Shakespeare begins, he feels the need of living, he is the Jack-at-all-trades at the Globe; he makes over old pieces and writes new ones in imitation of Plautus or the Italians: no originality as yet, and, oddly enough, no dramatic genius; he was, above all, the poet of *Venus and Adonis*, in whom it was difficult to foresee the writer of *Hamlet*. But the time of groping ceased: he wrote *Richard III*, and in that he discovered character; he wrote *Romeo and Juliet*, and in that he discovered drama. Still, the second part of his career is almost entirely devoted to comedy. If he attempts drama, it is through the national history; which gives him the chance of creating Falstaff, perhaps his best-rounded comic type. This was the time when he began his fortune and his glory. He is full of hope and gaiety; he takes delight in those adorable compositions *A Midsummer Night's Dream, The Merchant of Venice, Much Ado about Nothing*. Fancy is his queen, and if Melancholy seizes him, it is to draw him to that marvelous forest of Arden, where so many songs are sung that the wickedest become good and the things that seem the most difficult to arrange end there — as you like it.

To this period of youth succeeds the prime of life. Shakespeare is rich and seems happy; but his thoughts are more somber. He doubts, he despairs, "Man pleases him not," and if he forgives Woman it is to make her fall under the injustice of destiny. From 1601 to 1607 were written these dramas: *Julius Caesar, Hamlet, Measure for Measure, Othello, Lear, Macbeth, Antony and Cleopatra, Timon of Athens* — masterpieces, all of them, and all disconsolate; it is the triumph of evil; the more Hamlet thinks the more he is discouraged; and it finishes with the anathema of Timon giving society at large over to destruction.

But now what happens? Because he has so often shown Man as the miserable plaything of heredity and chance, Shakespeare takes pity on him; and pity engenders serenity. Then the last period opens, the period of *A Winter's Tale*, of *Cymbeline*, of *The Tempest*, of the fragments of *Pericles*. Always life and its troubles; but a dream mingles strangely with action, and it is Providence that settles the end. The drama loses in concentration; but, on the other hand, the poetry becomes wonderful: it attains to the ineffable in *The Tempest*, the most divine poem ever dreamed by man.

Is it now possible to discover in the work of Molière, as in that of his rival, a history of his private thought? And does the chronological sequence of his comedies reveal to us something of his views on man and of the secret leanings of his genius?

I think so; but only on one condition: the date of *Tartuffe* must be that of its composition, and not that of its first representation, as is generally taken. Then we find in the work of Molière, as in that of Shakespeare, four distinct periods.

The period of groping, first: Molière is likewise the Jack-at-all-trades of his company; he acts in tragedy, tinkers old plays with the help of Madeleine Béjart, and writes farces, most of them imitated from the Italian, many of them derived from our old stock of fabliaux. Then, as success comes, he attempts better things — writes *L'Étourdi* and *The Lovers' Quarrel*. We have there only his gaiety unfailing and full of *go*; his observation betrays itself only in comic touches, and does not rise as high as character drawing; but what an admirable choice of words — lively, alert, and full of savor! And he not only finds words but scenes, such as the delicious quarrel in the *Dépit*.

At last he is in Paris; and as though he became conscious of his genius upon touching his native soil, he throws the *Précieuses* at the society of the day. No imitation of the ancients this time, no more Italian comedy; he paints the times, but he paints only its absurdities.

It is a great step forward. No matter. The work is brave and alive; it begins the second period; but strange to relate, although the *Précieuses* was a success, Molière did not follow it up; he returned to bolder farce with *Sganarelle*, to tragi-comedy with *Don Garcia de Navarre*; and it is from the ancients, from Terence, that he borrows *The School for Husbands*. But these were still but gropings: the last was at all events a real work, and Molière became more confident. A lucky chance brings him to the notice of the king, for whom he prepares the *Fâcheux*, a sparkling improvisa-

tion; and then he is in favor, sure of himself, sure of the princes; and he writes *The School for Wives*.

It is the first of the great masterpieces, it is the beginning of the third period; Molière has discovered himself. He has the vocabulary, he has the daring and the invention; he creates; Arnolphe, Agnes are immortal. But there is still more, and this it is that to my mind characterizes this third manner: *The School for Wives* is a social comedy. I beg pardon for the word, which is modern, but I could replace it only by a long periphrase. What I mean is that *The School for Wives* shows society itself; Arnolphe has his own ideas on these eternally serious points, woman's education and marriage, and he calls religion to the aid of his ideas.

Molière is there on delicate ground, but it is by his own wish; and it is very valiantly that he takes part against Arnolphe's theories and turns them into ridicule. This causes a tempest; the bigots discover an enemy. Molière is censured, cast forth, vilified. He does not care. Ever since the *Critique of the School for Wives* one feels that he will not recede. In that play he attacks the marquises, and more than one anecdote shows that this needed courage. But what is this skirmish compared with the battle of *Tartuffe!* Here evidently is comedy as it was dreamed of by the master in full possession of his strength; it turns towards satire of society; it makes itself a power, and shows on the stage the secrets of social organization. What will he respect, this Molière? He touches the Church! And it is in the name of nature that he scoffs at the theories of the mystics. But what happens? This time he is beaten. *Tartuffe* is forbidden. Well! Molière does not give in. Such is then his ardor for the fray that, after having attacked false piety, he combats what next is most dangerous — false science. He begins his war on the physicians. But this is a mere episode: he meditates a revenge; he creates *Don Juan*. This is his most extraordinary work; we are stupefied by what he has dared to say in the scene with the Poor Man, and in that with Don Louis, and in the whole of the fifth act. After the Church, it is autocracy which he shakes. He was never so

free, or, as they said in those days, so libertine.

Unfortunately — others perhaps will say
fortunately — *Don Juan* was not enough of a
success, and the piece met much dangerous
hostility in high quarters; at the same time the
flood of insults increases. Molière, ill, perhaps
discouraged, and feeling, doubtless, that he
could not go farther on this road, that the
people of his century would not follow him
there — Molière reasons with himself. A contest arises within him: Molière the indignant
protests, wants to combat, and would let loose
"the vigorous hatreds"; Molière the philosopher puts reason first, which wishes that we be
wise with sobriety, and which counsels man,
being incorrigible, to accept fate without cursing him, and to observe him as one observes
the "evil apes" and the "mad wolves."

This profound mental debate gave birth to
The Misanthrope, another masterpiece, that
belongs to the third manner by Alceste and to
the last by Philinte. For it is Philinte who gets
the best of it. Certainly Molière does not renounce the correction of men, but he gives up
calling to judgment the powers of society. With
more sharpness than ever he studies character, but individual character, not the social
character. He avoids the soldier; he leaves the
speculator to Le Sage; while the judge will
await Beaumarchais.

He no longer fights — he contemplates.
Even after *Tartuffe* was authorized he persisted
in not giving a companion piece to *Tartuffe*.
He will come back to Plautus — *Amphitryon*,
The Miser; he will come back to Italian
comedy — *The Tricks of Scapin*; he will come
back to the satire of the provincials — *Pour-
ceaugnac, Georges Dandin*; and in each of
these returns he will create masterpieces, for
he is absolute master of his art, and not for
one instant does his genius pale. But he never
returns to *Don Juan*. Twice he approaches the
forbidden ground; but *The Would-be Gentleman* is not the whole of the burgher class; and
if you would see how much the new Molière
differs from the old, compare the youth, the
fierceness, the set purpose of *The School for
Wives* with the serene maturity, impartial and
profound, of *The Learned Ladies*.

We must say at once that Molière's self-
denial cost his vivacity nothing; this dazzles
us to the last moment, and it is with one of his
gayest farces that he ends. It is true that this
farce is, upon reflection, one of his strongest
comedies. He is, I repeat, in this last period
absolute master of his art; I would add that he
is much more careful of form; to such an
extent that not having time to give to his
verses that degree of perfection which he
desired, he wrote no more except in prose.
From *The Physician in Spite of Himself* to *The
Imaginary Invalid* there are ten plays in prose,
three in verse, in with which must be counted
Psyche, although *Psyche*, it is well known,
was principally by Corneille. But the other
two are the most finished works of Molière in
point of style. We may regret sometimes the
Rabelaisian freedom of the earlier manner,
the large and oily brush marks of *Tartuffe*;
but we must render homage to the adorable
workmanship of *Amphitryon* as well as to the
judicial and sustained grandeur of style of *The
Learned Ladies*.

After all, if he from preference used prose,
it was not that he might be negligent, for now
he cadences it and fills it with blank verse, and
now, as in *The Would-be Gentleman*, he gives
it such a variety of shading that the author
disappears, leaving only his characters to be
heard, each one speaking his own language,
like the good Madame Jourdain, according to
the frankness of their nature.

I will not enter upon the comparisons that
these historical portraits of the minds of the
two masters might suggest. I would insist on
but one point. It does not appear that, at any
moment of his career, Shakespeare thought it
possible to reform society by the stage. Neither
in his fantastic, optimistic comedy nor in the
merciless, pitiless drama of the somber period,
nor in the providential drama of the last
period, did he appear to occupy himself with
correcting men of their vices. He makes works
of art — that is all. If there be in them a
lesson, it is, in a way, unmeant by him, and as
there might be one in the spectacle of human
affairs. Molière, on the contrary, has taken
seriously his duty as a comic author. He has,
just like old Corneille, frankly wished to put

into practice Aristotle's principle of purging mankind of its faults. He has accepted comedy as a social power. And, even after he was forced to renounce *Tartuffe*, he renounced neither correcting nor instructing; and almost all his plays, if not all, have an aim and a moral. This difference is accounted for, I think, by another, which is to a certain extent primary: Molière was a Latin, Shakespeare was not. Shakespeare very probably received a much better education than Ben Jonson leads us believe. He loved and read the ancients much; many Latinisms have been found in his style. In his youth he imitated the *Menæchmi* of Plautus; and in his maturity he took from Plutarch not only the plots of dramas, but phrases, even whole discourses, to which he gave only the rhythm of verse, but which are absolutely opposed in tone to his poetry. Notwithstanding all this he remains free, original, and modern. It is with deliberation that he rejects the classic rules promulgated and put in use by the Ben Jonsons.

What connection is there between the spirit of antiquity and that of *Venus and Adonis*, his sensual poem, all sparkling with *concetti* of the Italian type? Has he not gone as far as to parody the *Iliad* in *Troilus and Cressida*? Finally, in his great Roman drama, are they real Romans that he shows us? The place, the costume, the speech, and the soil — all are contemporary with Shakespeare. Romans, no; but men surely! And that is enough. And as for the people, whom he loved to paint — though not to flatter — it is the populace that he has known and mingled with, the mob and not the plebeians, to such an extent that one might say that *Coriolanus* was one of the most English of Shakespeare's plays.

In short, the spirit of the Renaissance breathed upon Shakespeare, but did not transform him. Shakespeare was, in his country, the definite and supreme end of the Middle Ages. In France, on the contrary, the Middle Ages did not end. In the sixteenth century the Latin spirit seized the people once more, and instead of finding, with Shakespeare, their inspiration in the miracle plays, in the Gesta, in the Round Table, in the fabliaux, our authors turned back to Rome. Thus did Molière. It

was not that he despised our immense repertory of farces and moralities; he was too fond of Rabelais for that, and he borrowed from the fabliaux for his little pieces, now almost all lost; but for his great comedies it is Plautus, it is Terence, who are his models and his inspiration. He imitated them, one may say, up to his last hour. To this he was predisposed not only by race, but by education; we know what vigorous training he had received, and that one of his pastimes — if he ever had any pastimes — was translating Lucretius in verse.

It is the alliance of the Latin and the French genius that has given to our comedy its character and its superiority. The Frenchman has inherited from the Celt, at the same time with the love of combat and the love of speech-making, an admirable promptness in seizing the ridiculous and in imitating it. He has found in his Latin heritage the taste for generalizations, the sentiment of measure, and the cult of reason. French comedy has been born of all these. It is gay on its Celtic side, and on its Latin side realistic and practical. In its most dizzy flights you would never see it, like the comedy of Shakespeare, beat its wings and fly into pure fantasy and the dream of a midsummer's night; it would not leave the earth, it would observe, it would keep one shred of truth, it would wish to be of use, to serve, to *prove* something.

Castigat ridendo mores. It has a mission; later, we might call it a function. I have said that it is a power, and Beaumarchais is there to show it. It has not been lost. What is Augier? What is Dumas? They are reformers! What is Labiche? A moralist! Sterne has said and shown in his way that the French people is the most serious of peoples; for he who loved so much to laugh does not care to laugh for nothing. He wishes that something should stay in the mind after even the lightest of farces, and that after having laughed one should think. Musset went further: he wished us to weep. That is too much. And I ask myself if there be not a grain of exaggeration in our contempt for the useless laugh. To laugh is good in itself. What is left after a laugh? the philosophers ask. Ah! what remains of a beautiful day after it has passed? And yet happiness is made up of beautiful days. But, to be definite, it is this taste for truth, this respect for reason, even this pretension of lifting up human nature, that makes the force of our comedy, and this is why it would be unjust to compare the comedies of Shakespeare with those of Molière.

Shakespeare's comedies are mostly youthful works. We find in them humors rather than characters, and no comedy of situation. They are imaginings, often charming; equivoques; disguises; forest surprises, as in *As You Like It*, where everyone becomes good; islands, as in *The Tempest*, enchanted with invisible music, where life is painted like a soap bubble — iridescent and empty. What likeness can there be between these exquisite fairy tales, made of dreams, and the comedy of Molière, all kneaded with reality?

There are exceptions, however. There is one of Shakespeare's comedies that approaches the French manner: it is *The Taming of the Shrew.* This has a logical action and a moral. Petruchio tames his devilish wife by showing himself more of a devil than she. But they are both eccentrics rather than true characters; and the play is a farce, where caricature injures the truth. No matter, it is one of the gayest, and — see the power of the French form — it has remained one of the most popular.

He was less successful, to my mind, in *The Merry Wives of Windsor,* another exception in his works, for it is a contemporaneous satire, notwithstanding the date, and a portrait of middle-class manners. It has excellent scenes. Ford recalls our Arnolphe. Like Arnolphe he is jealous, like Arnolphe he is kept informed of all that is being prepared against him (at least he thinks so), and like Arnolphe he succeeds only in getting himself laughed at. But how feeble and brutal he is! What unreason in all his actions! In short, he is any husband, while Arnolphe, in representing the old sect which insists on the subjection of woman, is one of those faces in which the humanity of all times recognizes itself laughing at the recognition. Even in the Falstaff of *The Merry Wives* one can pick flaws. Is this the Falstaff of *Henry IV,* who was always brimming over with audacity and humor? Alas! how he is faded!

What a fall! No, no; this dupe is not Falstaff! Shakespeare was no more at ease in working on an idea of Elizabeth's than was Molière when he composed *The Magnificent Lovers* on an outline of Louis XIV's.

A few words must be added on the *wit* of Shakespeare, the sparkling of which fills the first plays. It is with double meaning, with puns, that he makes the laughter break out; counterfeit coin, doubtless, but so prettily struck off, so brilliant, so resonant! Recall the battles of wit between Beatrice and Benedict, and the loving chatter of Rosalind and the elegant babble of Mercutio. But all this has sadly cooled in three centuries.

Molière has no mere wit. Puns, points, the collocation of droll sounds, words taken one for another — all these are absent from his work. At most he permits himself, in his farces, some Gallic equivoques. He wishes to bring a laugh only by touches of nature. It is not from him as author that his witticisms come: it is from his characters, and they come naturally and by the force of things. He himself explains this in his criticism. "The author has not put this in as a clever saying of his own, but only as a thing that characterizes the man." So with him there is nothing unnecessary. Each touch brings out the character in the living reality.

Can we here say that from this point of view Molière has the better of his rival? But it would be easy to reply that Shakespeare in his mighty maturity renounced witticisms to seek effects only from nature. And it is by their masterpieces that these great men must be compared. Thus we admire in them the same creative fecundity, the same intensity of life, the same dramatic vigor. This latter is so great in Molière that it was able to lead astray his fervent admirer the great Goethe, who attributed to him tragic genius. This seems an error; but nothing shows better than this error the force of the situations in *The Misanthrope,* in *Tartuffe,* and elsewhere. They have suggested to Molière, as to Shakespeare, those phrases that suddenly shed light into the very depths of the soul. Pathetic in Shakespeare, comic in Molière, they are sublime in both. Sublime, you say? Can the comic be sublime?

Why not? After all, the sublime is but a stroke of truth, so brilliant, so deep, that it calls for no explanation or reasoning, leaves nothing to be said, and sometimes — like the "Let him die!" of the old Horace — attains a pure and simple absurdity.

Even in Shakespeare there are strokes of this kind of comedy; such is the famous acclamation of the "Brutus! Hail Brutus! Let Brutus be Cæsar." And another saying, in *Coriolanus*, "Let us kill Marcius, and we'll have corn at our own price." As for the pathetic cries, it is unnecessary for me to recall the apostrophe of Lear to the storm, "Nor rain, wind, thunder, fire, are my daughters!" Or the saying of Macduff, "He has no children!" Nor all those that spring from the troubled conscience of Hamlet. But is not the Poor Man in *Tartuffe* of the same caliber? Does not Alceste's "Morbleu! Faut-il que je vous aime?" spring from the same depths? And the innocent question of Arnolphe, "Why not love me, Madam Impudence?" But Molière has whole scenes written in this tone. Recall the scene before the last in the third act of *Tartuffe* between Orgon, Tartuffe, and Damis. There is not a line that does not carry. If it were not so funny it would be terrible. Never has human credulity been so truly painted, neither has the faculty which Tartuffes have of dishumanizing the best of us. If one forgets to laugh, the scene leaves an impression of stupefaction; and this I think is the duty of the sublime.

In Shakespeare Othello is less deeply duped by Iago. For from the moment that he has made the germ of jealousy tremble that had been sleeping in his breast, from the moment that this frightful passion is wakened; it is this that acts and governs; it is this that makes the unhappy creature believe what it will; it is this that, in one word, cheats him and makes him breathe blood and death.

Passion — this is the true domain of Shakespeare. It is the domain of the drama. (Shakespeare has the heart, Molière the head.) Shakespeare's personages are the *changing* and *differing* men, frequently made or unmade by the torrent of blood and of life. Those of Molière are man built all of a piece, born what he is, and dying as he was born. Could anything modify Tartuffe? Could Alceste have been different from what we see him? And was not Harpagon from his mother's womb a petty usurer? Did Arnolphe need to develop to become the pedant and the brute that he is? Scarcely has study added to the natural bent. And it is certainly not by philosophizing on a school bench that Don Juan came to the denying of all things. He came into the world unbelieving, and never admitted the existence of any other God but his own good pleasure. Molière shows us these unchanging characters in the most diverse situations; they remain there true to themselves and make their own fate.

Shakespeare likes to take an irreproachable man; he shows him coming straight from nature's hands, full of the milk of human kindness and seeking nobly all that he most ardently craves. But there is in him a germ, sometimes imperceptible; this germ circumstances, chance, the perfidy of an *Iago*, the meeting of the three old women on the heath, a dream, even less — a doubt — may cause suddenly to ferment; it rises up, swells, and becomes a devouring and irresistible passion; the end is fatal, it is crime, despair, death. Nothing can help it; the will of the man is the sport of chance and the heat of his blood. Even in the last works — in which the ending is happy — the man has had nothing to do with it; it is again chance which this time ends everything well; but Posthumus and Leontes are as miserably the prey of their imaginations as Othello or Lear.

Thus Molière's personages *are*; Shakespeare's *become*. I leave it to the philosophers to decide which are the more true. But we must not exaggerate; one finds likewise in Shakespeare innate characters. Iago, Lady Macbeth are certainly born what they are. Likewise it is a great wrong to Molière to reproach him with not knowing the contradictions of the human heart; his works are filled with it. See Alceste in love with Célimène, see Tartuffe at the same time so arrogant and so humble; see Argon, most tender of fathers and most humane of men, led by his bigotry to sacrifice his daughter and his whole house to the egotistic needs of his own salvation! These contradictions are marvelously natural; they do not indicate a single modification of man, they only reveal his complexity, and Molière knows how to render the comic side of this with his usual superiority.

This difference between the characters of drama and those of comedy has still another reason. To laugh one must be impersonal. He who sees that it is he himself who is on the stage and made fun of does not laugh willingly. Other people — that is all right; one can laugh at others without scruple. And this is why Molière shows us from the first his people well characterized, well possessed by their proper individuality, in a way resembling us as little as possible. After this, quite at our ease, sure of being neither Harpagon, nor M. Jourdain, nor Sganarelle, we can follow the master in laughing at them and at the same time at the Harpagons and the M. Jourdains and the Sganarelles that we know in real life and that we are delighted to find before us here.

The drama needs a contrary sentiment. To make us shudder or weep it must show us in its personages, if not the man that we are, at least the man that we flatter ourselves on being — good, valiant, and wise. Then we are interested in what happens to these men who are like us. It seems as though we were following our own possible history. And this is why Othello or Macbeth is at first neither ambitious nor jealous; they only become so after we have contracted a fellow feeling for them.

Hamlet has been compared to Alceste, but what ground can they offer for comparison? The one delicate, scant of breath, an obstinate dreamer, whom destiny makes a dispenser of justice in spite of himself; and the other robust, bristling, scolding, misanthropic — not as Hamlet is, in consequence of a melancholy that makes him see everything through a black veil, but from the effect of a vigorous nature full of itself and not understanding that all the world does not resemble him, and irritated by the differences as by so many personal injuries.

It would be easier to compare Alceste and Timon of Athens. They have common hatreds, and both end with the desert. But Alceste is born a misanthrope: Timon, on the contrary, begins with the love of man, as immeasured in this liberal tenderness as later he will be in his execrations. With all his faults Alceste is better balanced; he is a character. Timon is ill. (Note in passing as a matter of curiosity, that the repast of hot water offered by Timon to his lukewarm friends is found again in *Le Misanthrope et L'Auvergnat* of Labiche.)

It is remarkable that in *Timon* Shakespeare, who intended a drama, should have deprived himself of that powerful element, Woman, and that it should be the comic author who had that idea of genius, profoundly dramatic, of making his misanthrope in love with a coquette. Shakespeare had put his Célimènes elsewhere: as a young girl she is in Cressida; mature and sovereign, she is in Cleopatra. It would be pleasant to compare with each other these attractive and perverse figures, but let me note only this characteristic point: it is that Célimène is cold, and that Cressida and Cleopatra are sensual. Cressida, a maiden yet, has instinctively all the trickery of an accomplished coquette, but she is sensual and she succumbs. And as she belonged to Troilus, so she will belong to Diomede; she has wit, perfidy, and weakness; she is a courtesan.

As for Cleopatra, she is the enchantress, but the irresistible grace that emanates from her is sustained by a deep art, which experience has developed. Then, too, how she leads him on, her Antony! But she is sensual; she loves him. Célimène is cold: she neither loves nor is capable of loving; her heart is in her head. She is a flower special to society, selfish, despotic, charming, deceiving everybody to nobody's profit, for the pleasure of it.

In general Shakespeare's women are admired; and yet what diversity in this curious series — the young girls, Ophelia, Cordelia, sister Isabella, Juliet, Perdita, Rosalind, and Celia; Beatrice; and the wives, Portia, Desdemona, Hermione, Imogen, Catherine of Arragon. I pass over some, and not the least celebrated. But among these delicious types, either profound or sublime, it is strange that you meet neither an Agnes nor an Armande. In Shakespeare the most chaste maid is not without knowledge. Ignorance, so dear to Arnolphe, seems impossible to our poet. Juliet is fourteen years old and she is a woman. And Miranda, brought up in a desert island between her father and Caliban, and so like Agnes in so many ways — Miranda has not the innocence of Agnes. She feels for Frederick the same admiration that Agnes feels for Horace; when Prospero threatens the young prince and inflicts upon him a slave's duties, she gives the same cry that Agnes does when Arnolphe orders Horace to throw a stone from the window if the young man calls, "But he is such a fine fellow!" Finally, like Arnolphe's ward, she gives herself secretly to him whom she loves; but she reserves her chastity, as Agnes does not, not knowing enough.

I said there is no Armande in Shakespeare either. In truth, there is not a trace of that fine contempt of the flesh which the young philosopher boasts. Even sister Isabella, so rigid, has only a horror for the sin, and not aversion for the matter. The severe young girl recognized the sanctity of marriage, which Armande will not have mentioned; and in the end she marries the Duke. Armande, you will say, would have the same sort of yielding for Clitandre. I agree, but none the less does she feel the sentiment that she expresses; and it is rather strange that Shakespeare, although nearer than Molière to the mysticism of the Middle Ages, seems not to have known it. All his plays are of flesh and blood! Besides, Molière, who is the apostle of nature, laughs at the philosophical disgust of the beautiful Armande, and is careful not to give it to Henriette. Although his young girls are often quite adventurous, they have neither the ardent love of a Juliet nor the romantic intrepidity of a Rosalind. They are sweet and sentimental, like the adorable Marianne in *Tartuffe*; exquisitely sensible, like Henriette; very likely later to become sincere Eliantes, or wise and keen Elmires. As for those whom reading has spoiled, like Cathos and Madelon, it is not for the love of love that they would lose themselves, but for love of wit.

Other physiognomies might be compared. Harpagon and Shylock, for example — two misers. But it seems precisely as though in these two characters Shakespeare and Molière had two absolutely contrary aims; that Shakespeare, with a generosity not common in his day, wished to show the man in the Jew, and in the insulted man surviving the insult and bent on vengeance, the sacred feelings of a father and a husband; while Molière showed in Harpagon these same feelings and all the human sentiments, smothered by the encroaching vice. I fear that it is Molière who is right. But there is much to say in favor of Shylock, in whom avarice — being a fault of his race — has not the dominant and special character that it takes with Harpagon. Do we find a Tartuffe in Shakespeare? Iago has been cited: but Iago only seeks the satisfaction of a personal hate; Tartuffe, in the name of the Church, seeks complete dominion. Honest Iago knows what he wants and does not hide from himself the fact that he is a rascal. Tartuffe goes so far as to deceive himself; he believes in the goodness of his actions; they are only for the glory of Heaven. Iago is but a passing scamp, an individual. As for Tartuffe, he is legion; Tartuffe is eternal, perhaps indestructible.

There is more of Tartuffe in Richard III, I think. Richard has no illusions about himself, but he plays his part with a perfection worthy of Molière's character. We can even discover rather frequent resemblances between the scene of Richard with Anne (Act I) and those of Tartuffe with Elmire. Each proposes to seduce a woman who holds him in horror — Tartuffe, the wife of his host, whom he ruins and betrays; Richard, the wife of his king, whom he murders. Both plead marvelously, with the same catlike softness, the same captious theories, the same subtleties. In both scenes the husband is present: he is under the table with Molière, in his coffin with Shakespeare. The difference is not so great as might be supposed, since the corpse denounces the presence of its murderer by the bleeding of its wounds. But where the two scenes differ is in their ending. For Richard III succeeds, Tartuffe fails. Has, then, Tartuffe less wit than Richard? No, but he has to do with a stronger woman. Anne is the feminine character, feeble, vain, inconstant; Elmire is the lady, fashioned by society, who knows and guesses, a woman of taste and reason, who uses the advantages of her sex, but who watches herself and does not lose her head. As she has no vanity, no sensuality, Tartuffe has no hold on her.

Molière and Shakespeare both worked fast. Molière, however, retouched none of his plays, except *Tartuffe*. Shakespeare, on the contrary, rehandled, sometimes considerably, a number of his. *Hamlet*, for instance, was probably to him what *Faust* was to Goethe — the preoccupation of his whole artistic life. He did not ripen his plans, and in the rapidity of his work he was too easily contented with helping himself (from the novels or the histories from which he took his plays) to the scenes in the order in which he found them, adding, it is true, the characters and the poetry. From this comes a lack of simplicity, incoherencies, contradictions, that revision does not always efface and sometimes even augments. Molière has more art and more method; he graduates his effects better.

Volumnia and the Roman matrons arrive at the camp of Coriolanus. The fierce refugee is seized with respect; he bends the knee at once. But Volumnia wishes only to be the suppliant; she, in her turn, kneels and makes all those who have followed her kneel, and with them the wife and sons of Coriolanus. Here is surely a powerful dramatic effect, but it is not led up to — it ends in nothing. Coriolanus gets up, then Volumnia, and then long discourses are pronounced that Shakespeare takes almost word for word from Plutarch. The emotion evaporates, the impression disappears. Compare to this the double kneeling of Tartuffe and Orgon in the scene before the last of Act III. How well it all goes, how all is developed from it later, and how the effect is prepared and sustained up to the fall of the curtain! It is a marvel of skill, as well as a marvel of truth.

It must, however, be said that Molière, more careful of his plots, neglected his endings; whereas Shakespeare worked over his with a kind of predilection that has given us some of an unnecessary length. He stuffs them with emotions, makes royal personages appear and pronounce great words. Everything is cleared up, even what the public knows best. No

matter, the emotion is immense. See the catastrophe of *Lear*. The soul of the spectator is plunged into a kind of desolate annihilation with the unfortunate old man. In a different style, reread the endings of *Pericles* and of *A Winter's Tale*. The sweetest tears that earth can know will flow of themselves from your eyes. And again, that close of *The Merchant of Venice*, which one does not dare call an ending — for the play was finished in Act IV — and which is a tailing off of a comedy after a comedy. What ravishing poetry and what malicious grace!

Shakespeare delights in complexity. He has often two, sometimes three, plots in his plays. He likes to vary the place of action, which changes without one's knowing why. In *Antony and Cleopatra* the scene is the world. The poet leads us almost to the Parthians to present to us Ventidius, of whom afterward we shall hear no more, and who is of not the least importance to the play. He needs these vast distances. Yet he did not despise the power of concentration (see the last acts of *Othello* and *Macbeth*). But he then falls into the excess that our tragedians are reproached with. He hurries the events, makes them take place in too short a time. If we may trust the text, the duration of *Macbeth* is hardly eight days. Who will ever believe that this somber and terrible history developed itself in so short a time, and that the Lady Macbeth of the sleepwalking night was but one week more advanced in life than the Lady Macbeth of the night of the crime? Molière, on the contrary, fancies the greatest simplicity in his plots and expedients.

There is some resemblance between *The School for Wives* and *Romeo and Juliet*. A perfume of youth is exhaled from these two masterpieces, both of them love stories. It is impossible to listen to them without profound interest. But, to keep up this interest, how many incidents did not Shakespeare need? Duels, a secret marriage, a potion, poison, a final killing, where the County Paris takes part most unnecessarily! Molière does not ask so much. Hardly anything happens in his play: Horace loves Agnes, Agnes loves Horace; they let each other know it, notwithstanding Arnolphe; and by the help of some innocent ruses that Horace's manly experience suggests and that Arnolphe's jealousy cannot detect, they get married in the end, to our great content. The story has happened a thousand times. It has happened to us — or something like it. And this is why it touches us, and why we laugh with such good will at that jealous wretch, taken in by an innocent girl.

For the rest, poetry is not wanting in *The School for Wives*. The whole part of Agnes is as poetically naive as the words of children. And the part of Arnolphe is comic poetry, rich in color, and rising into humor. But on these two points, poetry and humor, the advantage is with Shakespeare.

Molière contents himself with humanity; he does not know nature. Shakespeare does not separate one from the other. There is in him no deed that has not an echo in things; no phenomenon of nature that is not prolonged in the soul. For him creation is one; the earth feels what man does, and shares his emotions. Is she not full of unknown forces? Are there not more things in heaven and earth than are dreamed of in all philosophy? From this union of the world and man, of the world of things and the world of mind or of forces, Shakespeare draws forth the most strange, the most mighty, the most bewildering poetry. I will not try to describe its thousand sides; it would be beyond my powers. Music has been called the art of expressing the inexpressible; it can be said too of Shakespeare's poetry. In fact, there is visibly too much of it in his last plays, as there was too much wit in the first ones. *Cymbeline, A Winter's Tale* are lengthened with episodes and descriptions admirable but parasitical, and almost all the characters in them are lyrical. The supernatural is introduced in the action; the gods it is who proclaim the innocence of Hermione, the gods bring about the climax (interminable besides) of *Cymbeline*. As for *The Tempest*, of which I have already said a word, we are there in full fairyland. There the exquisite and visionary poetry is in its true place.

Shakespeare likewise has humor, little known to Molière, although Molière was a grandson of Rabelais. It is to the humor of Shakespeare that we owe the incomparable Falstaff. Yet Shakespeare is not, strictly speaking, a humorist like Swift or Sterne. As it seems to me, humor is more literary than dramatic, with its hints, its ironies, and its intentional incoherencies. It is not always clear; and it is clearness that the playgoer demands.

Many definitions of humor have been attempted. It seems as though the true one were still to be found. It is, I think, that they attempt to make a quality of the mind out of what is rather a state of the spirit. There is the humorous state, just as there is the poetic state. He who is subject to it sees things in a special manner, out of proportion, out of place, upside down; then he discovers in them unexpected resemblances, and he expresses his sensations in appropriate language; that is to say, in affecting the tone contrary to that which he would have used were he in the ordinary state. This manner of seeing things does not absolutely disfigure them; it gives them a new aspect, striking and singular, comic because it is crazy, useful because by exaggerating the proportion it can bring to light certain points of truth that were not before suspected. You know the story of the husband who did not love his wife; he had no knowledge that she was pretty. Chance let him one day see her on the stage masquerading as a man, and he fell desperately in love with her. Humor sometimes renders this same service and ideas; by clothing them in what seems to be the least suitable it makes them most pleasing.

But this turning of things upside down, as the humorist does, to see what is in them, this dislocating of the thought and sentiment, is greatly against the spirit of reason; this is why we care but little for it. Yet, as it is a very Celtic taste, it comes back to us now and again. Witness Rabelais, whom I cited just now, and who is the universal father of humorists; witness also Voltaire's tales.

Molière knows not humor except on the extreme and extravagant side. It is certain that in this kind the ceremony in *The Would-be Gentleman*, and above all that of *The Imaginary Invalid* are masterpieces of humor in the Rabelaisian taste, full of vengeful irony and irresistible comedy. But, to be precise, Molière did not seek humor any more than he sought wit; one and both were for him too easy. "There is nothing common," said the great Goethe, "that does not appear humorous if you express it in a grotesque way." As for poetry, that of Shakespeare, it will be conceded, would be little in place in the comedy of Molière. But if the force and the delicacy of expression are elements of it, if the freshness or vivacity of the language, if the beautiful marriage of words, if this living breath of truth is poetic, then Molière is a poet. He has the "vigorous hates," "the well-placed soul," "the clearness of everything." He knows where is the "tenderness of the soul," and dictates to Agnes a delicious letter. He is, in more than one scene, as eloquent as Corneille, and he handles the popular proverb with the same vigor. There is as much lightness and grace in Acaste as in Mercutio. And the verses of Eliante are as charming as those of Rosalind, and truer. What is not in this poetry — what could not be in it — is the dreaming. It is the loyal reflection of the true depth of humanity.

Molière and Shakespeare had an entirely different conception of life. Shakespeare saw it moving, troubled, changing, uncircumscribed in its development by human will, subject to "the winds and the rain and all the breezes that blow." He says in one of those passages of *The Two Noble Kinsmen* that were evidently written by him:

This world's a city full of straying streets,
And death's the market-place where each one
    meets.

It is in these straying streets that Shakespeare moves, the obscure labyrinth where man goes blindly, meeting here an ambush, there a precipice, and where he changes fortune from a chance meeting. There is nothing certain, not one of his characters who could swear to what he will do an hour later. They do not belong to themselves. They are so much the plaything of a higher force that they do not even feel sure of their conscience. "I believe myself passably virtuous," says Hamlet.

But who shall explain Hamlet? Hamlet is an enigma. How far was he mad? When is he completely mad? But no one in these plays is quite sane. Lear is out of his senses long before he is demented; Macbeth has hallucinations; Othello sees blood at the first word; Brutus talks to a ghost; that terrible skeptic Richard III sees visions. Events themselves sometimes seem half crazy. What I have said of *Macbeth* might be said of *Romeo and Juliet*, where in five days Juliet sees, loves, marries, dies, resuscitates, and dies once more. All is falsehood, deceit, bewilderment. This cavalier, it is Rosalind; this page, Imogen; this judge, Portia; this statue, Hermione. One scene in *King Lear* makes Lear (who goes mad from sorrow) and an exile (who pretends to madness) and a fool (who is mad by profession) all talk together amid the thunder and lightning. We ask ourselves, Where are we? Who are we? Prospero tells us:

We are such stuff
As dreams are made on; and our little life
Is rounded with a sleep.

Shakespeare saw life as in a dream, and thus he has shown it. Molière saw things in their reality. He went down to the immutable. As for life, in his plays he sees it simple. Only those events happen which happen to all of us. We love, we marry, we have children, we consult the doctor, we die. The other incidents that may occur spring from the shock of character; they can be deduced logically one from another, and would remain in the control of man if he would but listen to reason.

And this is the great moral that can be drawn from Molière: Keep your head, and all will go well. His work is as clear as day; hatred of vice shows itself, and the love of truth — no platonic love, but an active love, armed and fighting to the last hour. For Molière is in the thick of the crowd; Shakespeare dwells in the Temples of Serenity; he observes, somber at first, peaceful later on; and he gives to our meditation and reflection the immense and painful spectacle of the world, but draws from it no rule, for what rule can be found used in a dream? Perhaps, to finish, it might be said that Shakespeare teaches us to think, but that Molière teaches us to live.

THE MISER

Molière

PERSONS OF THE PLAY

HARPAGON, *father of Cléante and Élise, suitor for the hand of Marianne*
CLÉANTE, *his son, in love with Marianne*
ÉLISE, *his daughter, in love with Valère*
VALÈRE, *son of Anselme and in love with Élise*
MARIANNE, *in love with Cléante and courted by Harpagon*
ANSELME, *father of Valère and Marianne*
FROSINE, *an adventuress*
MASTER SIMON, *an intermediary*
MASTER JACQUES, *cook and coachman to Harpagon*
BRINDAVOINE ⎫
LA MERLUCHE ⎬ *servants to Harpagon*
DAME CLAUDE ⎭
LA FLÈCHE, *valet to Cléante*
OFFICER
OFFICER'S CLERK

THE SCENE IS IN PARIS

(TIME: 1668)

ACT ONE

VALÈRE, ÉLISE.

VALÈRE: Come, my dear Élise, surely you are not feeling sad, after giving me such generous assurance of your love? Here am I, the happiest of men, and I find you sighing! Is it because you regret having made me happy? Do you repent the promise which my ardour has won from you?

ÉLISE: No, Valère. I could never regret anything I did for you. I cannot even bring myself to wish things were other than as they are, though I must confess I am concerned about the outcome and more than a little afraid that I may love you more dearly than I ought.

VALÈRE: But what can you possibly have to fear from loving me, Élise?

ÉLISE: Alas! A hundred and one things: my father's anger, the reproaches of my family, what people may say about me, but most of all, Valère, a change in your affection for me. I dread the cruel indifference with which men so often requite an innocent love too ardently offered them.

VALÈRE: Ah! Do not be so unjust as to judge me by other men. Believe me capable of anything, Élise, rather than of failure in my duty to you. I love you too dearly, and mine is a love which will last as long as life itself.

ÉLISE: Ah, Valère, you all talk like that. Men are all alike in their promises. It is only in their deeds that they differ.

VALÈRE: If deeds alone show what we are, then at least wait and judge my love by mine. Do not look for faults which only exist in your own fond forebodings. I implore you not to let such wounding and unjust suspicions destroy my happiness! Give me time to convince you and you shall have a thousand proofs of the sincerity of my love.

ÉLISE: Ah! How easy it is to let ourselves be persuaded by those we love! I am convinced that you would never deceive me, Valère. I do believe you love me truly and faithfully. I have not the least wish to doubt you, and my only concern is that other people may find cause to blame me.

VALÈRE: And why should that trouble you?

ÉLISE: Ah, if only everyone could see you as I do, I should have nothing to fear. The qualities I see in you justify everything I do for you. My love is founded on knowledge of your virtues and sustained by my gratitude, a gratitude which Heaven itself enjoins. How can I ever forget the dreadful danger which first brought us together, your noble courage in risking your life to snatch me from the fury of the waves, your tender solicitude when you had brought me to the shore and the unremitting ardour of your love which neither time nor adversity has diminished, a love for which you neglect your parents and your country, conceal your true rank and stoop to service in my father's household merely for the sake of being near me! These are the things which weigh with me, Valère, and justify, for me, my promises to you, but the justification may not seem sufficient to others — and I cannot be certain that they will share my feelings.

VALÈRE: Of all these things you have mentioned, only one gives me any claim on you, Élise, and that is my love. As for your scruples, surely your father has done everything he could to justify you in the eyes of the world! Surely his avarice and the miserable existence he makes his children lead, would justify still stranger things! Forgive me, my dear, for speaking of him in this way, but you know that on this issue there is nothing good one can say of him. However, if only I can find my parents again, as I hope I may, we shall have little difficulty in gaining his consent. I grow impatient for news of them, and if I do not hear soon I shall set out in search of them myself.

ÉLISE: Oh no, Valère. Do not go away, I beseech you! Stay and give your whole attention to gaining my father's confidence.

VALÈRE: Cannot you see how I am endeavouring to do so? You know what adroitness and subservience I had to show to get into his service, what a mask of sympathy and conformity with his feelings I assumed in order to ingratiate myself with him, how in his presence I am for ever playing a part with a view to gaining his favour. And am I not, indeed, making remarkable progress? I find that the best way to win people's favour is to pretend to agree with them, to fall in with their precepts, encourage their foibles and applaud whatever they do. One need have no fear of overdoing the subservience. One can play up to them quite openly, for, when it comes to flattery, the most cunning of men are the most easily deceived, and people can be induced to swallow anything, however absurd or ridiculous, provided it is sufficiently seasoned with praise. Such methods may impair one's integrity, but if one has need of people one must accom-

modate oneself to them, and if there is no other way of gaining their support, well then, the blame lies less with the flatterers than with those who want to be flattered.

ÉLISE: Why don't you try to win my brother's support in case the maidservant should take it into her head to betray us?

VALÈRE: No, I couldn't handle father and son at the same time. They are so utterly different that one could not be in the confidence of both simultaneously. Do what you can with your brother and make use of your mutual affection to win him to our side. He is coming in now. I will withdraw. Take this opportunity of speaking to him, but tell him only so much of our affairs as you think fit.

ÉLISE: I don't know whether I can bring myself to take him into my confidence.

(*Enter* CLÉANTE.)

CLÉANTE: I am delighted to find you alone, sister. I have been longing for a talk with you. I want to tell you a secret.

ÉLISE: Well, here I am, ready to listen, Cléante. What have you to tell me?

CLÉANTE: Lots of things, my dear, but — to sum it up in one word — I'm in love.

ÉLISE: *You* are in love?

CLÉANTE: Yes, I'm in love, and let me say before we go any further that I am fully aware that I am dependent on my father, that as a son I must submit to his wishes, that we should never give a promise of marriage without the consent of those who brought us into the world, that Heaven made them the arbiters of our choice, that it is our duty never to bestow our affections except as they may decide, that, not being blinded by passion, they are less likely to be deceived and better able to see what is good for us than we are ourselves, that it behoves us to trust to the light of their prudence rather than to our own blind desires, and that youthful impetuosity leads, as often as not, to disaster! I mention all this, my dear sister, to save you the trouble of saying it. The fact is that I am too much in love to listen to anything you have to say and I, therefore, ask you to spare your remonstrances.

ÉLISE: And have you actually given her your promise?

CLÉANTE: No, but I am determined to do so, and I ask you, once again, not to try to dissuade me.

ÉLISE: Am I such a strange person as that, Cléante?

CLÉANTE: No, Élise, but you aren't in love. You know nothing of the power of the tender passion over the hearts of us lovers. I am afraid you may take too prudent a view.

ÉLISE: Oh, don't talk of my prudence! There is no one who is not imprudent at some time or other, and if I were to reveal all that is in my own heart you might find I was even less prudent than you are.

CLÉANTE: Ah, if only you were like me — if only you loved —

ÉLISE: Let us deal with your troubles first. Tell me who she is.

CLÉANTE: A new-comer to our neighbourhood — the most charming person in the world. I was completely carried away from the first moment I saw her. Her name is Marianne and she lives with her invalid mother, to whom she is wonderfully devoted. She cares for and consoles her in her sufferings with the most touching devotion. She lends a charm to everything she touches and a grace to everything she does. She is so gentle, so kind, so modest — so adorable. Oh, Élise, I only wish you had seen her!

ÉLISE: Oh, I can see her very well from your description, and the fact that you love her tells me sufficiently what sort of person she is.

CLÉANTE: I have discovered, indirectly, that they are not very well off, and that, even living modestly, as they do, they are hard put to make ends meet. Just think, my dear, what a pleasure it would be if I could restore her fortunes or even discreetly supplement the modest needs of a virtuous family. Imagine, on the other hand, my despair at my inability to enjoy such a pleasure, thanks to my father's avarice, or even to offer a single token of my love.

ÉLISE: Yes, I can see how galling it must be for you.

CLÉANTE: Ah, my dear, it's worse than you could ever imagine. Could anything be more cruel than this rigorous economy he inflicts on us, this unnatural parsimony under which we perforce languish? What use will money be to us if it only comes when we are too old to enjoy it; if, to manage at all in the meantime, I have to run into debt on all sides, and, like you, am constantly reduced to going to tradesmen for help in order to clothe myself decently? I wanted to talk to you and ask you to help me to sound father about what I have in mind. If I find he is opposed to it, I'm determined to run away with my beloved and take whatever fortune Heaven may vouchsafe us. With this end in view I am trying to raise money everywhere. If you are in the same position as I am, my dear sister, and father opposes your wishes too, let us both leave him and free ourselves from the tyranny his intolerable avarice has so long imposed on us.

ÉLISE: He certainly gives us more and more cause every day to regret our dear mother's death.

CLÉANTE: I hear his voice. Let us go and discuss our plans somewhere else and later we can join forces in an attack on his obduracy.

(*They go out. Enter* HARPAGON *and* LA FLÈCHE.)

HARPAGON: Get out at once! I'll have no back answers! Go on! Clear out of my house, sworn thief and gallows-bird that you are!

LA FLÈCHE (*aside*): I never came across such a confounded old scoundrel. I reckon he is possessed of a devil, if you ask me!

HARPAGON: What are you muttering about?

LA FLÈCHE: What are you turning me out for?

HARPAGON: What right have you to ask me my reasons? Get out before I throw you out.

La Flèche: What have I done to you?

Harpagon: Enough for me to want to be rid of you.

La Flèche: Your son — my master — told me to wait for him!

Harpagon: Go wait in the street, then! Don't let me see you in the house any more, standing there keeping a watch on everything that goes on, and an eye for anything you can pick up. I want no spy for ever watching my affairs, a sneaking dog with his confounded eyes on everything I do, devouring everything I possess and rummaging everywhere to see if there's anything he can steal.

La Flèche: And how the deuce do you think anyone is going to steal from you? Is it likely anyone is going to steal from you when you keep everything under lock and key and stand guard day and night?

Harpagon: I'll lock up what I want and stand guard when I please. I never saw such a pack of prying scoundrels! They've an eye on everything one does! (aside) I'm only afraid he's got wind of my money. (to La Flèche) You are just the man to go spreading it round that I have got money hidden, aren't you?

La Flèche: You have money hidden?

Harpagon: No, you rogue — I never said so! (aside) Oh, it infuriates me! (to La Flèche) All I'm asking is that you shan't go spreading malicious rumours that I have!

La Flèche: What does it matter to us whether you have or you haven't? It's all the same either way.

Harpagon: So you'll argue, will you! (Raising his fist) I'll teach you to argue! Once again, get out of here!

La Flèche: All right! I'm going.

Harpagon: Wait! You are not taking anything with you?

La Flèche: What could I be taking?

Harpagon: Come here! Let me see! Show me your hands.

La Flèche: There!

Harpagon: Now the others.

La Flèche: The others?

Harpagon: Yes, the others.

La Flèche: There you are!

Harpagon (pointing to his breeches): Have you nothing in there?

La Flèche: See for yourself!

Harpagon (feeling at the bottom of his breeches): These wide breeches are the very things for hiding stolen property. They deserve hanging — whoever makes such things.

La Flèche (aside): A fellow like this deserves to get what he expects. I only wish I could have the pleasure of robbing him.

Harpagon: Eh?

La Flèche: What's that?

Harpagon: What did you say about robbing?

La Flèche: I said, 'Have a good look and make sure I am not robbing you'.

Harpagon: That's what I intend to do. (Harpagon feels in La Flèche's pockets.)

La Flèche (aside): A plague on all misers and their miserly ways.

Harpagon: What's that? What d'ye say?

La Flèche: What did I say?

Harpagon: Yes, what did you say about misers and miserly ways?

La Flèche: I said a plague on all misers and their miserly ways!

Harpagon: And who are you referring to?

La Flèche: Misers, of course.

Harpagon: And who are they?

La Flèche: Who are they? Stingy old scoundrels.

Harpagon: But who d'ye mean by that?

La Flèche: What are you worrying about?

HARPAGON: I am worrying about what I've a right to worry about.

LA FLÈCHE: Did you think I meant you?

HARPAGON: I think what I choose, but I want to know who you were talking to.

LA FLÈCHE: To — to my hat.

HARPAGON: Yes, and I'll talk to your thick skull.

LA FLÈCHE: Can't I say what I like about misers?

HARPAGON: Yes, you can if you like, but I can put a stop to your impudent nonsense! Hold your tongue.

LA FLÈCHE: I mentioned no names.

HARPAGON: If you say a word more, I'll leather you.

LA FLÈCHE: If the cap fits — I say —

HARPAGON: Will you be quiet?

LA FLÈCHE: Yes, if I must!

HARPAGON: Ah! You —

LA FLÈCHE (*shows a pocket in his jerkin*): Steady on! Here's another pocket! Will that satisfy you?

HARPAGON: Come on! Hand it over without my having to search you!

LA FLÈCHE: Hand over what?

HARPAGON: Whatever it is you've taken from me!

LA FLÈCHE: I've taken nothing from you.

HARPAGON: Sure?

LA FLÈCHE: Certain!

HARPAGON: Be off, then, and go to the devil!

LA FLÈCHE: That's a nice sort of leave taking.

HARPAGON: I leave you to your conscience. (*Alone.*) He's a confounded nuisance, this scoundrelly valet. I hate the sight of the limping cur! It is a terrible worry having a large sum of money in the house. Much better have one's money well invested and keep no more than is needed for current expenses. It's difficult to find a safe hiding-place in the house. I've no confidence in strong boxes. I don't trust 'em. They are just an invitation to thieves, I always think — the first things they go for. All the same I'm not sure I was wise to bury in the garden the ten thousand crowns I was paid yesterday. Ten thousand crowns in gold is a sum which . . . (*Enter* ÉLISE *and* CLÉANTE *talking in low voices.*) Oh Heavens! Have I given myself away? I let myself be carried away by my temper — I do believe I was talking aloud. (*to* CLÉANTE) What is it?

CLÉANTE: Nothing, father.

HARPAGON: Have you been here long?

ÉLISE: No, we have only just come.

HARPAGON: Did you hear — er —

CLÉANTE: Hear what, father?

HARPAGON: Just now —

ÉLISE: What was it?

HARPAGON: What I have just been saying.

CLÉANTE: No.

HARPAGON: Yes, you did, you did! You did!

CLÉANTE: Pardon me, we heard nothing.

HARPAGON: I can see you overheard something. The fact is I was just saying to myself how difficult it is nowadays to get hold of any money and how fortunate anybody is who has ten thousand crowns by him.

CLÉANTE: We hesitated to come near you for fear of interrupting you.

HARPAGON: I'm very glad of the chance to explain to you, in case you got the wrong impression and imagined I was saying that I had ten thousand crowns.

CLÉANTE: We don't concern ourselves with your affairs.

HARPAGON: I only wish I had ten thousand crowns.

CLÉANTE: I don't believe —

HARPAGON: It would be a good thing for me if I had.

ÉLISE: Such things —

HARPAGON: I could well do with a sum like that.

CLÉANTE: It would come in very useful.

ÉLISE: You are —

HARPAGON: I should have less cause to complain of hard times than I have.

CLÉANTE: Good Heavens, father! You have no cause to complain. Everybody knows you are well enough off!

HARPAGON: Me? Well off! What a lie! Nothing could be further from the truth! It's scandalous to spread such tales!

ÉLISE: Well, don't be angry.

HARPAGON: It's a queer thing when my own children betray me and turn against me.

CLÉANTE: Is it turning against you to say that you are well off?

HARPAGON: Yes. What with your saying things like that and your extravagant ways someone will be coming and cutting my throat one of these days in the belief that I'm made of money.

CLÉANTE: What extravagant ways have I got?

HARPAGON: What, indeed! What could be more scandalous than the sumptuous apparel you flaunt round the town? Only yesterday I was complaining of your sister — but you are far worse! It's a crying scandal! What you are wearing now, taking you as you stand, would add up to a nice competency. I have told you a score of times already, my lad, I don't like your goings on at all: this aping of the nobility and going about dressed up as you are can only mean that you are robbing me somehow.

CLÉANTE: But how can I be robbing you?

HARPAGON: How should I know? Where do you get the money to live as you do?

CLÉANTE: Where do I get the money? From cards. I happen to be lucky and I put my winnings on my back.

HARPAGON: That's no way to go on! No way at all! If you are lucky at cards you should take advantage of it and put your winnings into some sound investment. Then they'll be there when you want 'em. But what I would like to know, never mind anything else, is what's the use of all these ribbons that you are decked out with from head to foot? Wouldn't half a dozen pins do to fasten up your breeches? Why need you spend money on a wig, when you can wear your own hair —which costs nothing? I'm willing to bet that your perukes and ribbons cost you twenty guineas at least, and twenty guineas invested bring in one pound thirteen shillings and elevenpence farthing a year at no more than eight per cent.

CLÉANTE: That's true enough.

HARPAGON: Well now, suppose we leave that and come to something else — Eh? (aside) I believe they are making signs to each other to steal my purse. (to CLÉANTE) What do you mean by making signs like that?

ÉLISE: We are just arguing as to who should speak first. We both have something to tell you.

HARPAGON: Yes, and I have something to tell both of you.

CLÉANTE: We want to talk to you about marriage, father.

HARPAGON: Ay, and it's marriage I want to talk to you about.

ÉLISE: Oh, father!

HARPAGON: Why the 'Oh, father'? Is it the word marriage or the idea of getting married yourself you are afraid of, my girl?

CLÉANTE: The word marriage might well alarm both of us. It depends on what you understand by it. We are afraid that what *we* want may not agree with what *you* want.

HARPAGON: Now do be patient. Don't get alarmed. I know what is good for both of you. Neither of you shall have any cause to complain of what I am going to do for you. First of all, do you know a young lady named Marianne who lives not far from here?

CLÉANTE: Yes, father, I do.

HARPAGON (*to* ÉLISE): And you?

ÉLISE: I have heard of her.

HARPAGON: Well now, my boy, what is your opinion of this young lady?

CLÉANTE: She is a most charming person.

HARPAGON: Her looks?

CLÉANTE: Modest and intelligent.

HARPAGON: Her manner?

CLÉANTE: Admirable, beyond question.

HARPAGON: You think a girl like that is worth serious consideration?

CLÉANTE: I do, father.

HARPAGON: An eligible match, in fact?

CLÉANTE: Most eligible.

HARPAGON: And she looks as if she'd make a good housewife?

CLÉANTE: Without a doubt.

HARPAGON: And whoever marries her can count himself a lucky man, eh?

CLÉANTE: Assuredly.

HARPAGON: There's one little difficulty. I'm afraid she may not bring as much money as one would like.

CLÉANTE: Ah! What does money matter, father, when it is a question of marrying a good woman?

HARPAGON: Oh no, I don't agree with you there! But there *is* this to be said, that if she hasn't as much money as one would wish there may be some other way of making up for it.

CLÉANTE: Of course.

HARPAGON: Well now, I'm very pleased to find you agree with me, because her modest ways and gentle disposition have quite won my heart. Provided that I find she has *some* money — I've made up my mind to marry her.

CLÉANTE: Eh?

HARPAGON: What do you mean by 'Eh'?

CLÉANTE: You have made up your mind to — what did you say?

HARPAGON: Marry Marianne.

CLÉANTE: You mean — you — you yourself?

HARPAGON: Yes. Me! Me! Me myself. What about it?

CLÉANTE: I feel faint. I must get out of here.

HARPAGON: It will pass off. Go into the kitchen and have a good drink — of cold water. (*Exit* CLÉANTE.) There! You see what these effeminate young men are! They haven't the strength of a chicken! Well, there you are, my girl, that is what I've decided for myself. For your brother I have a certain widow in mind. Someone came to talk to me about her this morning. As for you, yourself, I mean to bestow you on Seigneur Anselme.

ÉLISE: Seigneur Anselme!

HARPAGON: Yes, he's a man of ripe experience, prudent and discreet, not more than fifty years of age and reputed to be very rich.

ÉLISE (*curtseying*): If you please, father, I don't want to marry.

HARPAGON (*imitating her*): If *you* please, my pet, I want you to marry.

ÉLISE: Excuse me, father —

HARPAGON: Excuse *me*, my dear —

ÉLISE: I am Seigneur Anselme's very humble servant but, if you don't mind, I won't marry him.

HARPAGON: And I am your very humble servant, my dear, but, if you don't mind, you *will* marry him, and this very evening too.

ÉLISE: This evening!

HARPAGON: This evening!

ÉLISE: No, father, I won't.

HARPAGON: Yes, daughter, you will.

ÉLISE: No!

HARPAGON: Yes!

ÉLISE: I tell you I shan't!

HARPAGON: But I say you shall!

ÉLISE: I will never agree to it!

HARPAGON: But I shall make you agree to it!

ÉLISE: I'll kill myself rather than marry such a man.

HARPAGON: You won't kill yourself and you shall marry him. The impertinence! Who ever heard of a daughter talking like this to her father!

ÉLISE: Who ever heard of a father requiring his daughter to make such a marriage!

HARPAGON: It is a most suitable match. I am willing to bet that everyone will approve of my choice.

ÉLISE: And I am willing to bet that no reasonable person would do any such thing.

HARPAGON: Here comes Valère. Will you agree to let him judge between us?

ÉLISE: Yes, I agree.

HARPAGON: You'll accept his decision?

ÉLISE: Yes, I'll abide by whatever he says.

HARPAGON: That's settled, then. Come here, Valère! We want you to decide which of us is in the right — my daughter here, or myself.

VALÈRE: Oh, you sir, beyond question.

HARPAGON: But you don't know what we are talking about!

VALÈRE: No, but you *couldn't* be wrong. You are always in the right.

HARPAGON: I intend to marry her this evening to a man who is both wealthy and wise, and the silly chit tells me to my face that she won't have him at any price. What d'ye say to that?

VALÈRE: What do I say to that?

HARPAGON: Yes.

VALÈRE: Ah well — I —

HARPAGON: Well?

VALÈRE: What I say is that fundamentally I agree with you — for of course you just must be right, but, on the other hand, she isn't altogether in the wrong.

HARPAGON: Why! Seigneur Anselme is an eligible match, well born, quiet, assured, prudent, and very well off and with no surviving children of his first marriage. What more could she want?

VALÈRE: That's true — though she might perhaps contend that it is rather precipitate and that she ought at least to be allowed time to see if she can reconcile herself to . . .

HARPAGON: No! An opportunity like this won't stand delay. What is more, there is a special, a unique advantage. He is willing to take her — without dowry!

VALÈRE: Without dowry?

HARPAGON: Yes.

VALÈRE: Oh! I say no more. There you are! One must agree — that's absolutely conclusive.

HARPAGON: It means a considerable saving for me.

VALÈRE: Of course, there's no gainsaying that. It is true that your daughter might contend that marriage is a more serious matter than people sometimes realize, that a lifetime's happiness or unhappiness may depend upon it and that one ought not to enter into a commitment for life without giving it serious consideration.

HARPAGON: But — without dowry!

VALÈRE: Yes, you are right! That's the important thing, of course — although there are people who would contend that in a case like this your daughter's own feelings should be considered, and that where there is such a great disparity of age, temperament, and opinions there is a risk that the marriage might turn out badly. . . .

HARPAGON: But — without dowry!

VALÈRE: Yes, one must admit there's no answer to that. There is no arguing against it. Not that there are not some fathers who would attach more importance to their daughter's happiness than the money they might have to part with and refuse to sacrifice it to mercenary considerations. They would rather seek to secure before everything else that union of mutual affection from which spring happiness, joy, and contentment —

HARPAGON: Without dowry!

VALÈRE: True. It is unanswerable. Without dowry! There's no countering that!

HARPAGON (*aside* — *looking offstage*): Ah, I thought I heard a dog barking. Can it be someone after my money? (*to* VALÈRE) Don't go away. I'll be back directly. (*Goes out.*)

ÉLISE: Surely you don't mean what you are saying, Valère?

VALÈRE: If we are to get what we want from him we must avoid rubbing him the wrong way. It would ruin everything to oppose him directly. There are some people you can't deal with except by humouring them. Impatient of opposition, restive by nature, they never fail to shy at the truth and won't go about things in a common-sense fashion. The only way to lead them is to turn them gently in the direction you want them to go. Pretend to give your consent and you'll find it's the best way to get what you want.

ÉLISE: But this marriage, Valère?

VALÈRE: We will find some excuse for breaking it off.

ÉLISE: But how — when it is to take place this evening?

VALÈRE: You must pretend to be ill and have it postponed.

ÉLISE: But they will discover the truth when they call in the doctor.

VALÈRE: Not they! What do those fellows know about anything? Have whatever malady you like, they'll explain how you got it.

HARPAGON (*returning* — *to himself*): It's nothing, thank Heaven!

VALÈRE: If the worst comes to the worst we must take refuge in flight, that is, if you love me well enough, my dear Élise, to face — (*seeing* HARPAGON) Yes, it's a daughter's duty to obey her father. It's not for her to worry about what her husband looks like; when it's a case of — without dowry — she must take what she's given.

HARPAGON: Good! That's the way to talk.

VALÈRE: Forgive me, sir, for letting my feelings run away with me and taking the liberty of talking to her in this way.

HARPAGON: Not at all. I am delighted. I give you a free hand with her. (*to* ÉLISE) It's no use running away. I invest him with full parental authority over you. You must do whatever he tells you.

VALÈRE (*to* ÉLISE): Now will you resist my remonstrances! (*to* HARPAGON) I'll follow her and continue the homily I was giving her.

HARPAGON: Do. I shall be grateful to you.

VALÈRE: It is as well to keep her on a tight rein.

HARPAGON: True. We must —

VALÈRE: Don't worry. I think I can deal with her.

HARPAGON: Do, by all means! I am just going to take a stroll in the town. I'll be back before long.

VALÈRE: Yes. Money is the most precious thing in all the world! You ought to thank Heaven you have such a good father. He knows the value of things. When a man offers to take a girl without dowry there's no point in looking any further. That's the only thing that matters. 'Without dowry' — it counts for more than good looks, youth, birth, honour, wisdom, and probity.

(*They go out together.*)

HARPAGON: Good lad! Spoken like an oracle! How lucky I am to have such a man in my service.

ACT TWO

CLÉANTE, LA FLÈCHE.

CLÉANTE: Now, you scoundrel! where have you been hiding yourself? Didn't I tell you to . . .

LA FLÈCHE: Yes, sir, and I came in here with every intention of waiting for you, but your father, who's a most awkward old man to deal with, would chase me out willy-nilly. I very nearly got myself a hiding.

CLÉANTE: How is our affair progressing? Things have become more pressing than ever, and since I last saw you I have found out that my father is my rival in love.

LA FLÈCHE: Your father in love?

CLÉANTE: Yes, and I had the greatest difficulty in the world in preventing him from seeing how upset I was by the discovery.

LA FLÈCHE: Fancy his being in love! What the devil is he thinking about? Is he trying to take a rise out of everybody? What use is love to a fellow like him, anyway?

CLÉANTE: It must be a judgment on me — his getting an idea like this into his head!

LA FLÈCHE: But why do you conceal your own love affair from him?

CLÉANTE: To give him less cause for suspicion, to keep myself in a position to prevent this marriage of his if it comes to the point. What reply did they give you?

LA FLÈCHE: Upon my word, sir, borrowing money is a miserable business. Anyone who has to go through the moneylender's hands, as you have, must put up with some pretty queer things.

CLÉANTE: So nothing will come of it?

LA FLÈCHE: Oh no! Master Simon, the agent they put us in touch with, is a keen business-like fellow, and he's moving Heaven and Earth for you. He assures me he has taken quite a fancy to you.

CLÉANTE: So I shall get the fifteen thousand I'm asking for?

LA FLÈCHE: Yes — subject to a few trifling conditions you'll have to accept if you want it to go through.

CLÉANTE: Has he put you in touch with the actual lender?

LA FLÈCHE: Now really, sir, that isn't the way these things are done! He's even more anxious to conceal his identity than you are. There is more involved in these jobs than you think. They won't give his name and he is to have an opportunity of talking to you to-day at a house hired for the purpose, so that he can learn from your own lips about your means and your family. I have no doubt at all that the mere mention of your father's name will make everything easy.

CLÉANTE: Especially as my mother is dead and they can't stop me getting her money.

LA FLÈCHE: There are a few conditions here which he himself has dictated to our go-between. He wants you to see them before going any further. 'Provided that the lender shall be satisfied as to the securities and that the borrower be of age and of a family with means sufficient, substantial and secure, free and quit of all encumbrance there shall be executed a proper and precise undertaking before a notary, of known probity, who to this end and purpose shall be nominated by the lender inasmuch as he is the more concerned that the instrument be executed in due form.'

CLÉANTE: I have nothing to say against that.

LA FLÈCHE: 'The lender, that his conscience may be free from all reproach, proposes to make his money available at no more than five and a half per cent.'

CLÈANTE: Five and a half per cent! My goodness, but that's very reasonable. There's nothing to complain of there!

LA FLÈCHE: True. 'But — whereas the lender aforesaid has not the sum in question by him and in order to oblige the borrower is himself obliged to borrow elsewhere at the rate of twenty per cent, the aforesaid borrower shall agree to meet this interest without prejudice to the five and a half per cent afore-mentioned in consideration of the fact that it is only to oblige the aforesaid borrower that the lender aforesaid undertakes to borrow the aforesaid amount.'

CLÉANTE: What the devil! What sort of Jew or Turk have we got hold of? That's more than twenty-five per cent!

LA FLÈCHE: True. That's what I said. You'd better think about it.

CLÉANTE: What's the use of thinking about it. I need the money, so I shall have to agree to everything.

LA FLÈCHE: That's what I told them.

CLÉANTE: Is there anything else?

LA FLÈCHE: Just one small clause. 'Of the fifteen thousand francs which the borrower re-quires, the lender can only dispose of twelve thousand in cash, and for the other three thousand the borrower shall undertake to take over the effects, clothing, and miscella-neous objects as set out in the following inventory and priced by the aforesaid lender at the most moderate valuation possible.'

CLÉANTE: What does that mean?

LA FLÈCHE: Listen to the inventory. 'Item — one four-poster bed complete with hangings of Hungarian lace, very handsomely worked upon an olive-coloured material, together with six chairs and a counterpane to match, the whole in very good condition and lined in red and blue shot silk: item — one tester bed with hangings of good Aumale serge in old rose with silk fringes and valance.'

CLÉANTE: What does he expect me to do with that?

LA FLÈCHE: Wait. 'Item — one set of hangings in tapestry representing the loves of Gom-baut and Macaea; item — one large table in walnut with twelve pedestal or turned legs with draw-out leaf at either end and fitted underneath with six stools.'

CLÉANTE: Confound it! What use is that to me?

LA FLÈCHE: Patience, please. 'Item — three muskets, inlaid in mother-of-pearl, with three assorted rests; item — one brick fur-nace with two retorts and three flasks, very useful for anyone interested in distilling; item — '

CLÉANTE: Oh! It's infuriating —

LA FLÈCHE: Now, now! 'Item — one Bologna lute complete with strings or nearly so; item — one fox-and-goose board, one draughts-board, one game of mother goose as derived from the ancient Greeks, very useful for passing the time when one has nothing else to do; item — one crocodile skin three feet six inches in length and stuffed with hay, a very attractive curio for suspension from the ceiling — all the aforementioned articles valued at upwards of four thousand five hundred francs and reduced to three thou-sand at the discretion of the lender.'

CLÈANTE: Confound him and his discretion! The miserable rogue! Did you ever hear of such usury! Not content with charging out-rageous interest, he must rook me three thousand francs for his collection of old junk. I shan't get two hundred for the lot, and yet I suppose I must just resign myself to agreeing to whatever he wants! He's in a position to make me put up with it. His dagger's at my throat, the scoundrel!

LA FLÈCHE: It seems to me, master, if you don't mind my saying so, that you are going the same road to ruin as Panurge — drawing your money in advance, buying dear, selling cheap, and eating your corn in the blade.

CLÉANTE: Well, what else can I do? That's what young men are driven to by the cursed niggardliness of their fathers. Can anyone wonder that their sons wish them dead!

LA FLÈCHE: I must admit that your father's be-havior would exasperate the mildest of men. I have no particular fancy for getting myself hanged, thank the Lord, and when I see some of my colleagues involving themselves in transactions of a certain sort I know when to keep out and steer clear of the little amusements which lead one too near the gallows, but I'm bound to say that I think his behavior is a sheer invitation to robbery. I should even consider it a praiseworthy action to rob him.

CLÉANTE: Give me the inventory a moment, I'll have another look at it.

(*Enter* MASTER SIMON *and* HARPAGON.)

MASTER SIMON: Yes, as I was saying, sir, the young man is in need of money. His affairs are such that he needs it urgently, and he will agree to any conditions you like to make.

HARPAGON: And you feel certain, Master Simon, that there's not the least risk? You know your client's name, means, and family?

MASTER SIMON: No, I can't tell you exactly. It was only by chance that he was put in touch with me, but he will tell you it all himself, and his servant assures me that you'll be completely satisfied when you make his acquaintance. All I can tell you is that his family is very wealthy, his mother is dead, and that he'll guarantee, if need be, that his father will die within six months!

HARPAGON: Well, that's something! After all, it's only charitable to assist people when we can, Master Simon.

MASTER SIMON: Of course.

LA FLÈCHE (*to* CLÉANTE *in a whisper*): What's the meaning of this — our Master Simon talking to your father?

CLÉANTE (*to* LA FLÈCHE *in a whisper*): Someone must have told him who I am. Could *you* betray me?

MASTER SIMON: You *are* in a hurry! Who told you this was the meeting-place? (*to* HARPAGON) I didn't disclose your name and address to them, sir, but I think there's no great harm done. They are people of discretion and you can discuss things between you here.

HARPAGON: What's this?

MASTER SIMON: This gentleman is the person I was speaking of sir, who wants to borrow fifteen thousand francs.

HARPAGON: So it's you, is it, you blackguard? You descend to this sort of thing, do you?

CLÉANTE: So it's you, is it, father? You stoop to this kind of trade, do you?

(MASTER SIMON *and* LA FLÈCHE *go out.*)

HARPAGON: So you are the man who is ruining himself by such outrageous borrowing?

CLÉANTE: And you are the man who is enriching himself by such criminal usury!

HARPAGON: How can you ever dare to face me after this?

CLÉANTE: How will you ever dare to face anyone at all?

HARPAGON: Aren't you ashamed to stoop to such extravagance, to involve yourself in such frightful expense, to squander in this disgraceful fashion the fortune your parents have toiled so hard to accumulate for you?

CLÉANTE: Don't you blush to disgrace your position by transactions of this kind, to sacrifice your honour and reputation to your insatiable lust for piling coin on coin and outdoing anything the most notorious usurers ever invented in the way of scandalous interest!

HARPAGON: Get out of my sight, you scoundrel! Get out of my sight!

CLÉANTE: I ask you, who commits the greater crime, the man who borrows to meet his necessities, or one who extorts money from people which he doesn't need?

HARPAGON: Go away, I tell you! You make my blood boil. (*Exit* CLÉANTE.) I'm not sorry this has happened! It's a warning to me to keep a closer watch on him than ever.

(*Enter* FROSINE.)

FROSINE: Sir —

HARPAGON: Just a minute. I'll come back and talk to you presently. (*aside*) It's time I had a look at my money!

(*He goes out. Enter* LA FLÈCHE.)

LA FLÈCHE (*to himself*): It's a most peculiar

business. He must have a regular furniture store somewhere. We didn't recognize any of the stuff in the inventory.

FROSINE: Ah, it's you, my poor La Flèche. Fancy meeting you!

LA FLÈCHE: Why, Frosine! What are you doing here?

FROSINE: Following my usual occupation — acting as go-between, making myself useful to people and picking up what I can from such small abilities as I possess. You have to live on your wits in this world, you know, and those of us who have no other resources must rely on scheming and hard work.

LA FLÈCHE: Have you some business with the master?

FROSINE: Yes, I'm handling a little transaction for him and hoping for some recompense.

LA FLÈCHE: From him? My goodness! You'll be clever if you get anything out of him! Money is hard to come by in this house I warn you.

FROSINE: But there *are* certain services which are wonderfully effective in opening the purse-strings.

LA FLÈCHE: Well I won't contradict you, but you don't know our Mr. Harpagon yet. He just isn't human at all, our Mr. Harpagon — he hasn't one scrap of humanity in him! He has the hardest heart and the closest fist of any man living. There's no service of any kind, sort, or description would make him grateful enough to put his hand in his pocket. Praise, compliments, fine words, friendliness, yes, as much as you like, but money — nothing doing! You may win his favour, be in his good graces — but nothing ever comes of it. He has such a dislike of the word 'giving' that he won't even give you 'good morning.'

FROSINE: Good Heavens! As if I don't know how to get round men! Why, I know all there is to be known about stroking them the right way, arousing their sympathy, and finding their soft spots.

LA FLÈCHE: Not the slightest use here. Where money's involved I defy you to make any impression. On that score he's adamant — absolutely past praying for. You could be at death's door but *he* wouldn't budge. He puts money before reputation, honour, or virtue, and the mere sight of anyone asking for money is enough to throw him into a fit. It's like inflicting a mortal wound on him, taking his heart's blood, tearing out his very entrails, and if — but he's coming back. I must be off. . . .

(*He goes out. Enter* HARPAGON.)

HARPAGON (*to himself*): Everything is all right. (*to* FROSINE) Well now, Frosine, what is it?

FROSINE: Goodness me, how well you are looking — the very picture of health.

HARPAGON: Who? Me!

FROSINE: I never saw you looking so fresh and so sprightly.

HARPAGON: Really?

FROSINE: Why, you've never looked so young in your life. I know fellows of twenty-five who are not half as youthful as you are.

HARPAGON: Nevertheless, I'm well over sixty, Frosine.

FROSINE: Well, what's sixty? What of it? It's the very flower of one's age. You are just coming to the prime of life.

HARPAGON: True, but I reckon I should be no worse for being twenty years younger.

FROSINE: What are you talking about! You need wish no such thing. You've the constitution to live to a hundred.

HARPAGON: Do you think so?

FROSINE: I'm certain. You have all the indications. Keep still a moment! Look what a sign of longevity that is — the line between the eyes!

HARPAGON: Is that really so?

FROSINE: Of course. Give me your hand. Heavens! What a line of life!

HARPAGON: What d'ye mean?

FROSINE: You see where that line goes to?

HARPAGON: Well, what does that mean?

FROSINE: Upon my word. Did I say a hundred? You'll live to a hundred and twenty!

HARPAGON: No! Is it possible?

FROSINE: I tell you they'll have to knock you on the head! You'll see your children buried, ay, and your children's children.

HARPAGON: So much the better! And how is our little business getting on?

FROSINE: Need you ask? Did you ever know me start a job and not finish it? I really have a wonderful talent for match-making. There's nobody I couldn't pair off, given a little time to arrange things. I really think, if I took it into my head, I could match the Grand Turk and the Venetian Republic! Not that there was anything very difficult about this little business of yours. I am friendly with the two ladies and have talked to them both about you and told the mother of the intentions you have formed in regard to Marianne from seeing her pass along the street and taking the air at her window.

HARPAGON: And her reply?

FROSINE: She was delighted by the proposal, and when I intimated that you would like her daughter to be present this evening at the signing of your own daughter's marriage contract she agreed without hesitation and put her in my charge.

HARPAGON: You see, I am committed to giving a supper for Seigneur Anselme, Frosine, and I shall be very pleased if she will join the party too.

FROSINE: Good. She is to visit your daughter after dinner and then go to the fair, which she wants to do, and return in time for supper.

HARPAGON: Very well. I'll lend them my carriage and they can go down together.

FROSINE: That's the very thing for her!

HARPAGON: Now, have you sounded the mother as to what dowry she can give her daughter, Frosine? Have you told her she must make an effort to contribute something and put herself to some pinching and scraping on an occasion like this? After all, nobody is going to marry a girl unless she brings something with her.

FROSINE: Why, this girl will bring you twelve thousand a year.

HARPAGON: Twelve thousand a year!

FROSINE: Yes. In the first place she's been brought up on a very spare diet. She is a girl who is used to living on salad and milk, apples and cheese, so she'll need no elaborate table, none of your rich broths or eternal barley concoctions, nor any of the delicacies other women would require, and that's no small consideration. It might well amount to three thousand francs a year at least. Moreover, her tastes are simple; she has not any hankering after extravagant dresses, expensive jewellery, or sumptuous furnishings which young women of her age are so fond of — and this item alone means more than four thousand a year. Then, again, she has a very strong objection to playing for money, a most unusual thing in a woman nowadays. I know one woman in our neighbourhood who has lost twenty thousand francs at cards this year. Suppose we reckon only a quarter of that — five thousand a year for cards and four thousand on clothes and jewellery, that's nine thousand, and another three thousand on food — that gives you your twelve thousand a year, doesn't it?

HARPAGON: Yes, it's not bad, but all these calculations don't amount to anything tangible.

FROSINE: Come, come! Do you mean to say that a modest appetite, a sober taste in dress, and a dislike of card playing don't amount to anything tangible? Why, they are a marriage portion and an inheritance rolled into one!

HARPAGON: No. It's just nonsense to try and make a dowry out of the expenses she won't incur. I'll give no credit for anything I don't actually receive. I really must have something I can get my hands on.

FROSINE: Heavens, man! You'll get your hands on plenty. They've mentioned that they have money abroad somewhere. That will come to you.

HARPAGON: Well, we shall have to look into that, but there's another thing worrying me, Frosine. The girl is young, as you know, and young people generally prefer those of their own age and don't fancy other society. I am afraid she may not take to a man as old as I am, and that might lead to certain little domestic complications which wouldn't please me at all.

FROSINE: How little you know her! It's another thing I was going to mention. She can't bear young men at all and keeps all her affection for old ones.

HARPAGON: Does she really?

FROSINE: Yes! I only wish you could have heard her on the subject. She can't bear the sight of a young man. She declares that nothing gives her more pleasure than to see a fine old man with a venerable beard. The older men are the better she likes them, so don't go making yourself look younger than you are. She wants someone in the sixties at least. She was on the point of being married when she suddenly broke it off because the man let it out that he was no more than fifty-six and he didn't put spectacles on to sign the marriage contract.

HARPAGON: That was the only reason?

FROSINE: Yes, she says fifty-six isn't old enough for her, and she likes a nose that wears spectacles.

HARPAGON: Well, that's something entirely new to me!

FROSINE: You wouldn't believe the lengths she goes to. She has a few pictures and engravings in her room, and what do you think they are? Adonis, Cephales, Paris, or Apollo? Not at all! Pictures of Saturn, King Priam, the aged Nestor, and good old father Anchises borne on the shoulders of his son.

HARPAGON: Well, that *is* remarkable! I should never have thought it. I'm delighted to hear that her tastes run that way. I must say if I'd been a woman I should never have fancied young men.

FROSINE: I can well believe you. What poor stuff young men are for anyone to fall in love with — a lot of snotty-nosed infants and fresh-faced country bumpkins. To think of anyone feeling any attraction towards them!

HARPAGON: I can never understand it myself. I don't know how it is that women are so fond of them.

FROSINE: They must be completely mad to find young men attractive. It doesn't make sense! These young fops aren't men. How can anyone take to such creatures?

HARPAGON: That's what I'm always saying. What with their effeminate voices and their two or three wisps of beard turned up like cat's whiskers, their tow wigs, their flowing breeches and unbuttoned coats!

FROSINE: Ay! They make a poor show compared with a man like you. You are something like a man, something worth looking at. You have the sort of figure women fall in love with, and you dress the part too.

HARPAGON: You think I'm attractive?

FROSINE: Why, you are quite irresistible. Your face is a picture. Turn round a little, if you please. What could be more handsome? Let me see you walk. There's a fine figure of a man — as limber and graceful as one could wish to see! Not a thing ails you.

HARPAGON: No, nothing very serious, Heaven be praised, except a bit of catarrh that catches me now and again.

FROSINE: Oh, that's nothing. Your catarrh is not unbecoming. Your cough is quite charming.

HARPAGON: Tell me now, has Marianne ever seen me? Has she not noticed me passing by?

FROSINE: No, but we've talked a lot about you. I've described you to her and I've not failed to sing your praises and tell her how fortunate she would be to have such a husband.

HARPAGON: You've done well. Thank you, Frosine.

FROSINE: I should like to make one small request to you, sir. (HARPAGON *looks grave.*) I'm involved in a lawsuit, and on the point of losing it for lack of a little money. You could easily ensure that I win my case if you were disposed to help me. You've no idea how pleased she will be to see you. (HARPAGON *looks cheerful.*) How delighted she will be with you. How she'll adore that old-fashioned ruff of yours! She will be absolutely charmed with your way of wearing your breeches pinned to your doublet. A lover with pinned-up breeches will be something quite out of the ordinary for her.

HARPAGON: I'm delighted to hear it.

FROSINE: This lawsuit is really a serious matter for me, sir — (HARPAGON *looks grave again.*) If I lose it I'm ruined, but a very little help would retrieve my position. I only wish you could have seen how delighted she was to hear me talking about you. (HARPAGON *looks cheerful again.*) As I recounted your good qualities, her eyes filled with pleasure and in the end I made her quite impatient to have the marriage all settled.

HARPAGON: You have been very kind, Frosine, and I can't say how much obliged I am to you.

FROSINE: I beseech you, sir, grant me the small assistance I'm asking. (HARPAGON *looks grave again.*) It will put me on my feet again and I shall be eternally grateful to you.

HARPAGON: Good-bye. I must finish my letters.

FROSINE: I do assure you, sir, I am in the most urgent need of your help.

HARPAGON: I'll give instructions for my carriage to be got ready to take you to the fair.

FROSINE: I wouldn't trouble you if I weren't absolutely obliged to.

HARPAGON: I'll see that we have supper early so that it won't upset any of you.

FROSINE: Please don't refuse me. You couldn't imagine, sir, how pleased —

HARPAGON: I'm off. There's somebody calling me. Until later — (*He goes.*)

FROSINE: May you rot, you stingy old cur! The skinflint held out against all my attempts. Devil take him! But I won't give it up. I can always count on getting something handsome out of the other party, whatever happens.

ACT THREE

HARPAGON, CLÉANTE, ÉLISE, VALÈRE, DAME CLAUDE, MASTER JACQUES, BRINDAVOINE, LA MERLUCHE.

HARPAGON: Come along. Let us have you all in here. I want to give you your instructions for this evening and see that everybody has his job. Come here, Dame Claude, we'll start with you. (*She carries a broom.*) Good, I see you are ready for the fray. Your job is to clean up all round, and do be careful not to rub the furniture too hard. I'm afraid of your wearing it out. Then, I'm putting you in charge of the bottles during the supper. If there's a single one missing or if anything is broken I shall hold you responsible and take it out of your wages.

MASTER JACQUES (*aside*): A shrewd penalty!

HARPAGON (*to* DAME CLAUDE): Off you go! (*She goes.*) Now you, Brindavoine, and you, La Merluche, I give you the job of rinsing the glasses and serving the wine, but mind, only when people are thirsty. Don't do, as some scoundrelly servants do, egg people on to drink, putting the idea into their heads when they would never have thought of it otherwise. Wait till they have asked several times and always remember to put plenty of water with it.

MASTER JACQUES (*aside*): Yes, wine without water goes to the head.

LA MERLUCHE: Be we to take off our aprons, master?

HARPAGON: Yes, when you see the guests arriving, but take care not to spoil your clothes.

BRINDAVOINE: You mind, master, that there be a great blotch of lamp oil on one side of my doublet.

LA MERLUCHE: And my breeches be that torn behind, master, that, saving your presence, they'll see my . . .

HARPAGON: That's enough. See that you keep it against the wall. Face the company all the time — and you — hold your hat in front of you like this when you are serving the guests. (*He shows* BRINDAVOINE *how to keep his hat over his doublet to hide the oil stain.*) As for you, my girl (*to* ÉLISE), you are to keep an eye on what is cleared away from the tables and see that nothing is wasted. That's the proper job for daughters to do. In the meantime get yourself ready to welcome my mistress. She is coming to call on you and take you to the fair. Do you hear what I'm telling you?

ÉLISE: Yes, father.

HARPAGON: And you, my effeminate fop of a son, I'm willing to forgive you for what happened just now, but don't you be giving her any of your black looks either.

CLÉANTE: I give her black looks, father? Whatever for?

HARPAGON: Oh Lord! We know very well how children carry on when their fathers marry again and what the usual attitude towards a stepmother is! If you want me to forget your last escapade, I'd advise you to put on a cheerful face for the young lady and make her as welcome as ever you can.

CLÉANTE: I really can't promise to be glad that she should become my stepmother. I couldn't truthfully say that I am, but I can promise to obey you to the letter in putting on a cheerful face to receive her.

HARPAGON: Well, mind that you do.

CLÉANTE: You will find you have no cause to complain on that score.

HARPAGON: Very well! (CLÉANTE *goes out.*) Valère, I want your help in this. Now then, Master Jacques, come along; I've kept you until last.

MASTER JACQUES: Do you want to speak to your cook or your coachman, sir? I'm both the one and the other.

HARPAGON: I want both.

MASTER JACQUES: But which d'ye want first?

HARPAGON: The cook.

MASTER JACQUES: Just a minute, then, if you don't mind. (*He takes off his coachman's overcoat and appears dressed as a cook.*)

HARPAGON: What the deuce is the meaning of this ceremony?

MASTER JACQUES: At your service now, sir.

HARPAGON: I am committed to giving a supper to-night, Master Jacques —

MASTER JACQUES: Wonders never cease!

HARPAGON: Now tell me, can you give us something good?

MASTER JACQUES: Yes, if you give me plenty of money.

HARPAGON: What the devil! It's always money. It seems to be all they can say. Money! Money! Money! It's the one word they know. Money! They are always talking of money. They can never do anything without money!

VALÈRE: I never heard such a fatuous answer. As if there's anything in providing good food if you have plenty of money. It's the easiest thing in the world. Any fool can do that much. The man who is really good at his job can put on a good meal without spending money.

MASTER JACQUES: Put on a good meal without spending money!

VALÈRE: Yes.

MASTER JACQUES: Upon my word, Mr. Steward, I would like you to show how it's done. You had better take on my job as cook since it seems you want to be managing everything.

HARPAGON: Be quiet! Just tell us what we shall need.

MASTER JACQUES: Ask Mr. Steward there. He is the man who can put on a meal without spending money.

HARPAGON: Hey! I want an answer from *you*.

MASTER JACQUES: How many will you be at table?

HARPAGON: We shall be eight or ten, but reckon on eight. Provide for eight and there's always plenty for ten.

VALÈRE: Of course.

MASTER JACQUES: Right. You need to provide four sorts of soup and five main courses — soups, entrées —

HARPAGON: The devil! You are not feeding the whole town.

MASTER JACQUES: Roasts —

HARPAGON (*putting his hand over his mouth*): You scoundrel. You'll eat me out of house and home.

MASTER JACQUES: Entremets —

HARPAGON: Still going on?

VALÈRE: Do you want them to burst themselves? Do you think the master is asking people to come and gorge themselves to death? Go study the rules of health! Ask the doctor whether there's anything does people more harm than overeating.

HARPAGON: How right he is!

VALÈRE: You need to learn, you, and folk like you, Master Jacques, that an overloaded table is a veritable death-trap. Anyone who is really concerned for the well-being of his guests should see that the meal that he offers them is distinguished by frugality. As the ancient philosopher has it, 'One should eat to live not live to eat.'

HARPAGON: Ah, well said, well said! Come, let me embrace you for that. It is the finest precept I've ever heard — 'One should live to eat and not eat to' — that's not it — how does it go?

VALÈRE: 'One should eat to live and not live to eat.'

HARPAGON: Yes. (*to* MASTER JACQUES) Do you hear that? (*to* VALÈRE) Who was the great man who said that?

VALÈRE: I don't remember his name just now.

HARPAGON: Remember to write the words down for me! I'll have them engraved in letters of gold over the chimney-piece in the dining-room.

VALÈRE: I won't fail to do so. As for the supper, just leave it to me. I will see that everything is as it should be.

HARPAGON: Yes, do.

MASTER JACQUES: So much the better. I shall have the less to worry about.

HARPAGON: We must have things people don't go in for much these days, things which soon fill them up — some good thick stew with dumplings and chestnuts. Have plenty of that.

VALÈRE: You may rely on me.

HARPAGON: And now, Master Jacques, I must have my carriage cleaned.

MASTER JACQUES: Just a minute. This is the coachman's job. (*Puts on his coat again.*) You were saying, sir?

HARPAGON: I must have my carriage cleaned and the horses made ready to go to the fair.

MASTER JACQUES: Your horses, master? Upon my word, they are in no state for work. I can't say that they are down on their litter because the poor creatures haven't a scrap, and that's the truth of it. You keep them on such short commons that they are no more than ghosts or shadows of horses.

HARPAGON: They are in a bad way, then — but they never do anything!

MASTER JACQUES: Because they never do anything are they never to eat anything? It would be far better for them to work more, poor creatures, if they could only eat in proportion. It fair breaks my heart to see them so thin — for the fact is, I'm fond of my horses and I suffer along with them. Not a day passes but I go short myself to feed them. A man must be very hard-hearted, master, not to have pity for his fellow-creatures.

HARPAGON: It's no great job to go as far as the fair.

MASTER JACQUES: No, I haven't the heart to drive them, master, and I should be ashamed to use the whip to them in the state they are in. How do you expect them to pull the coach when they can hardly drag themselves along?

VALÈRE: I will arrange for Le Picard next door to drive them, sir. We shall want his help in preparing the supper, too.

MASTER JACQUES: Right. I'd far rather they died under someone else's hand than mine.

VALÈRE: You are a great talker, Master Jacques.

MASTER JACQUES: And you are a great meddler, Master Steward!

HARPAGON: Be quiet!

MASTER JACQUES: I can't stand flatterers, master, and I can see that everything he does, all his everlasting prying into the bread and the wine and the wood and the salt and the candles is nothing but back-scratching, all done to curry favour with you. That's bad enough, but on top of it all I have to put up with hearing what folk say about you and, after all, I have a soft spot for you, in spite of myself. Next to my horses I think more of you than anybody else.

HARPAGON: Would you mind telling me what people say about me?

MASTER JACQUES: Yes, master — if I could be sure it wouldn't annoy you.

HARPAGON: Not in the least.

MASTER JACQUES: Excuse me, but I know very well you'll be angry.

HARPAGON: On the contrary. I shall enjoy it. I like to know what people are saying about me.

MASTER JACQUES: Well, since you will have it, master, I'll tell you straight then — they make a laughing stock of you everywhere; we have scores of jokes thrown at us about you; there's nothing folk like better than running you down and making game of your stinginess. One tale is that you've had special almanacs printed with double the number of fast days and vigils so that you can save money by making your household keep additional fasts; another is that you are always ready to pick a quarrel with your servants when they have a present due to them or when they are leaving your service so that you don't have to give them anything: one fellow tells how you had the law on your neighbour's cat for eating the remains of a leg of mutton, another how you were caught one night stealing oats from your own horses and how your coachman, the one before me, gave you a drubbing in the dark and you never said anything about it; in fact, I'll tell you what it is, there's no going anywhere without hearing you pulled to pieces. You are a butt and a byword for everybody, and nobody ever refers to you except as a miser, a skinflint, and a niggardly old usurer.

HARPAGON (beating him): And you are a silly, rascally, scoundrelly, impudent rogue!

MASTER JACQUES: Ah, well! Didn't I guess as much? You wouldn't believe me. I said you'd be angry if I told you the truth.

HARPAGON: I'll teach you to talk like that. (He goes out.)

VALÈRE: You seem to have got a poor reward for your frankness, Master Jacques.

MASTER JACQUES: Upon my word, Mr. Upstart, you are mighty self-important, but it's no affair of yours. Keep your laughter for your own hidings when you get 'em. Don't come laughing at mine.

VALÈRE: Ah, my dear Master Jacques, please don't be annoyed —

MASTER JACQUES (*aside*): He's climbing down. I'll put on a bold front and give him a beating if he's fool enough to be frightened. (*to* VALÈRE) *You* may laugh, but I'd have you know that I'm not laughing, and if you get me annoyed I'll make you laugh on the other side of your face. (*Drives him across stage, threatening him.*)

VALÈRE: Go easy!

MASTER JACQUES: How d'ye mean, go easy? Suppose I don't choose to go easy.

VALÈRE: Please —

MASTER JACQUES: You are an impudent fellow!

VALÈRE: My dear Master Jacques —

MASTER JACQUES: I don't care tuppence for your dear Master Jacques. If I once take my stick to you I'll beat you black and blue.

VALÈRE: How d'ye mean, your stick! (VALÈRE *makes him retreat in his turn.*)

MASTER JACQUES: I didn't mean anything.

VALÈRE: Just understand, my dear fat-head, that if anyone's going to feel the stick you are the one!

MASTER JACQUES: I don't doubt it.

VALÈRE: And that you are only a good-for-nothing cook when all's said and done.

MASTER JACQUES: Yes, I know I am.

VALÈRE: And that you don't half know me yet.

MASTER JACQUES: Please forgive me!

VALÈRE: Did you say that you'd beat me?

MASTER JACQUES: It was only a joke.

VALÈRE: Well, I don't like your jokes. (*Beats him.*) Your jokes are in very bad taste. Just understand that. (*He goes out.*)

MASTER JACQUES: So much for sincerity! It's a poor sort of trade. From now on I've done with it. No more telling the truth. I can put up with my master. He's got some right to beat me, but as for this precious steward, I'll have my own back on him if I can.

(*Enter* MARIANNE *and* FROSINE.)

FROSINE: Do you know if the master is in, Master Jacques?

MASTER JACQUES: Ay, indeed he is. I know only too well.

FROSINE: Please tell him that we are here. (*He goes out.*)

MARIANNE: What a strange position to be in, Frosine! I must say I am dreading the meeting.

FROSINE: Why? What is there to worry about?

MARIANNE: Oh, dear! How can you ask! Can't you imagine what a girl feels when she is about to confront the fate that's in store for her.

FROSINE: I agree that Harpagon isn't what you would choose if you wanted a pleasant sort of death, and I guess from your expression that your thoughts still turn to the young man you were telling me about.

MARIANNE: Yes, I won't pretend to deny it, Frosine. The respectful manner in which he paid his visits to us made a most favourable impression upon me.

FROSINE: But did you find out who he is?

MARIANNE: No, I don't know in the least, but I do know that he is very attractive, and that if I had my own choice I would as soon have him as another. Indeed he makes me loathe this husband they have chosen for me all the more.

FROSINE: Good Lord, yes! these young sparks are all attractive enough, and can tell a good tale, but most of them are as poor as church mice. You would do much better to take an old husband with plenty of money. I admit it may seem to fly in the face of nature and there may well be some distasteful things to put up with, but then it won't be for long. When he dies you may be sure he'll leave you in a position to choose one you like better, and he'll make up for everything.

MARIANNE: But it doesn't seem right, Frosine, that one should have to look forward to someone else dying before one can be happy. Moreover, death doesn't always fall in with our schemes.

FROSINE: Don't be silly. You only marry him on the strict understanding that he leaves you a widow before very long. That must be put in the contract. It would be most inconsiderate of him if he didn't die within, say, three months! — But here comes the man himself.

MARIANNE: Oh, Frosine! What a face!

HARPAGON: Don't be offended, my dear, if I come to meet you with my spectacles on. I know that your charms are striking enough, sufficiently visible; they need no glasses to discover them, but it is through glass that one observes the stars, you know, and you yourself are a star, I declare, the loveliest one in all the firmament. (to FROSINE) Frosine, she doesn't say a word, and from what I can see she doesn't seem at all pleased to see me.

FROSINE: She is a little overcome. Young girls are always shy of showing their feelings at first.

HARPAGON: Perhaps you are right (to MARIANNE) Now my dearie, here is my daughter coming to greet you.

(Enter ÉLISE.)

MARIANNE: I fear I am late in paying my respects.

ÉLISE: On the contrary, I should have come to you first.

HARPAGON: You see what a big lass she is, but ill weeds do grow fast.

MARIANNE (aside to FROSINE): What a horrible man!

HARPAGON: What did my pretty one say?

FROSINE: She was saying how much she admires you.

HARPAGON: That's very kind of you, my pet.

MARIANNE (aside): Oh, what a creature!

HARPAGON: Very gratifying sentiments indeed!

MARIANNE (aside): I can bear it no longer.

(Enter CLÉANTE.)

HARPAGON: This is my son. He has come to pay his respects too.

MARIANNE (aside to FROSINE): Ah, Frosine! What an encounter. This is the very young man I was telling you about.

FROSINE (to MARIANNE): How very remarkable!

HARPAGON: I see you are surprised to find I have a grown-up family, but I shall be rid of both of them before long.

CLÉANTE: I must say this is a most unexpected meeting. I was completely taken aback when my father told me of his intentions a little while ago.

MARIANNE: I am in the same position. The meeting is as much a surprise to me as to you. I was quite unprepared for such a coincidence.

CLÉANTE: Truly, madam, my father could have made no better choice, and it is indeed a pleasure to meet you. All the same I cannot bring myself to say that I should welcome your becoming my stepmother. I must admit that the honour is not one I appreciate. Indeed the title, if I may say so, is the last one I should wish you to assume. All this might appear rude to some people, but you, I am sure, will know in what sense to take it, understand how repugnant this marriage must be to me, and how contrary to all my intentions. In short, I am sure you will allow me to say, with my father's kind permission, that if I had my way this marriage would never take place.

HARPAGON: That's a fine way of paying your respects. What a tale to be telling her!

MARIANNE: My answer is that I feel as you do. If you are loath to see me as your stepmother I am no less opposed to having you as a stepson. Please do not think it is by any wish of mine that you are placed in such a dilemma. I should be grieved to cause you distress, and had I any freedom of choice I should never consent to a marriage which would cause you unhappiness.

HARPAGON: She's quite right. Answer a fool according to his folly. I must apologize, my dear, for my son's silliness. He is young and foolish and doesn't yet understand what he is saying.

MARIANNE: I am not the least offended, I assure you. On the contrary, it has been a pleasure to hear your son express his feelings so frankly. I value such an avowal coming from him. Had he spoken otherwise I should not esteem him so highly.

HARPAGON: It's very good of you to overlook his faults. He will get more sense as he grows older, and you'll find that his feelings will change.

CLÉANTE: Never, father! My feelings will not change. I ask the lady to believe that.

HARPAGON: You see what an absurd fellow he is. He gets worse and worse.

CLÉANTE: Would you have me be false to my love?

HARPAGON: Still at it? Kindly try a different tune!

CLÉANTE: Very well, then, since you wish me to speak in a different vein — permit me, madam, to put myself in my father's place and assure you that you are the most charming person I ever met, that the greatest happiness I could imagine would be to win your favour and that I would rather be your husband than the greatest king on earth. Yes, madam, to enjoy your love would be for me the height of good fortune, and that is indeed my only ambition. There is nothing that I would not do to achieve so enviable a purpose, and whatever the obstacles may be —

HARPAGON: Steady on, lad, if you don't mind.

CLÉANTE: I am addressing the lady on your behalf.

HARPAGON: Good Lord! I have a tongue of my own. I don't need you as my advocate. Here, bring some chairs.

FROSINE: No, I think it would be better if we set out for the fair at once, so as to get back earlier and have plenty of time to talk later.

HARPAGON: Have the horses put in the carriage, then. Please forgive me, my dear, for not having thought to provide some refreshment before you go.

CLÉANTE: I have arranged it, father. I told them to bring in a bowl of china oranges, lemons, and sweetmeats. I had them ordered on your behalf.

HARPAGON (in a whisper): Valère!

VALÈRE (to HARPAGON): He's out of his mind!

CLÉANTE: Do you think there is not enough, father? The lady will perhaps excuse any deficiency.

MARIANNE: There was no need to have troubled.

CLÉANTE: Did you ever see a finer diamond, madam, than the one my father has on his finger.

MARIANNE: It is very brilliant.

CLÉANTE (taking it from his father's finger and offering it to MARIANNE): You need to look at it from close to.

MARIANNE: It is certainly exquisite, so full of fire.

CLÉANTE (preventing MARIANNE from returning it): No, no, madam. It is in hands which are worthy of it now. My father has made a present of it to you.

HARPAGON: I have?

CLÉANTE: You do wish the lady to keep it for your sake, don't you, father?

HARPAGON (aside to CLÉANTE): What d'ye mean?

CLÉANTE (aside): What a question! (to MARIANNE) He means that I am to make you accept it.

MARIANNE: But I don't at all want to —

CLÉANTE: You really can't mean that! He would never hear of taking it back.

HARPAGON (aside): I can't bear it!

MARIANNE: It would be —

CLÉANTE (*still preventing her from returning it*): No, I assure you, he would be offended —

MARIANNE: Please —

CLÉANTE: Not at all!

HARPAGON (*aside*): Confound the —

CLÉANTE: You see how put out he is at your refusal.

HARPAGON (*aside*): You traitor!

CLÉANTE: You see! He's losing his patience.

HARPAGON (*whispers to* CLÉANTE, *threatening him*): You scoundrel!

CLÉANTE: It's not my fault, father; I'm doing the best I can to make her keep it, but she's very obstinate.

HARPAGON (*furious, whispers to* CLÉANTE): You blackguard!

CLÉANTE: You are making my father angry with me, madam.

HARPAGON (*as before*): You villain!

CLÉANTE: You will make him ill. Madam, please do not refuse any further.

FROSINE: Good Lord, what a fuss! Keep the ring since the gentleman wants you to.

MARIANNE: Rather than cause further annoyance I will keep it for the time being, but I will find another occasion to return it.

(*Enter* BRINDAVOINE.)

BRINDAVOINE: There's a man wanting to speak to you, sir.

HARPAGON: Tell him I'm busy. Tell him to come back another time.

BRINDAVOINE: He says he has some money for you.

HARPAGON: Excuse me. I'll be back presently.

(*Enter* LA MERLUCHE, *running. He knocks* HARPAGON *over.*)

LA MERLUCHE: Master!

HARPAGON: Oh! He's killed me.

CLÉANTE: What is it, father? Are you hurt?

HARPAGON: The scoundrel must have been bribed to break my neck by people who owe me money.

VALÈRE: It's nothing serious.

LA MERLUCHE: Master, I beg your pardon, I thought I was doing right to hurry.

HARPAGON: What did you come for, you scoundrel?

LA MERLUCHE: To tell you that your horses have cast their shoes.

HARPAGON: Have them taken to the smith at once.

CLÉANTE: While they are being shod I will do the honours of the house for you, father, and take the lady into the garden. I will have the refreshments taken out there.

HARPAGON: Valère, keep your eye on that stuff, and do, I implore you, save as much of it as you can so that it can go back to the shop.

VALÈRE: Very good, sir.

HARPAGON (*alone*): Oh what a scoundrel of a son! He's determined to ruin me!

ACT FOUR

CLÉANTE, MARIANNE, ÉLISE, FROSINE.

CLÉANTE: We'll do better to go in here. There's no one here to worry about, so we can talk openly.

ÉLISE: My brother has told me about his love for you. I know how trying your position must be and I assure you that you have my whole sympathy.

MARIANNE: It is a great comfort to know that one has the support of such a person as yourself, and I do hope you will always maintain the same friendliness for me. It is such a consolation in adversity.

FROSINE: Upon my word, it is most unlucky for both of you that you didn't let me into your secrets a bit earlier. I could have saved you all this trouble. I would never have let matters go the way they have done.

CLÉANTE: What's the use! It's my ill luck! It just had to happen this way. (*to* MARIANNE) What decisions have you come to, my dear?

MARIANNE: Alas! How can I come to any decisions? Dependent as I am on other people, what more can I do than hope for the best?

CLÉANTE: Is that all the help you can offer me? Just to hope for the best? No compassionate support? No helping hand? No positive token of your affection?

MARIANNE: What can I say? Put yourself in my place and tell me what I should do! Advise me! Command me! I will put myself in your hands, and I know that you will not ask more of me than honour and propriety permit.

CLÉANTE: But how can I do anything effective if you expect me to keep within the bounds of rigorous honour and scrupulous propriety?

MARIANNE: But what would you have me do? Even if I could disregard the scruples of my sex I must still consider my mother. She has always shown me the most tender affection. I could never bring myself to give her cause for sorrow. You must persuade her. Use every endeavour to gain her approval. I give you leave to say and do whatever you think necessary, and if the issue should depend on my declaring my love for you I shall be willing to avow to her all that I feel.

CLÉANTE: Frosine, dear Frosine, won't you help us out?

FROSINE: Goodness me! Need you ask? I should like to — with all my heart: I'm really quite kind-hearted, you know! I'm not hard by nature, and when I see people really and truly in love I'm only too willing to help them. The question is, what can we do?

CLÉANTE: Please, do think of something.

MARIANNE: Do make some suggestions.

ÉLISE: Find some way of undoing the mischief you've done.

FROSINE: It isn't so easy. (*to* MARIANNE) Your mother isn't altogether unreasonable. She might be persuaded to transfer to the son what she intended to bestow on the father. (*to* CLÉANTE) The real difficulty, as I see it, is that your father's your father!

CLÉANTE: Exactly!

FROSINE: What I mean is that he'll have a grievance if he finds his offer refused, and be in no mood to agree to your marriage. What we really need is that the refusal shall come from him. We must try to find some means of making him take a dislike to you, Marianne.

CLÉANTE: That's the idea.

FROSINE: Yes, I know it's the right idea. That's what we need, but how the deuce can we manage it? Wait a minute. Suppose we could produce someone, an elderly woman, say, with a touch of my sort of talent who could carry off the part of a lady of quality with the help of a few scratch retainers and some fancy title or other — a Marchioness or Viscountess of Lower Britanny, should we say — I might contrive to make your father believe she was a wealthy woman with a hundred thousand crowns in ready money and landed property as well, and that she was head over heels in love with him — so anxious to marry him that she would be willing to hand over all her money under the terms of the marriage contract. I don't doubt he'd listen to that proposition, for though I know he loves you very much (*to* MARIANNE) he loves money better. Once he has swallowed the bait and agreed to all that you want it wouldn't matter that he found out the truth when he came to examine our Marchioness's possessions more closely!

CLÉANTE: It sounds a most ingenious notion.

FROSINE: Leave it to me. I've just remembered a friend of mine who is the very person we want.

CLÉANTE: You can count on my showing my gratitude, Frosine, if you can carry it off.

Meanwhile, dear Marianne, let us make a start by winning over your mother. It would be a great deal accomplished if we could only break off the marriage. I do implore you to do all you can. Make use of her affection for you. Employ all your charm, and all the eloquence of looks and of speech that Heaven has endowed you with. Use all your gentle persuasions and tender entreaties, those endearing caresses of yours, and they will, I am sure, prove irresistible.

MARIANNE: I will do all I can. I won't forget anything you tell me.

(*Enter* HARPAGON.)

HARPAGON (*aside*): Ha! My son kissing the hand of his stepmother to be! And the stepmother to be doesn't seem to be offering much objection. Is there more in this than meets the eye?

ÉLISE: Here comes father.

HARPAGON: The carriage is ready. You can set out as soon as you like.

CLÉANTE: I will go with them, father, as you are not going.

HARPAGON: No, you stay here. They will get along very well by themselves, and I need you here.

(ÉLISE, MARIANNE, *and* FROSINE *go out*.)

HARPAGON: Well now, forget she's your stepmother and let me hear what you think of her?

CLÉANTE: What I think of her?

HARPAGON: Yes, her looks, her manners, her figure, her intelligence?

CLÉANTE: Oh — so so.

HARPAGON: Is that all you can say?

CLÉANTE: Well, frankly, she doesn't come up to what I expected. She's just a coquette — nothing more; her figure is not particularly graceful, her looks are no more than middling, and her intelligence is very ordinary. Don't think I'm trying to put you off, father. As stepmothers go I would as soon have her as anyone else.

HARPAGON: But you were telling her just now that —

CLÉANTE: Merely a few conventional compliments on your behalf, and purely to please you.

HARPAGON: So you wouldn't fancy her for yourself, then?

CLÉANTE: Me? Not in the least!

HARPAGON: I'm sorry about that. It cuts across an idea that was passing through my mind. Looking at her just now I began thinking about my age and the way people would talk about my marrying a girl so young, and I was on the point of giving up the idea, but as I had asked for her hand and pledged my word to her I would have let you have her, had you not taken a dislike to her.

CLÉANTE: You would have given her to me?

HARPAGON: Yes, to you.

CLÉANTE: In marriage?

HARPAGON: In marriage.

CLÉANTE: Listen. It's true that she's not exactly what I should choose, but, to please you, father, I am prepared to marry her if you want me to.

HARPAGON: No, I'm not so unreasonable as you think. I have no wish to make you marry a girl against your will.

CLÉANTE: No, but I'm willing to make the effort out of consideration for you.

HARPAGON: No, no! There's no happiness in marriage without love.

CLÉANTE: Well, perhaps that might come afterwards. They say that love often comes after marriage.

HARPAGON: No. I'm against taking chances where the man is concerned. I don't want to run any risk of things turning out badly. If you'd felt any inclination for her, that would have been fine and I'd have arranged for you to marry her instead of me, but, as it is, I'll stick to my original plan and marry her myself.

CLÉANTE: Very well, father, since that's how things stand I must disclose my real feelings and tell you our secret. The truth is that I have loved her since the first day I saw her. I was intending just now to ask your permission to marry her; it was only when you revealed your own feelings and for fear of displeasing you that I refrained from doing so.

HARPAGON: Have you visited her home?

CLÉANTE: Yes, father.

HARPAGON: Often?

CLÉANTE: Fairly often, considering what time there has been.

HARPAGON: And were you well received?

CLÉANTE: Very well, but without their knowing who I was. That was why Marianne was so surprised when she saw me just now.

HARPAGON: Did you tell her you loved her and that you intended to marry her?

CLÉANTE: Of course. I have even made some approach to her mother.

HARPAGON: And she entertained your proposals on her daughter's behalf?

CLÉANTE: Yes, she was very kind.

HARPAGON: And the daughter returns your affections?

CLÉANTE: If one may judge from appearances, I think she likes me a little.

HARPAGON (aside): I'm very pleased to have found all this out. It is just what I wanted to know. (to CLÉANTE) Right, my lad, you want to know what the position is? It's this. You'll just put this fancy of yours out of your head if you don't mind; you'll stop paying attentions to the lady I am intending to marry myself, and marry the woman I've chosen for you — and at once.

CLÉANTE: So that was your game, father! Very well! Since that's what things have come to, let me tell you this — I will never give up my love for Marianne, I will stop at nothing to prevent your having her, and even if you have the mother's consent I may find I have some resources on my side.

HARPAGON: What, you rascal! You have the audacity to trespass on my preserves!

CLÉANTE: It's you who are trespassing on mine. I was there first.

HARPAGON: Am I not your father? Aren't you bound to defer to my wishes?

CLÉANTE: This isn't a case where a son needs defer to his father. Love is no respecter of persons.

HARPAGON: I'll make *you* respect *me* — with a stick!

CLÉANTE: You will do no good with threats.

HARPAGON: You shall give up Marianne.

CLÉANTE: Never!

HARPAGON: Bring me a stick — at once!

(Enter MASTER JACQUES.)

MASTER JACQUES: Now, now, now, gentlemen! What *is* all this? What are you thinking about?

CLÉANTE: I'm beyond caring!

MASTER JACQUES: Steady, sir! Steady on!

HARPAGON: Talking to me like that! The impudence!

MASTER JACQUES (to HARPAGON): Now, master — please!

CLÉANTE: I won't budge an inch.

MASTER JACQUES (to CLÉANTE): What! to your father!

HARPAGON: Just let me get at him!

MASTER JACQUES: What! To your son! It would be different if you were talking to me!

HARPAGON: I'll make you the judge between us, Master Jacques, and prove that I'm right.

MASTER JACQUES: I agree. (to CLÉANTE) Just stand a bit farther away.

HARPAGON: I am in love with a young lady and mean to marry her, and now this scoundrel here has the impudence to fall in love with her too, and he wants to marry her, although I've told him he can't.

MASTER JACQUES: Oh! That's wrong of him.

HARPAGON: Don't you agree that it's shocking for a son to set up as his father's rival? Isn't he in duty bound, in respect for his father, to refrain from interfering with my intentions?

MASTER JACQUES: Oh yes, you are right, but let me have a word with him. Stay there! (He goes across stage to CLÉANTE.)

CLÉANTE: Very well. Since he has chosen you as the judge, I make no objection. It doesn't matter to me who it is, I'm quite willing to submit to your decision, Master Jacques.

MASTER JACQUES: That's very kind of you.

CLÉANTE: I'm in love with a young lady. She returns my affection and receives my offer of love sympathetically. Then my father decides to come along and upset everything by proposing to marry her himself.

MASTER JACQUES: Oh, that's very wrong of him!

CLÉANTE: Should he not be ashamed to be thinking of marriage at his age? Isn't it absurd for him to be falling in love? Wouldn't he do better to leave love-making to younger men, don't you think?

MASTER JACQUES: You are right. He can't really mean it! Just let me have a word with him. (Goes across to HARPAGON.) Now look, the lad isn't as bad as you make him out to be. He'll listen to reason. He says he knows the respect he owes to you — that he was carried away in the heat of the moment and that he is willing to do whatever you want, provided you show him more consideration and arrange for him to marry someone to his liking.

HARPAGON: Well then, Master Jacques, you can tell him that, on that understanding, he can count on me absolutely. I leave him free to choose any woman he likes — except Marianne.

MASTER JACQUES: Leave it to me. (Crosses to CLÉANTE.) Well now, your father is not so unreasonable as you make him out to be. He has given me to understand that it was your outburst of temper that annoyed him, and all he objects to is your method of going about things. He's ready to grant you anything you ask provided you do it nicely and show him the respect and obedience a son owes to his father.

CLÉANTE: Well then, Master Jacques, you can assure him that if only he will let me have Marianne he'll find me obedience itself and I'll do whatever he wishes in future.

MASTER JACQUES (to HARPAGON): It's all settled. He agrees to everything you said.

HARPAGON: That's splendid!

MASTER JACQUES (to CLÉANTE): Everything's settled. He's satisfied with your promises.

CLÉANTE: Thank Heaven for that!

MASTER JACQUES: Gentlemen! It only remains for you to talk it over together. You are now in complete agreement. You were going to fall out merely because you were misunderstanding each other.

CLÉANTE: My dear Master Jacques, I shall be eternally grateful to you.

MASTER JACQUES: Don't mention it, sir.

HARPAGON: I'm very pleased with you indeed, Master Jacques, and you deserve some reward. (He feels in his pocket. MASTER JACQUES holds out his hand, but HARPAGON pulls out his handkerchief and says) Well, be off. I shan't forget, I assure you.

MASTER JACQUES: Thank you kindly, sir. (He goes out.)

CLÉANTE: Father, I ask you to forgive me for having been so angry.

HARPAGON: It doesn't matter.

CLÉANTE: I am very sorry, I assure you.

HARPAGON: And I'm extremely pleased, for my part, to find you so reasonable.

CLÉANTE: It's very generous of you to forgive me so promptly.

HARPAGON: A father can always forgive his children's faults once they remember the duty they owe him.

CLÉANTE: What! Have you forgiven my outrageous behaviour?

HARPAGON: I *must* forgive it now that you show such obedience and respect.

CLÉANTE: I promise you, father, I shall remember your goodness to my dying day.

HARPAGON: And for my part I promise you shall have anything you want from me.

CLÉANTE: Why, father, what more can I ask now that you have given me Marianne?

HARPAGON: What's that?

CLÉANTE: I was saying how grateful I am, father, for what you have done for me. In giving me Marianne you have given me all I could wish for.

HARPAGON: Who said anything about giving you Marianne?

CLÉANTE: Why, you did, father!

HARPAGON: I did?

CLÉANTE: Of course!

HARPAGON: But it's you who promised to give her up.

CLÉANTE: Give her up?

HARPAGON: Yes.

CLÉANTE: Never!

HARPAGON: You've not given her up?

CLÉANTE: On the contrary, I'm more determined than ever to marry her.

HARPAGON: What! Are you starting all over again, you scoundrel!

CLÉANTE: Nothing shall ever make me change my mind.

HARPAGON: I'll see about that, you villain!

CLÉANTE: You can do what you like!

HARPAGON: Clear out of my sight!

CLÉANTE: With the greatest of pleasure.

HARPAGON: I've finished with you!

CLÉANTE: Right! Be finished, then.

HARPAGON: I renounce you!

CLÉANTE: Good!

HARPAGON: I disinherit you!

CLÉANTE: Anything you please.

HARPAGON: And I give you my curse!

CLÉANTE: Keep your gifts to yourself!

(*Exit* HARPAGON.)

LA FLÈCHE (*coming from the garden with a strong box*): Ah master, here you are, just in the nick of time. Quick! Follow me!

CLÉANTE: What is it?

LA FLÈCHE: Follow me, I tell you. We are in luck.

CLÉANTE: How d'ye mean?

LA FLÈCHE: Here's just what you are needing.

CLÉANTE: What is it?

LA FLÈCHE: I have had my eye on it all day.

CLÉANTE: But what is it?

LA FLÈCHE: Your father's treasure — I've lifted it!

CLÉANTE: How did you manage it?

LA FLÈCHE: I'll tell you all about it, but let us be off. I can hear him shouting.

(*They go.*)

HARPAGON (*calling 'Stop, thief!' in the garden. He enters hatless*): Thieves! Robbers! Assassins! Murderers! Justice! Merciful Heavens! I'm done for! I'm murdered! They've cut my throat; they've taken my money! Whoever can it be? Where's he gone to? Where is he now? Where is he hiding? How can I find him? Which way shall I go? Which way shan't I go? Is he here? Is he there? Who's that? Stop! (*Catching his own arm*) Give me my money back, you scoundrel! Ah, it's me! I'm going out of my mind! I don't know where I am or who I am or what I'm doing. Oh dear, my dear, darling money, my beloved, they've taken you away from me and now you are gone I have lost my strength, my joy and my consolation. It's all over with me. There's nothing left for me to do in the world. I can't go on living without you. It's the finish. I can't bear any more. I'm dying; I'm dead — and buried. Will nobody bring me to life again by giving me my beloved money back or telling me who has taken it? Eh? What d'ye say? There's nobody there! Whoever did it must have watched his opportunity well and chosen the very moment I was talking to my blackguard of a son. I must go. I'll demand justice. I'll have everyone in the house put to the torture, menservants, maidservants, son, daughter, everyone — myself included. What a crowd in here! I suspect the whole pack of 'em. They all look to me like the thief. Eh? What are they talking about over there? About the fellow that robbed me? What's that noise up there? Is the thief there? Please, I implore you, tell me if you know anything about him! Isn't he hiding among you? They are all looking at me. Now they are laughing. You'll see, they are all in it, beyond question, all involved in the robbery. Come on! Come quickly! Magistrates, police, provosts, judges, racks, gibbets, hangmen. I'll have everybody hanged, and, if I don't get my money back, I'll hang myself afterwards.

ACT FIVE

HARPAGON, *an* OFFICER *and his* CLERK.

OFFICER: You leave it to me! I know my job, thank the Lord! This isn't the first time I've had a case of theft to investigate. I only wish I'd as many bags of money as I've had people hanged.

HARPAGON: It's to the interest of every magistrate in the country to take hand in this case. If I don't get my money back I'll demand justice on justice itself.

OFFICER: We must go through the proper procedure. How much did you say there was in the box?

HARPAGON: Ten thousand crowns — in cash.

OFFICER: Ten thousand crowns!

HARPAGON: Ten thousand crowns!

OFFICER: A considerable theft.

HARPAGON: No punishment could be bad enough for a crime of this enormity. If it goes unpunished nothing, however sacred, will be safe.

OFFICER: In what denomination of coin was the money?

HARPAGON: In good *louis d'or* and *pistoles* of full weight.

OFFICER: And whom do you suspect of the theft?

HARPAGON: Everybody. Arrest the whole town and the suburbs as well.

OFFICER: If you'll take my advice, it's unwise to alarm people unduly. Let us try to go quietly and collect our evidence, and then — then we can proceed with the full rigour of the law to recover the sum you have lost.

MASTER JACQUES (*calling over his shoulder as he comes on stage*). I'll be coming back. Cut his throat at once and let them be singeing his feet for me and putting him in boiling water. Then string him up from the rafters.

HARPAGON: Who? The fellow who has stolen my money?

MASTER JACQUES: I was talking about the sucking pig your steward has just sent me. I mean to dress him for you according to my own special recipe.

HARPAGON: We aren't interested in all that. There are other things you have to talk to this gentleman about.

OFFICER: Now, don't be alarmed. I'm not the sort of fellow to get you into trouble. Everything shall be done quietly.

MASTER JACQUES: Is the gentleman one of your supper party?

OFFICER: In a case like this, friend, you must withhold nothing from your master.

MASTER JACQUES: Upon my word, sir, I'll show you all I know. I'll do the best that I can for you.

HARPAGON: We are not worrying about that!

MASTER JACQUES: If I don't give you as good a meal as I could wish, you must blame that steward of yours. He's clipped my wings with his economies.

HARPAGON: You scoundrel! It isn't supper we are concerned with. I want you to tell what you know about the money that has been stolen from me.

MASTER JACQUES: Has somebody stolen your money?

HARPAGON: Yes, you rogue, and I'll have you hanged if you don't give it back.

OFFICER: Good Lord! Don't be so hard on him. I can see by the look of him that he is an honest fellow, and he'll tell you what you want to know without need to put him in jail. Now, my lad, if you confess you'll come to no harm and you will get a suitable reward from your master. Someone has taken his money during the day and you must know something about it.

MASTER JACQUES (aside): Here's the very thing for getting my own back on that steward of ours. Ever since he arrived he's been the favourite. They won't listen to anybody but him. Moreover, I haven't forgotten the beating I had a while back.

HARPAGON: What are you muttering about now?

OFFICER: Let him alone. He's getting ready to tell you what you are wanting to know. I wasn't mistaken when I said he was an honest fellow.

MASTER JACQUES: If you want to know, master, I believe that precious steward of yours has done it.

HARPAGON: Valère?

MASTER JACQUES: Yes.

HARPAGON: He who seemed so trustworthy?

MASTER JACQUES: That's the man. I suspect he's the fellow who has robbed you.

HARPAGON: On what grounds do you suspect him?

MASTER JACQUES: On what grounds?

HARPAGON: Yes.

MASTER JACQUES: I suspect him on the grounds — that I suspect him.

OFFICER: But you must indicate what evidence you have.

HARPAGON: Did you see him hanging about the spot where I had put my money?

MASTER JACQUES: Yes, I did that! Where was your money?

HARPAGON: In the garden.

MASTER JACQUES: Exactly. He was hanging about the garden when I saw him. What was your money in?

HARPAGON: In a cash box.

MASTER JACQUES: The very thing! He had a cash box. I saw him with it.

HARPAGON: What sort of a cash box? I can easily tell if it was mine.

MASTER JACQUES: What sort of cash box?

HARPAGON: Yes, yes, yes.

MASTER JACQUES: Well — a sort of — like a cash box.

OFFICER: Yes, of course, but describe it a little so that we can see whether —

MASTER JACQUES: It was a big one.

HARPAGON: Mine was a small one.

MASTER JACQUES: Ay, it was small if you are going by size, but I meant it was big in that it had a big lot of money in it.

OFFICER: What colour was it?

MASTER JACQUES: What colour?

OFFICER: Yes.

MASTER JACQUES: A sort of — what's the word? Can't you help me to describe it?

HARPAGON: Eh?

MASTER JACQUES: It wasn't red, was it?

HARPAGON: No, grey.

MASTER JACQUES: That's it, a greyish red. That's what I meant.

HARPAGON: There's no doubt about it. It's certainly the same one. Write it down, sir, write down his evidence. Oh Lord! Whom can one trust after this? There's no certainty in anything any more. I shall begin to believe that I'm capable of robbing myself.

MASTER JACQUES: Here he comes, master. Whatever you do, don't go and tell him I told you.

(*Enter* VALÈRE.)

HARPAGON: Come here! Come and confess to the foulest, most dastardly crime that was ever committed.

VALÈRE: What can I do for you, sir?

HARPAGON: What, you scoundrel! Don't you blush for your crime?

VALÈRE: What crime are you talking about?

HARPAGON: What crime am I talking about! You infamous wretch! As if you didn't know very well what I'm talking about. It's no use your trying to hide it. The secret is out. I've just heard the whole story. To think of your taking advantage of my kindness and getting yourself into my household on purpose to betray me and play a trick like this on me.

VALÈRE: Well, sir, since you know all about it I won't attempt to excuse or deny it.

MASTER JACQUES (*aside*): So ho. Have I guessed better than I thought?

VALÈRE: I have been meaning to speak to you about it. I was waiting for a favourable opportunity, but since things have turned out as they have I can only ask you not to be angry, but be good enough to hear what I have to say in justification.

HARPAGON: And what sort of justification can you give, you scoundrelly thief?

VALÈRE: Ah sir, I hardly deserve epithets of that kind. It is true that I have put myself in the wrong with you, but, after all, my fault is a pardonable one.

HARPAGON: Pardonable! A stab in the back! A mortal injury!

VALÈRE: Please don't be angry. When you have heard what I have to say, you'll see that there is less harm done than you think.

HARPAGON: Less harm done than I think. My very heart's blood, you scoundrel!

VALÈRE: On a question of blood, sir, you haven't done badly. My rank is such that I shall not disgrace your blood and there's nothing in all this that I can't make amends for.

HARPAGON: And that's exactly what I intend that you shall do — you shall return what you've stolen from me.

VALÈRE: Your honour shall be fully satisfied, sir.

HARPAGON: There's no question of honour! Tell me, what on earth led you to do such a thing?

VALÈRE: Do you really need to ask?

HARPAGON: Of course I need ask!

VALÈRE: It was that little god who is always forgiven, whatever he makes people do. Love, I mean.

HARPAGON: Love!

VALÈRE: Of course.

HARPAGON: A pretty sort of love! Upon my word! Love of my gold pieces.

VALÈRE: No, sir, it was not your wealth that tempted me, not in the least. That's not what dazzled me! Let me assure you I have no aspirations whatever where your wealth is concerned, provided you let me keep the one treasure I already possess.

HARPAGON: No, indeed! By all the devils in Hell! You shan't keep it. The impudence! Wanting to keep what he's stolen.

VALÈRE: Do you really call it stealing?

HARPAGON: Do I really call it stealing? A treasure like that!

VALÈRE: Yes, a treasure indeed, and beyond question the most precious you have, but not lost to you in becoming mine. On my bended knees I beg you to accord me this most cherished of treasures. Surely you can't refuse your consent.

HARPAGON: I'll do nothing of the sort. What on earth are you talking about?

VALÈRE: We are promised to each other and sworn never to be parted.

HARPAGON: A wonderful promise! A very remarkable compact, I must say!

VALÈRE: Yes, we are bound to one another for ever.

HARPAGON: I'll put a stop to that, I promise you.

VALÈRE: Death alone shall part us.

HARPAGON: He must have my money on the brain!

VALÈRE: I have already told you, sir, that I was not moved to do what I have done by material considerations. My motive was not what you think, but a far nobler one.

HARPAGON: He'll be telling me next that it's sheer Christian charity set him wanting my money. But I'll see to that, and the law shall give me satisfaction on you, you impudent scoundrel.

VALÈRE: Do as you please. I am resigned to bear whatever violence you may resort to, but I do ask you to believe that if any fault has been committed I alone am guilty. Your daughter is in no way to blame.

HARPAGON: I should think not, indeed! It would be a queer thing if my daughter were involved in a crime like this. But I want to be seeing you make restoration. Where's the hiding-place?

VALÈRE: There's no question of restoration or of hiding-place since we have not left the house.

HARPAGON (aside): Oh, my treasure! (to VALÈRE) Not left the house, you say?

VALÈRE: No, sir.

HARPAGON: Now tell me — you haven't been tampering —

VALÈRE: Never! There you wrong both of us. My love is pure and honourable, and though I am so deeply in love —

HARPAGON (aside): Deeply in love — with my cash box?

VALÈRE: I would die sooner than harbour a single thought unworthy of one so kind and so modest as —

HARPAGON (aside): Modest — my cash box?

VALÈRE: I have asked nothing more than the pleasure of feasting my eyes upon her. Nothing base or unworthy has ever profaned the love which her beauty inspires in me.

HARPAGON (aside): Beauty — my cash box! You might think he was a lover talking of his mistress.

VALÈRE: Dame Claude knows the truth of the matter, sir. She can bear witness.

HARPAGON: Ha, so my servant is in the plot, is she?

VALÈRE: Yes, sir, she was a witness to our vows. Once she found that my intentions were honourable, she helped me to persuade your daughter to give me her promise and accept mine in return.

HARPAGON (aside): Fear of justice must have turned his brain! (to VALÈRE) What has my daughter to do with it?

VALÈRE: I am just saying, sir, that I had the greatest difficulty in persuading her to accept my advances.

HARPAGON: Accept your advances? Who?

VALÈRE: Why, your daughter, sir. It was not

until yesterday that she gave me her promise to marry me.

HARPAGON: *My* daughter has given her promise to marry *you?*

VALÈRE: Yes, sir — as I gave her mine in return.

HARPAGON: Heavens! Another disaster!

MASTER JACQUES (*to the* OFFICER): Write it down, mister! Write it all down!

HARPAGON: Trouble on trouble. Misfortune piled on misfortune. Come, sir, do your duty! Draw up the indictment and arrest him as a thief and a seducer as well.

VALÈRE: I have done nothing to deserve such a description. When you know who I am —

(*Enter* ÉLISE, MARIANNE, FROSINE.)

HARPAGON: Wretched girl! You are unworthy of a father like me. This is how you follow my precepts! You go and fall in love with a scoundrelly thief and promise to marry him without my consent. But you will both find you have made a mistake. (*to* ÉLISE) I'll keep you within four walls in future (*to* VALÈRE) and you shall pay for your audacity on the gallows.

VALÈRE: The question won't be decided by your getting angry. I shall at least be heard before I'm condemned.

HARPAGON: I was wrong when I said the gallows. You shall be broken on the wheel.

ÉLISE (*on her knees to* HARPAGON): Father, be merciful, I implore you. Do not push your parental rights to the limit. Don't let yourself be carried away in the first flush of anger. Take time to consider what you are doing. Take the trouble to find out a little more about the man you are so incensed against. He is not what he seems. You will be less surprised that I have given him my promise when you learn that you owe it to him that you haven't lost me already. Yes, it was he, father, who saved me from drowning. It is to him you owe your daughter's life and —

HARPAGON: All that amounts to nothing at all. I'd rather he had left you to drown than do what he has done.

ÉLISE: Father, I implore you by your love for me as a father —

HARPAGON: I won't hear any more. Justice must take its course.

MASTER JACQUES (*aside*): Now you shall pay for that beating you gave me.

FROSINE (*aside*): Here's a fine kettle of fish.

(*Enter* ANSELME.)

ANSELME: What is the trouble, Mr. Harpagon? You seem very much upset.

HARPAGON: Ah, Mr. Anselme. You see in me the most unlucky of men. All sorts of trouble and difficulty have arisen over the contract you have come to sign. I have suffered deadly blows both to my fortune and my reputation. This treacherous scoundrel here has wormed his way into my household in defiance of every sacred obligation, stolen my money and seduced my daughter.

VALÈRE: Who cares anything about your money that you keep making such a song about?

HARPAGON: They've got themselves engaged to be married — that's an insult to you, Mr. Anselme. You must bring an action against him, at your own expense, and get your revenge for his insolence with all the rigour of the law.

ANSELME: I have no intention of forcing anyone to marry me. I make no claim to any affection which is already given elsewhere, but, in so far as your own interests may be involved, you can count on me to support them as my own.

HARPAGON: This gentleman here is a very honest officer who has assured me he'll not fail to do everything his duty requires. (*to the* OFFICER) Charge him with everything he can be charged with and see that you make things black against him.

VALÈRE: I fail to see how loving your daughter

can be accounted a crime! As for the punishment you think will be meted out to me for aspiring to her hand, when you know who I am —

HARPAGON: I don't give a rap for your stories. The world is full of self-styled nobility nowadays, impostors who take advantage of their own obscurity to assume the first illustrious name that comes into their heads!

VALÈRE: I should scorn to lay claim to anything that doesn't belong to me, let me tell you. Anyone in Naples can bear witness to my birth and family.

ANSELME: Gently! Mind what you are saying. You are running more risk than you think. You are speaking in the presence of one who knows Naples well and will see through any tale you invent.

VALÈRE (*proudly putting on his hat*): I have nothing to fear. If you know Naples you know who Don Thomas d'Alburci was.

ANSELME: I knew him well! Few better!

HARPAGON: I care nothing for Don Thomas or Don Martin either! (*He notices two candles burning, and blows one out.*)

ANSELME: Please — let him speak. Let us hear what he has to say.

VALÈRE: I say that he was my father.

ANSELME: *Your* father?

VALÈRE: Yes.

ANSELME: Come now! You are joking. Try a fresh tale and you may do better. You will do yourself no good with this one.

VALÈRE: Take care what you say! This is no tale. I don't make statements that I cannot easily prove.

ANSELME: What! You dare pretend that you are Thomas d'Alburci's son?

VALÈRE: I do, and I will maintain it against all comers.

ANSELME: What astounding effrontery! Let me tell you that the man you refer to was lost at sea more than sixteen years ago with his wife and children while fleeing from the cruel persecutions which accompanied the disorders in Naples, when so many noble families were driven into exile.

VALÈRE: Yes, and let me tell *you* that his son, a boy of seven years of age, was saved from the wreck along with one servant by a Spanish ship, and that it is that son who is now speaking to you. Let me tell you also that the ship's captain took compassion upon me, brought me up as his own son, and that I have followed a career of arms from my earliest years. It is only recently that I learned that my father did not perish as I had always believed. I set out in search of him, and, passing through this town, I met, by a happy chance, my beloved Élise and fell under the spell of her beauty. Such was the effect of my love and her father's intransigence that I decided to take service in his household and send someone else in search of my parents.

ANSELME: But what proof can you offer beyond your own word that this is not just a story built upon some foundation of truth?

VALÈRE: The Spanish captain, a ruby signet ring which belonged to my father, an agate bracelet my mother clasped on my own arm, and lastly, old Pedro himself, who escaped from the shipwreck along with me.

MARIANNE: Now I myself can vouch for the truth of what you have told us. I realize now that you are my brother.

VALÈRE: Can you be my sister?

MARIANNE: Yes. My heart was strangely moved from the very moment you began to speak. My mother — how overjoyed she will be to see you — has recounted our family misfortunes to me a thousand times. Heaven so willed that we too survived that unhappy shipwreck, but we did so at the cost of our liberty. The men who saved my mother and myself from a fragment of wreckage were corsairs. After ten years of slavery we regained our freedom by a stroke of good fortune and returned to Naples. There we found that our possessions had been sold and that there was no news of my father. We took ship thence to Genoa where my mother went to collect the miserable remnants of a despoiled inheritance. Fleeing from the inhumanity of her family she came to these parts, where she has since languished.

ANSELME: Oh Lord! How wonderful are the manifestations of thy power! How true it is that Heaven alone can accomplish miracles! Come to my arms, my children, and mingle your happiness with your father's.

VALÈRE: You are our father?

MARIANNE: It was you my mother so lamented?

ANSELME: Yes, my daughter. Yes, my son. I am Don Thomas d'Alburci. By the mercy of Heaven I was saved from the waves with all the money I had with me. For sixteen years I have believed you all drowned. After many wanderings I was about to seek to renew the consolations of domestic felicity by marriage to a good woman. Uncertain of my safety if I returned to Naples, I renounced my country for ever and, having contrived to dispose of all I had there, I settled down in this place and sought, under the name of Anselme, to forget the misfortunes which the other name had brought upon me.

HARPAGON: Is this your son?

ANSELME: It is.

HARPAGON: Then I shall hold you responsible for paying me the ten thousand crowns he has stolen from me.

ANSELME: Stolen from you?

HARPAGON: Yes, this same fellow.

VALÈRE: Who told you that?

HARPAGON: Master Jacques.

MASTER JACQUES: Oh! You know I've never said a word!

HARPAGON: Oh, yes you did, and the officer here wrote it all down.

VALÈRE: Do you think me capable of such an action?

HARPAGON: Capable or incapable. I want my money back.

(*Enter* CLÉANTE *and* LA FLÈCHE.)

CLÉANTE: Don't worry any more, father. Don't accuse anybody. I have news of your money. I come to tell you you can have it all back, provided you let me marry Marianne.

HARPAGON: Where is the money?

CLÉANTE: Don't you worry. It is where I can answer for it. It rests entirely with me. Just say what you want to do. Take your choice. Either give me Marianne or give up your money.

HARPAGON: Is it all there?

CLÉANTE: Every bit. Decide whether you will agree to the marriage and join her mother in giving consent. She has left her daughter free to choose between us: you — or me.

MARIANNE: You are overlooking the fact that my mother's consent is now not sufficient. Heaven has restored my brother to me and my father. You need his consent now.

ANSELME: Heaven has not brought me back to you, dear children, to oppose your own wishes. Mr. Harpagon, you must be aware that a young girl is likely to prefer a son to his father. Come then, don't force me to say what I would much rather not. Join me in giving consent to this double marriage.

HARPAGON: I can't decide until I see my cash box again.

CLÉANTE: You shall — safe and sound.

HARPAGON: I have no money for marriage portions.

ANSELME: Well, I have enough for both, so that needn't worry you.

HARPAGON: And you'll undertake to meet the costs of both marriages?

ANSELME: Yes, I agree. Now are you satisfied?

HARPAGON: Provided you buy me new clothes for the wedding.

ANSELME: Agreed. Come, let us go and enjoy the pleasures of this happy day.

OFFICER: Heh! Gentlemen, just a minute, if you don't mind. Who is going to pay for my depositions?

HARPAGON: We want nothing to do with your depositions.

OFFICER: Yes, but I don't intend to work for nothing, not likely!

HARPAGON: There's that fellow there! (*Pointing to* MASTER JACQUES.) Take him and hang him for payment.

MASTER JACQUES: Oh dear! What's a fellow to do! First I'm beaten for telling the truth and now they are going to hang me for telling lies.

ANSELME: Come, Mr. Harpagon, we must forgive him his untruths.

HARPAGON: Will you pay the officer, then?

ANSELME: So be it, but let us go at once and share our joy with your mother.

HARPAGON: And let me go and see my beloved cash box again.

CURTAIN

The School For Scandal

The great hits of the London theatre in the eighteenth century were Joseph Addison's *Cato* (1713), which set the tone of elevated and emotional tragedy; John Gay's *Beggar's Opera* (1728), which was followed by a long line of ballad operas but was never equalled for good cheer combined with satiric bite; and George Lillo's *The London Merchant* (1730), which, though Charles Lamb later denounced it as making "uncle-murder too trivial," according to the theatre historians Freedley and Reeves "changed the whole course of English tragedy" and spawned the French *tragédie bourgeoise* (that angered Voltaire) and innumerable Dutch, German, and other imitations. But those, and the theatrical successes of the next century in England (which the reader can find in my *Nineteenth-Century British Drama*, which fills in the gap between Sheridan and Shaw), we have to omit and for a sample of Enlightened England's drama we offer not Gay's immortal "Newgate pastoral" nor Lillo's "nauseous sermon" but "the best comedy of manners in our language," as one critic raved, "and the best play of any kind since Shakespeare": *The School for Scandal*.

The comedy of manners, satirizing social and psychological types in an artificial and sophisticated society, employing clever plots and sparkling dialogue to betray people's aberrations from sensible behavior, we have seen in *The Country Wife* and might trace to Oscar Wilde's scintillating *The Importance of Being Earnest* and beyond. Our eighteenth-century example, one of the most often revived plays and among the most loved, is from Wilde's fellow Irishman Richard Brinsley Sheridan.

Much earlier playwrights like Ben Jonson (1572–1637) wanted in comedy "to mix profit with your pleasure" and (like Molière later) used exaggerated characters, driven by predominating "humours" and affectations, to satirize society, castigate folly, and improve morals. Even when the Restoration was more interested in wit than in wisdom, comedy had a bite to it. But then came Colley Cibber (1671–1757) and Sentimental Comedy. In reaction to Restoration rakes and raillery came writers who pronounced Restoration wit "disserviceable to probity and religion" and fed the new burghers in the theatres Cibber's *Love's Last Shift* (1696) and *The Careless Husband* (1704), Sir Richard Steele's *The Tender Husband* (1705) and *The Conscious Lovers* (1722) and a spate of saccharine successors, well-meant but dull comedies that succeeded in praising virtue without ridiculing vice and moving the audience to tears by "tender strokes of art." In Hugh

Kelly's *False Delicacy* (1768) and Richard Cumberland's *The West Indian* (1771), to name but a few of the comedies that kept pace with the sentimental tragedies of Nicholas Rowe, Edward Moore, and John Home, there were conscientious lovers, delicate sensibilities, noble and high-minded heroes, and pitiful vicissitudes crowned by happy endings that were as contrived as the conclusions of Victorian melodramas. Going to see a comedy through most of the eighteenth century, the prudent armed themselves with several handkerchiefs: it was not that one expected to laugh oneself to tears but rather that tears had replaced laughter.

Then two Irishmen, Oliver Goldsmith (1728–1774) author of a novel about his father called *The Vicar of Wakefield*, and Richard Brinsley Sheridan (1754–1816) decided it was time for Thalia, Muse of Comedy, to smile again. They re-introduced Laughing Comedy. With *The Good-Natur'd Man* (1768), Goldsmith had passable success with a protest against Sentimental Comedy; and *She Stoops to Conquer* (1773), a triumph of Laughing Comedy, is still stage-worthy. Sheridan's great contribution to the *genre* was *The School for Scandal* (1777). At the climax of Sheridan's play, tradition says, the delight of the audience was so deafening that passersby in Drury Lane feared for the fate of the old building, "so violent and tumultuous were the applause and laughter "

Sheridan had learned his theatre skills early: his father was a teacher of elocution and an actor; his mother had written a couple of plays. As a schoolboy, Sheridan himself penned a three-act farce and later parlayed success as a playwright (*The Rivals*, 1775, introducing the deathless Mrs. Malaprop) and financial management into control of The Theatre-Royal in Drury Lane, taking over from the celebrated actor-manager David Garrick. With a thorough understanding of the stage — and a sense of humor about it: see *The Critic* of 1779 — he was able to build in *The School for Scandal* (which Taine called "the most brilliant fireworks imaginable") a piece of dramatic machinery that is still running. Pulling together elements of romantic Shakespearian comedy and classical Jonsonian comedy, the wit of Restoration comedy, and what Lamb called the "sentimental incompatibilities" of Sentimental Comedy, the comedy of humours and the comedy of manners, comedy of character and comedy of situation, humor and farce, Sheridan produced a somewhat superficial but sparkling satire which though it could not entirely escape the sentimentalism of the period has long outlived it.

As these remarks suggest, the structure of the play is as complex as the tone is uneven: different scenes present simultaneous actions and the two brothers (Joseph and Charles Surface) are sharply contrasted: they are to be deprecated in one case and laughed at in the other. From scene to scene the tone changes but without the effect that the juxtaposition of farce and pathos creates in *The Cherry Orchard*. In one plot, the gossipy Lady Teazle and Lady Sneerwell (who is in love with Joseph Surface) are involved with him; in the other Joseph and his brother Charles are tested by their uncle, Sir Oliver. The two plots — "obstreperously fictional," says Louis Kronenberger — brilliantly come together in the famous "Screen Scene," while through it all run fully-realized minor characters (such as Maria) and Snake who, of course, snakes through the intrigues. Sneerwell counsels Joseph Surface in the last act to be "only constant in one roguery at a time," but Sheridan successfully juggles several. Examine how convincing are the motivations he provides for his various characters; how credible his manipulation of cause and effect, circumstances and coincidences; and how the secret of holding the whole dazzling display together is just this: the basic compatibility of his two subjects, gossip and hypocrisy. See if you can catch Sheridan playing with ironies and even taking short cuts in exposition by the use of old-fashioned devices such as soliloquies, which were still feasible in a theatre where the actors paraded in front of the scenery rather than in a box set, near to the audience in the pit and the boxes. In performance everything in *The School for Scandal* moves so swiftly and so distractingly that one abandons attempts to anatomize, but you can, in reading the play, take advantage of the opportunity to go backstage, as it were, and watch the performance from the wings. From this vantage point, as pointed out in the general introduction, some of the magic and the illusion are lost, but sometimes it is fun to uncover the conjurer's tricks so that the skill in his legerdemain can be better appreciated. Then, when you understand how the whole thing works, borrow a recorded version from the library and listen to it, all dancing and virtuoso twittering voices, dazzling and delightful, intoxicating.

The English producer Gilbert Miller told a teen-age Noël Coward, just beginning his career, that "the construction of a play is as important as the foundation of a house — whereas the dialogue, however good, can only be considered an interior decoration." *The School for Scandal* is as good a play as any to use as evidence in debating that remark. In the examination of these elements (*together*, "rather than," as Henry James would say, "as if they had a kind of internecine distinctness") the student will learn important facts about drama. Throughout this anthology we have stressed the relationship of drama and theatre. With *The School for Scandal* the need for anthologies is further justified: it is a play whose theatrical presentation can be so dazzling that for close structural and verbal analysis the study of printed text is essential. Remember, however, that drama and theatre have no "internecine distinctness" either.

THE SCHOOL FOR SCANDAL

Richard Brinsley Sheridan

DRAMATIS PERSONÆ

Sir PETER TEAZLE
Sir OLIVER SURFACE
JOSEPH SURFACE ⎫
CHARLES SURFACE ⎰ [*his nephews*]
CRABTREE
Sir BENJAMIN BACKBITE
ROWLEY
MOSES
TRIP
SNAKE
CARELESS
Sir TOBY BUMPER
Lady TEAZLE
MARIA
Lady SNEERWELL
Mrs. CANDOUR

The Scene: LONDON in the last quarter of the Eighteenth Century.

PROLOGUE

WRITTEN BY MR. [DAVID] GARRICK*

Spoken by Mr. Thomas King, the actor who played Sir PETER TEAZLE *in 1777.*

A school for scandal! tell me, I beseech you,
Needs there a school this modish art to teach
    you?
No need of lessons now, the knowing think;
We might as well be taught to eat and drink.

Caused by a dearth of scandal, should the
    vapors
Distress our fair ones, let them read the papers;
Their powerful mixtures such disorders hit,
Crave what you will, — there's *quantum
    sufficit.*[1]

"Lord!" cries my Lady Wormwood, who loves
    tattle

And puts much salt and pepper in her prattle,
Just risen at noon, all night at cards when
    threshing
Strong tea and scandal, — "Bless me, how
    refreshing!

Give me the papers, Lisp, — how bold and
    free! (*Sips*)
Last night Lord L. (*Sips*) *was caught with Lady
    D.*
For aching head what charming sal volatile!
    (*Sips*)

*If Mrs. B. will still continue flirting,
We hope she'll draw, or we'll undraw the
    curtain.*
Fine satire, poz![2] In public all abuse it,
But by ourselves (*Sips*) our praise we can't
    refuse it.

Now, Lisp, read you, — there at that dash and
    star."
"Yes, ma'am. *A certain lord had best beware,
Who lives not twenty miles from Grosvenor
    Square,
For, should he Lady W. find willing,
Wormwood is bitter* — " "Oh! that's me! the
    villain!

Throw it behind the fire and never more
Let that vile paper come within my door.
Thus at our friends we laugh, who feel the
    dart;
To reach our feelings, we ourselves must smart.

Is our young bard so young to think that he
Can stop the full spring-tide of calumny?
Knows he the world so little, and its trade?
Alas! the devil's sooner raised than laid.

So strong, so swift, the monster there's no
    gagging;
Cut Scandal's head off, still the tongue is
    wagging.
Proud of your smiles once lavishly bestowed,[3]
Again our young Don Quixote takes the road;

---

* An early editor, Rhodes, printed the text as it appeared in *The Town and Country Magazine* for June, 1777. He says Mr. King spoke it.
1 *quantum sufficit:* enough (as in a prescription). **2** *poz:* positively. **3** *bestowed:* for *The Rivals* (1775).

To show his gratitude he draws his pen
And seeks this hydra, Scandal, in his den.
For your applause all perils he would
   through, —
He'll fight (that's write) a cavalliero true,
Till every drop of blood (that's ink) is spilt
   for you.

ACT ONE

SCENE ONE   Lady Sneerwell's House.

Discovered, LADY SNEERWELL *at the dressing
table;* SNAKE *drinking chocolate.*

LADY SNEERWELL: The paragraphs, you say, Mr.
Snake, were all inserted?

SNAKE: They were, madam; and as I copied
them myself in a feigned hand, there can be
no suspicion whence they came.

LADY SNEERWELL: Did you circulate the report
of Lady Brittle's intrigue with Captain Boast-
all?

SNAKE: That's in as fine a train as your ladyship could wish. In the common course of
things, I think it must reach Mrs. Clackitt's
ears within four-and-twenty hours; and then,
you know, the business is as good as done.

LADY SNEERWELL: Why, truly, Mrs. Clackitt has
a very pretty talent and a great deal of
industry.

SNAKE: True, madam, and has been tolerably
successful in her day. To my knowledge, she
has been the cause of six matches being
broken off and three sons being disinherited;
of four forced elopements and as many close
confinements; nine separate maintenances
and two divorces. Nay, I have more than
once traced her causing a *tête-à-tête* in the
Town and Country Magazine[1] when the
parties, perhaps, had never seen each other's
face before in the course of their lives.

LADY SNEERWELL: She certainly has talents, but
her manner is gross.

SNAKE: 'Tis very true. She generally designs
well, has a free tongue and a bold invention;

but her coloring is too dark and her outlines
often extravagant.[2] She wants that delicacy
of tint and mellowness of sneer which distinguish your ladyship's scandal.

LADY SNEERWELL: You are partial, Snake.

SNAKE: Not in the least; everybody allows that
Lady Sneerwell can do more with a word or
look than many can with the most labored
detail, even when they happen to have a
little truth on their side to support it.

LADY SNEERWELL: Yes, my dear Snake; and I
am no hypocrite to deny the satisfaction I
reap from the success of my efforts. Wounded myself in the early part of my life by the
envenomed tongue of slander, I confess I
have since known no pleasure equal to the
reducing others to the level of my own reputation.

SNAKE: Nothing can be more natural. But, Lady
Sneerwell, there is one affair in which you
have lately employed me, wherein, I confess,
I am at a loss to guess your motives.

LADY SNEERWELL: I conceive you mean with
respect to my neighbor, Sir Peter Teazle, and
his family?[3]

SNAKE: I do. Here are two young men to whom
Sir Peter has acted as a kind of guardian
since their father's death, the eldest possessing the most amiable character and universally well spoken of, the youngest, the most
dissipated and extravagant young fellow in
the kingdom, without friends or character;
the former an avowed admirer of your ladyship and apparently your favorite; the latter
attached to Maria, Sir Peter's ward, and con-
fessedly beloved by her. Now, on the face
of these circumstances, it is utterly un-
accountable to me why you, the widow of
a city knight, with a good jointure, should

---

1 In January, 1777, one of these scandalous vignettes
was of a Mrs. Abington, the actress who created the
character of Lady Teazle (Rhodes). 2 *coloring,* etc.: it
is discussed as an art, like painting. 3 *my neighbor:*
an awkward piece of exposition. Look for other examples throughout the play but judge it by the standards and customs of its time, not ours.

not close with the passion of a man of such character and expectations as Mr. Surface; and more so, why you should be so uncommonly earnest to destroy the mutual attachment subsisting between his brother Charles and Maria.

LADY SNEERWELL: Then at once to unravel this mystery, I must inform you that love has no share whatever in the intercourse between Mr. Surface and me.

SNAKE: No!

LADY SNEERWELL: His real attachment is to Maria, or to her fortune; but finding in his brother a favored rival, he has been obliged to mask his pretensions and profit by my assistance.

SNAKE: Yet still I am more puzzled why you should interest yourself in his success.

LADY SNEERWELL: Heavens! how dull you are! Cannot you surmise the weakness which I hitherto, through shame, have concealed even from you? Must I confess that Charles, that libertine, that extravagant, that bankrupt in fortune and reputation, — that he it is for whom I am thus anxious and malicious, and to gain whom I would sacrifice everything?

SNAKE: Now, indeed, your conduct appears consistent; but how came you and Mr. Surface so confidential?

LADY SNEERWELL: For our mutual interest. I have found him out a long time since. I know him to be artful, selfish, and malicious, — in short, a sentimental knave, while with Sir Peter, and indeed with all his acquaintance, he passes for a youthful miracle of prudence, good sense, and benevolence.

SNAKE: Yes! Yet Sir Peter vows he has not his equal in England; and, above all, he praises him as a man of sentiment.

LADY SNEERWELL: True; and with the assistance of his sentiment and hypocrisy he has brought Sir Peter entirely into his interest with regard to Maria, while poor Charles has no friend in the house, though I fear he has a powerful one in Maria's heart, against whom we must direct our schemes.

(*Enter* SERVANT.)

SERVANT: Mr. Surface.

LADY SNEERWELL: Show him up.

(*Exit* SERVANT.)

(*Enter* JOSEPH SURFACE.)

JOSEPH SURFACE: My dear Lady Sneerwell, how do you do to-day? Mr. Snake, your most obedient.

LADY SNEERWELL: Snake has just been rallying me on our mutual attachment; but I have informed him of our real views. You know how useful he has been to us, and, believe me, the confidence is not ill placed.

JOSEPH SURFACE: Madam, it is impossible for me to suspect a man of Mr. Snake's sensibility and discernment.

LADY SNEERWELL: Well, well, no compliments now; but tell me when you saw your mistress, Maria, — or what is more material to me, your brother.

JOSEPH SURFACE: I have not seen either since I left you; but I can inform you that they never meet. Some of your stories have taken a good effect on Maria.

LADY SNEERWELL: Ah, my dear Snake, the merit of this belongs to you. But do your brother's distresses increase?

JOSEPH SURFACE: Every hour. I am told he has had another execution in the house yesterday. In short, his dissipation and extravagance exceed anything I have ever heard of.

LADY SNEERWELL: Poor Charles!

JOSEPH SURFACE: True, madam, notwithstanding his vices, one can't help feeling for him. Poor Charles! I'm sure I wish it were in my power to be of any essential service to him, for the man who does not share in the distress of a brother, even though merited by his own misconduct, deserves —

LADY SNEERWELL: O lud! you are going to be moral and forget that you are among friends.

JOSEPH SURFACE: Egad, that's true! I'll keep that sentiment till I see Sir Peter. However, it is certainly a charity to rescue Maria from such a libertine, who, if he is to be reclaimed, can be so only by a person of your ladyship's superior accomplishments and understanding.

SNAKE: I believe, Lady Sneerwell, here's company coming. I'll go and copy the letter I mentioned to you. Mr. Surface, your most obedient.

JOSEPH SURFACE: Sir, your very devoted. — (*Exit* SNAKE.) Lady Sneerwell, I am very sorry you have put any farther confidence in that fellow.

LADY SNEERWELL: Why so?

JOSEPH SURFACE: I have lately detected him in frequent conference with old Rowley, who was formerly my father's steward and has never, you know, been a friend of mine.

LADY SNEERWELL: And do you think he would betray us?

JOSEPH SURFACE: Nothing more likely. Take my word for 't, Lady Sneerwell, that fellow hasn't virtue enough to be faithful even to his own villainy. Ah, Maria!

(*Enter* MARIA.)

LADY SNEERWELL: Maria, my dear, how do you do? What's the matter?

MARIA: Oh! there's that disagreeable lover of mine, Sir Benjamin Backbite, has just called at my guardian's with his odious uncle, Crabtree; so I slipped out and ran hither to avoid them.

LADY SNEERWELL: Is that all?

JOSEPH SURFACE: If my brother Charles had been of the party, madam, perhaps you would not have been so much alarmed.

LADY SNEERWELL: Nay, now you are too severe, for I dare swear the truth of the matter is, Maria heard you were here. But, my dear, what has Sir Benjamin done that you should avoid him so?

MARIA: Oh, he has done nothing; but 'tis for what he has said. His conversation is a perpetual libel on all his acquaintance.

JOSEPH SURFACE: Ay, and the worst of it is, there is no advantage in not knowing him for he'll abuse a stranger just as soon as his best friend; and his uncle's as bad.[4]

LADY SNEERWELL: Nay, but we should make allowance; Sir Benjamin is a wit and a poet.

MARIA: For my part, I own, madam, wit loses its respect with me when I see it in company with malice. What do you think, Mr. Surface?

JOSEPH SURFACE: Certainly, madam. To smile at the jest which plants a thorn in another's breast is to become a principal in the mischief.

LADY SNEERWELL: Psha, there's no possibility of being witty without a little ill nature. The malice of a good thing is the barb that makes it stick. What's your opinion, Mr. Surface?

JOSEPH SURFACE: To be sure, madam, that conversation where the spirit of raillery is suppressed will ever appear tedious and insipid.

MARIA: Well, I'll not debate how far scandal may be allowable; but in a man, I am sure, it is always contemptible. We have pride, envy, rivalship, and a thousand motives to depreciate each other; but the male slanderer must have the cowardice of a woman before he can traduce one.

(*Enter* SERVANT.)

SERVANT: Madam, Mrs. Candour is below and, if your ladyship's at leisure, will leave her carriage.

LADY SNEERWELL: Beg her to walk in. (*Exit* SERVANT.) Now, Maria, here is a character to your taste, for though Mrs. Candour is a little talkative, everybody allows her to be the best natured and best sort of woman.

---

4 *abuse a stranger:* watch for sly (and sometimes not so sly) digs like this in the dialogue. The implication here is that the libeller has no loyalty to his "best friend," that being his "friend" is dangerous, etc.

MARIA: Yes, with a very gross affectation of good-nature and benevolence, she does more mischief than the direct malice of old Crabtree.

JOSEPH SURFACE: I' faith that's true, Lady Sneerwell. Whenever I hear the current running against the characters of my friends, I never think them in such danger as when Candour undertakes their defence.

LADY SNEERWELL: Hush! — Here she is.

(*Enter* MRS. CANDOUR.)

MRS. CANDOUR: My dear Lady Sneerwell, how have you been this century? Mr. Surface, what news do you hear, — though indeed it is no matter, for I think one hears nothing else but scandal.

JOSEPH SURFACE: Just so, indeed, ma'am.

MRS. CANDOUR: Oh, Maria, child! What, is the whole affair off between you and Charles? His extravagance, I presume — the town talks of nothing else.

MARIA: I am very sorry, ma'am, the town is not better employed.

MRS. CANDOUR: True, true, child; but there's no stopping people's tongues. I own I was hurt to hear it, as I indeed was to learn from the same quarter that your guardian, Sir Peter, and Lady Teazle have not agreed lately as well as could be wished.

MARIA: 'Tis strangely impertinent for people to busy themselves so.

MRS. CANDOUR: Very true, child, but what's to be done? People will talk; there's no preventing it. Why, it was but yesterday I was told that Miss Gadabout had eloped with Sir Filigree Flirt. But, Lord, there's no minding what one hears, though, to be sure, I had this from very good authority.

MARIA: Such reports are highly scandalous.

MRS. CANDOUR: So they are, child, — shameful, shameful! But the world is so censorious, no character escapes. Lord, now who would have suspected your friend, Miss Prim, of an indiscretion? Yet such is the ill nature of people that they say her uncle stopped her last week just as she was stepping into the York diligence with her dancing master.

MARIA: I'll answer for 't there are no grounds for that report.

MRS. CANDOUR: Ah, no foundation in the world, I dare swear; no more probably than for the story circulated last month of Mrs. Festino's affair with Colonel Cassino, — though, to be sure, that matter was never rightly cleared up.

JOSEPH SURFACE: The license of invention some people take is monstrous indeed.

MARIA: 'Tis so; but in my opinion those who report such things are equally culpable.

MRS. CANDOUR: To be sure they are; tale bearers are as bad as the tale makers. 'Tis an old observation and a very true one; but what's to be done, as I said before? How will you prevent people from talking? To-day, Mrs. Clackitt assured me Mr. and Mrs. Honeymoon were at last become mere man and wife like the rest of their acquaintance. She likewise hinted that a certain widow in the next street had got rid of her dropsy and recovered her shape in a most surprising manner. And at the same time Miss Tattle, who was by, affirmed that Lord Buffalo had discovered his lady at a house of no extraordinary fame; and that Sir H[arry] Boquet and Tom Saunter were to measure swords on a similar provocation. But, Lord, do you think I would report these things! No, no! Tale bearers as I said before, are just as bad as the tale makers.

JOSEPH SURFACE: Ah! Mrs. Candour, if everybody had your forbearance and good nature!

MRS. CANDOUR: I confess, Mr. Surface, I cannot bear to hear people attacked behind their backs; and when ugly circumstances come out against our acquaintance, I own I always love to think the best. By the by, I hope 'tis not true that your brother is absolutely ruined.

JOSEPH SURFACE: I am afraid his circumstances are very bad indeed, ma'am.

MRS. CANDOUR: Ah, I heard so; but you must tell him to keep up his spirits. Everybody almost is in the same way. Lord Spindle, Sir Thomas Splint, Captain Quinze, and Mr. Nickit, — all up,[5] I hear, within this week; so, if Charles is undone, he'll find half his acquaintance ruined too; and that, you know, is a consolation.

JOSEPH SURFACE: Doubtless, ma'am, a very great one.

(*Enter* SERVANT.)

SERVANT: Mr. Crabtree and Sir Benjamin Backbite. (*Exit.*)

LADY SNEERWELL: So, Maria, you see your lover pursues you. Positively you shan't escape.

(*Enter* CRABTREE *and* SIR BENJAMIN BACKBITE.)

CRABTREE: Lady Sneerwell, I kiss your hand. Mrs. Candour, I don't believe you are acquainted with my nephew, Sir Benjamin Backbite? Egad, ma'am, he has a pretty wit and is a pretty poet too, isn't he, Lady Sneerwell?

SIR BENJAMIN: Oh, fie, uncle!

CRABTREE: Nay, egad, it's true; I back him at a rebus or a charade against the best rhymer in the kingdom. Has your ladyship heard the epigram he wrote last week on Lady Frizzle's feather catching fire? — Do, Benjamin, repeat it, or the charade you made last night extempore at Mrs. Drowzie's *conversazione*. Come, now, your first is the name of a fish, your second a great naval commander, and —

SIR BENJAMIN: Uncle, now, prithee —

CRABTREE: I' faith, ma'am, 'twould surprise you to hear how ready he is at all these sort of things.

LADY SNEERWELL: I wonder, Sir Benjamin, you never publish anything.

SIR BENJAMIN: To say truth, ma'am, 'tis very vulgar to print; and, as my little productions are mostly satires and lampoons on particular people, I find they circulate more by giving copies in confidence to the friends of the parties. However, I have some love elegies, which, when favoured with this lady's smiles, I mean to give the public.

(*Indicating* MARIA.)

CRABTREE: 'Fore heaven, ma'am, they'll immortalize you! — You will be handed down to posterity like Petrarch's Laura or Waller's Sacharissa.[6]

SIR BENJAMIN: Yes, madam, I think you will like them when you shall see them on a beautiful quarto page, where a neat rivulet of text shall meander through a meadow of margin. 'Fore gad they will be the most elegant things of their kind!

CRABTREE: But, ladies, that's true — Have you heard the news?

MRS. CANDOUR: What, sir, do you mean the report of —

CRABTREE: No, ma'am, that's not it. Miss Nicely is going to be married to her own footman.

MRS. CANDOUR: Impossible!

CRABTREE: Ask Sir Benjamin.

SIR BENJAMIN: 'Tis very true, ma'am. Everything is fixed and the wedding liveries bespoke.

CRABTREE: Yes; and they do say there were pressing reasons for it.

LADY SNEERWELL: Why, I have heard something of this before.

MRS. CANDOUR: It can't be — And I wonder anyone should believe such a story of so prudent a lady as Miss Nicely.

SIR BENJAMIN: O lud! ma'am, that's the very reason 'twas believed at once. She has always been so cautious and so reserved that everybody was sure there was some reason for it at bottom.

---

5 *all up:* bankrupt. 6 Laura was the heroine and inspiration of the sonnets of Francesco Petrarca (1304–1374). "Sacharissa" — no pun intended on saccharine — was the name given to Lady Dorothy Sidney in the poems of Edmund Waller (1606–1687).

MRS. CANDOUR: Why, to be sure, a tale of scandal is as fatal to the credit of a prudent lady of her stamp as a fever is generally to those of the strongest constitutions. But there is a sort of puny, sickly reputation that is always ailing, yet will outlive the robuster characters of a hundred prudes.

SIR BENJAMIN: True, madam, there are valetudinarians in reputation as well as in constitution, who, being conscious of their weak part, avoid the least breath of air and supply their want of stamina by care and circumspection.

MRS. CANDOUR: Well, but this may be all a mistake. You know, Sir Benjamin, very trifling circumstances often give rise to the most injurious tales.

CRABTREE: That they do, I'll be sworn, ma'am. Did you ever hear how Miss Piper came to lose her lover and her character last summer at Tunbridge? Sir Benjamin, you remember it?

SIR BENJAMIN: Oh, to be sure, — the most whimsical circumstance.

LADY SNEERWELL: How was it, pray?

CRABTREE: Why, one evening at Mrs. Ponto's assembly the conversation happened to turn on the breeding of Nova Scotia sheep in this country. Says a young lady in company, "I have known instances of it, for Miss Letitia Piper, a first cousin of mine, had a Nova Scotia sheep that produced her twins." "What," cries the Lady Dowager Dundizzy, who, you know, is as deaf as a post, "has Miss Piper had twins?" This mistake, as you may imagine, threw the whole company into a fit of laughter. However, 'twas next morning everywhere reported, and in a few days believed by the whole town, that Miss Letitia Piper had actually been brought to bed of a fine boy and a girl; and in less than a week there were some people who could name the father and the farm-house where the babies were put to nurse.[7]

LADY SNEERWELL: Strange, indeed!

CRABTREE: Matter of fact, I assure you. — O lud, Mr. Surface, pray is it true that your uncle, Sir Oliver, is coming home?

JOSEPH SURFACE: Not that I know of, indeed, sir.

CRABTREE: He has been in the East Indies a long time. You can scarcely remember him, I believe? Sad comfort, whenever he returns, to hear how your brother has gone on.

JOSEPH SURFACE: Charles has been imprudent, sir, to be sure; but I hope no busy people have already prejudiced Sir Oliver against him. He may reform.

SIR BENJAMIN: To be sure, he may. For my part, I never believed him to be so utterly void of principle as people say; and, though he has lost all his friends, I am told nobody is better spoken of by the Jews.

CRABTREE: That's true, egad, nephew. If the Old Jewry was a ward, I believe Charles would be an alderman. No man is more popular there, 'fore gad! I hear he pays as many annuities as the Irish tontine;[8] and that whenever he is sick, they have prayers for the recovery of his health in all the synagogues.

SIR BENJAMIN: Yet no man lives in greater splendor. They tell me that when he entertains his friends he will sit down to dinner with a dozen of his own securities, have a score of tradesmen waiting in the antechamber, and an officer behind every guest's chair.

JOSEPH SURFACE: This may be entertaining to you, gentlemen, but you pay very little regard to the feelings of a brother.

MARIA (aside): Their malice is intolerable! — Lady Sneerwell, I must wish you a good morning; I'm not very well. (Exit.)

---

7 *put to nurse:* the practice of "baby-farming," or hiring women to suckle babies of the rich, continued into the nineteenth century. 8 *tontine:* The seventeenth-century Italian banker Lorenzo Tonti invented a type of insurance which, adapted by acts of the Irish Parliament (1773, 1775, 1777), provided annuities for subscribers at whose death the capital went to the government revenues.

MRS. CANDOUR: O dear, she changes color very much!

LADY SNEERWELL: Do, Mrs. Candour, follow her. She may want assistance.

MRS. CANDOUR: That I will, with all my soul, ma'am. Poor dear girl, who knows what her situation may be! (*Exit.*)

LADY SNEERWELL: 'Twas nothing but that she could not bear to hear Charles reflected on, notwithstanding their difference.

SIR BENJAMIN: The young lady's *penchant* is obvious.

CRABTREE: But, Benjamin, you must not give up the pursuit for that. Follow her and put her into good humour. Repeat her some of your own verses. Come, I'll assist you.

SIR BENJAMIN: Mr. Surface, I did not mean to hurt you; but depend on 't your brother is utterly undone.

CRABTREE: O lud, ay! Undone as ever man was! Can't raise a guinea!

SIR BENJAMIN: And everything sold, I'm told, that was moveable.

CRABTREE: I have seen one that was at his house. Not a thing left but some empty bottles that were overlooked and the family pictures, which I believe are framed in the wainscots.

SIR BENJAMIN: And I'm very sorry also to hear some bad stories against him. (*Going.*)

CRABTREE: Oh, he has done many mean things, that's certain.

SIR BENJAMIN: But, however, as he's your brother — (*Going.*)

CRABTREE: We'll tell you all another opportunity.

(*Exeunt* CRABTREE *and* SIR BENJAMIN.)

LADY SNEERWELL: Ha! ha! 'tis very hard for them to leave a subject they have not quite run down.

JOSEPH SURFACE: And I believe the abuse was no more acceptable to your ladyship than Maria.

LADY SNEERWELL: I doubt her affections are farther engaged than we imagine. But the family are to be here this evening; so you may as well dine where you are and we shall have an opportunity of observing farther. In the meantime, I'll go and plot mischief and you shall study sentiment. (*Exeunt.*)

SCENE TWO   Sir Peter's House.

Enter SIR PETER.

SIR PETER: When an old bachelor marries a young wife, what is he to expect? 'Tis now six months since Lady Teazle made me the happiest of men, — and I have been the most miserable dog ever since! We tiffed a little going to church and fairly quarreled before the bells had done ringing. I was more than once nearly choked with gall during the honeymoon and had lost all comfort in life before my friends had done wishing me joy. Yet I chose with caution, — a girl bred wholly in the country, who never knew luxury beyond one silk gown nor dissipation above the annual gala of a race ball. Yet she now plays her part in the extravagant fopperies of the fashion and the town with as ready a grace as if she never had seen a bush or a grass-plot out of Grosvenor Square. I am sneered at by all my acquaintance and paragraphed in the newspapers. She dissipates my fortune and contradicts all my humors; yet the worst of it is, I doubt [not] I love her, or I should never bear all this. However, I'll never be weak enough to own it.

(*Enter* ROWLEY.)

ROWLEY: Oh, Sir Peter, your servant! How is it with you, sir?

SIR PETER: Very bad, Master Rowley, very bad. I meet with nothing but crosses and vexations.

ROWLEY: What can have happened to trouble you since yesterday?

SIR PETER: A good question to a married man!

ROWLEY: Nay, I'm sure your lady, Sir Peter, can't be the cause of your uneasiness.

SIR PETER: Why, has anybody told you she was dead?

ROWLEY: Come, come, Sir Peter, you love her, notwithstanding your tempers don't exactly agree.

SIR PETER: But the fault is entirely hers, Master Rowley. I am myself the sweetest tempered man alive and hate a teasing temper; and so I tell her a hundred times a day.

ROWLEY: Indeed!

SIR PETER: Ay; and what is very extraordinary in all our disputes she is always in the wrong. But Lady Sneerwell and the set she meets at her house encourage the perverseness of her disposition. Then, to complete my vexation, Maria, my ward, whom I ought to have the power over, is determined to turn rebel too and absolutely refuses the man whom I have long resolved on for her husband, meaning, I suppose, to bestow herself on his profligate brother.

ROWLEY: You know, Sir Peter, I have always taken the liberty to differ with you on the subject of these two young gentlemen. I only wish you may not be deceived in your opinion of the elder. For Charles, my life on 't, he will retrieve his errors yet. Their worthy father, once my honored master, was at his years nearly as wild a spark; yet when he died, he did not leave a more benevolent heart to lament his loss.

SIR PETER: You are wrong, Master Rowley. On their father's death, you know, I acted as a kind of guardian to them both till their uncle Sir Oliver's liberality gave them an early independence. Of course, no person could have more opportunities of judging of their hearts, and I was never mistaken in my life. Joseph is indeed a model for the young men of the age. He is a man of sentiment and acts up to the sentiments he professes; but for the other, take my word for 't, if he had any grain of virtue by descent, he has dissipated it with the rest of his inheritance. Ah! my old friend Sir Oliver will be deeply mortified when he finds how part of his bounty has been misapplied.

ROWLEY: I am sorry to find you so violent against the young man, because this may be the most critical period of his fortune. I came hither with news that will surprise you.

SIR PETER: What? Let me hear!

ROWLEY: Sir Oliver is arrived and at this moment in town.

SIR PETER: How! You astonish me! I thought you did not expect him this month.

ROWLEY: I did not; but his passage has been remarkably quick.

SIR PETER: Egad, I shall rejoice to see my old friend. 'Tis fifteen years since we met. We have had many a day together. But does he still enjoin us not to inform his nephews of his arrival?

ROWLEY: Most strictly. He means, before it is known, to make some trial of their dispositions.

SIR PETER: Ah! There needs no art to discover their merits. He shall have his way; but, pray, does he know I am married?

ROWLEY: Yes, and will soon wish you joy.

SIR PETER: What, as we drink health to a friend in a consumption? Ah! Oliver will laugh at me. We used to rail at matrimony together, and he has been steady to his text. Well, he must be soon at my house, though — I'll instantly give orders for his reception. But, Master Rowley, don't drop a word that Lady Teazle and I ever disagree.

ROWLEY: By no means.

SIR PETER: For I should never be able to stand Noll's jokes; so I'll have him think, Lord forgive me! that we are a very happy couple.

ROWLEY: I understand you; but then you must be very careful not to differ while he is in the house with you.

SIR PETER: Egad, and so we must, — and that's impossible. Ah! Master Rowley, when an old bachelor marries a young wife,[1] he deserves

---

1 *old bachelor marries a young wife:* a typical subject of the Restoration comedy of wit. Find other examples of such in the play and contrast *The Country Wife* and *The School for Scandal*.

— No, the crime carries its punishment along with it. (*Exeunt.*)

ACT TWO

Scene One   Sir Peter's House.

Enter Sir Peter *and* Lady Teazle.

Sir Peter: Lady Teazle, Lady Teazle, I'll not bear it!

Lady Teazle: Sir Peter, Sir Peter, you may bear it or not as you please; but I ought to have my own way in everything, and, what's more, I will, too. What though I was educated in the country, I know very well that women of fashion in London are accountable to nobody after they are married.

Sir Peter: Very well, ma'am, very well; so a husband is to have no influence, no authority?

Lady Teazle: Authority! No, to be sure! If you wanted authority over me, you should have adopted me and not married me. I am sure you were old enough.

Sir Peter: Old enough! Ay, there it is. Well, well, Lady Teazle, though my life may be made unhappy by your temper, I'll not be ruined by your extravagance.

Lady Teazle: My extravagance! I'm sure I'm not more extravagant then a woman of fashion ought to be.

Sir Peter: No, no, madam, you shall throw away no more sums on such unmeaning luxury. 'Slife! to spend as much to furnish your dressing-room with flowers in winter as would suffice to turn the Pantheon[1] into a greenhouse and give a *fête champêtre*[2] at Christmas.

Lady Teazle: And am I now to blame, Sir Peter, because flowers are dear in cold weather? You should find fault with the climate and not with me. For my part, I'm sure I wish it was spring all the year round and that roses grew under our feet!

Sir Peter: Oons, madam! If you had been born to this, I shouldn't wonder at your talking thus; but you forget what your situation was when I married you.

Lady Teazle: No, no, I don't. 'Twas a very disagreeable one, or I should never have married you.

Sir Peter: Yes, yes, madam, you were then in somewhat a humbler style, — the daughter of a plain country squire. Recollect, Lady Teazle, when I saw you first, sitting at your tambour[3] in a pretty figured linen gown with a bunch of keys at your side, your hair combed smooth over a roll and your apartment hung round with fruits in worsted of your own working.

Lady Teazle: Oh, yes! I remember it very well, and a curious life I led. My daily occupation to inspect the dairy, superintend the poultry, make extracts from the family receipt-book, and comb my Aunt Deborah's lap-dog.

Sir Peter: Yes, yes, ma'am, 'twas so indeed.

Lady Teazle: And then you know, my evening amusements! To draw patterns for ruffles, which I had not materials to make up; to play Pope Joan[4] with the curate; to read a sermon to my aunt; or to be stuck down to an old spinet to strum my father to sleep after a fox-chase.

Sir Peter: I am glad you have so good a memory. Yes, madam, these were the recreations I took you from; but now you must have your coach, — *vis-à-vis*,[5] — and three powdered footmen before your chair, and in the summer a pair of white cats[6] to draw you to Kensington Gardens. No recollection, I suppose, when you were content to ride

---

1 *Pantheon*: a fashionable concert hall, with tea-rooms and other amenities, opened in Oxford Street in 1770. See Fanny Burney's *Evelina*. 2 *fête champêtre*: French, a picnic on the grass. 3 *tambour*: a ring for holding cloth to be embroidered. 4 *Pope Joan*: an old-fashioned, simple card game (cf. fish). 5 *vis-à-vis*: French, "face to face," referring to the seating arrangements for four people. 6 *cats*: probably should be "cobs," ponies (Rae).

double behind the butler on a docked coach-horse.

LADY TEAZLE: No — I swear I never did that. I deny the butler and the coach-horse.

SIR PETER: This, madam, was your situation; and what have I done for you? I have made you a woman of fashion, of fortune, of rank, — in short, I have made you my wife.

LADY TEAZLE: Well, then, and there is but one thing more you can make me to add to the obligation, that is —

SIR PETER: My widow, I suppose?

LADY TEAZLE: Hem! hem!

SIR PETER: I thank you, madam; but don't flatter yourself; for, though your ill conduct may disturb my peace, it shall never break my heart, I promise you. However, I am equally obliged to you for the hint.

LADY TEAZLE: Then why will you endeavor to make yourself so disagreeable to me and thwart me in every little elegant expense?

SIR PETER: 'Slife, madam, I say; had you any of these little elegant expenses when you married me?

LADY TEAZLE: Lud, Sir Peter, would you have me be out of the fashion?

SIR PETER: The fashion, indeed! What had you to do with the fashion before you married me?

LADY TEAZLE: For my part, I should think you would like to have your wife thought a woman of taste.

SIR PETER: Ay! There again! Taste! Zounds, madam, you had no taste when you married me!

LADY TEAZLE: That's very true, indeed, Sir Peter; and, having married you, I should never pretend to taste again, I allow. But now, Sir Peter, since we have finished our daily jangle, I presume I may go to my engagement at Lady Sneerwell's.

SIR PETER: Ay, there's another precious circumstance! A charming set of acquaintance you have made there!

LADY TEAZLE: Nay, Sir Peter, they are all people of rank and fortune and remarkably tenacious of reputation.

SIR PETER: Yes, egad, they are tenacious of reputation with a vengeance, for they don't choose anybody should have a character but themselves! Such a crew! Ah, many a wretch has rid on a hurdle[7] who has done less mischief than these utterers of forged tales, coiners of scandal, and clippers of reputation.

LADY TEAZLE: What, would you restrain the freedom of speech!

SIR PETER: Ah! they have made you just as bad as any one of the society.

LADY TEAZLE: Why, I believe I do bear a part with a tolerable grace. But I vow I bear no malice against the people I abuse. When I say an ill-natured thing, 'tis out of pure good humor; and I take it for granted they deal exactly in the same manner with me. But, Sir Peter, you know you promised to come to Lady Sneerwell's, too.

SIR PETER: Well, well, I'll call in just to look after my own character.

LADY TEAZLE: Then, indeed, you must make haste after me, or you'll be too late. So good by to ye!

(Exit.)

SIR PETER: So I have gained much by my intended expostulation! Yet with what a charming air she contradicts everything I say, and how pleasantly she shows her contempt for my authority! Well, though I can't make her love me, there is great satisfaction in quarreling with her; and I think she never appears to such advantage as when she is doing everything in her power to plague me.

(Exit.)

SCENE TWO   At Lady Sneerwell's.

Enter LADY SNEERWELL, MRS. CANDOUR, CRABTREE, SIR BENJAMIN BACKBITE, *and* JOSEPH SURFACE.

---

7 hurdle: "rail" say some editors, but what is meant is a rough cart or tumbril on which criminals were taken to execution.

LADY SNEERWELL: Nay, positively, we will hear it.

JOSEPH SURFACE: Yes, yes, the epigram, by all means.

SIR BENJAMIN: O plague on it, uncle! 'Tis mere nonsense.

CRABTREE: No, no! 'Fore gad, very clever for an extempore!

SIR BENJAMIN: But, ladies, you should be acquainted with the circumstance. You must know that one day last week as Lady Betty Curricle was taking the dust in Hyde Park in a sort of duodecimo phaëton,[1] she desired me to write some verses on her ponies, upon which I took out my pocketbook and in one moment produced the following: —

Sure never were seen two such beautiful
    ponies;
Other horses are clowns, but these
    macaronies.
To give them this title I'm sure can't be
    wrong,
Their legs are so slim and their tails are so
    long.

CRABTREE: There, ladies, done in the smack of a whip and on horseback too!

JOSEPH SURFACE: A very Phœbus mounted! Indeed, Sir Benjamin!

SIR BENJAMIN: Oh, dear sir! Trifles, trifles.

(*Enter* LADY TEAZLE *and* MARIA.)

MRS. CANDOUR: I must have a copy.

LADY SNEERWELL: Lady Teazle, I hope we shall see Sir Peter?

LADY TEAZLE: I believe he'll wait on your ladyship presently.

LADY SNEERWELL: Maria, my love, you look grave. Come, you shall sit down to piquet with Mr. Surface.

MARIA: I take very little pleasure in cards; however I'll do as you please.

LADY TEAZLE (*aside*): I am surprised Mr. Surface should sit down with her; I thought she would have embraced this opportunity of speaking to me before Sir Peter came.

MRS. CANDOUR: Now, I'll die; but you are so scandalous I'll forswear your society.

LADY TEAZLE: What's the matter, Mrs. Candour?

MRS. CANDOUR: They'll not allow our friend Miss Vermilion to be handsome.

LADY SNEERWELL: Oh, surely she is a pretty woman.

CRABTREE: I am very glad you think so, ma'am.

MRS. CANDOUR: She has a charming, fresh color.

LADY TEAZLE: Yes, when it is fresh put on.

MRS. CANDOUR: Oh, fie! I'll swear her color is natural. I have seen it come and go.

LADY TEAZLE: I dare swear you have, ma'am; it goes off at night and comes again in the morning.

SIR BENJAMIN: True, ma'am, it not only comes and goes; but what's more, egad, her maid can fetch and carry it!

MRS. CANDOUR: Ha, ha, ha! How I hate to hear you talk so! But surely, now, her sister is, or was, very handsome.

CRABTREE: Who? Mrs. Evergreen? O Lord! She's six-and-fifty if she's an hour!

MRS. CANDOUR: Now positively you wrong her; fifty-two or fifty-three in the utmost, — and I don't think she looks more.

SIR BENJAMIN: Ah! There's no judging by her looks unless one could see her face.

LADY SNEERWELL: Well, well, if Mrs. Evergreen does take some pains to repair the ravages of time, you must allow she effects it with great ingenuity; and surely that's better than

---

1 *duodecimo phaëton:* a phaëton is a carriage and "duodecimo" (taken from a size of books) means diminutive.

the careless manner in which the widow Ochre chalks her wrinkles.

SIR BENJAMIN: Nay, now, Lady Sneerwell, you are severe upon the widow. Come, come, 'tis not that she paints so ill; but, when she has finished her face, she joins it so badly to her neck that she looks like a mended statue in which the connoisseur may see at once that the head's modern though the trunk's antique.

CRABTREE: Ha! ha! ha! Well said, nephew!

MRS. CANDOUR: Ha! ha! ha! Well, you make me laugh; but I vow I hate you for it. What do you think of Miss Simper?

SIR BENJAMIN: Why, she has very pretty teeth.

LADY TEAZLE: Yes; and on that account, when she is neither speaking nor laughing, which very seldom happens, she never absolutely shuts her mouth, but leaves it always on a-jar, as it were; thus — (*Shows her teeth.*)

MRS. CANDOUR: How can you be so ill natured?

LADY TEAZLE: Nay, I allow even that's better than the pains Mrs. Prim takes to conceal her losses in front. She draws her mouth till it positively resembles the aperture of a poor's-box, and all her words appear to slide out edgewise, as it were; thus: *How do you do, madam? Yes, madam.*

LADY SNEERWELL: Very well, Lady Teazle. I see you can be a little severe.

LADY TEAZLE: In defence of a friend it is but justice. But here comes Sir Peter to spoil our pleasantry.

(*Enter* SIR PETER.)

SIR PETER: Ladies, your most obedient. — (*aside*) Mercy on me, here is the whole set! A character dead at every word, I suppose.

MRS. CANDOUR: I am rejoiced you are come, Sir Peter. They have been so censorious, and Lady Teazle as bad as any one.

SIR PETER: That must be very distressing to you, Mrs. Candour, I dare swear.

MRS. CANDOUR: Oh, they will allow good qualities to nobody, not even good nature to our friend Mrs. Pursy.

LADY TEAZLE: What, the fat dowager who was at Mrs. Quadrille's last night?

MRS. CANDOUR: Nay, her bulk is her misfortune; and, when she takes so much pains to get rid of it, you ought not to reflect on her.

LADY SNEERWELL: That's very true, indeed.

LADY TEAZLE: Yes, I know she almost lives on acids and small whey; laces herself by pulleys; and often in the hottest noon in summer you may see her on a little squat pony, with her hair plaited up behind like a drummer's and puffing round the Ring[2] on a full trot.

MRS. CANDOUR: I thank you, Lady Teazle, for defending her.

SIR PETER: Yes, a good defence, truly.

MRS. CANDOUR: Truly, Lady Teazle is as censorious as Miss Sallow.

CRABTREE: Yes, and she is a curious being to pretend to be censorious, an awkward gawky without any one good point under heaven.

MRS. CANDOUR: Positively you shall not be so very severe. Miss Sallow is a near relation of mine by marriage, and, as for her person, great allowance is to be made; for, let me tell you, a woman labors under many disadvantages who tries to pass for a girl of six-and-thirty.

LADY SNEERWELL: Though, surely, she is handsome still; and for the weakness in her eyes, considering how much she reads by candlelight, it is not to be wondered at.

MRS. CANDOUR: True, and then as to her manner; upon my word, I think it is particularly graceful, considering she never had the least education; for you know her mother was a Welsh milliner and her father a sugar-baker at Bristol.

---

2 *Ring:* The fashionable drive in Hyde Park laid out by King Charles II.

SIR BENJAMIN: Ah! you are both of you too good natured!

SIR PETER (*aside*): Yes, damned good natured! This their own relation! Mercy on me!

MRS. CANDOUR: For my part, I own I cannot bear to hear a friend ill spoken of.

SIR PETER: No, to be sure!

SIR BENJAMIN: Oh, you are of a moral turn. Mrs. Candour and I can sit for an hour and hear Lady Stucco talk sentiment.

LADY TEAZLE: Nay, I vow Lady Stucco is very well with the dessert after dinner, for she's just like the French fruit[3] one cracks for mottoes, made up of paint and proverb.

MRS. CANDOUR: Well, I never will join in ridiculing a friend; and so I constantly tell my cousin Ogle, and you all know what pretensions she has to be critical on beauty.

CRABTREE: Oh, to be sure, she has herself the oddest countenance that ever was seen; 'tis a collection of features from all the different countries of the globe.

SIR BENJAMIN: So she has, indeed! An Irish front —

CRABTREE: Caledonian locks —

SIR BENJAMIN: Dutch nose —

CRABTREE: Austrian lips —

SIR BENJAMIN: Complexion of a Spaniard —

CRABTREE: And teeth *à la Chinoise* —

SIR BENJAMIN: In short, her face resembles a *table d'hôte* at Spa, — where no two guests are of a nation —

CRABTREE: Or a congress at the close of a general war, — wherein all the members, even to her eyes, appear to have a different interest, and her nose and chin are the only parties likely to join issue.

MRS. CANDOUR: Ha! ha! ha!

SIR PETER (*aside*): Mercy on my life! A person they dine with twice a week!

LADY SNEERWELL: Go, go! You are a couple of provoking toads.

MRS. CANDOUR: Nay, but I vow you shall not carry the laugh off so, for give me leave to say that Mrs. Ogle —

SIR PETER: Madam, madam, I beg your pardon. There's no stopping these good gentlemen's tongues. But when I tell you, Mrs. Candour, that the lady they are abusing is a particular friend of mine, I hope you'll not take her part.

LADY SNEERWELL: Ha! ha! ha! Well said, Sir Peter! But you are a cruel creature, — too phlegmatic yourself for a jest, and too peevish to allow wit in others.

SIR PETER: Ah, madam, true wit is more nearly allied to good nature than your ladyship is aware of.

LADY TEAZLE: True, Sir Peter. I believe they are so near akin that they can never be united.

SIR BENJAMIN: Or rather, madam, suppose them to be man and wife because one seldom sees them together.

LADY TEAZLE: But Sir Peter is such an enemy to scandal I believe he would have it put down by parliament.

SIR PETER: 'Fore heaven, madam, if they were to consider the sporting with reputation of as much importance as poaching on manors and pass an act for the preservation of fame, [as well as game], I believe I would thank them for the bill.

LADY SNEERWELL: O lud, Sir Peter, would you deprive us of our privileges?

SIR PETER: Ay, madam; and then no person should be permitted to kill characters and run down reputations but qualified old maids and disappointed widows.

LADY SNEERWELL: Go, you monster!

MRS. CANDOUR: But, surely, you would not be quite so severe on those who only report what they hear!

---

3 *French fruit:* Artificial fruits containing sentiments on slips of paper, like the "crackers" or fortune cookies of today.

SIR PETER: Yes, madam, I would have law merchant[4] for them, too; and in all cases of slander currency, whenever the drawer of the lie was not to be found, the injured parties should have a right to come on any of the indorsers.

CRABTREE: Well, for my part, I believe there never was a scandalous tale without some foundation.

SIR PETER: O, nine out of ten of the malicious inventions are founded on some ridiculous misrepresentation.

LADY SNEERWELL: Come, ladies, shall we sit down to cards in the next room?

(*Enter* SERVANT, *who whispers* SIR PETER.)

SIR PETER (*to* SERVANT): I'll be with them directly. (*Exit* SERVANT. *Aside*) I'll get away unperceived.

LADY SNEERWELL: Sir Peter, you are not going to leave us?

SIR PETER: Your ladyship must excuse me; I'm called away by particular business. But I leave my character behind me. (*Exit.*)

SIR BENJAMIN: Well — certainly, Lady Teazle, that lord of yours is a strange being. I could tell you some stories of him would make you laugh heartily if he were not your husband.

LADY TEAZLE: Oh, pray don't mind that; come, do let's hear them.

(*Joins the rest of the company going into the next room,* [who] *exeunt, except* JOSEPH SURFACE *and* MARIA.)

JOSEPH SURFACE: Maria, I see you have no satisfaction in this society.

MARIA: How is it possible I should? If to raise malicious smiles at the infirmities or misfortunes of those who have never injured us be the province of wit or humor, Heaven grant me a double portion of dulness!

JOSEPH SURFACE: Yet they appear more ill-natured than they are; they have no malice at heart.

MARIA: Then is their conduct still more con-temptible; for, in my opinion, nothing could excuse the [intemperance][5] of their tongues but a natural and uncontrollable bitterness of mind.

JOSEPH SURFACE: Undoubtedly, madam; and it has always been a sentiment of mine that to propagate a malicious truth wantonly is more despicable than to falsify from revenge. But can you, Maria, feel thus for others and be unkind to me alone? Is hope to be denied the tenderest passion?

MARIA: Why will you distress me by renewing this subject?

JOSEPH SURFACE: Ah, Maria, you would not treat me thus and oppose your guardian, Sir Peter's will, but that I see that profligate Charles is still a favored rival.

MARIA: Ungenerously urged! But whatever my sentiments are for that unfortunate young man, be assured I shall not feel more bound to give him up because his distresses have lost him the regard even of a brother.

JOSEPH SURFACE: Nay, but Maria, do not leave me with a frown. By all that's honest I swear — (*Kneels. Enter* LADY TEAZLE. *Aside*) Gad's life, here's Lady Teazle. — You must not — no, you shall not — for though I have the greatest regard for Lady Teazle —

MARIA: Lady Teazle!

JOSEPH SURFACE: Yet were Sir Peter to suspect —

(LADY TEAZLE *comes forward.*)

LADY TEAZLE (*aside*): What is this, pray? Does he take her for me? — Child, you are wanted in the next room. (*Exit* MARIA.) What is all this, pray?

JOSEPH SURFACE: Oh, the most unlucky circumstance in nature! Maria has somehow suspected the tender concern I have for your happiness and threatened to acquaint Sir

---

4 *law merchant:* Mercantile law, which makes indorsers liable for debts the principals fail to pay. 5 *intemperance:* interference (Murray).

Peter with her suspicions, and I was just endeavoring to reason with her when you came in.

LADY TEAZLE: Indeed! but you seemed to adopt a very tender mode of reasoning. Do you usually argue on your knees?

JOSEPH SURFACE: Oh, she's a child and I thought a little bombast — But, Lady Teazle, when are you to give me your judgment on my library, as you promised?

LADY TEAZLE: No, no; I begin to think it would be imprudent, and you know I admit you as a lover no farther than fashion sanctions.

JOSEPH SURFACE: True — a mere Platonic *cicisbeo*,[6] — what every wife is entitled to.

LADY TEAZLE: Certainly, one must not be out of the fashion. However, I have so many of my country prejudices left that, though Sir Peter's ill humor may vex me ever so, it shall never provoke me to —

JOSEPH SURFACE: The only revenge in your power. Well, I applaud your moderation.

LADY TEAZLE: Go! You are an insinuating wretch! But we shall be missed. Let us join the company.

JOSEPH SURFACE: But we had best not return together.

LADY TEAZLE: Well, don't stay, for Maria shan't come to hear any more of your reasoning, I promise you. (*Exit.*)

JOSEPH SURFACE: A curious dilemma my politics have run me into! I wanted at first only to ingratiate myself with Lady Teazle that she might not be my enemy with Maria; and I have, I don't know how, become her serious lover. Sincerely I begin to wish I had never made such a point of gaining so very good a character, for it has led me into so many cursed rogueries that I doubt I shall be exposed at last.

(*Exit.*)

SCENE THREE   Sir Peter Teazle's House.

Enter ROWLEY *and* SIR OLIVER SURFACE.

SIR OLIVER: Ha! ha! ha! so my old friend is married, hey? A young wife from the country! Ha! ha! ha! that he should have stood bluff[1] to old bachelor so long and sink into a husband at last!

ROWLEY: But you must not rally him on the subject, Sir Oliver; 'tis a tender point, I assure you, though he has been married only seven months.

SIR OLIVER: Then he has been just half a year on the stool of repentance! Poor Peter! But you say he has entirely given up Charles — never sees him, hey?

ROWLEY: His prejudice against him is astonishing, and I am sure greatly increased by a jealousy of him with Lady Teazle, which he has industriously been led into by a scandalous society in the neighborhood who have contributed not a little to Charles's ill name. Whereas the truth is, I believe, if the lady is partial to either of them, his brother is the favorite.

SIR OLIVER: Ay, I know there are a set of malicious, prating, prudent gossips, both male and female, who murder characters to kill time and will rob a young fellow of his good name before he has years to know the value of it. But I am not to be prejudiced against my nephew by such, I promise you. No, no; if Charles has done nothing false or mean, I shall compound for his extravagance.

ROWLEY: Then, my life on 't, you will reclaim him. Ah, sir, it gives me new life to find that your heart is not turned against him and that the son of my good old master has one friend, however, left.

SIR OLIVER: What! Shall I forget, Master Rowley, when I was at his years myself? Egad, my brother and I were neither of us very prudent youths; and yet I believe you have not seen many better men than your old master was?

---

6 *cicisbeo:* Italian, lover of a married woman.

1 *bluff:* steadfast.

ROWLEY: Sir, 'tis this reflection gives me assurance that Charles may yet be a credit to his family. But here comes Sir Peter.

SIR OLIVER: Egad, so he does. Mercy on me, he's greatly altered and seems to have a settled, married look! One may read *husband* in his face at this distance.

(*Enter* SIR PETER.)

SIR PETER: Ha! Sir Oliver, my old friend! Welcome to England a thousand times!

SIR OLIVER: Thank you, thank you, Sir Peter! And i' faith I am glad to find you well, believe me!

SIR PETER: Oh, 'tis a long time since we met, — fifteen years, I doubt, Sir Oliver, and many a cross accident in the time.

SIR OLIVER: Ay, I have had my share. But, what! I find you are married, hey? Well, well, it can't be helped; and so — I wish you joy with all my heart!

SIR PETER: Thank you, thank you, Sir Oliver. Yes, I have entered into — the happy state; but we'll not talk of that now.

SIR OLIVER: True, true, Sir Peter. Old friends should not begin on grievances at first meeting. No, no, no.

ROWLEY (*aside to* SIR OLIVER): Take care, pray, sir.

SIR OLIVER: Well, so one of my nephews is a wild fellow, hey?

SIR PETER: Wild! Ah, my old friend, I grieve for your disappointment there. He's a lost young man, indeed. However, his brother will make you amends; Joseph is, indeed, what a youth should be, — everybody in the world speaks well of him.

SIR OLIVER: I am sorry to hear it; he has too good a character to be an honest fellow. "Everybody speaks well of him!" Psha! then he has bowed as low to knaves and fools as to the honest dignity of genius and virtue.

SIR PETER: What, Sir Oliver! Do you blame him for not making enemies?

SIR OLIVER: Yes, if he has merit enough to deserve them.

SIR PETER: Well, well — you'll be convinced when you know him. 'Tis edification to hear him converse; he professes the noblest sentiments.

SIR OLIVER: Oh, plague of his sentiments! If he salutes me with a scrap of morality in his mouth, I shall be sick directly. But, however, don't mistake me, Sir Peter; I don't mean to defend Charles's errors; but before I form my judgment of either of them, I intend to make a trial of their hearts; and my old friend Rowley and I have planned something for the purpose.

ROWLEY: And Sir Peter shall own for once he has been mistaken.

SIR PETER: Oh, my life on Joseph's honor!

SIR OLIVER: Well, come, give us a bottle of good wine, and we'll drink the lads' health and tell you our scheme.

SIR PETER: *Allons*, then!

SIR OLIVER: And don't, Sir Peter, be so severe against your old friend's son; Odds, my life! I am not sorry that he has run out of the course a little. For my part, I hate to see prudence clinging to the green suckers of youth; 'tis like ivy round a sapling and spoils the growth of the tree.

(*Exeunt.*)

ACT THREE

SCENE ONE   Sir Peter Teazle's House.

Enter SIR PETER TEAZLE, SIR OLIVER SURFACE, *and* ROWLEY.

SIR PETER: Well, then, we will see this fellow first and have our wine afterwards. But how is this, Master Rowley? I don't see the jet[1] of your scheme.

---

1 *jet:* thrust, point.

ROWLEY: Why, sir, this Mr. Stanley, whom I was speaking of, is nearly related to them by their mother. He was once a merchant in Dublin but has been ruined by a series of undeserved misfortunes. He has applied by letter to both Mr. Surface and Charles. From the former he has received nothing but evasive promises of future service, while Charles has done all that his extravagance has left him power to do; and he is at this time endeavoring to raise a sum of money, part of which, in the midst of his own distresses, I know he intends for the service of poor Stanley.

SIR OLIVER: Ah! he is my brother's son.

SIR PETER: Well, but how is Sir Oliver personally to —

ROWLEY: Why, sir, I will inform Charles and his brother that Stanley has obtained permission to apply personally to his friends; and, as they have neither of them ever seen him, let Sir Oliver assume his character and he will have a fair opportunity of judging at least of the benevolence of their dispositions. And, believe me, sir, you will find in the youngest brother one who, in the midst of folly and dissipation, has still, as our immortal bard expresses it, —

> a heart to pity and a hand,
> Open as day for melting charity.[2]

SIR PETER: Psha! What signifies his having an open hand or purse either when he has nothing left to give? Well, well, make the trial, if you please. But where is the fellow whom you brought for Sir Oliver to examine relative to Charles's affairs?

ROWLEY: Below, waiting his commands, and no one can give him better intelligence. This, Sir Oliver, is a friendly Jew, who, to do him justice, has done everything in his power to bring your nephew to a proper sense of his extravagance.

SIR PETER: Pray, let us have him in.

ROWLEY (*apart to* SERVANT): Desire Mr. Moses to walk upstairs.

SIR PETER: But, pray, why should you suppose he will speak the truth?

ROWLEY: Oh, I have convinced him that he has no chance of recovering certain sums advanced to Charles but through the bounty of Sir Oliver, who, he knows, has arrived, so that you may depend on his fidelity to his own interests. I have also another evidence in my power, one Snake, whom I have detected in a matter little short of forgery and shall speedily produce him to remove some of your prejudices.

SIR PETER: I have heard too much on that subject.

ROWLEY: Here comes the honest Israelite. (*Enter* MOSES.) This is Sir Oliver.

SIR OLIVER: Sir, I understand you have lately had great dealings with my nephew Charles.

MOSES: Yes, Sir Oliver, I have done all I could for him; but he was ruined before he came to me for assistance.

SIR OLIVER: That was unlucky, truly, for you have had no opportunity of showing your talents.

MOSES: None at all. I hadn't the pleasure of knowing his distresses till he was some thousands worse than nothing.

SIR OLIVER: Unfortunate, indeed! But I suppose you have done all in your power for him, honest Moses?

MOSES: Yes, he knows that. This very evening I was to have brought him a gentleman from the city who does not know him and will, I believe, advance him some money.

SIR PETER: What, one Charles has never had money from before!

MOSES: Yes. Mr. Premium, of Crutched Friars,[3] formerly a broker.

---

2 *a heart a pity:* a slight misquotation from Shakespeare's II Henry IV, IV, iv., 31–32: "a tear for pity . . .".
3 *Crutched Friars:* a street near the Tower of London named for a former monastery on the site ("crutched" = "crossed").

Sir Peter: Egad, Sir Oliver, a thought strikes me! Charles, you say, does not know Mr. Premium?

Moses: Not at all.

Sir Peter: Now then, Sir Oliver, you may have a better opportunity of satisfying yourself than by an old, romancing tale of a poor relation. Go with my friend Moses and represent Premium, and then, I'll answer for it, you'll see your nephew in all his glory.

Sir Oliver: Egad, I like this idea better than the other, and I may visit Joseph afterwards as old Stanley.

Sir Peter: True, — so you may.

Rowley: Well, this is taking Charles rather at a disadvantage, to be sure. However, Moses, you understand Sir Peter and will be faithful?

Moses: You may depend upon me. This is near the time I was to have gone.

Sir Oliver: I'll accompany you as soon as you please, Moses. But hold! I have forgot one thing, — how the plague shall I be able to pass for a Jew?

Moses: There's no need. The principal is Christian.

Sir Oliver: Is he? I'm very sorry to hear it; but then, again, an't I rather too smartly dressed to look like a money-lender?

Sir Peter: Not at all; 'twould not be out of character, if you went in your own carriage, would it, Moses?

Moses: Not in the least.

Sir Oliver: Well, but how must I talk? There's certainly some cant of usury and mode of treating that I ought to know.

Sir Peter: Oh, there's not much to learn. The great point, as I take it, is to be exorbitant enough in your demands. Hey, Moses?

Moses: Yes, that's a very great point.

Sir Oliver: I'll answer for 't I'll not be wanting in that. I'll ask him eight or ten per cent on the loan at least.

Moses: If you ask him no more than that, you'll be discovered immediately.

Sir Oliver: Hey! what, the plague! how much then?

Moses. If he appears not very anxious for the supply, you should require only forty or fifty per cent; but if you find him in great distress and want the moneys very bad, you may ask double.

Sir Peter: A good honest trade you're learning, Sir Oliver!

Sir Oliver: Truly, I think so, — and not unprofitable.

Moses: Then you know, you haven't the moneys yourself but are forced to borrow them of an old friend.

Sir Oliver: Oh! I borrow it of a friend, do I?

Moses: And your friend is an unconscionable dog; but you can't help that.

Sir Oliver: My friend an unconscionable dog, is he?

Moses: Yes, and he himself has not the moneys by him but is forced to sell stock at a great loss.

Sir Oliver: He is forced to sell stock at a great loss, is he? Well, that's very kind of him.

Sir Peter: I'faith, Sir Oliver — Mr. Premium, I mean — you'll soon be master of the trade. But, Moses, would not you have him run out a little against the annuity bill?[4] That would be in character, I should think.

Moses: Very much.

Rowley: And lament that a young man now must be at years of discretion before he is suffered to ruin himself?

Moses: Ay, great pity!

---

4 *the annuity bill:* passed by Parliament in May, 1777. This act was designed to protect minors against the sellers of annuities. It was under debate in Commons at the time *The School for Scandal* was first presented.

Sir Peter: And abuse the public for allowing merit to an act whose only object is to snatch misfortune and imprudence from the rapacious gripe of usury and give the minor a chance of inheriting his estate without being undone by coming into possession.

Sir Oliver: So, so — Moses shall give me farther particulars as we go together.

Sir Peter: You will not have much time, for your nephew lives hard by.

Sir Oliver: Oh, never fear! My tutor appears so able that though Charles lived in the next street, it must be my own fault if I am not a complete rogue before I turn the corner. (*Exit with* Moses.)

Sir Peter: So, now, I think Sir Oliver will be convinced. You are partial, Rowley, and would have prepared Charles for the other plot.

Rowley: No, upon my word, Sir Peter.

Sir Peter: Well, go bring me this Snake, and I'll hear what he has to say presently. I see Maria and want to speak with her. (*Exit* Rowley.) I should be glad to be convinced my suspicions of Lady Teazle and Charles were unjust. I have never yet opened my mind on this subject to my friend Joseph. I am determined I will do it; he will give me his opinion sincerely. (*Enter* Maria.) So, child, has Mr. Surface returned with you?

Maria: No, sir. He was engaged.

Sir Peter: Well, Maria, do you not reflect the more you converse with that amiable young man what return his partiality for you deserves?

Maria: Indeed, Sir Peter, your frequent importunity on this subject distresses me extremely. You compel me to declare that I know no man who has ever paid me a particular attention whom I would not prefer to Mr. Surface.

Sir Peter: So — here's perverseness! No, no, Maria, 'tis Charles only whom you would prefer. 'Tis evident his vices and follies have won your heart.

Maria: This is unkind, sir. You know I have obeyed you in neither seeing or corresponding with him. I have heard enough to convince me that he is unworthy my regard. Yet I cannot think it culpable, if, while my understanding severely condemns his vices, my heart suggests some pity for his distresses.

Sir Peter: Well, well, pity him as much as you please, but give your heart and hand to a worthier object.

Maria: Never to his brother.

Sir Peter: Go, perverse and obstinate! But take care, madam; you have never yet known what the authority of a guardian is. Don't compel me to inform you of it.

Maria: I can only say, you shall not have just reason. 'Tis true, by my father's will I am for a short period bound to regard you as his substitute, but must cease to think you so when you would compel me to be miserable. (*Exit.*)

Sir Peter: Was ever man so crossed as I am, everything conspiring to fret me! I had not been involved in matrimony a fortnight before her father, a hale and hearty man, died, on purpose, I believe, for the pleasure of plaguing me with the care of his daughter. — But here comes my helpmate! She appears in great good humor. How happy I should be if I could tease her into loving me, though but a little!

(*Enter* Lady Teazle.)

Lady Teazle: Lud, Sir Peter, I hope you haven't been quarreling with Maria? It is not using me well to be ill-humored when I am not by.

Sir Peter: Ah, Lady Teazle, you might have the power to make me good humored at all times.

Lady Teazle: I am sure I wish I had, for I want you to be in a charming, sweet temper at this moment. Do be good humored now and let me have two hundred pounds, will you?

Sir Peter: Two hundred pounds! What, ain't

I to be in a good humor without paying for it? But speak to me thus and, i' faith, there's nothing I could refuse you. You shall have it, but seal me a bond for the repayment.

Lady Teazle: Oh, no! There, — my note of hand will do as well. (*Offering her hand.*)

Sir Peter: And you shall no longer reproach me with not giving you an independent settlement. I mean shortly to surprise you. But shall we always live thus, hey?

Lady Teazle: If you please. I'm sure I don't care how soon we leave off quarreling provided you'll own you were tired first.

Sir Peter: Well, then let our future contest be who shall be most obliging.

Lady Teazle: I assure you, Sir Peter, good nature becomes you. You look now as you did before we were married, when you used to walk with me under the elms and tell me stories of what a gallant you were in your youth and chuck me under the chin and ask me if I thought I could love an old fellow who would deny me nothing — didn't you?

Sir Peter: Yes, yes, and you were as kind and attentive —

Lady Teazle: Ay, so I was, and would always take your part when my acquaintance used to abuse you and turn you into ridicule.

Sir Peter: Indeed!

Lady Teazle: Ay, and when my cousin Sophy has called you a stiff, peevish old bachelor and laughed at me for thinking of marrying one who might be my father, I have always defended you and said I didn't think you so ugly by any means; and I dared say you'd make a very good sort of husband.

Sir Peter: And you prophesied right; and we shall now be the happiest couple —

Lady Teazle: And never differ again?

Sir Peter: No, never. Though at the same time, indeed, my dear Lady Teazle, you must watch your temper very seriously, for in all our quarrels, my dear, if you recollect, my love, you always began first.

Lady Teazle: I beg your pardon, my dear Sir Peter. Indeed you always gave the provocation.

Sir Peter: Now see, my angel! Take care! Contradicting isn't the way to keep friends.

Lady Teazle: Then don't you begin it, my love.

Sir Peter: There, now, you — you — are going on. You don't perceive, my life, that you are just doing the very thing which you know always makes me angry.

Lady Teazle: Nay, you know if you will be angry without any reason, my dear —

Sir Peter: There, now you want to quarrel again.

Lady Teazle: No, I'm sure I don't; but if you will be so peevish —

Sir Peter: There now! Who begins first?

Lady Teazle: Why, you to be sure. I said nothing; but there's no bearing your temper.

Sir Peter: No, no, madam! The fault's in your own temper.

Lady Teazle: Ay, you are just what my cousin Sophy said you would be.

Sir Peter: Your cousin Sophy is a forward, impertinent gipsy.

Lady Teazle: You are a great bear, I'm sure, to abuse my relations.

Sir Peter: Now may all the plagues of marriage be doubled on me if ever I try to be friends with you any more!

Lady Teazle: So much the better.

Sir Peter: No, no, madam. 'Tis evident you never cared a pin for me and I was a madman to marry you, — a pert, rural coquette that had refused half the honest squires in the neighborhood.

Lady Teazle: And I am sure I was a fool to marry you, — an old dangling bachelor, who was single at fifty only because he never could meet with anyone who would have him.

SIR PETER: Ay, ay, madam; but you were pleased enough to listen to me. You never had such an offer before.

LADY TEAZLE: No? Didn't I refuse Sir Tivy Terrier, who everybody said would have been a better match, for his estate is just as good as yours and he has broke his neck since we have been married?

SIR PETER: I have done with you, madam! You are an unfeeling, ungrateful — But there's an end of everything. I believe you capable of everything that is bad. Yes, madam, I now believe the reports relative to you and Charles, madam. Yes, madam, you and Charles are, not without grounds —

LADY TEAZLE: Take care, Sir Peter! You had better not insinuate any such thing! I'll not be suspected without cause, I promise you.

SIR PETER: Very well, madam, very well! A separate maintenance as soon as you please. Yes, madam, or a divorce! I'll make an example of myself for the benefit of all old bachelors. Let us separate, madam.

LADY TEAZLE: Agreed, agreed! And now, my dear, Sir Peter, we are of a mind once more, we may be the happiest couple and never differ again, you know. Ha, ha, ha! Well, you are going to be in a passion, I see, and I shall only interrupt you; so bye, bye! (*Exit.*)

SIR PETER: Plagues and tortures! Can't I make her angry either? Oh, I am the most miserable fellow! But I'll not bear her presuming to keep her temper. No! She may break my heart, but she shan't keep her temper. (*Exit.*)

SCENE Two   Charles Surface's House.

Enter TRIP, MOSES, *and* SIR OLIVER SURFACE.

TRIP: Here, Master Moses! If you'll stay a moment, I'll try whether — What's the gentleman's name?

SIR OLIVER (*aside to* MOSES): Mr. Moses, what is my name?

MOSES: Mr. Premium.

TRIP: Premium. Very well.

(*Exit, taking snuff.*)

SIR OLIVER: To judge by the servants, one wouldn't believe the master was ruined. But what! Sure, this was my brother's house?

MOSES: Yes, sir; Mr. Charles bought it of Mr. Joseph, with the furniture, pictures, &c., just as the old gentleman left it. Sir Peter thought it a piece of extravagance in him.

SIR OLIVER: In my mind, the other's economy in selling it to him was more reprehensible by half.

(*Enter* TRIP.)

TRIP: My master says you must wait, gentlemen. He has company and can't speak with you yet.

SIR OLIVER: If he knew who it was wanted to see him, perhaps he would not send such a message?

TRIP: Yes, yes, sir; he knows you are here. I did not forget little Premium. No, no, no.

SIR OLIVER: Very well; and I pray, sir, what may be your name?

TRIP: Trip, sir; my name is Trip, at your service.

SIR OLIVER: Well, then, Mr. Trip, you have a pleasant sort of place here, I guess.

TRIP: Why, yes. Here are three or four of us pass our time agreeably enough; but then our wages are sometimes a little in arrear, and not very great either, but fifty pounds a year and find our own bags and bouquets.[1]

SIR OLIVER (*aside*): Bags and bouquets! Halters and bastinadoes!

TRIP: And *à propos*, Moses, have you been able to get me that little bill discounted?

SIR OLIVER (*aside*): Wants to raise money too! Mercy on me! has his distresses too, I warrant, like a lord and affects creditors and duns.

---

1 *bags and bouquets:* bag wigs and shoulder knots were worn by footmen.

MOSES: 'Twas not to be done, indeed, Mr. Trip.

TRIP: Good lack, you surprise me! My friend Brush has indorsed it, and I thought when he put his name at the back of a bill 'twas the same as cash.

MOSES: No, 'twouldn't do.

TRIP: A small sum, — but twenty pounds. Harkee, Moses, do you think you couldn't get it me by way of annuity?

SIR OLIVER (aside): An annuity! Ha, ha! A footman raise money by way of annuity! Well done, luxury, egad!

MOSES: Well, but you must insure your place.

TRIP: Oh, with all my heart! I'll insure my place and my life too, if you please.

SIR OLIVER (aside): It's more than I would your neck.

MOSES: But is there nothing you could deposit?

TRIP: Why, nothing capital of my master's wardrobe has dropped lately; but I could give you a mortgage on some of his winter clothes with equity of redemption before November; or you shall have the reversion of the French velvet or a post-obit[2] on the blue and silver. These I should think, Moses, with a few pairs of point ruffles as collateral security — Hey, my little fellow?

MOSES: Well, well.

(Bell rings.)

TRIP: Egad, I heard the bell! I believe, gentlemen, I can now introduce you. Don't forget the annuity, little Moses. This way, gentlemen; I'll insure my place, you know.

SIR OLIVER (aside): If the man be a shadow of the master, this is a temple of dissipation indeed.

(Exeunt.)

SCENE THREE   [Another room].

CHARLES SURFACE, CARELESS, &c., &c., at a table with wine, &c.

CHARLES: 'Fore heaven, 'tis true! There's the great degeneracy of the age. Many of our acquaintance have taste, spirit, and politeness; but, plague on't, they won't drink.

CARELESS: It is so, indeed, Charles. They go into all the substantial luxuries of the table and abstain from nothing but wine and wit. Oh, certainly society suffers by it intolerably, for now instead of the social spirit of raillery that used to mantle over a glass of bright Burgundy, their conversation is become just like the Spa-water they drink, which has all the pertness and flatulency of champagne without the spirit or flavor.

FIRST GENTLEMAN: But what are they to do who love play better than wine?

CARELESS: True! There's Sir Harry diets himself for gaming and is now under a hazard regimen.

CHARLES SURFACE: Then he'll have the worst of it. What! you wouldn't train a horse for the course by keeping him from corn?[1] For my part, egad, I am never so successful as when I am a little merry. Let me throw on a bottle of champagne and I never lose.

CARELESS: At least I never feel my losses, which is exactly the same thing.

SECOND GENTLEMAN: Ay, that I believe.

CHARLES: And then, what man can pretend to be a believer in love who is an abjurer of wine? 'Tis the test by which the lover knows his own heart. Fill a dozen bumpers to a dozen beauties and she that floats atop is the maid that has bewitched you.

CARELESS: Now then, Charles, be honest and give us your real favorite.

CHARLES: Why, I have withheld her only in compassion to you. If I toast her, you must give a round of her peers, which is impossible — on earth.

---

2 post-obit: legacy (after his death, Latin).

1 corn: in Britain this means wheat or other grains and what Americans call corn is termed "Indian corn" or "maize."

CARELESS: Oh, then, we'll find some canonized vestals or heathen goddesses that will do, I warrant!

CHARLES: Here, then, bumpers, you rogues! Bumpers! Maria! Maria!

SIR [TOBY] BUMPER: Maria who?

CHARLES: Oh, damn the surname! 'Tis too formal to be registered in love's calendar. But now, Sir [Toby], beware! We must have beauty superlative.

CARELESS: Nay, never study, Sir [Toby]. We'll stand to the toast though your mistress should want an eye and you know you have a song will excuse you.

SIR [TOBY]: Egad, so I have, and I'll give him the song instead of the lady. (*Sings*)

Here's to the maiden of bashful fifteen;
Here's to the widow of fifty;
Here's to the flaunting, extravagant quean,
And here's to the housewife that's thrifty.
CHORUS: Let the toast pass,
            Drink to the lass, —
I'll warrant she'll prove an excuse for the
     glass!

Here's to the charmer whose dimples we
     prize;
Now to the maid who has none, sir!
Here's to the girl with a pair of blue eyes,
And here's to the nymph with but one, sir!
CHORUS: Let the toast pass, &c.

Here's to the maid with a bosom of snow!
Now to her that's as brown as a berry!
Here's to the wife with a face full of woe,
And now to the girl that's merry!
CHORUS: Let the toast pass, &c.

For let 'em be clumsy, or let 'em be slim,
Young or ancient, I care not a feather:
So fill a pint bumper quite up to the brim,
And let us e'en toast them together!
CHORUS: Let the toast pass, &c.

ALL: Bravo! Bravo!

(*Enter* TRIP *and whispers* CHARLES SURFACE.)

CHARLES: Gentlemen, you must excuse me a little. Careless, take the chair, will you?

CARELESS: Nay, pr'ythee, Charles, what now? This is one of your peerless beauties, I suppose, has dropped in by chance?

CHARLES: No, faith! To tell you the truth, 'tis a Jew and a broker, who are come by appointment.

CARELESS: Oh, damn it, let's have the Jew in.

FIRST GENTLEMAN: Ay, and the broker too, by all means.

SECOND GENTLEMAN: Yes, yes, the Jew and the broker!

CHARLES: Egad, with all my heart! Trip, bid the gentlemen walk in. (*Exit* TRIP.) Though there's one of them a stranger, I can tell you.

CARELESS: Charles, let us give them some generous Burgundy and perhaps they'll grow conscientious.

CHARLES: Oh, hang 'em, no! Wine does but draw forth a man's natural qualities; and to make them drink would only be to whet their knavery.

(*Enter* TRIP, SIR OLIVER, *and* MOSES.)

CHARLES: So, honest Moses! Walk in, pray, Mr. Premium. That's the gentleman's name, isn't it, Moses?

MOSES: Yes, sir.

CHARLES: Set chairs, Trip. — Sit down, Mr. Premium. — Glasses, Trip. — Sit down, Moses. — Come, Mr. Premium, I'll give you a sentiment: here's *Success to usury!* Moses, fill the gentleman a bumper.

MOSES: Success to usury! (*Drinks.*)

CARELESS: Right, Moses! Usury is prudence and industry, and deserves to succeed.

SIR OLIVER: Then — here's — all the success it deserves! (*Drinks.*)

CARELESS: No, no, that won't do! Mr. Premium, you have demurred at the toast and must drink it in a pint bumper.

FIRST GENTLEMAN: A pint bumper at least!

MOSES: Oh, pray, sir, consider! Mr. Premium's a gentleman.

CARELESS: And therefore loves good wine.

SECOND GENTLEMAN: Give Moses a quart glass. This is mutiny and a high contempt for the chair.

CARELESS: Here, now for 't! I'll see justice done, to the last drop of my bottle.

SIR OLIVER: Nay, pray, gentlemen! I did not expect this usage.

CHARLES: No, hang it, you shan't. Mr. Premium's a stranger.

SIR OLIVER (aside): Odd! I wish I was well out of their company.

CARELESS: Plague on 'em then! If they won't drink, we'll not sit down with them. Come, Toby, the dice are in the next room. Charles, you'll join us when you have finished your business with the gentlemen?

CHARLES: I will! I will! (Exeunt [Gentlemen].) Careless!

CARELESS (returning): Well?

CHARLES: Perhaps I may want you.

CARELESS: Oh, you know I am always ready. Word, note, or bond, 'tis all the same to me! (Exit.)

MOSES: Sir, this is Mr. Premium, a gentleman of the strictest honor and secrecy, and always performs what he undertakes. Mr. Premium, this is —

CHARLES: Psha! Have done! Sir, my friend Moses is a very honest fellow but a little slow at expression. He'll be an hour giving us our titles. Mr. Premium, the plain state of the matter is this: I am an extravagant young fellow who wants to borrow money; you I take to be a prudent old fellow who have got money to lend. I am blockhead enough to give fifty per cent sooner than not have it; and you, I presume, are rogue enough to take a hundred if you can get it. Now, sir, you see we are acquainted at once and may proceed to business without farther ceremony.

SIR OLIVER: Exceeding frank, upon my word. I see, sir, you are not a man of many compliments.

CHARLES: Oh, no, sir! Plain dealing in business I always think best.

SIR OLIVER: Sir, I like you the better for it. However, you are mistaken in one thing. I have no money to lend, but I believe I could procure some of a friend; but then he's an unconscionable dog, isn't he, Moses?

MOSES: But you can't help that.

SIR OLIVER: And must sell stock to accommodate you, mustn't he, Moses?

MOSES: Yes, indeed! You know I always speak the truth and scorn to tell a lie.

CHARLES: Right! People that speak truth generally do. But these are trifles, Mr. Premium. What, I know money isn't to be bought without paying for 't!

SIR OLIVER: Well, but what security could you give? You have no land, I suppose?

CHARLES: Not a mole-hill, nor a twig, but what's in the bough-pots[2] out of the window!

SIR OLIVER: Nor any stock, I presume?

CHARLES: Nothing but live stock, — and that's only a few pointers and ponies. But, pray, Mr. Premium, are you acquainted at all with any of my connections?

SIR OLIVER: Why, to say truth, I am.

CHARLES: Then you must know that I have a devilish rich uncle in the East Indies, Sir Oliver Surface, from whom I have the greatest expectations.

SIR OLIVER: That you have a wealthy uncle, I have heard; but how your expectations will turn out is more, I believe, than you can tell.

CHARLES: Oh, no! There can be no doubt! They tell me I'm a prodigious favorite and that he talks of leaving me everything.

SIR OLIVER: Indeed! This is the first I've heard of it.

CHARLES: Yes, yes, 'tis just so. Moses knows 'tis true, don't you, Moses?

---

2 *bough-pots:* large ornamental flower-pots.

Moses: Oh, yes! I'll swear to 't.

Sir Oliver (aside): Egad, they'll persuade me presently I'm at Bengal.

Charles: Now I propose, Mr. Premium, if it's agreeable to you, a post-obit on Sir Oliver's life, though at the same time the old fellow has been so liberal to me that I give you my word I should be very sorry to hear that anything had happened to him.

Sir Oliver: Not more than I should, I assure you. But the bond you mention happens to be just the worst security you could offer me, — for I might live to a hundred and never see the principal.

Charles: Oh, yes, you would! The moment Sir Oliver dies, you know, you would come on me for the money.

Sir Oliver: Then I believe I should be the most unwelcome dun you ever had in your life.

Charles: What! I suppose you're afraid that Sir Oliver is too good a life?

Sir Oliver: No, indeed I am not, though I have heard he is as hale and healthy as any man of his years in Christendom.

Charles: There, again, now you are misinformed. No, no, the climate has hurt him considerably, poor uncle Oliver. Yes, yes, he breaks apace, I'm told, and is so much altered lately that his nearest relations don't know him.

Sir Oliver: No! Ha, ha, ha! So much altered lately that his nearest relations don't know him! Ha, ha, ha! Egad! Ha, ha, ha!

Charles: Ha, ha! You're glad to hear that, little Premium?

Sir Oliver: No, no, I'm not.

Charles: Yes, yes, you are! Ha, ha, ha! You know that mends your chance.

Sir Oliver: But I'm told Sir Oliver is coming over. Nay, some say he is actually arrived.

Charles: Psha! sure I must know better than you whether he's come or not. No, no, rely on 't, he's at this moment at Calcutta, isn't he, Moses?[3]

Moses: Oh, yes, certainly.

Sir Oliver: Very true, as you say, you must know better than I, though I have it from pretty good authority, haven't I, Moses?

Moses: Yes, most undoubted!

Sir Oliver: But, sir, as I understand you want a few hundreds immediately, is there nothing you could dispose of?

Charles: How do you mean?

Sir Oliver: For instance, now, I have heard that your father left behind him a great quantity of massy old plate.

Charles: O Lud! that's gone long ago. Moses can tell you how better than I can.

Sir Oliver (aside): Good lack, all the family race-cups and corporation bowls![4] Then it was also supposed that his library was one of the most valuable and compact.

Charles: Yes, yes, so it was — vastly too much so for a private gentleman. For my part, I was always of a communicative disposition; so I thought it a shame to keep so much knowledge to myself.

Sir Oliver (aside): Mercy upon me! Learning that had run in the family like an heirloom! — Pray what are become of the books?

Charles: You must inquire of the auctioneer, Master Premium, for I don't believe even Moses can direct you.

Moses: I know nothing of books.

Sir Oliver: So, so, nothing of the family property left, I suppose?

Charles: Not much, indeed, unless you have a mind to the family pictures. I have got a room full of ancestors above; and if you have a taste for paintings, egad, you shall have 'em a bargain.

---

3 *Calcutta:* after Clive annexed India for Britain, many *nabobs* of the East India Company and others grew rich on eastern trade. 4 *race-cups and corporation bowls:* trophies from horse races and loving cups presented by the Lord Mayor and Corporation of the City.

Sir Oliver: Hey! What the devil? Sure, you wouldn't sell your forefathers, would you?

Charles: Every man of them to the best bidder.

Sir Oliver: What! Your great-uncles and aunts?

Charles: Ay, and my great-grandfathers and grandmothers too.

Sir Oliver (aside): Now I give him up. — What the plague, have you no bowels for your own kindred? Odd's life, do you take me for Shylock in the play that you would raise money of me on your own flesh and blood?

Charles: Nay, my little broker, don't be angry. What need you care if you have your money's worth?

Sir Oliver: Well, I'll be the purchaser. I think I can dispose of the family canvas. (aside) Oh, I'll never forgive him for this, never!

(Enter Careless.)

Careless: Come, Charles; what keeps you?

Charles: I can't come yet. I' faith, we are going to have a sale above stairs. Here's little Premium will buy all my ancestors.

Careless: Oh, burn your ancestors!

Charles: No, he may do that afterwards if he pleases. Stay, Careless, we want you. Egad, you shall be auctioneer; so come along with us.

Careless: Oh, have with you, if that's the case. Handle a hammer as well as a dice-box!

Sir Oliver (aside): Oh, the profligates!

Charles: Come, Moses, you shall be appraiser if we want one. Gad's life, little Premium, you don't seem to like the business.

Sir Oliver: Oh, yes, I do, vastly! Ha, ha, ha! Yes, yes, I think it a rare joke to sell one's family by auction. Ha, ha! (aside) Oh, the prodigal!

Charles: To be sure! When a man wants money, where the plague should he get

assistance if he can't make free with his own relations? (Exeunt.)

ACT FOUR

Scene One   Picture room at Charles's.

Enter Charles Surface, Sir Oliver Surface, Moses, and Careless.

Charles: Walk in, gentlemen, pray walk in. Here they are, the family of the Surfaces up to the Conquest.[1]

Sir Oliver: And, in my opinion, a goodly collection.

Charles: Ay, ay, these are done in the true spirit of portrait-painting; no volontière grace[2] or expression. Not like the works of your modern Raphaels,[3] who give you the strongest resemblance, yet contrive to make your portrait independent of you, so that you may sink the original and not hurt the picture. No, no; the merit of these is the inveterate likeness, — all stiff and awkward as the originals and like nothing in human nature besides.

Sir Oliver: Ah! We shall never see such figures of men again.

Charles: I hope not! Well, you see, Master Premium, what a domestic character I am; here I sit of an evening surrounded by my family. But come, get into your pulpit, Mr. Auctioneer; here's an old, gouty chair of my grandfather's will answer the purpose.

Careless: Ay, ay, this will do. But, Charles, I haven't a hammer; and what's an auctioneer without his hammer!

Charles: Egad, that's true! What parchment have we here? Oh, our genealogy in full. Here, Careless, you shall have no common

---

1 up to the Conquest: surely since the Conquest (1066). 2 volontière grace: French, volunteer grace. 3 modern Raphaels: perhaps a crack at Sir Joshua Reynolds—or Gainsborough or Romney, other fashionable painters of the time.

bit of mahogany; here's the family tree for you, you rogue! This shall be your hammer, and now you may knock down my ancestors with their own pedigree.

SIR OLIVER (*aside*): What an unnatural rogue! An *ex post facto* parricide!

CARELESS: Yes, yes, here's a list of your generation, indeed. Faith, Charles, this is the most convenient thing you could have found for the business, for 'twill serve not only as a hammer but a catalogue into the bargain. Come, begin! A-going, a-going, a-going!

CHARLES: Bravo, Careless! Well, here's my great-uncle, Sir Richard Raveline, a marvellous good general in his day, I assure you. He served in all the Duke of Marlborough's wars and got that cut over his eye at the battle of Malplaquet.[4] What say you, Mr. Premium? Look at him. There's a hero! Not cut out of his feathers as your modern clipped captains are, but enveloped in wig and regimentals as a general should be. What do you bid?

MOSES: Mr. Premium would have you speak.

CHARLES: Why, then, he shall have him for ten pounds, and I'm sure that's not dear for a staff officer.

SIR OLIVER (*aside*): Heaven deliver me! His famous uncle Richard for ten pounds! — Very well, sir, I take him at that.

CHARLES: Careless, knock down my uncle Richard. — Here, now, is a maiden sister of his my great-aunt Deborah, done by Kneller,[5] thought to be in his best manner, and a very formidable likeness. There she is, you see, a shepherdess feeding her flock. You shall have her for five pounds ten, — the sheep are worth the money.

SIR OLIVER (*aside*): Ah, poor Deborah, a woman who set such a value on herself! — Five pounds ten — She's mine.

CHARLES: Knock down my aunt Deborah! Here, now, are two that were a sort of cousins of theirs. You see, Moses, these pictures were done some time ago when beaux wore wigs and the ladies their own hair.

SIR OLIVER: Yes, truly, head-dresses appear to have been a little lower in those days.

CHARLES: Well, take that couple for the same.

MOSES: 'Tis a good bargain.

CHARLES: Careless! — This now, is a grandfather of my mother's, a learned judge, well known on the western circuit. What do you rate him at, Moses?

MOSES: Four guineas.[6]

CHARLES: Four guineas! Gad's life, you don't bid me the price of his wig. Mr. Premium, you have more respect for the woolsack.[7] Do let us knock his lordship down at fifteen.

SIR OLIVER: By all means.

CARELESS: Gone!

CHARLES: And these are two brothers of his, William and Walter Blunt, Esquires, both members of parliament and noted speakers; and what's very extraordinary, I believe this is the first time they were ever bought or sold.

SIR OLIVER: That is very extraordinary, indeed! I'll take them at your own price for the honor of parliament.

CARELESS: Well said, little Premium! I'll knock them down at forty.

CHARLES: Here's a jolly fellow! I don't know what relation, but he was mayor of Manchester; take him at eight pounds.

SIR OLIVER: No, no; six will do for the mayor.

CHARLES: Come, make it guineas, and I'll throw you the two aldermen there into the bargain.

---

4 *Malplaquet:* the Duke of Marlborough's victory (1709) actually encouraged his enemies, for his losses were twice as great as the French. 5 *Kneller:* Sir Godfrey Kneller (1648–1723) was the most fashionable painter of his time. Watch the use of "formidable" in the rest of the sentence. 6 *guineas:* a guinea is 21 shillings, one shilling more than a pound, and a fashionable way of asking a trifle more. 7 *woolsack:* in the House of Lords, the Lord Chancellor sits on a woolsack, symbol of the source of Britain's traditional wealth. Here the symbolic seat of the highest legal officer is made to serve as token of the legal profession.

SIR OLIVER: They're mine.

CHARLES: Careless, knock down the mayor and aldermen. But, plague on 't, we shall be all day retailing in this manner. Do let us deal wholesale, what say you, little Premium? Give me three hundred pounds for the rest of the family in the lump.

CARELESS: Ay, ay, that will be the best way.

SIR OLIVER: Well, well, anything to accommodate you. They are mine. But there is one portrait which you have always passed over.

CARELESS: What, that ill-looking little fellow over the settee?

SIR OLIVER: Yes, sir, I mean that, though I don't think him so ill-looking a little fellow by any means.

CHARLES: What, that? Oh, that's my uncle Oliver. 'Twas done before he went to India.

CARELESS: Your uncle Oliver! Gad, then you'll never be friends, Charles. That, now, is as stern a looking rogue as ever I saw, an unforgiving eye and a damned disinheriting countenance! An inveterate knave, depend on 't, don't you think so, little Premium?

SIR OLIVER: Upon my soul, sir, I do not. I think it is as honest a looking face as any in the room, dead or alive. But I suppose uncle Oliver goes with the rest of the lumber?

CHARLES: No, hang it! I'll not part with poor Noll. The old fellow has been very good to me, and, egad, I'll keep his picture while I've a room to put it in.

SIR OLIVER (aside): The rogue's my nephew after all! — But, sir, I have somehow taken a fancy to that picture.

CHARLES: I'm sorry for't, for you certainly will not have it. Oons, haven't you got enough of them?

SIR OLIVER (aside): I forgive him for everything! — But, sir, when I take a whim in my head, I don't value money. I'll give you as much for that as for all the rest.

CHARLES: Don't tease me, master broker. I tell you I'll not part with it, and there's an end of it.

SIR OLIVER (aside): How like his father the dog is! — Well, well, I have done. (aside) I did not perceive it before, but I think I never saw such a striking resemblance. — Here's a draft for your sum.

CHARLES: Why, 'tis for eight hundred pounds!

SIR OLIVER: You will not let Sir Oliver go?

CHARLES: Zounds, no! I tell you once more.

SIR OLIVER: Then never mind the difference, we'll balance that another time. But give me your hand on the bargain. You are an honest fellow, Charles — I beg pardon, sir, for being so free. — Come, Moses.

CHARLES: Egad, this is a whimsical old fellow! — But hark'ee, Premium, you'll prepare lodgings for these gentlemen.

SIR OLIVER: Yes, yes, I'll send for them in a day or two.

CHARLES: But hold! Do, now, send a genteel conveyance for them, for, I assure you, they were most of them used to ride in their own carriages.

SIR OLIVER: I will, I will, — for all but little Oliver.

CHARLES: Ay, all but the little nabob.

SIR OLIVER: You're fixed on that?

CHARLES: Peremptorily.

SIR OLIVER (aside): A dear extravagant rogue! — Good day! Come, Moses. (aside) Let me hear now who dares call him profligate!

(Exeunt SIR OLIVER and MOSES.)

CARELESS: Why, this is the oddest genius of the sort I ever met with.

CHARLES: Egad, he's the prince of brokers, I think. I wonder how Moses got acquainted with so honest a fellow. Ha! here's Rowley. — Do, Careless, say I'll join the company in a few moments.

CARELESS: I will, but don't let that old blockhead persuade you to squander any of that money on old, musty debts or any such nonsense, for tradesmen, Charles, are the most exorbitant fellows.

CHARLES: Very true, and paying them is only encouraging them.

CARELESS: Nothing else.

CHARLES: Ay, ay, never fear. (*Exit* CARELESS.) So, this was an odd old fellow, indeed. Let me see, two-thirds of this is mine by right, five hundred and thirty odd pounds. 'Fore heaven, I find one's ancestors are more valuable relations than I took them for! (*Bowing to the pictures*) Ladies and gentlemen, your most obedient and very grateful servant. (*Enter* ROWLEY.) Ha, old Rowley! Egad, you are just come in time to take leave of your old acquaintance.

ROWLEY: Yes, I heard they were a-going. But I wonder you can have such spirits under so many distresses.

CHARLES: Why, there's the point, my distresses are so many that I can't afford to part with my spirits; but I shall be rich and splenetic, all in good time. However, I suppose you are surprised that I am not more sorrowful at parting with so many near relations. To be sure, 'tis very affecting; but you see they never move a muscle; so why should I?

ROWLEY: There's no making you serious a moment.

CHARLES: Yes, faith, I am so now. Here, my honest Rowley, here get me this changed directly and take a hundred pounds of it immediately to old Stanley.

ROWLEY: A hundred pounds! Consider only —

CHARLES: Gad's life, don't talk about it! Poor Stanley's wants are pressing and, if you don't make haste, we shall have someone call that has a better right to the money.

ROWLEY: Ah, there's the point! I never will cease dunning you with the old proverb —

CHARLES: "Be just before you're generous." — Why, so I would if I could; but Justice is an

old, lame, hobbling beldame, and I can't get her to keep pace with Generosity for the soul of me.

ROWLEY: Yet, Charles, believe me, one hour's reflection —

CHARLES: Ay, ay, that's very true; but hark'ee, Rowley, while I have, by heaven I'll give; so damn your economy. And now for hazard!

(*Exeunt.*)

SCENE TWO   The parlor.

Enter SIR OLIVER SURFACE *and* MOSES.

MOSES: Well, sir, I think, as Sir Peter said, you have seen Mr. Charles in high glory; 'tis great pity he's so extravagant.

SIR OLIVER: True, but he would not sell my picture.

MOSES: And loves wine and women so much.

SIR OLIVER: But he would not sell my picture.

MOSES: And games so deep.

SIR OLIVER: But he would not sell my picture. Oh, here's Rowley!

(*Enter* ROWLEY.)

ROWLEY: So, Sir Oliver, I find you have made a purchase —

SIR OLIVER: Yes, yes, our young rake has parted with his ancestors like old tapestry.[1]

ROWLEY: And here he has commissioned me to re-deliver you part of the purchase money. I mean, though, in your necessitous character of old Stanley.

MOSES: Ah, there's the pity of all; he is so damned charitable.

ROWLEY: And left a hosier and two tailors in the hall, who, I'm sure, won't be paid; and this hundred would satisfy them.

---

1 *like old tapestry:* extensive wall coverings, by the yard.

SIR OLIVER: Well, well, I'll pay his debts and his benevolence, too. But now I am no more a broker, and you shall introduce me to the elder brother as old Stanley.

ROWLEY: Not yet awhile. Sir Peter, I know, means to call there about this time.

(*Enter* TRIP.)

TRIP: Oh, gentlemen, I beg pardon for not showing you out. This way. — Moses, a word. (*Exit with* MOSES.)

SIR OLIVER: There's a fellow for you! Would you believe it, that puppy intercepted the Jew on our coming and wanted to raise money before he got to his master!

ROWLEY: Indeed!

SIR OLIVER: Yes, they are now planning an annuity business. Ah, Master Rowley, in my days servants were content with the follies of their masters when they were worn a little threadbare, but now they have their vices like their birthday clothes,[2] with the gloss on.

(*Exeunt.*)

SCENE THREE   A library [in Joseph Surface's house].

Enter JOSEPH SURFACE *and* SERVANT.

JOSEPH SURFACE: No letter from Lady Teazle?

SERVANT: No, sir.

JOSEPH SURFACE: I am surprised she has not sent if she is prevented from coming. Sir Peter certainly does not suspect me. Yet I wish I may not lose the heiress through the scrape I have drawn myself into with the wife. However, Charles's imprudence and bad character are great points in my favor.

(*Knocking heard without.*)

SERVANT: Sir, I believe that must be Lady Teazle.

JOSEPH SURFACE: Hold! See whether it is or not before you go to the door. I have a particular message for you if it should be my brother.

SERVANT: 'Tis her ladyship, sir. She always leaves her chair at a milliner's in the next street.

JOSEPH SURFACE: Stay, stay! Draw that screen before the window. That will do. My opposite neighbor is a maiden lady of so curious a temper. (SERVANT *draws the screen and exit*) I have a difficult hand to play in this affair. Lady Teazle has lately suspected my views on Maria, but she must by no means be let into that secret, — at least, till I have her more in my power.

(*Enter* LADY TEAZLE.)

LADY TEAZLE: What, sentiment in soliloquy now? Have you been very impatient? O lud! don't pretend to look grave. I vow I couldn't come before.

JOSEPH SURFACE: O madam, punctuality is a species of constancy very unfashionable in a lady of quality.

LADY TEAZLE: Upon my word, you ought to pity me. Do you know Sir Peter is grown so ill-natured to me of late, and so jealous of Charles too! That's the best of the story, isn't it?

JOSEPH SURFACE (*aside*): I am glad my scandalous friends keep that up.

LADY TEAZLE: I am sure I wish he would let Maria marry him and then, perhaps, he would be convinced don't you, Mr. Surface?

JOSEPH SURFACE (*aside*): Indeed I do not. — Oh, certainly I do! for then my dear Lady Teazle would also be convinced how wrong her suspicions were of my having any design on the silly girl.

LADY TEAZLE: Well, well, I'm inclined to believe you. But isn't it provoking to have the most ill-natured things said of one? And there's my friend Lady Sneerwell has circulated I

---

2 *birthday clothes:* elegant costumes for the celebration of the king's birthday, a traditional occasion for the creation of new peers and the announcement of other honors. They have their "gloss" because of infrequent wear.

don't know how many scandalous tales of me, and all without any foundation too. That's what vexes me.

JOSEPH SURFACE: Ay, madam, to be sure, that's the provoking circumstance, — without foundation. Yes, yes, there's the mortification, indeed; for, when a scandalous story is believed against one, there certainly is no comfort like the consciousness of having deserved it.

LADY TEAZLE: No, to be sure, then I'd forgive their malice. But to attack me, who am really so innocent and who never say an ill-natured thing of anybody — that is, of any friend; and then Sir Peter, too, to have him so peevish and so suspicious, when I know the integrity of my own heart — indeed, 'tis monstrous!

JOSEPH SURFACE: But, my dear Lady Teazle, 'tis your own fault if you suffer it. When a husband entertains a groundless suspicion of his wife and withdraws his confidence from her, the original compact is broken; and she owes it to the honor of her sex to endeavor to outwit him.

LADY TEAZLE: Indeed! So that, if he suspects me without cause, it follows that the best way of curing his jealousy is to give him reason for it?

JOSEPH SURFACE: Undoubtedly, — for your husband should never be deceived in you; and in that case it becomes you to be frail in compliment to his discernment.

LADY TEAZLE: To be sure, what you say is very reasonable, and when the consciousness of my innocence —

JOSEPH SURFACE: Ah, my dear madam, there is the great mistake! 'Tis this very conscious innocence that is of the greatest prejudice to you. What is it makes you negligent of forms and careless of the world's opinion? Why, the consciousness of your own innocence. What makes you thoughtless in your conduct and apt to run into a thousand little imprudences? Why, the consciousness of your own innocence. What makes you impatient of Sir Peter's temper and outrageous

at his suspicions? Why, the consciousness of your own innocence.

LADY TEAZLE: 'Tis very true.

JOSEPH SURFACE: Now, my dear Lady Teazle, if you would but make a trifling *faux pas*, you can't conceive how cautious you would grow and how ready to humor and agree with your husband.

LADY TEAZLE: Do you think so?

JOSEPH SURFACE: Oh, I am sure on't! And then you would find all scandal cease at once, for, in short, your character at present is like a person in a plethora, absolutely dying from too much health.

LADY TEAZLE: So, so; then I perceive your prescription is that I must sin in my own defense and part with my virtue to preserve my reputation?

JOSEPH SURFACE: Exactly so, upon my credit, ma'am.

LADY TEAZLE: Well, certainly this is the oddest doctrine and the newest receipt for avoiding calumny!

JOSEPH SURFACE: An infallible one, believe me. Prudence, like experience, must be paid for.

LADY TEAZLE: Why, if my understanding were once convinced —

JOSEPH SURFACE: Oh, certainly, madam, your understanding should be convinced. Yes, yes, — heaven forbid I should persuade you to do anything you thought wrong. No, no, I have too much honor to desire it.

LADY TEAZLE: Don't you think we may as well leave honor out of the question?

JOSEPH SURFACE: Ah, the ill effects of your country education, I see, still remain with you.

LADY TEAZLE: I doubt they do, indeed; and I will fairly own to you that if I could be persuaded to do wrong, it would be by Sir Peter's ill usage sooner than your honorable logic after all.

JOSEPH SURFACE: Then, by this hand, which he is unworthy of — (*Taking her hand. Enter*

SERVANT.) 'Sdeath, you blockhead, what do you want?

SERVANT: I beg your pardon, sir, but I thought you would not choose Sir Peter to come up without announcing him.

JOSEPH SURFACE: Sir Peter! Oons, — the devil!

LADY TEAZLE: Sir Peter! O lud! I'm ruined! I'm ruined!

SERVANT: Sir, 'twasn't I let him in.

LADY TEAZLE: Oh, I'm quite undone! What will become of me now, Mr. Logic? Oh, he's on the stairs — I'll get behind here, and if ever I'm so imprudent again —

(*Goes behind the screen.*)

JOSEPH SURFACE: Give me that book.

(*Sits down.* SERVANT *pretends to adjust his chair.*)

(*Enter* SIR PETER TEAZLE.)

SIR PETER: Ay, ever improving himself! Mr. Surface, Mr. Surface —

JOSEPH SURFACE: Oh, my dear Sir Peter, I beg your pardon. (*Gaping, throws away the book*) I have been dozing over a stupid book. Well, I am much obliged to you for this call. You haven't been here, I believe, since I fitted up this room. Books, you know, are the only things I am a coxcomb in.

SIR PETER: 'Tis very neat indeed. Well, well, that's proper; and you can make even your screen a source of knowledge, — hung, I perceive, with maps.

JOSEPH SURFACE: Oh, yes, I find great use in that screen.

SIR PETER: I dare say you must, certainly, when you want to find anything in a hurry.

JOSEPH SURFACE (*aside*): Ay, or to hide anything in a hurry either.

SIR PETER: Well, I have a little private business —

JOSEPH (*to* SERVANT): You need not stay.

SERVANT: No, sir. (*Exit.*)

JOSEPH SURFACE: Here's a chair, Sir Peter. I beg —

SIR PETER: Well, now we are alone, there's a subject, my dear friend, on which I wish to unburden my mind to you, a point of the greatest moment to my peace; in short, my good friend, Lady Teazle's conduct of late has made me very unhappy.

JOSEPH SURFACE: Indeed! I am very sorry to hear it.

SIR PETER: Ay, 'tis but too plain she has not the least regard for me; but, what's worse, I have pretty good authority to suppose she has formed an attachment to another.

JOSEPH SURFACE: Indeed! You astonish me!

SIR PETER: Yes, and, between ourselves, I think I've discovered the person.

JOSEPH SURFACE: How! You alarm me exceedingly.

SIR PETER: Ay, my dear friend, I knew you would sympathize with me!

JOSEPH SURFACE: Yes, believe me, Sir Peter, such a discovery would hurt me just as much as it would you.

SIR PETER: I am convinced of it. Ah, it is a happiness to have a friend whom we can trust even with one's family secrets. But have you no guess who I mean?

JOSEPH SURFACE: I haven't the most distant idea. It can't be Sir Benjamin Backbite!

SIR PETER: Oh, no! What say you to Charles?

JOSEPH SURFACE: My brother? Impossible!

SIR PETER: Oh, my dear friend, the goodness of your own heart misleads you. You judge of others by yourself.

JOSEPH SURFACE: Certainly, Sir Peter, the heart that is conscious of its own integrity is ever slow to credit another's treachery.

SIR PETER: True, but your brother has no sentiment. You never hear him talk so.

JOSEPH SURFACE: Yet I can't but think Lady Teazle herself has too much principle.

SIR PETER: Ay, but what is principle against the flattery of a handsome, lively young fellow?

JOSEPH SURFACE: That's very true.

SIR PETER: And then, you know, the difference of our ages makes it very improbable that she should have any great affection for me; and, if she were to be frail, and I were to make it public, why, the town would only laugh at me, the foolish old bachelor who had married a girl.

JOSEPH SURFACE: That's true, to be sure. They would laugh.

SIR PETER: Laugh, ay! And make ballads and paragraphs and the devil knows what of me.

JOSEPH SURFACE: No, you must never make it public.

SIR PETER: But then, again, that the nephew of my old friend, Sir Oliver, should be the person to attempt such a wrong, hurts me more nearly.

JOSEPH SURFACE: Ay, there's the point. When ingratitude barbs the dart of injury, the wound has double danger in it.

SIR PETER: Ay! I that was, in a manner, left his guardian, in whose house he had been so often entertained, who never in my life denied him — my advice!

JOSEPH SURFACE: Oh, 'tis not to be credited! There may be a man capable of such baseness, to be sure; but, for my part, till you can give me positive proofs, I cannot but doubt it. However, if it should be proved on him, he is no longer a brother of mine; I disclaim kindred with him; for the man who can break the laws of hospitality and tempt the wife of his friend, deserves to be branded as the pest of society.

SIR PETER: What a difference there is between you! What noble sentiments!

JOSEPH SURFACE: Yet I cannot suspect Lady Teazle's honor.

SIR PETER: I am sure I wish to think well of her and to remove all ground of quarrel between us. She has lately reproached me more than once with having made no settlement on her, and, in our last quarrel, she almost hinted that she should not break her heart if I was dead. Now, as we seem to differ in our ideas of expense, I have resolved she shall have her own way and be her own mistress in that respect for the future; and, if I were to die, she will find I have not been inattentive to her interest while living. Here, my friend, are the drafts of two deeds, which I wish to have your opinion on. By one, she will enjoy eight hundred a year independent while I live; and, by the other, the bulk of my fortune at my death.

JOSEPH SURFACE: This conduct, Sir Peter, is indeed truly generous. (*aside*) I wish it may not corrupt my pupil.

SIR PETER: Yes, I am determined she shall have no cause to complain, though I would not have her acquainted with the latter instance of my affection yet awhile.

JOSEPH SURFACE (*aside*): Nor I, if I could help it.

SIR PETER: And now, my dear friend, if you please, we will talk over the situation of your hopes with Maria.

JOSEPH SURFACE (*softly*): Oh, no, Sir Peter! Another time, if you please.

SIR PETER: I am sensibly chagrined at the little progress you seem to make in her affections.

JOSEPH SURFACE (*softly*): I beg you will not mention it. What are my disappointments when your happiness is in debate! (*aside*) 'Sdeath, I shall be ruined every way!

SIR PETER: And though you are averse to my acquainting Lady Teazle with your passion for Maria, I'm sure she's not your enemy in the affair.

JOSEPH SURFACE: Pray, Sir Peter, now oblige me. I am really too much affected by the subject we have been speaking of to bestow a thought on my own concerns. The man who is entrusted with his friend's distress can never — (*Enter* SERVANT.) Well, sir?

SERVANT: Your brother, sir, is speaking to a

gentleman in the street and says he knows you are within.

JOSEPH SURFACE: 'Sdeath, you blockhead! I'm not within. I'm out for the day.

SIR PETER: Stay — Hold! A thought has struck me. You shall be at home.

JOSEPH SURFACE: Well, well, let him up. (*Exit* SERVANT. *Aside*) He'll interrupt Sir Peter, however.

SIR PETER: Now, my good friend, oblige me, I entreat you. Before Charles comes, let me conceal my self somewhere; then do you tax him on the point we have been talking, and his answer may satisfy me at once.

JOSEPH SURFACE: Oh, fie, Sir Peter! Would you have me join in so mean a trick? To trepan³ my brother too!

SIR PETER: Nay, you tell me you are sure he is innocent. If so, you do him the greatest service by giving him an opportunity to clear himself, and you will set my heart at rest. Come, you shall not refuse me. Here, behind the screen will be — Hey! What the devil! There seems to be one listener here already! I'll swear I saw a petticoat!

JOSEPH SURFACE: Ha! ha! ha! Well, this is ridiculous enough. I'll tell you, Sir Peter, though I hold a man of intrigue to be a most despicable character, yet, you know, it does not follow that one is to be an absolute Joseph either.⁴ Hark'ee, 'tis a little French milliner, a silly rogue that plagues me; and having some character to lose, on your coming, sir, she ran behind the screen.

SIR PETER: Ah, you rogue, — But, egad, she has overheard all I have been saying of my wife.

JOSEPH SURFACE: Oh, 'twill never go any farther, you may depend upon it!

SIR PETER: No? Then, faith, let her hear it out. — Here's a closet will do as well.

JOSEPH SURFACE: Well, go in there.

SIR PETER: Sly rogue! Sly rogue!

(*Going into the closet.*)

JOSEPH SURFACE: A narrow escape, indeed! And a curious situation I'm in, to part man and wife in this manner.

LADY TEAZLE (*peeping*): Couldn't I steal off?

JOSEPH SURFACE: Keep close, my angel!

SIR PETER (*peeping*): Joseph, tax him home!

JOSEPH SURFACE: Back, my dear friend!

LADY TEAZLE (*peeping*): Couldn't you lock Sir Peter in?

JOSEPH SURFACE: Be still, my life!

SIR PETER (*peeping*): You're sure the little milliner won't blab?

JOSEPH SURFACE: In, in, my good Sir Peter! — 'Fore gad, I wish I had a key to the door!

(*Enter* CHARLES SURFACE.)

CHARLES: Holla, brother, what has been the matter? Your fellow would not let me up at first. What, have you had a Jew or a wench with you?

JOSEPH SURFACE: Neither, brother, I assure you.

CHARLES: But what has made Sir Peter steal off? I thought he had been with you.

JOSEPH SURFACE: He was, brother; but, hearing you were coming, he did not choose to stay.

CHARLES: What, was the old gentleman afraid I wanted to borrow money of him?

JOSEPH SURFACE: No, sir; but I am sorry to find, Charles, you have lately given that worthy man grounds for great uneasiness.

CHARLES: Yes, they tell me I do that to a great many worthy men. But how so, pray?

JOSEPH SURFACE: To be plain with you, brother, he thinks you are endeavoring to gain Lady Teazle's affections from him.

CHARLES: Who, I? O lud, not I, upon my word. Ha! ha! ha! so the old fellow has found

---

3 *trepan:* deceive. 4 *Joseph:* see the story of Joseph, who resisted the advances of Potiphar's wife, in Genesis 39.

out that he has got a young wife, has he? Or, what's worse, Lady Teazle has found out she has an old husband?

JOSEPH SURFACE: This is no subject to jest on, brother. He who can laugh —

CHARLES: True, true, as you were going to say — Then, seriously, I never had the least idea of what you charge me with, upon my honor.

JOSEPH SURFACE (aloud): Well, it will give Sir Peter great satisfaction to hear this.

CHARLES: To be sure, I once thought the lady seemed to have taken a fancy to me; but, upon my soul, I never gave her the least encouragement. Besides, you know my attachment to Maria.

JOSEPH SURFACE: But, sure, brother, even if Lady Teazle had betrayed the fondest partiality for you —

CHARLES: Why, look'ee, Joseph, I hope I shall never deliberately do a dishonorable action; but if a pretty woman was purposely to throw herself in my way, and that pretty woman married to a man old enough to be her father —

JOSEPH SURFACE: Well?

CHARLES: Why, I believe I should be obliged to borrow a little of your morality, that's all. But, brother, do you know now that you surprise me exceedingly by naming me with Lady Teazle; for, i' faith, I always understood you were her favorite.

JOSEPH SURFACE: Oh, for shame, Charles! This retort is foolish.

CHARLES: Nay, I swear I have seen you exchange such significant glances —

JOSEPH SURFACE: Nay, nay, sir, this is no jest.

CHARLES: Egad, I'm serious! Don't you remember one day when I called here —

JOSEPH SURFACE: Nay, pr'ythee, Charles —

CHARLES: And found you together —

JOSEPH SURFACE: Zounds, sir, I insist —

CHARLES: And another time when your servant —

JOSEPH SURFACE: Brother, brother, a word with you! (aside) Gad, I must stop him.

CHARLES: Informed, I say, that —

JOSEPH SURFACE: Hush! I beg your pardon, but Sir Peter has overhead all we have been saying. I knew you would clear yourself, or I should not have consented.

CHARLES: How, Sir Peter! Where is he?

JOSEPH SURFACE: Softly! There! (Points to the closet.)

CHARLES: Oh, 'fore heaven, I'll have him out. Sir Peter, come forth!

JOSEPH SURFACE: No, no —

CHARLES: I say, Sir Peter, come into court! (Pulls in SIR PETER) What! My old guardian! What, turn inquisitor and take evidence incog.?[5]

SIR PETER: Give me your hand, Charles. I believe I have suspected you wrongfully; but you mustn't be angry with Joseph. 'Twas my plan.

CHARLES: Indeed!

SIR PETER: But I acquit you. I promise you I don't think near so ill of you as I did. What I have heard has given me great satisfaction.

CHARLES: Egad, then, 'twas lucky you didn't hear any more. (apart to JOSEPH) Wasn't it, Joseph?

SIR PETER: Ah, you would have retorted on him.

CHARLES: Ah, ay, that was a joke.

SIR PETER: Yes, yes, I know his honor too well.

CHARLES: But you might as well have suspected him as me in this matter, for all that. (apart to JOSEPH) Mightn't he, Joseph?

SIR PETER: Well, well, I believe you.

JOSEPH SURFACE (aside): Would they were both out of the room!

(Enter SERVANT and whispers JOSEPH.)

---

5 incog.: Latin, incognito.

SIR PETER: And in future, perhaps, we may not be such strangers. (*Exit* SERVANT.)

JOSEPH SURFACE: Gentlemen, I beg pardon. I must wait on you down stairs. Here is a person come on particular business.

CHARLES: Well, you can see him in another room. Sir Peter and I have not met a long time, and I have something to say to him.

JOSEPH SURFACE (*aside*): They must not be left together. — I'll send this man away and return directly. (*Apart to* SIR PETER *and goes out*) Sir Peter, not a word of the French milliner.

SIR PETER (*apart to* JOSEPH): I! Not for the world. — Ah, Charles, if you associated more with your brother, one might indeed hope for your reformation. He is a man of sentiment. Well, there is nothing in the world so noble as a man of sentiment.[6]

CHARLES: Psha, he is too moral by half; and so apprehensive of his good name, as he calls it, that I suppose he would as soon let a priest into his house as a wench.

SIR PETER: No, no! Come, come! You wrong him. No, no, Joseph is no rake, but he is no such saint either, in that respect. (*aside*) I have a great mind to tell him. We should have such a laugh at Joseph.

CHARLES: Oh, hang him, he's a very anchorite, a young hermit.

SIR PETER: Hark'ee, you must not abuse him. He may chance to hear of it again, I promise you.

CHARLES: Why, you won't tell him?

SIR PETER: No, but — This way. (*aside*) Egad, I'll tell him. — Hark'ee, have you a mind to have a good laugh at Joseph?

CHARLES: I should like it, of all things.

SIR PETER: Then, i' faith, we will! I'll be quit with him for discovering me. He had a girl with him when I called.

CHARLES: What! Joseph? You jest.

SIR PETER: Hush! A little French milliner, and the best of the jest is she's in the room now.

CHARLES: The devil she is!

SIR PETER: Hush, I tell you! (*Points.*)

CHARLES: Behind the screen? 'Slife let's unveil her!

SIR PETER: No, no, he's coming. You shan't, indeed!

CHARLES: Oh, egad, we'll have a peep at the little milliner!

SIR PETER: Not for the world! Joseph will never forgive me.

CHARLES: I'll stand by you —

SIR PETER: Odds, here he is!

(JOSEPH SURFACE *enters just as* CHARLES SURFACE *throws down the screen.*)

CHARLES: Lady Teazle, by all that's wonderful!

SIR PETER: Lady Teazle, by all that's damnable!

CHARLES: Sir Peter, this is one of the smartest French milliners I ever saw. Egad, you seem all to have been diverting yourselves here at hide and seek, and I don't see who is out of the secret. Shall I beg your ladyship to inform me? Not a word! Brother, will you be pleased to explain this matter? What! Is morality dumb too? Sir Peter, though I found you in the dark, perhaps you are not so now! All mute! — Well, though I can make nothing of the affair, I suppose you perfectly understand one another; so I'll leave you to yourselves. (*Going*) Brother, I'm sorry to find you have given that worthy man grounds for so much uneasiness. Sir Peter, there's nothing in the world so noble as a man of sentiment!

(*Exit* CHARLES. *They stand for some time looking at each other.*)

JOSEPH SURFACE: Sir Peter, notwithstanding — I confess, that appearances are against me, — if you will afford me your patience, I

---

6 *a man of sentiment:* note in the play how the dramatist makes use of some of the very things he attacks in his satire.

make no doubt — but I shall explain everything to your satisfaction.

SIR PETER: If you please, sir.

JOSEPH SURFACE: The fact is, sir, that Lady Teazle, knowing my pretensions to your ward Maria, — I say, sir, Lady Teazle, being apprehensive of the jealousy of your temper, — and knowing my friendship to the family, — she, sir, I say — called here, — in order that — I might explain these pretensions; but on your coming, — being apprehensive, — as I said, — of your jealousy, she withdrew; and this, you may depend on it, is the whole truth of the matter.

SIR PETER: A very clear account, upon my word, and I dare swear the lady will vouch for every particle of it.

LADY TEAZLE: For not one word of it, Sir Peter.

SIR PETER: How! Don't you think it worth while to agree in the lie?

LADY TEAZLE: There is not one syllable of truth in what that gentleman has told you.

SIR PETER: I believe you, upon my soul, ma'am.

JOSEPH SURFACE (aside): 'Sdeath, madam, will you betray me?

LADY TEAZLE: Good Mr. Hypocrite, by your leave, I'll speak for myself.

SIR PETER: Ay, let her alone, sir; you'll find she'll make out a better story than you, without prompting.

LADY TEAZLE: Hear me, Sir Peter! I came here on no matter relating to your ward and even ignorant of this gentleman's pretensions to her. But I came, seduced by his insidious arguments, at least to listen to his pretended passion, if not to sacrifice your honor to his baseness.

SIR PETER: Now, I believe the truth is coming, indeed.

JOSEPH SURFACE: The woman's mad!

LADY TEAZLE: No, sir; she has recovered her senses and your own arts have furnished her with the means. Sir Peter, I do not expect you to credit me, but the tenderness you expressed for me when I am sure you could not think I was a witness to it has so penetrated to my heart that had I left this place without the shame of this discovery my future life should have spoken the sincerity of my gratitude. As for that smooth-tongued hypocrite, who would have seduced the wife of his too credulous friend while he affected honorable addresses to his ward, I behold him now in a light so truly despicable that I shall never again respect myself for having listened to him. (Exit.)

JOSEPH SURFACE: Notwithstanding all this, Sir Peter, heaven knows —

SIR PETER: That you are a villain, and so I leave you to your conscience. (Exit.)

JOSEPH SURFACE (following SIR PETER): You are too rash, Sir Peter. You shall hear me. The man who shuts out conviction by refusing to —

(Exit.)

ACT FIVE

SCENE ONE   The library.

Enter JOSEPH SURFACE and SERVANT.

JOSEPH SURFACE: Mr. Stanley! And why should you think I would see him? You must know he comes to ask something.

SERVANT: Sir, I should not have let him in, but that Mr. Rowley came to the door with him.

JOSEPH SURFACE: Psha, blockhead! To suppose that I should now be in a temper to receive visits from poor relations! Well, why don't you show the fellow up?

SERVANT: I will, sir. Why, sir, it was not my fault that Sir Peter discovered my lady —

JOSEPH SURFACE: Go, fool! (Exit SERVANT.) Sure, Fortune never played a man of my policy such a trick before. My character with Sir Peter, my hopes with Maria, destroyed in a moment! I'm in a rare humor to listen to other people's distresses. I shan't be able to bestow even a benevolent sentiment on Stanley. — So here he comes and Rowley with him. I must try to recover myself and put a little charity into my face, however. (*Exit.*)

(*Enter* SIR OLIVER SURFACE *and* ROWLEY.)

SIR OLIVER: What, does he avoid us? That was he, was it not?

ROWLEY: It was, sir. But I doubt you are come a little too abruptly. His nerves are so weak that the sight of a poor relation may be too much for him. I should have gone first to break it to him.

SIR OLIVER: Oh, plague of his nerves! Yet this is he whom Sir Peter extols as a man of the most benevolent way of thinking.

ROWLEY: As to his way of thinking, I cannot pretend to decide; for, to do him justice, he appears to have as much speculative benevolence as any private gentleman in the kingdom, though he is seldom so sensual as to indulge himself in the exercise of it.

SIR OLIVER: Yet he has a string of charitable sentiments at his fingers' ends.

ROWLEY: Or, rather, at his tongue's end, Sir Oliver, for I believe there is no sentiment he has such faith in as that "Charity begins at home."

SIR OLIVER: And his, I presume, is of that domestic sort which never stirs abroad at all.

ROWLEY: I doubt you'll find it so. But he's coming. I mustn't seem to interrupt you; and you know immediately as you leave him, I come in to announce your arrival in your real character.

SIR OLIVER: True, and afterwards you'll meet me at Sir Peter's.

ROWLEY: Without losing a moment. (*Exit.*)

SIR OLIVER: I don't like the complaisance of his features.

(*Enter* JOSEPH SURFACE.)

JOSEPH SURFACE: Sir, I beg you ten thousand pardons for keeping you a moment waiting. Mr. Stanley, I presume.

SIR OLIVER: At your service.

JOSEPH SURFACE: Sir, I beg you will do me the honor to sit down. — I entreat you, sir.

SIR OLIVER: Dear sir, — there's no occasion. (*aside*) Too civil by half.

JOSEPH SURFACE: I have not the pleasure of knowing you, Mr. Stanley, but I am extremely happy to see you look so well. You were nearly related to my mother, I think, Mr. Stanley?

SIR OLIVER: I was, sir; so nearly that my present poverty, I fear, may do discredit to her wealthy children, else I should not have presumed to trouble you.

JOSEPH SURFACE: Dear sir, there needs no apology! He that is in distress, though a stranger, has a right to claim kindred with the wealthy. I am sure I wish I was of that class and had it in my power to offer you even a small relief.

SIR OLIVER: If your uncle, Sir Oliver, were here, I should have a friend.

JOSEPH SURFACE: I wish he was, sir, with all my heart. You should not want an advocate with him, believe me, sir.

SIR OLIVER: I should not need one; my distresses would recommend me. But I imagined his bounty would enable you to become the agent of his charity.

JOSEPH SURFACE: My dear sir, you were strangely misinformed. Sir Oliver is a worthy man, a very worthy man; but avarice, Mr. Stanley, is the vice of age. I will tell you, my good sir, in confidence what he has done for me has been a mere nothing, though people I know have thought otherwise; and, for my part, I never chose to contradict the report.

SIR OLIVER: What! Has he never transmitted you bullion, rupees, pagodas?[1]

JOSEPH SURFACE: Oh, dear sir, nothing of the kind! No, no, a few presents now and then,

---

1 *rupees, pagodas:* silver and gold coins of India, valued at about two and eight shillings respectively.

— china, shawls, congou tea, avadavats,[2] and Indian crackers,[3] — little more, believe me.

SIR OLIVER (*aside*): Here's gratitude for twelve thousand pounds! Avadavats and Indian crackers!

JOSEPH SURFACE: Then, my dear sir, you have heard, I doubt not, of the extravagance of my brother. There are very few who would credit what I have done for that unfortunate young man.

SIR OLIVER (*aside*): Not I, for one!

JOSEPH SURFACE: The sums I have lent him! Indeed I have been exceedingly to blame; it was an amiable weakness; however, I don't pretend to defend it; and now I feel it doubly culpable since it has deprived me of the pleasure of serving you, Mr. Stanley, as my heart dictates.

SIR OLIVER (*aside*): Dissembler! — Then, sir, you can't assist me?

JOSEPH SURFACE: At present it grieves me to say I cannot; but whenever I have the ability, you may depend upon hearing from me.

SIR OLIVER: I am extremely sorry —

JOSEPH SURFACE: Not more than I, believe me. To pity without the power to relieve is still more painful than to ask and be denied.

SIR OLIVER: Kind sir, your most obedient, humble servant!

JOSEPH SURFACE: You leave me deeply affected, Mr. Stanley. — William, be ready to open the door.

SIR OLIVER: Oh, dear sir, no ceremony.

JOSEPH SURFACE: Your very obedient!

SIR OLIVER: Sir, your most obsequious!

JOSEPH SURFACE: You may depend upon hearing from me whenever I can be of service.

SIR OLIVER: Sweet sir, you are too good!

JOSEPH SURFACE: In the meantime I wish you health and spirits.

SIR OLIVER: Your ever grateful and perpetual humble servant!

JOSEPH SURFACE: Sir, yours as sincerely!

SIR OLIVER (*aside*): Charles, you are my heir! (*Exit.*)

JOSEPH SURFACE: This is one bad effect of a good character; it invites application from the unfortunate, and there needs no small degree of address to gain the reputation of benevolence without incurring the expense. The silver ore of pure charity is an expensive article in the catalogue of a man's good qualities, whereas the sentimental French plate I use instead of it, makes just as good a show and pays no tax.

(*Enter* ROWLEY.)

ROWLEY: Mr. Surface, your servant! I was apprehensive of interrupting you, though my business demands immediate attention, as this note will inform you.

JOSEPH SURFACE: Always happy to see Mr. Rowley. (*Reads the letter.*) Sir Oliver Surface! My uncle arrived!

ROWLEY: He is, indeed; we have just parted. Quite well after a speedy voyage and impatient to embrace his worthy nephew.

JOSEPH SURFACE: I am astonished! — William, stop Mr. Stanley, if he's not gone!

ROWLEY: Oh, he's out of reach, I believe.

JOSEPH SURFACE: Why did you not let me know this when you came in together?

ROWLEY: I thought you had particular business. But I must be gone to inform your brother and appoint him here to meet your uncle. He will be with you in a quarter of an hour.

JOSEPH SURFACE: So he says. Well, I am strangely overjoyed at his coming. (*aside*) Never, to be sure, was anything so damned unlucky!

ROWLEY: You will be delighted to see how well he looks.

---

2 *avadavats:* small singing birds of India with red and black plumage. 3 *Indian crackers:* firecrackers in colorful papers.

Joseph Surface: Ah, I'm overjoyed to hear it. — (*aside*) Just at this time!

Rowley: I'll tell him how impatiently you expect him.

Joseph Surface: Do, do! Pray give him my best duty and affection. Indeed, I cannot express the sensations I feel at the thought of seeing him. (*Exit* Rowley.) Certainly his coming just at this time is the cruellest piece of ill fortune.

(*Exit.*)

Scene Two   Sir Peter Teazle's.

Enter Mrs. Candour *and* Maid.

Maid: Indeed, ma'am, my lady will see nobody at present.

Mrs. Candour: Did you tell her it was her friend Mrs. Candour?

Maid: Yes, ma'am; but she begs you will excuse her.

Mrs. Candour: Do go again. I shall be glad to see her if it be only for a moment, for I am sure she must be in great distress. (*Exit* Maid.) Dear heart, how provoking! I'm not mistress of half the circumstances! We shall have the whole affair in the newspapers with the names of the parties at length before I have dropped the story at a dozen houses. (*Enter* Sir Benjamin Backbite.) Oh, Sir Benjamin, you have heard, I suppose —

Sir Benjamin: Of Lady Teazle and Mr. Surface —

Mrs. Candour: And Sir Peter's discovery —

Sir Benjamin: Oh, the strangest piece of business, to be sure!

Mrs. Candour: Well, I never was so surprised in my life. I am so sorry for all parties, indeed.

Sir Benjamin: Now, I don't pity Sir Peter at all; he was so extravagantly partial to Mr. Surface.

Mrs. Candour: Mr. Surface! Why, 'twas with Charles Lady Teazle was detected.

Sir Benjamin: No, no, I tell you; Mr. Surface is the gallant.

Mrs. Candour: No such thing! Charles is the man. 'Twas Mr. Surface brought Sir Peter on purpose to discover them.

Sir Benjamin: I tell you I had it from one —

Mrs. Candour: And I have it from one —

Sir Benjamin: Who had it from one, who had it —

Mrs. Candour: From one immediately. But here comes Lady Sneerwell; perhaps she knows the whole affair.

(*Enter* Lady Sneerwell.)

Lady Sneerwell: So, my dear Mrs. Candour, here's a sad affair of our friend Lady Teazle.

Mrs. Candour: Ay, my dear friend, who would have thought —

Lady Sneerwell: Well, there is no trusting appearances, though, indeed, she was always too lively for me.

Mrs. Candour: To be sure, her manners were a little too free; but then she was so young!

Lady Sneerwell: And had, indeed, some good qualities.

Mrs. Candour: So she had, indeed. But have you heard the particulars?

Lady Sneerwell: No; but everybody says that Mr. Surface —

Sir Benjamin: Ay, there, I told you Mr. Surface was the man.

Mrs. Candour: No, no; indeed, the assignation was with Charles.

Lady Sneerwell: With Charles? You alarm me, Mrs. Candour!

Mrs. Candour: Yes, yes; he was the lover. Mr. Surface, to do him justice, was only the informer.

Sir Benjamin: Well, I'll not dispute with you,

Mrs. Candour; but, be it which it may, I hope that Sir Peter's wound will not —

Mrs. Candour: Sir Peter's wound! Oh, mercy! I didn't hear a word of their fighting.

Lady Sneerwell: Nor I, not a syllable.

Sir Benjamin: No? What, no mention of the duel?

Mrs. Candour: Not a word.

Sir Benjamin: Oh, yes. They fought before they left the room.

Lady Sneerwell: Pray let us hear.

Mrs. Candour: Ay, do oblige us with the duel.

Sir Benjamin: "Sir," says Sir Peter, immediately after the discovery, "you are a most ungrateful fellow."

Mrs. Candour: Ay, to Charles —

Sir Benjamin: No, no, to Mr. Surface. "A most ungrateful fellow; and old as I am, sir," says he, "I insist on immediate satisfaction."

Mrs. Candour: Ay, that must have been to Charles, for 'tis very unlikely Mr. Surface should fight in his own house.

Sir Benjamin: Gad's life, ma'am, not at all, — "giving me immediate satisfaction!" On this, ma'am, Lady Teazle, seeing Sir Peter in such danger, ran out of the room in strong hysterics and Charles after her calling out for hartshorn and water; then, madam, they began to fight with swords —

(*Enter* Crabtree.)

Crabtree: With pistols, nephew, pistols! I have it from undoubted authority.

Mrs. Candour: Oh, Mr. Crabtree, then it is all true?

Crabtree: Too true, indeed, madam, and Sir Peter is dangerously wounded —

Sir Benjamin: By a thrust in second[1] quite through his left side —

Crabtree: By a bullet lodged in the thorax.

Mrs. Candour: Mercy on me! Poor Sir Peter!

Crabtree: Yes, madam, though Charles would have avoided the matter if he could.

Mrs. Candour: I knew Charles was the person.

Sir Benjamin: My uncle, I see, knows nothing of the matter.

Crabtree: But Sir Peter taxed him with the basest ingratitude —

Sir Benjamin: That I told you, you know —

Crabtree: Do, nephew, let me speak! And insisted on immediate —

Sir Benjamin: Just as I said —

Crabtree: Odd's life, nephew, allow others to know something too! A pair of pistols lay on the bureau (for Mr. Surface, it seems, had come home the night before late from Salt-hill,[2] where he had been to see the Montem with a friend who has a son at Eton) so, unluckily, the pistols were left charged.

Sir Benjamin: I heard nothing of this.

Crabtree: Sir Peter forced Charles to take one, and they fired, it seems, pretty nearly together. Charles's shot took effect, as I tell you, and Sir Peter's missed; but what is very extraordinary, the ball struck a little bronze Shakespeare that stood over the fireplace, grazed out of the window at a right angle and wounded the postman, who was just coming to the door with a double letter[3] from Northamptonshire.

Sir Benjamin: My uncle's account is more circumstantial, I confess; but I believe mine is the true one, for all that.

Lady Sneerwell (*aside*): I am more interested in this affair than they imagine and must have better information. (*Exit.*)

---

1 *second:* properly *seconde* (French), a parrying position in fencing.   2 *Salthill:* it was a custom for Eton schoolboys every third Whit-Tuesday to climb Salt Hill (*processus ad montem*) and charge spectators *salt-money*. The ceremony is described in detail in Benjamin Disraeli's *Coningsby*. The reference dates the action of the play about the first of June, Whitsun being fifty days after Easter.   3 *double letter:* a letter heavy enough to require double postage.

SIR BENJAMIN: Ah, Lady Sneerwell's alarm is very easily accounted for.

CRABTREE: Yes, yes, they certainly do say — But that's neither here nor there.

MRS. CANDOUR: But, pray, where is Sir Peter at present?

CRABTREE: Oh, they brought him home, and he is now in the house, though the servants are ordered to deny him.

MRS. CANDOUR: I believe so, and Lady Teazle, I suppose, attending him.

CRABTREE: Yes, yes; and I saw one of the faculty[4] enter just before me.

SIR BENJAMIN: Hey! Who comes here?

CRABTREE: Oh, this is he, the physician, depend on't.

MRS. CANDOUR: Oh, certainly, it must be the physician; and now we shall know.

(*Enter* SIR OLIVER SURFACE.)

CRABTREE: Well, doctor, what hopes?

MRS. CANDOUR: Ay, doctor, how's your patient?

SIR BENJAMIN: Now, doctor, isn't it a wound with a smallsword?

CRABTREE: A bullet lodged in the thorax, for a hundred!

SIR OLIVER: Doctor? A wound with a smallsword? And a bullet in the thorax? — Oons, are you mad, good people?

SIR BENJAMIN: Perhaps, sir, you are not a doctor?

SIR OLIVER: Truly, I am to thank you for my degree, if I am.

CRABTREE: Only a friend of Sir Peter's, then, I presume. But, sir, you must have heard of his accident.

SIR OLIVER: Not a word.

CRABTREE: Not of his being dangerously wounded?

SIR OLIVER: The devil he is!

SIR BENJAMIN: Run through the body —

CRABTREE: Shot in the breast —

SIR BENJAMIN: By one Mr. Surface —

CRABTREE: Ay, the younger —

SIR OLIVER: Hey, what the plague! You seem to differ strangely in your accounts; however you agree that Sir Peter is dangerously wounded.

SIR BENJAMIN: Oh, yes, we agree there.

CRABTREE: Yes, yes, I believe there can be no doubt of that.

SIR OLIVER: Then, upon my word, for a person in that situation he is the most imprudent man alive, for here he comes, walking as if nothing at all was the matter. (*Enter* SIR PETER TEAZLE.) Odd's heart, Sir Peter, you are come in good time, I promise you, for we had just given you over.

SIR BENJAMIN (*aside to* CRABTREE): Egad, uncle, this is the most sudden recovery!

SIR OLIVER: Why, man, what do you out of bed with a smallsword through your body and a bullet lodged in your thorax?

SIR PETER: A smallsword and a bullet!

SIR OLIVER: Ay! These gentlemen would have killed you without law or physic, and wanted to dub me a doctor to make me an accomplice.

SIR PETER: Why, what is all this?

SIR BENJAMIN: We rejoice, Sir Peter, that the story of the duel is not true and are sincerely sorry for your other misfortune.

SIR PETER (*aside*): So, so! All over the town already.

CRABTREE: Though, Sir Peter, you were certainly vastly to blame to marry at your years.

SIR PETER: Sir, what business is that of yours?

MRS. CANDOUR: Though, indeed, as Sir Peter made so good a husband, he's very much to be pitied.

---

4 *faculty*: medical profession.

SIR PETER: Plague on your pity, ma'am! I desire none of it.

SIR BENJAMIN: However, Sir Peter, you must not mind the laughing and jests you will meet with on the occasion.

SIR PETER: Sir, sir, I desire to be master in my own house.

CRABTREE: 'Tis no uncommon case, that's one comfort.

SIR PETER: I insist on being left to myself. Without ceremony, I insist on your leaving my house directly.

MRS. CANDOUR: Well, well, we are going; and depend on't, we'll make the best report of it we can. (*Exit.*)

SIR PETER: Leave my house!

CRABTREE: And tell how hardly you've been treated. (*Exit.*)

SIR PETER: Leave my house!

SIR BENJAMIN: And how patiently you bear it. (*Exit.*)

SIR PETER: Fiends! Vipers! Furies! Oh, that their own venom would choke them!

SIR OLIVER: They are very provoking indeed, Sir Peter.

(*Enter* ROWLEY.)

ROWLEY: I heard high words. What has ruffled you, sir?

SIR PETER: Psha, what signifies asking? Do I ever pass a day without my vexations?

ROWLEY: Well, I'm not inquisitive.

SIR OLIVER: Well, Sir Peter, I have seen both my nephews in the manner we proposed.

SIR PETER: A precious couple they are!

ROWLEY: Yes, and Sir Oliver is convinced that your judgment was right, Sir Peter.

SIR OLIVER: Yes, I find Joseph is indeed the man, after all.

ROWLEY: Ay, as Sir Peter says, he is a man of sentiment.

SIR OLIVER: And acts up to the sentiments he professes.

ROWLEY: It certainly is edification to hear him talk.

SIR OLIVER: Oh, he's a model for the young men of the age! But how's this, Sir Peter, you don't join us in your friend Joseph's praise as I expected?

SIR PETER: Sir Oliver, we live in a damned wicked world, and the fewer we praise the better.

ROWLEY: What, do you say so, Sir Peter, who were never mistaken in your life?

SIR PETER: Psha! Plague on you both! I see by your sneering you have heard the whole affair. I shall go mad among you!

ROWLEY: Then, to fret you no longer, Sir Peter, we are indeed acquainted with it all. I met Lady Teazle coming from Mr. Surface's so humbled that she deigned to request me to be her advocate with you.

SIR PETER: And does Sir Oliver know all this?

SIR OLIVER: Every circumstance.

SIR PETER: What? Of the closet and the screen, hey?

SIR OLIVER: Yes, yes, and the little French milliner. Oh, I have been vastly diverted with the story! Ha! ha! ha!

SIR PETER: 'Twas very pleasant.

SIR OLIVER: I never laughed more in my life, I assure you. Ah! ah! ah!

SIR PETER: Oh, vastly diverting! Ha! ha! ha!

ROWLEY: To be sure, Joseph with his sentiments! Ha! ha! ha!

SIR PETER: Yes, yes, his sentiments! Ha! ha! ha! Hypocritical villain!

SIR OLIVER: Ay, and that rogue Charles to pull Sir Peter out of the closet! Ha! ha! ha!

SIR PETER: Ha! ha! 'Twas devilish entertaining, to be sure!

SIR OLIVER: Ha! ha! ha! Egad, Sir Peter, I

should like to have seen your face when the screen was thrown down! Ha! ha!

SIR PETER: Yes, yes, my face when the screen was thrown down! Ha! ha! ha! Oh, I must never show my head again!

SIR OLIVER: But come, come, it isn't fair to laugh at you neither, my old friend, though, upon my soul, I can't help it.

SIR PETER: Oh, pray don't restrain your mirth on my account. It does not hurt me at all. I laugh at the whole affair myself. Yes, yes, I think being a standing jest for all one's acquaintance a very happy situation. Oh, yes, and then of a morning to read the paragraphs about Mr. S —, Lady T —, and Sir P — will be so entertaining.

ROWLEY: Without affectation, Sir Peter, you may despise the ridicule of fools. But I see Lady Teazle going towards the next room. I am sure you must desire a reconciliation as earnestly as she does.

SIR OLIVER: Perhaps my being here prevents her coming to you. Well, I'll leave honest Rowley to mediate between you; but he must bring you all presently to Mr. Surface's, where I am now returning, if not to reclaim a libertine, at least to expose hypocrisy.

SIR PETER: Ah, I'll be present at your discovering yourself there with all my heart, though 'tis a vile unlucky place for discoveries.

ROWLEY: We'll follow. (*Exit* SIR OLIVER.)

SIR PETER: She is not coming here, you see, Rowley.

ROWLEY: No, but she has left the door of that room open, you perceive. See, she is in tears.

SIR PETER: Certainly a little mortification appears very becoming in a wife. Don't you think it will do her good to let her pine a little?

ROWLEY: Oh, this is ungenerous in you!

SIR PETER: Well, I know not what to think. You remember the letter I found of hers evidently intended for Charles?

ROWLEY: A mere forgery, Sir Peter, laid in your way on purpose. This is one of the points which I intend Snake shall give you conviction of.

SIR PETER: I wish I were once satisfied of that. She looks this way. What a remarkably elegant turn of the head she has! Rowley, I'll go to her.

ROWLEY: Certainly.

SIR PETER: Though, when it is known that we are reconciled, people will laugh at me ten times more.

ROWLEY: Let them laugh and retort their malice only by showing them you are happy in spite of it.

SIR PETER: I' faith, so I will! And, if I'm not mistaken, we may yet be the happiest couple in the country.

ROWLEY: Nay, Sir Peter, he who once lays aside suspicion —

SIR PETER: Hold, Master Rowley! If you have any regard for me, never let me hear you utter anything like a sentiment. I have had enough of them to serve me the rest of my life.

(*Exeunt.*)

SCENE THREE   The library.

Enter JOSEPH SURFACE *and* LADY SNEERWELL.

LADY SNEERWELL: Impossible! Will not Sir Peter immediately be reconciled to Charles and, of course, no longer oppose his union with Maria? The thought is distraction to me!

JOSEPH SURFACE: Can passion furnish a remedy?

LADY SNEERWELL: No, nor cunning neither. Oh, I was a fool, an idiot, to league with such a blunderer!

JOSEPH SURFACE: Sure, Lady Sneerwell, I am the greatest sufferer; yet you see I bear the accident with calmness.

LADY SNEERWELL: Because the disappointment doesn't reach your heart; your interest only attached you to Maria. Had you felt for her what I have for that ungrateful libertine, neither your temper nor hypocrisy could prevent your showing the sharpness of your vexation.

JOSEPH SURFACE: But why should your reproaches fall on me for this disappointment?

LADY SNEERWELL: Are you not the cause of it? Had you not a sufficient field for your roguery in imposing upon Sir Peter and supplanting his brother but you must endeavor to seduce his wife? I hate such an avarice of crimes. 'Tis an unfair monopoly and never prospers.

JOSEPH SURFACE: Well, I admit I have been to blame. I confess I deviated from the direct road of wrong, but I don't think we're so totally defeated neither.

LADY SNEERWELL: No?

JOSEPH SURFACE: You tell me you have made a trial of Snake since we met and that you still believe him faithful to us?

LADY SNEERWELL: I do believe so.

JOSEPH SURFACE: And that he has undertaken, should it be necessary, to swear and prove that Charles is at this time contracted by vows and honor to your ladyship, which some of his former letters to you will serve to support?

LADY SNEERWELL: This, indeed, might have assisted.

JOSEPH SURFACE: Come, come; it is not too late yet. (*Knocking at the door.*) But hark! This is probably my uncle, Sir Oliver. Retire to that room; we'll consult farther when he is gone.

LADY SNEERWELL: Well, but if he should find you out, too?

JOSEPH SURFACE: Oh, I have no fear of that. Sir Peter will hold his tongue for his own credit's sake. And you may depend on it I shall soon discover Sir Oliver's weak side.

LADY SNEERWELL: I have no diffidence[1] of your abilities; only be constant to one roguery at a time. (*Exit.*)

JOSEPH SURFACE: I will, I will! So! 'Tis confounded hard, after such bad fortune, to be baited by one's confederate in evil. Well, at all events, my character is so much better than Charles's that I certainly — Hey! What! This is not Sir Oliver but old Stanley again. Plague on't that he should return to tease me just now! I shall have Sir Oliver come and find him here, and — (*Enter* SIR OLIVER SURFACE.) Gad's life, Mr. Stanley, why have you come back to plague me at this time? You must not stay now, upon my word.

SIR OLIVER: Sir, I hear your uncle Oliver is expected here and, though he has been so penurious to you, I'll try what he'll do for me.

JOSEPH SURFACE: Sir, 'tis impossible for you to stay now; so I must beg — Come any other time and I promise you, you shall be assisted.

SIR OLIVER: No. Sir Oliver and I must be acquainted.

JOSEPH SURFACE: Zounds, sir! Then I must insist on your quitting the room directly.

SIR OLIVER: Nay, sir —

JOSEPH SURFACE: Sir, I insist on 't! — Here William, show this gentleman out. Since you compel me, sir, not one moment — This is such insolence! (*Going to push him out.*)

(*Enter* CHARLES SURFACE.)

CHARLES: Heyday! What's the matter now? What the devil? Have you got hold of my little broker here! Zounds, brother, don't hurt little Premium. What's the matter, my little fellow?

JOSEPH SURFACE: So, he has been with you too, has he?

CHARLES: To be sure, he has. Why, he's as honest a little — But sure, Joseph, you have not been borrowing money too, have you?

JOSEPH SURFACE: Borrowing? No! But, brother, you know we expect Sir Oliver here every —

---

1 *diffidence:* doubt.

CHARLES: O Gad, that's true! Noll mustn't find the little broker here, to be sure!

JOSEPH SURFACE: Yet Mr. Stanley insists —

CHARLES: Stanley! Why his name's Premium.

JOSEPH SURFACE: No, sir, Stanley.

CHARLES: No, no, Premium!

JOSEPH SURFACE: Well, no matter which, but —

CHARLES: Ay, ay, Stanley or Premium, 'tis the same thing, as you say; for I suppose he goes by half a hundred names besides A. B. at the coffee-house.[2] (*Knocking.*)

JOSEPH SURFACE: 'Sdeath, here's Sir Oliver at the door! Now, I beg, Mr. Stanley —

CHARLES: Ay, ay, and I beg, Mr. Premium —

SIR OLIVER: Gentlemen —

JOSEPH SURFACE: Sir, by heaven, you shall go!

CHARLES: Ay, out with him, certainly!

SIR OLIVER: This violence —

JOSEPH SURFACE: Sir, 'tis your own fault.

CHARLES: Out with him, to be sure! (*Both forcing* SIR OLIVER *out.*)

(*Enter* SIR PETER *and* LADY TEAZLE, MARIA, *and* ROWLEY.)

SIR PETER: My old friend, Sir Oliver — Hey! What in the name of wonder? Here are two dutiful nephews! Assault their uncle at a first visit!

LADY TEAZLE: Indeed, Sir Oliver, 'twas well we came in to rescue you.

ROWLEY: Truly it was, for I perceive, Sir Oliver, the character of old Stanley was no protection to you.

SIR OLIVER: Nor of Premium either. The necessities of the former could not extort a shilling from that benevolent gentleman; and, now, egad, I stood a chance of faring worse than my ancestors and being knocked down without being bid for.

JOSEPH SURFACE: Charles!

CHARLES: Joseph!

JOSEPH SURFACE: 'Tis now complete!

CHARLES: Very!

SIR OLIVER: Sir Peter, my friend, and Rowley, too, look on that elder nephew of mine. You know what he has already received from my bounty; and you know how gladly I would have regarded half my fortune as held in trust for him. Judge then my disappointment in discovering him to be destitute of faith, charity, and gratitude!

SIR PETER: Sir Oliver, I should be more surprised at this declaration if I had not myself found him to be mean, treacherous, and hypocritical.

LADY TEAZLE: And if the gentleman pleads not guilty to these, pray let him call me to his character.

SIR PETER: Then, I believe, we need add no more. If he knows himself, he will consider it as the most perfect punishment that he is known to the world.

CHARLES (*aside*): If they talk this way to honesty, what will they say to me, by and by?

SIR OLIVER: As for that prodigal, his brother there —

CHARLES (*aside*): Ay, now comes my turn. The damned family pictures will ruin me!

JOSEPH SURFACE: Sir Oliver — uncle, will you honor me with a hearing?

CHARLES (*aside*): Now, if Joseph would make one of his long speeches, I might recollect myself a little.

SIR OLIVER (*to* JOSEPH): I suppose you would undertake to justify yourself entirely?

JOSEPH SURFACE: I trust I could.

SIR OLIVER (*to* CHARLES): Well, sir, and you could justify yourself, too, I suppose?

---

2 *A.B. at the coffee-house:* an allusion to the use of assumed names for assignations at these places.

CHARLES: Not that I know of, Sir Oliver.

SIR OLIVER: What? Little Premium has been let too much into the secret, I suppose?

CHARLES: True, sir; but they were family secrets and should not be mentioned again, you know.

ROWLEY: Come, Sir Oliver, I know you cannot speak of Charles's follies with anger.

SIR OLIVER: Odd's heart, no more I can, nor with gravity either. Sir Peter, do you know the rogue bargained with me for all his ancestors, sold me judges and generals by the foot and maiden aunts as cheap as broken china?

CHARLES: To be sure, Sir Oliver, I did make a little free with the family canvas, that's the truth on 't. My ancestors may rise in judgment against me, there's no denying it; but believe me sincere when I tell you, and upon my soul I would not say so if I was not, that if I do not appear mortified at the exposure of my follies, it is because I feel at this moment the warmest satisfaction in seeing you, my liberal benefactor.

SIR OLIVER: Charles, I believe you. Give me your hand again. The ill-looking little fellow over the settee has made your peace.

CHARLES: Then, sir, my gratitude to the original is still increased.

LADY TEAZLE: Yet I believe, Sir Oliver, here is one whom Charles is still more anxious to be reconciled to.

SIR OLIVER: Oh, I have heard of his attachment there; and, with the young lady's pardon, if I construe right, that blush —

SIR PETER: Well, child, speak your sentiments!

MARIA: Sir, I have little to say, but that I shall rejoice to hear that he is happy. For me, whatever claim I had to his attention, I willingly resign to one who has a better title.

CHARLES: How, Maria!

SIR PETER: Heyday! What's the mystery now? While he appeared an incorrigible rake, you would give your hand to no one else; and now that he is likely to reform I'll warrant you won't have him!

MARIA: His own heart and Lady Sneerwell know the cause.

CHARLES: Lady Sneerwell!

JOSEPH SURFACE: Brother, it is with great concern I am obliged to speak on this point, but my regard for justice compels me, and Lady Sneerwell's injuries can no longer be concealed. (*Opens the door.*)

(*Enter* LADY SNEERWELL.)

SIR PETER: So! Another French milliner! Egad, he has one in every room in the house, I suppose!

LADY SNEERWELL: Ungrateful Charles! Well may you be surprised and feel for the indelicate situation your perfidy has forced me into.

CHARLES: Pray, uncle, is this another plot of yours? For, as I have life, I don't understand it.

JOSEPH SURFACE: I believe, sir, there is but the evidence of one person more necessary to make it extremely clear.

SIR PETER: And that person, I imagine, is Mr. Snake. Rowley, you were perfectly right to bring him with us, and pray let him appear.

ROWLEY: Walk in, Mr. Snake (*Enter* SNAKE.) I thought his testimony might be wanted; however, it happens unluckily that he comes to confront Lady Sneerwell, not to support her.

LADY SNEERWELL: A villain! Treacherous to me at last! Speak, fellow, have you, too, conspired against me?

SNAKE: I beg your ladyship ten thousand pardons. You paid me extremely liberally for the lie in question, but I unfortunately have been offered double to speak the truth.

SIR PETER: Plot and counter-plot, egad!

LADY SNEERWELL: The torments of shame and disappointment on you all!

LADY TEAZLE: Hold, Lady Sneerwell! Before you go, let me thank you for the trouble you and that gentleman have taken in writing letters from me to Charles and answering them yourself; and let me also request you to make my respects to the scandalous college, of which you are president, and inform them that Lady Teazle, licentiate, begs leave to return the diploma they granted her, as she leaves off practice and kills characters no longer.

LADY SNEERWELL: You too, madam! Provoking! Insolent! May your husband live these fifty years! (*Exit.*)

SIR PETER: Oons, what a fury!

LADY TEAZLE: A malicious creature, indeed!

SIR PETER: Hey! Not for her last wish?

LADY TEAZLE: Oh, no!

SIR OLIVER: Well, sir, and what have you to say now?

JOSEPH SURFACE: Sir, I am so confounded to find that Lady Sneerwell could be guilty of suborning Mr. Snake in this manner to impose on us all that I know not what to say. However, lest her revengeful spirit should prompt her to injure my brother, I had certainly better follow her directly. (*Exit.*)

SIR PETER: Moral to the last drop!

SIR OLIVER: Ay, and marry her, Joseph, if you can. Oil and vinegar! Egad you'll do very well together.

ROWLEY: I believe we have no more occasion for Mr. Snake at present?

SNAKE: Before I go, I beg pardon once for all, for whatever uneasiness I have been the humble instrument of causing to the parties present.

SIR PETER: Well, well, you have made atonement by a good deed at last.

SNAKE: But I must request of the company that it shall never be known.

SIR PETER: Hey! What the plague! Are you ashamed of having done a right thing once in your life?

SNAKE: Ah, sir, consider. I live by the badness of my character. I have nothing but my infamy to depend on; and, if it were once known that I had been betrayed into an honest action, I should lose every friend I have in the world.

SIR OLIVER: Well, well, we'll not traduce you by saying anything in your praise, never fear. (*Exit* SNAKE.)

SIR PETER: There's a precious rogue!

LADY TEAZLE: See, Sir Oliver, there needs no persuasion now to reconcile your nephew and Maria.

SIR OLIVER: Ay, ay, that's as it should be; and, egad, we'll have the wedding tomorrow morning.

CHARLES: Thank you, dear uncle.

SIR PETER: What, you rogue! Don't you ask the girl's consent first?

CHARLES: Oh, I have done that a long time — a minute ago, and she has looked *yes*.

MARIA: For shame, Charles! I protest, Sir Peter, there has not been a word —

SIR OLIVER: Well then, the fewer the better. May your love for each other never know abatement!

SIR PETER: And may you live as happily together as Lady Teazle and I intend to do!

CHARLES: Rowley, my old friend, I am sure you congratulate me; and I suspect that I owe you much.

SIR OLIVER: You do, indeed, Charles.

ROWLEY: If my efforts to serve you had not succeeded, you would have been in my debt for the attempt; but deserve to be happy and you overpay me!

SIR PETER: Ay, honest Rowley always said you would reform.

CHARLES: Why, as to reforming, Sir Peter, I'll make no promises, and that I take to be a proof that I intend to set about it. But here shall be my monitor, my gentle guide. Ah,

can I leave the virtuous path those eyes
illumine?

Though thou, dear maid, shouldst waive thy
 beauty's sway,
Thou still must rule, because I will obey.
An humble fugitive from Folly view,
No sanctuary near but love and you.

(*to the audience*)

You can, indeed, each anxious fear remove,
For even *Scandal* dies, if *you* approve!

EPILOGUE

By Mr. [George] Colman

Spoken by Lady Teazle

I, who was late so volatile and gay,
Like a trade-wind must now blow all one way,
Bend all my cares, my studies, and my vows,
To one dull, rusty weathercock — my spouse!

So wills our virtuous bard,— the motley Bayes[1]
Of crying epilogues and laughing plays!
Old bachelors who marry smart young wives
Learn from our play to regulate your lives;

Each bring his dear to town, all faults upon
 her, —
London will prove the very source of honor.
Plunged fairly in, like a cold bath it serves,
When principles relax, to brace the nerves.

Such is my case; and yet I must deplore
That the gay dream of dissipation's o'er.
And say, ye fair, was ever lively wife,
Born with a genius for the highest life,

Like me untimely blasted in her bloom,
Like me condemned to such a dismal doom?
Save money, when I just knew how to waste it!
Leave London, just as I began to taste it!

Must I then watch the early-crowing cock,
The melancholy ticking of a clock;
In a lone rustic hall forever pounded,[2]
With dogs, cats, rats, and squalling brats
 surrounded?

With humble curate can I now retire,
(While good Sir Peter boozes with the squire)
And at backgammon mortify my soul,
That pants for loo or flutters at a vole?[3]

Seven's near the main![4] Dear sound that must
 expire,
Lost at hot cockles[5] round a Christmas fire.
The transient hour of fashion too soon spent,
Farewell the tranquil mind, farewell content![6]

Farewell the plumèd head, the cushioned *tête*,
That takes the cushion from its proper seat!
That spirit-stirring drum! Card drums, I mean,
Spadille, odd trick, pam, basto, king and
 queen![7]

And you, ye knockers that with brazen throat
The welcome visitors' approach denote,
Farewell all quality of high renown,
Pride, pomp, and circumstance of glorious
 town!

Farewell! Your revels I partake no more,
And Lady Teazle's occupation's o'er!
All this I told our bard; he smiled and said
 'twas clear,
I ought to play deep tragedy next year.

Meanwhile he drew wise morals from his play,
And in these solemn periods stalked away: —
"Blessed were the fair like you, her faults who
 stopped,
And closed her follies when the curtain
 dropped!

No more in vice or error to engage
Or play the fool at large on life's great stage."

---

1 *Bayes:* poet, dramatist (from a character in *The Rehearsal*, where John Dryden was satirized under this name by the Duke of Buckingham et al.). 2 *pounded:* in a pound, like an animal. 3 *loo, vole:* "loo" was a card game, "vole" taking all the tricks. 4 *near the main:* in hazard, the thrower of the dice called his "main" (point) by selecting a number between five and nine. Seven is a good number to try for with two dice. 5 *cockles:* a child's game in which you cover your eyes and guess who strikes you. 6 *Farewell,* etc.: here begins a parody of the Moor's soliloquy in *Othello*, III, iii, 347–357. 7 *drum, spadille, pam, basto:* card game, ace of spades, jack of clubs, ace of clubs.

Woyzeck

It was not until *Woyzeck* (written 1836, performed 1913) and *Danton's Death* (written 1835, performed 1916) were uncovered in this century that the world discovered the genius of Georg Büchner (1813–1837), one of the forerunners of modern expressionism. His influence, particularly the taut, episodic construction, was to be seen in the Lulu plays (*Erdgeist* of 1895 and *Die Büchse der Pandora* of 1903) of Frank Wederkind (1864–1918), Eugene O'Neill's *The Emperor Jones* (with which Jones first attracted attention outside the United States), and (most recently) the British playwright John Arden. What seemed so new in Germany, America and Britain in the twentieth century turned out to be much more than hinted at in the work of this romantic young man who burst out of the empty heroics of the *Sturm und Drang* ("Storm and Stress") period with a revolutionary new drama that was generations ahead of his time.

As a student of science and philosophy at Strassburg and Giessen, Büchner was caught up in the radical movement in Germany in the 1830's. His polemic pamphlet, *The Hessian Courtier* (1834), was really a manifesto of Marxist socialism well before Karl Marx' *Communist Manifesto* which did not appear until 1848. By the time he composed his play on the greatest victim of the French Revolution, the audacious Georges-Jacques Danton (1759–1794) — *"De l'audace, encore de l'audace, toujours de l'audace"* — Büchner had become disillusioned about the revolution that his mentor Karl Ferdinand Gutzkow (1811–1874) had championed for "Young Germany." In *Danton's Death* the hero perishes, shocked and disgusted by the flood of violence he has helped to unloose. Büchner had lost some of his faith in man's ability to control his destiny and was ready, while not entirely condemning the struggle, to face its final futility:

> Individuals are so much surf on a wave, greatest is the sheerest accident, the strength of genius a puppet play — a child's struggle against an iron law; to recognize it the supreme achievement, to control it impossible.

Büchner was never to renounce his radical ideas nor to grow up (or decline) into conservatism. He died too convinced, too young for that. But he did denounce extremism, revolution that becomes reactionary in the face of counter-revolutionary threats, terrorists who overthrow one tyranny only to replace it with another. He saw freedom as somehow connected with the power of the masses, but he realized that though they are a political force they are not politicians and know "no difference between weakness and moderation," that though the mob may cleanse the commonwealth of the bloodsucking aristocracy, they are thereafter very likely to steal their finery and thereby catch their leprosy. In a letter to his fiancée — a girl who destroyed his play *Pietro Aretino* because she thought it unorthodox — Büchner spoke of "the gruesome fatalism of history" and he frequently refers to men as marionettes. *Danton's Death* may suggest that the great man might have saved himself had he acted effectively enough and soon enough, but at the same time it makes us wonder if it lies in man to know how and when to act. "We are all villains and angels, fools and geniuses, all in one," says Camille Desmoulins, one of Danton's fellow deputies in the revolutionary Chamber, and too often we are the inappropriate character at the appropriate time or vice versa for we seldom have reliable control over ourselves and often little or no control over the times and circumstances in which we find ourselves.

None of the grandeur or the grandiloquence of the French Revolution is to be found in *Woyzeck*, any more than in the sophisticated satire of Büchner's charming little *Leonce and Lena*, but the sense of fate is there. The tragic end of the little man Woyzeck, who perishes without any of the opportunities for histrionics of Danton's defense before the Revolutionary Tribunal (which has been described as "sublime in its audacity, its incoherence, its heroism and magnificent buffoonery"), is more moving than the end of any political victim on the guillotine jesting in the moment of death. In *Woyzeck* the "topical" problems have been given, as another German expressionist, Ernst Toller (1893–1939), said, an "eternal" interpretation. They will not be staged by any Max Reinhardt in any Grosses Schauspielhaus extravaganza or self-indulgently expurgated and exploited by any Orson Welles production. Here is the stark story of a simple barber from Leipzig who murders his mistress in a jealous fit; a poor and insignificant man who looks good only in comparison with the unfeeling persons who surround him and who, despite their "superiority," offer neither help nor sympathy. In *The Theatre of Revolt* (1964), Robert Brustein found Woyzeck "the natural man, untaught, unmoral, incorrigible" and the message of the play this:

> To such born victims, morality is an extravagance and virtue a luxury — or as Brecht will put it a hundred years later, *Erst kommt das Fressen, dann kommt die Moral.*

This disillusion and fatality, this dislocation of the individual reflected in what Brustein calls "the accidental, unconnected form of the play," is discussed at some length in "A Note on Georg Büchner's Plays" in Ronald Peacock's collection of essays on *The Poet in the Theatre* (1960), which serious students should read for a guide to the "romantic lyricism that flowers amidst intimations of a new, socially realistic subject." Other students may wish to compare Büchner's *Woyzeck* with the best known opera of the Austrian composer Alban Berg (1885–1935), who wrote *Wozzeck* (1924); a comparison and contrast of the play and the libretto (as in the case of *The Lady of the Camelias* and its musical setting) will teach one much about both of the media. Even without going outside of the text presented here, however, the student can analyze important details. The translator, Walter Sorell, who prepared this text especially for *Mirrors for Man* (based on Büchner's *Gesammelte Verke* as edited by Carl Seeling for Artemis Verlag, Zürich, 1944), has included the postscript naturalistic scene (here number 24) in which Woyzeck passes his house and sees the Half-Wit play with his child, a scene which is often omitted from English versions of *Woyzeck*. The reader should consider what scene 24 contributes to the whole nightmare structure and how the symbol of the wooden horse, here and in scene 26, functions.

The great rule remains "only connect." See each play in terms of others you have read. Look back to *Macbeth*, and consider it with *Woyzeck* as a nonregenerative drama: "noble Macbeth," who might have been elected king on the death of Duncan and enjoyed the fulfillment of his ambitions within the system, is prodded to compass that death and eventually meets his own destruction, for Duncan nominates his son as his successor and throws the Establishment into disorder; Woyzeck's tragedy is humbler, for he is a simple man with little or nothing to hope for in any system. Both men seem to be foredoomed, but Woyzeck is more victimized than vile and more pathetic, less tragic than Macbeth, thus pointing to the redefinition of tragedy in our age of Willie Lomans. In one play a highly-placed personage is brought to destruction and prophecies give the audience foreknowledge; in the other, the audience is equally aware of dramatic ironies and just as certain of the outcome, but the flaws seem to be more in the society than in the protagonist. *Macbeth* and *Woyzeck* are milestones in the development (or, as one critic has called it, the death) of tragedy.

WOYZECK

Georg Büchner

Translated by Walter Sorell

SCENE ONE   At the Captain's.

The CAPTAIN *in a chair*, WOYZECK *shaving him.*

CAPTAIN: Easy, Woyzeck, easy. One thing at a time! You make me quite dizzy. You'll be through too soon today, and what will I do with the ten minutes left to me? Woyzeck, think of it, you still have a good thirty years to live . . . Thirty years, that comes to 360 months, and God knows how many days and hours and minutes! What will you do with such a tremendous amount of time? Organize yourself, Woyzeck!

WOYZECK: Aye, Captain.

CAPTAIN: I'm getting afraid for the world when I think about eternity. To be busy, Woyzeck, to be busy . . . That lasts forever, ever, ever . . . you can see that. But then again, it's not forever, and just a moment, a moment . . . Woyzeck, I'm frightened to think that the world turns around itself in one day! What a waste of time! What should become of it? Woyzeck, I can no longer look at a mill wheel without getting melancholy.

WOYZECK: Aye, Captain.

CAPTAIN: Woyzeck, you always look so harassed. A good man doesn't do that, not a good man with a good conscience . . . Say something, Woyzeck. What's the weather like today?

WOYZECK: Bad, Captain, bad. There's a wind.

CAPTAIN: I could feel it myself . . . there's something really fast going around outside. You know what such a wind reminds me of? A mouse. (*Slyly*) I think the wind is somehow blowing from the south-north.

WOYZECK: Aye, Captain.

CAPTAIN: Ha! Ha! Ha! South-north! Ha! Ha! Ha! Oh, are you stupid, quite horribly stupid! (*With a gentle tone*) Woyzeck, you're a good man, but . . . (*With dignity*) Woyzeck, you have no morals! Morals, that's what you have when you're moral. That's clear, isn't it? It's a good word. You have a child without the blessing of the Church, as our right reverend chaplain says, without the blessing of the Church. It's not I who said it.

WOYZECK: Captain, Our Good Lord won't be hard on my poor worm because no Amen was said before he was put into this world. The Good Lord said: "Suffer little children to come unto me."

CAPTAIN: What did he say? What kind of a funny answer is that? He got me all confused with his answer. And when I say "he" I mean him, him . . . See?

WOYZECK: With us, poor people, Captain . . . you see, it's money, money! If you have no money . . . you can't put someone like us into the world in a moral way. We're only made of flesh and blood. Our kind of people can't be blessed in this world or in the next. I'm sure if we ever get to heaven, they'll make us work on the thunder.

CAPTAIN: Woyzeck, you have no virtue. You're not a virtuous man. Flesh and blood, eh? You see, when I lean out of my window after the rain and watch those white stockings the way they jump along the street . . . why, damn it, Woyzeck, then love overcomes me. I'm flesh and blood, too. But, virtue, Woyzeck, virtue! Oh, all those things with which I could pass my time. But I always say to myself: You're a virtuous man . . . (*Moved*) a good man, a good man.

WOYZECK: Aye, Captain, the virtue. I didn't get quite behind it yet. You see, we common people have no virtue, with us it's just nature. But if I were a gentleman with a hat and watch and could dance a fine dance and talk like the noble people, I'd be virtuous too. There must be something beautiful about virtue, Captain. But I'm only a poor fellow.

CAPTAIN: You're good, Woyzeck. You're a good man. But you think too much. It wears you out. You always look so harassed. Well, our little discussion has pretty much exhausted me. Go now . . . but don't run. Slowly, nice and slowly, out in the street!

SCENE TWO   An open field.

The town can be seen in the distance. WOYZECK *and* ANDRES *cut sticks in the bushes.* ANDRES *whistles.*

WOYZECK: There's a curse on this place, Andres.

ANDRES: What is it?
(*He sings*)

That's the land for me,
That's where I want to be,
Where I can shoot and hunt,
Where I could fly.

WOYZECK: Yeah, Andres, there's a curse on it. You see that light streak over there on the grass . . . where the toadstools grow overnight? That's where a head rolls around in the dark. Once someone picked it up . . . thought it was a hedgehog. Three days and three nights later he was lying between four planks.

ANDRES: It's getting dark. I'm scared.
(*He sings*)

Two hares came jumping by,
Ask, will I hunt them, why.
Hares I must shoot and hunt,
Can't keep my powder dry.

WOYZECK: Quiet, Andres. That was the Freemasons. I've got it. The Freemasons, Andres.

ANDRES: You'd better sing with me.
(*He sings*)

Two hares were sitting in the grass,
Were biting bits of green, green grass . . .

WOYZECK: Listen, Andres . . . There's something moving there.

ANDRES: Were biting bits of green, green grass
      Down to the roots of all the grass . . .

WOYZECK: Now it's running behind me. Under me. (*He stamps on the ground*) Hollow. It's all hollow, you hear it? The Freemasons. Listen!

ANDRES: You sure scare me.

WOYZECK: Come out of here! (*He stops*) It's all so quiet and strange. Makes you want to hold your breath. Andres!

ANDRES: What?

WOYZECK: Say something! (*He stares into the distance*) Andres! How bright it is! The town's all in flames. There's a fire running around the sky and so much noise coming down like so many trumpets. It's coming closer and closer! Come on. Don't look behind you. (*He pulls him into the shrubbery*)

ANDRES (*after a while*): Woyzeck, can you still hear it?

WOYZECK: Quiet. It's all quiet again. As if all the world was dead.

ANDRES: You hear them? They're beating the drum. We must be gone!

SCENE THREE   The town.

MARIE *with her child at the window.* MARGARET, *a neighbor, is with her. The Retreat goes by, with the* DRUM-MAJOR *in front.*

MARIE (*dandling her child*): Hey, boy! Sa-ra-ra-ra! Hear them? Now they're coming!

MARGARET: What a man! Like a tree!

MARIE: He moves as if he were a lion.

DRUM-MAJOR: (*salutes her.*)

MARGARET: Ah, neighbor, how he looks at you with a friendly eye! I wouldn't have thought that of you.

MARIE (*singing*): Soldiers are such handsome boys
Shining like some pretty toys . . .

MARGARET: Also your eyes are shining all right.

MARIE: So what! You'd better take your eyes to the hawker and have them first polished. Maybe they would shine enough to be sold for a couple of buttons.

MARGARET: How dare you? You! Mrs. Virgin! I'm a decent person. But you . . . you know how to look through seven pairs of leather pants!

MARIE: You bitch! (*She slams the window*) Come, my little fellow! What do people want from us. You're a whore's son only, but your dishonest face gives your mother a lot of joy! Sa! sa! sa!
(*She sings*)

Girl, do you know what you are at?
You've got no man, but got a brat!
Why should I ask what is right?
I want to sing through the night.
Heio-popeio, my boy, hurray!
No one would help me anyway.

Hansel, your horses want to be fed,
To their trough they want to be led.
But they don't want their oats,
Nor water in their throats.
All what they want is some wine, hurray!
Cool wine, it's cool wine all the way.

(*Knock on the window*) Who's that? Is it you, Franz? Come in.

WOYZECK: Can't. Have got to go on roll-call.

MARIE: You got the wood all cut for the Captain?

WOYZECK: Yes. Marie . . .

MARIE: What's the matter with you? Franz, you look so scared.

WOYZECK (*mysteriously*): Marie . . . there was that thing there again . . . I found it all out . . . there's a lot of things which never gets written. But the Lord's Book says: "And behold, there was a smoke coming up from the land like the smoke of an oven."

MARIE: Oh, man . . . what?

WOYZECK: It kept following me all the way to the town. What will it all come to?

MARIE: Franz!

WOYZECK: I must go . . . Tonight at the fair. I've a bit saved again. (*He goes*)

MARIE: That man! He's going out of his mind. Didn't give a look at his own child. He'll crack up with so much thinking. Why so still, boy? Are you frightened?

(*She carries the child to the cradle.*)

It's getting so dark that it's like going blind. Wasn't the street light always shining in? I can't stand it any longer. It makes me shiver.

SCENE FOUR   Fairground.

Fair booths. Crowd. An Old Man sings and a Child dances to the sounds of a barrel-organ.

OLD MAN: Whatever lives must die one day,
Death will take us all away.
That's what the wise men say.

WOYZECK: It's nice here, Marie. A poor old man and a poor little boy. So much trouble and so much fun, Marie.

MARIE: Oh God, what a crazy world! If fools make sense, then we're all fools. What a beautiful world! Look!

BARKER (*in front of a booth, with his wife in trousers and a costumed monkey*): Gentlemen, gentlemen, look at this creature as God made him. What you see is nothing, nothing at all. And look now, look what art can do! He walks upright, he wears a jacket and trousers, he carries a sword. This monkey is real, and a real soldier. Now why don't you bow? That's it. He's an aristocrat, a perfect gentleman. Blow the ladies a kiss! (*The monkey trumpets*) And he's musical too, that rascal. And here, gentlemen, you can see the astronomical horse and the little love birds. They're the favorites of all crowned heads in Europe, Africa, Australia. The horse can tell you anything you don't know. The program is about to begin, and begin it must with the beginning. What you've seen so far is just an introduction to the introduction!

FIRST ONLOOKER: I'm fond of everything grotesque. I am an atheist.

SECOND ONLOOKER: I'm a Christian-dogmatical atheist. I think we ought to see those creatures of God.

(*Both enter the booth.*)

WOYZECK: Want to go in?

MARIE: Wouldn't mind. We should get to see a few nice things. Only look at the man's tassels. And the woman wearing pants.

(*They go in.*)

DRUM-MAJOR: Now stop for a moment! Did you see her? What a piece!

SERGEANT: The devil take me! She's made to propagate a whole regiment of cuirassiers.

DRUM-MAJOR: And to breed drum-majors.

SERGEANT: How she carries her head! You'd think all that black hair of hers would pull her down like a heavy weight. And those eyes . . . !

DRUM-MAJOR: It's like looking down into a well or up a chimney. Come on . . . after her!

SCENE FIVE   Inside the booth.

MARIE: Look at those lights!

WOYZECK: Yeah, like burning eyes of black cats. What a night!

BARKER (*leading a horse*): Show your talent! Show your beastly reasoning. Put human society to shame! Gentlemen, the animal

you see here with one tail on his body and four hoofs on the ground is a member of all learned societies and professor at our own university where he lectures his students on riding and kicking. . . . So far he showed simple reason. But now think with double intelligence! Let's see what you do when you use double your reason. Look around and tell us . . . do you see a single ass among these cultured people here?

(*The horse shakes his head.*)

Well, have you seen his double reasoning? That's beastology for you. Yes, that's no animal dumbness of an individual, this is a real person, a beastly human, in fact, a human beast . . .

(*The horse behaves indecently.*)

. . . and yet, as you can see for yourselves, a beast, une bête. Go ahead and put society to shame. Well, this beast is still all nature, though not ideal nature. And yet you may still learn from him. But consult your doctor first, otherwise it might be dangerous for you. All the time we have been told: Man, be natural! Dust, sand, and dirt thou art . . . do you want to be more than dust, sand, and dirt? Look here and watch his mind: He can calculate, even though he can't count on his fingers. Why? He simply can't express himself, he just can't explicate — he's a transformed man. Why don't you tell these gentlemen what time it is. Who of you, gentlemen and ladies, has a watch, a watch?

SERGEANT: A watch? (*He pulls a watch out of his pocket with a boastful and slow gesture*) Here it is, sir!

MARIE: I've got to see this! (*She climbs on one of the front seats. The* SERGEANT *helps her.*)

DRUM-MAJOR: What a woman!

SCENE SIX   Marie's room.

It is afternoon. MARIE, *sitting and holding her child in her lap, has a piece of a broken mirror in her hand. She looks at herself.*

MARIE: How those beads shine! What kind of

stones are they? What did he say . . . ? (*She puts the child to bed*) Sleep, my boy! Keep your eyes closed, baby, hold them closed . . . ! (*The child covers his eyes with his hands*) Tighter, still tighter. That's my boy. Just like that — or he'll come and get you! (*She sings*)

Girl, keep your windows down,
'Tis a gypsy boy in town.
He will take you by the hand
With him into gypsy land.

(*She looks into the mirror again.*) For sure they must be gold. What would I look like dancing with them? I wonder . . . A woman like me has little more than a corner of the world and a broken piece of mirror, but my lips are just as red as the lips of the finest ladies with mirror from top to bottom and their dandy gentlemen kissing their hands. I'm only a poor woman . . . (*The child raises himself.*) Hush, baby, close your eyes. The sandman! How he's running along the wall! (*She flashes the mirror.*) Shut your eyes . . . or he'll look at you till you get blind.

(Woyzeck *enters, steps behind her. Startled, she jumps up, her hands covering her ears.*)

Woyzeck: What's wrong?

Marie: Nothing . . .

Woyzeck: There's something shining through your fingers.

Marie: A little earring I picked up.

Woyzeck: I've never found anything like that. And two at a time.

Marie: Am I a whore?

Woyzeck: All right, Marie . . . Look how that kid sleeps! Lift him up . . . under his arms . . . the chair's hurting him. Those shiny drops on his forehead. Everything under the sun's work. Sweat even in sleep for poor folk like us! Here's some more money, Marie . . . my pay and a bit from the Captain . . . and something from the doctor.

Marie: God bless you, Franz.

Woyzeck: I must be going. Till tonight, Marie. Bye.

Marie (*alone, after a pause*): Oh God, what a bad woman I am! I could kill myself . . . ! Ah, what a world! At the end the devil will get us all, man and woman!

Scene Seven   The Doctor's room.

The Doctor, Woyzeck.

Doctor: What do I see, Woyzeck? That's how you keep your word!

Woyzeck: What is it, doctor?

Doctor: I saw you do it, Woyzeck. Pissing in the street, pissing against the wall like a dog . . . and for that you're getting three Groschen a day. Woyzeck, that's bad, the world's getting evil, very evil.

Woyzeck: But, doctor, if you can't help it, if nature . . .

Doctor: If nature, if nature, nature! Did I not prove that the *musculus constrictor vesicae* is subject to the human will? Nature! Woyzeck, man is free! Man's individuality becomes transfigured in his freedom to act. Can't hold his water! (*He shakes his head and, with his hands behind his back, paces up and down.*) Have you been eating your peas, Woyzeck? There will be a revolution in science, I'll blow it to bits. Urea 0, 10 . . . ammonium chloride . . . hydrogen . . . Woyzeck, don't you have to piss again? Just go inside and try.

Woyzeck: I can't, doctor.

Doctor (*with emphasis*): But to piss against a wall, that you can! I have it in writing, the agreement is right here in my hand! I saw it, saw it with my own eyes . . . I just stuck my nose out the window to let the sun's rays shine into it so that I can observe the genesis of sneezing. Nothing must be left unexamined. Did you bring me any frogs? Any spawn? Fresh water polyps? *Cristatellum?* Eh?! For God's sake, stay away from the microscope. There's the left back tooth of an infusorium under it. Science, man!

I'll blow it to bits! (*He bears down upon him.*) But pissing against a wall . . . ! No, Woyzeck, I won't get angry. Anger is unhealthy, is unscientific. I'm calm, quite calm. My pulse keeps its usual 60, and I'm speaking in the most controlled, cold-blooded manner. God forbid! Why get angry over a man? A man! At least if it were a Proteus going to the dogs! But, Woyzeck, you shouldn't have pissed against that wall.

WOYZECK: You see, doctor. . . . Sometimes there are folks with something like character, something like structure as you say . . . But you see, it's something else with nature. (*He snaps his fingers.*) It's like . . . how shall I say . . . like . . .

DOCTOR: Woyzeck, you're philosophizing again.

WOYZECK (*as if taking the* DOCTOR *into his confidence*): You see, doctor . . . When nature gives way . . .

DOCTOR: What's that again? When nature . . .

WOYZECK: . . . gives way . . . and the world turns all dark and you have to fumble around for things with your hands and then it feels as if nothing would be there any more . . . like going through a spider's web . . . when something's there but then it isn't there. Ah, Marie! When it's all dark with just a red spot in the West like out of a chimney . . . what are you doing if there's nothing you can hold on to then?

(*He paces the room.*)

DOCTOR: Don't shuffle around like that. You're not a spider.

WOYZECK: Doctor, have you ever seen nature double? When the sun's at noon, and it's like the whole world is burning? That's when a terrible voice spoke to me.

DOCTOR: Woyzeck, you've got an *aberratio.*

WOYZECK (*with the finger at his nose*): In toadstools, doctor, that's where it is. Did you ever see the figures toadstools make growing on the ground? If someone could only read what they mean!

DOCTOR: Woyzeck, you have a most beautiful *aberratio mentalis partialis*, secondary species, beautifully developed. Woyzeck, you're getting a raise . . . Secondary species, idée fixe with a generally reasonable condition. Still doing everything as usual, Woyzeck? Shaving your Captain?

WOYZECK: Aye, sir.

DOCTOR: Eating your peas?

WOYZECK: Everything the way it was, doctor. The money goes to her to keep the house.

DOCTOR: Going on duty?

WOYZECK: Aye, sir.

DOCTOR: You're an interesting case, Woyzeck. Now look at me. What was it I said?

WOYZECK: Ah, Marie!

DOCTOR: Eat your peas . . . then eat your mutton . . . clean your kit . . . we must cultivate our idée fixe! It's a beautiful theory. I'll be famous! Immortal, Woyzeck, immortal. I'll give you half a Groschen more each week. Now behave yourself. Let's have your pulse. Put out your tongue. Yes.

SCENE EIGHT   Marie's room.

MARIE, DRUM-MAJOR.

DRUM-MAJOR: Marie!

MARIE (*looks at him passionately*): Man! Walk up and down in front of me. With your chest like a bull and beard like a lion. No one's like you. I'm the proudest of all women.

DRUM-MAJOR: You wait till Sunday . . . when I'll wear my shako with the big plumes and my white gloves! Damn it! Know what the Prince always says? "Man, there's a real fellow for you!"

MARIE (*mocking him*): Does he? (*Steps in front of him.*) A real man!

DRUM-MAJOR: And you're a fine piece of a woman, too. The dickens! Let's breed a new race of drum-majors! Hey, shall we? (*He embraces her.*)

MARIE (*acting moodily*): Let me be!

DRUM-MAJOR: You wildcat!

MARIE (*suddenly with vehemence*): Take me!

DRUM-MAJOR: Isn't the devil looking out of your eyes?!

MARIE: For all I care. It's all the same to me.

SCENE NINE   The street.

The DOCTOR *enters, walking very fast. The* CAPTAIN *having difficulty in following him, stops, pants, looks around.*

CAPTAIN: Doctor, don't walk so fast! Take your time, doctor! Take your time. For heaven's sake, don't poke the air with your cane like that. Good man . . . You're running after your own death. A good man, with a clear conscience, doesn't walk so fast. You worry me . . . Doctor, permit me to save a human life.

(*He seizes the* DOCTOR *by the coat.*)

DOCTOR: I'm in a hurry, man, in a hurry.

CAPTAIN: It worries me to think of all those poor horses. They're always on their feet . . . and must run. Poor creatures! But you don't have to run so fast . . . I'm feeling melancholy, doctor. Sometimes I feel so romantic, so sentimental. I can't help crying when I see my coat hanging on the wall.

DOCTOR: It was a woman . . . dead in four weeks, stone dead. *Cancer uteri* . . . saw over twenty such cases . . . within four weeks dead . . . And what about you?

CAPTAIN: Oh God, doctor, I can't help crying when I see my coat hanging on the wall . . .

DOCTOR: Hm, bloated! Fat, thick neck! All the signs of an apoplectic condition. Yes, Captain, you can easily develop a nice case of apoplexia cerebri. But don't worry, you may only get it on one side, and then you'll be paralyzed just on one side, or if you're lucky only your mental faculties will be affected by it, and you can go on vegetating. Those, I would say, are your prospects for about the next four weeks. And I can assure you, Captain, you'll be one of my most interesting cases . . . anyway, if with the help of God your tongue should be only partially paralyzed, we'll do immortal experiments together.

(*He tries to leave.*)

CAPTAIN: Don't leave me now, you friend of the dead. About four weeks did you say? Don't frighten me, doctor. People have died from fright, from sheer fright . . . I can see them already, the mourners with the pomanders in their hands. Do you know what they'll say? He was a good man. A good man, they'll say, you devil of a coffin nail!

DOCTOR (*takes off his hat, greeting him as if he had just met him*): Ah, Captain, nice to run into you. (*Pointing to his hat.*) Do you know who that is? That's Mr. Blockhead.

CAPTAIN (*taking off his cap*): And who is this doctor? A man out of his head. Hahahaha! But no harm meant. I'm a good man, a good man. But if I want to, I can also play the joker.

(WOYZECK *enters and intends to pass by.*)

Hey, Woyzeck, why are you trying to rush by? Stay, Woyzeck! He runs through the world like an open razor blade. You could cut yourself on him. He runs as if he had to shave a regiment of castrates and would be hanged on the last hair if he didn't get away fast enough. But about long beards, Woyzeck . . . what was it I wanted to say? Long beards, Woyzeck . . .

DOCTOR: It must be said that Pliny already mentions that soldiers should be broken of the habit of wearing long beards under the chin . . .

CAPTAIN (*continuing*): Well, speaking of long beards, Woyzeck . . . have you not yet found a hair from a long beard in your soup bowl? Now you do know what I mean, don't you? A nice long hair from the beard of a sapper perhaps, or from a sergeant's beard, or, let's say, from the beard of a . . . a drum-major? Eh, Woyzeck? But he has a good woman. Things like that don't happen to him, not like to some of us . . .

WOYZECK: Yes, Captain. What do you want to say, Captain?

CAPTAIN: What a face that man's making . . . ! Could be there's no hair in the soup, but if you hurry and run around the corner, perhaps you can still find it on a pair of lips. What a pair of lips, Woyzeck! I also know what it means to love, Woyzeck. Man, you're white like chalk.

WOYZECK: Captain, I'm a poor devil . . . have nothing else in this world. Captain, if you make fun . . .

CAPTAIN: Fun, making fun . . . do I ever make fun, Woyzeck?

DOCTOR: Your pulse, Woyzeck, your pulse. Short, hard, jumpy, irregular.

WOYZECK: Captain, the earth is hot like hell, but to me it's ice cold, ice cold . . . hell is cold . . . You want to bet? Impossible. Whore. She a whore. Impossible.

CAPTAIN: Man, you don't really want . . . is he going to shoot himself? You keep stabbing at me with those eyes of yours, and I mean well by him, because he is a good man, Woyzeck, a good man.

DOCTOR: Facial muscles rigid, taut, jumpy at times. Carriage: excitable, tense.

WOYZECK: I'm going. Anything can happen. A man's only a man. Anything can happen. . . . We have nice weather, Captain. Look. Such a fine, clear, gray sky. A man might almost want to drive a nail through it so that he can hang himself on it. And only because of that little dash between yes and again yes and no. Yes and no, Captain? Must we blame the No for the Yes, or the Yes for the No? Let me think about it . . . think about it.

(*He leaves, taking long steps, slowly at first, then faster and faster.*)

DOCTOR: A phenomenon! (*Rushing after him.*) Woyzeck, another raise.

CAPTAIN: People can make me dizzy. How fast they are. The long one running as fast as the shadow of a spider's leg, and the little one limping after him. The long one is like lightning, the little one like thunder. Hahaha, grotesque. He can't keep up. It's all grotesque. A good man is careful how he walks and gives thanks to his Maker. A good man doesn't have courage. I joined the army to prove to myself that I have no courage.

SCENE TEN   Marie's room.

WOYZECK *enters.* MARIE, *at the window, goes to meet him. She stops, speechless, frightened.* WOYZECK *stares at her, shakes his head.*

MARIE: Good morning, Franz.

WOYZECK: Hm. I can't see it. But a man should be able to see it, to hold it in his fist.

MARIE (*timid*): What is it, Franz? You're mad, Franz.

WOYZECK: A sin, so big and so wide . . . It stinks so much that the angels can be smoked out of heaven. You've a red mouth, Marie. Can't see a blister on it anywhere. Marie, you're so beautiful as sin. Can a deadly sin be so beautiful?

MARIE: Franz, you talk like in a fever.

WOYZECK: The devil take him. Did he stand there? Or here? Like this?

MARIE: While the day's long and the world's getting older by the day, lots of people can stand on the same spot, one after the other.

WOYZECK: I saw him!

MARIE: There's a lot you can see if you have two eyes, you're not blind and the sun is shining.

WOYZECK (*he steps toward her*): You whore!

MARIE: Don't touch me, Franz! I'd rather have a knife in my ribs than your hands on me. When I was ten, my father didn't dare touch me any more. Not when I looked at him like that.

WOYZECK: Woman! No, it would have to show on you. There's a deep in all of us. One gets dizzy looking down. It could have been . . . ! She walks like innocence! Yeah, innocence, you've got to have some sign on you. Can I see it? Can I know it? Who knows?

(*He rushes out.*)

SCENE ELEVEN   The Guardroom.

ANDRES (*singing*): The landlady has an honest maid,
Who sits in the garden all night, all day,
Sits waiting in her garden . . .

WOYZECK (*enters*): Andres!

ANDRES: What?

WOYZECK: Where will they . . . ? What d'you think? Nice weather.

ANDRES: Sunny Sunday weather. Music plays outside the town. The skirts have already gone out there. The men will be sweating. It'll be great.

WOYZECK (*restless*): Dancing, Andres. They'll be dancing.

ANDRES: At The White Horse and at The Star.

WOYZECK: Dancing . . . dancing . . . !

ANDRES: So what! (*singing*)
Sits waiting in her garden
To hear the bell strike twelve at noon,
To see the soldiers coming soon . . .

WOYZECK: Andres, I can't get myself together.

ANDRES: Ass!

WOYZECK: I must get out there. It keeps turning in front of my eyes. Dancing! They'll be dancing! How hot her hands will be! Damn it, Andres.

ANDRES: What do you want?

WOYZECK: Must get going . . . must see it with my own eyes.

ANDRES: Because of that bitch?

WOYZECK: I've got to get out. It's so hot in here.

SCENE TWELVE   In front of an inn.

The windows are open. Dancing. Benches in front of the house. Apprentices and girls. WOYZECK, ANDRES, *a* HALF-WIT.

FIRST APPRENTICE (*singing*):
I have a shirt that is not mine,
My soul, it stinks of schnaps and wine.

SECOND APPRENTICE: Brother, for friendship's sake, let me make a hole in your nature. Come on! Let me make a hole in your nature. You know, I'm quite a man . . . I'll squash all fleas on your body.

FIRST APPRENTICE: My soul, my soul, it stinks of schnaps and wine. Even the money's rotting away. Forget me not, brother. How beautiful the world is! I could fill a rain barrel with my tears. I wish our noses were two bottles of wine, and we could pour them down into each other's throats.

ANDRES (*singing with a few others*):
A hunter from the Palatine
Is riding through fields and through the wood.
Hallee, hallo, where hunting is fine
Through the fields, through the wood,
Where hunting is good.

WOYZECK (*he stands by the window.* MARIE *and* DRUM-MAJOR *dance by without noticing him*): He! She! The devil take them!

MARIE (*dancing by*): Go on! Go on!

WOYZECK (*choking*): Go on . . . go on . . .

(*Jumps up and glides back on the bench.*)

Go on . . . go on . . .

(*Pounding his hands.*)

Turn around! Go on rolling. Why doesn't God blow out the sun so that they can all roll together in filth? Male and female, man and beast. They do it in broad daylight, they do it like flies on your hand. Woman, that woman is hot, hot. Go on . . . go on . . .

(*He jumps up.*)

That bastard! How he fingers her all over the body. He's . . . he's got her, like I did once. And she laughs, laughs, laughs.

(*He slumps down.*)

ANDRES (*coming from inside with soldiers and apprentices*): What are you doing here alone?

WOYZECK: What's the time?

ANDRES: Almost eleven.

WOYZECK: Thought it was later. With so much fun going on time passes. Andres, I wish it would be later . . . and would be all over . . . all over.

ANDRES: Why don't you go inside?

WOYZECK: I'm doing fine here. Some people are near a door and don't know it till they're dragged out, feet first.

ANDRES: Come along with us.

WOYZECK: I'm all right where I am. I'll be in the cool grave one day, and only then it may be better.

ANDRES: You're drunk.

WOYZECK: Not enough.

FIRST APPRENTICE (*he jumps on a table, with a priest's gestures, delivering a mock sermon*): Nevertheless, I say, behold the wanderer who standeth leaning against the stream of time or who, on the other hand, answereth himself with God's wisdom when asking: *Why* is man? Why is *man*? But verily I say unto you, how would the farmer farm, or the tanner tan, or the shoemaker make shoes, or the doctor kill if God had not created man? How would the tailor live, if God had not given man a sense of shame — how the soldier if God had not equipped him with the urge to kill himself? Brethren, therefore have faith and doubt not. Yes, verily I say unto you, everything that is is lovely and fine, but also, my brethren, everything on earth is evil, even the money's rotting in a man's hand. And in conclusion, my beloved brethren, now let us piss over the cross, so that somewhere a Jew may die.

(*The sermon is greeted with a howling. WOYZECK comes to.*)

HALF-WIT (*pushes past WOYZECK to the window*): He's a jolly good fellow . . . ! It's stinking jolly.

WOYZECK: What is it?

HALF-WIT: Can you smell? It smells.

WOYZECK: Yes. It smells all right. She had red, red lips. And he a long beard. Is it that you smell?

HALF-WIT: I smell blood.

WOYZECK: Blood! Blood! I see red before my eyes. Red. As if they were all rolling, one on the other, in a sea of blood.

SCENE THIRTEEN   An open field.

WOYZECK: Go on! Go on! Silence. The fiddles fiddle and the flutes flute. No more music. (*He stretches on the ground.*) Hey, what is it? What's that you say? Louder, louder. Stab, stab the goat-wolf dead? Stab, stab . . . the bitch of a goat-wolf dead. Shall I? Must I? There, it comes from there too! Wind, does the wind say it too? Go on, go on . . . Will I hear it forever, forever . . . go on, go on . . . stab her dead . . . stab her dead.

SCENE FOURTEEN   A room in the barracks.

It is night. WOYZECK *and* ANDRES *in one bed.*

WOYZECK (*softly*): Andres. (*Shakes* ANDRES.) Andres, I can't sleep! When I close my eyes, then everything turns round and round and the fiddles sing: Go on . . . go on . . . And then the voices . . . They're coming out of the wall . . . Can't you hear how everything fiddles and turns around?

ANDRES: Yeah . . . let them dance. I'm tired. God bless us all. Amen.

(*He tries to fall asleep again.*)

WOYZECK: It goes on saying, saying, saying: Stab, stab, stab. It's like a sharp knife passing by my eyes. I can see it, Andres. A knife on a counter. The street is dark. An old man sitting behind the counter. I can see the knife in front of me, Andres.

ANDRES: Drink some more schnaps with a powder in it. It cuts the fever.

WOYZECK: And lead us not into temptation, Lord. No, lead us not into temptation. Amen. The knife. It's still saying: go on . . . go on . . .

ANDRES: Go to sleep, you fool.

(*He falls asleep.*)

SCENE FIFTEEN   The Courtyard at the Doctor's.

The DOCTOR *at the garret window. Students and* WOYZECK *below.*

DOCTOR: Gentlemen, I am on the roof like David beholding his Bathsheba, but what I see are only the panties of the boarding-school girls drying in the garden. Gentlemen, we have arrived at the important question of the relationship of subject to object. If we isolate just one phenomenon in which the highest organic self-affirmation of the Divine Spirit manifests itself and investigate briefly its relation to space, earth and the planetary constellations . . . In short, gentlemen, if I throw this cat out of the window, how will this organism behave with respect to its center of gravity — its *centrum gravitationis* — and its own instincts? Hey, Woyzeck! (*Shouts*) Woyzeck!

WOYZECK (*has caught the cat*): Doctor, she's biting me.

DOCTOR: Ass! He handles the beast as gingerly as though she were his grandmother. (*He comes down into the courtyard.*)

WOYZECK: Doctor, I have the shakes.

DOCTOR (*bears down on him, delighted*): Ah, fine, Woyzeck, that's fine! (*He rubs his hands, then takes the cat.*) What do I see, gentlemen? A rare species of a louse, a beautiful species . . . (*He pulls out a magnifying glass. The cat escapes.*) Gentlemen, that animal has no instinct for scientific research. But you may see something else instead. Look at this man! For three months he has eaten nothing but peas. Make a note of the effect. Just check. Irregular pulse. And look at his eyes!

WOYZECK: Doctor, it's getting dark in front of my eyes!

(*He sits down.*)

DOCTOR: Courage, Woyzeck, courage. A few more days, and all will be over. Now, gentlemen, just feel, just feel his pulse.

(*The students check his pulse, touch his temples and listen to his chest.*)

By the way, Woyzeck, be good and move your ears for the gentlemen. I've always wanted to show you that. He does it with two muscles only. Come on now, Woyzeck, get on with it.

WOYZECK: Oh, doctor!

DOCTOR: Beast! Do you want me to wiggle your ears for you? Are you going to behave like that cat? Look, gentlemen, this is a perfect case of evolution into a donkey which so often is the consequence of being brought up by a woman. Also, the mother tongue may have something to do with it. Woyzeck, tell us, how much of your hair has your mother pulled out of pure love to keep as souvenirs? Your hair has thinned quite a bit in the last few days. Yeah, the peas, gentlemen, those peas!

SCENE SIXTEEN   The barracks yard.

WOYZECK: You didn't hear anything?

ANDRES: He's still in there with another fellow.

WOYZECK: He must have said something.

ANDRES: How do you know? What do you want me to say? If you must know, he laughed and then said: "A juicy bit of a woman! Thighs like that, and all hot!"

WOYZECK (*quite coldly*): So that's what he said. What was it I was dreaming last night? Wasn't it about a knife? What crazy dreams one can have!

(*He is about to leave.*)

ANDRES: Where are you going?

WOYZECK: Getting wine for my Captain. But, Andres, you know, she was an unusual girl.

ANDRES: Who was?

WOYZECK: Nothing, See you.

SCENE SEVENTEEN   The inn.

DRUM-MAJOR, WOYZECK, *people.*

DRUM-MAJOR: What a man I am!
(*He pounds his chest.*) A real man, I say. Anyone want anything? Keep off me who isn't drunk like a judge or I'll smash his nose into his arsehole for him. I'll . . . (*to* WOYZECK) Get drunk, you oaf! I wish the whole world was schnaps, schnaps . . . get drunk, man!

WOYZECK (*whistles.*)

DRUM-MAJOR: You bastard! Do you want me to pull out your tongue and twist it around your belly?

(*They wrestle.* WOYZECK *loses.*)

Shall I leave you enough wind for an old woman's fart? Shall I?

WOYZECK (*sits on a bench, exhausted, trembling.*)

DRUM-MAJOR: Now that lout can whistle himself blue in the face. Let him whistle:

Schnaps is all I need to live,
Schnaps is courage . . .

SOMEONE: He sure has his belly full.

ANDRES (*pointing at* WOYZECK): He's bleeding.

WOYZECK: One thing after the other.

SCENE EIGHTEEN   At the Pawnshop.

WOYZECK, *the* JEW.

WOYZECK: The pistol is too much.

JEW: So you take it or you don't.

WOYZECK: How much is the knife? (*He runs his finger down the blade.*)

JEW: It's a good knife. Straight and sharp. Good enough to cut your throat with it.

WOYZECK (*startled.*)

JEW: Well, so . . . what is it? I'll give it to you for a cheap price . . . as cheap as anyone else . . . You shall have your death at a cheap price. But not for nothing. So, what's the matter? Have a cut-rate death.

WOYZECK: That can cut more than bread.

JEW: Two Groschen.

WOYZECK: Here . . .

(*He leaves.*)

JEW: Here! As if it were nothing. And is good money. That swine!

SCENE NINETEEN   Marie's room.

MARIE (*turning over the pages of a Bible.*)

HALF-WIT (*sitting by her feet with the Child.*)

MARIE (*reading*): "He that is without sin among you, let him first cast a stone at her . . ."

(*She looks up.*)

O God, oh God! Don't look at me!

(*She turns the pages again.*)

"And there is no guile found in his mouth. And the Scribes and the Pharsees brought unto Him a woman taken in adultery, and set her in the midst. And Jesus said, Neither do I condemn thee; go, and sin no more."

(*She clasps her hands.*)

Oh God! Oh God! I can't. Help me to pray . . .

(*The Child nestles against her.*)

The child breaks my heart. Go away!

(*She pushes the Child away from her and goes to the window.*)

That man! There he struts and boasts in the sun!

HALF-WIT (*he tells the Child fairy tales on his fingers*): This one's got a golden crown. He's our Lord, the King. Tomorrow I'll bring the Queen her child . . . Blood pudding says to the liverwurst: Come on . . .

(*He takes the Child into his arms and becomes quiet.*)

MARIE: Franz hasn't been here, not yesterday, not today. It's getting hot in here.

(*She opens the window.*)

"And stood at His feet weeping, and began to wash His feet with tears, and did wipe them with the hairs of her head, and kissed his feet, and anointed them with ointment."

(*She beats her breast.*)

Everything's dead. Saviour! Saviour! How I would love to anoint your feet! Lord, you had pity on her. Have pity on me!

SCENE TWENTY   In the barracks.

ANDRES *with* WOYZECK *who rummages through his belongings.*

WOYZECK: This jacket, Andres, it isn't part of the equipment. I'm sure you can use it.

ANDRES: I sure can.

WOYZECK: This cross was my sister's, and this little ring, too.

ANDRES (*mechanically, matter-of-fact*): Sure . . .

WOYZECK: I've still got a holy picture. See? With two hearts and all gold. I found it in my mother's Bible, and there 'twas written:

Lord, like Thy body, sore and red,
So let my heart be till I'm dead.

Mother doesn't feel much any more, only the sun that shines on her hands. Nevermind.

ANDRES: Sure.

WOYZECK: Andres! You know . . . she was . . .

ANDRES: Who was . . . ?

WOYZECK: Forget it.

(*He pulls out a paper.*)

Friedrich Johann Franz Woyzeck, soldier. Rifleman, 2nd Regiment, 2nd Battalion, 4th Company. Born the day of Assumption of the Virgin Mary, July 20th. . . . Today I'm 30 years old, 7 months and 12 days . . .

ANDRES: Franz, you ought to go on sick-call. They'll give you some schnaps with a powder in it. That kills the fever for sure.

WOYZECK: Yeah, Andres. When the cabinetmaker has finished his job, no one knows whose head is going to lie in that wooden box.

SCENE TWENTY-ONE   The street.

Sunday afternoon. MARIE, *her child on her arm, in front of her door. Little girls. An Old Woman. Later,* WOYZECK.

GIRLS (*singing*):
At Candlemas the sun was bright,
The corn stood in blooming height.
They danced around the meadow dew,
They danced in couples, two and two,
The flutists led the little crew,
The fiddlers stayed behind,
With stockings of the reddest kind . . .

FIRST GIRL: That's silly.

SECOND GIRL: You always want to do something else.

FIRST GIRL: Marie, please sing for us.

MARIE: I can't.

SECOND GIRL: Why not?

MARIE: Because . . . that's why.

SECOND GIRL: Then dance with us!

FIRST GIRL: Dance with us!

MARIE (*forms a ring with the children, walks around in a circle, singing and dancing with them*):

Ring-around-a-rosy
A pocket full of posy.
Ashes, ashes, all fall down.

(*She breaks away from the children.*)

Grandma, tell them a story!

OLD WOMAN: Now come, you little rascals. Once upon a time there was a poor little girl, no father she had and had no mother. Everyone was dead, and there was no one left in the whole world. So the child went off and kept looking for someone all night long and all day long. And because there was no one on earth any more, she wanted to go to heaven. The moon looked at her with friendly eyes, but when she finally got to the moon it was nothing but a piece of rotten wood. So the little girl went on to the sun, but when she got there, it was just a shrivelled-up sun flower. And when she got to the stars, they were only little golden flies on thorns where the shrikes have stuck them up. And when our little girl wanted to go back to the earth, it was just an overturned mug. And so the child was quite alone and sat down and cried and cried. And she's still sitting there, all alone.

WOYZECK (*enters, standing behind* MARIE): Marie!

MARIE (*frightened*): What is it?

WOYZECK: Don't we want to go, Marie? It's time.

MARIE: Where d'you want to go?

WOYZECK: Don't know myself.

SCENE TWENTY-TWO A woodland path by a pond.

MARIE: Now where's the way into town? It's so dark.

WOYZECK: You've got to stay here. Come, sit down.

(*He pulls her down.*)

MARIE: No, I must go.

WOYZECK: Your feet will get sore from so much running.

MARIE: You've changed so much.

WOYZECK: Marie, do you know how long it's been?

MARIE: Two years, come Whitsunday.

WOYZECK: Marie, do you know how long it'll last?

MARIE: I must go . . . must get the supper ready.

WOYZECK (*catches her hand*): You're freezing, Marie . . . ? (*He laughs.*) And yet you're warm. How hot your lips are! Hot! The hot breath of a whore. And still . . . I'd like to give heaven to kiss them once more. Are you shivering? When you're all cold, one doesn't freeze any more. Lying in the morning damp you won't freeze.

MARIE: What are you talking about?

WOYZECK: Nothing.

(*Silence.*)

MARIE: How red that moon's coming up!

WOYZECK: Like a knife full of blood.

(*He grasps her wrist.*)

MARIE (*frightened*): What are you doing, Franz? You're all white.

WOYZECK (*he raises the knife.*)

MARIE: Franz, don't! In God's name, don't! Help! Help!

WOYZECK (*stabbing her in a blind rage*): Take that! And that! Can't you die? There! There! She's still moving . . . Not yet? Not yet? Still twitching?

(*He stabs her once more.*)

Now are you dead?

(*He drops the knife and runs off.*)

Dead! Dead . . . !

SCENE TWENTY-THREE The inn.

People are sitting at tables, others are dancing. WOYZECK *alone at a table.*

WOYZECK: Go on . . . dance around, everyone. Sweat . . . stink, in the end he'll get all of you.

(*He empties his glass and sings.*)

Oh, daughter, my daughter, dear,
Whatever came over you
To hang around with carters here
And there with coachmen too.

(*He dances with* KÄTHE.)

Sit, Käthe, sit down. I'm hot, hot . . .

(*He takes off his coat.*)

That's how it is . . . The devil will get hold of one and let another one get away. Käthe, you're hot. What has come over you? One day you'll be cold too . . . So be nice. Can't you sing something?

KÄTHE (*sings*):

To Swabia I will not go
Nor will I dress from top to toe
In fancy dress with pointed shoes
Which never a simple maid may choose.

WOYZECK: No . . . no shoes. You can get into hell without shoes all the same.

KÄTHE (*sings*):

Oh shame on you, my dear, that wasn't right.
You keep your coins and sleep alone tonight.

WOYZECK: I'd like a fight, I would . . . No, no. I don't want to get any blood on me.

KÄTHE: But then . . . what's that on your hand?

WOYZECK: On me? Me?

KÄTHE: Red! It's blood!

(*People gather around them.*)

WOYZECK: Blood? Blood?

INNKEEPER: O-Oh, blood!

WOYZECK: I must have cut myself. On my right hand.

INNKEEPER: How come then it's up there on your elbow?

WOYZECK: Wiped it off . . .

INNKEEPER: You can wipe your right hand on your right elbow? Quite some talent you have.

HALF-WIT: And then the giant said: "I smell, I smell the flesh of man!" It stinks, it stinks of human blood.

WOYZECK (*jumps up*): To hell with all of you! What d'you want? It's none of your business. Get out of my way, or the first one . . . Hell, do you think I killed someone? Am I a murderer? What d'you stare at me? Look at yourselves! Get out of my way!

(*He runs off.*)

SCENE TWENTY-FOUR   In front of Marie's house.

The HALF-WIT *with* MARIE's *Child on his lap. They play. Then,* WOYZECK.

HALF-WIT: He went and fell in the water . . . he fell in the water . . . fell in the water . . .

WOYZECK (*passes by. He bends down to touch the child*): Hey, little boy! Christian!

HALF-WIT (*stares at him*): He fell in the water . . . the water . . .

WOYZECK (*tries to caress the child. It turns from him and cries*): Oh, God!

HALF-WIT: He fell in the water . . .

WOYZECK: Christian, I'll buy you a little horsey . . . (*The child turns away again. To the* HALF-WIT) There, take this . . . and get the boy a little horsey.

HALF-WIT (*stares at him.*)

WOYZECK: Up, up, horsey . . .

HALF-WIT (*joyful*): Up, up, horsey, horsey . . . ! (*He rushes off with the child.*)

SCENE TWENTY-FIVE   At the pond.

Night. WOYZECK *alone.*

WOYZECK: The knife? Where's the knife? Here. I left it here. It'll give me away. Nearer. It was nearer. Was that the spot?

Noise, is there noise? Something was moving there. No, quiet. Here it must be. Marie? Hey, Marie! Quiet, everything's quiet. Why are you so pale, Marie? What's the red string around your neck? Who gave you that necklace and for what of your sins? You were black with sin, black! Did I wash you white again? Look at your black hair hanging down all wild. Didn't you braid your hair today? There's something . . .

(*He gropes for something.*)

Cold, wet, still! The knife, the knife . . . I've got it. Away from here.

(*He runs towards the water.*)

There . . .

(*He throws the knife into the pond.*)

Down it goes! It dives into the dark water like a stone. The moon's like a knife full of blood! Does the whole world talk about it? No, it's lying too close here. When they'll be going for a swim . . .?

(*He steps into the pond and throws the knife further.*)

Yes, that's it . . . But when it's summer and they'll dive for mussels . . . Bah, it'll be rusty by then . . . who can recognize it? I would have done better to break it. Am I still bloody? I've got to wash myself. There. There's a mark, and there's another.

(*He wades deeper into the water. People come.*)

FIRST PERSON: Stop where you are!

SECOND PERSON: You hear it? Be quiet. It's over there.

FIRST PERSON: Uh! There. What a sound!

SECOND PERSON: It's the water. It is calling. No one has drowned for quite some time. Let's go! I don't like to hear that sound.

FIRST PERSON: Uh, there it is again . . . Like a man, dying . . .

SECOND PERSON: It's eerie. It's so misty. That gray fog all around, and the humming of the bugs like cracked bells. Let's go!

FIRST PERSON: No, it's too clear, too loud. It must be up there. Come on, keep near me.

SCENE TWENTY-SIX   The street.

Children.

FIRST CHILD: Let's go and look at Marie!

SECOND CHILD: What happened?

FIRST CHILD: Don't you know? They're all gone out there. (*To* MARIE'S *Boy*) Hey, your mother's dead.

MARIE'S BOY (*riding on doorstep*): Gee-up, gee-up, horsey!

SECOND CHILD: Where is she?

FIRST CHILD: Left from the cross on the way to the pond.

SECOND CHILD: Let's run . . . that we can still see something before they'll take her away. (*They run off.*)

MARIE'S BOY: Gee-up . . . gee-up, horsey!

SCENE TWENTY-SEVEN   At the pond.

POLICEMAN, DOCTOR, JUDGE, COURT CLERK.

POLICEMAN: A fine murder, a genuine murder, a beautiful murder! As nice a murder as you can only wish for. We haven't had such a murder for quite a time.

The Subscription Scroll

It sounds a trifle strange in these days when Japan is becoming a more and more important and progressive world force, but it used to be said that Japan was, above all, an imitative nation, clever but utterly unoriginal, able to make anything cheaper but never better, and never first. This theory may be what lay behind the tradition that a Chinese (or a Japanese of Chinese extraction) composed the 33 dramas which constituted the foundation of the Japanese theatre.

In any case, the Japanese developed the *nō* drama (whose name puts the stress on a performance of skill), the *jōruri* (puppet drama) and the live actors of the *Kabuki*, which drew on the *nō* dramas as they in turn had drawn on the historical epics. In time, as the puppet theatre declined, Kabuki took over the puppet plays in revised form as well. On an open stage more decorated than set, more symbolic than realistic, the highly-trained, traditional actors of the Kabuki theatre present a classic repertory of ancient and highly respected plays, more literary than theatrical, which nonetheless are full of significance and excitement to the initiated, though perhaps baffling and static to the average Westerner.

The *nō* theatre has always been aristocratic, but the Kabuki is enormously popular even today and its realistic and *aragoto* (exaggerated) acting styles are still to be seen both in the classical plays and in the modern film, in which Japanese actors and directors have achieved world-wide recognition (such as the Japanese film of *Macbeth* entitled *Throne of Blood*).

The Kabuki theatre is said to have originated with dancing (a woman named O-Kuni, performing in male dress, is supposed to have originated it about 1600) and still, to the Occidental, looks more like ballet or opera with elaborate choreography than what we think of as drama. Certainly the varied repertory of the Kabuki theatre, which ranges from tragedy to farce and includes both ancient tales of *The Forty-Seven Ronin* and modern domestic dramas by Mokuami Kawatake (1816–1893), is a far cry, in its stylized traditions, from the more or less realistic stage presentations of the West. The foreigner, reading in translations or puzzled by his ignorance of the conventions at performances, finds it difficult to see the acting vehicles by Chikamatsu Monzayémon (1653?–1724, called "the Shakespeare of Japan") as great dramatic literature, misses the nuances of gesture and every other time-hallowed detail of presentation, and may fail to appre-

337

ciate the subtlety of even the most renowned *onnagata* (female imperson-
ator), trained from childhood in an age-old art. Audiences at New York's
City Center, for instance, viewing the Grand Kabuki on tour may have
been able to follow the story with earphones and simultaneous translation
but most were quite unaware that Nakamura Utaemon VI (born 1917,
whose name and number suggest the elaborate and long traditions of the
Kabuki) was a male, so strange and convincing was he in the role of Lady
Kaoyo in *Chushingura* (*The Forty-Seven Ronin*).*

Our example of oriental drama here — and there is, of course, a rich
mine of it, but little, because of its exoticism that is suitable for a general
and introductory anthology — is one of the most famous plays of the
Kabuki theatre, *The Subscription Scroll* (1840), on stage a gorgeous presentation of dance and ritualized gesture, sumptuously costumed. The clever
servant of Greek and Roman comedy appears here as a warrior-monk,
Benkei, a brave and resourceful figure also encountered in *Hashi-Benkei*
(*Benkei on the Bridge of Gōjo*) and other plays dating from the earliest
period of the classical Japanese drama. *The Subscription Scroll* might be
compared with some of these plays, especially the *nō* play *Ataka* by Namiki
Gohei III (1789–1855),** or one could trace Japanese elements in Western
playwrights as different as Yeats in Ireland, Brecht in Germany, and Thornton Wilder in America.

Students require, perhaps, much investigation into background before
they can fully visualize the brightly-lit and brilliantly decorated Kabuki
stage and the stylized posturings on it, but *The Subscription Scroll* may give
some hint, at least, of the elements which make this play popular with the
Japanese. The Westerner will not react as do the Japanese to Benkei beating
his disguised master to protect the fiction that he is just a servant — to the
Japanese this is, says G. L. Anderson, "a heinous breach of the samurai
code and certainly brought shudders to the Japanese audience." Still the
Westerner can see the opportunities the play offers for virtuoso acting and
dancing within the rigid traditions of the Kabuki. A closer examination will
show that there are more connections between the drama of East and West
than the adaptation of the "flower paths" (bridges through the audience to
the stage to formalize and facilitate the entrance of actors) to the runways
of our burlesque houses of yore and the gangways of the theatres in the
round of today. But let the translator himself tell us more.

----

* *Ronin* are masterless *samurai* (knights) of Kaoyo's husband, Hangan, who commits suicide.

** The English translation can be found in *Transactions of the Asiatic Society of Japan*, XXXVIII,
Part 3 (1911). Sir George Sansom, Arthur Walley, Donald Keene, Earle Ernst, Aubrey S. Halford
and Giovanna M. Halford are among English scholars and translators. *Benkei on the Bridge* is
conveniently found in G. L. Anderson's *The Genius of the Oriental Theater* (1966).

Introduction
A. C. SCOTT

The Subscription Scroll is considered one of the masterpieces of the Kabuki theatre. It was first staged in March 1840 by the actor Ichikawa Danjuro VII (1791–1859), who played the role of Benkei. *The Subscription Scroll* was adapted from a nō play, *Ataka*, and reflects much of the austere quality of its classical prototype. Emphasis is given to highly formalised gesture and movement used to create powerful choreographic compositions with almost an architectural quality. The playwright Namiki Gohei III (1789–1855) wrote *The Subscription Scroll*, although "devised" would probably be a more accurate term in a case like this.

The word Kabuki is a portmanteau term which literally means music, dance and artistic expression and implies, therefore, a total form of theatrical expression. A unique feature in any Kabuki theatre is the runway connecting the stage with an entry-exit at the rear of the auditorium. This gives its own special dimensions to a stylised acting technique in which the disparate elements of speech, movement and musical sound are fused to impose a sensory assault on the consciousness of the audience.

The plot of *The Subscription Scroll* revolves around a confrontation in which the samurai code of loyalty to a superior is resolved in novel fashion. Yoshitsune, a valiant feudal warrior, has incurred the implacable jealousy of his brother Yoritomo, leader of the clan. Yoshitsune flees into exile with a small band of devoted followers led by Benkei, his most faithful henchman and a one-time militant monk. Benkei orders the group to disguise them-

selves as mendicant priests soliciting contributions to restore a Buddhist temple. Yoshitsune poses as their humble mountain guide. They are stopped at a frontier barrier, one of many set up by the suspicious Yoritomo who has heard of their plans. Togashi, the captain of the barrier guard, sees through Benkei's ruse and tries to catch him by asking him to read aloud his list of pious subscribers. He follows this with a gruelling cross-questioning on the esoteric symbolism of the priestly costumes they wear. Benkei successfully bluffs his way through the ordeal and Togashi apologetically allows them to travel on. Just as they are going through the barrier, Yoshitsune is recognised by one of Togashi's soldiers and the little group is called back. The situation is tense but Benkei without more ado beats their "mountain guide" with his staff as a punishment for loitering behind and so bringing suspicion on the party. Such dire action is an unthinkable transgression of the samurai code and suspicion is apparently allayed. Once again Togashi allows them to go free after first offering Benkei wine.

The hero who extricates himself from a tight corner against all odds provides a universal theme, but there are deeper psychological implications in this play for the Japanese audience. Togashi, though seeming to call Benkei's bluff, is actually overwhelmed with inner admiration at such a supreme expression of loyalty and so allows the fugitives to escape, even though by so doing it means his own disgrace and eventual suicide. The physical portrayal of the inner anguish of both Benkei and Togashi in their different situations presents a supreme artistic challenge for the master kabuki actor.

The translation presented here is a revised version of one first published by the Hokuseido Press in 1953. It was prepared for a research project carried out by my students at the University of Wisconsin during 1972–73, when the Kabuki actor Onoe Kuroemon II worked with us on the campus. A few printing errors in the old version have been eliminated and some infelicities of style ironed out. Some Japanese technical terms and personal names have been eliminated as being merely confusing for the general reader.

THE SUBSCRIPTION SCROLL

(*Kanjinchō*)

Namiki Gohei III

Translated by A. C. Scott

CHARACTERS IN THE PLAY

TOGASHI SAEMON, *captain of the guard at the frontier barrier of Kaga*

THREE SOLDIERS, *Togashi's guards*

A SWORD BEARER, *page to Togashi*

YOSHITSUNE, *a warrior leader in disguise as a mountain guide*

BENKEI, *loyal henchman of Yoshitsune and a former Buddhist monk renowned for his swordsmanship*

FOUR RETAINERS, *faithful followers of Yoshitsune*

Before the play commences, the notes of flute and drum are heard for several minutes in a grave and sustained prelude. When the main stage curtain is drawn aside to the sharp sound of wooden clappers, the orchestra is revealed at the rear of the long stage. Twelve samisen players and eight narrators are seated in a row on a long dais which is covered with a scarlet drape and stretches the whole length of the stage. In front of the dais are seated five drummers and a flute player. Three of the drummers play hand drums, two holding their instruments on their right shoulders with their left hand and beating the drum head with the right hand, the third holding his drum against the left waist and beating the drum head with his right hand. The other two drummers play instruments which stand on the ground supported on low bamboo frames and are beaten with two short thick drumsticks. The arrangement of the orchestra and the controlled postures of the musicians intensifies the ritualistic atmosphere of the stage. A small entry curtain at right stage is suddenly flung upwards from

the base, being operated by two stage hands backstage, and TOGASHI *makes his slow entry with his page bearing his sword and the three soldiers.* TOGASHI *strides in a stately manner to front stage where he turns to address the audience. His sword-bearer takes up a position in the rear of his master and the three soldiers seat themselves to his right.*

TOGASHI: I am Togashi Saemon of Kaga province. The Minamoto leader, Yoritomo, is estranged from his younger brother Yoshitsune, who is reported to be in flight from the capital accompanied by retainers disguised as mountain priests. Knowing this, Yoritomo has erected new barriers in every province so that all travellers may be questioned. I am the guardian of this barrier. I want you to be careful that no mountain priests pass through without being examined.

FIRST SOLDIER: Only the other day we cut down some suspicious looking mountain priests and placed their heads on display.

THIRD SOLDIER: If any mountain priest comes along we will tie him up and kill him.

SECOND SOLDIER: We have been on guard. From now on any mountain priest will be held and brought before you.

THREE SOLDIERS (*in unison*): Each of us is ready.

TOGASHI: I am glad to know it. You are to be praised for your diligence. If any mountain priests appear I will seize them by strategy and so ease the mind of Yoritomo. All of you continue to be watchful.

THREE SOLDIERS (*in unison*): Your order shall be obeyed, sir.

(TOGASHI *now strides over to left stage and seats himself on a cylindrical lacquered tub. The soldiers sit to his right and his page in the left rear. The narrators in the orchestra begin to chant a song.*)

"Disguised as mountain priests we set out on a journey, we set out on a journey. Because our expedition is a sad one our sleeves are wet with tears as well as dew. So bright was the moon when we left the capital on that

February night, we crossed Mount Osaka and gazed back regretfully unable to see Kyoto through the spring mists. Crossing Lake Biwa we came by ship to Kaizu."

(*While this song is being played,* YOSHITSUNE *appears on the runway from the rear of the auditorium. He carries a stave and a large round bamboo straw hat. He has a pack on his back; it is covered with purple silk and actually represents a portable shrine of a kind that was carried by wandering priests of this particular sect. Two thirds of the way down the runway he strikes a dramatic pose for the audience and then turning his back to them waits erect and motionless as the four retainers enter from the rear of the auditorium in single file down the runway. They walk past their disguised master and take up their position facing the audience. Next* BENKEI *comes down the runway, a solitary and dramatic figure. The four retainers sit in ceremonial posture.* BENKEI *comes to a halt close to* YOSHITSUNE. *While this action has been going on,* TOGASHI *and his men remain seated like graven images on the stage.* YOSHITSUNE *now turns to address* BENKEI.)

YOSHITSUNE: Now Benkei, on the way here it was said that we should never be able to reach Michinoku if we are compelled to pass through one barrier after another. It would be shameful to be killed by nameless men and I am ready to die by my own hand first. However, I cannot ignore the loyalty of my retainers and on your advice, Benkei, I have disguised myself as a mountain guide. Have you contrived a plan for getting through?

FIRST RETAINER: Sir, why do we wear these swords? If we do not use them now we shall never do so. It is a critical moment for our master.

SECOND RETAINER: We must be ready to cut down the barrier guards and pass through.

THIRD RETAINER: Our master's kindness over many years must be repaid.

FOUR RETAINERS (*in unison and rising aggressively*): Let us brave this barrier now.

BENKEI: Stop! Wait a minute. This is a crucial

occasion; we must think carefully. If we are to face the same difficulties at each successive barrier, we shall only bring trouble on ourselves by using violence now and it will be harder still to reach our destination. That is why I asked my master to remove his priestly garb and disguise himself as a mountain guide carrying only a pack on his shoulders. Leave everything to me. I sympathise with you, my master. Pull your hat well down over your eyes and act as though you are weary, go through the barrier at some distance behind us. If you do this they will pay less attention to you so please keep in the rear.

YOSHITSUNE: I leave everything to Benkei. All of you follow his orders.

FOUR RETAINERS (*in unison*): We shall obey.

BENKEI: Then all of you go forward.

FOUR RETAINERS (*in unison*): We follow your instructions.

(*The narrators in the orchestra begin a new song*):

"They agree to pass the barrier and now they are before it."

(YOSHITSUNE *turns with his back to the audience and begins to fasten on his hat.* BENKEI *strides forcefully towards the stage followed by each retainer in turn with* YOSHITSUNE, *now in full disguise as a mountain guide, bringing up the rear.* TOGASHI *rises from his seat and moves to centre stage as* BENKEI *approaches. The four retainers seat themselves up right with* YOSHITSUNE *in front, his head bent and his face concealed beneath the shadow of his wide brimmed hat. Both hands clasp his stave which is supported on his right shoulder. A drum beats out slow taps emphasising the tension as* BENKEI *prepares to address* TOGASHI.)

BENKEI: We are mountain priests and wish to pass through this barrier.

FIRST SOLDIER: What! Mountain priests at the barrier?

THREE SOLDIERS (*in unison*): Are they here?

TOGASHI (*fiercely*): What! Mountain priests attempting to pass through this barrier? Well, I am ready for them. Now you mountain priests, this barrier is erected against you.

BENKEI: I have heard about it. Many priests have been sent out to all the provinces to solicit contributions for the construction of the Todai Temple at Nara. I am responsible for the Hokurokudo area and we are on our way there.

TOGASHI: Your efforts deserve praise in these times but this barrier is especially forbidden to mountain priests.

BENKEI: You speak strange words. For what reason?

TOGASHI: It is as follows. Yoritomo is now estranged from his brother Yoshitsune who is reported to be fleeing with his retainers disguised as mountain priests, to ask for Hidehira's help. Knowing this, Yoritomo has ordered barriers to be erected in every province in order to examine all travellers. I am the guardian of this barrier.

FIRST SOLDIER: We have been ordered to question all mountain priests and we are ready for them.

SECOND SOLDIER: Moreover as there are so many of you mountain priests . . .

THIRD SOLDIER: Not a single one of you may pass through.

THREE SOLDIERS (*in unison*): You shall not.

BENKEI: I have listened to all you have to say but I think you have only been ordered to stop false mountain priests and not true ones.

FIRST SOLDIER: Bah, only yesterday we beheaded three mountain priests.

SECOND SOLDIER: It matters not whether you are real mountain priests.

THIRD SOLDIER: Every man will pass through at the risk of his life.

THREE SOLDIERS (*in unison*): His life!

BENKEI: Well, now, was Yoshitsune among those you beheaded?

TOGASHI: I cannot discuss that question with you. You may not pass.

(*He turns sharply and angrily returns to his seat left stage.*)

BENKEI: What an abominable way to speak. I did not expect to meet with such sacrilege. There is nothing more we can do, we must perform our last rites and resign ourselves to death. Come closer all of you.

FOUR RETAINERS: Sir!

(*The music of samisens and drums is now heard and BENKEI goes to rear stage with his back to the audience while a stage assistant hands him a Buddhist rosary. The four retainers move to centre stage and kneel facing outwards as they form the four corners of a square. YOSHITSUNE remains where he is. BENKEI hastily moves forward and takes up a position in the centre of the retainers. Then follows a slow ritual dance with each of them rolling their rosaries between their palms. They conclude by kneeling in prayer with BENKEI standing defiantly in the centre of them. The narrators in the orchestra chant a song as the dance proceeds*):

"Mountain priests follow the teachings of Buddha whom they represent while they live. The gods guard our destiny and if you kill us here we know not what they may do but they will punish you instantly. We pray to them for help. So saying Benkei rolled his beads."

TOGASHI: I admire your brave preparations for death. You said you were soliciting subscriptions for the Todai Temple at Nara; if that is so you must carry a subscription scroll. Read it out please, let me hear you!

BENKEI (*off guard for a moment*): What, you wish me to read the subscription scroll?

TOGASHI (*ironically*): That is what I mean!

BENKEI: Um, very well.

(*The narrators chant*):

"Of course he has no subscription scroll but taking out a blank scroll from his pack he pretends to read."

(BENKEI *goes rear stage to be given a scroll by a stage assistant. The retainers have already returned rear stage after their dance.* BENKEI *returns and begins to unroll the scroll slowly with the deliberate bombast and exaggerated posture that is typical of kabuki. As he reads* TOGASHI *rises slowly and begins to move slowly toward* BENKEI. *Every movement is part of a deliberate choreographic pattern which contributes to the mounting tension. The atmosphere of the theatre is hushed and the audience waits expectantly.* TOGASHI *halts and leans forward in a posture of suspicious enquiry. Suddenly he peers forward at the scroll in* BENKEI's *hands and quickly draws back. He says nothing but his facial expression indicates his innermost thoughts.* BENKEI *turns aside clutching the scroll and assumes a bombastic and defiant pose. The scene is a triumph of the kabuki actor's art.* TOGASHI *is a man whose suspicions have been confirmed but who at the same time has decided to ignore his duty in deference to more complex reasons.* BENKEI *realises the moment is crucial but is prepared to see it through to the end, and match his mental skill against his adversary. It is open to the master actor to place a more delicate emphasis one way or the other on his interpretation of parts such as these, which require the great artists of kabuki to give the finesse needed. After this climax* BENKEI *turns to face* TOGASHI *again and commences to read from the scroll he holds aloft.*)

BENKEI: Listen to my words. Since the death of Buddha there has been no one to succour men amidst the perplexities of life and death. In another age there was an Emperor who was a sincere believer and took pity on the people. One night he had a dream and divine revelation came to him. He was so impressed that he built a temple in which to pray for the peace of the world as well as his own people. However, it was destroyed by fire in the Jisho era and it was regrettable that after its destruction people no longer observed the traditions of their faith in that place. Now the holy Shun Bo Chogen has been granted an Imperial mandate to rebuild the temple and has sent many of us out to different provinces. Those who contribute even a small coin will obtain great happiness on earth and find peace in the next world. Buddha hear my words.

(BENKEI *brusquely rolls up the scroll as he finishes his recital.*)

(*The narrators in the orchestra chant their comment*):

"He read so loudly that it echoed in the heavens."

TOGASHI: As I have heard you read the subscription list there are no grounds for suspicion any more. However, let me take this opportunity to ask a few more questions. Priestly costumes differ but only the dress of mountain priests has an intimidating appearance. I do not understand why such clothing is necessary to pious men. Is there a reason for it?

(*Next follows a battle of wits between the two men in which* TOGASHI *subjects* BENKEI *to a barrage of questions on the technicalities of Buddhist symbolism. The tension mounts under this verbal assault.*)

BENKEI: That is easily answered. Mountain priests must climb high peaks where others dare not pass and kill wild beasts and poisonous snakes. We take compassion on ordinary men and practice austerities over long years. We try to persuade lost souls and evil spirits as well to achieve the true stage of Buddha. We pray for the peace of the world. So, although mountain priests are peaceful men in themselves they must appear outwardly fierce. This string of beads symbolises the virtues of Buddhism in overcoming the evils of the world.

TOGASHI: You wear the scarf of an ordinary priest but why do you wear such a hat on your head?

BENKEI: This hat and scarf are comparable to the helmet and armour of a warrior. We carry stout swords and an iron staff blessed by Buddha with which we strike the ground as we cross high mountains and steep places.

TOGASHI: A temple priest carries a wooden staff only. Why do you defend yourselves with iron staves?

BENKEI: It is very easily explained. The iron staff is a divine object because it was used by an Indian mountain hermit under whom Buddha practised austerities in his youth.

TOGASHI: And how came the iron staff to be introduced into your religion?

BENKEI: The founder of our faith carried this staff when crossing fields or high mountains and his custom was handed down from generation to generation. Because of its origin it is a divine staff.

TOGASHI (*makes a subtle but highly dramatic gesture towards* BENKEI *with his fan*): You are a priest and yet you wear a sword. Is it only for appearance or do you really use it?

BENKEI: It may seem like a weapon worn by a scarecrow but we do not carry it just for effect. Besides wild beasts and poisonous snakes, we cut down any man who brings harm to the world or goes against the law of Buddha and the Imperial realm. We can dispatch him immediately for if we save many by killing the one we are in the right.

(BENKEI *is facing the audience at this point and makes a forceful downward gesture with the scroll in his hand.*)

TOGASHI: You can kill visible things but suppose invisible evils attack the Imperial realm. How do you destroy those?

BENKEI: We have no difficulty for we use spiritual weapons and pray to Buddha.

TOGASHI: What does the costume of the mountain priests symbolise?

BENKEI: The physical form of the immoveable god of our sect.

TOGASHI: What is the meaning of your hat?

BENKEI: It is a crown which symbolises the Five Wisdoms.

TOGASHI: What about your scarf?

BENKEI: It symbolises the scroll of enlightenment.

TOGASHI: What meaning have your leggings?

BENKEI: They represent the darkness of the inner world.

TOGASHI: What about your eight-knotted straw sandals?

BENKEI: They represent purification as they symbolise treading on the eight petals of the lotus flower.

TOGASHI: And what meaning is there when you draw breath?

BENKEI: It represents ah-un. Ah, the sound with an open mouth and un when the mouth is closed. It stands for the beginning and end of all things.

(*The pace has quickened under this barrage of questioning with its repetitious complexities as* TOGASHI *tries to confound* BENKEI *in an esoteric maze. A climax is reached as* TOGASHI *asks the next question and assumes a threatening pose with a spiral of movement ending in his right hand, clutching his fan, flung high above his head. Sound and movement merge here in a magnificent finale.*)

TOGASHI: What about the nine character prayer? Let me have a reply to that question. Answer me quickly.

BENKEI (*he is completely at ease and in a mounting torrent of explanation passes the final test which he caps with a forceful and melodramatic pose*): The meaning is subtle and very hard to explain but I will tell you to allay your suspicions. When you wish to make this prayer you must stand erect and strike your teeth thirty-six times with the thumb of your right hand, draw five vertical lines and four horizontal lines after that, then intone the nine character prayer. All kinds of evils as well as heretics may be destroyed. It is like pouring hot water on frost and acts as an invisible weapon more powerful than the famous sword of ancient China. If you have any further questions about our religion I will answer them for you. Its virtues are great and boundless. Remember this and keep it to yourself. I vow these words before all the gods in Great Japan as well as Buddha. We speak with reverence in our hearts.

(*The narrators in the orchestra chant*):

"He was regarded with admiration."

TOGASHI: I was wrong to suspect so reverent a priest even for a moment. Now I will be a contributor to your subscription fund. Bring my offerings here.

THREE SOLDIERS (*in unison*): Sir!

(*The narrators in the orchestra chant out the details of the ritual the soldiers now perform. The soldiers bearing a white ceremonial costume, silks from Kaga province and other things, place them on wooden stands.*)

TOGASHI: I fear these are poor gifts but I ask you to accept them in good faith.

BENKEI: Oh thank you, I am grateful, you are a generous donor. I am sure you will find happiness in this life and the next world. I have another favour to ask you. I must travel round the provinces soliciting contributions and returning here about mid-April. Until that time these gifts will be an encumbrance and I would like you to keep them for us. (*Turning to his party*) Now all of you go ahead!

FOUR RETAINERS (*in unison*): We respectfully obey!

BENKEI: Come, come we must hasten on our way.

FOUR RETAINERS (*in unison*): We are ready.

(*The narrators in the orchestra now chant*):

"The mountain priests rose and went on their way quietly rejoicing."

(*Next follows a tense sequence. The four retainers rise and troop round in single file to follow* BENKEI *with* YOSHITSUNE *in his disguise well in the rear.* BENKEI *has already reached the middle of the runway leading to the rear of the auditorium when one of* TOGASHI'S *soldiers suddenly calls his superior's attention to the mountain guide who is just approaching the runway.* TOGASHI *immediately calls upon him to stop as he poses with a threatening hand on his sword hilt. The mountain guide sinks to the ground instantly while* BENKEI *on the runway gives a mighty bound and rushes back on to stage followed by the four retainers.*)

TOGASHI: Hey you mountain guide, wait a moment.

(*The narrators in the orchestra chant*):

"They suspect our master. All the mountain priests step back in anxious suspense."

BENKEI (*backed up by the four retainers* BENKEI *is now face to face with* TOGASHI *and his soldiers*): Aiya! Wait a minute. Do not be too hasty in your actions. Mountain guide, you there, why don't you move along?

TOGASHI: I stopped him!

BENKEI: For what reason?

TOGASHI: I am informed he resembles a certain person. That is why I stopped him.

BENKEI: It is not unknown for someone to resemble another person, but who is he like?

TOGASHI: I am told he resembles Yoshitsune so I stopped him to question his identity.

BENKEI (*with feigned incredulity and anger*): What! It will be a never forgotten day in his life that he has been mistaken for Yoshitsune. It is exasperating. We hoped to reach Noto province by sundown if possible but this mountain guide carrying only a small burden on his shoulders lags behind. That is why he brings suspicion on us. What a useless fellow you are! You shall pay dearly for this. Because you were incompetent in your task you were mistaken for Yoshitsune.

(*The narrators in the orchestra chant*):

"He gave Yoshitsune a good beating with the staff."

(BENKEI *then seizes the staff from his disguised master's grasp and raising it aloft beats the crouching figure across the shoulders. The actor does not actually touch the victim, of course; the beating is a graphic example of choreographic symbolism and dextrous manipulation to a co-ordinated rhythm.*)

BENKEI: Now go ahead!

TOGASHI: Whatever explanation you give we cannot let him pass!

THREE SOLDIERS (*in unison*): He shall not!

BENKEI: Why do you keep eying his pack? Is he a thief?

(*The narrators in the orchestra chant*):

"Why do you all try to draw your swords to fight for such a mountain guide?"

(*At this point there ensues a scene full of great power and superb stagecraft.* BENKEI'*s four followers rush up to him forming a square behind him, pressing forward threateningly and swaying backwards as* BENKEI *restrains them with his staff.* TOGASHI, *with sword half drawn, and* BENKEI, *grasping his staff in both hands, move in to a confrontation which becomes a slow dance acted out to a musical rhythm. First* TOGASHI *and his soldiers with slow and measured stamping, almost feline in its suggestion of concealed power, press* BENKEI *and his group backwards only to have the action reversed as they in turn are compelled to retreat to their original starting point. The dance becomes a tremendous surge of threatening movement which has a unique visual appeal. At the conclusion of the dance the group become transfixed in a tableau as* BENKEI *raises his staff high over his head in a threat which he cries aloud.*)

BENKEI: If you are still suspicious I will leave the mountain guide in your charge with the gifts. Treat him as you like or shall I beat him to death on the spot?

TOGASHI (*he turns away in anguish at all the threat implies*): Your actions are violent. They belie so pious a leader.

BENKEI: Then why did you suspect him?

TOGASHI: One of my soldiers informed me about him.

BENKEI (*making a threatening gesture with his staff again*): I will beat him to death to allay your suspicions.

TOGASHI (*his anguish becomes overwhelming at this point and his emotions are complex*): Iya! Do not be rash. Just because my suspicious retainers mistook this man for Yoshitsune you beat him like that. Now my suspicions are allayed. You may take him with you and hasten on your way.

BENKEI: But for our generous contributor's words I would have beaten him to death and abandoned him here. What a lucky fellow you are. From now on be more careful!

TOGASHI: We will be on our guard more strictly yet!

THREE SOLDIERS (*in unison*): Ha!

(*The narrators in the orchestra chant*):

"The guardian of the barrier enters the gate accompanied by his soldiers."

(TOGASHI *turns away from* BENKEI *in a moment of suspended action, his head averted to indicate that he is blinded by his tears. He hastens offstage through the curtained door at the left of the stage followed by his men.* BENKEI *stands and watches them go and turns as they disappear.* YOSHITSUNE *rises and walks slowly from up right centre to left centre. The four retainers rise one after the other up right centre and go to up centre where they seat themselves in a row.* BENKEI, *who has moved to right centre, turns and moves towards* YOSHITSUNE, *who is seated facing the right of the stage, kneeling down to make a deep obeisance at some distance from his master. The dignified reserve of the scene that now ensues has considerable emotional depth for the Japanese playgoer. Slow samisen music and the intermittent taps of a drum.*)

YOSHITSUNE: You have acted with great presence of mind today. No man can compare with you. You saved my life by beating me like a humble menial. It was by divine protection and the will of the gods.

FIRST RETAINER: I thought it was a desperate moment for our master when he was stopped by the barrier guard.

SECOND RETAINER: It is a sign that the gods protect our master. We can now proceed to Michinoku more easily than we dared hope.

THIRD RETAINER: We owe everything to the resourcefulness of Benkei. Without him we should have been lost.

FOURTH RETAINER: We cannot compare with him.

FIRST RETAINER: That is so.

FOUR RETAINERS (*in unison*): We are filled with admiration.

BENKEI (*he has half raised his head to speak*): Although we live in a corrupt world, the sun and the moon are still in heaven. We are grateful that you were saved. Although I beat my master as a ruse I thought I should incur divine punishment. I can lift a thousand pounds weight but at that moment my arm seemed numb. How irreverent I was, how irreverent!

(*At this point BENKEI goes down with his face close to the ground as he expresses his shame.*)

(*The narrators in the orchestra chant a slow passage*):

"Benkei had never wept before but now he weeps. Yoshitsune takes his hand."

(YOSHITSUNE *moves slowly towards* BENKEI *with slowly extended hand although there is no actual contact. The passage is entirely symbolic and ritualistic in its performance.*)

YOSHITSUNE: I was born of a samurai family but I have not been favoured by the for-

tunes of war. I was prepared to give my life for my brother Yoritomo and leave my corpse floating on the waves.

(*The orchestra now begins a more spirited passage, the prelude to a vigorous dance mime scene.*)

BENKEI: We slept on mountains, in the fields and by the sea coast.

(*The line is taken up by the narrators in the orchestra as* BENKEI *raises himself on one knee and begins to mime out the words of the narrators' chant*):

Whenever we slept we were in armour, in constant danger of attack our sleep was fitful. Once, aboard a ship our fate was at the mercy of the waves and once, high in the mountains a storm drove the snow drifts as high as our horses' knees. For three years we helped Yoritomo to power yet you remain unfortunate. I weep tears of pity for you. Benkei was as a thistle beaten down by frost and rain.

FOUR RETAINERS: Hurry, hurry disperse!

(*The narrators in the orchestra chant*):

"Plucking each others' sleeves they were about to leave."

(*The voice of* TOGASHI *is heard off stage and the curtain right stage is flung back and he makes his entry followed by his sword bearer and his soldiers carrying flasks of sake.* TOGASHI *moves across the stage and takes up a seated position at the left with his sword bearer in his rear and the soldiers seated in a row up left centre. One of the soldiers rises and pours out sake for* TOGASHI *who drinks in ceremonial style and then orders sake to be offered to* BENKEI.)

TOGASHI (*making his entry*): No, no, you travelling priests, wait a moment wait. (*Then after he is seated*) As I was so abrupt with you I have brought some sake. Come, come let us drink, take this cup.

BENKEI: Oh thank you generous patron we will drink.

(Next follows some light hearted foolery which comes as a relief to the tension of the preceding scene and when performed by master actors offers some hilarious comic mime. BENKEI *is seated up centre and two soldiers kneel on either side of him armed with flasks of sake. After the first few drinks* BENKEI *is dissatisfied with the capacity of the cups and orders one of the soldiers to bring the lid of the lacquer tub on which* TOGASHI *sat in the earlier part of the play. Ordering the astonished soldiers to fill the lid with sake he quaffs the outsize draught. Mellowed with so much wine he directs the two soldiers to follow the direction of his finger pointing high in the air and having transfixed their gaping attention bowls them both over with a mighty clap of each hand. He bursts into a roar of laughter at their angry protests. After completely emptying both flasks which he seizes by force from the reluctant soldiers in turn, he drains the lid of the tub to its last drop and finishes by placing his outsize cup drunkenly on his head. This is the prelude to a long and complex dance which he now rises to perform. The chant of the narrators in the orchestra runs as follows):*

"Truly he knows how to accept both the sake and the hospitality of others."

(His dance moves through several phases in which romantic episodes in his past are used to express his present problems. The narrators continue as the drunken dance proceeds, BENKEI *giving their words choreographic expression.)*

"Because of a girl I met long ago I had to face the barrier of public criticism in the past. It is an old story and I am embarassed to speak of it. Now I am in trouble once more and face another barrier. In this transient world fortune or misfortune depend on mere chance."

(The next portion of the dance represents an ancient pastime that originated in China. Wine cups were set afloat on a winding stream at some distance between each other. The players sat on the banks of the stream and had to compose a short poem between the passing of each floating cup. BENKEI *dances this theme with his fan as the narrators chant):*

"It is interesting to float a cup on a mountain stream letting my sleeve dip the winding water."

(He climaxes the dance by going down on his knees in a pose.)

BENKEI: Let me offer you a cup of sake on behalf of us all!

TOGASHI *(who is half dozing)*: Dance for us please!

BENKEI: Congratulations and may you have long life like the turtle living on a rock.

*(*BENKEI *then rises to perform the longevity dance as the rhythm and tempo of the music quicken and the narrators chant):*

"Benkei had always been skilled in dancing and especially in the longevity dance."

(After a vigorous passage BENKEI *moves over towards the retainers and* YOSHITSUNE *and with a quick gesture of his hands and while still dancing he signals them to go. They hastily rise and in single file, with* YOSHITSUNE *bringing up the rear, scurry down the runway and disappear from the theatre. The narrators are chanting):*

"The mountains echo to the sound of the torrent dropping from crag to crag and the waterfall's roar, the roar of the waterfall, the waterfall's roar. The bright sun is above and the waters flow on. Quickly, quickly, hasten away, be watchful of the barrier guards, now this is our farewell. As though treading on the tail of a tiger or escaping the fangs of a serpent they slung their packs upon their shoulders and departed on their way and departed on their way."

*(*BENKEI *has gone to up right stage where an assistant helps him on with the pack formerly worn by* YOSHITSUNE *and with this in position he moves towards the runway with erratic steps as though physically overcome with relief.* TOGASHI *in the meantime strides to centre stage and takes a dominant pose, as with a*

violent twist of his voluminous sleeve he flings his right hand holding his fan above his head. His men are in a row behind him as the main stage curtain is pulled across hiding them from sight but leaving BENKEI *standing motionless at the head of the runway and in full view of the audience. The wooden clappers are heard and he assumes a bold posture tucking his staff beneath his left arm and moving his right arm in a sweeping flow of gesture. Then to the re-sonant beat of a large drum back stage he moves off down the runway using what may best be described as a gigantic hop. The whole body is inclined forward as the actor moves from one leg to the other, the right arm being flung out in a wide arc behind his head as he changes his foot position, gathering speed as he goes, and finally making his exit at the rear of the auditorium in a flurry of sound and magnificently controlled movement.)*

The Lady of the Camellias

The Lady of the Camellias is an old-fashioned play that still looks surprisingly modern, partly because of the indestructible popularity of sentiment and even sentimentality in many media, from soap operas' love stories to *Love Story* as a novel and a film, and partly because it has, as the most popular play of nineteenth-century France, maintained a life in the theatre. Victor Hugo's *Marion Delorme* may have been (as the critic Sarcey claimed) a true *"cri de passion,"* but Alexandre Dumas *fils' Lady of the Camellias* is even more theatrically effective and more rounded as a psychological study. Not a stereotype, the courtesan is more human than the *demi-mondaines* of *Les Filles de marbre, Les Femmes sans noms* and the rest of that army of mercenaries chronicled in such histories as Sidney D. Braun's *The 'Courtisane' in the French Theatre from Hugo to Becque (1831–1885)* (1947) and Grace Pauline Ihrig's *Heroines in the French Drama of the Romantic Period, 1829–1848* (1950).

The courtesan appealed to the romantics as a literary figure, and Dumas *fils* (that is, "the son") might well have written about one anyway; but he was fortunate, in a way, to have been able to write from personal experience. He based his heroine on Marie Duplessis, who died at twenty-three in 1847, after living a glittering and lavish life — some of the luxury having been provided by Dumas *fils* himself. Finally his finances forced him to break off the affair and to write her a touching letter which said in part:

> I am neither rich enough to love you as I should like nor poor enough to be loved as you would like. Let us forget each other — you a name that must leave you practically cold, I a happiness that I cannot afford.

After she died, Dumas *fils* made a novel of her life, then a play from his novel, recouping much of what he may be said to have laid out for research.

It is often said that the need for money drove Dumas *fils* to literature, that he yearned for the luxury that the voluminous publications of his father (author of *The Count of Monte Cristo* and about 1200 more works) had brought to Alexandre Dumas *père.* In fact, the father's rags-to-riches life had made him rather extravagant with his wealth, rich enough not only to recognize his illegitimate son (by a seamstress) but to give him the money associated with the name. The boy was not happy at school (as *L'Affaire Clémenceau* records) but his young manhood was lavish and libertine.

When he turned to literature it was not only for money — he always needed money — but largely for independence and fame like his father's.

He published some poetry. He published the novel *La Dame aux camélias*. Then he decided to make a play of it. In 1852 he shut himself up in his little house at Neuilly and in a few days wrote *The Lady of the Camellias*. It was harder to get the play staged, for the Board of Censors did not agree with Dumas *père* that his son's work had "a high moral purpose." *The Lady of the Camellias* was banned. Fortunately Morny — another illegitimate child, but this time the half-brother of Napoleon III — championed it and had it produced. After the triumph of opening night, the argument still raged over its morality, but never again was there to be any doubt about its theatrical effectiveness.

In *A Digest of 500 Plays*, a book superficially summarizing plays for would-be producers, *The Lady of the Camellias* is said to have these "difficulties" (apart from the expensive sets): "The minor characters are sketchily drawn; many scenes seem ragged and hastily conceived; the motivations are often intellectually unconvincing." Certainly this did not prevent the great Charles Fechter, who created the role of Armand, from making it impressive; as for the role of Marguerite Gauthier, generations of actresses have gloried in it. Sarah Bernhardt found tremendous theatricality in it; Eleanora Duse surpassed Bernhardt (as always) by discovering depth. Meyerhold directed his wife in the role in Russia in 1936 and found it could be played without affectation; Eva Le Gallienne proved it was a great vehicle. Actresses as good as Réjane and as poor as Ethel Barrymore succeeded in the role; Garbo (directed by George Cukor) made *Camille* one of the masterpieces of the cinema, investing the role with such beauty and power that one was ready to accept it in the place of all the great roles she never tried: Medea, Cleopatra, Hedda Gabler, Saint Joan, and the rest. What do the principal roles in this play have that make them so viable in more than one dramatic medium?

It was long ago demonstrated that the woman with a past had a future in the theatre. The modern drama is full of the lost, or the mislaid, woman. Suderman's Alma in *Honor* and heroines in Wilde, from the Duchess of Padua to Mrs. Erlynne, showed how staunch moralists could produce plays defective in moral logic. Agnes in *The Notorious Mrs. Ebbsmith* and Paula in *The Second Mrs. Tanqueray* showed how Pinero could forge problem plays: constructing well-made stage problems and "solving" them entirely in terms of well-motivated stage solutions, not applicable to or drawn from observation of real life. Henry Arthur Jones was ready to show a clergyman's daughter going astray in *Saints and Sinners* or trying to go straight after a wicked past (Drusilla Ives in *The Dancing Girl*), but he was far more likely to come up with a sermon than a solution. Ibsen's women with a past, the heart-of-gold wayward ladies in the works of Maeterlinck and Schnitzler, all the wayward, well-made women in all the stage-worthy, well-made plays from the sensational (such as Wilde's *Salome*) to the sedate (such as Galsworthy's *The Fugitive*) — all seemed to tempt dramatists to play with serious, contemporary problems (or problems like them) but to evade the essentials, to gloss over realities, to relegate the *scene à faire* of the well-made play to an off-stage suicide or something similar. It is interesting to consider how close Dumas *fils* came to tackling problems of prostitution in *The Lady of the Camellias* and how his work compares with Shaw's dramatic discussion of *Mrs. Warren's Profession*, "the presentation in parable of the conflict between man's will and his environment; in a word, of a problem." The place that money plays in both plays — Shaw thinks that the lack of money is the root of all evil — is very significant, while Marguerite and Mrs. Warren could hardly be more different. Shaw thinks economics explain it all. Dumas *fils* would tend to agree with G. K. Chesterton that sentimentality has to be taken into account: "The world has kept sentimentalities," wrote Chesterton, "simply because they are the most practical things in the world. They alone make men do things." And what better subject for sentimentalities than The Woman With A Past?

Dumas *fils* did not go quite as far as Maeterlinck — whose Sister Beatrice was forgiven by the Blessed Virgin making a personal appearance — but he did, sentimentally and with great theatricality, show Marguerite redeemed by love. (She was then promptly removed from the scene to avoid further complications.) In *La Femme de Claude* (1873) Dumas *fils* condemned the unregenerate fallen woman and suggested that her husband ought to kill her. (The best of them, like Clare in *The Fugitive* and Paula Tanqueray, obligingly commit suicide.) The prostitute, redeemed or unredeemed, was a perfect subject, both in drama and in moral interest, for the "useful theatre" which Dumas *fils* championed. In the Preface to *Un Père prodigue* (1859), Dumas *fils* defined the basis of that theatre: "All literature whose aim is not perfectability, morality — usefulness, in short — is a rickety and unhealthy, still-born literature." In *The Lady of the Camellias* the didacticism is kept more or less in check, as it is in his first play not adapted from a novel (*Le Demi-monde*, 1855, translated as *The Outer Edge of Society*) and his last play (*Francillon*, 1887). In general, however, Dumas *fils* tended to be quite as commonsensical as his rival in sparkling comedy, Émile Augier, and often more honestly concerned with reality (as in *Le Question d'argent*, 1857) than the "serious" writers of tragedy in the period. He makes a fascinating predecessor for Ibsen and Shaw and we may ask to what extent he uses what one critic has termed the Ibsenite approach: coming into a very stuffy room and throwing up all the windows so that everybody catches cold and dies.

The modern drama, of which Ibsen and Shaw were two of the giants, developed in reaction to romantic strains that are still strongly evident in Dumas *fils*. The Germans probably invented this elevated, exotic, escapist drama with their *Sturm und Drang* in the eighteenth century, but it reached its height in France in the nineteenth century after the six-hour bore of Hugo's *Cromwell* (1827) and the riots that greeted his *Hernani* (1830, largely because it was presented in that bastion of conservatism, the Comédie-Française). Escapist drama was still strong by the end of the century when Edmond Rostand wrote *Cyrano de Bergerac* (1898). Dumas *père* contributed significantly to it not only with *The Three Musketeers* and other swashbuckling novels but in plays like his *Antony* (1831) and *La Tour de Nesle* (1832), which was his best, at the Théâtre de Porte Saint-Martin. The stage version of *The Count of Monte Cristo* was influential world wide: Eugene O'Neill's father, for example, played it for a quarter of a century in America. There are plenty of romantic touches in *The Lady of the Camellias* by the younger Dumas, along with the devices of the well-made plays of Scribe and Sardou. He writes with *panache*, certainly, but Parigot's *Génie et métier* assures us that the manuscripts of the plays of Dumas *fils* (which some critics call "hastily conceived") are full of rewritten lines, rejected scenes, careful craftsmanship — and that they are about four times longer than the printed versions finally arrived at. From his own life Dumas *fils* took the romantic situation of his involvement with the charming Marie Duplessis, but then, as he said in introduction to *Le Supplice d'une femme,* he knew that "a situation is not an idea" and that "the art lies in preparing it, getting it accepted, rendering it possible, especially in untying the knot [*dénouement*]." In treating a romantic subject in a well-ordered way, Dumas *fils* helps to bridge between the old drama and the new. When this can be combined with the creation of a deathless dramatic heroine, it is something of an achievement.

To help you to appreciate this play, a new translation has been prepared for this book. Nigel Playfair and Edith Reynolds translated the play in 1930 and their work has recently reappeared, but despite their claim that it is "a translation, not an adaptation," it is a much truncated version. They confess to have "pruned it of some sentences and even passages which seemed to have merely a topical or local interest . . . and others that sounded, in English, priggish or long-winded." I hope that this translation sounds neither pompous nor tedious but it is a translation of the whole play. In a production, it might well be cut; perhaps you ought to consider where that might be necessary for a modern audience. But first you should have the opportunity to read the play in its entirety as close to the way Dumas *fils* wrote it as possible.

THE LADY OF THE CAMELLIAS

Alexandre Dumas *fils*

*Translated from the French
by L. R. N. Ashley*

DRAMATIS PERSONÆ

ARMAND DUVAL	MESSENGER
GEORGE DUVAL,	SERVANTS
his father	MARGUERITE GAUTHIER
GASTON RIEUX	NICHETTE
SAINT-GAUDENS	PRUDENCE
GUSTAVE	NANINE
Count de GIRAY	OLYMPE [DUVERNOY]
[Baron de] VARVILLE	ANAÏS
ARTHUR	GUESTS
DOCTOR	

PLACE: PARIS AND AUTEUIL

THE ACTION TAKES PLACE AROUND 1848.

ACT ONE

The drawing room of Marguerite. Paris.

SCENE ONE   Nanine sewing; Varville, sitting by the fireplace. [Nichette, later.] The bell rings.

VARVILLE: Someone rang.

NANINE: Valentine will open the door.

VARVILLE: It must be Marguerite.

NANINE: Not yet. She's not expected before half-past ten and it's not ten o'clock yet.

(*Enter* NICHETTE.)

Oh, it's Mademoiselle Nichette.

SCENE TWO   The same, Nichette.

NICHETTE: Isn't Marguerite here?

NANINE: No, mademoiselle. Did you wish to see her?

NICHETTE: I was just going by and I came up to say hello to her, but if she's not here I'll be running along.

NANINE: Wait a little, she'll be back.

NICHETTE: I haven't time, Gustave is downstairs. Is she well?

NANINE: Just the same.

NICHETTE: Tell her I'll come to see her in a day or so. Goodbye, Nanine. Goodbye, monsieur.

(*Exit* NICHETTE.)

SCENE THREE   Nanine, Varville.

VARVILLE: Who is that young lady?

NANINE: That's Mademoiselle Nichette.

VARVILLE: Nichette? That's a name for a cat, not for a woman!

NANINE: It's also a name, and they nicknamed her that because with her curly hair she's got the little head of a cat. She was a friend of madame, in the store where madame used to work.

VARVILLE: You mean Marguerite used to work in a store?

NANINE: She sold linen.

VARVILLE: Hmm!

NANINE: Didn't you know that? It's no secret.

VARVILLE: Little Nichette is pretty.

NANINE: And so good.

VARVILLE: What about this Monsieur Gustave?

NANINE: What Monsieur Gustave?

VARVILLE: The one she said was waiting downstairs.

NANINE: It's her husband.

VARVILLE: Monsieur Nichette?

NANINE: Well, he isn't her husband yet, but he will be.

VARVILLE: In a word, he's her lover. Well, well, she is a good girl, but she has a lover.

NANINE: Who loves nobody else, as she has never loved anybody but him, and who will marry her, mark my words. Mademoiselle Nichette is a very nice girl.

VARVILLE (*getting up and going to* NANINE): After all, of what concern is it to me. . . . I'm certainly not making much progress here.

NANINE: Not the least.

VARVILLE: I must say that Marguerite. . . .

NANINE: What?

VARVILLE: Is awfully silly to give up everybody else for Monsieur de Mauriac, who can't be much fun.

NANINE: Poor man, she's his only happiness. He is like her father, or just about.

VARVILLE: Ah, yes. There's a very sad story about that; unfortunately. . . .

NANINE: Unfortunately what?

VARVILLE: I don't believe a word of it.

NANINE (*getting up*): Listen, Monsieur de Varville, there are plenty of true things you could say about madame, which is all the more reason for not spreading lies. You see, I can speak with authority, and the Lord knows I wasn't prompted by madame, because she has no reason to fool you, either to get into your good graces or to anger you. I can tell you that two years ago madame, after a long illness, went to take the waters to recuperate. I went with her. Among the invalids at the spa there was a young lady of about the same age, with the same illness, only at the tertiary stage, who looked like

her twin sister. That young lady was Mademoiselle de Mauriac, the daughter of the duke.

VARVILLE: Mademoiselle de Mauriac died.

NANINE: Yes.

VARVILLE: And the duke, in despair, found in the mannerisms, in the age, even in the illness of Marguerite, the image of his own daughter, begged her to receive him and allow him to love her as his child. Well, Marguerite confessed to him what kind of a life she had been living.

NANINE: Because madame never tells a lie.

VARVILLE: Naturally. And because Marguerite was not so much mentally as physically like his daughter, the duke promised to give her anything she wanted, if she would consent to change her way of life, which Marguerite promised to do, and naturally she once again returned to Paris and kept her word; and the duke, as she then gave him only half of the happiness he had hoped for, cut her income in half, so that she's now fifty thousand francs in debt.[1]

NANINE: Which you are offering to pay. But it is better to owe money to other people than gratitude to you.

VARVILLE: Especially when the Count de Giray is there?

NANINE: You are really unbearable! All that I can tell you is that the story of the duke is true, I give you my word. As for the count, he is just a friend.

VARVILLE: Make that "and a lover."

NANINE: Yes, a friend. What a wicked tongue you have! — But there's the bell. It's madame. Must I tell her everything that you've been saying?

VARVILLE: Just be careful.

---

[1] Marie Duplessis, the real Marguerite, spent about $60,000 a year, André Maurois calculated (1954 rates). Dumas *fils* (her Armand) went deeply into debt buying her trinkets.

SCENE FOUR   The same, Marguerite.

MARGUERITE (*to* NANINE): Go tell them to prepare some supper. Olympe and Saint-Gaudens will be coming. I ran into them at the opera. (*to* VARVILLE) You're here, are you? (*She goes and sits by the fireplace.*)

VARVILLE: Am I not destined to wait for you?

MARGUERITE: Am I destined to find you here all the time?

VARVILLE: Until you bar your door against me, I'll keep coming.

MARGUERITE: Really, I can't come in a single time without finding you here. What is there left to say to me?

VARVILLE: You know very well.

MARGUERITE: Always the same thing! You get monotonous, Varville.

VARVILLE: Is it my fault that I love you?

MARGUERITE: Great argument! My dear, if I were to listen to everybody who loves me, I wouldn't even have time to eat. For the hundredth time, I'm telling you, you are wasting your time. I let you come here at all hours, to see me when I'm here and to wait for me when I'm out, I don't really know why, but if you must keep talking of your love, I'm going to have to cut you off.

VARVILLE: However, Marguerite, at Bagnères,[1] last year, you gave me some hope.

MARGUERITE: Oh, my dear, that was at Bagnères, I wasn't feeling well, I was bored. Here it's not the same thing at all; I'm feeling better and I'm not bored.

VARVILLE: I suppose so, when one is loved by the Duke de Mauriac. . . .

MARGUERITE: Idiot!

VARVILLE: And when you love Monsieur de Giray. . . .

MARGUERITE: I am free to love whom I please. It's nobody's business, yours least of all. So if you have nothing else to say, I repeat, you'd better go. (VARVILLE *paces back and forth.*) Aren't you going to go?

VARVILLE: No.

MARGUERITE: Well, sit down at the piano; the piano is your one redeeming quality.

VARVILLE: What shall I play? (NADINE *comes in as he begins to play.*)

MARGUERITE: Whatever you like.

SCENE FIVE   The same, Nadine.

MARGUERITE: You've ordered supper?

NADINE: Yes, madame.

MARGUERITE (*approaching* VARVILLE): What is that you're playing, Varville?

VARVILLE: A reverie by Rosellen.[1]

MARGUERITE: It's very pretty. . . .

VARVILLE: Listen, Marguerite, I have an income of eighty thousand francs a year.

MARGUERITE: And I have a hundred. (*to* NANINE) Have you seen Prudence?

NANINE: Yes, madame.

MARGUERITE: Is she coming this evening?

NANINE: Yes, madame, she'll be back. Mademoiselle Nichette was here too.

MARGUERITE: Why didn't she wait?

NANINE: Monsieur Gustave was waiting for her downstairs.

MARGUERITE: Dear little girl!

NANINE: The doctor dropped in.

MARGUERITE: What did he say?

NANINE: He recommended that madame rest.

MARGUERITE: The good doctor. Is that all?

NANINE: No, madame; this bouquet came for you.

VARVILLE: From me.

---

1 A spa, either Bagnères-de-Bigorre (Hautes-Pyrénées) or Bagnères-de-Luchon (Haute-Garonne).

1 Henri Rosellen (1811–1870), a popular minor composer.

MARGUERITE (*taking the bouquet*): Roses and white lilacs. Put this bouquet in your room, Nanine.

(*Exit* NANINE.)

VARVILLE (*stops playing the piano*): Don't you want them?

MARGUERITE: What do they call me?

VARVILLE: Marguerite Gauthier.

MARGUERITE: What name have they given me?

VARVILLE: The Lady of the Camellias.

MARGUERITE: Why?

VARVILLE: Because you never wear any other flowers.

MARGUERITE: Which means that I only like those and that it's useless to send me any others. If you think I'll make an exception for you, you're mistaken. The odor makes me sick.

VARVILLE: I have no luck. Goodbye, Marguerite.

MARGUERITE: Goodbye!

SCENE SIX   The same, Olympe, Saint-Gaudens, Nanine.

NANINE (*re-entering*): Madame, here are Mademoiselle Olympe and Monsieur Saint-Gaudens.

(*Enter* OLYMPE *and* SAINT-GAUDENS.)

MARGUERITE: Come on in, Olympe! I thought you weren't coming.

OLYMPE: It's Saint-Gaudens' fault.

SAINT-GAUDENS: It's always my fault. Good day, Varville.

VARVILLE: Good day, my dear friend.

SAINT-GAUDENS: You'll have supper with us?

VARVILLE: No, no.

SAINT-GAUDENS (*to* MARGUERITE): And you, my dear child, how are you?

MARGUERITE: Very well.

SAINT-GAUDENS: Well, so much the better. Shall we have a nice time here?

OLYMPE: One always has a nice time with you.

SAINT-GAUDENS: Naughty! — but I'm sorry to hear that dear Varville isn't supping with us. That's a terrible blow. (*to* MARGUERITE) Coming by the *Maison d'Or* I ordered some oysters and a special champagne that they keep only for me. It's perfect, perfect!

OLYMPE (*aside to* MARGUERITE): Why didn't you invite Edmond?

MARGUERITE (*aside*): Why didn't you bring him with you?

OLYMPE (*aside*): With Saint-Gaudens?

MARGUERITE (*aside*): Isn't he used to it?

OLYMPE (*aside*): Not yet, my dear. At his age it's very difficult to acquire a new habit, especially a good one.

MARGUERITE (*calling to* NADINE): Isn't supper ready?

NANINE: In five minutes, madame. Where do you want it served? In the dining room?

MARGUERITE: No, in here; we'll be more comfortable. — Well, Varville, haven't you gone yet?

VARVILLE: I'm going.

MARGUERITE (*at the window, calling*): Prudence!

OLYMPE: Prudence lives across the way?

MARGUERITE: You know she lives in the same building with only a little court separating us. It's very convenient when I need her.

SAINT-GAUDENS: Hmm, what does she do for a living?

OLYMPE: She sells hats.

MARGUERITE: And I'm the only one who buys them.

OLYMPE: And you never wear them.

MARGUERITE: They're frightful. But she's not a bad woman, and she needs the money. (*calling*) Prudence!

PRUDENCE (*offstage*): Here I am!

MARGUERITE: Why don't you come over now that you've returned?

PRUDENCE: I can't.

MARGUERITE: Why not?

PRUDENCE: I have a couple of young fellows here; they've invited me to supper.

MARGUERITE: Well invite them to supper here, that will be just as good. Who are they?

PRUDENCE: You know one of them, Gaston Rieux.

MARGUERITE: I certainly do! And the other one?

PRUDENCE: The other is a friend of his.

MARGUERITE: That's good enough; well, come right over ... It's cold this evening.... (*She coughs slightly.*) Varville, put a little wood on the fire; it's cold in here; make yourself useful, at least, since you can't be agreeable. (VARVILLE *obeys*.)

SCENE SEVEN   The same, Gaston, Armand, Prudence, a Servant.

A SERVANT (*announcing*): Monsieur Gaston Rieux, Monsieur Armand Duval, Madame Duvernoy.

OLYMPE: My, how people are announced here!

PRUDENCE: Well, I thought it was a fashionable party!

SAINT-GAUDENS: There goes Madame Duvernoy with her society manners.

GASTON (*ceremoniously to* MARGUERITE): How do you do, madame?

MARGUERITE (*in the same manner*): Very well; and you, sir?

PRUDENCE: The way they do go on here!

MARGUERITE: Gaston has become a man of the world; and besides, Eugénie would tear my eyes out if we were to say anything else.[1]

GASTON: Eugénie's hands are too small, and your eyes too big.

PRUDENCE: Enough flattery.[2] My dear Marguerite, permit me to present Monsieur Armand Duval (ARMAND *and* MARGUERITE *greet each other*), the man in Paris who is most in love with you.

MARGUERITE (*to* PRUDENCE): Tell them to lay two more places, in that case; I suppose that this love of his will prevent him from eating supper. (*She offers her hand to* ARMAND, *who kisses it.*)

SAINT-GAUDENS (*to* GASTON, *who has come up to him*): Ah, my dear Gaston, I'm very glad to see you.

GASTON: Young as ever, my dear old Saint-Gaudens.

SAINT-GAUDENS: Of course.

GASTON: And your love-life?

SAINT-GAUDENS (*pointing to* OLYMPE): As you see.

GASTON: My compliments.

SAINT-GAUDENS: Youth must give way. Poor Varville, who is not having supper with us, I feel so sorry for him.

GASTON (*going over to* MARGUERITE): He's superb!

MARGUERITE: It's only the old who don't age.

SAINT-GAUDENS (*to* ARMAND, *whom* OLYMPE *is*

---

1 This is not, of course, the Empress Eugénie (1826–1920), consort of Louis Napoléon in the Second Empire, beauty and arbiter of fashion. The play is set in 1848; Eugénie met and married Louis Napoléon in 1853 before which she was not well known, being simply Eugenia Maria de Montijo de Gúzman, daughter of the Spanish Conde de Teba.   **2** The French word *marivaudage* suggests not so much flattery as excessively refined mannerisms, style, or sentiments. The word derives from the name of Pierre Carlet de Chamblain de Marivaux (1688–1763), one of France's most famous playwrights (*Le Jeu de l'amour et du hasard* and more than 30 others) and novelists (*La Vie de Marianne*, 1731-1742), whose work was characterized by delicate nuances presented with meticulous precision and even preciosity.

presenting to him): Are you related, sir, to Monsieur Duval, the receiver-general?[3]

ARMAND: Yes, sir, he's my father. Do you know him?

SAINT-GAUDENS: I met him once, at the Baroness de Nersay's, and your mother, Madame Duval, too, a beautiful and charming lady.

ARMAND: She has been dead three years now.

SAINT-GAUDENS: Forgive me, sir, for having stirred that sorrowful memory.

ARMAND: One can always remind me of my mother. Great and pure affections have the merit that after having experienced them one has the added happiness of remembering them.

SAINT-GAUDENS: Are you the only child — ?

ARMAND: I have a sister. . . .

(*They walk away together to the back of the stage.*)

MARGUERITE (*aside, to* GASTON): Your friend is charming.

GASTON: Yes, I know. And, moreover, he's madly in love with you — isn't that true, Prudence?

PRUDENCE: What?

GASTON: I was telling Marguerite that Armand is crazy about her.

PRUDENCE: He's not lying. No doubt about that.

GASTON: He loves you so much, my dear, that he doesn't dare tell you about it.

MARGUERITE (*to* VARVILLE, *who has been playing the piano*): That's enough, Varville.

VARVILLE: You told me to keep on playing the piano.

MARGUERITE: When I'm alone with you, yes; but when there are people here, no!

OLYMPE: What's that she's whispering about there?

MARGUERITE: Listen and you'll find out.

PRUDENCE (*softly*): . . . and that love has been going on for two years now.

MARGUERITE: Well it's an old affair, then.

PRUDENCE: Armand spends all his time at Gustave's and Nichette's just to hear them talking of you.

GASTON: When you were ill last year, before you went to Bagnères, when you were confined to bed for three months, you know that every day a young man came, who wouldn't give his name, to find out how you were.

MARGUERITE: I remember. . . .

GASTON: It was he.

MARGUERITE: That was very nice. (*calling*) Monsieur Duval. . . .

ARMAND: Madame?

MARGUERITE: Do you know what they've just been telling me? They say that while I was sick you came every day for news of me.

ARMAND: That's the truth, madame.

MARGUERITE: The least I can do is thank you. Do you hear that, Varville? You never did anything like that for me.

VARVILLE: I've only known you for a year.

MARGUERITE: And this gentleman has only known me for five minutes. . . . You're always saying silly things.

(*Enter* NANINE *preceding the* SERVANTS, *who bring on a table.*)

PRUDENCE: Let's go to the table! I'm dying of hunger.

VARVILLE: Goodbye, Marguerite.

MARGUERITE: When shall I see you again?

VARVILLE: Whenever you wish!

MARGUERITE: Well, goodbye.

VARVILLE (*bowing himself out*): Gentlemen. . . .

OLYMPE: Goodbye, Varville! Goodbye, old boy!

---

3 Each governmental division (*département*) of France had a treasurer called *recevreur général*. Since 1865 the title has been *trésorier-payeur-général*. The elder Duval, then, was a rather high-ranking official (*fonctionnaire*).

(*During this the two* Servants *place the full set table around which the guests seat themselves.*)

Scene Eight   The same, minus Varville.

Prudence: My dear child, you are really very hard on the baron.

Marguerite: He's boring. He's always proposing to give me an allowance.

Olympe: Does that bother you? I wish someone would make a proposition like that to me.

Saint-Gaudens (*to* Olympe): That's alright with me, if you say so.

Olympe: I've asked you, my dear, not to be too familiar with me; I don't know you.

Marguerite: Now, children, help yourself, drink, eat, but don't quarrel just to be able to make up with each other right away.

Olympe (*to* Marguerite): Do you know what he gave me for my birthday?

Marguerite: Who?

Olympe: Saint-Gaudens.

Marguerite: No.

Olympe: He gave me a carriage.[1]

Saint-Gaudens: From Binder's.

Olympe: Yes, but I haven't been able to get him to give me horses for it.

Prudence: Nonetheless, it's a carriage.

Saint-Gaudens: I'm ruined. Love me for myself.

Olympe: The idea!

Prudence (*pointing to a plate*): What are those little creatures?

Gaston: Partridges.

Prudence: Give me one.

Gaston: She only asks for one partridge at a time. Such an appetite! She's probably the one who has ruined Saint-Gaudens.

Prudence: "She"! "She"! Is that the way to speak of a lady? In my day. . . .

Gaston: Oh, that would be the reign of Louis XV.[2] — Marguerite, pour some wine for Armand; he's very sad, as sad as a drinking song.

Marguerite: Well, Monsieur Armand, drink to my health!

All: Marguerite's health!

Prudence: Speaking of drinking songs, won't somebody give us one?

Gaston: Always the old traditions. I'm sure that Prudence had a passion for someone in the old Cave tavern.[3]

Prudence: What fun! Such fun!

Gaston: Always singing at supper. How absurd!

Prudence: I like it, it's merry. Alright, Marguerite, sing us the song by Philogène, a poet who writes verses. . . .

Gaston: What would you want him to do?

Prudence: Who writes verses for Marguerite! It's his specialty. Alright, the song!

Gaston: I protest in the name of the younger generation.

Prudence: Let's take a vote! (*All of them raise their hands except* Gaston.) The song is passed. Gaston, go along with the majority.

Gaston: Very well. But I know Philogène's verses, and I don't like them. I'd rather sing . . . well . . . if I must (*he sings.*)

I

Mahomet's paradise is made
Of flashing eyes and lemonade.

---

1 The French says *coupé*, a kind of diligence then fashionable. 2 Louis XV (1710–1774) became King of France in 1715. 3 *Le Caveau* was a literary café, founded in 1729 by Crébillion *père* and revived 1837; Joseph L. Borgerhoff says "Light poetry and drinking songs were its specialty."

Reject what Prophets proffer us!
We'd rather that you offer us
  Those flashing eyes
  In other guise,
  Their lightnings dancing in
  And more entrancing in
Our glasses of wine, our glasses of wine!

God made the wine as he made love
Both for our earth and up above.
Let's live in joyful ways, therefore,
And quaff our glasses ever more
  And raise our glass
  To every lass,
  Their charms elating with
  And celebrating with
Our glasses of wine, our glasses of wine!

(*The others applaud* GASTON.)

GASTON (*sitting down again*): Well, it's certainly true that life is as gay as Prudence is fat.

OLYMPE: That's been true for thirty years.

PRUDENCE: That's enough of that. How old do you think I am?

OLYMPE: I think you're an obvious forty.

PRUDENCE: Her and her "forty years" again! I was thirty-five my last birthday.

GASTON: Which makes you thirty-six already. Well, word of honor, you don't look a day over forty.

MARGUERITE: Speaking of which, Saint-Gaudens, on the subject of age, I heard a little story about you.

OLYMPE: Me too.

SAINT-GAUDENS: What story?

MARGUERITE: It concerns a yellow hackney coach.

OLYMPE: It's true, my dear.

PRUDENCE: Let's have the story of the yellow hackney coach.

GASTON: Yes, but let me go sit next to Marguerite; I'm tired of Prudence.

PRUDENCE: What a nicely brought up young man!

MARGUERITE: Gaston, try to sit still.

SAINT-GAUDENS: Oh, an excellent supper!

OLYMPE: I see what he's up to, he wants to avoid the story of the yellow . . .

MARGUERITE: Hackney coach!

SAINT-GAUDENS: Oh, I don't care.

OLYMPE: Well, you must all know that once upon a time Saint-Gaudens was in love with Amanda.

GASTON: I am deeply moved — I must kiss Marguerite.

OLYMPE: You are really too much, my dear!

GASTON: Olympe is furious because I made her lose her effect.

MARGUERITE: Olympe is right. Gaston is just as boring as Varville and ought to be put in the corner, like a naughty child.

OLYMPE: Yes, go put yourself there.

GASTON: On the condition that at the end all the girls will kiss me.

MARGUERITE: Prudence will take up a collection and kiss you for all of us.

GASTON: Not fair, not fair, I want to be kissed by you yourselves.

OLYMPE: Alright, we'll kiss you; go sit down and be quiet. One day, or rather one night . . .

GASTON (*playing* Malbrouck [s'en va't-en guerre][4] *on the piano*): This piano's out of tune.

MARGUERITE: Don't answer him.

GASTON: This story bores me.

SAINT-GAUDENS: Gaston is right.

GASTON: And anyway, what's this story going to prove? I know it and it's as old as Pru-

---

4 This is a song that originally was a satire on the Duke of Marlborough (1650-1752), who soundly defeated the French in the War of the Spanish Succession, but now is more of a nursery song. The modern equivalent would be playing something like "Chopsticks."

dence. The point is that Saint-Gaudens followed on foot a yellow hackney coach that he saw dropping Agénor at Amanda's door; it proves that Amanda was deceiving Saint-Gaudens. What else is new? Who has not been deceived? One knows that one is always deceived by one's friends and one's mistresses. And so it ends — to the tune of "The Carillon of Dunkirk."

(*He plays the tune on the piano.*)[5]

SAINT-GAUDENS: And I knew very well that Amanda was deceiving me with Agénor just as I know that Olympe is cheating on me with Edmond.

MARGUERITE: Bravo, Saint-Gaudens! You are a hero! We are all crazy about Saint-Gaudens! Those who are crazy about Saint-Gaudens, raise your hands. (*Everyone raises his hand.*) What unanimity! Hurrah for Saint-Gaudens! Gaston, play us something for Saint-Gaudens to dance to.

GASTON: I don't know anything but a polka.

MARGUERITE: Well, let's have a polka! Come on, Saint-Gaudens and Armand, move the table.

PRUDENCE: I'm not finished.

OLYMPE: Gentlemen, Marguerite said Armand only.

GASTON (*playing*): Hurry up — here's the part where I get confused.

OLYMPE: Do I have to dance with Saint-Gaudens?

MARGUERITE: No, I'll dance with him. Come on, my little Saint-Gaudens, come on!

OLYMPE: Let's go, Armand, let's go!

(MARGUERITE *polkas for a moment and stops suddenly.*)

SAINT-GAUDENS: What's the matter?

MARGUERITE: Nothing. I choked a little.

ARMAND (*approaching her*): Are you in pain, madame?

MARGUERITE: Oh, it's nothing. Continue.

(GASTON *plays with all his might*, MARGUERITE *tries again and once more stops.*)

ARMAND: Stop, Gaston.

PRUDENCE: Marguerite is ill.

MARGUERITE (*choking*): Give me a glass of water.

PRUDENCE: What's wrong?

MARGUERITE: Always the same thing. But it's nothing, really. Go into the other room and light up a cigar; I'll be with you in a moment.

PRUDENCE: Let's go in; she prefers to be alone when she's like this.

MARGUERITE: Go ahead, I'll join you.

PRUDENCE: Come on. (*Aside*) You never can enjoy yourself for a minute here.

ARMAND: Poor girl! (*Exit with the others.*)

SCENE NINE   Marguerite alone, trying to catch her breath.

MARGUERITE: Ah! . . . (*She looks at herself in the mirror.*) How pale I am! . . . Ah! . . . (*She puts her head in her hands and rests her elbows on the mantlepiece.*)

SCENE TEN   Marguerite, Armand.

ARMAND (*returning*): Well, how are you, madame?

MARGUERITE: It's you, Monsieur Armand! Thank you, I'm feeling better. . . . Besides, I'm used to. . . .

ARMAND: You're killing yourself! I wish I were your friend, your brother, to prevent you from doing yourself harm like this.

MARGUERITE: You wouldn't succeed. Let's go. What's the matter with you?

ARMAND: What I see. . . .

---

5 *Le Carillon de Dunkerque* is a folk tune which imitates the bells of that city. Here it furnishes a mocking accompaniment, like the American "Shave and a haircut—two bits!"

MARGUERITE: Oh, you are sweet! Look at the others, not bothering about me.

ARMAND: The others don't love you the way I love you.

MARGUERITE: That's so; I'd forgotten that great love of yours.

ARMAND: You're making fun of it.

MARGUERITE: Heaven forbid. Every day I hear the same thing; I'm not making fun of it any more.

ARMAND: Very well. But this love merits a promise from you.

MARGUERITE: What, exactly?

ARMAND: That you'll take care of yourself.

MARGUERITE: Me take care of myself? Is it possible?

ARMAND: Why not?

MARGUERITE: Because if I took care of myself, I would die, my dear. Don't you see that it's only the hectic life that I lead that keeps me alive? And then, taking care of oneself is easy for women who have a family and friends; but when we can no longer serve the pleasure or the vanity of anyone, we are abandoned, and the long nights follow the long days; I know all about it; I was sick in bed two months; after three weeks not a soul came to see me.

ARMAND: It's true that I'm nothing to you, but, if you would let me, Marguerite, I'd take care of you like a brother, I would never leave your side and I would cure you. Then, when you had got your strength back, you could return to this life you lead, if it seemed good to you; but I'm sure you'd then prefer a quieter existence.

MARGUERITE: That's sad wine you offer.

ARMAND: Have you no heart, Marguerite?

MARGUERITE: Heart! That's the only thing that shipwrecks you in a journey such as I am making. (*A pause.*) Are you really serious?

ARMAND: Perfectly serious.

MARGUERITE: Prudence wasn't deceiving me when she said that you'd be sentimental. So you'd take care of me?

ARMAND: Yes!

MARGUERITE: You'd stay with me every day all day long?

ARMAND: As long as I didn't weary you.

MARGUERITE: And what do you call that?

ARMAND: Devotion.

MARGUERITE: And what is the source of this devotion?

ARMAND: An irresistible sympathy I have for you.

MARGUERITE: Since when?

ARMAND: For two years now; since the day I saw you for the very first time, beautiful, proud, smiling. Since that very day I have watched you from a distance, silently.

MARGUERITE: How is it that you didn't tell me that until today?

ARMAND: I didn't know you, Marguerite.

MARGUERITE: You should have got to know me. Why when I was sick and you so faithfully came every day for news of me, why didn't you come up?

ARMAND: What right would I have had to come up to your place?

MARGUERITE: Is one usually so thoughtful with a woman like me?

ARMAND: One is always considerate with a woman. . . . And then. . . .

MARGUERITE: And then . . . ?

ARMAND: I was afraid of the influence that you might have over my life.

MARGUERITE: Is *this* your way of making love to me!

ARMAND (*looking at her and seeing that she is laughing*): If I must tell it to you, today is not the day.

MARGUERITE: Don't ever tell it to me.

ARMAND: Why?

MARGUERITE: Because nothing could come of that avowal but that I wouldn't believe it and you would resent me or else I would believe it and you would have a tragic life with a woman who is nervous and sick and depressed or gay with a forced gaiety sadder than sorrow. A woman who runs through a hundred thousand francs a year may suit a rich old man like the duke, but it's boring for a young man like you. There, we've been babbling such nonsense! Give me your hand and let's go into the dining room; the others must not know what your absence means.

ARMAND: You go if you think you should, but let me stay here.

MARGUERITE: Why?

ARMAND: Because your gaiety has made me sad.

MARGUERITE: Shall I give you some good advice?

ARMAND: Go ahead.

MARGUERITE: Go away and save yourself, if what you tell me is true, or love me as a friend, but nothing more. Come and see me and we'll laugh and chat, but don't have any illusions about me because I'm not worth much. You have a good heart. You need love, but you are too young and too sensitive to live in our world. Fall in love with another woman, get married. You'll see that I'm being kind and speaking frankly to you.

SCENE ELEVEN   The same, Prudence.

PRUDENCE (*opening the door*): Ah, ha! What the devil are you doing in here?

MARGUERITE: Talking reason. Leave us alone a moment. We'll be right with you.

PRUDENCE: Well, well — chatter on, children.

SCENE TWELVE   Marguerite, Armand.

MARGUERITE: It's settled then, you won't be in love with me anymore?

ARMAND: I'll take your advice and go away.

MARGUERITE: That's the way it is?

ARMAND: Yes.

MARGUERITE: How many others have said the same thing to me and wouldn't go.

ARMAND: You held on to them.

MARGUERITE: Certainly not.

ARMAND: Haven't you ever loved anyone?

MARGUERITE: Never, thank God!

ARMAND: Wonderful — thank you!

MARGUERITE: For what?

ARMAND: For what you've just said. You couldn't have made me happier.

MARGUERITE: You're a strange boy!

ARMAND: If I were to tell you that I have spent whole nights beneath your windows, that for six months I've treasured a button you lost from a glove. . . .

MARGUERITE: I wouldn't believe you.

ARMAND: You're right, I'm a fool. Laugh at me, it's the best thing to do. . . . Goodbye.

MARGUERITE: Armand!

ARMAND: Yes? You're calling me back?

MARGUERITE: I don't want to see you go away angry.

ARMAND: I couldn't be angry with you.

MARGUERITE: Tell me, in all that you've said, is there any truth at all?

ARMAND: You ask me that?

MARGUERITE: Well, here's my hand. Come to see me sometimes, often; we'll talk about it some more.

ARMAND: That's too much — and not enough.

MARGEURITE: Well then suit yourself, ask what you like, because it seems that I do owe you something.

ARMAND: Don't talk like that. I can't bear to have you laugh at serious things any more.

MARGUERITE: I'm not laughing any more.

ARMAND: Tell me.

MARGUERITE: What?

ARMAND: Would you like to be loved?

MARGUERITE: It depends. By whom?

ARMAND: By me.

MARGUERITE: What then?

ARMAND: To be loved deeply, eternally.

MARGUERITE: Eternally? . . .

ARMAND: Yes.

MARGUERITE: And if I suddenly were to believe you, what would you say?

ARMAND (*passionately*): I would say. . . .

MARGUERITE: You'd say what everyone says of me. What does it matter? If I am to live a shorter time than others I have to live more quickly. But never mind, however brief my life is to be it will outlast your "eternal" love.

ARMAND: Marguerite! . . .

MARGUERITE: Meanwhile you are deeply touched, sincere, convinced of what you're saying; all that deserves something. . . . Take this flower. (*She gives him a camellia.*)

ARMAND: What shall I do with this?

MARGUERITE: Bring it back to me.

ARMAND: When?

MARGUERITE: When it fades.

ARMAND: How long will that take?

MARGUERITE: The time it takes for any flower to fade, an evening or a morning.

ARMAND: Oh, Marguerite, I'm so happy!

MARGUERITE: Well, tell me again that you love me.

ARMAND: Oh, I love you!

MARGUERITE: Now, go.

ARMAND (*lingering at the closed door*): I'm going.

(*He retraces his steps, kisses her hand, then exits. Laughter and singing are heard from the next room [as he opens and closes the door behind him].*)

SCENE THIRTEEN   Marguerite, then Gaston, Saint-Gaudens, Olympe, Prudence.

MARGUERITE (*alone, looking at the closed door*): Why not? What for? My life gets used up trying to answer those questions.

GASTON (*opening the door*): Chorus of villagers! (*Sings*)

It's a happy time now!
Let's, this joyful day,
Sing the praise of Hymen
And of marriage gay. . . .

SAINT-GAUDENS: Long live Monsieur and Madame Duval!

OLYMPE: Let's have the marriage celebration!

MARGUERITE: May I have the pleasure of this dance?

SAINT-GAUDENS: The pleasure is all mine!

(PRUDENCE *puts on a man's hat,* GASTON *a woman's hat, etc., etc. [Someone plays the piano.] They dance.*)

CURTAIN

ACT TWO

Marguerite's dressing room. Paris.

SCENE ONE   Marguerite, Prudence, Nanine.

MARGUERITE (*seated at a dressing table, to* PRUDENCE, *who enters*): Good evening, my dear. Have you seen the duke?

PRUDENCE: Yes.

MARGUERITE: Did he give you anything?

PRUDENCE (*giving banknotes to* MARGUERITE): Here you are. Could you lend me three or four hundred francs?

MARGUERITE: Take it. . . . Did you tell the duke that I intend to go away to the country?

PRUDENCE: Yes.

MARGUERITE: What did he say?

PRUDENCE: That it's a good idea and can only do you good. Are you going?

MARGUERITE: I hope so. I took another look at the house today.

PRUDENCE: What's the rent?

MARGUERITE: Four thousand francs.

PRUDENCE: Oh, my! That's what I call love, my dear!

MARGUERITE: I'm afraid of it. It may be a passion and it may only be a caprice, but whatever it is it's something.

PRUDENCE: Was *he* here yesterday?

MARGUERITE: Need you ask?

PRUDENCE: And he'll be back this evening.

MARGUERITE: Certainly.

PRUDENCE: I know. He stayed three or four hours.

MARGUERITE: He spoke to you about me?

PRUDENCE: What would we speak about?

MARGUERITE: What did he say to you?

PRUDENCE: My goodness — that he loves you!

MARGUERITE: You've known that for a long time.

PRUDENCE: Yes.

MARGUERITE: Has he ever seemed to be in love before?

PRUDENCE: Never.

MARGUERITE: Your word!

PRUDENCE: Seriously.

MARGUERITE: If you only knew what a tender heart he has, how he speaks of his mother and his sister!

PRUDENCE: It's too bad that men like that don't have a hundred thousand a year.

MARGUERITE: On the contrary, it's lucky they

don't! At least they are sure that they are loved for themselves. (*Taking* PRUDENCE's *hand and placing it on her breast*) Look!

PRUDENCE: What?

MARGUERITE: My heart's beating, don't you feel it?

PRUDENCE: Why is your heart beating?

MARGUERITE: Because it's ten o'clock and *he* is coming.

PRUDENCE: All that much? I'd better be off. Imagine! Suppose it's catching!

MARGUERITE (*to* NANINE *who comes in and straightens up the room*): Go open the door, Nanine.

NANINE: Nobody rang.

MARGUERITE: I tell you he did.

(*Exit* NANINE.)

SCENE TWO   Prudence, Marguerite.

PRUDENCE: My dear, I'm going to pray for you.

MARGUERITE: Why?

PRUDENCE: Because you are in danger.

MARGUERITE: Perhaps I am.

SCENE THREE   The same, Armand.

ARMAND: Marguerite! (*He runs to* MARGUERITE.)

PRUDENCE: Aren't you even going to say hello to me, ingrate?

ARMAND: I'm sorry, my dear Prudence. How are you?

PRUDENCE: About time! . . . Children, I'm going to leave you. I happen to have someone waiting for me at home. — Goodbye. (*Exit.*)

SCENE FOUR   Armand, Marguerite.

MARGUERITE: Well, come right over here, monsieur.

ARMAND (*kneeling at her feet*): And then?

MARGUERITE: Do you love me as much as ever?

ARMAND: No.

MARGUERITE: What?

ARMAND: I love you a thousand times more than before, madame.

MARGUERITE: What have you been doing to-day? . . .

ARMAND: I went to see Prudence, Gustave and Nichette, I've been everywhere where they would listen to me talk about you.

MARGUERITE: And this evening?

ARMAND: I had a letter from my father who is waiting for me at Tours and I answered that I couldn't get there. Should I get ready to go to Tours?

MARGUERITE: Still I don't want you to quarrel with your father.

ARMAND: No danger of that. And you, what have you been up to? Tell me.

MARGUERITE: I've been thinking of you.

ARMAND: Really and truly?

MARGUERITE: Yes. I have made some lovely plans.

ARMAND: Really?

MARGUERITE: Yes.

ARMAND: Tell me about them.

MARGUERITE: Later on.

ARMAND: Why not right now?

MARGUERITE: Perhaps you don't love me enough yet; when they are completed it will be time enough to tell you; just be sure now that it's you that I'm occupied with.

ARMAND: Me?

MARGUERITE: Yes, you, whom I love too much.

ARMAND: Come on, what is it?

MARGUERITE: Now why?

ARMAND: I beg you.

MARGUERITE (*after a little hesitation*): How can I hide anything from you?

ARMAND: I'm listening.

MARGUERITE: I've been able to manage something for us.

ARMAND: What is it?

MARGUERITE: I can only tell you what the results are going to be.

ARMAND: And what results will there be?

MARGUERITE: Would it make you happy to spend the summer in the country with me?

ARMAND: How can you ask?

MARGUERITE: Well, if my scheme works, (and it will), in a couple of weeks I'll be free of this place, nothing to keep me here, and the two of us can go and spend the summer in the country.

ARMAND: And you can't tell me how you are going to manage it?

MARGUERITE: No.

ARMAND: Marguerite, this scheme is all your own idea?

MARGUERITE: Why do you ask?

ARMAND: Answer me.

MARGUERITE: Of course, yes, just mine.

ARMAND: And you alone are going to carry it out?

MARGUERITE (*hesitating again*): By myself.

ARMAND (*getting up*): Have you ever read *Manon Lescaut*, Marguerite?[1]

---

1 The popular novelist Antoine François Prévost (d'Exiles) (1697-1763) concluded his seven-volume novel *Mémoires et aventures d'un homme de qualité qui s'est retiré du monde* (1728-1731) with a brief *Histoire du Chevalier des Grieux et de Manon Lescaut* in which the moralizing of his training as a Benedictine monk and the experiences of his later career as a libertine were neatly blended in what might possibly be described as sentimentalized pornography, the story of a gentleman of good family ruined by an affair with a courtesan. Two operas have been made of this melodramatic material: *Manon*, by Jules Massenet (1842-1912), and *Manon Lescaut* by Giacomo Puccini (1858-1924). Neither

MARGUERITE: Yes, the book is in the *salon*.

ARMAND: What do you think of Des Grieux?

MARGUERITE: Why do you ask?

ARMAND: There's a moment when Manon, who has also worked out a scheme, which is to contrive to get money from Monsieur de B...... and to spend it with Des Grieux. ... Marguerite, I know you have more heart than she, and I have more integrity than he!

MARGUERITE: Meaning what?

ARMAND: Meaning that if your scheme is anything like that I won't go along with it.

MARGUERITE: Very well, my friend, we'll say no more about it. . . . (*A pause.*) Lovely day today, isn't it?

ARMAND: Yes, beautiful.

MARGUERITE: Were there many people on the Champs Elysées?

ARMAND: A lot.

MARGUERITE: It will be like this until the new moon?

ARMAND (*in an outburst*): Oh, what do I care about the moon!

MARGUERITE: Well, what do you want to talk about? When I tell you that I love you, when I prove it, you start pouting; so I talk about the moon.

ARMAND: What do you want of me, Marguerite? I'm jealous of every little thought of yours. What you suggested to me just now. . . .

MARGUERITE: Oh, we're going back to that?

ARMAND: My God, yes, we're going back to that. . . . Well, what you proposed would make me jump with joy, but the mystery that precedes the execution of this plan. . . .

MARGUERITE: Look, let's talk about it for a minute. You love me and you'd like to spend some time with me in some corner out of this frightful Paris.

ARMAND: Yes, I'd like that.

MARGUERITE: So would I. I love you and want the same thing; but, in order to do that, I must have something that I haven't got now. You are not jealous of the duke, you know what pure feelings he has for me. Then let me do it.

ARMAND: And yet. . . .

MARGUERITE: I love you. Now, is it settled?

ARMAND: But. . . .

MARGUERITE (*cajoling*): Is it settled? . . .

ARMAND: Not yet.

MARGUERITE: Then you'll come back to see me tomorrow and we'll talk about it.

ARMAND: Come back tomorrow? Are you sending me away already?

MARGUERITE: I'm not sending you away. You can stay a little longer.

ARMAND: "A little longer"? Are you expecting someone else?

MARGUERITE: Are you starting again?

ARMAND: Marguerite — you are deceiving me!

MARGUERITE: Just how long is it I've known you?

ARMAND: Four days.

MARGUERITE: What forced me to see you?

ARMAND: Nothing.

MARGUERITE: If I didn't love you wouldn't I have the right to show you the door, as I've done with Varville and so many others?

existed, of course, at the time this play was set or written. It is interesting to trace the resemblances, however, between the Abbé Prévost's original story and the works of Dumas *fils*, Massenet, and Puccini, while, of course, Giuseppe Verdi (1813–1901) produced one of the most popular operas of all, *La Traviata*, based on *La Dame aux camélias* itself. Verdi's libretto ought to be compared with *Camille*. It was a failure at the first performance (La Fenice, Venice, 6 March, 1853) but only because the audience jeered a fat soprano dying of consumption. Revived about a year later—and set in 1700 instead of 1850—it began its triumphant career.

ARMAND: Certainly.

MARGUERITE: Well then, my friend, go right on loving, I won't begrudge you.

ARMAND: Forgive me, I'm very sorry.

MARGUERITE: If this goes on, I'm going to spend the rest of my life forgiving you.

ARMAND: No, this is the very last time. See, I'm going now.

MARGUERITE: Good. Come back tomorrow, at noon; we'll have lunch together.

ARMAND: Till tomorrow, then.

MARGUERITE: Till tomorrow.

ARMAND: At noon?

MARGUERITE: At noon.

ARMAND: You swear to me. . . .

MARGUERITE: What?

ARMAND: That you're not expecting someone else.

MARGUERITE: Again! I swear to you that I love you and that you're the only one in the whole wide world I love!

ARMAND: Goodnight!

MARGUERITE: Goodnight, you big baby!

(ARMAND *hesitates for a moment and then exits*.)

SCENE FIVE   Marguerite alone, in the same place.

MARGUERITE: A week ago if anyone had told me that this man, of whose existence I didn't have an inkling, would involve my whole heart and mind like this, so quickly . . . and does he love me? Do I know if I love him, I who have never loved anyone. . . . But why reject happiness? Why not follow the dictates of our hearts? What am I? A creature of fate! Alright then, let fate do with me as it will. It's all the same, it seems to me that I am happier than I have ever been before. Perhaps that's a bad sign. We women are always sensing we shall be loved, never that we shall love, so much so that the first time something like this happens to us we don't know where we are any more.

SCENE SIX   Marguerite, Nanine, the Comte de Giray.

NANINE (*announcing the count, who follows her in*): Monsieur le comte!

MARGUERITE (*without disturbing herself*): Good evening, count. . . .

THE COUNT (*going to kiss her hand*): Good evening, dear friend. How are you this evening.

MARGUERITE: Fine, thank you.

THE COUNT (*going to sit by the fireplace*): It's as cold as hell outside. You wrote me to come at half-past ten. You see I'm right on time.

MARGUERITE: Thank you. We have something to talk over, my dear count.

THE COUNT: Have you had supper? . . .

MARGUERITE: Why?

THE COUNT: Because we could have gone somewhere to eat and chatted over supper.

MARGUERITE: Are you hungry?

THE COUNT: One is always hungry for a little supper. I dined badly at my club!

MARGUERITE: What were they up to?

THE COUNT: Gambling, when I left.

MARGUERITE: Was Saint-Gaudens losing?

THE COUNT: He had lost twenty-five *louis* and was howling as if it were a thousand *écus*.[1]

MARGUERITE: He was here for supper the other evening with Olympe.

THE COUNT: And who else?

MARGUERITE: Gaston Rieux. Do you know him?

---

1 The *écu* ("shield") was a silver coin worth five francs and the *louis* (named for the king in whose reign it was adopted) was a gold coin worth twenty francs.

THE COUNT: Yes.

MARGUERITE: Monsieur Armand Duval. . . .

THE COUNT: Who is this Monsieur Armand Duval?

MARGUERITE: A friend of Gaston. Prudence and I, that was the group . . . We had a lot of fun.

THE COUNT: Had I known, I would have come. By the way, did someone leave here, just a moment ago, as I came in?

MARGUERITE: No, no one.

THE COUNT: Because just at the moment that I was getting out of my carriage someone ran up to see who I was and, when he saw me, ran away.

MARGUERITE (*aside*): Could it have been Armand? (*She rings [the bell for the maid].*)

THE COUNT: Do you need anything?

MARGUERITE: Yes, I have to say a word to Nanine (*to* NANINE, *sotto voce*) Go down to the street and without attracting any attention see if Monsieur Armand Duval is there, and come back and tell me.

NANINE: Yes, madame. (*Exit.*)

THE COUNT: There's some news.

MARGUERITE: What?

THE COUNT: Gagouki is getting married.

MARGUERITE: Our Polish prince?

THE COUNT: The same.

MARGUERITE: Who is he going to marry?

THE COUNT: Guess.

MARGUERITE: How should I know?

THE COUNT: He's going to marry little Adèle.

MARGUERITE: She's making a big mistake!

THE COUNT: On the contrary — he is.

MARGUERITE: My dear, when a man of the world marries a girl like Adèle, he's not the one who's being foolish but she who's getting into a bad business. Your Pole is ruined,

he had a detestable reputation, and if he marries Adèle it's for the twelve or fifteen thousand a year income that you all have given her.

NANINE (*re-entering, softly to* MARGUERITE): No, madame, there's no one there.

MARGUERITE: Now let's talk of serious things, my dear count . . .

THE COUNT: Serious things! I prefer to talk of pleasant things.

MARGUERITE: We'll soon see whether you take the matter pleasantly.

THE COUNT: I'm listening.

MARGUERITE: Have you any ready cash?

THE COUNT: I? Never.

MARGUERITE: Then you must borrow it for me.

THE COUNT: Do you really need it badly?

MARGUERITE: Alas, I need fifteen thousand francs!

THE COUNT: The devil! That's a pretty little sum. And why precisely fifteen thousand francs?

MARGUERITE: Because I owe it.

THE COUNT: You don't mean to say you pay your creditors?

MARGUERITE: They insist.

THE COUNT: You absolutely need it? . . .

MARGUERITE: Yes.

THE COUNT: Well . . . that's it. I'll sign for it.

SCENE SEVEN   The same, Nanine.

NANINE (*entering*): Madame this letter has come for your immediate reply.

MARGUERITE: Who could be writing me at this hour? (*Opening the letter*) Armand! What does this mean? (*Reading*) "I do not choose to play a ridiculous role, especially in front of the woman I love. The very moment that I left your house Monsieur le comte de Giray walked in. I lack both the age and the character of Saint-Gaudens; forgive the sole fault that I may have, that is not to be a millionaire, and let us both forget that we ever knew each other and that for a moment believed we were in love. By the time you receive this letter, I shall already have left Paris. ARMAND."

NANINE: Madame wishes to send a reply?

MARGUERITE: No, say it's alright.

(*Exit* NANINE.)

SCENE EIGHT   The Count, Marguerite.

MARGUERITE (*to herself*): Well, there's a dream shattered. It's too bad.

THE COUNT: What was that letter?

MARGUERITE: What was it, my friend? Good news for you.

THE COUNT: How's that?

MARGUERITE: Because of that letter you have saved fifteen thousand francs.

THE COUNT: It's the first one that ever brought me as much.

MARGUETITE: I no longer need what I asked you for.

THE COUNT: Your creditors have returned your notes, cancelled? That was sweet of them!

MARGUERITE: No, my dear, I was in love.

THE COUNT: You?

MARGUERITE: I.

THE COUNT: For God's sake, with whom?

MARGUERITE: With a man who didn't love me, as it sometimes happens; with a man without any fortune, as it always happens.

THE COUNT: Oh yes, it's with love affairs like that you think you can make up for the others.

MARGUERITE: And here is what he wrote me.

(*She gives the letter to* THE COUNT.)

THE COUNT (*reading*): "My dear Marguerite . . ." Well, well, it's from Monsieur Duval. He's very jealous, that one. Ah, now I understand the usefulness of letters of exchange. That was a neat little trick of yours! (*He gives back the letter.*)

MARGUERITE (*ringing [the bell] and throwing the letter on the table*): You did invite me to supper.

THE COUNT: And I repeat the invitation. You are never going to eat fifteen thousand francs worth, so I'll still be saving money.

MARGUERITE: Well, let's go to supper; I need a little air.

THE COUNT: It seems to have been serious; you're very agitated, my dear.

MARGUERITE: Don't worry about it. (*to* NANINE, *who comes in*) Get me a shawl and a hat.

NANINE: Which one, madame?

MARGUERITE: Any hat you like and a light shawl. (*to* THE COUNT) You'll have to take us as we are, my poor friend.

THE COUNT: Oh, I'm used to all that.

NANINE (*giving her the shawl*): Madame will be cold!

MARGUERITE: No.

NANINE: Shall I wait up for madame? . . .

MARGUERITE: No, go to bed; perhaps I shall not be back until late . . . Are you coming, count? (*Exeunt.*)

SCENE NINE   Nanine, alone.

NANINE: Something's going on; madame is very disturbed; it's that letter that just arrived that's bothering her, of course. (*Taking the letter*) Here's the letter. (*She reads it.*) The devil! Monsieur Armand doesn't dilly-dally with things. Chosen two days ago, dismissed today, he survives (as the poem says) only as long as roses and politicians.[1] Well! (*Enter* PRUDENCE.) Madame Duvernoy.

---

1 The French is "*il a vécu ce que vivent les roses et les hommes d'Etat,*" but it was thought that English readers and audiences might require an adaptation of this quotation from *Consolation à M. du Périer* by François de Malherbe (1555-1628).

SCENE TEN *Nanine, Prudence, later a Servant.*

PRUDENCE: Has Marguerite gone out?

NANINE: Just this moment.

PRUDENCE: Where?

NANINE: To supper.

PRUDENCE: With Monsieur de Giray?

NANINE: Yes.

PRUDENCE: She received a letter just now. . . .

NANINE: From Monsieur Armand.

PRUDENCE: What was in it?

NANINE: Nothing.

PRUDENCE: When will she be back?

NANINE: Late, undoubtedly. I thought that you had gone to bed long ago.

PRUDENCE: I had. I was fast asleep when I was awakened by somebody repeatedly ringing the bell. I got up and answered it. . . .

(Someone knocks at the door.)

NANINE: Come in!

A SERVANT: Madame wants her cloak; she's cold.

PRUDENCE: Is madame downstairs?

A SERVANT: Yes, madame is in the carriage.

PRUDENCE: Ask her to step upstairs, please; tell her that it is I who asked for her.

A SERVANT: But madame is not alone in the carriage.

PRUDENCE: No matter, go ahead!

(Exit the SERVANT.*)*

ARMAND *(outside)*: Prudence!

PRUDENCE *(opening the window)*: Well, let's go, there's the other one who's impatient! Oh these jealous lovers, they're all the same!

ARMAND *(outside)*: Well?

PRUDENCE: Just wait a minute, for Heaven's sake! I'll call you in a moment!

SCENE ELEVEN The same, *Marguerite, later Nanine.*

MARGUERITE: What do you want, Prudence dear?

PRUDENCE: Armand is at my house.

MARGUERITE: So what?

PRUDENCE: He wants to speak with you.

MARGUERITE: And I don't want to see him; and also, I couldn't, somebody's waiting for me downstairs. Tell him that.

PRUDENCE: I'll do nothing of the kind. He would only go and pick a fight with the count.

MARGUERITE: Well, what does he want?

PRUDENCE: How do I know? Does he know himself? But we know all too well what a man is like when he's in love.

NANINE *(the cloak in her hand)*: Does Madame want her cloak?

MARGUERITE: No, not any more.

PRUDENCE: Well, what have you decided?

MARGUERITE: That boy will make me unhappy.

PRUDENCE: Then don't see him any more, my dear. — It would be best to leave things just as they are.

MARGUERITE: Is that your advice?

PRUDENCE: Certainly.

MARGUERITE *(after a pause)*: What else did he say to you?

PRUDENCE: I see that you want him to come. I'll go get him. What about the count?

MARGUERITE: The count! He'll wait.

PRUDENCE: It might be better to send him on his way right now.

MARGUERITE: You're right. Nanine, go down and tell Monsieur de Giray that I definitely feel ill and will not be able to go to supper; apologize for me.

NANINE: Yes, madame.

PRUDENCE (*at the window*): Armand. Come on! Oh! He didn't need to be told twice!

MARGUERITE: You stay here when he comes.

PRUDENCE: Not me. The moment will come when you'll tell me to go anyway, so I might as well go right now.

NANINE (*returning*): *Monsieur le comte* has gone, madame.

MARGUERITE: Did he say anything?

NANINE: No. (*Exit.*)

SCENE TWELVE   Marguerite, Armand, Prudence.

ARMAND (*coming in*): Marguerite! At last!

PRUDENCE: Children, this is where I leave. (*Exit.*)

SCENE THIRTEEN   Marguerite, Armand.

ARMAND (*throwing himself on his knees at the feet of* MARGUERITE): Marguerite!

MARGUERITE: What do you want?

ARMAND: I want you to forgive me.

MARGUERITE: You don't deserve it! (ARMAND *reacts.*) I can see perfectly well that you could be jealous and write me an angry letter, but not an ironic and impudent one. You've caused me a lot of pain and done me a great disservice.

ARMAND: And you, Marguerite, haven't you done anything to me?

MARGUERITE: If I've done anything to you it wasn't deliberately.

ARMAND: When I saw the count arrive and realized that it was for him that you had sent me away, I went mad, I lost my head, I wrote you a letter. But when, instead of answering my letter as I had hoped, when instead of apologizing you said to Nanine that it was alright, I asked myself what would become of me if I never saw you again. The abyss instantly opened before me. Don't forget, Marguerite, that though I have only known you for a few days I have been in love with you for two years!

MARGUERITE: Well, my friend, you arrived at a wise decision.

ARMAND: What's that?

MARGUERITE: To go away. Isn't that what you wrote me?

ARMAND: How could I?

MARGUERITE: You must.

ARMAND: Must?

MARGUERITE: Yes, for my sake as well as your own. My position prevents me from seeing any more of you and everything stands in the way of my love.

ARMAND: But you still love me a little, Marguerite?

MARGUERITE: I did love you.

ARMAND: And now?

MARGUERITE: Now I have thought it over, and what I was hoping for is impossible.

ARMAND: If you had really loved me you wouldn't have seen the count, especially tonight.

MARGUERITE: That's precisely why we'll be better off apart. I am young, I am pretty, I pleased you, I'm a nice girl and you are a boy with spirit, you had to take the best of me, leave what's bad, and not worry about the rest.

ARMAND: That's not how you spoke to me a while ago, Marguerite, when you talked of the months that I was going to spend with you alone, far from Paris, far from everyone; that hope has been crushed for me by a cruel reality.

MARGUERITE (*sadly*): It's true. I told myself, "A little rest would do me good; he cares about my health; if there were a way to spend the summer peacefully with him somewhere in the country, deep in the country, there always would be that against the bad days." At the end of three or four months we would have returned to Paris, shaken hands, and made a friendship out of the remains of our love; that would have been more than enough, but the love you have for me is so strong that you couldn't in the end bring yourself to make a friendship out of it. You wouldn't want that; your heart is a great lord that will not bow to anything! Let's say no more about it. You've been coming here for four days, you've had supper here — send me a jewel with your card and we shall be even.

ARMAND: Marguerite, you're crazy; I love you! That doesn't mean you're just pretty and would amuse me for three or four months. You are all my hope, all my thoughts, all my life; in a word: I love you! What more can I say?

MARGUERITE: Then you're right; it's better that we don't see each other any more.

ARMAND: Of course, because *you* don't love me!

MARGUERITE: Because.... You don't know what you're saying!

ARMAND: Why, then!

MARGUERITE: Why? Do you want to know? Because there have been moments when I have had this dream and followed it through to the end; because there have been days when I have grown tired of the life I lead and envisioned another; because in the midst of our troubled lives our minds, our pride, our senses live but our hearts are stifled, and not finding an outlet for their emotion they suffocate us. We seem happy; people envy us. In fact we have lovers who ruin themselves, not for our sakes, as they claim, but for their own vanity; we are first in their self-love, last in their esteem. We have friends, friends like Prudence, whose friendship does not go so far as being unself-seeking and disinterested. They care little enough what we do so long as they are seen in our boxes at the theatre or riding along in our carriages. So all around us is ruin, shame, and deceit. I used to dream sometimes of being able, without daring to tell anyone of it, to meet a man heroic enough not to call me to account for anything, who would want to be the lover of my dreams. This man I found in the duke; but old age neither protects nor consoles, and my spirit had other needs. Then I met you — you, young, ardent, happy. The tears you shed for me, the interest you took in my health, the mysterious visits you made when I was sick, your openness, your enthusiasm, all led me to see in you what I had been crying for from the depths of my noisy solitude. In a moment, like a fool, I built my whole future on your love, I dreamed of the countryside, of purity; I remembered the innocence of my youth — we all have a childhood, whatever we may become — an impossible wish; a word from you substantiated that. . . . You wanted to know everything. Now you know!

ARMAND: And do you believe that after what you have just told me I could think of leaving you? When happiness comes to us shall we hide to escape from it? No, Marguerite, no; your dream shall come true, I swear to you. Don't let us argue any more: we are young, we love each other, let us follow our love.

MARGUERITE: Don't lie to me, Armand, you know that a violent emotion could kill me; think well who I am — and what I am.

ARMAND: You are an angel, and I love you!

NANINE (*outside, knocking on the door*): Madame! . . .

MARGUERITE: What is it?

NANINE: There's a letter for you!

MARGUERITE (*laughing*): Oh, is this a night for letters? . . . From whom?

NANINE: From *Monsieur le comte*.

MARGUERITE: Does he ask for an answer?

NANINE: Yes, madame.

MARGUERITE (*hanging around* ARMAND'S *neck*): Well, tell him there is none!

CURTAIN

ACT THREE

Auteuil [a suburb of Paris]. The *salon* of a country house. At the back, a fireplace; a door on either side of it. A view of the garden.

SCENE ONE Nanine, carrying out a tea tray after lunch; Prudence, later Armand.

PRUDENCE (*entering*): Where's Marguerite?

NANINE: Madame is in the garden with Mademoiselle Nichette and Monsieur Gustave. They've just had lunch and are spending the day with her.

PRUDENCE: I'll join them.

ARMAND (*entering as* NANINE *exits*): Prudence, I want a word with you. Two weeks ago you left here in Marguerite's carriage.

PRUDENCE: That's true.

ARMAND: Since then we haven't seen the carriage or the horses again. A week ago when you left you appeared to be afraid of being chilly and Marguerite lent you a cashmere that you haven't returned. Finally, yesterday she gave you some bracelets and some diamonds that she said needed to be reset. Where are the horses and the carriage and the cashmere and the diamonds?

PRUDENCE: Shall I be frank?

ARMAND: I wish you would.

PRUDENCE: The horses went back to the seller for a partial refund.

ARMAND: The cashmere?

PRUDENCE: Sold.

ARMAND: The diamonds?

PRUDENCE: Pawned this morning. I brought back the tickets with me.

ARMAND: And why did you never mention any of this to me?

PRUDENCE: Marguerite didn't want me to.

ARMAND: And why are you selling and pawning things?

PRUDENCE: To pay expenses! Ah, my dear, you think all one has to do is to fall in love and go out and live, outside Paris, a pastoral, ethereal existence? Not on your life! Right along with the poetic life is the life of reality. The duke, whom I've just seen, be-cause I wanted if possible to avoid these sacrifices, won't give Marguerite another penny unless she leaves you, and God knows she doesn't want to do that!

ARMAND: Good old Marguerite!

PRUDENCE: Yes, good old Marguerite; too good Marguerite, because who knows how all this will end? Not to mention that to pay what she still owes she wants to give up every-thing she now owns. Right in my pocket here is a plan of sale that her agent has just transmitted to me.

ARMAND: How much is needed?

PRUDENCE: At least fifty thousand francs.

ARMAND: Ask the creditors for a couple of weeks' grace; in two weeks I'll pay off every-thing.

PRUDENCE: You'll borrow money? . . .

ARMAND: Yes.

PRUDENCE: Oh, that'll be fine. You'll just get into an argument with your father and risk your whole future.

ARMAND: I thought something like this would happen. I've already written to my lawyer to say that I'd like to make over to someone a legacy that I have from my mother and I have just had a response: the document is all prepared, there are only a few formalities to comply with, and during the day I must go to Paris to give them my signature. Mean-while, stop Marguerite from. . . .

PRUDENCE: But what about the papers I have?

ARMAND: Once I'm gone you give them back to her as if you hadn't heard anything, be-cause I don't want her to know of our con-versation. Here she is; silence!

SCENE TWO Marguerite, Nichette, Gustave, Armand, Prudence.

MARGUERITE (*enters with a finger to her lips to signify to* PRUDENCE *to be quiet.*)

ARMAND (*to* MARGUERITE): Dear child, scold Prudence.

MARGUERITE: Why?

ARMAND: I asked her yesterday to drop by my place and to bring me any letters there might be because for two weeks now I haven't been in Paris; the first thing she did was to forget all about it, so that now I'm going to have to leave you for an hour or two. I haven't written to my father for a month. Nobody knows where I am, not even my servant, because I wanted to avoid intruders. It's a nice day, you have Nichette and Gustave to keep you company; I'll jump in a carriage, drop by my place, and be right back.

MARGUERITE: Go, my friend, go; but if you haven't written your father it's not my fault. I've asked you to write him often enough. Hurry back. You'll find us chatting and working here, Gustave, Nichette, and I.

ARMAND: I'll be back in an hour. (MARGUERITE *accompanies him to the door.*)

MARGUERITE (*coming back, to* PRUDENCE): Is it all arranged?

PRUDENCE: Yes.

MARGUERITE: You have the papers?

PRUDENCE: Here they are. The agent will be along soon to talk things over with you. I'm going to get some lunch; I'm dying of hunger.

MARGUERITE: Go ahead; Nanine will give you everything you want.

SCENE THREE   The same, without Armand and Prudence.

MARGUERITE (*to* NICHETTE *and* GUSTAVE): You see, this is how we've been living for three months.

NICHETTE: Are you happy?

MARGUERITE: Am I!

NICHETTE: I always told you, Marguerite, that true happiness depends on peace and quiet and in the habits of the heart . . . How many times Gustave and I have said, "When will Marguerite ever fall in love with someone and settle down to a peaceful existence?"

MARGUERITE: Well, your wish has come true: I'm in love and I'm happy; it's the love and the happiness of the two of you that I've envied and emulated.

GUSTAVE: The fact is that we two really are happy, aren't we, Nichette?

NICHETTE: I think so, and it's not dearly bought. You yourself are a great lady and you never come to see us; otherwise you'd be content to live as we do. You think you live very simply here; what would you say if you could see my two little rooms in the rue Blanche, on the fifth floor, where the windows overlook gardens where those who own them never go for a walk! — How can it be that people who have gardens never go walking in them?

GUSTAVE: We're like a German novel or one of Goethe's idylls, with music by Schubert.

NICHETTE: Oh, it's a good thing you're joking because Marguerite's here. When we're alone you never make jokes, and you are as gentle as a lamb, tender as a turtle-dove. You know that he'd like us to move? He finds our existence too simple.

GUSTAVE: No, I just find our apartment too high.

NICHETTE: You never go out so you don't know what floor we're on.

MARGUERITE: You're charming, both of you.

NICHETTE: On the pretext that he has six thousand a year in income from rents, he doesn't want me to work any more. One of these days he'll be wanting to buy me a carriage.

GUSTAVE: Perhaps that will come.

NICHETTE: We can wait. First your uncle has to look at me in a better light and make you his heir and me his niece.

GUSTAVE: He's beginning to change his mind about you.

MARGUERITE: Then he doesn't know you? If he did, he'd be crazy about you.

NICHETTE: No, his uncle has never wanted to see me. He's still of that breed of uncles who believe that smart working girls are made to ruin nephews; he would like him to marry a society lady. Am I not of society?

GUSTAVE: He'll let up; since I became a lawyer he's been more indulgent about the rest.

NICHETTE: Oh, yes, I forgot to tell you: Gustave is a lawyer.

MARGUERITE: I shall give him my next case.

NICHETTE: He's pleaded already! I was in the audience.

MARGUERITE: Did he win?

GUSTAVE: I lost, completely. My client was condemned to ten years hard labor.

NICHETTE: Fortunately.

MARGUERITE: Why fortunately?

NICHETTE: The man he was defending was an absolute scoundrel. What a rascally job being a lawyer is! You see a lawyer become a great man when he can tell himself: "I had in my hands a villain who had murdered his father, his mother and his children; well, I had so much talent that I was able to get him off scot free, and I have restored to society this ornament it needed."

MARGUERITE: And shall we soon be going to a marriage with this lawyer of yours?

GUSTAVE: If I get married.

NICHETTE: What do you mean, if you get married? I certainly hope you are going to get married, and moreover with me! You'll never marry a better woman or one who loves you more.

MARGUERITE: When, then?

NICHETTE: Soon.

MARGUERITE: You're very lucky!

NICHETTE: Aren't you going to finish up like us? . . .

MARGUERITE: Whom should I marry?

NICHETTE: Armand.

MARGUERITE: Armand? He has the right to love

me, but not to marry me; I want very much to have his heart, but I'll never take his name. There are things in a woman's life that cannot be erased, you know, Nichette, and that she must not give her husband the right to reproach her about. If I wanted it Armand would marry me. He would marry me tomorrow. But I love him too much to ask him to make a sacrifice like that! Monsieur Gustave, am I right?

GUSTAVE: You're a good girl, Marguerite.

MARGUERITE: No I'm not, but I think like a gentleman. At least there's that. I'm delighted with a happiness that I would never have expected to enjoy; I thank God and I do not wish to tempt Providence.

NICHETTE: Gustave talks big and he'd marry you if he were in Armand's place; wouldn't you, Gustave?

GUSTAVE: Maybe.

NICHETTE (*to* MARGUERITE): Well, so long as you are happy, what does anything else matter?

MARGUERITE: I am happy. But who would have predicted that I, Marguerite Gauthier, would some day be content with the love of one man, to spend her days by his side, working, reading, listening to him?

NICHETTE: Like us.

MARGUERITE: I can speak frankly to you and you'll both believe me, for you listen with your hearts: there are moments when I completely forget what I used to be and when the Marguerite of the past is so separated from the Marguerite of today that they seem like two different human beings and that the second hardly remembers the first. When, in a white dress and a big straw hat, carrying on my arm a cloak against the chill of the evening, I get into a boat with Armand that will take us out into the current and only stop when we rest by ourselves under the willows of the nearby island, no one could suspect, not even myself, that this white shadow is Marguerite Gauthier. I have thrown away more money on bouquets than it would take to support an ordinary family for a year; now a single flower such as Armand gave me this morning is enough to perfume my entire day. You yourselves know what love is like: how the hours are short when you are alone together and how they run into weeks and months without disturbance or fatigue. Yes, I am very happy, but I want to be happier still; for you don't know everything. . . .

NICHETTE: Tell us.

MARGUERITE: You told me just now that I don't live like you; you won't be able to say that to me much longer.

NICHETTE: How do you mean?

MARGUERITE: Without a word to Armand I'm going to sell everything I own in my apartment in Paris that I never want to go back to. I'm going to pay all my debts, rent a little place near yours, and furnish it very simply, and we'll live together forgetting and forgotten. In the summertime we'll come back to the country, but in a little house more modest than this one. Where are the people who want to know what happiness is? You have taught me and now I could teach them if they liked.

NANINE: Madame, there's a gentleman here who would like to speak with you. . . .

MARGUERITE (to NICHETTE and GUSTAVE): Very likely the agent I've been expecting; go and wait for me in the garden, will you? I'll join you and we'll go to Paris all together, as a group. . . . (to NANINE) Have him come in.

(After a gesture toward NICHETTE and GUSTAVE, who go out, she turns toward the door where the person announced enters.)

SCENE FOUR Monsieur Duval, Marguerite, later Nanine.

M. DUVAL (at the threshold): Mademoiselle Marguerite Gauthier?

MARGUERITE: Yes, monsieur. Whom do I have the honor of addressing?

M. DUVAL: Monsieur Duval.

MARGUERITE: Monsieur Duval!

M. DUVAL: Yes, mademoiselle, Armand's father.

MARGUERITE (disturbed): Armand is not here, monsieur.

M. DUVAL: That I know, mademoiselle . . . and it's with you that I want to have a little talk. Please listen to what I have to say. My son, mademoiselle, has compromised and ruined himself for you.

MARGUERITE: You are mistaken, monsieur. Thank God there's no more gossip about me, and I have accepted nothing from Armand.

M. DUVAL: Which means, for your luxury and expenditures are well-known, that my son is foolish enough to help you spend what you accept from others?

MARGUERITE: Excuse me, monsieur; but I am a lady and I am in my own house, two reasons which should plead in my favor for courtesy from you; the tone in which you address me is hardly the one I would expect from a man of the world whom I have the honor of meeting for the first time, and. . . .

M. DUVAL: And? . . .

MARGUERITE: I beg you to permit me to withdraw, more for your sake than for mine.

M. DUVAL: In truth when one hears this language and sees these manners one finds it painful to say the language is borrowed and the manners put on. They were right when they told me that you would be a dangerous individual.

MARGUERITE: I may be dangerous, monsieur, but to myself, not to others.

M. DUVAL: Dangerous or not, it is nonetheless true, madame, that Armand is ruining himself, for you.

MARGUERITE: I repeat to you, monsieur, with all the respect that I owe Armand's father. I repeat that you are making a mistake.

M. DUVAL: Well then, what is the meaning of this letter from my lawyer that informs me that Armand wants to settle his property on you?

MARGUERITE: I assure you, monsieur, that if Armand has done that he did it without my knowledge, for he knew very well that whatever he offered to me I should have rejected.

M. DUVAL: It seems, however, that that has not always been your method of operation.

MARGUERITE: That, monsieur, is true. But I wasn't in love then.

M. DUVAL: And now?

MARGUERITE: Now I love with all the purity that a woman can find at the botton of her heart when God takes pity on her and shows her the way to repent.

M. DUVAL: Fine phrases, indeed.

MARGUERITE: Listen to me, monsieur. . . . My God, I know that one is not predisposed to believe the oaths of women like me; but by all that I hold dear in the world, by my love for Armand, I swear to you that I knew nothing of that settlement.

M. DUVAL: Nevertheless, mademoiselle, you have to live on something.

MARGUERITE: You compel me to tell you what I would have preferred to keep from you, monsieur; but because I value over everything else the esteem of Armand's father, I shall speak. Ever since I met your son, so that this love of mine which should not resemble for an instant anything which I have ever called love before, I have been pawning and selling cashmeres, diamonds, jewelry, carriages; and a moment ago, when I was told that someone wanted to see me, I fully expected to see the very agent to whom I am going to sell the furniture, the pictures, the tapestries, and all the rest of the luxurious things with which you reproach me. As a matter of fact, if you doubt my word, have a look at this. I was not expecting you, monsieur, and consequently you cannot believe that these papers were prepared especially for you. If you have any doubts, read this document. (*She gives him the act of sale which* PRUDENCE *has brought back to her.*)

M. DUVAL (*he reads it*): A bill of sale of your furniture with an order to the buyer to pay your creditors and to remit the surplus to you. (*He looks at her with astonishment.*) Can I have been mistaken?

MARGUERITE: Yes, monsieur, you have been mistaken, or rather misled. Yes, I have been foolish; yes, I have had a sad past; but to wash that away, since I fell in love, I have given to the last drop of my blood. Oh, whatever they may have told you, I have a heart; I am a good person really: you will see when you know me better. . . . Armand has transformed me! He has loved me. He loves me now. You are his father, you must be as good as he. I beg you, don't speak ill of me to him for he would believe you; he loves you; and I respect and love you too, because you are his father.

M. DUVAL: Forgive me, madame, for my discourtesy just now; I did not know you, I could not foresee what I would discover in you. I arrived angered by the silence and ingratitude of my son and I thought you were responsible for that. Forgive me, madame.

MARGUERITE: I thank you for those kind words, monsieur.

M. DUVAL: Moreover, it is in the name of the noble sentiments you have expressed that I am going to ask you to give Armand the greatest proof of your love that you could give.

MARGUERITE: Oh, monsieur, be silent, I beg you; you are going to ask a terrible thing, all the more terrible, because it is something I have always dreaded. You had to come — I was too happy!

M. DUVAL: I am no longer angry. Two honest hearts are speaking to each other, with the same affection in different ways, and we are both jealous, aren't we, to prove our affection to the one dear to us?

MARGUERITE: Yes, monsieur, yes.

M. DUVAL: Your soul has depths of generosity which most women lack, and I speak to you as a father, Marguerite, as a father who comes to beg for the happiness of his two children.

MARGUERITE: Two children?

M. DUVAL: Yes, Marguerite, two children. I have a daughter, young, beautiful, pure as an angel. She loves a young man and he loves her; she has set her heart on this love; but she has the right to her love. I want her to marry; I had written to Armand, but Armand, all because of you, has not received my letter; I might have died and he would never have known. Well, my daughter Blanche became the dearly-loved *fiancée* of a respectable man; she entered an honorable family which expects mine to be honorable too. Society is exacting, especially provincial society. However pure you may seem in the eyes of Armand, or in my eyes because of the sentiments you express, you are not so in the eyes of the world, which sees nothing but your past and pitilessly closes its doors to you. My prospective son-in-law's family has found out how Armand is living and has declared it will break off the engagement if he goes on in that life. The whole future of a young girl who has never done you any harm may therefore be shattered by you. Marguerite, in the name of your love, grant me the happiness of my daughter.

MARGUERITE: You are so good, monsieur, to deign to speak to me like this, how can I refuse your good words? Yes, I understand; you are right. I shall leave Paris; I shall stay away from Armand for a while. This will bring me misery; but I want to do that for you and give you nothing with which to reproach me. . . . Besides, the joy of our reunion will help us to forget the sadness of our parting. You will permit me to write to him now and then and, later, when his sister is married. . . .

M. DUVAL: Thank you, Marguerite, thank you; but there is something else I want to ask of you.

MARGUERITE: Something else! and what more could you ask of me?

M. DUVAL: Listen carefully to me, my child,

and face up honestly to what must be done; a temporary break will not suffice.

MARGUERITE: You mean you want me to leave Armand for ever?

M. DUVAL: You must!

MARGUERITE: Never! . . . You cannot know how much we love each other! You do not know that I have no friends, no parents, no family; that forgiving me, he swore to be all of that to me and that I placed my life in his. You don't know that in fact I am suffering from a mortal disease and have only a few years left to live. To leave Armand, monsieur, would kill me immediately.

M. DUVAL: Now, now, let's be calm and not exaggerate. . . . You are young and beautiful, and what you think an illness is only the fatigue of a rather hectic life; you certainly are not going to die before the age at which one is content to die. I am asking you to make an enormous sacrifice, I know, but I am forced to do it. Listen to me; you have known Armand for three months, and you love him! Can a love so young be allowed to shatter a whole future? You will wreck the whole future of my son! Are you certain that this love will endure for ever? Are you not mistaken in this already? Suppose that all of a sudden — and too late — you come to see that you do not love my son and you fall in love with another. Forgive me, Marguerite, but your past lends color to these suppositions.

MARGUERITE: Never, monsieur! I never have loved and I never shall love the way I love him.

M. DUVAL: So be it! But if it is not you who will deceive him, perhaps he will deceive you. At his age can the heart swear eternal passion? Doesn't the heart perpetually alter its affections? It is the same heart which, in the son, loves the parents above all others, which, in the husband, loves the wife more than the parents, which later in the father, loves the children more than the parents, and the wife — and the mistresses. Nature is demanding because she is prodigal. There could be deception: there you have the probabilities. Now would you like to hear the realities and the certainties. Are you listening to me?

MARGUERITE: Am I listening? Oh, my God!

M. DUVAL: You are ready to sacrifice everything for my son; but what equal sacrifice, if he accepts yours, could he make in exchange? He will take the best years of your life and, much later, when surfeit comes, as it will, what will happen? Either he will be an ordinary man who will throw your past in your face and walk out on you saying that he isn't doing anything that other men would not do; or he will be an honorable man and marry you or at least keep you close to him. This affair, or this marriage, which cannot be founded on chastity and cannot have the support of religion nor be blessed by a family, may perhaps be excusable in a young man's life, but what will it be for a mature man? What ambition shall he be permitted? What career will be open to him? What consolation shall I draw from my son after twenty years of dedication to his happiness? Your attachment is not the fruit of two pure sympathies, the union of two innocent affections; it's the most earthly and the most human of passions, born of the caprice of one and the fantasies of the other. What will remain when both of you are old? Who is to say that the first wrinkles on your brow will not snatch the veil from his eyes and that his illusion will not vanish with your youth?

MARGUERITE: Oh, reality!

M. DUVAL: Can't you see what your old age will be together, doubly deserted, doubly isolated, doubly useless? What memory will remain? What good will you have accomplished? You and my son have two very different paths to follow, that chance has brought together for a little while but that reason separates for ever. In the life that you have chosen for yourselves you have not looked ahead to the future. You have been happy together for three months, do not blight that happiness which cannot continue, but keep the memory of that always

in your heart, where it will give you strength, which is all you have the right to demand of it. Some day you will be proud of what you shall have done and for the rest of your life you will have your self-respect. I speak to you as a man who knows about life, and I implore you as a father. Come, Marguerite, prove to me that you truly love my son, and have courage!

MARGUERITE (*to herself*): And so the poor woman who has fallen cannot, whatever she may do, ever rise again! Perhaps God will pardon her, but society is relentless. In fact, by what right do you ask a place in the heart of families that virtue alone should occupy? . . . You are in love! What does it matter? And that is a reason! Whatever proofs you give of your love, no one will believe them. That's justice. What good is it to speak of love or of the future? What do these new words mean? Look at the degradation of your past! What man would want to call you his wife? What child would want to call you its mother? (*to* M. DUVAL) You are right, monsieur; everything that you have said to me I have said to myself before in terror; but when I said it to myself I did not come to face it fully. Now that you have repeated it to me, it has become inescapably real; I must obey. You speak to me in the name of your son and in the name of your daughter and it is well for you to invoke both these names. Very well, monsieur, one day you must say to this beautiful and pure young girl, for it is for her sake that I sacrifice my happiness, you would say to her that there once was a woman who had but one hope, one thought, one dream in the world, and that at the invocation of her name this woman renounced all of that, crushed her heart between her hands and died of it, for I shall die of it, monsieur, and then, perhaps, God will pardon me.

M. DUVAL (*moved in spite of himself*): Poor woman!

MARGUERITE: You pity me, monsieur, and I think you're crying; thank you for your tears; they will strengthen me enough to do what you wish. You ask me to leave your son for his peace, for his honor, for the sake of his future; what must I do? Tell me; I am ready.

M. DUVAL: You must tell him that you do not love him any more.

MARGUERITE (*with a sad smile*): He won't believe me.

M. DUVAL: You must go away from him.

MARGUERITE: He'll follow me.

M. DUVAL: In that case. . . .

MARGUERITE: Look, monsieur, do you believe that I love Armand, that my love for him is truly unselfish?

M. DUVAL: Yes, Marguerite.

MARGUERITE: Do you believe that I have invested in this love the joy and the pardon of my life?

M. DUVAL: I do.

MARGUERITE: Then, monsieur, kiss me once as you would kiss your daughter, and I swear to you that that kiss, the only truly pure one that I have ever received, shall make me triumph over my love and that within a week your son will be returned to you, perhaps unhappy for a certain amount of time, but cured forever; I swear also that he will never know what has passed between us.

M. DUVAL (*embracing* MARGUERITE): You are a noble girl, Marguerite, but I really fear. . . .

MARGUERITE: Oh, fear nothing, monsieur; he will hate me. (*She rings* [*the bell*], NANINE *appears*.) Ask Madame Duvernoy to come in here.

NANINE: Yes, madame. (*Exit.*)

MARGUERITE (*to* M. DUVAL): One last favor, monsieur!

M. DUVAL: Ask, madame, ask it.

MARGUERITE: Within a few hours Armand will experience one of the greatest sorrows of his life, perhaps the greatest he will ever know. He will then need a heart who loves him; be there, monsieur, be near him. And now,

let us part; he will be here any moment; all will be lost if he sees you.

M. DUVAL: But what are you going to do?

MARGUERITE: If I told you, monsieur, it would be your duty to prevent it.

M. DUVAL: Then is there nothing I can do to repay you for what I shall owe you?

MARGUERITE: You might, when I am dead and Armand curses my memory, avow that I loved him truly and that I have proved it well. I hear a noise; goodbye, monsieur, undoubtedly we shall never see each other again, be happy!

(*Exit* M. DUVAL.)

SCENE FIVE   Marguerite, alone; later Prudence.

MARGUERITE (*aside*): Oh, God! Give me strength. (*She writes a letter.*)

PRUDENCE (*entering*): You sent for me, Marguerite dear?

MARGUERITE: Yes, I'd like you to do something for me.

PRUDENCE: What?

MARGUERITE: Take this letter.

PRUDENCE: To whom?

MARGUERITE: Look! (PRUDENCE *is astonished to read the address.*) Hush, go at once.

SCENE SIX   Marguerite, later Armand.

MARGUERITE (*alone, continuing to write*): And now a letter to Armand. What shall I say? I'm dreaming or I'm losing my mind — this can't be true. I'll never have the courage. . . . You can't ask a human being to do more than he can!

ARMAND (*who during this time has entered and has come near* MARGUERITE): What are you up to there, Marguerite?

MARGUERITE (*rising and crumpling the letter*): Nothing, my dear!

ARMAND: You're writing to someone?

MARGUERITE: No. . . . yes.

ARMAND: Why are you so agitated, so pale? To whom are you writing, Marguerite? Give me that letter.

MARGUERITE: The letter was for you, Armand; but I beg you, in the name of heaven, not to ask for it.

ARMAND: I thought that we were done with secrets and mystery.

MARGUERITE: But not with suspicions, it seems.

ARMAND: I'm sorry, but I myself am worried.

MARGUERITE: About what?

ARMAND: My father has arrived!

MARGUERITE: You've seen him?

ARMAND: No, but he left a severe letter for me at my place. He has learned of my retreat here, my life with you. He's coming here tonight. There will be a long discussion, for God knows what he has been told or what I shall have to dissuade him from; but he will see you, and when he has seen you he will love you! So what does it matter? I depend on him as it is, but I can work if I have to.

MARGUERITE (*aside*): How he loves me! (*Aloud*) But don't get into an argument with your father, my dear. He's coming, you say? Well, I must get out of the way, for he won't want to see me right away; but I'll be back, and I'll be there, near you. I shall throw myself at his feet and implore him not to force us apart.

ARMAND: How oddly you say that. There's something the matter. It's not the news I've brought that has agitated you like this. You can hardly stand up. There's trouble here. . . . That letter. . . . (*He reaches out his hand.*)

MARGUERITE (*she refuses him the letter*): This letter contains something I can't tell you about; you know, there are some things a person can't say face to face or let someone read in his presence. This letter, my Armand, is proof of the love I have for you, I swear by our love; don't press me any more.

ARMAND: Keep the letter, Marguerite, I know all about it. Prudence told me everything this morning, which is why I went to Paris. I know what sacrifice you want to make for me. While you were busy planning our happiness, I was busy too. Now everything is arranged. And that's the secret you didn't want to tell me, isn't it? How can I ever show enough gratitude for your love, good, dear Marguerite?

MARGUERITE: Well, now that you know everything, let me go.

ARMAND: Go!

MARGUERITE: Only for a little while. Isn't your father due to arrive at any moment? I'll just be out there in the garden a few steps away from you, with Gustave and Nichette. You have only to call for me to return. How could I separate myself from you? You'll calm your father, if he's angry, and afterwards we can go on with our plans, can't we? The two of us will live together and we'll love each other as we always have and we'll be as happy as we have been these last three months! You are happy, aren't you? You have nothing to reproach me with? If so tell me, and I'll make it good. If I have caused you any pain at all, forgive me, it wasn't my fault, for I love you more than all the world. You too, you love me, don't you? And, whatever proof of my love I shall give you, you'll never mistake or condemn me. . . .

ARMAND: Why these tears?

MARGUERITE: I had to cry a little; now, you see, I'm alright. I'm going back to Nichette and Gustave. I'll be there, always yours, always ready to come back to you, always in love with you. See, I'm smiling; we shall meet again soon, for ever. (*She throws him kisses as she exits.*)

SCENE SEVEN   Armand, later Nanine.

ARMAND: Dear Marguerite! How frightened she is at the thought of a separation! (*He rings [the bell].*) How she loves me! (*to* NANINE, *who appears*) If a gentleman comes to speak with me, it's my father, show him right in.

NANINE: Very well, monsieur. (*Exit*.)

ARMAND: I was wrong to be alarmed. My father will understand. The past is dead. Besides, what difference is there between Marguerite and other women? This Olympe whom I've met is always busy with a round of parties and pleasures; women who are not in love have to fill up the emptiness of their hearts with excitement like that. In a few days she's going to give a ball and she's invited me, Marguerite and me, as if Marguerite and I would ever return to that world! Oh, time passes so slowly when she's not here! . . . What's this book? *Manon Lescaut!* A woman who loves cannot do as you did, Manon! . . . How does this book happen to be here? (NANINE *enters with a lamp. Exit. He reads at random.*) "I give you my oath, my dear *chevalier*, that you are the idol of my heart, and that there is no one in the world whom I could love in the way that I love you; but cannot you see, my poor dear soul, that, in the state to which we have been reduced, fidelity is a foolish ideal? Do you believe that one can afford the luxury of tenderness when one lacks bread? It was hunger that caused me my fatal mistake and one day I gave up the last gasp believing that I was heaving a sigh of love. I adore you, note that down, but leave to me for some time the management of our fortune; bad luck to him who falls into my net! I struggle to make my lover rich and happy. My brother will bring you news of your Manon; he will tell you how she has wept at the necessity of leaving you. . . ." (ARMAND *replaces the book and stands a few moments uneasily.*) She was reasonable, but she was not in love, for love knows no reason. . . . (*He goes to the window.*) Reading that has made me feel bad; that book is not true! . . . (*He rings [the bell].*) Seven o'clock. My father is not coming tonight. (*To* NANINE, *who enters.*) Ask madame to come back here.

NANINE (*embarrassed*): Madame is not here, monsieur.

ARMAND: Well where is she?

NANINE: On the road. She asked me to tell you she'd be back soon.

ARMAND: Has Madame Duvernoy gone out with her?

NANINE: Madame Duvernoy went a little before madame.

ARMAND: That's alright. . . . (*Exit* NANINE.) (*Alone*) She's capable of going to Paris to concern herself with that sale! Luckily Prudence, who is warned, will find a means of putting a stop to it! . . . (*He gazes out the window.*) I seem to see a shadow in the garden. It must be she. (*Calling*) Marguerite! Marguerite! Marguerite! No one there. . . . (*Exit, calling*) Nanine! Nanine! (*He comes back and rings [the bell].*) Nanine doesn't answer either. What can that mean? This emptiness makes me feel cold. There's something ominous in this silence. Why did I ever let Marguerite go out? She was hiding something from me. She was crying. Would she deceive me? . . . *She* deceive me! Just at the moment when she was thinking of sacrificing everything for me! . . . Something may have happened to her! She could be hurt, perhaps dead. I must know! (*He turns toward the garden. A* MESSENGER *meets him face to face at the door.*)

SCENE EIGHT   Armand, a Messenger.

MESSENGER: Monsieur Armand Duval?

ARMAND: Yes.

MESSENGER: Here is a letter for you.

ARMAND: From where?

MESSENGER: From Paris.

ARMAND: Who gave it to you?

MESSENGER: A lady.

ARMAND: And how did you get in this way?

MESSENGER: The garden gate was open, I didn't see anyone around, I saw the light in here, and I thought. . . .

ARMAND: Very well; you can go! (*Exit* MESSENGER.)

SCENE NINE   Armand, later M. Duval.

ARMAND: It's from Marguerite. . . . Why am I so disturbed? Surely she's waiting for me somewhere and has written for me to come and get her. . . . (*He begins to open the letter.*) My hands are trembling. Oh, how childish! (*During this,* M. DUVAL *enters and stands behind his son.* ARMAND *reads.*) "By the time you receive this letter, Armand. . . ." (*He lets out a cry of anger. He turns and sees his father. He throws himself into his father's arms, sobbing.*) Oh, father, father!

CURTAIN

ACT FOUR

A very elegant *salon* in Olympe's house. — The sound of an orchestra [offstage]; dancing, movement, lights.

SCENE ONE   Gaston, Arthur, the Doctor, Prudence, Anaïs, Guests; later Saint-Gaudens and Olympe.

GASTON (*acting as banker in* baccarat[1]): Now then, play, *messieurs.*

ARTHUR:[2] How much in the bank?

GASTON: A hundred *louis.*

ARTHUR: Five francs on the right.

GASTON: Was your question really worth the trouble in the light of five francs?

ARTHUR: Would you like it better if I played ten francs on credit?

GASTON: No, no, no. (*To the* DOCTOR) You, doctor, aren't you playing?

THE DOCTOR: No.

GASTON: What are you doing over there?

THE DOCTOR: I'm chatting with some charming ladies, introducing myself.

GASTON: To know you is to love.

THE DOCTOR: But what good does it do me? (*The talking continues and laughter runs around the table.*)

GASTON: If this is the way you're going to play, I'll pass this hand.

PRUDENCE: Wait, I'll bet five francs.

GASTON: Where are they?

PRUDENCE: In my pocket.

GASTON (*laughing*): I'll give you fifteen francs if you can show them to me.

PRUDENCE: Oh my, I've forgotten my purse!

GASTON: Now there's a purse that knows its business. Here, take these twenty francs.

PRUDENCE: I'll pay you back.

GASTON: Don't be foolish. (*Dealing cards*) I have nine. (*He pulls in the money.*)

PRUDENCE: He always wins.

ARTHUR: That makes fifty *louis* that I've lost.

ANAÏS: Would you cure Arthur, doctor, of the malady of making a fuss?

THE DOCTOR: That's a disease of youth that will go with age.

ANAÏS: He's pretending to have lost a thousand francs; he had two *louis* in his pocket when he arrived.

ARTHUR: How do you know?

ANAÏS: If you look at a pocket for a long time you know what's in it.

ARTHUR: So what? It only proves that I owe nine hundred and sixty francs.

---

1 Olympe's guests are gambling. *Baccarat* is a card game described in the Abbé Bellecour's "French Hoyle," *L'Académie de jeu* (1768) which reached the height of its popularity in France in the 1830's. A version of it, called *chemin de fer,* is better known in Britain and the United States, but the original game, *baccarat banque,* as played in the scene here, is still to be found in Continental casinos. Here Gaston has bought the bank by outbidding the others for the privilege— among other advantages the banker wins ties—and has to play by covering the bets of the others up to the limit of the "pot," here a hundred *louis d'or.*   2 His name is supposed to suggest the traditional sentimental lover, as in French fiction.

ANAÏS: I pity those you owe money to.

ARTHUR: You're wrong, my dear; I pay my debts, you know that.

GASTON: Let's go, *messieurs*, play up; we're not here just for the fun of it.

OLYMPE (*coming in with* SAINT-GAUDENS): Still playing?

ARTHUR: Still.

OLYMPE: Give me ten *louis*, Saint-Gaudens, I want to play a little.

GASTON: Olympe, this is a charming party.

ARTHUR: Saint-Gaudens knows what it will cost him.

OLYMPE: He doesn't — but his lady does!

SAINT-GAUDENS: Well said! Ah, there you are, doctor. (*Sotto voce*) I'd like to consult you. I have this dizziness sometimes. . . .

THE DOCTOR: Lady!

OLYMPE: What does he want?

THE DOCTOR: He thinks there's something wrong with his brain.

OLYMPE: The fop! I've lost, Saint-Gaudens, play for me and try to win.

PRUDENCE: Saint-Gaudens lend me three *louis* . . . (*He gives them to her.*)

ANAÏS: Saint-Gaudens, go and get me an ice-cream.

SAINT-GAUDENS: In a minute!

ANAÏS: Well, tell us the story of the yellow hackney coach.

SAINT-GAUDENS: I'm going, I'm going.

PRUDENCE (*to* GASTON): Do you remember the story of the yellow hackney coach?

GASTON: Do I remember! I know it well; Olympe wanted to tell it that night at Marguerite's. By the way, is Marguerite here?

OLYMPE: She's coming.

GASTON: And Armand?

PRUDENCE: Armand is not in Paris. . . . Didn't you hear what happened?

GASTON: No.

PRUDENCE: They're separated.

ANAÏS: Bah!

PRUDENCE: Yes, Marguerite left him.

GASTON: When?

ANAÏS: A month ago, and it was a good idea!

GASTON: How so?

ANAÏS: One always ought to leave men before they walk out on you.

ARTHUR: Well, *messieurs*, are we playing or aren't we?

GASTON: Oh, you really are a bore! Do you think I want to wear my fingers to the bone dealing cards for a hundred *sous*[3] such as you bet? All sentimental lovers are the same. Luckily, you are the last Arthur.

SAINT-GAUDENS (*coming back [with the ice-cream]*): Anaïs, here's the ice-cream you asked for.

ANAÏS: You've been long enough getting it, my dear old boy; after all, at your age. . . .

GASTON (*getting up*): Messieurs, the bank is broken. — You know, if anyone had said to me: "Gaston, my friend, I'll give you five hundred francs on the condition that you deal all evening," I would have said nothing doing. Well, I've now been dealing for two full hours and I've lost two thousand francs. Ah, gambling is certainly an odd way of enjoying oneself.

(*Another* GUEST *takes the bank.*)

SAINT-GAUDENS: You won't go on playing?

GASTON: No.

SAINT-GAUDENS (*showing two players the bottom card*): Shall we play with these gentlemen?

———————————

3 A hundred *sous* equal only one franc.

GASTON: No confidence. Are you the one who invited them?

SAINT-GAUDENS: They are friends of Olympe. She knew them abroad.

GASTON: Charming fellow.

PRUDENCE: Look! It's Armand!

SCENE TWO   The same, Armand.

GASTON (*to* ARMAND): We were just talking about you.

ARMAND: And what were you saying?

PRUDENCE: We were saying that you were in Tours and would not be coming.

ARMAND: You were wrong.

GASTON: When did you get here?

ARMAND: An hour ago.

PRUDENCE: Well, my dear Armand, what news have you got to tell me?

ARMAND: Nothing at all, my dear; and you?

PRUDENCE: Have you seen Marguerite?

ARMAND: No.

PRUDENCE: She's going to be here.

ARMAND (*coldly*): Well then I'll see her.

PRUDENCE: How you said that!

ARMAND: How would you want me to say it?

PRUDENCE: Your heart is cured, then?

ARMAND: Complete recovery.

PRUDENCE: And you don't think about her any more?

ARMAND: To tell you I don't think about her any more would be lying: but Marguerite gave me my walking papers in so brisk a fashion that I thought myself pretty silly to have been so in love with her, for I really was very much in love with her.

PRUDENCE: She loved you very much too, and she'll always love you a little, but it was time for you two to call it quits. She was ready to sell her home.

ARMAND: And now it's paid for.

PRUDENCE: Entirely.

ARMAND: Is it Monsieur de Varville who has put up the money?

PRUDENCE: Yes.

ARMAND: All for the best, then.

PRUDENCE: That's what men are for. In short, he has made his point, he has returned her horses, jewels to her, — all her previous luxury! . . . As far as happiness goes, she is happy.

ARMAND: And she is back in Paris?

PRUDENCE: Naturally. She never wanted to go back to Auteuil, my dear, after you left there. I'm the one who had to go and look after everything, your affairs too. By the way, that reminds me that I have some things to return to you; you can come and get them at my place. There's only a little pocketbook with your initials on it that Marguerite wanted to keep; if you want it, I'll get it back from her.

ARMAND (*with emotion*): Let her keep it!

PRUDENCE: As for the rest, I've never seen her as she is now; she hardly sleeps any more; she goes to all the balls, stays up all night. Lately she had to go to bed after one supper and stayed three days in bed, and, when the doctor gave her permission to get up, she started in again, at the risk of death. If she goes on like that she won't last long. Do you plan on going to see her?

ARMAND: No, I'd just as soon avoid all kinds of explanations. The past is dead of apoplexy, may God rest its soul, if it had one!

PRUDENCE: You are really being reasonable. I'm charmed.

ARMAND (*noticing* GUSTAVE): My dear Prudence, here is a friend of mine I have something to say to. You'll excuse me?

PRUDENCE: Well really! (*She returns to play.*) I bet five francs!

SCENE THREE   The same, Gustave.

ARMAND: At last! Did you get my letter?

GUSTAVE: Yes, and here I am.

ARMAND: You're asking yourself why I begged you to come to one of these parties that you're not in the habit of attending?

GUSTAVE: Yes, I am.

ARMAND: You haven't seen Marguerite for a long time?

GUSTAVE: No, not since I last saw her with you.

ARMAND: Then you know nothing of what's happened?

GUSTAVE: Not a thing; tell me.

ARMAND: You believed that Marguerite was in love with me, didn't you?

GUSTAVE: I believe she still is.

ARMAND (*handing him* MARGUERITE's *letter*): Read this.

GUSTAVE (*having read it*): Marguerite wrote that?

ARMAND: She did.

GUSTAVE: When?

ARMAND: A month ago.

GUSTAVE: Have you answered this letter?

ARMAND: What would you have me say? The blow was so sudden, so unexpected, that I thought I would lose my mind. Do you understand? Marguerite deceiving me! I was so much in love with her! These bitches have no souls. I needed real affection to help me survive after what happened. I let my father lead me around like an inert thing. We finally got to Tours, where I hoped I could live, but it was impossible; I couldn't sleep any more, I was suffocating. I had been too much in love with this woman to be able to become indifferent to her all of a sudden; I had either to love her or to hate her! In the end I couldn't stay there any longer; it seemed to me that I'd die if I didn't see her again, if I didn't hear from her own lips what she had written to me. I came here because she's coming here. I have no idea what's going to happen, but I wanted you here, because I may need a friend.

GUSTAVE: I'm completely with you, my dear Armand; but in the name of heaven consider that a woman is involved; to do evil to a woman is very much like an act of cowardice.

ARMAND: Alright! She has a lover; he can challenge me. If I do something cowardly, I have blood enough to pay for it!

A SERVANT (*announcing*): Mademoiselle Marguerite Gauthier! Monsieur le Baron de Varville!

ARMAND: There they are!

SCENE FOUR   The same, Varville, Marguerite.

OLYMPE (*going up to* MARGUERITE): How late you are!

VARVILLE: We've just left the opera.

(VARVILLE *shakes hands with the men nearby*.)

PRUDENCE (*to* MARGUERITE): How are things?

MARGUERITE: Fine!

PRUDENCE (*sotto voce*): Armand is here.

MARGUERITE (*troubled*): Armand?

PRUDENCE: Yes!

(*At this moment,* ARMAND, *approaching the gaming table, sees* MARGUERITE; *she smiles timidly at him; he greets her coldly.*)

MARGUERITE: I was wrong to come to this party.

PRUDENCE: On the contrary; one time or another you had to run into Armand again, better sooner than later.

MARGUERITE: Has he spoken with you?

PRUDENCE: Yes.

MARGUERITE: About me?

PRUDENCE: Naturally.

MARGUERITE: And he said? . . .

PRUDENCE: That he's not angry with you and that you were right.

MARGUERITE: So much the better, if that's how it is; but it couldn't be that; he greeted me too coldly and he's too pale.

VARVILLE (*sotto voce to* MARGUERITE): Monsieur Duval is here, Marguerite.

MARGUERITE: I know.

VARVILLE: Do you swear to me that you didn't know when you came that he was going to be here?

MARGUERITE: I swear to you.

VARVILLE: And you promise me not to speak to him?

MARGUERITE: I promise; but I can't promise not to answer him if he speaks to me. Prudence, you stay near me.

THE DOCTOR (*to* MARGUERITE): Good evening, madame.

MARGUERITE: Oh, it's you, doctor. Why are you looking at me like that?

THE DOCTOR: When I'm face to face with such beauty, what better thing is there to do?

MARGUERITE: You find me changed, don't you?

THE DOCTOR: Take care of yourself, please take care of yourself. I'll come to see you tomorrow to scold you at my leisure.

MARGUERITE: That's it; scold me, I'll love you all the more for it. Are you leaving now?

THE DOCTOR: No, but soon; I have the same invalid to look in on every day at the same hour for six months now.

MARGUERITE: What fidelity! (*He presses her hand and goes away.*)

GUSTAVE (*approaching* MARGUERITE): Good evening, Marguerite.

MARGUERITE: Oh, how happy I am to see you, my good Gustave! Is Nichette here?

GUSTAVE: No.

MARGUERITE: Of course not! Nichette mustn't come here. — Love her dearly. Gustave, it's so good to be loved! (*She wipes her eyes.*)

GUSTAVE: What's wrong?

MARGUERITE: I'm very unhappy, go!

GUSTAVE: There, don't cry! Why did you come?

MARGUERITE: Am I my own mistress; and, besides, haven't I cares of my own?

GUSTAVE: Well, if you take my advice, you'll leave the party soon.

GUSTAVE: Because who knows who'll arrive. . . . Armand. . . .

MARGUERITE: Armand hates and despises me, doesn't he?

GUSTAVE: No, Armand loves you. See how restless he is! He's not in control of himself. He wants to cause trouble with Monsieur de Varville. Say you're not feeling very well, and go.

MARGUERITE: A duel for me, between Varville and Armand! You're right, I must leave. (*She gets up.*)

VARVILLE (*approaching her*): Where are you going?

MARGUERITE: My dear, I'm in pain and I want to retire.

VARVILLE: No, you're not in pain, Marguerite; you want to leave because Monsieur Duval is there and doesn't seem to be paying any attention to you; but you must understand that I myself neither want to nor must leave where I am just because he's there. We are at this party and here we stay.

OLYMPE (*loudly*): What was playing at the opera tonight?

VARVILLE: *La Favorite.*[1]

---

1 *La Favorite* (The Mistress [of the King]) by Gaetano Donizetti (1797–1848) was an opera in four acts developed out of the original three-act *L'Ange de Niside*. One of the librettists was the famous French playwright (Augustin) Eugène Scribe and the opera was a favorite of Parisian audiences after its première in Paris on 2 December, 1840, though today Donizetti is best known for such romantic vehicles for vocal virtuosity as *L'Elisir d'Amore* (1832) and *Lucia di Lammermoor* (1835) or even the comic *opera buffa* called *Don Pasquale* (1843). Armand's next speech makes clear the aptness of the choice of *La Favorite*'s mention in this scene.

ARMAND: The story of a woman who deceives her lover.

PRUDENCE: Oh, it happens all the time!

ANAÏS: Of course women never betray their lovers — it's not true.

ARMAND: Let me tell you there are some who do.

ANAÏS: Where, for instance?

ARMAND: Everywhere.

OLYMPE: Yes, but there are lovers and lovers.

ARMAND: Just as there are women and women.

GASTON: Ah, look at that! My dear Armand, you're playing a devilish game.

ARMAND: To see if the old proverb is true; "Unlucky in love, lucky at cards."

GASTON: Ah, you must be particularly unlucky in love, because you're terrifically lucky at cards.

ARMAND: My boy, I'm counting on making my fortune this evening, and, when I've won a lot of money I'm going to go live in the country.

OLYMPE: All alone?

ARMAND: No, with someone who has already accompanied me once and who left me. Maybe when I'm richer. . . . (*Aside*) She won't respond to anything!

GUSTAVE: Be quiet, Armand; Look at the state the poor girl's in!

ARMAND: It's a good story; I must tell it to you. In it there's a gentleman who appears at the end, a sort of *Deus ex machina*[2] who's an adorable fellow.

VARVILLE: Monsieur.

MARGUERITE (*sotto voce to* VARVILLE): If you provoke Monsieur Duval you'll never see me again as long as you live.

ARMAND (*to* VARVILLE): Didn't you address me, monsieur?

VARVILLE: Indeed, monsieur; your luck tonight tempts me to try my own, and I understand so well the use you propose to make of your winnings that I have decided to help you to increase them by having a game with you.

ARMAND (*facing up to him*): I accept with all my heart, monsieur.

VARVILLE (*passing in front of* ARMAND): I wager a hundred *louis*, monsieur.

ARMAND (*surprised, haughtily*): Playing for a hundred *louis!* Which side do you want, monsieur?

VARVILLE: The side you don't take.

ARMAND: One hundred *louis* on the left.

VARVILLE: A hundred *louis* on the right.[3]

GASTON (*acting as banker and dealing*): On the right, four; on the left, nine. Armand wins!

VARVILLE: Two hundred *louis*, then.

ARMAND: Playing for two hundred *louis*; but be careful, monsieur; if the proverb says: "Unlucky in love, lucky at cards" it also says: "Lucky in love, unlucky at cards."

GASTON: Six! Eight! Armand wins again.

OLYMPE: Well, it looks as if the baron will be financing Monsieur Duval's life in the country.

MARGUERITE (*to* OLYMPE): My God, what is going to happen now?

OLYMPE (*to distract them*): Let's go, gentlemen; to the table, supper is served.

ARMAND: Shall we continue to play, monsieur?

VARVILLE: No, not just now.

---

2 The phrase is Latin but it was the Greeks who originated the "god out of the machine," letting down onto the stage a god who extricated the mortals in the play from a perplexing or insoluble plot complication by an unexpected and often improbable means. Varville, it is suggested, might conveniently make things turn out right. 3 In *baccarat* the banker deals both to his left and right and the other players bet on which of these will beat the dealer, so that left and right are in effect opponents.

ARMAND: You are entitled to your return match; I promise to play whenever you choose.

VARVILLE: Rest assured, monsieur, that I shall take advantage of your good will!

OLYMPE (*taking* ARMAND'S *arm*): You are not too lucky, my dear.

ARMAND: You only "my dear" me when I'm winning.

VARVILLE: Are you coming, Marguerite?

MARGUERITE: Not yet. I have a few things to say to Prudence.

VARVILLE: I'll give you ten minutes and, if you haven't come to join us by then, I'll come back here looking for you, Marguerite, I warn you.

MARGUERITE: Very well, go!

SCENE FIVE   Prudence, Marguerite.

MARGUERITE: Go find Armand, and, in the name of all that's holy, beg him to come here to listen to me; I have to speak with him.

PRUDENCE: Suppose he refuses?

MARGUERITE: He won't refuse. He detests me too much not to seize the opportunity of telling me so. Go on!

SCENE SIX   Marguerite.

MARGUERITE (*alone*): Let's try to be calm; he must continue to believe what he does. Have I the strength to keep the promise I made to his father? My God, make him despise and hate me, for that's the only way of preventing a misfortune. . . . Here he is!

SCENE SEVEN   Marguerite, Armand.

ARMAND: You sent for me, madame?

MARGUERITE: Yes, Armand, I have to talk with you.

ARMAND: Go ahead, I'm listening. Are you going to excuse your behavior?

MARGUERITE: No, Armand, there will be no

question of that. I shall even beg you not to bring up the past all over again.

ARMAND: You're right; there's too much shame in it for you.

MARGUERITE: Don't heap that on me, Armand. Listen to me without hatred, without anger, without recrimination! Look, Armand, give me your hand.

ARMAND: Never, madame; If that's all you have to say to me. . . . (*He makes a move to withdraw.*)

MARGUERITE: Who would ever have thought that you'd refuse the hand that I offered you? But that's not what it's all about, Armand, it's that you must leave.

ARMAND: I must leave?

MARGUERITE: Yes! That you must return to your father, and right away.

ARMAND: And why, madame?

MARGUERITE: Because Monsieur de Varville is going to provoke you to a duel, and I don't want anything unpleasant to happen. I want to be the only one to suffer.

ARMAND: And so you advise me to run away from a provocation! You're advising me to commit an act of cowardice! What other advice, indeed, could one expect from a woman like you?

MARGUERITE: Armand, I swear to you that for the past month I have suffered so deeply that I hardly have the strength to admit it; I know very well the evil that grows and consumes me. In the name of our past love, in the name of what I suffer still, Armand, in the name of your mother and your sister, flee from me, return to your father and forget my very name, if you can.

ARMAND: I understand, madame; you are afraid for your lover who represents your means of support. I could ruin you with a pistol shot or the stroke of a sword. That indeed would certainly be a terrible misfortune!

MARGUERITE: You might be killed, Armand, and that would be the real misfortune!

ARMAND: What do you care if I live or die? Did you care at all for my life when you wrote me: "Armand, forget me, I am the mistress of another!"? If I'm not dead after that letter it's because I had to get my revenge. Oh, you thought it would happen like that, that you could just break my heart and that I'd take no further notice of you and your accomplice. No, madame, no. I have returned to Paris, and between Monsieur de Varville and myself there is a serious matter to settle! Whether you die too or not, I shall kill him, I swear!

MARGUERITE: Monsieur de Varville is innocent of everything that has happened.

ARMAND: You love him, madame! That's reason enough for me to hate him.

MARGUERITE: You know very well that I do not love him, that I could never love a man like that!

ARMAND: Then why have you given yourself to him?

MARGUERITE: Don't ask me that, Armand; I can't tell you that.

ARMAND: I'll tell you that myself. You've given yourself to him because you're a girl without heart or loyalty, because your love belongs to anyone who can pay for it, for you have put your soul on sale; because when you found yourself face to face with the sacrifice you were going to make for my sake, your courage failed you, and your base instincts brought you down; because in the long run this man to whom you were devoting your life and who gave up his honor for you was not worth in your estimation the horses for your carriage or the diamonds around your neck.

MARGUERITE: Well, yes, I did all that. Yes, I'm an infamous, miserable creature, who is not in love with you; I was deceiving you. But the more infamous I am the less reason you have to endanger your life and the life of those who love you, for me. Armand, on my knees, I beg you, get out of Paris and don't look back!

ARMAND: That's fine with me, on one condition.

MARGUERITE: Whatever it is, I accept it.

ARMAND: You will come with me.

MARGUERITE (*taken aback*): Never!

ARMAND: Never!

MARGUERITE: Oh, my God, give me courage.

ARMAND (*running to the door and back*): Listen to me, Marguerite; I've gone mad, overexcited, my blood boils, my mind reels, I'm in that state of passion in which a man is capable of anything, even of infamy. I thought for a moment that it was hate that propelled me back to you; but it was love, invincible love, angry, hateful, remorseful, full of scorn and shame, for I hate myself for still being in love, after what has happened. Well now, give me one word of repentance, blame your mistake on chance, on fate, on your weakness, and I'll forget everything. What do I care about this man? I can only hate him if you love him. Tell me only that you still love me and I'll pardon you, Marguerite, we shall flee Paris (which is to say the past) together, we shall flee to the ends of the earth if we must, where we shall not see a single human face and where we shall be all alone in the world with our love.

MARGUERITE (*drained of emotion*): I would give my life for an hour of happiness such as you describe, but such happiness is impossible.

ARMAND: Still!

MARGUERITE: An abyss separates us; we would be too unhappy together. We can no longer love each other; go, forget me, it must be so, I have sworn it.

ARMAND: To whom?

MARGUERITE: To the one who had the right to demand it.

ARMAND (*getting angry*): To Monsieur de Varville?

MARGUERITE: Yes.

ARMAND (*seizing* MARGUERITE's *arm*): To Monsieur de Varville because you love him; tell me that you are in love with him and I'll go.

MARGUERITE: Well then, yes, I love Monsieur de Varville.

ARMAND (*throws her to the ground, raises his hands as if to strike her, dashes to the door and, seeing the other guests who are in the other salon, cries*): Come in here, all of you!

MARGUERITE: What are you doing?

ARMAND: You see this woman?

ALL: Marguerite Gauthier! . . .

ARMAND: Yes! Marguerite Gauthier. Do you know what she's done? She sold everything she possessed to live with me, she loved me so much. Isn't that nice? Do you know what I did? I acted miserably: I accepted her sacrifice without giving her anything in exchange. But it is never too late: I repent and I have come back to make restitution. You all are witnesses that I owe this woman nothing more. (*He throws her a number of banknotes.*)

MARGUERITE (*giving a cry and falling over*): Ah!

VARVILLE (*to* ARMAND, *with contempt, throwing his gloves in his face*): Without a doubt, monsieur, you are a coward! (*The others* [GUESTS] *throw themselves between them* [*and separate them*].)

CURTAIN

ACT FIVE

MARGUERITE's bedroom. Bed at the back; curtains partly drawn. Fireplace on the right; in front of it a sofa, on which GASTON is stretched out. No light except that from a night-lamp [beside the bed].

SCENE ONE Marguerite in bed, asleep; Gaston.

GASTON (*raising his head and listening*): I dozed off for a moment. . . . I hope she didn't need me in the meanwhile! No, she's sleeping. . . . What time is it? Seven o'clock. . . . It's not day yet. . . . I'll rekindle the fire. (*He pokes it.*)

MARGUERITE (*waking up*): Nanine, bring me something to drink.

GASTON: Here you are, my dear child.

MARGUERITE (*lifting her head*): Who is that?

GASTON (*preparing a tisane*[1]): Gaston.

MARGUERITE: How do you happen to be in my room?

GASTON (*giving her a cup*): Drink this first and I'll tell you afterwards. Is there enough sugar in it?

MARGUERITE: Yes.

GASTON: I was born to be a nurse for you.

MARGUERITE: Where is Nanine?

GASTON: Asleep. When I arrived at eleven o'clock to get some news of you, the poor girl was dead on her feet; on the other hand, I was wide awake. You were already asleep. . . . I told her to go to bed. I lay down there, on the sofa, near the fire, and I've spent a very good night. That did me good to stretch out and rest; it was just as if I myself was sleeping. How do you feel this morning?

MARGUERITE: I'm fine, my brave Gaston; but what good is it for you to tire yourself out like this? . . .

GASTON: I've spent enough nights staying up at parties that I can manage a few looking after the sick! And besides, I had something to tell you.

MARGUERITE: What do you want to say?

GASTON: Are you short of cash?

MARGUERITE: Short of cash?

GASTON: Yes, do you need money? When I came here yesterday I saw a bailiff in the *salon*. I showed him the door and paid him. But that's not all; there isn't any money here, and you must have some. Now, I don't have much. I've lost quite a lot gambling and I've bought a lot of useless New Year's presents.

---

1 a herbal drink for invalids, a tonic.

(*He embraces her.*) And I'd like to wish you a very happy New Year. . . . But in any case there will always be twenty-five *louis* that I'm going to put in the drawer over there. And there's more where that came from.

MARGUERITE (*deeply touched*): What a heart! And to think that it's you, whom they used to call a scatterbrain, and who never was anything more than a friend of mine, who should come and take care of me. . . .

GASTON: It's always like that. . . . Now, do you know what we're going to do?

MARGUERITE: Tell me.

GASTON: It's going to be a beautiful day! You've had eight good hours' sleep; you're going to get a little more sleep. Between one and three the sun will be brightly shining; I'll come and get you; you'll wrap up well; we'll go out for a ride; and who will sleep soundly tonight? Marguerite. Until then, I'm going to see my mother and who knows what kind of reception I'll get: it's more than two weeks since I saw her! I'll have breakfast with her and in an hour I'll be back here. How's that?

MARGUERITE: I'll try to get my strength together. . . .

GASTON: You'll have enough, you will! (NANINE *opens the door.*) Come in! Marguerite is awake.

SCENE TWO   The same, Nanine.

MARGUERITE: You were very tired then, my poor Nanine?

NANINE: A little, madame.

MARGUERITE: Open the window and let a little daylight in. I want to get up.

NANINE (*opening the window and looking into the street*): Madame, the doctor is here.

MARGUERITE: Good doctor! His first visit of the day is always to me. Gaston, open the front door for him as you go out. Nanine, help me to get up.

NANINE: But, madame. . . .

MARGUERITE: I want to.

GASTON: See you in a while. (*Exit.*)

MARGUERITE: In a little while. (*She tries to rise and falls back; finally, supported by* NANINE, *she walks toward the sofa,* THE DOCTOR *enters in time to help her sit down.*)

SCENE THREE   Marguerite, Nanine, The Doctor.

MARGUERITE: Good morning, doctor dear; how kind of you to think of me so early in the morning! Nanine, go see if there are any letters.

THE DOCTOR: Give me your hand. (*He takes it.*) How are you feeling?

MARGUERITE: Ill but a little better. Sick of body but better in spirit. Last night I was so afraid of dying that I sent for a priest. I was sad, full of despair, afraid of death; this man came, talked an hour with me, and when he left he took with him all the despair, terror, and remorse. And so I fell asleep and have just now awakened.

THE DOCTOR: Everything is going well, madame, and I promise you'll be completely cured by the first days of Spring.

MARGUERITE: Thank you, doctor. . . . It's your duty to speak to me like that. When God decreed that it is a sin to lie He made an exception for doctors, and He permitted them to lie each time that they see a patient. (*To* NANINE, *who comes back in.*) What are you carrying there?

NANINE: These are some presents, madame.

MARGUERITE: Ah, yes, today is New Year's! . . . How many things have happened in the last year! A year ago at this time we were sitting at a table, singing, we were giving to the year then being born the same smile that we give now to the dying year. Where are the days, my good doctor, when we still laughed? (*Opening the packages*) A ring sent by Saint-Gaudens. What a dear heart! A bracelet sent by the Count de Giray, who sends it to me from London. How he would gasp if he could see me the way I am now! . . . and candy too. . . . Well, men are not as forget-ful as I used to think! Do you have a little niece, doctor?

THE DOCTOR: Yes, madame.

MARGUERITE: Take this candy to the dear little child; it's a long time now since I ate candy. (*to* NANINE) Is that all that you have?

NANINE: I have a letter.

MARGUERITE: Who can be writing me? (*Taking the letter and opening it*) Take this package down to the doctor's carriage. (*Exit* NANINE *with the box of candy.*) (*Reading*) "My dearest Marguerite, I have come twenty times to see you and was never allowed in; nevertheless, I would not wish to fail to have you share the happiest day of my life; I am being married New Year's Day; it is my New Year's present that Gustave was keep-ing for me; I hope that you will not be the last to come to the wedding, a simple cere-mony, very plain, which will be held at nine o'clock in the morning in the chapel of St. Theresa in the church of The Magdalene.[1] I kiss you with all the strength of a happy heart, NICHETTE." There shall be happiness for everybody in the world except me! No, I'm being ungrateful. Doctor, I'm cold. Would you close that window, and give me something to write with? (*She drops her head in her hands;* THE DOCTOR *takes the inkstand from the mantlepiece and gives a writing portfolio* [*from a nearby table*] *to* MARGUERITE.)

NANINE (*sotto voce, to* THE DOCTOR, *while he is at a distance* [*from* MARGUERITE]): How is she, doctor?

THE DOCTOR (*shaking his head* [*aside*]): She's very ill!

MARGUERITE (*aside*): They think I don't hear them. . . . (*Aloud*) Doctor, do me the favor, as you go, of dropping off this letter at the church where Nichette is to be married, and ask them not to give it to her until after the ceremony. (*She writes, folds the letter, and seals it* [*with wax*].) Take this, and thank you. (*She presses his hand.*) Don't forget, and come back as soon as you can. . . . (*Exit* THE DOCTOR.)

SCENE FOUR   Marguerite, Nanine.

MARGUERITE: Now, now let's have a little order in this room. (*The bell rings.*) Someone's ringing, go see who it is. (*Exit* NANINE.)

NANINE (*coming back*): It's Madame Duvernoy who wants to see madame.

MARGUERITE: Have her come in!

SCENE FIVE   The same, Prudence.

PRUDENCE: Well, my dear Marguerite, how are you this morning?

MARGUERITE: Better, my dear Prudence, thank you.

PRUDENCE: Send Nanine away for a moment, I want to talk with you — alone.

MARGUERITE: Nanine, you can do another room first. I'll call you when I need you. . . .

(*Exit* NANINE.)

PRUDENCE: There's something I want you to do for me if you will, my dear Marguerite.

MARGUERITE: What is it?

PRUDENCE: You have some money? . . .

MARGUERITE: You know that I've been short of money for some time now; but go on, ask away.

PRUDENCE: Today is the first of the year and I have some presents to buy; I absolutely need two hundred francs; could you be a dear and lend them to me, just until the end of the month?

---

1 The *Madeleine* is a large Parisian church begun in 1764. Construction was halted by the French Revolution and it was converted (at the command of Napoleon) into a Temple of Glory, on which the architect Bart-hélemy Vignon worked 1807–1828. It was completed by J.-J.-M. Huvé in 1842 and after the Bourbon restora-tion became a church once more, though of course it looks like an overly-tall Roman temple rather than a Christian church. The fact that it was fashionable for weddings and also that it was dedicated to St. Mary Magdalene (by tradition the repentant prostitute of Luke 7: 36–50) make it a very suitable choice for *The Lady of the Camellias.*

MARGUERITE (*lifting her eyes to heaven*): "The end of the month!"

PRUDENCE: Of course if you haven't. . . .

MARGUERITE: I really did need the money that's there. . . .

PRUDENCE: Oh well, don't say any more of it.

MARGUERITE: Never mind! Open that drawer. . . .

PRUDENCE: Which one? (*She opens several drawers.*) Oh, this one in the middle!

MARGUERITE: How much is there?

PRUDENCE: Five hundred francs.

MARGUERITE: Very well, take the two hundred francs you need.

PRUDENCE: Are you sure you'll be alright with the rest?

MARGUERITE: I have what I need; don't you worry about me.

PRUDENCE (*taking the money*): You're really doing me a big favor.

MARGUERITE: So much the better, my dear Prudence!

PRUDENCE: I'll run along now and come back later to see you. You're looking better.

MARGUERITE: Actually I am better.

PRUDENCE: The fine weather is coming soon. A little country air will cure you.

MARGUERITE: That's it.

PRUDENCE (*going out*): Thank you again!

MARGUERITE: Send Nanine back to me.

PRUDENCE: Of course. (*Exit.*)

NANINE (*coming in*): Has she come again asking for money?

MARGUERITE: Yes.

NANINE: And have you given her any?

MARGUERITE: Money is such a little thing to give, and she needed it badly, so she said. But we need some too, however; we have some presents to give. Take this bracelet that has just arrived, go sell it and hurry right back.

NANINE: But in the meantime. . . .

MARGUERITE: I can get on by myself, I won't need anything; and you won't be gone very long. Heaven knows you know the way to the merchant: he's bought enough from me over the last three months. (*Exit* NANINE.)

SCENE SIX   Marguerite.

MARGUERITE (*reading a letter which she takes from her bosom*): "Madame, I have learned of the duel between Armand and the Baron de Varville, but not from my son, who went away without even saying goodbye to me. Can you believe that, madame? For a while I thought you guilty of the duel and of his departure. Now, thank God, Monsieur de Varville is out of danger and I know the truth about it all. You have kept your word to me to the utmost of your strength and all these efforts have injured your health. I wrote the whole truth to Armand. He is far away, but he will come back to beg pardon not only for himself but for me, for I was compelled to force you to do yourself an injury and I want to set it right. Take good care of yourself and live in hope; your courage and your self-sacrifice merit a better future; and you shall have one, I promise you. In the meantime, accept the assurance of my feelings and sympathy, of my esteem and my devotion. GEORGE DUVAL. — November 15." It's six weeks since I received this letter and I have read it over and over to give me a little courage. If I only would receive some word from Armand, if I could only last until Spring! (*She raises herself and looks at herself in a mirror.*) Oh, how I've changed! However the doctor has promised to cure me. I shall be patient. But just now, talking with Nanine, didn't he expect the worst? I heard him distinctly: he said that I was very ill. Very ill! Just a little more hope and once again only a few months to live, but, if during that time Armand should come, I would be saved. The New Year — the least one can do is to hope! Besides, my mind is clear. If I were in real danger, Gaston would not have the courage to be laughing at my bedstead as he was doing just now. The doctor wouldn't be leaving me. (*At the window*) What happy families! Oh, what a pretty child, laughing and gamboling with his toys. I should like to kiss that child.

SCENE SEVEN   Nanine, Marguerite.

NANINE (*coming to* MARGUERITE, *having first placed on the mantlepiece the money she has brought*): Madame. . . .

MARGUERITE: What is it, Nanine?

NANINE: Do you feel any better today?

MARGUERITE: Yes; why?

NANINE: Promise me you'll be calm.

MARGUERITE: What's happening?

NANINE: I wanted to warn you. . . . too sudden a joy is so difficult to bring.

MARGUERITE: Joy, you say?

NANINE: Yes, madame.

MARGUERITE: Armand! You've seen Armand? . . . Armand is coming to see me! . . . (NANINE *shakes her head affirmatively.* — [MARGUERITE] *runs to the door*) Armand! (*She seems pale; she throws her arms around his neck and crushes him to her.*) Oh, it's not you; it's impossible that God could be so kind!

SCENE EIGHT   Marguerite, Armand.

ARMAND: It's I, Marguerite, I, so repentant, so disturbed, so guilty, that I dared not cross the threshold of this door. If I had not met Nanine, I would have stayed in the street, praying and crying. Marguerite, don't curse me! My father has written me everything! I was very far away from you, I did not know where to go to flee my love and my remorse. . . . I fled like a fool, traveling night and day, without rest, without peace, without sleep, pursued by sinister presentiments, seeing from afar the house hung with black. Oh, if I had not found you, I would have died, for I am the one who would have

killed you! I have not seen my father yet. Marguerite, tell me that you forgive us both. Oh, it's so good to see you again!

MARGUERITE: Forgive you, my darling! I alone am guilty! But what else could I have done? I wanted your happiness so much more than my own. But now, your father won't separate us any more, will he? It's no longer the Marguerite that you used to know whom you find here; however, I am still young, I shall be beautiful again, for I am so happy. You will forget everything. From today on we'll begin to live.

ARMAND: I'll never leave you again. Listen, Marguerite, this very moment we are going to leave this house. We shall never return. We shall never return to Paris. My father knows who you are. He will love you as the guardian angel of his son. My sister is married. The future is ours.

MARGUERITE: Oh, speak to me, go on speaking to me! I feel my soul reviving with your words, my health reborn with your sighs. I said it this morning: only one thing could save me. I dared not hope for it — and here you are! Let us waste no time, go, as my life goes by I shall catch it as it flies. Don't you know? Nichette is getting married. She marries Gustave this morning. We'll go see her. It will do us good to enter a church, to pray God to bless the happiness of others. What a surprise Providence had in store for me to mark the New Year! But tell me now once more that you love me!

ARMAND: Oh, I love you, Marguerite, you are my whole life.

MARGUERITE (*to* NANINE, *who comes in*): Bring me everything I need to go out.

ARMAND: Good Nanine! You've taken such good care of her; thank you!

MARGUERITE: Every day the two of us used to speak of you; for no one dared to mention your name anymore. It was she who consoled me, who told me that you would come back! She wasn't lying. You have seen beautiful countries. You will take me there. (*She sways.*)

ARMAND: What's wrong, Marguerite? You look pale! . . .

MARGUERITE (*with effort*): Nothing, my darling, nothing! You know that happiness cannot rush so suddenly into a heart that has long been desolate without overcoming it a little. (*She sits down and throws back her head.*)

ARMAND: Marguerite, speak to me! I beg you!

MARGUERITE (*coming to herself*): Don't be afraid, darling; you know I've always had these moments of weakness. But they quickly pass; look, I'm smiling, I feel strong. It's the shock of living that overcame me.

ARMAND (*taking her hand*): You're trembling.

MARGUERITE: It's nothing! Nanine, give me a shawl; a hat. . . .

ARMAND (*terrified*): My God! Oh, my God!

MARGUERITE (*throwing down her shawl, having tried to walk*): I just can't. (*She falls on the sofa.*)

ARMAND: Nanine, go fetch the doctor!

MARGUERITE: Yes, yes; tell him that Armand has come back, that I want to live, I must live. . . . (*Exit* NANINE.) But if your return does not save me, nothing can save me. Sooner or later a human being must die of life itself. I have lived for love, now I am dying of it.

ARMAND: Hush, Marguerite; you will live, you must!

MARGUERITE: Sit near me, as close as you can, Armand dear, and listen closely to me. Just now I had a moment of anger with death, which I regret; death must come, and I loved the idea of it because it waited for you first before it struck me. If my death had not been certain, your father would not have written you to return. . . .

ARMAND: Please, Marguerite, don't talk any more like that, you will drive me to distraction. Don't say any more that you are going to die, tell me that you don't believe it, that it cannot be, that you will not let it be!

MARGUERITE: Even if I do not wish it to be so, darling, it must happen, for God wills it. If I were a holy girl, completely chaste, perhaps I might cry at the idea of leaving a world where you remain, because the future would be full of promise, to which all my past would grant me a right. With me dead, everything that you have of me will be kept pure; with me alive, there would always be a stain on our love. . . . Believe me, God is right to do as He does. . . .

ARMAND (*getting up*): Oh, I'm suffocating.

MARGUERITE (*holding him*): What! Must I be the one to give you courage? Look, obey me. Open that drawer and take the medallion which you find there . . . it's my portrait, from the time when I was pretty! I had it made for you: keep it, it will help your memory later. But if, some day, a beautiful young girl should fall in love with you and marry you, as it must be, as I wish it to be. And if she were to find this portrait tell her that it's a picture of a dear friend who (if God permits her to dwell in the most obscure corner of heaven) prays to God every day for her and for you. If she should be jealous of the past, as we women sometimes are, if she demands that you put this picture away from you, do so without fear and without remorse; that will only be just, and I forgive you in advance. — A woman suffers too much when she feels she is not loved. . . . Are you listening, Armand dear, do you understand me well?

SCENE NINE   The same, Nanine, later Nichette, Gustave and Gaston.

(*Enter* NICHETTE, *terrified but becoming bolder as she sees* MARGUERITE *smiling at her and* ARMAND *at her feet.*)

NICHETTE: My dearest Marguerite, you wrote me that you were dying and I find you smiling and receiving visitors.

ARMAND (*sotto voce*): Oh, Gustave, I am so unhappy!

MARGUERITE: I am dying, but I am happy too, and my happiness eclipses my death. So you two are married! What a strange life this first one is, whatever can the life to come be like? . . . You will be even happier than you were before. Speak of me sometimes, won't you? Armand, give me your hand . . . Believe me, it is not difficult to die. (*Enter* GASTON.) Here's Gaston come to look for me. . . . I'm glad to see you again, my dear Gaston. Happiness is ungrateful: I had forgotten you. . . . (*to* ARMAND) He has been so good to me. . . . Ah, that's strange. (*She raises herself up.*)

ARMAND: What is?

MARGUERITE: I feel no more pain. One could say that life is coming back to me . . . I feel so much better than I have ever felt before. . . . And I shall live! . . . Ah! I feel so well! (*She sits down and seems to fall asleep.*)

GASTON: She's asleep!

ARMAND (*anxious, then terrified*): Marguerite! Marguerite! Marguerite! (*A great cry. — He is compelled to make an effort in order to draw his hand out of* MARGUERITE'S *grip.*) Oh! (*He recoils, stunned.*) Dead! (*Running to* GUSTAVE) My God! my God! what's to become of me? . . .

GUSTAVE (*to* ARMAND): She loved you dearly, the poor girl.

NICHETTE (*who is kneeling beside her*): Sleep in peace, Marguerite! Much will be forgiven you, for you loved much![1]

TABLEAU. CURTAIN

---

[1] In Luke: 7 (already mentioned in connection with the *Madeleine*) verse 47 has Jesus say of Mary Magdalene: "Wherefore I say unto thee, Her sins, which are many, are forgiven; for she loved much. . . ." The suggestion only made the play less attractive to conventional moralists and Comte Horace de Viel-Castel confided to his diary that "the entire play is dedicated to vice and debauchery." The theatricality of the scene (and of the whole play), however, brought down the curtain to deafening applause on opening night. Dumas *fils* telegraphed to his father (exiled in Belgium): "Great, great success! So great that I thought I was attending the *première* of one of your works." The father replied with wit and grace: "My finest work, dear child, is you." Even the cast had expected a theatrical disaster, but it certainly was not that. If Dumas *fils* expected his sentiments to please conventional, bourgeois morality, however, he was much mistaken. The whole subject, let alone the treatment, caused a *frisson* in Respectable Paris (which may have contributed to the play's lasting appeal on stage). When Dumas *fils* overly stressed the moral (as in *The Ideas of Madame Aubray*) he was not at his best, as he was with the psychology of this play or the sparkle of his witty comedies.

The Wild Duck

Henrik Ibsen (1828–1906) became the father of modern drama when, after writing five expansive romantic dramas and a play in 1857 rather in the style of the great German romantic Schiller, he then put the well-made machinery of the plays of the French dramaturgical technicians Eugène Scribe (1791–1861) and Victorien Sardou (1831–1908) to a serious purpose. Though he claimed rightly in a speech of 1898 to have been "more poet and less social philosopher than people generally seem inclined to believe," Ibsen made the drama of ideas, set in contemporary surroundings, the dominant drama of his time. His pervasive influence was strongly felt not only in his native Norway but also in Russia with Chekhov, in Britain with Shaw, in France with Eugène Brieux (1858–1946), in Germany with Gerhardt Hauptmann (1862–1946), and elsewhere with others. He became the "master builder" of problem plays that came to grips honestly with social evils and preached "the capacity for procreation and development of ideals." Grappling with "the temporal and eternal questions which are astir in the age," challenging "dead ideas," and making Heredity and Environment the implacable gods of a modern tragedy, Ibsen mixed realism and symbolism to create such masterpieces as *A Doll's House* (1879), *Ghosts* (1881), *An Enemy of the People* (1882), *The Wild Duck* (1884), *Rosmersholm* (1886), *John Gabriel Borkman* (1896), *Hedda Gabler* (1890), and *The Master Builder* (1892).

He thought his historical drama *Emperor and Galilean* (1873) his *chef d'oeuvre*, but the moral and social insights of *The Wild Duck*, with its "life lies" (echoed in the "pipe dreams" of Eugene O'Neill's *The Iceman Cometh*) and its marvelous handling of exposition, and ethical and psychological problems, make it our choice as his best work. Reflecting the beliefs of the existentialist philosopher Søren Kierkegaard (1813–1855), Ibsen said: "I do not complain that mankind is wicked, I complain that it is abject." He went on to enlighten his fellow men, sometimes with a messianic zeal like Gregers Werle in *The Wild Duck*, sometimes with humor, and sometimes in great earnest. What Ibsen really was doing may be best expressed in a few lines of his poetry:

> What is life? a fighting
>   In heart and brain with Trolls.
> Poetry? that means writing
>   Doomsday-accounts of our souls.

He was great because he was as honest as he was perceptive and made his dramatic characters humanly grey, not melodramatically black and white; because he could see both sides of every question even when he was certain of his own position. (His dying words were: "On the contrary.")

Rather than take up more space with introduction to Ibsen, for you can find many books on the subject (Shaw, Jaeger, Koht, Bradbrook, Tennant, Knight, McFarlane, etc.), following the final version of *The Wild Duck* we will present Ibsen's "Notes and Jottings" so that you can see the master at work, jotting down working notes, and drafting scenes of the play.

In England at this time, the actor-managers and "The Theatre Theatrical" were still firmly in control; the intellectuals had more or less deserted the stage and the pit; the dramatists were derivatives or (as Sir W. S. Gilbert more kindly put it) "steady and stolidly"; and J. J. Grein was saying that "so long as Shakespeare draws the crowd we need not bewail the poverty of our contemporary drama." In America, with farce and melodrama and, at the best, touring stars from Britain, things were worse. In Norway, Ibsen's efforts to create a national theatre and to modernize the drama were to have far-reaching effects upon the world theatre. To understand what happened when Ibsen's *Ghosts* was played, first in Chicago (in Norwegian), then in Paris (produced by André Antoine, 1890) and in London (by J. J. Grein's Independent Theatre, 1891), we can study the best-constructed of all Ibsen's masterpieces, *The Wild Duck*. The French critic Sarcey greeted it as "obscure, incoherent, intolerable." Since then it has come to be regarded as the perfect example of the way in which "the new poet" (as Rilke called him) was able, in Muriel Bradbrook's words, "to infuse the particular, drab, limited fact with a halo and a glory," to mix comedy and tragedy, to master exposition and to bring symbolism to the service of realism. We can see the finished product and something of the process in the play and these notes which record Ibsen's progress. "Many of the details only occur to me during the process of composition, bit by bit as I go along." Ibsen once said: "I don't like people seeing what stupidities I was guilty of before I got my work into the shape I wanted." But what an insight we can gain by seeing genius at work, "playing upon the human conscience" in the problem play at its most artistic.

THE WILD DUCK

Henrik Ibsen

*Translated from the Norwegian
by Frances E. Archer*

DRAMATIS PERSONÆ

HÅKON WERLE, *Businessman, Industrialist*
GREGERS WERLE, *his Son*
Old EKDAL
HIALMAR EKDAL, *his Son, Photographer*
GINA EKDAL, *his Wife*
HEDVIG, *their fourteen-year-old Daughter*
Mrs. BERTA SØRBY, *Housekeeper to* HÅKON WERLE
Dr. RELLING, *Physician*
MOLVIK, *a former Theological Student*
PETTERSEN, *Servant to* HÅKON WERLE
GRÅBERG, *Bookkeeper to* HÅKON WERLE
JENSEN, *hired Waiter*
A FLABBY GENTLEMAN ⎫
A SHORTSIGHTED GENTLEMAN ⎬ *Guests of*
Six OTHER GENTLEMEN ⎭ HÅKON WERLE

SCENE:

ACT I: THE HOUSE OF HÅKON WERLE

ACTS II-V: THE HOUSE OF HIALMAR EKDAL

A NORWEGIAN VILLAGE

TIME: THE PRESENT [1880's]

ACT ONE

Scene — At WERLE's *house. A richly and comfortably furnished study; bookcases and upholstered furniture; a writing table, with papers and documents, in the center of the room; lighted lamps with green shades, giving a subdued light. At the back open folding doors with curtains drawn back. Within is seen a large and handsome room, brilliantly lighted with lamps and branching candlesticks.*

In front, on the right (in the study), a small baize door leads into WERLE's *office. On the left, in front, a fireplace with a glowing coal fire and farther back a double door leading into the dining room.*

WERLE's *servant* PETTERSEN, *in livery and* JENSEN, *the hired waiter, in black, are putting the study in order. In the large room two or three other hired waiters are moving about arranging things and lighting more candles. From the dining room the hum of conversation and laughter of many voices are heard; a glass is tapped with a knife; silence follows, and a toast is proposed; shouts of "Bravo!" and then again a buzz of conversation.*

PETTERSEN (*lights a lamp on the chimney place and places a shade over it*): Hark to them, Jensen! Now the old man's on his legs holding a long palaver about Mrs. Sørby.

JENSEN (*pushing forward an armchair*): Is it true, what folks say, that they're — very good friends, eh?

PETTERSEN: Lord knows.

JENSEN: I've heard tell as he's been a lively customer in his day.

PETTERSEN: May be.

Note on the names: GREGERS WERLE: pronounced "Grayghers Verlë," the surname being slightly changed from a word meaning "wall-eyed," stressing the imagery of sight in the play; HIALMAR EKDAL: "Yalmar Aykdoll"; GINA: "Cheena"; GRABERG: "Growberg"; PETTERSEN: "Paytersen"; JENSEN: "Yensen."
[*The Wild Duck* was planned in part as early as 1882, actively written between mid-April and 13 June in 1884, revised between 15 June and 30 August and published 11 November, 1884. Ibsen wrote to Frederik Hegel on 2 September, 1884: "For the last four months I have worked on it every day, and I part with it not without a certain feeling of regret. Long daily contact with the characters in this play has endeared them to me, despite their manifold failings. And I hope that they may find good and kind friends among the vast reading public and more especially among the tribe of actors—for all the roles, without exception, are rewarding." The play was seen in leading Norwegian theatres as early as January 1885 and soon had great effect abroad, particularly in Russia.]

JENSEN: And he's giving this spread in honor of his son, they say.

PETTERSEN: Yes. His son came home yesterday.

JENSEN: This is the first time I ever heard as Mr. Werle had a son.

PETTERSEN: Oh yes, he has a son right enough. But he's a fixture, as you might say, up at the Höidal works. He's never once come to town all the years I've been in service here.

A WAITER (*in the doorway of the other room*): Pettersen, here's an old fellow wanting —

PETTERSEN (*mutters*): The devil — who's this now?

(OLD EKDAL *appears from the right, in the inner room. He is dressed in a threadbare overcoat with a high collar; he wears woolen mittens and carries in his hand a stick and a fur cap. Under his arm a brown paper parcel. Dirty red-brown wig and small gray mustache.*)

PETTERSEN (*goes toward him*): Good lord! — what do you want here?

EKDAL (*in the doorway*): Must get into the office, Pettersen.

PETTERSEN: The office was closed an hour ago, and —

EKDAL: So they told me at the front door. But Gråberg's in there still. Let me slip in this way, Pettersen; there's a good fellow. (*Points toward the baize door.*) It's not the first time I've come this way.

PETTERSEN: Well, you may pass. (*Opens the door.*) But mind you go out again the proper way, for we've got company.

EKDAL: I know, I know — h'm! Thanks, Pettersen, good old friend! Thanks! (*Mutters softly.*) Ass! (*He goes into the office; PETTERSEN shuts the door after him.*)

JENSEN: Is he one of the office people?

PETTERSEN: No, he's only an outside hand that does odd jobs of copying. But he's been a tiptopper in his day, has old Ekdal.

JENSEN: You can see he's been through a lot.

PETTERSEN: Yes; he was an army officer, you know.

JENSEN: You don't say so?

PETTERSEN: No mistake about it. But then he went into the timber trade or something of the sort. They say he once played Mr. Werle a very nasty trick. They were partners in the Höidal works at the time. Oh, I know old Ekdal well, I do. Many a nip of bitters and bottle of ale we two have drunk at Madam Eriksen's.

JENSEN: He don't look as if he'd much to stand treat with.

PETTERSEN: Why, bless you, Jensen, it's me that stands treat. I always think there's no harm in being a bit civil to folks that have seen better days.

JENSEN: Did he go bankrupt then?

PETTERSEN: Worse than that. He went to prison.

JENSEN: To prison!

PETTERSEN: Or perhaps it was the penitentiary. (*Listens*) Sh! They're leaving the table.

(*The dining room door is thrown open from within by a couple of waiters. MRS. SØRBY comes out conversing with two gentlemen. Gradually the whole company follows, amongst them WERLE. Last come HIALMAR EKDAL and GREGERS WERLE.*)

MRS. SØRBY (*in passing, to the servant*): Tell them to serve the coffee in the music room, Pettersen.

PETTERSEN: Very well, madam.

(*She goes with the two gentlemen into the inner room and thence out to the right. PETTERSEN and JENSEN go out the same way.*)

A FLABBY GENTLEMAN (*to a THIN-HAIRED GENTLEMAN*): Whew! What a dinner! It was no joke to do it justice.

THE THIN-HAIRED GENTLEMAN: Oh, with a little good will one can get through a lot in three hours.

THE FLABBY GENTLEMAN: Yes, but afterward, afterward, my dear Chamberlain!

A THIRD GENTLEMAN: I hear the coffee and maraschino are to be served in the music room.

THE FLABBY GENTLEMAN: Bravo! Then perhaps Mrs. Sørby will play us something.

THE THIN-HAIRED GENTLEMAN (*in a low voice*): I hope Mrs. Sørby mayn't play us a tune we don't like, one of these days!

THE FLABBY GENTLEMAN: Oh no, not she! Bertha will never turn against her old friends.

(*They laugh and pass into the inner room.*)

WERLE (*in a low voice, dejectedly*): I don't think anybody noticed it, Gregers.

GREGERS (*looks at him*): Noticed what?

WERLE: Did you not notice it either?

GREGERS: What do you mean?

WERLE: We were thirteen at table.

GREGERS: Indeed? Were there thirteen of us?

WERLE (*glances toward* HIALMAR EKDAL): Our usual party is twelve. (*to the others*) This way, gentlemen!

(WERLE *and the others, all except* HIALMAR *and* GREGERS, *go out by the back, to the right.*)

HIALMAR (*who has overheard the conversation*): You ought not to have invited me, Gregers.

GREGERS: What! Not ask my best and only friend to a party supposed to be in my honor?

HIALMAR: But I don't think your father likes it. You see, I am quite outside his circle.

GREGERS: So I hear. But I wanted to see you and have a talk with you, and I certainly shan't be staying long. Ah, we two old school-fellows have drifted apart from each other. It must be sixteen or seventeen years since we met.

HIALMAR: Is it so long?

GREGERS: It is indeed. Well, how goes it with you? You look well. You have put on flesh and grown almost stout.

HIALMAR: Well, "stout" is scarcely the word, but I daresay I look a little more of a man than I used to.

GREGERS: Yes, you do; your outer man is in first-rate condition.

HIALMAR (*in a tone of gloom*): Ah, but the inner man! That is a very different matter, I can tell you! Of course you know of the terrible catastrophe that has befallen me and mine since we last met.

GREGERS (*more softly*): How are things going with your father now?

HIALMAR: Don't let us talk of it, old fellow. Of course my poor unhappy father lives with me. He hasn't another soul in the world to care for him. But you can understand that this is a miserable subject for me. Tell me, rather, how you have been getting on up at the works.

GREGERS: I have had a delightfully lonely time of it — plenty of leisure to think and think about things. Come over here; we may as well make ourselves comfortable. (*He seats himself in an armchair by the fire and draws* HIALMAR *down into another alongside of it.*)

HIALMAR (*sentimentally*): After all, Gregers, I thank you for inviting me to your father's table; for I take it as a sign that you have got over your feeling against me.

GREGERS (*surprised*): How could you imagine I had any feeling against you?

HIALMAR: You had at first, you know.

GREGERS: How at first?

HIALMAR: After the great misfortune. It was natural enough that you should. Your father was within an ace of being drawn into that — well, that terrible business.

GREGERS: Why should that give me any feeling against you? Who can have put that into your head?

HIALMAR: I know it did, Gregers; your father told me so himself.

GREGERS (*starts*): My father! Oh, indeed. H'm. Was that why you never let me hear from you? — not a single word.

HIALMAR: Yes.

GREGERS: Not even when you made up your mind to become a photographer?

HIALMAR: Your father said I had better not write to you at all, about anything.

GREGERS (*looking straight before him*): Well, well, perhaps he was right. But tell me now, Hialmar: are you pretty well satisfied with your present position?

HIALMAR (*with a little sigh*): Oh yes, I am; I have really no cause to complain. At first, as you may guess, I felt it a little strange. It was such a totally new state of things for me. But of course my whole circumstances were totally changed. Father's utter, irretrievable ruin — the shame and disgrace of it, Gregers —

GREGERS (*affected*): Yes, yes; I understand.

HIALMAR: I couldn't think of remaining at college; there wasn't a shilling to spare; on the contrary, there were debts — mainly to your father, I believe —

GREGERS: H'm.

HIALMAR: In short, I thought it best to break, once for all, with my old surroundings and associations. It was your father that specially urged me to it, and since he interested himself so much in me —

GREGERS: My father did?

HIALMAR: Yes, you surely knew that, didn't you? Where do you suppose I found the money to learn photography and to furnish a studio and make a start? All that costs a pretty penny, I can tell you.

GREGERS: And my father provided the money?

HIALMAR: Yes, my dear fellow, didn't you know? I understood him to say he had written to you about it.

GREGERS: Not a word about his part in the business. He must have forgotten it. Our correspondence has always been purely a business one. So it was my father that —

HIALMAR: Yes, certainly. He didn't wish it to be generally known, but he it was. And of course it was he, too, that put me in a position to marry. Don't you — don't you know about that either?

GREGERS: No, I haven't heard a word of it. (*Shakes him by the arm.*) But, my dear Hialmar, I can't tell you what pleasure all this gives me — pleasure and self-reproach. I have perhaps done my father injustice after all — in some things. This proves that he has a heart. It shows a sort of compunction —

HIALMAR: Compunction?

GREGERS: Yes, yes — whatever you like to call it. Oh, I can't tell you how glad I am to hear this of Father. So you are a married man, Hialmar! That is further than I shall ever get. Well, I hope you are happy in your married life?

HIALMAR: Yes, thoroughly happy. She is as good and capable a wife as any man could wish for. And she is by no means without culture.

GREGERS (*rather surprised*): No, of course not.

HIALMAR: You see, life is itself an education. Her daily intercourse with me — And then we know one or two rather remarkable men who come a good deal about us. I assure you, you would hardly know Gina again.

GREGERS: Gina?

HIALMAR: Yes; had you forgotten that her name was Gina?

GREGERS: Whose name? I haven't the slightest idea —

HIALMAR: Don't you remember that she used to be in service here?

GREGERS (*looks at him*): Is it Gina Hansen?

HIALMAR: Yes, of course it is Gina Hansen.

GREGERS: — who kept house for us during the last year of my mother's illness?

HIALMAR: Yes, exactly. But, my dear friend, I'm quite sure your father told you I was married.

GREGERS (*who has risen*): Oh yes, he mentioned it, but not that — (*Walking about the room.*) Stay — perhaps he did — now that I think of it. My father always writes such short letters. (*Half seats himself on the arm of the chair.*) Now tell me, Hialmar — this is interesting — how did you come to know Gina — your wife?

HIALMAR: The simplest thing in the world. You know Gina did not stay here long; everything was so much upset at that time, owing to your mother's illness and so forth, that Gina was not equal to it all; so she gave notice and left. That was the year before your mother died — or it may have been the same year.

GREGERS: It was the same year. I was up at the works then. But afterward?

HIALMAR: Well, Gina lived at home with her mother, Madam Hansen, an excellent, hard-working woman who kept a little eating house. She had a room to let too, a very nice comfortable room.

GREGERS: And I suppose you were lucky enough to secure it?

HIALMAR: Yes; in fact, it was your father that recommended it to me. So it was there, you see, that I really came to know Gina.

GREGERS: And then you got engaged?

HIALMAR: Yes. It doesn't take young people long to fall in love — h'm.

GREGERS (*rises and moves about a little*): Tell me: was it after your engagement — was it then that my father — I mean was it then that you began to take up photography?

HIALMAR: Yes, precisely. I wanted to make a start and to set up house as soon as possible, and your father and I agreed that this photography business was the readiest way. Gina thought so too. Oh, and there was another thing in its favor, by the bye; it happened luckily, that Gina had learned to retouch.

GREGERS: That chimed in marvelously.

HIALMAR (*pleased, rises*): Yes, didn't it? Don't you think it was a marvelous piece of luck?

GREGERS: Oh, unquestionably. My father seems to have been almost a kind of providence to you.

HIALMAR (*with emotion*): He did not forsake his old friend's son in the hour of his need. For he has a heart, you see.

MRS. SØRBY (*enters arm in arm with* WERLE): Nonsense, my dear Mr. Werle; you musn't stop there any longer staring at all the lights. It's very bad for you.

WERLE (*lets go her arm and passes his hand over his eyes*): I daresay you are right.

(PETTERSEN *and* JENSEN *carry round refreshment trays.*)

MRS. SØRBY (*to the guests in the other room*): This way, if you please, gentlemen. Whoever wants a glass of punch must be so good as to come in here.

THE FLABBY GENTLEMAN (*comes up to* MRS. SØRBY): Surely it isn't possible that you have suspended our cherished right to smoke?

MRS. SØRBY: Yes. No smoking here, in Mr. Werle's sanctum, Chamberlain.

THE THIN-HAIRED GENTLEMAN: When did you enact these stringent amendments on the cigar law, Mrs. Sørby?

MRS. SØRBY: After the last dinner, Chamberlain, when certain persons permitted themselves to overstep the mark.

THE THIN-HAIRED GENTLEMAN: And may one never overstep the mark a little bit, Madame Bertha? Not the least little bit?

MRS. SØRBY: Not in any respect whatsoever, Mr. Balle.

(*Most of the guests have assembled in the study; servants hand round glasses of punch.*)

WERLE (*to* HIALMAR, *who is studying beside a table*): What are you studying so intently, Ekdal?

HIALMAR: Only an album, Mr. Werle.

THE THIN-HAIRED GENTLEMAN (*who is wandering about*): Ah, photographs! They are quite in your line of course.

THE FLABBY GENTLEMAN (*in an armchair*): Haven't you brought any of your own with you?

HIALMAR: No, I haven't.

THE FLABBY GENTLEMAN: You ought to have; it's very good for the digestion to sit and look at pictures.

THE THIN-HAIRED GENTLEMAN: And it contributes to the entertainment, you know.

THE SHORTSIGHTED GENTLEMAN: And all contributions are thankfully received.

MRS. SØRBY: The chamberlains think that when one is invited out to dinner one ought to exert oneself a little in return, Mr. Ekdal.

THE FLABBY GENTLEMAN: Where one dines so well, that duty becomes a pleasure.

THE THIN-HAIRED GENTLEMAN: And when it's a case of the struggle for existence, you know —

MRS. SØRBY: I quite agree with you!

(*They continue the conversation with laughter and joking.*)

GREGERS (*softly*): You must join in, Hialmar.

HIALMAR (*writhing*): What am I to talk about?

THE FLABBY GENTLEMAN: Don't you think, Mr. Werle, that Tokay may be considered one of the more wholesome sorts of wine?

WERLE (*by the fire*): I can answer for the Tokay you had today, at any rate; it's one of the very finest seasons. Of course you would notice that.

THE FLABBY GENTLEMAN: Yes, it had a remarkably delicate flavor.

HIALMAR (*shyly*): Is there any difference between the seasons?

THE FLABBY GENTLEMAN (*laughs*): Come! That's good!

WERLE (*smiles*): It really doesn't pay to set fine wine before you.

THE THIN-HAIRED GENTLEMAN: Tokay is like photographs, Mr. Ekdal; they both need sunshine. Am I not right?

HIALMAR: Yes, light is important, no doubt.

MRS. SØRBY: And it's exactly the same with the chamberlains — they, too, depend very much on sunshine, as the saying is.

THE THIN-HAIRED GENTLEMAN: Oh, fie! That's a very threadbare sarcasm!

THE SHORTSIGHTED GENTLEMAN: Mrs. Sørby is coming out —

THE FLABBY GENTLEMAN: — and at our expense too. (*Holds up his finger reprovingly.*) Oh, Madame Bertha, Madame Bertha!

MRS. SØRBY: Yes, and there's not the least doubt that the seasons differ greatly. The old vintages are the finest.

THE SHORTSIGHTED GENTLEMAN: Do you reckon me among the old vintages?

MRS. SØRBY: Oh, far from it.

THE THIN-HAIRED GENTLEMAN: There now! But me, dear Mrs. Sørby —

THE FLABBY GENTLEMAN: Yes, and me? What vintage should you say that we belong to?

MRS. SØRBY: Why, to the sweet vintages, gentlemen. (*She sips a glass of punch. The gentlemen laugh and flirt with her.*)

WERLE: Mrs. Sørby can always find a loophole — when she wants to. Fill your glasses, gentlemen! Pettersen, will you see to it? Gregers, suppose we have a glass together. (GREGERS *does not move.*) Won't you join us, Ekdal? I found no opportunity of drinking with you at table.

(GRÅBERG, *the bookkeeper, looks in at the baize door.*)

GRÅBERG: Excuse me, sir, but I can't get out.

WERLE: Have you been locked in again?

GRÅBERG: Yes, and Flakstad has carried off the keys.

WERLE: Well, you can pass out this way.

GRÅBERG: But there's someone else —

WERLE: All right; come through, both of you. Don't be afraid.

(GRÅBERG *and* OLD EKDAL *come out of the office.*)

WERLE (*involuntarily*): Ugh!

(*The laughter and talk among the guests cease. HIALMAR starts at the sight of his father, puts down his glass and turns toward the fireplace.*)

EKDAL (*does not look up but makes little bows to both sides as he passes, murmuring*): Beg pardon, come the wrong way. Door locked— door locked. Beg pardon. (*He and* GRÅBERG *go out by the back, to the right.*)

WERLE (*between his teeth*): That idiot Gråberg.

GREGERS (*open-mouthed and staring, to* HIALMAR): Why, surely that wasn't —

THE FLABBY GENTLEMAN: What's the matter? Who was it?

GREGERS: Oh, nobody; only the bookkeeper and someone with him.

THE SHORTSIGHTED GENTLEMAN (*to* HIALMAR): Did you know that man?

HIALMAR: I don't know — I didn't notice —

THE FLABBY GENTLEMAN: What the deuce has come over everyone? (*He joins another group who are talking softly.*)

MRS. SØRBY (*whispers to the* SERVANT): Give him something to take with him — something good, mind.

PETTERSEN (*nods*): I'll see to it. (*Goes out.*)

GREGERS (*softly and with emotion, to* HIALMAR): So that was really he!

HIALMAR: Yes.

GREGERS: And you could stand there and deny that you knew him.

HIALMAR (*whispers vehemently*): But how could I —

GREGERS: — acknowledge your own father?

HIALMAR (*with pain*): Oh, if you were in my place —

(*The conversation amongst the guests, which has been carried on in a low tone, now swells into constrained joviality.*)

THE THIN-HAIRED GENTLEMAN (*approaching* HIALMAR *and* GREGERS *in a friendly manner*): Ah! Reviving old college memories, eh? Don't you smoke, Mr. Ekdal? May I give you a light? Oh, by the bye, we musn't —

HIALMAR: No, thank you, I won't —

THE FLABBY GENTLEMAN: Haven't you a nice little poem you could recite us, Mr. Ekdal? You used to recite so charmingly.

HIALMAR: I am sorry, I can't remember anything.

THE FLABBY GENTLEMAN: Oh, that's a pity. Well, what shall we do, Balle?

(*Both gentlemen move and pass into the other room.*)

HIALMAR (*gloomily*): Gregers — I am going! When a man has felt the crushing hand of Fate, you see — Say good-by to your father for me.

GREGERS: Yes, yes. Are you going straight home?

HIALMAR: Yes. Why?

GREGERS: Oh, because I may perhaps look in on you later.

HIALMAR: No, you musn't do that. You must not come to my home. Mine is a melancholy abode, Gregers; especially after a splendid banquet like this. We can always arrange to meet somewhere in the town.

MRS. SØRBY (*who has quietly approached*): Are you going, Ekdal?

HIALMAR: Yes.

MRS. SØRBY: Remember me to Gina.

HIALMAR: Thanks.

MRS. SØRBY: And say I am coming up to see her one of these days.

HIALMAR: Yes, thank you. (*to* GREGERS) Stay here; I will slip out unobserved. (*He saunters away, then into the other room and so out to the right.*)

MRS. SØRBY (*softly to the* SERVANT, *who has come back*). Well, did you give the old man something?

PETTERSEN: Yes; I sent him off with a bottle of cognac.

MRS. SØRBY: Oh, you might have thought of something better than that.

PETTERSEN: Oh no, Mrs. Sørby; cognac is what he likes best in the world.

THE FLABBY GENTLEMAN (*in the doorway with a sheet of music in his hand*): Shall we play a duet, Mrs. Sørby?

MRS. SØRBY: Yes, suppose we do.

THE GUESTS: Bravo, bravo!

(*She goes with all the guests through the back room out to the right.* GREGERS *remains standing by the fire.* WERLE *is looking for something on the writing table and appears to wish that* GREGERS *would go; as* GREGERS *does not move* WERLE *goes toward the door.*)

GREGERS: Father, won't you stay a moment?

WERLE (*stops*): What is it?

GREGERS: I must have a word with you.

WERLE: Can it not wait until we are alone?

GREGERS: No, it cannot, for perhaps we shall never be alone together.

WERLE (*drawing nearer*): What do you mean by that?

(*During what follows the pianoforte is faintly heard from the distant music room.*)

GREGERS: How has that family been allowed to go so miserably to the wall?

WERLE: You mean the Ekdals, I suppose.

GREGERS: Yes, I mean the Ekdals. Lieutenant Ekdal was once so closely associated with you.

WERLE: Much too closely; I have felt that to my cost for many a year. It is thanks to him that I — yes *I* — have had a kind of slur cast upon my reputation.

GREGERS (*softly*): Are you sure that he alone was to blame?

WERLE: Who else do you suppose?

GREGERS: You and he acted together in that affair of the forests —

WERLE: But was it not Ekdal that drew the map of the tracts we had bought — that fraudulent map! It was he who felled all that timber illegally on government ground. In fact, the whole management was in his hands. I was quite in the dark as to what Lieutenant Ekdal was doing.

GREGERS: Lieutenant Ekdal himself seems to have been very much in the dark as to what he was doing.

WERLE: That may be. But the fact remains that he was found guilty and I acquitted.

GREGERS: Yes, I know that nothing was proved against you.

WERLE: Acquittal is acquittal. Why do you rake up these old miseries that turned my hair gray before its time? Is that the sort of thing you have been brooding over up there, all these years? I can assure you, Gregers, here in the town the whole story has been forgotten long ago — as far as *I* am concerned.

GREGERS: But that unhappy Ekdal family —

WERLE: What would you have me do for the people? When Ekdal came out of prison he was a broken-down being, past all help. There are people in the world who dive to the bottom the moment they get a couple of slugs in their body and never come to the surface again. You may take my word for it, Gregers, I have done all I could without positively laying myself open to all sorts of suspicion and gossip.

GREGERS: Suspicion? Oh, I see.

WERLE: I have given Ekdal copying to do for the office, and I pay him far, far more for it than his work is worth.

GREGERS (*without looking at him*): H'm; that I don't doubt.

WERLE: You laugh? Do you think I am not telling you the truth? Well, I certainly can't refer you to my books, for I never enter payments of that sort.

GREGERS (*smiles coldly*): No, there are certain payments it is best to keep no account of.

WERLE (*taken aback*): What do you mean by that?

GREGERS (*mustering up courage*): Have you entered what it cost you to have Hialmar Ekdal taught photography?

WERLE: I? How "entered" it?

GREGERS: I have learned that it was you who paid for his training. And I have learned, too, that it was you who enabled him to set up house so comfortably.

WERLE: Well, and yet you talk as though I had done nothing for the Ekdals! I can assure you these people have cost me enough in all conscience.

GREGERS: Have you entered any of these expenses in your books?

WERLE: Why do you ask?

GREGERS: Oh, I have my reasons. Now tell me: when you interested yourself so warmly in your old friend's son — it was just before his marriage, was it not?

WERLE: Why, deuce take it — after all these years how can I —

GREGERS: You wrote me a letter about that time — a business letter, of course — and in a postscript you mentioned — quite briefly — that Hialmar Ekdal had married a Miss Hansen.

WERLE: Yes, that was quite right. That was her name.

GREGERS: But you did not mention that this Miss Hansen was Gina Hansen — our former housekeeper.

WERLE (*with a forced laugh of derision*): No; to tell the truth, it didn't occur to me that you were so particularly interested in our former housekeeper.

GREGERS: No more I was. But (*lowers his voice*) there were others in this house who were particularly interested in her.

WERLE: What do you mean by that? (*Flaring up.*) You are not alluding to me, I hope?

GREGERS (*softly but firmly*): Yes, I am alluding to you.

WERLE: And you dare — You presume to — How can that ungrateful hound — that photographer fellow — how dare he go making such insinuations!

GREGERS: Hialmar has never breathed a word about this. I don't believe he has the faintest suspicion of such a thing.

WERLE: Then where have you got it from? Who can have put such notions in your head?

GREGERS: My poor unhappy mother told me, and that the very last time I saw her.

WERLE: Your mother! I might have known as much! You and she — you always held together. It was she who turned you against me from the first.

GREGERS: No, it was all that she had to suffer and submit to until she broke down and came to such a pitiful end.

WERLE: Oh, she had nothing to suffer or submit to; not more than most people, at all events. But there's no getting on with morbid, overstrained creatures — that I have learned to my cost. And you could go on nursing such a suspicion — burrowing into all sorts of slanders against your own father! I must say Gregers, I really think at your age you might find something more useful to do.

GREGERS: Yes, it is high time.

WERLE: Then perhaps your mind would be easier than it seems to be now. What can be your object in remaining up at the works year out and year in, drudging away like a common clerk and not drawing a farthing more than the ordinary monthly wage? It is downright folly.

GREGERS: Ah, if I were only sure of that.

WERLE: I understand you well enough. You want to be independent; you won't be beholden to me for anything. Well, now there happens to be an opportunity for you to become independent, your own master in everything.

GREGERS: Indeed? In what way?

WERLE: When I wrote you insisting on your coming to town at once — h'm —

GREGERS: Yes, what is it you really want of me? I have been waiting all day to know.

WERLE: I want to propose that you should enter the firm as partner.

GREGERS: I! Join your firm? As partner?

WERLE: Yes. It would not involve our being constantly together. You could take over the business here in town, and I should move up to the works.

GREGERS: You would?

WERLE: The fact is, I am not so fit for work as I once was. I am obliged to spare my eyes, Gregers; they have begun to trouble me.

GREGERS: They have always been weak.

WERLE: Not as they are now. And besides, circumstances might possibly make it desirable for me to live up there — for a time, at any rate.

GREGERS: That is certainly quite a new idea to me.

WERLE: Listen, Gregers, there are many things that stand between us; but we are father and son after all. We ought surely to be able to come to some sort of understanding with each other.

GREGERS: Outwardly, you mean, of course?

WERLE: Well, even that would be something. Think it over, Gregers. Don't you think it ought to be possible? Eh?

GREGERS (*looking at him coldly*): There is something behind all this.

WERLE: How so?

GREGERS: You want to make use of me in some way.

WERLE: In such a close relationship as ours the one can always be useful to the other.

GREGERS: Yes, so people say.

WERLE: I want very much to have you at home with me for a time. I am a lonely man, Gregers; I have always felt lonely all my life through, but most of all now that I am getting up in years. I feel the need of someone about me —

GREGERS: You have Mrs. Sørby.

WERLE: Yes, I have her, and she has become, I may say, almost indispensable to me. She is lively and even tempered; she brightens up the house; and that is a very great thing for me.

GREGERS: Well, then, you have everything as you wish it.

WERLE: Yes, but I am afraid it can't last. A woman so situated may easily find herself in a false position in the eyes of the world. For that matter, it does a man no good either.

GREGERS: Oh, when a man gives such dinners as you give he can risk a great deal.

WERLE: Yes, but how about the woman, Gregers? I fear she won't accept the situation much longer, and even if she did — even if, out of attachment to me, she were to take her chance of gossip and scandal and all that — do you think, Gregers, you with your strong sense of justice —

GREGERS (*interrupts him*): Tell me in one word: are you thinking of marrying her?

WERLE: Suppose I were thinking of it? What then?

GREGERS: That's what I say: What then?

WERLE: Should you be inflexibly opposed to it?

GREGERS: Not at all. Not by any means.

WERLE: I was not sure whether your devotion to your mother's memory —

GREGERS: I am not overstrained.

WERLE: Well, whatever you may or not be, at all events you have lifted a great weight from my mind. I am extremely pleased that I can reckon on your concurrence in this matter.

GREGERS (*looking intently at him*): Now I see the use you want to put me to.

WERLE: Use to put you to? What an expression!

GREGERS: Oh, don't let us be nice in our choice of words — not when we are alone together, at any rate. (*With a short laugh.*) Well, well. So this is what made it absolutely essential that I should come to town in person. For the sake of Mrs. Sørby we are to get up a pretense at family life in the house — a tableau of filial affection. That will be something new, indeed.

WERLE: How dare you speak in that tone!

GREGERS: Was there ever any family life here? Never since I can remember. But now, forsooth, your plans demand something of the sort. No doubt it will have an excellent effect when it is reported that the son has hastened home, on the wings of filial piety, to the gray-haired father's wedding feast. What will then remain of all the rumors as to the wrongs the poor dead mother had to submit to? Not a vestige. Her son annihilates them at one stroke.

WERLE: Gregers — I believe there is no one in the world you detest as you do me.

GREGERS (*softly*): I have seen you at too close quarters.

WERLE: You have seen me with your mother's eyes. (*Lowers his voice a little.*) But you should remember that her eyes were — clouded now and then.

GREGERS (*quivering*): I see what you are hinting at. But who was to blame for mother's unfortunate weakness? Why, you and all those — The last of them was this woman that you palmed off upon Hialmar Ekdal when you were — Ugh!

WERLE (*shrugs his shoulders*): Word for word as if it were your mother speaking!

GREGERS (*without heeding*): And there he is now, with his great, confiding childlike mind, compassed about with all this treachery — living under the same roof with such a creature and never dreaming that what he calls his home is built up on a lie! (*Comes a step nearer.*) When I look back upon your past I seem to see a battlefield with shattered lives on every hand.

WERLE: I begin to think that the chasm that divides us is too wide.

GREGERS (*bowing with self-command*): So I have observed, and therefore I take my hat and go.

WERLE: You are going? Out of the house?

GREGERS: Yes. For at last I see my mission in life.

WERLE: What mission?

GREGERS: You would only laugh if I told you.

WERLE: A lonely man doesn't laugh so easily. Gregers.

GREGERS (*pointing toward the background*): Look, Father — the chamberlains are playing blindman's buff with Mrs. Sørby. Good night and good-by. (*He goes out by the back to the right. Sound of laughter and merriment from the company, who are now visible in the outer room.*)

WERLE (*muttering contemptuously after GREGERS*): Ha! Poor wretch — and he says he is not overstrained!

ACT TWO

Scene — HIALMAR EKDAL's *studio, a good-sized room, evidently in the top story of the building. On the right a sloping roof of large panes of glass half covered by a blue curtain. In the right-hand corner, at the back, the entrance door; farther forward, on the same side, a door leading to the sitting room. Two doors on the opposite side and between them an iron stove. At the back a wide double sliding door. The studio is plainly but comfortably fitted up and furnished. Between the door on the right, stand-*

ing out a little from the wall, a sofa with a table and some chairs; on the table a lighted lamp with a shade; beside the stove an old armchair. Photographic instruments and apparatus of different kinds lying about the room. Against the back wall, to the left of the double door, stands a bookcase containing a few books, boxes and bottles of chemicals, instruments, tools and other objects. Photographs and small articles, such as camel's-hair pencils, paper and so forth, lie on the table.

GINA EKDAL sits on a chair by the table, sewing. HEDVIG is sitting on the sofa, with her hands shading her eyes and her thumbs in her ears, reading a book.

GINA (glances once or twice at HEDVIG, as if with secret anxiety, then says): Hedvig!

(HEDVIG does not hear.)

GINA (repeats more loudly): Hedvig!

HEDVIG (takes away her hands and looks up): Yes, Mother?

GINA: Hedvig dear, you musn't sit reading any longer now.

HEDVIG: Oh, Mother, mayn't I read a little more? Just a little bit?

GINA: No, no, you must put away your book now. Father doesn't like it; he never reads himself in the evening.

HEDVIG (shuts the book): No, Father doesn't care much about reading.

GINA (puts aside her sewing and takes up a lead pencil and a little account book from the table): Can you remember how much we paid for the butter today?

HEDVIG: It was one crown sixty-five.

GINA: That's right (Puts it down.) It's terrible what a lot of butter we get through in this house. Then there was the smoked sausage and the cheese — let me see (writes) — and the ham (adds up). Yes, that makes just —

HEDVIG: And then the beer.

GINA: Yes, to be sure. (Writes.) How it do

mount up! But we can't manage with no less.

HEDVIG: And then you and I didn't need anything hot for dinner, as Father was out.

GINA: No, that was so much to the good. And then I took eight crowns fifty for the photographs.

HEDVIG: Really! So much as that?

GINA: Exactly eight crowns fifty.

(Silence. GINA takes up her sewing again; HEDVIG takes paper and pencil and begins to draw, shading her eyes with her left hand.)

HEDVIG: Isn't it jolly to think that Father is at Mr. Werle's big dinner party?

GINA: You know he's not really Mr. Werle's guest. It was the son invited him. (After a pause.) We have nothing to do with that Mr. Werle.

HEDVIG: I'm longing for Father to come home. He promised to ask Mrs. Sørby for something nice for me.

GINA: Yes, there's plenty of good things going in that house, I can tell you.

HEDVIG (goes on drawing): And I believe I'm a little hungry too.

(OLD EKDAL, with the paper parcel under his arm and another parcel in his coat pocket, comes in by the entrance door.)

GINA: How late you are today, Grandfather!

EKDAL: They had locked the office door. Had to wait in Gråberg's room. And then they let me through — h'm.

HEDVIG: Did you get some more copying to do, Grandfather?

EKDAL: This whole packet. Just look.

GINA: That's capital.

HEDVIG: And you have another parcel in your pocket.

EKDAL: Eh? Oh, never mind, that's nothing. (Puts his stick away in a corner.) This work will keep me going a long time, Gina. (Opens one of the sliding doors in the back wall a little.) Hush! (*Peeps into the room for a moment, then pushes the door carefully to again.*) Hee-hee! They're fast asleep, all the lot of them. And she's gone into the basket herself. Hee-hee!

HEDVIG: Are you sure she isn't cold in the basket, Grandfather?

EKDAL: Not a bit of it! Cold? With all that straw? (*Goes toward the farther door on the left.*) There are matches in here, I suppose.

GINA: The matches is on the drawers.

(EKDAL *goes into his room.*)

HEDVIG: It's nice that Grandfather has got all that copying.

GINA: Yes, poor old Father; it means a bit of pocket money for him.

HEDVIG: And he won't be able to sit the whole forenoon down at that horrid Madam Eriksen's.

GINA: No more he won't. (*Short silence.*)

HEDVIG: Do you suppose they are still at the dinner table?

GINA: Goodness knows; as like as not.

HEDVIG: Think of all the delicious things Father is having to eat! I'm certain he'll be in splendid spirits when he comes. Don't you think so, Mother?

GINA: Yes; and if only we could tell him that we'd got the room let —

HEDVIG: But we don't need that this evening.

GINA: Oh, we'd be none the worst of it, I can tell you. It's no use to us as it is.

HEDVIG: I mean we don't need it this evening, for Father will be in good humor at any rate. It is best to keep the letting of the room for another time.

GINA (*looks across at her*): You like having some good news to tell Father when he comes home in the evening?

HEDVIG: Yes, for then things are pleasanter somehow.

GINA (*thinking to herself*): Yes, yes, there's something in that.

(OLD EKDAL *comes in again and is going out by the foremost door to the left.*)

GINA (*half turning in her chair*): Do you want something in the kitchen, Grandfather?

EKDAL: Yes, yes, I do. Don't you trouble. (*Goes out*).

GINA: He's not poking away at the fire, is he? (*Waits a moment.*) Hedvig, go and see what he's about.

(EKDAL *comes in again with a small jug of steaming hot water.*)

HEDVIG: Have you been getting some hot water, Grandfather?

EKDAL: Yes, hot water. Want it for something. Want to write, and the ink has got as thick as porridge — h'm.

GINA: But you'd best have your supper first, Grandfather. It's laid in there.

EKDAL: Can't be bothered with supper, Gina. Very busy, I tell you. No one's to come to my room. No one — h'm. (*He goes into his room; GINA and HEDVIG look at each other.*)

GINA (*softly*): Can you imagine where he's got money from.

HEDVIG: From Gråberg, perhaps.

GINA: Not a bit of it. Gråberg always sends the money to me.

HEDVIG: Then he must have got a bottle on credit somewhere.

GINA: Poor Grandfather, who'd give him credit?

(HIALMAR EKDAL, *in an overcoat and gray felt hat, comes in from the right.*)

GINA (*throws down her sewing and rises*): Why, Ekdal, is that you already?

HEDVIG (*at the same time jumping up*): Fancy your coming so soon, Father!

HIALMAR (*taking off his hat*): Yes, most of the people were coming away.

HEDVIG: So early?

HIALMAR: Yes, it was a dinner party, you know. (*Takes off his overcoat.*)

GINA: Let me help you.

HEDVIG: Me too.

(*They draw off his coat; GINA hangs it up on the back wall.*)

HEDVIG: Were there many people there, Father?

HIALMAR: Oh no, not many. We had about twelve or fourteen at table.

GINA: And you had some talk with them all?

HIALMAR: Oh yes, a little; but Gregers took me up most of the time.

GINA: Is Gregers as ugly as ever?

HIALMAR: Well, he's not very much to look at. Hasn't the old man come home?

HEDVIG: Yes, Grandfather is in his room, writing.

HIALMAR: Did he say anything?

GINA: No, what should he say?

HIALMAR: Did he say anything about — I heard something about his having been with Gråberg. I'll go in and see him for a moment.

GINA: No no, better not.

HIALMAR: Why not? Did he say he didn't want me to go in?

GINA: I don't think he wants to see anybody this evening.

HEDVIG (*making signs*): H'm — h'm!

GINA (*not noticing*): He has been in to fetch hot water —

HIALMAR: Aha! Then he's —

GINA: Yes, I suppose so.

HIALMAR: Oh God! My poor old white-haired father! Well, well, there let him sit and get all the enjoyment he can.

(OLD EKDAL, *in an indoor coat and with a lighted pipe, comes from his room.*)

EKDAL: Got home? Thought it was you I heard talking.

HIALMAR: Yes, I have just come.

EKDAL: You didn't see me, did you?

HIALMAR: No, but they told me you had passed through — so I thought I would follow you.

EKDAL: H'm, good of you, Hialmar. Who were they, all those fellows?

HIALMAR: Oh, all sorts of people. There was Chamberlain Flor and Chamberlain Balle and Chamberlain Kaspersen and Chamberlain — this, that and the other — I don't know who all.

EKDAL (*nodding*): Hear that, Gina! Chamberlains every one of them!

GINA: Yes, I hear as they're terrible genteel in that house nowadays.

HEDVIG: Did the chamberlains sing, Father? Or did they read aloud?

HIALMAR: No, they only talked nonsense. They wanted me to recite something for them, but I knew better than that.

EKDAL: You weren't to be persuaded, eh?

GINA: Oh, you might have done it.

HIALMAR: No; one mustn't be at everybody's beck and call. (*Walks about the room.*) That's not my way, at any rate.

EKDAL: No, no; Hialmar's not to be had for the asking, he isn't.

HIALMAR: I don't see why I should bother myself to entertain people on the rare occasions when I go into society. Let the others exert themselves. These fellows go from one great dinner table to the next and gorge and guzzle day out and day in. It's for them to bestir themselves and do something in return for all the good feeding they get.

GINA: But you didn't say that?

HIALMAR (*humming*): Ho-ho-ho; faith, I gave them a bit of my mind.

EKDAL: Not the chamberlains?

HIALMAR: Oh, why not? (*Lightly.*) After that we had a little discussion about Tokay.

EKDAL: Tokay! There's a fine wine for you!

HIALMAR (*comes to a standstill*): It may be a fine wine. But of course you know the vintages differ; it all depends on how much sunshine the grapes have had.

GINA: Why, you know everything, Ekdal.

EKDAL: And did they dispute that?

HIALMAR: They tried to, but they were requested to observe it was just the same with chamberlains — that with them, too, different batches were of different qualities.

GINA: What things you do think of!

EKDAL: Hee-hee! So they got that in their pipes too?

HIALMAR: Right in their teeth.

EKDAL: Do you hear that, Gina? He said it right in the very teeth of all the chamberlains.

GINA: Fancy! Right in their teeth!

HIALMAR: Yes, but I don't want it talked about. One doesn't speak of such things. The whole affair passed off quite amicably, of course. They were nice genial fellows; I didn't want to wound them — not I!

EKDAL: Right in their teeth, though!

HEDVIG (*caressingly*): How nice it is to see you in a dress coat! It suits you so well, Father.

HIALMAR: Yes, don't you think so? And this one really fits to perfection. It fits almost as if it had been made for me — a little tight in the armholes, perhaps; help me, Hedvig (*takes off the coat*). I think I'll put on my jacket. Where is my jacket, Gina?

GINA: Here it is. (*Brings the jacket and helps him.*)

HIALMAR: That's it! Don't forget to send the coat back to Molvik first thing tomorrow morning.

GINA (*laying it away*): I'll be sure and see to it.

HIALMAR (*stretching himself*): After all, there's a more homely feeling about this. A free-and-easy indoor costume suits my whole personality better. Don't you think so, Hedvig?

HEDVIG: Yes, Father.

HIALMAR: When I loosen my necktie into a pair of flowing ends — like this — eh?

HEDVIG: Yes, and that goes so well with your mustache and the sweep of your curls.

HIALMAR: I should not call them curls exactly; I should rather say locks.

HEDVIG: Yes, they are too big for curls.

HIALMAR: Locks describes them better.

HEDVIG (*after a pause, twitching his jacket*): Father!

HIALMAR: Well, what is it?

HEDVIG: Oh, you know very well.

HIALMAR: No, really I don't.

HEDVIG (*half laughing, half whispering*): Oh yes, Father; now don't tease me any longer!

HIALMAR: Why, what do you mean?

HEDVIG (*shaking him*): Oh, what nonsense! Come, where are they, Father? All the good things you promised me, you know?

HIALMAR: Oh — if I haven't forgotten all about them!

HEDVIG: Now you're only teasing me, Father! Oh, it's too bad of you! Where have you put them?

HIALMAR: No, I positively forgot to get anything. But wait a little! I have something else for you, Hedvig. (*Goes and searches in the pockets of the coat.*)

HEDVIG (*skipping and clapping her hands*): Oh, Mother, Mother!

HIALMAR (*with a paper*): Look, here it is.

GINA: There, you see; if you only give him time —

HEDVIG: That? Why, that's only a paper.

HIALMAR: That is the bill of fare, my dear; the whole bill of fare. Here you see "Menu" — that means bill of fare.

HEDVIG: Haven't you anything else?

HIALMAR: I forgot the other things, I tell you. But you may take my word for it, these dainties are very unsatisfying. Sit down at the table and read the bill of fare, and then I'll describe to you how the dishes taste. Here you are, Hedvig.

HEDVIG (*gulping down her tears*): Thank you. (*She seats herself but does not read; GINA makes signs to her; HIALMAR notices it.*)

HIALMAR (*pacing up and down the room*): It's monstrous what absurd things the father of a family is expected to think of, and if he forgets the smallest trifle he is treated to sour faces at once. Well, well, one gets used to that too. (*Stops near the stove by the old man's chair.*) Have you peeped in there this evening, Father?

EKDAL: Yes, to be sure I have. She's gone into the basket.

HIALMAR: Ah, she has gone into the basket. Then she's beginning to get used to it.

EKDAL: Yes, just as I prophesied. But you know there are still a few little things —

HIALMAR: A few improvements, yes.

EKDAL: They've got to be made, you know.

HIALMAR: Yes, let us have a talk about the improvements, Father. Come, let us sit on the sofa.

EKDAL: All right. H'm — think I'll just fill my pipe first. Must clean it out too. H'm. (*He goes into his room.*)

GINA (*smiling to HIALMAR*): His pipe!

HIALMAR: Oh yes, yes, Gina; let him alone — the poor shipwrecked old man. Yes, these improvements — we had better get them out of hand tomorrow.

GINA: You'll hardly have time tomorrow, Ekdal.

HEDVIG (*interposing*): Oh yes, he will, Mother!

GINA: — for remember them prints that has to be retouched; they've sent for them time after time.

HIALMAR: There now! Those prints again! I shall get them finished all right. Have any orders come in?

GINA: No, worse luck; tomorrow I have nothing to do but those two sittings, you know.

HIALMAR: Nothing else? Oh no, if people won't set about things with a will —

GINA: But what more can I do? Don't I advertise in the papers as much as we can afford?

HIALMAR: Yes, the papers; you see how much good they do. And I suppose no one has been to look at the room either?

GINA: No, not yet.

HIALMAR: That was only to be expected. If people won't keep their eyes open — Nothing can be done without a real effort, Gina!

HEDVIG (*going toward him*): Shall I fetch you the flute, Father?

HIALMAR: No; no flute for me; *I* want no pleasures in this world. (*Pacing about.*) Yes indeed, I will work tomorrow; you shall see if I don't. You may be sure I shall work as long as my strength holds out.

GINA: But, my dear good Ekdal, I didn't mean it in that way.

HEDVIG: Father, mayn't I bring in a bottle of beer?

HIALMAR: No, certainly not. I require nothing, nothing. (*Comes to a standstill.*) Beer? Was it beer you were talking about?

HEDVIG (*cheerfully*): Yes, Father; beautiful fresh beer.

HIALMAR: Well — since you insist upon it, you may bring in a bottle.

GINA: Yes, do; and we'll be nice and cosy.

(HEDVIG *runs toward the kitchen door.*)

HIALMAR (*by the stove, stops her, looks at her, puts his arm round her neck and presses her to him*): Hedvig, Hedvig!

HEDVIG (*with tears of joy*): My dear, kind father!

HIALMAR: No, don't call me that. Here have I

been feasting at the rich man's table — battening at the groaning board! And I couldn't even —

GINA (*sitting at the table*): Oh, nonsense, nonsense, Ekdal.

HIALMAR: It's not nonsense! And yet you mustn't be too hard upon me. You know that I love you for all that.

HEDVIG (*throwing her arms round him*): And we love you, oh, so dearly, Father!

HIALMAR: And if I am unreasonable once in a while — why, then — you must remember that I am a man beset by a host of cares. There, there! (*Dries his eyes.*) No beer at such a moment as this. Give me the flute.

(HEDVIG *runs to the bookcase and fetches it.*)

HIALMAR: Thanks! That's right. With my flute in my hand and you two at my side — ah!

(HEDVIG *seats herself at the table near* GINA; HIALMAR *paces backward and forward, pipes up vigorously and plays a Bohemian peasant dance, but in a slow plaintive tempo and with sentimental expression.*)

HIALMAR (*breaking off the melody, holds out his left hand to* GINA *and says with emotion*): Our roof may be poor and humble, Gina, but it is home. And with all my heart I say: here dwells my happiness. (*He begins to play again; almost immediately after a knocking is heard at the entrance door.*)

GINA (*rising*): Hush, Ekdal — I think there's someone at the door.

HIALMAR (*laying the flute on the bookcase*): There! Again!

(GINA *goes and opens the door.*)

GREGERS (*in the passage*): Excuse me —

GINA (*starting back slightly*): Oh!

GREGERS: — does not Mr. Ekdal, the photographer, live here?

GINA: Yes, he does.

HIALMAR (*going toward the door*): Gregers! You here after all? Well, come in then.

GREGERS (*coming in*): I told you I would come and look you up.

HIALMAR: But this evening — Have you left the party?

GREGERS: I have left both the party and my father's house. Good evening, Mrs. Ekdal. I don't know whether you recognize me?

GINA: Oh yes, it's not difficult to know young Mr. Werle again.

GREGERS: No, I am like my mother, and no doubt you remember her.

HIALMAR: Left your father's house, did you say?

GREGERS: Yes, I have gone to a hotel.

HIALMAR: Indeed. Well, since you're here, take off your coat and sit down.

GREGERS: Thanks. (*He takes off his overcoat. He is now dressed in a plain gray suit of a countrified cut.*)

HIALMAR: Here on the sofa. Make yourself comfortable.

GREGERS (*looking around him*): So these are your quarters, Hialmar — this is your home.

HIALMAR: This is the studio, as you see.

GINA: But it's the largest of our rooms, so we generally sit here.

HIALMAR: We used to live in a better place, but this flat has one great advantage: there are such capital outer rooms —

GINA: And we have a room on the other side of the passage that we can let.

GREGERS (*to* HIALMAR): Ah — so you have lodgers too?

HIALMAR: No, not yet. They're not so easy to find, you see; you have to keep your eyes open. (*to* HEDVIG) How about that beer, eh?

(HEDVIG *nods and goes out into the kitchen.*)

GREGERS: So that is your daughter?

HIALMAR: Yes, that is Hedvig.

GREGERS: And she is your only child?

HIALMAR: Yes, the only one. She is the joy of our lives, and (*lowering his voice*) at the same time our deepest sorrow, Gregers.

GREGERS: What do you mean?

HIALMAR: She is in serious danger of losing her eyesight.

GREGERS: Becoming blind?

HIALMAR: Yes. Only the first symptoms have appeared as yet, and she may not feel it much for some time. But the doctor has warned us. It is coming inexorably.

GREGERS: What a terrible misfortune! How do you account for it?

HIALMAR (*sighs*): Hereditary, no doubt.

GREGERS (*starting*): Hereditary?

GINA: Ekdal's mother had weak eyes.

HIALMAR: Yes, so my father says; I can't remember her.

GREGERS: Poor child! And how does she take it?

HIALMAR: Oh, you can imagine we haven't the heart to tell her of it. She dreams of no danger. Gay and careless and chirping like a little bird, she flutters onward into a life of endless night. (*Overcome.*) Oh, it is cruelly hard on me, Gregers.

(HEDVIG *brings a tray with beer and glasses which she sets upon the table.*)

HIALMAR (*stroking her hair*): Thanks, thanks, Hedvig.

(HEDVIG *puts her arm around his neck and whispers in his ear.*)

HIALMAR: No, no bread and butter just now. (*Looks up.*) But perhaps you would like some, Gregers?

GREGERS (*with a gesture of refusal*): No, no thank you.

HIALMAR (*still melancholy*): Well, you can bring in a little all the same. If you have a crust, that is all I want. And plenty of butter on it, mind.

(HEDVIG *nods gaily and goes out into the kitchen again.*)

GREGERS (*who has been following her with his eyes*): She seems quite strong and healthy otherwise.

GINA: Yes. In other ways there's nothing amiss with her, thank goodness.

GREGERS: She promises to be very like you, Mrs. Ekdal. How old is she now?

GINA: Hedvig is close on fourteen; her birthday is the day after tomorrow.

GREGERS: She is pretty tall for her age then.

GINA: Yes, she's shot up wonderful this last year.

GREGERS: It makes one realize one's own age to see these young people growing up. How long is it now since you were married?

GINA: We've been married — let me see — just on fifteen years.

GREGERS: Is it so long as that?

GINA (*becomes attentive, looks at him*): Yes, it is indeed.

HIALMAR: Yes, so it is. Fifteen years, all but a few months. (*Changing his tone.*) They must have been long years for you up at the works, Gregers.

GREGERS: They seemed long while I was living them; now they are over, I hardly know how the time has gone.

(OLD EKDAL *comes from his room without his pipe but with his old-fashioned uniform cap on his head; his gait is somewhat unsteady.*)

EKDAL: Come now, Hialmar, let's sit down and have a good talk about this — h'm — what was it again?

HIALMAR (*going toward him*): Father, we have a visitor here — Gregers Werle — I don't know if you remember him.

EKDAL (*looking at* GREGERS, *who has risen*): Werle? Is that the son? What does he want with me?

HIALMAR: Nothing! It's me he has come to see.

EKDAL: Oh! Then there's nothing wrong?

HIALMAR: No, no, of course not.

EKDAL (*with a large gesture*): Not that I'm afraid, you know; but —

GREGERS (*goes over to him*): I bring you a greeting from your old hunting grounds, Lieutenant Ekdal.

EKDAL: Hunting grounds?

GREGERS: Yes, up in Höidal, about the works, you know.

EKDAL: Oh, up there. Yes, I knew all those places well in the old days.

GREGERS: You were a great sportsman then.

EKDAL: So I was, I don't deny it. You're looking at my uniform cap. I don't ask anybody's leave to wear it in the house. So long as I don't go out in the streets with it —

(HEDVIG *brings a plate of bread and butter which she puts upon the table.*)

HIALMAR: Sit down, Father, and have a glass of beer. Help yourself, Gregers.

(EKDAL *mutters and stumbles over to the sofa. GREGERS seats himself on the chair nearest to him, HIALMAR on the other side of GREGERS. GINA sits a little way from the table, sewing; HEDVIG stands beside her father.*)

GREGERS: Can you remember, Lieutenant Ekdal, how Hialmar and I used to come up and visit you in the summer and at Christmas?

EKDAL: Did you? No, no, no; I don't remember it. But, sure enough, I've been a tidy bit of sportsman in my day. I've shot bears too. I've shot nine of 'em no less.

GREGERS (*looking sympathetically at him*): And now you never get any shooting?

EKDAL: Can't say that, sir. Get a shot now and then, perhaps. Of course not in the old way. For the woods, you see — the woods, the woods — (*Drinks.*) Are the woods fine up there now?

GREGERS: Not so fine as in your time. They have been thinned out a good deal.

EKDAL: Thinned? (*More softly and as if afraid.*) It's dangerous work, that. Bad things come of it. The woods revenge themselves.

HIALMAR (*filling up his glass*): Come — a little more, Father.

GREGERS: How can a man like you — such a man for the open air — live in the midst of a stuffy town, boxed within four walls?

EKDAL (*laughs quietly and glances at* HIALMAR): Oh, it's not so bad here. Not at all so bad.

GREGERS: But don't you miss all the things that used to be a part of your very being — the cool sweeping breezes, the free life in the woods and on the uplands, among beasts and birds?

EKDAL (*smiling*): Hialmar, shall we let him see it?

HIALMAR (*hastily and a little embarrassed*): Oh no, no, Father; not this evening.

GREGERS: What does he want to show me?

HIALMAR: Oh, it's only something — you can see it another time.

GREGERS (*continues, to the old man*): You see, I have been thinking, Lieutenant Ekdal, that you should come up with me to the works; I am sure to be going back soon. No doubt you could get some copying there too. And here you have nothing on earth to interest you — nothing to liven you up.

EKDAL (*stares in astonishment at him*): Have I nothing on earth to —

GREGERS: Of course you have Hialmar, but then he has his own family. And a man like you, who has always had such a passion for what is free and wild —

EKDAL (*thumps the table*): Hialmar, he shall see it!

HIALMAR: Oh, do you think it's worth while, Father? It's all dark.

EKDAL: Nonsense; it's moonlight. (*Rises.*) He shall see it, I tell you. Let me pass! Come on and help me, Hialmar.

HEDVIG: Oh yes, do, Father!

HIALMAR (*rising*): Very well then.

GREGERS (*to* GINA): What is it?

GINA: Oh, nothing so wonderful after all.

(EKDAL *and* HIALMAR *have gone to the back wall and are each pushing back a side of the sliding door;* HEDVIG *helps the old man;* GREGERS *remains standing by the sofa;* GINA *sits still and sews. Through the open doorway a large, deep irregular garret is seen with odd nooks and corners, a couple of stovepipes running through it from rooms below. There are skylights through which clear moonbeams shine in on some parts of the great room; others lie in deep shadow.*)

EKDAL (*to* GREGERS): You may come close up if you like.

GREGERS (*going over to them*): Why, what is it?

EKDAL: Look for yourself, h'm.

HIALMAR (*somewhat embarrassed*): This belongs to Father, you understand.

GREGERS (*at the door, looks into the garret*): Why, you keep poultry, Lieutenant Ekdal.

EKDAL: Should think we did keep poultry. They've gone to roost now. But you should see our fowls by daylight, sir!

HEDVIG: And there's a —

EKDAL: Sh — sh! Don't say anything about it yet.

GREGERS: And you have pigeons too, I see.

EKDAL: Oh yes, haven't we just got pigeons! They have their nest boxes up there under the rooftree; for pigeons like to roost high, you see.

HIALMAR: They aren't all common pigeons.

EKDAL: Common! Should think not, indeed! We have tumblers and a pair of pouters too. But come here! Can you see that hutch down there by the wall?

GREGERS: Yes; what do you use it for?

EKDAL: That's where the rabbits sleep, sir.

GREGERS: Dear me, so you have rabbits too?

EKDAL: Yes, you may take my word for it, we have rabbits! He wants to know if we have rabbits, Hialmar! H'm! But now comes the thing, let me tell you! Here we have it! Move away, Hedvig. Stand here; that's right — and now look down there. Don't you see a basket with straw in it?

GREGERS: Yes. And I can see a fowl lying in the basket.

EKDAL: H'm — "a fowl" —

GREGERS: Isn't it a duck?

EKDAL (*hurt*): Why, of course it's a duck.

HIALMAR: But what kind of a duck, do you think?

HEDVIG: It's not just a common duck.

EKDAL: Sh!

GREGERS: And it's not a Muscovy duck either.

EKDAL: No, Mr. — Werle; it's not a Muscovy duck, for it's a wild duck!

GREGERS: Is it really? A wild duck?

EKDAL: Yes, that's what it is. That "fowl" — as you call it — is the wild duck. It's our wild duck, sir.

HEDVIG: My wild duck. It belongs to me.

GREGERS: And can it live up here in the garret? Does it thrive?

EKDAL: Of course it has a trough of water to splash about in, you know.

HIALMAR: Fresh water every other day.

GINA (*turning toward* HIALMAR): But, my dear Ekdal, it's getting icy cold here.

EKDAL: H'm, we had better shut up then. It's as well not to disturb their night's rest too. Close up, Hedvig.

(HIALMAR *and* HEDVIG *push the garret doors together.*)

EKDAL: Another time you shall see her properly. (*Seats himself in the armchair by the stove.*) Oh, they're curious things, these wild ducks, I can tell you.

GREGERS: How did you manage to catch it, Lieutenant Ekdal?

EKDAL: *I* didn't catch it. There's a certain man in this town whom we have to thank for it.

GREGERS (*starts slightly*): That man was not my father, was he?

EKDAL: You've hit it. Your father and no one else. H'm.

HIALMAR: Strange that you should guess that, Gregers.

GREGERS: You were telling me that you owed so many things to my father, and so I thought perhaps —

GINA: But we didn't get the duck from Mr. Werle himself.

EKDAL: It's Håkon Werle we have to thank for her, all the same, Gina. (*to* GREGERS) He was shooting from a boat, you see, and he brought her down. But your father's sight is not very good now. H'm; she was only wounded.

GREGERS: Ah! She got a couple of slugs in her body, I suppose?

HIALMAR: Yes, two or three.

HEDVIG: She was hit under the wing so that she couldn't fly.

GREGERS: And I suppose she dived to the bottom, eh?

EKDAL (*sleepily, in a thick voice*): Of course. Always do that, wild ducks do. They shoot to the bottom as deep as they can get, sir — and bite themselves fast in the tangle and seaweed — and all the devil's own mess that grows down there. And they never come up again.

GREGERS: But your wild duck came up again, Lieutenant Ekdal.

EKDAL: He had such an amazingly clever dog, your father had. And that dog — he dived in after the duck and fetched her up again.

GREGERS (*who has turned to* HIALMAR): And then she was sent to you here?

HIALMAR: Not at once; at first your father took her home. But she wouldn't thrive there, so Pettersen was told to put an end to her.

EKDAL (*half asleep*): H'm — yes — Pettersen — that ass —

HIALMAR (*speaking more softly*): That was how we got her, you see; for Father knows Pettersen a little, and when he heard about the wild duck he got him to hand her over to us.

GREGERS: And now she thrives as well as possible in the garret there?

HIALMAR: Yes, wonderfully well. She has got fat. You see, she has lived in there so long now that she has forgotten her natural wild life, and it all depends on that.

GREGERS: You are right there, Hialmar. Be sure you never let her get a glimpse of the sky and the sea. But I mustn't stay any longer; I think your father is asleep.

HIALMAR: Oh, as for that —

GREGERS: But by the bye — you said you had a room to let — a spare room?

HIALMAR: Yes; what then? Do you know of anybody?

GREGERS: Can *I* have that room?

HIALMAR: You?

GINA: Oh no, Mr. Werle, you —

GREGERS: May I have the room? If so, I'll take possession first thing tomorrow morning.

HIALMAR: Yes, with the greatest pleasure.

GINA: But, Mr. Werle, I'm sure it's not at all the sort of room for you.

HIALMAR: Why, Gina! how can you say that?

GINA: Why, because the room's neither large enough nor light enough, and —

GREGERS: That really doesn't matter, Mrs. Ekdal.

HIALMAR: I call it quite a nice room, and not at all badly furnished either.

GINA: But remember the pair of them underneath.

GREGERS: What pair?

GINA: Well, there's one as has been a tutor.

HIALMAR: That's Molvik — Mr. Molvik, B.A.

GINA: And then there's a doctor by the name of Relling.

GREGERS: Relling? I know him a little; he practiced for a time up in Höidal.

GINA: They're a regular rackety pair, they are. As often as not they're out on the loose in the evenings, and then they come home at all hours, and they are not always just —

GREGERS: One soon gets used to that sort of thing. I daresay I shall be like the wild duck.

GINA: H'm; I think you ought to sleep upon it first, anyway.

GREGERS: You seem very unwilling to have me in the house, Mrs. Ekdal.

GINA: Oh no! What makes you think that?

HIALMAR: Well, you really behave strangely about it, Gina. (to GREGERS) Then I suppose you intend to remain in town for the present?

GREGERS (putting on his overcoat): Yes, now I intend to remain here.

HIALMAR: And yet not at your father's? What do you propose to do then?

GREGERS: Ah, if I only knew that, Hialmar, I shouldn't be so badly off! But when one has the misfortune to be called Gregers! — "Gregers" — and then "Werle" after it; did you ever hear of anything so hideous?

HIALMAR: Oh, I don't think so at all.

GREGERS: Ugh! Bah! I feel I should like to spit on the fellow that answers to such a name. But when a man is once for all doomed to be Gregers Werle — in this world — as I am —

HIALMAR (laughs): Ha, ha! If you weren't Gregers Werle, what would you like to be?

GREGERS: If I should choose, I should like best to be a clever dog.

GINA: A dog!

HEDVIG (involuntarily): Oh no!

GREGERS: Yes, an amazingly clever dog; one that goes to the bottom after wild ducks when they dive and bite themselves fast in tangle and seaweed down among the ooze.

HIALMAR: Upon my word now, Gregers — I don't in the least know what you are driving at.

GREGERS: Oh well, you might not be much the wiser if you did. It's understood, then, that I move in early tomorrow morning. (to GINA) I won't give you any trouble; I do everything for myself. (to HIALMAR) We will talk about the rest tomorrow. Good night, Mrs. Ekdal. (Nods to HEDVIG.) Good night.

GINA: Good night, Mr. Werle.

HEDVIG: Good night.

HIALMAR (who has lighted a candle): Wait a moment; I must show you a light; the stairs are sure to be dark.

(GREGERS and HIALMAR go out by the passage door.)

GINA (looking straight before her with her sewing in her lap): Wasn't that queer-like talk about wanting to be a dog?

HEDVIG: Do you know, Mother — I believe he meant something quite different by that.

GINA: Why, what should he mean?

HEDVIG: Oh, I don't know, but it seemed to me he meant something different from what he said — all the time.

GINA: Do you think so? Yes, it was sort of queer.

HIALMAR (comes back): The lamp was still burning. (Puts out the candle and sets it down.) Ah, now one can get a mouthful of food at last. (Begins to eat the bread and butter.) Well, you see, Gina — if only you keep your eyes open —

GINA: How keep your eyes open?

HIALMAR: Why, haven't we at last had the luck

to get the room let? And just think — to a person like Gregers — a good old friend.

GINA: Well, I don't know what to say about it.

HEDVIG: Oh, Mother, you'll see; it'll be such fun!

HIALMAR: You're very strange. You were so bent upon getting the room let before, and now you don't like it.

GINA: Yes, I do, Ekdal; if it had only been to someone else. But what do you suppose Mr. Werle will say?

HIALMAR: Old Werle? It doesn't concern him.

GINA: But surely you can see that there's something amiss between them again, or the young man wouldn't be leaving home. You know very well those two can't get on with each other.

HIALMAR: Very likely not, but —

GINA: And now Mr. Werle may fancy it's you that has edged him on —

HIALMAR: Let him fancy so, then! Mr. Werle has done a great deal for me; far be it from me to deny it. But that doesn't make me everlastingly dependent upon him.

GINA: But, my dear Ekdal, maybe Grandfather'll suffer for it. He may lose the little bit of work he gets from Gråberg.

HIALMAR: I could almost say: so much the better! Is it not humiliating for a man like me to see his grayhaired father treated as a pariah? But now I believe the fullness of time is at hand. (*Takes a fresh piece of bread and butter.*) As sure as I have a mission in life, I mean to fulfill it now!

HEDVIG: Oh yes, Father, do!

GINA: Hush! Don't wake him!

HIALMAR (*more softly*): I will fulfill it, I say. The day shall come when — And that is why I say it's a good thing we have let the room, for that makes me more independent. The man who has a mission in life must be independent. (*By the armchair, with emotion.*) Poor old white-haired Father! Rely on

your Hialmar. He has broad shoulders — strong shoulders, at any rate. You shall yet wake up some fine day and — (*to* GINA) Do you not believe it?

GINA (*rising*): Yes, of course I do, but in the meantime suppose we see about getting him to bed.

HIALMAR: Yes, come.

(*They take hold of the old man carefully.*)

ACT THREE

Scene — HIALMAR EKDAL'S *studio. It is morning; the daylight shines through the large window in the slanting roof; the curtain is drawn back.*
HIALMAR *is sitting at the table, busy retouching a photograph; several others lie before him. Presently* GINA, *wearing her hat and cloak, enters by the passage door; she has a covered basket on her arm.*

HIALMAR: Back already, Gina?

GINA: Oh yes, one can't let the grass grow under one's feet. (*Sets her basket on a chair and takes off her things.*)

HIALMAR: Did you look in at Gregers' room?

GINA: Yes, that I did. It's a rare sight, I can tell you; he's made a pretty mess to start off with.

HIALMAR: How so?

GINA: He was determined to do everything for himself, he said; so he sets to work to light the stove, and what must he do but screw down the damper till the whole room is full of smoke. Ugh! There was a smell fit to —

HIALMAR: Well, really!

GINA: But that's not the worst of it; for then he thinks he'll put out the fire and goes and empties his water jug into the stove and so makes the whole floor one filthy puddle.

HIALMAR: How annoying!

GINA: I've got the porter's wife to clear up

after him, pig that he is! But the room won't be fit to live in till the afternoon.

HIALMAR: What's he doing with himself in the meantime?

GINA: He said he was going out for a little while.

HIALMAR: I looked in upon him too, for a moment — after you had gone.

GINA: So I heard. You've asked him to lunch.

HIALMAR: Just to a little bit of early lunch, you know. It's his first day — we can hardly do less. You've got something in the house, I suppose?

GINA: I shall have to find something or other.

HIALMAR: And don't cut it too fine, for I fancy Relling and Molvik are coming up too. I just happened to meet Relling on the stairs, you see; so I had to —

GINA: Oh, are we to have those two as well?

HIALMAR: Good lord — a couple more or less can't make any difference.

OLD EKDAL (opens his door and looks in): I say, Hialmar — (Sees GINA.) Oh!

GINA: Do you want anything, Grandfather?

EKDAL: Oh no, it doesn't matter. H'm! (Retires again.)

GINA (takes up the basket): Be sure you see that he doesn't go out.

HIALMAR: All right, all right. And, Gina, a little herring salad wouldn't be a bad idea. Relling and Molvik were out on the loose again last night.

GINA: If only they don't come before I'm ready for them —

HIALMAR: No, of course they won't; take your own time.

GINA: Very well, and meanwhile you can be working a bit.

HIALMAR: Well, I am working! I am working as hard as I can!

GINA: Then you'll have that job off your hands, you see. (She goes out to the kitchen with her basket. HIALMAR sits for a time penciling away at the photograph in an indolent and listless manner.)

EKDAL (peeps in, looks round the studio and says softly): Are you busy?

HIALMAR: Yes, I'm toiling at these wretched pictures.

EKDAL: Well, well, never mind — since you're so busy — h'm! (He goes out again; the door stands open.)

HIALMAR (continues for some time in silence, then he lays down his brush and goes over to the door): Are you busy, Father?

EKDAL (in a grumbling tone within): If you're busy, I'm busy too. H'm!

HIALMAR: Oh, very well then. (Goes to his work again.)

EKDAL (presently coming to the door again): H'm; I say Hialmar, I'm not so very busy, you know.

HIALMAR: I thought you were writing.

EKDAL: Oh, devil take it! Can't Gråberg wait a day or two? After all, it's not a matter of life and death.

HIALMAR: No, and you're not his slave either.

EKDAL: And about that other business in there —

HIALMAR: Just what I was thinking of. Do you want to go in? Shall I open the door for you?

EKDAL: Well, it wouldn't be a bad notion.

HIALMAR (rises): Then we'd have that off our hands,

EKDAL: Yes, exactly. It's got to be ready first thing tomorrow. It is tomorrow, isn't it? H'm?

HIALMAR: Yes, of course it's tomorrow.

(HIALMAR and EKDAL push aside each his half of the sliding door. The morning sun is shining in through the skylights; some doves are *flying about; others sit cooing upon the perches; the hens are heard clucking now and then further back in the garret.*)

HIALMAR: There; now you can get to work, Father.

EKDAL (*goes in*): Aren't you coming too?

HIALMAR: Well, really, do you know — I almost think — (*Sees* GINA *at the kitchen door.*) I? No; I haven't time; I must work — But now for our new contrivance — (*He pulls a cord; a curtain slips down inside, the lower part consisting of a piece of old sail-cloth, the upper part of a stretched fishing net. The floor of the garret is thus no longer visible.*)

HIALMAR (*goes to the table*): So! Now perhaps I can sit in peace for a little while.

GINA: Is he rampaging in there again?

HIALMAR: Would you rather have him slip down to Madam Eriksen's? (*Seats himself.*) Do you want anything? You know you said —

GINA: I only wanted to ask if you think we can lay the table for lunch here?

HIALMAR: Yes; we have no early appointment, I suppose?

GINA: No, I expect no one today except those two sweethearts that are to be taken together.

HIALMAR: Why the deuce couldn't they be taken together another day?

GINA: Don't you know, I told them to come in the afternoon, when you are having your nap.

HIALMAR: Oh, that's capital. Very well, let us have lunch here then.

GINA: All right, but there's no hurry about laying the cloth; you can have the table for a good while yet.

HIALMAR: Do you think I am not sticking at my work? I'm at it as hard as I can!

GINA: Then you'll be free later on, you know.

(*Goes out into the kitchen again. Short pause.*)

EKDAL (*in the garret doorway, behind the net*): Hialmar!

HIALMAR: Well?

EKDAL: Afraid we shall have to move the water trough after all.

HIALMAR: What else have I been saying all along?

EKDAL: H'm — h'm — h'm. (*Goes away from the door again.* HIALMAR *goes on working a little, glances toward the garret and half rises.* HEDVIG *comes in from the kitchen.*)

HIALMAR (*sits down again hurriedly*): What do you want?

HEDVIG: I only wanted to come in beside you, Father.

HIALMAR (*after a pause*): What makes you go prying around like that? Perhaps you are told off to watch me?

HEDVIG: No, no.

HIALMAR: What is your mother doing out there?

HEDVIG: Oh, Mother's in the middle of making the herring salad. (*Goes to the table.*) Isn't there any little thing I could help you with, Father?

HIALMAR: Oh no. It is right that I should bear the whole burden — so long as my strength holds out. Set your mind at rest, Hedvig; if only your father keeps his health —

HEDVIG: Oh no, Father! You mustn't talk in that horrid way. (*She wanders about a little, stops by the doorway and looks into the garret.*)

HIALMAR: Tell me, what is he doing?

HEDVIG: I think he's making a new path to the water trough.

HIALMAR: He can never manage that by himself! And here am I doomed to sit!

HEDVIG (*goes to him*): Let me take the brush, Father! I can do it quite well.

HIALMAR: Oh, nonsense; you will only hurt your eyes.

HEDVIG: Not a bit. Give me the brush.

HIALMAR (*rising*): Well, it won't take more than a minute or two.

HEDVIG: Pooh, what harm can it do then? (*Takes the brush.*) There! (*Seats herself.*) I can begin upon this one.

HIALMAR: But mind you don't hurt your eyes! Do you hear? *I* won't be answerable; you do it on your own responsibility — understand that.

HEDVIG (*retouching*): Yes, yes, I understand.

HIALMAR: You are quite clever at it, Hedvig. Only a minute or two, you know. (*He slips through by the edge of the curtain into the garret. HEDVIG sits at her work. HIALMAR and EKDAL are heard disputing inside.*)

HIALMAR (*appears behind the net*): I say, Hedvig — give me those pincers that are lying on the shelf. And the chisel. (*Turns away inside.*) Now you shall see, Father. Just let me show you first what I mean!

(*HEDVIG has fetched the required tools from the shelf and hands them to him through the net.*)

HIALMAR: Ah, thanks. I didn't come a moment too soon.

(*Goes back from the curtain again; they are heard carpentering and talking inside. HEDVIG stands looking in at them. A moment later there is a knock at the passage door; she does not notice it.*)

GREGERS WERLE (*bareheaded, in indoor dress, enters and stops near the door*): H'm!

HEDVIG (*turns and goes toward him*): Good morning. Please come in.

GREGERS: Thank you. (*Looking toward the garret.*) You seem to have work-people in the house.

HEDVIG: No, it's only Father and Grandfather. I'll tell them you are here.

GREGERS: No, no, don't do that; I would rather wait a little. (*Seats himself on the sofa.*)

HEDVIG: It looks so untidy here — (*Begins to clear away the photographs.*)

GREGERS: Oh, don't take them away. Are those prints that have to be finished off?

HEDVIG: Yes, they are a few I was helping Father with.

GREGERS: Please don't let me disturb you.

HEDVIG: Oh no. (*She gathers the things to her and sits down to work; GREGERS looks at her meanwhile in silence.*)

GREGERS: Did the wild duck sleep well last night?

HEDVIG: Yes, I think so, thanks.

GREGERS (*turning toward the garret*): It looks quite different by day from what it did last night in the moonlight.

HEDVIG: Yes, it changes ever so much. It looks different in the morning and in the afternoon, and it's different on rainy days from what it is in fine weather.

GREGERS: Have you noticed it?

HEDVIG: Yes, how could I help it?

GREGERS: Are you too fond of being in there with the wild duck?

HEDVIG: Yes, when I can manage it.

GREGERS: But I suppose you haven't much spare time; you go to school, no doubt.

HEDVIG: No, not now; Father is afraid of my hurting my eyes.

GREGERS: Oh, then he reads with you himself?

HEDVIG: Father has promised to read with me, but he has never had time yet.

GREGERS: Then is there nobody else to give you a little help?

HEDVIG: Yes, there is Mr. Molvik, but he is not always exactly — quite —

GREGERS: Sober?

HEDVIG: Yes, I suppose that's it!

GREGERS: Why, then, you must have any

amount of time on your hands. And in there I suppose it is a sort of world by itself?

HEDVIG: Oh yes, quite. And there are such lots of wonderful things.

GREGERS: Indeed?

HEDVIG: Yes, there are big cupboards full of books, and a great many of the books have pictures in them.

GREGERS: Aha!

HEDVIG: And there's an old bureau with drawers and flaps and a big clock with figures that go out and in. But the clock isn't going now.

GREGERS: So time has come to a standstill in there — in the wild duck's domain?

HEDVIG: Yes. And then there's an old paintbox and things of that sort, and all the books.

GREGERS: And you read the books, I suppose.

HEDVIG: Oh yes, when I get the chance. Most of them are English, though, and I don't understand English. But then I look at the pictures. There is one great book called *Harrison's History of London*. It must be a hundred years old, and there are such heaps of pictures in it. At the beginning there is Death with an hourglass and a woman. I think that is horrid. But then there are all the other pictures of churches and castles and streets and great ships sailing on the sea.

GREGERS: But tell me, where did all those wonderful things come from?

HEDVIG: Oh, an old sea captain once lived here, and he brought them home with him. They used to call him "The Flying Dutchman." That was curious, because he wasn't a Dutchman at all.

GREGERS: Was he not?

HEDVIG: No. But at last he was drowned at sea, and so he left all those things behind him.

GREGERS: Tell me now — when you are sitting in there looking at the pictures don't you wish you could travel and see the real world for yourself?

HEDVIG: Oh no! I mean always to stay at home and help Father and Mother.

GREGERS: To retouch photographs?

HEDVIG: No, not only that. I should love above everything to learn to engrave pictures like those in the English books.

GREGERS: H'm. What does your father say to that?

HEDVIG: I don't think Father likes it; Father is strange about such things. Only think, he talks of my learning basketmaking and straw plaiting! But I don't think that would be much good.

GREGERS: Oh no, I don't think so either.

HEDVIG: But Father was right in saying that if I had learned basketmaking I could have made the new basket for the wild duck.

GREGERS: So you could; and it was you that ought to have done it, wasn't it?

HEDVIG: Yes, for it's my wild duck.

GREGERS: Of course it is.

HEDVIG: Yes, it belongs to me. But I lend it to Father and Grandfather as often as they please.

GREGERS: Indeed? What do they do with it?

HEDVIG: Oh, they look after it and build places for it and so on.

GREGERS: I see; for no doubt the wild duck is by far the most distinguished inhabitant of the garret?

HEDVIG: Yes, indeed she is; for she is a real wild fowl, you know. And then she is so much to be pitied; she has no one to care for, poor thing.

GREGERS: She has no family, as the rabbits have.

HEDVIG: No. The hens too, many of them, were chickens together; but she has been taken right away from all her friends. And then there is so much that is strange about the wild duck. Nobody knows her, and nobody knows where she came from either.

GREGERS: And she has been down in the depths of the sea.

HEDVIG (*with a quick glance at him, represses a smile and asks*): Why do you say "depths of the sea"?

GREGERS: What else should I say?

HEDVIG: You could say "the bottom of the sea."

GREGERS: Oh, mayn't I just as well say the depths of the sea?

HEDVIG: Yes, but it sounds so strange to me when other people speak of the depths of the sea.

GREGERS: Why so? Tell me why?

HEDVIG: No, I won't; it's so stupid.

GREGERS: Oh no, I am sure it's not. Do tell me why you smiled.

HEDVIG: Well, this is the reason: whenever I come to realize suddenly — in a flash — what is in there, it always seems to me that the whole room and everything in it should be called "the depths of the sea." But that is so stupid.

GREGERS: You mustn't say that.

HEDVIG: Oh yes, for you know it is only a garret.

GREGERS (*looks fixedly at her*): Are you so sure of that?

HEDVIG (*astonished*): That it's a garret?

GREGERS: Are you quite certain of it?

(HEDVIG *is silent and looks at him open-mouthed.* GINA *comes in from the kitchen with the table things.*)

GREGERS (*rising*): I have come in upon you too early.

GINA: Oh, you must be somewhere, and we're nearly ready now anyway. Clear the table, Hedvig.

(HEDVIG *clears away her things; she and* GINA *lay the cloth during what follows.* GREGERS *seats himself in the armchair and turns over an album.*)

GREGERS: I hear you can retouch, Mrs. Ekdal.

GINA (*with a side glance*): Yes, I can.

GREGERS: That was exceedingly lucky.

GINA: How — lucky?

GREGERS: Since Ekdal took to photography, I mean.

HEDVIG: Mother can take photographs too.

GINA: Oh yes, I was bound to learn that.

GREGERS: So it is really you that carry on the business, I suppose?

GINA: Yes, when Ekdal hasn't time himself —

GREGERS: He is a great deal taken up with his old father, I daresay.

GINA: Yes; and then you can't expect a man like Ekdal to do nothing but take car-de-visits of Dick, Tom and Harry.

GREGERS: I quite agree with you, but having once gone in for the thing —

GINA: You can surely understand, Mr. Werle, that Ekdal's not like one of your common photographers.

GREGERS: Of course not, but still —

(*A shot is fired within the garret.*)

GREGERS (*starting up*): What's that?

GINA: Ugh! Now they're firing again!

GREGERS: Have they firearms in there?

HEDVIG: They are out shooting.

GREGERS: What! (*At the door of the garret.*) Are you shooting, Hialmar?

HIALMAR (*inside the net*): Are you there? I didn't know; I was so taken up — (*to* HEDVIG) Why did you not let us know? (*Comes into the studio.*)

GREGERS: Do you go shooting in the garret?

HIALMAR (*showing a double-barreled pistol*): Oh, only with this thing.

GINA: Yes, you and Grandfather will do yourselves a mischief someday with that there pigstol.

HIALMAR (*with irritation*): I believe I have told you that this kind of firearm is called a pistol.

GINA: Oh, that doesn't make it much better that I can see.

GREGERS: So you have become a sportsman too, Hialmar?

HIALMAR: Only a little rabbit shooting now and then. Mostly to please Father, you understand.

GINA: Men are strange beings; they must always have something to pervert theirselves with.

HIALMAR (*snappishly*): Just so; we must always have something to divert ourselves with.

GINA: Yes, that's just what I say.

HIALMAR: H'm. (*to* GREGERS) You see, the garret is fortunately so situated that no one can hear us shooting. (*Lays the pistol on the top shelf of the bookcase.*) Don't touch the pistol, Hedvig! One of the barrels is loaded; remember that.

GREGERS (*looking through the net*): You have a fowling piece too, I see.

HIALMAR: That is Father's old gun. It's of no use now. Something has gone wrong with the lock. But it's fun to have it all the same, for we can take it to pieces now and then and clean and grease it and screw it together again. Of course it's mostly Father that fiddle-faddles with all that sort of thing.

HEDVIG (*beside* GREGERS): Now you can see the wild duck properly.

GREGERS: I was just looking at her. One of her wings seems to me to droop a bit.

HEDVIG: Well, no wonder; her wing was broken, you know.

GREGERS: And she trails one foot a little. Isn't that so?

HIALMAR: Perhaps a very little bit.

HEDVIG: Yes, it was by that foot the dog took hold of her.

HIALMAR: But otherwise she hasn't the least thing the matter with her, and that is simply marvelous for a creature that has a charge of shot in her body and has been between a dog's teeth —

GREGERS (*with a glance at* HEDVIG): — and that has lain in the depths of the sea — so long.

HEDVIG (*smiling*): Yes.

GINA (*laying the table*): That blessed wild duck! What a lot of fuss you do make over her.

HIALMAR: H'm — will lunch soon be ready?

GINA: Yes, directly. Hedvig, you must come and help me now.

(GINA *and* HEDVIG *go out into the kitchen.*)

HIALMAR (*in a low voice*): I think you had better not stand there looking in at Father; he doesn't like it. (GREGERS *moves away from the garret door.*) Besides, I may as well shut up before the others come. (*Claps his hands to drive the fowls back.*) Shh-shh, in with you! (*Draws up the curtain and pulls the doors together.*) All the contrivances are my own invention. It's really quite amusing to have things of this sort to potter with and to put to rights when they get out of order. And it's absolutely necessary too, for Gina objects to having rabbits and fowls in the studio.

GREGERS: To be sure, and I suppose the studio is your wife's special department?

HIALMAR: As a rule I leave the everyday details of business to her, for then I can take refuge in the parlor and give my mind to more important things.

GREGERS: What things may they be, Hialmar?

HIALMAR: I wonder you have not asked that question sooner. But perhaps you haven't heard of the invention?

GREGERS: The invention? No.

HIALMAR: Really? Have you not? Oh no, out there in the wilds —

GREGERS: So you have invented something, have you?

HIALMAR: It is not quite completed yet, but I am working at it. You can easily imagine that when I resolved to devote myself to photography it wasn't simply with the idea of taking likenesses of all sorts of commonplace people.

GREGERS: No; your wife was saying the same thing just now.

HIALMAR: I swore that if I concentrated my powers to this handicraft I would so exalt it that it should become both an art and a science. And to that end I determined to make this great invention.

GREGERS: And what is the nature of the invention? What purpose does it serve?

HIALMAR: Oh, my dear fellow, you mustn't ask for details yet. It takes time, you see. And you must not think that my motive is vanity. It is not for my own sake that I am working. Oh no; it is my life's mission that stands before me night and day.

GREGERS: What is your life's mission?

HIALMAR: Do you forget the old man with the silver hair?

GREGERS: Your poor father? Well, but what can you do for him?

HIALMAR: I can raise up his self-respect from the dead by restoring the name of Ekdal to honor and dignity.

GREGERS: Then that is your life's mission?

HIALMAR: Yes. I will rescue the shipwrecked man. For shipwrecked he was, by the very first blast of the storm. Even while those terrible investigations were going on he was no longer himself. That pistol there — the one we used to shoot rabbits with — has played its part in the tragedy of the house of Ekdal.

GREGERS: The pistol? Indeed?

HIALMAR: When the sentence of imprisonment was passed — he had the pistol in his hand.

GREGERS: Had he?

HIALMAR: Yes, but he dared not use it. His courage failed him. So broken, so demoralized was he even then! Oh, can you understand it? He, a soldier; he who had shot nine bears and who was descended from two lieutenant colonels — one after the other, of course. Can you understand it, Gregers?

GREGERS: Yes, I understand it well enough.

HIALMAR: I cannot. And once more the pistol played a part in the history of our house. When he had put on the gray clothes and was under lock and key — oh, that was a terrible time for me, I can tell you. I kept the blinds drawn down over both my windows. When I peeped out I saw the sun shining as if nothing had happened. I could not understand it. I saw people going along the street, laughing and talking about indifferent things. I could not understand it. It seemed to me that the whole of existence must be at a standstill — as if under an eclipse.

GREGERS: I felt that too, when my mother died.

HIALMAR: It was in such an hour that Hialmar Ekdal pointed the pistol at his own breast.

GREGERS: You, too, thought of —

HIALMAR: Yes.

GREGERS: But you did not fire?

HIALMAR: No. At the decisive moment I won the victory over myself. I remained in life. But I can assure you it takes some courage to choose life under circumstances like those.

GREGERS: Well, that depends on how you look at it.

HIALMAR: Yes indeed, it takes courage. But I am glad I was firm, for now I shall soon perfect my invention; and Doctor Relling thinks, as I do myself, that Father may be allowed to wear his uniform again. I will demand that as my sole reward.

GREGERS: So that is what he meant about his uniform?

HIALMAR: Yes, that is what he most yearns for. You can't think how my heart bleeds for him. Every time we celebrate any little family festival — Gina's and my wedding day or whatever it may be — in comes the old man in the lieutenant's uniform of happier days. But if he only hears a knock at the door — for he daren't show himself to strangers, you know — he hurries back to his room again as fast as his old legs can carry him. Oh, it's heart-rending for a son to see such things!

GREGERS: How long do you think it will take you to finish your invention?

HIALMAR: Come now, you mustn't expect me to enter into particulars like that. An invention is not a thing completely under one's own control. It depends largely on inspiration — on intuition — and it is almost impossible to predict when the inspiration may come.

GREGERS: But it's advancing?

HIALMAR: Yes, certainly it is advancing. I turn it over in my mind every day; I am full of it. Every afternoon, when I have had my dinner, I shut myself up in the parlor where I can ponder undisturbed. But I can't be goaded to it; it's not a bit of good. Relling says so too.

GREGERS: And you don't think that all that business in the garret draws you off and distracts too much?

HIALMAR: No, no, no; quite the contrary. You mustn't say that. I cannot be everlastingly absorbed in the same laborious train of thought. I must have something alongside of it to fill up the time of waiting. The inspiration, the intuition, you see — when it comes it comes, and there's an end of it.

GREGERS: My dear Hialmar, I almost think you have something of the wild duck in you.

HIALMAR: Something of the wild duck? How do you mean?

GREGERS: You have dived down and bitten yourself fast in the undergrowth.

HIALMAR: Are you alluding to the well-nigh fatal shot that has broken my father's wing — and mine too?

GREGERS: Not exactly to that. I don't say that your wing has been broken, but you have strayed into a poisonous marsh, Hialmar; an insidious disease has taken hold of you, and you have sunk down to die in the dark.

HIALMAR: I? To die in the dark? Look here, Gregers, you must really leave off talking such nonsense.

GREGERS: Don't be afraid; I shall find a way to help you up again. I, too, have a mission in life now; I found it yesterday.

HIALMAR: That's all very well, but you will please leave me out of it. I can assure you that — apart from my very natural melancholy, of course — I am as contented as anyone can wish to be.

GREGERS: Your contentment is an effect of the marsh poison.

HIALMAR: Now, my dear Gregers, pray do not go on about disease and poison; I am not used to that sort of talk. In my house nobody ever speaks to me about unpleasant things.

GREGERS: Ah, that I can easily believe.

HIALMAR: It's not good for me, you see. And there are no marsh poisons here, as you express it. The poor photographer's roof is lowly, I know — and my circumstances are narrow. But I am an inventor, and I am the breadwinner of a family. That exalts me above my mean surroundings. Ah, here comes lunch!

(GINA and HEDVIG bring bottles of ale, a decanter of brandy, glasses, etc. At the same time RELLING and MOLVIK enter from the passage; they are both without hat or overcoat. MOLVIK is dressed in black.)

GINA (placing the things upon the table): Ah, you two have come in the nick of time.

RELLING: Molvik got it into his head that he could smell herring salad, and then there was no holding him. Good morning again, Ekdal.

HIALMAR: Gregers, let me introduce you to Mr. Molvik — Doctor — Oh, you know Relling, don't you?

GREGERS: Yes, slightly.

RELLING: Oh, Mr. Werle junior! Yes, we two have had one or two little skirmishes up at the Höidal works. You've just moved in?

GREGERS: I moved in this morning.

RELLING: Molvik and I live right under you, so you haven't far to go for the doctor and the clergyman if you should need anything in that line.

GREGERS: Thanks; it's not quite unlikely, for yesterday we were thirteen at table.

HIALMAR: Oh, come now, don't let us get upon unpleasant subjects again!

RELLING: You may make your mind easy, Ekdal; I'll be hanged if the finger of fate points to you.

HIALMAR: I should hope not, for the sake of my family. But let us sit down now and eat and drink and be merry.

GREGERS: Shall we not wait for your father?

HIALMAR: No, his lunch will be taken in to him later. Come along!

(*The men seat themselves at table and eat and drink.* GINA *and* HEDVIG *go in and out and wait upon them.*)

RELLING: Molvik was frightfully screwed yesterday, Mrs. Ekdal.

GINA: Really? Yesterday again?

RELLING: Didn't you hear him when I brought him home last night?

GINA: No, I can't say I did.

RELLING: That was a good thing, for Molvik was disgusting last night.

GINA: Is that true, Molvik?

MOLVIK: Let us draw a veil over last night's proceedings. That sort of thing is totally foreign to my better self.

RELLING (*to* GREGERS): It comes over him like a sort of possession, and then I have to go out on the loose with him. Mr. Molvik is demonic, you see.

GREGERS: Demonic?

RELLING: Molvik is demonic, yes.

GREGERS: H'm.

RELLING: And demonic natures are not made to walk straight through the world; they must meander a little now and then. Well, so you still stick up there at those horrible grimy works?

GREGERS: I have stuck there until now.

RELLING: And did you ever manage to collect that claim you went about presenting?

GREGERS: Claim? (*Understands him.*) Ah, I see.

HIALMAR: Have you been presenting claims, Gregers?

GREGERS: Oh, nonsense.

RELLING: Faith, but he has, though! He went round to all the cotters' cabins presenting something he called "the claim of the ideal."

GREGERS: I was young then.

RELLING: You're right; you were very young. And as for the claim of the ideal — you never got it honored while *I* was up there.

GREGERS: Nor since either.

RELLING: Ah, then you've learned to knock a little discount off, I expect.

GREGERS: Never, when I have a true man to deal with.

HIALMAR: No, I should think not, indeed. A little butter, Gina.

RELLING: And a slice of bacon for Molvik.

MOLVIK: Ugh! not bacon!

(*A knock at the garret door.*)

HIALMAR: Open the door, Hedvig; Father wants to come out.

(HEDVIG *goes over and opens the door a little way;* EKDAL *enters with a fresh rabbitskin; she closes the door after him.*)

EKDAL: Good morning, gentlemen! Good sport today. Shot a big one.

HIALMAR: And you've gone and skinned it without waiting for me!

EKDAL: Salted it too. It's good tender meat, is rabbit; it's sweet; it tastes like sugar. Good appetite to you, gentlemen! (*Goes into his room.*)

MOLVIK (*rising*): Excuse me — I can't — I must get downstairs immediately —

RELLING: Drink some soda water, man!

MOLVIK (*hurrying away*): Ugh — ugh. (*Goes out by the passage door.*)

RELLING (*to* HIALMAR): Let us drain a glass to the old hunter.

HIALMAR (*clinks glasses with him*): To the undaunted sportsman who has looked death in the face!

RELLING: To the gray-haired — (*Drinks.*) By the bye, is his hair gray or white?

HIALMAR: Something between the two, I fancy; for that matter, he has very few hairs left of any color.

RELLING: Well, well, one can get through the world with a wig. After all, you are a happy man, Ekdal; you have your noble mission to labor for —

HIALMAR: And I do labor, I can tell you.

RELLING: And then you have your excellent wife, shuffling quietly in and out in her felt slippers, with that seesaw walk of hers, and making everything cosy and comfortable about you.

HIALMAR: Yes, Gina (*nods to her*) — you were a good helpmate on the path of life.

GINA: Oh, don't sit there cricketizing me.

RELLING: And your Hedvig too, Ekdal!

HIALMAR (*affected*): The child, yes! The child before everything! Hedvig, come here to me. (*Strokes her hair.*) What day is it tomorrow, eh?

HEDVIG (*shaking him*): Oh no, you're not to say anything, Father.

HIALMAR: It cuts me to the heart when I think

what a poor affair it will be; only a little festivity in the garret.

HEDVIG: Oh, but that's just what I like!

RELLING: Just you wait till the wonderful invention sees the light, Hedvig!

HIALMAR: Yes indeed — then you shall see! Hedvig, I have resolved to make your future secure. You shall live in comfort all your days. I will demand something or other — on your behalf. That shall be the poor inventor's sole reward.

HEDVIG (*whispering, with her arms round his neck*): Oh, you dear, kind father!

RELLING (*to* GREGERS): Come now, don't you find it pleasant, for once in a way, to sit at a well-spread table in a happy family circle?

HIALMAR: Ah yes, I really prize these social hours.

GREGERS: For my part, I don't thrive in marsh vapors.

RELLING: Marsh vapors?

HIALMAR: Oh, don't begin with that stuff again!

GINA: Goodness knows there's no vapors in this house, Mr. Werle; I give the place a good airing every blessed day.

GREGERS (*leaves the table*): No airing you can give will drive out the taint I mean.

HIALMAR: Taint!

GINA: Yes, what do you say to that, Ekdal!

RELLING: Excuse me — may it not be you yourself that have brought the taint from those mines up there?

GREGERS: It is like you to call what I bring into this house a taint.

RELLING (*goes up to him*): Look here, Mr. Werle junior: I have a strong suspicion that you are still carrying about that "claim of the ideal" large as life in your coattail pocket.

GREGERS: I carry it in my breast.

RELLING: Well, wherever you carry it, I advise you not to come dunning us with it here as long as *I* am on the premises.

GREGERS: And if I do so nonetheless?

RELLING: Then you'll go headforemost down the stairs; now I've warned you.

HIALMAR (*rising*): Oh, but, Relling —

GREGERS: Yes, you may turn me out.

GINA (*interposing between them*): We can't have that, Relling. But I must say, Mr. Werle, it ill becomes you to talk about vapors and taints after all the mess you made with your stove.

(*A knock at the passage door.*)

HEDVIG: Mother, there's somebody knocking.

HIALMAR: There now, we're going to have a whole lot of people!

GINA: I'll go. (*Goes over and opens the door, starts and draws back.*) Oh — oh dear!

(WERLE, *in a fur coat, advances one step into the room.*)

WERLE: Excuse me, but I think my son is staying here.

GINA (*with a gulp*): Yes.

HIALMAR (*approaching him*): Won't you do us the honor to —

WERLE: Thank you, I merely wish to speak to my son.

GREGERS: What is it? Here I am.

WERLE: I want a few words with you in your room.

GREGERS: In my room? Very well. (*About to go.*)

GINA: No, no, your room's not in a fit state.

WERLE: Well, then, out in the passage here; I want to have a few words with you alone.

HIALMAR: You can have them here, sir. Come into the parlor, Relling.

(HIALMAR *and* RELLING *go off to the right;* GINA *takes* HEDVIG *with her into the kitchen.*)

GREGERS (*after a short pause*): Well, now we are alone.

WERLE: From something you let fall last evening, and from your coming to lodge with the Ekdals, I can't help inferring that you intend to make yourself unpleasant to me in one way or another.

GREGERS: I intend to open Hialmar Ekdal's eyes. He shall see his position as it really is — that is all.

WERLE: Is that the mission in life you spoke of yesterday?

GREGERS: Yes. You have left me no other.

WERLE: Is it I, then, that have crippled your mind, Gregers?

GREGERS: You have crippled my whole life. I am not thinking of all that about Mother — but it's thanks to you that I am continually haunted and harassed by a guilty conscience.

WERLE: Indeed! It is your conscience that troubles you, is it?

GREGERS: I ought to have taken a stand against you when the trap was set for Lieutenant Ekdal. I ought to have cautioned him, for I had a misgiving as to what was in the wind.

WERLE: Yes, that was the time to have spoken.

GREGERS: I did not dare to, I was so cowed and spiritless. I was mortally afraid of you — not only then, but long afterward.

WERLE: You have got over that fear now, it appears.

GREGERS: Yes, fortunately. The wrong done to old Ekdal, both by me and by others, can never be undone; but Hialmar I can rescue from all the falsehood and deception that are bringing him to ruin.

WERLE: Do you think that will be doing him a kindness?

GREGERS: I have not the least doubt of it.

WERLE: You think our worthy photographer is the sort of man to appreciate such friendly offices?

GREGERS: Yes, I do.

WERLE: H'm — we shall see.

GREGERS: Besides, if I am to go on living, I must try to find some cure for my sick conscience.

WERLE: It will never be sound. Your conscience has been sickly from childhood. That is a legacy from your mother, Gregers — the only one she left you.

GREGERS (*with a scornful half-smile*): Have you not yet forgiven her for the mistake you made in supposing she would bring you a fortune?

WERLE: Don't let us wander from the point. Then you hold to your purpose of setting young Ekdal upon what you imagine to be the right scent?

GREGERS: Yes, that is my fixed resolve.

WERLE: Well, in that case I might have spared myself this visit, for of course it is useless to ask whether you will return home with me?

GREGERS: Quite useless.

WERLE: And I suppose you won't enter the firm either?

GREGERS: No.

WERLE: Very good. But as I am thinking of marrying again, your share in the property will fall to you at once.

GREGERS (*quickly*): No, I do not want that.

WERLE: You don't want it?

GREGERS: No, I dare not take it, for conscience' sake.

WERLE (*after a pause*): Are you going up to the works again?

GREGERS: No; I consider myself released from your service.

WERLE: But what are you going to do?

GREGERS: Only to fulfill my mission, nothing more.

WERLE: Well, but afterward? What are you going to live upon?

GREGERS: I have laid by a little out of my salary.

WERLE: How long will that last?

GREGERS: I think it will last my time.

WERLE: What do you mean?

GREGERS: I shall answer no more questions.

WERLE: Good-by, then, Gregers.

GREGERS: Good-by.

(WERLE *goes.*)

HIALMAR (*peeping in*): He's gone, isn't he?

GREGERS: Yes.

(HIALMAR *and* RELLING *enter; also* GINA *and* HEDVIG *from the kitchen.*)

RELLING: That luncheon party was a failure.

GREGERS: Put on your coat, Hialmar; I want you to come for a long walk with me.

HIALMAR: With pleasure. What was it your father wanted? Had it anything to do with me?

GREGERS: Come along. We must have a talk. I'll go and put on my overcoat. (*Goes by the passage door.*)

GINA: You shouldn't go out with him, Ekdal.

RELLING: No, don't you do it. Stay where you are.

HIALMAR (*gets his hat and overcoat*): Oh, nonsense! When a friend of my youth feels impelled to open his mind to me in private —

RELLING: But devil take it — don't you see that the fellow's mad, cracked, demented!

GINA: There, what did I tell you! His mother before him had crazy fits like that sometimes.

HIALMAR: The more need for a friend's watchful eye. (*to* GINA) Be sure you have dinner ready in good time. Good-by for the present. (*Goes out by the passage door.*)

RELLING: It's a thousand pities the fellow didn't go to hell through one of the Höidal mines.

GINA: Good lord! What makes you say that?

RELLING (*muttering*): Oh, I have my own reasons.

GINA: Do you think young Werle is really mad?

RELLING: No, worse luck; he's no madder than most other people. But one disease he has certainly got in his system.

GINA: What is it that's the matter with him?

RELLING: Well, I'll tell you, Mrs. Ekdal. He is suffering from an acute attack of integrity.

GINA: Integrity?

HEDVIG: Is that a kind of disease?

RELLING: Yes, it's a national disease, but it only appears sporadically. (*Nods to* GINA.) Thanks for your hospitality. (*He goes out by the passage door.*)

GINA (*moving restlessly to and fro*): Ugh, that Gregers Werle — he was always a wretched creature.

HEDVIG (*standing by the table and looking searchingly at her*): I think all this is very strange.

ACT FOUR

SCENE — HIALMAR EKDAL's *studio. A photograph has just been taken; a camera with the cloth over it, a pedestal, two chairs, a folding table, etc., are standing out in the room. Afternoon light; the sun is going down; a little later it begins to grow dusk.*
GINA *stands in the passage doorway with a little box and a wet glass plate in her hand and is speaking to somebody outside.*

GINA: Yes, certainly. When I make a promise I keep it. The first dozen shall be ready on Monday. Good afternoon.

(*Someone is heard going downstairs.* GINA *shuts the door, slips the plate into the box and puts it into the covered camera.*)

HEDVIG (*comes in from the kitchen*): Are they gone?

GINA (*tidying up*): Yes, thank goodness. I've got rid of them at last.

HEDVIG: But can you imagine why Father hasn't come home yet?

GINA: Are you sure he's not down in Relling's room?

HEDVIG: No, he's not; I ran down the kitchen stair just now and asked.

GINA: And his dinner standing and getting cold too.

HEDVIG: Yes, I can't understand it. Father's always so careful to be home to dinner!

GINA: Oh, he'll be here directly, you'll see.

HEDVIG: I wish he would come; everything seems so queer today.

GINA (*calls out*): There he is!

(HIALMAR EKDAL *comes in at the passage door.*)

HEDVIG (*going to him*): Father! Oh, what a time we've been waiting for you!

GINA (*glancing sidelong at him*): You've been out a long time, Ekdal.

HIALMAR (*without looking at her*): Rather long, yes. (*He takes off his overcoat;* GINA *and* HEDVIG *go to help him; he motions them away.*)

GINA: Perhaps you've had dinner with Werle?

HIALMAR (*hanging up his coat*): No.

GINA (*going toward the kitchen door*): Then I'll bring some in for you.

HIALMAR: No; let the dinner alone. I want nothing to eat.

HEDVIG (*going nearer to him*): Are you not well, Father?

HIALMAR: Well? Oh yes, well enough. We have had a tiring walk, Gregers and I.

GINA: You didn't ought to have gone so far, Ekdal; you're not used to it.

HIALMAR: H'm; there's many a thing a man must get used to in this world. (*Wanders about the room.*) Has anyone been here whilst I was out?

GINA: Nobody but the two sweethearts.

HIALMAR: No new orders?

GINA: No, not today.

HEDVIG: There will be some tomorrow, Father, you'll see.

HIALMAR: I hope there will, for tomorrow I am going to set to work in real earnest.

HEDVIG: Tomorrow! Don't you remember what day it is tomorrow?

HIALMAR: Oh yes, by the bye — Well, the day after, then. Henceforth I mean to do everything myself; I shall take all the work into my own hands.

GINA: Why, what can be in good of that, Ekdal? It'll only make your life a burden to you. I can manage the photography all right, and you can go on working at your invention.

HEDVIG: And think of the wild duck, Father, and all the hens and rabbits and —

HIALMAR: Don't talk to me of all that trash! From tomorrow I will never set foot in the garret again.

HEDVIG: Oh, but, Father, you promised that we should have a little party.

HIALMAR: H'm, true. Well, then, from the day after tomorrow. I should almost like to wring that cursed wild duck's neck!

HEDVIG (*shrieks*): The wild duck!

GINA: Well, I never!

HEDVIG (*shaking him*): Oh no, Father; you know it's my wild duck!

HIALMAR: That is why I don't do it. I haven't the heart to — for your sake, Hedvig. But in my inmost soul I feel that I ought to do it. I ought not to tolerate under my roof a creature that has been through those hands.

GINA: Why, good gracious, even if Grandfather did get it from that poor creature Pettersen —

HEDVIG (*going after him*): But think of the wild duck — the poor wild duck!

HIALMAR (*stops*): I tell you I will spare it — for your sake. Not a hair of its head shall be — I mean, it shall be spared. There are greater problems than that to be dealt with. But you should go out a little now, Hedvig, as usual; it is getting dusk enough for you now.

HEDVIG: No, I don't care about going out now.

HIALMAR: Yes, do; it seems to me your eyes are blinking a great deal; all these vapors in here are bad for you. The air is heavy under this roof.

HEDVIG: Very well then, I'll run down the kitchen stair and go for a little walk. My cloak and hat? Oh, they're in my own room. Father — be sure you don't do the wild duck any harm whilst I'm out.

HIALMAR: Not a feather of its head shall be touched. (*Draws her to him*) You and I, Hedvig — we two — Well, go along.

(HEDVIG *nods to her parents and goes out through the kitchen.*)

HIALMAR (*walks about without looking up*): Gina.

GINA: Yes?

HIALMAR: From tomorrow — or say from the day after tomorrow — I should like to keep the household account book myself.

GINA: Do you want to keep the accounts too now?

HIALMAR: Yes; or to check the receipts at any rate.

GINA: Lord help us; that's soon done.

HIALMAR: One would hardly think so; at any rate you seem to make the money go a very long way. (*Stops and looks at her.*) How do you manage it?

GINA: It's because me and Hedvig, we need so little.

HIALMAR: Is it the case that Father is very liberally paid for the copying he does for Mr. Werle?

GINA: I don't know as he gets anything out of the way. I don't know the rates for that sort of work.

HIALMAR: Well, what does he get, about? Let me hear!

GINA: Oh, it varies; I daresay it'll come to about as much as he costs us, with a little pocket money over.

HIALMAR: As much as he costs us! And you have never told me this before.

GINA: No, how could I tell you? It pleased you so much to think he got everything from you.

HIALMAR: And he gets it from Mr. Werle.

GINA: Oh well, he has plenty and to spare, he has.

HIALMAR: Light the lamp for me, please!

GINA (lighting the lamp): And of course we don't know as it's Mr. Werle himself; it may be Gråberg.

HIALMAR: Why attempt such an evasion?

GINA: I don't know; I only thought —

HIALMAR: H'm!

GINA: It wasn't me that got Grandfather that copying. It was Bertha, when she used to come about us.

HIALMAR: It seems to me your voice is trembling.

GINA (putting the lamp shade on): Is it?

HIALMAR: And your hands are shaking, are they not?

GINA (firmly): Come right out with it, Ekdal. What has he been saying about me?

HIALMAR: Is it true — can it be true that — that there was an — an understanding between you and Mr. Werle while you were in service there?

GINA: That's not true. Not at that time. Mr. Werle did come after me, that's a fact. And his wife thought there was something in it, and then she made such a hocus-pocus and hurly-burly, and she hustled me and bustled me about so that I left her service.

HIALMAR: But afterward, then?

GINA: Well, then I went home. And Mother — well, she wasn't the woman you took her for, Ekdal; she kept on worrying and worrying at me about one thing and another — for Mr. Werle was a widower by that time.

HIALMAR: Well, and then?

GINA: I suppose you've got to know it. He gave me no peace until he'd had his way.

HIALMAR (striking his hands together): And this is the mother of my child! How could you hide this from me?

GINA: Yes, it was wrong of me; I ought certainly to have told you long ago.

HIALMAR: You should have told me at the very first — then I should have known the sort of woman you were.

GINA: But would you have married me all the same?

HIALMAR: How can you dream that I would?

GINA: That's just why I didn't dare tell you anything then. For I'd come to care for you so much, you see, and I couldn't go and make myself utterly miserable.

HIALMAR (walks about): And this is my Hedvig's mother! And to know that all I see before me (kicks at chair) — all that I call my home — I owe to a favored predecessor! Oh, that scoundrel Werle!

GINA: Do you repent of the fourteen — the fifteen years we've lived together?

HIALMAR (placing himself in front of her): Have you not every day, every hour, repented of the spider's web of deceit you have spun around me? Answer me that!

How could you help writhing with penitence and remorse?

GINA: Oh, my dear Ekdal, I've had all I could do to look after the house and get through the day's work.

HIALMAR: Then you never think of reviewing your past?

GINA: No; heaven knows I'd almost forgotten those old stories.

HIALMAR: Oh, this dull, callous contentment! To me there is something revolting about it. Think of it — never so much as a twinge of remorse!

GINA: But tell me, Ekdal — what would have become of you if you hadn't had a wife like me?

HIALMAR: Like you!

GINA: Yes; for you know I've always been a bit more practical and wide awake than you. Of course I'm a year or two older.

HIALMAR: What would have become of me!

GINA: You'd got into all sorts of bad ways when first you met me; that you can't deny.

HIALMAR: "Bad ways," do you call them? Little do you know what a man goes through when he is in grief and despair — especially a man of my fiery temperament.

GINA: Well, well, that may be so. And I've no reason to crow over you neither, for you turned a moral of a husband, that you did, as soon as ever you had a house and home of your own. And now we'd got everything so nice and cosy about us, and me and Hedvig was just thinking we'd soon be able to let ourselves go a bit in the way of both food and clothes.

HIALMAR: In the swamp of deceit, yes.

GINA: I wish to goodness that detestable thing had never set his foot inside our doors!

HIALMAR: And I, too, thought my home such a pleasant one. That was a delusion. Where shall I now find the elasticity of spirit to bring my invention into the world of reality?

Perhaps it will die with me, and then it will be your past, Gina, that will have killed it.

GINA (nearly crying): You mustn't say such things, Ekdal. Me, that has only wanted to do the best I could for you all my days!

HIALMAR: I ask you, what becomes of the breadwinner's dream? When I used to lie in there on the sofa and brood over my invention I had a clear enough presentiment that it would sap my vitality to the last drop. I felt even then that the day when I held the patent in my hand — that day — would bring my — release. And then it was my dream that you should live on after me, the dead inventor's well-to-do widow.

GINA (drying her tears): No, you mustn't talk like that, Ekdal. May the Lord never let me see the day I am left a widow!

HIALMAR: Oh, the whole dream has vanished. It is all over now. All over!

(GREGERS WERLE opens the passage door cautiously and looks in.)

GREGERS: May I come in?

HIALMAR: Yes, come in.

GREGERS (comes forward, his face beaming with satisfaction, and holds out both his hands to them): Well, dear friends! (Looks from one to the other and whispers to HIALMAR.) Have you not done it yet?

HIALMAR (aloud): It is done.

GREGERS: It is?

HIALMAR: I have passed through the bitterest moments of my life.

GREGERS: But also, I trust, the most ennobling.

HIALMAR: Well, at any rate, we have got through it for the present.

GINA: God forgive you, Mr. Werle.

GREGERS (in great surprise): But I don't understand this.

HIALMAR: What don't you understand?

GREGERS: After so great a crisis — a crisis that

is to be the starting point of an entirely new life — of a communion founded on truth and free from all taint of deception —

HIALMAR: Yes, yes, I know; I know that quite well.

GREGERS: I confidently expected, when I entered the room, to find the light of transfiguration shining upon me from both husband and wife. And now I see nothing but dullness, oppression, gloom —

GINA: Oh, is that it? (*Takes off the lamp shade.*)

GREGERS: You will not understand me, Mrs. Ekdal. Ah well, you, I suppose, need time to — But you, Hialmar? Surely you feel a new consecration after the great crisis?

HIALMAR: Yes, of course I do. That is — in a sort of way.

GREGERS: For surely nothing in the world can compare with the joy of forgiving one who has erred and raising her up to oneself in love.

HIALMAR: Do you think a man can so easily throw off the bitter cup I have drained?

GREGERS: No, not a common man, perhaps. But a man like you —

HIALMAR: Good God! I know that well enough. But you must keep me up to it, Gregers. It takes time, you know.

GREGERS: You have much of the wild duck in you, Hialmar.

(RELLING *has come in at the passage door.*)

RELLING: Oho! Is the wild duck to the fore again?

HIALMAR: Yes; Mr. Werle's wing-broken victim.

RELLING: Mr. Werle? So it's him you are talking about?

HIALMAR: Him and — ourselves.

RELLING (*in an undertone to* GREGERS): May the devil fly away with you!

HIALMAR: What is that you are saying?

RELLING: Only uttering a heartfelt wish that this quacksalver would take himself off. If he stays here he is quite equal to making an utter mess of life for both of you.

GREGERS: These two will not make a mess of life, Mr. Relling. Of course I won't speak to Hialmar — him we know. But she too, in her innermost heart, has certainly something loyal and sincere —

GINA (*almost crying*): You might have let me alone for what I was then.

RELLING (*to* GREGERS): Is it rude to ask what you really want in this house?

GREGERS: To lay the foundations of a true marriage.

RELLING: So you don't think Ekdal's marriage is good enough as it is?

GREGERS: No doubt it is as good a marriage as most others, worse luck. But a true marriage it has yet to become.

HIALMAR: You have never had eyes for the claims of the ideal, Relling.

RELLING: Rubbish, my boy! But excuse me, Mr. Werle; how many — in round numbers — how many true marriages have you seen in the course of your life?

GREGERS: Scarcely a single one.

RELLING: Nor I either.

GREGERS: But I have seen innumerable marriages of the opposite kind. And it has been my fate to see at close quarters what ruin such a marriage can work in two human souls.

HIALMAR: A man's whole moral basis may give away beneath his feet; that is the terrible part of it.

RELLING: Well, I can't say I've ever been exactly married, so I don't pretend to speak with authority. But this I know, that the child enters into the marriage problem. And you must leave the child in peace.

HIALMAR: Oh — Hedvig! My poor Hedvig!

RELLING: Yes, you must be good enough to

keep Hedvig outside of all this. You two are grown-up people; you are free, in God's name, to make what mess and muddle you please of your life. But you must deal cautiously with Hedvig, I tell you; else you may do her a great injury.

HIALMAR: An injury!

RELLING: Yes, or she may do herself an injury — and perhaps others too.

GINA: How can you know that, Relling?

HIALMAR: Her sight is in no immediate danger, is it?

RELLING: I am not talking about her sight. Hedvig is at a critical age. She may be getting all sorts of mischief into her head.

GINA: That's true — I've noticed it already! She's taken to carrying on with the fire out in the kitchen. She calls it playing at house on fire. I'm often scared for fear she really sets fire to the house.

RELLING: You see, I thought as much.

GREGERS (to RELLING): But how do you account for that?

RELLING (sullenly): Her constitution's changing, sir.

HIALMAR: So long as the child has me — so long as I am above ground —(A knock at the door.)

GINA: Hush, Ekdal, there's someone in the passage. (Calls out.) Come in!

(MRS. SØRBY, in walking dress, comes in.)

MRS. SØRBY: Good evening.

GINA (going toward her): Is it really you, Bertha?

MRS. SØRBY: Yes, of course it is. But I'm disturbing you, I'm afraid.

HIALMAR: No, not at all; an emissary from that house —

MRS. SØRBY (to GINA): To tell the truth, I hoped your menfolk would be out at this time. I just ran up to have a little chat with you and to say good-by.

GINA: Good-by? Are you going away then?

MRS. SØRBY: Yes, tomorrow morning — up to Höidal. Mr. Werle started this afternoon. (Lightly to GREGERS.) He asked me to say good-by for him.

GINA: Only fancy!

HIALMAR: I say: beware!

GREGERS: I must explain the situation. My father and Mrs. Sørby are going to be married.

HIALMAR: Going to be married!

GINA: Oh, Bertha! So it's come to that at last!

RELLING (his voice quivering a little): This is surely not true?

MRS. SØRBY: Yes, my dear Relling, it's true enough.

RELLING: You are going to marry again?

MRS. SØRBY: Yes, it looks like it. Werle has got a special license, and we are going to be married quietly up at the works.

GREGERS: Then I must wish you all happiness, like a dutiful stepson.

MRS. SØRBY: Thank you very much — if you mean what you say. I certainly hope it will lead to happiness, both for Werle and for me.

RELLING: You have every reason to hope that. Mr. Werle never gets drunk — so far as I know; and I don't suppose he's in the habit of thrashing his wives, like the late lamented doctor.

MRS. SØRBY: Come now, let Sørby rest in peace. He had his good points too.

RELLING: Mr. Werle has better ones, I have no doubt.

MRS. SØRBY: He hasn't frittered away all that was good in him, at any rate. The man who does that must take the consequences.

RELLING: I shall go out with Molvik this evening.

MRS. SØRBY: You mustn't do that, Relling. Don't do it — for my sake.

RELLING: There's nothing else for it. (*to* HIAL-MAR) If you're going with us, come along.

GINA: No, thank you. Ekdal doesn't go in for that sort of dissertation.

HIALMAR (*half aloud, in vexation*): Oh, do hold your tongue!

RELLING: Good-by, Mrs. — Werle. (*Goes out through the passage door.*)

GREGERS (*to* MRS. SØRBY): You seem to know Doctor Relling pretty intimately.

MRS. SØRBY: Yes, we have known each other for many years. At one time it seemed as if things might have gone further between us.

GREGERS: It was surely lucky for you that they did not.

MRS. SØRBY: You may well say that. But I have always been wary of acting on impulse. A woman can't afford absolutely to throw herself away.

GREGERS: Are you not in the least afraid that I may let my father know about this old friendship?

MRS. SØRBY: Why, of course I have told him all about it myself.

GREGERS: Indeed?

MRS. SØRBY: Your father knows every single thing that can, with any truth, be said about me. I have told him all; it was the first thing I did when I saw what was in his mind.

GREGERS: Then you have been franker than most people, I think.

MRS. SØRBY: I have always been frank. We women find that the best policy.

HIALMAR: What do you say to that, Gina?

GINA: Oh, we're not all alike, us women aren't. Some are made one way, some another.

MRS. SØRBY: Well, for my part, Gina, I believe it's wisest to do as I've done. And Werle has no secrets either, on his side. That's really the great bond between us, you see. Now he can talk to me as openly as a child. He

has never had the chance to do that before. Fancy a man like him, full of health and vigor, passing his whole youth and the best years of his life in listening to nothing but penitential sermons! And very often the sermons had for their text the most imaginary offenses — at least so I understand.

GINA: That's true enough.

GREGERS: If you ladies are going to follow up this topic, I had better withdraw.

MRS. SØRBY: You can stay as far as that's concerned. I shan't say a word more. But I wanted you to know that I had done nothing secretly or in an underhand way. I may seem to have come in for a great piece of luck, and so I have, in a sense. But after all, I don't think I am getting any more than I am giving. I shall stand by him always, and I can tend and care for him as no one else can, now that he is getting helpless.

HIALMAR: Getting helpless?

GREGERS (*to* MRS. SØRBY): Hush, don't speak of that here.

MRS. SØRBY: There is no disguising it any longer, however much he would like to. He is going blind.

HIALMAR (*starts*): Going blind? That's strange. He, too, going blind!

GINA: Lots of people do.

MRS. SØRBY: And you can imagine what that means to a businessman. Well, I shall try as well as I can to make my eyes take the place of his. But I mustn't stay any longer; I have heaps of things to do. Oh, by the bye, Ekdal, I was to tell you that if there is anything Werle can do for you, you must just apply to Gråberg.

GREGERS: That offer I am sure Hialmar Ekdal will decline with thanks.

MRS. SØRBY: Indeed? I don't think he used to be so —

GINA: No, Bertha, Ekdal doesn't need anything from Mr. Werle now.

HIALMAR (*slowly and with emphasis*): Will you

present my compliments to your future husband and say that I intend very shortly to call upon Mr. Gråberg —

GREGERS: What! You don't really mean that?

HIALMAR: To call upon Mr. Gråberg, I say, and obtain an account of the sum I owe his principal. I will pay that debt of honor — ha, ha, ha! a debt of honor, let us call it! In any case I will pay the whole with five per cent interest.

GINA: But, my dear Ekdal, God knows we haven't got the money to do it.

HIALMAR: Be good enough to tell your future husband that I am working assiduously at my invention. Please tell him that what sustains me in this laborious task is the wish to free myself from a torturing burden of debt. That is my reason for proceeding with the invention. The entire profits shall be devoted to releasing me from my pecuniary obligations to your future husband.

MRS. SØRBY: Something has happened here.

HIALMAR: Yes, you are right.

MRS. SØRBY: Well, good-by. I had something else to speak to you about, Gina, but it must keep till another time. Good-by.

(HIALMAR and GREGERS bow silently. GINA follows MRS. SØRBY to the door.)

HIALMAR: Not beyond the threshold, Gina!

(MRS. SØRBY goes; GINA shuts the door after her.)

HIALMAR: There now, Gregers, I have got that burden of debt off my mind.

GREGERS: You soon will, at all events.

HIALMAR: I think my attitude may be called correct.

GREGERS: You are the man I have always taken you for.

HIALMAR: In certain cases it is impossible to disregard the claim of the ideal. Yes, as the breadwinner of a family, I cannot but writhe and groan under it. I can tell you it is no joke for a man without capital to attempt the repayment of a long-standing obligation over which, so to speak, the dust of oblivion has gathered. But it cannot be helped; the man in me demands his rights.

GREGERS (laying his hand on HIALMAR's shoulder): My dear Hialmar — was it not a good thing I came?

HIALMAR: Yes.

GREGERS: Are you not glad to have had your true position made clear to you?

HIALMAR (somewhat impatiently): Yes, of course I am. But there is one thing that is revolting to my sense of justice.

GREGERS: And what is that?

HIALMAR: It is that — But I don't know whether I ought to express myself so unreservedly about your father.

GREGERS: Say what you please so far as I am concerned.

HIALMAR: Well, then, is it not exasperating to think that it is not I, but he, who will realize the true marriage?

GREGERS: How can you say such a thing?

HIALMAR: Because it is clearly the case. Isn't the marriage between your father and Mrs. Sørby founded upon complete confidence, upon entire and unreserved candor on both sides? They hide nothing from each other, they keep no secrets in the background; their relation is based, if I may put it so, on mutual confession and absolution.

GREGERS: Well, what then?

HIALMAR: Well, is not that the whole thing? Did you not yourself say that this was precisely the difficulty that had to be overcome in order to found a true marriage?

GREGERS: But this is a totally different matter, Hialmar. You surely don't compare either yourself or your wife with those two — Oh, you understood me well enough.

HIALMAR: Say what you like, there is something in all this that hurts and offends my sense of justice. It really looks as if there were no just Providence to rule the world.

GINA: Oh no, Ekdal; for God's sake don't say such things.

GREGERS: H'm; don't let us get upon those questions.

HIALMAR: And yet, after all, I cannot but recognize the guiding finger of Fate. He is going blind.

GINA: Oh, you can't be sure of that.

HIALMAR: There is no doubt about it. At all events there ought not to be, for in that very fact lies the righteous retribution. He has hoodwinked a confiding fellow creature in days gone by —

GREGERS: I fear he has hoodwinked many.

HIALMAR: And now comes inexorable, mysterious Fate and demands Werle's own eyes.

GINA: Oh, how dare you say such dreadful things! You make me quite scared.

HIALMAR: It is profitable, now and then, to plunge deep into the night side of existence.

(HEDVIG, in her hat and cloak, comes in by the passage door. She is pleasurably excited and out of breath.)

GINA: Are you back already?

HEDVIG: Yes, I didn't care to go any farther. It was a good thing, too, for I've just met someone at the door.

HIALMAR: It must have been that Mrs. Sørby.

HEDVIG: Yes.

HIALMAR (walks up and down): I hope you have seen her for the last time.

(Silence. HEDVIG, discouraged, looks first at one and then at the other, trying to divine their frame of mind.)

HEDVIG (approaching, coaxingly): Father.

HIALMAR: Well — what is it, Hedvig?

HEDVIG: Mrs. Sørby had something with her for me.

HIALMAR (stops): For you?

HEDVIG: Yes. Something for tomorrow.

GINA: Bertha has always given you some little thing on your birthday.

HIALMAR: What is it?

HEDVIG: Oh, you mustn't see it now. Mother is to give it to me tomorrow morning before I'm up.

HIALMAR: What is all this hocus-pocus that I am to be in the dark about?

HEDVIG (quickly): Oh no, you may see it if you like. It's a big letter. (Takes the letter out of her cloak pocket.)

HIALMAR: A letter too?

HEDVIG: Yes, it is only a letter. The rest will come afterward, I suppose. But fancy — a letter! I've never had a letter before. And there's "Miss" written upon it. (Reads.) "Miss Hedvig Ekdal." Only fancy — that's me!

HIALMAR: Let me see that letter.

HEDVIG (hands it to him): There it is.

HIALMAR: That is Mr. Werle's hand.

GINA: Are you sure of that, Ekdal?

HIALMAR: Look for yourself.

GINA: Oh, what do I know about suchlike things?

HIALMAR: Hedvig, may I open the letter — and read it?

HEDVIG: Yes, of course you may, if you want to.

GINA: No, not tonight, Ekdal; it's to be kept till tomorrow.

HEDVIG (softly): Oh, can't you let him read it! It's sure to be something good, and then Father will be glad and everything will be nice again.

HIALMAR: I may open it then?

HEDVIG: Yes, do, Father. I'm so anxious to know what it is.

HIALMAR: Well and good. (*Opens the letter, takes out a paper, reads it through and appears bewildered.*) What is this?

GINA: What does it say?

HEDVIG: Oh yes, Father — tell us!

HIALMAR: Be quiet. (*Reads it through again; he has turned pale but says with self-control.*) It is a deed of gift, Hedvig.

HEDVIG: Is it? What sort of gift am I to have?

HIALMAR: Read for yourself.

(HEDVIG *goes over and reads for a time by the lamp.*)

HIALMAR (*half aloud, clenching his hands*): The eyes! The eyes — and then that letter!

HEDVIG (*leaves off reading*): Yes, but it seems to me that it's Grandfather that's to have it.

HIALMAR (*takes letter from her*): Gina — can you understand this?

GINA: I know nothing whatever about it; tell me what's the matter.

HIALMAR: Mr. Werle writes to Hedvig that her old grandfather need not trouble himself any longer with the copying but that he can henceforth draw on the office for a hundred crowns a month —

GREGERS: Aha!

HEDVIG: A hundred crowns, Mother! I read that.

GINA: What a good thing for Grandfather!

HIALMAR: — a hundred crowns a month so long as he needs it—that means, of course, so long as he lives.

GINA: Well, so he's provided for, poor dear.

HIALMAR: But there is more to come. You didn't read that, Hedvig. Afterward this gift is to pass on to you.

HEDVIG: To me! The whole of it?

HIALMAR: He says the same amount is assured to you for the whole of your life. Do you hear that, Gina?

GINA: Yes, I hear.

HEDVIG: Fancy — all that money for me! (*Shakes him.*) Father, Father, aren't you glad?

HIALMAR (*eluding her*): Glad! (*Walks about.*) Oh, what vistas — what perspectives open up before me! It is Hedvig, Hedvig that he showers these benefactions upon!

GINA: Yes, because it's Hedvig's birthday.

HEDVIG: And you'll get it all the same, Father! You know quite well I shall give all the money to you and Mother.

HIALMAR: To Mother, yes! There we have it.

GREGERS: Hialmar, this is a trap he is setting for you.

HIALMAR: Do you think it's another trap?

GREGERS: When he was here this morning he said: Hialmar Ekdal is not the man you imagine him to be.

HIALMAR: Not the man —

GREGERS: That you shall see, he said.

HIALMAR: He meant you should see that I would let myself be bought off!

HEDVIG: Oh, Mother, what does all this mean?

GINA: Go and take off your things.

(HEDVIG *goes out by the kitchen door, half crying.*)

GREGERS: Yes, Hialmar — now is the time to show who was right, he or I.

HIALMAR (*slowly tears the paper across, lays both pieces on the table and says*): Here is my answer.

GREGERS: Just what I expected.

HIALMAR (*goes over to* GINA, *who stands by the stove and says in a low voice*): Now please make a clean breast of it. If the connection between you and him was quite over when you — came to care for me, as you call it — why did he place us in a position **to** marry?

GINA: I suppose he thought as he could come and go in our house.

HIALMAR: Only that? Was he not afraid of a possible contingency?

GINA: I don't know what you mean.

HIALMAR: I want to know whether — your child has the right to live under my roof.

GINA (draws herself up; her eyes flash): You ask that!

HIALMAR: You shall answer me this one question: Does Hedvig belong to me — or — ? Well?

GINA (looking at him with cold defiance): I don't know.

HIALMAR (quivering a little): You don't know!

GINA: How should I know. A creature like me —

HIALMAR (quietly turning away from her): Then I have nothing more to do in this house.

GREGERS: Take care, Hialmar! Think what you are doing!

HIALMAR (puts on his overcoat): In this case there is nothing for a man like me to think twice about.

GREGERS: Yes indeed, there are endless things to be considered. You three must be together if you are to attain the true frame of mind for self-sacrifice and forgiveness.

HIALMAR: I don't want to attain it. Never, never! My hat! (Takes his hat.) My home has fallen into ruins about me. (Bursts into tears.) Gregers, I have no child!

HEDVIG (who has opened the kitchen door): What is that you're saying? (Coming to him.) Father, Father!

GINA: There, you see!

HIALMAR: Don't come near me, Hedvig! Keep far away. I cannot bear to see you. Oh! those eyes! Good-by. (Makes for the door.)

HEDVIG (clinging close to him and screaming loud): No! No! Don't leave me!

GINA (cries out): Look at the child, Ekdal! Look at the child!

HIALMAR: I will not! I cannot! I must get out — away from all this! (He tears himself away from HEDVIG and goes out by the passage door.)

HEDVIG (with despairing eyes): He is going away from us, Mother! He is going away from us! He will never come back again!

GINA: Don't cry, Hedvig. Father's sure to come back again.

HEDVIG (throws herself sobbing on the sofa): No, no, he'll never come home to us any more.

GREGERS: Do you believe I meant all for the best, Mrs. Ekdal?

GINA: Yes, I daresay you did, but God forgive you all the same.

HEDVIG (lying on the sofa): Oh, this will kill me! What have I done to him? Mother, you must fetch him home again!

GINA: Yes, yes, yes; only be quiet, and I'll go out and look for him. (Puts on her outdoor things.) Perhaps he's gone into Relling's. But you mustn't lie there and cry. Promise me.

HEDVIG (weeping convulsively): Yes, I'll stop, I'll stop; if only Father comes back!

GREGERS (to GINA, who is going): After all, had you not better leave him to fight out his bitter fight to the end?

GINA: Oh, he can do that afterward. First of all we must get the child quieted. (Goes out by the passage door.)

HEDVIG (sits up and dries her tears): Now you must tell me what all this means. Why doesn't Father want me any more?

GREGERS: You mustn't ask that till you are a big girl — quite grown up.

HEDVIG (sobs): But I can't go on being as miserable as this till I'm grown up. I think I know what it is. Perhaps I'm not really Father's child.

GREGERS (*uneasy*): How could that be?

HEDVIG: Mother might have found me. And perhaps Father has just got to know it; I've read of such things.

GREGERS: Well, but if it were so —

HEDVIG: I think he might be just as fond of me for all that. Yes, fonder almost. We got the wild duck in a present, you know, and I love it so dearly all the same.

GREGERS (*turning the conversation*). Ah, the wild duck, by the bye! Let us talk about the wild duck a little, Hedvig.

HEDVIG: The poor wild duck! He doesn't want to see it any more either. Only think, he wanted to wring its neck!

GREGERS: Oh, he won't do that.

HEDVIG: No, but he said he would like to. And I think it was horrid of Father to say it, for I pray for the wild duck every night and ask that it may be preserved from death and all that is evil.

GREGERS (*looking at her*): Do you say your prayers every night?

HEDVIG: Yes.

GREGERS: Who taught you to do that?

HEDVIG: I myself — one time when Father was very ill and had leeches on his neck and said that death was staring him in the face.

GREGERS: Well?

HEDVIG: Then I prayed for him as I lay in bed, and since then I have always kept it up.

GREGERS: And now you pray for the wild duck too?

HEDVIG: I thought it best to bring in the wild duck, for she was so weakly at first.

GREGERS: Do you pray in the morning too?

HEDVIG: No, of course not.

GREGERS: Why not in the morning as well?

HEDVIG: In the morning it's light, you know, and there's nothing in particular to be afraid of.

GREGERS: And your father was going to wring the neck of the wild duck that you love so dearly?

HEDVIG: No; he said he ought to wring its neck but he would spare it for my sake, and that was kind of Father.

GREGERS (*coming a little nearer*): But suppose you were to sacrifice the wild duck of your own free will for his sake?

HEDVIG (*rising*): The wild duck!

GREGERS: Suppose you were to make a free-will offering, for his sake, of the dearest treasure you have in the world?

HEDVIG: Do you think that would do any good?

GREGERS: Try it, Hedvig.

HEDVIG (*softly, with flashing eyes*): Yes, I will try it.

GREGERS: Have you really the courage for it, do you think?

HEDVIG: I'll ask Grandfather to shoot the wild duck for me.

GREGERS: Yes, do. But not a word to your mother about it.

HEDVIG: Why not?

GREGERS: She doesn't understand us.

HEDVIG: The wild duck! I'll try it tomorrow morning.

(GINA *comes in by the passage door.*)

HEDVIG (*going toward her*): Did you find him, Mother?

GINA: No, but I heard as he had called and taken Relling with him.

GREGERS: Are you sure of that?

GINA: Yes, the porter's wife said so. Molvik went with them too, she said.

GREGERS: This evening, when his mind so sorely needs to wrestle in solitude!

GINA (*takes off her things*): Yes, men are strange creatures, so they are. The Lord only knows where Relling has dragged him to! I ran over to Madam Eriksen's, but they weren't there.

HEDVIG (*struggling to keep back her tears*): Oh, if he should never come home any more!

GREGERS: He will come home again. I shall have news to give him tomorrow, and then you shall see how he comes home. You may rely upon that, Hedvig, and sleep in peace. Good night. (*He goes out by the passage door.*)

HEDVIG (*throws herself sobbing on* GINA's *neck*): Mother, Mother!

GINA (*pats her shoulder and sighs*): Ah yes, Relling was right, he was. That's what comes of it when crazy creatures go about presenting the claim of the — what-you-may-call-it.

ACT FIVE

SCENE—HIALMAR EKDAL's *studio. Cold gray morning light. Wet snow lies upon the large panes of the sloping roof window.*
GINA *comes in from the kitchen with an apron and bib on and carrying a dusting brush and a duster; she goes toward the sitting-room door. At the same moment* HEDVIG *comes hurriedly in from the passage.*

GINA (*stops*): Well?

HEDVIG: Oh, Mother, I almost think he's down at Relling's —

GINA: There, you see!

HEDVIG: — because the porter's wife says she could hear that Relling had two people with him when he came home last night.

GINA: That's just what I thought.

HEDVIG: But it's no use his being there if he won't come up to us.

GINA: I'll go down and speak to him at all events.

(OLD EKDAL, *in dressing gown and slippers and with a lighted pipe, appears at the door of his room.*)

EKDAL: Hialmar — isn't Hialmar at home?

GINA: No, he's gone out.

EKDAL: So early? And in such a tearing snow-storm? Well, well, just as he pleases; I can take my morning walk alone. (*He slides the garret door aside;* HEDVIG *helps him; he goes in; she closes it after him.*)

HEDVIG (*in an undertone*): Only think, Mother, when poor Grandfather hears that Father is going to leave us.

GINA: Oh, nonsense; Grandfather mustn't hear anything about it. It was a heaven's mercy he wasn't at home yesterday in all that hurly-burly.

HEDVIG: Yes, but —

(GREGERS *comes in by the passage door.*)

GREGERS: Well, have you any news of him?

GINA: They say he's down at Relling's.

GREGERS: At Rellings! Has he really been out with those creatures?

GINA: Yes, like enough.

GREGERS: When he ought to have been yearning for solitude, to collect and clear his thoughts —

GINA: Yes, you may well say so.

(RELLING *enters from the passage.*)

HEDVIG (*going to him*): Is Father in your room?

GINA (*at the same time*): Is he there?

RELLING: Yes, to be sure he is.

HEDVIG: And you never let us know!

RELLING: Yes, I'm a brute. But in the first place I had to look after the other brute; I mean our demonic friend, of course; and then I fell so dead asleep that —

GINA: What does Ekdal say today?

RELLING: He says nothing whatever.

HEDVIG: Does he speak?

RELLING: Not a blessed word.

GREGERS: No, no; I can understand that very well.

GINA: But what's he doing then?

RELLING: He's lying on the sofa snoring.

GINA: Oh, is he? Yes, Ekdal's a rare one to snore.

HEDVIG: Asleep? Can he sleep?

RELLING: Well, it certainly looks like it.

GREGERS: No wonder, after the spiritual conflict that has rent him —

GINA: And then he's never been used to gadding about out of doors at night.

HEDVIG: Perhaps it's a good thing that he's getting sleep, Mother.

GINA: Of course it is, and we must take care we don't wake him up too early. Thank you, Relling. I must get the house cleaned up a bit now, and then — Come and help me, Hedvig.

(GINA and HEDVIG *go into the sitting-room.*)

GREGERS (*turning to* RELLING): What is your explanation of the spiritual tumult that is now going on in Hialmar Ekdal?

RELLING: Devil a bit of a spiritual tumult have I noticed in him.

GREGERS: What! Not at such a crisis, when his whole life has been placed on a new foundation? How can you think that such an individuality as Hialmar's —

RELLING: Oh, individuality—he! If he ever had any tendency to the abnormal developments you call individuality, I can assure you it was rooted out of him while he was still in his teens.

GREGERS: That would be strange indeed — considering the loving care with which he was brought up.

RELLING: By those two high-flown, hysterical maiden aunts, you mean?

GREGERS: Let me tell you that they were women who never forgot the claim of the ideal — but of course you will only jeer at me again.

RELLING: No, I'm in no humor for that. I know all about those ladies, for he has ladled out no end of rhetoric on the subject of his "two soul mothers." But I don't think he has much to thank them for. Ekdal's misfortune is that in his own circle he has always been looked upon as a shining light.

GREGERS: Not without reason, surely. Look at the depth of his mind!

RELLING: I have never discovered it. That his father believed in it I don't so much wonder; the old lieutenant has been an ass all his days.

GREGERS: He has had a childlike mind all his days; that is what you cannot understand.

RELLING: Well, so be it. But then when our dear sweet Hialmar went to college he at once passed for the great light of the future amongst his comrades too! He was handsome, the rascal — red and white — a shopgirl's dream of manly beauty; and with his superficially emotional temperament and his sympathetic voice and his talent for declaiming other people's verses and other people's thoughts —

GREGERS (*indignantly*): Is it Hialmar Ekdal you are talking about in this strain?

RELLING: Yes, with your permission; I am simply giving you an inside view of the idol you are groveling before.

GREGERS: I should hardly have thought I was quite stone-blind.

RELLING: Yes, you are — or not far from it. You are a sick man too, you see.

GREGERS: You are right there.

RELLING: Yes. Yours is a complicated case. First of all there is that plaguy integrity fever, and then — what's worse — you are always in a delirium of hero worship; you must always have something to adore, outside yourself.

GREGERS: Yes, I must certainly seek it outside myself.

RELLING: But you make such shocking mistakes about every new phoenix you think you have discovered. Here again you have come to a cotter's cabin with your claim of the ideal, and the people of the house are insolvent.

GREGERS: If you don't think better than that of Hialmar Ekdal, what pleasure can you find in being everlastingly with him?

RELLING: Well, you see, I'm supposed to be a sort of a doctor — save the mark! I can't but give a hand to the poor sick folk who live under the same roof with me.

GREGERS: Oh, indeed! Hialmar Ekdal is sick too, is he?

RELLING: Most people are, worse luck.

GREGERS: And what remedy are you applying in Hialmar's case?

RELLING: My usual one. I am cultivating the life illusion in him.

GREGERS: Life — illusion? I didn't catch what you said.

RELLING: Yes, I said illusion. For illusion, you know, is the stimulating principle.

GREGERS: May I ask with what illusion Hialmar is inoculated?

RELLING: No, thank you; I don't betray professional secrets to quacksalvers. You would probably go and muddle his case still more than you have already. But my method is infallible. I have applied it to Molvik as well. I have made him "demonic." That's the blister I have to put on his neck.

GREGERS: Is he not really demonic then?

RELLING: What the devil do you mean by demonic? It's only a piece of gibberish I've invented to keep up a spark of life in him. But for that, the poor harmless creature would have succumbed to self-contempt and despair many a long year ago. And then the old lieutenant! But he has hit upon his own cure, you see.

GREGERS: Lieutenant Ekdal? What of him?

RELLING: Just think of the old bear hunter shutting himself up in that dark garret to shoot rabbits! I tell you there is not a happier sportsman in the world than that old man pottering about in there among all that rubbish. The four or five withered Christmas trees he has saved up are the same to him as the whole great fresh Höidal forest; the cock and the hens are big game birds in the fir tops, and the rabbits that flop about the garret floor are the bears he has to battle with — the mighty hunter of the mountains!

GREGERS: Poor unfortunate old man! Yes, he has indeed had to narrow the ideals of his youth.

RELLING: While I think of it, Mr. Werle junior — don't use that foreign word: ideals. We have the excellent native word: lies.

GREGERS: Do you think the two things are related?

RELLING: Yes, just about as closely as typhus and putrid fever.

GREGERS: Doctor Relling, I shall not give up the struggle until I have rescued Hialmar from your clutches!

RELLING: So much the worse for him. Rob the average man of his life illusion and you rob him of his happiness at the same stroke. (*to* HEDVIG, *who comes in from the sitting room*) Well, little wild-duck mother. I'm just going down to see whether Papa is still lying meditating upon that wonderful invention of his. (*Goes out by passage door.*)

GREGERS (*approaches* HEDVIG): I can see by your face that you have not yet done it.

HEDVIG: What? Oh, that about the wild duck! No.

GREGERS: I suppose your courage failed when the time came?

HEDVIG: No, that wasn't it. But when I awoke this morning and remembered what he had been talking about it seemed so strange.

GREGERS: Strange?

HEDVIG: Yes, I don't know — Yesterday evening, at the moment, I thought there was something so delightful about it; but since I have slept and thought of it again, it somehow doesn't seem worth while.

GREGERS: Ah, I thought you could not have grown up quite unharmed in this house.

HEDVIG: I don't care about that, if only Father would come up —

GREGERS: Oh, if only your eyes had been opened to that which gives life its value — if you possessed the true, joyous, fearless spirit of sacrifice you would soon see how he would come up to you. But I believe in you still, Hedvig. (*He goes out by the passage door. HEDVIG wanders about the room for a time; she is on the point of going into the kitchen when a knock is heard at the garret door. HEDVIG goes out and opens it a little; OLD EKDAL comes out; she pushes the door to again.*)

EKDAL: H'm, it's not much fun to take one's morning walk alone.

HEDVIG: Wouldn't you like to go shooting, Grandfather?

EKDAL: It's not the weather for it today. It's so dark there you can scarcely see where you're going.

HEDVIG: Do you never want to shoot anything besides the rabbits?

EKDAL: Do you think the rabbits aren't good enough?

HEDVIG: Yes, but what about the wild duck?

EKDAL: Ho-ho! Are you afraid I shall shoot your wild duck? Never in the world. Never!

HEDVIG: No, I suppose you couldn't; they say it's very difficult to shoot wild ducks.

EKDAL: Couldn't! Should rather think I could.

HEDVIG: How would you set about it, Grandfather? I don't mean with my wild duck, but with others.

EKDAL: I should take care to shoot them in the breast, you know; that's the surest place. And then you must shoot against the feathers, you see — not the way of the feathers.

HEDVIG: Do they die then, Grandfather?

EKDAL: Yes they die right enough — when you shoot properly. Well, I must go and brush up a bit. H'm — understand — h'm. (*Goes into his room.*)

(*HEDVIG waits a little, glances toward the sitting-room door, goes over to the bookcase, stands on tiptoe, takes the double-barreled pistol down from the shelf and looks at it. GINA, with brush and duster, comes from the sitting room. HEDVIG hastily lays down the pistol unobserved.*)

GINA: Don't stand raking amongst Father's things, Hedvig.

HEDVIG (*goes away from the bookcase*): I was only going to tidy up a little.

GINA: You'd better go into the kitchen and see if the coffee's keeping hot; I'll take his breakfast on a tray when I go down to him.

(*HEDVIG goes out. GINA begins to sweep and clean up the studio. Presently the passage door is opened with hesitation and HIALMAR EKDAL looks in. He has on his overcoat but not his hat; he is unwashed, and his hair is disheveled and unkempt. His eyes are dull and heavy.*)

GINA (*standing with the brush in her hand and looking at him*): Oh, there now, Ekdal — so you've come after all?

HIALMAR (*comes in an answers in a toneless voice*): I come — only to depart immediately.

GINA: Yes, yes, I suppose so. But, Lord help us! what a sight you are!

HIALMAR: A sight?

GINA: And your nice winter coat too! Well, that's done for.

HEDVIG (*at the kitchen door*): Mother, hadn't I better — (*Sees HIALMAR, gives a loud scream of joy and runs to him.*) Oh, Father, Father!

HIALMAR (*turns away and makes a gesture of repulsion*): Away, away, away! (*to GINA*) Keep her away from me, I say!

GINA (*in a low tone*): Go into the sitting room, Hedvig. (*HEDVIG does so without a word.*)

HIALMAR (*fussily pulls out the table drawer*): I must have my books with me. Where are my books?

GINA: Which books?

HIALMAR: My scientific books, of course; the technical magazines I require for my invention.

GINA (*searches in the bookcase*): Is it these here paper-covered ones?

HIALMAR: Yes, of course.

GINA (*lays a heap of magazines on the table*): Shan't I get Hedvig to cut them for you?

HIALMAR: I don't require to have them cut for me. (*Short silence.*)

GINA: Then you're still set on leaving us, Ekdal?

HIALMAR (*rummaging amongst the books*): Yes, that is a matter of course, I should think.

GINA: Well, well.

HIALMAR (*vehemently*): How can I live here, to be stabbed to the heart every hour of the day?

GINA: God forgive you for thinking such vile things of me.

HIALMAR: Prove —

GINA: I think it's you as has got to prove.

HIALMAR: After a past like yours? There are certain claims — I may almost call them claims of the ideal —

GINA: But what about Grandfather? What's to become of him, poor dear?

HIALMAR: I know my duty; my helpless father will come with me. I am going out into the town to make arrangements — H'm (*hesitatingly*) — has anyone found my hat on the stairs?

GINA: No. Have you lost your hat?

HIALMAR: Of course I had it on when I came in last night — there's no doubt about that — but I couldn't find it this morning.

GINA: Lord help us! Where have you been to with those two ne'er-do-wells?

HIALMAR: Oh, don't bother me about trifles. Do you suppose I am in the mood to remember details?

GINA: If only you haven't caught cold, Ekdal — (*Goes out into the kitchen.*)

HIALMAR (*talks to himself in a low tone of irritation while he empties the table drawer*): You're a scoundrel, Relling! You're a low fellow! Ah, you shameless tempter! I wish I could get someone to stick a knife into you! (*He lays some old letters on one side, finds the torn document of yesterday, takes it up and looks at the pieces, puts it down hurriedly as* GINA *enters.*)

GINA (*sets a tray with coffee, etc., on the table*): Here's a drop of something hot, if you'd fancy it. And there's some bread and butter and a snack of salt meat.

HIALMAR (*glancing at the tray*): Salt meat? Never under this roof! It's true I have not had a mouthful of solid food for nearly twenty-four hours, but no matter. My memoranda! The commencement of my autobiography! What has become of my diary and all my important papers? (*Opens the sitting-room door but draws back.*) She is there too!

GINA: Good lord! the child must be somewhere!

HIALMAR: Come out. (*He makes room;* HEDVIG *comes, scared, into the studio.*)

HIALMAR (*with his hand on the door handle, says to* GINA): In these, the last moments I spend in my former home, I wish to be spared from interlopers. (*Goes into the room.*)

HEDVIG (*with a bound toward her mother, asks softly, trembling*): Does that mean me?

GINA: Stay out in the kitchen, Hedvig; or, no — you'd best go into your own room. (*Speaks to* HIALMAR *as she goes to him.*) Wait a bit, Ekdal; don't rummage so in the drawers. I know where everything is.

HEDVIG (*stands a moment immovable, in terror and perplexity, biting her lips to keep back the tears; then she clenches her hands convulsively and says softly*): The wild duck! (*She steals over and takes the pistol from the shelf, opens the garret door a little way, creeps in and draws the door to after her.* HIALMAR *and* GINA *can be heard disputing in the sitting room.*)

HIALMAR (*comes in with some manuscript books and old loose papers which he lays upon the table*): That portmanteau is of no use! There are a thousand and one things I must drag with me.

GINA (*following with the portmanteau*): Why not leave all the rest for the present and only take a shirt and a pair of woolen drawers with you?

HIALMAR: Whew! All these exhausting preparations! (*pulls off his overcoat and throws it upon the sofa.*)

GINA: And there's the coffee getting cold.

HIALMAR: H'm. (*Drinks a mouthful without thinking of it and then another.*)

GINA (*dusting the backs of the chairs*): A nice job you'll have to find such another big garret for the rabbits.

HIALMAR: What! Am I to drag all those rabbits with me too?

GINA: You don't suppose Grandfather can get on without his rabbits.

HIALMAR: He must get used to doing without them. Have not *I* to sacrifice very much greater things than rabbits!

GINA (*dusting the bookcase*): Shall I put the flute in the portmanteau for you?

HIALMAR: No. No flute for me. But give me the pistol!

GINA: Do you want to take the pistol with you?

HIALMAR: Yes. My loaded pistol.

GINA (*searching for it*): It's gone. He must have taken it in with him.

HIALMAR: Is he in the garret?

GINA: Yes, of course he's in the garret.

HIALMAR: H'm — poor lonely old man. (*He takes a piece of bread and butter, eats it and finishes his cup of coffee.*)

GINA: And if we hadn't have let that room, you could have moved in there.

HIALMAR: And continued to live under the same roof with — Never — never!

GINA: But couldn't you put up with the sitting room for a day or two? You could have it all to yourself.

HIALMAR: Never within these walls!

GINA: Well, then, down with Relling and Molvik.

HIALMAR: Don't mention those wretches' names to me! The very thought of them almost takes away my appetite. Oh no, I must go out into the storm and the snowdrift — go from house to house and seek shelter for my father and myself.

GINA: But you've got no hat, Ekdal! You've been and lost your hat, you know.

HIALMAR: Oh, those two brutes, those slaves of all the vices! A hat must be procured. (*Takes another piece of bread and butter.*) Some arrangements must be made. For I have no mind to throw away my life either. (*Looks for something on the tray.*)

GINA: What are you looking for?

HIALMAR: Butter.

GINA: I'll get some at once. (*Goes out into the kitchen.*)

HIALMAR (*calls after her*): Oh, it doesn't matter; dry bread is good enough for me.

GINA (*brings a dish of butter*): Look here; this is fresh churned. (*She pours out another cup of coffee for him; he seats himself on the sofa, spreads more butter on the already buttered bread and eats and drinks a while in silence.*)

HIALMAR: Could I, without being subject to

intrusion—intrusion of any sort—could I live in the sitting room there for a day or two?

GINA: Yes, to be sure you could, if you only would.

HIALMAR: For I see no possibility of getting all Father's things out in such a hurry.

GINA: And, besides, you've surely got to tell him first as you don't mean to live with us others no more.

HIALMAR (*pushes away his coffee cup*): Yes, there is that too; I shall have to lay bare the whole tangled story to him — I must turn matters over; I must have breathing time. I cannot take all these burdens on my shoulders in a single day.

GINA: No, especially in such horrible weather as it is outside.

HIALMAR (*touching* WERLE's *letter*): I see that paper still lying about here.

GINA: Yes, I haven't touched it.

HIALMAR: So far as I am concerned it is mere waste-paper —

GINA: Well, I have certainly no notion of making any use of it.

HIALMAR: — but we had better not let it get lost all the same; in all the upset when I move it might easily —

GINA: I'll take good care of it, Ekdal.

HIALMAR: The donation is in the first instance made to Father, and it rests with him to accept or decline it.

GINA (*sighs*): Yes, poor old Father —

HIALMAR: To make quite safe — Where shall I find some gum?

GINA (*goes to the bookcase*): Here's the gum pot.

HIALMAR: And a brush?

GINA: The brush is here too. (*Brings him the things.*)

HIALMAR (*takes a pair of scissors*): Just a strip

of paper at the back — (*Clips and gums.*) Far be it from me to lay hands upon what is not my own — and least of all upon what belongs to a destitute old man — and to — the other as well. There now! Let it lie there for a time, and when it is dry take it away. I wish never to see that document again. Never!

(GREGERS WERLE *enters from the passage.*)

GREGERS (*somewhat surprised*): What — are you sitting here, Hialmar?

HIALMAR (*rises hurriedly*): I had sunk down from fatigue.

GREGERS: You had been having breakfast, I see.

HIALMAR: The body sometimes makes its claims felt too.

GREGERS: What have you decided to do?

HIALMAR: For a man like me there is only one course possible. I am just putting my most important things together. But it takes time, you know.

GINA (*with a touch of impatience*): Am I to get the room ready for you or am I to pack your portmanteau?

HIALMAR (*after a glance of annoyance at* GREGERS): Pack — and get the room ready!

GINA (*takes the portmanteau*): Very well; then I'll put in the shirt and other things. (*Goes into the sitting room and draws the door to after her.*)

GREGERS (*after a short silence*): I never dreamed that this would be the end of it. Do you really feel it a necessity to leave house and home?

HIALMAR (*wanders about restlessly*): What would you have me do? I am not fitted to bear unhappiness, Gregers. I must feel secure and at peace in my surroundings.

GREGERS: But can you not feel that here? Just try it. I should have thought you had firm ground to build upon — if only you start afresh. And, remember, you have your invention to live for.

HIALMAR: Oh, don't talk about my invention. It's perhaps still in the dim distance.

GREGERS: Indeed!

HIALMAR: Why, great heavens, what would you have one invent? Other people have invented almost everything already. It becomes more and more difficult every day —

GREGERS: And you have devoted so much labor to it.

HIALMAR: It was that blackguard Relling that urged me to it.

GREGERS: Relling?

HIALMAR: Yes, it was he that first made me realize my aptitude for making some notable discovery in photography.

GREGERS: Aha — it was Relling!

HIALMAR: Oh, I have been so truly happy over it! Not so much for the sake of the invention itself as because Hedvig believed in it — believed in it with a child's whole eagerness of faith. At least I have been fool enough to go and imagine that she believed in it.

GREGERS: Can you really think Hedvig has been false toward you?

HIALMAR: I can think anything now. It is Hedvig that stands in my way. She will blot out the sunlight from my whole life.

GREGERS: Hedvig! Is it Hedvig you are talking of? How should she blot out your sunlight?

HIALMAR (*without answering*): How unutterably I have loved that child! How unutterably happy I have felt every time I came home to my humble room and she flew to meet me with her sweet little blinking eyes. Oh, confiding fool that I have been! I loved her unutterably — and I yielded myself up to the dream, the delusion, that she loved me unutterably in return.

GREGERS: Do you call that a delusion?

HIALMAR: How should I know? I can get nothing out of Gina; and besides, she is totally blind to the ideal side of these complications. But to you I feel impelled to open my mind, Gregers. I cannot shake off this frightful doubt — perhaps Hedvig has never really and honestly loved me.

GREGERS: What would you say if she were to give you a proof of her love? (*Listens.*) What's that? I thought I heard the wild duck —

HIALMAR: It's the wild duck quacking. Father's in the garret.

GREGERS: Is he? (*His face lights up with joy.*) I say you may yet have proof that your poor misunderstood Hedvig loves you!

HIALMAR: Oh, what proof can she give me? I dare not believe in any assurance from that quarter.

GREGERS: Hedvig does not know what deceit means.

HIALMAR: Oh, Gregers, that is just what I cannot be sure of. Who knows what Gina and that Mrs. Sørby may many a time have sat here whispering and tattling about? And Hedvig usually has her ears open, I can tell you. Perhaps the deed of gift was not such a surprise to her after all. In fact, I'm not sure but that I noticed something of the sort.

GREGERS: What spirit is this that has taken possession of you?

HIALMAR: I have had my eyes opened. Just you notice — you'll see, the deed of gift is only a beginning. Mrs. Sørby has always been a good deal taken up with Hedvig, and now she has the power to do whatever she likes for the child. They can take her from me whenever they please.

GREGERS: Hedvig will never, never leave you.

HIALMAR: Don't be so sure of that. If only they beckon to her and throw out a golden bait — And oh! I have loved her so unspeakably! I would have counted it my highest happiness to take her tenderly by the hand and lead her, as one leads a timid child through a great dark empty room! I am cruelly certain now that the poor photographer in his humble attic has never really and truly been anything to her. She has only cunningly contrived to keep on a good footing with him until the time came.

GREGERS: You don't believe that yourself, Hialmar.

HIALMAR: That is just the terrible part of it — I don't know what to believe — I never can know it. But can you really doubt that it must be as I say? Ho-ho, you have far too much faith in the claim of the ideal, my good Gregers! If those others came, with the glamour of wealth about them, and called to the child: "Leave him; come to us; here life awaits you — "

GREGERS (*quickly*): Well, what then?

HIALMAR: If I then asked her: "Hedvig are you willing to renounce that life for me?" (*Laughs scornfully.*) No, thank you! You would soon hear what answer I should get.

(*A pistol shot is heard from within the garret.*)

GREGERS (*loudly and joyfully*): Hialmar!

HIALMAR: There now; he must needs go shooting too.

GINA (*comes in*): Oh, Ekdal, I can hear Grandfather blazing away in the garret by himself.

HIALMAR: I'll look in —

GREGERS (*eagerly, with emotion*): Wait a moment! Do you know what that was?

HIALMAR: Yes, of course I know.

GREGERS: No, you don't know. But *I* do. That was the proof!

HIALMAR: What proof?

GREGERS: It was a child's free-will offering. She has got your father to shoot the wild duck.

HIALMAR: To shoot the wild duck!

GINA: Oh, think of that!

HIALMAR: What was that for?

GREGERS: She wanted to sacrifice to you her most cherished possession, for then she thought you would surely come to love her again.

HIALMAR (*tenderly, with emotion*): Oh, poor child!

GINA: What things she does think of!

GREGERS: She only wanted your love again, Hialmar. She could not live without it.

GINA (*struggling with her tears*): There, you can see for yourself, Ekdal.

HIALMAR: Gina, where is she?

GINA (*sniffs*): Poor dear, she's sitting out in the kitchen, I daresay.

HIALMAR (*goes over, tears open the kitchen door and says*): Hedvig, come, come in to me! (*Looks around.*) No, she's not here.

GINA: Then she must be in her own little room.

HIALMAR (*without*): No, she's not here either. (*Comes in.*) She must have gone out.

GINA: Yes, you wouldn't have her anywhere in the house.

HIALMAR: Oh, if she would only come home quickly, so that I can tell her — Everything will come right now, Gregers; now I believe we can begin life afresh.

GREGERS (*quietly*): I knew it; I knew the child would make amends.

(OLD EKDAL *appears at the door of his room; he is in full uniform and is busy buckling on his sword.*)

HIALMAR (*astonished*): Father! Are you there?

GINA: Have you been firing in your room?

EKDAL (*resentfully approaching*): So you go shooting alone, do you, Hialmar?

HIALMAR (*excited and confused*): Then it wasn't you that fired that shot in the garret?

EKDAL: Me that fired? H'm.

GREGERS (*calls out to* HIALMAR): She has shot the wild duck herself!

HIALMAR: What can it mean? (*Hastens to the garret door, tears it aside, looks in and calls loudly.*) Hedvig!

GINA (*runs to the door*): Good God! what's that?

HIALMAR (*goes in*): She's lying on the floor!

GREGERS: Hedvig! Lying on the floor! (*Goes to* HIALMAR.)

GINA (*at the same time*): Hedvig! (*Inside the garret.*) No, no, no!

EKDAL: Ho-ho! Does she go shooting too now?

(HIALMAR, GINA *and* GREGERS *carry* HEDVIG *into the studio; in her dangling right hand she holds the pistol fast clasped in her fingers.*)

HIALMAR (*distracted*): The pistol has gone off. She has wounded herself. Call for help! Help!

GINA (*runs into the passage and calls down*): Relling! Relling! Doctor Relling, come up as quick as you can!

(HIALMAR *and* GREGERS *lay* HEDVIG *down on the sofa.*)

EKDAL (*quietly*): The woods avenge themselves.

HIALMAR (*on his knees beside* HEDVIG): She'll soon come to now. She's coming to; yes, yes, yes.

GINA (*who has come in again*): Where has she hurt herself? I can't see anything.

(RELLING *comes hurriedly, and immediately after him* MOLVIK; *the latter without his waistcoat and necktie and with his coat open.*)

RELLING: What's the matter here?

GINA: They say Hedvig shot herself.

HIALMAR: Come and help us!

RELLING: Shot herself! (*He pushes the table aside and begins to examine her.*)

HIALMAR (*kneeling and looking anxiously up at him*): It can't be dangerous? Speak, Relling! She is scarcely bleeding at all. It can't be dangerous?

RELLING: How did it happen?

HIALMAR: Oh, we don't know —

GINA: She wanted to shoot the wild duck.

RELLING: The wild duck?

HIALMAR: The pistol must have gone off.

RELLING: H'm. Indeed.

EKDAL: The woods avenge themselves. But I'm not afraid all the same. (*Goes into the garret and closes the door after him.*)

HIALMAR: Well, Relling, why don't you say something?

RELLING: The ball has entered the breast.

HIALMAR: Yes, but she's coming to!

RELLING: Surely you can see that Hedvig is dead.

GINA (*bursts into tears*): Oh, my child, my child—

GREGERS (*huskily*): In the depths of the sea —

HIALMAR (*jumps up*): No, no, she must live! Oh, for God's sake, Relling — only a moment — only just till I can tell her how unspeakably I loved her all the time.

RELLING: The bullet has gone through her heart. Internal hemorrhage. Death must have been instantaneous.

HIALMAR: And I! I hunted her from me like an animal! And she crept terrified into the garret and died for love of me! (*Sobbing.*) I can never atone to her! I can never tell her — (*Clenches his hands and cries upward.*) Oh, Thou above — if Thou be indeed! Why hast Thou done this thing to me?

GINA: Hush, hush, you mustn't go on that awful way. We had no right to keep her, I suppose.

MOLVIK: The child is not dead but sleepeth.

RELLING: Bosh!

HIALMAR (*becomes calm, goes over to the sofa, folds his arms and looks at* HEDVIG): There she lies so stiff and still.

RELLING (*tries to loosen the pistol*): She's holding it so tight, so tight.

GINA: No, no, Relling; don't break her fingers; let the pistol be.

HIALMAR: She shall take it with her.

GINA: Yes, let her. But the child mustn't lie here for a show. She shall go to her own room, so she shall. Help me, Ekdal.

(HIALMAR *and* GINA *take* HEDVIG *between them.*)

HIALMAR (*as they are carrying her*): Oh, Gina, Gina, can you survive this?

GINA: We must help each other to bear it. For now, at least, she belongs to both of us.

MOLVIK (*stretches out his arms and mumbles*): Blessed be the Lord; to earth thou shalt return; to earth thou shalt return —

RELLING (*whispers*): Hold your tongue, you fool; you're drunk.

(HIALMAR *and* GINA *carry the body out through the kitchen door.* RELLING *shuts it after them.* MOLVIK *slinks out into the passage.*)

RELLING (*goes over to* GREGERS *and says*): No one shall ever convince me that the pistol went off by accident.

GREGERS (*who has stood terrified, with conculsive twitching*): Who can say how the dreadful thing happened?

RELLING: The powder has burned the body of her dress. She must have pressed the pistol right against her breast and fired.

GREGERS: Hedvig has not died in vain. Did you not see how sorrow set free what is noble in him?

RELLING: Most people are ennobled by the actual presence of death. But how long do you suppose this nobility will last in him?

GREGERS: Why should it not endure and increase throughout his life?

RELLING: Before a year is over, little Hedvig will be nothing to him but a pretty theme for declamation.

GREGERS: How dare you say that of Hialmar Ekdal?

RELLING: We will talk of this again, when the grass has first withered on her grave. Then you'll hear him spouting about "the child too early torn from her father's heart"; then you'll see him steep himself in a syrup of sentiment and self-admiration and self-pity. Just you wait!

GREGERS: If you are right and I am wrong, then life is not worth living.

RELLING: Oh, life would be quite tolerable, after all, if only we could be rid of the confounded duns that keep on pestering us, in our poverty, with the claim of the ideal.

GREGERS (*looking straight before him*): In that case I am glad that my destiny is what it is.

RELLING: May I inquire — what is your destiny?

GREGERS (*going*): To be the thirteenth at table.

RELLING: The devil it is.

CURTAIN

Notes and Jottings

Nine separate sets of notes relevant to The Wild Duck *have survived, of varying length, and dating from probably early 1883, before the drama had begun to take proper shape, to about April 1884, when Ibsen was actively working on the first draft of Act I. Of these A1–5 are on the same kind of paper watermarked 'Imperial Treasury de la Rue'; but it is not at all certain that all the sides of any one folded sheet were always written on one and the same occasion; A6 and 7 also share the same kind of paper, the former being a folded sheet octavo, the latter a single leaf, being the torn half of such a folded sheet; they are also both in pencil, and the character of the rapid handwriting is the same on each. A8 and 9 also share the same kind of paper, the former being written in a pencilled hand similar to that of A6 and 7; A9 is more carefully written in ink.*

In addition there is one fragmentary and one fuller draft of the play, the latter containing many interleaved emendations.

A1. *Written on four sides of a folded sheet octavo, probably in early 1883, possibly as early as December 1882. Some of the ideas mentioned here are echoed in Ibsen's correspondence: e.g., sheep in a community of wolves, letter of 23 March 1884; Holger Drachmann's volte-face, letters of 27 Dec. 1883 and 17 Jan. 1884; an echo also of his views on the 'new nobility' in his Trondheim speech of 1885 and in* Rosmersholm. *For a note on 'E.L.' and 'A.K.' see A4 below; 'A. the printer' is no doubt a reference to the figure of Aslaksen, who appears in* The League of Youth *and* An Enemy of the People.

'Free-born men' is cant. They do not exist. Marriage, the relationship between man and woman, has ruined the human race, set the brand of slavery on everybody.

E.L. has come to the conclusion that no improvement is possible by emancipation. The work of creation has been a failure from the start. He is a half-baked pessimist, without any initiative, a futile dreamer.

Patriotism and such things are but passing phases.

Scientists should not be allowed to torture animals to death; let doctors experiment on journalists and politicians.

Modern society is not a society of people; it is merely a society of males.

When liberal-minded men want to bring about some improvement in the position of women in society, they first inquire whether public opinion — men — will approve. It is the same as asking wolves whether they favour new measures for the protection of sheep.

Many a doctrinaire agitator has gradually gone over to become his own grandfather (Drachmann, for example).

E. L.'s marrying beneath him has in one way become a 'true marriage' in that during his married life he has sunk down or in any case has not grown. Now he cannot dispense with his wife — With her, things have gone likewise.

He has to spend the evening with some distinguished people, but he finds it tiring and a strain. He returns to his narrow home surroundings.

Rather like A. the printer, he has had a glimpse of a higher world; that is his misfortune.

In becoming civilized, man undergoes

461

the same change as when a child grows up. Instinct weakens, but powers of logical thought are developed. Adults have lost the ability to play with dolls.

'The sixth sense.' E.L.'s favourite thought is of hypnotic influence.

We make fun of Germany's 34 fatherlands; but having just as many in Europe is equally ludicrous. North America manages with one or — for the moment — with two.

His refined nature will not allow him to confess openly that he does not believe in patriotism and things like that.

The pity is that our best thoughts are thought by our worst scoundrels.

E.L., the photographer, the unsuccessful poet, dreams of a socialist revolution, the revolution of the future, of science. Poison in the breakfast. . . .

A.K., the sybarite, enjoys an aesthetic indignation at poverty and misery. He enjoys his visits to his one-time school friend, now starving, without being conscious of the real reason.

To wish and to will. Our worst faults are the consequences of confusing the two things.

What devil! They maintain the right of the majority, and yet those with the vote represent only a small arbitrarily limited minority.

All existing things, art, poetry, etc., break down into new categories as does the mind of the child in the spirit of the adult.

Liberty consists of giving the individual the right to liberate himself, each according to his personal needs.

Introduce the episode of the mortally sick person. Use Deininger as a model.

Women artists and business women try to conceal their sex. On their pictures, their nameplates, etc., they put only the initial of their first name so that people will think they are men — e.g. M.Sm., E.Zogb., etc.

E.L. is socialist-minded; but he dare not confess it; he has a family, and is therefore not independent.

Those among us having the vote are in a minority. Is then the minority right?

Conscience is not a stable thing. It varies in different individuals and with time. That of the country folk is old-fashioned, obsolescent. It is between obsolescent and developing consciences that party battles are fought.

A new nobility will take shape. It will not be one of birth or of money, nor of ability or knowledge. The nobility of the future will be a nobility of mind and will.

Christianity in various ways demoralizes and hinders both men and women.

They say suicide is immoral. But what of a life of slow suicide — out of regard for one's surroundings?

A.K.-d: to be well-fed, tucked up in a soft bed, and listening to the pouring rain and thinking about difficult journeys in bad weather and cold — that is a great delight.

A2. *Written on four sides of a folded sheet, octavo:*

CHARACTERS

(a) first side

The old dismissed official.
  White haired, broken in spirit by his prison sentence. Earns a little by clerical work.

His vain wife.
  Half crazy as a result of the family's misfortunes. Herself partly to blame without realizing it. Stupid idolatry of son. Moaning and complaining.

The son with the wasted talents.
  Feeling of piety towards his parents holds him, the family shame oppresses him.

The son's wife.
  Slightly older than him; practical gifts, prosaic, from simple home.

The rich old ship-owner and merchant.
  An old roué in secret.

His son, the rich social writer.
  Widower; fights for the rights of the poor; regards it as a sport.

(b) second and third sides

The host: Yes, my dear Chamberlain, what have you to say about the Liebfraumilch? Chamb. Yes indeed, I must say it was faultless. 2nd Chamb. Huh, I suppose it cost you a pretty penny? Eh? The host: You can take your oath on that. It's one of the very very best vintages, I can tell you. Gregers. Is there any sort of difference among the vintages. The host: Well, you are a fine one! It's not much good putting good wine in front of you. 2nd Cham. It's the same with hock as it is with . . . with photographs, Mr. . . ., it's a matter of sunlight. Or am I wrong? Gregers. No indeed, the light certainly has something to do with it. . . . H.L. The past few years haven't been particularly good for the production of chamberlains. 1st Chamb. No, the weather's been a bit cloudy as you might say; not enough sunshine. — Gregers. So it is a bit with chamberlains as it is with different sorts of wine. 2nd Chamb. How do you mean, my dear sir? Gregers. Not all the vintages are equally good. The host: Just listen to *him*, gentlemen! Graaberg (from the office) I beg your pardon, but there's somebody here who wants to be out. The host: Don't worry. (Here comes the episode with the old man. Hired servant. Don't forget the cognac, Pettersen. Embarrassed pause. 2nd Chamb. makes sarcastic remarks. Gregers is offended [(] Al.K. That isn't very nice of you. Chamb. But I ['but' *crossed out*] assure you; I didn't mean the slightest thing by that. Mrs. M (with cigarette) No, the chamberlain is very good at heart. But, heavens, all of us have to work for a living. (N.B.

this topic has been mentioned before by the host to Gregers.)

H.L. 'the capon' goes and 'enjoys' all the 'little girls' he is on familiar terms with.

In Act I, the merchant finishes by abusing the photographer after they have drunk too much. Halfdan leaves. At home he gives nothing away, he gives a different account of the events at the party, has been the centre of attraction, etc. — The next day the more noble-minded ones visit him — His mother is in the asylum. She went mad as a result of the family misfortunes. Possibility that the son also, etc.

Old Ekdahl keeps pigeons and other birds. Passion for hunting. . . . He has an old gun. . . . Hedvig — decision. . . .

Mrs. S. Slip him something outside, something good. P. Certainly (goes).

Mrs. S. Well, did he get anything? P. Yes, I slipped him a bottle of cognac. Mrs. S. Oh, you might have found something a bit better than that. P. No, Mrs. S., cognac is the best thing he knows.

(c) fourth page discusses the character of A.K. (eventually Gregers Werle, see note A4 below)

Al.K. has no objection to his father marrying Mrs. M. First because that would be better than possible scandals with the servant girls, and also because when his father marries, he must make a settlement on his son.

A.K. would not mind marrying Mrs. M. himself, but in that case his father would presumably not marry, and not make any settlement either, and 'it is not good for capital to stay too long in the hands of old people. 400,000 kroner in the hands of a man of 34 is more productive than a million in the hands of a man in his sixties['].

Nor would the chamberlain have any objection to marrying Mrs. M. But his income is not adequate, so —

A3. *One folded sheet, octavo; the first side*

has a list of characters, with an indication of the age of some; on the fourth side, some notes and draft dialogue, probably written down on some later occasion, perhaps whilst drafting Act I.

(a) *first side*

THE CHARACTERS

63   Walle, merchant, factory owner, etc.
35   [*originally* 37] Halfdan Walle, his son
67   Ekdahl, former bailiff
      ['Mrs. Ekdahl' *crossed out*], his wife
37   [*originally* 35] Gregers Ekdahl, their
      son, photographer
      ['Hedvig, his wife' *crossed out*]
38   Gina, his wife
14   Hedvig, their eldest daughter, 14–15
      years
      ['Their three' *crossed out*] younger
      children
35   Mrs. Berta [*originally* Lövstad] Sörby,
      the merchant's housekeeper
      Nanne, a teacher
      Flor, a chamberlain the one with the
      anecdotes)
      Rasmussen, a chamberlain (satirical)
      Sæther, a chamberlain (gallant, stupid)
      Graaberg, the merchant's chief clerk
      Pettersen, the merchant's personal servant
      Flasrud, his driver
      Guests, hired servants, etc.
      (The action takes place in Kristiania)

(b) *fourth side*

Comparison with wild ducks: when they are wounded —, they go to the bottom, the stubborn devils, and bite on fast —; but if you have a good dog, and it is in shallow water[?], then — Hedvig like the wild duck,— Gregers's knowledge of children's first and deepest sorrows. They are not cares about love; no, they are family sorrows — painful home circumstances —

———

Gregers: But is Molvik's religious preach-

ing any good? 'The Doctor': Well, it isn't up to much, you know. But it can always serve quite well for the poor and people like that.

———

Hedvig's description of what it was like the first time she saw a big expanse of water looking down from a height.

———

People are sea-creatures — like the wild duck — not land creatures — Gregers was made for the sea. All people will in time live on it when the dry land is inundated. Then family life will stop.

A.4. *One folded sheet, octavo, written on the first side only:*

MODELS

Edvard Larsen/Alexander Kjelland/Mrs. Colban/Rektor Steen/Miss Riis/Hartvig Lassen / Chamberlain Gran / Chamberlain Christenssen/Assessor Saxlund/Professor Lochmann/Udvig/Midling/Ross, the painter.
[Edvard Larsen, (i.e. Edward Larssen), a poetaster and photographer who took the first known photograph of Ibsen. Alexander Kielland (1849–1906), Norwegian novelist, with a highly articulate (but, perhaps in Ibsen's view, not altogether genuinely felt) sense of social indignation; Ibsen was never personally acquainted with him. Rector Steen (1827–1906), leading left-wing politician, was later Prime Minister 1898–1902. Hartvig Lassen (1824–97) literary critic and historian, was attached to Kristiania Theatre from 1873. Miss Riis, Mrs. Colban and C. M. Ross belong to Ibsen's circle of acquaintances in Rome. F. Lochmann was a professor of medicine whom Ibsen met in Uppsala in 1877 when both received honorary degrees. Udvig had probably been a fellow student of Ibsen's.]

A5. *Written on the first and part of the second side of a folded sheet, octavo; dated 20 April 1884:*

In the house of the rich old factory owner. Elegant and comfortable smoking-room; upholstered sofas and easy chairs; lighted lamps and candelabra. At the rear, a large open door with curtains drawn back. Within can be seen the billiard-room, similarly lit up. Right, front, in the smoking-room is the door leading into the office; left beyond the fireplace is a double door leading to the dining-room. Loud conversation of many guests is heard within; somebody taps a knife on a glass; silence follows; a toast is proposed; shouts of 'hurrah' and 'bravo'; again the noise and buzz of conversation.

A couple of liveried servants and two or three hired servants in black are putting the smoking-room and billiard-room in order.

A hired servant comes with the old 'former' . . . from the right in the billiard-room.— Hired servant (to house servant): Pettersen, there's a man here, who —— P. Lord, are you here at this time? The fmr. I have to get into the office. P. Oh, but it was shut over an hour ago. The fmr. Yes, I saw that, but — (looks towards the door on the right) P. Yes, you can come through here; because Graaberg is still sitting in there. The fmr. Thanks (moves to go in). The other servant. Here, you, give me a hand with this table. The fmr. Who, me? Oh, yes, the table (helps). The servant. Thanks. The fmr. Perhaps I can go in now. P. Yes, just go in. (He goes in to the right.)

A6. *Written in pencil on four sides of a folded sheet, octavo; same kind of paper as A7. Ink entry at head of first side: 'Act I/In the house of Walle, the merchant' crossed out.*

(a) first side

The danger of undermining the ideals. The irony of fate in belonging to another generation. Hedvig's drawings are not her own creations; the moment she realizes this, she does not draw any more. All happiness is past once she discovers that her father's suspicions of her admiration are roused, fights, evasions, observations, etc.

——

There is always one ideal left remaining —— Gregers, who denies all the others, believes in 'friendship' —— Hjalmar sees through the egoistic reasons.

——

Hjalmar is also admired in the family because he supports his father; but this he doesn't do!

(b) second side

Every family runs 'to the end of the line' in one generation, and in it in a certain individual. The Werle family has reached its peak: the old merchant. The son represents something new. ['The same is the case' *crossed out.*] The case is different with Hedvig —

——

Hjalmar was regarded by his parents as being very handsome; believes it himself; is not.

——

Act I finishes with Gregers reproaching the members present concerning Hjalmar, whereupon he breaks with his father.

——

Act II finishes like this: It is the family that has ruined him!

(c) third side

GREGERS. Do you think I have invented all this? Oh no, I have given up inventing things. But it exists out there, concealed —— Patiotism is dead —— etc. ——

(d) fourth side

The doctor is lying. (Dahl), it is a lie — well, then let us let this bird go — Theologian (Schibsted) I — Sch — Mr. Sch — Mr. Sch the graduate —— etc.

——

In Gregers there remains one element of superstition. At dinner there are 13 at table.

———

In Act I Hjalmar tells a highly romantic story of how his mother went mad with grief because his future had been ruined, and that his father committed his crimes out of love for his son. Gregers becomes attentive; — later another explanation, prosaic but true.

A7. *Written rapidly in pencil on one side of a loose sheet, the torn half of a folded sheet similar to A6.*

E.L.
   Yes, but let us just look at all this business about ideals. Do you believe in religion?
   No
E.L. In morals — no ( ) Science (no) ———
E.L. Well — but you believe in patriotism, don't you? In good old Norway?
   Yes, of course.

A8. *Written on the first side of a folded sheet, small octavo, in rapid pencilled handwriting similar in character to that in A6 and 7.*

The complication of what is inherited and what is habitual

———

Hedvig's attraction to the sea

———

her shyness

———

the need to keep her in on account of her weak eyes

A9. *Carefully written in ink on the first side of a folded sheet, small octavo, same sort of paper as A8.*

Act I

Introduction by means of the servants; Old Ekdal. The merchant Werle and Mrs. Sörby; the merchant and Gregers (?).

Gregers and Hjalmar. The guests; Old Ekdal. Gregers and Werle.

Act II

Gina and Hedvig: Old Ekdal. The former and Hjalmar. Old Ekdal and the former. Gina, Hedvig, Hjalmar and Gregers; conversation about how things are at Werle's house. The former and Old Ekdal; conversation about the old days up at the works, then about the wild duck. Gregers rents the room.

SELECTIONS FROM THE DRAFTS

FIRST DRAFT OF THE WILD DUCK

Act I is dated 20.4.84–28.4.84. The setting is a smoking-room (i.e., not a study) beyond which can be glimpsed a billiard room (i.e., not a sitting-room); otherwise the disposition of the room and its furniture is not greatly dissimilar from the final text.
The opening moments of the Act, until the point where the guests emerge from the dining-room, differ slightly from the final text at a few points: (a) there is no reference to the party as being given in Gregers's honour; (b) Pettersen abruptly asks Ekdahl [sic] to give a hand with moving a table; (c) Ekdahl is described here as 'white-haired' and is reported to have earlier been 'an attorney' (i.e., not a lieutenant); and (d) there is no reference to the dirty trick he is supposed to have played on Werle. The draft continues:

(A couple of servants open the dining-room doors from within. The whole party comes out gradually WALLE Senior first, with MRS. SÖRBY [originally 'an elderly lady'] on his arm. He takes her through the billiard room to the adjoining room on the right; groups of gentlemen, both young and old, follow and stand about the billiard room and smoking-room. Chamberlains FLOR, KASPERSEN and SÆTHER come out conversing with GREGERS WALLE.

HALFDAN EKDAHL *comes last.*)

FLOR: Whew! What a dinner! Took a bit of getting through!

KASPERSEN: Oh, if you put your mind to it, it's incredible what you can manage in three hours. What do you say, Mr. Sæther?

SÆTHER: Where there's a will there's a way, he-he!

FLOR: That's all right if you've got a stomach like yours, Mr. Kaspersen.

KASPERSEN (*stroking* FLOR's *waistcoat*): I fancy your own should take a fair amount.

FLOR: Ah, if it could only digest all it can take, then . . .

GREGERS WALLE: There are remedies for everything, Mr. Flor; why else do you suppose a wise Providence made mineral waters?

KASPERSEN: Tut, tut, now you're being all Parisian again.

GREGERS WALLE: It's difficult to get out of the habit, I'm afraid. I have just returned from Paris.

WALLE (*returns* ['with MRS. SÖRBY' *added later*]): What is that you are so engrossed in, Ekdahl?

HALFDAN: It is just an album, Mr. Walle.

WALLE: Well now, photographs. That's right up your street.

KASPERSEN: Have you brought any of your own with you? Any you've done yourself? Eh?

HALFDAN: No, I haven't.

WALLE: You should have done, then you could have contributed to the entertainment, you see.

MRS. SÖRBY: Everybody has to work for his supper in this house, Mr. Ekdahl.

EKDAHL (*error for* WALLE): Ha, ha, ha! That's very true.

FLOR: And *that*, where the food is good, is sheer pleasure.

MRS. SÖRBY: Mr. Flor does his work for the ladies until the sweat pours off him.

FLOR: For the lady, Mrs. Sörby; the lady of the house.

MRS. SÖRBY: Well that's easy today. And Mr. Kaspersen . . . now what does he do?

FLOR: He produces jokes . . .

MRS. SÖRBY: Did you say *re*-produces. . . .

KASPERSEN (*laughs*): Now you're getting rather naughty.

FLOR: I did say produces right enough, but . . .

KASPERSEN: Good heavens, you can only use the talents you've got.

MRS. SÖRBY: But of course! That's why Mr. Sæther is always willing to turn over the music.

SÆTHER: Ha, ha!

GREGERS (*quietly*): You must join in, Hjalmar.

HJALMAR EKDAHL (*shrugs his shoulders*): What do you expect me to say?

WALBERG (*i.e.* WALLE/WERLE): Throw your cigarette-end away and help yourself to a proper cigar.

KASPERSEN: Well now, has Mrs. Sörby been properly smoked-in?

MRS. SÖRBY (*lighting a cigarette*): I'll attend to that myself.

SÆTHER: Well, just look at that.

FLOR: Remarkably fine Tokay.

VALBERG (*i.e.* WALLE/WERLE): You're right there. But it's cost a pretty penny; it's one of the finest vintages, don't you know.

HJALMAR EKDAHL (*sic*): Does the vintage make any difference?

VALBERG: By heavens, that's good. There's obviously not much point in putting good wine in front of *you*.

KASPERSEN: It's the same with Tokay as with photographs, Mr. Ekdahl. There has to be sunlight, or am I wrong?

HJALMAR EKDAHL: No, indeed. Light certainly plays a part.

MRS. SÖRBY: Well then it's exactly the same with your court officials. You have to have a place in the sun as well.

KASPERSEN: Come, come, that joke's a bit ancient.

FLOR: Mrs. Sörby is reproducing.

MRS. SÖRBY: That's as may be. But it's a fact that vintages vary tremendously.

KASPERSEN: But you surely rank me with the fine vintages, Mrs. Sörby?

MRS. SÖRBY: I'm sure you're the same vintage, all three of you.

VALBERG: Ha, ha, ha! There's one in the eye for you. Drink up and have another, gentlemen. In such swinishly cold weather (*originally the speech ended here*). A good drink, a warm comfortable home . . . or so I believe it to be, at least. Look no further than your own four walls for true well-being.

(*The guests touch glasses and drink.*)

GRAABERG (*at the baize door*): Excuse me, sir, but I can't get out.

WALLE: What, you locked in again?

GRAABERG: Yes, and Flaksrud's gone off with the keys.

WALLE: Well, you had better come through this way.

GRAABERG: But there's somebody else as well. . . .

WALLE: Come on, come on, both of you. Don't be shy.

(GRAABERG *and* OLD EKDAHL *come out through the baize door.*)

WERLE (*involuntarily*): Ah!

(*The laughter and chatter of the guests stop abruptly.* HJALMAR *starts up at the sight of his father and turns away.* GRAABERG *and* OLD EKDAHL *go out through the billiard room.* ['*Off to the right*' *added later.*])

WERLE (*mumbling*): Damn that Graaberg!

GREGERS: Surely that was never . . .

SÆTHER: What was that? Who was it?

GREGERS: Oh, nobody.

SÆTHER (*to* HJALMAR): Did *you* know the man?

HJALMAR: I don't know . . . I didn't notice. . . .

SÆTHER: Coming in past locked doors? I must find out about this.

(*Goes over to the others.*)

MRS. SÖRBY (*whispers to the servant*): Slip him something outside, something really good.

PETTERSEN: Certainly.

(*Goes out.*)

GREGERS (*softly*): Then it really *was* him!

HJALMAR: Yes it was.

GREGERS: And you denied him!

HJALMAR: How could I . . . ?

GREGERS: I'm very much afraid you've grown up a coward, Hjalmar.

HJALMAR: Or, if you were in my shoes, then . . .

(*The conversation among the guests which has been conducted in low voices, now changes over to forced conviviality.*)

KASPERSEN (*approaching* HJALMAR *and* GREGERS *in friendly fashion*): Ah! Here you are standing reviving old memories. Won't you have a light for your cigar, Mr. Ekdahl? (*Reaching him a candle.*) Here.

HJALMAR: Thank you, but I won't smoke now.

FLOR: Haven't you some poem or other to read to us, Mr. Ekdahl? There was a time once when you wrote such charming poems.

HJALMAR: No, I have none here.

FLOR: All well at home? Your children—you have children . . . ?

HJALMAR: I have a daughter.

FLOR: And what does she do?

HJALMAR: Hedvig draws.

FLOR: Indeed. She has inherited the artistic temperament, then.

SÆTHER (*joining them*): No, it wasn't past locked doors. He came on legitimate business.

KASPERSEN (*amiably turns him round*): My dear Sæther, you're talking nonsense.

(*Leads him away.*)

FLOR: God knows what *he's* chattering about. (*Goes away.*)

HJALMAR (*whispers*): I'll go now, Gregers. Say goodbye to your father for me.

GREGERS: Yes, of course. Are you going straight home?

HJALMAR: Yes, why?

GREGERS: Nothing . . . just that I'll look in and see you later.

HJALMAR: No, don't do that. Not my home. We can always meet somewhere in town.

MRS. SÖRBY: Are you leaving, Ekdahl?

HJALMAR: Yes.

MRS. SÖRBY: Give my regards to Gina.

HJALMAR: Thank you.

(*He tries to steal out as unobtrusively as possible, to the right.*)

MRS. SÖRBY (*softly to* PETTERSEN): Well, did the old fellow get anything?

PETTERSEN: Yes, I slipped him a bottle of brandy.

MRS. SÖRBY: Oh, you might have found him something a bit better than that.

PETTERSEN: Not at all Mrs. Sörby. Brandy is the best thing he knows.

FLOR (*in the doorway of the billiard room, with a sheet of music in his hand*): Shall we play something for you, Mrs. Sörby?

MRS. SÖRBY: Yes indeed, let's do that.

GUESTS: Bravo! Bravo!

(*They all go right, through the billiard room. During what follows, a piano can be faintly heard.*)

GREGERS: Just a moment, Father.

WERLE: What is it?

GREGERS: I want a word with you.

WERLE: Can't it wait until the others have gone?

GREGERS: No, it can't. It may turn out that I shall leave before the others.

WERLE: Leave? You want to leave? What do you mean by *that*?

GREGERS: How could people here let that family go to the dogs like that?

WERLE: Do you mean the Ekdahls?

GREGERS: Yes, I mean the Ekdahls. Old Ekdahl was such a close friend of yours once. And in any case there was one occasion in his life when he was very useful to you.

WERLE: Oh, you're thinking of that old business of the court case. That account was settled long ago. You can rest assured he got proper recompense.

GREGERS: Let that pass. But since then, Father. Everything else. . . .

WERLE: I don't know what you mean by 'else.' There isn't anything else! Not one word did he address to me while there was still time. He didn't know himself what a mess he was in until it all came to light, and then of course it was too late.

GREGERS: It's not that either I was talking about. It's since, afterwards. . . .

WERLE: Yes afterwards. When he came out, he was a broken man. You can take my word for it, Gregers, I have done everything in my power to help him. I've put him on doing copying for the office and I've paid him far, far more for his work than it's worth. You smile at that? Perhaps you think I'm not telling you the truth? I admit there's nothing in my books to account for it, I never enter expenses of that kind. . . .

GREGERS (*smiles*): No, there are some expenses better not accounted for.

[*Then not greatly dissimilar from the final version—except that instead of Werle being unable to remember the details of Hjalmar's wedding 'after all these years,' he says here: 'It must be about eighteen or nineteen years ago,' to which Gregers replies: 'It is now about seventeen years ago — until:*]

WERLE: You surely never intended to go raking up old rumours and gossip. I honestly think at your age, you might find something a bit more useful to do.

GREGERS: We two have always had divided opinions on what was useful.

WERLE: Both on what was useful and on everything else. Gregers, I don't think there's any man in this world you hate as much as me.

GREGERS (*whispering*): I've seen you at far too close quarters.

WERLE: The truth is, you've seen me with your mother's eyes.

GREGERS: And you have never been able to forgive me for taking after my mother . . . and for feeling sorry for her.

WERLE: Listen now, Gregers. There are a lot of things where we don't exactly hit it off, but all the same, we are father and son. I think we should be able to reach some sort of understanding between us. On the surface at any rate.

GREGERS: In the eyes of the world, as they say. Is that what you mean?

WERLE: Yes, if you like to put it that way. Think it over, Gregers. Don't you think something like that might be done? Eh?

GREGERS (*looking at him coldly*): Now you obviously want to make use of me for something.

WERLE: When two people are as closely connected as we are, one always has some use for the other, Gregers.

GREGERS: Yes. That's what they say.

WERLE: When I wrote to you to come home, I'll not deny I had something extra in mind.

GREGERS: Hm!

WERLE: Yes, because our affairs generally, the settlement of your mother's legacy and all the rest, could have been dealt with by letter, of course. But now that — unfortunately — it is no longer necessary for you to live down there . . .

GREGERS: Well?

WERLE: I should like to have you home for a while. I am a lonely man, Gregers. I've always felt lonely, all my life, but especially now I'm getting on a bit in years. I need somebody near me.

[*Then not greatly dissimilar from the final version until:*]

GREGERS: When has there ever been any family life here? But now there's a sudden need for something of that kind. Yes, indeed that's quite clear. Think of the good impression it must create when it is rumoured how the son hurried home — on wings of devotion — to his aged father's wedding feast. So there is a perfectly happy relationship between the two of them then, after all! Yes of course. Father and son — in heaven's name, could it be otherwise! It's the natural order.

WERLE: Yes, it ought to be the natural order, Gregers.

GREGERS: I don't care a jot for either nature or her order.

WERLE: Listen here. I admit there's a great deal to find fault with in my way of life — (*With raised voice.*) but there are some things I insist on having respected in my house.

GREGERS (*bows slightly*): So I have observed. And so I take my hat and go.

WERLE: Go . . . ? Leave the house?

GREGERS: Yes. There is only one thing in this world for which *I* have any respect.

WERLE: And what may that be?

GREGERS: You would laugh if you knew.

WERLE: Laughter doesn't come so easily to a lonely man, Gregers.

GREGERS (*points towards the billiard room*): Look, Father, your guests are playing Blind Man's Buff with Mrs. Sörby. Good night and goodbye.

(*He goes out to the right.*)

WERLE (*smiling scornfully after him*): Huh . . . ! And he says he's not neurotic.

[*The beginning of Act I is dated 2.5.84. The setting is largely as in the final version, except that there is only one door on the right wall (the main entrance) instead of two as ultimately; otherwise the arrangement of the fixtures and furniture is roughly the same. Mrs. Ekdahl sits sewing at the table, Hedvig sits on the sofa, drawing. The scene opens:*]

MRS. EKDAHL: How much did you pay for the butter today?

HEDVIG: It was 45 öre.

MRS. EKDAHL: And then there's the beer as well. You see . . . straight off there's more than one crown.

HEDVIG: Yes, but Father got four crowns fifty for the photographs.

MRS. EKDAHL: Was it all that much?

HEDVIG: Yes, it was exactly four crowns fifty.

(*Silence.*)

MRS. EKDAHL: Hm . . . wouldn't I like to know how your father's getting on at the party.

HEDVIG: Yes, wouldn't it be fun if we could see him?

(OLD EKDAHL *comes in through the door right* [*originally left*] *with a paper parcel under his arm.*)

HEDVIG: You're very late home today, Grandfather.

EKDAHL: Graaberg held me up, he always makes such a fuss about things, that man.

MRS. EKDAHL: Did you get any more copying to bring home, Father?

EKDAHL: Yes, all this lot.

MRS. EKDAHL: That was nice.

EKDAHL (*sets his umbrella down*): There's enough to keep me going for a long time here, Gina. (*Draws one of the sliding doors in the rear wall, a little to one side.*) Hush! (*Peeps into the dark room; closes the door.*) He! He! They're all sitting sleeping nicely together. (*Goes towards the furthest door on the left.*) Will I find some matches in here?

MRS. EKDAHL: The matches are on the chest of drawers.

(EKDAHL *goes in.*)

HEDVIG: It was jolly good, Grandfather getting all that copying to do.

MRS. EKDAL: Yes, poor old soul; he can earn himself a few coppers.

HEDVIG: And besides, he'll not be able to sit all morning down at that horrid Ma Eriksen's place.

MRS. EKDAHL: Yes, that's another thing. I wonder though — I don't really know — but I sometimes wonder if men aren't nicer when they've had a drink. . . .

HEDVIG: Ugh, no! They may be nicer; but it's so uncertain. . . .

MRS. EKDAHL: How do you mean, uncertain?

HEDVIG: I mean it's uncertain for other people. You're never quite sure how you have them.

MRS. EKDAHL (*looks at her*): When have you noticed *that*?

HEDVIG: Oh, you can always see it. Molstad and Riser are often tipsy, both of them.

MRS. EKDAHL: It was those two you meant, then?

(OLD EKDAL [*sic*] *comes in again and makes for the door front, left.*)

MRS. EKDAHL (*half turning on her chair*): Do you want something in the kitchen, Father?

EKDAHL: Yes, I do. But don't get up.

(*Goes out.*)

MRS. EKDAHL: I hope he isn't messing about with the fire in there! Just go and see what he's up to, Hedvig.

(EKDAHL *comes in again with a little jug of steaming water.*)

HEDVIG: Have you been getting some hot water, Grandfather?

EKDAHL: Yes, I have. I want it for something. I've got some writing to do and the ink's gone all thick like porridge.

MRS. EKDAHL: But you mustn't sit up late and ruin your eyes, Father.

EKDAHL: I haven't time to worry about eyes, Gina. I'm busy I tell you. I don't want anybody coming into my room.

(*Goes into his room.*)

[*Then not greatly dissimilar from the final version — except that there is no reference by Hjalmar to the fact of Gregers having monopolized him at the dinner, nor Gina's question as to whether Gregers was still as nasty as ever — until:*]

EKDAHL: No, no! You don't catch Hjalmar as easily as that, not him!

HJALMAR: I don't see why *I* should be expected to be the one to provide the entertainment when I happen to have an evening out. I gave them to understand that, too. Yes, I even found myself having to put a couple of the gentlemen firmly in their places.

MRS. EKDAHL: No . . . did you really!

EKDAHL: Some of the Court officials?

HJALMAR: Yes, it was indeed. We were having an argument about Tokay. . . .

EKDAHL: To be sure, it's a good wine.

HJALMAR: But, you know the different vintages are not equally good; it all depends on how much sunshine the grapes have had. . . .

MRS. EKDAHL: Why, Hjalmar, the things you know!

EKDAHL: And that's what they started arguing with you about?

HJALMAR: They tried it on, but they were given to understand (*originally 'I let them know'*) that it was exactly the same with Court officials. Not all *their* vintages were equally good either, I said.

MRS. EKDAHL: Really, the things you think of!

EKDAHL: And you said that to them. . . .

HJALMAR: Straight to their faces.

EKDAHL: There you are, Gina, he let them have it straight to their faces.

MRS. EKDAHL: Well, fancy! Straight to their faces.

HJALMAR (*posing by the pedestal*): Yes, I stood so, you see — leaning against the fireplace and I played with my right glove, and then I told them.

EKDAHL: Straight to their faces.

HEDVIG: What fun it is to see Daddy in evening dress. You look so nice in evening dress, Daddy.

HJALMAR: Yes, I do don't I? And it's almost as if it had been made for me. A little tight under the arms perhaps — (*Takes the coat off.*) But I'll have my jacket on now — (*Does so.*) it feels more homely. (*to* GINA.) Don't forget to let Molvik have the coat back first thing in the morning.

MRS. EKDAHL: We'll see to that all right.

HJALMAR (*sits down on the sofa*): Ah, there's nothing as comfortable as a corner of your own sofa, with your feet under your own table. . . .

MRS. EKDAHL: And with a glass of beer to have with your pipe. . . .

HJALMAR: Have we some beer in?

MRS. EKDAHL: Yes, we haven't forgotten it.

(*Goes out into the kitchen.*)

HEDVIG: Here's your pipe and tobacco. . . .

HJALMAR: Thanks. I've really been longing for my pipe. Werle's cigars are all right, but there's nothing to beat a good pipe in the long run.

MRS. EKDAHL (*comes in from the kitchen with beer bottles and glasses*): Here, now you can quench your thirst.

HJALMAR: Splendid. Come along now, Father, we'll have a glass of beer together.

EKDAHL: Hm, I think I'll just fill my pipe first.

(*Goes into his room.*)

MRS. EKDAHL (*smiles*): He wants to fill his pipe.

HJALMAR: I know, I know, leave him alone, poor old Father.

(*There is a knock on the door to the right.*)

MRS. EKDAHL: Hush, wasn't that a knock at the door? Who can it be?

(*Goes and opens the door.*)

GREGERS (*in the passage*): Excuse me, doesn't Ekdahl the photographer live here?

MRS. EKDAHL: Yes, he does.

HJALMAR (*gets up*): Gregers! Is that you after all? Come along in.

GREGERS (*comes in*): I told you I'd be looking in, didn't I?

HJALMAR: But tonight . . . ? Have you left the party?

GREGERS: Both the party and the house. Good evening, Mrs. Ekdahl. Do you remember me from the old days? Do you recognize me again?

MRS. EKDAHL: Oh yes, of course.

HJALMAR: You say you've left the house . . . ?

GREGERS: Yes, I'll stay in a hotel tonight and tomorrow I'll find myself some lodgings. You have a couple of rooms to rent, haven't you, Hjalmar?

HJALMAR: Yes, we have, but. . . .

MRS. EKDAHL: But it really wouldn't be suitable for you, Mr. Werle.

GREGERS: Don't worry about that, I'm sure I'll like it and I think we should be able to agree about the rent.

HJALMAR: Well, that was a stroke of luck for us. . . . Now that you're here, won't you sit down?

GREGERS: Thanks. You live like real artists here.

HJALMAR: As you see, it's the studio. . . .

MRS. EKDAHL: But there's more room here, so we prefer to be in here.

[*This draft breaks off abruptly at this point, undated.*]

SECOND DRAFT OF THE WILD DUCK

Act I is undated; the 'fat,' 'balding' and 'near-sighted' guests of the final version are here variously Chamberlains Flor and Kaspersen; there is no exchange of remarks between Werle père and Gregers about there having been thirteen at table and the opening of the immediately following conversation between Gregers and Hjalmar is rather less circumstantial; otherwise Act I in this draft is not greatly dissimilar from the final version.

Act II, the end of which is dated 24.5.84, still has a setting which lacks the second (i.e., living-room) door in the right wall. From the beginning of this Act until the conversation given below the development is not greatly dissimilar from the final version, except that the following details and exchanges are different or lacking: (a) the 'eye-strain' motif is still attached to Old Ekdahl [sic] (see p. 97 in the first draft) and not yet to Hedvig; (b) the whole of the conversation between Hedvig and Hjalmar about the latter's wavy hair and the menu is lacking; (c) Hjalmar's flute-playing with the attendant sentimental conversation from his 'Hedvig! Hedvig!' to Gregers's entrance is lacking; and (d) there is no reference to Hedvig's approaching hereditary blindness. Then:

GREGERS: You were a great sportsman then, Lieutenant Ekdal.

EKDAL: I was, yes, I was. Went shooting every day. (*'The uniform' inserted later.*)

GREGERS: But you don't go shooting any more?

EKDAL: I don't go shooting any more, no. That is to say, not even in that way.

HJALMAR: Sit down now, Father, and get yourself a glass of beer. Won't you sit down, Gregers?

(EKDAL *and* GREGERS *take the seats on the sofa, the others sit at the table.*)

GREGERS: Do you remember that Christmas I came up to visit you with Hjalmar, Lieutenant?

EKDAL: At the works? That must be a long time ago.

GREGERS: That must surely be more than twenty years ago. It was the winter there were so many wolves up there.

EKDAL: Ah, was it that winter! Then perhaps you were with us the nights we lay in the stables on the look-out for them?

GREGERS: To be sure, I was. Hjalmar was also with us on the first night, but he got fed-up with it. But I stuck it out. Don't you remember you'd put a dead horse outside the stable door?

EKDAL: Yes, indeed. It was lying just beside a big hawthorn bush.

GREGERS: That's quite true.

EKDAL: And then there was a pile of stones alongside that cast a shadow in the moon-light —

GREGERS: Yes, the moon *was* shining those nights as bright as it is tonight.

EKDAL: But wolves don't like moonlight. But do you remember that morning in the half-light, after the moon had gone down. . . . ?

GREGERS: When thirteen of them came in a pack . . . ?

EKDAL: No, do you remember that! I shot one of them beside the carcase, and another as they ran away.

GREGERS: Yes, there's no doubt about it, you were a great sportsman, Lieutenant Ekdal.

EKDAL: Ah yes, ah yes. Not so bad. I've shot bears; shot all kinds of things, both animals and birds. For the forest you see . . . the forest, the forest . . . ! What are the forests like up there now?

[*Then not greatly dissimilar from the final version, until:*]

HJALMAR: How could you guess that?

GREGERS: You told me before you owed such a lot of different things to my father and so I thought . . .

GINA: We didn't get the duck straight from Mr. Werle himself. . . .

EKDAL: But it's him we have to thank for it just the same. He was out shooting, you see, and he shot at her, but she was only winged. . . .

GREGERS: Aha! she got a slug or two in her, did she?

HJALMAR: Yes, she got a couple from behind.

GREGERS: Aha! From behind?

EKDAL: Wild duck must always be shot from behind.

GREGERS: Naturally. There's a better chance of hitting from behind.

EKDAL: It's quite understandable; if you shoot at the breast, it glances off.

HEDVIG: It was in the wing, so she couldn't fly.

GREGERS: And then she dived right down to the bottom, eh?

EKDAL (*sleepily*): Yes, that's the way with wild ducks. They go plunging right to the bottom . . . as deep as they can get, hold on with their beaks to the weeds at the bottom and then they never come up again.

GREGERS: But Lieutenant Ekdal, *your* wild duck came up again.

EKDAL: Yes, because your father had such an absurdly good dog, you see. One of those dogs that are all the latest fashion, long-haired and web-footed. It dived down and brought the wild duck up again.

GREGERS: And then you got it?

HJALMAR: We didn't get it straight away. First it was taken to your father's, but it didn't really thrive there.

GREGERS: No, it isn't the right sort of place for wild ducks.

HJALMAR: No, you can imagine, amongst all the tame ones. They were always at her and stole her food so she didn't get a chance to recover. So Pettersen was told to put it down.

EKDAL (*half asleep*): Hmm . . . yes . . . Pettersen . . . yes.

HJALMAR (*softly*): That was the way we got it, you see, through Father knowing Pettersen; and when he heard all the business about the wild duck, he got it turned over to him.

GREGERS: And now it's thriving perfectly well there in the loft.

HJALMAR: Excellently. It's been so long in there now, it's forgotten what real wild life is like. And that's the only thing that counts.

GREGERS: I'm sure you are right, Hjalmar. If you want to keep wild ducks . . . and have them thrive and grow big and fat . . . I think you have to keep them locked up in a loft so that they never catch sight of the clouds or the sea.

HJALMAR: Yes, yes, that way they forget, you see. And, heavens, what they've forgotten they don't miss either.

GREGERS: No, and in time they grow fat. But, I say Hjalmar, you said you had some rooms to let — vacant rooms.

[*Then, apart from Gregers's disgust at the sound of his own name, not greatly dissimilar from the final version, to the end of the Act.*]

[*Act III is dated 25.5.84–30.5.84. The opening exchanges lack any reference to the mess in Gregers's room, thus:*]

HJALMAR: Are you back again already, Gina? Did you look in on Gregers?

GINA: Yes. He's arranged everything the way he wants. He says he'll look after himself.

HJALMAR: I've been in to see him too.

GINA: So I heard. And you've asked him to lunch.

[*Then not greatly dissimilar from the final version, until:*]

HJALMAR (*getting up*): And then we'd have *that* off our hands.

EKDAL: Exactly, yes, exactly.

(HJALMAR *and* EKDAL *open the upper half of the door to the loft; the morning sun is shining in through the skylights; pigeons are flying about in all directions and some sit cooing on the rafters; the cocks and hens crow and cackle occasionally.*)

HJALMAR (*opens one of the lower half-doors a little*): Make yourself thin, Father.

EKDAL (*crawls through the opening*): Aren't you coming?

HJALMAR: Yes, I rather think . . . (*Sees* GINA *at the kitchen door.*) No, I haven't time. I must work. And what about the net. . . . (*He pulls a string; a piece of fishing net, stretched taut, falls down in front of the door opening.*) There now. (*Goes over to the table.*)

GINA: Is he in there again?

HJALMAR: Would you rather he'd gone running off to Ma Eriksen's? Is there anything you want? You said . . .

GINA: I just wanted to ask if you thought we could lay the table in here?

HJALMAR: Yes. I take it we haven't got anybody booked for today?

GINA: No.

HJALMAR: Well, it's to be hoped there won't be any callers either, and then we can eat in here.

GINA: All right, but there's no hurry now. There's nothing to stop you using it a while yet.

HJALMAR (*sits down again*): Oh, Lord, I'll be using the table right enough.

(GINA *goes out into the kitchen.*)

EKDAL (*appears behind the net*): I'm afraid we'll have to move the water trough after all, Hjalmar.

HJALMAR: Yes, that's just what I've been saying all along.

EKDAL: Hm, hm, hm!

(*Can no longer be seen.* HJALMAR *does a little work, glances over at the loft and half gets up.* HEDVIG *comes in from the kitchen.*)

HJALMAR (*sits down again quickly*): What do you want? Are you supposed to be keeping an eye on me, or something?

HEDVIG: No, of course not. Isn't there something I could help you with?

HJALMAR: No, no. I'd best see to it myself . . . as long as my strength lasts.

(HEDVIG *goes over to the opening and looks into the loft a while.*)

HJALMAR: What's he doing, Hedvig?

HEDVIG: Looks like a new way up to the water trough.

HJALMAR (*gets up*): He'll never manage *that* alone, never in this world. Look Hedvig, there's a clever girl, you take the brush. . . .

HEDVIG: Yes of course, Daddy.

HJALMAR: It'll only take a minute. It's this retouching . . . here's one to copy from.

HEDVIG: Yes, I know how to do it. I've done some of the others, you know.

HJALMAR: Only a minute and I'll have *this* off my hands.

(*He pushes one of the lower half-doors open a little way, crawls into the loft and pulls the door to after him.* HEDVIG *sits retouching.* HJALMAR *and* EKDAL *can be heard arguing within.*)

[*Then not greatly dissimilar from the final version, but with some omissions — no reference to Hedvig's weak eyes and that she has left school supposedly to be coached by Hjalmar and Molvik; nor to the 'Flying Dutchman'; nor to Hjalmar's insistence on Hedvig's going to learn basketwork; lacking also are a number of Gina's malapropisms—until the moment when Gina and Hedvig go into the kitchen leaving Hjalmar and Gregers together alone:*]

HJALMAR (*crawls through the lower half-door and comes into the studio*): I won't ask you to go in to see Father, he doesn't like it. I'd better shut it up before the others arrive. (*He draws the netting and shuts the upper half-doors.*) All these gadgets are very necessary, you see, because Gina doesn't like having the rabbits and the hens in the studio.

GREGERS: Naturally. A good housewife like her . . .

HJALMAR: This thing with the fishing net is my own invention. Really it's great fun having something like this to look after, and mending it when it gets broken now and again.

GREGERS: We have certainly got on in the world, we two, Hjalmar.

HJALMAR: What do you mean by that?

GREGERS: I have got on most, because I'll soon have reached the point where I'm no damned use for anything.

HJALMAR: You don't have to be of use for anything. You can live perfectly well without that.

GREGERS: Do you believe that?

HJALMAR: Yes, I shouldn't think you need have any worries.

GREGERS: But what about yourself?

HJALMAR (*more quietly*): Can I help it that things turned out as they did . . . that I was thrown off my course . . . ?

GREGERS: It's not that I mean. . . .

HJALMAR: Perhaps you mean I don't work hard enough to better myself. Perhaps you think I don't put my back into things enough.

GREGERS: I haven't the faintest idea how hard you put your back into things.

HJALMAR: Yes, of course you are thinking there's too much time wasted on useless things.

GREGERS: Not time, but will.

HJALMAR: But can I leave my poor old father absolutely on his own? Isn't it understandable that I should spare a bit of thought for the little things that keep *him* happy.

GREGERS: Is it entirely for your father's sake?

HJALMAR: Oh no, it is perhaps for my own as well. I need something to distract me from reality.

GREGERS: Then you are not happy, after all?

HJALMAR: Happy, happy? Yes, in a way I am. I'm all right — up to a point. But you must realize that for a man like me, a photographer's job is just a passing phase.

GREGERS: Indeed.

HJALMAR: Naturally. And therefore . . . to put it plainly, Gregers, I need something that can fill in the interval. . . .

GREGERS: Can work not do that?

HJALMAR: No, no, no! Not work alone. I need to dream the intervening time away . . . leap across it.

GREGERS: And when that time is passed, what then?

HJALMAR: Ah, then comes the big moment, I hope.

GREGERS: What big moment?

HJALMAR: Well, I have a mission.

GREGERS: What kind?

HJALMAR: A mission — an aim in life. I am the one who will raise the family name to honour again. Who else could do it?

GREGERS: Is that your mission, then?

HJALMAR: Yes, of course.

GREGERS: And what line do you intend to take?

HJALMAR: But my dear fellow, how can I tell you that beforehand. It depends so enormously on how things stand when the moment comes.

GREGERS: And you have no doubt the moment will come?

HJALMAR: That would be to doubt my whole destiny in life.

GREGERS: Are you so certain you *have* a destiny?

HJALMAR: Are you mad?

GREGERS: You know, Hjalmar, there's a bit of the wild duck about you. You were once wounded and you have plunged down and bit fast to the weeds.

HJALMAR: That's ludicrous.

GREGERS: But now I'm going to see if I can get you up again. For I think I too have a sort of mission, you know. Not in the way you think of it . . . not because I feel it is a destiny or an obligation to others, but because I feel it is necessary for *me*.

HJALMAR: No, my dear Gregers, I don't understand a word of all this. . . . Ah, we'll soon be having lunch now.

(GINA *and* HEDVIG *carry in bottles of beer, a decanter of brandy, glasses and other things for the table; at the same time* RELLING *and* MOLVIK *enter from the right.*)

[*Then, except that there is no mention of Relling and Gregers having known each other before, not greatly dissimilar from the final version until:*]

RELLING: Molvik has a demonic nature.

GREGERS: Hm.

MOLVIK: Yes, people will insist on saying that about me.

RELLING: And demonic natures can't keep on the straight and narrow, you see. Such people have to kick over the traces now and then. You must have lived a very long time up there at the works, Mr. Werle.

GREGERS: I've lived there a good many years.

RELLING: How the devil did you stick it out?

GREGERS: Oh, when one has books, then . . .

RELLING: Books! You just drive yourself silly, reading them.

GREGERS: But there are people up there as well.

RELLING: Yes, the workpeople. You know, my dear sir, I dare bet you have a mission in life.

GREGERS: I believe I have.

HJALMARS: And it is a belief that gives strength, Relling.

RELLING: Yes, that's something you could tell him a thing or two about.

HJALMAR: Ah, yes.

(*There is a knock on the loft door.*)

GINA: Hedvig, open up for Grandfather.

(HEDVIG *opens the door a little.* OLD EKDAL *crawls out.*)

EKDAL (*mumbles*): Good morning, gentlemen. Enjoy your lunch. Hm.

(*He goes into his room.*)

RELLING: Let us drink to him, Ekdal, and may he soon wear his uniform again.

HJALMAR: Thank you.

GREGERS: Uniform?

RELLING: His lieutenant's uniform, of course.

GREGERS (*looks at* HJALMAR): Is that the only thing you think about?

HJALMAR: Well, his restitution goes with it. But it's the uniform that's important to Father. An old soldier . . .

GREGERS: Yes, but what about you? You yourself, Hjalmar, surely you have no patience with the likes of that.

RELLING: What more should he want, damn it?

GREGERS: Then it is only the stigma you want to get rid of?

RELLING: I don't see anything wrong with that myself.

GREGERS: And here was I thinking it was the guilt you wanted to clear him of.

RELLING: Now we're for it.

HJALMAR: What's done can't be undone.

GREGERS: Do you think he was as guilty as it appeared?

HJALMAR: I don't think he had any idea what he'd done.

GREGERS (*gets up*): And yet you have lived here all these years, gone numbly through life, waiting and waiting . . . or perhaps not even that.

RELLING: You've been brooding too long up there in the forests, Mr. Werle.

GREGERS: If I'd had the good fortune to have a father like yours . . .

HJALMAR: The good fortune. . . .

GREGERS: . . . then I'd have been a different son to him. . . . But it's your environment that has dragged you down in the mud.

RELLING: Well, what do you know!

MOLVIK: Are you referring to me?

HJALMAR: What have you to say about my environment?

GINA: Hush, hush, Hjalmar. Don't say any more about it.

GREGERS: I have this to say, that anybody who lives his life, his most intimate domestic life, in a swamp of lies and deceit and secrecy . . .

HJALMAR: Have you gone mad!

RELLING (*jumps up*): Shut up, Mr. Werle.

HJALMAR: His most intimate domestic life . . .

(*There is a knock at the door, right.*)

GINA: Hush, be quiet, there's someone there.

(*She goes to the door.*)

HJALMAR: Have you gone completely mad, Gregers?

GINA (*opens the door and draws back*): Oh, what on earth!

(HAAKON WERLE, *wearing a fur coat, takes a step into the room.*)

WERLE: I beg your pardon, but I believe my son is supposed to be living here.

GINA (*gulping*): Yes.

HJALMAR (*who has got up*): Won't you . . . ?

WERLE: Thanks. I wish to speak to my son.

GREGERS: Yes, what is it? Here I am.

WERLE: I wish to speak with you in your room.

GREGERS: And I, for my part, prefer to have witnesses.

WERLE: What I want to speak to you about is not the sort of thing that . . .

GREGERS: To begin with, I am not interested in discussing anything but the Ekdals' affairs.

WERLE: The Ekdals' affairs?

GREGERS: And these two gentlemen are almost a part of the household.

WERLE: What I have to discuss with you, concerns only you and me.

GREGERS: Since Mother died, I think there is only one thing in the world that concerns me, and that is the affairs of the Ekdals.

HJALMAR: I don't know what else there is to discuss about our affairs.

WERLE: Nor I.

GREGERS: But I do, and I intend to shout it at every street corner. Every manjack in the country will know that Lieutenant Ekdal

was not the guilty one, but somebody who has gone scot free from that day to this.

WERLE: You dare, you crazy fool . . . ! I suppose it's me you are referring to.

GREGERS: No, I refer more particularly to myself.

WERLE: What are you thinking about? You knew nothing about it. . . .

GREGERS: I had my doubts at the time it was all going on up there. If I had spoken to Ekdal then, while there was still time . . .

WERLE: Then why didn't you speak?

GREGERS: I didn't dare because of you.

WERLE: Excuses, stories, sheer fantasy. You gave evidence in court yourself. . . .

GREGERS: Ah, what a coward I was. I was afraid to take my share of the blame.

WERLE: Oh, it's this desperate sick conscience of yours.

GREGERS: You are the one who made my conscience sick.

WERLE: You are mistaken, it's a heritage from your mother, Gregers. The one thing she did leave you.

GREGERS: You still haven't been able to forget that you ['made a mistake when you' *inserted later*] thought she would bring you a fortune.

WERLE: Let's not talk about that. I have come to ask you if you will come home with me again.

GREGERS: No.

WERLE: And you won't come into the firm either?

GREGERS: No.

[*Then, except for the reappearance of Molvik in addition to the other characters at the end of the Act, not greatly dissimilar from the final version.*]

[*Act IV is dated 2.6.84–8.6.84. It is given below in full.*]

(HJALMAR EKDAL's *studio. Afternoon. It is growing dusk.* HEDVIG *is moving about the studio.* GINA *comes in from the kitchen.*)

GINA: Still no sign?

HEDVIG: No.

GINA: Are you sure he's not in with Werle?

HEDVIG: No, it's locked.

GINA: And not with Relling either?

HEDVIG: No, I've been down twice to ask.

GINA: And his dinner's standing there getting cold.

HEDVIG: Yes. Can you think what's become of him, Mother? Daddy's generally on the dot for dinner.

GINA: Oh, don't fret, he'll be here soon.

HEDVIG (*after a pause*): Do you think it's a good thing Werle's come to live with us?

GINA: Why shouldn't it be?

HEDVIG: Well, I don't know, but it was nice when we were on our own. And I think Relling is better for Daddy than Werle – Dear, what has become of him?

GINA (*shouts*): There he is.

(HJALMAR EKDAL *comes in from the right.*)

HEDVIG (*going to meet him*): Daddy, you've come home at last!

GINA: We've waited ages for you, Hjalmar.

HJALMAR: Yes, I have been rather a long time.

GINA: Have you had something to eat with Gregers Werle?

HJALMAR: No.

GINA: Then I'll bring your dinner in for you.

HJALMAR: No, don't bother. I won't eat anything now.

HEDVIG: Are you all right, Daddy?

HJALMAR: Oh yes, not so bad. We went for a very long walk. . . .

GINA: You shouldn't have, Hjalmar; you're not used to it.

HJALMAR: One can get used to a great many things. Have there been any bookings today?

GINA: No, not today.

HEDVIG: There's sure to be some tomorrow, Daddy, you'll see.

HJALMAR: That would be very nice. For tomorrow I'm going to get down to things. I want to do everything myself. I want to manage things alone.

GINA: But why do you want to do that, Hjalmar? You'll only make your life a misery.

HJALMAR: That's my affair. And I think I would like to keep proper accounts, too.

GINA: You?

HJALMAR: Yes, you *do* keep accounts?

HEDVIG: But Mother's so good at it.

HJALMAR: And that's how she gets the money to stretch so far, I imagine. Remarkable that we can live so well on the pittance I've earned this winter.

HEDVIG: Yes, Daddy, but think of all that copying for Graaberg.

HJALMAR: The copying, yes.

GINA: Nonsense, nonsense, that doesn't amount to much. . . .

HEDVIG: Oh, but it does. It's mostly that we live on.

GINA: Oh, how can you say such a thing!

HEDVIG: Why mustn't Daddy know that, Mother?

HJALMAR: So, that's what we live on. Copying for Mr. Werle.

GINA: But you know very well it's Graaberg who pays for it.

HJALMAR: Out of his own pocket?

GINA: Yes, presumably.

HEDVIG: But it's all the same to us, Daddy.

HJALMAR: Of course! It's all the same to us where the money comes from.

GINA: I agree. But since we're on the subject . . . ! Hedvig, you haven't done a thing all day today. . . .

HEDVIG: I'd better go in and . . .

GINA: Yes, go on.

(HEDVIG *goes into the living-room.*)

GINA: What happened to you, Hjalmar?

HJALMAR: Do you think Gregers is in his right mind?

GINA: How should I know? I hardly know him.

HJALMAR: If only I knew.

GINA: You heard what Relling said about him.

HJALMAR: Oh Relling, Relling. . . . Let's have the lamp lit.

GINA (*lights it*): All his life Gregers Werle has been a bit strange.

HJALMAR: Your voice seems to be trembling.

GINA: Is it?

HJALMAR: And your hands are shaking. Aren't they?

GINA: Yes. I don't know why.

HJALMAR: Now you're going to hear what Gregers has said about you.

GINA (*puts her hands over her ears, in horror*): No, no, I won't listen!

HJALMAR (*pulls her hands away*): You will hear it.

GINA: You needn't tell me.

HJALMAR: You know what it is.

GINA: I can guess.

HJALMAR: It's true, then. True, true. This is dreadful!

GINA: I realize I ought to have told you long ago.

HJALMAR: You should have told me immediately while there was still time.

GINA: What would you have done?

HJALMAR: Then, of course, I wouldn't have wanted anything to do with you.

GINA: That's what I thought too, at the time. So I said nothing.

HJALMAR: Simple-minded fool that I was, I imagined you were very much in love with me.

GINA: That has come with time, Hjalmar, as sure as I stand here. Oh yes, my dear, I care a great deal for you, more than anyone else does.

HJALMAR: I don't want to hear about it. How do you think I see you now, giving yourself like that to a middle-aged married man?

GINA: Yes. I can't really think how I could do it.

HJALMAR: Can't you now? Perhaps you've grown respectable with time. But then — how on earth could you get yourself mixed up in a thing like that?

GINA: Oh, believe me, Hjalmar, it isn't easy for poor girls. These rich men start in a small way with presents and then . . .

HJALMAR: Yes, cash! That's what you think's important.

GINA: It was mostly jewellery and dress material and that sort of thing.

HJALMAR: And you've sent it all back long ago, of course.

GINA: I've worn out the dresses and I sold the gold things bit by bit when we needed money.

HJALMAR: We have lived on that man's money. Everything we have in the house we owe to him!

GINA: I've never had a penny off him from the day we were married and I don't believe I've even clapped eyes on him since.

HJALMAR: But the copying!

GINA: Berta fixed that for me when she started in the house.

HJALMAR: You and Berta, yes, you are both the same.

GINA: Tell me, Hjalmar, haven't I been a good wife to you?

HJALMAR: But what about all the things *you* owe me? Didn't I take you away from that menial job? Haven't I given you a name to bear — yes, a name — for it *shall* be restored to respect and honour again.

GINA: It doesn't make any difference to me.

HJALMAR: Really? Ah yes, I dare say.

GINA: Yes, because I like you just as you are, Hjalmar, even if you never do all the great things you talk about.

HJALMAR: That's your baser nature showing itself. Misunderstood in my own home! You have always misunderstood me.

GINA: But I've been a good wife to you all the same.

(GREGERS WERLE *enters through the hall door.*)

GREGERS (*at the hall door*): May I come in.

HJALMAR: Yes, come in.

GREGERS: So you haven't done it yet, then?

HJALMAR: I *have* done it.

GREGERS: You *have?*

HJALMAR: I have experienced the bitterest moment in my life.

GREGERS: But also the most sublime, I should think.

HJALMAR: Well, so far we've got it off our chests anyway.

GINA: May God forgive you, Mr. Werle.

GREGERS: But I don't understand.

HJALMAR: What don't you understand?

GREGERS: After laying bare your souls like that . . . so completely . . . this exchange on which you can now build a completely new mode of life . . . a way of living in truth.

HJALMAR: Yes, I know, I know all that.

GREGERS: I was absolutely convinced that when I came in after this, I would find, as it were, a purer light of regeneration over your home, and here I am confronted by this dull, gloomy, miserable . . .

GINA: Very well then. (*She turns up the lamp.*)

GREGERS: Tell me honestly though, Mrs. Ekdal, isn't it a joy for you to be relieved of this burden of deceit?

GINA: I can tell you, Mr. Werle, I haven't had the time to think about the past.

GREGERS: I would have thought it would have been with you every minute of the day.

GINA: I've really had far too much to think of in running the house. And since I've been married, nobody can say but what I haven't been respectable and honest.

GREGERS: Your whole attitude to life baffles me — so different, so fundamentally different, from mine. But *you* now Hjalmar, all this must have brought you some higher resolve.

HJALMAR: Yes, of course it has. That is . . . in a sort of way.

GREGERS: To forgive one who has sinned, to raise up again in love one who has strayed. . . .

HJALMAR: Do you think a man so easily recovers from what I have just been through.

GREGERS: No, not an *ordinary* man, I dare say. But a man like *you* . . . !

HJALMAR: Yes, I know, but it takes time, you know.

GREGERS: You have been too long at the bottom, Hjalmar, bit yourself fast down there. And of course it's always difficult, when you first come up again into the clear light of day.

HJALMAR: You're right there, it is difficult.

GREGERS: Yes, because you do have some of the spirit of the wild duck in you.

(RELLING *comes in from the hall.*)

RELLING: What's this, the wild duck on the carpet again?

GREGERS: Yes, it's the evil spirit of the house. And it's not for nothing that it came back from Haakon Werle.

RELLING: Ah, it's Mr. Werle who's under discussion.

HJALMAR: Him . . . and certain others.

RELLING (*turns to* GREGERS): God damn you!

HJALMAR: You know about it too, then!

RELLING: It doesn't matter what I do or don't know. If it concerns that quarter, you can believe anything.

GREGERS: But I am not supposed to speak . . . I who know all about these things? Could I stand by and see these two dearly beloved people ruined because they were basing their lives in a false foundation?

RELLING: But it has nothing whatsoever to do with you. You can leave my patients alone with your quackery.

HJALMAR: Patients?

RELLING: Oh yes, everybody has need of a doctor sometimes. But you are no judge of that, Mr. Werle.

GREGERS: I know from experience what it is to live with a gnawing conscience, such as has poisoned my life. But here I've found my mission. Now I'm happy, so happy. Why shouldn't I open the eyes of two people who need so desperately to see?

RELLING: What is it they are going to see?

GREGERS: The truth, the revelation that until today their union has not been a true marriage.

RELLING: Do you think it's going to be any more true hereafter?

GREGERS: I sincerely hope so.

RELLING: Naturally, your sort are always so damned hopeful. Time and again you get led by the nose . . . made fool of. Hasn't that ever happened to you?

GREGERS: To be sure; I've suffered many disappointments.

RELLING: But, nevertheless you go on sincerely hoping.

GREGERS: This is different, quite out of the ordinary. A character like Hjalmar Ekdal.

RELLING: Ekdal . . . !

HJALMAR: That may very well be true, but . . .

RELLING: Oh well, Ekdal, yes. But he already has his mission in life elsewhere, he doesn't need any better marriage than the one he has had up to now.

GINA: Ah, you believe that too, Relling. We used to get on so well. . . .

HJALMAR: You don't understand the claims of the ideal at all.

RELLING: But don't you see, Hjalmar Ekdal can manage things all right, he can't sink right to the bottom. Hasn't he got his great project to grapple with . . . ?

HJALMAR: Yes, the project . . . it's true, I have that.

RELLING: And when it is solved, he will again have brought glory and honour to the name of Ekdal.

HJALMAR: It's to be hoped so anyway.

GREGERS: Yes, this project is all very well, but it is something which is *outside* the individual; a scientific problem pure and simple, a technical thing or whatever you like to call it. And it is inconceivable that such a project could satisfy an individual like Hjalmar. Or do you think perhaps it *does* satisfy you?

HJALMAR: No, I don't altogether. . . .

GREGERS: Now you see, Doctor Relling. And if it does not fully occupy his personality *now*, when it still hasn't developed to complete freedom . . . Well let me put this question to you. Do you think a great problem can ever be solved by an immature personality?

RELLING: Do you mean that photography cannot be raised to the level of an art as long as the relationship between the photographer and his wife is not a true marriage?

GREGERS: You put it rather crudely. But I have such utter faith in the regenerative powers of a true marriage. . . .

RELLING: Excuse me, Mr. Werle, have you seen many true marriages?

GREGERS: No, I hardly think I've seen a single one.

RELLING: Nor have I.

GREGERS: But I have seen the opposite sort of marriage, and what damage it can do to a person. . . .

RELLING: And it's from these that you draw your conclusions. Well, well, Ekdal, now you know then what it takes to make a great invention.

GINA: But you shouldn't talk so much about this invention, Relling. Because nothing will ever come of it anyway.

HJALMAR: Nothing ever come of it!

RELLING: Now what are you saying!

HJALMAR: You say nothing will come of my project!

GINA: No, I'm pretty sure it won't. You've been waiting all this time to invent something; but you never get any further. . . .

RELLING: These things often happen through a kind of revelation, Mrs. Ekdal.

HJALMAR: She doesn't understand that.

GINA: Yes, revelations are all very well, but surely you need something else too. I think it would be better if you worked with those instruments we have, Hjalmar, and then the others can find the new things.

HJALMAR: Not understood; not understood in one's own home. (*Sees* HEDVIG.) Yes, she

understands me. Or don't you believe in me either, Hedvig?

HEDVIG: What am I to believe in, Daddy?

HJALMAR: Naturally you must believe generally in me, believe in my mission in life and believe in my project.

HEDVIG: Yes, I think you'll find it sometime all right.

HJALMAR: Hm. . . .

GINA: Hush, there's a knock.

(*She goes over to the hall door*, MRS. SÖRBY *comes in.*)

GINA: Why Berta, it's you!

MRS. SÖRBY: Yes, it's me.

HJALMAR: If it's something you've got to talk to Gina about, wouldn't you like to . . . (*He points to the living-room.*)

MRS. SÖRBY: Thank you, I'd rather stay here. I've come with a message from Mr. Werle.

HJALMAR: What does he want with us?

GREGERS: Perhaps it's something about me.

MRS. SÖRBY: He wants you to hear it in any case. The first thing is there's going to be a fairly big change in Mr. Werle's domestic and other arrangements.

GREGERS: Aha!

MRS. SÖRBY: Mr. Werle has decided to hand over the business here in town to Graaberg and then he himself is going to move up to the works.

GREGERS: Is he!

HJALMAR: Well, well. So Mr. Werle's going to move up to the works.

RELLING: He won't stand that long, it's so lonely up there.

MRS. SÖRBY: Well, he won't be completely alone, actually.

GREGERS: So he's going through with it after all.

MRS. SÖRBY: Yes.

RELLING: What's he going through with?

HJALMAR: I don't understand a word.

GREGERS: I'll explain. My father is marrying Mrs. Sörby.

HJALMAR: Marrying!

GINA: Well, at last!

RELLING: Surely this is never true.

MRS. SÖRBY: Yes, it is true. He has a special license and is leaving for up there this evening and I mean to go tomorrow. Well, I've told you; now it's over.

RELLING: So this is the end of the affair.

GREGERS: What do you think will become of all this, Mrs. Sörby?

MRS. SÖRBY: Nothing but good, I think. Mr. Werle is by no means as difficult to get on with as some people imagine.

GREGERS: You surely have no grounds for complaint.

MRS. SÖRBY: Oh, no. He can be a bit unreasonable at times, but I have been through worse things than that, Mr. Werle. And it's nice to be provided for.

RELLING: And Mr. Werle is the man to provide for you. He's no beggar.

MRS. SÖRBY: There are plenty who wouldn't need to be beggars if only they'd really put their minds to something.

RELLING: Put their minds . . . Tell me, what good do you think that does?

MRS. SÖRBY: Oh yes, a person can be so far gone that he no longer has a mind for anything.

RELLING: Tonight I'm going out with Molvik.

MRS. SÖRBY: You shouldn't, Relling.

RELLING: There's nothing else for it.

(*He goes out through the hall door.*)

MRS. SÖRBY: There's one thing more. There are probably some people who think that Mr.

Werle should have done a bit more for an old friend like Lieutenant Ekdal.

HJALMAR: Mr. Werle does a great deal for Father. He pays so generously. . . .

MRS. SÖRBY: Yes, you mean for the copying. But your father's getting old now and soon his eyes won't be able to stand it, so here is a banker's draft as a final settlement. You or Gina can draw 100 crowns every month for your father. . . .

HJALMAR: Gina can?

MRS. SÖRBY: Yes, or you, just as you will. And when your father, well . . . when he doesn't need anything any more, then it passes to Hedvig.

HJALMAR (*recoils as though stabbed*): To Hedvig?

HEDVIG: Fancy! All that money!

HJALMAR: Hedvig! What do you say to that, Gina?

GINA: Mr. Werle probably thought that . . .

MRS. SÖRBY: He thought this was the nicest way of doing it . . . after all Hedvig is still a child, and she can quite well accept it.

HJALMAR: Yes, she has the greatest right to it, if Gina herself won't . . .

MRS. SÖRBY: Gina herself!

HJALMAR: But what about me, me!

HEDVIG: I don't want anything. You can have it all, Daddy.

MRS. SÖRBY: What's happened here?

HJALMAR: Something should have happened long, long ago.

MRS. SÖRBY: Already.

GREGERS: I quite understand why Father has made this arrangement. He wanted to convince me Hjalmar Ekdal is not the man I imagined.

HJALMAR: Then, he's made a mistake there. Look, Gregers! (*He tears the paper in two.*)

There you are, Mrs. Sörby. Will you please give Mr. Werle that back?

MRS. SÖRBY: I won't take it.

HJALMAR (*throws it on the table*): Then let it be. But tell him anyway that I've torn his deed of gift in little pieces.

GREGERS: And ask your future husband who was wrong — he or I.

MRS. SÖRBY: I shall. Goodbye, Gina, I do hope things turn out all right.

GINA: Same to you, Berta. Goodbye.

(MRS. SÖRBY *goes.*)

HJALMAR (*in a whisper*): Now you must answer me as if you were on oath: Is Hedvig mine or is she not?

GINA: I don't know.

HJALMAR: You don't know!

GINA: How should *I* know . . . the kind of woman I am?

HJALMAR: And brazen about it, too. Gregers, tomorrow I leave this house.

HEDVIG (*screams*): No, Daddy, no.

GINA: Surely you'll never do that, Hjalmar!

GREGERS: Must you, Hjalmar?

HJALMAR: I must. I'm going immediately. (*He puts on his topcoat.*) I won't be home tonight. . . .

HEDVIG: Oh, no, no Daddy, you mustn't go.

HJALMAR: Go away. I want nothing to do with you. Ask your mother . . . if you want to. So! (*He takes his hat.*) I'm going now and I'll never set foot here again.

(*He goes out right.*)

HEDVIG (*throws herself on the sofa*): He's leaving us! Daddy, Daddy's leaving us! Oh Mother, Mother!

GINA: Don't cry, Hedvig. He'll come back.

HEDVIG: No, he'll never come back. He said so.

GINA: Do you think he'll come back, Mr. Werle?

GREGERS: I sincerely believe so. Hjalmar will come back to his home, and you'll see how uplifted he'll be when he returns.

HEDVIG: But what have we done to him? Mother, tell me, what is it? Why doesn't he want anything to do with me? Tell me that. Oh, tell me that!

GINA: Hush, hush, you'll know all about it when you're older.

HEDVIG: Yes, but I won't ever be older if Daddy won't have anything to do with me.

(*She bursts out sobbing.*)

GINA: You mustn't cry, Hedvig. You really mustn't cry. It's bad for you, Dr. Relling said so.

HEDVIG: I can't help it. Oh Mother, Mother get him to come back home again. . . .

GINA: Yes, I'll go after him. Perhaps he's only down below with Relling. (*She throws her shawl round her.*) But you must be quiet, Hedvig, promise me?

HEDVIG: Yes, yes.

GREGERS: Wouldn't it be better to let him fight his bitter fight to the end . . . ?

GINA: Oh, he can do that afterwards. The first thing is to get the child quietened down.

(*She goes out through the hall door.*)

GREGERS: Come on now, cheer up, Hedvig. It may be all right yet.

HEDVIG: Why doesn't Daddy want anything to do with me any more, Mr. Werle? You must tell me that.

GREGERS: I can only say the same as your mother. You'll find out one day.

HEDVIG: But I can't go on waiting and being as miserable as I am now.

GREGERS: What right have you or anybody else to be happy? What right, I say?

HEDVIG: Oh, I don't bother myself about that. Because it's so lovely to be happy and gay.

GREGERS: There are higher things than that in life, Hedvig.

HEDVIG: Yes, but that doesn't mean a thing so long as everything comes all right here again at home between Daddy and Mother and me. Do you think everything will be all right again between us?

GREGERS: I hope most sincerely that everything will be all right again in time between your father and mother.

HEDVIG: Yes, but what about me!

GREGERS: You must remember one thing, Hedvig. You are not bound to stay at home for ever.

HEDVIG: Yes, yes I am. I'm always going to stay at home. I'd never dream of leaving Daddy and Mother. Ah, but . . . just think . . . Daddy doesn't want anything to do with me!

GREGERS: You must wait and hope. Your father must first fight out his battle.

HEDVIG: But I can't wait, all miserable like this. Why won't Daddy have anything to do with me any more? Perhaps I'm not Daddy's and Mother's real child? Perhaps they only found me?

GREGERS: Found you? Well, it could be that your father thinks something of the sort.

HEDVIG: Yes, but then Mother could tell him it wasn't true.

GREGERS: But what if he doesn't believe her now?

HEDVIG: But even if it *was* true, couldn't Daddy be just as fond of me for all that? We don't know where the wild duck came from either, and yet we're terribly fond of her.

GREGERS: The wild duck. Yes, you're terribly fond of the wild duck, Hedvig.

HEDVIG: Yes, terribly.

GREGERS: And the wild duck belongs to *you.* Doesn't it?

HEDVIG: Yes, it belongs to *me.* But why . . . ?

GREGERS: Have you anything else you're equally fond of?

HEDVIG: Oh no, definitely not! Nothing in the world.

GREGERS: Then you must sacrifice the most precious thing you have. . . .

HEDVIG: The wild duck!

GREGERS: Yes, and get back your father's love instead.

HEDVIG: But how can you know . . . ?

GREGERS: He said it himself before he left. Neither you nor the old man would make such a sacrifice for his sake. It is your love for him he doubts, that's why he won't have anything to do with you.

HEDVIG: Oh, if it were no more than that. . . .

GREGERS: Show him that it means more to you than anything else on earth to win him back. Give, give gladly the most precious thing you have in the world.

HEDVIG: Yes, if only that could put everything right again.

GREGERS: You must not doubt the powers of self-sacrifice, it is the real ideal in family life, you see. . . .

HEDVIG: Oh, but I can't be bothered about *that.* I don't understand it.

GREGERS: But can't you understand that this would be a deed that would impress itself as something most unusual. And that's just what would make your father see the kinship between you and him.

HEDVIG: Do you think so?

GREGERS: Yes. I certainly think so. And then your father will say: Hedvig is my child in spirit and truth, though she came from the far ends of the earth.

HEDVIG: Or from the briny deep.

GREGERS: Or from the briny deep, if you prefer it.

HEDVIG: And then everything would be all

right between Daddy and me again? Oh, that would be so very wonderful.

GREGERS: Everything is so very wonderful when one's life is lifted to a more sublime plane. Well, Hedvig, that which is most precious must be sacrificed. Confide in your grandfather, and get him to do it. Wait until he feels he wants to go hunting, you know. . . .

HEDVIG: Yes, yes, I know all right. . . .

GREGERS: But keep your mother out of it. . . .

HEDVIG: Why Mother?

GREGERS: Well, because she's not likely to understand us.

(GINA *comes in from the hall.*)

HEDVIG: Did you find him, Mother?

GINA: No, I heard he'd called and gone out with Relling.

GREGERS: Are you sure?

GINA: Yes, the woman down in the yard told me. Molvik was with them as well.

GREGERS: At a time like this, when his soul desperately needs to wrestle in solitude. . . .

GINA: Yes, I would have thought so too. God knows where they've gone. Not to Ma Eriksen's anyway.

HEDVIG (*bursts into tears*): Oh, suppose he never comes home again.

GREGERS: He will come back. And then you'll see just *how* he'll come. Good evening, and sleep peacefully.

(*He goes out through the hall door.*)

HEDVIG (*throws herself on* GINA's *neck in tears*): Mother, Mother!

GINA: Ugh! This is what happens when you get mad people in the house.

[*Act V is dated 9.6.84–13.6.84; the beginning is not greatly dissimilar from the final version, until:*]

GREGERS: Can you explain to me the mental turmoil going on in Ekdal?

RELLING: I'm damned if I think there's any mental turmoil going on in him.

GREGERS: But do you really think that a personality like his . . . ?

RELLING: Oh, personality, personality! I don't know what personality is. Hjalmar Ekdal is a good, kind, decent person whose chief desire is to live as good and comfortable and carefree a life as possible.

GREGERS: Him . . . who has his name and his family honour to reinstate.

RELLING: Oh yes, I know that sort of talk; he gabbled something about it last night. How the devil can he make reparation for what's happened? Tell me that.

GREGERS: Aren't you forgetting the marvellous invention he's working on.

RELLING: Don't say you seriously believe in this invention?

GREGERS: Yes, most certainly I do. Surely you yourself believe in it too.

RELLING: Well, Mr. Werle, you know . . . I may be a bit of a swine, but I'm not a bit of a fool.

GREGERS: But you spoke highly enough yesterday about his efforts.

RELLING: Well, damn it, can't you see why? All this about a remarkable invention, that's the life-lie he lives by.

GREGERS: Life-lie?

RELLING: Yes, of course. Most people go around clinging to an illusion, it helps them to live their lives.

GREGERS: That would be very sad.

RELLING: Who says it ought to be pleasant? That's just the way it is. The remarkable invention is for Ekdal what the demonic is for Molvik.

GREGERS: Isn't it true with him then, either?

RELLING: An idiot like him — demonic? How the devil could you imagine a thing like that? And what's more there isn't even anything like it. But if I hadn't put that idea into his mind, he would have succumbed miserably to self-contempt long ago.

GREGERS: So it's you perhaps who gave him this idea.

RELLING: Yes, I'm his doctor after all; curing him is impossible, but a little lie injected now and again . . . that alleviates things.

GREGERS: That may be. But this is not the case with Hjalmar Ekdal.

RELLING: Isn't it? Take that lie away from Hjalmar Ekdal and straight away you take away his happiness.

GREGERS: Oh, the lie, the lie — possibly. But what about his idealism?

RELLING: Good Lord, man, they are just two different names for the same thing. (*To* HEDVIG *who comes in.*) Well, Hedvig, I'm just going down to see your father.

(*He goes out right.*)

GREGERS: Have you the courage and the strength today?

HEDVIG: Well, I don't know; I don't really think I believe in a thing like that.

GREGERS: Then let it be. Without the proper strength of mind there's nothing to be done.

(*He goes out right.* HEDVIG *goes towards the kitchen; at that moment there is a knock on the door of the loft; she goes over and opens it, and* OLD EKDAL *comes out; she shuts the door after him.*)

EKDAL: There's no fun in being alone in there. What's happened to Hjalmar?

HEDVIG: Wouldn't you like to shoot the wild duck today, Grandfather?

EKDAL: Hush, hush, don't talk like that. It's just that something comes over me. Old sportsman, you know.

HEDVIG: Isn't it in the breast they have to be shot?

EKDAL: Under the wing, if that can be managed. And preferably a little from behind.

HEDVIG: Do you often feel like taking a shot at her?

EKDAL: Needn't be afraid. I can make do with a rabbit.

(*He goes into his room.* GINA *comes from the living-room and begins to tidy up the studio. After a moment the hall door slowly opens;* ['HJALMAR *appears' inserted later*]; *he is without hat or top-coat, unwashed and with tousled hair.*)

GINA: Well, so you've come at last!

HJALMAR (*enters*): I'm going straight off again.

GINA: Yes, yes, I suppose that's all right.

HEDVIG (*from the kitchen*): Oh, Daddy!

HJALMAR (*turns aside and waves her away*): Go away, go away!

GINA: Go into the other room, Hedvig.

(HEDVIG *goes.*)

HJALMAR: I must have my books with me. Where are my books?

GINA: What books?

HJALMAR: My scientific books, of course; the technical periodicals I use for my invention.

GINA (*looks in the bookcase*): Are these them, the ones in paper backs?

HJALMAR: Of course they are.

GINA (*placing them in the table*): Shouldn't I get Hedvig to cut the pages for you?

HJALMAR: I don't need any cutting done.

GINA: So you haven't changed your mind about moving out and leaving us?

HJALMAR: I should think that was pretty evident.

GINA: What about Grandfather?

HJALMAR: He'll come with me. I shall go to town and make the necessary arrangements. . . . Hm. . . . Has anybody seen my hat on the stairs?

GINA: No, have you lost your hat?

HJALMAR: I had it when I got back, I'm quite certain of that. But I couldn't find it again today.

GINA: As long as you haven't caught cold, Hjalmar.

(*She goes out into the kitchen.* HJALMAR *rakes about in the papers and photographs, finds the torn document of the day before, picks it up and looks at it; he sees* GINA *and puts it down.*)

GINA (*with a breakfast tray from the kitchen*): Just a bit of something to warm you up, if you fancy it.

HJALMAR (*glances across*): Coffee! . . . Oh yes, I am in just the right mood for drinking coffee! My manuscripts, my letters and my important papers. (*Opens the living-room door.*) Is she there again? Get out. (HEDVIG *comes.*) Spending these last moments here, I wish to remain undisturbed by people who have no business to be here.

(*He goes into the living-room.*)

GINA: Stay in the kitchen, Hedvig. (GINA *goes into the living-room.*)

(HEDVIG *stands motionless for a moment, biting her lip to stop herself from crying and clenches her hands.*)

HEDVIG (*softly*): The wild duck!

(*She crosses to the door of the loft, pushes it a little to one side, slips in and shuts the door behind her.*)

HJALMAR (*with some writing books which he puts on the table*): Oh, there are thousands of things I've got to hump away with me.

GINA: Yes, it won't be easy for you getting things in order again. But now your coffee's standing there getting cold.

HJALMAR: Hm.

(*He takes a mouthful or two without thinking.*)

GINA: Your worst job will be finding a room for the rabbits.

HJALMAR: What! Have I to take all the rabbits with me?

GINA: Yes, you know Father wouldn't live without his rabbits.

HJALMAR: He'll have to get used to it. The pigeons will have to stay here for the time being, too. I must try and dispense with them. There are many things I'll have to dispense with after this.

(*He takes a piece of bread and butter, eats a little and drinks some coffee.*)

GINA: If only we hadn't let that room, you could have moved in there.

HJALMAR: Me live under the same roof as you and her . . . her . . . that . . .

GINA: Hush, don't talk so loud. Father's in the loft.

HJALMAR: So he's in the loft again?

GINA: But couldn't you move into the living-room for a day or two? You could be all on your own there.

HJALMAR: Never within these walls.

GINA: What about going in with Relling then?

HJALMAR: Don't mention those people to me. It makes me feel sick just to think of them. Ah, no, I must go out into the snow and seek shelter for my father and myself.

[*Then not greatly dissimilar from the final version, until:*]

HJALMAR: Of course I shall leave this house as soon as possible. I'm busy packing my things. I cannot live in a broken home.

GINA: Will you give me the key to the chest of drawers, Hjalmar?

HJALMAR: What do you want with it?

GINA: I want to put your shirts in the valise.

HJALMAR: Here! And keep it. I don't need it any more.

(GINA *goes into the living-room.*)

GREGERS: Must you do this?

HJALMAR: Don't you know me well enough to realize that I can't live in a shattered home?

GREGERS: But now is just the time when that home could be built up again on foundations ten times firmer than before — on truth, on forgiveness, on reconciliation.

HJALMAR: Could you really approve of that?

GREGERS: Yes, my dear fellow, isn't that just what I was wanting?

HJALMAR: Yes, but the terrible thing — the absolutely desperate thing about it you see — is that happiness is gone for good! Just think of Hedvig, and how terribly fond of her I was.

GREGERS: And who is so fond of you, too.

HJALMAR: But that's something I just can't believe in after today. Whatever she says, whatever she does, I'll never be able to know whether she isn't behaving like that just because she feels insecure, worrying herself and feeling that she has become a stranger in the house, so to speak.

GREGERS: Hedvig knows nothing of deceit. Supposing she were now to bring you, as a sacrifice, the best thing she possessed — would you still not believe her?

HJALMAR: Oh, what sacrifice could she possibly make which . . . ?

GREGERS: Some small thing perhaps; but for her, the most precious. Let us suppose that for your sake she gave up the wild duck.

HJALMAR: The wild duck? What would be the point of that?

GREGERS: To give up the most precious thing she knew in the world.

HJALMAR: This is hysterical talk. Even if she gave up the wild duck ten times over, there would still be a sort of hidden gulf between us. Both Hedvig and I would feel it and suffer under it. No, for us, happiness is past. Never again can Hedvig and I be together as father and child.

(*A shot is heard inside the loft.*)

HJALMAR: What! Is he shooting again!

GINA (*comes in*): I hope he doesn't end up by doing himself an injury.

HJALMAR: I'll look in. . . .

GREGERS: Wait a minute. Do you know what that was?

HJALMAR: What what was?

GREGERS: That was a futile sacrifice which poor Hedvig has made. She got him to shoot the wild duck.

GINA: Are you sure of that?

GREGERS: I know it.

HJALMAR: The wild duck.

GINA: Yes; she's been so wretched and dejected, Hjalmar.

GREGERS: And she couldn't think of anything else but to sacrifice to you the best thing she had.

HJALMAR: And to think that I could have been so hard on her. Where is she, Gina?

GINA (*fighting her tears*): She's sitting out in the kitchen.

HJALMAR: Things must and shall be put right again. (*He walks over and opens the kitchen door.*) Come here, I want you, Hedvig! — No, she isn't here.

GINA: Isn't she? Then she must have gone out.

HJALMAR: Oh, I do hope she comes back again soon, so that I could tell her properly . . . because really I didn't mean anything by it at all.

GREGERS: You didn't mean anything by it at all?

GINA: It wasn't like you, either, Hjalmar.

HJALMAR: No, it was mostly on your account, Gregers. Coming here and making these unreasonably large demands upon me. . . .

GREGERS: Do you think that?

HJALMAR: Yes, you don't know me properly, you see; I'm not quite as you imagine me to be — must have everything nice and easy and comfortable. . . .

GINA: Hjalmar just isn't made to be unhappy. . . .

GREGERS: I'm almost beginning to believe that.

HJALMAR: Yes, and that's why I'm going to stay here, together with Gina and Hedvig, just as things were before. . . .

GINA: That's right.

GREGERS: But my dear fellow, that's exactly what I've been fighting for.

HJALMAR: Yes, but you wanted to make it happen by a lot of hocuspocus, which I didn't understand at all.

GREGERS: Oh, there's no doubt that I'm the one who got things wrong.

HJALMAR: Yes, you see, because we're not like that, neither Gina nor I; but what's become of Hedvig? Oh Lord, I do wish she would come. And then I'll tell her how much I love her. . . .

GINA: Just as much as she loves you, Hjalmar.

HJALMAR: And as much as she loved the wild duck.

GREGERS: The sacrifice has after all not been in vain.

HJALMAR: No. After this, Hedvig shall be the wild duck in our house. . . .

(OLD EKDAL appears at the door of his room.)

HJALMAR: Father!

GINA: Was he shooting in *there*!

EKDAL: What do you mean by going off shooting alone, Hjalmar?

HJALMAR: Wasn't it you who was shooting?

EKDAL: Me shooting?

GREGERS: She's shot it herself, then!

HJALMAR: What is this! (*He runs to the door of the loft, tears it open, looks in and screams.*) Hedvig!

GINA (*going towards the door*): What is it?

HJALMAR: She's lying on the floor!

(*He goes into the loft.*)

GREGERS: Hedvig!

GINA: Hedvig! (*From within the loft.*) No, no, no.

EKDAL: What is it? Was it Hedvig . . . ?

HJALMAR (*carries HEDVIG into the studio*): She's shot herself! Call for help!

GINA (*runs out into the hall and is heard shouting*): Relling! Relling! Dr. Relling!

HJALMAR (*lays HEDVIG down on the sofa*): She's coming round. . . . She'll come round soon. The pistol's gone off. . . .

EKDAL: There were bullets in it. She didn't know that. Didn't know it was loaded.

GINA (*who has come in again*): Where's she been shot? I can't see anything.

(RELLING *comes in from the hall, closely followed by* MOLVIK, *the latter has neither waistcoat nor collar and his coat is flying open.*)

RELLING: What's going on here?

GINA: Hedvig has shot herself.

HJALMAR: Come here and help!

RELLING: Shot herself!

(*He goes over to the sofa and examines her.*)

HJALMAR: It can't be anything serious; she's hardly bleeding, it can't be. . . .

RELLING: How did this happen?

HJALMAR: Oh, how do I know . . . !

GINA: She wanted to shoot the wild duck.

RELLING: The wild duck?

HJALMAR: The pistol must have gone off.

RELLING: Hm!

EKDAL: Shoot the wild duck. Don't understand a word of it. Don't want to hear any more.

(*He goes into the loft.*)

RELLING: The bullet hit her in the breast. . . .

HJALMAR: Yes, but she's alive!

GINA: Can't you see that Hedvig is dead. . . .

HJALMAR: No, no, she *must* live. Just for a moment. Just long enough for me to tell her. . . .

RELLING: She was hit in the heart. Internal hæmorrhage. She died instantaneously.

HJALMAR: Oh, Gina, Gina. What have I done to you!

GINA: Perhaps I didn't have any right to keep her.

HJALMAR: Did I have any right to take her away from you? From you, after what you have been to us all these years?

GINA: She must be carried in and laid on her own bed. Help me with her, Hjalmar.

(*She and* HJALMAR *take* HEDVIG *between them.*)

HJALMAR (*as they carry her*): Oh, Gina, can you bear this?

GINA: We must help one another. I brought her into the world, and you took her out of the world—so *now* she's as much yours as mine.

['*They carry her into the living-room*' crossed out.]

MOLVIK (*stretches out his arms and mutters*): Praised be the Lord! Earth to earth . . . earth to earth. . . .

RELLING (*in an undertone*): Shut up, Molvik; you're drunk. Go downstairs.

(HJALMAR *and* GINA *carry the body into the living-room.*)

RELLING (*shuts the door after them, crosses to* GREGERS): That was no accident.

GREGERS: Are you quite certain of that?

RELLING: No doubt about it. After the way the powder burnt her dress. She pressed the pistol right against her dress and fired.

GREGERS: I can almost believe that was the way it happened.

RELLING: And can you claim to be altogether free from blame?

GREGERS: I meant everything for the best.

RELLING: Yes, you wanted to make something you call a true marriage in this house; and then you calculated only for the man and the wife, but the child you forgot [*altered to* 'you cancelled out']

GREGERS: She couldn't stand the light of truth; it burnt into her eyes.

RELLING: For most people, truth is not always a good thing. Take the lie out of any particular situation, and at once you take away happiness as well.

GREGERS: If that were so, life would not be worth living.

RELLING: Do *you* think it is so important then that life should be lived?

GREGERS: I don't. On the contrary. But my fate isn't to live my life, either. I have another mission.

RELLING: What mission is that?

GREGERS: To be thirteenth at table.

(*He goes.*)

RELLING: The devil it is.

[*The text of this draft was subsequently heavily revised, both by alterations on the pages of the manuscript itself and by more extensive deletions and additional substitute passages on separate sheets of paper, which then served as the basis for the final text.*]

Miss Julie

August Strindberg (1849–1912) was a schoolteacher, an actor and theatre innovator, a painter, a medical student, a librarian, an alchemist, a short-story writer, a novelist and journalist, an essayist and critic, a biographer and historian, and a dramatist. Despite a miserable childhood, disastrous marriages, and even bouts of madness, without typist or tape-recorders, secretaries and research assistance, without even (until the last years of his life) real acclaim from the public to help him on, he persevered and filled 55 volumes with his sufferings and his achievements.

He never won the Nobel Prize for Literature — he had an enemy on the committee — but he earned it over and over. When Shaw won the prize he gave the money to underwrite English translations of Strindberg's works. Emile Zola hailed Strindberg as a master of naturalism, saying that *The Father* was "one of the few dramatic works to have moved me profoundly." Friedrich Nietzsche rejoiced to see in Strindberg's plays the realization of his own theories about love, "with war as its means and the deathly hate of the sexes as its fundamental law." Ibsen, who hung a portrait of Strindberg over his desk to goad himself to work, said "He will be greater than I." In the long run Strindberg, "deficient in balance and consistent rationality," was probably surpassed by Ibsen, but the Strindbergian psychological intensity is still felt in drama, from Joseph Kramm to Tennessee Williams and Edward Albee. Eugene O'Neill, whose work Strindberg deeply affected, hailed him as "the most modern of moderns, the greatest interpreter of the characteristic spiritual conflicts that constitute the drama. . . ."

Strindberg, whose history, *The Swedish People,* became standard, wrote plays about such figures as Queen Christina, Gustav Vasa, and Erik XIV and became the greatest writer of historical plays since Shakespeare, a fact which (in spite of excellent translations by Walter Johnson) is hardly known in the English-speaking world. Strindberg, though little known as a painter, actually pioneered in abstract art and even in action painting, and was a bold experimenter in theatrical art as well in such expressionistic plays as *The Keys of the Kingdom of Heaven* (1892), *A Dream Play* (1902), *The Ghost Sonata* (1907), *The Great Highway* (1909), and *To Damascus* (1898–1904). A multifaceted man, Strindberg constantly strove to get beyond mere surface realism and produced a stunning variety of works: a classic Swedish novel (*The People of Hemsö*, 1887), short stories which brought him up on charges of blasphemy, "chamber plays" for his Intimate Theatre and the expansive and romantic *The Wanderings of Lucky Per* (1882), the mystical and idealistic *Easter* (1901) and the dark comedy *There are Crimes and Crimes* (1899), the folk play *The Bridal Crown* (1902) and the fairytale *Swanwhite*, and desperate diatribes on domesticity, debt, and doubt in devastating naturalistic plays touched with symbolism and expressionism. The naturalists' attempt to photograph reality without distortion is combined with clever devices to bring out and emphasize the reality that is caught.

These last-mentioned plays, demanding "savagery" in presentation said Strindberg, are driven by sexual strife as if by a dynamo. They made his fame and saddled him with a reputation as a misogynist who alternated between morose brooding and near-hysterical ire. He wrote these plays at a time when he was laying the foundations for a Scandinavian experimental theatre and, indeed, the modern drama itself, before he descended at the height of his power into the "inferno" of madness. These plays include an overwhelming amalgam of autobiography and the Agamemnon myth in *The Father* (1887), a merciless analysis of a competing couple in *Comrades* (1888), brief biopsies of love and divorce in *The Stronger* (1890) and *The Bond* (1893), and the naturalistic masterpiece *Dance of Death* (1901), which makes Albee's *Who's Afraid of Virginia Woolf?* look almost placid and relaxing in comparison. Perhaps the greatest of these naturalistic plays is the unrelenting chronicle of the war to the death between the sexes — with strong overtones of Ibsen's and Chekhov's interest in society and in political change — called *Miss Julie* (1888), "a work of such resolute realism that only a strong stomach can endure it." It is the case history, sparing no details, of a man-hating nymphomaniac.

The temptation is strong for the editor to go into detail about *Miss Julie* as a milestone in dramatic history (combining as it does the concept of tragedy as a struggle of wills in Ferdinand Brunetière [1849–1906] with the idea of economy and the obligatory *scene à faire* in Franscisque Sarcey [1827–1899]) or as a work of art of itself or as related to tragedy rooted in character (as in *Antigone*) and influenced by the inexorable workings of fate (or, as in *The Wild Duck*, by the modern gods: heredity and environment), etc., etc. At the least (at the worst?) *Miss Julie* might well serve as an opportunity for critics to air their own views on all their favorite subjects, for Strindberg has traditionally been subjected to the sort of treatment that Professor Simon Karlingsky of Berkeley refers to in an article entitled "Dostoevsky as Rorschach Test" (*New York Times Book Review*, 13 June, 1971). Professor Karlingsky notes that the famous author of *Crime and Punishment* and other Russian classics — much like Strindberg in his way of picking up all the "isms" of his time, in his irrational passions and spiritual insights — was, after all, first and foremost a literary artist, though:

much of what one gets to read and hear on the subject of Dostoevsky could very easily lead one to believe, if one didn't know better, that he was a theologian, a political analyst, an existential philosopher or some sort of revolutionary.

It is always perilous, when discussing a dramatist, to lose sight of the play: the play's the thing. Let us, then, permit Strindberg to speak for himself in connection with *Miss Julie*. The play is prefaced by Strindberg's Foreword, both sensitively translated by Elizabeth Sprigge.

Foreword to Miss Julie
AUGUST STRINDBERG

Theatre has long seemed to me — in common with much other art — a *Biblia Pauperum*, a Bible in pictures for those who cannot read what is written or printed; and I see the playwright as a lay preacher peddling the ideas of his time in popular form, popular enough for the middle-classes, mainstay of theatre audiences, to grasp the gist of the matter without troubling their brains too much. For this reason theatre has always been an elementary school for the young, the semi-educated and for women who still have a primitive capacity for deceiving themselves and letting themselves be deceived — who, that is to say, are susceptible to illusion and to suggestion from the author. I have therefore thought it not unlikely that in these days, when that rudimentary and immature thought-process operating through fantasy appears to be developing into reflection, research and analysis, that theatre, like religion, might be discarded as an outworn form for whose appreciation we lack the necessary conditions. This

opinion is confirmed by the major crisis still prevailing in the theatres of Europe, and still more by the fact that in those countries of culture, producing the greatest thinkers of the age, namely England and Germany, drama — like other fine arts — is dead.

Some countries, it is true, have attempted to create a new drama by using the old forms with up-to-date contents, but not only has there been insufficient time for these new ideas to be popularized, so that the audience can grasp them, but also people have been so wrought up by the taking of sides that pure, disinterested appreciation has become impossible. One's deepest impressions are upset when an applauding or a hissing majority dominates as forcefully and openly as it can in the theatre. Moreover, as no new form has been devised for these new contents, the new wine has burst the old bottles.

In this play I have not tried to do anything new, for this cannot be done, but only to modernize the form to meet the demands which may, I think, be made on this art today. To this end I chose — or surrendered myself to — a theme which claims to be outside the controversial issues of today, since questions of social climbing or falling, of higher or lower, better or worse, of man and woman, are, have been and will be of lasting interest. When I took this theme from a true story told me some years ago, which made a deep impression, I saw it as a subject for tragedy, for as yet it is tragic to see one favoured by fortune go under, and still more to see a family heritage die out, although a time may come when we have grown so developed and enlightened that we shall view with indifference life's spectacle, now seeming so brutal, cynical and heartless. Then we shall have dispensed with those inferior, unreliable instruments of thought called feelings, which become harmful and superfluous as reasoning develops.

The fact that my heroine rouses pity is solely due to weakness; we cannot resist fear of the same fate overtaking us. The hyper-sensitive spectator may, it is true, go beyond this kind of pity, while the man with belief in the future may actually demand some suggestion for remedying the evil — in other words some kind of policy. But, to begin with, there is no such thing as absolute evil; the downfall of one family is the good fortune of another, which thereby gets a chance to rise, and, fortune being only comparative, the alternation of rising and falling is one of life's principal charms. Also, to the man of policy, who wants to remedy the painful fact that the bird of prey devours the dove, and lice the bird of prey, I should like to put the question: why should it be remedied? Life is not so mathematically idiotic as only to permit the big to eat the small; it happens just as often that the bee kills the lion or at least drives it mad.

That my tragedy depresses many people is their own fault. When we have grown strong as the pioneers of the French revolution, we shall be happy and relieved to see the national parks cleared of ancient rotting trees which have stood too long in the way of others equally entitled to a period of growth — as relieved as we are when an incurable invalid dies.

My tragedy *The Father* was recently criticised for being too sad — as if one wants cheerful tragedies! Everybody is clamouring for this supposed "joy of life," and theatre managers demand farces, as if the joy of life consisted in being ridiculous and portraying all human beings as suffering from St. Vitus's dance or total idiocy. I myself find the joy of life in its strong and cruel struggles, and my pleasure in learning, in adding to my knowledge. For this reason I have chosen for this play an unusual situation, but an instructive one — an exception, that is to say, but a great exception, one proving the rule, which will no doubt annoy all lovers of the commonplace. What will offend simple minds is that my plot is not simple, nor its point of view single. In real life an action — this, by the way, is a somewhat new discovery — is generally caused by a whole series of motives, more or less fundamental, but as a rule the spectator chooses just one of these — the one which his mind can most easily grasp or that does most credit to his intelligence. A suicide is committed. Business troubles, says the man of affairs. Unrequited love, say the women. Sickness, says the invalid. Despair, says the down-and-out. But it is possible that the motive lay in all or none of these directions, or that the dead man concealed his actual motive by revealing quite another, likely to reflect more to his glory.

I see Miss Julie's tragic fate to be the result of many circumstances: the mother's character, the father's mistaken upbringing of the girl, her own nature, and the influence of her fiancé on a weak, degenerate mind. Also, more directly, the festive mood of Midsummer Eve, her father's absence, her monthly indisposition, her pre-occupation with animals, the excitement of dancing, the magic of dusk, the strongly aphrodisiac influence of flowers, and finally the chance that drives the couple into a room alone — to which must be added the urgency of the excited man.

My treatment of the theme, moreover, is neither exclusively physiological nor psychological. I have not put the blame wholly on the inheritance from her mother, nor on her physical condition at the time, nor on immorality. I have not even preached a moral sermon; in the absence of a priest I leave this to the cook.

I congratulate myself on this multiplicity of motives as being up-to-date, and if others have done the same thing before me, then I congratulate myself on not being alone in my "paradoxes," as all innovations are called.

In regard to the drawing of the characters, I have made my people somewhat "characterless" for the following reasons. In the course of time the word character has assumed manifold meanings. It must have originally signified the dominating trait of the soul-complex, and this was confused with temperament. Later it became the middle-class term for the automaton, one whose nature had become fixed or who had adapted himself to a particular rôle in life. In fact a person who had ceased to grow was called a character, while one continuing to develop — the skilful navigator of life's river, sailing not with sheets set fast, but veering before the wind to luff again — was called characterless, in a derogatory sense, of course, because he was so hard to catch, classify and keep track of. This middle-class conception of the immobility of the soul was transferred to the stage where the middle-class has al-

ways ruled. A character came to signify a man fixed and finished: one who invariably appeared either drunk or jocular or melancholy, and characterization required nothing more than a physical defect such as a club-foot, a wooden leg, a red nose; or the fellow might be made to repeat some such phrase as: "That's capital!" or: "Barkis is willin'!" This simple way of regarding human beings still survives in the great Molière. Harpagon is nothing but a miser, although Harpagon might have been not only a miser, but also a first-rate financier, an excellent father and a good citizen. Worse still, his "failing" is a distinct advantage to his son-in-law and his daughter, who are his heirs, and who therefore cannot criticise him, even if they have to wait a while to get to bed. I do not believe, therefore, in simple stage characters; and the summary judgments of authors — this man is stupid, that one brutal, this jealous, that stingy, and so forth — should be challenged by the Naturalists who know the richness of the soul-complex and realise that vice has a reverse side very much like virtue.

Because they are modern characters, living in a period of transition more feverishly hysterical than its predecessor at least, I have drawn my figures vacillating, disintegrated, a blend of old and new. Nor does it seem to me unlikely that, through newspapers and conversations, modern ideas may have filtered down to the level of the domestic servant.

My souls (characters) are conglomerations of past and present stages of civilization, bits from books and newspapers, scraps of humanity, rags and tatters of fine clothing, patched together as is the human soul. And I have added a little evolutionary history by making the weaker steal and repeat the words of the stronger, and by making the characters borrow ideas or "suggestions" from one another.

Miss Julie is a modern character, not that the half-woman, the man-hater, has not existed always, but because now that she has been discovered she has stepped to the front and begun to make a noise. The half-woman is a type who thrusts herself forward, selling herself nowadays for power, decorations, distinctions, diplomas, as formerly for money. The type implies degeneration; it is not a good type and it does not endure; but it can unfortunately transmit its misery, and degenerate men seem instinctively to choose their mates from among such women, and so they breed, producing offspring of indeterminate sex to whom life is torture. But fortunately they perish, either because they cannot come to terms with reality, or because their repressed instincts break out uncontrollably, or again because their hopes of catching up with men are shattered. The type is tragic, revealing a desperate fight against nature, tragic too in its Romantic inheritance now dissipated by Naturalism, which wants nothing but happiness — and for happiness strong and sound species are required.

But Miss Julie is also a relic of the old warrior nobility now giving way to the new nobility of nerve and brain. She is a victim of the discord which a mother's "crime" has produced in a family, a victim too of the day's complaisance, of circumstances, of her own defective constitution, all of which are equivalent to the Fate or Universal Law of former days. The Naturalist has abolished guilt with God, but the consequences of the action — punishment, imprisonment or the fear of it — he cannot abolish, for the simple reason that they remain whether he is acquitted or not. An injured fellow-being is not so complacent as outsiders, who have not been injured, can afford to be. Even if the father had felt impelled to take no vengeance, the daughter would have taken vengeance on herself, as she does here, from that innate or acquired sense of honour which the upper-classes inherit — whether from Barbarism or Aryan forebears, or from the chivalry of the Middle Ages, who knows? It is a very beautiful thing, but it has become a danger nowadays to the preservation of the race. It is the nobleman's *hara kiri*, the Japanese law of inner conscience which compels him to cut his own stomach open at the insult of another, and which survives in modified form in the duel, a privilege of the nobility. And so the valet Jean lives on, but Miss Julie cannot live without honour. This is the thrall's advantage over the nobleman, that he lacks this fatal preoccupation with honour. And in all of us Aryans there is something of the nobleman, or the Don Quixote, which makes us sympathize with the man who commits suicide because he has done something ignoble and lost his honour. And we are noblemen enough to suffer at the sight of fallen greatness littering the earth like a corpse — yes, even if the fallen rise again and make restitution by honourable deeds. Jean, the valet, is a race-builder, a man of marked characteristics. He was a labourer's son who has educated himself towards becoming a gentleman. He has learnt easily, through his well-developed senses (smell, taste, vision) — and he also has a sense of beauty. He has already bettered himself, and is thick-skinned enough to have no scruples about using other people's services. He is already foreign to his associates, despising them as part of the life he has turned his back on, yet also fearing and fleeing from them because they know his secrets, pry into his plans, watch his rise with envy, and look forward with pleasure to his fall. Hence his dual, indeterminate character, vacillating between love of the heights and hatred of those who have already achieved them. He is, he says himself, an aristocrat; he has learned the secrets of good society. He is polished, but vulgar within; he already wears his tails with taste, but there is no guarantee of his personal cleanliness.

He has some respect for his young lady, but he is frightened of Kristin, who knows his dangerous secrets, and he is sufficiently callous not to allow the night's events to wreck his plans for the future. Having both the slave's brutality and the master's lack of squeamishness, he can see blood without fainting and take disaster by the horns. Consequently he emerges from the battle unscathed, and probably ends his days as a hotel-keeper. And even if *he* does not become a Roumanian Count, his son will doubtless go to the university and perhaps become a county attorney.

The light which Jean sheds on a lower-class conception of life, life seen from below, is on the whole illuminating — when he speaks the truth, which is not often, for he says what is favourable to himself rather than what is true. When Miss Julie suggests that the lower-classes must be oppressed by the attitude of their superiors, Jean naturally agrees, as his object is to gain her sympathy; but when he perceives the advantage of separating himself from the common herd, he at once takes back his words.

It is not because Jean is now rising that he has the upper hand of Miss Julie, but because he is a man. Sexually he is the aristocrat because of his virility, his keener senses and his capacity for taking the initiative. His inferiority is mainly due to the social environment in which he lives, and he can probably shed it with his valet's livery.

The slave mentality expresses itself in his worship of the Count (the boots), and his religious superstition; but he worships the Count chiefly because he holds that higher position for which Jean himself is striving. And this worship remains even

when he has won the daughter of the house and seen how empty is that lovely shell.

I do not believe that a love relationship in the "higher" sense could exist between two individuals of such different quality, but I have made Miss Julie imagine that she is in love, so as to lessen her sense of guilt, and I let Jean suppose that if his social position were altered he would truly love her. I think love is like the hyacinth which has to strike roots in darkness *before* it can produce a vigorous flower. In this case it shoots up quickly, blossoms and goes to seed all at the same time, which is why the plant dies so soon.

As for Kristin, she is a female slave, full of servility and sluggishness acquired in front of the kitchen fire, and stuffed full of morality and religion, which are her cloak and scapegoat. She goes to church as a quick and easy way of unloading her household thefts on to Jesus and taking on a fresh cargo of guiltlessness. For the rest she is a minor character, and I have therefore sketched her in the same manner as the Pastor and the Doctor in *The Father*, where I wanted ordinary human beings, as are most country pastors and provincial doctors. If these minor characters seem abstract to some people this is due to the fact that ordinary people are to a certain extent abstract in pursuit of their work; that is to say, they are without individuality, showing, while working, only one side of themselves. And as long as the spectator does not feel a need to see them from other sides, there is nothing wrong with my abstract presentation.

In regard to the dialogue, I have departed somewhat from tradition by not making my characters catechists who ask stupid questions in order to elicit a smart reply. I have avoided the symmetrical, mathematical construction of French dialogue, and let people's minds work irregularly, as they do in real life where, during a conversation, no topic is drained to the dregs, and one mind finds in another a chance cog to engage in. So too the dialogue wanders, gathering in the opening scenes material which is later picked up, worked over, repeated, expounded and developed like the theme in a musical composition.

The plot speaks for itself, and as it really only concerns two people, I have concentrated on these, introducing only one minor character, the cook, and keeping the unhappy spirit of the father above and behind the action. I have done this because it seems to me that the psychological process is what interests people most today. Our inquisitive souls are no longer satisfied with seeing a thing happen; we must also know how it happens. We want to see the wires themselves, to watch the machinery, to examine the box with the false bottom, to take hold of the magic ring in order to find the join, and look at the cards to see how they are marked.

In this connection I have had in view the documentary novels of the brothers de Goncourt, which appeal to me more than any other modern literature.

As far as the technical side of the work is concerned I have made the experiment of abolishing the division into acts. This is because I have come to the conclusion that our capacity for illusion is disturbed by the intervals, during which the audience has time to reflect and escape from the suggestive influence of the author-hypnotist. My play will probably take an hour and a half, and as one can listen to a lecture, a sermon or a parliamentary debate for as long as that or longer, I do not think a theatrical performance will be fatiguing in the same length of time. As early as 1872, in one of my first dramatic attempts, *The Outlaw*, I tried this concentrated form, although with scant success. The play was

written in five acts, and only when finished did I become aware of the restless, disjointed effect that it produced. The script was burnt and from the ashes rose a single well-knit act — fifty pages of print, playable in one hour. The form of the present play is, therefore, not new, but it appears to be my own, and changing tastes may make it timely. My hope is one day to have an audience educated enough to sit through a whole evening's entertainment in one act, but one would have to try this out to see. Meanwhile, in order to provide respite for the audience and the players, without allowing the audience to escape from the illusion, I have introduced three art forms: monologue, mime and ballet. These are all part of drama, having their origins in classic tragedy, monody having become monologue and the chorus, ballet.

Monologue is now condemned by our realists as unnatural, but if one provides motives for it one makes it natural, and then can use it to advantage. It is, surely, natural for a public speaker to walk up and down the room practicing his speech, natural for an actor to read his part aloud, for a servant girl to talk to her cat, a mother to prattle to her child, an old maid to chatter to her parrot, and a sleeper to talk in his sleep. And in order that the actor may have a chance, for once, of working independently, free from the author's direction, it is better that the monologue should not be written, but only indicated. For since it is of small importance what is said in one's sleep or to the parrot or to the cat — none of it influences the action — a talented actor, identifying himself with the atmosphere and the situation, may improvise better than the author, who cannot calculate how much may be said or how long taken without waking the audience from the illusion.

Some Italian theatres have, as we know, returned to improvisation, thereby producing actors who are creative, although within the bounds set by the author. This may well be a step forward, or even the beginning of a new art-form worthy to be called *productive*.

In places where monologue would be unnatural I have used mime, leaving here an even wider scope for the actor's imagination, and more chance for him to win independent laurels. But so as not to try the audience beyond endurance, I have introduced music — fully justified by the Midsummer Eve dance — to exercise its powers of persuasion during the dumb show. But I beg the musical director to consider carefully his choice of compositions, so that conflicting moods are not induced by selections from the current operetta or dance show, or by folk-tunes of too local a character.

The ballet I have introduced cannot be replaced by the usual kind of "crowd-scene," for such scenes are too badly played — a lot of grinning idiots seizing the opportunity to show off and thus destroying the illusion. And as peasants cannot improvise their taunts, but use ready-made phrases with a double meaning, I have not composed their lampoon, but taken a little-known song and dance which I myself noted down in the Stockholm district. The words are not quite to the point, but this too is intentional, for the cunning, i.e., weakness, of the slave prevents him from direct attack. Nor can there be clowning in a serious action, or coarse joking in a situation which nails the lid on a family coffin.

As regards the scenery, I have borrowed from impressionist painting its asymmetry and its economy; thus, I think, strengthening the illusion. For the fact that one does not see the whole room and all the furniture leaves scope of conjecture — that is to say imagination is roused and complements what is seen. I have succeeded too

in getting rid of those tiresome exits through doors, since scenery doors are made of canvas, and rock at the slightest touch. They cannot even express the wrath of an irate head of the family who, after a bad dinner, goes out slamming the door behind him, "so that the whole house shakes." On the stage it rocks. I have also kept to a single set, both in order to let the characters develop in their métier and to break away from over-decoration. When one has only one set, one may expect it to be realistic; but as a matter of fact nothing is harder than to get a stage room that looks something like a room, however easily the scene painter can produce flaming volcanoes and water-falls. Presumably the walls must be of canvas; but it seems about time to dispense with painted shelves and cooking utensils. We are asked to accept so many stage conventions that we might at least be spared the pain of painting pots and pans.

I have set the back wall and the table diagonally so that the actors may play full-face and in half-profile when they are sitting opposite one another at the table. In the opera AIDA I saw a diagonal background, which led the eye to unfamiliar perspectives and did not look like mere reaction against boring straight lines.

Another much needed innovation is the abolition of footlights. This lighting from below is said to have the purpose of making the actors' faces fatter. But why, I ask, should all actors have fat faces? Does not this underlighting flatten out all the subtlety of the lower part of the face, specially the jaw, falsify the shape of the nose and throw shadows up over the eyes? Even if this were not so, one thing is certain: that the lights hurt the performers' eyes, so that the full play of their expression is lost. The foot-lights strike part of the retina usually protected — except in sailors who have to watch sunlight on water — and therefore one seldom sees anything other than a crude rolling of the eyes, either sideways or up towards the gallery, showing their whites. Perhaps this too causes that tiresome blinking of the eyelashes, especially by actresses. And when anyone on the stage wants to speak with his eyes, the only thing he can do is to look straight at the audience, with whom he or she then gets into direct communication, outside the framework of the set — a habit called, rightly or wrongly, "greeting one's friends."

Would not sufficiently strong side-lighting, with some kind of reflectors, add to the actor's powers of expression by allowing him to use the face's greatest asset: — the play of the eyes?

I have few illusions about getting the actors to play *to* the audience instead of *with* it, although this is what I want. That I shall see an actor's back throughout a critical scene is beyond my dreams, but I do wish crucial scenes could be played, not in front of the prompter's box, like duets expecting applause, but in the place required by the action. So, no revolutions, but just some small modifications, for to make the stage into a real room with the fourth wall missing would be too upsetting altogether.

I dare not hope that the actresses will listen to what I have to say about make-up, for they would rather be beautiful than life-like, but the actor might consider whether it is to his advantage to create an abstract character with grease-paints, and cover his face with it like a mask. Take the case of a man who draws a choleric charcoal line between his eyes and then, in this fixed state of wrath, has to smile at some repartee. What a frightful grimace the result is! And equally, how is that false forehead, smooth as a billiard ball, to wrinkle when the old man loses his temper?

In a modern psychological drama, where the subtlest reactions of a character need to be mirrored in the face rather than expressed by sound and gesture, it would be worth while experimenting with powerful side-lighting on a small stage and a cast without make-up, or at least with the minimum.

If, in addition, we could abolish the visible orchestra, with its distracting lamps and its faces turned toward the audience; if we could have the stalls raised so that the spectators' eyes were higher than the players' knees; if we could get rid of the boxes (the centre of my target), with their tittering diners and supper-parties, and have total darkness in the auditorium during the performance; and if, first and foremost, we could have a *small* stage and a *small* house, then perhaps a new dramatic art might arise, and theatre once more become a place of entertainment for educated people. While waiting for such a theatre it is as well for us to go on writing so as to stock that repertory of the future.

I have made an attempt. If it has failed, there is time enough to try again.

MISS JULIE

August Strindberg

CHARACTERS

MISS JULIE, *aged 25*
JEAN, *the valet, aged 30*
KRISTIN, *the cook, aged 35*

Scene: The large kitchen of a Swedish manor house in a country district in the eighties. Midsummer eve.
The kitchen has three doors, two small ones into JEAN's and KRISTIN's bedrooms, and a large, glass-fronted double one, opening on to a courtyard. This is the only way to the rest of the house.
Through these glass doors can be seen part of a fountain with a cupid, lilac bushes in flower and the tops of some Lombardy poplars. On one wall are shelves edged with scalloped paper on which are kitchen utensils of copper, iron and tin.
To the left is the corner of a large tiled range and part of its chimney-hood, to the right the end of the servants' dinner table with chairs beside it.
The stove is decorated with birch boughs, the floor strewn with twigs of juniper. On the end of the table is a large Japanese spice jar full of lilac.
There are also an ice-box, a scullery table and a sink. Above the double door hangs a big old-fashioned bell; near it is a speaking-tube.
A fiddle can be heard from the dance in the barn near-by. KRISTIN is standing at the stove, frying something in a pan. She wears a light-coloured cotton dress and a big apron.
JEAN enters, wearing livery and carrying a pair of large riding-boots with spurs, which he puts in a conspicuous place.

JEAN: Miss Julie's crazy again to-night, absolutely crazy.

KRISTIN: Oh, so you're back, are you?

JEAN: When I'd taken the Count to the station, I came back and dropped in at the Barn for a dance. And who did I see there but our young lady leading off with the gamekeeper. But the moment she sets eyes on me, up she rushes and invites me to waltz with her. And how she waltzed — I've never seen anything like it! She's crazy.

KRISTIN: Always has been, but never so bad as this last fortnight since the engagement was broken off.

JEAN: Yes, that was a pretty business, to be sure. He's a decent enough chap, too, even if he isn't rich. Oh, but they're choosy! (*Sits down at the end of the table.*) In any case, it's a bit odd that our young — er — lady would rather stay at home with the yokels than go with her father to visit her relations.

KRISTIN: Perhaps she feels a bit awkward, after that bust-up with her fiancé.

JEAN: Maybe. That chap had some guts, though. Do you know the sort of thing that was going on, Kristin? I saw it with my own eyes, though I didn't let on I had.

KRISTIN: You saw them . . . ?

JEAN: Didn't I just! Came across the pair of them one evening in the stable-yard. Miss Julie was doing what she called "training" him. Know what that was? Making him jump over her riding-whip — the way you teach a dog. He did it twice and got a cut each time for his pains, but when it came to the third go, he snatched the whip out of her hand and broke it into smithereens. And then he cleared off.

KRISTIN: What goings on! I never did!

JEAN: Well, that's how it was with that little affair . . . Now, what have you got for me, Kristin? Something tasty?

KRISTIN (*serving from the pan to his plate*): Well, it's just a little bit of kidney I cut off their joint.

JEAN (*smelling it*): Fine! That's my special delice. (*Feels the plate.*) But you might have warmed the plate.

KRISTIN: When you choose to be finicky you're worse than the Count himself. (*Pulls his hair affectionately.*)

JEAN (*crossly*): Stop pulling my hair. You know how sensitive I am.

KRISTIN: There, there! It's only love, you know.

(JEAN *eats.* KRISTIN *brings a bottle of beer.*)

JEAN: Beer on Midsummer Eve? No thanks! I've got something better than that. (*From a drawer in the table brings out a bottle of red wine with a yellow seal.*) Yellow seal, see! Now get me a glass. You use a glass with a stem of course when you're drinking it straight.

KRISTIN (*Giving him a wine-glass*): Lord help the woman who gets you for a husband, you old fusser! (*She puts the beer in the ice-box and sets a small saucepan on the stove.*)

JEAN: Nonsense! You'll be glad enough to get a fellow as smart as me. And I don't think it's done you any harm people calling me your fiancé. (*Tastes the wine.*) Good. Very good indeed. But not quite warmed enough. (*Warms the glass in his hand.*) We bought this in Dijon. Four francs the litre without the bottle, and duty on top of that. What are you cooking now? It stinks.

KRISTIN: Some bloody muck Miss Julie wants for Diana.

JEAN: You should be more refined in your speech, Kristin. But why should you spend a holiday cooking for that bitch? Is she sick or what?

KRISTIN: Yes, she's sick. She sneaked out with the pug at the lodge and got in the usual mess. And that, you know, Miss Julie won't have.

JEAN: Miss Julie's too high-and-mighty in some respects, and not enough in others, just like her mother before her. The Countess was more at home in the kitchen and cowsheds than anywhere else, but would she ever go driving with only one horse? She went round with her cuffs filthy, but she had to have the coronet on the cuff-links. Our young lady — to come back to her — hasn't any proper respect for herself or her position. I mean she isn't refined. In the Barn just now she dragged the gamekeeper away from Anna and made him dance with her — no waiting to be asked. We wouldn't do a thing like that. But that's what happens when the gentry try to behave like the common people — they become common . . . Still she's a fine girl. Smashing! What shoulders! And what — er — etcetera!

KRISTIN: Oh come off it! I know what Clara says, and she dresses her.

JEAN: Clara? Pooh, you're all jealous! But I've been out riding with her . . . and as for her dancing!

KRISTIN: Listen, Jean. You will dance with me, won't you, as soon as I'm through.

JEAN: Of course I will.

KRISTIN: Promise?

JEAN: Promise? When I say I'll do a thing I do it. Well, thanks for the supper. It was a real treat. (*Corks the bottle.*)

(JULIE *appears in the doorway, speaking to someone outside.*)

JULIE: I'll be back in a moment. Don't wait.

(JEAN *slips the bottle into the drawer and rises respectfully.* JULIE *enters and joins* KRISTIN *at the stove.*)

Well, have you made it? (KRISTIN *signs that* JEAN *is near them.*)

JEAN (*gallantly*): Have you ladies got some secret?

JULIE (*flipping his face with her handkerchief*): You're very inquisitive.

JEAN: What a delicious smell! Violets.

JULIE (*coquettishly*): Impertinence! Are you an expert of scent too? I must say you know how to dance. Now don't look. Go away. (*The music of a schottische begins.*)

JEAN (*with impudent politeness*): Is it some witches' brew you're cooking on Midsummer

Eve? Something to tell your stars by, so you can see your future?

JULIE (*sharply*): If you could see that you'd have good eyes. (*to* KRISTIN) Put it in a bottle and cork it tight. Come and dance this schottische with me, Jean.

JEAN (*hesitating*): I don't want to be rude, but I've promised to dance this one with Kristin.

JULIE: Well, she can have another, can't you, Kristin? You'll lend me Jean, won't you?

KRISTIN (*bottling*): It's nothing to do with me. When you're so condescending, Miss, it's not his place to say no. Go on, Jean, and thank Miss Julie for the honour.

JEAN: Frankly speaking, Miss, and no offence meant, I wonder if it's wise for you to dance twice running with the same partner, specially as those people are so ready to jump to conclusions.

JULIE (*flaring up*): What did you say? What sort of conclusions? What do you mean?

JEAN (*meekly*): As you choose not to understand, Miss Julie, I'll have to speak more plainly. It looks bad to show a preference for one of your retainers when they're all hoping for the same unusual favour.

JULIE: Show a preference! The very idea! I'm surprised at you. I'm doing the people an honour by attending their ball when I'm mistress of the house, but if I'm really going to dance, I mean to have a partner who can lead and doesn't make me look ridiculous.

JEAN: If those are your orders, Miss, I'm at your service.

JULIE (*gently*): Don't take it as an order. To-night we're all just people enjoying a party. There's no question of class. So now give me your arm. Don't worry, Kristin. I shan't steal your sweetheart.

(JEAN *gives* JULIE *his arm and leads her out.*)

(*Left alone,* KRISTIN *plays her scene in an unhurried, natural way, humming to the tune of the schottische, played on a distant violin. She*

clears JEAN'S *place, washes up and puts things away, then takes off her apron, brings out a small mirror from a drawer, props it against the jar of lilac, lights a candle, warms a small pair of tongs and curls her fringe. She goes to the door and listens, then turning back to the table finds* MISS JULIE'S *forgotten handkerchief. She smells it, then meditatively smooths it out and folds it.*)

(*Enter* JEAN.)

JEAN: She really *is* crazy. What a way to dance! With people standing grinning at her too from behind the doors. What's got into her, Kristin?

KRISTIN: Oh, it's just her time coming on. She's always queer then. Are you going to dance with me now?

JEAN: Then you're not wild with me for cutting that one.

KRISTIN: You know I'm not — for a little thing like that. Besides, I know my place.

JEAN (*putting his arm round her waist*): You're a sensible girl, Kristin, and you'll make a very good wife . . .

(*Enter* JULIE, *unpleasantly surprised.*)

JULIE (*with forced gaiety*): You're a fine beau — running away from your partner.

JEAN: Not away, Miss Julie, but as you see back to the one I deserted.

JULIE (*changing her tone*): You really can dance you know. But why are you wearing your livery on a holiday. Take it off at once.

JEAN: Then I must ask you to go away for a moment, Miss. My black coat's here. (*Indicates it hanging on the door to his room.*)

JULIE: Are you so shy of me — just over changing a coat? Go into your room then — or stay here and I'll turn my back.

JEAN: Excuse me then, Miss. (*He goes to his room and is partly visible as he changes his coat.*)

JULIE: Tell me, Kristin, is Jean your fiancé? You seem very intimate.

KRISTIN: My fiancé? Yes, if you like. We call it that.

JULIE: Call it?

KRISTIN: Well, you've had a fiancé yourself, Miss, and . . .

JULIE: But we really were engaged.

KRISTIN: All the same it didn't come to anything.

(JEAN *returns in his black coat.*)

JULIE: Très gentil, Monsieur Jean. Très gentil.

JEAN: Vous voulez plaisanter, Madame.

JULIE: Et vous voulez parler français. Where did you learn it?

JEAN: In Switzerland, when I was sommelier at one of the biggest hotels in Lucerne.

JULIE: You look quite the gentleman in that get-up. Charming. (*Sits at the table.*)

JEAN: Oh, you're just flattering me!

JULIE (*annoyed*): Flattering you?

JEAN: I'm too modest to believe you would pay real compliments to a man like me, so I must take it you are exaggerating — that this is what's known as flattery.

JULIE: Where on earth did you learn to make speeches like that? Perhaps you've been to the theatre a lot.

JEAN: That's right. And travelled a lot too.

JULIE: But you come from this neighbourhood, don't you?

JEAN: Yes, my father was a labourer on the next estate — the District Attorney's place. I often used to see you, Miss Julie, when you were little, though you never noticed me.

JULIE: Did you really?

JEAN: Yes. One time specially I remember . . . but I can't tell you about that.

JULIE: Oh do! Why not? This is just the time.

JEAN: No, I really can't now. Another time perhaps.

JULIE: Another time means never. What harm in now?

JEAN: No harm, but I'd rather not. (*Points to* KRISTIN, *now fast asleep.*) Look at her.

JULIE: She'll make a charming wife, won't she? I wonder if she snores.

JEAN: No, she doesn't, but she talks in her sleep.

JULIE (*cynically*): How do you know she talks in her sleep?

JEAN (*brazenly*): I've heard her. (*Pause. They look at one another.*)

JULIE: Why don't you sit down?

JEAN: I can't take such a liberty in your presence.

JULIE: Supposing I order you to.

JEAN: I'll obey.

JULIE: Then sit down. No, wait a minute. Will you get me a drink first?

JEAN: I don't know what's in the ice-box. Only beer, I expect.

JULIE: There's no only about it. My taste is so simple I prefer it to wine.

(JEAN *takes a bottle from the ice-box, fetches a glass and plate and serves the beer.*)

JEAN: At your service.

JULIE: Thank you. Won't you have some yourself?

JEAN: I'm not really a beer-drinker, but if it's an order . . .

JULIE: Order? I should have thought it was ordinary manners to keep your partner company.

JEAN: That's a good way of putting it.

(*He opens another bottle and fetches a glass.*)

JULIE: Now drink my health. (*He hesitates.*) I believe the man really is shy.

(JEAN *kneels and raises his glass with mock ceremony.*)

JEAN: To the health of my lady!

JULIE: Bravo! Now kiss my shoe and everything will be perfect. (*He hesitates, then boldly takes hold of her foot and lightly kisses it.*) Splendid. You ought to have been an actor.

JEAN (*rising*): We can't go on like this, Miss Julie. Someone might come in and see us.

JULIE: Why would that matter?

JEAN: For the simple reason that they'd talk. And if you knew the way their tongues were wagging out there just now, you . . .

JULIE: What were they saying? Tell me. Sit down.

JEAN (*sitting*): No offence meant, Miss, but . . . well, their language wasn't nice, and they were hinting . . . oh, you know quite well what. You're not a child, and if a lady's seen drinking alone at night with a man — and a servant at that — then . . .

JULIE: Then what? Besides, we're not alone. Kristin's here.

JEAN: Yes, asleep.

JULIE: I'll wake her up. (*Rises.*) Kristin, are you asleep? (KRISTIN *mumbles in her sleep.*) Kristin! Goodness, how she sleeps!

KRISTIN (*in her sleep*): The Count's boots are cleaned — put the coffee on — yes, yes, at once. . . . (*Mumbles incoherently.*)

JULIE (*tweaking her nose*): Wake up, can't you!

JEAN (*sharply*): Let her sleep.

JULIE: What?

JEAN: When you've been standing at the stove all day you're likely to be tired at night. And sleep should be respected.

JULIE (*changing her tone*): What a nice idea. It does you credit. Thank you for it. (*Holds out her hand to him.*) Now come out and pick some lilac for me.

(*During the following* KRISTIN *goes sleepily in to her bedroom.*)

JEAN: Out with you, Miss Julie?

JULIE: Yes.

JEAN: It wouldn't do. It really wouldn't.

JULIE: I don't know what you mean. You can't possibly imagine that . . .

JEAN: I don't, but others do.

JULIE: What? That I'm in love with the valet?

JEAN: I'm not a conceited man, but such a thing's been known to happen, and to these rustics nothing's sacred.

JULIE: You, I take it, are an aristocrat.

JEAN: Yes, I am.

JULIE: And I am coming down in the world.

JEAN: Don't come down, Miss Julie. Take my advice. No one will believe you came down of your own accord. They'll all say you fell.

JULIE: I have a higher opinion of our people than you. Come and put it to the test. Come on. (*Gazes into his eyes.*)

JEAN: You're very strange, you know.

JULIE: Perhaps I am, but so are you. For that matter everything is strange. Life, human beings, everything, just scum drifting about on the water until it sinks — down and down. That reminds me of a dream I sometimes have, in which I'm on top of a pillar and can't see any way of getting down. When I look down I'm dizzy; I have to get down but I haven't the courage to jump. I can't stay there and I long to fall, but I don't fall. There's no respite. There can't be any peace at all for me until I'm down, right down on the ground. And if I did get to the ground I'd want to be under the ground . . . Have you ever felt like that?

JEAN: No. In my dream I'm lying under a great tree in a dark wood. I want to get up, up to the top of it, and look out over the bright landscape where the sun is shining and rob that high nest of its golden eggs. And I climb and climb, but the trunk is so thick and smooth and it's so far to the first branch. But I know if I can once reach that first branch I'll go to the top just as if I'm on a ladder. I haven't reached it yet, but I shall get there, even if only in my dreams.

JULIE: Here I am chattering about dreams with you. Come on. Only into the park. (*She takes his arm and they go towards the door.*)

JEAN: We must sleep on nine midsummer flowers tonight; then our dreams will come true, Miss Julie. (*They turn at the door. He has a hand to his eye.*)

JULIE: Have you got something in your eye? Let me see.

JEAN: Oh, it's nothing. Just a speck of dust. It'll be gone in a minute.

JULIE: My sleeve must have rubbed against you. Sit down and let me see to it. (*Takes him by the arm and makes him sit down, bends his head back and tries to get the speck out with the corner of her handkerchief.*) Keep still now, quite still. (*Slaps his hand.*) Do as I tell you. Why, I believe you're trembling, big, strong man though you are! (*Feels his biceps.*) What muscles!

JEAN (*warning*): Miss Julie!

JULIE: Yes, Monsieur Jean?

JEAN: Attention. Je ne suis qu'un homme.

JULIE: Will you stay still! There now. It's out. Kiss my hand and say thank you.

JEAN (*rising*): Miss Julie, listen. Kristin's gone to bed now. Will you listen?

JULIE: Kiss my hand first.

JEAN: Very well, but you'll have only yourself to blame.

JULIE: For what?

JEAN: For what! Are you still a child at twenty-five? Don't you know it's dangerous to play with fire?

JULIE: Not for me. I'm insured.

JEAN (*bluntly*): No, you're not. And even if you are, there's still stuff here to kindle a flame.

JULIE: Meaning yourself?

JEAN: Yes. Not because I'm me, but because I'm a man and young and . . .

JULIE: And good-looking? What incredible conceit! A Don Juan perhaps? Or a Joseph? Good Lord, I do believe you are a Joseph!

JEAN: Do you?

JULIE: I'm rather afraid so.

(JEAN *goes boldly up and tries to put his arms round her and kiss her. She boxes his ears.*)

JULIE: How dare you!

JEAN: Was that in earnest or a joke?

JULIE: In earnest.

JEAN: Then what went before was in earnest too. You take your games too seriously and that's dangerous. Anyhow I'm tired of playing now and beg leave to return to my work. The Count will want his boots first thing and it's past midnight now.

JULIE: Put those boots down.

JEAN: No. This is my work, which it's my duty to do. But I never undertook to be your playfellow and I never will be. I consider myself too good for that.

JULIE: You're proud.

JEAN: In some ways—not all.

JULIE: Have you even been in love?

JEAN: We don't put it that way, but I've been gone on quite a few girls. And once I went sick because I couldn't have the one I wanted. Sick, I mean, like those princes in the Arabian Nights who couldn't eat or drink for love.

JULIE: Who was she? (*No answer.*) Who was she?

JEAN: You can't force me to tell you that.

JULIE: If I ask as an equal, ask as a — friend? Who was she?

JEAN: You.

JULIE (*sitting*): How absurd!

JEAN: Yes, ludicrous if you like. That's the story I wouldn't tell you before, see, but now I will . . . Do you know what the world looks like from below? No, you don't. No more than the hawks and falcons do whose backs one hardly ever sees because they're always soaring up aloft. I lived in a labourer's hovel with seven other children and a pig, out in the grey fields where there isn't a single tree. But from the window I could see the wall round the Count's park with apple-trees above it. That was the Garden of Eden, guarded by many terrible angels with flaming swords. All the same I and the other boys managed to get to the tree of life. Does all this make you despise me?

JULIE: Goodness, all boys steal apples!

JEAN: You say that now, but all the same you do despise me. However, one time I went into the Garden of Eden with my mother to weed the onion beds. Close to the kitchen garden there was a Turkish pavilion hung all over with jasmine and honeysuckle. I hadn't any idea what it was used for, but I'd never seen such a beautiful building. People used to go in and then come out again, and one day the door was left open. I crept up and saw the walls covered with pictures of kings and emperors, and the windows had red curtains with fringes — you know now what the place was, don't you? I. . . . (*Breaks off a piece of lilac and holds it for* JULIE *to smell. As he talks, she takes it from him.*) I had never been inside the manor, never seen anything but the church, and this was more beautiful. No matter where my thoughts went, they always came back — to that place. The longing went on growing in me to enjoy it fully, just once. Enfin, I sneaked in, gazed and admired. Then I heard someone coming. There was only one way out for the gentry, but for me there was another and I had no choice but to take it. (JULIE *drops the lilac on the table.*) Then I took to my heels, plunged through the raspberry canes, dashed across the strawberry beds and found my-self on the rose terrace. There I saw a pink

dress and a pair of white stockings — it was you. I crawled into a weed pile and lay there right under it among prickly thistles and damp rank earth. I watched you walking among the roses and said to myself: "If it's true that a thief can get to heaven and be with the angels, it's pretty strange that a labourer's child here on God's earth mayn't come in the park and play with the Count's daughter."

JULIE (*sentimentally*): Do you think all poor children feel the way you did?

JEAN (*taken aback, then rallying*): *All* poor children? . . . Yes, of course they do. Of course.

JULIE: It must be terrible to be poor.

JEAN (*with exaggerated distress*): Oh yes, Miss Julie, yes. A dog may lie on the Countess's sofa, a horse may have his nose stroked by a young lady, but a servant. . . . (*Change of tone.*) well, yes, now and then you meet one with guts enough to rise in the world, but how often? Anyhow, do you know what I did? Jumped in the millstream with my clothes on, was pulled out and got a hiding. But the next Sunday, when Father and all the rest went to Granny's, I managed to get left behind. Then I washed with soap and hot water, put my best clothes on and went to church so as to see you. I did see you and went home determined to die. But I wanted to die beautifully and peacefully, without any pain. Then I remembered it was dangerous to sleep under an elder bush. We had a big one in full bloom, so I stripped it and climbed into the oats-bin with the flowers. Have you ever noticed how smooth oats are? Soft to touch as human skin . . . Well, I closed the lid and shut my eyes, fell asleep, and when they woke me I was very ill. But I didn't die, as you see. What I meant by all that I don't know. There was no hope of winning you — you were simply a symbol of the hopelessness of ever getting out of the class I was born in.

JULIE: You put things very well, you know. Did you go to school?

JEAN: For a while. But I've read a lot of novels

and been to the theatre. Besides, I've heard educated folk talking — that's what's taught me most.

JULIE: Do you stand round listening to what we're saying?

JEAN: Yes, of course. And I've heard quite a bit too! On the carriage box or rowing the boat. Once I heard you, Miss Julie, and one of your young lady friends . . .

JULIE: Oh! Whatever did you hear?

JEAN: Well, it wouldn't be nice to repeat it. And I must say I was pretty startled. I couldn't think where you had learnt such words. Perhaps, at bottom, there isn't as much difference between people as one's led to believe.

JULIE: How dare you! We don't behave as you do when we're engaged.

JEAN (looking hard at her): Are you sure? It's no use making out so innocent to me.

JULIE: The man I gave my love to was a rotter.

JEAN: That's what you always say — afterwards.

JULIE: Always?

JEAN: I think it must be always. I've heard the expression several times in similar circumstances.

JULIE: What circumstances?

JEAN: Like those in question. The last time.

JULIE (rising): Stop. I don't want to hear any more.

JEAN: Nor did she — curiously enough. May I go to bed now please?

JULIE (gently): Go to bed on Midsummer Eve?

JEAN: Yes. Dancing with that crowd doesn't really amuse me.

JULIE: Get the key of the boathouse and row me out on the lake. I want to see the sun rise.

JEAN: Would that be wise?

JULIE: You sound as though you're frightened for your reputation.

JEAN: Why not? I don't want to be made a fool of, nor to be sent packing without a character when I'm trying to better myself. Besides, I have Kristin to consider.

JULIE: So now it's Kristin.

JEAN: Yes, but it's you I'm thinking about too. Take my advice and go to bed.

JULIE: Am I to take orders from you?

JEAN: Just this once, for your own sake. Please. It's very late and sleepiness goes to one's head and makes one rash. Go to bed. What's more, if my ears don't deceive me, I hear people coming this way. They'll be looking for me, and if they find us here, you're done for.

(The CHORUS approaches, singing. During the following dialogue the song is heard in snatches, and in full when the peasants enter.)

Out of the wood two women came,
Tridiri-ralla, tridiri-ra.
The feet of one were bare and cold,
Tridiri-ralla-la.

The other talked of bags of gold,
Tridiri-ralla, tridiri-ra.
But neither had a sou to her name,
Tridiri-ralla-la.

The bridal wreath I give to you,
Tridiri-ralla, tridiri-ra.
But to another, I'll be true,
Tridiri-ralla-la.

JULIE: I know our people and I love them, just as they do me. Let them come. You'll see.

JEAN: No, Miss Julie, they don't love you. They take your food, then spit at it. You must believe me. Listen to them, just listen to what they're singing . . . No, don't listen.

JULIE (listening): What are they singing?

JEAN: They're mocking — you and me.

JULIE: Oh no! How horrible! What cowards!

JEAN: A pack like that's always cowardly. But against such odds there's nothing we can do but run away.

JULIE: Run away? Where to? We can't get out and we can't go in to Kristin's room.

JEAN: Into mine then. Necessity knows no rules. And you can trust me. I really am your true and devoted friend.

JULIE: But supposing . . . supposing they were to look for you in there?

JEAN: I'll bolt the door, and if they try to break in I'll shoot. Come on. (*Pleading.*) Please come.

JULIE (*tensely*): Do you promise . . . ?

JEAN: I swear!

(JULIE *goes quickly into his room and he excitedly follows her.*)
(*Led by the fiddler, the peasants enter in festive attire with flowers in their hats. They put a barrel of beer and a keg of spirits, garlanded with leaves, on the table, fetch glasses and begin to carouse. The scene becomes a ballet. They form a ring and dance and sing and mime:* "Out of the wood two women came." *Finally they go out, still singing.*)
(JULIE *comes in alone. She looks at the havoc in the kitchen, wrings her hands, then takes out her powder puff and powders her face.*)
(JEAN *enters in high spirits.*)

JEAN: Now you see! And you heard, didn't you? Do you still think it's possible for us to stay here?

JULIE: No, I don't. But what can we do?

JEAN: Run away. Far away. Take a journey.

JULIE: Journey? But where to?

JEAN: Switzerland. The Italian lakes. Ever been there?

JULIE: No. Is it nice?

JEAN: Ah! Eternal summer, oranges, evergreens . . . ah!

JULIE: But what would we do there?

JEAN: I'll start a hotel. First-class accommodation and first-class customers.

JULIE: Hotel?

JEAN: There's life for you. New faces all the time, new languages — no time for nerves or worries, no need to look for something to do — work rolling up of its own accord. Bells ringing night and day, trains whistling, buses coming and going, and all the time gold pieces rolling on to the counter. There's life for you!

JULIE: For *you*. And I?

JEAN: Mistress of the house, ornament of the firm. With your looks, and your style . . . oh, it's bound to be a success! Terrific! You'll sit like a queen in the office and set your slaves in motion by pressing an electric button. The guests will file past your throne and nervously lay their treasure on your table. You've no idea the way people tremble when they get their bills. I'll salt the bills and you'll sugar them with your sweetest smiles. Ah, let's get away from here! (*Produces a time-table.*) At once, by the next train. We shall be at Malmö at six-thirty, Hamburg eight-forty next morning, Frankfurt-Basle the following day, and Como by the St. Gothard pass in — let's see — three days. Three days!

JULIE: That's all very well. But Jean, you must give me courage. Tell me you love me. Come and take me in your arms.

JEAN (*reluctantly*): I'd like to, but I daren't. Not again in this house. I love you — that goes without saying. You can't doubt that, Miss Julie, can you?

JULIE (*shyly, very feminine.*): Miss? Call me Julie. There aren't any barriers between us now. Call me Julie.

JEAN (*uneasily*): I can't. As long as we're in this house, there *are* barriers between us. There's the past and there's the Count. I've never been so servile to anyone as I am to him. I've only got to see his gloves on a chair to feel small. I've only to hear his bell and I shy like a horse. Even now, when I look at his boots, standing there so proud and stiff, I feel my back beginning to bend. (*Kicks the boots.*) It's those old, narrow-

minded notions drummed into us as children
. . . but they can soon be forgotten. You've
only got to get to another country, a republic,
and people will bend themselves double before my porter's livery. Yes, double they'll
bend themselves, but I shan't. I wasn't born
to bend. I've got guts, I've got character, and
once I reach that first branch, you'll watch
me climb. Today I'm valet, next year I'll be
proprietor, in ten years I'll have made a
fortune, and then I'll go to Roumania, get
myself decorated and I may, I only say *may*,
mind you, end up as a Count.

JULIE (*sadly*): That would be very nice.

JEAN: You see in Roumania one can buy a title,
and then you'll be a Countess after all. My
Countess.

JULIE: What do I care about all that? I'm
putting those things behind me. Tell me you
love me, because if you don't . . . if you
don't, what am I?

JEAN: I'll tell you a thousand times over —
later. But not here. No sentimentality now or
everything will be lost. We must consider
this thing calmly like reasonable people.
(*Takes a cigar, cuts and lights it.*) You sit
down there and I'll sit here and we'll talk as
if nothing has happened.

JULIE: My God, have you no feelings at all?

JEAN: Nobody has more. But I know how to
control them.

JULIE: A short time ago you were kissing my
shoe. And now . . .

JEAN (*harshly*): Yes, that was then. Now we
have something else to think about.

JULIE: Don't speak to me so brutally.

JEAN: I'm not. Just sensibly. One folly's been
committed, don't let's have more. The Count
will be back at any moment and we've got
to settle our future before that. Now, what
do you think of my plans? Do you approve?

JULIE: It seems a very good idea — but just
one thing. Such a big undertaking would
need a lot of capital. Have you got any?

JEAN (*chewing his cigar*): I certainly have. I've
got my professional skill, my wide experience
and my knowledge of foreign languages.
That's capital worth having, it seems to me.

JULIE: But it won't buy even one railway ticket.

JEAN: Quite true. That's why I need a backer
to advance some ready cash.

JULIE: How could you get that at a moment's
notice?

JEAN: You must get it, if you want to be my
partner.

JULIE: I can't. I haven't any money of my own.
(*Pause.*)

JEAN: Then the whole thing's off.

JULIE: And . . . ?

JEAN: We go on as we are.

JULIE: Do you think I'm going to stay under
this roof as your mistress? With everyone
pointing at me. Do you think I can face my
father after this? No. Take me away from
here, away from this shame, this humiliation.
Oh my God, what have I done? My God, my
God! (*Weeps.*)

JEAN: So that's the tune now, is it? What have
you done? Same as many before you.

JULIE (*hysterically*): And now you despise me.
I'm falling, I'm falling.

JEAN: Fall as far as me and I'll lift you up
again.

JULIE: Why was I so terribly attracted to you?
The weak to the strong, the falling to the
rising? Or was it love? Is that love? Do you
know what love is?

JEAN: Do I? You bet I do. Do you think I never
had a girl before?

JULIE: The things you say, the things you
think!

JEAN: That's what life's taught me, and that's
what I am. It's no good getting hysterical or
giving yourself airs. We're both in the same
boat now. Here, my dear girl, let me give

you a glass of something special. (*Opens the drawer, takes out the bottle of wine and fills two used glasses.*)

JULIE: Where did you get that wine?

JEAN: From the cellar.

JULIE: My father's burgundy.

JEAN: Why not, for his son-in-law?

JULIE: And I drink beer.

JEAN: That only shows your taste's not so good as mine.

JULIE: Thief!

JEAN: Are you going to tell on me?

JULIE: Oh God! The accomplice of a petty thief! Was I blind drunk? Have I dreamt this whole night? Midsummer Eve, the night for innocent merrymaking.

JEAN: Innocent, eh?

JULIE: Is anyone on earth as wretched as I am now?

JEAN: Why should *you* be? After such a conquest. What about Kristin in there? Don't you think she has any feelings?

JULIE: I did think so, but I don't any longer. No. A menial is a menial . . .

JEAN: And a whore is a whore.

JULIE (*falling to her knees, her hands clasped*): O God in heaven, put an end to my miserable life! Lift me out of this filth in which I'm sinking. Save me! Save me!

JEAN: I must admit I'm sorry for you. When I was in the onion bed and saw you up there among the roses, I . . . yes, I'll tell you now . . . I had the same dirty thoughts as all the boys.

JULIE: You, who wanted to die because of me?

JEAN: In the oats-bin? That was just talk.

JULIE: Lies, you mean.

JEAN (*getting sleepy*): More or less. I think I read a story in some paper about a chimney-sweep who shut himself up in a chest full of

lilac because he'd been summonsed for not supporting some brat . . .

JULIE: So this is what you're like.

JEAN: I had to think up something. It's always the fancy stuff that catches the women.

JULIE: Beast!

JEAN: Merde!

JULIE: Now you have seen the falcon's back.

JEAN: Not exactly it's *back*.

JULIE: I was to be the first branch.

JEAN: But the branch was rotten.

JULIE: I was to be a hotel sign.

JEAN: And I the hotel.

JULIE: Sit at your counter, attract your clients and cook their accounts.

JEAN: I'd have done that myself.

JULIE: That any human being can be so steeped in filth!

JEAN: Clean it up then.

JULIE: Menial! Lackey! Stand up when I speak to you.

JEAN: Menial's whore, lackey's harlot, shut your mouth and get out of here! Are you the one to lecture me for being coarse? Nobody of my kind would ever be as coarse as you were tonight. Do you think any servant girl would throw herself at a man that way? Have you ever seen a girl of my class asking for it like that? I haven't. Only animals and prostitutes.

JULIE (*broken*): Go on. Hit me, trample on me — it's all I deserve. I'm rotten. But help me! If there's any way out at all, help me.

JEAN (*more gently*): I'm not denying myself a share in the honour of seducing you, but do you think anybody in my place would have dared look in your direction if you yourself hadn't asked for it? I'm still amazed . . .

JULIE: And proud.

JEAN: Why not? Though I must admit the victory was too easy to make me lose my head.

JULIE: Go on hitting me.

JEAN (*rising*): No. On the contrary I apologise for what I've said. I don't hit a person who's down — least of all a woman. I can't deny there's a certain satisfaction in finding that what dazzled one below was just moonshine, that the falcon's back is grey after all, that there's powder on the lovely cheek, that polished nails can have black tips, that the handkerchief is dirty although it smells of scent. On the other hand it hurts to find that what I was struggling to reach wasn't high and isn't real. It hurts to see you fallen so low you're far lower than your own cook. Hurts like when you see the last flowers of summer lashed to pieces by rain and turned to mud.

JULIE: You're talking as if you're already my superior.

JEAN: I am. I might make you a Countess, but you could never make me a Count, you know.

JULIE: But I am the child of a Count, and you could never be that.

JEAN: True, but I might be the father of Counts if. . . .

JULIE: You're a thief. I'm not.

JEAN: There are worse things than being a thief — much lower. Besides, when I'm in a place I regard myself as a member of the family to some extent, as one of the children. You don't call it stealing when children pinch a berry from overladen bushes. (*His passion is roused again.*) Miss Julie, you're a glorious woman, far too good for a man like me. You were carried away by some kind of madness, and now you're trying to cover up your mistake by persuading yourself you're in love with me. You're not, although you may find me physically attractive, which means your love's no better than mine. But I wouldn't be satisfied with being nothing but an animal for you, and I could never make you love me.

JULIE: Are you sure?

JEAN: You think there's a chance? Of my loving you, yes, of course. You're beautiful, refined (*Takes her hand.*), educated, and you can be nice when you want to be. The fire you kindle in a man isn't likely to go out. (*Puts his arm round her.*) You're like mulled wine, full of spices, and your kisses. . . . (*He tries to pull her to him, but she breaks away.*)

JULIE: Let go of me! You won't win me that way.

JEAN: Not that way, how then? Not by kisses and fine speeches, not by planning the future and saving you from shame? How then?

JULIE: How? How? I don't know. There isn't any way. I loathe you — loathe you as I loathe rats, but I can't escape from you.

JEAN: Escape with me.

JULIE (*pulling herself together*): Escape? Yes, we must escape. But I'm so tired. Give me a glass of wine. (*He pours it out. She looks at her watch.*) First we must talk. We still have a little time. (*Empties the glass and holds it out for more.*)

JEAN: Don't drink like that. You'll get tipsy.

JULIE: What's that matter?

JEAN: What's it matter? It's vulgar to get drunk. Well, what have you got to say?

JULIE: We've got to run away, but we must talk first — or rather, I must, for so far you've done all the talking. You've told me about your life, now I want to tell you about mine, so that we really know each other before we begin this journey together.

JEAN: Wait. Excuse my saying so, but don't you think you may be sorry afterwards if you give away your secrets to me?

JULIE: Aren't you my friend?

JEAN: On the whole. But don't rely on me.

JULIE: You can't mean that. But anyway everyone knows my secrets. Listen. My mother wasn't well-born; she came of quite humble people, and was brought up with all those new ideas of sex-equality and women's rights and so on. She thought marriage was quite wrong. So when my father proposed to her, she said she would never become his *wife* . . . but in the end she did. I came into the world, as far as I can make out, against my mother's will, and I was left to run wild, but I had to do all the things a boy does — to prove women are as good as men. I had to wear boys' clothes; I was taught to handle horses — and I wasn't allowed in the dairy. She made me groom and harness and go out hunting; I even had to try to plough. All the men on the estate were given the women's jobs, and the women the men's, until the whole place went to rack and ruin and we were the laughing-stock of the neighbourhood. At last my father seems to have come to his senses and rebelled. He changed everything and ran the place his own way. My mother got ill — I don't know what was the matter with her, but she used to have strange attacks and hide herself in the attic or the garden. Sometimes she stayed out all night. Then came the great fire which you have heard people talking about. The house and the stables and the barns — the whole place burnt to the ground. In very suspicious circumstances. Because the accident happened the very day the insurance had to be renewed, and my father had sent the new premium, but through some carelessness of the messenger it arrived too late. (*Refills her glass and drinks.*)

JEAN: Don't drink any more.

JULIE: Oh, what does it matter? We were destitute and had to sleep in the carriages. My father didn't know how to get money to rebuild, and then my mother suggested he should borrow from an old friend of hers, a local brick manufacturer. My father got the loan and, to his surprise, without having to pay interest. So the place was rebuilt. (*Drinks.*) Do you know who set fire to it?

JEAN: Your lady mother.

JULIE: Do you know who the brick manufacturer was?

JEAN: Your mother's lover?

JULIE: Do you know whose the money was?

JEAN: Wait . . . no, I don't know that.

JULIE: It was my mother's.

JEAN: In other words the Count's, unless there was a settlement.

JULIE: There wasn't any settlement. My mother had a little money of her own which she didn't want my father to control, so she invested it with her — friend.

JEAN: Who grabbed it.

JULIE: Exactly. He appropriated it. My father came to know all this. He couldn't bring an action, couldn't pay his wife's lover, nor prove it was his wife's money. That was my mother's revenge because he made himself master in his own house. He nearly shot himself then — at least there's a rumour he tried and didn't bring it off. So he went on living, and my mother had to pay dearly for what she'd done. Imagine what those five years were like for me. My natural sympathies were with my father, yet I took my mother's side, because I didn't know the facts. I'd learnt from her to hate and distrust men — you know how she loathed the whole male sex. And I swore to her I'd never become the slave of any man.

JEAN: And so you got engaged to that attorney.

JULIE: So that he should be my slave.

JEAN: But he wouldn't be.

JULIE: Oh yes, he wanted to be, but he didn't have the chance. I got bored with him.

JEAN: Is that what I saw — in the stableyard?

JULIE: What did you see?

JEAN: What I saw was him breaking off the engagement.

JULIE: That's a lie. It was I who broke it off. Did he say it was him? The cad.

JEAN: He's not a cad. Do you hate men, Miss Julie?

JULIE: Yes . . . most of the time. But when that weakness comes, oh . . . the shame!

JEAN: Then do you hate me?

JULIE: Beyond words, I'd gladly have you killed like an animal.

JEAN: Quick as you'd shoot a mad dog, eh?

JULIE: Yes.

JEAN: But there's nothing here to shoot with — and there isn't a dog. So what do we do now?

JULIE: Go abroad.

JEAN: To make each other miserable for the rest of our lives?

JULIE: No, to enjoy ourselves for a day or two, for a week, for as long as enjoyment lasts, and then — to die . . .

JEAN: Die? How silly! I think it would be far better to start a hotel.

JULIE (without listening): . . . die on the shores of Lake Como, where the sun always shines and at Christmas time there are green trees and glowing oranges.

JEAN: Lake Como's a rainy hole and I didn't see any oranges outside the shops. But it's a good place for tourists. Plenty of villas to be rented by — er honeymoon couples. Profitable business that. Know why? Because they all sign a lease for six months and all leave after three weeks.

JULIE (naïvely): After three weeks? Why?

JEAN: They quarrel, of course. But the rent has to be paid just the same. And then it's let again. So it goes on and on, for there's plenty of love although it doesn't last long.

JULIE: You don't want to die with me?

JEAN: I don't want to die at all. For one thing I like living and for another I consider suicide's a sin against the Creator who gave us life.

JULIE: You believe in God — you?

JEAN: Yes, of course. And I go to church every Sunday. Look here, I'm tired of all this. I'm going to bed.

JULIE: Indeed! And do you think I'm going to leave things like this? Don't you know what you owe the woman you've ruined?

JEAN (taking out his purse and throwing a silver coin on the table): There you are. I don't want to be in anybody's debt.

JULIE (pretending not to notice the insult): Don't you know what the law is?

JEAN: There's no law unfortunately that punishes a woman for seducing a man.

JULIE: But can you see anything for it but to go abroad, get married and then divorce?

JEAN: What if I refuse this mésalliance?

JULIE: Mésalliance?

JEAN: Yes, for me. I'm better bred than you, see! Nobody in my family committed arson.

JULIE: How do you know?

JEAN: Well, you can't prove otherwise, because we haven't any family records outside the Registrar's office. But I've seen your family tree in that book on the drawing-room table. Do you know who the founder of your family was? A miller who let his wife sleep with the King one night during the Danish war. I haven't any ancestors like that. I haven't any ancestors at all, but I might become one.

JULIE: This is what I get for confiding in someone so low, for sacrificing my family honour . . .

JEAN: Dishonour! Well, I told you so. One shouldn't drink, because then one talks. And one shouldn't talk.

JULIE: Oh, how ashamed I am, how bitterly ashamed! If at least you loved me!

JEAN: Look here — for the last time — what do you want? Am I to burst into tears? Am I to jump over your riding whip? Shall I kiss you and carry you off to Lake Como for three weeks, after which . . . What am I to do? What do you want? This is getting unbearable, but that's what comes of playing around with women. Miss Julie, I can see how miserable you are; I know you're going through hell, but I don't understand you. We don't have scenes like this; we don't go in for hating each other. We make love for fun in our spare time, but we haven't all day and all night for it like you. I think you must be ill. I'm sure you're ill.

JULIE: Then you must be kind to me. You sound almost human now.

JEAN: Well, be human yourself. You spit at me, then won't let me wipe it off — on you.

JULIE: Help me, help me! Tell me what to do, where to go.

JEAN: Jesus, as if I knew!

JULIE: I've been mad, raving mad, but there must be a way out.

JEAN: Stay here and keep quiet. Nobody knows anything.

JULIE: I can't. People do know. Kristin knows.

JEAN: They don't know and they wouldn't believe such a thing.

JULIE (hesitating): But — it might happen again.

JEAN: That's true.

JULIE: And there might be — consequences.

JEAN (in panic): Consequences! Fool that I am I never thought of that. Yes, there's nothing for it but to go. At once. I can't come with you. That would be a complete giveaway. You must go alone — abroad — anywhere.

JULIE: Alone? Where to? I can't.

JEAN: You must. And before the Count gets back. If you stay, we know what will happen. Once you've sinned you feel you might as well go on, as the harm's done. Then you get more and more reckless and in the end you're found out. No. You must go abroad. Then write to the Count and tell him everything, except that it was me. He'll never guess that — and I don't think he'll want to.

JULIE: I'll go if you come with me.

JEAN: Are you crazy, woman? "Miss Julie elopes with valet." Next day it would be in the headlines, and the Count would never live it down.

JULIE: I can't go. I can't stay. I'm so tired, so completely worn out. Give me orders. Set me going. I can't think any more, can't act . . .

JEAN: You see what weaklings you are. Why do you give yourselves airs and turn up your noses as if you're the lords of creation? Very well, I'll give you your orders. Go upstairs and dress. Get money for the journey and come down here again.

JULIE (Softly): Come up with me.

JEAN: To your room? Now you've gone crazy again. (Hesitates a moment.) No! Go along at once. (Takes her hand and pulls her to the door.)

JULIE (As she goes): Speak kindly to me, Jean.

JEAN: Orders always sound unkind. Now you know. Now you know.

(Left alone, JEAN sighs with relief, sits down at the table, takes out a note-book and pencil and adds up figures, now and then aloud. Dawn begins to break. KRISTIN enters dressed for church, carrying his white dickey and tie.)

KRISTIN: Lord Jesus, look at the state the place is in! What have you been up to? (Turns out the lamp.)

JEAN: Oh, Miss Julie invited the crowd in. Did you sleep through it? Didn't you hear anything?

KRISTIN: I slept like a log.

JEAN: And dressed for church already.

KRISTIN: Yes, you promised to come to Communion with me today.

JEAN: Why, so I did. And you've got my bib and tucker, I see. Come on then. (Sits. KRISTIN begins to put his things on. Pause. Sleepily.) What's the lesson today?

KRISTIN: It's about the beheading of John the Baptist, I think.

JEAN: That's sure to be horribly long. Hi, you're choking me! Oh Lord, I'm so sleepy, so sleepy!

KRISTIN: Yes, what have you been doing up all night? You look absolutely green.

JEAN: Just sitting here talking with Miss Julie.

KRISTIN: She doesn't know what's proper, that one (*Pause.*)

JEAN: I say, Kristin.

KRISTIN. What?

JEAN: It's queer really, isn't it, when you come to think of it? Her.

KRISTIN: What's queer?

JEAN: The whole thing. (*Pause.*)

KRISTIN (*looking at the half-filled glasses on the table*): Have you been drinking together too?

JEAN: Yes.

KRISTIN: More shame you. Look me straight in the face.

JEAN: Yes.

KRISTIN: Is it possible? Is it possible?

JEAN (*after a moment*): Yes, it is.

KRISTIN: Oh! This I would never have believed. How low!

JEAN: You're not jealous of her, surely?

KRISTIN: No, I'm not. If it had been Clara or Sophie I'd have scratched your eyes out. But not of her. I don't know why; that's how it is though. But it's disgusting.

JEAN: You're angry with her then.

KRISTIN: No. With you. It was wicked of you, very very wicked. Poor girl. And, mark my words, I won't stay here any longer now — in a place where one can't respect one's employers.

JEAN: Why should one respect them?

KRISTIN: You should know since you're so smart. But you don't want to stay in the ser-

vice of people who aren't respectable, do you? I wouldn't demean myself.

JEAN: But it's rather a comfort to find out they're no better than us.

KRISTIN: I don't think so. If they're no better there's nothing for us to live up to. Oh and think of the Count! Think of him. He's been through so much already. No, I won't stay in the place any longer. A fellow like you too! If it had been that attorney now or somebody of her own class . . .

JEAN: Why, what's wrong with . . .

KRISTIN: Oh, you're all right in your own way, but when all's said and done there is a difference between one class and another. No, this is something I'll never be able to stomach. That our young lady who was so proud and so down on men you'd never believe she'd let one come near her should go and give herself to one like you. She who wanted to have poor Diana shot for running after the lodgekeeper's pug. No, I must say . . . ! Well, I won't stay here any longer. On the twenty-fourth of October I quit.

JEAN: And then?

KRISTIN: Well, since you mention it, it's about time you began to look around, if we're ever going to get married.

JEAN: But what am I to look for? I shan't get a place like this when I'm married.

KRISTIN: I know you won't. But you might get a job as porter or caretaker in some public institution. Government rations are small but sure, and there's a pension for the widow and children.

JEAN: That's all very fine, but it's not in my line to start thinking at once about dying for my wife and children. I must say I had rather bigger ideas.

KRISTIN: You and your ideas! You've got obligations too, and you'd better start thinking about them.

JEAN: Don't *you* start pestering me about obligations. I've had enough of that. (*Listens to a sound upstairs.*) Anyway we've plenty of time to work things out. Go and get ready now and we'll be off to church.

KRISTIN: Who's that walking about upstairs?

JEAN: Don't know — unless it's Clara.

KRISTIN (*going*): You don't think the Count could have come back without our hearing him?

JEAN (*scared*): The Count? No, he can't have. He'd have rung for me.

KRISTIN: God help us! I've never known such goings on. (*Exits.*)

(*The sun has now risen and is shining on the treetops. The light gradually changes until it slants in through the windows.* JEAN *goes to the door and beckons.* JULIE *enters in travelling clothes, carrying a small bird-cage covered with a cloth which she puts on a chair.*)

JULIE: I'm ready.

JEAN: Hush! Kristin's up.

JULIE (*in a very nervous state*): Does she suspect anything?

JEAN: Not a thing. But, my God, what a sight you are!

JULIE: Sight? What do you mean?

JEAN: You're white as a corpse and — pardon me — your face is dirty.

JULIE: Let me wash then. (*Goes to the sink and washes her face and hands.*) There. Give me a towel. Oh! The sun is rising!

JEAN: And that breaks the spell.

JULIE: Yes. The spell of Midsummer Eve . . . But listen, Jean. Come with me. I've got the money.

JEAN (*sceptically*): Enough?

JULIE: Enough to start with. Come with me. I can't travel alone today. It's Midsummer Day, remember. I'd be packed into a suffocating train among crowds of people who'd all stare at me. And it would stop at every station while I yearned for wings. No, I can't do that, I simply can't. There will be

memories too; memories of Midsummer Days when I was little. The leafy church — birch and lilac — the gaily spread dinner table, relatives, friends — evening in the park — dancing and music and flowers and fun. Oh, however far you run away — there'll always be memories in the baggage car — and remorse and guilt.

JEAN: I will come with you, but quickly now then, before it's too late. At once.

JULIE: Put on your things. (*Picks up the cage.*)

JEAN: No luggage, mind. That would give us away.

JULIE: No, only what we can take with us in the carriage.

JEAN (*fetching his hat*): What on earth have you got there? What is it?

JULIE: Only my greenfinch. I don't want to leave it behind.

JEAN: Well, I'll be damned! We're to take a bird-cage along, are we? You're crazy. Put that cage down.

JULIE: It's the only thing I'm taking from my home. The only living creature who cares for me since Diana went off like that. Don't be cruel. Let me take it.

JEAN: Put that cage down, I tell you — and don't talk so loud. Kristin will hear.

JULIE: No, I won't leave it in strange hands. I'd rather you killed it.

JEAN: Give the little beast here then and I'll wring its neck.

JULIE: But don't hurt it, don't . . . no, I can't.

JEAN: Give it here. I *can*.

JULIE (*taking the bird out of the cage and kissing it*): Dear little Serena, must you die and leave your mistress?

JEAN: Please don't make a scene. It's *your* life and future we're worrying about. Come on, quick now!

(*He snatches the bird from her, puts it on a board and picks up a chopper.* JULIE *turns away.*)

You should have learnt how to kill chickens instead of target-shooting. Then you wouldn't faint at a drop of blood.

JULIE (*screaming*): Kill me too! Kill me! You who can butcher an innocent creature without a quiver. Oh, how I hate you, how I loathe you! There is blood between us now. I curse the hour I first saw you. I curse the hour I was conceived in my mother's womb.

JEAN: What's the use of cursing. Let's go.

JULIE (*going to the chopping-block as if drawn against her will*): No, I won't go yet. I can't . . . I must look. Listen! There's a carriage. (*Listens without taking her eyes off the board and chopper.*) You don't think I can bear the sight of blood. You think I'm so weak. Oh, how I should like to see your blood and your brains on a chopping-block! I'd like to see the whole of your sex swimming like that in a sea of blood. I think I could drink out of your skull, bathe my feet in your broken breast and eat your heart roasted whole. You think I'm weak. You think I love you, that my womb yearned for your seed and I want to carry your offspring under my heart and nourish it with my blood. You think I want to bear your child and take your name. By the way, what is your name? I've never heard your surname. I don't suppose you've got one. I should be "Mrs. Hovel" or "Madam Dunghill." You dog wearing my collar, you lackey with my crest on your buttons! I share you with my cook; I'm my own servant's rival! Oh! Oh! Oh! . . . You think I'm a coward and will run away. No, now I'm going to stay — and let the storm break. My father will come back . . . find his desk broken open . . . his money gone. Then he'll ring that bell — twice for the valet — and then he'll send for the police . . . and I shall tell everything. Everything. Oh how wonderful to make an end of it all — a real end! He has a stroke and dies and that's the end of all of us. Just peace and quietness . . . eternal rest. The coat of arms broken on the coffin and the Count's line extinct . . . But the valet's line goes on in an orphanage, wins laurels in the gutter and ends in jail.

JEAN: There speaks the noble blood! Bravo, Miss Julie. But now, don't let the cat out of the bag.

(KRISTIN *enters dressed for church, carrying a prayer-book.* JULIE *rushes to her and flings herself into her arms for protection.*)

JULIE: Help me, Kristin! Protect me from this man!

KRISTIN (*unmoved and cold*): What goings-on for a feast day morning! (*Sees the board.*) And what a filthy mess. What's it all about? Why are you screaming and carrying on so?

JULIE: Kristin, you're a woman and my friend. Beware of that scoundrel!

JEAN (*embarrassed*): While you ladies are talking things over, I'll go and shave. (*Slips into his room.*)

JULIE: You must understand. You must listen to me.

KRISTIN: I certainly don't understand such loose ways. Where are you off to in those travelling clothes? And he had his hat on, didn't he, eh?

JULIE: Listen, Kristin. Listen, I'll tell you everything.

KRISTIN: I don't want to know anything.

JULIE: You must listen.

KRISTIN: What to? Your nonsense with Jean? I don't care a rap about that; it's nothing to do with me. But if you're thinking of getting him to run off with you, we'll soon put a stop to that.

JULIE (*very nervously*): Please try to be calm, Kristin, and listen. I can't stay here, nor can Jean — so we must go abroad.

KRISTIN: Hm, hm!

JULIE (*brightening*): But you see, I've had an idea. Supposing we all three go — abroad — to Switzerland and start a hotel together . . . I've got some money, you see . . . and Jean and I could run the whole thing — and I thought you would take charge of the kitchen. Wouldn't that be splendid? Say yes, do. If you come with us everything will be fine. Oh do say yes! (*Puts her arms round* KRISTIN.)

KRISTIN (*coolly thinking*): Hm, hm.

JULIE (*presto tempo*): You've never travelled, Kristin. You should go abroad and see the world. You've no idea how nice it is travelling by train — new faces all the time and new countries. On our way through Hamburg we'll go to the zoo — you'll love that — and we'll go to the theatre and the opera too . . . and when we get to Munich there'll be the museums, dear, and pictures by Rubens and Raphael — the great painters, you know . . . You've heard of Munich, haven't you? Where King Ludwig lived — you know, the king who went mad. . . . We'll see his castles — some of his castles are still just like in fairy-tales . . . and from there it's not far to Switzerland — and the Alps. Think of the Alps, Kristin dear, covered with snow in the middle of summer . . . and there are oranges there and trees that are green the whole year round . . .

(JEAN *is seen in the door of his room, sharpening his razor on a strop which he holds with his teeth and his left hand. He listens to the talk with satisfaction and now and then nods approval.* JULIE *continues, tempo prestissimo.*)

And then we'll get a hotel . . . and I'll sit at the desk, while Jean receives the guests and goes out marketing and writes letters . . . There's life for you! Trains whistling, buses driving up, bells ringing upstairs and downstairs . . . and I shall make out the bills — and I shall cook them too . . . you've no idea how nervous travellers are when it comes to paying their bills. And you — you'll sit like a queen in the kitchen . . . of course there won't be any standing at the stove for you. You'll always have to be nicely dressed and ready to be seen, and with your looks — no, I'm not flattering you — one fine day you'll catch yourself a husband . . . some rich Englishman, I shouldn't wonder — they're the ones who are easy (*Slowing down.*) to catch . . . and then we'll get rich and build

ourselves a villa on Lake Como . . . of course it rains there a little now and then — but — (*Dully.*) — the sun must shine there too sometimes — even though it seems gloomy — and if not — then we can come home again — come back (*Pause.*) here — or somewhere else . . .

KRISTIN: Look here, Miss Julie, do you believe all that yourself?

JULIE (*exhausted*): Do I believe it?

KRISTIN: Yes.

JULIE (*wearily*): I don't know. I don't believe anything any more. (*Sinks down on the bench; her head in her arms on the table.*) Nothing. Nothing at all.

KRISTIN (*turning to* JEAN): So you meant to beat it, did you?

JEAN (*disconcerted, putting the razor on the table*): Beat it? What are you talking about? You've heard Miss Julie's plan, and though she's tired now with being up all night, it's a perfectly sound plan.

KRISTIN: Oh, is it? If you thought I'd work for that . . .

JEAN (*interrupting*): Kindly use decent language in front of your mistress. Do you hear?

KRISTIN: Mistress?

JEAN: Yes.

KRISTIN: Well, well, just listen to that!

JEAN: Yes, it would be a good thing if you did listen and talked less. Miss Julie is your mistress and what's made you lose your respect for her now ought to make you feel the same about yourself.

KRISTIN: I've always had enough self-respect —

JEAN: To despise other people.

KRISTIN: — not to go below my own station. Has the Count's cook ever gone with the groom or the swineherd? Tell me that.

JEAN: No, you were lucky enough to have a high-class chap for your beau.

KRISTIN: High-class all right — selling the oats out of the Count's stable.

JEAN: You're a fine one to talk — taking a commission on the groceries and bribes from the butcher.

KRISTIN: What the devil . . . ?

JEAN: And now you can't feel any respect for your employers. You, you!

KRISTIN: Are you coming to church with me? I should think you need a good sermon after your fine deeds.

JEAN: No, I'm not going to church today. You can go alone and confess your own sins.

KRISTIN: Yes, I'll do that and bring back enough forgiveness to cover yours too. The Saviour suffered and died on the cross for all our sins, and if we go to Him with faith and a penitent heart, He takes all our sins upon Himself.

JEAN: Even grocery thefts?

JULIE: Do you believe that, Kristin?

KRISTIN: That is my living faith, as sure as I stand here. The faith I learnt as a child and have kept ever since, Miss Julie. "But where sin abounded, grace did much more abound."

JULIE: Oh, if I had your faith! Oh, if . . .

KRISTIN: But you see you can't have it without God's special grace, and it's not given to all to have that.

JULIE: Who is it given to then?

KRISTIN: That's the great secret of the workings of grace, Miss Julie. God is no respecter of persons, and with Him the last shall be first . . .

JULIE: Then I suppose He does respect the last.

KRISTIN (continuing): . . . and it is easier for a camel to go through the eye of a needle than for a rich man to enter into the kingdom of God. That's how it is, Miss Julie. Now I'm going — alone, and on my way I shall tell the groom not to let any of the horses out, in case anyone should want to leave before the Count gets back. Goodbye. (Exit.)

JEAN: What a devil! And all on account of a greenfinch.

JULIE (wearily): Never mind the greenfinch. Do you see any way out of this, any end to it?

JEAN (pondering): No.

JULIE: If you were in my place, what would you do?

JEAN: In your place? Wait a bit. If I was a woman — a lady of rank who had — fallen. I don't know. Yes, I do know now.

JULIE (picking up the razor and making a gesture): This?

JEAN: Yes. But I wouldn't do it, you know. There's a difference between us.

JULIE: Because you're a man and I'm a woman? What is the difference?

JEAN: The usual difference — between man and woman.

JULIE (holding the razor): I'd like to. But I can't. My father couldn't either, that time he wanted to.

JEAN: No, he didn't want to. He had to be revenged first.

JULIE: And now my mother is revenged again, through me.

JEAN: Didn't you ever love your father, Miss Julie?

JULIE: Deeply, but I must have hated him too — unconsciously. And he let me be brought up to despise my own sex, to be half woman, half man. Whose fault is what's happened? My father's, my mother's or my own? My own? I haven't anything that's my own. I haven't one single thought that I didn't get from my father, one emotion that didn't come from my mother, and as for this last idea — about all people being equal — I got that from him, my fiancé — that's why I call him a cad. How can it be my fault? Push the responsibility on to Jesus, like Kristin does? No, I'm too proud and — thanks to my father's teaching — too intelligent. As for all that about a rich person not being able to get into heaven, it's just a lie, but Kristin, who has money in the savings-bank, will certainly not get in. Whose fault is it? What does it matter whose fault it is? In any case I must take the blame and bear the consequences.

JEAN: Yes, but . . . (*There are two sharp rings on the bell.* JULIE *jumps to her feet.* JEAN *changes into his livery.*) The Count is back. Supposing Kristin . . . (*Goes to the speaking-tube, presses it and listens.*)

JULIE: Has he been to his desk yet?

JEAN: This is Jean, sir. (*Listens.*) Yes, sir. (*Listens.*) Yes, sir, very good, sir. (*Listens.*) At once, sir? (*Listens.*) Very good, sir. In half an hour.

JULIE (*in panic*): What did he say? My God, what did he say?

JEAN: He ordered his boots and his coffee in half an hour.

JULIE: Then there's half an hour . . . Oh, I'm so tired! I can't do anything. Can't be sorry, can't run away, can't stay, can't live — can't die. Help me. Order me, and I'll obey like a dog. Do me this last service — save my honour, save his name. You know what I ought to do, but haven't the strength to do. Use your strength and order me to do it.

JEAN: I don't know why — I can't now — I don't understand . . . It's just as if this coat made me — I can't give you orders — and now that the Count has spoken to me — I can't quite explain, but . . . well, that devil of a lackey is bending my back again. I believe if the Count came down now and ordered me to cut my throat, I'd do it on the spot.

JULIE: Then pretend you're him and I'm you. You did some fine acting before, when you knelt to me and played the aristocrat. Or . . . Have you ever seen a hypnotist at the theatre? (*He nods.*) He says to the person "Take the broom," and he takes it. He says "Sweep," and he sweeps . . .

JEAN: But the person has to be asleep.

JULIE (*as if in a trance*): I am asleep already . . . the whole room has turned to smoke — and you look like a stove — a stove like a man in black with a tall hat — your eyes are glowing like coals when the fire is low — and your face is a white patch like ashes. (*The sunlight has now reached the floor and lights up* JEAN.) How nice and warm it is! (*She holds out her hands as though warming them at a fire.*) And so light — and so peaceful.

JEAN (*putting the razor in her hand*): Here is the broom. Go now while it's light — out to the barn — and. . . . (*Whispers in her ear.*)

JULIE (*waking*): Thank you. I am going now — to rest. But just tell me that even the first can receive the gift of grace.

JEAN: The first? No, I can't tell you that. But wait . . . Miss Julie, I've got it! You aren't one of the first any longer. You're one of the last.

JULIE: That's true. I'm one of the very last. I *am* the last. Oh! . . . But now I can't go. Tell me again to go.

JEAN: No, I can't now either. I can't.

JULIE: And the first shall be last.

JEAN: Don't think, don't think. You're taking my strength away too and making me a coward. What's that? I thought I saw the bell move . . . To be so frightened of a bell! Yes, but it's not just a bell. There's somebody behind it — a hand moving it — and something else moving the hand — and if you stop your ears — if you stop your ears — yes, then it rings louder than ever. Rings and rings until you answer — and then it's too late. Then the police come and . . . and . . . . . (*The bell rings twice loudly.* JEAN *flinches, then straightens himself up.*) It's horrible. But there's no other way to end it . . . Go!

(JULIE *walks firmly out through the door.*)

CURTAIN

Mrs. Warren's Profession

George Bernard Shaw (1856–1950), like Andrew Undershaft in his *Major Barbara*, hated "poverty and slavery worse than any other crimes whatsoever." He thought something could be done, gradually (thus his Fabian or gradual socialism); in fact would be done, inevitably, through the working of the Life Force and creative evolution (*Man and Superman*). He liked to work in paradox, to shock with the truth, to play the clown ("the best part of the circus"), to propagandize ("All great art and Literature is propaganda") while entertaining (as did Bunyan, Dickens, Mozart, and others whom he thanked, for their influence upon him, in *The Perfect Wagnerite*). He confessed to "no taste for what is called popular art, no respect for popular morality, no belief in popular religion, no admiration for popular heroics" — and yet he turned to the theatre, where these things so often prevail, for his platform.

This, like his championing of Ibsen before he was generally accepted (*The Quintessence of Ibsenism*), often put him in the position of his Confucius in his vast play of *Back to Methuselah*:

> Nobody likes me: I am held in awe. Capable persons are never liked. I am not likeable; but I am indispensable.

In the end he became the village iconoclast and world prophet:

> I am myself by profession what is called an original thinker, my business being to question and test all the established creeds and codes to see how far they are still valid and how far worn out or superseded, and even to draft new creeds and codes.

Now, as the dust of controversy clears in arenas as diverse as English spelling, vegetarianism, the nineteenth century's "carboniferous capitalism" (for which he had a "kindly dislike"), sainthood and vaccination, it is becoming clearer that, whatever one may think of this idea or that, the 35 volumes of his collected criticism, essays, political tracts, and plays (he achieved fame as a dramatist at fifty) enshrine the work of one of the greatest writers in English since Shakespeare. "Nobody has ever called me a god," he wrote in *Everybody's Political What's What*. "I am at best a sage." It turns out that he was at best an artist, a dramatic genius.

To great works, such as *Saint Joan*, he often attached prolegomena, commentaries, sermons, dissertations, harangues, bulls, "eking out a penn'orth of play with a pound of preface." One dare not attempt to write a more stimulating preface to Shaw's "unpleasant" play *Mrs. Warren's Profession* than he did himself, so here in the words of the Master are some of the materials he had "left over" from the play and some of the characteristic comments he made on its career in the period from 1894 to 1933.

Preface

Mrs. Warren's Profession was written in 1894 to draw attention to the truth that prostitution is caused, not by female depravity and male licentiousness, but simply by underpaying, undervaluing, and overworking women so shamefully that the poorest of them are forced to resort to prostitution to keep body and soul together. Indeed all attractive unpropertied women lose money by being infallibly virtuous or contracting marriages that are not more or less venal. If on the large social scale we get what we call vice instead of what we call virtue it is simply because we are paying more for it. No normal woman would be a professional prostitute if she could better herself by being respectable, nor marry for money if she could afford to marry for love.

Also I desired to expose the fact that prostitution is not only carried on without organization by individual enterprise in the lodgings of solitary women, each her own mistress as well as every customer's mistress, but organized and exploited as a big international commerce for the profit of capitalists like any other commerce, and very lucrative to great city estates, including Church estates, through the rents of the houses in which it is practised.

I could not have done anything more injurious to my prospects at the outset of my career. My play was immediately stigmatized by the Lord Chamberlain, who by Act of Parliament has despotic and even supermonarchical power over our theatres, as "immoral and otherwise improper for the stage." Its performance was prohibited, I myself being branded by implication, to my great damage, as an unscrupulous and blackguardly author. True, I have lived this defamation down, and am apparently none the worse. True too that the stage under the censorship became so licentious after the war that the ban on a comparatively prudish play like mine became ridiculous and had to be lifted. Also I admit that my career as a revolutionary critic of our most respected social institutions kept me so continually in hot water that the addition of another jugful of boiling fluid by the Lord Chamberlain troubled me too little to entitle me to personal commiseration, especially as the play greatly strengthened my repute among serious readers. Besides, in 1894 the ordinary commercial theatres would have nothing to say to me, Lord Chamberlain or no Lord Chamberlain. None the less the injury done me, now admittedly indefensible, was real and considerable, and the injury to society much greater; for when the White Slave Traffic, as Mrs. Warren's profession came to be called, was dealt with legislatively, all that Parliament did was to enact that prostitutes' male bullies and parasites should be flogged, leaving Mrs. Warren in complete command of the situation, and its true nature more effectually masked than ever. It was the fault of the Censorship that our legislators and journalists were not better instructed.

In 1902 the Stage Society, technically a club giving private performances for the entertainment of its own members, and therefore exempt from the Lord Chamberlain's jurisdiction, resolved to perform the play. None of the public theatres dared brave his displeasure (he has absolute power to close them if they offend him) by harboring the performance; but another club which had a little stage, and which rather courted a pleasantly scandalous reputation, opened its doors for one night and one afternoon. Some idea of the resultant sensation may be gathered from the following polemic, which appeared as a preface to a special edition of the play, and was headed: THE AUTHOR'S APOLOGY.

Mrs. Warren's Profession has been performed at last, after a delay of only eight years; and I have once more shared with Ibsen the triumphant amusement of startling all but the strongest-headed of the London theatre critics clean out of the practice of their profession. No author who has ever known the exultation of sending the Press into an hysterical tumult of protest, of moral panic, of involuntary and frantic confession of sin, of a horror of conscience in which the power of distinguishing between the work of art on the stage and the real life of the spectator is confused and overwhelmed, will ever care for the stereotyped compliments which every successful farce or melodrama elicits from the newspapers. Give me that critic who rushed from my play to declare furiously that Sir George Crofts ought to be kicked. What a triumph for the actor, thus to reduce a jaded London journalist to the condition of the simple sailor in the Wapping gallery, who shouts execrations at Iago and warnings to Othello not to believe him! But dearer still than such simplicity is that sense of the sudden earthquake shock to the foundations of morality which sends a pallid crowd of critics into the street shrieking that the pillars of society are cracking and the ruin of the State at hand. Even the Ibsen champions of ten years ago remonstrate with me just as the veterans of those brave days remonstrated with them. Mr. Grein, the hardy iconoclast who first launched my plays on the stage alongside *Ghosts* and *The Wild Duck*, exclaims that I have shattered his ideals. Actually his ideals! What would Dr. Relling say? And Mr. William Archer himself disowns me because I "cannot touch pitch without wallowing in it." Truly my play must be more needed than I knew; and yet I thought I knew how little the others know.

Do not suppose, however, that the consternation of the Press reflects any consternation among the general public. Anybody can upset the theatre critics, in a turn of the wrist, by substituting for the romantic commonplaces of the stage the moral commonplaces of the pulpit, the platform, or the library. Play *Mrs. Warren's Profession* to an audience of clerical members of the Christian Social Union and of women well experienced in Rescue, Temperance, and Girls' Club work, and no moral panic will arise: every man and woman present will know that as long as poverty makes virtue hideous and the spare pocket-money of rich bachelordom makes vice dazzling, their daily hand-to-hand fight against prostitution with prayer and persuasion, shelters and scanty alms, will be a losing one. There was a time when they were able to urge that though "the white-lead factory where Anne Jane was poisoned" may be a far more terrible place than Mrs. Warren's house, yet hell is still more dreadful. Nowadays they no longer believe in hell; and the girls among whom they are working know that they do not believe in it, and would laugh at them if they did. So well have the rescuers learnt that Mrs. Warren's defence of herself and indictment of society is the thing that most needs saying, that those who know me personally reproach me, not for writing this play, but for wasting my energies on "pleasant plays" for the amusement of frivolous people, when I can build up such excellent stage sermons on their own work. *Mrs. Warren's Profession* is the one play of mine which I could submit to a censorship without doubt of the result; only, it must not be the censorship of the minor theatre critic, nor of an innocent court official like the Lord Chamberlain's Examiner, much less of people who consciously profit by Mrs. Warren's profession, or who personally make use of it, or who hold the widely whispered view that it is an indispensable safety-valve for the protection of domestic virtue, or, above all, who are smitten with a sentimental affection for our fallen sister, and would "take her up tenderly, lift her with care, fashioned so slenderly, young, and *so* fair." Nor am I prepared to accept the verdict of the medical gentlemen who would compulsorily examine and register Mrs. Warren, whilst leaving Mrs. Warren's patrons, especially her military patrons, free to destroy her health and

anybody else's without fear of reprisals. But I should be quite content to have my play judged by, say, a joint committee of the Central Vigilance Society and the Salvation Army. And the sterner moralists the members of the committee were, the better.

Some of the journalists I have shocked reason so unripely that they will gather nothing from this but a confused notion that I am accusing the National Vigilance Association and the Salvation Army of complicity in my own scandalous immorality. It will seem to them that people who would stand this play would stand anything. They are quite mistaken. Such an audience as I have described would be revolted by many of our fashionable plays. They would leave the theatre convinced that the Plymouth Brother who still regards the playhouse as one of the gates of hell is perhaps the safest adviser on the subject of which he knows so little. If I do not draw the same conclusion, it is not because I am one of those who claim that art is exempt from moral obligations, and deny that the writing or performance of a play is a moral act, to be treated on exactly the same footing as theft or murder if it produces equally mischievous consequences. I am convinced that fine art is the subtlest, the most seductive, the most effective instrument of moral propaganda in the world, excepting only the example of personal conduct; and I waive even this exception in favor of the art of the stage, because it works by exhibiting examples of personal conduct made intelligible and moving to crowds of unobservant unreflecting people to whom real life means nothing. I have pointed out again and again that the influence of the theatre in England is growing so great that private conduct, religion, law, science, politics, and morals are becoming more and more theatrical, whilst the theatre itself remains impervious to common sense, religion, science, politics, and morals. That is why I fight the theatre, not with pamphlets and sermons and treatises, but with plays; and so effective do I find the dramatic method that I have no doubt I shall at last persuade even London to take its conscience and its brains with it when it goes to the theatre, instead of leaving them at home with its prayer-book as it does at present. Consequently, I am the last man to deny that if the net effect of performing *Mrs. Warren's Profession* were an increase in the number of persons entering that profession or employing it, its performance might well be made an indictable offence.

Now let us consider how such recruiting can be encouraged by the theatre. Nothing is easier. Let the Lord Chamberlain's Examiner of Plays, backed by the Press, make an unwritten but perfectly well understood regulation that members of Mrs. Warren's profession shall be tolerated on the stage only when they are beautiful, exquisitely dressed, and sumptuously lodged and fed; also that they shall, at the end of the play, die of consumption to the sympathetic tears of the whole audience, or step into the next room to commit suicide, or at least be turned out by their protectors and passed on to be "redeemed" by old and faithful lovers who have adored them in spite of all their levities. Naturally the poorer girls in the gallery will believe in the beauty, in the exquisite dresses, and the luxurious living, and will see that there is no real necessity for the consumption, the suicide, or the ejectment: mere pious forms, all of them to save the Censor's face. Even if these purely official catastrophes carried any conviction, the majority of English girls remain so poor, so dependent, so well aware that the drudgeries of such honest work as is within their reach are likely enough to lead them eventually to lung disease, premature death,

and domestic desertion or brutality, that they would still see reason to prefer the primrose path to the stony way of virtue, since both, vice at worst and virtue at best, lead to the same end in poverty and overwork. It is true that the Elementary School mistress will tell you that only girls of a certain kind will reason in this way. But alas! that certain kind turns out on inquiry to be simply the pretty, dainty kind: that is, the only kind that gets the chance of acting on such reasoning. Read the first report of the Commission on the Housing of the Working Classes [Bluebook C 4402, 1889]; read the Report on Home Industries (sacred word, Home!) issued by the Women's Industrial Council [Home Industries of Women in London, 1897, 1s.]; and ask yourself whether, if the lot in life therein described were your lot in life, you would rather be a jewelled Vamp. If you can go deep enough into things to be able to say no, how many ignorant half-starved girls will believe you are speaking sincerely? To them the lot of the stage courtesan is heavenly in comparison with their own. Yet the Lord Chamberlain's Examiner, being an officer of the Royal Household, places the King in the position of saying to the dramatist "Thus, and thus only, shall you present Mrs. Warren's profession on the stage, or you shall starve. Witness Shaw, who told the untempting truth about it, and whom We, by the Grace of God, accordingly disallow and suppress, and do what in Us lies to silence." Fortunately, Shaw cannot be silenced. "The harlot's cry from street to street" is louder than the voices of all the kings. I am not dependent on the theatre, and cannot be starved into making my play a standing advertisement of the attractive side of Mrs. Warren's business.

Here I must guard myself against a misunderstanding. It is not the fault of their authors that the long string of wanton's tragedies, from Antony and Cleopatra to Iris, are snares to poor girls, and are objected to on that account by many earnest men and women who consider *Mrs. Warren's Profession* an excellent sermon. Pinero is in no way bound to suppress the fact that his Iris is a person to be envied by millions of better women. If he made his play false to life by inventing fictitious disadvantages for her, he would be acting as unscrupulously as any tract-writer. If society chooses to provide for its Irises better than for its working women, it must not expect honest playwrights to manufacture spurious evidence to save its credit. The michief lies in the deliberate suppression of the other side of the case: the refusal to allow Mrs. Warren to expose the drudgery and repulsiveness of plying for hire among coarse tedious drunkards. All that, says the Examiner in effect, is horrifying, loathsome. Precisely: what does he expect it to be? would he have us represent it as beautiful and gratifying? His answer to this question amounts, I fear, to a blunt Yes; for it seems impossible to root out of an Englishman's mind the notion that vice is delightful, and that abstention from it is privation. At all events, as long as the tempting side of it is kept towards the public, and softened by plenty of sentiment and sympathy, it is welcomed by our Censor, whereas the slightest attempt to place it in the light of the policeman's lantern or the Salvation Army shelter is checkmated at once as not merely disgusting, but, if you please, unnecessary.

Everybody will, I hope, admit that this state of things is intolerable; that the subject of Mrs. Warren's profession must be either tabu altogether, or else exhibited with the warning side as freely displayed as the tempting side. But many persons will vote for a complete tabu, and an impartial clean sweep from the boards of Mrs. Warren and Gretchen and the rest:

in short, for banishing the sexual instincts from the stage altogether. Those who think this impossible can hardly have considered the number and importance of the subjects which are actually banished from the stage. Many plays, among them *Lear, Hamlet, Macbeth, Coriolanus, Julius Cæsar*, have no sex complications: the thread of their action can be followed by children who could not understand a single scene of *Mrs. Warren's Profession* or *Iris*. None of our plays rouse the sympathy of the audience by an exhibition of the pains of maternity, as Chinese plays constantly do. Each nation has its particular set of tabus in addition to the common human stock; and though each of these tabus limits the scope of the dramatist, it does not make drama impossible. If the Examiner were to refuse to license plays with female characters in them, he would only be doing to the stage what our tribal customs already do to the pulpit and the bar. I have myself written a rather entertaining play with only one woman in it, and she quite heartwhole; and I could just as easily write a play without a woman in it at all. I will even go as far as to promise the Examiner my support if he will introduce this limitation for part of the year, say during Lent, so as to make a close season for that dullest of stock dramatic subjects, adultery, and force our managers and authors to find out what all great dramatists find out spontaneously: to wit, that people who sacrifice every other consideration to love are as hopelessly unheroic on the stage as lunatics or dipsomaniacs. Hector and Hamlet are the world's heroes; not Paris and Antony.

But though I do not question the possibility of a drama in which love should be as effectively ignored as cholera is at present, there is not the slightest chance of that way out of the difficulty being taken by the Examiner. If he attempted it there would be a revolt in which he would be swept away in spite of my singlehanded efforts to defend him. A complete tabu is politically impossible. A complete toleration is equally impossible to the Examiner, because his occupation would be gone if there were no tabu to enforce. He is therefore compelled to maintain the present compromise of a partial tabu, applied, to the best of his judgment, with a careful respect to persons and to public opinion. And a very sensible English solution of the difficulty, too, most readers will say. I should not dispute it if dramatic poets really were what English public opinion generally assumes them to be during their lifetime: that is, a licentiously irregular group to be kept in order in a rough and ready way by a magistrate who will stand no nonsense from them. But I cannot admit that the class represented by Eschylus, Sophocles, Aristophanes, Euripides, Shakespeare, Goethe, Ibsen, and Tolstoy, not to mention our own contemporary playwrights, is as much in place in the Examiner's office as a pickpocket is in Bow Street. Further, it is not true that the Censorship, though it certainly suppresses Ibsen and Tolstoy, and would suppress Shakespeare but for the absurd rule that a play once licensed is always licensed (so that Wycherly is permitted and Shelley prohibited), also suppresses unscrupulous playwrights. I challenge the Examiner to mention any extremity of sexual misconduct which any manager in his senses would risk presenting on the London stage that has not been presented under his license and that of his predecessor. The compromise, in fact, works out in practice in favor of loose plays as against earnest ones.

To carry conviction on this point, I will take the extreme course of narrating the plots of two plays witnessed within the last ten years by myself at London West End theatres, one licensed under Queen Victoria, the other under her successor. Both plots conform to the strictest rules of the period when *La Dame aux Camellias* was still a forbidden play, and when *The Second Mrs. Tanqueray* would have been tolerated only on condition that she carefully explained to the audience that when she met Captain Ardale she sinned "but in intention."

Play number one. A prince is compelled by his parents to marry the daughter of a neighboring king, but loves another maiden. The scene represents a hall in the king's palace at night. The wedding has taken place that day; and the closed door of the nuptial chamber is in view of the audience. Inside, the princess awaits her bridegroom. A duenna is in attendance. The bridegroom enters. His sole desire is to escape from a marriage which is hateful to him. A means occurs to him. He will assault the duenna, and be ignominiously expelled from the palace by his indignant father-in-law. To his horror, when he proceeds to carry out this stratagem, the duenna, far from raising an alarm, is flattered, delighted, and compliant. The assaulter becomes the assaulted. He flings her angrily to the ground, where she remains placidly. He flies. The father enters; dismisses the duenna; and listens at the keyhole of his daughter's nuptial chamber, uttering various pleasantries, and declaring, with a shiver, that a sound of kissing, which he supposes to proceed from within, makes him feel young again.

Story number two. A German officer finds himself in an inn with a French lady who has wounded his national vanity. He resolves to humble her by committing a rape upon her. He announces his purpose. She remonstrates, implores, flies to the doors and finds them locked, calls for help and finds none at hand, runs screaming from side to side, and, after a harrowing scene, is overpowered and faints. Nothing further being possible on the stage without actual felony, the officer then relents and leaves her. When she recovers, she believes that he has carried out his threat; and during the rest of the play she is represented as vainly vowing vengeance upon him, whilst she is really falling in love with him under the influence of his imaginary crime against her. Finally she consents to marry him; and the curtain falls on their happiness.

This story was certified by the Examiner, acting for the Lord Chamberlain, as void in its general tendency of "anything immoral or otherwise improper for the stage." But let nobody conclude therefore that the Examiner is a monster, whose policy it is to deprave the theatre. As a matter of fact, both the above stories are strictly in order from the official point of view. The incidents of sex which they contain, though carried in both to the extreme point at which another step would be dealt with, not by the Examiner, but by the police, do not involve adultery, nor any allusion to Mrs. Warren's profession, nor to the fact that children of any polyandrous group will, when they grow up, inevitably be confronted, as those of Mrs. Warren's group are in my play, with the insoluble problem of their own possible consanguinity. In short, by depending wholly on the coarse humors and the physical fascination of sex, they comply with all the formulable requirements of the Censorship, whereas plays in which these humors and fascinations are discarded, and the social problems created by sex seriously faced and dealt with, inevitably ignore the official formula and are suppressed. If the old rule against the exhibition of illicit sex relations on the stage were revived, and the subject absolutely barred, the only result would be that *Antony and Cleopatra, Othello* (because of the Bianca episode), *Troilus and Cressida, Henry IV, Measure for Measure, Timon of Athens, La Dame aux Camel-*

lias, *The Profligate, The Second Mrs. Tanqueray, The Notorious Mrs. Ebbsmith, The Gay Lord Quex, Mrs. Dane's Defence,* and *Iris* would be swept from the stage, and placed under the same ban as Tolstoy's *Dominion of Darkness* and *Mrs. Warren's Profession,* whilst such plays as the two described above would have a monopoly of the theatre as far as sexual interest is concerned.

What is more, the repulsiveness of the worst of the certified plays would protect the Censorship against effective exposure and criticism. Not long ago an American Review of high standing asked me for an article on the Censorship of the English Stage. I replied that such an article would involve passages too disagreeable for publication in a magazine for general family reading. The editor persisted nevertheless; but not until he had declared his readiness to face this, and had pledged himself to insert the article unaltered (the particularity of the pledge extending even to a specification of the exact number of words in the article) did I consent to the proposal. What was the result? The editor, confronted with the two stories given above, threw his pledge to the winds, and, instead of returning the article, printed it with the illustrative examples omitted, and nothing left but the argument from political principle against the Censorship. In doing this he fired my broadside after withdrawing the cannon balls; for neither the Censor nor any other Englishman, except perhaps a few veterans of the dwindling old guard of Benthamism, cares a dump about political principle. The ordinary Briton thinks that if every other Briton is not under some form of tutelage, the more childish the better, he will abuse his freedom viciously. As far as its principle is concerned, the Censorship is the most popular institution in England; and the playwright who criticizes it is slighted as a blackguard agitating for impunity. Consequently nothing can really shake the confidence of the public in the Lord Chamberlain's department except a remorseless and unbowdlerized narration of the licentious fictions which slip through its net, and are hallmarked by it with the approval of the royal household. But as such stories cannot be made public without great difficulty, owing to the obligation an editor is under not to deal unexpectedly with matters that are not *virginibus puerisque* [for girls and boys], the chances are heavily in favor of the Censor escaping all remonstrance. With the exception of such comments as I was able to make in my own critical articles in *The World* and *The Saturday Review* when the pieces I have described were first produced, and a few ignorant protests by churchmen against much better plays which they confessed they had not seen nor read, nothing has been said in the press that could seriously disturb the easygoing notion that the stage would be much worse than it admittedly is but for the vigilance of the Examiner. The truth is, that no manager would dare produce on his own responsibility the pieces he can now get royal certificates for at two guineas per piece.

I hasten to add that I believe these evils to be inherent in the nature of all censorship, and not merely a consequence of the form the institution takes in London. No doubt there is a staggering absurdity in appointing an ordinary clerk to see that the leaders of European literature do not corrupt the morals of the nation, and to restrain Sir Henry Irving from presuming to impersonate Samson or David on the stage, though any other sort of artist may daub these scriptural figures on a signboard or carve them on a tombstone without hindrance. If the General Medical Council, the Royal College of Physicians, the Royal Academy of Arts, the Incorporated Law Society, and Convocation were abolished, and their functions handed over to the Examiner, the Concert of Europe would presumably certify England as mad. Yet, though neither medicine nor painting nor law nor the Church moulds the character of the nation as potently as the theatre does, nothing can come on the stage unless its dimensions admit of its first passing through the Examiner's mind! Pray do not think that I question his honesty. I am quite sure that he sincerely thinks me a blackguard, and my play a grossly improper one, because, like Tolstoy's *Dominion of Darkness*, it produces, as they are both meant to produce, a very strong and very painful impression of evil. I do not doubt for a moment that the rapine play which I have described, and which he licensed, was quite incapable in manuscript of producing any particular effect on his mind at all, and that when he was once satisfied that the ill-conducted hero was a German and not an English officer, he passed the play without studying its moral tendencies. Even if he had undertaken that study, there is no more reason to suppose that he is a competent moralist than there is to suppose that I am a competent mathematician. But truly it does not matter whether he is a moralist or not. Let nobody dream for a moment that what is wrong with the Censorship is the shortcoming of the gentleman who happens at any moment to be acting as Censor. Replace him tomorrow by an Academy of Letters and an Academy of Dramatic Poetry, and the new filter will still exclude original and epoch-making work, whilst passing conventional, old-fashioned, and vulgar work. The conclave which compiles the expurgatory index of the Roman Catholic Church is the most august, ancient, learned, famous, and authoritative censorship in Europe. Is it more enlightened, more liberal, more tolerant than the comparatively unqualified office of the Lord Chamberlain? On the contrary, it has reduced itself to a degree of absurdity which makes a Catholic university a contradiction in terms. All censorships exist to prevent anyone from challenging current conceptions and existing institutions. All progress is initiated by challenging current conceptions and executed by supplanting existing institutions. Consequently the first condition of progress is the removal of censorships. There is the whole case against censorships in a nutshell.

It will be asked whether theatrical managers are to be allowed to produce what they like, without regard to the public interest. But that is not the alternative. The managers of our London music-halls are not subject to any censorship. They produce their entertainments on their own responsibility, and have no two-guinea certificates to plead if their houses are conducted viciously. They know that if they lose their character, the County Council will simply refuse to renew their license at the end of the year; and nothing in the history of popular art is more amazing than the improvement in music-halls that this simple arrangement has produced within a few years. Place the theatres on the same footing, and we shall promptly have a similar revolution: a whole class of frankly blackguardly plays, in which unscrupulous low comedians attract crowds to gaze at bevies of girls who have nothing to exhibit but their prettiness, will vanish like the obscene songs which were supposed to enliven the squalid dullness, incredible to the younger generation, of the music-halls fifteen years ago. On the other hand, plays which treat sex questions as problems for thought instead of as aphrodisiacs will be freely performed. Gentlemen of the Examiner's way of thinking will have plenty of opportunity of protesting against them in Council; but the result will be that the

Examiner will find his natural level; Ibsen and Tolstoy theirs; so no harm will be done.

This question of the Censorship reminds me that I have to apologize to those who went to the recent performance of *Mrs. Warren's Profession* expecting to find it what I have just called an aphrodisiac. That was not my fault: it was the Examiner's. After the specimens I have given of the tolerance of his department, it was natural enough for thoughtless people to infer that a play which overstepped his indulgence must be a very exciting play indeed. Accordingly, I find one critic so explicit as to the nature of his disappointment as to say candidly that "such airy talk as there is upon the matter is utterly unworthy of acceptance as being a representation of what people with blood in them think or do on such occasions." Thus am I crushed between the upper millstone of the Examiner, who thinks me a libertine, and the nether popular critic, who thinks me a prude. Critics of all grades and ages, middle-aged fathers of families no less than ardent young enthusiasts, are equally indignant with me. They revile me as lacking in passion, in feeling, in manhood. Some of them even sum the matter up by denying me any dramatic power: a melancholy betrayal of what dramatic power has come to mean on our stage under the Censorship! Can I be expected to refrain from laughing at the spectacle of a number of respectable gentlemen lamenting because a playwright lures them to the theatre by a promise to excite their senses in a very special and sensational manner, and then, having successfully trapped them in exceptional numbers, proceeds to ignore their senses and ruthlessly improve their minds? But I protest again that the lure was not mine. The play had been in print for four years; and I have spared no pains to make known that my plays are built to induce, not voluptuous reverie but intellectual interest, not romantic rhapsody but humane concern. Accordingly, I do not find those critics who are gifted with intellectual appetite and political conscience complaining of want of dramatic power. Rather do they protest, not altogether unjustly, against a few relapses into staginess and caricature which betray the young playwright and the old playgoer in this early work of mine. As to the voluptuaries, I can assure them that the playwright, whether he be myself or another, will always disappoint them. The drama can do little to delight the senses: all the apparent instances to the contrary are instances of the personal fascination of the performers. The drama of pure feeling is no longer in the hands of the playwright: it has been conquered by the musician, after whose enchantments all the verbal arts seem cold and tame. *Romeo and Juliet* with the loveliest Juliet is dry, tedious, and rhetorical in comparison with Wagner's *Tristan*, even though Isolde be both fourteen stone and forty, as she often is in Germany. Indeed, it needed no Wagner to convince the public of this. The voluptuous sentimentality of Gounod's *Faust* and Bizet's *Carmen* has captured the common playgoer; and there is, flatly, no future now for any drama without music except the drama of thought. The attempt to produce a genus of opera without music (and this absurdity is what our fashionable theatres have been driving at for a long time past without knowing it) is far less hopeful than my own determination to accept problem as the normal material of the drama.

That this determination will throw me into a long conflict with our theatre critics, and with the few playgoers who go to the theatre as often as the critics, I well know; but I am too well equipped for the strife to be deterred by it, or to bear malice towards the losing side. In trying to produce the sensuous effects of opera, the fashionable drama has become so flaccid in its sentimentality, and the intellect of its frequenters so atrophied by disuse, that the reintroduction of problem, with its remorseless logic and iron framework of fact, inevitably produces at first an overwhelming impression of coldness and inhuman rationalism. But this will soon pass away. When the intellectual muscle and moral nerve of the critics has been developed in the struggle with modern problem plays, the pettish luxuriousness of the clever ones, and the sulky sense of disadvantaged weakness in the sentimental ones, will clear away; and it will be seen that only in the problem play is there any real drama, because drama is no mere setting up of the camera to nature: it is the presentation in parable of the conflict between Man's will and his environment: in a word, of problem. The vapidness of such drama as the pseudo-operatic plays contain lies in the fact that in them animal passion, sentimentality diluted, is shewn in conflict, not with real circumstances, but with a set of conventions and assumptions half of which do not exist off the stage, whilst the other half can either be evaded by a pretence of compliance or defied with complete impunity by any reasonably strong-minded person. Nobody can feel that such conventions are really compulsory; and consequently nobody can believe in the stage pathos that accepts them as an inexorable fate, or in the reality of the figures who indulge in such pathos. Sitting at such plays we do not believe: we make-believe. And the habit of make-believe becomes at last so rooted, that criticism of the theatre insensibly ceases to be criticism at all, and becomes more and more a chronicle of the fashionable enterprises of the only realities left on the stage: that is, the performers in their own persons. In this phase the playwright who attempts to revive genuine drama produces the disagreeable impression of the pedant who attempts to start a serious discussion at a fashionable at-home. Later on, when he has driven the tea services out and made the people who had come to use the theatre as a drawing-room understand that it is they and not the dramatists who are the intruders, he has to face the accusation that his plays ignore human feeling, and illusion produced by that very resistance of fact and law to human feeling which creates drama. It is the *deus ex machina* who, by suspending that resistance, makes the fall of the curtain an immediate necessity, since drama ends exactly where resistance ends. Yet the introduction of this resistance produces so strong an impression of heartlessness nowadays that a distinguished critic has summed up the impression made on him by *Mrs. Warren's Profession*, by declaring that "the difference between the spirit of Tolstoy and the spirit of Mr. Shaw is the difference between the spirit of Christ and the spirit of Euclid." But the epigram would be as good if Tolstoy's name were put in place of mine and D'Annunzio's in place of Tolstoy's. At the same time I accept the enormous compliment to my reasoning powers with sincere complacency; and I promise my flatterer that when he is sufficiently accustomed to and therefore undazzled by problem on the stage to be able to attend to the familiar factor of humanity in it as well as to the unfamiliar one of a real environment, he will both see and feel that *Mrs. Warren's Profession* is no mere theorem, but a play of instincts and temperaments in conflict with each other and with a flinty social problem that never yields an inch to mere sentiment.

I go further than this. I declare that the real secret of the cynicism and inhumanity of which shallower critics accuse me is the unexpectedness with which my charac-ters behave like human beings, instead of conforming to the romantic logic of the stage. The axioms and postulates of that dreary mimanthropometry are so well known that it is almost impossible for its slaves to write tolerable last acts to their plays, so conventionally do their conclusions follow from their premises. Because I have thrown this logic ruthlessly overboard, I am accused of ignoring, not stage logic, but, of all things, human feeling. People with completely theatrified imaginations tell me that no girl would treat her mother as Vivie Warren does, meaning that no stage heroine would in a popular sentimental play. They say this just as they might say that no two straight lines would enclose a space. They do not see how completely inverted their vision has become even when I throw its preposterousness in their faces, as I repeatedly do in this very play. Praed, the sentimental artist (fool that I was not to make him a theatre critic instead of an architect!) burlesques them by expecting all through the piece that the feelings of the others will be logically deducible from their family relationships and from his "conventionally unconventional" social code. The sarcasm is lost on the critics: they, saturated with the same logic, only think him the sole sensible person on the stage. Thus it comes about that the more completely the dramatist is emancipated from the illusion that men and women are primarily reasonable beings, and the more powerfully he insists on the ruthless indifference of their great dramatic antagonist, the external world, to their whims and emotions, the surer he is to be denounced as blind to the very distinction on which his whole work is built. Far from ignoring idiosyncrasy, will, passion, impulse, whim, as factors in human action, I have placed them so nakedly on the stage that the elderly citizen, accustomed to see them clothed with the veil of manufactured logic about duty, and to disguise even his own impulses from himself in this way, finds the picture as unnatural as Carlyle's suggested painting of parliament sitting without its clothes.

I now come to those critics who, intellectually baffled by the problem in *Mrs. Warren's Profession,* have made a virtue of running away from it on the gentlemanly ground that the theatre is frequented by women as well as by men, and that such problems should not be discussed or even mentioned in the presence of women. With that sort of chivalry I cannot argue: I simply affirm that *Mrs. Warren's Profession* is a play for women; that it was written for women; that it has been performed and produced mainly through the determination of women that it should be performed and produced; that the enthusiasm of women made its first performance excitingly successful; and that not one of these women had any inducement to support it except their belief in the timeliness and the power of the lesson the play teaches. Those who were "surprised to see ladies present" were men; and when they proceeded to explain that the journals they represented could not possibly demoralize the public by describing such a play, their editors cruelly devoted the space saved by their delicacy to reporting at unusual length an exceptionally abominable police case.

My old Independent Theatre manager, Mr. Grein, besides that reproach to me for shattering his ideals, complains that Mrs. Warren is not wicked enough, and names several romancers who would have clothed her black soul with all the terrors of tragedy. I have no doubt they would; but that is just what I did not want to do. Nothing would please our sanctimonious British public more than to throw the whole guilt of Mrs. Warren's profession on Mrs. Warren herself. Now the whole aim of my play is to throw that guilt on the British public itself. Mr. Grein may remember that when he produced my first play, *Widower's Houses,* exactly the same misunderstanding arose. When the virtuous young gentleman rose up in wrath against the slum landlord, the slum landlord very effectually shewed him that slums are the product, not of individual Harpagons, but of the indifference of virtuous young gentlemen to the condition of the city they live in provided they live at the west end of it on money earned by somebody else's labor. The notion that prostitution is created by the wickedness of Mrs. Warren is as silly as the notion — prevalent, nevertheless, to some extent in Temperance circles — that drunkenness is created by the wickedness of the publican. Mrs. Warren is not a whit a worse woman than the reputable daughter who cannot endure her. Her indifference to the ultimate social consequences of her means of making money, and her discovery of that means by the ordinary method of taking the line of least resistance to getting it, are too common in English society to call for any special remark. Her vitality, her thrift, her energy, her outspokenness, her wise care of her daughter, and the managing capacity which has enabled her and her sister to climb from the fried fish shop down by the Mint to the establishments of which she boasts, are all high English social virtues. Her defence of herself is so overwhelming that it provokes the St. James's Gazette to declare that "the tendency of the play is wholly evil" because "it contains one of the boldest and most specious defences of an immoral life for poor women that has ever been penned." Happily the St. James's Gazette here speaks in its haste. Mrs. Warren's defence of herself is not only bold and specious, but valid and unanswerable. But it is no defence at all of the vice which she organizes. It is no defence of an immoral life to say that the alternative offered by society collectively to poor women is a miserable life, starved, overworked, fetid, ailing, ugly. Though it is quite natural and *right* for Mrs. Warren to choose what is, according to her lights, the least immoral alternative, it is none the less infamous of society to offer such alternatives. For the alternatives offered are not morality and immorality, but two sorts of immorality. The man who cannot see that starvation, overwork, dirt, and disease are as anti-social as prostitution — that they are the vices and crimes of a nation, and not merely its misfortunes — is (to put it as politely as possible) a hopelessly Private Person.

The notion that Mrs. Warren must be a fiend is only an example of the violence and passion which the slightest reference to sex rouses in undisciplined minds, and which makes it seem natural to our law-givers to punish silly and negligible inde-cencies with a ferocity unknown in dealing with, for example, ruinous financial swind-ling. Had my play been entitled *Mr. War-ren's Profession*, and Mr. Warren been a bookmaker, nobody would have expected me to make him a villain as well. Yet gambling is a vice, and bookmaking an institution, for which there is absolutely nothing to be said. The moral and econ-omic evil done by trying to get other people's money without working for it (and this is the essence of gambling) is not only enormous but uncompensated. There are no two sides to the question of gamb-ling, no circumstances which force us to tolerate it lest its suppression lead to worse things, no consensus of opinion among responsible classes, such as magistrates and military commanders, that it is a necessity, no Athenian records of gambling made splendid by the talents of its professors, no contention that instead of violating morals it only violates a legal institution which is

in many respects oppressive and unnatural, no possible plea that the instinct on which it is founded is a vital one. Prostitution can confuse the issue with all these excuses: gambling has none of them. Consequently, if Mrs. Warren must needs be a demon, a bookmaker must be a cacodemon. Well, does anybody who knows the sporting world really believe that bookmakers are worse than their neighbors? On the con-trary, they have to be a good deal better; for in that world nearly everybody whose social rank does not exclude such an occu-pation would be a bookmaker if he could; but the strength of character required for handling large sums of money and for strict settlements and unflinching payment of losses is so rare that successful book-makers are rare too. It may seem that at least public spirit cannot be one of a book-maker's virtues; but I can testify from personal experience that excellent public work is done with money subscribed by bookmakers. It is true that there are abys-ses in bookmaking: for example, welshing. Mr. Grein hints that there are abysses in Mrs. Warren's profession also. So there are in every profession: the error lies in supposing that every member of them sounds these depths. I sit on a public body which prosecutes Mrs. Warren zealously; and I can assure Mr. Grein that she is often leniently dealt with because she has con-ducted her business "respectably" and held herself above its vilest branches. The de-grees in infamy are as numerous and as scrupulously observed as the degrees in the peerage: the moralist's notion that there are depths at which the moral atmosphere ceases is as delusive as the rich man's no-tion that there are no social jealousies or snobberies among the very poor. No: had I drawn Mrs. Warren as a fiend in human form, the very people who now rebuke me for flattering her would probably be the first to deride me for deducing character logically from occupation instead of observing it accurately in society.

One critic is so enslaved by this sort of logic that he calls my portraiture of the Reverend Samuel Gardner an attack on religion. According to this view Subaltern Iago is an attack on the army, Sir John Falstaff an attack on knighthood, and King Claudius an attack on royalty. Here again the clamor for naturalness and human feeling, raised by so many critics when they are confronted by the real thing on the stage, is really a clamor for the most mechanical and superficial sort of logic. The dramatic reason for making the clergyman what Mrs. Warren calls "an old stick-in-the-mud," whose son, in spite of much capacity and charm, is a cynically worthless member of society, is to set up a mordant contrast between him and the woman of infamous profession, with her well brought-up, straightforward, hardworking daughter. The critics who have missed the contrast have doubtless observed often enough that many clergymen are in the Church through no genuine calling, but simply because, in circles which can command preferment, it is the refuge of the fool of the family; and that clergymen's sons are often conspicuous reactionists against the restraints imposed on them in childhood by their father's profession. These critics must know, too, from history if not from experience, that women as unscrupulous as Mrs. Warren have distinguished themselves as administrators and rulers, both commercially and politically. But both observation and knowledge are left behind when journalists go to the theatre. Once in their stalls, they assume that it is "natural" for clergymen to be saintly, for soldiers to be heroic, for lawyers to be hard-hearted, for sailors to be simple and generous, for doctors to perform miracles with little

bottles, and for Mrs. Warren to be a beast and a demon. All this is not only not natural, but not dramatic. A man's profession only enters into the drama of his life when it comes into conflict with his nature. The result of this conflict is tragic in Mrs. Warren's case, and comic in the clergyman's case (at least we are savage enough to laugh at it); but in both cases it is illogical, and in both cases natural. I repeat, the critics who accuse me of sacrificing nature to logic are so sophisticated by their profession that to them logic is nature, and nature absurdity.

Many friendly critics are too little skilled in social questions and moral discussions to be able to conceive that respectable gentlemen like themselves, who would instantly call the police to remove Mrs. Warren if she ventured to canvass them personally, could possibly be in any way responsible for her proceedings. They remonstrate sincerely, asking me what good such painful exposures can possibly do. They might as well ask what good Lord Shaftesbury did by devoting his life to the exposure of evils (by no means yet remedied) compared to which the worst things brought into view or even into surmise in this play are trifles. The good of mentioning them is that you make people so extremely uncomfortable about them that they finally stop blaming "human nature" for them, and begin to support measures for their reform. Can anything be more absurd than the copy of *The Echo* which contains a notice of the performance of my play? It is edited by a gentleman who, having devoted his life to work of the Shaftesbury type, exposes social evils and clamors for their reform in every column except one; and that one is occupied by the declaration of the paper's kindly theatre critic, that the performance left him "wondering what useful purpose the play was intended to serve." The balance has to be redressed by the more fashionable papers, which usually combine capable art criticism with West-End solecism on politics and sociology. It is very noteworthy, however, on comparing the press explosion produced by *Mrs. Warren's Profession* in 1902 with that produced by *Widowers' Houses* about ten years earlier, that whereas in 1892 the facts were frantically denied and the persons of the drama flouted as monsters of wickedness, in 1902 the facts are admitted, and the characters recognized, though it is suggested that this is exactly why no gentleman should mention them in public. Only one writer has ventured to imply this time that the poverty mentioned by Mrs. Warren has since been quietly relieved, and need not have been dragged back to the footlights. I compliment him on his splendid mendacity, in which he is unsupported, save by a little plea in a theatrical paper which is innocent enough to think that ten guineas a year with board and lodging is an impossibly low wage for a barmaid. It goes on to cite Mr. Charles Booth as having testified that there are many laborers' wives who are happy and contented on eighteen shillings a week. But I can go further than that myself. I have seen an Oxford agricultural laborer's wife looking cheerful on eight shillings a week; but that does not console me for the fact that agriculture in England is a ruined industry. If poverty does not matter as long as it is contented, then crime does not matter as long as it is unscrupulous. The truth is that it is only then that it does matter most desperately. Many persons are more comfortable when they are dirty than when they are clean; but that does not recommend dirt as a national policy.

In 1905 Arnold Daly produced *Mrs. Warren's Profession* in New York. The press of that city instantly raised a cry that such persons as Mrs. Warren are "ordure" and should not be mentioned in the presence of decent people. This hideous repudiation of humanity and social conscience so took possession of the New York journalists that the few among them who kept their feet morally and intellectually could do nothing to check the epidemic of foul language, gross suggestion, and raving obscenity of word and thought that broke out. The writers abandoned all self-restraint under the impression that they were upholding virtue instead of outraging it. They infected each other with their hysteria until they were for all practical purposes indecently mad. They finally forced the police to arrest Daly and his company, and led the magistrate to express his loathing of the duty thus forced upon him of reading an unmentionable and abominable play. Of course the convulsion soon exhausted itself. The magistrate, naturally somewhat impatient when he found that what he had to read was a strenuously ethical play forming part of a book which had been in circulation unchallenged for eight years, and had been received without protest by the whole London and New York Press, gave the journalists a piece of his mind as to their moral taste in plays. By consent, he passed the case on to a higher court, which declared that the play was not immoral; acquitted Daly; and made an end of the attempt to use the law to declare living women to be "ordure," and thus enforce silence as to the far-reaching fact that you cannot cheapen women in the market for industrial purposes without cheapening them for other purposes as well. I hope *Mrs. Warren's Profession* will be played everywhere, in season and out of season, until Mrs. Warren has bitten that fact into the public conscience, and shamed the newspapers which support a tariff to keep up the price of every American commodity except American manhood and womanhood.

Unfortunately, Daly had already suffered the usual fate of those who direct public attention to the profits of the sweater or the pleasures of the voluptuary. He was morally lynched side by side with me. Months elapsed before the decision of the courts vindicated him; and even then, since his vindication implied the condemnation of the Press, which was by that time sober again, and ashamed of its orgie, his triumph received a rather sulky and grudging publicity. In the meantime he had hardly been able to approach an American city, including even those cities which had heaped applause on him as the defender of hearth and home when he produced *Candida*, without having to face articles discussing whether mothers could allow their daughters to attend such plays as *You Never Can Tell*, written by the infamous author of *Mrs. Warren's Profession*, and acted by the monster who produced it. What made this harder to bear was that though no fact is better established in theatrical business than the financial disastrousness of moral discredit, the journalists who had done all the mischief kept paying vice the homage of assuming that it is enormously popular and lucrative, and that Daly and I, being exploiters of vice, must therefore be making colossal fortunes out of the abuse heaped on us, and had in fact provoked it and welcomed it with that express object. Ignorance of real life could hardly go further.

I was deeply disgusted by this unsavory mobbing. And I have certain sensitive places in my soul: I do not like that word "ordure." Apply it to my work, and I can afford to smile, since the world, on the whole, will smile with me. But to apply it to the woman in the street, whose spirit is of one substance with your own and her body no less holy: to look your women folk in the face afterwards and not go out and hang yourself: that is not on the list of pardonable sins.

Shortly after these events a leading New York newspaper, which was among the most abusively clamorous for the suppression of *Mrs. Warren's Profession*, was fined heavily for deriving part of its revenue from advertisements of Mrs. Warren's houses.

Many people have been puzzled by the fact that whilst stage entertainments which are frankly meant to act on the spectators as aphrodisiacs are everywhere tolerated, plays which have an almost horrifying contrary effect are fiercely attacked by persons and papers notoriously indifferent to public morals on all other occasions. The explanation is very simple. The profits of Mrs. Warren's profession are shared not only by Mrs. Warren and Sir George Crofts, but by the landlords of their houses, the newspapers which advertize them, the restaurants which cater for them, and, in short, all the trades to which they are good customers, not to mention the public officials and representatives whom they silence by complicity, corruption, or blackmail. Add to these the employers who profit by cheap female labor, and the shareholders whose dividends depend on it (you find such people everywhere, even on the judicial bench and in the highest places in Church and State) and you get a large and powerful class with a strong pecuniary incentive to protect Mrs. Warren's profession, and a correspondingly strong incentive to conceal, from their own consciences no less than from the world, the real sources of their gain. These are the people who declare that it is feminine vice and not poverty that drives women to the streets, as if vicious women with independent incomes ever went there. These are the people who, indulgent or indifferent to aphrodisiac plays, raise the moral hue and cry against performances of *Mrs. Warren's Profession*, and drag actresses to the police court to be insulted, bullied, and threatened for fulfilling their engagements. For please observe that the judicial decision in New York State in favor of the play did not end the matter. In Kansas City, for instance, the municipality, finding itself restrained by the courts from preventing the performance, fell back on a local bye-law against indecency. It summoned the actress who impersonated Mrs. Warren to the police court, and offered her and her colleagues the alternative of leaving the city or being prosecuted under this bye-law.

Now nothing is more possible than that the city councillors who suddenly displayed such concern for the morals of the theatre were either Mrs. Warren's landlords, or employers of women at starvation wages, or restaurant keepers, or newspaper proprietors, or in some other more or less direct way sharers of the profits of her trade. No doubt it is equally possible that they were simply stupid men who thought that indecency consists, not in evil, but in mentioning it. I have, however, been myself a member of a municipal council, and have not found municipal councillors quite so simple and inexperienced as this. At all events I do not propose to give the Kansas councillors the benefit of the doubt. I therefore advise the public at large, which will finally decide the matter, to keep a vigilant eye on gentlemen who will stand anything at the theatre except a performance of *Mrs. Warren's Profession*, and who assert in the same breath that (*a*) the play is too loathsome to be bearable by civilized people, and (*b*) that unless its performance is prohibited the whole town will throng to see it. They may be merely excited and foolish; but I am bound to warn the public that it is equally likely that they may be collected and knavish.

At all events, to prohibit the play is to protect the evil which the play exposes; and in view of that fact, I see no reason for assuming that the prohibitionists are disinterested moralists, and that the author, the managers, and the performers, who depend for their livelihood on their personal reputations and not on rents, advertisements, or dividends, are grossly inferior to them in moral sense and public responsibility.

It is true that in *Mrs. Warren's Profession*, Society, and not any individual, is the villain of the piece; but it does not follow that the people who take offence at it are all champions of society. Their credentials cannot be too carefully examined.

PICCARD'S COTTAGE, *January* 1902.

P.S. (1930) On reading the above after a lapse of 8 years, with the ban on Mrs. Warren withdrawn and forgotten, I should have discarded it as an overdone fuss about nothing that now matters were it not for a recent incident. Before describing this I must explain that with the invention of the cinematograph a new censorship has come into existence, created, not this time by Act of Parliament, but by the film manufacturers to provide themselves with the certificates of propriety which have proved so useful to the theatre managers. This private censorship has acquired public power through its acceptance by the local authorities, without whose licence the films cannot be exhibited in place of public entertainment.

A lady who has devoted herself to the charitable work of relieving the homeless and penniless people who are to be found every night in London on the Thames Embankment had to deal largely with working men who had come to London from the country under the mistaken impression that there is always employment there for everybody, and with young women, also from the provinces, who had been lured to London by offers of situations which were really traps set for them by the agents of the White Slave traffic. The lady rightly concluded that much the best instrument for warning the men, and making known to the women the addresses of the organization for befriending unprotected girl travellers, is the cinema. She caused a film to be made for this purpose. The Film Censor immediately banned the part of the film which gave the addresses to the girls and shewed them the risks they ran. The lady appealed to me to help her to protest. After convincing myself by witnessing a private exhibition of the film that it was quite innocent I wrote to the Censor, begging him to examine the film personally, and remedy what seemed to be a rule-of-thumb mistake by his examiners. He not only confirmed their veto, but left uncontradicted a report in all the papers that he had given as his reason that the lady had paraded the allurements of vice, and that such parades could not be tolerated by him. The sole allurements were the smart motor car in which the heroine of the film was kidnapped, and the fashionable clothes

of the two very repulsive agents who drugged her in it. In every other respect her experiences were as disagreeable as the sternest moralist could desire.

I then made a tour of the picture houses to see what the Film Censor considers allowable. Of the films duly licensed by him two were so nakedly pornographic that their exhibition could hardly have been risked without the Censor's certificate of purity. One of them presented the allurements of a supposedly French brothel so shamelessly that I rose and fled in disgust long before the end, though I am as hardened to vulgar salacity in the theatre as a surgeon is to a dissecting room.

The only logical conclusion apparent is that the White Slave traffickers are in complete control of our picture theatres, and can close them to our Rescue workers as effectively as they can reserve them for advertisements of their own trade. I spare the Film Censor that conclusion. The conclusion I press upon him and on the public is my old one of twenty-eight years ago: that all the evil effects of such corrupt control are inevitably produced gratuitously by Censors with the best intentions.

MRS. WARREN'S PROFESSION

George Bernard Shaw

ACT ONE

Summer afternoon in a cottage garden on the eastern slope of a hill a little south of Hasle-mere in Surrey. Looking up the hill, the cottage is seen in the left hand corner of the garden, with its thatched roof and porch, and a large latticed window to the left of the porch. A paling completely shuts in the garden, except for a gate on the right. The common rises uphill beyond the paling to the sky line. Some folded canvas garden chairs are leaning against the side bench in the porch. A lady's bicycle is propped against the wall, under the window. A little to the right of the porch a hammock is slung from two posts. A big canvas umbrella, stuck in the ground, keeps the sun off the hammock, in which a young lady lies reading and making notes, her head towards the cottage and her feet towards the gate. In front of the hammock, and within reach of her hand, is a common kitchen chair, with a pile of serious-looking books and a supply of writing paper on it.

A gentleman walking on the common comes into sight from behind the cottage. He is hardly past middle age, with something of the artist about him, unconventionally but carefully dressed, and clean-shaven except for a moustache, with an eager susceptible face and very amiable and considerate manners. He has silky black hair, with waves of grey and white in it. His eyebrows are white, his moustache black. He seems not certain of his way. He looks over the palings; takes stock of the place; and sees the young lady.

THE GENTLEMAN (*taking off his hat*): I beg your pardon. Can you direct me to Hindhead View — Mrs. Alison's?

THE YOUNG LADY (*glancing up from her book*): This is Mrs. Alison's. (*She resumes her work.*)

THE GENTLEMAN: Indeed! Perhaps — may I ask are you Miss Vivie Warren?

THE YOUNG LADY (*sharply, as she turns on her elbow to get a good look at him*): Yes.

THE GENTLEMAN (*daunted and conciliatory*): I'm afraid I appear intrusive. My name is Praed. (VIVIE *at once throws her books upon the chair, and gets out of the hammock.*) Oh, pray dont let me disturb you.

VIVIE (*striding to the gate and opening it for him*): Come in, Mr. Praed. (*He comes in.*) Glad to see you. (*She proffers her hand and takes his with a resolute and hearty grip. She is an attractive specimen of the sensible, able, highly-educated young middle-class Englishwoman. Age 22. Prompt, strong, confident, self-possessed. Plain business-like dress, but not dowdy. She wears a chatelaine at her belt, with a fountain pen and a paper knife among its pendants.*)

PRAED: Very kind of you indeed, Miss Warren. (*She shuts the gate with a vigorous slam. He passes in to the middle of the garden, exercising his fingers, which are slightly numbed by her greeting.*) Has your mother arrived?

VIVIE (*quickly, evidently scenting aggression*): Is she coming?

PRAED (*surprised*): Didnt you expect us?

VIVIE: No.

PRAED: Now, goodness me, I hope Ive not mistaken the day. That would be just like me, you know. Your mother arranged that she was to come down from London and that I was to come over from Horsham to be introduced to you.

VIVIE (*not at all pleased*): Did she? Hm! My mother has rather a trick of taking me by surprise — to see how I behave myself when she's away, I suppose. I fancy I shall take my mother very much by surprise one of these days, if she makes arrangements that concern me without consulting me beforehand. She hasnt come.

PRAED (*embarrassed*): I'm really very sorry.

VIVIE (*throwing off her displeasure*): It's not your fault, Mr. Praed, is it? And I'm very glad youve come. You are the only one of my mother's friends I have ever asked her to bring to see me.

PRAED (*relieved and delighted*): Oh, now this is really very good of you, Miss Warren!

VIVIE: Will you come indoors; or would you rather sit out here and talk?

PRAED: It will be nicer out here, dont you think?

VIVIE: Then I'll go and get you a chair. (*She goes to the porch for a garden chair.*)

PRAED (*following her*): Oh, pray, pray! Allow me. (*He lays hands on the chair.*)

VIVIE (*letting him take it*): Take care of your fingers: theyre rather dodgy things, those chairs. (*She goes across to the chair with the books on it; pitches them into the hammock; and brings the chair forward with one swing.*)

PRAED (*who has just unfolded his chair*): Oh, now do let me take that hard chair. I like hard chairs.

VIVIE: So do I. Sit down, Mr. Praed. (*This invitation she gives with genial peremptoriness, his anxiety to please her clearly striking her as a sign of weakness of character on his part. But he does not immediately obey.*)

PRAED: By the way, though, hadnt we better go to the station to meet your mother?

VIVIE (*coolly*): Why? She knows the way.

PRAED (*disconcerted*): Er — I suppose she does (*he sits down*).

VIVIE: Do you know, you are just like what I expected. I hope you are disposed to be friends with me.

PRAED (*again beaming*): Thank you, my dear Miss Warren: thank you. Dear me! I'm so glad your mother hasnt spoilt you!

VIVIE: How?

PRAED: Well, in making you too conventional. You know, my dear Miss Warren, I am a born anarchist. I hate authority. It spoils the relations between parent and child: even between mother and daughter. Now I was always afraid that your mother would strain her authority to make you very conventional. It's such a relief to find that she hasnt.

VIVIE: Oh! have I been behaving unconventionally?

PRAED: Oh no: oh dear no. At least not conventionally unconventionally, you understand. (*She nods and sits down. He goes on, with a cordial outburst.*) But it was so charming of you to say that you were disposed to be friends with me! You modern young ladies are splendid: perfectly splendid!

VIVIE (*dubiously*): Eh? (*watching him with dawning disappointment as to the quality of his brains and character*).

PRAED: When I was your age, young men and women were afraid of each other: there was no good fellowship. Nothing real. Only gallantry copied out of novels, and as vulgar and affected as it could be. Maidenly reserve! gentlemanly chivalry! always saying no when you meant yes! simple purgatory for shy and sincere souls.

VIVIE: Yes, I imagine there must have been a frightful waste of time. Especially women's time.

PRAED: Oh, waste of life, waste of everything. But things are improving. Do you know, I have been in a positive state of excitement about meeting you ever since your magnificent achievements at Cambridge: a thing unheard of in my day. It was perfectly splendid, your tieing with the third wrangler. Just the right place, you know. The first wrangler is always a dreamy, morbid fellow, in whom the thing is pushed to the length of a disease.

VIVIE: It doesnt pay. I wouldnt do it again for the same money.

PRAED (*aghast*): The same money!

VIVIE: I did it for £50.

PRAED: Fifty pounds!

VIVIE: Yes. Fifty pounds. Perhaps you dont know how it was. Mrs. Latham, my tutor at Newnham, told my mother that I could distinguish myself in the mathematical tripos if I went in for it in earnest. The papers were full just then of Phillipa Summers beating the senior wrangler. You remember about it, of course.

PRAED (*shakes his head energetically*): !!!

VIVIE: Well anyhow she did; and nothing would please my mother but that I should do the same thing. I said flatly it was not worth my while to face the grind since I was not going in for teaching; but I offered to try for fourth wrangler or thereabouts for £50. She closed with me at that, after a little grumbling; and I was better than my bargain. But I wouldnt do it again for that. £200 would have been nearer the mark.

PRAED (*much damped*): Lord bless me! Thats a very practical way of looking at it.

VIVIE: Did you expect to find me an unpractical person?

PRAED: But surely it's practical to consider not only the work these honors cost, but also the culture they bring.

VIVIE: Culture! My dear Mr. Praed: do you know what the mathematical tripos means? It means grind, grind, grind for six to eight hours a day at mathematics, and nothing but mathematics. I'm supposed to know something about science; but I know nothing except the mathematics it involves. I can make calculations for engineers, electricians, insurance companies, and so on; but I know next to nothing about engineering or electricity or insurance. I dont even know arithmetic well. Outside mathematics, lawn-tennis, eating, sleeping, cycling, and walking, I'm a more ignorant barbarian than any woman could possibly be who hadnt gone in for the tripos.

PRAED (*revolted*): What a monstrous, wicked, rascally system! I knew it! I felt at once that it meant destroying all that makes womanhood beautiful.

VIVIE: I dont object to it on that score in the least. I shall turn it to very good account, I assure you.

PRAED: Pooh! In what way?

VIVIE: I shall set up in chambers in the City, and work at actuarial calculations and conveyancing. Under cover of that I shall do some law, with one eye on the Stock Exchange all the time. Ive come down here by myself to read law: not for a holiday, as my mother imagines. I hate holidays.

PRAED: You make my blood run cold. Are you to have no romance, no beauty in your life?

VIVIE: I dont care for either, I assure you.

PRAED: You cant mean that.

VIVIE: Oh yes I do. I like working and getting paid for it. When I'm tired of working, I like a comfortable chair, a cigar, a little whisky, and a novel with a good detective story in it.

PRAED (*rising in a frenzy of repudiation*): I dont believe it. I am an artist; and I cant believe it: I refuse to believe it. It's only that you havnt discovered yet what a wonderful world art can open up to you.

VIVIE: Yes I have. Last May I spent six weeks in London with Honoria Fraser. Mamma thought we were doing a round of sightseeing together; but I was really at Honoria's chambers in Chancery Lane every day, working away at actuarial calculations for her, and helping her as well as a greenhorn could. In the evenings we smoked and talked, and never dreamt of going out except for exercise. And I never enjoyed myself more in my life. I cleared all my expenses, and got initiated into the business without a fee into the bargain.

PRAED: But bless my heart and soul, Miss Warren, do you call that discovering art?

VIVIE: Wait a bit. That wasnt the beginning. I went up to town on an invitation from some artistic people in Fitzjohn's Avenue; one of the girls was a Newnham chum. They took me to the National Gallery —

PRAED (*approving*): Ah!! (*He sits down, much relieved.*)

VIVIE (*continuing*): — to the Opera —

PRAED (*still more pleased*): Good!

VIVIE: — and to a concert where the band played all the evening: Beethoven and Wagner and so on. I wouldnt go through that experience again for anything you could offer me. I held out for civility's sake until the third day; and then I said, plump out, that I couldnt stand any more of it, and went off to Chancery Lane. Now you know the sort of perfectly splendid modern young lady I am. How do you think I shall get on with my mother?

PRAED (*startled*): Well, I hope — er —

VIVIE: It's not so much what you hope as what you believe, that I want to know.

PRAED: Well, frankly, I am afraid your mother will be a little disappointed. Not from any shortcoming on your part, you know: I dont mean that. But you are so different from her ideal.

VIVIE: Her what?!

PRAED: Her ideal.

VIVIE: Do you mean her ideal of ME?

PRAED: Yes.

VIVIE: What on earth is it like?

PRAED: Well, you must have observed, Miss Warren, that people who are dissatisfied with their own bringing-up generally think that the world would be all right if everybody were to be brought up quite differently. Now your mother's life has been — er — I suppose you know —

VIVIE: Dont suppose anything, Mr. Praed. I hardly know my mother. Since I was a child I have lived in England, at school or college, or with people paid to take charge of me. I have been boarded out all my life. My mother has lived in Brussels or Vienna and never let me go to her. I only see her when she visits England for a few days. I dont complain: it's been very pleasant; for people have been very good to me; and there has always been plenty of money to make things smooth. But dont imagine I know anything about my mother. I know far less than you do.

PRAED (*very ill at ease*): In that case — (*He stops, quite at a loss. Then, with a forced attempt at gaiety.*) But what nonsense we are talking! Of course you and your mother will get on capitally. (*He rises, and looks abroad at the view.*) What a charming little place you have here!

VIVIE (*unmoved*): Rather a violent change of subject, Mr. Praed. Why wont my mother's life bear being talked about?

PRAED: Oh, you really mustnt say that. Isnt it natural that I should have a certain delicacy in talking to my old friend's daughter about her behind her back? You and she will have plenty of opportunity of talking about it when she comes.

VIVIE: No: she wont talk about it either. (*Rising.*) However, I daresay you have good reasons for telling me nothing. Only, mind this, Mr. Praed. I expect there will be a battle royal when my mother hears of my Chancery Lane project.

PRAED (*ruefully*): I'm afraid there will.

VIVIE: Well, I shall win, because I want nothing but my fare to London to start there to-morrow earning my own living by devilling for Honoria. Besides, I have no mysteries to keep up; and it seems she has. I shall use that advantage over her if necessary.

PRAED (*greatly shocked*). Oh no! No, pray. Youd not do such a thing.

VIVIE: Then tell me why not.

PRAED: I really cannot. I appeal to your good feeling. (*She smiles at his sentimentality.*) Besides, you may be too bold. Your mother is not to be trifled with when she's angry.

VIVIE: You cant frighten me, Mr. Praed. In that month at Chancery Lane I had opportunities of taking the measure of one or two women very like my mother. You may back me to win. But if I hit harder in my ignorance than I need, remember that it is you who refuse to enlighten me. Now, let us drop the subject. (*She takes her chair and replaces it near the hammock with the same vigorous swing as before.*)

PRAED (*taking a desperate resolution*): One word, Miss Warren. I had better tell you. It's very difficult; but —

(MRS. WARREN *and* SIR GEORGE CROFTS *arrive at the gate.* MRS. WARREN *is between 40 and 50, formerly pretty, showily dressed in a brilliant hat and a gay blouse fitting tightly over her bust and flanked by fashionable sleeves. Rather spoilt and domineering, and decidedly vulgar, but, on the whole, a genial and fairly presentable old blackguard of a woman.*
CROFTS *is a tall powerfully-built man of about 50, fashionably dressed in the style of a young man. Nasal voice, reedier than might be expected from his strong frame. Clean-shaven bulldog jaws, large flat ears, and thick neck: gentlemanly combination of the most brutal types of city man, sporting man, and man about town.*)

VIVIE: Here they are. (*Coming to them as they enter the garden.*) How do, mater? Mr. Praed's been here this half hour, waiting for you.

MRS. WARREN: Well, if youve been waiting, Praddy, it's your own fault: I thought youd have had the gumption to know I was coming by the 3.10 train. Vivie: put your hat on, dear: youll get sunburnt. Oh, I forgot to introduce you. Sir George Crofts: my little Vivie.

(CROFTS *advances to* VIVIE *with his most courtly manner. She nods, but makes no notion to shake hands.*)

CROFTS: May I shake hands with a young lady whom I have known by reputation very long as the daughter of one of my oldest friends?

VIVIE (*who has been looking him up and down sharply*): If you like. (*She takes his tenderly proffered hand and gives it a squeeze that makes him open his eyes; then turns away, and says to her mother.*) Will you come in, or shall I get a couple more chairs? (*She goes into the porch for the chairs.*)

MRS. WARREN: Well, George, what do you think of her?

CROFTS (*ruefully*): She has a powerful fist. Did you shake hands with her, Praed?

PRAED: Yes: it will pass off presently.

CROFTS: I hope so. (VIVIE *reappears with two more chairs. He hurries to her assistance.*) Allow me.

MRS. WARREN (*patronizingly*): Let Sir George help you with the chairs, dear.

VIVIE (*pitching them into his arms*): Here you are. (*She dusts her hands and turns to* MRS. WARREN.) Youd like some tea, wouldnt you?

MRS. WARREN (*sitting in* PRAED's *chair and fanning herself*): I'm dying for a drop to drink.

VIVIE: I'll see about it. (*She goes into the cottage.*)

(SIR GEORGE *has by this time managed to unfold a chair and plant it beside* MRS. WARREN, *on her left. He throws the other on the grass and sits down, looking dejected and rather foolish, with the handle of his stick in his mouth.* PRAED, *still very uneasy, fidgets about the garden on their right.*)

MRS. WARREN (*to* PRAED, *looking at* CROFTS): Just look at him, Praddy: he looks cheerful, dont he? He's been worrying my life out these three years to have that little girl of mine shewn to him; and now that Ive done it, he's quite out of countenance. (*Briskly.*) Come! sit up, George; and take your stick out of your mouth. (CROFTS *sulkily obeys.*)

PRAED: I think, you know — if you dont mind my saying so — that we had better get out of the habit of thinking of her as a little girl. You see she has really distinguished herself; and I'm not sure, from what I have seen of her, that she is not older than any of us.

MRS. WARREN (*greatly amused*): Only listen to him, George! Older than any of us! Well, she has been stuffing you nicely with her importance.

PRAED: But young people are particularly sensitive about being treated in that way.

MRS. WARREN: Yes; and young people have to get all that nonsense taken out of them, and a good deal more besides. Dont you interfere, Praddy: I know how to treat my own child as well as you do. (PRAED, *with a grave shake of his head, walks up the garden with his hands behind his back.* MRS. WARREN *pretends to laugh, but looks after him with perceptible concern. Then she whispers to* CROFTS.) Whats the matter with him? What does he take it like that for?

CROFTS (*morosely*): Youre afraid of Praed.

MRS. WARREN: What! Me! Afraid of dear old Praddy! Why, a fly wouldnt be afraid of him.

CROFTS: Youre afraid of him.

MRS. WARREN (*angry*): I'll trouble you to mind your own business, and not try any of your sulks on me. I'm not afraid of you, anyhow. If you cant make yourself agreeable, youd better go home. (*She gets up, and turning her back on him, finds herself face to face with* PRAED.) Come, Praddy, I know it was only your tender-heartedness. Youre afraid I'll bully her.

PRAED: My dear Kitty: you think I'm offended. Dont imagine that: pray dont. But you know I often notice things that escape you; and though you never take my advice, you sometimes admit afterwards that you ought to have taken it.

MRS. WARREN: Well, what do you notice now?

PRAED: Only that Vivie is a grown woman. Pray, Kitty, treat her with every respect.

MRS. WARREN (*with genuine amazement*): Respect! Treat my own daughter with respect! What next, pray!

VIVIE (*appearing at the cottage door and calling to* MRS. WARREN): Mother: will you come to my room before tea.

MRS. WARREN: Yes, dearie. (*She laughs indulgently at* PRAED'S *gravity, and pats him on the cheek as she passes him on her way to the porch.*) Dont be cross, Praddy. (*She follows* VIVIE *into the cottage.*)

CROFTS (*furtively*): I say, Praed.

PRAED: Yes.

CROFTS: I want to ask you a rather particular question.

PRAED: Certainly. (*He takes* MRS. WARREN'S *chair and sits close to* CROFTS.)

CROFTS: That's right: they might hear us from the window. Look here: did Kitty ever tell you who that girl's father is?

PRAED: Never.

CROFTS: Have you any suspicion of who it might be?

PRAED: None.

CROFTS (*not believing him*): I know, of course, that you perhaps might feel bound not to tell if she had said anything to you. But it's very awkward to be uncertain about it now that we shall be meeting the girl every day. We dont exactly know how we ought to feel towards her.

PRAED: What difference can that make? We take her on her own merits. What does it matter who her father was?

CROFTS (*suspiciously*): Then you know who he was?

PRAED (*with a touch of temper*): I said no just now. Did you not hear me?

CROFTS: Look here, Praed. I ask you as a particular favor. If you do know (*movement of protest from* PRAED) — I only say, if you know, you might at least set my mind at rest about her. The fact is, I feel attracted.

PRAED (*sternly*): What do you mean?

CROFTS: Oh, dont be alarmed: it's quite an

innocent feeling. Thats what puzzles me about it. Why, for all I know, *I* might be her father.

PRAED: You! Impossible!

CROFTS (*catching him up cunningly*): You know for certain that I'm not?

PRAED: I know nothing about it, I tell you, any more than you. But really, Crofts — oh no, it's out of the question. Theres not the least resemblance.

CROFTS: As to that, theres no resemblance between her and her mother that I can see. I suppose she's not your daughter, is she?

PRAED (*rising indignantly*): Really, Crofts — !

CROFTS: No offence, Praed. Quite allowable as between two men of the world.

PRAED (*recovering himself with an effort and speaking gently and gravely*): Now listen to me, my dear Crofts. (*He sits down again.*) I have nothing to do with that side of Mrs. Warren's life, and never had. She has never spoken to me about it; and of course I have never spoken to her about it. Your delicacy will tell you that a handsome woman needs some friends who are not — well, not on that footing with her. The effect of her own beauty would become a torment to her if she could not escape from it occasionally. You are probably on much more confidential terms with Kitty than I am. Surely you can ask her the question yourself.

CROFTS: I have asked her, often enough. But she's so determined to keep the child all to herself that she would deny that it ever had a father if she could. (*Rising.*) I'm thoroughly uncomfortable about it, Praed.

PRAED (*rising also*): Well, as you are, at all events, old enough to be her father, I dont mind agreeing that we both regard Miss Vivie in a parental way, as a young girl whom we are bound to protect and help. What do you say?

CROFTS (*aggressively*): I'm no older than you, if you come to that.

PRAED: Yes you are, my dear fellow: you were born old. I was born a boy: Ive never been able to feel the assurance of a grown-up man in my life. (*He folds his chair and carries it to the porch.*)

MRS. WARREN (*calling from within the cottage*): Prad-dee! George! Tea-ea-ea-ea!

CROFTS (*hastily*): She's calling us. (*He hurries in.*)

(PRAED *shakes his head bodingly, and is following* CROFTS *when he is hailed by a young gentleman who has just appeared on the common, and is making for the gate. He is pleasant, pretty, smartly dressed, cleverly good-for-nothing, not long turned 20, with a charming voice and agreeably disrespectful manner. He carries a light sporting magazine rifle.*)

THE YOUNG GENTLEMAN: Hallo! Praed!

PRAED: Why, Frank Gardner! (FRANK *comes in and shakes hands cordially.*) What on earth are you doing here?

FRANK: Staying with my father.

PRAED: The Roman father?

FRANK: He's rector here. I'm living with my people this autumn for the sake of economy. Things came to a crisis in July: the Roman father had to pay my debts. He's stony broke in consequence; and so am I. What are you up to in these parts? Do you know the people here?

PRAED: Yes: I'm spending the day with a Miss Warren.

FRANK (*enthusiastically*): What! Do you know Vivie? Isnt she a jolly girl? I'm teaching her to shoot with this (*putting down the rifle*). I'm so glad she knows you: youre just the sort of fellow she ought to know. (*He smiles, and raises the charming voice almost to a singing tone as he exclaims.*) It's ever so jolly to find you here, Praed.

PRAED: I'm an old friend of her mother. Mrs. Warren brought me over to make her daughter's acquaintance.

FRANK: The mother! Is she here?

PRAED: Yes: inside, at tea.

Mrs. Warren (*calling from within*): Prad-dee-ee-ee-eee! The tea-cake'll be cold.

Praed (*calling*): Yes, Mrs. Warren. In a moment. Ive just met a friend here.

Mrs. Warren: A what?

Praed (*louder*): A friend.

Mrs. Warren: Bring him in.

Praed: All right. (*to* Frank) Will you accept the invitation?

Frank (*incredulous, but immensely amused*): Is that Vivie's mother?

Praed: Yes.

Frank: By Jove! What a lark! Do you think she'll like me?

Praed: Ive no doubt youll make yourself popular, as usual. Come in and try (*moving towards the house*).

Frank: Stop a bit. (*Seriously.*) I want to take you into my confidence.

Praed: Pray dont. It's only some fresh folly, like the barmaid at Redhill.

Frank: It's ever so much more serious than that. You say youve only just met Vivie for the first time?

Praed: Yes.

Frank (*rhapsodically*): Then you can have no idea what a girl she is. Such character! Such sense! And her cleverness! Oh, my eye, Praed, but I can tell you she is clever! And — need I add? — she loves me.

Crofts (*putting his head out of the window*): I say, Praed: what are you about? Do come along. (*He disappears.*)

Frank: Hallo! Sort of chap that would take a prize at a dog show, aint he? Who's he?

Praed: Sir George Crofts, an old friend of Mrs. Warren's. I think we had better come in.

(*On their way to the porch they are interrupted by a call from the gate. Turning, they see an elderly clergyman looking over it.*)

The Clergyman (*calling*): Frank!

Frank: Hallo! (*to* Praed) The Roman father. (*to the* Clergyman) Yes, gov'nor: all right: presently. (*to* Praed) Look here, Praed: youd better go in to tea. I'll join you directly.

Praed: Very good. (*He goes into the cottage.*)

(*The* Clergyman *remains outside the gate, with his hands on the top of it. The* Rev. Samuel Gardner, *a beneficed clergyman of the Established Church, is over 50. Externally he is pretentious, booming, noisy, important. Really he is that obsolescent social phenomenon the fool of the family dumped on the Church by his father the patron, clamorously asserting himself as father and clergyman without being able to command respect in either capacity.*)

Rev. S.: Well, sir. Who are your friends here, if I may ask?

Frank: Oh, it's all right, gov'nor! Come in.

Rev. S.: No, sir; not until I know whose garden I am entering.

Frank: It's all right. It's Miss Warren's.

Rev. S.: I have not seen her at church since she came.

Frank: Of course not: she's a third wrangler. Ever so intellectual. Took a higher degree than you did; so why should she go to hear you preach?

Rev. S.: Dont be disrespectful, sir.

Frank: Oh, it dont matter: nobody hears us. Come in. (*He opens the gate, unceremoniously pulling his father with it into the garden.*) I want to introduce you to her. Do you remember the advice you gave me last July, gov'nor?

Rev. S. (*severely*): Yes. I advised you to conquer your idleness and flippancy, and to work your way into an honorable profession and live on it and not upon me.

Frank: No: thats what you thought of afterwards. What you actually said was that since I had neither brains nor money, I'd better turn my good looks to account by marrying somebody with both. Well, look here. Miss Warren has brains: you cant deny that.

REV. S.: Brains are not everything.

FRANK: No, of course not: theres the money —

REV. S. (*interrupting him austerely*): I was not thinking of money, sir. I was speaking of higher things. Social position, for instance.

FRANK: I dont care a rap about that.

REV. S.: But I do, sir.

FRANK: Well, nobody wants you to marry her. Anyhow, she has what amounts to a high Cambridge degree; and she seems to have as much money as she wants.

REV. S. (*sinking into a feeble vein of humor*): I greatly doubt whether she has as much money as you will want.

FRANK: Oh, come: I havent been so very extravagant. I live ever so quietly; I dont drink; I dont bet much; and I never go regularly on the razzle-dazzle as you did when you were my age.

REV. S. (*booming hollowly*): Silence, sir.

FRANK: Well, you told me yourself, when I was making ever such an ass of myself about the barmaid at Redhill, that you once offered a woman £50 for the letters you wrote to her when —

REV. S. (*terrified*): Sh-sh-sh, Frank, for Heaven's sake! (*He looks round apprehensively. Seeing no one within earshot he plucks up courage to boom again, but more subduedly.*) You are taking an ungentlemanly advantage of what I confided to you for your own good, to save you from an error you would have repented all your life long. Take warning by your father's follies, sir; and dont make them an excuse for your own.

FRANK: Did you ever hear the story of the Duke of Wellington and his letters?

REV. S.: No, sir; and I dont want to hear it.

FRANK: The old Iron Duke didn't throw away £50: not he. He just wrote: "Dear Jenny: publish and be damned! Yours affectionately, Wellington." Thats what you should have done.

REV. S. (*piteously*): Frank, my boy: when I wrote those letters I put myself into that woman's power. When I told you about them I put myself, to some extent, I am sorry to say, in your power. She refused my money with these words, which I shall never forget. "Knowledge is power" she said; "and I never sell power." Thats more than twenty years ago; and she has never made use of her power or caused me a moment's uneasiness. You are behaving worse to me than she did, Frank.

FRANK: Oh yes I dare say! Did you ever preach at her the way you preach at me every day?

REV. S. (*wounded almost to tears*). I leave you, sir. You are incorrigible. (*He turns towards the gate.*)

FRANK (*utterly unmoved*): Tell them I shant be home to tea, will you, guv'nor, like a good fellow? (*He moves towards the cottage door and is met by* PRAED *and* VIVIE *coming out.*)

VIVIE (*to* FRANK): Is that your father, Frank? I do so want to meet him.

FRANK: Certainly. (*Calling after his father*) Gov'nor. Youre wanted. (*The parson turns at the gate, fumbling nervously at his hat.* PRAED *crosses the garden to the opposite side, beaming in anticipation of civilities.*) My father: Miss Warren.

VIVIE (*going to the clergyman and shaking his hand*): Very glad to see you here, Mr. Gardner. (*Calling to the cottage*) Mother: come along: youre wanted.

(MRS. WARREN *appears on the threshold, and is immediately transfixed, recognizing the clergyman.*)

VIVIE (*continuing*): Let me introduce —

MRS. WARREN (*swooping on the* REVEREND SAMUEL): Why, it's Sam Gardner, gone into the Church! Well, I never! Dont you know us, Sam? This is George Crofts, as large as life and twice as natural. Dont you remember me?

Rev. S. (*very red*): I really — er —

Mrs. Warren: Of course you do. Why, I have a whole album of your letters still: I came across them only the other day.

Rev. S. (*miserably confused*): Miss Vavasour, I believe.

Mrs. Warren (*correcting him quickly in a loud whisper*): Tch! Nonsense! Mrs. Warren: dont you see my daughter there?

ACT TWO

Inside the cottage after nightfall. Looking eastward from within instead of westward from without, the latticed window, with its curtains drawn, is now seen in the middle of the front wall of the cottage, with the porch door to the left of it. In the left-hand side wall is the door leading to the kitchen. Farther back against the same wall is a dresser with a candle and matches on it, and Frank's *rifle standing beside them, with the barrel resting in the plate-rack. In the centre a table stands with a lighted lamp on it.* Vivie's *books and writing materials are on a table to the right of the window, against the wall. The fireplace is on the right, with a settle: there is no fire. Two of the chairs are set right and left of the table.*

The cottage door opens, showing a fine starlit night without; and Mrs. Warren, *her shoulders wrapped in a shawl borrowed from* Vivie, *enters, followed by* Frank, *who throws his cap on the window seat. She has had enough of walking, and gives a gasp of relief as she unpins her hat; takes it off, sticks the pin through the crown; and puts it on the table.*

Mrs. Warren: O Lord! I dont know which is the worst of the country, the walking or the sitting at home with nothing to do. I could do with a whisky and soda now very well, if only they had such a thing in this place.

Frank: Perhaps Vivie's got some.

Mrs. Warren: Nonsense! What would a young girl like her be doing with such things! Never mind: it dont matter. I wonder how she passes her time here! I'd a good deal rather be in Vienna.

Frank: Let me take you there. (*He helps her to take off her shawl, gallantly giving her shoulders a very preceptible squeeze as he does so.*)

Mrs. Warren: Ah! would you? I'm beginning to think youre a chip of the old block.

Frank: Like the guv'nor, eh? (*He hangs the shawl on the nearest chair, and sits down.*)

Mrs. Warren: Never you mind. What do you know about such things? Youre only a boy. (*She goes to the hearth, to be farther from temptation.*)

Frank: Do come to Vienna with me? It'd be ever such larks.

Mrs. Warren: No, thank you. Vienna is no place for you — at least not until youre a little older. (*She nods at him to emphasize this piece of advice. He makes a mock-piteous face, belied by his laughing eyes. She looks at him; then comes back to him.*) Now, look here, little boy (*taking his face in her hands and turning it up to her*) I know you through and through by your likeness to your father, better than you know yourself. Dont you go taking any silly ideas into your head about me. Do you hear?

Frank (*gallantly wooing her with his voice*): Cant help it, my dear Mrs. Warren: it runs in the family.

(*She pretends to box his ears; then looks at the pretty laughing upturned face for a moment, tempted. At last she kisses him, and immediately turns away, out of patience with herself.*)

Mrs. Warren: There! I shouldnt have done that. I am wicked. Never you mind, my dear: it's only a motherly kiss. Go and make love to Vivie.

Frank: So I have.

Mrs. Warren (*turning on him with a sharp note of alarm in her voice*): What!

Frank: Vivie and I are ever such chums.

MRS. WARREN: What do you mean? Now see here: I wont have any young scamp tampering with my little girl. Do you hear? I wont have it.

FRANK (*quite unabashed*): My dear Mrs. Warren: dont you be alarmed. My intentions are honorable: ever so honorable; and your little girl is jolly well able to take care of herself. She dont need looking after half so much as her mother. She aint so handsome, you know.

MRS. WARREN (*taken aback by his assurance*): Well, you have got a nice healthy two inches thick of cheek all over you. I dont know where you got it. Not from your father, anyhow.

CROFTS (*in the garden*): The gipsies, I suppose?

REV. S. (*replying*): The broomsquires are far worse.

MRS. WARREN (*to* FRANK): S-sh! Remember! youve had your warning.

(CROFTS *and the* REVEREND SAMUEL *come in from the garden, the clergyman continuing his conversation as he enters.*)

REV. S.: The perjury at the Winchester assizes is deplorable.

MRS. WARREN: Well? what became of you two? And wheres Praddy and Vivie?

CROFTS (*putting his hat on the settle and his stick in the chimney corner.*) They went up the hill. We went to the village. I wanted a drink. (*He sits down on the settle, putting his legs up along the seat.*)

MRS. WARREN: Well, she oughtnt to go off like that without telling me. (*to* FRANK) Get your father a chair, Frank: where are your manners? (FRANK *springs up and gracefully offers his father his chair; then takes another from the wall and sits down at the table, in the middle, with his father on his right and* MRS. WARREN *on his left.*) George: where are you going to stay to-night? You cant stay here. And whats Praddy going to do?

CROFTS: Gardner'll put me up.

MRS. WARREN: Oh, no doubt youve taken care of yourself! But what about Praddy?

CROFTS: Dont know. I suppose he can sleep at the inn.

MRS. WARREN: Havent you room for him, Sam?

REV. S.: Well — er — you see, as rector here, I am not free to do as I like. Er — what is Mr. Praed's social position?

MRS. WARREN: Oh, he's all right: he's an architect. What an old stick-in-the-mud you are, Sam!

FRANK: Yes, it's all right, guv'nor. He built that place down in Wales for the Duke. Caernarvon Castle they call it. You must have heard of it. (*He winks with lightning smartness at* MRS. WARREN, *and regards his father blandly.*)

REV. S.: Oh, in that case, of course we shall only be too happy. I suppose he knows the Duke personally.

FRANK: Oh, ever so intimately! We can stick him in Georgina's old room.

MRS. WARREN: Well, thats settled. Now if those two would only come in and let us have supper. Theyve no right to stay out after dark like this.

CROFTS (*aggressively*): What harm are they doing you?

MRS. WARREN: Well, harm or not, I dont like it.

FRANK: Better not wait for them, Mrs. Warren. Praed will stay out as long as possible. He has never known before what it is to stray over the heath on a summer night with my Vivie.

CROFTS (*sitting up in some consternation*): I say, you know! Come!

REV. S. (*rising startled out of his professional manner into real force and sincerity*): Frank, once for all, it's out of the question. Mrs. Warren will tell you that it's not to be thought of.

CROFTS: Of course not.

FRANK (*with enchanting placidity*): Is that so, Mrs. Warren?

MRS. WARREN (*reflectively*): Well, Sam, I dont know. If the girl wants to get married, no good can come of keeping her unmarried.

REV. S. (*astounded*): But married to him! — your daughter to my son! Only think: it's impossible.

CROFTS: Of course it's impossible. Dont be a fool, Kitty.

MRS. WARREN (*nettled*): Why not? Isnt my daughter good enough for your son?

REV. S.: But surely, my dear Mrs. Warren, you know the reasons —

MRS. WARREN (*defiantly*): I know no reasons. If you know any, you can tell them to the lad, or to the girl, or to your congregation, if you like.

REV. S. (*collapsing helplessly into his chair*): You know very well that I couldnt tell anyone the reasons. But my boy will believe me when I tell him there are reasons.

FRANK: Quite right, Dad: he will. But has your boy's conduct ever been influenced by your reasons?

CROFTS: You cant marry her; and thats all about it. (*He gets up and stands on the hearth, with his back to the fireplace, frowning determinedly.*)

MRS. WARREN (*turning on him sharply*): What have you got to do with it, pray?

FRANK (*with his prettiest lyrical cadence*): Precisely what I was going to ask, myself, in my own graceful fashion.

CROFTS (*to* MRS. WARREN): I suppose you dont want to marry the girl to a man younger than herself and without either a profession or twopence to keep her on. Ask Sam, if you dont believe me. (*to the parson*) How much more money are you going to give him?

REV. S.: Not another penny. He has had his patrimony; and he spent the last of it in July. (MRS. WARREN'S *face falls.*)

CROFTS (*watching her*): There! I told you. (*He resumes his place on the settle and puts up his legs on the seat again, as if the matter were finally disposed of.*)

FRANK (*plaintively*): This is ever so mercenary. Do you suppose Miss Warren's going to marry for money? If we love one another —

MRS. WARREN: Thank you. Your love's a pretty cheap commodity, my lad. If you have no means of keeping a wife, that settles it: you cant have Vivie.

FRANK (*much amused*): What do you say, gov'nor, eh?

REV. S.: I agree with Mrs. Warren.

FRANK: And good old Crofts has already expressed his opinion.

CROFTS (*turning angrily on his elbow*): Look here: I want none of your cheek.

FRANK (*pointedly*): I'm ever so sorry to surprise you, Crofts, but you allowed yourself the liberty of speaking to me like a father a moment ago. One father is enough, thank you.

CROFTS (*contemptuously*): Yah! (*He turns away again.*)

FRANK (*rising*): Mrs. Warren: I cannot give my Vivie up, even for your sake.

MRS. WARREN (*muttering*): Young scamp!

FRANK (*continuing*): And as you no doubt intend to hold out other prospects to her, I shall lose no time in placing my case before her. (*They stare at him; and he begins to declaim gracefully*)

He either fears his fate too much,
Or his deserts are small,
That dares not put it to the touch
To gain or lose it all.

(*The cottage door opens whilst he is reciting; and* VIVIE *and* PRAED *come in. He breaks off.* PRAED *puts his hat on the dresser. There is an immediate improvement in the company's behavior.* CROFTS *takes down his legs from the settle and pulls himself together as* PRAED joins him at the fireplace. MRS. WARREN loses her ease of manner and takes refuge in querulousness.)

MRS. WARREN: Wherever have you been, Vivie?

VIVIE (taking off her hat and throwing it carelessly on the table): On the hill.

MRS. WARREN: Well, you shouldnt go off like that without letting me know. How could I tell what had become of you? And night coming on too!

VIVIE (going to the door of the kitchen and opening it, ignoring her mother): Now, about supper? (All rise except MRS. WARREN.) We shall be rather crowded in here, I'm afraid.

MRS. WARREN: Did you hear what I said, Vivie?

VIVIE (quietly): Yes, mother. (Reverting to the supper difficulty.) How many are we? (Counting) One, two, three, four, five, six. Well, two will have to wait until the rest are done: Mrs. Alison has only plates and knives for four.

PRAED: Oh, it doesn't matter about me. I —

VIVIE: You have had a long walk and are hungry, Mr. Praed: you shall have your supper at once. I can wait myself. I want one person to wait with me. Frank: are you hungry?

FRANK: Not the least in the world. Completely off my peck, in fact.

MRS. WARREN (to CROFTS): Neither are you, George. You can wait.

CROFTS: Oh, hang it, Ive eaten nothing since tea-time. Cant Sam do it?

FRANK: Would you starve my poor father?

REV. S. (testily): Allow me to speak for myself, sir. I am perfectly willing to wait.

VIVIE (decisively): Theres no need. Only two are wanted. (She opens the door of the kitchen.) Will you take my mother in, Mr. Gardner. (The parson takes MRS. WARREN;

and they pass into the kitchen. PRAED and CROFTS follow. All except PRAED clearly disapprove of the arrangement, but do not know how to resist it. VIVIE stands at the door looking in at them.) Can you squeeze past to that corner, Mr. Praed: it's rather a tight fit. Take care of your coat against the white-wash: thats right. Now, are you all comfortable?

PRAED (within): Quite, thank you.

MRS. WARREN (within): Leave the door open, dearie. (VIVIE frowns; but FRANK checks her with a gesture, and steals to the cottage door, which he softly sets wide open.) Oh Lor, what a draught! Youd better shut it, dear.

(VIVIE shuts it with a slam, and then, noting with disgust that her mother's hat and shawl are lying about, takes them tidily to the window seat, whilst FRANK noiselessly shuts the cottage door.)

FRANK (exulting): Aha! Got rid of em. Well, Vivvums: what do you think of my governor?

VIVIE (preoccupied and serious): Ive hardly spoken to him. He doesnt strike me as being a particularly able person.

FRANK: Well, you know, the old man is not altogether such a fool as he looks. You see, he was shoved into the Church rather; and in trying to live up to it he makes a much bigger ass of himself than he really is. I dont dislike him as much as you might expect. He means well. How do you think youll get on with him?

VIVIE (rather grimly): I dont think my future life will be much concerned with him, or with any of that old circle of my mother's, except perhaps Praed. (She sits down on the settle.) What do you think of my mother?

FRANK: Really and truly?

VIVIE: Yes, really and truly.

FRANK: Well, she's ever so jolly. But she's rather a caution, isnt she? And Crofts! Oh, my eye, Crofts! (He sits beside her.)

VIVIE: What a lot, Frank!

FRANK: What a crew!

VIVIE (*with intense contempt for them*): If I thought that *I* was like that — that I was going to be a waster, shifting along from one meal to another with no purpose, and no character, and no grit in me, I'd open an artery and bleed to death without one moment's hesitation.

FRANK: Oh no, you wouldnt. Why should they take any grind when they can afford not to? I wish I had their luck. No: what I object to is their form. It isnt the thing: it's slovenly, ever so slovenly.

VIVIE: Do you think your form will be any better when youre as old as Crofts, if you dont work?

FRANK: Of course I do. Ever so much better. Vivvums mustnt lecture: her little boy's incorrigible. (*He attempts to take her face caressingly in his hands.*)

VIVIE (*striking his hands down sharply*): Off with you: Vivvums is not in a humor for petting her little boy this evening. (*She rises and comes forward to the other side of the room.*)

FRANK (*following her*): How unkind!

VIVIE (*stamping at him*): Be serious. I'm serious.

FRANK: Good. Let us talk learnedly. Miss Warren: do you know that all the most advanced thinkers are agreed that half the diseases of modern civilization are due to starvation of the affections in the young. Now, I —

VIVIE (*cutting him short*): You are very tiresome. (*She opens the inner door.*) Have you room for Frank there? He's complaining of starvation.

MRS. WARREN (*within*): Of course there is (*clatter of knives and glasses as she moves the things on the table.*) Here! theres room now beside me. Come along, Mr. Frank.

FRANK: Her little boy will be ever so even with his Vivvums for this. (*He passes into the kitchen.*)

MRS. WARREN (*within*): Here, Vivie: come on you too, child. You must be famished. (*She enters, followed by* CROFTS, *who holds the door open for* VIVIE *with marked deference. She goes out without looking at him; and he shuts the door after her.*) Why, George, you cant be done: youve eaten nothing. Is there anything wrong with you?

CROFTS: Oh, all I wanted was a drink. (*He thrusts his hands in his pockets, and begins prowling about the room, restless and sulky.*)

MRS. WARREN: Well, I like enough to eat. But a little of that cold beef and cheese and lettuce goes a long way. (*With a sigh of only half repletion she sits down lazily on the settle.*)

CROFTS: What do you go encouraging that young pup for?

MRS. WARREN (*on the alert at once*): Now see here, George: what are you up to about that girl? Ive been watching your way of looking at her. Remember: I know you and what your looks mean.

CROFTS: Theres no harm in looking at her, is there?

MRS. WARREN: I'd put you out and pack you back to London pretty soon if I saw any of your nonsense. My girl's little finger is more to me than your whole body and soul. (CROFTS *receives this with a sneering grin.* MRS. WARREN, *flushing a little at her failure to impose on him in the character of a theatrically devoted mother, adds in a lower key.*) Make your mind easy: the young pup has no more chance than you have.

CROFTS: Maynt a man take an interest in a girl?

MRS. WARREN: Not a man like you.

CROFTS: How old is she?

MRS. WARREN: Never you mind how old she is.

CROFTS: Why do you make such a secret of it?

MRS. WARREN: Because I choose.

CROFTS: Well, I'm not fifty yet; and my property is as good as ever it was—

MRS. WARREN (*interrupting him*): Yes; because youre as stingy as youre vicious.

CROFTS (*continuing*): And a baronet isnt to be picked up every day. No other man in my position would put up with you for a mother-in-law. Why shouldnt she marry me?

MRS. WARREN: You!

CROFTS: We three could live together quite comfortably. I'd die before her and leave her a bouncing widow with plenty of money. Why not? It's been growing in my mind all the time Ive been walking with that fool inside there.

MRS. WARREN (*revolted*): Yes: it's the sort of thing that would grow in your mind.

(*He halts in his prowling; and the two look at one another, she steadfastly, with a sort of awe behind her contemptuous disgust: he stealthily, with a carnal gleam in his eye and a loose grin.*)

CROFTS (*suddenly becoming anxious and urgent as he sees no sign of sympathy in her*): Look here, Kitty: youre a sensible woman: you neednt put on any moral airs. I'll ask no more questions; and you need answer none. I'll settle the whole property on her; and if you want a cheque for yourself on the wedding day, you can name any figure you like—in reason.

MRS. WARREN: So it's come to that with you, George, like all the other worn-out old creatures!

CROFTS (*savagely*): Damn you!

(*Before she can retort the door of the kitchen is opened; and the voices of the others are heard returning. CROFTS, unable to recover his presence of mind, hurries out of the cottage. The clergyman appears at the kitchen door.*)

REV. S. (*looking round*): Where is Sir George?

MRS. WARREN: Gone out to have a pipe. (*The clergyman takes his hat from the table, and joins MRS. WARREN at the fireside. Meanwhile VIVIE comes in, followed by FRANK, who collapses into the nearest chair with an air of extreme exhaustion. MRS. WARREN looks round at VIVIE and says, with her affection of maternal patronage even more forced than usual*) Well, dearie: have you had a good supper?

VIVIE: You know what Mrs. Alison's suppers are. (*She turns to FRANK and pets him.*) Poor Frank! was all the beef gone? did it get nothing but bread and cheese and ginger beer? (*Seriously, as if she had done quite enough trifling for one evening*) Her butter is really awful. I must get some down from the stores.

FRANK: Do, in Heaven's name!

(*VIVIE goes to the writing-table and makes a memorandum to order the butter. PRAED comes in from the kitchen, putting up his handkerchief, which he has been using as a napkin.*)

REV. S.: Frank, my boy: it is time for us to be thinking of home. Your mother does not know yet that we have visitors.

PRAED: I'm afraid we're giving trouble.

FRANK (*rising*): Not the least in the world: my mother will be delighted to see you. She's a genuinely intellectual artistic woman; and she sees nobody here from one year's end to another except the gov'nor; so you can imagine how jolly dull it pans out for her. (*to his father*) Youre not intellectual or artistic: are you, pater? So take Praed home at once; and I'll stay here and entertain Mrs. Warren. Youll pick up Crofts in the garden. He'll be excellent company for the bull-pup.

PRAED (*taking his hat from the dresser, and coming close to FRANK*): Come with us, Frank. Mrs. Warren has not seen Miss Vivie for a long time; and we have prevented them from having a moment together yet.

FRANK (*quite softened, and looking at PRAED with romantic admiration*): Of course. I forgot. Ever so thanks for reminding me. Perfect gentleman, Praddy. Always were. My ideal through life. (*He rises to go, but pauses a moment between the two older men, and puts his hand on PRAED's shoulder.*) Ah, if you had only been my father instead of this unworthy old man! (*He puts his other hand on his father's shoulder.*)

Rev. S. (*blustering*): Silence, sir, silence: you are profane.

Mrs. Warren (*laughing heartily*): You should keep him in better order, Sam. Good-night. Here: take George his hat and stick with my compliments.

Rev. S. (*taking them*): Good-night. (*They shake hands. As he passes* Vivie *he shakes hands with her also and bids her good-night. Then, in booming command, to* Frank) Come along, sir, at once. (*He goes out.*)

Mrs. Warren: Byebye, Praddy.

Praed: Byebye, Kitty.

(*They shake hands affectionately and go out together, she accompanying him to the garden gate.*)

Frank (*to* Vivie): Kissums?

Vivie (*fiercely*): No. I hate you. (*She takes a couple of books and some paper from the writing-table, and sits down with them at the middle table, at the end next the fireplace.*)

Frank (*grimacing*): Sorry. (*He goes for his cap and rifle.* Mrs. Warren *returns. He takes her hand.*) Good-night, dear Mrs. Warren. (*He kisses her hand. She snatches it away, her lips tightening, and looks more than half disposed to box his ears. He laughs mischievously and runs off, clapping-to the door behind him.*)

Mrs. Warren (*resigning herself to an evening of boredom now that the men are gone*): Did you ever in your life hear anyone rattle on so? Isnt he a tease? (*She sits at the table.*) Now that I think of it, dearie, dont you go encouraging him. I'm sure he's a regular good-for-nothing.

Vivie (*rising to fetch more books*): I'm afraid so. Poor Frank! I shall have to get rid of him; but I shall feel sorry for him, though he's not worth it. That man Crofts does not seem to me to be good for much either: is he? (*She throws the books on the table rather roughly.*)

Mrs. Warren (*galled by* Vivie's *indifference*):

What do you know of men, child, to talk that way about them? Youll have to make up your mind to see a good deal of Sir George Crofts, as he's a friend of mine.

Vivie (*quite unmoved*): Why? (*She sits down and opens a book.*) Do you expect that we shall be much together? You and I, I mean?

Mrs. Warren (*staring at her*): Of course: until youre married. Youre not going back to college again.

Vivie: Do you think my way of life would suit you? I doubt it.

Mrs. Warren: Your way of life! What do you mean?

Vivie (*cutting a page of her book with the paper knife on her chatelaine*): Has it really never occurred to you, mother, that I have a way of life like other people?

Mrs. Warren: What nonsense is this youre trying to talk? Do you want to shew your independence, now that youre a great little person at school? Dont be a fool, child.

Vivie (*indulgently*): Thats all you have to say on the subject, is it, mother?

Mrs. Warren (*puzzled, then angry*): Dont you keep on asking me questions like that. (*Violently*) Hold your tongue. (Vivie *works on, losing no time, and saying nothing.*) You and your way of life, indeed! What next? (*She looks at* Vivie *again. No reply.*) Your way of life will be what I please, so it will. (*Another pause.*) Ive been noticing these airs in you ever since you got that tripos or whatever you call it. If you think I'm going to put up with them youre mistaken; and the sooner you find it out, the better. (*Muttering*) All I have to say on the subject, indeed! (*Again raising her voice angrily*) Do you know who you are speaking to, Miss?

Vivie (*looking across at her without raising her head from her book*): No. Who are you? What are you?

Mrs. Warren (*rising breathless*): You young imp!

VIVIE: Everybody knows my reputation, my social standing, and the profession I intend to pursue. I know nothing about you. What is that way of life which you invite me to share with you and Sir George Crofts, pray?

MRS. WARREN: Take care. I shall do something I'll be sorry for after, and you too.

VIVIE (*putting aside her books with cool decision*): Well, let us drop the subject until you are better able to face it. (*Looking critically at her mother*) You want some good walks and a little lawn tennis to set you up. You are shockingly out of condition: you were not able to manage twenty yards uphill today without stopping to pant; and your wrists are mere rolls of fat. Look at mine. (*She holds out her wrists.*)

MRS. WARREN (*after looking at her helplessly, begins to whimper*): Vivie —

VIVIE (*springing up sharply*): Now pray dont begin to cry. Anything but that. I really cannot stand whimpering. I will go out of the room if you do.

MRS. WARREN (*piteously*): Oh, my darling, how can you be so hard on me? Have I no rights over you as your mother?

VIVIE: Are you my mother?

MRS. WARREN (*appalled*): Am I your mother! Oh, Vivie!

VIVIE: Then where are our relatives? my father? our family friends? You claim the rights of a mother: the right to call me fool and child; to speak to me as no woman in authority over me at college dare speak to me; to dictate my way of life; and to force on me the acquaintance of a brute whom anyone can see to be the most vicious sort of London man about town. Before I give myself the trouble to resist such claims, I may as well find out whether they have any real existence.

MRS. WARREN (*distracted, throwing herself on her knees*): Oh no, no. Stop, stop. I am your mother: I swear it. Oh, you cant mean to turn on me — my own child! it's not natural.

You believe me, dont you? Say you believe me.

VIVIE: Who was my father?

MRS. WARREN: You dont know what your asking. I cant tell you.

VIVIE (*determined*): Oh yes you can, if you like. I have a right to know; and you know very well that I have that right. You can refuse to tell me, if you please; but if you do, you will see the last of me tomorrow morning.

MRS. WARREN: Oh, it's too horrible to hear you talk like that. You wouldnt — you couldnt leave me.

VIVIE (*ruthless*): Yes, without a moment's hesitation, if you trifle with me about this. (*Shivering with disgust*) How can I feel sure that I may not have the contaminated blood of that brutal waster in my veins?

MRS. WARREN: No, no. On my oath it's not he, nor any of the rest that you have ever met. I'm certain of that, at least.

(VIVIE's *eyes fasten sternly on her mother as the significance of this flashes on her.*)

VIVIE (*slowly*): You are certain of that, at least. Ah! You mean that that is all you are certain of. (*Thoughtfully*) I see. (MRS. WARREN *buries her face in her hands.*) Dont do that, mother: you know you dont feel it a bit. (MRS. WARREN *takes down her hands and looks up deplorably at* VIVIE, *who takes out her watch and says*) Well, that is enough for tonight. At what hour would you like breakfast? Is half-past eight too early for you?

MRS. WARREN (*wildly*): My God, what sort of woman are you?

VIVIE (*coolly*): The sort the world is mostly made of, I should hope. Otherwise I dont understand how it gets its business done. Come (*taking her mother by the wrist, and pulling her up pretty resolutely*): pull yourself together. Thats right.

MRS. WARREN (*querulously*): Youre very rough with me, Vivie.

VIVIE: Nonsense. What about bed? It's past ten.

MRS. WARREN (*passionately*): Whats the use of my going to bed? Do you think I could sleep?

VIVIE: Why not? I shall.

MRS. WARREN: You! youve no heart. (*She suddenly breaks out vehemently in her natural tongue — the dialect of a woman of the people — with all her affectations of maternal authority and conventional manners gone, and an overwhelming inspiration of true conviction and scorn in her*) Oh, I wont bear it: I wont put up with the injustice of it. What right have you to set yourself up above me like this? You boast of what you are to me — to me, who gave you the chance of being what you are. What chance had I? Shame on you for a bad daughter and a stuck-up prude!

VIVIE (*sitting down with a shrug, no longer confident; for her replies, which have sounded sensible and strong to her so far, now begin to ring rather woodenly and even priggishly against the new tone of her mother*): Dont think for a moment I set myself above you in any way. You attacked me with the conventional authority of a mother: I defended myself with the conventional superiority of a respectable woman. Frankly, I am not going to stand any of your nonsense; and when you drop it I shall not expect you to stand any of mine. I shall always respect your right to your own opinions and your own way of life.

MRS. WARREN: My own opinions and my own way of life! Listen to her talking! Do you think I was brought up like you? able to pick and choose my own way of life? Do you think I did what I did because I liked it, or thought it right, or wouldnt rather have gone to college and been a lady if I'd had the chance.

VIVIE: Everybody has some choice, mother. The poorest girl alive may not be able to choose between being Queen of England or Principal of Newnham; but she can choose between ragpicking and flowerselling, according to her taste. People are always blaming their circumstances for what they are. I dont believe in circumstances. The people who get on in this world are the people who get up and look for the circumstances they want, and, if they cant find them, make them.

MRS. WARREN: Oh, it's easy to talk, very easy, isnt it? Here! would you like to know what my circumstances were?

VIVIE: Yes: you had better tell me. Wont you sit down?

MRS. WARREN: Oh, I'll sit down: dont you be afraid. (*She plants her chair farther forward with brazen energy, and sits down. VIVIE is impressed in spite of herself.*) D'you know what your gran'mother was?

VIVIE: No.

MRS. WARREN: No you dont. I do. She called herself a widow and had a fried-fish shop down by the Mint, and kept herself and four daughters out of it. Two of us were sisters: that was me and Liz; and we were both good-looking and well made. I suppose our father was a well-fed man: mother pretended he was a gentleman; but I dont know. The other two were only half sisters: undersized, ugly, starved looking, hard working, honest poor creatures: Liz and I would have half-murdered them if mother hadnt half-murdered us to keep our hands off them. They were the respectable ones. Well, what did they get by their respectability? I'll tell you. One of them worked in a whitelead factory twelve hours a day for nine shillings a week until she died of lead poisoning. She only expected to get her hands a little paralyzed; but she died. The other was always held up to us as a model because she married a Government laborer in the Deptford victualling yard, and kept his room and the three children neat and tidy on eighteen shilling a week — until he took to drink. That was worth being respectable for, wasnt it?

VIVIE (*now thoughtfully attentive*): Did you and your sister think so?

MRS. WARREN: Liz didnt, I can tell you: she had more spirit. We both went to a church school — that was part of the ladylike airs we gave ourselves to be superior to the children that knew nothing and went nowhere — and we stayed there until Liz went out one night and never came back. I know the schoolmistress thought I'd soon follow her example; for the clergyman was always warning me that Lizzie'd end by jumping off Waterloo Bridge. Poor fool: that was all he knew about it! But I was more afraid of the whitelead factory than I was of the river; and so would you have been in my place. That clergyman got me a situation as scullery maid in a temperance restaurant where they sent out for anything you liked. Then I was waitress; and then I went to the bar at Waterloo station: fourteen hours a day serving drinks and washing glasses for four shillings a week and my board. That was considered a great promotion for me. Well, one cold, wretched night, when I was so tired I could hardly keep myself awake, who should come up for a half of Scotch but Lizzie, in a long fur cloak, elegant and comfortable, with a lot of sovereigns in her purse.

VIVIE (grimly): My aunt Lizzie!

MRS. WARREN: Yes; and a very good aunt to have, too. She's living down at Winchester now, close to the cathedral, one of the most respectable ladies there. Chaperones girls at the county ball, if you please. No river for Liz, thank you! You remind me of Liz a little: she was a first-rate business woman — saved money from the beginning — never let herself look too like what she was — never lost her head or threw away a chance. When she saw I'd grown up good-looking she said to me across the bar "What are you doing there, you little fool? wearing out your health and your appearance for other people's profit!" Liz was saving money then to take a house for herself in Brussels; and she thought we two could save faster than one. So she lent me some money and gave me a start: and I saved steadily and first paid her back, and then went into business with her as her partner. Why shouldnt I have done it? The house in Brussels was real high class: a much better place for a woman to be in than the factory where Anne Jane got poisoned. None of our girls were ever treated as I was treated in the scullery of that temperance place, or at the Waterloo bar, or at home. Would you have had me stay in them and become a worn out old drudge before I was forty?

VIVIE (intensely interested by this time): No; but why did you choose that business? Saving money and good management will succeed in any business.

MRS. WARREN: Yes, saving money. But where can a woman get the money to save in any other business? Could you save out of four shillings a week and keep yourself dressed as well? Not you. Of course, if youre a plain woman and cant earn anything more; or if you have a turn for music, or the stage, or newspaper-writing: thats different. But neither Liz nor I had any turn for such things: all we had was our appearance and our turn for pleasing men. Do you think we were such fools as to let other people trade in our good looks by employing us as shop-girls, or barmaids, or waitresses, when we could trade in them ourselves and get all the profits instead of starvation wages? Not likely.

VIVIE: You were certainly quite justified — from the business point of view.

MRS. WARREN: Yes; or any other point of view. What is any respectable girl brought up to do but to catch some rich man's fancy and get the benefit of his money by marrying him? — as if a marriage ceremony could make any difference in the right or wrong of the thing! Oh, the hypocrisy of the world makes me sick! Liz and I had to work and save and calculate just like other people; elseways we should be as poor as any good-for-nothing drunken waster of a woman that thinks her luck will last for ever. (With great energy) I despise such people: theyve no character; and if theres a thing I hate in women, it's want of character.

VIVIE: Come now, mother: frankly! Isnt it part of what you call character in a woman that she should greatly dislike such a way of making money?

MRS. WARREN: Why, of course. Everybody dislikes having to work and make money; but they have to do it all the same. I'm sure Ive often pitied a poor girl, tired out and in low spirits, having to try to please some man that she doesn't care two straws for — some half-drunken fool that thinks he's making himself agreeable when he's teasing and worrying and disgusting a woman so that hardly any money could pay her for putting up with it. But she has to bear with disagreeables and take the rough with the smooth, just like a nurse in a hospital or anyone else. It's not work that any woman would do for pleasure, goodness knows; though to hear the pious people talk you would suppose it was a bed of roses.

VIVIE: Still, you consider it worth while. It pays.

MRS. WARREN: Of course it's worth while to a poor girl, if she can resist temptation and is good-looking and well conducted and sensible. It's far better than any other employment open to her. I always thought that oughtnt to be. It cant be right, Vivie, that there shouldnt be better opportunities for women. I stick to that: it's wrong. But it's so, right or wrong; and a girl must make the best of it. But of course it's not worth while for a lady. If you took to it youd be a fool; but I should have been a fool if I'd taken to anything else.

VIVIE (more and more deeply moved): Mother: suppose we were both as poor as you were in those wretched old days, are you quite sure that you wouldnt advise me to try the Waterloo bar, or marry a laborer, or even go into the factory?

MRS. WARREN (indignantly): Of course not. What sort of mother do you take me for! How could you keep your self-respect in such starvation and slavery? And whats a woman worth? whats life worth? without self-respect! Why am I independent and able to give my daughter a first-rate education, when other women that had just as good opportunities are in the gutter? Because I always knew how to respect myself and control myself. Why is Liz looked up to in a cathedral town? The same reason. Where would we be now if we'd minded the clergyman's foolishness? Scrubbing floors for one and sixpence a day and nothing to look forward to but the workhouse infirmary. Dont you be led astray by people who dont know the world, my girl. The only way for a woman to provide for herself decently is for her to be good to some man that can afford to be good to her. If she's in his own station of life, let her make him marry her; but if she's far beneath him she cant expect it: why should she? it wouldnt be for her own happiness. Ask any lady in London society that has daughters; and she'll tell you the same, except that I tell you straight and she'll tell you crooked. Thats all the difference.

VIVIE (fascinated, gazing at her): My dear mother: you are a wonderful woman: you are stronger than all England. And you are really and truly not one wee bit doubtful — or — or — ashamed?

MRS. WARREN: Well, of course, dearie, it's only good manners to be ashamed of it: it's expected from a woman. Women have to pretend to feel a great deal that they dont feel. Liz used to be angry with me for plumping out the truth about it. She used to say that when every woman could learn enough from what was going on in the world before her eyes, there was no need to talk about it to her. But then Liz was such a perfect lady! She had the true instinct of it; while I was always a bit of a vulgarian. I used to be so pleased when you sent me your photos to see that you were growing up like Liz: youve just her ladylike, determined way. But I cant stand saying one thing when everyone knows I mean another. Whats the use in such hypocrisy? If people arrange the world that way for women, theres no good pretending it's arranged the other way. No: I never was a bit ashamed really. I consider I had a right to be proud of how we managed everything so respectably, and never had a word against us, and how the girls were so well taken care of. Some of them did very well: one of them married an ambassador. But of course now I darent talk about such things: whatever would they think of us! (*She yawns.*) Oh dear! I do believe I'm getting sleepy after all. (*She stretches herself lazily, thoroughly relieved by her explosion, and placidly ready for her night's rest.*)

VIVIE: I believe it is I who will not be able to sleep now. (*She goes to the dresser and lights the candle. Then she extinguishes the lamp, darkening the room a good deal.*) Better let in some fresh air before locking up. (*She opens the cottage door, and finds that it is broad moonlight.*) What a beautiful night! Look! (*She draws aside the curtains of the window. The landscape is seen bathed in the radiance of the harvest moon rising over Blackdown.*)

MRS. WARREN (*with a perfunctory glance at the scene*): Yes, dear; but take care you dont catch your death of cold from the night air.

VIVIE (*contemptuously*): Nonsense.

MRS. WARREN (*querulously*): Oh yes: everything I say is nonsense, according to you.

VIVIE (*turning to her quickly*): No: really that is not so, mother. You have got completely the better of me tonight, though I intended it to be the other way. Let us be good friends now.

MRS. WARREN (*shaking her head a little ruefully*): So it has been the other way. But I suppose I must give in to it. I always got the worst of it from Liz; and now I suppose it'll be the same with you.

VIVIE: Well, never mind. Come: good-night, dear old mother. (*She takes her mother in her arms.*)

MRS. WARREN (*fondly*): I brought you up well, didnt I, dearie?

VIVIE: You did.

MRS. WARREN: And youll be good to your poor old mother for it, wont you?

VIVIE: I will, dear. (*Kissing her*) Good-night.

MRS. WARREN (*with unction*): Blessings on my own dearie darling! a mother's blessing!

(*She embraces her daughter protectingly, instinctively looking upward for a divine sanction.*)

ACT THREE

In the rectory garden next morning, with the sun shining from a cloudless sky. The garden wall has a five-barred wooden gate, wide enough to admit a carriage, in the middle. Beside the gate hangs a bell on a coiled spring, communicating with a pull outside. The carriage drive comes down the middle of the garden and then swerves to its left, where it ends in a little gravelled circus opposite the Rectory porch. Beyond the gate is seen the dusty high road, parallel with the wall, bounded on the farther side by a strip of turf and an unfenced pine wood. On the lawn, between the house and the drive, is a clipped yew tree, with a garden bench in its shade. On the opposite side the garden is shut in by a box hedge; and there is a sundial on the turf, with an iron chair near it. A little path leads off through the box hedge, behind the sundial.

FRANK, *seated on the chair near the sundial, on which he has placed the morning papers, is reading The Standard. His father comes from the house, red-eyed and shivery, and meets* FRANK's *eye with misgiving.*

FRANK (*looking at his watch*): Half-past eleven. Nice hour for a rector to come down to breakfast!

REV. S.: Dont mock, Frank: dont mock. I am a little — er — (*Shivering*) —

FRANK: Off color?

REV. S. (*repudiating the expression*): No, sir: unwell this morning. Wheres your mother?

FRANK: Dont be alarmed: she's not here. Gone to town by the 11.13 with Bessie. She left several messages for you. Do you feel equal to receiving them now, or shall I wait til youve breakfasted?

REV. S.: I have breakfasted, sir. I am surprised at your mother going to town when we have people staying with us. Theyll think it very strange.

FRANK: Possibly she has considered that. At all events, if Crofts is going to stay here, and you are going to sit up every night with him until four, recalling the incidents of your fiery youth, it is clearly my mother's duty, as a prudent housekeeper, to go up to the stores and order a barrel of whisky and a few hundred siphons.

REV. S.: I did not observe that Sir George drank excessively.

FRANK: You were not in a condition to, gov'nor.

REV. S.: Do you mean to say that I — ?

FRANK (calmly): I never saw a beneficed clergyman less sober. The anecdotes you told about your past career were so awful that I really dont think Praed would have passed the night under your roof if it hadnt been for the way my mother and he took to one another.

REV. S.: Nonsense, sir. I am Sir George Crofts' host. I must talk to him about something; and he has only one subject. Where is Mr. Praed now?

FRANK: He is driving my mother and Bessie to the station.

REV. S.: Is Crofts up yet?

FRANK: Oh, long ago. He hasnt turned a hair: he's in much better practice than you. Has kept it up ever since, probably. He's taken himself off somewhere to smoke.

(FRANK resumes his paper. The parson turns disconsolately towards the gate; then comes back irresolutely.)

REV. S.: Er — Frank.

FRANK: Yes.

REV. S.: Do you think the Warrens will expect to be asked here after yesterday afternoon?

FRANK: Theyve been asked already.

REV. S. (appalled): What!!!

FRANK: Crofts informed us at breakfast that you told him to bring Mrs. Warren and Vivie over here to-day, and to invite them to make this house their home. My mother then found she must go to town by the 11.13 train.

REV. S. (with despairing vehemence): I never gave any such invitation. I never thought of such a thing.

FRANK (compassionately): How do you know, gov'nor, what you said and thought last night?

PRAED (coming in through the hedge): Good morning.

REV. S.: Good morning. I must apologize for not having met you at breakfast. I have a touch of — of —

FRANK: Clergyman's sore throat, Praed. Fortunately not chronic.

PRAED (changing the subject): Well, I must say your house is in a charming spot here. Really most charming.

REV. S.: Yes: it is indeed. Frank will take you for a walk, Mr. Praed, if you like. I'll ask you to excuse me: I must take the opportunity to write my sermon while Mrs. Gardner is away and you are all amusing yourselves. You wont mind, will you?

PRAED: Certainly not. Dont stand on the slightest ceremony with me.

REV. S.: Thank you. I'll — er — er — (He stammers his way to the porch and vanishes into the house.)

PRAED: Curious thing it must be writing a sermon every week.

FRANK: Ever so curious, if he did it. He buys em. He's gone for some soda water.

PRAED: My dear boy: I wish you would be

more respectful to your father. You know you can be so nice when you like.

FRANK: My dear Praddy: you forget that I have to live with the governor. When two people live together — it dont matter whether theyre father and son or husband and wife or brother and sister — they cant keep up the polite humbug thats so easy for ten minutes on an afternoon call. Now the governor, who unites to many admirable domestic qualities the irresoluteness of a sheep and the pompousness and aggressiveness of a jackass —

PRAED: No, pray, pray, my dear Frank, remember! He is your father.

FRANK: I give him due credit for that. (*Rising and flinging down his paper.*) But just imagine his telling Crofts to bring the Warrens over here! He must have been ever so drunk. You know, my dear Praddy, my mother wouldnt stand Mrs. Warren for a moment. Vivie mustnt come here until she's gone back to town.

PRAED: But your mother doesnt know anything about Mrs. Warren, does she? (*He picks up the paper and sits down to read it.*)

FRANK: I dont know. Her journey to town looks as if she did. Not that my mother would mind in the ordinary way: she has stuck like a brick to lots of women who had got into trouble. But they were all nice women. Thats what makes the real difference. Mrs. Warren, no doubt, has her merits; but she's ever so rowdy; and my mother simply wouldnt put up with her. So — hallo! (*This exclamation is provoked by the reappearance of the clergyman, who comes out of the house in haste and dismay.*)

REV. S.: Frank: Mrs. Warren and her daughter are coming across the heath with Crofts: I saw them from the study windows. What am I to say about your mother?

FRANK: Stick on your hat and go out and say how delighted you are to see them; and that Frank's in the garden: and that mother and Bessie have been called to the bedside of a sick relative, and were ever so sorry they couldnt stop; and that you hope Mrs. Warren slept well; and — and — say any blessed thing except the truth, and leave the rest to Providence.

REV. S.: But how are we to get rid of them afterwards?

FRANK: Theres no time to think of that now. Here! (*He bounds into the house.*)

REV. S.: He's so impetuous. I dont know what to do with him, Mr. Praed.

FRANK (*returning with a clerical felt hat, which he claps on his father's head*): Now: off with you. (*Rushing him through the gate.*) Praed and I'll wait here, to give the thing an unpremeditated air. (*The clergyman, dazed but obedient, hurries off.*)

FRANK: We must get the old girl back to town somehow, Praed. Come! Honestly, dear Praddy, do you like seeing them together?

PRAED: Oh, why not?

FRANK (*his teeth on edge*): Dont it make your flesh creep ever so little? that wicked old devil, up to every villainy under the sun, I'll swear, and Vivie — ugh!

PRAED: Hush, pray. Theyre coming.

(*The clergyman and* CROFTS *are seen coming along the road, followed by* MRS. WARREN *and* VIVIE *walking affectionately together.*)

FRANK: Look: she actually has her arm round the old woman's waist. It's her right arm: she began it. She's gone sentimental, by God! Ugh! ugh! Now do you feel the creeps? (*The clergyman opens the gate; and* MRS. WARREN *and* VIVIE *pass him and stand in the middle of the garden looking at the house.* FRANK, *in an ecstasy of dissimulation, turns gaily to* MRS. WARREN, *exclaiming*) Ever so delighted to see you, Mrs. Warren. This quiet old rectory garden becomes you perfectly.

MRS. WARREN: Well, I never! Did you hear that, George? He says I look well in a quiet old rectory garden.

REV. S. (*still holding the gate for* CROFTS, *who*

loafs through it, heavily bored): You look well everywhere, Mrs. Warren.

FRANK: Bravo, gov'nor! Now look here: lets have a treat before lunch. First lets see the church. Everyone has to do that. It's a regular old thirteenth century church, you know: the gov'nor's ever so fond of it, because he got up a restoration fund and had it completely rebuilt six years ago. Praed will be able to shew its points.

PRAED (*rising*): Certainly, if the restoration has left any to shew.

REV. S. (*mooning hospitably at them*): I shall be pleased, I'm sure, if George and Mrs. Warren really care about it.

MRS. WARREN: Oh, come along and get it over.

CROFTS (*turning back towards the gate*): Ive no objection.

REV. S.: Not that way. We go through the fields, if you dont mind. Round here. (*He leads the way by the little path through the box hedge.*)

CROFTS: Oh, all right. (*He goes with the parson.*)

(PRAED *follows with* MRS. WARREN. VIVIE *does not stir: she watches them until they have gone, with all the lines of purpose in her face marking it strongly.*)

FRANK: Aint you coming?

VIVIE: No, I want to give you a warning, Frank. You were making fun of my mother just now when you said that about the rectory garden. That is barred in future. Please treat my mother with as much respect as you treat your own.

FRANK: My dear Viv: she wouldnt appreciate it: the two cases require different treatment. But what on earth has happened to you? Last night we were perfectly agreed as to your mother and her set. This morning I find you attitudinizing sentimentally with your arm round your parent's waist.

VIVIE (*flushing*): Attitudinizing!

FRANK: That was how it struck me. First time I ever saw you do a second-rate thing.

VIVIE (*controlling herself*): Yes, Frank: there has been a change; but I dont think it a change for the worse. Yesterday I was a little prig.

FRANK: And today?

VIVIE (*wincing; then looking at him steadily*): Today I know my mother better than you do.

FRANK: Heaven forbid!

VIVIE: What do you mean?

FRANK: Viv: theres a freemasonry among thoroughly immoral people that you know nothing of. Youve too much character. Thats the bond between your mother and me: thats why I know her better than youll ever know her.

VIVIE: You are wrong: you know nothing about her. If you knew the circumstances against which my mother had to struggle —

FRANK (*adroitly finishing the sentence for her*): I should know why she is what she is, shouldnt I? What difference would that make? Circumstances or no circumstances, Viv, you wont be able to stand your mother.

VIVIE (*very angry*): Why not?

FRANK: Because she's an old wretch, Viv. If you ever put your arm round her waist in my presence again, I'll shoot myself there and then as a protest against an exhibition which revolts me.

VIVIE: Must I choose between dropping your acquaintance and dropping my mother's?

FRANK (*gracefully*): That would put the old lady at ever such a disadvantage. No, Viv: your infatuated little boy will have to stick to you in any case. But he's all the more anxious that you shouldnt make mistakes. It's no use, Viv: your mother's impossible. She may be a good sort; but she's a bad lot, a very bad lot.

VIVIE (*hotly*): Frank — ! (*He stands his ground, she turns away and sits down on the bench under the yew tree, struggling to recover her self-command. Then she says)* Is she to be deserted by all the world because she's what you call a bad lot? Has she no right to live?

FRANK: No fear of that, Viv: she wont ever be deserted. *(He sits on the bench beside her.)*

VIVIE: But I am to desert her, I suppose.

FRANK *(babyishly lulling her and making love to her with his voice)*: Mustnt go live with her. Little family group of mother and daughter wouldnt be a success. Spoil our little group.

VIVIE *(falling under the spell)*: What little group?

FRANK: The babes in the wood: Vivie and little Frank. *(He nestles against her like a weary child.)* Lets go and get covered up with leaves.

VIVIE *(rhythmically, rocking him like a nurse)*: Fast asleep, hand in hand, under the trees.

FRANK: The wise little girl with her silly little boy.

VIVIE: The dear little boy with his dowdy little girl.

FRANK: Ever so peaceful, and relieved from the imbecility of the little boy's father and the questionableness of the little girl's —

VIVIE *(smothering the word against her breast)*: Sh-sh-sh-sh! little girl wants to forget all about her mother. *(They are silent for some moments, rocking one another. Then VIVIE wakes up with a shock exclaiming)* What a pair of fools we are! Come: sit up. Gracious! your hair. *(She smoothes it.)* I wonder do all grown up people play in that childish way when nobody is looking. I never did it when I was a child.

FRANK: Neither did I. You are my first playmate. *(He catches her hand to kiss it, but checks himself to look round first. Very unexpectedly, he sees CROFTS emerging from the box hedge.)* Oh damn!

VIVIE: Why damn, dear?

FRANK *(whispering)*: Sh! Here's this brute Crofts. *(He sits farther away from her with an unconcerned air.)*

CROFTS: Could I have a few words with you, Miss Vivie?

VIVIE: Certainly.

CROFTS *(to FRANK)*: Youll excuse me, Gardner. Theyre waiting for you in the church, if you dont mind.

FRANK *(rising)*: Anything to oblige you, Crofts — except church. If you should happen to want me, Vivvums, ring the gate bell. *(He goes into the house with unruffled suavity.)*

CROFTS *(watching him with a crafty air as he disappears, and speaking to VIVIE with an assumption of being on privileged terms with her)*: Pleasant young fellow that, Miss Vivie. Pity he has no money, isnt it?

VIVIE: Do you think so?

CROFTS: Well, whats he to do? No profession. No property. Whats he good for?

VIVIE: I realize his disadvantages, Sir George.

CROFTS *(a little taken aback at being so precisely interpreted)*: Oh, it's not that. But while we're in this world we're in it; and money's money. *(VIVIE does not answer.)* Nice day, isnt it?

VIVIE *(with scarcely veiled contempt for this effort at conversation)*: Very.

CROFTS *(with brutal good humor, as if he liked her pluck)*: Well, thats not what I came to say. *(Sitting down beside her)* Now listen, Miss Vivie. I'm quite aware that I'm not a young lady's man.

VIVIE: Indeed, Sir George?

CROFTS: No; and to tell you the honest truth I dont want to be either. But when I say a thing I mean it; when I feel a sentiment I feel it in earnest; and what I value I pay hard money for. Thats the sort of man I am.

VIVIE: It does you great credit, I'm sure.

CROFTS: Oh, I dont mean to praise myself. I have my faults, Heaven knows: no man is more sensible of that than I am. I know I'm not perfect: thats one of the advantages of being a middle-aged man; for I'm not a young man, and I know it. But my code is a simple one, and, I think, a good one. Honor between man and man; fidelity between man and woman; and no cant about this religion or that religion, but an honest belief that things are making for good on the whole.

VIVIE (*with biting irony*): "A power, not ourselves, that makes for righteousness," eh?

CROFTS (*taking her seriously*): Oh certainly. Not ourselves, of course. You understand what I mean. Well, now as to practical matters. You may have an idea that Ive flung my money about; but I havnt: I'm richer today than when I first came into the property. Ive used my knowledge of the world to invest my money in ways that other men have overlooked; and whatever else I may be, I'm a safe man from the money point of view.

VIVIE: It's very kind of you to tell me all this.

CROFTS: Oh well, come, Miss Vivie: you neednt pretend you dont see what I'm driving at. I want to settle down with a Lady Crofts. I suppose you think me very blunt, eh?

VIVIE: Not at all: I am much obliged to you for being so definite and business-like. I quite appreciate the offer: the money, the position, Lady Crofts, and so on. But I think I will say no, if you dont mind. I'd rather not. (*She rises, and strolls across to the sundial to get out of his immediate neighborhood.*)

CROFTS (*not at all discouraged, and taking advantage of the additional room left him on the seat to spread himself comfortably, as if a few preliminary refusals were part of the inevitable routine of courtship*): I'm in no hurry. It was only just to let you know in case young Gardner should try to trap you. Leave the question open.

VIVIE (*sharply*): My no is final. I wont go back from it.

(CROFTS *is not impressed. He grins; leans forward with his elbows on his knees to prod with his stick at some unfortunate insect in the grass; and looks cunningly at her. She turns away impatiently.*)

CROFTS: I'm a good deal older than you. Twenty-five years: quarter of a century. I shant live for ever; and I'll take care that you shall be well off when I'm gone.

VIVIE: I am proof against even that inducement, Sir George. Dont you think youd better take your answer? There is not the slightest chance of my altering it.

CROFTS (*rising, after a final slash at a daisy, and coming nearer to her*): Well, no matter. I could tell you some things that would change your mind fast enough; but I wont, because I'd rather win you by honest affection. I was a good friend to your mother: ask her whether I wasnt. She'd never have made the money that paid for your education if it hadn't been for my advice and help, not to mention the money I advanced her. There are not many men would have stood by her as I have. I put not less than £40,000 into it, from first to last.

VIVIE (*staring at him*): Do you mean to say you were my mother's business partner?

CROFTS: Yes. Now just think of all the trouble and the explanations it would save if we were to keep the whole thing in the family, so to speak. Ask your mother whether she'd like to have to explain all her affairs to a perfect stranger.

VIVIE: I see no difficulty, since I understand that the business is wound up, and the money invested.

CROFTS (*stopping short, amazed*): Wound up! Wind up a business thats paying 35 per cent in the worst years! Not likely. Who told you that?

VIVIE (*her color quite gone*): Do you mean that it is still—? (*She stops abruptly, and puts her hand on the sundial to support herself. Then she gets quickly to the iron chair and sits down.*) What business are you talking about?

CROFTS: Well, the fact is it's not what would be considered exactly a high-class business in my set — the county set, you know — our set it will be if you think better of my offer. Not that theres any mystery about it: dont think that. Of course you know by your mother's being in it that it's perfectly straight and honest. Ive known her for many years; and I can say of her that she'd cut off her hands sooner than touch anything that was not what it ought to be. I'll tell you all about it if you like. I dont know whether youve found in travelling how hard it is to find a really comfortable private hotel.

VIVIE (*sickened, averting her face*): Yes: go on.

CROFTS: Well, thats all it is. Your mother has a genius for managing such things. We've got two in Brussels, one in Ostend, one in Vienna, and two in Budapest. Of course there are others besides ourselves in it; but we hold most of the capital; and your mother's indispensable as managing director. Youve noticed, I daresay, that she travels a good deal. But you see you cant mention such things in society. Once let out the word hotel and everybody says you keep a public-house. You wouldnt like people to say that of your mother, would you? Thats why we're so reserved about it. By the way, youll keep it to yourself, wont you? Since it's been a secret so long, it had better remain so.

VIVIE: And this is the business you invite me to join you in?

CROFTS: Oh no. My wife shant be troubled with business. Youll not be in it more than youve always been.

VIVIE: *I* always been! What do you mean?

CROFTS: Only that youve always lived on it. It paid for your education and the dress you have on your back. Dont turn up your nose at business, Miss Vivie: where would your Newnhams and Girtons be without it?

VIVIE (*rising, almost beside herself*): Take care. I know what this business is.

CROFTS (*starting, with a suppressed oath*): Who told you?

VIVIE: Your partner. My mother.

CROFTS (*black with rage*): The old —

VIVIE: Just so.

(*He swallows the epithet and stands for a moment swearing and raging foully to himself. But he knows that his cue is to be sympathetic. He takes refuge in generous indignation.*)

CROFTS: She ought to have had more consideration for you. *I'd* never have told you.

VIVIE: I think you would probably have told me when we were married: it would have been a convenient weapon to break me in with.

CROFTS (*quite sincerely*): I never intended that. On my word as a gentleman I didnt.

(VIVIE *wonders at him. Her sense of the irony of his protest cools and braces her. She replies with contemptuous self-possession.*)

VIVIE: It does not matter. I suppose you understand that when we leave here today our acquaintance ceases.

CROFTS: Why? Is it for helping your mother?

VIVIE: My mother was a very poor woman who had no reasonable choice but to do as she did. You were a rich gentleman; and you did the same for the sake of 35 per cent. You are a pretty common sort of scoundrel, I think. That is my opinion of you.

CROFTS (*after a stare: not at all displeased, and much more at his ease on these frank terms than on their former ceremonious ones*): Ha! ha! ha! ha! Go it, little missie, go it: it doesnt hurt me and it amuses you. Why the devil shouldnt I invest my money that way? I take the interest on my capital like other people: I hope you dont think I dirty my own hands with the work. Come! you wouldnt refuse the acquaintance of my mother's cousin the Duke of Belgravia because some of the rents he gets are earned in queer ways. You wouldnt cut the Archbishop of Canterbury, I suppose, because the Ecclesiastical Commissioners have a few publicans and sinners among their tenants. Do you remember your Crofts scholarship at

Newnham? Well, that was founded by my brother the M.P. He gets his 22 per cent out of a factory with 600 girls in it, and not one of them getting wages enough to live on. How d'ye suppose they manage when they have no family to fall back on? Ask your mother. And do you expect me to turn my back on 35 per cent when all the rest are pocketing what they can, like sensible men? No such fool! If youre going to pick and choose your acquaintances on moral principles, youd better clear out of this country, unless you want to cut yourself out of all decent society.

VIVIE (*conscience stricken*): You might go on to point out that I myself never asked where the money I spent came from. I believe I am just as bad as you.

CROFTS (*greatly reassured*): Of course you are; and a very good thing too! What harm does it do after all? (*Rallying her jocularly*) So you think me such a scoundrel now you come to think it over. Eh?

VIVIE: I have shared profits with you; and I admitted you just now to the familiarity of knowing what I think of you.

CROFTS (*with serious friendliness*): To be sure you did. You wont find me a bad sort: I dont go in for being superfine intellectually; but Ive plenty of honest human feeling; and the old Crofts breed comes out in a sort of instinctive hatred of anything low, in which I'm sure youll sympathize with me. Believe me, Miss Vivie, the world isnt such a bad place as the croakers make out. As long as you dont fly openly in the face of society, society doesnt ask any inconvenient questions; and it makes precious short work of the cads who do. There are no secrets better kept than the secrets everybody guesses. In the class of people I can introduce you to, no lady or gentleman would so far forget themselves as to discuss my business affairs or your mother's. No man can offer you a safer position.

VIVIE (*studying him curiously*): I suppose you really think youre getting on famously with me.

CROFTS: Well, I hope I may flatter myself that you think better of me than you did at first.

VIVIE (*quietly*): I hardly find you worth thinking about at all now. When I think of the society that tolerates you, and the laws that protect you! when I think of how helpless nine out of ten young girls would be in the hands of you and my mother! the unmentionable woman and her capitalist bully —

CROFTS (*livid*): Damn you!

VIVIE: You need not. I feel among the damned already.

(*She raises the latch of the gate to open it and go out. He follows her and puts his hand heavily on the top bar to prevent its opening.*)

CROFTS (*panting with fury*): Do you think I'll put up with this from you, you young devil?

VIVIE (*unmoved*): Be quiet. Someone will answer the bell.

(*Without flinching a step she strikes the bell with the back of her hand. It clangs harshly; and he starts back involuntarily. Almost immediately* FRANK *appears at the porch with his rifle.*)

FRANK (*with cheerful politeness*): Will you have the rifle, Viv; or shall I operate?

VIVIE: Frank: have you been listening?

FRANK (*coming down into the garden*): Only for the bell, I assure you; so that you shouldnt have to wait. I think I shewed great insight into your character, Crofts.

CROFTS: For two pins I'd take that gun from you and break it across your head.

FRANK (*stalking him cautiously*): Pray dont. I'm ever so careless in handling firearms. Sure to be a fatal accident, with a reprimand from the coroner's jury for my negligence.

VIVIE: Put the rifle away, Frank; it's quite unnecessary.

FRANK: Quite right, Viv. Much more sportsmanlike to catch him in a trap. (CROFTS, *understanding the insult, makes a threatening movement.*) Crofts: there are fifteen cartridges in the magazine here; and I am a dead shot at the present distance and at an object of your size.

CROFTS: Oh, you neednt be afraid. I'm not going to touch you.

FRANK: Ever so magnanimous of you under the circumstances! Thank you.

CROFTS: I'll just tell you this before I go. It may interest you, since youre so fond of one another. Allow me, Mister Frank, to introduce you to your half-sister, the eldest daughter of the Reverend Samuel Gardner. Miss Vivie: your half-brother. Good morning. (*He goes out through the gate and along the road.*)

FRANK (*after a pause of stupefaction, raising the rifle*): Youll testify before the coroner that it's an accident, Viv. (*He takes aim at the retreating figure of* CROFTS. VIVIE *seizes the muzzle and pulls it round against her breast.*)

VIVIE: Fire now. You may.

FRANK (*dropping his end of the rifle hastily*): Stop! take care. (*She lets it go. It falls on the turf.*) Oh, youve given your little boy such a turn. Suppose it had gone off! ugh! (*He sinks on the garden seat, overcome.*)

VIVIE: Suppose it had: do you think it would not have been a relief to have some sharp physical pain tearing through me?

FRANK (*coaxingly*): Take it ever so easy, dear Viv. Remember: even if the rifle scared that fellow into telling the truth for the first time in his life, that only makes us the babes in the wood in earnest. (*He holds out his arm to her.*) Come and be covered up with leaves again.

VIVIE (*with a cry of disgust*): Ah, not that, not that. You make all my flesh creep.

FRANK: Why, whats the matter?

VIVIE: Goodbye. (*She makes for the gate.*)

FRANK (*jumping up*): Hallo! Stop! Viv! Viv! (*She turns in the gateway*) Where are you going to? Where shall we find you?

VIVIE: At Honoria Fraser's chambers, 67 Chancery Lane, for the rest of my life. (*She goes off quickly in the opposite direction to that taken by* CROFTS.)

FRANK: But I say — wait — dash it! (*He runs after her.*)

ACT FOUR

Honoria Fraser's chambers in Chancery Lane. An office at the top of New Stone Buildings, with a plate-glass window, distempered walls, electric light, and a patent stove. Saturday afternoon. The chimneys of Lincoln's Inn and the western sky beyond are seen through the window. There is a double writing table in the middle of the room, with a cigar box, ash pans, and a portable electric reading lamp almost snowed up in heaps of papers and books. This table has knee holes and chairs right and left and is very untidy. The clerk's desk, closed and tidy, with its high stool, is against the wall, near a door communicating with the inner rooms. In the opposite wall is the door leading to the public corridor. Its upper panel is of opaque glass, lettered in black on the outside, FRASER AND WARREN. *A baize screen hides the corner between this door and the window.* FRANK, *in a fashionable light-colored coaching suit, with his stick, gloves, and white hat in his hands, is pacing up and down the office. Somebody tries the door with a key.*

FRANK (*calling*): Come in. It's not locked.

(VIVIE *comes in, in her hat and jacket. She stops and stares at him.*)

VIVIE (*sternly*): What are you doing here?

FRANK: Waiting to see you. Ive been here for hours. Is this the way you attend to your business? (*He puts his hat and stick on the table, and perches himself with a vault on the clerk's stool, looking at her with every appearance of being in a specially restless, teasing, flippant mood.*)

VIVIE: Ive been away exactly twenty minutes for a cup of tea. (*She takes off her hat and jacket and hangs them up behind the screen.*) How did you get in?

FRANK: The staff had not left when I arrived. He's gone to play cricket on Primrose Hill. Why dont you employ a woman, and give your sex a chance?

VIVIE: What have you come for?

FRANK (*springing off the stool and coming close to her*): Viv: lets go and enjoy the Saturday half-holiday somewhere, like the staff. What do you say to Richmond, and then a music hall, and a jolly supper?

VIVIE: Cant afford it. I shall put in another six hours work before I go to bed.

FRANK: Cant afford it, cant we? Aha! Look here. (*He takes out a handful of sovereigns and makes them chink.*) Gold, Viv: gold!

VIVIE: Where did you get it?

FRANK: Gambling, Viv: gambling. Poker.

VIVIE: Pah! It's meaner than stealing it. No: I'm not coming. (*She sits down to work at the table, with her back to the glass door, and begins turning over the papers.*)

FRANK (*remonstrating piteously*): But, my dear Viv, I want to talk to you ever so seriously.

VIVIE: Very well: sit down in Honoria's chair and talk here. I like ten minutes chat after tea. (*He murmurs.*) No use groaning: I'm inexorable. (*He takes the opposite seat disconsolately.*) Pass that cigar box, will you?

FRANK (*pushing the cigar box across*): Nasty womanly habit. Nice men dont do it any longer.

VIVIE: Yes: they object to the smell in the office; and weve had to take to cigarets. See! (*She opens the box and takes out a cigaret, which she lights. She offers him one; but he shakes his head with a wry face. She settles herself comfortably in her chair, smoking.*) Go ahead.

FRANK: Well, I want to know what youve done — what arrangements youve made.

VIVIE: Everything was settled twenty minutes after I arrived here. Honoria has found the business too much for her this year; and she was on the point of sending for me and proposing a partnership when I walked in and told her I hadnt a farthing in the world. So I installed myself and packed her off for a fortnight's holiday. What happened at Haslemere when I left?

FRANK: Nothing at all. I said youd gone to town on particular business.

VIVIE: Well?

FRANK: Well, either they were too flabbergasted to say anything, or else Crofts had prepared your mother. Anyhow, she didnt say anything; and Crofts didnt say anything; and Praddy only stared. After tea they got up and went; and Ive not seen them since.

VIVIE (*nodding placidly with one eye on a wreath of smoke*): Thats all right.

FRANK (*looking round disparagingly*): Do you intend to stick in this confounded place?

VIVIE (*blowing the wreath decisively away, and sitting straight up*): Yes. These two days have given me back all my strength and self-possession. I will never take a holiday again as long as I live.

FRANK (*with a very wry face*): Mps! You look quite happy. And as hard as nails.

VIVIE (*grimly*): Well for me that I am!

FRANK (*rising*): Look here, Viv: we must have an explanation. We parted the other day under a complete misunderstanding. (*He sits on the table, close to her.*)

VIVIE (*putting away the cigaret*): Well: clear it up.

FRANK: You remember what Crofts said?

VIVIE: Yes.

FRANK: That revelation was supposed to bring about a complete change in the nature of our feelings for one another. It placed us on the footing of brother and sister.

VIVIE: Yes.

FRANK: Have you ever had a brother?

VIVIE: No.

FRANK: Then you dont know what being brother and sister feels like? Now I have lots of sisters; and the fraternal feeling is quite familiar to me. I assure you my feeling for you is not the least in the world like it. The girls will go their way; I will go mine; and we shant care if we never see one another again. Thats brother and sister. But as to you, I cant be easy if I have to pass a week without seeing you. Thats not brother and sister. It's exactly what I felt an hour before Crofts made his revelation. In short, dear Viv, it's love's young dream.

VIVIE (*bitingly*): The same feeling, Frank, that brought your father to my mother's feet. Is that it?

FRANK (*so revolted that he slips off the table for a moment*): I very strongly object, Viv, to have my feelings compared to any which the Reverend Samuel is capable of harboring; and I object still more to a comparison of you to your mother. (*Resuming his perch.*) Besides, I dont believe the story. I have taxed my father with it, and obtained from him what I consider tantamount to a denial.

VIVIE: What did he say?

FRANK: He said he was sure there must be some mistake.

VIVIE: Do you believe him?

FRANK: I am prepared to take his word as against Crofts'.

VIVIE: Does it make any difference? I mean in your imagination or conscience; for of course it makes no real difference.

FRANK (*shaking his head*): None whatever to me.

VIVIE: Nor to me.

FRANK (*staring*): But this is ever so surprising! (*He goes back to his chair.*) I thought our whole relations were altered in your imagination and conscience, as you put it, the moment those words were out of that brute's muzzle.

VIVIE: No; it was not that. I didn't believe him. I only wish I could.

FRANK: Eh?

VIVIE: I dont think brother and sister would be a very suitable relation for us.

FRANK: You really mean that?

VIVIE: Yes. It's the only relation I care for, even if we could afford any other. I mean that.

FRANK (*raising his eyebrows like one on whom a new light has dawned, and rising with quite an effusion of chivalrous sentiment*): My dear Viv: why didnt you say so before? I am ever so sorry for persecuting you. I understand, of course.

VIVIE (*puzzled*): Understand what?

FRANK: Oh, I'm not a fool in the ordinary sense: only in the Scriptural sense of doing all the things the wise man declared to be folly, after trying them himself on the most extensive scale. I see I am no longer Vivvums's little boy. Dont be alarmed: I shall never call you Vivvums again — at least unless you get tired of your new little boy, whoever he may be.

VIVIE: My new little boy!

FRANK (*with conviction*): Must be a new little boy. Always happens that way. No other way, in fact.

VIVIE: None that you know of, fortunately for you.

(*Someone knocks at the door.*)

FRANK: My curse upon yon caller, whoe'er he be!

VIVIE: It's Praed. He's going to Italy and wants to say goodbye. I asked him to call this afternoon. Go and let him in.

FRANK: We can continue our conversation after his departure for Italy. I'll stay him out. (*He goes to the door and opens it.*) How are you, Praddy? Delighted to see you. Come in.

(PRAED, *dressed for travelling, comes in, in high spirits.*)

PRAED: How do you do, Miss Warren? (*She presses his hand cordially, though a certain sentimentality in his high spirits jars on her.*) I start in an hour from Holborn Viaduct. I wish I could persuade you to try Italy.

VIVIE: What for?

PRAED: Why, to saturate yourself with beauty and romance, of course.

(VIVIE *with a shudder, turns her chair to the table, as if the work waiting for her there were a support to her.* PRAED *sits opposite to her.* FRANK *places a chair near* VIVIE, *and drops lazily and carelessly into it, talking at her over his shoulder.*)

FRANK: No use, Praddy. Viv is a little Philistine. She is indifferent to my romance, and insensible to my beauty.

VIVIE: Mr. Praed: once and for all, there is no beauty and no romance in life for me. Life is what it is; and I am prepared to take it as it is.

PRAED (*enthusiastically*): You will not say that if you come with me to Verona and on to Venice. You will cry with delight at living in such a beautiful world.

FRANK: This is most eloquent, Praddy. Keep it up.

PRAED: Oh, I assure you *I* have cried — I shall cry again, I hope — at fifty! At your age, Miss Warren, you would not need to go so far as Verona. Your spirits would absolutely fly up at the mere sight of Ostend. You would be charmed with the gaiety, the vivacity, the happy air of Brussels.

VIVIE (*springing up with an exclamation of loathing*): Agh!

PRAED (*rising*): Whats the matter?

FRANK (*rising*): Hallo, Viv!

VIVIE (*to* PRAED, *with deep reproach*): Can you find no better example of your beauty and romance than Brussels to talk to me about?

PRAED (*puzzled*): Of course it's very different from Verona. I dont suggest for a moment that —

VIVIE (*bitterly*): Probably the beauty and romance comes to much the same in both places.

PRAED (*completely sobered and much concerned*): My Dear Miss Warren: I — (*looking enquiringly at* FRANK) Is anything the matter?

FRANK: She thinks your enthusiasm frivolous, Praddy. She's had ever such a serious call.

VIVIE (*sharply*): Hold your tongue, Frank. Dont be silly.

FRANK (*sitting down*): Do you call this good manners, Praed?

PRAED (*anxious and considerate*): Shall I take him away, Miss Warren? I feel sure we have disturbed you at your work.

VIVIE: Sit down: I'm not ready to go back to work yet. (PRAED *sits.*) You both think I have an attack of nerves. Not a bit of it. But there are two subjects I want dropped, if you dont mind. One of them (*to* FRANK) is love's young dream in any shape or form: the other (*to* PRAED) is the romance and beauty of life, especially Ostend and the gaiety of Brussels. You are welcome to any illusions you may have left on these subjects: I have none. If we three are to remain friends, I must be treated as a woman of business, permanently single (*to* FRANK) and permanently unromantic (*to* PRAED.)

FRANK: I shall also remain permanently single until you change your mind. Praddy: change the subject. Be eloquent about something else.

PRAED (*diffidently*): I'm afraid theres nothing else in the world that I can talk about. The Gospel of Art is the only one I can preach. I know Miss Warren is a great devotee of the Gospel of Getting On; but we cant discuss that without hurting your feelings, Frank, since you are determined not to get on.

FRANK: Oh, dont mind my feelings. Give me some improving advice by all means: it does me ever so much good. Have another try to make a successful man of me, Viv. Come: lets have it all: energy, thrift, foresight, self-respect, character. Dont you hate people who have no character, Viv?

VIVIE (*wincing*): Oh, stop, stop: let us have no more of that horrible cant. Mr. Praed: if there are really only those two gospels in the world, we had better all kill ourselves; for the same taint is in both, through and through.

FRANK (*looking critically at her*): There is a touch of poetry about you today, Viv, which has hitherto been lacking.

PRAED (*remonstrating*): My dear Frank: arnt you a little unsympathetic?

VIVIE (*merciless to herself*): No: it's good for me. It keeps me from being sentimental.

FRANK (*bantering her*): Checks your strong natural propensity that way, dont it?

VIVIE (*almost hysterically*): Oh yes: go on: dont spare me. I was sentimental for one moment in my life — beautifully sentimental — by moonlight; and now —

FRANK (*quickly*): I say, Viv: take care. Dont give yourself away.

VIVIE: Oh, do you think Mr. Praed does not know all about my mother? (*Turning on PRAED*) You had better have told me that morning, Mr. Praed. You are very old fashioned in your delicacies, after all.

PRAED: Surely it is you who are a little old fashioned in your prejudices, Miss Warren. I feel bound to tell you, speaking as an artist, and believing that the most intimate human relationships are far beyond and above the scope of the law, that though I know that your mother is an unmarried woman, I do not respect her the less on that account. I respect her more.

FRANK (*airily*): Hear! hear!

VIVIE (*staring at him*): Is that all you know?

PRAED: Certainly that is all.

VIVIE: Then you neither of you know anything. Your guesses are innocence itself compared to the truth.

PRAED (*rising, startled and indignant, and preserving his politeness with an effort*): I hope not. (*More emphatically*) I hope not, Miss Warren.

FRANK (*whistles*): Whew!

VIVIE: You are not making it easy for me to tell you, Mr. Praed.

PRAED (*his chivalry drooping before their conviction*): If there is anything worse — that is, anything else — are you sure you are right to tell us, Miss Warren?

VIVIE: I am sure that if I had the courage I should spend the rest of my life in telling everybody — stamping and branding it into them until they all felt their part in its abomination as I feel mine. There is nothing I despise more than the wicked convention that protects these things by forbidding a woman to mention them. And yet I cant tell you. The two infamous words that describe what my mother is are ringing in my ears and struggling on my tongue; but I cant utter them: the shame of them is too horrible for me. (*She buries her face in her hands. The two men, astonished, stare at one another and then at her. She raises her head again desperately and snatches a sheet of paper and a pen.*) Here: let me draft you a prospectus.

FRANK: Oh, she's mad. Do you hear, Viv? mad. Come! pull yourself together.

VIVIE: You shall see. (*She writes.*) "Paid up capital: not less than £40,000 standing in the name of Sir George Crofts, Baronet, the chief shareholder. Premises at Brussels, Ostend, Vienna and Budapest. Managing director: Mrs. Warren"; and now dont let us forget her qualifications: the two words. (*She writes the words and pushes the paper to them.*) There! Oh no: dont read it: dont! (*She snatches it back and tears it to pieces; then seizes her head in her hands and hides her face on the table.*)

(FRANK, *who has watched the writing over her shoulder, and opened his eyes very widely at it, takes a card from his pocket; scribbles the two words on it; and silently hands it to* PRAED, *who reads it with amazement, and hides it hastily in his pocket.*)

FRANK (*whispering tenderly*): Viv, dear: thats all right. I read what you wrote: so did Praddy. We understand. And we remain, as this leaves us at present, yours ever so devotedly.

PRAED: We do indeed, Miss Warren. I declare you are the most splendidly courageous woman I ever met.

(*This sentimental compliment braces* VIVIE. *She throws it away from her with an impatient shake, and forces herself to stand up, though not without some support from the table.*)

FRANK: Dont stir, Viv, if you dont want to. Take it easy.

VIVIE: Thank you. You can always depend on me for two things: not to cry and not to faint. (*She moves a few steps towards the door of the inner room, and stops close to* PRAED *to say*) I shall need much more courage than that when I tell my mother that we have come to the parting of the ways. Now I must go into the next room for a moment to make myself neat again, if you dont mind.

PRAED: Shall we go away?

VIVIE: No: I'll be back presently. Only for a moment. (*She goes into the other room,* PRAED *opening the door for her.*)

PRAED: What an amazing revelation! I'm extremely disappointed in Crofts: I am indeed.

FRANK: I'm not in the least. I feel he's perfectly accounted for at last. But what a facer for me, Praddy! I cant marry her now.

PRAED (*sternly*): Frank! (*The two look at one another,* FRANK *unruffled,* PRAED *deeply indignant.*) Let me tell you, Gardner, that if you desert her now you will behave very despicably.

FRANK: Good old Praddy! Ever chivalrous! But

you mistake: it's not the moral aspect of the case: it's the money aspect. I really cant bring myself to touch the old woman's money now.

PRAED: And was that what you were going to marry on?

FRANK: What else? *I* havnt any money, nor the smallest turn for making it. If I married Viv now she would have to support me; and I should cost her more than I am worth.

PRAED: But surely a clever bright fellow like you can make something by your own brains.

FRANK: Oh yes, a little. (*He takes out his money again.*) I made all that yesterday in an hour and a half. But I made it in a highly speculative business. No, dear Praddy: even if Bessie and Georgina marry millionaires and the governor dies after cutting them off with a shilling, I shall have only four hundred a year. And he wont die until he's three score and ten: he hasnt originality enough. I shall be on short allowance for the next twenty years. No short allowance for Viv, if I can help it. I withdraw gracefully and leave the field to the gilded youth of England. So thats settled. I shant worry about it: I'll just send her a little note after we're gone. She'll understand.

PRAED (*grasping his hand*): Good fellow, Frank! I heartily beg your pardon. But must you never see her again?

FRANK: Never see her again! Hang it all, be reasonable. I shall come along as often as possible, and be her brother. I can not understand the absurd consequences you romantic people expect from the most ordinary transactions. (*A knock at the door.*) I wonder who this is. Would you mind opening the door? If it's a client it will look more respectable than if I appeared.

PRAED: Certainly. (*He goes to the door and opens it.* FRANK *sits down in* VIVIE's *chair to scribble a note.*) My dear Kitty: come in: come in.

(MRS. WARREN *comes in, looking apprehen-*

sively round for VIVIE. *She has done her best to make herself matronly and dignified. The brilliant hat is replaced by a sober bonnet, and the gay blouse covered by a costly black silk mantle. She is pitiably anxious and ill at ease: evidently panic-stricken.*)

MRS. WARREN (*to* FRANK): What! Youre here, are you?

FRANK (*turning in his chair from his writing, but not rising*): Here, and charmed to see you. You come like a breath of spring.

MRS. WARREN: Oh, get out with your nonsense. (*In a low voice*) Wheres Vivie?

(FRANK *points expressively to the door of the inner room, but says nothing.*)

MRS. WARREN (*sitting down suddenly and almost beginning to cry*): Praddy: wont she see me, dont you think?

PRAED: My dear Kitty: dont distress yourself. Why should she not?

MRS. WARREN: Oh, you never can see why not: youre too innocent. Mr. Frank: did she say anything to you?

FRANK (*folding his note*): She must see you, if (*very expressively*) you wait til she comes in.

MRS. WARREN (*frightened*): Why shouldnt I wait?

(FRANK *looks quizzically at her; puts his note carefully on the ink-bottle, so that* VIVIE *cannot fail to find it when next she dips her pen; then rises and devotes his attention entirely to her.*)

FRANK: My dear Mrs. Warren: suppose you were a sparrow — ever so tiny and pretty a sparrow hopping in the roadway — and you saw a steam roller coming in your direction, would you wait for it?

MRS. WARREN: Oh, dont bother me with your sparrows. What did she run away from Haslemere like that for?

FRANK: I'm afraid she'll tell you if you rashly await her return.

MRS. WARREN: Do you want me to go away?

FRANK: No: I always want you to stay. But I advise you to go away.

MRS. WARREN: What! And never see her again!

FRANK: Precisely.

MRS. WARREN (*crying again*): Praddy: dont let him be cruel to me. (*She hastily checks her tears and wipes her eyes.*) She'll be so angry if she sees Ive been crying.

FRANK (*with a touch of real compassion in his airy tenderness*): You know that Praddy is the soul of kindness, Mrs. Warren. Praddy: what do you say? Go or stay?

PRAED (*to* MRS. WARREN): I really should be very sorry to cause you unnecessary pain; but I think perhaps you had better not wait. The fact is — (VIVIE *is heard at the inner door.*)

FRANK: Sh! Too late. She's coming.

MRS. WARREN: Dont tell her I was crying. (VIVIE *comes in. She stops gravely on seeing* MRS. WARREN, *who greets her with hysterical cheerfulness.*) Well, dearie. So here you are at last.

VIVIE: I'm glad you have come: I want to speak to you. You said you were going, Frank, I think.

FRANK: Yes. Will you come with me, Mrs. Warren? What do you say to a trip to Richmond, and the theatre in the evening? There is safety in Richmond. No steam roller there.

VIVIE: Nonsense, Frank. My mother will stay here.

MRS. WARREN (*scared*): I dont know: perhaps I'd better go. We're disturbing you at your work.

VIVIE (*with quiet decision*): Mr. Praed: please take Frank away. Sit down, mother. (MRS. WARREN *obeys helplessly.*)

PRAED: Come, Frank. Goodbye, Miss Vivie.

VIVIE (*shaking hands*): Goodbye. A pleasant trip.

PRAED: Thank you: thank you. I hope so.

FRANK (to MRS. WARREN): Goodbye: youd ever so much better have taken my advice. (*He shakes hands with her. Then airily to* VIVIE) Byebye, Viv.

VIVIE: Goodbye. (*He goes out gaily without shaking hands with her.*)

PRAED (*sadly*): Goodbye, Kitty.

MRS. WARREN (*snivelling*): — oobye!

(PRAED *goes.* VIVIE, *composed and extremely grave, sits down in Honoria's chair, and waits for her mother to speak.* MRS. WARREN, *dreading a pause, loses no time in beginning.*)

MRS. WARREN: Well, Vivie, what did you go away like that for without saying a word to me? How could you do such a thing! And what have you done to poor George? I wanted him to come with me; but he shuffled out of it. I could see that he was quite afraid of you. Only fancy: he wanted me not to come. As if (*trembling*) I should be afraid of you, dearie. (VIVIE's *gravity deepens.*) But of course I told him it was all settled and comfortable between us, and that we were on the best of terms. (*She breaks down.*) Vivie: whats the meaning of this? (*She produces a commercial envelope, and fumbles at the enclosure with trembling fingers.*) I got it from the bank this morning.

VIVIE: It is my month's allowance. They sent it to me as usual the other day. I simply sent it back to be placed to your credit, and asked them to send you the lodgment receipt. In future I shall support myself.

MRS. WARREN (*not daring to understand*): Wasnt it enough? Why didnt you tell me? (*With a cunning gleam in her eye*) I'll double it: I was intending to double it. Only let me know how much you want.

VIVIE: You know very well that that has nothing to do with it. From this time I go my own way in my own business and among my own friends. And you will go yours. (*She rises.*) Goodbye.

MRS. WARREN (*rising, appalled*): Goodbye?

VIVIE: Yes: goodbye. Come: dont let us make a useless scene: you understand perfectly well. Sir George Crofts has told me the whole business.

MRS. WARREN (*angrily*): Silly old — (*She swallows an epithet, and turns white at the narrowness of her escape from uttering it.*)

VIVIE: Just so.

MRS. WARREN: He ought to have his tongue cut out. But I thought it was ended: you said you didnt mind.

VIVIE (*steadfastly*): Excuse me: I do mind.

MRS. WARREN: But I explained —

VIVIE: You explained how it came about. You did not tell me that it is still going on. (*She sits.*)

(MRS. WARREN, *silenced for a moment, looks forlornly at* VIVIE, *who waits, secretly hoping that the combat is over. But the cunning expression comes back into* MRS. WARREN's *face; and she bends across the table, sly and urgent, half whispering.*)

MRS. WARREN: Vivie: do you know how rich I am?

VIVIE: I have no doubt you are very rich.

MRS. WARREN: But you dont know all that that means: youre too young. It means a new dress every day; it means theatres and balls every night; it means having the pick of all the gentlemen in Europe at your feet; it means a lovely house and plenty of servants; it means the choicest of eating and drinking; it means everything you like, everything you want, everything you can think of. And what are you here? A mere drudge, toiling and moiling early and late for your bare living and two cheap dresses a year. Think over it. (*Soothingly*) Youre shocked, I know. I can enter into your feelings; and I think they do you credit; but trust me, nobody will blame you: you may take my word for that. I know what young girls are; and I know youll think better of it when youve turned it over in your mind.

VIVIE: So that's how it's done, is it? You must

have said all that to many a woman, mother, to have it so pat.

MRS. WARREN (*passionately*): What harm am I asking you to do? (VIVIE *turns away contemptuously*. MRS. WARREN *continues desperately*) Vivie: listen to me: you dont understand: youve been taught wrong on purpose: you dont know what the world is really like.

VIVIE (*arrested*): Taught wrong on purpose! What do you mean?

MRS. WARREN: I mean that youre throwing away all your chances for nothing. You think that people are what they pretend to be: that the way you were taught at school and college to think right and proper is the way things really are. But it's not: it's all only a pretence, to keep the cowardly slavish common run of people quiet. Do you want to find that out, like other women, at forty, when youve thrown yourself away and lost your chances; or wont you take it in good time now from your own mother, that loves you and swears to you that it's truth: gospel truth? (*Urgently*) Vivie: the big people, the clever people, the managing people, all know it. They do as I do, and think what I think. I know plenty of them. I know them to speak to, to introduce you to, to make friends of for you. I dont mean anything wrong: thats what you dont understand: your head is full of ignorant ideas about me. What do the people that taught you know about life or about people like me? When did they ever meet me, or speak to me, or let anyone tell them about me? the fools! Would they ever have done anything for you if I hadnt paid them? Havnt I told you that I want you to be respectable? Havnt I brought you up to be respectable? And how can you keep it up without my money and my influence and Lizzie's friends? Cant you see that youre cutting your own throat as well as breaking my heart in turning your back on me?

VIVIE: I recognize the Crofts philosophy of life, mother. I heard it all from him that day at the Gardners'.

MRS. WARREN: You think I want to force that played-out old sot on you! I dont, Vivie: on my oath I dont.

VIVIE: It would not matter if you did: you would not succeed. (MRS. WARREN *winces, deeply hurt by the implied indifference towards her affectionate intention*. VIVIE, *neither understanding this nor concerning herself about it, goes on calmly*) Mother: you dont at all know the sort of person I am. I dont object to Crofts more than to any other coarsely built man of his class. To tell you the truth, I rather admire him for being strongminded enough to enjoy himself in his own way and make plenty of money instead of living the usual shooting, hunting, dining-out, tailoring, loafing life of his set merely because all the rest do it. And I'm perfectly aware that if I'd been in the same circumstances as my aunt Liz, I'd have done exactly what she did. I dont think I'm more prejudiced or straitlaced than you: I think I'm less. I'm certain I'm less sentimental. I know very well that fashionable morality is all a pretence, and that if I took your money and devoted the rest of my life to spending it fashionably, I might be as worthless and vicious as the silliest woman could possibly want to be without having a word said to me about it. But I dont want to be worthless. I shouldnt enjoy trotting about the park to advertize my dressmaker and carriage builder, or being bored at the opera to shew off a shopwindowful of diamonds.

MRS. WARREN (*bewildered*): But —

VIVIE: Wait a moment: Ive not done. Tell me why you continue your business now that you are independent of it. Your sister, you told me, has left all that behind her. Why dont you do the same?

MRS. WARREN: Oh, it's all very easy for Liz: she likes good society, and has the air of being a lady. Imagine me in a cathedral town! Why, the very rooks in the trees would find me out even if I could stand the dulness of it. I must have work and excitement, or I should go melancholy mad. And what else is there for me to do? The life suits me: I'm fit for it and not for anything else. If I didn't do it somebody else would;

so I dont do any real harm by it. And then it brings in money; and I like making money. No: it's no use: I cant give it up — not for anybody. But what need you know about it? I'll never mention it. I'll keep Crofts away. I'll not trouble you much: you see I have to be constantly running about from one place to another. Youll be quit of me altogether when I die.

VIVIE: No: I am my mother's daughter. I am like you: I must have work, and must make more money than I spend. But my work is not your work, and my way not your way. We must part. It will not make much difference to us: instead of meeting one another for perhaps a few months in twenty years, we shall never meet: thats all.

MRS. WARREN (*her voice stifled in tears*): Vivie: I meant to have been more with you: I did indeed.

VIVIE: It's no use, mother: I am not to be changed by a few cheap tears and entreaties any more than you are, I daresay.

MRS. WARREN (*wildly*): Oh, you call a mother's tears cheap.

VIVIE: They cost you nothing; and you ask me to give you the peace and quietness of my whole life in exchange for them. What use would my company be to you if you could get it? What have we two in common that could make either of us happy together?

MRS. WARREN (*lapsing recklessly into her dialect*): We're mother and daughter. I want my daughter. I've a right to you. Who is to care for me when I'm old? Plenty of girls have taken to me like daughters and cried at leaving me; but I let them all go because I had you to look forward to. I kept myself lonely for you. Youve no right to turn on me now and refuse to do your duty as a daughter.

VIVIE (*jarred and antagonized by the echo of the slums in her mother's voice*): My duty as a daughter! I thought we should come to that presently. Now once for all, mother, you want a daughter and Frank wants a wife. I dont want a mother; and I dont want a husband. I have spared neither Frank nor myself in sending him about his business. Do you think I will spare you?

MRS. WARREN (*violently*): Oh, I know the sort you are: no mercy for yourself or anyone else. *I* know. My experience has done that for me anyhow: I can tell the pious, canting, hard, selfish woman when I meet her. Well, keep yourself to yourself: *I* dont want you. But listen to this. Do you know what I would do with you if you were a baby again? aye, as sure as there's a Heaven above us.

VIVIE: Strangle me, perhaps.

MRS. WARREN: No: I'd bring you up to be a real daughter to me, and not what you are now, with your pride and your prejudices and the college education you stole from me: yes, stole: deny it if you can: what was it but stealing? I'd bring you up in my own house, I would.

VIVIE (*quietly*): In one of your own houses.

MRS. WARREN (*screaming*): Listen to her! listen to how she spits on her mother's grey hairs! Oh, may you live to have your own daughter tear and trample on you as you have trampled on me. And you will: you will. No woman ever had luck with a mother's curse on her.

VIVIE: I wish you wouldn't rant, mother. It only hardens me. Come: I suppose I am the only young woman you ever had in your power that you did good to. Dont spoil it all now.

MRS. WARREN: Yes, Heaven forgive me, it's true; and you are the only one that ever turned on me. Oh, the injustice of it! the injustice! the injustice! I always wanted to be a good woman. I tried honest work; and I was slave-driven until I cursed the day I ever heard of honest work. I was a good mother; and because I made my daughter a good woman she turns me out as if I was a leper. Oh, if I only had my life to live over again! I'd talk to that lying clergyman in the school. From this time forth, so help me Heaven in my last hour, I'll do wrong and nothing but wrong. And I'll prosper on it.

VIVIE: Yes, it's better to choose your line and go through with it. If I had been you, mother, I might have done as you did; but I should not have lived one life and believed in another. You are a conventional woman at heart. That is why I am bidding you goodbye now. I am right, am I not?

MRS. WARREN (*taken aback*): Right to throw away all my money!

VIVIE: No: right to get rid of you? I should be a fool not to? Isnt that so?

MRS. WARREN (*sulkily*): Oh well, yes, if you come to that, I suppose you are. But Lord help the world if everybody took to doing the right thing! And now I'd better go than stay where I'm not wanted. (*She turns to the door.*)

VIVIE (*kindly*): Wont you shake hands?

MRS. WARREN (*after looking at her fiercely for a moment with a savage impulse to strike her*): No, thank you. Goodbye.

VIVIE (*matter-of-factly*): Goodbye. (MRS. WARREN *goes out, slamming the door behind her. The strain on* VIVIE's *face relaxes; her grave expression breaks up into one of joyous content; her breath goes out in a half sob, half laugh of intense relief. She goes buoyantly to her place at the writing-table; pushes the electric lamp out of the way; pulls over a great sheaf of paper; and is in the act of dipping her pen in the ink when she finds* FRANK's *note. She opens it unconcernedly and reads it quickly, giving a little laugh at some quaint turn of expression in it.*) And goodbye, Frank. (*She tears the note up and tosses the pieces into the wastepaper basket without a second thought. Then she goes at her work with a plunge, and soon becomes absorbed in its figures.*)

Ubu the King

Alfred Jarry (1873–1907) in his grotesque and violent farce of *Ubu Roi*, which was first presented as a *guignolade* or puppet play (1888) and premièred at the Théâtre de l'Œuvre (1896), broke with the heroic traditions of the romantic theatre and the newer realistic and naturalistic movements to lay the foundations of the modern Theatre of the Absurd.

Under Lugné-Poë, whose assistant Jarry was, the Théâtre de l'Œuvre strove to make the spectator feel that "not only his spirit but his senses are at stake." Its manifesto declared:

> He will go henceforth to the theatre as he goes to the dentist or the surgeon. In the same state of mind, with the thought that he will evidently not die of it, but that it is a serious matter, and he will not come out of it intact.

After the first night of *Ubu Roi*, a "serious matter" which led to a riot — a friend told William Butler Yeats, who was in the audience, "There are often duels after these performances" — the French theatre was never quite the same. In *Modern French Theatre* (1964), Michael Benedikt and George E. Wellwarth have put together a whole anthology to show the influence of Jarry on the *avant-garde* theatre since *Ubu Roi* and on the work of such well-known later writers as Guillaume Apollinaire [Wilhelm de Kostrowitzky], Jean Cocteau, Raymond Radiguet, Tristan Tzara, André Breton, Louis Aragon, Antonin Artaud, Roger Vitrac, Jean Anouilh, Eugène Ionesco, and others. They write:

> When Alfred Jarry wrote *King Ubu,* first performed in 1896, he effected what in literature amounts to a miraculous event. With no immediate literary antecedents, he created a genre of drama in which many of the most advanced poets and dramatists of his country — and many of the most talented — have worked; a genre which, indeed, has achieved a prominence today that Jarry himself could hardly have imagined.

The play that did this was originally a schoolboy skit, written when Jarry was at the *lycée* in Rennes to caricature his physics teacher, one M. Hébert, whom the boys nicknamed Hébé. Called *Les Polonais*, it was put on as a puppet show in the attic of his chums Charles and Henri Morin and only later "restored" and augmented to make *Ubu Roi*. Though other Ubu plays followed, such as *Ubu Enchaîné and Ubu Cocu* (collected by Maurice Saillet

583

as *Tout Ubu*, 1962), and the works of Jarry were eventually collected in eight volumes (*Œuvres complètes*, 1948), *Ubu Roi* remained his masterpiece and his great contribution to the modern theatre. Roger Shattuck in his history of the period (*The Banquet Years*, 1960) and Martin Esslin in *The Theatre of the Absurd* (1962) rightly describe it as a milestone.

On opening night, even its scenery and other production details baffled or enraged the audience. Working for "a sure comic effect," Jarry put a mask and an enormous paunch on his King Ubu and hung a cardboard horse's head around his neck to represent him on horseback. He gave him a special and very unreal voice to speak in and both petulant babytalk and pompous rhetoric to spout. He opened his play with "Merdre" (which we have rendered as "schit" in translation) and from the beginning shocked and stunned his audience with a burlesque of the theatre they knew and understood, all the while damning the bourgeois morality and mercantile ethic in which they believed. One man played "The Whole Polish Army," and, as for the staging, Arthur Symons in *Studies in Seven Arts* (1906) recorded:

> The scenery was painted to represent, by a child's convention, indoors and out of doors, and even the torrid, temperate, and arctic zones at once. Opposite to you, at the back of the stage, you saw apple trees in bloom, under a blue sky, and against the sky a small closed window and a fireplace . . . through the very midst of which trooped in and out these clamorous and sanguinary persons of the drama. On the left was painted a bed, and at the foot of the bed a bare tree, and snow falling. On the right were palm trees, about one of which coiled a boa constrictor; a door opened against the sky, and beside the door a skeleton dangled from a gallows. Changes of scene were announced by the simple Elizabethan method of a placard. . . . A venerable gentleman in evening dress . . . trotted across the stage on the points of his toes between every scene and hung the new placard on its nail.

One can see from this description that Jarry has formed the roots of many of the important movements in modern art, including the absurdists, the Dadaists, and the surrealists. In the play itself, the student of modern drama may find much more that was invented by that strange and debauched man Jarry who lived in an attic with owls and drank himself to death at an early age before he ever realized what an immense effect he was to have on modern art as well as modern theatre. To list them in more or less random order, you might consider such devices of *Ubu Roi* as these: the attack on capitalist avarice and cowardice; the burlesque of the romantic and the operatic; the use of the mask and other elements of the expressionist theatre; the use of modern dress (to create "relevance") with symbolic or fantastic costume; the revival of the poetic "open stage" and other devices of the Elizabethan theatre; the traces of the *guignol* (puppet theatre) and the *commedia dell'arte*, not to mention the *Grand Guignol* (horror theatre) and the comedy of Aristophanes; the anti-hero, Jarry's crass and craven "*être ignoble*" Ubu himself; the influence of the Shakespearian panoramic and episodic drama, and even of Ibsen's *Peer Gynt*; the deliberate and even self-indulgent irrationality which some people now equate with the *avant-garde*'s very nature; the black comedy and the tragedy in farce; the satire that goes beyond excoriating the object to a world so fantastic that, in the words of Apollinaire, it is "so high that Poetry itself can hardly keep up with it"; the merging of the play with a message (the old thesis play) with the new symbolist play to create what Cocteau said was related to realism but beyond it — what Apollinaire coined the word *surrealist* to describe; the artificiality of casting, costuming, acting, with the actor as *Übermarionette*; the collapsing of language (as in Beckett and Ionesco) as it is racked to make it confess the truth; the use of bits of Shakespeare (*Macbeth, Lear, Julius Caesar, Hamlet*, etc.) and other playwrights as *objets trouvés* (ready-made bits) for combination into strange new constructions; the inspired madness, reminiscent of Tzara's nihilistic Dada movement in art and of Marcel Duchamps and other artists right up to Claes Oldenburg; the sense of improvisation that we like so much in modern "happenings"; the nightmare quality we have come to know so well in the works of Kafka and others and the sense that the unconscious has been tapped to create a "real dream"; the aggression (*schit, the unmentionable brush*, and the rest) now called The Theatre of Cruelty; the stage as circus, as in Meyerhold and Peter Weiss' *Marat/Sade*; the cerebral subtlety and dynamism of Marinetti's Theatre of Variety; the "alienation effect," even the placards of Brecht's Epic Theatre; the sense that "men and objects play together" as in Barrault's Total Theatre; the logic beyond logic of Ionesco's *The Bald Soprano* and the manipulation of language as in *The Lesson*, a mad Marx Brothers jumble that recalls the favorite joke of e. e. cummings: "Would you hit a woman with a baby?", "No, I'd hit her with a brick"; an attack on things as they are, as in Adamov's *Le Ping-Pong* and an attack on theatre itself by anti-theatre, as in Artaud's Théâtre Alfred Jarry, founded "to contribute by strictly theatrical means to the ruin of the theatre as it exists today"; the profundity of Beckett in *Waiting for Godot* and the fooling around (is it foolishness or not?) of André Breton and Philippe Soupault in *S'il vous plaît,* in which the third act is followed by "a long intermission" and then the note "The authors of *S'il vous plaît,* do not want the fourth act printed." Indeed, when you think about it, you can relate Jarry's work to the vaudeville of Brendan Behan's *The Hostage* and the bleak world of Harold Pinter, Jarry's nonsensically verbal Poles to the grim, grunting Poles of Grotowsky. The riot that greeted *Ubu Roi*, like the riot that greeted Stravinsky's *Le Sacre du Printemps* (1913), was epoch-making, and the effects are still with us, as new as the latest "experimental" play off Broadway (in the tradition of Jean-Claude van Itallie's *America Hurrah*! or even modern composer John Cage), as lasting as the combination of cruelty and mirth in Punch and Judy.

In a world of *Angst*, Alienation, and Atomic Warfare, there probably is even a message in Father Ubu, whom the perceptive critic Cyril Connolly once called "the Santa Claus of the Atomic Age." Jarry certainly is at least as inventive as Dadaist Tristan Tzara (whose play *The Gas Heart* has the characters Eye, Mouth, Nose, Ear, Neck, and Eyebrow) and probably more serious (Tzara called another of his plays "the greatest swindle of the century in three acts"), even if he was, as Roger Shattuck suggested in *Selected Works of Alfred Jarry* (1965), "writing over everyone's head, including his own." Behind all the *play*, there is a real concern with what it has become fashionable now to call "the absurdity of the human condition." Jarry would agree with Adamov's insistence that the theatre must show "both the curable and incurable aspect of things. The incurable aspect, as we all know, is that of the inevitability of death. The curable aspect is the social one." Although Jarry in his Pataphysics devised a "science of imaginary solutions" and mocked rationality, he may possibly be giving us more than schoolboy slang and trenchant satire in *Ubu Roi*. Many think that in this play he laid some of the foundations for the modern theatre called for by the Nobel Prize winner Pablo Neruda, "a theatre that is simple without being simplistic, critical but not inhuman, advancing like a river of the Andes whose only limits are those it itself imposes."

UBU THE KING

A Drama in Five Acts
in prose
Restored in its entirety
as it was played
by the marionettes of
The Théâtre des Phynances
in 1888

Alfred Jarry

Translated from the French by
Margaret Ganz and L. R. N. Ashley

Dedicated to MARCEL SCHWOB

Thereatte FATHER UBU *shooke hys peare-shapt heade, wherefore by the Englysshe he was since yclept* SHAKESPEARE, *and from hym ye hath hadde vnder that name diuers goodlie tragœdies in hys owne hande.*

COMPOSITION OF THE ORCHESTRA

OBOES

PIPES

BRATWURST

DOUBLE BASS

FLAGEOLETS   TRANSVERSE FLUTES

LARGE FLUTE

SMALL BASSOON   DOUBLE BASSOON

TRIPLE BASSOON   SMALL BLACK CORNETS

SHRILL WHITE CORNETS

HORNS   SACKBUTS   TROMBONES

GREEN IVORY HUNTING HORNS   TABOR PIPES

BAGPIPES

BOMBARDS   TIMPANI

DRUM   BASS DRUM

GRAND ORGANS

DRAMATIS PERSONÆ

FATHER UBU
MOTHER UBU

Captain OR d'URE
WENCESLAS, *King of Poland*
ROSAMONDE, *Queen of Poland*
BOLESLAS ⎫
LADISLAS ⎬ *sons to the King*
BUGGERLAS ⎭
General LASKI
STANISLAS LECZINSKI
JOHN SOBIESKI
NICHOLAS RENSKY
ALEXIS, *Czar of Russia*
BOOZUMPALADIN ⎫
GUILDENCRANZ ⎬ *ubulings*
ROSENSTERN ⎭
CONSPIRATORS *and* SOLDIERS
PEOPLE
MICHAEL FEDEROVITCH
NOBLES
JUDGES
SHADES OF THE ANCESTORS OF THE ROYAL HOUSE
OF POLAND
COUNSELLORS TO THE KING
FINANCIERS
PHYNANCIAL PHLUNKIES
PEASANTRY
THE WHOLE RUSSIAN ARMY
THE WHOLE POLISH ARMY
THE QUEEN'S GUARDS
A RUSSIAN SOLDIER
A CAPTAIN
A BEAR
A PHYNANCIAL HORSE
A DEBRAINING DEVICE
THE CREW OF A SHIP
THE SEA CAPTAIN

INVENTORY OF COSTUMES FOR
*UBU THE KING**

FATHER UBU Suit with iron-grey vest, always a cane stuck in the right-hand pocket, derby. Crown on top of his hat, from scene ii of Act II. Bareheaded from the beginning of scene vi, Act II. Scene ii, Act III, crown and white cape in the shape of a royal mantle. Scene iv, Act III large cape, traveling cap with ear-flaps, same costume but bareheaded in scene vii. Scene viii, cape, helmet, a sabre at the belt, a hook, scissors, a knife, still the cane in the right-hand pocket. A bottle bumping against his rump. Scene v, Act IV, cape and cap without weapons or baton. A suitcase in his hand in the shipboard scene.

MOTHER UBU Costume of concierge and wash-room attendant. Pink bonnet or hat with flowers and feathers, at her side a shopping bag of cloth or netting. An apron in the banquet scene. Royal mantle from the beginning of scene vi, Act II.

Captain OR d'URE Costume of Hungarian musician, skin-tight, red. Greatcoat, big sword, jackboots, chapska [hat].

KING WENCESLAS The royal mantle and crown which UBU will wear after the KING's murder.

QUEEN ROSAMONDE The mantle and crown that MOTHER UBU will wear.

BOLESLAS, LADISLAS Grey Polish costumes with frogs, short trousers.

BUGGERLAS Dressed as a baby in a little skirt and bonnet with [*two words effaced*].

General LASKI Polish costume, with a cocked hat with white feathers and a sword.

STANISLAS LECZINSKI In Polish costume. White beard.

JOHN SOBIESKI, N[ICHOLAS] RENSKY In Polish costume.

CZAR (*or* EMPEROR) ALEXIS Black costume, big yellow sash, dagger and decorations, big boots. Terrific beard encircling face. Head-gear [*word crossed out*: pointed] in the form of a black cone.

THE UBULINGS Very bearded, lined cloaks color of schit; in green or red as a last resort; tights.

ROSENSTERN [*word crossed out*: Tights.]

PEOPLE In Polish costume.

M[ICHAEL] FEDEROVITCH The same. Fur hat instead of the chapska.

NOBLES In Polish costume, with fur-bordered and embroidered cloaks.

JUDGES Black robes, toques. [French judges wear a peculiar flat-topped round hat.]

COUNSELLORS, FINANCIERS Black robes, astro-logers' hats [conical], glasses, pointed noses.

PHYNANCIAL PHLUNKIES The UBULINGS.

PEASANTS In Polish costume.

THE POLISH ARMY In grey with furs and frogs. At least three men with guns.

THE RUSSIAN ARMY Two horsemen: costume resembling that of the Poles, but green with fur hat. Horses' heads of cardboard.

A RUSSIAN INFANTRYMAN In green, with a cap.

THE GUARDS *of* MOTHER UBU In Polish costume, with halberds.

A CAPTAIN. GENERAL LASKI.

THE BEAR. OR d'URE in a bear skin.

THE PHYNANCIAL HORSE Wooden horse on wheels or cardboard horse's head, according to the particular scene.

THE CREW Two men in sailors' costumes, in blue, with a sailor's collar, etc.

---

* *Inventory:* These notes by Jarry were published from a manuscript by J. H. Sainment in the "notebooks of the College of Pataphysics," nos. 3–4 (22 HaHa 78 E.P.). Consider what they add to the tone of the play and how they further carry out Jarry's intentions for *Ubu the King.* What would be lost by presenting the play in "serious" costumes or modern dress? How are some of Jarry's ideas echoed in modern experimental plays you know?

THE SEA CAPTAIN   In costume of an officer of the French navy.

ACT ONE

SCENE ONE   Father Ubu, Mother Ubu.

FATHER UBU: Schit!

MOTHER UBU: That's a fine way to talk, Father Ubu. What a great big scoundrel you are!

FATHER UBU: Wouldn't I like to clobber you, Mother Ubu!

MOTHER UBU: It's not me, Father Ubu, but someone else who ought to be assassinated.

FATHER UBU: By my candle of green, I don't understand.

MOTHER UBU: What, Father Ubu, are you satisfied with your lot?

FATHER UBU: By my candle of green, schit, Madam, indeed yes, I am content. Even less would do: captain of dragoons, aide de camp to King Wenceslas, decorated with the Order of the Red Eagle of Poland, and former King of Aragon — what more do you want?

MOTHER UBU: What! After being King of Aragon, you are satisfied to lead in review a measly fifty followers with cabbage slicers when on your noggin the crown of Poland might succeed that of Aragon?

FATHER UBU: But, Mother Ubu, I don't understand anything you are saying.

MOTHER UBU: You are so dense.

FATHER UBU: By my candle of green, King Wenceslas is still very much alive, and even if he goes, doesn't he leave legions of children behind?

MOTHER UBU: What's to keep you from butchering the whole family and taking over?

FATHER UBU: Really, Mother Ubu, you do me wrong and I'm going to cook your goose.

MOTHER UBU: You poor wretch, if you cook my goose who will sew the seat of your pants?

FATHER UBU: Really? So what? Have I not an ass like other men?

MOTHER UBU: If I were you, I should firmly deposit that ass upon a throne. You could multiply riches indefinitely, munch sausages quite often, and ride in triumph through the streets in your state coach.

FATHER UBU: If I were king, I could have a flowing cape tailored for myself, like the one I had in Aragon and which those damned Spaniards had the impudence to filch from me.

MOTHER UBU: You might also get yourself an umbrella and a fine overcoat down to your heels.

FATHER UBU: Ah! To temptation I yield. A cartload of schit, a schitload of cart, if I ever meet him in a dark neck of the woods he's in for a bad time.

MOTHER UBU: Well said, Father Ubu. At last you dare do all that doth become a man.

FATHER UBU: Oh, no! Me, a captain of dragoons, massacre the King of Poland! I'd rather die!

MOTHER UBU (aside): Oh, schit! (aloud) Then you are going to stay as poor as a churchmouse, Father Ubu?

FATHER UBU: 'Odsblood, by my candle of green, better to be poor like a noble, skinny mouse than rich like a mean fat cat.

MOTHER UBU: And the cape? the umbrella? the big overcoat?

FATHER UBU: What about it, Mother Ubu?

(Exit, slamming the door.)

MOTHER UBU (alone): Crap, schit, he was hard to move, but crap, schit, I think I've got him going. Thanks to God (and Yours Truly) maybe next week I shall be Queen of Poland.

SCENE TWO   The scene represents a room in the house of Father Ubu where a dining table is splendidly set. Father Ubu, Mother Ubu.

MOTHER UBU: Our guests are very late.

FATHER UBU: Yes, by my candle of green, I'm starving. You're very ugly today, Mother Ubu. Is it because we are having company?

MOTHER UBU (*shrugging her shoulders*): Schit!

FATHER UBU (*seizing a roast chicken*): I'm famished. I'm going to bite into this bird. It's a chicken, I think. Not bad.

MOTHER UBU: What are you up to, you wretch? What will our guests eat?

FATHER UBU: There'll still be quite enough for them. I won't touch another thing. Mother Ubu, go look out the window and see if our guests are coming.

MOTHER UBU (*going*): I don't see anything.

(*Meanwhile* FATHER UBU *snatches a roast of veal.*)

MOTHER UBU: Ah, here come Captain Or d'Ure and his men. What are you eating, Father Ubu?

FATHER UBU: Nothing, a little veal.

MOTHER UBU: Oh, the veal, the veal! He's eaten the veal! Help!

FATHER UBU: By my candle of green, I'll tear your eyes out!

(*The door opens.*)

SCENE THREE   Father Ubu, Mother Ubu, Captain Or d'Ure and his Followers.

MOTHER UBU: Good day, gentlemen, we've been awaiting you impatiently. Be seated.

OR d'URE: Good day, Madam. But where is Father Ubu?

FATHER UBU: Here I am, here! Egad, by my candle of green, I'm certainly fat enough to be visible.

OR d'URE: Good day, Father Ubu. Sit down, men.

(*They all sit.*)

FATHER UBU: Ouch! A little more and I'd have gone through my chair.

OR d'URE: Well, Mother Ubu, what goodies have you got for us today?

MOTHER UBU: Here's the menu.

FATHER UBU: Well, this interests me.

MOTHER UBU: Polish soup, side of bison, veal, chicken, paté de dog, turkey tails, *charlotte russian. . . .*

FATHER UBU: Well, that's plenty, I guess. Anything else?

MOTHER UBU (*continuing*): *Bombe surprise,* salad, fruit, boiled beef, articroaks, cauliflowers à la crap, and crap *suzette.*

FATHER UBU: What? Do you think I'm the Emperor of China to spend that much money?

MOTHER UBU: Don't listen to him, he's an idiot.

FATHER UBU: I'm going to sharpen my fangs on your flanks.

MOTHER UBU: Eat instead, Father Ubu. Have some Polish soup.

FATHER UBU: Crap, that's awful!

OR d'URE: It does leave something to be desired.

MOTHER UBU: What do you want, you conniving crew?

FATHER UBU (*striking his forehead*): Oh, I have an idea! I'll be back soon.

(*Exit.*)

MOTHER UBU: Gentlemen, let's try the veal.

OR d'URE: It's very good, but I'm finished.

MOTHER UBU: Now on to the turkey rumps.

OR d'URE: Exquisite, exquisite. Long live Mother Ubu!

ALL: Long live Mother Ubu!

FATHER UBU (*returning*): And you'll soon shout all hail Father Ubu.

(*He holds an unmentionable* [toilet] *brush in his hand and throws it on the food.*)

MOTHER UBU: Villain, what you doing?

FATHER UBU: Try a little of that!

(*Several taste and fall down poisoned.*)

FATHER UBU: Mother Ubu, pass me the ram chops so that I can serve them.

MOTHER UBU: Here they are.

FATHER UBU: Stand not upon the order of your going — get out. Captain Or d'Ure, I must have a word with you.

THE OTHERS: We haven't eaten yet!

FATHER UBU: What do you mean you haven't eaten yet? Everybody clear out. Or d'Ure, you stay.

(*No one budges.*)

FATHER UBU: You have not left. By my candle of green, I'll clobber you with bison chops.

(*He begins to throw some.*)

ALL: Oh! Ouch! Help! Let's make a stand. Woe is me, I'm done for!

FATHER UBU: Schit, schit, and schit! Out — of — here! I believe I am making myself clear.

ALL: Every man for himself. Wretched Father Ubu! Traitor and cheapskate scoundrel!

(OR d'URE's *men flee.*)

FATHER UBU: Well, they've gone. I breathe once again — but I must say that I have dined rather badly. Come on, Or d'Ure.

(*Exeunt with* MOTHER UBU.)

SCENE FOUR   Father Ubu, Mother Ubu, Captain Or d'Ure.

FATHER UBU: Well, Captain, did you enjoy your dinner?

OR d'URE: It was awfully good, sir, except for the schit.

FATHER UBU: Oh, I don't know, it really wasn't too bad, that schit.

MOTHER UBU: *Chacun à son gout.*

FATHER UBU: Captain Or d'Ure, I have decided to create you duke of Lithuania.

OR d'URE: Oh, really? I thought you were flat broke, Father Ubu.

FATHER UBU: In a few days, if you consent, I shall reign in Poland.

OR d'URE: You're going to kill Wenceslas?

FATHER UBU: He's not so dumb, the bugger. He guessed.

OR d'URE: If it's a question of killing Wenceslas, count me in. I am his mortal enemy.

FATHER UBU (*thrusting himself on him for an embrace*): Oh, oh! You know, I *like* you, Or d'Ure.

OR d'URE: Hey, you stink, Father Ubu. Don't you ever wash?

FATHER UBU: Only on very rare occasions.

MOTHER UBU: Never.

FATHER UBU: I am going to step on your feet.

MOTHER UBU: Fat schit.

FATHER UBU: Leave us, Or d'Ure. That's it for now. But, by my candle of green, I swear by Mother Ubu to make you duke of Lithuania.

MOTHER UBU: But . . .

FATHER UBU: Shut up, my gentle child . . . .

SCENE FIVE   Father Ubu, Mother Ubu, a Messenger.

FATHER UBU: What do you want, sir? Piss off, I weary of you.

MESSENGER: Sir, you are summoned by the King.

(*Exit.*)

FATHER UBU: Oh, schit! Goldarnit, by my candle of green, I am found out, my head has had it! Alas, alack!

MOTHER UBU: What a lily-livered loon! and time is running out.

FATHER UBU: Ah, I've got it! I'll say it's Mother Ubu and Or d'Ure.

MOTHER UBU: Oh, you booby, Ubu, if you do that . . .

FATHER UBU: I'm going to do it this very minute.

(*Exit.*)

MOTHER UBU (*running after him*): Oh, Father Ubu, Father Ubu, come back, I'll give you some meat.

FATHER UBU (*offstage*): Oh, schit! You're some meathead you are, alright. You certainly are.

SCENE SIX   The palace. King Wenceslas, attended by his Officers; Or d'Ure; the King's sons: Boleslas, Ladislas, and Buggerlas. Then Ubu.

FATHER UBU (*entering*): Hey, listen, it's not me, it's Mother Ubu, you know, it's Mother Ubu and Or d'Ure.

WENCESLAS: What's the matter with you, Father Ubu?

OR d'URE: He's drunk.

WENCESLAS: Like me this morning.

FATHER UBU: Yes, I am drunk, it's because I've drunk too much French wine.

WENCESLAS: We wish to reward your many services as captain of dragoons, and therefore today we create you Earl of Sandomir.

FATHER UBU: Oh, Mr. Wenceslas, I don't know how to thank you.

WENCESLAS: Don't thank me, Father Ubu, and be present tomorrow morning at the grand review.

FATHER UBU: I'll be there, but meanwhile do me the honor of accepting this party favor.

(*He presents the King with a toy that whistles and unrolls when one blows into it.*)

WENCESLAS: What do you want me, at my age, to do with that? I'll give it to Buggerlas.

BUGGERLAS: He's so dumb, that Father Ubu!

FATHER UBU: And now I'm getting the hell out. (*He falls as he turns around.*) Oh, ow, help! By my candle of green, I've ruptured my gut and busted my — bowels!

WENCESLAS (*lifting him up*): You have not, perchance, done yourself some injury, have you, Father Ubu?

FATHER UBU: Indeed I have, and I'm going to croak, sure as hell. What will become of Mother Ubu?

WENCESLAS: We ourselves shall provide for her upkeep.

FATHER UBU: You are kindness itself. (*As he leaves*) Yes, but King Wenceslas, you will nonetheless be wiped out for all that.

SCENE SEVEN   Ubu's House. Boozumpaladin, Guildencranz, Rosenstern, Father Ubu, Mother Ubu, Conspirators and Soldiers, Or d'Ure.

FATHER UBU: My good friends, the time has come to settle the plan of the conspiracy. Let each man speak his mind. If you don't mind, I'll give my opinion first.

OR d'URE: Speak up, Father Ubu.

FATHER UBU: Well, my friends, I am for neatly poisoning the King by stuffing arsenic in his breakfast. When munchtime comes, he'll drop dead — and I'll be King.

ALL: Fie, what a pig!

FATHER UBU: What? The plan does not meet with your unqualified approval? Let Or d'Ure give his opinion then.

OR d'URE: I'm for giving a good swift swipe with my sword that will split him from brain to belt buckle.

ALL: Now there's a noble and valiant scheme!

FATHER UBU: And what if he kicks you? It occurs to me now that he wears iron shoes for military review that really hurt. If I could, I would run to denounce you to get myself out of this dirty business, and methinks I might even pick up a tidy bit of change out of it.

MOTHER UBU: Oh! that traitor, that coward, that villainous coarse skinflint.

ALL: Hoot him down!

FATHER UBU: Calm down, gentlemen, if you don't want me to get the lot of you. Well, I agree to risk my own skin for all of you. So then, Or d'Ure, you'll be responsible for cleaving the King in twain.

OR d'URE: Wouldn't it be better if all of us three throw ourselves on him howling and screaming? We'd have a better chance of winning over the troops.

FATHER UBU: That settles it. I'll try to step on his toes, he will demur, then I'll say *SCHIT* to him, and at that signal you'll throw yourselves upon him.

MOTHER UBU: Yes, and as soon as he is dead you will take his scepter and his crown.

OR d'URE: And I and my men will set off in pursuit of the royal family.

FATHER UBU: Right. And I commend young Buggerlas to your special attention.

(*Exeunt.*)

FATHER UBU (*running after them and getting them to return*): Gentlemen we have forgotten an indispensible ceremony: we must swear to conduct ourselves with valor.

OR d'URE: How are we to manage that? We lack a priest.

FATHER UBU: Mother Ubu will officiate.

ALL: So be it!

FATHER UBU: And so you all swear to kill the King?

ALL: We swear! Long live Father Ubu!

(*Exeunt.*)

ACT TWO

SCENE ONE   The palace. Wenceslas, Queen Rosamonde, Boleslas, Ladislas, Buggerlas.

WENCESLAS: Master Buggerlas, you were strongly impertinent this morning to my lord Ubu, knight of my Orders and Earl of Sandomir. Wherefore I forbid you to appear at my review.

ROSAMONDE: And yet, Wenceslas, your whole family is needed to protect you there.

WENCESLAS: Madam, I choose never to alter my pronouncements. You weary me with your nonsensical chatter.

BUGGERLAS: I submit, dear father.

ROSAMONDE: Well, Sire, are you yourself still bent on attending that review?

WENCESLAS: And why not, Madam?

ROSAMONDE: But, I tell you again, have I not dreamt that I saw him strike you with armed power, hurl you into the Vistula, and that an eagle such as graces Poland's arms settled on his head the kingdom's crown?

WENCESLAS: On whose head?

ROSAMONDE: Father Ubu's.

WENCESLAS: How absurd! My lord Ubu is an awfully nice fellow who'd knock himself out to do me a favor.

ROSAMONDE
BUGGERLAS } How wrong you are!

WENCESLAS: Shut up, you little monkey. And you, Madam, to prove to you how little I fear my lord Ubu, I shall attend the review as I am, with neither armor nor a sword.

ROSAMONDE: Oh, fatal imprudence! I shall not look upon you in this life again.

WENCESLAS: Come, Ladislas. Come, Boleslas.

(*Exeunt. The* QUEEN *and* BUGGERLAS *go to the window.*)

ROSAMONDE
BUGGERLAS } May God and the great Saint Nicholas keep you!

ROSAMONDE: Buggerlas, come with me to the chapel to pray for your father and your brothers.

(*Exeunt.*)

SCENE TWO   The parade ground. The Whole Polish Army, King Wenceslas, Boleslas, Ladislas, Father Ubu, Captain Or d'Ure and his men, Boozumpaladin, Guildencranz, Rosenstern.

WENCESLAS: My noble Father Ubu, join me, with your retinue, to inspect the troops.

FATHER UBU (*to his followers*): Watch out, all of you. (*to the* KING) Coming, sir, coming.

(Ubu's *men surround the* KING.)

WENCESLAS: Ah! Here is the regiment of the Danziger horse guards. They are very handsome indeed.

FATHER UBU: You really think so? They seem a wretched ragtail lot to me. (*to a* SOLDIER) How long since you washed your face, you disgraceful dolt?

WENCESLAS: But that soldier is immaculate. What's the matter with you, Father Ubu?

FATHER UBU: There!

(*He crushes his foot.*)

WENCESLAS: Wretch!

FATHER UBU: *Schit!* Rally round me, men!

OR d'URE: Hurrah! Onward!

(*All strike the* KING. *A firecracker explodes.*)

WENCESLAS: Help! Help! Holy Virgin, I'm dead!

BOLESLAS (*to* LADISLAS): What's up? Let's draw our swords.

FATHER UBU: I've got the crown! Let's get the others now.

OR d'URE: Get the traitors!

(*The* KING's *sons flee. All pursue them.*)

SCENE THREE   Queen Rosamonde and Buggerlas.

ROSAMONDE: I begin to feel reassured.

BUGGERLAS: You have no reason to fear.

(*A frightful clamor is heard outside.*)

Ah, what do mine eyes behold? My two brothers pursued by Father Ubu and his henchmen!

ROSAMONDE: Oh, my goodness! Mother of God, they are losing, they are losing ground!

BUGGERLAS: The whole army follows Father Ubu. The King is no longer there. Horrors! Help!

ROSAMONDE: Look, Boleslas is dead! He has been hit by a bullet.

BUGGERLAS: Ladislas!

(LADISLAS *turns around.*)

Defend yourself! Hurrah, Ladislas!

ROSAMONDE: Oh, he is surrounded!

BUGGERLAS: He's done for. Or d'Ure has just sliced him in two like a sausage.

ROSAMONDE: Alas, this crazy mob is penetrating my — palace! They are coming up the stairs!

(*The clamor swells.*)

ROSAMONDE ⎱ (*kneeling*): God protect us!
BUGGERLAS ⎰

BUGGERLAS: Oh, that Father Ubu! That scoundrel, that wretch, if I could lay my hands on him. . . .

SCENE FOUR   The same. The door is smashed in. Father Ubu and a wild mob enter.

FATHER UBU: What are you trying to do, Buggerlas?

BUGGERLAS: Praise God, I shall defend my mother to the death. The first one who steps forward is dead.

FATHER UBU: Oh, Or d'Ure, I'm so scared! Let me out of here.

A SOLDIER (*steps forward*): Give yourself up, Buggerlas!

BUGGERLAS: There, villain! Take that!

(*He splits his skull.*)

ROSAMONDE: Hold fast, Buggerlas, hold fast!

SEVERAL (*advancing*): Buggerlas, we promise to spare your life.

BUGGERLAS: Scoundrels, wineskins, mercenary riffraff!

(*He makes a windmill motion with his sword and massacres them.*)

FATHER UBU: Oh well, I'll still win in the end anyway.

BUGGERLAS: Save yourself, Mother, by the secret staircase.

ROSAMONDE: And you, my son, and you?

BUGGERLAS: I follow.

FATHER UBU: Try to seize the Queen. Ah! She got away. As for you, you wretch. . . .

(*He steps toward* BUGGERLAS.)

BUGGERLAS: Ah! Thank heaven, here is my vengeance!

(*With a fierce sword thrust he rips open* FATHER UBU's *stomacher.*)

Mother, I follow!

(*He disappears by way of the secret staircase*)

(*Exeunt.*)

SCENE FIVE   A cave in the mountains. Buggerlas enters, followed by Queen Rosamonde.

BUGGERLAS: Here we shall be safe.

ROSAMONDE: I do believe it. Bear me up, Buggerlas!

(*She sinks down in the snow.*)

BUGGERLAS: What ails you, Mother dear?

ROSAMONDE: Believe me, Buggerlas, I am very ill. I have but two bare hours to live.

BUGGERLAS: What? Have you caught a chill?

ROSAMONDE: How can I sustain so many blows? The King massacred, our family destroyed, and you, the scion of the most noble race that ever bore sword, forced to flee like a smuggler into the mountains!

BUGGERLAS: And thanks to whom, good heavens, thanks to whom? A vulgar Father Ubu, an adventurer come from who knows where, a tawdry toad, a vile vagabond! And when I think that my father decorated him and made him an earl and the very next day that villain has not been ashamed to raise his hand against his King!

ROSAMONDE: O Buggerlas, when I recall our happiness before the arrival of this Father Ubu! But now, alas!, all is altered!

BUGGERLAS: What can we do? We must wait in hope and never renounce our rights.

ROSAMONDE: I hope for you, my dear child, but as for me, my eyes shall never see that happy day.

BUGGERLAS: Oh, what's wrong? She pales, she falls. Help! But I am alone, deserted in a desert. O God. Her heart has ceased to beat! She is dead! Can it be? Another victim of Father Ubu? (*Hiding his face in his hands and weeping.*) How sad it is, O my God, to see oneself at fourteen years of age with such a terrible vengeance to pursue!

(*He falls prey to the most violent despair. Meanwhile, the souls of* WENCESLAS, BOLESLAS, LADISLAS, *and* ROSAMONDE *enter the grotto. The* ANCESTORS *accompany them and fill the grotto. The oldest approaches* BUGGERLAS *and gently rouses him.*)

BUGGERLAS: What do mine eyes behold? My whole family, my ancestors. . . . What miracle has been wrought?

THE SHADE: Know, Buggerlas, that in my days of nature I was the ruler Matthias of Königsberg, first King and founder of our dynasty. I hereby entrust to you the task of our revenge. (*Giving him a great sword.*) And may this sword never sleep till it strikes the usurper dead.

(*All the Shades disappear and* BUGGERLAS *remains alone, wrapt in an attitude of ecstasy.*)

SCENE SIX   The palace. Father Ubu, Mother Ubu, Captain Or d'Ure.

FATHER UBU: No! Me, I don't want to! Do you want to ruin me for those clowns?

OR d'URE: But don't you see, Father Ubu, that the people are counting on a joyful coronation largesse?

MOTHER UBU: If you don't have food and gold distributed, you won't last two hours.

FATHER UBU: Food, yes. Gold, no. Slaughter three old horses. That's good enough for that rabble.

MOTHER UBU: Rabble yourself! How did I ever get myself involved with a pig like that?

FATHER UBU: I'm telling you once more, I want to get rich, you won't get a penny out of me.

MOTHER UBU: And that man's got all the treasure of Poland in his hands!

OR d'URE: Yes, I happen to know there's an immense treasure in the chapel. We'll distribute it.

FATHER UBU: Wretch, don't you dare do that.

OR d'URE: But, Father Ubu, if you don't distribute something the people won't want to pay taxes.

FATHER UBU: Is that really true?

MOTHER UBU: Yes, indeed.

FATHER UBU: Oh! Then I agree to everything. Bring up three millions and cook up one hundred and fifty beeves and sheep — especially since I'll have some myself.

(Exeunt.)

SCENE SEVEN The courtyard of the palace, thronged with People. Father Ubu (crowned), Mother Ubu, Captain Or d'Ure, Phlunkies laden with viands.

PEOPLE: Here comes the King! Long live the King! Hurrah!

FATHER UBU (throwing gold coins): There, that's for you. I didn't think it much fun to give away money but, you know, Mother Ubu put her foot down. At least promise me to pay taxes.

PEOPLE: Yes, yes!

OR d'URE: Look, Mother Ubu, how they scramble for the gold. What a battle!

MOTHER UBU: It is really horrible. Ugh! One just got his skull split.

FATHER UBU: What an edifying spectacle! Bring more chests of gold!

OR d'URE: Why don't we make a race of it?

FATHER UBU: That's an idea. (to the PEOPLE) My friends, do you see this chest? It contains three hundred thousand rose nobles of gold in money both Polish coin of the realm and worth something. Let those who wish to race for it go to the end of the courtyard. You'll start when I wave my handkerchief and the first one to arrive back here will have the chest. As for those who don't win, they will be able to share in another chest as a consolation prize.

ALL: Yeah! Long live Father Ubu! We never saw such things in King Wenceslas' reign.

FATHER UBU (joyfully): Mother Ubu, listen to them.

(The PEOPLE all go to line themselves up at the end of the courtyard.)

FATHER UBU: One, two, three. Ready?

PEOPLE: Yes! Yes!

FATHER UBU: Go!

(The PEOPLE start, jostling each other. Shouts and tumult.)

OR d'URE: Here they come! They're coming closer!

FATHER UBU: Hey! The one in front is losing ground!

MOTHER UBU: No, he's regained his lead now.

OR d'URE: He's losing, he's losing. That's the end! The other one wins!

(The one who was second has come in first.)

PEOPLE: Long live Michael Federovitch! Long live Michael Federovitch!

FEDEROVITCH: Sire, I hardly know how to thank Your Majesty. . . .

FATHER UBU: My dear friend, think nothing of it. Take your chest with you, Michael, and the rest of you divide the other one, each taking a piece in turn until there's nothing left.

PEOPLE: Long live Michael Federovitch! Long live Father Ubu!

FATHER UBU: And you, my friends, come and dine with me. The doors of my palace are open to you today. Do me the favor of honoring my table.

PEOPLE: Let's go! Let's go! Long live Father Ubu! The Most Noble of Sovereigns!

(*They troop into the palace. The noise of the orgy lasts into the next day. The curtain falls.*)

ACT THREE

SCENE ONE   The palace. Father Ubu, Mother Ubu.

FATHER UBU: By my candle of green, here I am King of the realm, I'm already stuck with a stomach ache, and they're bringing my flowing cape.

MOTHER UBU: What is it made of, Father Ubu? For economies are in order, even if we are monarchs.

FATHER UBU: Madam female of mine, it is of lambskin with a clasp and drawstrings of dog.

MOTHER UBU: Not a bad thing, that — but not as good as being monarchs.

FATHER UBU: Yes, you were certainly right about that, Mother Ubu.

MOTHER UBU: We owe a great debt of gratitude to the Duke of Lithuania.

FATHER UBU: Who's he?

MOTHER UBU: Captain Or d'Ure, of course.

FATHER UBU: For heaven's sake, Mother Ubu, don't talk to me about that ape. Now that I don't need him, he can go climb a tree. He won't get his dukedom.

MOTHER UBU: You're making a big mistake, Father Ubu. He'll turn against you.

FATHER UBU: I should worry about that pip-squeak. I worry as little about him as about Buggerlas.

MOTHER UBU: Oh, so you think you are through with Buggerlas?

FATHER UBU: By my financial sabre, of course! What can he do to me, this fourteen-year-old boy?

MOTHER UBU: Father Ubu, listen to me. Believe me, try to keep Or d'Ure your ally by favors.

FATHER UBU: More money to give away? No, I've had it! You've already made me squander at least twenty-two millions.

MOTHER UBU: Follow your instincts, Father Ubu, and you will be a cooked goose.

FATHER UBU: Well, you and I will share the pot.

MOTHER UBU: Listen to me one more time. I'm sure Buggerlas will prevail because he has right on his side.

FATHER UBU: You filthy wretch! Is not wrong every bit as precious as right? Madam, you do *me* wrong and I'll chop you into little tiny bits.

(MOTHER UBU *runs off, pursued by* FATHER UBU.)

SCENE TWO   The great hall of the palace. Father Ubu, Mother Ubu, Officers and Soldiers, Boozumpaladin, Guildencranz, Rosenstern, Nobles in chains, Financiers, Judges, Clerks.

FATHER UBU: Bring in the chest for nobles, the hook for nobles, the knife for nobles, and the account book for nobles. Then — bring on the nobles.

(*The nobles are brutally pushed forward.*)

MOTHER UBU: For heaven's sake, restrain yourself, Father Ubu.

FATHER UBU: I have the signal honor to inform you that, to enrich the realm, I am going to have the nobles killed and confiscate their goods.

NOBLES: Horrors! People and soldiers, help us!

FATHER UBU: Bring on the first noble and then pass me the hook for nobles. Those who are condemned to death I shall assist into the trap. They will fall into the basement of Pinch-Pig and the Sub-Treasury, where they will be debrained. (*to the* FIRST NOBLE) Who are you, clown?

FIRST NOBLE: The Count of Vitebsk.

FATHER UBU: How large are your revenues?

FIRST NOBLE: Three million rixdals.

FATHER UBU: You stand condemned.

(*He seizes the* FIRST NOBLE *with a hook and drops him into the trap.*)

MOTHER UBU: Such base ferocity!

FATHER UBU: Second noble: who are you?

(*The* SECOND NOBLE *does not answer.*)

Will you answer me, clown?

SECOND NOBLE: The Grand Duke of Posen.

FATHER UBU: Excellent, excellent! That's good enough for me. Into the trap!

(*He seizes the* SECOND NOBLE *with the hook and drops him into the trap.*)

Third noble: who are you? That's an ugly mug you've got there.

THIRD NOBLE: The Duke of Courlande and of the cities of Riga, Revel, and Mitau.

FATHER UBU: Very good, very good! You don't have any other titles, do you?

THIRD NOBLE: Nothing.

FATHER UBU: Nothing will come of nothing. Into the trap!

(*He seizes the* THIRD NOBLE *with the hook and drops him into the trap.*)

Fourth noble: who are you?

FOURTH NOBLE: The Prince of Podolia.

FATHER UBU: What revenues do you have?

FOURTH NOBLE: I'm flat broke.

FATHER UBU: For that unwelcome news, into the trap!

(*He seizes the* FOURTH NOBLE *with the hook and drops him into the trap.*)

Fifth noble: who are you?

FIFTH NOBLE: The Margrave of Thorn, Count Palatine of Polock.

FATHER UBU: Not very impressive. Have you nothing else to your name?

FIFTH NOBLE: It was good enough for me.

FATHER UBU: Well, better little than nothing. Into the trap!

(*He seizes the* FIFTH NOBLE *with the hook and drops him into the trap.*)

What's bugging you, Mother Ubu?

MOTHER UBU: You're too ferocious, Father Ubu.

FATHER UBU: I'm getting wealthy, that's what I am. I'm going to draw up *my* list of *my* goods. Clerk, read me *my* list of *my* goods.

CLERK: The Earldom of Sandomir. . . .

FATHER UBU: Pray begin with the princely titles, you stupid bugger!

CLERK: The Principality of Podolia, the Grand Duchy of Posen, the Duchy of Courlande, the Earldom of Sandomir, the County of Vitebsk, the Palatinate of Polock, the Margravation of Thorn. . . .

FATHER UBU: What else?

CLERK: That's it.

FATHER UBU: What do you mean "that's it"? Well then, bring on more nobles, and since I don't propose to stop getting wealthier, I shall execute *all* the nobles and thus have all the properties vacant. Come on, all the nobles into the trap!

(*The* NOBLES *are piled into the trap.*)

Hurry up, faster! I want to make some laws now.

SEVERAL [JUDGES]: That remains to be seen.

FATHER UBU: First off I shall reform the judicial system, after which we shall tackle the financial questions.

JUDGES: We are unalterably opposed to any alterations.

FATHER UBU: Schit! Firstly, judges will no longer be paid.

JUDGE: And how shall we live? We are poor men.

MOTHER UBU: You can keep the fines you levy and the goods of those you condemn to death.

FIRST JUDGE: Horror!

SECOND JUDGE: Infamy!

THIRD JUDGE: Scandal!

FOURTH JUDGE: Indignity!

ALL [THE JUDGES]: We absolutely refuse to judge under such conditions!

FATHER UBU: Into the trap with the judges!

(They struggle in vain. The JUDGES go down the trap.)

MOTHER UBU: What have you done, Father Ubu? Who will render justice now?

FATHER UBU: Me, as a matter of fact. You'll see how efficiently it will work.

MOTHER UBU: I'll bet.

FATHER UBU: Keep your trap shut, clowness! And now, gentlemen, we proceed to matters of finance.

FINANCIERS: There is no need to change anything.

FATHER UBU: What do you mean? I want to change everything. First of all, I want to keep half the taxes for myself.

FINANCIERS: He's a cool one.

FATHER UBU: Gentlemen, we shall levy a tax of ten percent on real property, another on commerce and industry. Moreover, nobody will be permitted to marry or to die without first paying fifteen francs a head.

FIRST FINANCIER: But that's absurd, Father Ubu.

SECOND FINANCIER: That is absurd.

THIRD FINANCIER: It doesn't seem to make any sense.

FATHER UBU: What do you take me for? Into the trap with the financiers!

(The FINANCIERS are shoved in.)

MOTHER UBU: But really, Father Ubu, what kind of a king are you, massacring everybody?

FATHER UBU: Oh, schit!

MOTHER UBU: No more justice, no more finances!

FATHER UBU: Fear not, sweet child, I shall go from village to village and collect the taxes myself.

SCENE THREE   A peasant's hut on the outskirts of Warsaw. Several Peasants are gathered.

A PEASANT (entering): There's great news. The King is dead along with the dukes, and young Buggerlas has escaped into the mountains with his mother. And Father Ubu has grabbed the throne!

ANOTHER PEASANT: I know even more. I come from Cracow, where I have seen them carry away the bodies of more than three hundred nobles and five hundred judges that have been killed, and I hear that taxes are going to be doubled and that Father Ubu is going to come and collect them in person.

ALL [THE PEASANTS]: Good gracious, what is to become of us? Father Ubu is a vile pig, and his family (they say) is absolutely loathsome.

A PEASANT: But listen: isn't that someone knocking at the door.

(A knock is heard at the door.)

THE VOICE [of FATHER UBU] (offstage): Horncock! Open up, by my schit, by Saint John, Saint Peter, and Saint Nicholas! Open up, by my financial sabre, by my financial horn, I have come to collect the taxes!

(The door is smashed in. UBU enters, followed by a legion of TAX-GRABBERS.)

SCENE FOUR   The same. Father Ubu, Tax-Grabbers, Peasants, Stanislas Leczinski.

FATHER UBU: Who is the oldest here?

(A PEASANT [STANISLAS LECZINSKI] comes forward.)

STANISLAS LECZINSKI: Stanislas Leczinski.

FATHER UBU: Well, horncock, listen to me carefully, or these gentlemen will snip off your ears. Are you or are you not going to listen?

STANISLAS LECZINSKI: But Your Excellency hasn't said anything yet.

FATHER UBU: What do you mean? I have been talking for an hour. Do you imagine that I have come all this way to preach in the desert?

STANISLAS LECZINSKI: Perish the thought.

FATHER UBU: I have come to express to order and to signify to you that it behooves you promptly to produce and cough up your valuables, or you will be slaughtered. Come, my lords the moneyrotters, convey hither the phynancial conveyance.

(*They bring in a little wagon.*)

STANISLAS LECZINSKI: Sire, we are registered for only 152 rixdals, which we have already paid, about six weeks ago, on the Feast of Saint Matthew.

FATHER UBU: That's a strong possibility. But I have changed the government and placed an advertisement in the newspapers to the effect that all taxes have to be paid twice. Any that I may happen to think up later will have to be paid three times. With that system, I shall make my fortune quickly. And then I'll kill everybody and go away.

PEASANTS: Mr. Ubu, for pity's sake, have mercy on us. We are poor citizens.

FATHER UBU: I don't give a damn. Pay up.

PEASANTS: We cannot. We have paid.

FATHER UBU: Pay up! Or I'll do you in with torture and decapitation of the neck and head. Horncock, am I not King?

ALL [THE PEASANTS]: Well, if that's the way it is — TO ARMS! Long live Buggerlas, by the Grace of God, King of Poland and Lithuania!

FATHER UBU: Come on, Lords of Finance, do your duty!

(*A struggle ensues. The hut is destroyed. Old STANISLAS flees alone across the plain. FATHER UBU stays behind to sweep up the money [that was in the wagon].*)

SCENE FIVE   A dungeon in the fortifications of Thorn. Or d'Ure in chains, Father Ubu.

FATHER UBU: Well, citizen, here's how things are: you wanted me to pay you what I owed you, then you rebelled because I refused to do so, you conspired against me, and now you are in the coop. Hornloot, the deed is well done and the trick so well played that you yourself must find it much to your taste.

OR d'URE: Have a care, Father Ubu. In the five days that you have been King you have committed more than enough murders to damn all the saints in Paradise. The blood of the King and the nobles cries for vengeance and shall speak with most miraculous organ!

FATHER UBU: Well, my fine fettered friend, you have quite a glib tongue. I have no doubt that, were you to escape, complications might result therefrom, but I doubt that the dungeons of Thorn have ever released one of the honest lads who were consigned to them. That is why I bid you good night. I strongly suggest that you had best sleep on both ears, because the rats dance a rather tidy sarabande around here.

(*Exit. The PHLUNKIES come and secure all the doors.*)

SCENE SIX   The palace at Moscow. The Czar Alexis and his Court, Or d'Ure.

ALEXIS: Infamous adventurer, have you not conspired in the death of our cousin Wenceslas?

OR d'URE: Forgive me, Sire, I was led astray against my will by Father Ubu.

ALEXIS: Oh, what a fearful liar! Well, what do you want?

OR d'URE: Father Ubu had me imprisoned on the pretext of conspiracy. I managed to escape and have raced five days and five nights — on horseback — across the steppes to come and implore your gracious mercy.

ALEXIS: What do you bring me as a token of submission?

OR d'URE: My sword as a soldier of fortune and — a detailed map of the city of Thorn.

ALEXIS: I'll accept the sword. But, by Saint George, burn that map. I do not wish to owe my victory to a betrayal.

OR d'URE: One of the sons of Wenceslas, young Buggerlas, still lives. I'll do everything to restore him to the throne.

ALEXIS: What rank did you hold in the Polish Army?

OR d'URE: I commanded the Fifth Regiment of Vilna Dragoons and a company of mercenaries in the service of Father Ubu.

ALEXIS: Very well. I appoint you second in command of the Tenth Regiment of Cossacks, and you had better not prove a traitor. If you fight well, you shall be rewarded.

OR d'URE: I am not lacking in courage, Sire.

ALEXIS: Very well. You may take your leave.

(*Exit.*)

SCENE SEVEN   Father Ubu's council chamber. Father Ubu, Mother Ubu, Phynancial Counsellors.

FATHER UBU: Gentlemen, the meeting is called to order, so try to listen carefully and keep quiet. First, we shall settle the matter of finances, then we shall discuss a little system I have dreamed up to bring good weather and exorcise the rain.

A COUNSELLOR: Very good indeed, Lord Ubu.

MOTHER UBU: What a nitwit!

FATHER UBU: My lady of schit, just watch it! For I shall not put up with your nonsense. I can tell you now, gentlemen, that the finances are going fairly well. A goodly number of our louts spread out into the streets every morning and the bastards are doing great. On all sides there are only burnt-out houses and people bent under the weight of our phynances.

THE COUNSELLOR: And the new taxes, Lord Ubu, are they doing well?

MOTHER UBU: Not well at all. The marriage tax has only produced 11 cents, and this despite the fact that Father Ubu pursues people all over the place to force them to get married.

FATHER UBU: By my financial sabre, horn of my cock, madam financial wizard, I have ears to speak with and you a mouth to listen! (*Bursts of laughter.*) That's not what I meant. You're making me go wrong and it's your fault if I am dumb. But, by the horn of Ubu!

(*A* MESSENGER *enters.*)

Well, what's the matter with him? Get out, pig, or I'll do you in with decapitation and twisting of legs.

(*Exit the* MESSENGER.)

MOTHER UBU: Ah, there he goes! But he's left a letter.

FATHER UBU: Read it. I'm either losing my mind or I don't know how to read. Hurry up, clowness, it must be from Or d'Ure.

MOTHER UBU: Precisely. He says that the czar has received him cordially, that he is going to invade your territories to reestablish Buggerlas, and that as for you, you are going to be killed.

FATHER UBU: Oh, oh! I'm scared! I'm scared! Oh, I think I'll die of fright! Wretch that I am, good God, what shall I do? That wicked man is going to kill me. Saint Anthony and all the saints, protect me, I'll give you phynances and burn votive candles for you. Heavens, what shall I do?

(*He weeps and sobs.*)

MOTHER UBU: There's only one course to take, Father Ubu.

FATHER UBU: Which, my love?

MOTHER UBU: War! ! !

ALL [THE COUNSELLORS]: Praise God! A noble plan!

FATHER UBU: Oh, sure, and I'll get clobbered again.

A COUNSELLOR: Hurry, hurry, let's mobilize the army!

SECOND COUNSELLOR: And collect provisions!

THIRD COUNSELLOR: And prepare the artillery and the fortifications!

FOURTH COUNSELLOR: And take the money to pay the troops!

FATHER UBU: Not so fast. I'm going to kill you for that. I don't want to give any money. A fine thing! I used to be paid to make war and now I have to do it at my own expense. No, by my candle of green, let's have a war, since you're so hot for it — but let's not spend a cent.

ALL [THE COUNSELLORS]: Make war not love!

SCENE EIGHT   The camp before Warsaw. Father Ubu, Mother Ubu, Soldiers and Ubulings.

SOLDIERS *and* UBULINGS: Long live Poland! Long live Father Ubu!

FATHER UBU: Listen, Mother Ubu, give me my breastplate and my little wooden stick. I'm going to be so loaded down that I won't be able to walk if they start to chase me.

MOTHER UBU: Fie, my lord, a soldier and afeared?

FATHER UBU: Ah, there's that schitty sword that won't stay put and the phynancial hook which won't hold! I'll never be ready, and the Russians are headed this way and are out to kill me.

A SOLDIER: My lord Ubu, your ear-snipper is falling off.

FATHER UBU: I weel keel you with my schit-hook and my phiz-ical knife.

MOTHER UBU: How handsome he looks with his helmet and breastplate: just like a pumpkin in full armor.

FATHER UBU: Ah, now I shall mount my steed. Gentlemen, bring on the phynancial horse!

MOTHER UBU: Father Ubu, that horse will never be able to carry you. He hasn't eaten in five days and is nearly dead.

FATHER UBU: That's a fine thing! They bilk me 12 cents a day for that nag and he can't even carry me. By the horn of Ubu, are you fooling me or are you stealing from me?

(MOTHER UBU *blushes and lowers her eyes.*)

No, bring me another beast. I will not go on foot, horncock!

(*They bring on an enormous horse.*)

I'm going to sit on it. Or rather, get up on it, because I am going to fall off for sure.

(*The horse starts to go as* FATHER UBU *gets on.*)

Help, stop the beast! Great heavens, I'll fall and be dead!

MOTHER UBU: He really is an idiot. Ah, he's up again! No, he's fallen off.

FATHER UBU: By my physical horn, I'm half dead! But who cares? I'm off to war and I shall kill everybody. Anybody who doesn't toe the line, just watch out! I weel do heem een with twisting of nose and teeth and extraction of the tongue.

MOTHER UBU: Good luck, Father Ubu!

FATHER UBU: I forgot to mention: I entrust you with the Regency. But I am taking with me my book of finances, so too bad for you if you steal from me. I leave you my ubuling Boozumpaladin to assist you. Goodbye, Mother Ubu.

MOTHER UBU: Farewell, Father Ubu: Kill the czar nicely!

FATHER UBU: Damn right! Twisting of the nose and teeth, extraction of the tongue, and thrusting of the little wooden stick into the earwholes.

(*The army marches off to the sound of trumpets.* [Manet MOTHER UBU.])

MOTHER UBU (*alone*): Now that that big oaf is off, let's try to get things done, kill Buggerlas, and get our hands on the treasure.

(*Exit.*)

ACT FOUR

SCENE One   The crypt of the ancient Kings of Poland in the Cathedral of Warsaw. Mother Ubu, The voice of John Sobieski.

MOTHER UBU: Where the hell is that treasure? None of these paving stones sounds hollow. After all, I have counted thirteen stones from the tomb of Ladislas the Great, moving along the wall, and there's nothing here. I must have been fooled. Here's a spot: this stone sounds hollow. To work, Mother Ubu. Courage, pry up that stone. It holds tight. Let's take the end of the phynancial hook which will again prove useful. There! There lies the gold in the midst of the bones of kings. Everything into our sack. What is that noise? Is there still life in these old vaults? No, it's nothing. Let's hurry. Let's take everything. That money will do better in the light of day than among the tombs of ancient princes. Let's put that stone back. Hark! Still that noise? My presence in this place makes me strangely afraid. I'll take the rest of the gold another time: I'll come back tomorrow.

A VOICE issuing from the tomb of JOHN SOBIESKI: Never, Mother Ubu!

(MOTHER UBU runs off in terror, carrying the stolen gold, through the secret door.)

SCENE Two   The Main Square of Warsaw. Buggerlas and his followers, People and Soldiers, Mother Ubu, Guards, Boozumpaladin.

BUGGERLAS: Onward, my friends! Long live Wenceslas and Poland! That old scoundrel Father Ubu has fled. Only that witch Mother Ubu and her ubuling remain. I offer myself to march at your head to re-establish the dynasty of my fathers.

ALL: Long live Buggerlas!

BUGGERLAS: And we shall abolish all the taxes imposed by that odious Father Ubu.

ALL: Forward! Hurrah! Let's run to the palace and massacre that breed of scoundrels!

BUGGERLAS: There is Mother Ubu with her guards coming out on the steps.

MOTHER UBU: What do you want, gentlemen? Ah — it's Buggerlas!

(The mob throws stones.)

FIRST GUARD: All the windows are broken.

SECOND GUARD: By Saint George, I'm done for.

THIRD GUARD: Heavenly horns, I die!

BUGGERLAS: Keep throwing stones, my friends!

BOOZUMPALADIN: Oh, so that's the way things are!

(He unsheathes his sword and rushes into the fray, causing tremendous carnage.)

BUGGERLAS: Lay on! Defend yourself, you cowardly clown!

(They duel. [BOOZUMPALADIN is struck down.])

BOOZUMPALADIN: I'm dead. (He dies. MOTHER UBU flees.)

BUGGERLAS: Victory, my friends! Down with Mother Ubu!

(A fanfare of trumpets is heard.)

BUGGERLAS: Ah, the nobles are arriving! Run, let us seize that horrid harpy!

ALL [THE REST]: . . . Until we can strangle the old bandit himself!

(MOTHER UBU escapes pursued by all the Poles. Gunshots and hail of stones.)

SCENE THREE   The Polish Army on the march in the Ukraine. Father Ubu, Guildencranz, Rosenstern, Nicholas Rensky, General Laski, the whole Polish army, and Ubulings.

FATHER UBU: 'Odshorn, 'odsfoot, 'odshead! We shall perish, for we are dying of thirst and we are a trifle tired too. Sir Soldier, be so obliging as to carry our phynancial helmet, and you, Sir Lancer, take charge of the schit scissors and the physical stick to relieve our person, for (we repeat) we are exhausted.

(The SOLDIERS obey.)

GUILDENCRANZ: Hey! Monsewer! It is astonishing that we have seen neither hide nor hair of the Russians.

FATHER UBU: It is regrettable that the state of our finances is such as to deny us a conveyance suitable to our stature; for, through fear that our mount would collapse under us, we have journeyed the whole road on foot, dragging our horse by the bridle. But once back in Poland, by means of our skill in physics and assisted by the illuminating insights of our counsellors, we shall invent a wind-driven chariot to transport the entire army.

ROSENSTERN: Here comes Nicholas Rensky on the run.

FATHER UBU: What's wrong with that lad?

NICHOLAS RENSKY: All is lost! Sire, the Poles are revolting. Boozumpaladin has been killed and Mother Ubu has fled to the mountains!

FATHER UBU: Dread raven, bird of ill omen, night owl in spats! Where did you fish up that story? What next? And who is responsible? Buggerlas, I'll wager. Where do you come from?

NICHOLAS RENSKY: From Warsaw, noble sovereign.

FATHER UBU: Boy after my own schit, if I believed you, I would make the whole army about face. But, sirrah, you have more plumes on your hat than brains in your head, and you have dreamt up sheer nonsense. Go to the front lines, my boy. The Russians are not far off, and soon we shall have to unleash our weaponry, whether schittical, phynancial, or physical.

GENERAL LASKI: Father Ubu, do you not see the Russians on the plain?

FATHER UBU: You're right! The Russians! That does it! If only there were some way out, but there isn't. We are on a hilltop and open to blows from all sides.

THE WHOLE POLISH ARMY: The Russians! The enemy!

FATHER UBU: Come, gentlemen, let us take our battle stations. We shall remain on the hill and shall not commit the blunder of descending. I shall keep in your midst like a living keep and thus keep living as you gravitate around me. I recommend that you put as many bullets in your rifles as they can hold, for 8 bullets can kill 8 Russians, and that would be that many more off my back. We shall station the infantry at the bottom of the hill to engage the Russians and kill them a little, the cavalry to throw themselves into the fray indiscriminately, and the artillery around this windmill here to fire at will into the heap. As for ourselves, we shall take our stand in the windmill and will fire out the window with our phynancial pistol, place a physical stick across the door — and if anyone tries to get in, let him watch out for the dreaded schithook! ! !

OFFICERS: Your orders shall be executed, Sire Ubu.

FATHER UBU: Things are going well. Victory shall be ours. What time is it?

GENERAL LASKI: Eleven o'clock in the morning.

FATHER UBU: Alright, we are going to lunch. The Russians never attack before noon. Tell the soldiers, my lord general, to answer nature's call if they have to and to strike up *The Anthem of Phynances.*

(*Exit* LASKI.)

SOLDIERS *and* UBULINGS: Long live Father Ubu, our great Financier! *Taran, ta, ta; taran-ta-ta; taran, taran, tarantara!*

(*Exeunt.*)

FATHER UBU: Oh these dear lads, I adore them! (*A Russian cannonball hurtles in and breaks an arm off the windmill.*) Ah, I'm scared! Great God, I'm dead! Whew! No, I'm all right after all.

SCENE FOUR   The same. Father Ubu, General Laski, Nicholas Rensky, The Whole Polish Army with the Ubulings, The Whole Russian Army, Captain Or d'Ure in disguise, Alexis the Czar of Russia and his attendants.

A [POLISH] CAPTAIN (*entering*): Sire Ubu, the Russians are attacking.

FATHER UBU: Oh yeah? Well what do you want me to do about it? I didn't tell them to. Nevertheless, prepare for combat, my Gentlemen of Finances! (*A cannonball hurtles in.*)

GENERAL LASKI: A second cannonball!

FATHER UBU: I've had it. It's raining lead and steel here and our august person might well be adversely affected. Let us descend.

(*They all trot down the slope. The battle has just begun. They disappear into clouds of smoke at the foot of the hill.*)

A RUSSIAN (*striking out at them*): For God and the Czar!

NICHOLAS RENSKY: Oh, I am dead!

FATHER UBU: Forward! Ah, you, sir, let me get my hands on you, 'cause you hurt me, you know that? Wineskin! You with your rusty Rusky musket!

THE RUSSIAN: Take that. (*He shoots at* FATHER UBU *with a revolver.*)

FATHER UBU: Ahhhh! Oh, I'm wounded, I'm punctured, I'm perforated, I'm administered, I'm in-terred! Enough is enough! Now I've got hold of him! (FATHER UBU *tears* THE RUSSIAN *to pieces.*) Now try to start something again!

GENERAL LASKI: Forward, press on regardless, across the trench! Victory is ours!

FATHER UBU: You think so? So far my forehead bears more lumps than laurels.

A RUSSIAN CAVALRYMAN: Hurrah! Make way for the Czar!

(*Czar* ALEXIS *arrives, accompanied by Captain* OR d'URE *in disguise.*)

A POLE: Oh lord! Every man for himself — it's the Czar!

ANOTHER [POLE]: Oh, my God, he's crossing the trench!

ANOTHER [POLE]: Bing, bang! There go four of our men, clobbered by that big bugger of a lieutenant!

OR d'URE: Haven't you had enough? There now, John Sobieski, that takes care of you! (*He clobbers him.*) Now for the rest of them! (*He massacres Poles.*)

FATHER UBU: On, on, my friends! Seize that cad. Make borschit out of the Muscovites! Victory is ours! Long live the Red Eagle!

ALL [THE POLES]: Forward! Hurrah! 'Odslegs, get that big bugger!

OR d'URE (*on the ground*): By Saint George, I'm down!

FATHER UBU (*recognizing him*): Oh, so it's you, Or d'Ure, my friend! We are delighted to see you again, and so is the rest of this company. I am going to cook your goose — over a slow fire. Gentlemen of Finance, light a fire. Oooh, aah, ooh, I'm dead! It must be at least a cannon shot that got me. Ah, God, forgive me my sins! It certainly was a cannon shot that did it!

OR d'URE: It was in fact a shot from a blank pistol.

FATHER UBU: So — you're making fun of me! Again! You have *had* it! (*He rushes upon him and tears him to pieces.*)

GENERAL LASKI: We are advancing on all fronts, Father Ubu!

FATHER UBU: So I see. I can do no more. I have been kicked all over. For God's sake let us sit upon the ground and — oh, for my bottle!

GENERAL LASKI: Take the czar's, Father Ubu.

FATHER UBU: That's just where I am headed. Let's go. Sword of schit, do your work! And you, phynancial hook, be not far behind! May the physical baton work just as well and vie with the little wooden stick for the honor of massacring, eviscerating and exploiting the Muscovite Emperor! Onward, our noble Phynancial Horse! (*He rushes upon the Czar.*)

A RUSSIAN OFFICER: On guard, Your Majesty!

FATHER UBU (*attacking the Czar*): Take THAT! (ALEXIS *strikes back*) Oooh, ouch, hey! just a minute! Excuse me, sir, oh please leave me alone. Oh, but I didn't do it on purpose! (*He flees with the Czar in pursuit.*)

FATHER UBU: Holy Mother of God, that madman is after me! Good God, what have I started? Ah, good, there's still a trench to cross. Ah! I've got him on my heels and the ditch ahead! Courage! Let me close my eyes! (*He jumps the ditch. The Czar falls into it.*)

ALEXIS: A fine thing! I've fallen in!

THE POLES: Hurrah! The Czar is down!

FATHER UBU: Ah, I hardly dare look back. He's really in it. Very well done, and they are thumping him. Keep on, Poles, give your all, he's got a broad back for it, the wretch. Me, I'm afraid to look back at him. And yet, our previous prediction has been fully fulfilled. The physical baton has wrought wonders, and doubtless we should have killed him completely had not an inexplicable terror welled up in us to disarm and nullify the effects of our courage. For we were suddenly obliged to turn tail and have owed our safety not only to our skill as an equestrian but also to the solidity of the legs of our phynancial horse, whose celerity is equalled only by his solidity and whose agility has earned him his celebrity — as well as to the depth of the ditch which found itself fortuitously beneath the feet of the enemy of ourselves, the here-present Master of Phynances. A rather elegant speech, this — but there isn't a goddam soul listening to me. Fine thing! It's starting again!

(*The Russian dragoons charge and rescue the Czar.*)

GENERAL LASKI: This time it's a rout.

FATHER UBU: Ah, the time has come for one to take to one's heels. Therefore, my Polish gentlemen, onward! or rather — advance to the rear!

THE POLES: Every man for himself!

FATHER UBU: Come on, let's go. What a rabble, what a rout, what a multitude! How can I get out of this mess? (*As he is jostled*) Hey

there you, watch out, or you will sample the ardent valor of the Master of Phynances! Ah, he's gone! Let's get out of here, and quickly, while Laski isn't watching.

(*Exit.*)

(*Then the Czar and the Russian Army pass by in pursuit of the Poles.*)

SCENE FIVE   A cave in Lithuania. It is snowing. Father Ubu, Guildencranz, Rosenstern.

FATHER UBU: Filthy weather! It's hailing hard enough to split rocks and the person of the Master of Phynances finds itself excessively damaged thereby.

GUILDENCRANZ: Monsewer Ubu, have you recovered from your funk and your flight?

FATHER UBU: The terror is gone, but the flight is still with me.

ROSENSTERN (*aside*): What a pig!

FATHER UBU: How does your earwhole, my lord Rosenstern?

ROSENSTERN: Well enough, Monsewer, considering that it is not doing well at all. In conzekvenze of vitch, the bullet is bending it toward the ground and I have not been able to get the lead out.

FATHER UBU: Well done, indeed. You also were always ready to fight. As for myself, I have displayed remarkable valor and, without exposing myself to danger, have massacred four of the enemy with my own hand, not counting those who were already dead when I dispatched them.

ROSENSTERN: Do you know what happened to little Rensky, Guildencranz?

GUILDENCRANZ: He got a bullet in the head.

FATHER UBU: Even as the poppy and the dandelion are mowed down in the flower of their youth by the pitiless mower who pitilessly mows down their pitiful mugs, so little Rensky has played the poppy's part, yet he fought very well — and, besides, there were too many Russians for him.

GUILDENCRANZ ⎱ (*grunting in disgust*):
ROSENSTERN ⎰ Monsewer.

AN ECHO (*echoing their groans*): Hrrron!

GUILDENCRANZ: What is that? Let's look through our field grasses.

FATHER UBU: Oh no, come on now! More Russians, I'll bet. I've had enough of them! What's more, if they were to catch up with me — I'd simply polish them off!

SCENE SIX   The same. (*Enter A BEAR.*)

ROSENSTERN: Uh — Monsewer of Phynances. . . .

FATHER UBU: Oh, look at the nice bowwow. My goodness, isn't he darling!

GUILDENCRANZ: Watch out! What an enormous bear! My cartridges!

FATHER UBU: A BEAR! Oh, the atrocious beast! Oh, poor little me, I feel eaten already. Heaven protect me! And he's coming at me! No, he is seizing Rosen's stern! Ah, I breathe freely again!

(*The BEAR throws itself on ROSENSTERN. GUILDENCRANZ attacks it with a knife. FATHER UBU seeks refuge on a rock.*)

ROSENSTERN: Help, GUILDENCRANZ! Help me! To my rescue, Monsewer Ubu!

FATHER UBU: Forget it! Fend for yourself, my friend; just now I happen to be reciting my *Pater Noster*. Each one will have his turn to be devoured.

GUILDENCRANZ: I've got him. I'm holding him!

ROSENSTERN: Hang on, friend, he's beginning to let go of me.

FATHER UBU: *Santificetur nomen tuum.*

ROSENSTERN: Cowardly bugger!

GUILDENCRANZ: Ah — he's biting me! Heavens, save us, I am dead.

FATHER UBU: *Fiat voluntas tua!*

ROSENSTERN: Ah, I've managed to wound him!

GUILDENCRANZ: Hurrah! He's losing blood.

(*In the midst of the ubulings' cries the BEAR bellows in pain and FATHER UBU continues to mumble.*)

ROSENSTERN: Hold firm, while I ready my special exploding uppercut.

FATHER UBU: *Panem nostrum quotidianum da nobis hodie.*

GUILDENCRANZ: Have you got him? I can't hold out much longer.

FATHER UBU: *Sicut et nos dimittibus debitoribus nostris.*

ROSENSTERN: Here goes!

(*An explosion resounds and the BEAR falls dead.*)

GUILDENCRANZ ⎱ Victory!
ROSENSTERN ⎰

FATHER UBU: *Sed libera nos a malo. Amen.* Well, is he good and dead? Can I get down from my rock now?

GUILDENCRANZ (*contemptuously*): Do whatever you like.

FATHER UBU (*descending*): You may rest assured that if you are still alive and still tread the snows of Lithuania you owe it to the magnanimous virtue of the Master of Phynances, who knocked himself out, wore himself thin, and screamed himself hoarse declaiming *pater nosters* for your deliverance, and who has wielded the spiritual sword of prayer with a courage equal to the dexterity with which you have wielded the temporal weapon of the here-present ubuling Rosenstern's celebrated explosive uppercut. We have carried our devotion even further, for we have not hesitated to clamber onto a more solid rock so that our prayers might have a shorter journey to heaven.

GUILDENCRANZ: Revolting donkey!

FATHER UBU: What a fat beast! Thanks to me, you have something for supper. What a belly, gentlemen! The Greeks would have been more comfortable in there than in the wooden horse, and it lacked but a little, dear friends, for us to have verified with our own eyes its interior capacity.

GUILDENCRANZ: I'm starving. What shall we eat?

ROSENSTERN: The bear!

FATHER UBU: Poor fellows, are you going to eat it raw? We have nothing to make a fire with.

GUILDENCRANZ: Haven't we got the flints of our rifles?

FATHER UBU: That's right. And then I think that not far from here there is a little wood where there just might be some dry branches. Go fetch some, Sire Rosenstern.

(ROSENSTERN *trudges off across the snow.*)

GUILDENCRANZ: And now, Sire Ubu, you carve up the bear.

FATHER UBU: Oh, no, maybe he's not dead yet! It's much more a task for you — after all, you're already half eaten and bitten all over. I'll light the fire while waiting for him to bring the wood.

(GUILDENCRANZ *begins to carve up the bear.*)

FATHER UBU: Oh, watch out! He moved!

GUILDENCRANZ: But Sire Ubu, he's already stone cold.

FATHER UBU: What a pity. It would have been better to eat him warm. This bodes indigestion for the Master of Phynances.

GUILDENCRANZ (*aside*): He's disgusting. (*aloud*) Give us a hand, Lord Ubu, I can't do it all by myself.

FATHER UBU: No, not me, I don't feel like doing anything. I'm tired out.

ROSENSTERN (*returning*): What snow, my friends! We could be in Castille or at the North Pole. Night is beginning to fall. In an hour it will be pitch black. Let's hurry while we still have enough light.

FATHER UBU: Do you hear, Guildencranz, hurry up. Hurry up both of you! Spit the beast, cook the beast. I'm famished.

GUILDENCRANZ: That's the limit! If you don't work, you don't eat. Get it, you glutton?

FATHER UBU: Oh, it's all the same to me. I'd just as soon eat it raw. You're the ones who will mind. Besides, I'm sleepy.

ROSENSTERN: What can you expect from him? Let's make the dinner ourselves. He won't have any, that's all. Or maybe we can give him some bones.

GUILDENCRANZ: Right. Ah, the fire is catching. . . .

FATHER UBU: Oh, that's nice. The fire is warm now. But I see Russians behind every tree. What a rout, good heavens! Ahhhh! (*He falls asleep.*)

ROSENSTERN: I'd like to know if what Rensky was saying is true, if Mother Ubu is really deposed. It isn't at all impossible.

GUILDENCRANZ: Let's finish making supper.

ROSENSTERN: No, we have to talk about more important matters. I think it would be a good idea for us to look into the truth of these rumors.

GUILDENCRANZ: That's true, should we abandon Father Ubu or stick with him?

ROSENSTERN: Let's sleep on it. Tomorrow we shall see what we should do.

GUILDENCRANZ: No. It would be better to take advantage of the cover of night to get away.

ROSENSTERN: Let's go.

(*Exeunt.*)

SCENE SEVEN   The same. Father Ubu.

FATHER UBU (*talking in his sleep*): Ah, Sire Russian Dragoon, watch out, don't shoot in this direction, it's rather crowded over here. Ah, there's Or d'Ure, isn't he mean, like a bear. And Buggerlas is coming at me. Is this a bear which I see before me? Ah, he's down! How tough he is, good heavens! No, not me, I don't feel like doing anything. Go away, Buggerlas! Do you hear me, dolt? Now here is Rensky and the Czar — oh, they're going to hit me! And Mother Ubu! Where did you get all that gold? You have taken my gold, you miserable woman, you have been poking around in my tomb which is in the cathedral at Warsaw, near the moon. I've been dead for a long time — Buggerlas killed me — and I am buried at Warsaw near Vladislas the Great, and also at Cracow, near John Sigismond, and also at Thorn, in the dungeon with Or d'Ure. Look where he comes again! Go, damned bear! You look like Or d'Ure. Do you hear me, you beast of Satan? No, he does not hear: the rotters have snipped his ears. Brain, kill, cut off ears, tear out finances, and drink until death — that is the rotter's life, that is the joy of the Master of Phynances.

(*He becomes quiet and goes* [deeper] *to sleep.*)

ACT FIVE

SCENE ONE   It is night. Father Ubu is asleep. Mother Ubu enters without seeing him. The stage is in total darkness.

MOTHER UBU: Safe at last. I'm alone here and none the worse for it, but what a frantic race I've had: crossing the whole of Poland in four days! Every possible misfortune has assailed me at once. No sooner is that fat donkey gone than I go to the crypt to make myself rich. Right afterwards I barely escape being stoned by that Buggerlas and his lunatic mob. I lose my cavalier, the ubuling Boozumpaladin, who was so enamoured of my charms that he swooned with delight on seeing me and even, I have been assured, on not seeing me — which is surely the height of tenderness. He would have cut himself in two for me, the poor boy. The proof of it is that he was cut in four — by Buggerlas. Bing, bang, bong! Oh, I thought I would die. Then after that I flee, pursued by a furious mob. I leave the palace, I arrive at the Vistula — all the bridges are guarded. I swim across the river, hoping thereby to shake my persecutors. From all sides the nobility gathers and chases me. A thousand times I have hair-breadth escapes from death, strangling in a circle of Poles dedicated to my annihilation. Finally I elude their fury

and after four days of flight through the snows of what was once my realm I come to seek refuge here. I have not had a drink or a bite to eat these four days. Buggerlas was close on my heels. . . . Finally, I am safe. Ah, I am nearly dead of fatigue and cold. But I'd really like to know what has happened to my big fat buffoon — my most respectable spouse, I mean to say. My, have I ever filched finances from him! Have I ever robbed him of rixdals! Have I ever bamboozled him! And his phynancial horse that was dying of malnutrition: it didn't see hay very often, the poor devil. Ah, those were the days! But alas, I have lost my treasure. It's in Warsaw, and anybody who wants it can just go and get it.

FATHER UBU (*beginning to awake*): Seize Mother Ubu! Snip off her ears!

MOTHER UBU: Oh God, where am I? I'm all confused. Ah, no, good heavens!

Thanks to heaven
I can see
Father Ubu
Sleeps by me.

Let's act nice. Well, my fine fellow, have you slept well?

FATHER UBU: Very badly. That bear was mighty indigestible. A combat of the detestable against the indigestible, but the voracious has completely and neatly consumed the tenacious, as you will see when day dawns. Do you hear, noble ubulings?

MOTHER UBU: What's he mumbling about? He's even dumber now than when he left. What is the matter with him?

FATHER UBU: Rosenstern, Guildencranz, answer me, by my bag of schit! Where are you? Ah, I'm scared. But after all, somebody spoke. Who spoke? Not the bear, I presume. Schit! Where are my matches? Ah, I lost them in the battle.

MOTHER UBU (*aside*): Let us profit from the situation and the night, simulate a supernatural visitation, and make him promise to forgive us our little larcenies.

FATHER UBU: By Saint Anthony, somebody is talking! 'Odsleg! Well I'll be hanged!

MOTHER UBU: (*swelling her voice*): True, Lord Ubu, someone is indeed speaking, and the angels trumpet-tongued which shall quicken the dead from the final ashes and dust would not speak otherwise. Harken to this awful voice. It is that of Saint Gabriel who cannot help telling you things for your own good.

FATHER UBU: Yeah, is that so?

MOTHER UBU: Don't interrupt me or I'll stop talking and that will fix your wagon.

FATHER UBU: Oh, bitch! I'll shut up. I won't say another word. Pray continue, Madam Apparition.

MOTHER UBU: We were speaking of you, Lord Ubu, as a sort of — fat fellow. . . .

FATHER UBU: Extremely fat, yes, that's quite true.

MOTHER UBU: For God's sake, shut up!

FATHER UBU: Oh, oh! Angels don't swear!

MOTHER UBU (*aside*): Schit! (*continuing*) Do you happen to be married, Lord Ubu?

FATHER UBU: Extremely. To the last of the chippies, in fact.

MOTHER UBU: You mean that she is a charming woman.

FATHER UBU: A veritable horror. She's got claws all over — one does not know where to have her.

MOTHER UBU: One ought to treat her with gentleness, Lord Ubu, and if you use her thus you will find her at least the equal of the Venus of Asphlece.

FATHER UBU: Who has fleas?

MOTHER UBU: You are not listening. Lord Ubu, I insist upon your undivided attention. But let us hurry, for day is about to break. Lord Ubu, your wife is adorable and delicious — she does not have a single defect.

FATHER UBU: You're wrong. There is no defect that she does not have.

MOTHER UBU: Be still! Your wife is not unfaithful to you.

FATHER UBU: I'd very much like to see who would want to make love to her, that harpy.

MOTHER UBU: For one thing, she doesn't drink.

FATHER UBU: Not since I took away the key to the cellar. Before that, at eight o'clock in the morning she was plastered and she dabbed brandy behind her ears. Now that she perfumes herself with heliotrope she doesn't smell as bad any more. It's all the same to me, but now I am the only one who can get pickled.

MOTHER UBU: Stupid creature, your wife is not taking your gold.

FATHER UBU: That's pretty funny.

MOTHER UBU: She does not divert a penny to herself.

FATHER UBU: Not much. As witness our noble and unfortunate phynancial horse who, not being nourished for three months, was so weak he had for the entire campaign to be dragged across the Ukraine by the bridle. Thus he died in harness, the poor thing.

MOTHER UBU: Lies, lies. Your wife is a paragon of virtue and you — what a monster you make of yourself!

FATHER UBU: Truths, truths. My wife is a vixen and you — are a meathead.

MOTHER UBU: Watch yourself, Father Ubu!

FATHER UBU: Ah, true enough. I forgot whom I was addressing. No, I didn't say that.

MOTHER UBU: You have murdered Wenceslas.

FATHER UBU: It's not really my fault, it isn't, not me. It was Mother Ubu who insisted on it.

MOTHER UBU: You had Boleslas and Ladislas killed.

FATHER UBU: Too bad for them. They wanted to hit me.

MOTHER UBU: You broke your word to Or d'Ure and later you killed him.

FATHER UBU: I'd rather rule Lithuania than let him do it. For the moment neither of us does. So you see, I'm not to blame, not me.

MOTHER UBU: You have only one way to be pardoned for your foul misdeeds.

FATHER UBU: Which way? I am quite disposed to become a saintly man. I wouldn't mind being a bishop and having my name on all the calendars.

MOTHER UBU: You yourself will have to grant pardon — to Mother Ubu, for having pocketed a little money.

FATHER UBU: Well, then! I shall pardon her when she has made restitution, has been roundly thrashed, and has revived my phynancial horse.

MOTHER UBU: He's got a thing about that horse! Ah, all is lost — day is breaking!

FATHER UBU: But I'm happy to know for sure that my dear spouse was stealing from me. I now have the information from an authoritative source. *Omnis a Deo scientia*, which translated means: *omnis*, all; *a Deo*, science; *scientia*, comes from God. Here is the explanation of the phenomenon. But Madam Apparition speaks no more. Oh, that I might offer her a crumb of comfort. What she said was most entertaining. Hey — it's day. Ah, gracious heavens, by my phynancial horse, if it isn't Mother Ubu herself!

MOTHER UBU (*with effrontery*): No it isn't. I shall excommunicate you for that!

FATHER UBU: Carrion!

MOTHER UBU: What impiety!

FATHER UBU: Oh, this is too much. I can see it's you, you stupid chippie! What the devil are you doing here?

MOTHER UBU: Boozumpaladin is defunct and the Poles have chased me out.

FATHER UBU: And me, the Russians have chased me out: a meeting of great minds!

MOTHER UBU: You might say that a great mind has met a great ass.

FATHER UBU: Well that great mind will now meet a major ursa. (*He throws the bear at her.*)

MOTHER UBU (*falling under the bear's weight*): Ugh! Good heavens, what a horror! Ah, I perish, I suffocate! I am bitten, swallowed, digested!

FATHER UBU: He's dead, you caricature! Oh, but suppose he isn't. Oh, heavens — no, he's not dead, let's get out of here! (*Climbing up on his rock*) Pater noster qui es. . . .

MOTHER UBU (*extricating herself*): Where is that man now?

FATHER UBU: Great heavens, there she is again! Isn't there any way to get rid of that stupid creature? Is that bear dead or isn't he?

MOTHER UBU: You dumb ass, he's cold already. How did he get in here anyway?

FATHER UBU (*confused*): I haven't a clue. Oh, yes, I do know. He wanted to devour Guildencranz and Rosenstern and I myself polished him off with one blow of my *Pater Noster*.

MOTHER UBU: Guildencranz, Rosenstern, *Pater Noster?* What is all this? He is crazy, that financial wizard of mine.

FATHER UBU: What I tell you is the honest-to-God truth. And you are an idiot, my little bitch.

MOTHER UBU: Fill me in about your campaign, Father Ubu.

FATHER UBU: Oh, no, it's a long story. All I know is that despite my incontestable valor everyone beat the hell out of me.

MOTHER UBU: What, even the *Poles?*

FATHER UBU: They shouted "Long Live Wenceslas and Buggerlas"! I thought they wanted to draw and quarter me. Absolute lunatics! And then they killed little Rensky.

MOTHER UBU: I couldn't care less. Do you know that Buggerlas killed the ubuling Boozumpaladin?

FATHER UBU: I couldn't care less. And then they killed poor Laski.

MOTHER UBU: I couldn't care less.

FATHER UBU: Look here, carrion, come over here — on your knees before your master. (*He seizes her and forces her to her knees.*) You will endure the final torture.

MOTHER UBU: Anything but that, Lord Ubu!

FATHER UBU: Oh, oh, oh. Have you finished yet? Me, I'm just getting started; twisting of the neck, tearing out of hair, penetration of the little wooden stick into the earwholes, extraction of the brain through the heels, laceration of the posterior, partial (or perhaps total) kneading of the spinal cord — if only that could rid one of her spiny nature — not forgetting the puncturing of the air bladder and finally, the great, ever-renewed decapitation à la Saint John the Baptist, the whole drawn from the most holy Scriptures, both the Old and New Testaments, directed and perfected, with *addenda* and *corrigenda*, by Yours Truly, the Master of Phynances. Does that meet with your approval? You dumb bitch! (*He tears her apart.*)

MOTHER UBU: For pity's sake, Lord Ubu!

(*A great noise* [is heard] *at the entrance to the cave.*)

SCENE TWO The same. Buggerlas, rushing into the cave with his Soldiers.

BUGGERLAS: Forward, my friends! Long live Poland!

FATHER UBU: Oh, oh, just a minute, my fine Polish friend. Wait until I get through with my better half.

BUGGERLAS (*hitting him*): Take that, yellow-belly, blackguard, whited sepulchre, miscreant, infidel!

FATHER UBU (*retorting*): Hold it, Polack, plastered bastard, Tartar hussar, soused louse, Italian rapscallion, communist!

MOTHER UBU (*joining the battle*): Hold it, malfactor, actor, nut, slut, blighter, schytter, pillow-fighter!

(*The* SOLDIERS *rush upon the* UBUS, *who defend themselves as best they can.*)

FATHER UBU: Ye gods, what an assault!

MOTHER UBU: Watch out for our feet, we are not without them, my precious Poles.

FATHER UBU: By my candle of green, is this thing ever going to be over once and for all? Here comes another one of them. A horse! a horse! my kingdom for a phynancial horse!

BUGGERLAS: Bop him, keep bopping him!

A VOICE [ROSENSTERN] *offstage:* Long live Father Ubu, our great financier!

FATHER UBU: Ah, there they are! Hurrah, the ubulings to the rescue! Forward, come on, we need you, Gentlemen of Finance! Smite the dreaded Polacks in a thrice!

(*Enter the ubulings* [including GUILDENCRANZ and ROSENSTERN], *who throw themselves into the fray.*)

ROSENSTERN: To the door, all you Poles!

GUILDENCRANZ: So we meet again, Monsewer of Phynance. Forward, push out again vigorously, get to the door. Once outside, one need only run away.

FATHER UBU: Now running away is where I shine. Oooh, how hard he's hitting!

BUGGERLAS: Good God, I'm wounded.

STANISLAS LECZINSKI: It is nothing, Sire.

BUGGERLAS: No, I am only stunned.

JOHN SOBIESKI: Keep hitting at them. They are gaining the door, the rascals!

ROSENSTERN: We're getting there. Follow the crowd — that's me! As a conzeqvenze of vitch, I behold the sky!

GUILDENCRANZ: Courage, Ubu, Sire!

FATHER UBU: I have schit in my pants. Forward, horncock! Killim, bleedim, scratchim, mazzakerim, by the horn of Ubu! Oh, look: the crowd seems to be thinning out.

ROSENSTERN: Only two of them are guarding the door!

FATHER UBU (*flailing them with the bear*): And a-one, and a-two! Ooof! I am outside! Let's save ourselves! Come on, the rest of you, make it snappy!

SCENE THREE The scene represents the Province of Livonia, deep in snow. The Ubus and their retinue in full flight.

FATHER UBU: Well, I think they have given up trying to catch us.

MOTHER UBU: Yes, Buggerlas has gone to get himself crowned.

FATHER UBU: Uneasy lies the head that wears that crown.

MOTHER UBU: How right you are, Father Ubu!

(*They disappear into the distance.*)

SCENE FOUR The bridge of a close-hauled schooner on the Baltic Sea. On the bridge, Father Ubu and all his retinue. Guildencranz, Rosenstern, and a Sea Captain.

SEA CAPTAIN: Oh, what a spanking breeze!

FATHER UBU: It is true that we are running with a rapidity that approximates the prodigious. We must be making at least a million knots an hour, with the peculiar advantage that, once knotted, those knots cannot be unknotted. It is true that we have a big wind at our rear.

GUILDENCRANZ: What a pathetic imbecile!

(*A light squall blows up. The ship heels over and the sea foams white.*)

FATHER UBU: Oh, ah! My God, we are capsized! This ship of yours is going every which way and it's going to fall right over.

SEA CAPTAIN: All hands to leeward! Close haul the mizzen-mast!

FATHER UBU: Oh, for goodness' sake, don't everybody go over to the same side, that's imprudent! And just suppose the wind should shift direction? Everybody would land up at the bottom of the sea and be fish food.

SEA CAPTAIN: Don't rush around. Line up and close ranks.

FATHER UBU: Yes, yes, do rush! I am in a hurry. Rush, do you hear me, rush! It's all your fault, you brute of a captain, that we are not rushing. We should already have got there. Oh, oh, I'm going to take command here. Prepare to tack. With the grace of God, here goes: drop anchor, tack into the wind, tack against the wind. Hoist the sails, raise the boom, lower the boom, swing the boom over. You see, everything's shipshape. Go broadside to the waves and everything will be Bristol fashion.

(*All writhe with laughter. The breeze freshens.*)

SEA CAPTAIN: Strike the main-jib. Take a reef in the topsails!

FATHER UBU: Not bad. It's even good. Do you hear that, Gentlemen of the Crew? Bring in the main cock and take a turn at the coxswain!

(*Many are convulsed with laughter. A wave washes over.*)

The deluge is after me! This is precisely the result of the maneuvres that he wanted.

MOTHER UBU   Oh for a life on the bounding
GUILDENCRANZ   wave.

(*A second wave washes over.*)

GUILDENCRANZ (*inundated*): Beware of Satan and all his works and pomps.

FATHER UBU: Sirrah, bring us something to wet our whistle.

(*They all settle down to drinking.*)

MOTHER UBU: Ah, the delight of beholding once again sweet France, my friends of yore, and our castle of Mondragon!

FATHER UBU: Ah, we shall soon be there. We are passing at this moment beneath the battlements of Elsinor.

GUILDENCRANZ: I am rejuvenated at the thought of beholding my beloved Spain again.

ROSENSTERN: Yes, we shall astonish our countrymen with the tales of our marvelous adventures and moving accidents of flood and field.

FATHER UBU: Yes, of course. And I shall get myself appointed Master of Phynance in Paris.

MOTHER UBU: Oh, that's it! Oooh, what a jolt that was!

ROSENSTERN: That's nothing. We have just made the point of Elsinore.

GUILDENCRANZ: And now our noble bark bounds at full speed over the somber waves of the North Sea.

FATHER UBU: O sinister and inhospitable ocean that laves the land called Germany, whose name is germane because all its inhabitants are cousins-german.

MOTHER UBU: Now that's what I call erudition. It is said that it is nice country thereabouts.

FATHER UBU: Ah, Gentlemen, beautiful as it may be, it is not the equal of Poland. If there were no Poland — there would be no Poles!

THE END

[CURTAIN]

The Cherry Orchard

The greatest name in Russian theatre and one of the greats of world drama is Anton Pavlovich Chekhov (1860–1904) and his fame overshadows that of all the other Russian dramatists. Alexander Ostrovsky was the most prolific of Russian playwrights, with some 80 plays (including *The Thunderstorm*) to his credit. The novelists Nikolai Gogol, Ivan Turgenev, and Count Leo Tolstoy also wrote for the theatre: Gogol the brilliant comedies of *The Inspector-General* and *The Marriage*, Turgenev the psychological comedy of *A Month in the Country* (suppressed for two decades), and Tolstoy the stark peasant drama of *The Power of Darkness*, reminiscent of *A Hard Lot* (banned as "in poor taste") by the novelist Alexei Pisemsky. Other names known in the West are those of Nikolai Evreinov, Maxim Gorki ("Maxim the Bitter"), Leonid Andreyev, Vladimir Mayakovsky, Isaac Babel, Nikolai Pogodin, and the poet Pushkin, major figures in a long list that dates from the time of Czar Alexei (who reigned from 1645 to 1676) who sent to Germany for actors and who financed Russian productions of German religious plays translated and presented by Johann Gregory, the pastor of the German Lutheran church in Moscow.

Chekhov began in the early 1880's with one-act farces in the style of Gogol — *The Marriage Proposal* and *The Bear* are still frequently produced. Like Babel he went on to add full-length plays to his accomplishments in the art of the short story, presenting people in "all the greyness of their everyday life" but never losing compassion and always with a wry humor and sometimes even a boisterous farce. He stands head and shoulders above the rest for a series of plays that grew increasingly better: *Ivanov, The Sea Gull, Uncle Vanya, The Three Sisters,* and *The Cherry Orchard.*

Chekhov is often admired for the wrong reasons. He is described as the master of the "drama of inaction" and it is said that nothing ever happens in his plays or, at the most, it happens offstage, while onstage time is given over to "three parts tea and one part conversation." Moreover, it is alleged, his characters never communicate, talking past each other and failing to make explicitly any of the points the dramatist is trying to convey. He is acceptable to the Soviets as a "critical realist" and yet is known for subtle psychological studies expressed in the most symbolic and impressionistic ways. He is hailed as the chief exponent of the most futile and despondent view of life, the author of tear-drenched dramas full of extravagantly self-pitying and wildly ineffectual people stagnating in desperate and hopeless situations.

No wonder Tolstoy misunderstood Chekhov and characterized his dramatic inventions as "worthless creatures . . . their suffering cannot therefore be worthy of our attention." No wonder Sir Desmond MacCarthy dismissed *The Sea Gull* as "a beautiful study in human nature, penetrating, detached, and compassionate" but added that "it has no theme."

For an example of how the critics and producers of Chekhov have gone wrong, consider the strange case of his greatest play, *The Cherry Orchard*.

The play was written in the Aristotelian tradition of comedy: "an imitation of characters of a lower type who are not bad in themselves but whose faults possess something ludicrous in them." Chekhov was sure it was going to be a laugh sensation. He sent it off to Konstantin Stanislavski (1863–1938) and Vladimir Nemirovich-Danchenko (1858–1943), leaders of the famed Moscow Art Theatre in the capital. (Chekhov was living in the milder climate of Yalta, attempting to delay the death from tuberculosis which overtook him soon after the première of *The Cherry Orchard*.) They gave it the full Stanislavski Method, designed to make "the spectator forget he is sitting in the theatre" as a result of actors who were trained in psychological realism ("The right thought will evoke the right emotion and the right emotion will evoke the right action"), loosely termed "living the part," actually meticulous technique developed from close study of the text and a role built from "feelings drawn from our actual experiences, and transferred to our part." That in itself threw a very serious pall over the whole proceeding.

Moreover Stanislavski (born Alexeyev) took himself, as well as the play, very seriously. He decided that it was a tragedy, not a comedy, and despatched a telegram to Yalta to that effect. Chekhov wrote to his wife, Olga Knipper, who was in Moscow and deeply involved in the arguments about how the play ought to be presented: "Nemirovich-Danchenko and Alexeyev positively see in my play something I have not written, and I am ready to bet anything you like that neither of them has ever read my play through carefully." Actually they had read it carefully; they had just read it wrong. How could it be comedy, they asked, when these poor aristocrats were losing their beautiful cherry orchard — from the beginning of the play there is no doubt about that outcome — and everyone is crying? Chekhov retorted that only Varya weeps and she does it so often that it is funny: she is, in fact, a cry-baby. What about the farce? The Moscow Art Theatre people didn't see that. Chekhov wrote to a fellow writer: "You tell me that people cry at my plays. I've heard others say the same. But that was not why I wrote them. It is Alexeyev who made my characters into cry-babies. All I wanted was to say honestly to people: 'Have a look at yourselves and see how bad and dreary your lives are!' The important thing is that people should realize that, for when they do, they will most certainly create another and a better life for themselves. I will not live to see it, but I know that it will be quite different, quite unlike our present life. And so long as this different life does not exist, I shall go on saying to people again and again: 'Please understand that your life is bad and dreary.' "

Chekhov was too compassionate a man to present characters as black and white, but the greyness of his characters does not mean that we are to be plunged into gloom because of them. Chekhov was no revolutionary of the sort that was to end the Czarist regime and leave him as the last and leading dramatist of that epoch of Russian history, but he did see that a new order was on the way and he felt deeply both for the old order that was passing and for the new one that was inexorably coming to take its place. The situation in *The Cherry Orchard* is one of the decay of the aristocracy, which was nothing new in Russian literature by any means but the future is not bleak: a housing development will replace the beautiful but useless orchard now that the recipe for preserving the cherries has been lost. It is a situation even more hopeful than that in Strindberg's *Miss Julie*. What was new was that Chekhov transcended, as did Strindberg, the political events on the horizon at the time and wrote with penetrating psychological insight of the permanent and universal tragedy of people everywhere, using specifics but going far beyond the realistic to the representative. And he did it with humor, with a combination of pathos and farce that make his characters touchingly human and, because such clashing colors are placed side by side, a sense of movement is created, even in this so-called "drama of inaction" in which the plot revolves about the fact that the central characters (like so many later in the plays of Samuel Beckett) are unable to move. See how much *Waiting for Godot* owes to Chekhov:

ESTRAGON: Well, shall we go?
VLADIMIR: Yes, let's go.
    They do not move.

The Moscow Art Theatre did not see the humor. At the end of their production, Firs dies (which is pitiful) rather than sitting there in stupid incomprehension (doing what vaudeville comedians used to call a "double take"). Somehow they got past the dropped bouquets, the non-sequiturs, the knocked-over furniture, the funny props, the proposal never quite made and the solution to the problem never quite heard. They made the speech to the bookcase sound so grave and nostalgic that no one dared to laugh. And they put their mark on the play so thoroughly that from its original production (1904) to 1958 (just before the Moscow Art Theatre ended) the gloomy rendition of this comedy was driven into the public consciousness, 1209 performances of the Stanislavski production over those years. (After 1958 there were some 64 performances of a new production, no whit lighter in tone.) Throughout the world, Chekhov's comedy of *The Cherry Orchard* was played with dead earnestness and nobody dared to laugh or even, since the critics had told them it was a "drama of inaction," to notice that much was happening in the play or that this collection of people was oddly representative of many different classes of society, much more so than was "realistic" to imagine would be gathered in Mme. Ranevskaya's house.

"With the exception of two or three parts," thundered Chekhov, a mild and modest man but serious about his art, "nothing is mine. I am describing life, ordinary life, and not blank despondency. They either make me into a cry-baby or a bore. They invent something about me out of their own heads, anything they like, something I never thought or dreamed about. This is beginning to make me angry." Clearly Chekhov saw the truth of Hegel's statement that history repeats itself, first as tragedy, then as farce.

David Magarshack, the best critic of this great playwright, explains in *Chekhov the Dramatist* how "they" got Chekhov wrong and what the right interpretation is; he undertakes to provide a key to the study of Chekhov's plays, each of which he sees as a "dramatic score whose manifold themes and climaxes must be carefully studied" the way a conductor studies a symphony he is going to conduct. He adds that "a Chekhov play . . . cannot be read, for its superb technique can only be given shape and form on the stage," but read this new translation of *The Cherry Orchard* and study it until you can perform it, like a symphony, in your head in all its richness and complexity. When you read this play, try playing it in your mind the way the composer wrote it: play it lightly, as a comedy, a bittersweet comedy, if you will, but not a tear-drenched one, for Chekhov would want you to see in the plight and paradox — today we would say "absurdity" — of human lives a ray of hope, a tender compassion and kind amusement, not "a cry-baby or a bore" but an objective, yet very sympathetic, observer of the human scene who wants you to see that "life is bad and dreary" only because he knows that then you will create "a new and better life."

THE CHERRY ORCHARD

Anton Pavlovich Chekhov

Translated from the Russian by
L. R. N. Ashley

DRAMATIS PERSONÆ

MADAME RANEVSKAYA (LYUBOV ANDREEVNA) [LYUBA], *the owner of the Cherry Orchard*
ANYA [ANECHKA], *her daughter* [aged 17]
VARYA [VARVARA MIKHAILOVNA], *her adopted daughter, aged 24*
GAEV, LEONID ANDREEVICH [LYONYA], *brother of Madame Ranevskaya*
LOPAKHIN, YERMOLAY ALEXEEVICH, *a Businessman*
TROFIMOV, PYOTR SERGEEVICH [PETYA], *a Student*
SIMYONOV-PISHCHIK [BORIS BORISOVICH], *a Landowner*
CHARLOTTA IVANOVNA, *a [German] Governess*
YEPIKHODOV, SEMYON PANTELEEVICH, *a Clerk* [on the Ranevsky estate]
DUNYASHA [AVODTYA FYODOROVNA], *a Maid*
FIRS [NIKOLAEVICH], *a Valet, aged* 87
YASHA, *a young Valet*
A PASSER-BY
THE STATION MASTER
A POST-OFFICE CLERK
GUESTS, SERVANTS

The action takes place on the estate of L. A. Ranevskaya.

[*Time: The play, first performed 17 January, 1904, in Moscow, is set a few years earlier, about the turn of the century, between the Emancipation of the Serfs (1861) and the then forthcoming Russian revolution.*]

ACT ONE

A room which even now is still called the nursery. One of the doors [up stage left] leads into ANYA's *room. Dawn: the sun will rise soon. It is May, the cherry trees are in bloom, but it is cold in the garden with the frost of early morning. The windows in the room [facing the audience] are closed.*

(*Enter* DUNYASHA *with a candle and* LOPAKHIN *with a book in his hand.*)

LOPAKHIN: The train is in, thank God. What time is it?

DUNYASHA: Nearly two. (*Puts out the candle.*) It's light already.

LOPAKHIN: Well how late is that? At least two hours. (*Yawns and stretches.*) I'm a fine one: what a fool I've been! Came here on purpose to meet them at the station and suddenly went back to sleep . . . dozed off sitting in the chair. It's annoying. . . . You might have waked me.

[NOTE: Russians ordinarily have three names: a given name (*Leonid*), a variation of the father's given name (*Andreevich:* son of *Andrei*), and a surname (*Gaev*). A woman might be *Lyubov Andreevna* (the daughter of *Andrei*) *Gaevna* and on marriage to a man named *Ranevsky* would take the feminine version of his surname (*Ranevskaya*), if the name was considered of Russian origin. In addition, familiar or nicknames (*Lyuba* for *Lyubov, Anechka* for *Anya, Lyonya* for *Leonid, Petya* for *Pyotr*) might be used among intimates, instead of the usual names (*Yermolay Alexeevich*). With the names of the characters listed above it might be noted that the second half of the hyphenated Simyonov-Pishchik is a funny anti-climax (suggesting in Russian the squeal of a pig) and that the stresses should fall as follows: Madame Lyu*BOV* An*DRE*evna Ran*EV*skaya, *AN*ya, *VAR*ya, Leon*ID* An*DRE*evich *GA*ev, Yermo*LAY* Alex*Ee*vich Lo*PAK*hin, Py*Otr* Ser*GE*evich Tro*FI*mov, Bor*IS* Bor*IS*ovich Sim*YON*ov-*PISH*chik, Char*LOT*ta *IVAN*ovna, Sem*YON* Pante*LEE*vich Yepik*HOD*ov, Dun*YAsha* Av*DOT*ya Fy*Odorovna*, *YAsha*, and Firs — pronounced *fierce* — Nikol*Ae*vich.]

DUNYASHA: I thought you had gone. (*Listens*) There, it sounds as if they're coming!

LOPAKHIN (*listening*): No, they have to get baggage and one thing and another. (*a pause*) Lyubov Andreevna has been living abroad for five years. I don't know what she's like now. . . . She's a good person, an easygoing, simple human being. I remember when I was a boy of fifteen, my poor father — he used to have a little shop here in the village in those days — punched me in the face with his fist and made my nose bleed. We had come here together for something in the yard — he had been drinking. Lyubov Andreevna — I can see her now — she was still young, and so slim then — took me to wash my face and then brought me into this very room, into the nursery. "Don't cry, little peasant," she says, 'it will be well in time for your wedding day". . . . (*a pause*) "Little peasant". . . . My father was a peasant, it's true, but here am I in a white waistcoat and yellow shoes, like some lucky bull in a china shop. Only that I'm a rich man — there's a lot of money. . . . Come to think and consider, a peasant I was and a peasant I am. (*Turning over the pages of the book*) Here, I've been reading this book and I can't make head or tail of it. I fell asleep over it. (*a pause.*)

DUNYASHA: But the dogs have been awake all night: they sense that their mistress is coming.

LOPAKHIN: What's the matter with you, Dunyasha? You're so. . . .

DUNYASHA: My hands are shaking. I am going to faint.

LOPAKHIN: You're too delicate a creature, Dunyasha. You dress like a lady too, and your hair's done up like one. That won't do. You must remember your place.

(*Enter* YEPIKHODOV *with a bouquet. He wears a suit jacket and high, highly polished boots that squeak loudly. He* [*inadvertently*] *drops the bouquet as he comes in.*)

YEPIKHODOV (*picking up the bouquet*): Here, the gardener sent this, says to put it in the dining-room. *Handing* DUNYASHA *the bouquet.*)

LOPAKHIN: And bring me some *kvass*.[1]

DUNYASHA: Yes, sir. (*Goes out.*)

YEPIKHODOV: There's frost this morning, three degrees, though the cherry trees are all in bloom. I can't say much for our climate, (*sighs*) no, I can't. Our climate is not often precisely conducive to. . . . Yermolay Alexeevich, permit me to venture to add the fact that the day before yesterday I purchased a pair of boots and I assure you that they squeak so much that there is no possibility of. . . . What should I grease them with?

LOPAKHIN: Oh, be quiet. You bore me.

YEPIKHODOV: Every day some misfortune befalls me. But I don't complain. I'm used to it, and I even smile.

(DUNYASHA *enters and hands* LOPAKHIN *the kvass.*)

I am going. (*Stumbles against a chair, which falls over.*) There! (*as if triumphant.*) There, you see now? Excuse the expression, what a situation. By the way. . . . It's positively remarkable. (*Goes out.*)

DUNYASHA: Do you know, Yermolay Alexeevich, I must confess that Yepikhodov has proposed to me.

LOPAKHIN: Ah!

DUNYASHA: I simply don't know. . . . He's a quiet man, but sometimes when he begins talking there's no making any sense out of it. It sounds very fine and expressive, only there's no understanding it. I seem to like him. He's madly in love with me. But he's an unfortunate man, every day something. They tease him about it: "two and twenty misfortunes."

LOPAKHIN (*listening*): There! I think I hear them coming!

DUNYASHA: They are coming! What's the matter with me? I'm cold all over.

---

1 Russian beer made from malt, barley, and rye.

LOPAKHIN: They really are coming. Let's go and meet them. Will she recognize me? It's five years since we've seen each other.

DUNYASHA (*in a flutter*): I'm going to faint this very minute. Oh, I'm going to faint.

(*Two carriages are heard driving up to the house.* LOPAKHIN *and* DUNYASHA *go out quickly. The stage is left empty. A noise begins in the adjoining rooms.* FIRS, *who has driven to meet* MADAME RANEVSKAYA, *hobbles across the stage hurriedly, leaning on a stick. He is wearing old-fashioned livery and a top hat. He mutters something to himself, but not a word can be distinguished. The noise offstage increases. The voice* [*of* LYUBOV ANDREEVNA]: "*Come, let's go through here.*" *Enter* LYUBOV ANDREEVNA, ANYA, *and* CHARLOTTA IVANOVNA *with a little dog on a chain. The women are in traveling dresses.* VARYA [*enters*] *with a coat, and a kerchief on her head,* GAEV, SIMYONOV-PISHCHIK, LOPAKHIN, DUNYASHA *with a bundle and an umbrella, servants with other baggage. All walk across the room.*)

ANYA: Let's come in here. Do you remember, mamma, what room this is?

LYUBOV (*joyfully, through her tears*): The nursery!

VARYA: It's so cold, my hands are numb. (*to* LYUBOV ANDREEVNA) Your rooms, the white room and the lavender one, are just as you left them, mamma.

LYUBOV: My nursery, dear, delightful room. . . . I used to sleep here when I was little . . . (*cries.*) And here I am, like a little child. . . . (*kisses her brother* [GAEV] *and* VARYA *and then her brother again.*) Varya's just the same as ever: she still looks like a nun. And I recognized Dunyasha (*kisses* DUNYASHA).

GAEV: The train was two hours late. What do you think of that? What a state of things!

CHARLOTTA (*to* PISHCHIK): My dog even eats nuts.

PISHCHIK (*astonished*): Imagine that!

(*They all go out except* ANYA *and* DUNYASHA.)

DUNYASHA: We've been waiting for you so long. (*Takes* ANYA's *hat and coat.*)

ANYA: I didn't sleep for four nights on the journey. Now I feel extremely cold.

DUNYASHA: When you went away it was Lent, there was snow and frost then, but now. . . . My darling! (*Laughs and kisses her.*) I really have missed you, my precious, my joy. I must tell you right away: I can't wait a minute. . . .

ANYA (*listlessly*): What now?

DUNYASHA: Yepikhodov, the clerk, proposed to me just after Easter.

ANYA: You're always talking about the same subject . . . (*Straightening her hair.*) I've lost all my hairpins . . . (*She is so exhausted that she even sways.*)

DUNYASHA: I don't know what to think, really. He loves me, he loves me so!

ANYA (*looking tenderly toward the door to her room*): My own room, my windows! It's just as though I had never gone away. I'm home! Tomorrow morning I shall get up and run into the orchard. . . . Oh, if I could get to sleep! I didn't sleep on the whole trip, I was so anxious and worried.

DUNYASHA: Pyotr Sergeevich arrived the day before yesterday.

ANYA (*joyfully*): Petya!

DUNYASHA: The gentleman is asleep in the bath house. He has settled in there. "I'm afraid of being in their way," he said. (*She glances at her pocket-watch.*) I was supposed to wake him up, but Varvara Mikhailovna told me not to. "Don't you wake him," she says.

(*Enter* VARYA *with a bunch of keys at her waist.*)

VARYA: Dunyasha, coffee, right away. . . . Mamma's asking for coffee.

DUNYASHA: This very minute. (*goes out.*)

VARYA: Well, thank God, you've come back. You're home again. (*embracing her.*) My little darling has returned, my beauty has come back again!

ANYA: I have been through so much!

VARYA: I can imagine!

ANYA: I left in Holy Week. It was so cold then, and all the way Charlotta would not stop talking and showing off her magic tricks. Why did you want to saddle me with Charlotta?

VARYA: You couldn't have traveled all alone, darling, at seventeen!

ANYA: At last we get to Paris. It is cold there — snowing. I speak French awfully badly. Mamma is living on the fifth floor, I go up to see her and there are certain French people, ladies and an old priest with a little book. The place is full of tobacco smoke, not cozy at all — and suddenly I felt so sorry, oh! so sorry for mamma. I put my arms around her head and hugged her and couldn't let her go. Mamma fondled me over and over — she cried.

VARYA (*through tears*): Don't talk about it, don't speak of it!

ANYA: She had already sold her villa near Mentone. She had nothing left, nothing. I hadn't a *kopek*[2] left either — we barely had enough to get there. But mamma doesn't understand! When we have dinner at the stations she always orders the most expensive things and tips each of the waiters a whole *rouble*. Charlotta's just the same. And Yasha insists upon ordering a portion for himself — it's simply awful. You know Yasha is mamma's valet now. We brought him here with us.

VARYA: Yes, I've seen the young rogue.

ANYA: Well tell me, have you paid the interest on the mortgage?

VARYA: How could we?

ANYA: Oh, my God! Oh, my God!

VARYA: In August they will be selling the place off.

ANYA: My God!

LOPAKHIN (*pokes his head in at the door and moos like a cow*): Moo! (*Disappears.*)

VARYA (*crying*): There! Oh, how I would like to. . . . (*Shakes her fist.*)

ANYA (*embracing* VARYA, *quietly*): Varya, has he proposed to you? (VARYA *shakes her head* [no].) But he loves you. Why is it you two don't come to an understanding? What are you waiting for?

VARYA: I don't think that there ever will be anything between us. He's too busy. He can't be bothered with me. He takes no notice of me. God bless him, it makes me miserable to see him. . . . Everyone's talking of our getting married, everyone's congratulatory, and actually there's really nothing there; it's all like a dream. (*In another tone.*) You have a brooch like a bee.

ANYA (*mournfully*): Mamma bought it. (*Goes into her room and in a light-hearted, childish tone calls back.*) In Paris I went up in a balloon.

VARYA: My darling is home again, my beauty is home again!

(DUNYASHA *returns with the coffee pot and makes coffee.*)

VARYA (*standing at the door* [*of* ANYA's *room*]): All day long, darling, as I'm busy running the house, I keep dreaming all the time. If only we could marry you to a rich man, then I'd rest more secure. Then I would go off all alone to a convent . . . then to Kiev . . . then to Moscow . . . and so I'd spend my life, going from one holy place to another. . . . I would go on and on. . . . What blissful beauty![3]

ANYA: The birds are singing in the orchard. What time is it?

---

2 A *rouble* was a Russian silver coin then worth about fifty cents and a *kopek* was a copper coin, worth only one-hundredth of a *rouble*. 3 A loose rendering of a conventional expression in the language of the Orthodox church.

VARYA: It must be after two. It's time you were asleep, darling. (*Going into* ANYA's *room.*) What blissful beauty!

(YASHA *enters with a traveling rug and a suitcase.*)

YASHA (*crosses the room, mincingly*): May one come through here, pray?

DUNYASHA: I should hardly recognize you, Yasha. How you have changed abroad!

YASHA: Hmm! . . . And who are you?

DUNYASHA: When you went away I was only that high. (*Indicates distance from the floor.*) Dunyasha, Fyodor Kozoedov's daughter. . . . You don't remember me?

YASHA: Hmm! . . . You're a little cucumber! (*Looks around and embraces her. She shrieks and drops a saucer.* YASHA *goes out hastily.*)

VARYA (*in the doorway [to* ANYA's *room], in a displeased tone*): What now?

DUNYASHA (*through her tears*): I have broken a saucer.

VARYA: Well, that's good luck.

ANYA (*coming out of her room*): We ought to prepare mamma. Petya is here.

VARYA: I gave orders not to wake him up.

ANYA (*pensively*): It's six years since father died, and only a month later little brother Grisha was drowned in the river, such a pretty little boy he was, only seven years old. It was more than mamma could bear, so she went away, went away without looking back (*shuddering*). . . . How well I understand her, if she only knew! (*a pause.*) And Petya Trofimov was Grisha's tutor, he may remind her. . . .

(*Enter* FIRS *wearing a jacket and a white waistcoat.*)

FIRS (*going up to the coffee-pot, perturbed*): The mistress will be served here. (*Puts on white gloves.*) Is the coffee ready? (*Sternly, to* DUNYASHA.) You — what about the cream?

DUNYASHA: Oh, my goodness! (*Runs out quickly.*)

FIRS (*fussing around the coffee-pot*): Ah, you half-baked[4]. . . . (*Muttering to himself.*) They have come back from Paris. And the old master used to go to Paris too . . . with horses. (*Laughs.*)

VARYA: What is it, Firs?

FIRS: What is your pleasure? (*Joyfully*) My mistress has come home. I have lived to see her once more! Now I can die. (*Weeps with joy.*)

(*Enter* LYUBOV ANDREEVNA, GAEV, SIMYONOV-PISHCHIK; SIMYONOV-PISHCHIK *is in [peasant costume] long-waisted full coat of fine cloth and ballooning trousers.* GAEV *as he comes on goes through the motions of shooting billiards.*)

LYUBOV: How does it go? Let me see if I can remember: the yellow one into the corner and double into the side pocket.

GAEV: Put a little English on the cue-ball. Why, once, sister, we used to sleep together in this very room, and now I'm fifty-one, strange as that may seem.

LOPAKHIN: Yes, time flies.

GAEV: What's that you say?

LOPAKHIN: Time, I say, flies.

GAEV: It smells of patchouli[5] here!

ANYA: I'm going to bed. Good night, mamma. (*Kisses her mother.*)

LYUBOV: My precious little child. (*Kisses her hands.*) Aren't you glad to be home? I can't come to my senses.

ANYA: Good night, uncle.

---

4 Chekhov invented the word *nedotëpa*, literally "not finished chopping," which has now become part of the Russian common speech. The implication for the cherry orchard and the axes cannot be carried over into English, only the pejorative feeling. 5 A perfume made from the fragrant oil of an East Indian plant of the mint family. It seems to be Lopakhin's cologne.

GAEV (*kissing her face and hands*): God bless you, how like your mother you are! (*to his sister.*) At her age you were exactly like her, Lyuba.

(ANYA *shakes hands with* LOPAKHIN *and* PISHCHIK *and goes out, closing the door* [*to her room*] *after her.*)

LYUBOV: She's exhausted.

PISHCHIK: It must have been a long journey, to be sure.

VARYA (*to* LOPAKHIN *and* PISHCHIK): Well, gentlemen? It's past two o'clock and high time to say goodbye.

LYUBOV (*laughing*): You're just the same as ever, Varya. (*Draws her to herself and kisses her.*) I'll just drink my coffee and then we shall all go to bed. (FIRS *puts a cushion under her feet.*) Thank you, my dear. I have got used to coffee. I drink it day and night. Thanks, dear old man. (*Kisses* FIRS.)

VARYA: I'd better see to it that all the baggage has arrived. (*Goes out.*)

LYUBOV: Is this really me sitting here? (*Laughs.*) I feel like dancing and waving my arms. (*Covers her face with her hands.*) Who knows, maybe I am asleep. God knows I love my country, I love it dearly; I couldn't look out of the window of the train, I was crying so. (*Through her tears.*) But I must drink my coffee, though. Thank you, Firs, thanks, dear old man. I'm so glad to find you still alive.

FIRS: The day before yesterday.

GAEV: He doesn't hear well.

LOPAKHIN: I have to leave for Kharkov shortly after four this morning. . . . It is annoying! I wanted to have a look at you and a little talk. . . . You look splendid, as always.

PISHCHIK (*breathing heavily*): More beautiful, in fact. . . . Dressed like a Parisienne . . . as the song says, you fixed my wagon completely.

LOPAKHIN: Your brother, this here Leonid Andreevich, is always saying that I'm a boor, that I'm a money-grubber. But I don't mind. Let him talk. All I want is for you to trust in me as you used to. I want your wonderful, pathetic eyes to look at me as they used to in the old days. Merciful God! My father was a serf of your grandfather and of your father, but you yourself did so much for me once that I've forgotten all that. I love you as though you were my own family . . . more than my own family.

LYUBOV: I can't sit still, I simply cannot. (*Jumps up and walks around, violently agitated.*) I shall not be able to live through this happiness. . . . You may laugh at me. I am silly. . . . My dear bookcase. (*Kisses the bookcase.*) My little table.

GAEV: Nurse died while you were away.

LYUBOV (*sitting down and drinking her coffee*): Yes, God rest her soul. They wrote me of her death.

GAEV: And Anastasy is dead. Squinting Petrushka has left me and he lives now at the police captain's in town. (*Takes a box of hard candies out of his pocket and sucks one.*)

PISHCHIK: My daughter, Dashenka, wishes to be remembered to you.

LOPAKHIN: I would like to tell you something very pleasant and cheering. (*Glancing at his watch.*) I must go now. . . . There's no time to say much . . . well, I can say it in two or three words. As you know, your cherry orchard is to be sold to pay your debts; the twenty-second of August is the date fixed for the auction; but don't worry, my dear lady, you may sleep in peace, there is a way out. . . . This is my plan. I beg your attention. Your estate is only twenty *versts*[6] from town, the railway now runs nearby, and if the cherry orchard and the land along the river bank were cut up into building plots and then leased for summer cottages, you would make an income of at the very least 25,000 *roubles* a year out of it.

---

6 A *verst* is 3500 feet.

GAEV: Excuse me, that's nonsense.

LYUBOV: I don't quite understand you, Yermolay Alexeevich.

LOPAKHIN: You will be able to get a rent of at the very least twenty-five *roubles* a year for a plot of about three acres from summer residents, and if you announce it now I'll bet you whatever you like there won't be one square foot of ground left by autumn — everything will be snapped up. In brief, I congratulate you — you are saved. It's a perfect site. The river is deep. Only of course the ground must be put in order and cleaned up — all the old buildings, for example, must be torn down, this house too, which is really worthless, and the old cherry orchard must be cut down.

LYUBOV: Cut down? My dear fellow, forgive me, but you don't know what you are talking about. If there is one thing that is interesting — remarkable, indeed — in the whole province, it's our cherry orchard.

LOPAKHIN: The only thing remarkable about the orchard is that it's very big. There's a crop of cherries every second year and then you can't dispose of it. Nobody will buy them.

GAEV: This orchard is mentioned in the *Encyclopedia.*

LOPAKHIN (*glancing at his watch*): If we don't decide on something and don't take some steps, on the twenty-second of August the cherry orchard and the entire estate will be auctioned off. Make up your minds! There is no other way out. I'll swear to that. No, no!

FIRS: In the old days, forty or fifty years ago, they used to dry the cherries, soak them, pickle them, make them into jam, and they used to. . . .

GAEV: Be quiet, Firs.

FIRS: And they used to send the preserved cherries to Moscow and to Kharkov by the cartload. That brought in money. And the preserved cherries in those days were soft and juicy, sweet, fragrant. . . . They had a way to do them then. . . .

LYUBOV: And where is that method now?

FIRS: Forgotten. Nobody remembers it.

PISHCHIK (*to* LYUBOV ANDREEVNA): What's it like in Paris? Did you eat frogs?

LYUBOV: I ate crocodiles.

PISHCHIK: Imagine that now!

LOPAKHIN: There used to be only the gentry and the peasants living in the country, but now there are these summer people. All the towns, even the smallest ones, are surrounded nowadays by summer cottages. And one can say that in another twenty years the summer residents will multiply to an extraordinary degree. Now the summer resident only drinks tea on his porch, but maybe he'll take to working his bit of land too, and then your cherry orchard would become happy, rich, prosperous. . . .

GAEV (*indignantly*): What nonsense!

(*Enter* VARYA *and* YASHA.)

VARYA: There are two telegrams for you, mamma. (*Takes out a key and opens an old-fashioned bookcase with a loud noise.*) Here they are.

LYUBOV (*taking the telegrams*): From Paris. (*Tears up the telegrams without finishing reading them.*) With Paris — things are finished.

GAEV: Do you know, Lyuba, how old that bookcase is? Last week I pulled out the bottom drawer. I look — there is a date burned into it. The bookcase was made exactly a hundred years ago. What do you think of that? Well? We could have celebrated its jubilee. It is an inanimate object, but nevertheless it is a *book*case.

PISHCHIK (*amazed*): A hundred years! Imagine that now!

GAEV: Yes . . . that is something . . . (*feeling the bookcase*) dear, honored bookcase! I salute the existence of that which for more than a hundred years has served the pure ideals of goodness and justice! Your silent call to fruitful labor has never flagged in a hundred years, maintaining (*in tears*) in the generations of our family courage and faith in a brighter future and fostering in us ideals of goodness and social consciousness. (*A pause.*)

LOPAKHIN: Yes. . . .

LYUBOV: You are just the same as ever, Lyonya.

GAEV (*a little embarrassed*): A little English on the ball into the corner pocket. I am cutting into the middle.

LOPAKHIN (*glancing at his watch*): Well, it's time I was going.

YASHA (*handing medicine to* LYUBOV AND-REEVNA): Perhaps you will take your pills now.

PISHCHIK: You shouldn't take medicines, my dear Madame . . . they do neither harm nor good. Let me have them, honored lady. (*Takes the pillbox, pours the pills into the palm of his hand, blows on them, puts them into his mouth, and drinks some kvass.*) There!

LYUBOV (*alarmed*): Why, you must be out of your mind!

PISHCHIK: I have taken all the pills.

LOPAKHIN: What a glutton! (*Everybody laughs.*)

FIRS: The gentleman stayed with us during Easter week, ate half a bucket of cucumbers. . . . (*Mutters.*)

LYUBOV: What is he saying?

VARYA: He's been muttering like that for the last three years. We are used to it.

YASHA: Venerable age!

(CHARLOTTA IVANOVNA, *in a white dress, a very thin, tightly-corseted figure with a lorgnette at her belt, walks across the room.*)

LOPAKHIN: I beg your pardon, Charlotta Ivanovna, I have not had time to greet you yet. (*Trying to kiss her hand.*)

CHARLOTTA (*pulling away her hand*): If I permit you to kiss my hand, you'll be wanting to kiss my elbow, and then my shoulder.

LOPAKHIN: I have no luck today! (*Everybody laughs.*) Charlotta Ivanovna, show us a trick!

LYUBOV: Charlotta, show us a trick!

CHARLOTTA (*having some trouble with the Russian language*): It is necessary — not. I'm desire to sleep. (*Goes out.*)

LOPAKHIN: In three weeks we'll meet again. (*Kisses* LYUBOV ANDREEVNA'S *hand.*) Goodbye until then — I must go. (*to* GAEV) Goodbye. (*Kisses* PISHCHIK.) Goodbye. (*Shakes hands with* VARYA, *then with* FIRS *and* YASHA.) I don't want to go. (*to* LYUBOV AN-DREEVNA) If you think over my plan for the cottages and come to a decision, let me know. I will get you 50,000 *roubles* or so. Think it over seriously.

VARYA (*angrily*): Well, aren't you going, for goodness' sake?

LOPAKHIN: I'm going, I'm going. (*Goes out.*)

GAEV: Boor! I beg pardon, though . . . Varya's going to marry him, he's Varya's intended.

VARYA: Don't talk useless nonsense, uncle.

LYUBOV: Well, Varya, I shall be delighted. He's a good man.

PISHCHIK: He is, one must acknowledge, a most worthy gentleman. And my Dashenka . . . she also says that . . . she says . . . all sorts of things. (*Snores, but wakes up immediately.*) But all the same, honored lady, could you oblige me . . . with a loan of 240 *roubles* . . . to pay the interest on my mortgage tomorrow?

VARYA (*dismayed*): No, no!

LYUBOV: Really, I have absolutely nothing.

PISHCHIK: It will turn up. (*laughs.*) I never lose hope. Just when I think everything is lost, I am a ruined man, lo and behold — the railway line ran right across my land and . . . they paid me for it. And, behold, something else will turn up again, if not today, then to-morrow. . . . Dashenka will win 200,000 . . . she's got a lottery ticket.

LYUBOV: Well, we've finished our coffee, we can go to bed.

FIRS (*brushing* GAEV [*'s clothes*], *reprovingly*): You've got on the wrong trousers again! What am I to do with you?

VARYA (*softly*): Anya's asleep. (*quietly opening the window*) Now that the sun is up it's not a bit cold. Look, mamma, what exquisite trees! My goodness! Lord, the air! The starlings are singing!

GAEV (*opening another window*): The orchard is all white. You've not forgotten it, Lyuba? That long avenue that runs straight, straight as a belt, how it shines on a moonlight night. You remember? You haven't forgotten?

LYUBOV (*looking out of the window into the orchard*): Oh, my childhood, my innocence! I used to sleep in this nursery, from here I looked out into the orchard, happiness awoke with me every morning, and in those days the orchard was just as it is now, nothing has changed (*laughs with delight.*) All, all white! Oh, my orchard! After the dark, nasty autumn, and the cold winter, you are young again, and full of happiness, the heavenly angels have not deserted you. . . . If I could cast off the heavy stone that weighs on my breast, the burden on my shoulders, if I could forget my past!

GAEV: Yes, and the orchard will be sold to pay our debts, strange as it may seem. . . .

LYUBOV: See — our dead mother walking . . . all in white, in the orchard! (*laughing with delight.*) It is she!

GAEV: Where?

VARYA: Mamma, what are you saying?

LYUBOV: There is no one there. It was my imagination. On the right there, by the path to the bower, there is a white tree. It is bent over, like a woman. . . .

(*Enter* TROFIMOV *wearing a shabby student's uniform and glasses.*)

What a wonderful orchard! The white clouds of blossom, the blue sky. . . .

TROFIMOV: Lyubov Andreevna! (*she turns and looks at him.*) I only want to pay my respects to you and then leave at once. (*Kisses her hand warmly.*) I was told to wait until morning, but I didn't have the patience to wait any longer.

(LYUBOV ANDREEVNA *looks at him, perplexed.*)

VARYA (*through her tears*): This is Petya Trofimov.

TROFIMOV: Petya Trofimov. The former tutor of your Grisha. Have I really changed so much?

(LYUBOV ANDREEVNA *embraces him and weeps quietly.*)

GAEV (*flustered*): There, there, Lyuba.

VARYA (*crying*): I *told* you, Petya, to wait until tomorrow.

LYUBOV: My Grisha . . . my boy . . . Grisha . . . my son!

VARYA: What can one do, mamma? It is God's will.

TROFIMOV (*gently, through his tears*): There, there. . . .

LYUBOV (*weeping quietly*): My little boy was lost . . . drowned. Why? Oh, dear Petya, why? (*more quietly.*) Anya is asleep in there, and I'm talking loudly . . . making all this noise. . . . But, Petya, why have you grown uglier? Why do you look older?

TROFIMOV: A peasant woman in the train called me a mangy-looking gentleman.

LYUBOV: You were still a little boy then, a nice little student, and now your hair is thin — and you wear spectacles. Are you really still a student? (*Goes toward the door.*)

TROFIMOV: I seem likely to be a perpetual student.

LYUBOV (*kisses her brother, then* VARYA): Well, go to bed. You are older too, Leonid.

PISHCHIK (*following her*): I suppose it's time

we were asleep. . . . Ooh, my gout! I'm staying the night. Lyubov Andreevna, my dear soul, if you could manage . . . tomorrow morning . . . 240 *roubles.*

GAEV: This one goes on and on with the same old story.

PISHCHIK: 240 *roubles* . . . to pay the interest on my mortgage.

LYUBOV: My dear man, I have no money.

PISHCHIK: I'll pay it back, my dear . . . it's a small sum.

LYUBOV: Oh, well, Leonid will give it to you. . . . You give him the money, Leonid.

GAEV: Me give it to him? (*Ironically*) Let him keep his pocket open!

LYUBOV: It can't be helped. Give it to him. He needs it. He'll pay it back.

(LYUBOV ANDREEVNA, TROFIMOV, PISHCHIK *and* FIRS *go out.* GAEV, VARYA *and* YASHA *remain.*)

GAEV: Sister hasn't got out of the habit of throwing her money around. (*to* YASHA) Get away, young fellow, you smell of the chicken coop.

YASHA (*with a smirk*): And you, Leonid Andreevich, are just the same as ever.

GAEV: What's that? (*to* VARYA) What did he say?

VARYA (*to* YASHA): Your mother has come from the village; she has been sitting in the servants' room since yesterday, waiting to see you.

YASHA: Let her wait.

VARYA: Aren't you ashamed of yourself?

YASHA: What's the hurry? She could just as well have come tomorrow. (*Goes out.*)

VARYA: Mamma's just the same as ever. She hasn't changed a bit. If she had her way, she'd give away everything.

GAEV: Yes. (*a pause*) If a great many remedies are suggested for some disease, it means that the disease is incurable. I keep thinking,

racking my brains; I have many remedies, a great many, and that really adds up to none. If someone would only leave us a legacy, or if we could marry our Anya to a very rich man, or if we could go to Yaroslavl and try our luck with my old aunt, the countess. She's very, very rich, you know.

VARYA (*crying*): If God would only help us!

GAEV: Stop blubbering. My aunt's very rich, but she doesn't like us. In the first place, sister married a lawyer instead of a nobleman. . . . (ANYA *appears in the doorway.*) She married a commoner and one could not say that she behaved very virtuously. She is good, and kind, and nice, and I love her dearly, but, however much one allows for extenuating circumstances, there's no denying that she's a sinful woman. One feels it in her slightest gesture.

VARYA (*whispering*): Anya's in the doorway.

GAEV: What's that? (*a pause*) It's funny, there seems to be something wrong with my right eye. I don't see as well as I did. And Thursday, when I was in the district court. . . .

(*Enter* ANYA.)

VARYA: Why aren't you asleep, Anya?

ANYA: I can't get to sleep.

GAEV: My little darling! (*Kisses* ANYA's *face and hands.*) My child. (*Weeps.*) You are not my niece, you are my angel. You are everything to me, believe me. Believe me. . . .

ANYA: I believe you, uncle. Everyone loves and respects you . . . but, uncle dear, you must keep quiet . . . simply be quiet. What were you saying just now about my mother, about your very own sister? What made you say that?

GAEV: Yes, yes . . . (*puts his hand over his face.*) Really, that was awful! My God, help me! And today I made a speech to the bookcase . . . so stupid! And it was only after I had finished that I saw how silly it was.

VARYA: It's true, uncle dear, you ought to keep quiet. Don't talk, that's all.

ANYA: If you could keep from talking, it would make things quieter for you, too.

GAEV: I won't speak. (*Kisses* ANYA's *hand and* VARYA's *hands.*) I am silent. Only this is about business: on Thursday I was in the district court; well, there was a large party of us there and we began talking of this and that, and you know, I believe it will be possible to raise a loan on a promissory note to pay the interest to the bank.

VARYA: If only God would help us!

GAEV: I'm going on Tuesday and I'll talk it over again. (*to* VARYA) Don't blubber. (*to* ANYA) Your mamma will talk to Lopakhin; he, of course, will not refuse her. And as soon as you are rested you shall go to Yaroslavl to the countess, to your grandmother. So we shall all set to work from three directions at once and the business is in the hat: we shall pay off the interest. I'm convinced of that. (*Puts a hard candy into his mouth.*) I swear on my honor — I swear by anything you like — the estate shall not be sold. (*Excitedly.*) By my happiness, I swear it! Here's my hand on it. Call me the basest, the most dishonest of men if I let it come up for auction. I swear by my whole being!

ANYA (*her calm has returned, she is happy*): How good you are, uncle, and how clever! (*Embraces her uncle.*) I'm at peace now! Quite content! I'm happy!

(*Enter* FIRS.)

FIRS (*reproachfully*): Leonid Andreevich, have you no fear of God? When is one going to sleep?

GAEV: Right away. You can go, Firs. I'll . . . yes, I will undress myself after all. Well, children, beddy-bye. We'll go into the details tomorrow, but now go to bed. (*kisses* ANYA *and* VARYA.) I'm a man of the 'Eighties. They don't think much of that period nowadays, but still I can say that in the course of my life I have had to suffer not a little for my convictions. It's not for nothing that the peasant loves me. You have to understand

the peasant! You have to know from which. . . .

ANYA: There you go, uncle!

VARYA: Uncle dear, you'd better be quiet.

FIRS (*angrily*): Leonid Andreevich!

GAEV: I'm coming, I'm coming. Go to bed. Off the two rails I'm sinking one. A beauty of a shot!

(*He goes out,* FIRS *hobbling after him.*)

ANYA: My mind is at rest now. Certainly I don't want to go to Yaroslavl, I don't like my grandmother, but still my mind's at rest, thanks to uncle (*sits down*).

VARYA: We must get some sleep. I'm going now. Something unpleasant happened while you were away. In the old servants' quarters, as you know, there are only the old servants — Yefimyushka, Polya, and Yevstigney — and Karp, too. They began to let in all sorts of rascals to spend the night. I said nothing. But then I heard that they had been spreading a rumor that I had given an order for them to be fed nothing but peas. Out of stinginess, you know . . . And it was all Yevstigney's doing. . . . Very well, I said to myself. . . . If that's the way it is, I thought, wait a minute. I sent for Yevstigney . . . (*yawns*) he comes . . . "What's this, Yevstigney?" I said. "You fool, you". . . . (*Looking at* ANYA) Anechka! (*a pause.*) She's asleep. (*Puts her arm around* ANYA.) Come to bed . . . come along. (*Leads her.*) My darling has fallen asleep! Come. (*They go.*)

(*In the distance, beyond the orchard, a shepherd plays on a pipe.* TROFIMOV *crosses the room and, seeing* VARYA *and* ANYA, *stops.*)

VARYA: Shh! asleep, asleep. Come, my darling.

ANYA (*softly, half asleep*): I'm so tired. Still those bells. Uncle . . . dear . . . mamma and uncle. . . .

VARYA: Come, my darling, come along.

(*They go into* ANYA's *room.*)

TROFIMOV (*deeply moved*): My sunshine! My spring!

CURTAIN

ACT TWO

A meadow. An old shrine, long abandoned and lopsided; near it a well, large stones that apparently once were tombstones, and an old garden seat. The road to GAEV's house is seen. On one side rise poplars darkening [against the sky] and there the cherry orchard begins. In the distance is seen a row of telegraph poles, and far, far away on the horizon there is the faint outline of a large town, only visible in fine clear weather. It is almost sunset. CHARLOTTA, YASHA and DUNYASHA are sitting on the garden seat. YEPIKHODOV is standing nearby, playing the guitar [mournfully]. All sit lost in thought. CHARLOTTA wears an old forage cap;[1] she has taken a gun from her shoulder and is adjusting the buckle on the sling.

CHARLOTTA (*musing*): I don't have a real passport of my own, and I don't know how old I am, and I always feel that I'm a young thing. When I was a little girl, my father and mother used to travel around to fairs and give performances — very good ones. And I used to perform the *salto-mortale*[2] and all sorts of things. And then when papa and mamma died, a German lady took me in and started to educate me. Good. So I grew up and became a governess. But where I come from, and who I am, I don't know. . . . Who are my parents? . . . perhaps they weren't even married . . . I don't know. (*Takes a cucumber out of her pocket and eats.*) I don't know anything. (*a pause*) One wants to talk and has no one to talk to. . . . I have nobody.

YEPIKHODOV (*playing the guitar and singing*):

"What do I care for the noisy world?
What do I care for friends or foes?"
How pleasant it is to play the mandoline!

DUNYASHA: That's a guitar, not a mandoline.

(*Looks in a pocket-mirror and powders her nose.*)

YEPIKHODOV: To a man mad with love, it's a mandoline. (*Sings*)

"I only wish my heart were warmed
By love's sweet shared, requited flame."

(*YASHA joins in.*)

CHARLOTTA: How very badly people sing! Ach! like jackals!

DUNYASHA (*to YASHA*): What happiness, though, to be able to visit foreign lands!

YASHA: Ah, yes, I cannot but agree with you there. (*Yawns, then lights a cigar.*)

YEPIKHODOV: That stands to reason. Abroad, everything has long since reached full consum — . . . completion.

YASHA: That's true, of course.

YEPIKHODOV: I'm a cultivated man. I read all sorts of remarkable books, but I can never make out just what I personally, precisely am inclined for, whether (exactly) to go on living or to shoot myself. But nevertheless I always carry a revolver. Here it is . . . (*Shows a revolver.*)

CHARLOTTA: I've had enough. I'm going now. (*Puts the gun over her shoulder.*) Yepikhodov, you're a very clever fellow, and a very terrifying one, too. Women must be wild about you. Brrrrrrr! (*Goes.*) These clever people are all so stupid. There's not a creature for me to talk to. . . . Always alone, alone. I have nobody . . . and who I am, what I am for, I don't know. (*Walks slowly away.*)

YEPIKHODOV: Strictly speaking, everything else aside, I'm bound to say about myself, besides, that destiny behaves mercilessly to me, as a storm does to a little boat. If, let

---

1 *Furazhka*, a peaked cap (like our yachting caps) then the commonest man's headgear in Russia. 2 Italian, "leap of death."

us assume, I am mistaken, then why (to cite one example) do I wake up this morning and look around and there on my chest is a spider of fearful magnitude . . . this big. (*Gestures with both hands.*) And then I take up a jug of *kvass* to quench my thirst and in it there is something in the highest degree unseemly, along the lines of a cockroach. (*a pause*) Have you read Buckle?[3] (*a pause*) I am desirous of troubling you a trifle, Avodtya Fyodorovna, with a couple of words.

DUNYASHA: Speak up.

YEPIKHODOV: I should be desirous with you alone . . . (*Sighs.*)

DUNYASHA (*embarrassed*): Well — just bring me my cloak first. It's by the cupboard. It's rather damp here.

YEPIKHODOV: Most certainly will I fetch it. Now I know what to do with my revolver. (*Picks up guitar and goes off playing it.*)

YASHA: "Two and twenty misfortunes." Between ourselves, he's a fool. (*yawns.*)

DUNYASHA: God forbid he should shoot himself! (*a pause*) I've become so nervous, I'm always worried. I was a little girl when I was taken into our mistress' house and now I have completely grown out of my simple life and my hands are white, as white as a lady's. I have become so sensitive. I'm so delicate and genteel that I'm afraid of everything. I am so frightened. And if you deceive me, Yasha, I don't know what will become of my nerves.

YASHA (*kisses her*): You are a little cucumber.[4] Of course a girl must never forget herself; what I dislike more than anything else is a girl being badly behaved.

DUNYASHA: I'm passionately in love with you. You are cultured. You can give your opinion about anything. (*a pause.*)

YASHA (*yawns*): Yes, that's true. My opinion is this: if a girl loves somebody, that means she is immoral (*a pause*). It's really nice smoking a cigar in the open air (*listens*).

Someone's coming this way . . . it's the gentry. (DUNYASHA *embraces him impulsively.*) Go home, as though you had been to the river to bathe; go by that path, or else they'll meet you and suppose I made an appointment with you here. That I can't bear.

DUNYASHA (*coughing softly*): That cigar has made my head ache. . . . (*Goes off.*)

(YASHA *remains sitting near the shrine. Enter* LYUBOV ANDREEVNA, GAEV *and* LOPAKHIN.)

LOPAKHIN: You have to make up your mind once and for all — there's no time to lose. It's quite a simple question, you know: will you consent to leasing the land for summer cottages or not? Just answer in one word: yes or no. One word!

LYUBOV: Who is smoking such disgusting cigars around here? (*Sits down.*)

GAEV: Now that the railway has been brought near it has made things very convenient. (*Sits down.*) We have been over and lunched in town. The yellow into the side pocket! I should like to go home and have a game.

LYUBOV: You have plenty of time.

LOPAKHIN: Just one word! (*Pleading*) Give me an answer!

GAEV (*yawns*): What do you say?

LYUBOV (*looks in her purse*): Yesterday I had quite a lot of money here and today there's scarcely any left. My poor Varya feeds us all on milk soup for the sake of economy, in the kitchen they get nothing but peas, and all the time I'm squandering my money

---

3 Henry Thomas Buckle (1821–1862) by 1853 had conceived of an elaborate *History of Civilisation in England.* He published two volumes (1857, 1861) before his death (at Damascus, while traveling) and they were very popular in Russia in the later nineteenth century.
4 Intended as a term of endearment or approval. The American equivalent would be something between "You're a peach," and "You're outasight."

recklessly. (*Drops her purse, scattering gold pieces.*) There now, they've all fallen out! (*Annoyed.*)

YASHA: Allow me. I'll soon pick them up. (*Collects the coins.*)

LYUBOV: Please do, Yasha. And why did I go to town for lunch? That restaurant is a wretched place, with its music and the table-cloth smelling of soap. . . . Why drink so much, Leonid? And eat so much? And talk so much? Today in the restaurant you talked a great deal again, and all so pointless — about the period of the 'Seventies, about the decadents. And to whom? Talking to waiters about decadents!

LOPAKHIN: Yes.

GAEV (*waving his hand*): I'm incorrigible, that's obvious. (*Irritably, to* YASHA) Why do you keep fidgeting around in front of us?

YASHA (*laughing*): I can't help laughing when I hear you talk.

GAEV (*to his sister*): Either I or he. . . .

LYUBOV: Run along. Go away, Yasha.

YASHA (*giving* LYUBOV ANDREEVNA *her purse*): Right away. (*Barely able to suppress his laughter.*) This minute . . . (*Goes off.*)

LOPAKHIN: The millionaire Deriganov intends to buy your estate. They say he is coming to the auction himself.

LYUBOV: Where did you hear that?

LOPAKHIN: That's what they say in town.

GAEV: My aunt in Yaroslavl has promised to send us something, but when, and how much she will send, we don't know.

LOPAKHIN: How much will she send? 100,000? 200,000?

LYUBOV: Oh, well! . . . 10 or 15,000 — and we must be thankful to get that.

LOPAKHIN: Forgive me, but such reckless people as you are — such odd, unbusiness-like people — I never met in my life. In plain Russian one tells you your estate is going to be sold — and you don't seem to understand it at all.

LYUBOV: Well what are we to do? Teach us what to do.

LOPAKHIN: I teach you every day. Every day I say the same thing. You absolutely must lease the cherry orchard and the land for summer cottages, and do it immediately, as fast as you can. The auction is close upon us! Do you understand? Once you make up your mind to build cottages you will be given as much money as you wish and then you are saved.

LYUBOV: Cottages and summer residents — forgive me saying so — it's so vulgar.

GAEV: There I completely agree with you.

LOPAKHIN: I'm going to burst into tears, or scream, or fall into a fit. I can't stand it! You drive me crazy! (*to* GAEV) You are an old woman!

GAEV: What's that?

LOPAKHIN: An old woman! (*Gets up to go.*)

LYUBOV (*in dismay*): No, don't go, stay, my dear friend! I beseech you. Perhaps we shall think of something.

LOPAKHIN: What is there to think of?

LYUBOV: Don't go, I beg you. With you here it's more cheerful somehow. (*a pause*) I keep expecting something, as if the house were going to tumble down around us.

GAEV (*profoundly dejected*): A carom into the side pocket, kiss in the middle.

LYUBOV: We have been sinning too much.

LOPAKHIN: You have no real sins.

GAEV (*puts a hard candy into his mouth*): They say I've eaten up my entire fortune in candy. (*Laughs.*)

LYUBOV: Oh, my sins! I've always thrown my money away like a lunatic, recklessly. I married a man who did nothing but amass debts. My husband died of champagne — he drank dreadfully. To my sorrow, I fell in love with another man and became his mistress and immediately — it was my first punishment — the blow fell upon me, here, by the river . . . my little boy was drowned and I went abroad — went away for ever, never to return, not to see this river ever again. . . . I shut my eyes and fled, beside myself, and *he* after me, pitilessly, brutally. I bought a villa near Mentone, for *he* fell ill there, and for three years I had no rest day or night. The sick man wore me out, my soul was sucked dry. And last year, when my villa was sold to pay my debts, I went to Paris and there he robbed me of everything and abandoned me for another woman . . . and I tried to poison myself. . . . So stupid, so shameful! . . . And suddenly I felt a longing for Russia, for my country, for my little girl. . . . (*Dries her tears.*) Lord, Lord, be merciful, forgive my sins! Do not punish me any more! (*Taking a telegram out of her pocket*) I got this today from Paris. He implores forgiveness, begs me to return. (*Tears up the telegram.*) I think I hear music somewhere. (*Listens.*)

GAEV: That's our famous Jewish orchestra. You remember: four violins, a flute, and a double bass.

LYUBOV: Is that still in existence? We ought to send for them some evening and give a party.

LOPAKHIN (*listening*): I can't hear . . . (*sings softly* [*a snatch of song*]).

"The Germans for money
Will take any Russian
And make him a Frenchman
At once."

(*Laughing.*) What a play I saw yesterday! It was very funny.

LYUBOV: And most likely there is not a thing funny in it. You shouldn't look at plays, you should look at yourselves a little oftener. How grey your lives are! How much futile nonsense you talk!

LOPAKHIN: That's true. I must say, honestly, we live a fool's existence. (*a pause*) My father was a peasant, an idiot: he knew nothing and taught me nothing, only beat me with his stick when he was drunk. As a matter of fact, I'm as much of a blockhead and idiot as he was. I have learned nothing properly. My handwriting is wretched. I write so badly that I feel ashamed before people, like a pig.

LYUBOV: You ought to be married, my dear friend.

LOPAKHIN: Yes . . . that's true.

LYUBOV: You should marry our Varya, she's a good girl.

LOPAKHIN: Yes.

LYUBOV: She's uncomplicated, she's busy from morn 'til night, and the most important thing is that she loves you. Besides, you have liked her for a long time.

LOPAKHIN: Well, I'm not opposed to it. . . . She's a good girl. (*a pause*)

GAEV: I've been offered a position in the bank — 6,000 *roubles* a year. Did you hear about it?

LYUBOV: How could you? Forget about that.

(*Enter* FIRS *with an overcoat.*)

FIRS: Put this on, sir. It's damp.

GAEV (*putting it on*): You pester me, old man.

FIRS: You can't go on like this. You went away this morning without leaving word, sir.

LYUBOV (*looking him over*): You look older, Firs.

FIRS: What do you wish, madame?

LOPAKHIN: She said you look older.

FIRS: I've lived a long life. They were arranging my wedding before your papa was born . . . (*Laughs.*) I was the head footman before the emancipation came. I would not consent to be set free then. I stayed on with my old master . . . (*a pause*) I remember how they celebrated and didn't themselves have any idea what they were celebrating.

LOPAKHIN (*ironically*): Oh those were the good old days. There was flogging then, anyway.

FIRS (*not hearing*): That's right! The peasants were with the masters and the masters were with the peasants, but now they are all separate, everything's confused.

GAEV: Hold your tongue, Firs. I must go to town tomorrow. I have been promised an introduction to a general, who might let us have a loan.

LOPAKHIN: That won't lead to anything. And you won't be able to pay your interest, you can rest assured of that.

LYUBOV: That's all his nonsense. There are no such generals.

(*Enter* TROFIMOV, ANYA *and* VARYA.)

GAEV: Here come our girls.

ANYA: Mamma's sitting here.

LYUBOV (*tenderly*): Come along, come along, my darlings! (*Embraces* ANYA *and* VARYA.) If you only knew how much I love you both. Sit down beside me, there, like that. (*All sit down.*)

LOPAKHIN: Our perpetual student is perpetually with the ladies.

TROFIMOV: That's none of your business.

LOPAKHIN: He'll soon be fifty, and he's still a student.

TROFIMOV: Cut out your idiotic jokes.

LOPAKHIN: Why are you so cross, you odd fellow?

TROFIMOV: Oh, don't keep pestering me!

LOPAKHIN (*laughs*): Let me ask you, what's your idea of me?

TROFIMOV: I'll tell you my idea of you, Yermolay Alexeevich: you are a rich man, you'll soon be a millionaire. Well, just as in the economy of nature a wild beast is useful because it gobbles up everything that comes its way, so you too have your purpose.

(*Everybody laughs.*)

VARYA: Better tell us something about the planets, Petya.

LYUBOV: No, let us go on with the conversation we had yesterday.

TROFIMOV: What was it about?

GAEV: About the proud man.

TROFIMOV: We had a long conversation yesterday but we came to no conclusion. The proud man, in your sense of the thing, is something mystical. Perhaps you are right, from your point of view, but if one looks at it simply, without sublety, what sort of pride can there be — what sense is there in it — if man in his physiological composition is very poorly constructed, if in the vast majority of cases he is coarse, dull-witted, profoundly unhappy? One must abandon glorification of self. One should work, that's all.

GAEV: One must die, in any case.

TROFIMOV: Who knows? And what does it mean — dying? Perhaps man has a hundred senses and only the five we know about are lost at death, while the other ninety-five go on living.

LYUBOV: How clever you are, Petya!

LOPAKHIN (*ironically*): Terribly clever!

TROFIMOV: Humanity progresses, perfecting its powers. Everything that is beyond its ken at this time will some day become comprehensible and familiar. Only we must work, we must with all our might aid the seeker after truth. Among us here in Russia such workers are few, so far. The vast majority of the intellectuals I know are after nothing, are doing nothing, are not yet fit for work of any kind. They call themselves the intelligensia, but they talk down to their servants, treat the peasants as if they were animals, learn little, read nothing serious, do absolutely nothing, only talk about science and have a smattering about art. They all look like serious people, they all have severe expressions, they all chatter of weighty matters and philosophize, and meanwhile the vast majority of us — ninety-nine percent — live like savages, at the least excuse turn to violence and abuse, eat disgustingly, sleep in filth and stuffiness, bedbugs everywhere, stench and damp and moral turpitude. And it's obvious that all our fine talk is only to divert our attention and other people's from the truth. Show me where to find the day-nurseries there's so much talk about, and the reading-rooms! They are only in novels — in real life there aren't any of them! There is nothing but filth, vulgarity, Asiatic backwardness. I fear and dislike very serious faces. I'm afraid of serious conversations. We'd be far better off to be silent.

LOPAKHIN: You know, I get up before five o'clock every morning and I work from morning to night. And I have money, my own and other people's, always passing through my hands and I see what people are made of, all around me. One has only to begin to do anything to see how few honest, decent people there are. Sometimes when I lie awake at night I think: "Oh Lord, thou hast given us immense forests, boundless plains, the broadest horizons, and living here we ourselves ought really to be giants."

LYUBOV: Now you ask for giants! They are no good except in fairy tales; in real life they frighten us.

(YEPIKHODOV *advances in the background, playing the guitar.*)

LYUBOV (*dreamily*): There goes Yepikhodov.

ANYA (*dreamily*): There goes Yepikhodov.

GAEV: My friends, the sun has set.

TROFIMOV: Yes.

GAEV (*not loudly, but in a declamatory way*): O Nature, divine Nature, thou art bright with eternal radiance, beautiful and indifferent! Thou, whom we call Mother, dost quicken and destroy!

VARYA (*beseechingly*): Uncle dear!

ANYA: Uncle, you are doing it again!

TROFIMOV: You'd be much better off playing billiards.

GAEV: I am silent. I am silent.

(*All sit wrapt in thought. Perfect stillness. Only the muttering of* FIRS *is audible. Suddenly there is a sound in the distance, as if from the sky: the sound of a harp-string snapping, mournfully dying away.*)

LYUBOV: What is that?

LOPAKHIN: I don't know. Somewhere far away in a mine a bucket has fallen and broken in the pits. But somewhere very far away.

GAEV: It might be some sort of bird — such as a heron.

TROFIMOV: Or an owl.

LYUBOV (*shuddering*): I don't know why exactly, but it's unpleasant. (*a pause*)

FIRS: It was the same before the calamity — the owl hooted and the *samovar*[5] hissed all day long.

GAEV: Before what calamity?

FIRS: Before the emancipation. (*a pause*)

LYUBOV: Come along, my friends, let's be going. Evening is falling. (*to* ANYA) There are tears in your eyes. What is it, darling? (*Embraces her.*)

ANYA: Nothing, mamma; it's nothing.

TROFIMOV: There's somebody coming.

(*A* PASSER-BY *appears in a shabby white forage cap and an overcoat. He is slightly drunk.*)

PASSER-BY: Permit me to inquire, can I get directly to the station this way?

GAEV: Yes, go along that road.

PASSER-BY: I am deeply grateful. (*After coughing*) The weather is superb. (*declaiming*) My brother, my suffering brother! . . . Come to the Volga! Whose groan do you hear? . . . (*to* VARYA) Mademoiselle, vouchsafe a hungry Russian thirty *kopeks*.

---

5 Literally in Russian a "self-boiler," a *samovar* is a metal urn with an internal tube which can be filled with hot coals to boil water for tea.

(VARYA *shrieks with alarm.*)

LOPAKHIN (*angrily*): To every indecency there's a propriety!

LYUBOV (*flustered*): Here, take this. (*Looks in her purse.*) I've no silver. Never mind — here's a gold piece for you.

PASSER-BY: I am deeply grateful to you. (*Goes off.*)

(*Laughter.*)

VARYA (*frightened*): I'm going home. I'm going. . . . Oh, mamma, the servants have nothing to eat, and you gave him a gold piece!

LYUBOV: There's no doing anything with a silly like me. When we get home, I'll give you everything I have. Yermolay Alexeevich, you will lend me some more. . . !

LOPAKHIN: I will.

LYUBOV: Come, friends, it's time to be going. Oh, Varya, we have made a match for you. I congratulate you.

VARYA (*through her tears*): Mamma, that's not anything to joke about.

LOPAKHIN: "Ophelia, get thee to a nunnery!" [6]

GAEV: My hands are trembling. It's a long time since I had a game of billiards.

LOPAKHIN: "Ophelia! Nymph, in thy orisons be all my sins remember'd."

LYUBOV: Let's go. It will soon be supper-time.

VARYA: How he frightened me! My heart's simply throbbing.

LOPAKHIN: Let me remind you, ladies and gentlemen: on the twenty-second of August the cherry orchard will be sold. Think about that! Think about that!

(*All go off except* TROFIMOV *and* ANYA.)

ANYA (*laughing*): I'm grateful to that passer-by. He frightened Varya off and we are alone.

TROFIMOV: Varya's afraid we are going to fall in love with each other, and for days she hasn't left us alone. With her narrow mind she can't grasp that we are above love. To eliminate the petty and transitory which hinders us from being free and happy — that is the meaning of our life. Forward! We march forward inexorably toward the bright star that shines yonder in the distance. Forward! Do not lag behind, my friends!

ANYA (*claps her hands*): How beautifully you speak! (*a pause*) It's marvelous here today.

TROFIMOV: Yes, it is astonishing weather.

ANYA: Somehow, Petya, you've made me so that I don't love the cherry orchard the way I used to. I used to love it so dearly. I used to think there was no spot on earth like our orchard.

TROFIMOV: All Russia is our orchard. The land is great and beautiful — there are many beautiful places in it. (*a pause*) Just think, Anya, your grandfather, your great-grandfather, and all your ancestors were slave-owners — the owners of living souls — and from every cherry in the orchard, from every leaf, from every tree trunk there are human creatures looking at you. Don't you hear their voices? Oh, it's awful! Your orchard is a frightful thing, and when in the evening or late at night one walks around in the orchard, the old bark on the trees glimmers dimly and the old cherry trees seem to be dreaming of what used to be a hundred or two hundred years ago, tormented by fearful visions. Of course, we have remained at least two hundred years behind the times, we have really achieved nothing yet, we have no definite attitude toward the past, we do nothing but philosophize or complain of boredom or drink vodka. It is clear that to begin to live in the present we must first expiate the past, we must break with it, and

---

6 Lopakhin is quoting, almost exactly, Shakespeare's *Hamlet*, but in English it is impossible to render the pun (or more likely Lopakhin's unconscious error) derived from the confusion of the name *Ophelia* with the verb ОХМеЛеТЬ, to become tipsy. In a subsequent line Lopakhin once again quotes *Hamlet* and gets the name *Ophelia* slightly wrong.

we can atone for it only by suffering, by extraordinary, unceasing labor. Understand that, Anya.

ANYA: The house we live in has long since ceased to be our own, and I shall leave it, I give you my word.

TROFIMOV: If you have the keys to the house, fling them into the well and go away. Be free as the wind.

ANYA (*ecstatically*): How beautifully you said that!

TROFIMOV: Believe me, Anya, believe me! I am not thirty yet — I am young — I am still a student, but I have gone through so much already! As soon as winter comes I am hungry, sick, loaded with cares, poor as a beggar, and what ups and downs of fortune have I not experienced at the hands of fate! And my soul has always, every minute, day and night, been full of inexplicable forebodings. But I have a foreboding of happiness, Anya. I see glimpses of it already.

ANYA (*pensively*): The moon is rising.

(YEPIKHODOV *is heard still playing the same mournful song on the guitar. The moon rises. Somewhere near the poplars* VARYA *is looking for* ANYA *and calling:* "Anya! Where are you?")

TROFIMOV: Yes, the moon is rising. (*a pause*) Here is happiness — here it comes now! It's coming nearer and nearer; already I can hear its footsteps. And if we never see it — or if we do not recognize it — what does that matter? Others will see it after us!

VARYA'S VOICE (*offstage*): Anya! Where are you?

TROFIMOV: That's Varya again. (*Angrily*) It's revolting!

ANYA: Well, let's go down to the river. It's lovely there.

TROFIMOV: Yes, let's go. (*They go off.*)

VARYA'S VOICE (*offstage*): Anya! Anya!

CURTAIN

ACT THREE

A drawing-room separated by an arch from a larger drawing-room. The chandelier burning. The Jewish orchestra, the same that was mentioned in ACT II, *is heard playing in the anteroom. It is evening. In the larger drawing-room they are dancing the* grand rond[1] *The* VOICE OF SIMYONOV-PISHCHIK: "Promenade à une paire!" *They enter the drawing-room in couples: first* PISHCHIK *and* CHARLOTTA IVANOVNA, *second* TROFIMOV *and* LYUBOV ANDREEVNA, *third* ANYA *with the* POST-OFFICE CLERK, *fourth* VARYA *with the* STATION MASTER, *etc.* [*other guests in pairs*]. VARYA *is quietly weeping and wipes away tears as she dances.* DUNYASHA *is in the last couple. As they move through the drawing-room,* PISHCHIK *shouts:* "Grand rond, balancez!" *and* "Les cavaliers à genou et remerciez vos dames."

(FIRS *in a dress coat brings in seltzer water on a tray.* PISHCHIK *and* TROFIMOV *enter the drawing-room.*)

PISHCHIK: I am a full-blooded man; I've already had two strokes. Dancing is hard work for me, but (as the old saying goes) if you run with the pack, whether you bark or not you have to wag your tail! I'm as strong, I may say, as a horse. My late father, who would have his joke — may God rest his soul! — used to say about our origin that the ancient line of Simyonov-Pishchik was descended from the very horse that Caligula made a member of the Senate.[2] (*Sits down.*) But I have no money — that's where the trouble lies. A hungry dog believes in nothing but meat . . . (*snores but immediately wakes up*)

---

1 The *grand rond* is danced by pairs in a circle. Pishchik calls "March around in couples," "Form the large circle and balance," and "Gentlemen kneel and thank your ladies." The use of French suggests a desire for cultivated elegance. 2 Under the name of Caligula, Caius Cæsar Germanicus (A.D. 12–41) ruled as Roman emperor (A.D. 37–41) after Tiberius. Perhaps to show his contempt for those offices, he is said to have made his horse a consul and a member of a priestly college.

And myself too . . . I'm capable of nothing when it comes to money except . . .

TROFIMOV: There really is something horsey about your appearance.

PISHCHIK: Well, a horse is a fine beast. . . . A horse can be sold.

(*There is the sound of billiards being played in an adjoining room.* VARYA *appears in the archway leading to the larger drawing-room.*)

TROFIMOV (*teasing*): Madame Lopakhina! Madame Lopakhina!

VARYA (*angrily*): Mangy-looking gentleman!

TROFIMOV: Yes, I'm a mangy-looking gentleman — and proud of it!

VARYA (*musing bitterly*): Here we have hired musicians and we have nothing to pay them with. (*Goes out.*)

TROFIMOV (*to* PISHCHIK): If you put the energy you have wasted in your life in trying to find the money to pay your interest into something else, you probably would have turned the world upside down.

PISHCHIK: Neitzsche — the philosopher — a very great and very famous man . . . of enormous intellect . . . says in his writings that one can forge banknotes.

TROFIMOV: You mean you have read Neitzsche?

PISHCHIK: Well, Dashenka told me. . . . Right now I'm in such a predicament I might just as well forge banknotes. The day after tomorrow I have to pay 310 *roubles* — and I've found only 130. (*Feels in his pockets, alarmed.*) The money's gone! I've lost my money! (*Through tears*) Where's the money? (*Joyfully*) Oh here it is, inside the lining. . . . That made me break out in perspiration!

(*Enter* LYUBOV ANDREEVNA *and* CHARLOTTA IVANOVNA.)

LYUBOV (*hums the* Lezginka)[3]: What's keeping Leonid? What can he be doing in town? (*to* DUNYASHA) Offer the musicians some tea.

TROFIMOV: Most likely the auction hasn't taken place.

LYUBOV: And the musicians have come at the wrong time. It's no time to give a ball. Well, never mind. (*Sits down and hums softly.*)

CHARLOTTA (*offering* PISHCHIK *a deck of cards*): Here's a deck of cards. Think of any card you like.

PISHCHIK: I've thought of one.

CHARLOTTA: Now shuffle the pack. That's right. Give it here, my dear Mr. Pishchik. *Ein, zwei, drei*[4] — now look for the card — it's in your side pocket.

PISHCHIK (*taking the card out of his side pocket*): The eight of spades! Absolutely right! (*Astonished*) Imagine that now!

CHARLOTTA (*holding the deck of cards in her hands, to* TROFIMOV): Quickly, tell me which is the top card.

TROFIMOV: Well . . . the queen of spades.

CHARLOTTA: It is. (*Showing it.*) (*to* PISHCHIK) Well, which card is on top now?

PISHCHIK: The ace of hearts.

CHARLOTTA: It is. (*Showing it.*) (*She claps her hands and the deck of cards disappears.*) Ah, what lovely weather it is today.

(*A mysterious feminine voice which seems to come out of the floor answers her:* "Yes, indeed, it's magnificent weather, madam.")

You are my perfect ideal.

(*The voice:* "And I greatly admire you, too, madam.")

(*The* STATION MASTER *has witnessed this through the archway and comes forward.*)

STATION MASTER (*applauding*): The lady ventriloquist — *bravo*!

PISHCHIK (*astonished*): Imagine that now! Most enchanting, Charlotta Ivanovna. I'm simply in love with you!

---

3 The *Lezginka* is a lively dance of the Caucasus in 2/4 time, popularized by Glinka. 4 German: "One, two, three. . . ."

CHARLOTTA: In love? (*shrugging her shoulders*) What do you know of love? — *guter Mensch, aber schlechter Musikant.*[5]

TROFIMOV (*patting* PISHCHIK *on the shoulder*): You old horse, you. . . .

CHARLOTTA: Attention, please! One more trick! (*Takes a traveling rug from a chair.*) Now here's a rug, a very pretty rug. I'm going to sell it. (*Shaking it out.*) Who will buy it?

PISHCHIK (*astonished*): Imagine that!

CHARLOTTA: *Ein, zwei, drei!* (*She lifts the rug and behind it stands* ANYA, *who curtsies, runs to her mother, embraces her, and runs back into the larger room amid general applause.*)

LYUBOV (*applauding*): *Brava, brava!*[6]

CHARLOTTA: Once more. *Ein, zwei, drei!* (*She lifts the rug and behind it stands* VARYA, *bowing.*)

PISHCHIK (*astonished*): Well, I never!

CHARLOTTA: That's all. (*She throws the rug at* PISHCHIK, *curtsies, and runs into the larger drawing-room.*)

PISHCHIK (*hurrying after her*): You mischievous rascal! Imagine! (*Goes out.*)

LYUBOV: And Leonid still isn't here. I can't understand what's keeping him in town so long. Why, everything must be over by now. The estate is sold, or the sale has not taken place. Why keep us so long in suspense?

VARYA (*trying to console her*): Uncle has bought it, I feel sure of that.

TROFIMOV (*ironically*): Oh, yes!

VARYA: Grandmamma sent him power of attorney to buy it in her name and transfer the debt. She's doing it for Anya's sake. I'm sure God will help uncle buy it.

LYUBOV: Your grandmother in Yaroslavl sent 15,000 to buy the estate in her name — she doesn't trust us — but that wouldn't even cover the interest due. (*Hides her face in her hands.*) My fate is being sealed today, my fate. . . .

TROFIMOV (*teasing* VARYA): Madame Lopakhina.

VARYA (*angrily*): Perpetual student! You've already been expelled from the university twice!

LYUBOV: Why are you so angry, Varya? He's teasing you about Lopakhin. Well, what about it? Marry Lopakhin if you want to — he's a good man, an interesting man — and if you don't want to, don't. Nobody is forcing you, my pet.

VARYA: I tell you plainly, mamma, I'm taking it seriously; he's a good man and I like him.

LYUBOV: Then marry him. I can't see what you are waiting for.

VARYA: Mamma! I can't propose to him myself. For two whole years everybody's been talking to me about him. But he either says nothing or makes a joke out of it. I see what it means. He's getting rich, he's involved in his business, he can't be bothered with me. If I only had a little money, no matter how little, even a hundred *roubles*, I'd drop everything and go as far away as possible. I'd go into a nunnery.

TROFIMOV: "What blissful beauty!"

VARYA (*to* TROFIMOV): A student ought to be sensible! (*In a gentler voice, through tears.*) How ugly you have grown, Petya; how you have aged! (*to* LYUBOV ANDREEVNA, *having stopped crying*) But I can't live without work, mamma. I must have something to keep me busy every minute.

(*Enter* YASHA.)

YASHA (*barely suppressing his laughter*):

<hr>

5 German: "a good man but a bad musician." 6 Italian: "Hurrah, hurrah!" To shout "well done" to men, one says *bravo*, to women *brava* (feminine), and to groups *bravi* (plural). Lyubov gets it correct; we allow the Station Master to get it wrong. Other characters, such as Yepikhodov in his statement about how everything abroad is perfected, also make errors throughout the play, but these cannot all be translated. Charlotta has some trouble with Russian, for example.

Yepikhodov has broken a billiard cue! (*Goes out.*)

VARYA: What is Yepikhodov doing here anyway? Who gave him permission to play billiards? I don't understand these people (*goes out*).

LYUBOV: Don't tease her, Petya. Don't you see that she's unhappy enough already?

TROFIMOV: She is so very officious, meddling in other people's business. All summer long she has given Anya and me no peace; she's afraid of a romance between us. What has that got to do with her? I have given her no grounds for that; such triviality is far from me. We are above love!

LYUBOV: And I suppose I must be beneath love. (*Very agitated*) Why isn't Leonid here? If only I knew whether the estate is sold or not! It seems such an impossible calamity that I really don't know what to think. . . . I'm bewildered. . . . I shall scream in a minute, I shall do something foolish. . . . Petya, save me; say something to me, talk to me!

TROFIMOV: What does it matter whether the estate is sold today or not? It was all over with long ago; there's no turning back; the path is overgrown. Don't worry, dear Lyubov Andreevna. You mustn't deceive yourself; for once in your life you must look the facts in the face.

LYUBOV: What facts? You see where the truth lies and where the lack of truth, but I seem to have lost my sight. I see nothing. You settle every important problem so boldly, but tell me, my dear boy, isn't that because you are young, because you have not yet had to solve a single one of your problems by suffering? You look forward boldly, and isn't it true that you don't see and don't expect anything terrible because life is still hidden from your young eyes? You are bolder, more honest, deeper than we are, but think, be just a pinch more magnanimous, take pity on me. I was born here, you know, my father and mother lived here, my grandfather lived here. I love this house.

Without the cherry orchard my life has no meaning for me and, if it really must be sold, then sell me with it! (*Embraces* TROFIMOV, *kisses him on the forehead.*) My son was drowned here. (*Weeps.*) Pity me, my dear, kind man.

TROFIMOV: You know I sympathize with all my heart.

LYUBOV: But you should have said that some other way, so differently. (*Takes out her handkerchief, a telegram falls on the floor.*) I am so unhappy today, you cannot imagine. It's so noisy here; my heart jumps at every sound. I tremble all over, but I can't go to my room. I'm afraid to be alone in the silence. Don't be hard on me, Petya . . . I love you as though you were one of ourselves. I would gladly let you marry Anya — I swear I would — only, my dear boy, you must work and finish your degree. You do nothing; fate tosses you around from place to place; that's not right. That's true, isn't it? And you must do something with your beard to make it grow somehow. (*Laughs.*) You look so funny!

TROFIMOV (*picking up the telegram*): I have no desire to be an Adonis.

LYUBOV: That's a telegram from Paris. I get one every day, one yesterday and another today. That savage creature is ill again; things are bad for him. . . . He begs forgiveness, beseeches me to come, and really I ought to go to Paris to be with him for a while. You look stern, Petya. What am I to do, dear boy, what am I to do? He is ill, alone and unhappy, and who will look after him, who is to keep him from doing something stupid? Who is to give him his medicine at the right time? After all, why hide it or be silent: I love him, that's obvious, I love him! He's a millstone around my neck, I'm going to the bottom with him, but I love that stone and I cannot live without it. (*Presses* TROFIMOV's *hand.*) Don't think badly of me, Petya, don't say anything, don't tell me. . . .

TROFIMOV (*through his tears*): For God's sake forgive my bluntness: but he robbed you!

LYUBOV: No, no, no! (*She covers her ears.*) You mustn't say such things!

TROFIMOV: He's a scoundrel. Everybody sees that but you. He's a petty villain, a despicable person!

LYUBOV (*angry but restraining herself*): You are twenty-six or twenty-seven years old, but you're still a little schoolboy.[7]

TROFIMOV: So what?

LYUBOV: You ought to be grown up at your age. You ought to understand what love means. And you ought to be in love yourself. You ought to fall in love! (*Angrily*) Yes, yes; it's not purity with you, you're simply a smug prude, a ridiculous fool, a freak. . . .

TROFIMOV (*horrified*): The things she's saying!

LYUBOV: "I am above love!" You are not above love but simply, as our Firs here says, "half-baked." At your age, not to have a mistress!

TROFIMOV (*horrified*): This is awful! The things she's saying! (*Goes quickly into the larger drawing-room, clutching his head.*) This is awful! I can't stand it! I'm getting out of here! (*Goes off quickly and quickly returns.*) All is over between us! (*Goes off into the ante-room.*)

LYUBOV (*calling after him*): Petya! Stop! You funny creature, I was only joking! Petya!

(*There is the sound of someone running quickly down the stairs and suddenly falling with a crash. ANYA and VARYA scream, but there is an immediate peal of laughter.*)

LYUBOV: What's happening?

(ANYA *runs in.*)

ANYA (*laughing*): Petya's fallen down the stairs! (*She runs out.*)

LYUBOV: What a ridiculous fellow Petya is!

(*The STATION MASTER stands in the middle of the larger drawing-room and reads "The Sinner" by Alexei Tolstoy:*[8]

"Thou art the one who teaches self-denial. Thy teachings move me not, for mine contain

More hope, more truth. My thoughts are not confused. . . ."

(*They listen to him, but scarcely has he recited several lines when the sound of a waltz is heard from the ante-room and the reading is broken off. They all dance.*)

(TROFIMOV, ANYA, VARYA *and* LYUBOV ANDREEVNA *enter from the ante-room.*)

LYUBOV: Come, Petya, come, you pure heart! I beg your pardon. Let's dance. (*Dances with* PETYA.)

(ANYA *and* VARYA *dance together.* FIRS *enters, puts his stick down by the side door.* YASHA *also comes into the drawing-room and watches the dancing.*)

YASHA: What is it, granddad?

FIRS: I don't feel well. In the old days we used to have generals, barons and admirals dancing at our balls, and now we send for the post-office clerk and the station master and even they are not too pleased to come. I am getting feeble. The dead master, their grandfather, used to give us sealing wax for all complaints.[9] I have been taking sealing wax now for twenty years or more. Perhaps that is what has kept me alive.

---

7 Literally, a sophomore in a gymnasium. 8 Alexei Konstantinovich Tolstoi (1817–1875) wrote this poem about 1857 in which Mary Magdalene encounters Christ who comes among a group of rich people, and says: "Thou art the one who teaches denial. I do not believe in Thy teaching. Mine has more hope and truth in it. My thoughts are not confused by a wanderer in the desert who fasted for forty days. I am drawn only to pleasure; prayer and fasting are unknown to me. I believe only in beauty. I serve wine and kisses. My soul is not troubled by Thee. Thy purity fills me with scorn. . . ." It would be difficult for a non-Russian audience to grasp the significance of this recitation or to see the relevance to Lyubov Andreevna or Trofimov, whose sins and whose purity of heart have already been mentioned in the play. Indeed, no English translation I have seen presents even the few lines from the poem that are called for in the text. As the poem continues the Magdalene, at first defiant, repents before the kindly gaze of Christ. 9 Sealing wax, sometimes gilded, used to be given as a *placebo* to the ignorant.

YASHA: You bore me, granddad. (*Yawns.*) It's time you croaked.

FIRS: Ah, you half-baked . . . (*Mutters.*)

(TROFIMOV *and* LYUBOV ANDREEVNA *dance in the larger room and then down into the drawing-room.*)

LYUBOV: *Merci.* I'll sit down a while. (*Sits.*) I'm tired.

(*Enter* ANYA.)

ANYA (*excitedly*): There's man in the kitchen who has been saying that the cherry orchard was sold today.

LYUBOV: Sold to whom?

ANYA: He didn't say to whom. He's gone away now.

(*She dances with* TROFIMOV *and they dance off into the larger drawing-room.*)

YASHA: It was some old man chattering, a stranger.

FIRS: Leonid Andreevich is not here yet; he has not come back. He has his spring and fall overcoat on; he'll catch cold for sure. Ah, young and green!

LYUBOV: I am going to die now. Go, Yasha, find out to whom it has been sold.

YASHA: Why, he went away long ago, the old man. (*Laughs.*)

LYUBOV (*vexed*): What are you laughing at? What are you so pleased about?

YASHA: Yepikhodov — he's so ridiculous, silly, "two and twenty misfortunes."

LYUBOV: Firs, if the estate is really sold, where will you go?

FIRS: Wherever you say to go, I'll go.

LYUBOV: Why do you look like that? Are you ill? You ought to be in bed.

FIRS (*ironically*): Yes, I'll go to bed and who will wait on you? Who's to look after things without me? I have the whole house to handle alone.

YASHA: Lyubov Andreevna, permit me to ask a favor of you; if you go back to Paris again, I beg you to take me with you. It's completely impossible for me to stay here. (*Looking around him, in a whisper.*) There's no need to say it — you can see for yourself: an uncivilized country, the people have no morals, and on top of it all the boredom! The food in the kitchen is abominable and then Firs runs after one muttering all sorts of nonsense. Take me with you, please!

(*Enter* PISHCHIK.)

PISHCHIK: May I have the pleasure of a waltz, my dear lady? (LYUBOV ANDREEVNA *goes with him.*) Enchanting lady, I really must borrow from you just 180 *roubles* (*dances*) . . . only 180 *roubles*. (*They move into the larger room.*)

YASHA (*singing to himself*):

"Oh, wilt thou know
My soul's emotion. . . ."

(*In the larger drawing-room a figure in a grey top hat and check trousers is gesticulating and cavorting. Shouts of "Bravo, Charlotta Ivanovna!"*)

DUNYASHA (*stopping to powder her nose*): My young mistress orders me to dance. There are a lot of gentlemen and too few ladies, but dancing makes me giddy and makes my heart pound, Firs Nikolaevich; the post-office clerk said something to me just now that took my breath away.

(*The music stops.*)

FIRS: What did he say to you?

DUNYASHA: He said, "You are like a flower."

YASHA (*yawning*): Boor! (*Goes out.*)

DUNYASHA: "Like a flower. . . ." I am a girl of such delicate feelings, I'm awfully fond of tender words.

FIRS: Your head is being turned.

(*Enter* YEPIKHODOV.)

YEPIKHODOV: You have no desire to see me,

Avdotya Fyodorovna, any more than an insect. (*sighs*) Ah, life!

DUNYASHA: What do you want?

YEPIKHODOV: Undoubtedly you may be right. (*sighs*) But of course, if one looks at it from that point of view, if I may so express myself, you have (excuse my putting it plainly) reduced me to a complete state of mind. I know my fate. Every day some misfortune befalls me and I have long since grown accustomed to it, so that I face my fate with a smile. You gave me your word, though. . . .

DUNYASHA: Let us talk it over later, please, but now leave me in peace, for I am busy meditating. (*Plays with her fan.*)

YEPIKHODOV: Every day some misfortune befalls me and, if I may venture so to express myself, I merely smile at it — I even laugh.

(*Enter* VARYA *from the larger drawing-room.*)

VARYA: You still haven't gone, Semyon? What a disrespectful creature you are! (*to* DUNYASHA) Run along, Dunyasha. (*to* YEPIKHODOV) First you play billiards and break the cue, then you go wandering around the drawing-room as if you were invited.

YEPIKHODOV: You really cannot — if I may so express myself — call me to account like this.

VARYA: I'm not calling you to account. I'm telling you. You do nothing but wander from place to place and you don't do your work; we keep you as an accountant, but what use you are to us I can't imagine.

YEPIKHODOV (*offended*): Whether I work or whether I wander around, whether I eat or whether I play billiards, is a matter to be decided by persons of discernment and my elders.

VARYA: You dare to talk to me like that? (*Blushing with anger*) You dare? You mean to say I have no discernment? Get out of here, this minute!

YEPIKHODOV (*intimidated*): I must beg you to express yourself with more delicacy.

VARYA (*enraged*): This minute! Get out! Out! (*He goes toward the door and she follows.*) "Two and twenty misfortunes," take yourself out of here! Don't let me see you again!

(YEPIKHODOV *has gone out, but behind the door his voice [is heard]*: "I shall lodge a complaint against you.") What? You're coming back? (*She snatches up the stick* FIRS *has left near the door.*) Come on, come on! I'll show you! What, you're coming back? Then take *that!* (*She swings the stick at the very moment that* LOPAKHIN *enters.*)

LOPAKHIN: Very much obliged to you! Thank you very much!

VARYA (*angry but ironically*): I beg your pardon.

LOPAKHIN: Don't mention it, madam. I humbly thank you for your kind reception.

VARYA (*moves away, then turns and asks gently*): I didn't hurt you, did I?

LOPAKHIN: Oh, no, not at all. There's a huge bump going to come up, that's all.

VOICES (*from the larger drawing-room*): Lopakhin has arrived. Yermolay Alexeevich!

PISHCHIK: "Here he is, beheld by the eyes, heard by the ears." [10] (*He kisses* LOPAKHIN *[peasant fashion].*) There's a whiff of cognac on you, my dear man, and we are making merry here too.

(*Enter* LYUBOV ANDREEVNA.)

LYUBOV: Is it you, Yermolay Alexeevich? Why have you been so long? Where is Leonid?

LOPAKHIN: Leonid Andreevich came back with me. He's coming.

LYUBOV (*agitated*): Well? Well? Was there an auction? Tell me!

LOPAKHIN (*embarrassed, afraid of betraying his pleasure*): The auction was over by four o'clock. We missed the train — had to wait until half-past nine. (*Sighing heavily*) Ah, I'm feeling a little giddy. . . .

---

10 A formula from ancient Russian epics.

(*Enter* GAEV. *In one hand he carries parcels and with the other he is wiping away his tears.*)

LYUBOV: Well, Lyonya, what's the news? (*Impatiently, in tears*) For heaven's sake, hurry up!

GAEV (*does not answer, simply waves his hand. To* FIRS, *weeping*): Here take these: some anchovies and Kerchensky[11] herrings. I haven't had a thing to eat all day. What I have been through!

(*The door into the billiard room is open and there is heard the clicking of balls and the voice of* YASHA: "Seven, eighteen!" GAEV's *expression changes. He stops crying.*)

I'm dreadfully tired. Firs, come and help me change. (*Goes to his room across the larger drawing-room,* FIRS *behind him.*)

PISHCHIK: What happened at the auction? Tell us about it!

LYUBOV: Is the cherry orchard sold?

LOPAKHIN: Sold!

LYUBOV: Who bought it?

LOPAKHIN: I did. (*A pause.* LYUBOV ANDREEVNA *is overwhelmed; she would have fallen down had she not been standing near a chair and table.* VARYA *snatches keys from her waist and flings them on the floor in the middle of the drawing-room and goes out.*)

LOPAKHIN: I bought it. Please wait a minute, ladies and gentlemen. My head is in a whirl, I can't speak (*laughs*). When we came to the auction Deriganov was already there. Leonid Andreevich only had 15,000 and right away Deriganov bid 30,000, over and above the interest. I saw how things stood, so I bid against him. I bid 40,000, he bid 45,000, I bid 55,000, and so it went on, he raising by 5,000 and I by 10,000. Well, it soon ended. I bid 90,000 more than the interest and it was knocked down to me. Now the cherry orchard is mine, mine! (*Laughing*) My God, the cherry orchard is mine! Tell me that I'm drunk; tell me that I'm out of my head; tell me that it's all a dream! (*Stamping his feet*) Don't laugh at me! If my father and my grandfather could only rise from their graves and see all that's happened! How their Yermolay, beaten, ignorant Yermolay, who used to run around barefoot in the wintertime, how that very same Yermolay has bought the finest estate in the whole world! I have bought the estate where my father and my grandfather were serfs, where they weren't even allowed into the kitchen! I'm asleep, it must be a dream, it's all imagination! It's all imagination shrouded in the darkness of ignorance. (*Picks up the keys, affectionately smiling.*) She's thrown down the keys to signify that she's not the mistress here any more! (*He jingles the keys.*) Well, never mind. (*The orchestra is heard tuning up.*) Hey, musicians! Play! I want to hear you. Come, all of you, and see how Yermolay Lopakhin will take his axe to the cherry orchard, how the trees will all fall down! We will build cottages and our grandsons and great-grandsons will see a new life here! Music! Play!

(*The music begins to play.* LYUBOV ANDREEVNA *sinks into a chair and weeps bitterly.*)

LOPAKHIN (*reproachfully*): Why, oh why didn't you listen to me? My poor friend! Dear lady, there's no turning back now. (*Through tears*) Oh, if only this could be all over, if only our miserable, disjointed life could somehow be changed!

PISHCHIK (*taking him by the arm, in a low voice*): She's crying. Let's go into the drawing-room and leave her alone to. . . . Come on. (*Takes him by the arm and leads him into the larger drawing-room.*)

LOPAKHIN: What's that? Music! Play your best! Everything must be as I want it! (*Ironically*) Here comes the new master, the owner of the cherry orchard! (*He accidentally bumps into a little table, almost upsetting the candelabra.*) I can pay for everything!

---

11 Kerch, on the Strait of Kerch, is on the Black Sea. Gaev's purchases seem a trifle extravagant, for these are delicacies.

(He goes out with PISHCHIK. *Nobody remains in the drawing-rooms except* LYUBOV AND-REEVNA, *who sits huddled up, weeping bitterly. The music plays softly. Enter* ANYA *and* TROFI-MOV; *quickly.* ANYA *goes up to her mother and kneels before her.* TROFIMOV *stands in the archway to the larger drawing-room.)*

ANYA: Mamma! Mamma you're crying, dear, kind, good mamma! My precious! I love you! I bless you! The cherry orchard is sold. It's gone, that's true, that's true! But don't you cry, mamma! You still have your life before you and you still have your good, pure heart. Let's go, let's go, darling, away from this place! We'll plant a new orchard, more splendid than this one, you'll see, and understand. And joy, tranquil, deep joy, will sink into your soul like the sun in the evening, and you'll smile, mamma! Come, darling, let's go.

CURTAIN

ACT FOUR

Same scene as Act I. There are no curtains on the windows or pictures on the walls. The little furniture remaining is stacked in a corner, as if for sale. There is a feeling of emptiness. By the door to the ante-room and at the back of the scene are trunks, bundles, etc. Through the open door stage left are heard the voices of VARYA *and* ANYA. *Lopakhin stands waiting.* YASHA *holds a tray with little glasses of champagne. In the ante-room* YEPIKHODOV *is tying up a box. A murmur of voices offstage: the peasants have come to say goodbye. The voice of* GAEV: *"Thanks, brothers, thank you."*

YASHA: The peasants have come to say goodbye. In my opinion, Yermolay Alexeevich, they are good people but they understand very little.

(The murmur offstage dies away. Enter from the ante-room LYUBOV ANDREEVNA *and* GAEV. *She is not crying, but she is pale, her face twitches, and she cannot speak.)*

GAEV: You gave them your purse, Lyuba. That was wrong, wrong.

LYUBOV: I couldn't help it! I couldn't help it! *(They both go out.)*

LOPAKHIN *(calling after them from the doorway):* Please. I beg you, take a little glass at parting. I didn't think of bringing any from the town and at the station I could only find one bottle. Please. *(a pause)* What, you don't want any? *(Returns from the door.)* If I had known that, I wouldn't have bought any. I'm not going to drink any either. *(YASHA carefully sets the tray down on a chair.)* At least take a glass yourself, Yasha.

YASHA: Here's to the travelers and good luck to those who stay behind! *(Drinks)* This champagne isn't the real thing, take my word for it.

LOPAKHIN: It cost eight *roubles* a bottle. *(a pause)* It's cold as hell here.

YASHA: They haven't lit the stove today. It doesn't matter, since we're going. *(laughs.)*

LOPAKHIN: What are you laughing at?

YASHA: I'm pleased.

LOPAKHIN: Though it's October it's still as calm and sunny as summer. Perfect weather for building. *(Looking at his watch, in the doorway)* Don't forget, ladies and gentlemen, that the train goes in 47 minutes, so you must leave for the station in twenty minutes. Better hurry up!

(TROFIMOV comes in from out of doors wearing an overcoat.)

TROFIMOV: I think it is time we were leaving. The carriages are at the door. The devil only knows what's become of my goloshes; they're lost. *(In the doorway)* Anya, my goloshes aren't here. I can't find them.

LOPAKHIN: I've got to go to Kharkov. I'm taking the same train as you. I'm going to spend the winter at Kharkov. I've been wasting my time loitering with you and I'm worn out with not working. I can't live without work. I don't know what to do with my hands; they dangle so oddly, as if they didn't belong to me.

TROFIMOV: Well, we'll soon be underway and

you will be able to take up your profitable labors again.

LOPAKHIN: Please drink a little glass.

TROFIMOV: I'm not going to.

LOPAKHIN: So you're off to Moscow now?

TROFIMOV: Yes, I'll see them as far as the town and tomorrow I'll go to Moscow.

LOPAKHIN: Well, I suppose the professors aren't giving any lectures yet — they're waiting for your arrival.

TROFIMOV: That's no concern of yours.

LOPAKHIN: How many years have you been studying at the university?

TROFIMOV: Can't you be more original than that — that joke is stale and flat. (*looking for his goloshes*) You know, I suppose that most likely we'll never see each other again, so just let me give you one piece of advice as we part: don't wave your arms around; get out of the habit of waving. And another thing, building cottages, predicting that the summer residents will turn into independent little farmers — planning like that, that's waving around too. When all is said and done, I like you: you have fine, delicate fingers, like an artist; you have a fine, delicate soul.

LOPAKHIN (*embracing him*): Goodbye, my dear fellow. Thanks for everything. Let me give you some money for the journey, if you need it.

TROFIMOV: What for? I don't need it.

LOPAKHIN: But you haven't got any.

TROFIMOV: Yes, I have. Thank you. I got a little for a translation. Here it is in my pocket. (*Anxiously*) But where are my goloshes?

VARYA (*from the next room*): Here, take the nasty things!

(*She flings a pair of goloshes onto the stage.*)

TROFIMOV: Why are you so cross, Varya? Hmm . . . but those are not *my* goloshes!

LOPAKHIN: I sowed 2700 acres with poppies in the spring and now I have cleared 40,000 profit. And when my poppies were in bloom, it was a sight to behold! So here, as I say, I made 40,000 and I'm offering you a little loan because I have some to spare. Why turn up your nose at it? I'm a peasant — I speak bluntly.

TROFIMOV: Your father was a peasant and mine was a pharmacist — which proves absolutely nothing. (LOPAKHIN *takes out his wallet.*) Stop that — stop that! If you were to offer me 200,000 I wouldn't take it. I am a free man, and everything that all of you, rich and poor alike, prize so highly and cherish so dearly, hasn't the slightest power over me — it's like a fluffy feather fluttering in the air. I can manage without you. I can go right on past you. I am strong and proud. Mankind is advancing toward the highest truth, the greatest happiness which is attainable on earth, and I am in the vanguard.

LOPAKHIN: Will you get there?

TROFIMOV: I shall get there. (*a pause*) I shall get there or I shall show others how to get there.

(*In the distance is heard the stroke of an axe on a tree.*)

LOPAKHIN: Goodbye, my friend; it's time to go. We turn up our noses at each other, but life goes on all the same. When I work hard without getting tired my mind seems more at ease, as if I also know the reason for my existence. But there are many people in Russia, my friend, and nobody knows what they exist for . . . Well, it doesn't matter anyhow: it doesn't keep the wheels from turning. They tell me that Leonid Andreevich has taken a position. He's going to be a clerk in the bank . . . 6,000 *roubles* a year. Only he won't stick at it; he's too lazy.

ANYA (*in the doorway*): Mamma begs you to stop them from cutting down the cherry orchard until she has gone.

TROFIMOV: Really, haven't you got any tact?

([*He turns from* LOPAKHIN] *and walks out into the ante-room.*)

LOPAKHIN: Just a moment! Just a moment! What stupid fellows!

(*He goes out after him.*)

ANYA (*in the doorway*): Has Firs been taken to the hospital?

YASHA: I told them this morning. They must have taken him.

ANYA (*to* YEPIKHODOV *as he crosses the drawing room*): Semyon Panteleevich, please find out if Firs has been taken to the hospital.

YASHA (*offended*): I told Yegor this morning. Why ask a dozen times?

YEPIKHODOV: Firs, who is so aged, it's my conclusive opinion that no treatment would effect a repair: it's time he was gathered to his fathers. I can only envy him. (*Puts a suitcase down on a cardboard hat-box and crushes it.*) There! Now, of course . . . I knew it!

YASHA (*jeering*): "Two and twenty misfortunes"!

VARYA (*offstage*): Has Firs been taken to the hospital?

ANYA: Yes.

VARYA: Why didn't they take the note to the doctor too?

ANYA (*from the doorway*): We must send it after him. (*Goes out.*)

VARYA (*from the adjoining room*): Where is Yasha? Tell him his mother has come to say goodbye to him.

YASHA (*with a wave of the hand*): They really try my patience.

(DUNYASHA *has been busying herself with the baggage. Seeing* YASHA *alone, she approaches him.*)

DUNYASHA: You might give me one little glance, Yasha. You're going away. You're leaving me.

(*She cries and throws herself on his neck.*)

YASHA: Why are you crying? (*He drinks some champagne.*) In six days I'll be back in Paris. Tomorrow we get on the express train, off we go, and that's the last of us! I can hardly believe it. *Vive la France!* This place doesn't suit me; I can't bear it. It can't be helped. I have had enough of the ignorance here. I've had my fill of it. (*Drinks champagne.*) Why are you crying? Behave yourself properly and then you won't have to cry.

DUNYASHA (*powders her nose, looking in a pocket mirror*): Send me a letter from Paris. You know how I have loved you, Yasha — how I have loved you. I am a delicate creature, Yasha.

YASHA: Here they come!

(*He busies himself with the baggage, humming softly. Enter* LYUBOV ANDREEVNA, GAEV, ANYA *and* CHARLOTTA IVANOVNA.)

GAEV: We ought to be going. There's not much time left. (*Looking at* YASHA) Who is it smells of herrings?

LYUBOV: In ten minutes we must get into the carriages. (*Looks around the room.*) Farewell, my dear house, my old grandfather! Winter will pass and spring will come and you will disappear; they will tear you down! How much these walls have seen! (*Kissing* ANYA *passionately*) My treasure, how radiant you look! Your eyes are sparkling like diamonds! Are you happy? Very happy?

ANYA: Very happy. A new life is just beginning, mamma.

GAEV: So it is; everything is all right now. Before the cherry orchard was sold, we were all worried and miserable, but afterwards, when the problem was finally settled conclusively, once and for all, we all calmed down and even cheered up. I am a bank clerk now — a financier — into the side pocket! And you, Lyuba, after all, you are looking so much better, no question about it.

LYUBOV: Yes, my nerves are better; that's true. (*Her hat and coat are given to her.*) I'm sleeping well. Carry out my things, Yasha. It's time to go. (*to* ANYA) My darling, we shall see each other soon again. I am off to

Paris. I can get by there on the money your grandmother in Yaroslavl sent us to buy the estate — hurray for your grandmother — but it won't last long.

ANYA: You'll come back very soon, won't you, mamma? I'll study for my examination in the *gymnasium*[12] and then I shall work and be a help to you. We shall read all sorts of books together, won't we, mamma? (*She kisses her mother's hands.*) We'll read in the autumn evenings. We'll read lots of books and a brave new world will open out before us (*dreamily*). . . . Come back soon, mamma!

LYUBOV: I'll come back, my golden one. (*Embraces her.*)

(*Enter* LOPAKHIN. CHARLOTTA *sings softly.*)

GAEV: Charlotta's happy — she's singing!

CHARLOTTA (*picking up a bundle that resembles a swaddled infant*). Lullaby, baby. (*The "baby" answers:* "Wah! wah!") Hushaby, my sweet, hushaby, my little one. ([*The "baby" repeats:*] "Wah! wah!") Poor little thing! (*She throws the bundle down again.*) You must find me a new situation, won't you? I can't go on without one.

LOPAKHIN: We'll find you something, Charlotta Ivanovna. Don't you worry.

GAEV: Everybody's leaving us. Varya's going away. Suddenly we have become of no use.

CHARLOTTA: There's no place for me in town. I have to go away. (*Sings softly*) Well, it doesn't matter. . . .

(*Enter* PISHCHIK.)

LOPAKHIN: A prodigy of nature!

PISHCHIK (*gasping for breath*): Oh . . . let me catch my breath. . . . I'm worn out . . . my most honored friends. . . . Give me a drink of water.

GAEV: Wants some money, I suppose. Excuse me — I'll get out of the way of temptation. (*Goes out.*)

PISHCHIK: It's a long while since I've been to see you, dearest lady. . . . (*to* LOPAKHIN)

You here! Good to see you . . . a man of immense intellect . . . take this . . . here. (*Gives* LOPAKHIN [*money*].) 400 *roubles*. I still owe you 840.

LOPAKHIN (*amazed, shrugging his shoulders*): It's like a dream! Where did you get it?

PISHCHIK: Wait a minute. . . . I'm hot . . . a most extraordinary thing! Some Englishmen came along and discovered some sort of white clay on my land. (*to* LYUBOV ANDREEVNA) And 400 for you . . . lovely, wonderful woman. (*Gives* [*her*] *money*.) The rest later. (*Takes a sip of water.*) A young man on the train just now was saying that some great philosopher advises us to jump off roofs. . . . "Jump!," he says, "the whole problem is settled just like that. . . ." (*Astonished*) Just imagine that! More water, please.

LOPAKHIN: Who were these Englishmen?

PISHCHIK: I signed over to them the rights to dig the clay for 24 years . . . and now . . . excuse me . . . I can't stay . . . I must be running along. I'm going to Znoikov's . . . to Kardamanov's. . . . I owe money everywhere! (*Sipping*) to your health! Goodbye, everyone . . . I'll come back on Thursday.

LYUBOV: We are just going into town and tomorrow I go abroad.

PISHCHIK: What? (*Agitated*) What are you going to town for? Oh . . . the furniture . . . the suitcases. . . . Well, never mind. (*Through his tears*) It's all right . . . never mind . . . men of enormous intellect, these Englishmen . . . never mind . . . be happy. God will help you . . . no matter . . . everything in the world has to come to an end (*kisses* LYUBOV ANDREEVNA's *hand*). If ever the news should reach you that I have come to my end, think of this . . . old horse . . . and say: "There was once such a bad man

---

12 If it is thought that this word will not be understood in its European sense, the words *high school* (the American equivalent) might be substituted, but that weakens the necessary sense of time and place.

in the world as Simyonov-Pishchik. . . . May God rest his soul!" Ah . . . splendid weather . . . yes. (*He goes out deeply moved but immediately returns and says from the doorway*) Dashenka wishes to be remembered to you! (*He goes out.*)

LYUBOV: Now we can go. I leave with two worries on my mind. The first is that Firs is ill. (*Looking at her watch*) We still have five minutes or so.

ANYA: Mamma, Firs has been taken to the hospital. Yasha sent him off this morning.

LYUBOV: My second worry is Varya. She is used to getting up early and working, and now that she has no work to do she's like a fish out of water. She has become pale and thin and cries, poor dear! (*a pause*) You know very well, Yermolay Alexeevich, I have been hoping . . . to marry her to you . . . and everything seemed to point to your getting married. (*Whispers to* ANYA *and motions to* CHARLOTTA *and both go out.*) She loves you; you must be fond of her . . . And I don't know . . . I don't know . . . why you seem, more or less, to avoid each other. I can't understand it!

LOPAKHIN: I don't understand it myself, to tell you the truth. It all seems so odd. If there's still time, I'll do it this minute. Let's settle it right away and get it over; without you I feel I'd never be able to bring myself to propose to her.

LYUBOV: Excellent! Why a single moment is all that it takes! I'll call her right in.

LOPAKHIN: And here's the champagne all ready. (*Looking into the glasses.*) Empty! Someone's emptied them already! (YASHA *coughs.*) That's what I call lapping it up!

LYUBOV (*eagerly*): Wonderful! We'll all go. . . . *Allez,*[13] Yasha! I'll call her in. (*At the door*) Varya, leave all that and come in here. Come along! (*She goes out with* YASHA.)

LOPAKHIN (*looking at his watch*): Yes.

(*A pause. Behind the door, stifled laughter and whispering; at last, enter* VARYA.)

VARYA (*looking over the baggage*): That's odd; I can't find it anywhere.

LOPAKHIN: What are you looking for?

VARYA: I packed it myself, and I can't remember. . . . (*a pause*)

LOPAKHIN: Where are you going today, Varvara Mikhailovna?

VARYA: Me? To the Ragulins. I have agreed to go to them to look after the house . . . as a sort of housekeeper.

LOPAKHIN: That's in Yashnevo? It'll be 70 *versts* from here. (*a pause*) So this is the end of life in this house.

VARYA (*looking at the baggage*): Where can it be? Perhaps I put it in the trunk. Yes, life here is over now; there will be no more of it. . . .

LOPAKHIN: And I'm going to Kharkov now — on the same train. I have a lot of business there. I'm leaving Yepikhodov here. I've hired him.

VARYA: Really?

LOPAKHIN: Last year at this time snow was already falling, if you remember; but now it's fine and sunny. Still, it's cold, to be sure — three degrees of frost.

VARYA: I haven't looked. (*a pause*) Besides, our thermometer's broken. (*a pause*)

(*A* VOICE *at the outer door;* "Yermolay Alexeevich!")

LOPAKHIN (*as though he had been waiting for a long time to be called*): Right away!

(LOPAKHIN *goes out quickly.* VARYA *sits on the floor, puts her head on a bundle and sobs quietly. The door opens. Enter* LYUBOV ANDREEVNA *quietly.*)

LYUBOV: Well? (*a pause*) We must be going.

---

13 French: "Go!" The use of French was very common among the Russian upper classes, even those who had not visited Paris.

VARYA (*wiping her eyes, no longer crying*): Yes, mamma, it's time to go. I shall have time to get to the Ragulins today as long as we are not late for the train.

LYUBOV (*in the doorway*): Anya, put on your things.

(*Enter* ANYA, *then* GAEV *and* CHARLOTTA IVANOVNA. GAEV *has on a warm coat with a hood.*)

(*Enter servants and carriage drivers.* YEPIKHODOV [*enters and*] *busies himself with the baggage.*)

LYUBOV: Now we can start on our trip.

ANYA (*joyfully*): We can start on our trip!

GAEV: My friends, my dear, beloved friends! Leaving this house forever, can I be silent? Can I refrain from giving utterance to those emotions which now well up in my heart?

ANYA (*pleading*): Uncle!

VARYA: Uncle, what use is it?

GAEV (*dejectedly*): Double the ball into the side pocket! . . . I'll be quiet. . . .

(*Enter* TROFIMOV *and after him* LOPAKHIN.)

TROFIMOV: Well, come along please, it's time to go.

LOPAKHIN: Yepikhodov, my coat!

LYUBOV: I'll stay just another minute. It is as though I had never seen the walls and ceilings of this house before. Now I look at them with such longing, such tender affection. . . .

GAEV: I remember, when I was six years old, how I sat in that window on Trinity Sunday, watching my father go off to church.

LYUBOV: Has everything been taken?

LOPAKHIN: Everything, I think. (*Putting on his overcoat, to* YEPIKHODOV) You, Yepikhodov, see that everything is alright.

YEPIKHODOV (*in a hoarse voice*): Don't worry, Yermolay Alexeevich.

LOPAKHIN: What's the matter with your voice?

YEPIKHODOV: I just had a drink of water. I swallowed something.

YASHA (*contemptuously*): What ignorance!

LYUBOV: We are going, and not a soul will be left here.

LOPAKHIN: Not until spring.

(VARYA *pulls an umbrella out of a bundle of clothes as though about to hit someone with it.* LOPAKHIN *pretends to be alarmed.*)

VARYA: What is it? I never thought of such a thing!

TROFIMOV: Let us get into the carriages, please. It's time. The train will be in soon.

VARYA: Petya, your goloshes, here they are, by that suitcase. (*Through tears*) And what dirty old things they are!

TROFIMOV (*putting on his goloshes*): Come along, please.

GAEV (*deeply moved, afraid of crying*): The train . . . the station . . . double the ball into the side pocket, doublet to sink the white in the corner. . . .

LYUBOV: Let us go.

LOPAKHIN: Everyone here? Nobody in there? (*He locks the door on the left.*) There are some things stored in there; they have to be locked up. Let's go.

ANYA: Goodbye, home! Goodbye, old life!

TROFIMOV: Welcome to the new life!

(TROFIMOV *goes out with* ANYA. VARYA *looks around the room and goes out, slowly.* YASHA *and* CHARLOTTA IVANOVNA, *with her dog, go out.*)

LOPAKHIN: Until spring! Go on, friends. Till we meet again. (*He goes out.*)

(LYUBOV ANDREEVNA *and* GAEV *are left alone. As though they had been waiting for this, they throw themselves on each other's necks and sob restrainedly, afraid of being overheard.*)

GAEV (*despairingly*): Sister, my sister!

LYUBOV: Oh, my orchard! My sweet, beautiful

orchard! My life, my youth, my happiness, farewell, farewell!

VOICE OF ANYA ([*offstage*] *calling gaily*): Mamma!

VOICE OF TROFIMOV ([*offstage*] *happily, excitedly*): Ah — oo!

LYUBOV: One last look at the walls, at the windows. My dear mother loved to walk around in this room.

GAEV: Sister, my sister!

VOICE OF ANYA (*as before*): Mamma!

VOICE OF TROFIMOV (*as before*): Aaa-oo!

LYUBOV: We're coming!

(*They go out. The stage is empty. There is the sound of all the doors being locked and then the carriages driving away. Silence. In the silence the thud of the axes on the trees clangs sadly, lonely. Footsteps are heard. FIRS appears in the doorway stage right. He is dressed, as usual, in a jacket and white waistcoat. He is wearing slippers. He is ill.*)

FIRS (*going up to the doors and trying the handles*): Locked! They have gone. . . . (*He sits down on the sofa.*) They have forgotten all about me. . . . Never mind . . . I'll just sit here a while. . . . I'll bet Leonid Andreevich hasn't put on his fur coat and has gone off in his thin overcoat. (*Sighs anxiously.*) I didn't look after him. . . . Young and green. . . . (*Mutters something indistinguishable.*) My life has gone by as if I had never lived. (*Lies down* [*on the sofa*]) I'll lie down a while. . . . There's no strength left in you; nothing, all gone. . . . Ah, you . . . half-baked. . . . (*Lies motionless.*)

(*A distant sound is heard that seems to come from the sky, like a harp-string snapping, with a mournful, dying fall. Stillness descends. Nothing is heard but the sound, far away in the orchard, of the axe thudding against the tree.*)

CURTAIN

Riders to the Sea

John Millington Synge (1871–1909) once remarked:

> Part of the misfortune of Ireland is that nearly all the characteristics which give colour and attractiveness to Irish life are bound up with a social condition near penury.

In *Riders to the Sea* (1904) he made of people rich in nothing but a brave, singing language and a brave, soaring spirit heroes of the most lyrical and emotionally charged tragedy of the modern theatre. In a few minutes Synge presents us, through the miracle of his language, proof of his assertion in another play that "the heart's a wonder" and a vignette which captures all the pain and triumph of the fate of a few Irish peasants who suffer the tragic lot of many millions the world over and, resigning themselves to the inevitable with fatalism but dignity, achieve the release and exaltation that follows.

Synge reminds us of John Berger's answer to the question of why art gives us pleasure:

> Because . . . it increases our awareness of our own potentiality. . . . The important point is that a valid work of art promises in some way or another the possibility of an increase, of an improvement. Nor need the work be optimistic to achieve this; indeed, its subject may be tragic. For it is not the subject that makes the promise, it is the artist's way of viewing his subject.

In *Riders to the Sea* there is an affirmation of human potential, a celebration of humanity. The subject matter is tragic, but because of the way Synge handles it we leave the theatre not depressed, as after Theatre of the Absurd, but proud.

In this, the finest of all folk plays in English, certainly the high point of modern tragedy, the simple Maurya is only a peasant woman, vanquished by natural forces (the sea; not supernatural forces, such as the gods), but in her noble acceptance she towers above the common lot. Many attempts have been made in the recent theatre to elevate the "little man" to the tragic stature of the heroes of old — in Clifford Odets' maunderings about the juggernaut of The System, in Arthur Miller's Willy, the low man (Loman) on the totem-pole who could never have succeeded in any system, in Elmer Rice's expressionistic Mr. Zero and Paddy Chayevsky's realistic Marty—but no one so far has surpassed this conception.

What makes Synge's play succeed here is the same factor which enabled him in his *The Playboy of the Western World* (1907) to pen, as Frank O'Connor says, "the greatest love scene since Shakespeare": a poetic language which soars to take the characters aloft on equal wings of melodious monologue and intensity of emotion. Synge will tell us in some words he prefaced to *The Playboy of the Western World* that his characters speak essentially the language of the peasants which he himself learned by keeping his ear to a crack in the floor above the kitchen in a cottage in the Aran Islands, but this is by no means the product of the tape-recorder school of dialogue. Tape recorders only give us exchanges like these:

A: Whadda ya wanna do?
B: I dunno. Whadda *you* wanna do?
A: I dunno. How 'bout you?
B: I dunno . . . .
or
A: What's it like?
B: What like?
A: You know.
B: No.

And so on. What Synge produces is a prose more "poetic" than most poetry, realizing the full potential of what the American critic Stark Young described as the "marvels of English — often declared unsingable by those who have studied with German gurglers or Parisian adenoiders. . . ." This is not the fiddling with prose to make it "poetic" of which Mary McCarthy complains in Tennessee Williams at his worst and O'Neill and Arthur Miller at their most characteristic — which McCarthy rightly compares to rouge on a pitted complexion — but rather a heightening of color and rhythm sensed there, not falsifying by touching up but giving fuller expression through development. That Synge did tinker with his tinkers' language is clear from the dialogue. Lajos Egri comments in *The Art of Dramatic Writing* (1946) that:

> In *Riders to the Sea*, John Millington Synge sways us to the tragic yet lovely rhythm of people who employ harmonious rhythms which are not identical. Maurya, Nora, Cathleen, and Bartley all use the accent of the Aran Islanders. But Bartley is swaggering, Cathleen patient, Nora quick with youth, and Maurya slow with age. The combination is one of the most beautiful in English.

Examine the dialogue and see if you agree with Mr. Egri's opinion or whether he is allowing his concept of the characters to color his estimate of their speech patterns.

A minority opinion on Synge's language is this from critic Kenneth Tynan who, reviewing *The Playboy of the Western World* at The Picadilly Theatre in London in 1960, wrote acidly:

Synge is often praised for his mastery of cadence, and for the splendour of his dying falls. Dying they may well be, but they take an unconscionable time doing it. Synge seldom lets a simple, declarative sentence alone. To its tail there must be pinned some such trailing tin can of verbiage as — to improvise an example — "the way you'd be roaring and moiling in the lug of a Kilkenny ditch, and she with a shift on her would destroy a man entirely, I'm thinking, and him staring till the eyes would be leaping surely from the holes in his head."

Writers like O'Casey, Behan and J. P. Donleavy have ruined my taste for Synge; and that taste, once lost, is not easily recovered. I acknowledge a handful of magical speeches. . . . For the rest, put me down as a saturation victim.

Riders to the Sea, being brief and perhaps your first experience of the lilt of this sort of speech, will hardly leave you saturated. You might examine it in a book with more care than you could in a performance and see what you think of the tricks that have created it.

You ought not to object to them *qua* tricks, however. As Guillaume Apollinaire wrote in the Preface to *Les Mamelles du Tirésias* in which he departed from poetic traditions of his time in diction as well as direction:

For the theatre should not be an imitation of reality
It is fitting that the dramatist should use
All the illusions at his disposal . . .
It is fitting that he should let crowds speak, even inanimate objects
If he so pleases
And that he no longer has to reckon
With time and space
His universe is the play
Within which he is God the Creator
Who disposes at will
Of sounds gestures movements masses colors
Not merely in order
To photograph what is called a slice of life
But to bring forth life itself in all its truth. . . .

If the theatre is magic it is also legerdemain.

It is my contention that if and when "The Great American Tragedy" ever is written, assuming that the stammering, "fogbound" O'Neill did not achieve it even in *A Long Day's Journey into Night* (which some would debate), its language will be some colorful native American speech heightened with taste and skill by someone who knows that though the theatre deals in truth it must distort reality somewhat in making it larger than life and that in this process the "tricks of the trade" revealed to the sharp student of Synge's monumental little tragedy are invaluable. The diction, more than the simple images and the stark setting (irresistibly inviting comparison with the plays of García Lorca), gives the play its power and ensures that (in the words of Synge about the drama in general) it "can no more go out of fashion than the blackberries on the hedges."

The scholarly may search Synge's book on *The Aran Islands* for the bits of folklore Synge used to make the play or seek parallels to the story, or the economy of its telling, in the ballads of long ago. The sympathetic may be wounded deeply by the compassion that wells up in them for the islanders who work so hard and have so little, who live and perforce must die by the sea, and whose lives must be as rocky as the three tiny puddles of land that form their home. The clever may see in Cathleen's busy wheel the image of the spinning of the thread of man's life and in the door, thrown open by the wind, the way that natural forces burst into the cosy life of the cottagers. Others will look for Synge's political views or his estimate of religion (the sup of holy water on the dresser and its use, the priest who is so young and so secure while Maurya is old and has a deeper knowledge of life through suffering: "there isn't anything more the sea can do to me"), the structure or the moral of the play (though Synge insisted that "the drama, like the symphony, does not teach or prove anything"). But no one will read or see the play who will not experience the nobility and fortitude of Maurya. Her personal tragedy and illumination of soul is all the essential action of the drama. Also, no one can fail to be intoxicated by the superb language in which it is expressed.

Of the nature and origin of this language Synge himself wrote in a famous passage prefaced to *The Playboy of the Western World:*

In writing *The Playboy of the Western World*, as in my other plays, I have used one or two words only that I have not heard among the country people of Ireland, or spoken in my own nursery before I could read the newspapers. A certain number of the phrases I employ I have heard also from herds and fishermen along the coast from Kerry to Mayo, or from beggar-women and ballad singers near Dublin; and I am glad to acknowledge how much I owe to the folk imagination of these fine people. Anyone who has lived in real intimacy with the Irish peasantry will know that the wildest sayings and ideas in this play are tame indeed, compared with the fancies one may hear in any little hillside cabin in Geesala, or Carraroe, or Dingle Bay. All art is a collaboration; and there is little doubt that in the happy ages of literature, striking and beautiful phrases were as ready to the storyteller's or the playwright's hand, as the rich cloaks and dresses of his time. It is probable that when the Elizabethan dramatist took his inkhorn and sat down to his work he used many phrases that he had just heard, as he sat at dinner, from his mother or his children. In Ireland, those of us who know the people have the same privilege. When I was writing *The Shadow of the Glen*, some years ago, I got more aid than any learning could have given me from a chink in the floor of the old Wicklow house where I was staying, that let me hear what was being said by the servant girls in the kitchen. This matter, I think, is of importance, for in countries where the imagination of the people, and the language they use, is rich and living, it is possible for a writer to be rich and copious in his words, and at the same time to give the reality, which is the root of all poetry, in a comprehensive and natural form. In the modern literature of towns, however, richness is found only in sonnets, or prose poems, or in one or two elaborate books that are far away from the profound and common interests of life. One has, on one side, Mallarmé and Huysmans producing this literature; and, on the other, Ibsen and

Zola dealing with the reality of life in joyless and pallid words. On the stage one must have reality, and one must have joy; and that is why the intellectual modern drama has failed, and people have grown sick of the false joy of the musical comedy that has been given them in place of the rich joy found only in what is superb and wild in reality. In a good play every speech should be as fully flavored as a nut or apple, and such speeches cannot be written by anyone who works among people who have shut their lips on poetry. In Ireland, for a few years more, we have a popular imagination that is fiery and magnificent, and tender; so that those who wish to write start with a chance that is not given to writers in places where the springtime of the local life has been forgotten, and the harvest is a memory only, and the straw has been turned into bricks.

RIDERS TO THE SEA

A Play in One Act

John Millington Synge

CHARACTERS

MAURYA, *an old woman*
BARTLEY, *her son*
CATHLEEN, *her daughter*
NORA, *a younger daughter*
MEN AND WOMEN

An Island off the west of Ireland.
Cottage kitchen, with nets, oil-skins, spinning-wheel, some new boards standing by the wall, etc. CATHLEEN, *a girl of about twenty, finishes kneading cake, and puts it down on the pot-oven by the fire; then wipes her hands, and begins to spin at the wheel.* NORA, *a young girl, puts her head in at the door.*

NORA (*in a low voice*): Where is she?

CATHLEEN: She's lying down, God help her, and may be sleeping, if she's able.

(NORA *comes in softly, and takes a bundle from under her shawl.*)

CATHLEEN (*spinning the wheel rapidly*): What is it you have?

NORA: The young priest is after bringing them. It's a shirt and a plain stocking were got off a drowned man in Donegal.

(CATHLEEN *stops her wheel with a sudden movement, and leans out to listen.*)

NORA: We're to find out if it's Michael's they are, some time herself will be down looking by the sea.

CATHLEEN: How would they be Michael's, Nora? How would he go the length of that way to the Far North?

NORA: The young priest says he's known the like of it. "If it's Michael's they are," says

he, "you can tell herself he's got a clean burial by the grace of God, and if they're not his, let no one say a word about them, for she'll be getting her death," says he, "with crying and lamenting."

(*The door which* NORA *half closed is blown open by a gust of wind.*)

CATHLEEN (*looking out anxiously*): Did you ask him would he stop Bartley going this day with the horses to the Galway fair?

NORA: "I won't stop him," says he, "but let you not be afraid. Herself does be saying prayers half through the night, and the Almighty God won't leave her destitute," says he, "with no son living."

CATHLEEN: Is the sea bad by the white rocks, Nora?

NORA: Middling bad, God help us. There's a great roaring in the west, and it's worse it'll be getting when the tide's turned to the wind. (*She goes over to the table with the bundle.*) Shall I open it now?

CATHLEEN: Maybe she'd wake up on us, and come in before we'd done. (*Coming to the table.*) It's a long time we'll be, and the two of us crying.

NORA (*goes to the inner door and listens*): She's moving about on the bed. She'll be coming in a minute.

CATHLEEN: Give me the ladder, and I'll put them up in the turf-loft, the way she won't know of them at all, and maybe when the tide turns she'll be going down to see would he be floating from the east.

(*They put the ladder against the gable of the chimney;* CATHLEEN *goes up a few steps and hides the bundle in the turf-loft.* MAURYA *comes from the inner room.*)

MAURYA (*looking up at* CATHLEEN *and speaking querulously*): Isn't it turf enough you have for this day and evening?

CATHLEEN: There's a cake baking at the fire for a short space (*throwing down the turf*) and Bartley will want it when the tide turns if he goes to Connemara.

(NORA *picks up the turf and puts it round the pot-oven.*)

MAURYA (*sitting down on a stool at the fire*): He won't go this day with the wind rising from the south and west. He won't go this day, for the young priest will stop him surely.

NORA: He'll not stop him, Mother, and I heard Eamon Simon and Stephen Pheety and Colum Shawn saying he would go.

MAURYA: Where is he itself?

NORA: He went down to see would there be another boat sailing in the week, and I'm thinking it won't be long till he's here now, for the tide's turning at the green head, and the hooker's[1] tacking from the east.

CATHLEEN: I hear some one passing the big stones.

NORA (*looking out*): He's coming now, and he in a hurry.

BARTLEY (*comes in and looks round the room; speaking sadly and quietly*): Where is the bit of new rope, Cathleen, was bought in Connemara?

CATHLEEN (*coming down*): Give it to him, Nora; It's on a nail by the white boards. I hung it up this morning, for the pig with the black feet was eating it.

NORA (*giving him a rope*): Is that it, Bartley?

MAURYA: You'd do right to leave that rope, Bartley, hanging by the boards. (BARTLEY *takes the rope.*) It will be wanting in this place, I'm telling you, if Michael is washed up tomorrow morning, or the next morning, or any morning in the week, for it's a deep grave we'll make him by the grace of God.

BARTLEY (*beginning to work with the rope*): I've no halter the way I can ride down on the mare, and I must go now quickly. This is the one boat going for two weeks or beyond it, and the fair will be a good fair for horses I heard them saying below.

MAURYA: It's a hard thing they'll be saying below if the body is washed up and there's no man in it to make the coffin, and I after giving a big price for the finest white boards you'd find in Connemara. (*She looks round at the boards.*)

BARTLEY: How would it be washed up, and we after looking each day for nine days, and a strong wind blowing a while back from the west and south?

MAURYA: If it wasn't found itself, that wind is raising the sea, and there was a star up against the moon, and it rising in the night. If it was a hundred horses, or a thousand horses you had itself, what is the price of a thousand horses against a son where there is one son only?

BARTLEY (*working at the halter, to* CATHLEEN): Let you go down each day, and see the sheep aren't jumping in on the rye, and if the jobber comes you can sell the pig with the black feet if there is a good price going.

MAURYA: How would the like of her get a good price for a pig?

BARTLEY (*to* CATHLEEN): If the west wind holds with the last bit of the moon let you and Nora get up weed enough for another cock[2] for the kelp. It's hard set we'll be from this day with no one in it but one man to work.

MAURYA: It's hard set we'll be surely the day you're drownd'd with the rest. What way will I live and the girls with me, and I an old woman looking for the grave?

(BARTLEY *lays down the halter, takes off his old coat, and puts on a newer one of the same flannel.*)

BARTLEY (*to* NORA): Is she coming to the pier?

NORA (*looking out*): She's passing the green head and letting fall her sails.

BARTLEY (*getting his purse and tobacco*): I'll have half an hour to go down, and you'll see me coming again in two days, or in three days, or maybe in four days if the wind is bad.

---

1 A single-masted fishing boat.   2 A stack for burning seaweed into the ashes (kelp) useful as fertilizer.

MAURYA (*turning round to the fire, and putting her shawl over her head*): Isn't it a hard and cruel man won't hear a word from an old woman, and she holding him from the sea?

CATHLEEN: It's the life of a young man to be going on the sea, and who would listen to an old woman with one thing and she saying it over?

BARTLEY (*taking the halter*): I must go now quickly. I'll ride down on the red mare, and the gray pony'll run behind me. . . . The blessing of God on you. (*He goes out.*)

MAURYA (*crying out as he is in the door*): He's gone now, God spare us, and we'll not see him again. He's gone now, and when the black night is falling I'll have no son left me in the world.

CATHLEEN: Why wouldn't you give him your blessing and he looking round in the door? Isn't it sorrow enough is on every one in this house without your sending him out with an unlucky word behind him, and a hard word in his ear?

(MAURYA *takes up the tongs and begins raking the fire aimlessly without looking round.*)

NORA (*turning toward her*): You're taking away the turf from the cake.

CATHLEEN (*crying out*): The Son of God forgive us, Nora, we're after forgetting his bit of bread. (*She comes over to the fire.*)

NORA: And it's destroyed he'll be going till dark night, and he after eating nothing since the sun went up.

CATHLEEN (*turning the cake out of the oven*): It's destroyed he'll be, surely. There's no sense left on any person in a house where an old woman will be talking forever.

(MAURYA *sways herself on her stool.*)

CATHLEEN (*cutting off some of the bread and rolling it in a cloth; to* MAURYA): Let you go down now to the spring well and give him this and he passing. You'll see him then and the dark word will be broken, and you can say "God speed you," the way he'll be easy in his mind.

MAURYA (*taking the bread*): Will I be in it as soon as himself?

CATHLEEN: If you go now quickly.

MAURYA (*standing up unsteadily*): It's hard set I am to walk.

CATHLEEN (*looking at her anxiously*): Give her the stick, Nora, or maybe she'll slip on the big stones.

NORA: What stick?

CATHLEEN: The stick Michael brought from Connemara.

MAURYA (*taking a stick* NORA *gives her*): In the big world the old people do be leaving things after them for their sons and children, but in this place it is the young men do be leaving things behind for them that do be old.

(*She goes out slowly.* NORA *goes over to the ladder.*)

CATHLEEN: Wait, Nora, maybe she'd turn back quickly. She's that sorry, God help her, you wouldn't know the thing she'd do.

NORA: Is she gone round by the bush?

CATHLEEN (*looking out*): She's gone now. Throw it down quickly, for the Lord knows when she'll be out of it again.

NORA (*getting the bundle from the loft*): The young priest said he'd be passing tomorrow, and we might go down and speak to him below if it's Michael's they are surely.

CATHLEEN (*taking the bundle*): Did he say what way they were found?

NORA (*coming down*): "There were two men," says he, "and they rowing round with poteen[3] before the cocks crowed, and the oar of one of them caught the body, and they passing the black cliffs of the north."

CATHLEEN (*trying to open the bundle*): Give me a knife, Nora, the string's perished with the

---

3 A strong whiskey illegally brewed and sold.

salt water, and there's a black knot on it you wouldn't loosen in a week.

NORA (*giving her a knife*): I've heard tell it was a long way to Donegal.

CATHLEEN (*cutting the string*): It is surely. There was a man in here a while ago — the man sold us that knife — and he said if you set off walking from the rocks beyond, it would be seven days you'd be in Donegal.

NORA: And what time would a man take, and he floating?

(CATHLEEN *opens the bundle and takes out a bit of a stocking. They look at them eagerly.*)

CATHLEEN (*in a low voice*): The Lord spare us, Nora! isn't it a queer hard thing to say if it's his they are surely?

NORA: I'll get his shirt off the hook the way we can put the one flannel on the other. (*She looks through some clothes hanging in the corner.*) It's not with them, Cathleen, and where will it be?

CATHLEEN: I'm thinking Bartley put it on him in the morning, for his own shirt was heavy with the salt in it. (*Pointing to the corner.*) There's a bit of a sleeve was of the same stuff. Give me that and it will do.

(NORA *brings it to her and they compare the flannel.*)

CATHLEEN: It's the same stuff, Nora; but if it is itself aren't there great rolls of it in the shops of Galway, and isn't it many another man may have a shirt of it as well as Michael himself?

NORA (*who has taken up the stocking and counted the stitches, crying out*): It's Michael, Cathleen, it's Michael; God spare his soul, and what will herself say when she hears this story, and Bartley on the sea?

CATHLEEN (*taking the stocking*): It's a plain stocking.

NORA. It's the second one of the third pair I knitted, and I put up threescore stitches, and I dropped four of them.

CATHLEEN (*counts the stitches*): It's that number is in it. (*crying out.*) Ah, Nora, isn't it a bitter thing to think of him floating that way to the Far North, and no one to keen him but the black hags that do be flying on the sea?

NORA (*swinging herself round, and throwing out her arms on the clothes*): And isn't it a pitiful thing when there is nothing left of a man who was a great rower and fisher, but a bit of an old shirt and a plain stocking?

CATHLEEN (*after an instant*): Tell me is herself coming, Nora? I hear a little sound on the path.

NORA (*looking out*): She is, Cathleen. She's coming up to the door.

CATHLEEN: Put these things away before she'll come in. Maybe it's easier she'll be after giving her blessing to Bartley, and we won't let on we've heard anything the time he's on the sea.

NORA (*helping* CATHLEEN *to close the bundle*): We'll put them here in the corner.

(*They put them into a hole in the chimney corner.* CATHLEEN *goes back to the spinning-wheel.*)

NORA: Will she see it was crying I was?

CATHLEEN: Keep your back to the door the way the light'll not be on you.

(NORA *sits down at the chimney corner, with her back to the door.* MAURYA *comes in very slowly, without looking at the girls, and goes over to her stool at the other side of the fire. The cloth with the bread is still in her hand. The girls look at each other, and* NORA *points to the bundle of bread.*)

CATHLEEN (*after spinning for a moment*): You didn't give him his bit of bread? (MAURYA *begins to keen softly, without turning round.*)

CATHLEEN: Did you see him riding down?

(MAURYA *goes on keening.*)

CATHLEEN (*a little impatiently*): God forgive

you; isn't it a better thing to raise your voice and tell what you seen, than to be making lamentation for a thing that's done? Did you see Bartley I'm saying to you.

MAURYA (*with a weak voice*): My heart's broken from this day.

CATHLEEN (*as before*): Did you see Bartley?

MAURYA: I seen the fearfulest thing.

CATHLEEN (*leaves her wheel and looks out*): God forgive you; he's riding the mare now over the green head, and the gray pony behind him.

MAURYA (*starts, so that her shawl falls back from her head and shows her white tossed hair. With a frightened voice*): The gray pony behind him.

CATHLEEN (*coming to the fire*): What is it ails you, at all?

MAURYA (*speaking very slowly*): I've seen the fearfulest thing any person has seen, since the day Bride Dara seen the dead man with a child in his arms.

CATHLEEN AND NORA: Uah.

(*They crouch down in front of the old woman at the fire.*)

NORA: Tell us what it is you seen.

MAURYA: I went down to the spring well, and I stood there saying a prayer to myself. Then Bartley came along, and he riding on the red mare with the gray pony behind him. (*She puts up her hands, as if to hide something from her eyes*). The Son of God spare us, Nora!

CATHLEEN: What is it you seen?

MAURYA: I seen Michael himself.

CATHLEEN (*speaking softly*): You did not, Mother; it wasn't Michael you seen, for his body is after being found in the Far North, and he's got a clean burial by the grace of God.

MAURYA (*a little defiantly*): I'm after seeing him this day, and he riding and galloping.

Bartley came first on the red mare; and I tried to say, "God speed you," but something choked the words in my throat. He went by quickly; and "the blessing of God on you, says he, and I could say nothing. I looked up then, and I crying, at the gray pony, and there was Michael upon it — with fine clothes on him, and new shoes on his feet.

CATHLEEN (*begins to keen*): It's destroyed we are from this day. It's destroyed, surely.

NORA: Didn't the young priest say the Almighty God wouldn't leave her destitute with no son living?

MAURYA (*in a low voice, but clearly*): It's little the like of him knows of the sea. . . . Bartley will be lost now, and let you call in Eamon and make me a good coffin out of the white boards, for I won't live after them. I've had a husband, and a husband's father, and six sons in this house — six fine men, though it was a hard birth I had with every one of them and they coming to the world — and some of them were found and some of them were not found, but they're gone now the lot of them. . . . There were Stephen, and Shawn, were lost in the great wind, and found after in the Bay of Gregory of the Golden Mouth, and carried up the two of them on the one plank, and in by that door.

(*She pauses for a moment, the girls start as if they heard something through the door that is half open behind them.*)

NORA (*in a whisper*): Did you hear that, Cathleen? Did you hear a noise in the northeast?

CATHLEEN (*in a whisper*): There's some one after crying out by the seashore.

MAURYA (*continues without hearing anything*): There was Sheamus and his father, and his own father again, were lost in a dark night, and not a stick or sign was seen of them when the sun went up. There was Patch after was drowned out of a curagh that turned over. I was sitting here with Bartley, and he a baby, lying on my two knees, and I seen two women, and three women, and four women coming in, and they crossing themselves, and not saying a word. I looked out then, and there were men coming after them, and they holding a thing in the half of a red sail, and water dripping out of it — it was a dry day, Nora — and leaving a track to the door.

(*She pauses again with her hand stretched out toward the door. It opens softly and old women begin to come in, crossing themselves on the threshold, and kneeling down in front of the stage with red petticoats over their heads.*)

MAURYA (*half in a dream, to* CATHLEEN): Is it Patch, or Michael, or what is it at all?

CATHLEEN: Michael is after being found in the Far North, and when he is found there how could he be here in this place?

MAURYA: There does be a power of young men floating round in the sea, and what way would they know if it was Michael they had, or another man like him, for when a man is nine days in the sea, and the wind blowing, it's hard set his own mother would be to say what man was it.

CATHLEEN: It's Michael, God spare him, for they're after sending us a bit of his clothes from the Far North.

(*She reaches out and hands* MAURYA *the clothes that belonged to Michael.* MAURYA *stands up slowly, and takes them in her hands.* NORA *looks out.*)

NORA: They're carrying a thing among them and there's water dripping out of it and leaving a track by the big stones.

CATHLEEN (*in a whisper to the women who have come in*): Is it Bartley it is?

ONE OF THE WOMEN: It is surely, God rest his soul.

(*Two younger women come in and pull out the table. Then men carry in the body of* BARTLEY, *laid on a plank, with a bit of a sail over it, and lay it on the table.*)

CATHLEEN (*to the women, as they are doing so*): What way was he drowned?

ONE OF THE WOMEN: The gray pony knocked him into the sea, and he was washed out where there is a great surf on the white rocks.

(MAURYA *has gone over and knelt down at the head of the table. The women are keening softly and swaying themselves with a slow movement.* CATHLEEN *and* NORA *kneel at the other end of the table. The men kneel near the door.*)

MAURYA (*raising her head and speaking as if she did not see the people around her*): They're all gone now, and there isn't anything more the sea can do to me. . . . I'll have no call now to be up crying and praying when the wind breaks from the south, and you can hear the surf is in the east, and the surf is in the west, making a great stir with the two noises, and they hitting one on the other. I'll have no call now to be going down and getting Holy Water in the dark nights after Samhain,[4] and I won't care what way the sea is when the other women will be keening. (*to* NORA) Give me the Holy Water, Nora, there's a small sup still on the dresser.

(NORA *gives it to her.*)

MAURYA (*drops Michael's clothes across Bartley's feet, and sprinkles the Holy Water over him*): It isn't that I haven't prayed for you, Bartley, to the Almighty God. It isn't that I haven't said prayers in the dark night till you wouldn't know what I'd be saying; but it's a great rest I'll have now, and it's time surely. It's a great rest I'll have now, and great sleeping in the long nights after Samhain, if it's only a bit of wet flour we do have to eat, and maybe a fish that would be stinking.

(*She kneels down again, crossing herself, and saying prayers under her breath.*)

CATHLEEN (*to an old man*): Maybe yourself and Eamon would make a coffin when the sun rises. We have fine white boards herself

---

4 The equivalent of Allhallows. It falls on November 1 and marks the beginning of winter; it is celebrated with harvest rites and a Feast of the Dead.

bought, God help her, thinking Michael would be found, and I have a new cake you can eat while you'll be working.

THE OLD MAN (*looking at the boards*): Are there nails with them?

CATHLEEN: There are not, Colum; we didn't think of the nails.

ANOTHER MAN: It's a great wonder she wouldn't think of the nails, and all the coffins she's seen made already.

CATHLEEN: It's getting old she is, and broken.

(MAURYA *stands up again very slowly and spreads out the pieces of Michael's clothes beside the body, sprinkling them with the last of the Holy Water.*)

NORA (*in a whisper to* CATHLEEN): She's quiet now and easy, but the day Michael was drowned you could hear her crying out from this to the spring well. It's fonder she was of Michael, and would any one have thought that?

CATHLEEN (*slowly and clearly*): An old woman will be soon tired with anything she will do, and isn't it nine days herself is after crying and keening, and making great sorrow in the house?

MAURYA (*puts the empty cup mouth downwards on the table and lays her hands together on Bartley's feet*): They're all together this time, and the end is come. May the Almighty God have mercy on Bartley's soul, and on Michael's soul, and on the souls of Sheamus and Patch, and Stephen and Shawn; (*bending her head*) and may He have mercy on my soul, Nora, and on the soul of every one is left living in the world.

(*She pauses, and the keen rises a little more loudly from the women, then sinks away.*)

MAURYA (*continuing*): Michael has a clean burial in the Far North, by the grace of the Almighty God. Bartley will have a fine coffin out of the white boards, and a deep grave surely. What more can we want than that? No man at all can be living forever, and we must be satisfied.

(*She kneels down again and the curtain falls slowly.*)

The Long Voyage Home

There are many who think that Eugene O'Neill (1888–1953) is the greatest dramatist that America has thus far produced. Oscar Cargill, for example, hits upon O'Neill's *Lazarus Laughed* (1928) — which he likes not for its humanist affirmation of the conquest over death but because it embodies the principles of Carl Jung's *Psychological Types* (1923) — and calls it "the supreme piece of drama of modern times." This in spite of the fact (or perhaps because of the fact) that the play has sunk like a stone and it is almost impossible to find anyone who clearly recalls having seen its first and only production. Eric Bentley may be, as the title of an interesting essay suggests, "trying to like O'Neill," but many people have succeeded in doing so and, with more or less qualification, touting him as the great American playwright.

Despite his Nobel Prize, O'Neill is no Shakespeare or Strindberg and when writers like Benjamin de Casseres proclaim in *Theatre* (February, 1928) that "Eugene O'Neill has brought Tragic Terror and Tragic Beauty back to the literature and stage of the English-speaking world" something stirs within the judicious to prompt some impolite retort. We recall with Robert Benchley that O'Neill was the son in more ways than one of the man who for a generation played the Count of Monte Cristo, that (as H. G. Kemelman said) he wrote "highbrow melodrama:"

> This experimentation is intended only to hide defective craftsmanship and to tickle the fancy of the audience. It is mere pandering to the taste of the moment. The intelligentsia whose patronage has raised O'Neill to his present eminence, blinded by their intellectual and emotional romanticism, mistake these little tricks of the showman for bold originality. O'Neill shows them a succession of thin-skinned poeticules and they hail them as tragic heroes. He paints a picture of a chimerical, daydream world and they shout, "It is true reality." They mistake extravagant "purple passages" for poetry and a maudlin bathos for power. In short, they call that tragedy which is merely violent and unbalanced melodrama.

But then we think of the very uncharacteristic comedy *Ah, Wilderness!* (1933). "If Mr. O'Neill can write with as much clarity as this, it is hard to understand why he has held up the grim mask so long," said Brooks Atkinson on opening night. We think of what many consider the masterpiece he had been working toward all his life, the posthumously-produced* *A Long Day's Journey into Night*, and we consider this criticism is perhaps too harsh. In fact, honest critics tend to do what Allardyce Nichol did in *World Drama*: he praised O'Neill very highly and then, one by one, showed why he really didn't like most of his plays.** We tend to have toward O'Neill the feeling that we have for the massive "biography to end all biographies" of him by Barbara and Arthur Gelb (1962): impressed by the magnitude of the work, we cannot help thinking more artistry would have produced less matter and that size alone is not the measure of greatness.

O'Neill himself was always concerned with magnitude; big ideas, big effects, big patterns, big ambitions, big obsessions that made him (Shaw said) "a banshee Shakespeare." His plays came "out of a bigger head," says Eric Bentley, than other people's. His becoming a playwright, say some unkindly persons, was not simply a mistake — it was a big mistake. Witness Mary McCarthy:

> O'Neill belongs to that group of American authors, which includes [James T.] Farrell and [Theodore] Dreiser, whose choice of vocation was a kind of triumphant catastrophe; none of these men possessed the slightest ear for the word, the sentence, the speech, the paragraph. . . . How is one to judge the great logical symphony of a tone-deaf musician?

But that word "great" again, even to describe the yawps of the prosiest poetry, the most tin-eared dialect, the lack in almost all his work of "great language to lift it beyond itself. I haven't got that. . . . The best one can do is to be pathetically eloquent by one's moving, dramatic inarticulations!" as O'Neill wrote to Arthur Hobson Quinn. O'Neill himself made a confession of his big intentions which is as revealing as it is characteristically clumsy: O'Neill wrote to George Jean Nathan that his subject was

> the death of an old God and the failure of science and materialism to give any satisfying new one for the surviving primitive religious instinct to find a meaning for life in, and to comfort its fears of death with.

Not for O'Neill was the attraction of little things clearly seen. Nor did he specialize in little things grossly inflated as has Arthur Miller ("His name was never in the paper. He's not the finest character that ever lived. But

---

* *A Long Day's Journey into Night* had its world première at The Royal Dramatic Theatre, Stockholm, 10 February, 1955, and opened on Broadway on 7 November of the same year. It is best known to the younger generation through the film which starred Katharine Hepburn and an all-star cast.
** The student can learn much not only about the dramatist but also about critics by consulting one of the collections on O'Neill such as Jordan Y. Miller's *Playwright's Progress* (1965), John Gassner's *O'Neill* in Prentice-Hall's Twentieth Century Views series (1964), or the Cargill, Fagin, and Fisher *O'Neill and His Plays* (1961), which is more extensive.

he's a human being, and a terrible thing is happening to him. So attention must be paid."). From the beginning, O'Neill exhibited the ponderousness that was to run from *Beyond the Horizon* (1920) on; from the beginning his work was characterized by theatricality combined with a distaste, even a defiance, of theatrical limitations: *Strange Interlude* (1927) and *Lazarus Laughed* (1928), too big, too long, too rambling, to *The Iceman Cometh* (1946). From the beginning the man who would not worry about box office (author of *Dynamo* and *The Great God Brown*, *Welded* and *Marco Millions* and others) sold out to the intellectuals, striving to impress, trying to earn from St. John Irvine such accolades as "immeasurably the most interesting man of letters that America has produced since the death of Walt Whitman." Always the "Big Grand Opus" which never materialized: "There'll be nine separate plays, to be acted on nine successive nights; together they will form a sort of dramatic autobiography, something in the style of *War and Peace* or *Jean Christophe*." And *By Way of Obit*, conceived as eight one-acters, which (if "Hughie" is the sample) the world will not much miss, plus *The Last Conquest*, featuring Christ and Satan and concluding (Mrs. Charlotta Monterey O'Neill confessed) with "all the world's church bells ringing," an abandoned project. Always like Yank in *The Hairy Ape*:

> I ain't on oith and I ain't in heaven, get me? I'm in de middle tryin' to separate 'em, takin' all the worst [shouldn't that be "woist"?] punches from bot' of 'em.

Though he became in time the high priest of what he himself called "unmitigated gloom," expressed in vast works, we have chosen to represent O'Neill here with a one-act play from the early years when O'Neill was learning his trade among the bobbed Bohemians of Greenwich Village, off-Broadway, as we would say today. O'Neill began with some short plays (*Thirst, Fog, Warnings*) based on stories that sailors told him. Then he wrote some plays based on his own experience on the tramp steamer *S.S. Ikalis* (which he called *S.S. Glencairn*): with "the typical mixed crew of the average British tramp steamer." Two of these he set in the ship's forecastle (*Bound East for Cardiff* and *In the Zone*) and one on its deck while the ship lay at anchor off the West Indies (*The Moon of the Caribees*). The fourth, the powerful little play here, he set in a London waterfront dive, but it is an *S.S. Glencairn* play nonetheless, its shanghaied sailor Olson a Norwegian on the *S.S. Ikalis*, its setting really a notorious saloon in Liverpool frequented by a Shanghai Brown "who would have shipped his own father to China for two pounds."

The Moon of the Caribees was O'Neill's favorite one-acter and could well be compared in mood with *The Glass Menagerie*, but unable to present *A Long Day's Journey into Night* here because of its length we think *The Long Voyage Home* the best. It contains the talent (and part of the story) that made *Beyond the Horizon* and won O'Neill the first of his four Pulitzer

Prizes. It was one of the earliest public announcements of his career when published by H. L. Mencken and George Jean Nathan in their "magazine of cleverness," *The Smart Set*. As a film it was, O'Neill said, "the best picture ever made from my stuff." It was one of the few plays, he told George Jean Nathan, by which he "would like to stand or fall," a little play ("an incident, scarcely more") with some of the marks of O'Neill's style (perhaps more characteristic of O'Neill than *Ile* and *In the Zone* because more melodramatic: "seduction, poisoned drink, robbery") and touched with the greatness of the brooding genius who, however flawed this work or that, whether he stands as the American playwright *par excellence* or not, grimly and devotedly strove to find "a meaning for life and comfort for the fears of death," some nobility in the tragic ironies of the human lot. Also the play demonstrates that at least in one way O'Neill was the theatre poet he so fervently wished to be, the one he describes in the character of Edmund in *A Long Day's Journey into Night* (which was, after all, a great American play):

> The *makings* of a poet. No, I'm afraid I'm like the guy who is always panhandling for a smoke. He hasn't even got the makings. He's only got the habit. I couldn't touch what I tried to tell you now [he has been speaking to his father of the mystical experience of the sea]. I just stammered. That's the best I'll ever do. I mean, if I live. Well, it will be faithful realism at least. Stammering is the native eloquence of us fog people.

The Long Voyage Home is not unworthy to be placed beside that other short and shattering tragedy of the sea, *Riders to the Sea*. It has its poetry too. It shows that at the beginning of his career, before his period of myth and monumentality, O'Neill had the greatness he was so long to seek. As Kenneth Tynan writes:

> Not until his fifties did this grievously haunted man overcome his personal shame and his artistic pretensions; when he did, he wrote the two auto-biographical masterpieces by which his name will be durably remembered — *The Iceman Cometh* [based on his experiences of 1909] and *A Long Day's Journey into Night* [set in 1912]. Serious theatre in O'Neill's heyday was discernibly splitting into two branches — one rooted in naturalistic fact, and the other in fable and fantasy. In the nick of time, O'Neill chose American fact. It was a prosaic choice, but it made him a poet.

THE LONG VOYAGE HOME

A play in one act

Eugene O'Neill

CHARACTERS

FAT JOE, *proprietor of a dive*
NICK, *a crimp*
MAG, *a barmaid*
KATE
FREDA
TWO ROUGHS

OLSON
DRISCOLL } *seamen of the British*
COCKY   } *tramp steamer, Glencairn*
IVAN

The bar of a low dive on the London water front — a squalid, dingy room dimly lighted by kerosene lamps placed in brackets on the walls. On the left, the bar. In front of it, a door leading to a side room. On the right, tables with chairs around them. In the rear, a door leading to the street.

A slovenly barmaid with a stupid face sodden with drink is mopping off the bar. Her arm moves back and forth mechanically and her eyes are half shut as if she were dozing on her feet. At the far end of the bar stands Fat Joe, the proprietor, a gross bulk of a man with an enormous stomach. His face is red and bloated, his little piggish eyes being almost concealed by rolls of fat. The thick fingers of his big hands are loaded with cheap rings and a gold watch chain of cable-like proportions stretches across his checked waistcoat.

At one of the tables, front, a round-shouldered young fellow is sitting, smoking a cigarette. His face is pasty, his mouth weak, his eyes shifting and cruel. He is dressed in a shabby suit, which must have once been cheaply flashy, and wears a muffler and cap.

It is about nine o'clock in the evening.

JOE (*yawning*): Blimey if bizness ain't 'arf slow to-night. I dunnow wot's 'appened. The place is like a bleedin' tomb. Where's all the sailor men, I'd like to know? (*Raising his voice*) Ho, you Nick! (NICK *turns around listlessly.*) Wot's the name o' that wessel put in at the dock below jest arter noon?

NICK (*laconically*): Glencairn — from Bewnezerry (Buenos Aires).

JOE: Ain't the crew been paid orf yet?

NICK: Paid orf this arternoon, they tole me. I 'opped on board of 'er an' seen 'em. 'Anded 'em some o' yer cards, I did. They promised faithful they'd 'appen in to-night — them as whose time was done.

JOE: Any two-year men to be paid orf?

NICK: Four — three Britishers an' a square-'ead.

JOE (*indignantly*): An' yer popped orf an' left 'em? An' me a-payin' yer to 'elp an' bring 'em in 'ere!

NICK (*grumbling*): Much you pays me! An' I ain't slingin' me 'ook abaht the 'ole bleedin' town fur now man. See?

JOE: I ain't speakin' on'y fur meself. Down't I always give yer yer share, fair an' square, as man to man?

NICK (*with a sneer*): Yus — b'cause you 'as to.

JOE: 'As to? Listen to 'im! There's many'd be 'appy to 'ave your berth, me man!

NICK: Yus? Wot wiv the peelers li'ble to put me away in the bloody jail fur crimpin', an' all?

JOE (*indignantly*): We down't do no crimpin'.

NICK (*sarcastically*): Ho, now! Not arf!

JOE (*a bit embarrassed*): Well, on'y a bit now an' agen when there ain't no reg'lar trade. (*To hide his confusion he turns to the barmaid angrily. She is still mopping off the bar, her chin on her breast, half-asleep.*) 'Ere, me gel, we've 'ad enough o' that. You been a-moppin', an' a-moppin', an' a-moppin' the blarsted bar fur a 'ole 'our. 'Op it aht o' this! You'd fair guv a bloke the shakes a-watchin' yer.

MAG (*beginning to sniffle*): Ow, you do frighten me when you 'oller at me, Joe. I ain't a bad gel, I ain't. Gawd knows I tries to do me best fur you. (*She bursts into a tempest of sobs.*)

JOE (*roughly*): Stop yer grizzlin'! An' 'op it aht of 'ere!

NICK (*chuckling*): She's drunk, Joe. Been 'ittin' the gin, eh, Mag?

MAG (*ceases crying at once and turns on him furiously*): You little crab, you! Orter wear a muzzle, you ort! A-openin' of your ugly mouth to a 'onest woman what ain't never done you no 'arm. (*Commencing to sob again*) H'abusin' me like a dawg cos I'm sick an' orf me oats, an' all.

JOE: Orf yer go, me gel! Go hupstairs and 'ave a sleep. I'll wake yer if I wants yer. An' wake the two gels when yer goes hup. It's 'arpas' nine an' time as some one was a-comin' in, tell 'em. D'yer 'ear me?

MAG (*stumbling around the bar to the door on left — sobbing*): Yus, yus, I 'ears you. Gawd knows wot's goin' to 'appen to me, I'm that sick. Much you cares if I dies, down't you? (*She goes out.*)

JOE (*still brooding over NICK's lack of diligence — after a pause*): Four two-year men paid orf wiv their bloody pockets full o' sovereigns — an' yer lorst 'em. (*He shakes his head sorrowfully.*)

NICK (*impatiently*): Stow it! They promised faithful they'd come, I tells yer. They'll be walkin' in in 'arf a mo'. There's lots o' time yet. (*In a low voice*) 'Ave yer got the drops? We might wanter use 'em.

JOE (*taking a small bottle from behind the bar*): Yus; 'ere it is.

NICK (*with satisfaction*): Righto! (*His shifty eyes peer about the room searchingly. Then he beckons to JOE, who comes over to the table and sits down.*) Reason I arst yer about the drops was 'cause I seen the capt'n of the Amindra this arternoon.

JOE: The Amindra? Wot ship is that?

NICK: Bloody windjammer — skys'l yarder — full rigged — painted white — been layin' at the dock above 'ere fur a month. You knows 'er.

JOE: Ho, yus. I knows now.

NICK: The capt'n says as 'e wants a man special bad — ter-night. They sails at daybreak ter-morrer.

JOE: There's plenty o' 'ands lyin' abaht waitin' fur ships, I should fink.

NICK: Not fur this ship, ole buck. The capt'n an' mate are bloody slave-drivers, an' they're bound down round the 'Orn. They 'arf starved the 'ands on the last trip 'ere, an' no one'll dare ship on 'er. (*After a pause*) I promised the capt'n faithful I'd get 'im one, and ter-night.

JOE (*doubtfully*): An' 'ow are yer goin' to git 'im?

NICK (*with a wink*): I was thinkin' as one of 'em from the Glencairn'd do — them as was paid orf an' is comin' 'ere.

JOE (*with a grin*): It'd be a good 'aul, that's the troof. (*Frowning*) If they comes 'ere.

NICK: They'll come, an' they'll all be rotten drunk, wait an' see.

(*There is the noise of loud, boisterous singing from the street.*)

NICK: Sounds like 'em, now. (*He opens the street door and looks out.*) Gawd blimey if it ain't the four of 'em! (*Turning to JOE in triumph*) Naw, what d'yer say? They're lookin' for the place. I'll go aht an' tell 'em. (*He goes out.*)

(*JOE gets into position behind the bar, assuming his most oily smile. A moment later the door is opened, admitting DRISCOLL, COCKY, IVAN and OLSON. DRISCOLL is a tall, powerful Irishman; COCKY, a wizened runt of a man with a straggling gray mustache; IVAN, a hulking oaf of a peasant; OLSON, a stocky, middle-aged Swede with round, childish blue eyes. The first three are all very drunk, especially*

IVAN, *who is managing his legs with difficulty.* OLSON *is perfectly sober. All are dressed in their ill-fitting shore clothes and look very uncomfortable.* DRISCOLL *has unbuttoned his stiff collar and its ends stick out sideways. He has lost his tie.* NICK *slinks into the room after them and sits down at a table in rear. The seamen come to the table, front.*)

JOE (*with affected heartiness*): Ship ahoy, mates! 'Appy to see yer 'ome safe an' sound.

DRISCOLL (*turns round, swaying a bit, and peers at him across the bar*): So ut's you, is ut? (*He looks about the place with an air of recognition.*) An' the same damn rat's-hole, sure enough. I remimber foive or six years back 'twas here I was sthripped av me last shillin' whin I was aslape. (*With sudden fury*) God stiffen ye, come none av your dog's thricks on me this trip or I'll — (*He shakes his fist at* JOE.)

JOE (*hastily interrupting*): Yer must be mistaiken. This is a 'onest place, this is.

COCKY (*derisively*): Ho, yus! An' you're a bleedin' angel, I s'pose?

IVAN (*vaguely taking off his derby hat and putting it on again — plaintively*): I don' li-ike dis place.

DRISCOLL (*going over to the bar — as genial as he was furious a moment before*): Well, no matter, 'tis all past an' gone an' forgot. I'm not the man to be holdin' harrd feelin's on me first night ashore, an' me dhrunk as a lord. (*He holds out his hand, which* JOE *takes very gingerly.*) We'll all be havin' a dhrink, I'm thinkin'. Whiskey for the three av us — *Irish* whiskey!

COCKY (*mockingly*): An' a glarse o' ginger beer fur our blarsted love-child 'ere. (*He jerks his thumb at* OLSON.)

OLSON (*with a good-natured grin*): I bane a good boy dis night, for one time.

DRISCOLL (*bellowing, and pointing to* NICK *as* JOE *brings the drinks to the table*): An' see what that crimpin' son av a crimp'll be wantin' — an' have your own pleasure. (*He pulls*

a sovereign out of his pocket and slams it on the bar.*)

NICK: Guv me a pint o' beer, Joe.

(JOE *draws the beer and takes it down to the far end of the bar.* NICK *comes over to get it and* JOE *gives him a significant wink and nods toward the door on the left.* NICK *signals back that he understands.*)

COCKY (*drink in hand — impatiently*): I'm that bloody dry! (*Lifting his glass to* DRISCOLL) Cheero, ole dear, cheero!

DRISCOLL (*pocketing his change without looking at it*): A toast for ye: Hell roast that divil av a bo'sun! (*He drinks.*)

COCKY: Righto! Gawd strike 'im blind! (*He drains his glass.*)

IVAN (*half-asleep*): Dot's gude. (*He tosses down his drink in one gulp.*)

(OLSON *sips his ginger ale.* NICK *takes a swallow of his beer and then comes round the bar and goes out the door on left.*)

COCKY (*producing a sovereign*): Ho there, you Fatty! Guv us another!

JOE: The saime, mates?

COCKY: Yus.

DRISCOLL: No, ye scut! I'll be havin' a pint av beer. I'm dhry as a loime kiln.

IVAN (*suddenly getting to his feet in a befuddled manner and nearly upsetting the table*): I don' li-ike dis place! I wan' see girls — plenty girls. (*Pathetically*) I don' li-ike dis place. I wan' dance with girl.

DRISCOLL (*pushing him back on his chair with a thud*): Shut up, ye Rooshan baboon! A foine Romeo you'd make in your condishun.

(IVAN *blubbers some incoherent protest — then suddenly falls asleep.*)

JOE (*bringing the drinks — looks at* OLSON): An' you, matey?

OLSON (*shaking his head*): Noting dis time, thank you.

COCKY (*mockingly*): A-savin' of 'is money, 'e is! Goin' back to 'ome an' mother. Goin' to buy a bloomin' farm an' punch the blarsted dirt, that's wot 'e is! (*Spitting disgustedly*) There's a funny bird of a sailor man for yer, Gawd blimey!

OLSON (*wearing the same good-natured grin*): Yust what I like, Cocky. I wus on farm long time when I wus kid.

DRISCOLL: Lave him alone, ye bloody insect! 'Tis a foine sight to see a man wid some sense in his head instead av a damn fool the loike av us. I only wisht I'd a mother alive to call me own. I'd not be dhrunk in this divil's hole this minute, maybe.

COCKY (*commencing to weep dolorously*): Ow, down't talk, Drisc! I can't bear to 'ear you. I ain't never 'ad no mother, I ain't —

DRISCOLL: Shut up, ye ape, an' don't be makin' that squealin'. If ye cud see your ugly face, wid the big red nose av ye all screwed up in a knot, ye'd never shed a tear the rist av your loife. (*Roaring into song*) We ar-re the byes av We-e-exford who fought wid hearrt an' hand! (*Speaking*) To hell wid Ulster! (*He drinks and the others follow his example.*) An' I'll strip to any man in the city av London won't dhrink to that toast.

(*He glares truculently at* JOE, *who immediately downs his beer.* NICK *enters again from the door on the left and comes up to* JOE *and whispers in his ear. The latter nods with satisfaction.*)

DRISCOLL (*glowering at them*): What divil's thrick are ye up to now, the two av ye? (*He flourishes a brawny fist.*) Play fair wid us or ye deal wid me!

JOE (*hastily*): No trick, shipmate! May Gawd kill me if that ain't troof!

NICK (*indicating* IVAN, *who is snoring*): On'y your mate there was arskin' fur gels an I thorght as 'ow yer'd like 'em to come dawhn and 'ave a wet wiv yer.

JOE (*with a smirking wink*): Pretty, 'olesome gels they be, ain't they, Nick?

NICK: Yus.

COCKY: Aar! I knows the gels you 'as, not 'arf! They'd fair blind yer, they're that 'omely. None of yer bloomin' gels fur me, ole Fatty. Me and Drisc knows a place, down't we, Drisc?

DRISCOLL: Divil a lie, we do. An' we'll be afther goin' there in a minute. There's music there an' a bit av a dance to liven a man.

JOE: Nick, 'ere, can play yer a tune, can't yer, Nick?

NICK: Yus.

JOE: An' yer can 'ave a dance in the side room 'ere.

DRISCOLL: Hurroo! Now you're talkin'.

(*The two women,* FREDA *and* KATE *enter from the left.* FREDA *is a little, sallow-faced blonde.* KATE *is stout and dark.*)

COCKY (*in a loud aside to* DRISCOLL): Gawd blimey, look at 'em! Ain't they 'orrible?

(*The women come forward to the table, wearing their best set smiles.*)

FREDA (*in a raspy voice*): 'Ullo mates.

KATE: 'Ad a good voyage?

DRISCOLL: Rotten; but no matther. Welcome, as the sayin' is, an' sit down an' what'll ye be takin' for your thirst? (*to* KATE) You'll be sittin' by me, darlin' — what's your name?

KATE (*with a stupid grin*): Kate. (*She stands by his chair.*)

DRISCOLL (*putting his arm around her*): A good Irish name, but you're English by the trim av ye, an' be damned to you. But no matther. Ut's fat ye are, Katy dear, an' I never cud endure skinny wimin. (FREDA *favors him with a viperish glance and sits down by* OLSON.) What'll ye have?

OLSON: No, Drisc. Dis one bane on me. (*He takes out a roll of notes from his inside pocket and lays one on the table.*)

(JOE, NICK, *and the women look at the money*

with greedy eyes. IVAN *gives a particularly violent snore.*)

FREDA: Waike up your fren'. Gawd, 'ow I 'ates to 'ear snorin'.

DRISCOLL (*springing to action, smashes* IVAN'S *derby over his ears*): D'you hear the lady talkin' to ye, ye Rooshan swab?

(*The only reply is a snore.* DRISCOLL *pulls the battered remains of the derby off* IVAN'S *head and smashes it back again.*)

DRISCOLL: Arise an' shine, ye dhrunken swine!

(*Another snore. The women giggle.* DRISCOLL *throws the beer left in his glass into* IVAN'S *face. The Russian comes to in a flash, spluttering. There is a roar of laughter.*)

IVAN (*indignantly*): I tell you — dot's something I don' li-ike!

COCKY: Down't waste good beer, Drisc.

IVAN (*grumblingly*): I tell you — dot is not ri-ight.

DRISCOLL: Ut's your own doin', Ivan. Ye was moanin' for girrls an' whin they come you sit gruntin' loike a pig in a sty. Have ye no manners?

(IVAN *seems to see the women for the first time and grins foolishly.*)

KATE (*laughing at him*): Cheero, ole chum, 'ows Russha?

IVAN (*greatly pleased — putting his hand in his pocket*): I buy a drink.

OLSEN: No, dis one bane on me. (*to* JOE) Hey, you faller!

JOE: Wot'll it be, Kate?

KATE: Gin.

FREDA: Brandy.

DRISCOLL: An' Irish whiskey for the rist av us — wid the excipshun av our timperance friend, God pity him!

FREDA (*to* OLSON): You ain't drinkin'?

OLSON (*half-ashamed*): No.

FREDA (*with a seductive smile*): I down't blame yer. You got sense, you 'ave. I on'y tike a nip o' brandy now an' agen fur my 'ealth.

(JOE *brings the drinks and* OLSON'S *change.* COCKY *gets unsteadily to his feet and raises his glass in the air.*)

COCKY: 'Ere's a toff toast for yer: The ladies, Gawd — (*He hesitates — then adds in a grudging tone*) — bless 'em.

KATE (*with a silly giggle*): Oo'er! That wasn't what you was goin' to say, you bad Cocky, you!

(*They all drink.*)

DRISCOLL (*to* NICK): Where's the tune ye was promisin' to give us?

NICK: Come ahn in the side 'ere an' you'll 'ear it.

DRISCOLL (*getting up*): Come on, all av ye. We'll have a tune an' a dance if I'm not too dhrunk to dance, God help me.

(COCKY *and* IVAN *stagger to their feet.* IVAN *can hardly stand. He is leering at* KATE *and snickering to himself in a maudlin fashion. The three, led by* NICK, *go out the door on the left.* KATE *follows them.* OLSON *and* FREDA *remain seated.*)

COCKY (*calling over his shoulder*): Come on an' dance, Ollie.

OLSON: Yes, I come. (*He starts to get up. From the side room comes the sound of an accordion and a boisterous whoop from* DRISCOLL, *followed by a heavy stamping of feet.*)

FREDA: Ow, down't go in there. Stay 'ere an' 'ave a talk wiv me. They're all drunk an' you ain't drinkin'. (*With a smile up into his face*) I'll think yer don't like me if yer goes in there.

OLSON (*confused*): You wus wrong, Miss Freda. I don't — I mean I do like you.

FREDA (*smiling — puts her hand over his on the table*): An' I likes you. Yer a genelman. You don't get drunk an' hinsult poor gels wot 'as a 'ard an' uneppy life.

OLSON (*pleased but still more confused —
wriggling his feet*): I bane drunk many time,
Miss Freda.

FREDA: Then why ain't yer drinkin' now? (*She
exchanges a quick, questioning glance with*
JOE, *who nods back at her — then she continues persuasively*) Tell me somethin'
abaht yeself.

OLSON (*with a grin*): There ain't noting to say,
Miss Freda. I bane poor devil sailor man,
dat's all.

FREDA: Where was you born — Norway?
(OLSON *shakes his head.*) Denmark?

OLSON: No. You guess once more.

FREDA: Then it must be Sweden.

OLSON: Yes. I wus born in Stockholm.

FREDA (*pretending great delight*): Ow, ain't
that funny! I was born there, too — in
Stockholm.

OLSON (*astonished*): You wus born in Sweden?

FREDA: Yes; you wouldn't think it, but it's
Gawd's troof. (*She clasps her hands de-
lightedly.*)

OLSON (*beaming all over*): You speak Swedish?

FREDA (*trying to smile sadly*): Now. Y'see my
ole man an' woman come 'ere to England
when I was on'y a baby an' they was speakin' English b'fore I was old enough to learn.
Sow I never knew Swedish. (*Sadly*) Wisht I
'ad! (*With a smile*) We'd 'ave a bloomin'
lark of it if I 'ad, wouldn't we?

OLSON: It sound nice to hear the old talk yust
once in a time.

FREDA: Righto! No place like yer 'ome, I says.
Are yer goin' up to — to Stockholm b'fore
yer ships away agen?

OLSON: Yes. I go home from here to Stockholm. (*Proudly*) As passenger!

FREDA: An' you'll git another ship up there
arter you've 'ad a vacation?

OLSON: No. I don't never ship on sea no more.
I got all sea I want for my life — too much

hard work for little money. Yust work,
work, work on ship. I don't want more.

FREDA: Ow, I see. That's why you give up
drinkin'.

OLSON: Yes. (*With a grin*) If I drink I yust get
drunk and spend all money.

FREDA: But if you ain't gointer be a sailor no
more, what'll yer do? You been a sailor all
yer life, ain't yer?

OLSON: No. I work on farm till I am eighteen.
I like it, too — it's nice — work on farm.

FREDA: But ain't Stockholm a city same's
London? Ain't no farms there, is there?

OLSON: We live — my brother and mother live
— my father iss dead — on farm yust a little
way from Stockholm. I have plenty money,
now. I go back with two years' pay and buy
more land yet; work on farm. (*Grinning*)
No more sea, no more bum grub, no more
storms — yust nice work.

FREDA: Ow, ain't that luv'ly! I s'pose you'll
be gittin' married, too?

OLSON (*very much confused*): I don't know. I
like to, if I find nice girl, maybe.

FREDA: Ain't yer got some gel back in Stockholm? I bet yer 'as.

OLSON: No. I got nice girl once before I go on
sea. But I go on ship, and I don't come back,
and she marry other faller. (*He grins
sheepishly.*)

FREDA: Well, it's nice for yer to be goin' 'ome,
anyway.

OLSON: Yes. I tank so.

(*There is a crash from the room on left and
the music abruptly stops. A moment later
COCKY and DRISCOLL appear, supporting the
inert form of IVAN between them. He is in the
last stage of intoxication, unable to move a
muscle. NICK follows them and sits down at
the table in rear.*)

DRISCOLL (*as they zigzag up to the bar*): Ut's
dead he is, I'm thinkin', for he's as limp as a
blarsted corpse.

COCKY (*puffing*): Gawd, 'e ain't 'arf 'eavy!

DRISCOLL (*slapping* IVAN'S *face with his free hand*): Wake up, ye divil, ye. Ut's no use. Gabriel's trumpet itself cudn't rouse him. (*to* JOE) Give us a dhrink for I'm perishing wid the thirst. 'Tis hard worrk, this.

JOE: Whiskey?

DRISCOLL: *Irish* whiskey, ye swab. (*He puts down a coin on the bar.*)

(JOE *serves* COCKY *and* DRISCOLL. *They drink and then swerve over to* OLSON'S *table.*)

OLSON: Sit down and rest for time, Drisc.

DRISCOLL: No, Ollie, we'll be takin' this lad home to his bed. Ut's late for wan so young to be out in the night. An' I'd not trust him in this hole as dhrunk as he is, an' him wid a full pay day on him. (*Shaking his fist at* JOE) Oho, I know your games, me sonny bye!

JOE (*with an air of grievance*): There yer goes again — hinsultin' a 'onest man!

COCKY: Ho, listen to 'im! Guv 'im a shove in the marf, Drisc.

OLSON (*anxious to avoid a fight — getting up*): I help you take Ivan to boarding house.

FREDA (*protestingly*): Ow, you ain't gointer leave me, are yer? An' we 'aving sech a nice talk an' all.

DRISCOLL (*with a wink*): Ye hear what the lady says, Ollie. Ye'd best stay here, me timperance lady's man. An' we need no help. 'Tis only a bit av a way and we're two strong men if we are dhrunk. Ut's no hard shift to take the remains home. But ye can open the door for us, Ollie. (OLSON *goes to the door and opens it.*) Come on, Cocky, an' don't be fallin' aslape yourself. (*They lurch toward the door. As they go out* DRISCOLL *shouts back over his shoulder.*) We'll be comin' back in a short time, surely. So wait here for us, Ollie.

OLSON: All right. I wait here, Drisc. (*He stands in the doorway uncertainly.*)

(JOE *makes violent signs to* FREDA *to bring*

him back. She goes over and puts her arm around OLSON'S shoulder. JOE motions to NICK to come to the bar. They whisper together excitedly.)

FREDA (*coaxingly*): You ain't gointer leave me, are yer, dearie? (*Then irritably*) Fur Gawd's sake, shet that door! I'm fair freezin' to death wiv the fog.

(OLSON *comes to himself with a start and shuts the door.*)

OLSON (*humbly*): Excuse me, Miss Freda.

FREDA (*leading him back to the table — coughing*): Buy me a drink o' brandy, will yer? I'm sow cold.

OLSON: All you want, Miss Freda, all you want. (*to* JOE, *who is still whispering instructions to* NICK) Hey, Yoe! Brandy for Miss Freda. (*He lays a coin on the table.*)

JOE: Righto! (*He pours out her drink and brings it to the table.*) 'Avin' something yerself, shipmate?

OLSON: No. I don't tank so. (*He points to his glass with a grin.*) Dis iss only belly-wash, no? (*He laughs.*)

JOE (*hopefully*): 'Ave a man's drink.

OLSON: I would like to — but no. If I drink one I want drink one tousand. (*He laughs again.*)

FREDA (*responding to a vicious nudge from* JOE'S *elbow*): Ow, tike somethin'. I ain't gointer drink all be meself.

OLSON: Den give me a little yinger beer — small one.

(JOE *goes back of the bar, making a sign to* NICK *to go to their table.* NICK *does so and stands so that the sailor cannot see what* JOE *is doing.*)

NICK (*to make talk*): Where's yer mates popped off ter?

(JOE *pours the contents of the little bottle into* OLSON'S *glass of ginger beer.*)

OLSON: Dey take Ivan, dat drunk faller, to bed. Dey come back.

(JOE *brings* OLSON's *drink to the table and sets it before him.*)

JOE (*to* NICK — *angrily*): 'Op it, will yer? There ain't no time to be dawdlin'. See? 'Urry!

NICK: Down't worry, ole bird, I'm orf. (*He hurries out the door.*)

(JOE *returns to his place behind the bar.*)

OLSON (*after a pause — worriedly*): I tank I should go after dem. Cocky iss very drunk, too, and Drisc —

FREDA: Aar! The big Irish is all right. Don't yer 'ear 'im say as 'ow they'd surely come back 'ere, an' fur you to wait fur 'em?

OLSON: Yes; but if dey don't come soon I tank I go see if dey are in boarding house all right.

FREDA: Where is the boardin' 'ouse?

OLSON: Yust little way back from street here.

FREDA: You stayin' there, too?

OLSON: Yes — until steamer sail for Stockholm — in two days.

FREDA (*alternately looking at* JOE *and feverishly trying to keep* OLSON *talking so he will forget about going away after the others*): Yer mother won't be arf glad to see yer agen, will she? (OLSON *smiles.*) Does she know yer comin'?

OLSON: No. I tought I would yust give her surprise. I write to her from Bonos Eres but I don't tell her I come home.

FREDA: Must be old, ain't she, yer ole lady?

OLSON: She iss eighty-two. (*He smiles reminiscently.*) You know, Miss Freda, I don't see my mother or my brother in — let me tank — (*He counts laboriously on his fingers.*) must be more than ten year. I write once in a while and she write many time; and my brother he write me, too. My mother say in all letter I should come home right away. My brother he write same ting, too. He want me to help him on farm. I write back always I come soon; and I mean all time to go back home at end of voyage. But

I come ashore, I take one drink, I take many drinks, I get drunk, I spend all money, I have to ship away for other voyage. So dis time I say to myself: Don't drink one drink, Ollie, or, sure, you don't get home. And I want go home dis time. I feel homesick for farm and to see my people again. (*He smiles.*) Yust like little boy, I feel homesick. Dat's why I don't drink noting to-night but dis — belly-wash! (*He roars with childish laughter, then suddenly becomes serious.*) You know, Miss Freda, my mother get very old, and I want see her. She might die and I would never —

FREDA (*moved a lot in spite of herself*): Ow, don't talk like that! I jest 'ates to 'ear any one speakin' abaht dyin'.

(*The door to the street is opened and* NICK *enters, followed by two rough-looking, shabbily-dressed men, wearing mufflers, with caps pulled down over their eyes. They sit at the table nearest to the door.* JOE *brings them three beers, and there is a whispered consultation, with many glances in the direction of* OLSON.)

OLSON (*starting to get up — worriedly*): I tank I go round to boarding house. I tank someting go wrong with Drisc and Cocky.

FREDA: Ow, down't go. They kin take care of theyselves. They ain't babies. Wait 'arf a mo'. You ain't 'ad yer drink yet.

JOE (*coming hastily over to the table, indicates the men in the rear with a jerk of his thumb*): One of them blokes wants yer to 'ave a wet wiv 'im.

FREDA: Righto! (*to* OLSON) Let's drink this. (*She raises her glass. He does the same.*) 'Ere's a toast fur yer: Success to yer bloomin' farm an' may yer live long an' 'appy on it. Skoal!

(*She tosses down her brandy.*)

(*He swallows half of his glass of ginger beer and makes a wry face.*)

OLSON: Skoal! (*He puts down his glass.*)

FREDA (*with feigned indignation*): Down't yer like my toast?

OLSON (*grinning*): Yes. It iss very kind, Miss Freda.

FREDA: Then drink it all like I done.

OLSON: Well—— (*He gulps down the rest.*) Dere! (*He laughs.*)

FREDA: Done like a sport!

ONE OF THE ROUGHS (*with a laugh*): Amindra, ahoy!

NICK (*warningly*): Sssshh!

OLSON (*turns around in his chair*): Amindra? Iss she in port? I sail on her once long time ago — three mast, full rig, skys'l yarder? Iss dat ship you mean?

THE ROUGH (*grinning*): Yus; right you are.

OLSON (*angrily*): I know dat damn ship — worst ship dat sail to sea. Rotten grub and dey make you work all time — and the Captain and Mate wus Bluenose devils. No sailor who know anyting ever ship on her. Where iss she bound from here?

THE ROGUE: Round Cape 'Orn — sails at daybreak.

OLSON: Py yingo, I pity poor fallers make dat trip round Cape Stiff dis time year. I bet you some of dem never see port once again. (*He passes his hand over his eyes in a dazed way. His voice grows weaker.*) Py golly, I feel dizzy. All the room go round and round like I was drunk. (*He gets weakly to his feet.*) Good night, Miss Freda. I bane feeling sick. Tell Drisc — I go home. (*He takes a step forward and suddenly collapses over a chair, rolls to the floor, and lies there unconscious.*)

JOE (*from behind the bar*): Quick, nawh!

(NICK *darts forward with* JOE *following.* FREDA *is already beside the unconscious man and has taken the roll of money from his inside pocket. She strips off a note furtively and shoves it into her bosom, trying to conceal her action, but* JOE *sees her. She hands the roll to* JOE, *who pockets it.* NICK *goes through all the other pockets and lays a handful of change on the table.*)

JOE (*impatiently*): 'Urry, 'urry, can't yer? The other blokes'll be 'ere in 'arf a mo'. (*The two roughs come forward.*) 'Ere, you two, tike 'im in under the arms like 'e was drunk. (*They do so.*) Tike 'im to the Amindra — yer knows that, don't yer? — two docks above. Nick'll show yer. An' you, Nick, down't yer leave the bleedin' ship till the capt'n guvs yer this bloke's advance — full month's pay — five quid, d'yer 'ear?

NICK: I knows me bizness, ole bird.

(*They support* OLSON *to the door.*)

THE ROUGH (*as they are going out*): This silly bloke'll 'ave the s'prise of 'is life when 'e wakes up on board of 'er.

(*They laugh. The door closes behind them.* FREDA *moves quickly for the door on the left but* JOE *gets in her way and stops her.*)

JOE (*threateningly*): Guv us what yer took!

FREDA: Took? I guv yer all 'e 'ad.

JOE: Yer a liar! I seen yer a-playin' yer sneakin' tricks, but yer can't fool Joe. I'm too old a 'and. (*Furiously*) Guv it to me, yer bloody cow! (*He grabs her by the arm.*)

FREDA: Lemme alone! I ain't got no——

JOE (*hits her viciously on the side of the jaw; she crumples up on the floor*): That'll learn yer!

(*He stoops down and fumbles in her bosom and pulls out the banknote, which he stuffs into his pocket with a grunt of satisfaction.*)

(KATE *opens the door on the left and looks in — then rushes to* FREDA *and lifts her head up in her arms.*)

KATE (*gently*): Pore dearie! (*Looking at* JOE *angrily*) Been 'ittin 'er agen, 'ave yer, yer cowardly swine!

JOE: Yus; an' I'll 'it you, too, if yer don't keep yer marf shut. Tike 'er aht of 'ere!

(KATE *carries* FREDA *into the next room.* JOE *goes behind the bar. A moment later the outer door is opened and* DRISCOLL *and* COCKY *come in.*)

DRISCOLL: Come on, Ollie. (*He suddenly sees that* OLSON *is not there, and turns to* JOE.) Where is ut he's gone to?

JOE (*with a meaning wink*): 'E an' Freda went aht t'gether 'bout five minutes past. 'E's fair gone on 'er, 'e is.

DRISCOLL (*with a grin*): Oho, so that's ut, is ut? Who'd think Ollie'd be sich a divil wid the wimin? 'Tis lucky he's sober or she'd have him stripped to his last ha'penny. (*Turning to* COCKY, *who is blinking sleepily.*) What'll ye have, ye little scut? (*to* JOE) Give me whiskey, *Irish* whiskey!

Six Characters in Search of an Author

One of the giants of modern theatre, Italy's best modern playwright and a pervasive influence on world drama, was Luigi Pirandello (1867–1936). He began as a writer of poems and short stories in the *verismo* (realistic) style and eventually gave his name to *pirandellismo*, a somewhat grotesque version of German expressionism which puts on the stage philosophical problems of illusion and reality in a drama of masks and faces.

After the birth of their third child, Pirandello's wife went insane. Unable to pay for a private hospital and unwilling to commit her to a public institution, he was compelled to keep her at home and to live, day by day, with her groundless jealousy and wild imaginings. After a while he realized that her reality, however fantastic, was real to *her*, that she suffered from her delusions just as much as if her suspicions were well founded, that "each in his own way" makes his world and "right you are, if you think you are." The great German poet Heine said that out of his great sorrows he made his little songs. Pirandello, out of his sad life, came to important conclusions about the nature of all men's lives, their illusions and delusions, their reality and their truth, their "naked masks."

Beginning by dramatizing some of his own short stories, he went on to write some 30 plays, to found his own theatre (*Teatro Odescalchi*), to tour Europe and the United States, and to change the whole course of modern drama with a highly intellectual drama of crisis. In unforgettably theatrical plays he examined paradoxes that previously were thought unsuited to the theatre in which characters had to be either consistent or consistently inconsistent, fixed. His characters find that there is no permanent personality, that humans are always in flux, that we are the sum of all the impressions that others have of us, that nothing may be behind the mask or that the mask may be become the face. What is reality? he asks. Can there be any tragedy or comedy when what seems to one person to be tragic may be to another ridiculous, or vice versa?

In *Six Characters in Search of an Author*, he discusses the relative nature of illusion and reality and catches up the audience in his theatrical game in which the humorous is deadly serious and the tragic only a play. Reality and theatricality battle before our eyes and we are transported from the workaday world of the Stage Manager and his actors into the world of the six characters who, in a way, are more real than we are, for they have a definite and unchanging reality and role.

Pirandello's deft manipulation of these seemingly unpromising dramatic elements earned him the Nobel Prize for literature (1934) and, with plays like *Six Characters in Search of an Author* (1921), *Right You Are, If You Think You Are* (1916), *Henry IV* (1922), *As You Desire Me* and *Tonight We Improvise* (both 1930), a permanent place in modern theatre and thought.

Here is his own Preface to *Six Characters in Search of an Author*:

Preface

It seems like yesterday but is actually many years ago that a nimble little maidservant entered the service of my art. However, she always comes fresh to the job.

She is called Fantasy.

A little puckish and malicious, if she likes to dress in black no one will wish to deny that she is often positively bizarre and no one will wish to believe that she always does everything in the same way and in earnest. She sticks her hand in her pocket, pulls out a cap and bells, sets it on her head, red as a cock's comb, and dashes away. Here today, there tomorrow. And she amuses herself by bringing to my house — since I derive stories and novels and plays from them — the most disgruntled tribe in the world, men, women, children, involved in strange adventures which they can find no way out of; thwarted in their plans; cheated in their hopes; with whom, in short, it is often torture to deal.

Well, this little maidservant of mine, Fantasy, several years ago, had the bad inspiration or ill-omened caprice to bring a family into my house. I wouldn't know where she fished them up or how, but, according to her, I could find in them the subject for a magnificent novel.

I found before me a man about fifty years old, in a dark jacket and light trousers, with a frowning air and ill-natured, mortified eyes; a poor woman in widow's weeds leading by one hand a little girl of four and by the other a boy of rather more than ten; a cheeky and "sexy" girl, also clad in black but with an equivocal and brazen pomp, all atremble with a lively, biting contempt for the mortified old man and for a young fellow of twenty who stood on one side closed in on himself as if he despised them all. In short, the six characters who are seen coming on stage at the beginning of the play. Now one of them and now another — often beating down one another — embarked on the sad story of their adventures, each shouting his own reasons, and projecting in my face his disordered passions, more or less as they do in the play to the unhappy Manager.

What author will be able to say how and why a character was born in his fantasy? The mystery of artistic creation is the same as that of birth. A woman who loves may desire to become a mother; but the desire by itself, however intense, cannot suffice. One fine day she will find herself a mother without having any precise intimation when it began. In the same way an artist imbibes very many germs of life and can never say how and why, at a certain moment, one of these vital germs inserts itself into his fantasy, there to become a living creature on a plane of life superior to the changeable existence of every day.

I can only say that, without having made any effort to seek them out, I found before me, alive — you could touch them and even hear them breathe — the six characters now seen on the stage. And they stayed there in my presence, each with his secret torment and all bound together by the one common origin and mutual entanglement of their affairs, while I had them enter the world of art, constructing from their persons, their passions, and their adventures a novel, a drama, or at least a story.

Born alive, they wished to live.

To me it was never enough to present a man or a woman and what is special and characteristic about them simply for the pleasure of presenting them; to narrate a particular affair, lively or sad, simply for the pleasure of narrating it; to describe a landscape simply for the pleasure of describing it.

There are some writers (and not a few) who do feel this pleasure and, satisfied, ask no more. They are, to speak more precisely, historical writers.

But there are others who, beyond such pleasure, feel a more profound spiritual need on whose account they admit only figures, affairs, landscapes which have been soaked, so to speak, in a particular sense of life and acquire from it a universal value. These are, more precisely, philosophical writers.

I have the misfortune to belong to these last.

I hate symbolic art in which the presentation loses all spontaneous movement in order to become a machine, an allegory — a vain and misconceived effort because the very fact of giving an allegorical sense to a presentation clearly shows that we have to do with a fable which by itself has no truth either fantastic or direct; it was made for the demonstration of some moral truth. The spiritual need I speak of cannot be satisfied — or seldom, and that to the end of a superior irony, as for example in Ariosto — by such allegorical symbolism. This latter starts from a concept, and from a concept which creates or tries to create for itself an image. The former, on the other hand, seeks in the image — which must remain alive and free throughout — a meaning to give it value.

Now, however much I sought, I did not succeed in uncovering this meaning in the six characters. And I concluded therefore that it was no use making them live.

I thought to myself: "I have already afflicted my readers with hundreds and hundreds of stories. Why should I afflict them now by narrating the sad entanglements of these six unfortunates?"

And, thinking thus, I put them away from me. Or rather I did all I could to put them away.

But one doesn't give life to a character for nothing.

Creatures of my spirit, these six were already living a life which was their own and not mine any more, a life which it was not in my power any more to deny them.

Thus it is that while I persisted in desiring to drive them out of my spirit, they, as if completely detached from every narrative support, characters from a novel miraculously emerging from the pages of the book that contained them, went on living on their own, choosing certain moments of the day to reappear before me in the solitude of my study and coming — now one, now the other, now two together — to tempt me, to propose that I present or describe this scene or that, to explain the effects that could be secured with them, the new interest which a certain unusual situation could provide, and so forth.

For a moment I let myself be won over. And this condescension of mine, thus letting myself go for a while, was enough, because they drew from it a new increment of life, a greater degree of clarity and addition, consequently a greater degree of persuasive power over me. And thus as it became gradually harder and harder for me to go back and free myself from them, it became easier and easier for them to come back and tempt me. At a certain point I actually became obsessed with them. Until, all of a sudden, a way out of the difficulty flashed upon me.

"Why not," I said to myself, "present this highly strange fact of an author who refuses to let some of his characters live though they have been born in his fantasy, and the fact that these characters, having by now life in their veins, do not resign themselves to remaining excluded from the world of art? They are detached from me; live on their own; have acquired voice and movement; have by themselves — in this struggle for existence that they have had to wage with me — become dramatic characters, characters that can move and talk on their own initiative; already see themselves as such; have learned to defend themselves against me; will even know how to defend themselves against others. And so let them go where dramatic characters do go to have life: on a stage. And let us see what will happen."

That's what I did. And, naturally, the result was what it had to be: a mixture of tragic and comic, fantastic and realistic, in a humorous situation that was quite new and infinitely complex, a drama which is conveyed by means of the characters, who carry it within them and suffer it, a drama, breathing, speaking, self-propelled, which seeks at all costs to find the means of its own presentation; and the comedy of the vain attempt at an improvised realization of the drama on stage. First, the surprise of the poor actors in a theatrical company rehearsing a play by day on a bare stage (no scenery, no flats). Surprise and incredulity at the sight of the six characters announcing themselves as such in search of an author. Then, immediately afterward, through that sudden fainting fit of the Mother veiled in black, their instinctive interest in the drama of which they catch a glimpse in her and in the other members of the strange family, an obscure, ambiguous drama, coming about so unexpectedly on a stage that is empty and unprepared to receive it. And gradually the growth of this interest to the bursting forth of the contrasting passions of Father, of Stepdaughter, of Son, of that poor Mother, passions seeking, as I said, to overwhelm each other with a tragic, lacerating fury.

And here is the universal meaning at first vainly sought in the six characters, now that, going on stage of their own accord, they succeed in finding it within themselves in the excitement of the desperate struggle which each wages against the other and all wage against the Manager and the actors, who do not understand them.

Without wanting to, without knowing

it, in the strife of their bedeviled souls, each of them, defending himself against the accusations of the others, expresses as his own living passion and torment the passion and torment which for so many years have been the pangs of my spirit: the deceit of mutual understanding irremediably founded on the empty abstraction of the words, the multiple personality of everyone corresponding to the possibilities of being to be found in each of us, and finally the inherent tragic conflict between life (which is always moving and changing) and form (which fixes it, immutable).

Two above all among the six characters, the Father and the Stepdaughter, speak of that outrageous, unalterable fixity of their form in which he and she see their essential nature expressed permanently and immutably, a nature that for one means punishment and for the other revenge; and they defend it against the factitious affectations and unaware volatility of the actors, and they try to impose it on the vulgar Manager who would like to change it and adapt it to the so-called exigencies of the theatre.

If the six characters don't all seem to exist on the same plane, it is not because some are figures of first rank and others of the second, that is, some are main characters and others minor ones — the elementary perspective necessary to all scenic or narrative art — nor is it that any are not completely created — for their purpose. They are all six at the same point of artistic realization and on the same level of reality, which is the fantastic level of the whole play. Except that the Father, the Stepdaughter, and also the Son are realized as mind; the Mother as nature; the Boy as a presence watching and performing a gesture and the Baby unaware of it all. This fact creates among them a perspective of a new sort. Unconsciously I had had the impression that some of them needed to be fully realized (artistically speaking), others

less so, and others merely sketched in as elements in a narrative or presentational sequence: the most alive, the most completely created, are the Father and the Stepdaughter who naturally stand out more and lead the way, dragging themselves along beside the almost dead weight of the others — first, the Son, holding back; second, the Mother, like a victim resigned to her fate, between the two children who have hardly any substance beyond their appearance and who need to be led by the hand.

And actually! actually they had each to appear in that stage of creation which they had attained in the author's fantasy at the moment when he wished to drive them away.

If I now think about these things, about having intuited that necessity, having unconsciously found the way to resolve it by means of a new perspective, and about the way in which I actually obtained it, they seem like miracles. The fact is that the play was really conceived in one of those spontaneous illuminations of the fantasy when by a miracle all the elements of the mind answer to each other's call and work in divine accord. No human brain, working "in the cold," however stirred up it might be, could ever have succeeded in penetrating far enough, could ever have been in a position to satisfy all the exigencies of the play's form. Therefore the reasons which I will give to clarify the values of the play must not be thought of as intentions that I conceived beforehand when I prepared myself for the job and which I now undertake to defend, but only as discoveries which I have been able to make afterward in tranquility.

I wanted to present six characters seeking an author. Their play does not manage to get presented — precisely because the author whom they seek is missing. Instead is presented the comedy of their vain attempt with all that it contains of tragedy by virtue of the fact that the six characters have been rejected.

But can one present a character while rejecting him? Obviously, to present him one needs, on the contrary, to receive him into one's fantasy before one can express him. And I have actually accepted and realized the six characters: I have, however, accepted and realized them as rejected: in search of *another* author.

What have I rejected of them? Not themselves, obviously, but their drama, which doubtless is what interests them above all but which did not interest me — for the reasons already indicated.

And what is it, for a character — his drama?

Every creature of fantasy and art, in order to exist, must have his drama, that is, a drama in which he may be a character and for which he *is* a character. This drama is the character's *raison d'être*, his vital function, necessary for his existence.

In these six, then, I have accepted the "being" without the reason for being. I have taken the organism and entrusted to it, not its own proper function, but another more complex function into which its own function entered, if at all, only as a datum. A terrible and desperate situation especially for the two — Father and Stepdaughter — who more than the others crave life and more than the others feel themselves to be characters, that is, absolutely need a drama and therefore their own drama .. the only one which they can envisage for themselves yet which meantime they see rejected: an "impossible" situation from which they feel they must escape at whatever cost; it is a matter of life and death. True, I have given them another *raison d'être*, another function: precisely that "impossible" situation, the drama of being in search of an author and rejected. But that this should be a *raison*

d'être, that it should have become their real function, that it should be necessary, that it should suffice, they can hardly suppose; for they have a life of their own. If someone were to tell them, they wouldn't believe him. It is not possible to believe that the sole reason for our living should lie in a torment that seems to us unjust and inexplicable.

I cannot imagine, therefore, why the charge was brought against me that the Father was not what it should have been because it stepped out of its quality and position as a character and invaded at times the author's province and took it over. I who understand those who don't quite understand me see that the charge derives from the fact that the character expresses and makes his own a torment of spirit which is recognized as mine. Which is entirely natural and of absolutely no significance. Aside from the fact that this torment of spirit in the character of the Father derives from causes, and is suffered and lived for reasons that have nothing to do with the drama of my personal experience, a fact which alone removes all substance from the criticism, I want to make it clear that the inherent torment of my spirit is one thing, a torment which I can legitimately — provided that it be organic — reflect in a character, and that the activity of my spirit as revealed in the realized work, the activity that succeeds in forming a drama out of the six characters in search of an author is another thing. If the Father participated in this latter activity, if he competed in forming the drama of the six characters without an author, then and only then would it by all means be justified to say that he was at times the author himself and therefore not the man he should be. But the Father suffers and does not create his existence as a character in search of an author. He suffers it as an inexplicable fatality and as a situation which he tries with all his powers to rebel against, which he tries to remedy; hence it is that he is a character in search of an author and nothing more, even if he expresses as his own the torment of my spirit. If he, so to speak, assumed some of the author's responsibilities, the fatality would be completely explained. He would, that is to say, see himself accepted, if only as a rejected character, accepted in the poet's heart of hearts, and he would no longer have any reason to suffer the despair of not finding someone to construct and affirm his life as a character. I mean that he would quite willingly accept the *raison d'être* which the author gives him and without regrets would forgo his own, throwing over the Manager and the actors to whom in fact he runs as his only recourse.

There is one character, that of the Mother, who on the other hand does not care about being alive (considering being alive is an end in itself). She hasn't the least suspicion that she is *not* alive. It has never occurred to her to ask how and why and in what manner she lives. In short, she is not aware of being a character inasmuch as she is never, even for a moment, detached from her role. She doesn't know she has a role.

This makes her perfectly organic. Indeed, her role of Mother does not of itself, in its natural essence, embrace mental activity. And she does not exist as a mind. She lives in an endless continuum of feeling, and therefore she cannot acquire awareness of her life — that is, of her existence as a character. But with all this, even she, in her own way and for her own ends, seeks an author, and at a certain stage seems happy to have been brought before the Manager. Because she hopes to take life from him, perhaps? No: because she hopes the Manager will have her present a scene with the Son in which she would put so much of her own life. But it is a scene which

does not exist, which never has and never could take place. So unaware is she of being a character, that is, of the life that is possible to her, all fixed and determined, moment by moment, in every action, every phrase.

She appears on stage with the other characters but without understanding what the others make her do. Obviously, she imagines that the itch for life with which the husband and the daughter are afflicted and for which she herself is to be found on stage is no more than one of the usual incomprehensible extravagances of this man who is both tortured and torturer and — horrible, most horrible — a new equivocal rebellion on the part of that poor erring girl. The Mother is completely passive. The events of her own life and the values they assume in her eyes, her very character, are all things which are "said" by the others and which she only once contradicts, and that because the maternal instinct rises up and rebels within her to make it clear that she didn't at all wish to abandon either the son or the husband: the Son was taken from her and the husband forced her to abandon him. She is only correcting data; she explains and knows nothing.

In short, she is nature. Nature fixed in the figure of a mother.

This character gave me a satisfaction of a new sort, not to be ignored. Nearly all my critics, instead of defining her, after their habit, as "unhuman" — which seems to be the peculiar and incorrigible characteristic of all my creatures without exception — had the goodness to note "with real pleasure" that at last a *very human* figure had emerged from my fantasy. I explain this praise to myself in the following way: since my poor Mother is entirely limited to the natural attitude of a Mother with no possibility of free mental activity, being, that is, little more than a lump of flesh completely alive in all its functions — procreation, lactation, caring for and loving its young — without any need therefore of exercising her brain, she realizes in her person the true and complete "human type." That must be how it is, since in a human organism nothing seems more superfluous than the mind.

But the critics have tried to get rid of the Mother with this praise without bothering to penetrate the nucleus of poetic values which the character in the play represents. A very human figure, certainly, because mindless, that is, unaware of being what she is or not caring to explain it to herself. But not knowing that she is a character doesn't prevent her from being one. That is her drama in my play. And the most living expression of it comes spurting out in her cry to the Manager, who wants her to think all these things have happened already and therefore cannot now be a reason for renewed lamentations: "No, it's happening now, it's happening always! My torture is not a pretense, signore! I am alive and present, always, in every moment of my torture: it is renewed, alive, and present always!" This she *feels*, without being conscious of it, and feels it therefore as something inexplicable: but she feels it so terribly that she doesn't think it *can* be something to explain either to herself or to others. She feels it and that is that. She feels it as pain and this pain is immediate; she cries it out. Thus she reflects the growing fixity of life in a form — the same thing, which in another way, tortures the Father and the Stepdaughter. In them, mind. In her, nature. The mind rebels and, as best it may, seeks an advantage; nature, if not aroused by sensory stimuli, weeps.

Conflict between life-in-movement and form is the inexorable condition not only of the mental but also of the physical order. The life which in order to exist has become fixed in our corporeal form little by little kills that form. The tears of a nature thus fixed lament the irreparable, continuous aging of our bodies. Hence the tears of the Mother are passive and perpetual. Revealed in three faces, made significant in three distinct and simultaneous dramas, this inherent conflict finds in the play its most complete expression. More: the Mother declares also the particular value of artistic form — a form which does not delimit or destroy its own life and which life does not consume — in her cry to the Manager. If the Father and Stepdaughter began their scene a hundred thousand times in succession, always, at the appointed moment, at the instant when the life of the work of art must be expressed with that cry, it would always be heard, unaltered and unalterable in its form, not as a mechanical repetition, not as a return determined by external necessities, but, on the contrary, alive every time and as new, suddenly born *thus forever!* embalmed alive in its incorruptible form. Hence, always, as we open the book, we shall find Francesca alive and confessing to Dante her sweet sin and if we turn to the passage a hundred thousand times in succession, Francesca will speak her words, never repeating them mechanically, but saying them as though each time were the first time with such living and sudden passion that Dante every time will turn faint. All that lives, by the fact of living, has a form, and by the same token must die — except the work of art which lives forever in so far as it *is* form.

The birth of a creature of human fantasy, a birth which is a step across the threshold between nothing and eternity, can also happen suddenly, occasioned by some necessity. An imagined drama needs a character who does or says a certain necessary thing; accordingly this character is born and is precisely what he had to be. In this way Madame Pace is born among the six characters and seems a miracle, even a trick, realistically portrayed on the stage. It is no trick. The birth is real. The new character is alive not because she was alive already but because she is now happily born as is required by the fact of her being a character — she is obliged to be as she is. There is a break here, a sudden change in the level of reality of the scene, because a character can be born in this way only in the poet's fancy and not on the boards of a stage. Without anyone's noticing it, I have all of a sudden changed the scene: I have gathered it up again into my own fantasy without removing it from the spectator's eyes. That is, I have shown them, instead of the stage, my own fantasy in the act of creating — my own fantasy in the form of this same stage. The sudden and uncontrollable changing of a visual phenomenon from one level of reality to another is a miracle comparable to those of the saint who sets his own statue in motion: it is neither wood nor stone at such a moment. But the miracle is not arbitrary. The stage — a stage which accepts the fantastic reality of the six characters — is no fixed, immutable datum. Nothing in this play exists as given and preconceived. Everything is in the making, is in motion, is a sudden experiment: even the place in which this unformed life, reaching after its own form, changes and changes again, contrives to shift position organically. The level of reality changes. When I had the idea of bringing Madame Pace to birth right there on the stage, I felt I could do it and I did it. Had I noticed that this birth was unhinging and silently, unnoticed, in a second, giving another shape, another reality to my scene, I certainly wouldn't have brought it about. I would have been afraid of the apparent lack of logic. And I would have committed an ill-omened assault on the beauty of my work. The fervor of my mind saved me from doing so. For, despite appearances, with their specious logic, this fantastic birth is sustained by a real necessity in mysterious, organic relation with the whole life of the work.

That someone now tells me it hasn't all the value it could have because its expression is not constructed but chaotic, because it smacks of romanticism, makes me smile.

I understand why this observation was made to me: because in this work of mine the presentation of the drama in which the six characters are involved appears tumultuous and never proceeds in an orderly manner. There is no logical development, no concatenation of the events. Very true. Had I hunted it with a lamp I couldn't have found a more disordered, crazy, arbitrary, complicated, in short, romantic way of presenting "the drama in which the six characters are involved." Very true. But I have not presented that drama. I have presented another — and I won't undertake to say again what! — in which, among the many fine things that everyone, according to his tastes, can find, there is a discreet satire on romantic procedures: in the six characters thus excited to the point where they stifle themselves in the roles which each of them plays in a certain drama while I present them as characters in another play which they don't know and don't suspect the existence of, so that this inflammation of their passions — which belongs to the realm of romantic procedures — is humorously "placed," located in the void. And the drama of the six characters presented not as it would have been organized by my fantasy had it been accepted but in this way, as a rejected drama, could not exist in the work except as a "situation," with some little development and could not come out except in indications, stormily, disorderly, in violent foreshortenings, in a chaotic manner: continually interrupted, sidetracked, contradicted (by one of its characters), denied, and (by two others) not even seen.

There is a character indeed — he who

denies the drama which makes him a character, the Son — who draws all his importance and value from being a character not of the comedy in the making — which as such hardly appears — but from the presentation that I made of it. In short, he is the only one who lives solely as "a character in search of an author" — inasmuch as the author he seeks is not a dramatic author. Even this could not be otherwise. The character's attitude is an organic product of my conception, and it is logical that in the situation it should produce greater confusion and disorder and another element of romantic contrast.

But I had precisely to *present* this organic and natural chaos. And to present a chaos is not at all to present chaotically, that is, romantically. That my presentation is the reverse of confused, that it is quite simple, clear, and orderly, is proved by the clarity which the intrigue, the characters, the fantastic and realistic, dramatic and comic levels of the work have had for every public in the world and by the way in which, for those with more searching vision, the unusual values enclosed within it come out.

Great is the confusion of tongues among men if criticisms thus made find words for their expression. No less great than this confusion is the intimate law of order which, obeyed in all points, makes this work of mine classical and typical and at its catastrophic close forbids the use of words. Though the audience eventually understands that one does not create life by artifice and that the drama of the six characters cannot be presented without an author to give them value with his spirit, the Manager remains vulgarly anxious to know how the thing turned out, and the "ending" is remembered by the Son in its sequence of actual moments, but without any sense and therefore not needing a human voice for its expression. It happens stupidly, uselessly, with the going off of a mechanical weapon on stage. It breaks up and disperses the sterile experiment of the characters and the actors, which has apparently been made without the assistance of the poet.

The poet, unknown to them, as if looking on at a distance during the whole period of the experiment, was at the same time busy creating — with it and of it — his own play.

SIX CHARACTERS IN SEARCH OF AN AUTHOR

A comedy in the making

Luigi Pirandello

English version by
Edward Storer

CHARACTERS OF THE COMEDY IN THE MAKING

THE FATHER
THE MOTHER
THE STEP-DAUGHTER
THE SON
THE BOY
THE CHILD (*The last two do not speak*)
MADAME PACE

ACTORS OF THE COMPANY

THE MANAGER
LEADING LADY
LEADING MAN
SECOND LADY
LEAD
L'INGÉNUE
JUVENILE LEAD
OTHER ACTORS AND ACTRESSES
PROPERTY MAN
PROMPTER
MACHINIST
MANAGER'S SECRETARY
DOOR-KEEPER
SCENE-SHIFTERS

DAYTIME. THE STAGE OF A THEATRE

N.B. The Comedy is without acts or scenes. The performance is interrupted once, without the curtain being lowered, when the manager and the chief characters withdraw to arrange the scenario. A second interruption of the action takes place when, by mistake, the stage hands let the curtain down.

ACT ONE

The spectators will find the curtain raised and the stage as it usually is during the day time. It will be half dark, and empty, so that from the beginning the public may have the impression of an impromptu performance.
Prompter's box and a small table and chair for the manager.
Two other small tables and several chairs scattered about as during rehearsals.
The ACTORS *and* ACTRESSES *of the company enter from the back of the stage:*
first one, then another, then two together; nine or ten in all. They are about to rehearse a Pirandello play: Mixing It Up.* Some of the company move off towards their dressing rooms. The PROMPTER *who has the "book" under his arm, is waiting for the manager in order to begin the rehearsal.*
The ACTORS *and* ACTRESSES, *some standing, some sitting, chat and smoke. One perhaps reads a paper; another cons his part.*
Finally, the MANAGER *enters and goes to the table prepared for him. His* SECRETARY *brings him his mail, through which he glances. The* PROMPTER *takes his seat, turns on a light, and opens the "book."*

THE MANAGER (*throwing a letter down on the table*): I can't see. (*to* PROPERTY MAN) Let's have a little light, please!

PROPERTY MAN: Yes sir, yes, at once. (*A light comes down on to the stage.*)

THE MANAGER (*clapping his hands*): Come along! Come along! Second act of "Mixing It Up." (*Sits down.*)

(*The* ACTORS *and* ACTRESSES *go from the front of the stage to the wings, all except the three who are to begin the rehearsal.*)

THE PROMPTER (*reading the "book"*): "Leo Gala's house. A curious room serving as dining-room and study."

THE MANAGER (*to* PROPERTY MAN): Fix up the old red room.

---

* i.e. *Il giuoco delle parti.*

PROPERTY MAN (*noting it down*): Red set. All right!

THE PROMPTER (*continuing to read from the "book"*): "Table already laid and writing desk with books and papers. Book-shelves. Exit rear to Leo's bedroom. Exit left to kitchen. Principal exit to right."

THE MANAGER (*energetically*): Well, you understand: The principal exit over there; here, the kitchen. (*Turning to actor who is to play the part of* SOCRATES.) You make your entrances and exits here. (*to* PROPERTY MAN) The baize doors at the rear, and curtains.

PROPERTY MAN (*noting it down*): Right!

PROMPTER (*reading as before*): "When the curtain rises, Leo Gala, dressed in cook's cap and apron is busy beating an egg in a cup. Philip, also dressed as a cook, is beating another egg. Guido Venanzi is seated and listening."

LEADING MAN (*to* MANAGER): Excuse me, but must I absolutely wear a cook's cap?

THE MANAGER (*annoyed*): I imagine so. It says so there anyway. (*Pointing to the "book."*)

LEADING MAN: But it's ridiculous!

THE MANAGER (*jumping up in a rage*): Ridiculous? Ridiculous? Is it my fault if France won't send us any more good comedies, and we are reduced to putting on Pirandello's works, where nobody understands anything, and where the author plays the fool with us all? (*The* ACTORS *grin. The* MANAGER *goes to* LEADING MAN *and shouts.*) Yes sir, you put on the cook's cap and beat eggs. Do you suppose that with all this egg-beating business you are on an ordinary stage? Get that out of your head. You represent the shell of the eggs you are beating! (*Laughter and comments among the* ACTORS.) Silence! and listen to my explanations, please! (*to* LEADING MAN) "The empty form of reason without the fullness of instinct, which is blind." — You stand for reason, your wife is instinct. It's a mixing up of the parts, according to which you who act your own part become the puppet of yourself. Do you understand?

LEADING MAN: I'm hanged if I do.

THE MANAGER: Neither do I. But let's get on with it. It's sure to be a glorious failure anyway. (*Confidentially*) But I say, please face three-quarters. Otherwise, what with the abstruseness of the dialogue, and the public that won't be able to hear you, the whole thing will go to hell. Come on! come on!

PROMPTER: Pardon sir, may I get into my box? There's a bit of a draught.

THE MANAGER: Yes, yes, of course!

(*At this point, the* DOOR-KEEPER *has entered from the stage door and advances towards the manager's table, taking off his braided cap. During this manoeuvre, the* SIX CHARACTERS *enter, and stop by the door at back of stage, so that when the* DOOR-KEEPER *is about to announce their coming to the* MANAGER, *they are already on the stage. A tenuous light surrounds them, almost as if irradiated by them — the faint breath of their fantastic reality.*

This light will disappear when they come forward towards the actors. They preserve, however, something of the dream lightness in which they seem almost suspended; but this does not detract from the essential reality of their forms and expressions.

He who is known as THE FATHER *is a man of about 50: hair, reddish in colour, thin at the temples; he is not bald, however; thick moustaches, falling over his still fresh mouth, which often opens in an empty and uncertain smile. He is fattish, pale; with an especially wide forehead. He has blue, oval-shaped eyes, very clear and piercing. Wears light trousers and a dark jacket. He is alternatively mellifluous and violent in his manner.*

THE MOTHER *seems crushed and terrified as if by an intolerable weight of shame and abasement. She is dressed in modest black and wears a thick widow's veil of crêpe. When she lifts this, she reveals a wax-like face. She always keeps her eyes downcast.*

THE STEP-DAUGHTER, *is dashing, almost impudent, beautiful. She wears mourning too, but with great elegance. She shows contempt for the timid half-frightened manner of the wretched* BOY (*14 years old, and also dressed in black); on the other hand, she displays a lively tenderness for her little sister,* THE CHILD *(about four), who is dressed in white, with a black silk sash at the waist.*

THE SON *(22) tall, severe in his attitude of contempt for* THE FATHER, *supercilious and indifferent to* THE MOTHER. *He looks as if he had come on the stage against his will.)*

DOOR-KEEPER *(cap in hand)*: Excuse me, sir . . .

THE MANAGER *(rudely)*: Eh? What is it?

DOOR-KEEPER *(timidly)*: These people are asking for you, sir.

THE MANAGER *(furious)*: I am rehearsing, and you know perfectly well no one's allowed to come in during rehearsals! *(turning to the* CHARACTERS*)* Who are you, please? What do you want?

THE FATHER *(coming forward a little, followed by the others who seem embarrassed)*: As a matter of fact . . . we have come here in search of an author . . .

THE MANAGER *(half angry, half amazed)*: An author? What author?

THE FATHER: Any author, sir.

THE MANAGER: But there's no author here. We are not rehearsing a new piece.

THE STEP-DAUGHTER *(vivaciously)*: So much the better, so much the better! We can be your new piece.

AN ACTOR *(coming forward from the others)*: Oh, do you hear that?

THE FATHER *(to* STEP-DAUGHTER*)*: Yes, but if the author isn't here . . . *(to* MANAGER*)* unless you would be willing . . .

THE MANAGER: You are trying to be funny.

THE FATHER: No, for Heaven's sake, what are you saying? We bring you a drama, sir.

THE STEP-DAUGHTER: We may be your fortune.

THE MANAGER: Will you oblige me by going away? We haven't time to waste with mad people.

THE FATHER *(mellifluously)*: Oh sir, you know

well that life is full of infinite absurdities, which, strangely enough, do not even need to appear plausible, since they are true.

THE MANAGER: What the devil is he talking about?

THE FATHER: I say that to reverse the ordinary process may well be considered a madness: that is, to create credible situations, in order that they may appear true. But permit me to observe that if this be madness, it is the sole *raison d'être* of your profession, gentlemen. *(The* ACTORS *look hurt and perplexed.)*

THE MANAGER *(getting up and looking at him)*: So our profession seems to you one worthy of madmen then?

THE FATHER: Well, to make seem true that which isn't true . . . without any need . . . for a joke as it were . . . Isn't that your mission, gentlemen: to give life to fantastic characters on the stage?

THE MANAGER *(interpreting the rising anger of the* COMPANY*)*: But I would beg you to believe, my dear sir, that the profession of the comedian is a noble one. If today, as things go, the playwrights give us stupid comedies to play and puppets to represent instead of men, remember we are proud to have given life to immortal works here on these very boards! *(The* ACTORS, *satisfied, applaud their* MANAGER.*)*

THE FATHER *(interrupting furiously)*: Exactly, perfectly, to living beings more alive than those who breathe and wear clothes: beings less real perhaps, but truer! I agree with you entirely. *(The* ACTORS *look at one another in amazement.)*

THE MANAGER: But what do you mean? Before, you said . . .

THE FATHER: No, excuse me, I meant it for you, sir, who were crying out that you had no time to lose with madmen, while no one better than yourself knows that nature uses the instrument of human fantasy in order to pursue her high creative purpose.

THE MANAGER: Very well, — but where does all this take us?

THE FATHER: Nowhere! It is merely to show you that one is born to life in many forms, in many shapes, as tree, or as stone, as water, as butterfly, or as woman. So one may also be born a character in a play.

THE MANAGER (*with feigned comic dismay*): So you and these other friends of yours have been born characters?

THE FATHER: Exactly, and alive as you see! (MANAGER *and* ACTORS *burst out laughing.*)

THE FATHER (*hurt*): I am sorry you laugh, because we carry in us a drama, as you can guess from this woman here veiled in black.

THE MANAGER (*losing patience at last and almost indignant*): Oh, chuck it! Get away please! Clear out of here! (*to* PROPERTY MAN) For Heaven's sake, turn them out!

THE FATHER (*resisting*): No, no, look here, we . . .

THE MANAGER (*roaring*): We come here to work, you know.

LEADING ACTOR: One cannot let oneself be made such a fool of.

THE FATHER (*determined, coming forward*): I marvel at your incredulity, gentlemen. Are you not accustomed to see the characters created by an author spring to life in yourselves and face each other? Just because there is no "book" (*pointing to the* PROMPTER'S *box*) which contains us, you refuse to believe . . .

THE STEP-DAUGHTER (*advances towards* MANAGER, *smiling and coquettish*): Believe me, we are really six most interesting characters, sir; side-tracked however.

THE FATHER: Yes, that is the word! (*to* MANAGER *all at once*) In the sense, that is, that the author who created us alive no longer wished, or was no longer able, materially to put us into a work of art. And this was a real crime, sir; because he who has had the luck to be born a character can laugh even at death. He cannot die. The man, the writer, the instrument of the creation will die, but his creation does not die. And to live for ever, it does not need to have extraordinary gifts or to be able to work wonders. Who was Sancho Panza? Who was Don Abbondio? Yet they live eternally because — live germs as they were — they had the fortune to find a fecundating matrix, a fantasy which could raise and nourish them: make them live for ever!

THE MANAGER: That is quite all right. But what do you want here, all of you?

THE FATHER: We want to live.

THE MANAGER (*ironically*): For Eternity?

THE FATHER: No, sir, only for a moment . . . in you.

AN ACTOR: Just listen to him!

LEADING LADY: They want to live, in us . . . !

JUVENILE LEAD (*pointing to the* STEP-DAUGHTER): I've no objection, as far as that one is concerned!

THE FATHER: Look here! look here! The comedy has to be made. (*to the* MANAGER) But if you and your actors are willing, we can soon concert it among ourselves.

THE MANAGER (*annoyed*): But what do you want to concert? We don't go in for concerts here. Here we play dramas and comedies!

THE FATHER: Exactly! That is just why we have come to you.

THE MANAGER: And where is the "book"?

THE FATHER: It is in us! (*The* ACTORS *laugh.*) The drama is in us, and we are the drama. We are impatient to play it. Our inner passion drives us on to this.

THE STEP-DAUGHTER (*disdainful, alluring, treacherous, full of impudence*): My passion, sir! Ah, if you only knew! My passion for him! (*Points to the* FATHER *and makes a pretence of embracing him. Then she breaks out into a loud laugh.*)

THE FATHER (*angrily*): Behave yourself! And please don't laugh in that fashion.

THE STEP-DAUGHTER: With your permission,

gentlemen, I, who am a two months' orphan, will show you how I can dance and sing. (*Sings and then dances* Prenez garde à Tchou-Tchin-Tchou.)

Les chinois sont un peuple malin,
De Shangaî à Pekin.
Ils ont mis des écriteaux partout:
Prenez garde à Tchou-Tchin-Tchou.

ACTORS AND ACTRESSES: Bravo! Well done! Tip-top!

THE MANAGER: Silence! This isn't a café concert, you know! (*turning to the* FATHER *in consternation*) Is she mad?

THE FATHER: Mad? No, she's worse than mad.

THE STEP-DAUGHTER (*to* MANAGER): Worse? Worse? Listen! Stage this drama for us at once! Then you will see that at a certain moment I . . . when this little darling here . . . (*Takes the* CHILD *by the hand and leads her to the* MANAGER.) Isn't she a dear? (*Takes her up and kisses her.*) Darling! Darling! (*Puts her down again and adds feelingly.*) Well, when God suddenly takes this dear little child away from that poor mother there; and this imbecile here (*Seizing hold of the* BOY *roughly and pushing him forward.*) does the stupidest things, like the fool he is, you will see me run away. Yes, gentlemen, I shall be off. But the moment hasn't arrived yet. After what has taken place between him and me (*indicates the* FATHER *with a horrible wink.*) I can't remain any longer in this society, to have to witness the anguish of this mother here for that fool . . . (*indicates the* SON.) Look at him! Look at him! See how indifferent, how frigid he is, because he is the legitimate son. He despises me, despises him (*pointing to the* BOY), despises this baby here; because . . . we are bastards. (*Goes to the* MOTHER *and embraces her.*) And he doesn't want to recognize her as his mother — she who is the common mother of us all. He looks down upon her as if she were only the mother of us three bastards. Wretch! (*She says all this very rapidly, excitedly. At the word "bastards" she raises her voice, and almost spits out the final "Wretch!"*)

THE MOTHER (*to the* MANAGER, *in anguish*): In the name of these two little children, I beg you . . . (*She grows faint and is about to fall.*) Oh God!

THE FATHER (*coming forward to support her as do some of the* ACTORS): Quick, a chair, a chair for this poor widow!

THE ACTORS: Is it true? Has she really fainted?

THE MANAGER: Quick, a chair! Here!

(*One of the* ACTORS *brings a chair, the* OTHERS *proffer assistance. The* MOTHER *tries to prevent the* FATHER *from lifting the veil which covers her face.*)

THE FATHER: Look at her! Look at her!

THE MOTHER: No, no; stop it please!

THE FATHER (*raising her veil*): Let them see you!

THE MOTHER (*rising and covering her face with her hands, in desperation*): I beg you, sir, to prevent this man from carrying out his plan which is loathsome to me.

THE MANAGER (*dumbfounded*): I don't understand at all. What is the situation? Is this lady your wife? (*to the* FATHER.)

THE FATHER: Yes, gentlemen: my wife!

THE MANAGER: But how can she be a widow if you are alive? (*The* ACTORS *find relief for their astonishment in a loud laugh.*)

THE FATHER: Don't laugh! Don't laugh like that, for Heaven's sake. Her drama lies just here in this: she has had a lover, a man who ought to be here.

THE MOTHER (*with a cry*): No! No!

THE STEP-DAUGHTER: Fortunately for her, he is dead. Two months ago as I said. We are in mourning, as you see.

THE FATHER: He isn't here you see, not because he is dead. He isn't here — look at her a moment and you will understand — because her drama isn't a drama of the love of two men for whom she was incapable of feeling anything except possibly a little gratitude — gratitude not for me but for the other. She isn't a woman, she is a mother, and her drama — powerful sir, I assure you — lies, as a matter of fact, all in these four children she has had by two men.

THE MOTHER: I had them? Have you got the courage to say that I wanted them? (*to the* COMPANY) It was his doing. It was he who gave me that other man, who forced me to go away with him.

THE STEP-DAUGHTER: It isn't true.

THE MOTHER (*startled*): Not true, isn't it?

THE STEP-DAUGHTER: No, it isn't true, it just isn't true.

THE MOTHER: And what can you know about it?

THE STEP-DAUGHTER: It isn't true. Don't believe it. (*to* MANAGER) Do you know why she says so? For that fellow there. (*indicates the* SON) She tortures herself, destroys herself on account of the neglect of that son there; and she wants him to believe that if she abandoned him when he was only two years old, it was because he (*indicates the* FATHER) made her do so.

THE MOTHER (*vigorously*): He forced me to it, and I call God to witness it. (*to the* MANAGER) Ask him (*indicates* HUSBAND) if it isn't true. Let him speak. You (*to* DAUGHTER) are not in a position to know anything about it.

THE STEP-DAUGHTER: I know you lived in peace and happiness with my father while he lived. Can you deny it?

THE MOTHER: No, I don't deny it . . .

THE STEP-DAUGHTER: He was always full of affection and kindness for you. (*to the* BOY, *angrily*) It's true, isn't it? Tell them! Why don't you speak, you little fool?

THE MOTHER: Leave the poor boy alone. Why do you want to make me appear ungrateful, daughter? I don't want to offend your father. I have answered him that I didn't abandon my house and my son through any fault of mine, nor from any wilful passion.

THE FATHER: It is true. It was my doing.

LEADING MAN (*to the* COMPANY): What a spectacle!

LEADING LADY: We are the audience this time.

JUVENILE LEAD: For once, in a way.

THE MANAGER (*beginning to get really interested*): Let's hear them out. Listen!

THE SON: Oh yes, you're going to hear a fine bit now. He will talk to you of the Demon of Experiment.

THE FATHER: You are a cynical imbecile. I've told you so already a hundred times. (*to the* MANAGER) He tries to make fun of me on account of this expression which I have found to excuse myself with.

THE SON (*with disgust*): Yes, phrases! phrases!

THE FATHER: Phrases! Isn't everyone consoled when faced with a trouble or fact he doesn't understand, by a word, some simple word, which tells us nothing and yet calms us?

THE STEP-DAUGHTER: Even in the case of remorse. In fact, especially then.

THE FATHER: Remorse? No, that isn't true. I've done more than use words to quieten the remorse in me.

THE STEP-DAUGHTER: Yes, there was a bit of money too. Yes, yes, a bit of money. There were the hundred lire he was about to offer me in payment, gentlemen . . . (*Sensation of horror among the* ACTORS.)

THE SON (*to the* STEP-DAUGHTER): This is vile.

THE STEP-DAUGHTER: Vile? There they were in a pale blue envelope on a little mahogany table in the back of Madame Pace's shop. You know Madame Pace — one of those ladies who attract poor girls of good family into their ateliers, under the pretext of their selling *robes et manteaux*.

THE SON: And he thinks he has bought the right to tyrannize over us all with those hundred lire he was going to pay; but which, fortunately — note this, gentlemen — he had no chance of paying.

THE STEP-DAUGHTER: It was a near thing, though, you know! (*Laughs ironically*.)

THE MOTHER (*protesting*): Shame, my daughter, shame!

THE STEP-DAUGHTER: Shame indeed! This is my revenge! I am dying to live that scene . . . The room . . . I see it . . . Here is the window with the mantles exposed, there the divan, the looking-glass, a screen, there in front of the window the little mahogany table with the blue envelope containing one hundred lire. I see it. I see it. I could take hold of it . . . But you, gentlemen, you ought to turn your backs now: I am almost nude, you know. But I don't blush: I leave that to him. (*indicating* FATHER.)

THE MANAGER: I don't understand this at all.

THE FATHER: Naturally enough. I would ask you, sir, to exercise your authority a little here, and let me speak before you believe all she is trying to blame me with. Let me explain.

THE STEP-DAUGHTER: Ah yes, explain it in your own way.

THE FATHER: But don't you see that the whole trouble lies here. In words, words. Each one of us has within him a whole world of things, each man of us his own special world. And how can we ever come to an understanding if I put in the words I utter the sense and value of things as I see them; while you who listen to me must inevitably translate them according to the conception of things each one of you has within himself. We think we understand each other, but we never really do. Look here! This woman (*indicating the* MOTHER) takes all my pity for her as a specially ferocious form of cruelty.

THE MOTHER: But you drove me away.

THE FATHER: Do you hear her? I drove her away! She believes I really sent her away.

THE MOTHER: You know how to talk, and I don't; but, believe me, sir (*to* MANAGER), after he had married me . . . who knows why? . . . I was a poor insignificant woman . . .

THE FATHER: But, good Heavens! it was just for your humility that I married you. I loved this simplicity in you. (*He stops when he sees she makes signs to contradict him, opens his arms wide in sign of desperation, seeing how hopeless it is to make himself understood.*) You see she denies it. Her mental deafness, believe me, is phenomenal, the limit: (*Touches his forehead.*) deaf, deaf, mentally deaf! She has plenty of feeling. Oh yes, a good heart for the children; but the brain — deaf, to the point of desperation ——!

THE STEP-DAUGHTER: Yes, but ask him how his intelligence has helped us.

THE FATHER: If we could see all the evil that may spring from good, what should we do? (*At this point the* LEADING LADY *who is biting her lips with rage at seeing the* LEADING MAN *flirting with the* STEP-DAUGHTER, *comes forward and says to the* MANAGER.)

LEADING LADY: Excuse me, but are we going to rehearse today?

MANAGER: Of course, of course; but let's hear them out.

JUVENILE LEAD: This is something quite new.

L'INGÉNUE: Most interesting!

LEADING LADY: Yes, for the people who like that kind of thing. (*Casts a glance at* LEADING MAN.)

THE MANAGER (*to* FATHER): You must please explain yourself quite clearly. (*Sits down.*)

THE FATHER: Very well then: listen! I had in my service a poor man, a clerk, a secretary of mine, full of devotion, who became friends with her. (*indicating the* MOTHER) They understood one another, were kindred souls in fact, without, however, the least suspicion of any evil existing. They were incapable even of thinking of it.

THE STEP-DAUGHTER: So he thought of it — for them!

THE FATHER: That's not true. I meant to do good to them — and to myself, I confess, at the same time. Things had come to the point that I could not say a word to either of them without their making a mute appeal, one to the other, with their eyes. I could see them silently asking each other how I was to be kept in countenance, how I was to be kept quiet. And this, believe me, was just about enough of itself to keep me in a constant rage, to exasperate me beyond measure.

THE MANAGER: And why didn't you send him away then — this secretary of yours?

THE FATHER: Precisely what I did, sir. And then I had to watch this poor woman drifting forlornly about the house like an animal without a master, like an animal one has taken in out of pity.

THE MOTHER: Ah yes . . . !

THE FATHER (*suddenly turning to the* MOTHER): It's true about the son anyway, isn't it?

THE MOTHER: He took my son away from me first of all.

THE FATHER: But not from cruelty. I did it so that he should grow up healthy and strong by living in the country.

THE STEP-DAUGHTER (*pointing to him ironically*): As one can see.

THE FATHER (*quickly*): Is it my fault if he has grown up like this? I sent him to a wet nurse in the country, a peasant, as *she* did not seem to me strong enough, though she is of humble origin. That was, anyway, the reason I married her. Unpleasant all this may be, but how can it be helped? My mistake possibly, but there we are! All my life I have had these confounded aspirations towards a certain moral sanity. (*At this point the* STEP-DAUGHTER *bursts into a noisy laugh.*) Oh, stop it! Stop it! I can't stand it.

THE MANAGER: Yes, please stop it, for Heaven's sake.

THE STEP-DAUGHTER: But imagine moral sanity from him, if you please — the client of certain ateliers like that of Madame Pace!

THE FATHER: Fool! That is the proof that I am a man! This seeming contradiction, gentlemen, is the strongest proof that I stand here a live man before you. Why, it is just for this very incongruity in my nature that I have had to suffer what I have. I could not live by the side of that woman (*indicating the* MOTHER) any longer; but not so much for the boredom she inspired me with as for the pity I felt for her.

THE MOTHER: And so he turned me out — .

THE FATHER: — well provided for! Yes, I sent her to that man, gentlemen . . . to let her go free of me.

THE MOTHER: And to free himself.

THE FATHER: Yes, I admit it. It was also a liberation for me. But great evil has come of it. I meant well when I did it; and I did it more for her sake than mine. I swear it. (*Crosses his arms on his chest; then turns suddenly to the* MOTHER.) Did I ever lose sight of you until that other man carried you off to another town, like the angry fool he was? And on account of my pure interest in you . . . my pure interest, I repeat, that had no base motive in it . . . I watched with the tenderest concern the new family that grew up around her. She can bear witness to this. (*Points to the* STEP-DAUGHTER.)

THE STEP-DAUGHTER: Oh yes, that's true enough. When I was a kiddie, so so high, you know, with plaits over my shoulders and knickers longer than my skirts, I used to see him waiting outside the school for me to come out. He came to see how I was growing up.

THE FATHER: This is infamous, shameful.

THE STEP-DAUGHTER: No. Why?

THE FATHER: Infamous! infamous! (*Then excitedly to* MANAGER *explaining*) After she (*indicating* MOTHER) went away, my house seemed suddenly empty. She was my incubus, but she filled my house. I was like a dazed fly alone in the empty rooms. This boy here (*indicating the* SON) was educated away from home, and when he came back, he seemed to me to be no more mine. With no mother to stand between him and me, he grew up entirely for himself, on his own, apart, with no tie of intellect or affection binding him to me. And then — strange but true — I was driven, by curiosity at first and then by some tender sentiment, towards her family, which had come into being through my will. The thought of her began gradually to fill up the emptiness I felt all around me. I wanted to know if she were happy in living out the simple daily duties of life. I wanted to think of her as fortunate and happy because far away from the complicated torments of my spirit. And so, to have proof of this, I used to watch that child coming out of school.

THE STEP-DAUGHTER: Yes, yes. True. He used to follow me in the street and smiled at me, waved his hand, like this. I would look at him with interest, wondering who he might be. I told my mother, who guessed at once. (*The* MOTHER *agrees with a nod.*) Then she didn't want to send me to school for some days; and when I finally went back, there he was again — looking so ridiculous — with a paper parcel in his hands. He came close to me, caressed me, and drew out a fine straw hat from the parcel, with a bouquet of flowers — all for me!

THE MANAGER: A bit discursive this, you know!

THE SON (*contemptuously*): Literature! Literature!

THE FATHER: Literature indeed! This is life, this is passion!

THE MANAGER: It may be, but it won't act.

THE FATHER: I agree. This is only the part leading up. I don't suggest this should be staged. She (*pointing to the* STEP-DAUGHTER), as you see, is no longer the flapper with plaits down her back — .

THE STEP-DAUGHTER: — and the knickers showing below the skirt!

THE FATHER: The drama is coming now, sir; something new, complex, most interesting.

THE STEP-DAUGHTER: As soon as my father died . . .

THE FATHER: — there was absolute misery for them. They came back here, unknown to me. Through her stupidity! (*pointing to the* MOTHER) It is true she can barely write her own name; but she could anyhow have got

her daughter to write to me that they were in need . . .

THE MOTHER: And how was I to divine all this sentiment in him?

THE FATHER: That is exactly your mistake, never to have guessed any of my sentiments.

THE MOTHER: After so many years apart, and all that had happened . . .

THE FATHER: Was it my fault if that fellow carried you away? It happened quite suddenly; for after he had obtained some job or other, I could find no trace of them; and so, not unnaturally, my interest in them dwindled. But the drama culminated unforeseen and violent on their return, when I was impelled by my miserable flesh that still lives . . . Ah! what misery, what wretchedness is that of the man who is alone and disdains debasing *liaisons!* Not old enough to do without women, and not young enough to go and look for one without shame. Misery? It's worse than misery; it's a horror; for no woman can any longer give him love; and when a man feels this . . . One ought to do without, you say? Yes, yes, I know. Each of us when he appears before his fellows is clothed in a certain dignity. But every man knows what unconfessable things pass within the secrecy of his own heart. One gives way to the temptation, only to rise from it again, afterwards, with a great eagerness to re-establish one's dignity, as if it were a tombstone to place on the grave of one's shame, and a monument to hide and sign the memory of our weaknesses. Everybody's in the same case. Some folks haven't the courage to say certain things, that's all.

THE STEP-DAUGHTER: All appear to have the courage to do them though.

THE FATHER: Yes, but in secret. Therefore, you want more courage to say these things. Let a man but speak these things out, and folks at once label him a cynic. But it isn't true. He is like all the others, better indeed, because he isn't afraid to reveal with the light of the intelligence the red shame of human bestiality on which most men close their eyes so as not to see it.

Woman — for example, look at her case! She turns tantalizing inviting glances on you. You seize her. No sooner does she feel herself in your grasp than she closes her eyes. It is the sign of her mission, the sign by which she says to man: "Blind yourself, for I am blind."

THE STEP-DAUGHTER: Sometimes she can close them no more: when she no longer feels the need of hiding her shame to herself, but dry-eyed and dispassionately, sees only that of the man who has blinded himself without love. Oh, all these intellectual complications make me sick, disgust me — all this philosophy that uncovers the beast in man, and then seeks to save him, excuse him . . . I can't stand it, sir. When a man seeks to "simplify" life bestially, throwing aside every relic of humanity, every chaste aspiration, every pure feeling, all sense of ideality, duty, modesty, shame . . . then nothing is more revolting and nauseous than a certain kind of remorse — crocodiles' tears, that's what it is.

THE MANAGER: Let's come to the point. This is only discussion.

THE FATHER: Very good, sir! But a fact is like a sack which won't stand up when it is empty. In order that it may stand up, one has to put into it the reason and sentiment which have caused it to exist. I couldn't possibly know that after the death of that man, they had decided to return here, that they were in misery, and that she (*pointing to the* MOTHER) had gone to work as a modiste, and at a shop of the type of that of Madame Pace.

THE STEP-DAUGHTER: A real high-class modiste, you must know, gentlemen. In appearance, she works for the leaders of the best society; but she arranges matters so that these elegant ladies serve her purpose . . . without prejudice to other ladies who are . . . well . . . only so so.

THE MOTHER: You will believe me, gentlemen, that it never entered my mind that the old hag offered me work because she had her eye on my daughter.

THE STEP-DAUGHTER: Poor mamma! Do you know, sir, what that woman did when I brought her back the work my mother had finished? She would point out to me that I had torn one of my frocks, and she would give it back to my mother to mend. It was I who paid for it, always I; while this poor creature here believed she was sacrificing herself for me and these two children here, sitting up at night sewing Madame Pace's robes.

THE MANAGER: And one day you met there . . .

THE STEP-DAUGHTER: Him, him. Yes sir, an old client. There's a scene for you to play! Superb!

THE FATHER: She, the Mother arrived just then . . .

THE STEP-DAUGHTER (*treacherously*): Almost in time!

THE FATHER (*crying out*): No, in time! in time! Fortunately I recognized her . . . in time. And I took them back home with me to my house. You can imagine now her position and mine; she, as you see her; and I who cannot look her in the face.

THE STEP-DAUGHTER: Absurd! How can I possibly be expected — after that — to be a modest young miss, a fit person to go with his confounded aspirations for "a solid moral sanity"?

THE FATHER: For the drama lies all in this — in the conscience that I have, that each one of us has. We believe this conscience to be a single thing, but it is many-sided. There is one for this person, and another for that. Diverse consciences. So we have this illusion of being one person for all, of having a personality that is unique in all our acts. But it isn't true. We perceive this when, tragically perhaps, in something we do, we are as it were, suspended, caught up in the air on a kind of hook. Then we perceive that all of us was not in that act, and that it would be an atrocious injustice to judge us by that action alone, as if all our existence were summed up in that one deed. Now do you understand the perfidy of this girl? She surprised me in a place, where she ought not to have known me, just as I could not exist for her; and she now seeks to attach to me a reality such as I could never suppose I should have to assume for her in a shameful and fleeting moment of my life. I feel this above all else. And the drama, you will see, acquires a tremendous value from this point. Then there is the position of the others ... his ... (*indicating the* SON.)

THE SON (*shrugging his shoulders scornfully*): Leave me alone! I don't come into this.

THE FATHER: What? You don't come into this?

THE SON: I've got nothing to do with it, and don't want to have; because you know well enough I wasn't made to be mixed up in all this with the rest of you.

THE STEP-DAUGHTER: We are only vulgar folk! He is the fine gentleman. You may have noticed, Mr. Manager, that I fix him now and again with a look of scorn while he lowers his eyes — for he knows the evil he has done me.

THE SON (*scarcely looking at her*): I?

THE STEP-DAUGHTER: You! you! I owe my life on the streets to you. Did you or did you not deny us, with your behaviour, I won't say the intimacy of home, but even that mere hospitality which makes guests feel at their ease? We were intruders who had come to disturb the kingdom of your legitimacy. I should like to have you witness, Mr. Manager, certain scenes between him and me. He says I have tyrannized over everyone. But it was just his behaviour which made me insist on the reason for which I had come into the house, — this reason he calls "vile" — into his house, with my mother who is his mother too. And I came as mistress of the house.

THE SON: It's easy for them to put me always in the wrong. But imagine, gentlemen, the position of a son, whose fate it is to see arrive one day at his home a young woman of impudent bearing, a young woman who inquires for his father, with whom who knows what business she has. This young man has then to witness her return bolder than ever, accompanied by that child there. He is obliged to watch her treat his father in an equivocal and confidential manner. She asks money of him in a way that lets one suppose he must give it her, *must,* do you understand, because he has every obligation to do so.

THE FATHER: But I have, as a matter of fact, this obligation. I owe it to your mother.

THE SON: How should I know? When had I ever seen or heard of her? One day there arrive with her (*indicating* STEP-DAUGHTER) that lad and this baby here. I am told: "This is *your* mother too, you know." I divine from her manner (*indicating* STEP-DAUGHTER *again*) why it is they have come home. I had rather not say what I feel and think about it. I shouldn't even care to confess to myself. No action can therefore be hoped for from me in this affair. Believe me, Mr. Manager, I am an "unrealized" character, dramatically speaking; and I find myself not at all at ease in their company. Leave me out of it, I beg you.

THE FATHER: What? It is just because you are so that ...

THE SON: How do you know what I am like? When did you ever bother your head about me?

THE FATHER: I admit it. I admit it. But isn't that a situation in itself? This aloofness of yours which is so cruel to me and to your mother, who returns home and sees you almost for the first time grown up, who doesn't recognize you but knows you are her son ... (*pointing out the* MOTHER *to the* MANAGER) See, she's crying!

THE STEP-DAUGHTER (*angrily, stamping her foot*): Like a fool!

THE FATHER (*indicating* STEP-DAUGHTER): She can't stand him you know. (*then referring again to the* SON) He says he doesn't come into the affair, whereas he is really the hinge of the whole action. Look at that lad who is always clinging to his mother, frightened and humiliated. It is on account of this fellow here. Possibly his situation is the most painful of all. He feels himself a stranger more than the others. The poor little chap feels mortified, humiliated at being brought into a home out of charity as it were. (*in confidence*) He is the image of his father. Hardly talks at all. Humble and quiet.

THE MANAGER: Oh, we'll cut him out. You've no notion what a nuisance boys are on the stage . . .

THE FATHER: He disappears soon, you know. And the baby too. She is the first to vanish from the scene. The drama consists finally in this: when that mother re-enters my house, her family born outside of it, and shall we say superimposed on the original, ends with the death of the little girl, the tragedy of the boy and the flight of the elder daughter. It cannot go on, because it is foreign to its surroundings. So after much torment, we three remain: I, the mother, that son. Then, owing to the disappearance of that extraneous family, we too find ourselves strange to one another. We find we are living in an atmosphere of mortal desolation which is the revenge, as he (*indicating* SON) scornfully said of the Demon of Experiment, that unfortunately hides in me. Thus, sir, you see when faith is lacking, it becomes impossible to create certain states of happiness, for we lack the necessary humility. Vaingloriously, we try to substitute ourselves for this faith, creating thus for the rest of the world a reality which we believe after their fashion, while, actually, it doesn't exist. For each one of us has his own reality to be respected before God, even when it is harmful to one's very self.

THE MANAGER: There is something in what you say. I assure you all this interests me very much. I begin to think there's the stuff for a drama in all this, and not a bad drama either.

THE STEP-DAUGHTER (*coming forward*): When you've got a character like me.

THE FATHER (*shutting her up, all excited to learn the decision of the* MANAGER): You be quiet!

THE MANAGER (*reflecting, heedless of interruption*): It's new . . . hem . . . yes . . .

THE FATHER: Absolutely new!

THE MANAGER: You've got a nerve though, I must say, to come here and fling it at me like this . . .

THE FATHER: You will understand, sir, born as we are for the stage . . .

THE MANAGER: Are you amateur actors then?

THE FATHER: No. I say born for the stage, because . . .

THE MANAGER: Oh, nonsense. You're an old hand, you know.

THE FATHER: No sir, no. We act that rôle for which we have been cast, that rôle which we are given in life. And in my own case, passion itself, as usually happens, becomes a trifle theatrical when it is exalted.

THE MANAGER: Well, well, that will do. But you see, without an author . . . I could give you the address of an author if you like . . .

THE FATHER: No, no. Look here! You must be the author.

THE MANAGER: I? What are you talking about?

THE FATHER: Yes, you, you! Why not?

THE MANAGER: Because I have never been an author: that's why.

THE FATHER: Then why not turn author now? Everybody does it. You don't want any special qualities. Your task is made much easier by the fact that we are all here alive before you . . .

THE MANAGER: It won't do.

THE FATHER: What? When you see us live our drama . . .

THE MANAGER: Yes, that's all right. But you want someone to write it.

THE FATHER: No, no. Someone to take it down, possibly, while we play it, scene by scene! It will be enough to sketch it out at first, and then try it over.

THE MANAGER: Well . . . I am almost tempted. It's a bit of an idea. One might have a shot at it.

THE FATHER: Of course. You'll see what scenes will come out of it. I can give you one, at once . . .

THE MANAGER: By Jove, it tempts me. I'd like to have a go at it. Let's try it out. Come with me to my office. (*turning to the* ACTORS) You are at liberty for a bit, but don't step out of the theatre for long. In a quarter of an hour, twenty minutes, all back here again! (*to the* FATHER) We'll see what can be done. Who knows if we don't get something really extraordinary out of it?

THE FATHER: There's no doubt about it. They (*indicating the* CHARACTERS) had better come with us too, hadn't they?

THE MANAGER: Yes, yes. Come on! come on! (*Moves away and then turning to the* ACTORS) Be punctual, please! (MANAGER *and the* SIX CHARACTERS *cross the stage and go off. The other* ACTORS *remain, looking at one another in astonishment.*)

LEADING MAN: Is he serious? What the devil does he want to do?

JUVENILE LEAD: This is rank madness.

THIRD ACTOR: Does he expect to knock up a drama in five minutes?

JUVENILE LEAD: Like the improvisers!

LEADING LADY: If he thinks I'm going to take part in a joke like this . . .

JUVENILE LEAD: I'm out of it anyway.

FOURTH ACTOR: I should like to know who they are. (*Alludes to* CHARACTERS.)

THIRD ACTOR: What do you suppose? Madmen or rascals!

JUVENILE LEAD: And he takes them seriously!

L'INGÉNUE: Vanity! He fancies himself as an author now.

LEADING MAN: It's absolutely unheard of. If the stage has come to this . . . well I'm . . .

FIFTH ACTOR: It's rather a joke.

THIRD ACTOR: Well, we'll see what's going to happen next.

(*Thus talking, the* ACTORS *leave the stage; some going out by the little door at the back; others retiring to their dressing-rooms.*
The curtain remains up.
The action of the play is suspended for twenty minutes.)

ACT TWO

The stage call-bells ring to warn the company that the play is about to begin again.

The STEP-DAUGHTER *comes out of the* MANAGER'S *office along with the* CHILD *and the* BOY. *As she comes out of the office, she cries: —*

Nonsense! nonsense! Do it yourselves! I'm not going to mix myself up in this mess. (*Turning to the* CHILD *and coming quickly with her on to the stage.*) Come on, Rosetta, let's run!

(*The* BOY *follows them slowly, remaining a little behind and seeming perplexed.*)

THE STEP-DAUGHTER (*stops, bends over the* CHILD *and takes the latter's face between her hands*): My little darling! You're frightened, aren't you? You don't know where we are, do you? (*Pretending to reply to a question of the* CHILD.) What is the stage? It's a place, baby, you know, where people play at being serious, a place where they act comedies. We've got to act a comedy now, dead serious, you know; and you're in it also, little one. (*embraces her, pressing the little head to her breast, and rocking the* CHILD *for a moment*) Oh darling, darling, what a horrid comedy you've got to play! What a wretched part they've found for you! A garden . . . a fountain . . . look . . . just suppose, kiddie, it's here. Where, you say? Why, right here in the middle. It's all pretence you know. That's the trouble, my pet: it's all make-believe here. It's better to imagine it though, because if they fix it up for you, it'll only be painted cardboard, painted cardboard for the rockery, the water, the plants . . . Ah, but I think a baby like this one would sooner have a make-believe fountain than a real one, so she could play with it. What a joke it'll be for the others! But for you, alas! not quite such a joke: you who are real, baby dear, and really play by a real fountain that is big and green and beautiful, with ever so many bamboos around it that are reflected in the water, and a whole lot of little ducks swimming about . . . No, Rosetta, no, your mother doesn't bother about you on account of that wretch of a son there. I'm in the devil of a temper, and as for that lad . . . (*Seizes* BOY *by the arm to force him to take one of his hands out of his pockets.*) What have you got there? What are you hiding? (*pulls his hand out of his pocket, looks into it and catches the glint of a revolver*) Ah! where did you get this? (*The* BOY, *very pale in the face, looks at her, but does not answer.*) Idiot! If I'd been in your place, instead of killing myself, I'd have shot one of those two, or both of them: father and son.

(*The* FATHER *enters from the office, all excited from his work. The* MANAGER *follows him.*)

THE FATHER: Come on, come on dear! Come here for a minute! We've arranged everything. It's all fixed up.

THE MANAGER (*also excited*): If you please, young lady, there are one or two points to settle still. Will you come along?

THE STEP-DAUGHTER (*following him towards the office*): Ouff! what's the good, if you've arranged everything.

(*The* FATHER, MANAGER *and* STEP-DAUGHTER *go back into the office again* [*off*] *for a moment. At the same time, The* SON *followed by The* MOTHER, *comes out.*)

THE SON (*looking at the three entering office*): Oh this is fine, fine! And to think I can't even get away!

(*The* MOTHER *attempts to look at him, but lowers her eyes immediately when* HE *turns away from her.* SHE *then sits down. The* BOY *and The* CHILD *approach her.* SHE *casts a* glance *again at the* SON, *and speaks with humble tones, trying to draw him into conversation.*)

THE MOTHER: And isn't my punishment the worst of all? (*Then seeing from the* SON'S *manner that he will not bother himself about her.*) My God! Why are you so cruel? Isn't it enough for one person to support all this torment? Must you then insist on others seeing it also?

THE SON (*half to himself, meaning the* MOTHER *to hear, however*): And they want to put it on the stage! If there was at least a reason for it! He thinks he has got at the meaning of it all. Just as if each one of us in every circumstance of life couldn't find his own explanation of it! (*pauses*) He complains he was discovered in a place where he ought not to have been seen, in a moment of his life which ought to have remained hidden and kept out of the reach of that convention which he has to maintain for other people. And what about my case? Haven't I had to reveal what no son ought ever to reveal: how father and mother live and are man and wife for themselves quite apart from that idea of father and mother which we give them? When this idea is revealed, our life is then linked at one point only to that man and that woman; and as such it should shame them, shouldn't it?

(*The* MOTHER *hides her face in her hands. From the dressing-rooms and the little door at the back of the stage the* ACTORS *and* STAGE MANAGER *return, followed by the* PROPERTY MAN, *and the* PROMPTER. *At the same moment, The* MANAGER *comes out of his office, accompanied by the* FATHER *and the* STEP-DAUGHTER.)

THE MANAGER: Come on, come on, ladies and gentlemen! Heh! you there, machinist!

MACHINIST: Yes sir?

THE MANAGER: Fix up the white parlor with the floral decorations. Two wings and a drop with a door will do. Hurry up!

(*The* MACHINIST *runs off at once to prepare the scene, and arranges it while The* MANAGER *talks with the* STAGE MANAGER, *the* PROPERTY MAN, *and the* PROMPTER *on matters of detail.*)

THE MANAGER (*to* PROPERTY MAN): Just have a look, and see if there isn't a sofa or divan in the wardrobe . . .

PROPERTY MAN: There's the green one.

THE STEP-DAUGHTER: No no! Green won't do. It was yellow, ornamented with flowers — very large! and most comfortable!

PROPERTY MAN: There isn't one like that.

THE MANAGER: It doesn't matter. Use the one we've got.

THE STEP-DAUGHTER: Doesn't matter? It's most important!

THE MANAGER: We're only trying it now. Please don't interfere. (*to* PROPERTY MAN) See if we've got a shop window — long and narrowish.

THE STEP-DAUGHTER: And the little table! The little mahogany table for the pale blue envelope!

PROPERTY MAN (*to* MANAGER): There's that little gilt one.

THE MANAGER: That'll do fine.

THE FATHER: A mirror.

THE STEP-DAUGHTER: And the screen! We must have a screen. Otherwise how can I manage?

PROPERTY MAN: That's all right, Miss. We've got any amount of them.

THE MANAGER (*to the* STEP-DAUGHTER): We want some clothes pegs too, don't we?

THE STEP-DAUGHTER: Yes, several, several!

THE MANAGER: See how many we've got and bring them all.

PROPERTY MAN: All right!

(*The* PROPERTY MAN *hurries off to obey his orders. While he is putting the things in their places, the* MANAGER *talks to the* PROMPTER *and then with the* CHARACTERS *and the* ACTORS.)

THE MANAGER (*to* PROMPTER): Take your seat.

Look here: this is the outline of the scenes, act by act. (*hands him some sheets of paper*) And now I'm going to ask you to do something out of the ordinary.

PROMPTER: Take it down in shorthand?

THE MANAGER (*pleasantly surprised*): Exactly! Can you do shorthand?

PROMPTER: Yes, a little.

THE MANAGER: Good! (*turning to a* STAGE HAND) Go and get some paper from my office, plenty, as much as you can find.

(*The* STAGE HAND *goes off, and soon returns with a handful of paper which he gives to the* PROMPTER.)

THE MANAGER (*to* PROMPTER): You follow the scenes as we play them, and try and get the points down, at any rate the most important ones. (*then addressing the* ACTORS) Clear the stage, ladies and gentlemen! Come over here (*pointing to the left*) and listen attentively.

LEADING LADY: But, excuse me, we . . .

THE MANAGER (*guessing her thought*): Don't worry! You won't have to improvise.

LEADING MAN: What have we to do then?

THE MANAGER: Nothing. For the moment you just watch and listen. Everybody will get his part written out afterwards. At present we're going to try the thing as best we can. They're going to act now.

THE FATHER (*as if fallen from the clouds into the confusion of the stage*): We? What do you mean, if you please, by a rehearsal?

THE MANAGER: A rehearsal for them. (*points to the* ACTORS.)

THE FATHER: But since we are the characters . . .

THE MANAGER: All right: "characters" then, if you insist on calling yourselves such. But here, my dear sir, the characters don't act. Here the actors do the acting. The characters are there, in the "book" (*pointing towards* PROMPTER'S *box*) — when there is a "book"!

THE FATHER: I won't contradict you; but excuse

me, the actors aren't the characters. They want to be, they pretend to be, don't they? Now if these gentlemen here are fortunate enough to have us alive before them . . .

THE MANAGER: Oh this is grand! You want to come before the public yourselves then?

THE FATHER: As we are . . .

THE MANAGER: I can assure you it would be a magnificent spectacle!

LEADING MAN: What's the use of us here anyway then?

THE MANAGER: You're not going to pretend that you can act? It makes me laugh! (*The* ACTORS *laugh.*) There, you see, they are laughing at the notion. But, by the way, I must cast the parts. That won't be difficult. They cast themselves. (*to the* SECOND LADY LEAD) You play the Mother. (*to the* FATHER) We must find her a name.

THE FATHER: Amalia, sir.

THE MANAGER: But that is the real name of your wife. We don't want to call her by her real name.

THE FATHER: Why ever not, if it is her name? . . . Still, perhaps, if that lady must . . . (*Makes a slight motion of the hand to indicate the* SECOND LADY LEAD) I see this woman here (*Means the* MOTHER) as Amalia. But do as you like. (*Gets more and more confused*) I don't know what to say to you. Already, I begin to hear my own words ring false, as if they had another sound . . .

THE MANAGER: Don't you worry about it. It'll be our job to find the right tones. And as for her name, if you want her Amalia, Amalia it shall be; and if you don't like it, we'll find another! For the moment though, we'll call the characters in this way: (*to* JUVENILE LEAD) You are the Son. (*to the* LEADING LADY) You naturally are the Step-Daughter . . .

THE STEP-DAUGHTER (*excitedly*): What? what? I, that woman there? (*Bursts out laughing.*)

THE MANAGER (*angry*): What is there to laugh at?

LEADING LADY (*indignant*): Nobody has ever dared to laugh at me. I insist on being treated with respect; otherwise I go away.

THE STEP-DAUGHTER: No, no, excuse me . . . I am not laughing at you . . .

THE MANAGER (*to* STEP-DAUGHTER): You ought to feel honored to be played by . . .

LEADING LADY (*at once, contemptuously*): "That woman there" . . .

THE STEP-DAUGHTER: But I wasn't speaking of you, you know. I was speaking of myself — whom I can't see at all in you! That is all. I don't know . . . but . . . you . . . aren't in the least like me . . .

THE FATHER: True. Here's the point. Look here, sir, our temperaments, our souls . . .

THE MANAGER: Temperament, soul, be hanged! Do you suppose the spirit of the piece is in you? Nothing of the kind!

THE FATHER: What, haven't we our own temperaments, our own souls?

THE MANAGER: Not at all. Your soul or whatever you like to call it takes shape here. The actors give body and form to it, voice and gesture. And my actors — I may tell you — have given expression to much more lofty material than this little drama of yours, which may or may not hold up on the stage. But if it does, the merit of it believe me, will be due to my actors.

THE FATHER: I don't dare contradict you, sir; but, believe me, it is a terrible suffering for us who are as we are, with these bodies of ours, these features to see . . .

THE MANAGER (*cutting him short and out of patience*): Good heavens! The make-up will remedy all that, man, the make-up . . .

THE FATHER: Maybe. But the voice, the gestures . . .

THE MANAGER: Now, look here! On the stage, you as yourself, cannot exist. The actor here acts you, and that's an end to it!

THE FATHER: I understand. And now I think I

see why our author who conceived us as we are, all alive, didn't want to put us on the stage after all. I haven't the least desire to offend your actors. Far from it! But when I think that I am to be acted by . . . I don't know by whom . . .

LEADING MAN (*on his dignity*): By me, if you've no objection!

THE FATHER (*humbly, mellifluously*): Honored, I assure you, sir. (*Bows*) Still, I must say that try as this gentleman may, with all his good will and wonderful art, to absorb me into himself . . .

LEADING MAN: Oh chuck it! "Wonderful art!" Withdraw that, please!

THE FATHER: The performance he will give, even doing his best with make-up to look like me . . .

LEADING MAN: It will certainly be a bit difficult! (*The* ACTORS *laugh.*)

THE FATHER: Exactly! It will be difficult to act me as I really am. The effect will be rather — apart from the make-up — according as to how he supposes I am, as he senses me — if he does sense me — and not as I inside of myself feel myself to be. It seems to me then that account should be taken of this by everyone whose duty it may become to criticize us . . .

THE MANAGER: Heavens! The man's starting to think about the critics now! Let them say what they like. It's up to us to put on the play if we can. (*looking around*) Come on! come on! Is the stage set? (*to the* ACTORS *and* CHARACTERS) Stand back — stand back! Let me see, and don't let's lose any more time! (*to the* STEP-DAUGHTER) Is it all right as it is now?

THE STEP-DAUGHTER: Well, to tell the truth, I don't recognize the scene.

THE MANAGER: My dear lady, you can't possibly suppose that we can construct that shop of Madame Pace piece by piece here? (*to the* FATHER) You said a white room with flowered wall paper, didn't you?

THE FATHER: Yes.

THE MANAGER: Well then. We've got the furniture right more or less. Bring that little table a bit further forward. (*The* STAGE HANDS *obey the order. To* PROPERTY MAN) You go and find an envelope, if possible, a pale blue one; and give it to that gentleman. (*indicates* FATHER)

PROPERTY MAN: An ordinary envelope?

MANAGER AND FATHER: Yes, yes, an ordinary envelope.

PROPERTY MAN: At once, sir. (*Exit.*)

THE MANAGER: Ready, everyone! First scene — the Young Lady. (*The* LEADING LADY *comes forward.*) No, no, you must wait. I meant her (*indicating the* STEP-DAUGHTER) You just watch —

THE STEP-DAUGHTER (*adding at once*): How I shall play it, how I shall live it! . . .

LEADING LADY (*offended*): I shall live it also, you may be sure, as soon as I begin!

THE MANAGER (*with his hands to his head*): Ladies and gentlemen, if you please! No more useless discussions! Scene I: the young lady with Madame Pace: Oh! (*Looks around as if lost.*) And this Madame Pace, where is she?

THE FATHER: She isn't with us, sir.

THE MANAGER: Then what the devil's to be done?

THE FATHER: But she is alive too.

THE MANAGER: Yes, but where is she?

THE FATHER: One minute. Let me speak! (*turning to the* ACTRESSES) If these ladies would be so good as to give me their hats for a moment . . .

THE ACTRESSES (*half surprised, half laughing, in chorus*): What?
Why?
Our hats?
What does he say?

THE MANAGER: What are you going to do with the ladies' hats? (*The* ACTORS *laugh.*)

THE FATHER: Oh nothing. I just want to put them on these pegs for a moment. And one of the ladies will be so kind as to take off her mantle . . .

THE ACTORS: Oh, what d'you think of that?
Only the mantle?
He must be mad.

SOME ACTRESSES: But why?
Mantles as well?

THE FATHER: To hang them up here for a moment. Please be so kind, will you?

THE ACTRESSES (*taking off their hats, one or two also their cloaks, and going to hang them on the racks*): After all, why not?
There you are!
This is really funny.
We've got to put them on show.

THE FATHER: Exactly; just like that, on show.

THE MANAGER: May we know why?

THE FATHER: I'll tell you. Who knows if, by arranging the stage for her, she does not come here herself, attracted by the very articles of her trade? (*Inviting the* ACTORS *to look towards the exit at back of stage.*) Look! Look!

(*The door at the back of stage opens and* MADAME PACE *enters and takes a few steps forward. She is a fat, oldish woman with puffy oxygenated hair. She is rouged and powdered, dressed with a comical elegance in black silk. Round her waist is a long silver chain from which hangs a pair of scissors. The* STEP-DAUGHTER *runs over to her at once amid the stupor of the actors.*)

THE STEP-DAUGHTER (*turning towards her*): There she is! There she is!

THE FATHER (*radiant*): It's she! I said so, didn't I? There she is!

THE MANAGER (*conquering his surprise, and then becoming indignant*): What sort of a trick is this?

LEADING MAN (*almost at the same time*): What's going to happen next?

JUVENILE LEAD: Where does *she* come from?

L'INGÉNUE: They've been holding her in reserve, I guess.

LEADING LADY: A vulgar trick!

THE FATHER (*dominating the protests*): Excuse me, all of you! Why are you so anxious to destroy in the name of a vulgar, commonplace sense of truth, this reality which comes to birth attracted and formed by the magic of the stage itself, which has indeed more right to live here than you, since it is much truer than you — if you don't mind my saying so? Which is the actress among you who is to play Madame Pace? Well, here is Madame Pace herself. And you will allow, I fancy, that the actress who acts her will be less true than this woman here, who is herself in person. You see my daughter recognized her and went over to her at once. Now you're going to witness the scene!

(*But the scene between the* STEP-DAUGHTER *and* MADAME PACE *has already begun despite the protest of the actors and the reply of The* FATHER. *It has begun quietly, naturally, in a manner impossible for the stage. So when the actors, called to attention by The* FATHER, *turn round and see* MADAME PACE, *who has placed one hand under the* STEP-DAUGHTER's *chin to raise her head, they observe her at first with great attention, but hearing her speak in an unintelligible manner their interest begins to wane.*)

THE MANAGER: Well? well?

LEADING MAN: What does she say?

LEADING LADY: One can't hear a word.

JUVENILE LEAD: Louder! Louder please!

THE STEP-DAUGHTER (*leaving* MADAME PACE, *who smiles a Sphinx-like smile, and advancing towards the actors*): Louder? Louder? What are you talking about? These aren't matters which can be shouted at the top of one's voice. If I have spoken them out loud, it was to shame him and have my revenge. (*indicates* FATHER) But for Madame it's quite a different matter.

THE MANAGER: Indeed? indeed? But here, you know, people have got to make themselves heard, my dear. Even we who are on the stage can't hear you. What will it be when the public's in the theatre? And anyway, you can very well speak up now among yourselves, since we shan't be present to listen to you as we are now. You've got to pretend to be alone in a room at the back of a shop where no one can hear you.

(*The* STEP-DAUGHTER *coquettishly and with a touch of malice makes a sign of disagreement two or three times with her finger.*)

THE MANAGER: What do you mean by no?

THE STEP-DAUGHTER (*sotto voce, mysteriously*): There's someone who will hear us if she (*indicating* MADAME PACE) speaks out loud.

THE MANAGER (*in consternation*): What? Have you got someone else to spring on us now? (*The* ACTORS *burst out laughing.*)

THE FATHER: No, no sir. She is alluding to me. I've got to be here — there behind that door, in waiting; and Madame Pace knows it. In fact, if you will allow me, I'll go there at once, so I can be quite ready. (*Moves away.*)

THE MANAGER (*stopping him*): No! Wait! wait! We must observe the conventions of the theatre. Before you are ready . . .

THE STEP-DAUGHTER (*interrupting him*): No, get on with it at once! I'm just dying, I tell you, to act this scene. If he's ready, I'm more than ready.

THE MANAGER (*shouting*): But, my dear young lady, first of all, we must have the scene between you and this lady . . . (*indicates* MADAME PACE) Do you understand? . . .

THE STEP-DAUGHTER: Good Heavens! She's been telling me what you know already: that mamma's work is badly done again, that the material's ruined; and that if I want her to continue to help us in our misery I must be patient . . .

MADAME PACE (*coming forward with an air of great importance*): Yes indeed, sir, I no wanta take advantage of her, I no wanta be hard . . .

(*Note.* MADAME PACE *is supposed to talk in a jargon half Italian, half English.*)

THE MANAGER (*alarmed*): What? What? She talks like that? (*The* ACTORS *burst out laughing again.*)

THE STEP-DAUGHTER (*also laughing*): Yes yes, that's the way she talks, half English, half Italian! Most comical it is!

MADAME PACE: Itta seem not verra polite gentlemen laugha atta me eef I trya best speaka English.

THE MANAGER: *Diamine!* Of course! Of course! Let her talk like that! Just what we want. Talk just like that, Madame, if you please! The effect will be certain. Exactly what was wanted to put a little comic relief into the crudity of the situation. Of course she talks like that! Magnificent!

THE STEP-DAUGHTER: Magnificent? Certainly! When certain suggestions are made to one in language of that kind, the effect is certain, since it seems almost a joke. One feels inclined to laugh when one hears her talk about an "old signore" "who wanta talka nicely with you." Nice old signore, eh, Madame?

MADAME PACE: Not so old my dear, not so old! And even if you no lika him, he won't make any scandal!

THE MOTHER (*jumping up amid the amazement and consternation of the actors who had not been noticing her.* THEY *move to restrain her*). You old devil! You murderess!

THE STEP-DAUGHTER (*running over to calm her* MOTHER): Calm yourself, Mother, calm yourself! Please don't . . .

THE FATHER (*going to her also at the same time*): Calm yourself! Don't get excited! Sit down now!

THE MOTHER: Well then, take that woman away out of my sight!

THE STEP-DAUGHTER (*to* MANAGER): It is impossible for my mother to remain here.

THE FATHER (*to* MANAGER): They can't be here

together. And for this reason, you see: that woman there was not with us when we came . . . If they are on together, the whole thing is given away inevitably, as you see.

THE MANAGER: It doesn't matter. This is only a first rough sketch — just to get an idea of the various points of the scene, even confusedly . . . (*turning to the* MOTHER *and leading her to her chair*) Come along, my dear lady, sit down now, and let's get on with the scene . . .

(*Meanwhile, the* STEP-DAUGHTER, *coming forward again, turns to* MADAME PACE.)

THE STEP-DAUGHTER: Come on, Madame, come on!

MADAME PACE (*offended*): No, no, *grazie*. I not do anything witha your mother present.

THE STEP-DAUGHTER: Nonsense! Introduce this "old signore" who wants to talk nicely to me. (*addressing the* COMPANY *imperiously*) We've got to do this scene one way or another, haven't we? Come on! (*to* MADAME PACE) You can go!

MADAME PACE: Ah yes! I go'way! I go'way! Certainly! (*Exits furious.*)

THE STEP-DAUGHTER (*to the* FATHER): Now you make your entry. No, you needn't go over here. Come here. Let's suppose you've already come in. Like that, yes! I'm here with bowed head, modest like. Come on! Out with your voice! Say "Good morning, Miss" in that peculiar tone, that special tone . . .

THE MANAGER: Excuse me, but are you the Manager, or am I? (*to the* FATHER, *who looks undecided and perplexed*) Get on with it, man! Go down there to the back of the stage. You needn't go off. Then come right forward here.

(*The* FATHER *does as he is told, looking troubled and perplexed at first. But as soon as he begins to move, the reality of the action affects him, and he begins to smile and to be more natural. The* ACTORS *watch intently.*)

THE MANAGER (*sotto voce, quickly to the*

PROMPTER *in his box*). Ready! ready? Get ready to write now.

THE FATHER (*coming forward and speaking in a different tone*): Good afternoon, Miss!

THE STEP-DAUGHTER (*head bowed down slightly, with restrained disgust*): Good afternoon!

THE FATHER (*looks under her hat which partly covers her face. Perceiving she is very young, he makes an exclamation, partly of surpise, partly of fear lest he compromise himself in a risky adventure*): Ah . . . but . . . ah . . . I say . . . this is not the first time that you have come here, is it?

THE STEP-DAUGHTER (*modestly*): No sir.

THE FATHER: You've been here before, eh? (*Then seeing her nod agreement.*) More than once? (*Waits for her to answer, looks under her hat, smiles, and then says*) Well then, there's no need to be so shy, is there? May I take off your hat?

THE STEP-DAUGHTER (*anticipating him and with veiled disgust*): No sir . . . I'll do it myself. (*Takes it off quickly.*)

(*The* MOTHER, *who watches the progress of the scene with* the SON *and the other two children who cling to her, is on thorns; and follows with varying expressions of sorrow, indignation, anxiety, and horror the words and actions of the other two. From time to time* SHE *hides her face in her hands and sobs.*)

THE MOTHER: Oh, my God, my God!

THE FATHER (*playing his part with a touch of gallantry*): Give it to me! I'll put it down. (*Takes hat from her hands*) But a dear little head like yours ought to have a smarter hat. Come and help me choose one from the stock, won't you?

L'INGÉNUE (*interrupting*): I say . . . those are our hats you know.

THE MANAGER (*furious*): Silence! silence! Don't try and be funny, if you please . . . We're playing the scene now I'd have you notice. (*to the* STEP-DAUGHTER) Begin again, please!

THE STEP-DAUGHTER (*continuing*): No thank you, sir.

THE FATHER: Oh, come now. Don't talk like that. You must take it. I shall be upset if you don't. There are some lovely little hats here; and then — Madame will be pleased. She expects it, anyway, you know.

THE STEP-DAUGHTER: No, no! I couldn't wear it!

THE FATHER: Oh, you're thinking about what they'd say at home if they saw you come in with a new hat? My dear girl, there's always a way round these little matters, you know.

THE STEP-DAUGHTER (*all keyed up*): No, it's not that. I couldn't wear it because I am . . . as you see . . . you might have noticed . . . (*showing her black dress.*)

THE FATHER: . . . in mourning! Of course: I beg your pardon: I'm frightfully sorry . . .

THE STEP-DAUGHTER (*forcing herself to conquer her indignation and nausea*): Stop! Stop! It's I who must thank you. There's no need for you to feel mortified or specially sorry. Don't think any more of what I've said. (*tries to smile*) I must forget that I am dressed so . . .

THE MANAGER (*interrupting and turning to the PROMPTER*): Stop a minute! Stop! Don't write that down. Cut out that last bit. (*then to the FATHER and STEP-DAUGHTER*) Fine! it's going fine! (*to the FATHER only*) And now you can go on as we arranged. (*to the ACTORS*) Pretty good that scene, where he offers her the hat, eh?

THE STEP-DAUGHTER: The best's coming now. Why can't we go on?

THE MANAGER: Have a little patience! (*to the ACTORS*) Of course, it must be treated rather lightly.

LEADING MAN: Still, with a bit of go in it!

LEADING LADY: Of course! It's easy enough! (*to LEADING MAN*) Shall you and I try it now?

LEADING MAN: Why, yes! I'll prepare my entrance. (*Exit in order to make his entrance.*)

THE MANAGER (*to LEADING LADY*): See here!

The scene between you and Madame Pace is finished. I'll have it written out properly after. You remain here . . . oh, where are you going?

LEADING LADY: One minute. I want to put my hat on again. (*goes over to hat-rack and puts her hat on her head.*)

THE MANAGER: Good! You stay here with your head bowed down a bit.

THE STEP-DAUGHTER: But she isn't dressed in black.

LEADING LADY: But I shall be, and much more effectively than you.

THE MANAGER (*to STEP-DAUGHTER*): Be quiet please, and watch! You'll be able to learn something. (*clapping his hands*) Come on! come on! Entrance, please!

(*The door at rear of stage opens, and the LEADING MAN enters with the lively manner of an old gallant. The rendering of the scene by the ACTORS from the very first words is seen to be quite a different thing, though it has not in any way the air of a parody. Naturally, the STEP-DAUGHTER and the FATHER, not being able to recognize themselves in the LEADING LADY and the LEADING MAN, who deliver their words in different tones and with a different psychology, express, sometimes with smiles, sometimes with gestures, the impression they receive.*)

LEADING MAN: Good afternoon, Miss . . .

THE FATHER (*at once unable to contain himself*): No! no!

(*The STEP-DAUGHTER noticing the way the LEADING MAN enters, bursts out laughing.*)

THE MANAGER (*furious*): Silence! And you please just stop that laughing. If we go on like this, we shall never finish.

THE STEP-DAUGHTER: Forgive me, sir, but it's natural enough. This lady (*indicating LEADING LADY*) stands there still; but if she is supposed to be me, I can assure you that if I heard anyone say "Good afternoon" in that manner and in that tone, I should burst out laughing as I did.

THE FATHER: Yes, yes, the manner, the tone . . .

THE MANAGER: Nonsense! Rubbish! Stand aside and let me see the action.

LEADING MAN: If I've got to represent an old fellow who's coming into a house of an equivocal character . . .

THE MANAGER: Don't listen to them, for Heaven's sake! Do it again! It goes fine. (*Waiting for the* ACTORS *to begin again.*) Well?

LEADING MAN: Good afternoon, Miss.

LEADING LADY: Good afternoon.

LEADING MAN (*imitating the gesture of the* FATHER *when he looked under the hat, and then expressing quite clearly first satisfaction and then fear*): Ah, but . . . I say . . . this is not the first time that you have come here, is it?

THE MANAGER: Good, but not quite so heavily. Like this. (*acts himself*) "This isn't the first time that you have come here" . . . (*to* LEADING LADY) And you say: "No, sir."

LEADING LADY: No, sir.

LEADING MAN: You've been here before, more than once.

THE MANAGER: No, no, stop! Let her nod "yes" first. "You've been here before, eh?" (*The* LEADING LADY *lifts up her head slightly and closes her eyes as though in disgust. Then* SHE *inclines her head twice.*)

THE STEP-DAUGHTER (*unable to contain herself*): Oh my God! (*puts a hand to her mouth to prevent herself from laughing.*)

THE MANAGER (*turning round*): What's the matter?

THE STEP-DAUGHTER: Nothing, nothing!

THE MANAGER (*to* LEADING MAN): Go on!

LEADING MAN: You've been here before, eh? Well then, there's no need to be so shy, is there? May I take off your hat?

(*The* LEADING MAN *says this last speech in such a tone and with such gestures that the* STEP-DAUGHTER, *though she has her hand to her mouth, cannot keep from laughing.*)

LEADING LADY (*indignant*): I'm not going to stop here to be made a fool of by that woman there.

LEADING MAN: Neither am I! I'm through with it!

THE MANAGER (*shouting to* STEP-DAUGHTER): Silence! for once and all, I tell you!

THE STEP-DAUGHTER: Forgive me! forgive me!

THE MANAGER: You haven't any manners: that's what it is! You go too far.

THE FATHER (*endeavouring to intervene*): Yes, it's true, but excuse her . . .

THE MANAGER: Excuse what? It's absolutely disgusting.

THE FATHER: Yes, sir, but believe me, it has such a strange effect when . . .

THE MANAGER: Strange? Why strange? Where is it strange?

THE FATHER: No, sir; I admire your actors — this gentleman here, this lady; but they are certainly not us!

THE MANAGER: I should hope not. Evidently they cannot be you, if they are actors.

THE FATHER: Just so: actors! Both of them act our parts exceedingly well. But, believe me, it produces quite a different effect on us. They want to be us, but they aren't, all the same.

THE MANAGER: What is it then anyway?

THE FATHER: Something that is . . . that is theirs — and no longer ours . . .

THE MANAGER: But naturally, inevitably. I've told you so already.

THE FATHER: Yes, I understand . . . I understand . . .

THE MANAGER: Well then, let's have no more of it! (*turning to the* ACTORS) We'll have the rehearsals by ourselves, afterwards, in the ordinary way. I never could stand rehearsing with the author present. He's never satisfied! (*turning to* FATHER *and* STEP-DAUGHTER) Come on! Let's get on with it again; and try and see if you can't keep from laughing.

THE STEP-DAUGHTER: Oh, I shan't laugh any more. There's a nice little bit coming for me now: you'll see.

THE MANAGER: Well then: when she says "Don't think any more of what I've said. I must forget, etc.," you (*addressing the* FATHER) come in sharp with "I understand, I understand"; and then you ask her . . .

THE STEP-DAUGHTER (*interrupting*): What?

THE MANAGER: Why she is in mourning.

THE STEP-DAUGHTER: Not at all! See here: when I told him that it was useless for me to be thinking about my wearing mourning, do you know how he answered me? "Ah well," he said, "then let's take off this little frock."

THE MANAGER: Great! Just what we want, to make a riot in the theatre!

THE STEP-DAUGHTER: But it's the truth!

THE MANAGER: What does that matter? Acting is our business here. Truth up to a certain point, but no further.

THE STEP-DAUGHTER: What do you want to do then?

THE MANAGER: You'll see, you'll see! Leave it to me.

THE STEP-DAUGHTER: No sir! What you want to do is to piece together a little romantic sentimental scene out of my disgust, out of all the reasons, each more cruel and viler than the other, why I am what I am. He is to ask me why I'm in mourning; and I'm to answer with tears in my eyes, that it is just two months since papa died. No sir, no! He's got to say to me; as he did say: "Well, let's take off this little dress at once." And I; with my two months' mourning in my heart, went there behind that screen, and with these fingers tingling with shame . . .

THE MANAGER (*running his hands through his hair*): For Heaven's sake! What are you saying?

THE STEP-DAUGHTER (*crying out excitedly*): The truth! The truth!

THE MANAGER: It may be. I don't deny it, and I can understand all your horror; but you must surely see that you can't have this kind of thing on the stage. It won't go.

THE STEP-DAUGHTER: Not possible, eh? Very well! I'm much obliged to you — but I'm off!

THE MANAGER: Now be reasonable! Don't lose your temper!

THE STEP-DAUGHTER: I won't stop here! I won't! I can see you've fixed it all up with him in your office. All this talk about what is possible for the stage . . . I understand! He wants to get at his complicated "cerebral drama," to have his famous remorses and torments acted; but I want to act my part, *my part!*

THE MANAGER (*annoyed, shaking his shoulders*): Ah! Just *your* part! But, if you will pardon me, there are other parts than yours: His (*indicating the* FATHER) and hers! (*indicating the* MOTHER) On the stage you can't have a character becoming too prominent and overshadowing all the others. The thing is to pack them all into a neat little framework and then act what is actable. I am aware of the fact that everyone has his own interior life which he wants very much to put forward. But the difficulty lies in this fact: to set out just so much as is necessary for the stage, taking the other characters into consideration, and at the same time hint at the unrevealed interior life of each. I am willing to admit, my dear young lady, that from your point of view it would be a fine idea if each character could tell the public all his troubles in a nice monologue or a regular one hour lecture. (*good humoredly*) You must restrain yourself, my dear, and in your own interest, too; because this fury of yours, this exaggerated disgust you show, may make a bad impression, you know. After you have confessed to me that there were others before him at Madame Pace's and more than once . . .

THE STEP-DAUGHTER (*bowing her head, im-*

pressed): It's true. But remember those others mean him for me all the same.

THE MANAGER (*not understanding*):What? The others? What do you mean?

THE STEP-DAUGHTER: For one who has gone wrong, sir, he who was responsible for the first fault is responsible for all that follow. He is responsible for my faults, was, even before I was born. Look at him, and see if it isn't true!

THE MANAGER: Well, well! And does the weight of so much responsibility seem nothing to you? Give him a chance to act it, to get it over!

THE STEP-DAUGHTER: How? How can he act all his "noble remorses," all his "moral torments," if you want to spare him the horror of being discovered one day — after he had asked her what he did ask her — in the arms of her, that already fallen woman, that child, sir, that child he used to watch come out of school? (SHE *is moved*.)

(*The* MOTHER *at this point is overcome with emotion, and breaks out into a fit of crying. ALL are touched. A long pause.*)

THE STEP-DAUGHTER (*as soon as the* MOTHER *becomes a little quieter, adds resolutely and gravely*): At present, we are unknown to the public. Tomorrow, you will act us as you wish, treating us in your own manner. But do you really want to see drama, do you want to see it flash out as it really did?

THE MANAGER: Of course! That's just what I do want, so I can use as much of it as is possible.

THE STEP-DAUGHTER: Well then, ask that Mother there to leave us.

THE MOTHER (*changing her low plaint into a sharp cry*): No! No! Don't permit it, sir, don't permit it!

THE MANAGER: But it's only to try it.

THE MOTHER: I can't bear it. I can't.

THE MANAGER: But since it has happened already . . . I don't understand!

THE MOTHER: It's taking place now. It happens all the time. My torment isn't a pretended one. I live and feel every minute of my torture. Those two children there — have you heard them speak? They can't speak any more. They cling to me to keep up my torment actual and vivid for me. But for themselves, they do not exist, they aren't any more. And she (*indicating the* STEP-DAUGHTER) has run away, she has left me, and is lost. If I now see her here before me, it is only to renew for me the tortures I have suffered for her too.

THE FATHER: The eternal moment! She (*indicating the* STEP-DAUGHTER) is here to catch me, fix me, and hold me eternally in the stocks for that one fleeting and shameful moment of my life. She can't give it up! And you sir, cannot either fairly spare me it.

THE MANAGER: I never said I didn't want to act it. It will form, as a matter of fact, the nucleus of the whole first act right up to her surprise. (*indicates the* MOTHER.)

THE FATHER: Just so! This is my punishment: the passion in all of us that must culminate in her final cry.

THE STEP-DAUGHTER: I can hear it still in my ears. It's driven me mad, that cry! — You can put me on as you like; it doesn't matter. Fully dressed, if you like — provided I have at least the arm bare; because, standing like this (*She goes close to the* FATHER *and leans her head on his breast.*) with my head so, and my arms round his neck, I saw a vein pulsing in my arm here; and then, as if that live vein had awakened disgust in me, I closed my eyes like this, and let my head sink on his breast. (*turning to the* MOTHER.) Cry out mother! Cry out! (*buries head in* FATHER'S *breast, and with her shoulders raised as if to prevent her hearing the cry, adds in tones of intense emotion.*) Cry out as you did then!

THE MOTHER (*coming forward to separate them*): No! My daughter, my daughter! (*and after having pulled her away from him*) You brute! you brute! She is my daughter! Don't you see she's my daughter?

THE MANAGER (*walking backwards towards footlights*): Fine! fine! Damned good! And then, of course — curtain!

THE FATHER (*going towards him excitedly*): Yes, of course, because that's the way it really happened.

THE MANAGER (*convinced and pleased*): Oh, yes, no doubt about it. Curtain here, curtain!

(*At the reiterated cry of the* MANAGER, *the* MACHINIST *lets the curtain down, leaving the* MANAGER *and the* FATHER *in front of it before the footlights.*)

THE MANAGER: The darned idiot! I said "curtain" to show the act should end there, and he goes and lets it down in earnest. (*to the* FATHER, *while he pulls the curtain back to go on to the stage again.*) Yes, yes, it's all right. Effect certain! That's the right ending. I'll guarantee the first act at any rate.

ACT THREE

When the curtain goes up again, it is seen that the stage hands have shifted the bit of scenery used in the last part, and have rigged up instead at the back of the stage a drop, with some trees, and one or two wings. A portion of a fountain basin is visible. The MOTHER *is sitting on the right with the two children by her side. The* SON *is on the same side, but away from the others. He seems bored, angry, and full of shame. The* FATHER *and the* STEP-DAUGHTER *are also seated towards the right front. On the other side (left) are the* ACTORS, *much in the positions they occupied before the curtain was lowered. Only the* MANAGER *is standing up in the middle of the stage, with his hand closed over his mouth in the act of meditating.*

THE MANAGER (*shaking his shoulders after a brief pause*): Ah yes: the second act! Leave it to me, leave it all to me as we arranged, and you'll see! It'll go fine!

THE STEP-DAUGHTER: Our entry into his house (*indicates* FATHER) in spite of him . . . (*indicates the* SON)

THE MANAGER (*out of patience*): Leave it to me, I tell you!

THE STEP-DAUGHTER: Do let it be clear, at any rate, that it is in spite of my wishes.

THE MOTHER (*from her corner, shaking her head*): For all the good that's come of it . . .

THE STEP-DAUGHTER (*turning towards her quickly*): It doesn't matter. The more harm done us, the more remorse for him.

THE MANAGER (*impatiently*): I understand! Good Heavens! I understand! I'm taking it into account.

THE MOTHER (*supplicatingly*): I beg you, sir, to let it appear quite plain that for conscience' sake I did try in every way . . .

THE STEP-DAUGHTER (*interrupting indignantly and continuing for the* MOTHER): . . . to pacify me, to dissuade me from spiting him. (*to* MANAGER) Do as she wants: satisfy her, because it is true! I enjoy it immensely. Anyhow, as you can see, the meeker she is, the more she tries to get at his heart, the more distant and aloof does he become.

THE MANAGER: Are we going to begin this second act or not?

THE STEP-DAUGHTER: I'm not going to talk any more now. But I must tell you this: you can't have the whole action take place in the garden, as you suggest. It isn't possible!

THE MANAGER: Why not?

THE STEP-DAUGHTER: Because he (*indicates the* SON *again*) is always shut up alone in his room. And then there's all the part of that poor dazed-looking boy there which takes place indoors.

THE MANAGER: Maybe! On the other hand, you will understand — we can't change scenes three or four times in one act.

THE LEADING MAN: They used to once.

THE MANAGER: Yes, when the public was up to the level of that child there.

THE LEADING LADY: It makes the illusion easier.

THE FATHER (*irritated*): The illusion! For Heaven's sake, don't say illusion. Please don't use that word, which is particularly painful for us.

THE MANAGER (*astounded*): And why, if you please?

THE FATHER: It's painful, cruel, really cruel; and you ought to understand that.

THE MANAGER: But why? What ought we to say then? The illusion, I tell you, sir, which we've got to create for the audience . . .

THE LEADING MAN: With our acting.

THE MANAGER: The illusion of a reality.

THE FATHER: I understand; but you, perhaps, do not understand us. Forgive me! You see . . . here for you and your actors, the thing is only — and rightly so . . . a kind of game . . .

THE LEADING LADY (*interrupting indignantly*): A game! We're not children here, if you please! We are serious actors.

THE FATHER: I don't deny it. What I mean is the game, or play, of your art, which has to give, as the gentleman says, a perfect illusion of reality.

THE MANAGER: Precisely — !

THE FATHER: Now, if you consider the fact that we (*indicates himself and the other five* CHARACTERS), as we are, have no other reality outside of this illusion . . .

THE MANAGER (*astonished, looking at his* ACTORS, *who are also amazed*): And what does that mean?

THE FATHER (*after watching them for a moment with a wan smile*): As I say, sir, that which is a game of art for you is our sole reality. (*Brief pause. He goes a step or two nearer the* MANAGER *and adds*) But not only for us, you know, by the way. Just you think it over well. (*Looks him in the eyes.*) Can you tell me who you are?

THE MANAGER (*perplexed, half smiling*): What? Who am I? I am myself.

THE FATHER: And if I were to tell you that that isn't true, because you and I . . . ?

THE MANAGER: I should say you were mad — ! (*The* ACTORS *laugh.*)

THE FATHER: You're quite right to laugh: be-cause we are all making believe here. (*to* MANAGER) And you can therefore object that it's only for a joke that that gentleman there (*indicates the* LEADING MAN), who naturally is himself, has to be me, who am on the contrary myself — this thing you see here. You see I've caught you in a trap! (*The* ACTORS *laugh.*)

THE MANAGER (*annoyed*): But we've had all this over once before. Do you want to begin again?

THE FATHER: No, no! That wasn't my meaning! In fact, I should like to request you to aban-don this game of art (*looking at the* LEADING LADY *as if anticipating her*) which you are accustomed to play here with your actors, and to ask you seriously once again: who are you?

THE MANAGER (*astonished and irritated, turn-ing to his* ACTORS): If this fellow here hasn't got a nerve! A man who calls himself a character comes and asks me who I am!

THE FATHER (*with dignity, but not offended*): A character, sir, may always ask a man who he is. Because a character has really a life of his own, marked with his especial charac-teristics; for which reason he is always "somebody." But a man — I'm not speaking of you now — may very well be "nobody."

THE MANAGER: Yes, but you are asking these questions of me, the boss, the manager! Do you understand?

THE FATHER: But only in order to know if you, as you really are now, see yourself as you once were with all the illusions that were yours then, with all the things both inside and outside of you as they seemed to you — as they were then indeed for you. Well, sir, if you think of all those illusions that mean nothing to you now, of all those things which don't even *seem* to you to exist any more, while once they *were* for you, don't you feel that — I won't say these boards — but the very earth under your feet is sinking away from you when you reflect that in the same way this *you* as you feel it today — all this present reality of yours — is fated to seem a mere illusion to you tomorrow?

THE MANAGER (*without having understood much, but astonished by the specious argument*): Well, well! And where does all this take us anyway?

THE FATHER: Oh, nowhere! It's only to show you that if we (*indicating the* CHARACTERS) have no other reality beyond the illusion, you too must not count overmuch on your reality as you feel it today, since, like that of yesterday, it may prove an illusion for you tomorrow.

THE MANAGER (*determining to make fun of him*): Ah, excellent! Then you'll be saying next that you, with this comedy of yours that you brought here to act, are truer and more real than I am.

THE FATHER (*with the greatest seriousness*): But of course; without doubt!

THE MANAGER: Ah, really?

THE FATHER: Why, I thought you'd understand that from the beginning.

THE MANAGER: More real than I?

THE FATHER: If your reality can change from one day to another . . .

THE MANAGER: But everyone knows it can change. It is always changing, the same as anyone else's.

THE FATHER (*with a cry*): No, sir, not ours! Look here! That is the very difference! Our reality doesn't change: it can't change! It can't be other than what it is, because it is already fixed for ever. It's terrible. Ours is an immutable reality which should make you shudder when you approach us if you are really conscious of the fact that your reality is a mere transitory and fleeting illusion, taking this form today and that tomorrow, according to the conditions, according to your will, your sentiments, which in turn are controlled by an intellect that shows them to you today in one manner and tomorrow . . . who knows how? . . . Illusions of reality represented in this fatuous comedy of life that never ends, nor can ever end! Because if tomorrow it were to end . . . then why, all would be finished.

THE MANAGER: Oh for God's sake, will you *at least* finish with this philosophizing and let us try and shape this comedy which you yourself have brought me here? You argue and philosophize a bit too much, my dear sir. You know you seem to me almost, almost . . . (*stops and looks him over from head to foot.*) Ah, by the way, I think you introduced yourself to me as a — what shall . . . we say — a "character," created by an author who did not afterward care to make a drama of his own creations.

THE FATHER: It is the simple truth, sir.

THE MANAGER: Nonsense! Cut that out, please! None of us believes it, because it isn't a thing, as you must recognize yourself, which one can believe seriously. If you want to know, it seems to me you are trying to imitate the manner of a certain author whom I heartily detest — I warn you — although I have unfortunately bound myself to put on one of his works. As a matter of fact, I was just starting to rehearse it, when you arrived. (*turning to the* ACTORS) And this is what we've gained — out of the frying-pan into the fire!

THE FATHER: I don't know to what author you may be alluding, but believe me I feel what I think; and I seem to be philosophizing only for those who do not think what they feel, because they blind themselves with their own sentiment. I know that for many people this self-blinding seems much more "human"; but the contrary is really true. For man never reasons so much and becomes so introspective as when he suffers; since he is anxious to get at the cause of his sufferings, to learn who has produced them, and whether it is just or unjust that he should have to bear them. On the other hand, when he is happy, he takes his happiness as it comes and doesn't analyze it, just as if happiness were his right. The animals suffer without reasoning about their sufferings. But take the case of a man who suffers and begins to reason about it. Oh no! it can't be allowed! Let him suffer like an animal, and then — ah yet, he is "human"!

THE MANAGER: Look here! Look here! You're off again, philosophizing worse than ever.

THE FATHER: Because I suffer, sir! I'm not philosophizing: I'm crying aloud the reason of my sufferings.

THE MANAGER (*makes brusque movement as he is taken with a new idea*): I should like to know if anyone has ever heard of a character who gets right out of his part and perorates and speechifies as you do. Have you ever heard of a case? I haven't.

THE FATHER: You have never met such a case, sir, because authors, as a rule, hide the labour of their creations. When the characters are really alive before their author, the latter does nothing but follow them in their action, in their words, in the situations which they suggest to him; and he has to will them the way they will themselves — for there's trouble if he doesn't. When a character is born, he acquires at once such an independence, even of his own author, that he can be imagined by everybody even in many other situations where the author never dreamed of placing him; and so he acquires for himself a meaning which the author never thought of giving him.

THE MANAGER: Yes, yes, I know this.

THE FATHER: What is there then to marvel at in us? Imagine such a misfortune for characters as I have described to you: to be born of an author's fantasy, and be denied life by him; and then answer me if these characters left alive, and yet without life, weren't right in doing what they did do and are doing now, after they have attempted everything in their power to persuade him to give them their stage life. We've all tried him in turn, I, she (*indicating the* STEP-DAUGHTER) and she. (*indicating the* MOTHER.)

THE STEP-DAUGHTER: It's true. I too have sought to tempt him, many, many times, when he has been sitting at his writing table, feeling a bit melancholy, at the twilight hour. He would sit in his armchair too lazy to switch on the light, and all the shadows that crept into his room were full of our presence com-ing to tempt him. (*as if she saw herself still there by the writing table, and was annoyed by the presence of the* ACTORS) Oh, if you would only go away, go away and leave us alone — mother here with that son of hers — I with that Child — that Boy there always alone — and then I with him (*just hints at the* FATHER) — and then I alone, alone . . . in those shadows! (*makes a sudden movement as if in the vision she has of herself illuminating those shadows she wanted to seize hold of herself*) Ah! my life! my life! Oh, what scenes we proposed to him — and I tempted him more than any of the others!

THE FATHER: Maybe. But perhaps it was your fault that he refused to give us life: because you were too insistent, too troublesome.

THE STEP-DAUGHTER: Nonsense! Didn't he make me so himself? (*goes close to the* MANAGER *to tell him as if in confidence*) In my opinion he abandoned us in a fit of depression, of disgust for the ordinary theatre as the public knows it and likes it.

THE SON: Exactly what it was, sir; exactly that!

THE FATHER: Not at all! Don't believe it for a minute. Listen to me! You'll be doing quite right to modify, as you suggest, the excesses both of this girl here, who wants to do too much, and of this young man, who won't do anything at all.

THE SON: No, nothing!

THE MANAGER: You too get over the mark occasionally, my dear sir, if I may say so.

THE FATHER: I? When? Where?

THE MANAGER: Always! Continuously! Then there's this insistence of yours in trying to make us believe you are a character. And then too, you must really argue and philo-sophize less, you know, much less.

THE FATHER: Well, if you want to take away from me the possibility of representing the torment of my spirit which never gives me peace, you will be suppressing me: that's all. Every true man, sir, who is a little above the level of the beasts and plants does not live for the sake of living, without knowing how to live; but he lives so as to give a meaning and a value of his own to life. For me this is *everything*. I cannot give up this, just to represent a mere fact as she (*indicating the* STEP-DAUGHTER) wants. It's all very well for her, since her "vendetta" lies in the "fact." I'm not going to do it. It destroys my *raison d'être*.

THE MANAGER: Your *raison d'être!* Oh, we're going ahead fine! First she starts off, and then you jump in. At this rate, we'll never finish.

THE FATHER: Now, don't be offended! Have it your own way — provided, however, that within the limits of the parts you assign us each one's sacrifice isn't too great.

THE MANAGER: You've got to understand that you can't go on arguing at your own pleasure. Drama is action, sir, action and not confounded philosophy.

THE FATHER: All right. I'll do just as much arguing and philosophizing as everybody does when he is considering his own torments.

THE MANAGER: If the drama permits! But for Heaven's sake, man, let's get along and come to the scene.

THE STEP-DAUGHTER: It seems to me we've got too much action with our coming into his house. (*indicating* FATHER) You said, before, you couldn't change the scene every five minutes.

THE MANAGER: Of course not. What we've got to do is to combine and group up all the facts in one simultaneous, close-knit, action. We can't have it as you want, with your little brother wandering like a ghost from room to room, hiding behind doors and meditating a project which — what did you say it did to him?

THE STEP-DAUGHTER: Consumes him, sir, wastes him away!

THE MANAGER: Well, it may be. And then at the same time, you want the little girl there to be playing in the garden . . . one in the house, and the other in the garden: isn't that it?

THE STEP-DAUGHTER: Yes, in the sun, in the sun! That is my only pleasure: to see her happy and careless in the garden after the misery and squalor of the horrible room where we all four slept together. And I had to sleep with her — I, do you understand? — with my vile contaminated body next to hers; with her holding me fast in her loving little arms. In the garden, whenever she spied me, she would run to take me by the hand. She didn't care for the big flowers, only the little ones; and she loved to show me them and pet me.

THE MANAGER: Well then, we'll have it in the garden. Everything shall happen in the garden; and we'll group the other scenes there. (*calls a* STAGE HAND) Here, a back-cloth with trees and something to do as a fountain basin. (*turning round to look at the back of the stage*) Ah, you've fixed it up. Good! (*to* STEP-DAUGHTER) This is just to give an idea, of course. The Boy, instead of hiding behind the doors, will wander about here in the garden, hiding behind the trees. But it's going to be rather difficult to find a child to do that scene with you where she shows you the flowers. (*turning to the* BOY) Come forward a little, will you please? Let's try it now! Come along! come along! (*Then seeing him come shyly forward, full of fear and looking lost.*) It's a nice business, this lad here. What's the matter with him? We'll have to give him a word or two to say. (*Goes close to him, puts a hand on his shoulders, and leads him behind one of the trees.*) Come on! come on! Let me see you a little! Hide here . . . yes, like that. Try and show your head just a little as if you were looking for someone . . . (*Goes back to observe the effect, when the* BOY *at once goes through the action.*) Excellent! fine! (*turning to* STEP-DAUGHTER) Suppose the little girl there were to surprise him as he looks round, and run over to him, so we could give him a word or two to say?

THE STEP-DAUGHTER: It's useless to hope he will speak, as long as that fellow there is here . . . (*indicates the* SON) You must send him away first.

THE SON (*jumping up*): Delighted! Delighted! I don't ask for anything better. (*Begins to move away.*)

THE MANAGER (*at once stopping him*): No! No! Where are you going? Wait a bit!

(*The* MOTHER *gets up alarmed and terrified at the thought that he is really about to go away. Instinctively she lifts her arms to prevent him, without, however, leaving her seat.*)

THE SON (*to* MANAGER *who stops him*): I've got nothing to do with this affair. Let me go please! Let me go!

THE MANAGER: What do you mean by saying you've got nothing to do with this?

THE STEP-DAUGHTER (*calmly, with irony*): Don't bother to stop him: he won't go away.

THE FATHER: He has to act the terrible scene in the garden with his mother.

THE SON (*suddenly resolute and with dignity*): I shall act nothing at all. I've said so from the very beginning. (*to the* MANAGER) Let me go!

THE STEP-DAUGHTER (*going over to the* MANAGER): Allow me? (*Puts down the* MANAGER'S *arm which is restraining the* SON.) Well, go away then, if you want to! (*The* SON *looks at her with contempt and hatred. She laughs and says*) You see, he can't, he can't go away! He is obliged to stay here, indissolubly bound to the chain. If I, who fly off when that happens which has to happen, because I can't bear him — if I am still here and support that face and expression of his, you can well imagine that he is unable to move. He has to remain here, has to stop with that nice father of his, and that mother whose only son he is. (*turning to the* MOTHER) Come on, mother, come along! (*turning to* MANAGER *to indicate her*) You see, she was getting up to keep him back. (*to the* MOTHER, *beckoning her with her hand.*) Come on! come on! (*then to* MANAGER) You can imagine how little she wants to show these actors of yours what she really feels; but so eager is she to

get near him that . . . There, you see? She is willing to act her part. (*And in fact, the* MOTHER *approaches him; and as soon as the* STEP-DAUGHTER *has finished speaking, opens her arms to signify that she consents.*)

THE SON (*suddenly*): No! no! If I can't go away, then I'll stop here; but I repeat: I act nothing!

THE FATHER (*to* MANAGER *excitedly*): You can force him, sir.

THE SON: Nobody can force me.

THE FATHER: I can.

THE STEP-DAUGHTER: Wait a minute, wait . . . First of all, the baby has to go to the fountain . . . (*runs to take the* CHILD *and leads her to the fountain.*)

THE MANAGER: Yes, yes of course; that's it. Both at the same time.

(*The second* LADY LEAD *and the* JUVENILE LEAD *at this point separate themselves from the group of* ACTORS. *One watches the* MOTHER *attentively; the other moves about studying the movements and manner of the* SON *whom he will have to act.*)

THE SON (*to* MANAGER): What do you mean by both at the same time? It isn't right. There was no scene between me and her. (*indicates the* MOTHER) Ask her how it was!

THE MOTHER: Yes, it's true. I had come into his room . . .

THE SON: Into my room, do you understand? Nothing to do with the garden.

THE MANAGER: It doesn't matter. Haven't I told you we've got to group the action?

THE SON (*observing the* JUVENILE LEAD *studying him*): What do you want?

THE JUVENILE LEAD: Nothing! I was just looking at you.

THE SON (*turning towards the second* LADY LEAD): Ah! she's at it too: to re-act her part! (*indicating the* MOTHER.)

THE MANAGER: Exactly! And it seems to me

that you ought to be grateful to them for their interest.

THE SON: Yes, but haven't you yet perceived that it isn't possible to live in front of a mirror which not only freezes us with the image of ourselves, but throws our likeness back at us with a horrible grimace?

THE FATHER: That is true, absolutely true. You must see that.

THE MANAGER (to second LADY LEAD and JUVENILE LEAD): He's right! Move away from them!

THE SON: Do as you like. I'm out of this!

THE MANAGER: Be quiet, you, will you? And let me hear your mother! (to MOTHER) You were saying you had entered . . .

THE MOTHER: Yes, into his room, because I couldn't stand it any longer. I went to empty my heart to him of all the anguish that tortures me . . . But as soon as he saw me come in . . .

THE SON: Nothing happened! There was no scene. I went away, that's all! I don't care for scenes!

THE MOTHER: It's true, true. That's how it was.

THE MANAGER: Well now, we've got to do this bit between you and him. It's indispensable.

THE MOTHER: I'm ready . . . when you are ready. If you could only find a chance for me to tell him what I feel here in my heart.

THE FATHER (going to SON in a great rage): You'll do this for your mother, for your mother, do you understand?

THE SON (quite determined): I do nothing!

THE FATHER (taking hold of him and shaking him): For God's sake, do as I tell you! Don't you hear your mother asking you for a favor? Haven't you even got the guts to be a son?

THE SON (taking hold of the FATHER): No! No! And for God's sake stop it, or else . . . (General agitation. The MOTHER, frightened, tries to separate them.)

THE MOTHER (pleading): Please! please!

THE FATHER (not leaving hold of the SON): You've got to obey, do you hear?

THE SON (almost crying from rage): What does it mean, this madness you've got? (They separate.) Have you no decency, that you insist on showing everyone our shame? I won't do it! I won't! And I stand for the will of our author in this. He didn't want to put us on the stage, after all!

THE MANAGER: Man alive! You came here . . .

THE SON (indicating FATHER): He did! I didn't!

THE MANAGER: Aren't you here now?

THE SON: It was his wish, and he dragged us along with him. He's told you not only the things that did happen, but also things that have never happened at all.

THE MANAGER: Well, tell me then what did happen. You went out of your room without saying a word?

THE SON: Without a word, so as to avoid a scene!

THE MANAGER: And then what did you do?

THE SON: Nothing . . . walking in the garden . . . (Hesitates for a moment with expression of gloom.)

THE MANAGER (coming closer to him, interested by his extraordinary reserve): Well, well . . . walking in the garden . . .

THE SON (exasperated): Why on earth do you insist? It's horrible! (The MOTHER trembles, sobs, and looks towards the fountain.)

THE MANAGER (slowly observing the glance and turning towards the SON with increasing apprehension): The baby?

THE SON: There in the fountain . . .

THE FATHER (pointing with tender pity to the MOTHER): She was following him at the moment . . .

THE MANAGER (to the SON anxiously): And then you . . .

THE SON: I ran over to her; I was jumping in to

drag her out when I saw something that froze my blood . . . the boy standing stock still, with eyes like a madman's, watching his little drowned sister, in the fountain! (*The* STEP-DAUGHTER *bends over the fountain to hide the* CHILD. *She sobs.*) Then . . . (*A revolver shot rings out behind the trees where the* BOY *is hidden.*)

THE MOTHER (*with a cry of terror runs over in that direction together with several of the* ACTORS *amid general confusion*): My son! My son! (*Then amid the cries and exclamations one hears her voice.*) Help! Help!

THE MANAGER (*pushing the* ACTORS *aside while*

THEY *lift up the* BOY *and carry him off*): Is he really wounded?

SOME ACTORS: He's dead! dead!

OTHER ACTORS: No, no, it's only make believe, it's only pretence!

THE FATHER (*with a terrible cry*): Pretence? Reality, sir, reality!

THE MANAGER: Pretence? Reality? To hell with it all! Never in my life has such a thing happened to me. I've lost a whole day over these people, a whole day!

CURTAIN

The Threepenny Opera

Bertolt Brecht (1898–1956) was probably Germany's greatest dramatist, certainly its most socially concerned one. He turned his poetic gifts to propaganda and in 1928 he established his reputation as the author of *Dreigroschenoper*, with music by Kurt Weill (1900–1950), adapting Gay's *The Beggar's Opera* to criticize the evils in German society just before Hitler. Though he set the play in Victorian London, his mordant satire was directed straight at the German audience and he hoped to keep them alert to its message and convince them to act upon it by the devices of what he called "epic" (or "narrative") theatre. Where the Aristotelian or regular theatre involved the spectator in the action, made him feel with the characters, created empathy and illusion, the Epic Theatre of Brecht dealt in *Verfremdung* ("alienation"): it attempted to keep the spectator aware of the ideas presented in a narrative way, constantly judging them, eventually acting on them, his feelings transformed into realizations and his understanding into decisions to act. The old theatre, as Brecht saw it, assumed that man was known and unalterable; Brecht wanted to examine him and to find ways of changing him. Eschewing the organic development of Aristotelian "imitations of an action," Brecht presented a montage of ideas, a series of discrete episodes, illustrations for his argument which made sudden leaps, not connections, between things. His polemics were supposed to appeal because they touched the reason, not the heart. He wanted the spectators to remain aware that they were in the theatre, not to lose themselves out there in the dark but to "awaken their energy" and to leave the theatre not purged but charged.

The whole subject of "epic realism" is complicated enough and interesting enough to warrant an extended discussion and, for that purpose, the play is prefaced by an article from *Modern Language Quarterly* by Heinz Politzer. You will see from this article how scholars relate one play by a dramatist to others and how they determine and discuss patterns in a playwright's work. Though you may be unfamiliar with other plays mentioned in the text, Politzer's descriptions will make them clear enough and his whole argument will cast *The Threepenny Opera* into a new light. It will help the student in understanding the technique of a great dramatist whom Harold Clurman in *Lies Like Truth* (1958) described this way:

> Brecht is a classicist. He seeks that form of artistic truth which emphasizes the thing created above the creator, a manner which allows the spectator

to appreciate the play with that repose and refinement of attention which liberate the spirit without drugging the senses. Brecht's programmatic antiromanticism is against art as magic as it is against faith as superstition. But, more deeply, Brecht's technique is a form of discipline undertaken by the artist to convey as devotedly and self-abnegatingly as possible his perception of reality. The goal is wisdom rather than excitement. It has always been the aspiration of the highest art.

In the end, after thinking about Brecht and his work, you may conclude that Brecht is great because he is a poet, despite his propaganda; that his genius overrides his technique and makes him succeed in spite of his theories, rather than because of them; that he touches the emotions even as he speaks to the reason; and that, above all, in his skill he enhances, whether he wishes to or not, the magic of the theatrical illusion and makes his puppets live for us.

How Epic Is Bertolt Brecht's Epic Theater?
HEINZ POLITZER

When Bertolt died in East Berlin, on August 14, 1956, he left behind an impressive literary work, a new method of producing and acting plays, as well as a theory of the drama. Even his enemies admit that his better poetry and drama has made an impact on the contemporary literary scene. However, his most ardent admirers cannot close their eyes to the often fantastic unevenness of his performance as a writer. He was as erratic as the era of revolution and war which he witnessed and depicted. Since he saw himself living in the "jungle of cities," he more than once adopted the law of the jungle as an aesthetic principle.

He succeeded, to some degree. Today, nearly six years after his death, Brecht's theatrical style is being perpetuated by the Berlin Ensemble am Schiffbauerdamm.

There the actress Helene Weigel, Brecht's widow, guards the practical techniques and theoretical policies which Brecht developed for modern stage production. Guest performances around Western Europe have established the fame of the Brecht troupe as a potent germinating force in the theater of today. To be sure, this style — which is both austere and grotesque — has remained a very personal achievement of its creator and defies any easy imitation. Therefore, Brecht's followers have to rely on his theory, the idea of the epic theater.

Brecht claimed that his idea was universally valid. "Modern theater is epic theater," he announced as early as 1930 when, still gropingly, he sketched the general principles of his theory in the notes to the opera, *Rise and Fall of the Town of*

Mahagonny.[1] After his return, twenty-five years later, from an exile which had driven him across half the globe, he asked more modestly: "Is it possible to reproduce the modern world in the theater?" To this he answered:

> I have (before me) all the possibilities but I cannot say that the dramaturgical ideas which I . . . call non-Aristotelian, and the epic manner of acting they entail, represent the one and only solution. However, one thing has become clear: the modern world can be described to modern men only when it is described as an alterable world.[2]

It was the old and somewhat tired Brecht who spoke; furthermore, since his statement was directed to a group of people who were discussing the theater outside of Eastern Germany, it had to be toned down considerably. Nevertheless, Brecht made it perfectly clear how he wanted the rather elastic term, "alterable world," to be understood. To him, "alterable" indicated no more nor less than the state of readiness for a change in the structure of society. Therefore, he wrote: "You will not be surprised to hear from me that I consider the question: can the world be described, to be a sociological issue."[3] Since it is Brecht in East Berlin who has raised the issue, the nature of this sociological description will be determined by Marxist theory. We know from his biography that Brecht's conversion from a bitterly exuberant anarchist to an orthodox Marxist preceded his first declaration of the principles of the epic theater by only two years. After this he was adamant in stressing the organic connection between dialectical materialism and his aesthetic theory.

No one knew better than Brecht himself that the influence of his epic theater reached much farther than the Communist countries. In fact, the activities of the Berlin Ensemble and its leader were tolerated rather than approved by the East German regime, whereas the (London) *Times Literary Supplement* — certainly no Marxist outpost — declared editorially in 1956: "The broad aims in which Brecht believes are sound and good and of general relevance: and where he sticks to them he is unmistakably a great writer."[4]

In spite of the Cold War and the Berlin crisis, we seem to be headed today for a Brecht boom as bullish as was the Kafka craze ten or fifteen years ago. For five consecutive years a not altogether authentic version of *The Threepenny Opera* had been running off Broadway, to be replaced recently by a *Brecht on Brecht* show. College and university theaters have tried their hands at *Mother Courage* and *The Caucasian Chalk Circle*. There are two full-fledged critical studies of Brecht in English,[5] and a highly ornate edition of seven of his plays has recently been published in this country by Eric Bentley.[6]

How are we to reconcile Brecht's political creed with the interest in his work which is displayed by the West? The vast majority of his critics have declared themselves firmly opposed to the political consequences he appears to draw in his didactic plays. Is it possible then that Brecht's non-Aristotelian poetics do not rest as solidly on Marxist grounds as he himself proclaimed time and again? Or do his plays continue to fascinate their audiences in spite of his theory rather than because of it? The following remarks attempt to sketch preliminary answers to both these questions.

---

1 Bertolt Brecht, *Schriften zum Theater* (Frankfurt, 1959), p. 13. Hereafter *SCH*. Translations are my own, unless otherwise indicated. 2 Ibid., p. 8. 3 *SCH*, p. 9. 4 *TLS* (March 17, 1956), p. 142. 5 John Willett, *The Theatre of Bertolt Brecht: A Study from Eight Aspects* (New York, 1959); Martin Esslin, *Brecht: The Man and His Works* (Garden City, 1960). 6 *Seven Plays by Bertolt Brecht*, edited and with an introduction by Eric Bentley (New York, 1961). Hereafter *SP*.

What is the epic theater? First and most important, it is, as Eric Bentley noted, a "misnomer."[7] It is certainly non-Aristotelian in so far as it upsets the sequence of time which Aristotle presupposed as one of the constituents of tragedy. As the early Brecht stated in the notes to *Mahagonny*, "narrative" is to replace "plot." Instead of being "a part of the whole" each scene is to be "an entity in itself," moving in "jerks" rather than in the "evolutionary necessity by which one follows from the other" (*evolutionäre Zwangsläufigkeit*).[8] But the negation of Aristotle's sequence of time does not yet turn the dramatic theater into an epic one. If Aristotle defined the epic as a narrative form in which "many events simultaneously transacted can be represented," he did not exclude coherence and consistency. The epic, Aristotle notes, "should have for its subject a single action, whole and complete, with a beginning, a middle and an end."[9] Yet this is precisely what Brecht attacked when, in the notes to *The Round Heads and the Pointed Heads* (1931–34), he demanded that "certain incidents in the play should be treated as self-contained scenes and raised — by means of inscriptions, music, and sound effects, and the actor's way of playing — above the level of the everyday, the obvious, the expected."[10] It is here that he mentions the *Verfremdungseffekt*, or Alienation Effect, which propels the spectator from a merely passive — or, as Brecht was fond of saying "culinary" — attitude into one of genuine participation. Instead of resting comfortably in his seat, the spectator is expected to take a stand, both literally and figuratively. Or, as Brecht put it, by the "culinary" theater "the audience is entangled in the action on stage," a process which is bound to "exhaust their power of action." The epic theater, on the other hand, arouses their power of action and "extorts decisions from them."[11]

It cannot be denied that some of the shock techniques of his Alienation Effect have contributed greatly to the success of his plays both am Schiffbauerdamm and off Broadway. He uses boards and streamers across the stage to indicate the time and place of the action, to give summaries of the action which is to follow (thus eliminating the "culinary" element of suspense), to contradict the action on stage (thus forcing the spectator to think for himself), or to address the audience in the way a street orator addresses a crowd. The dramatic action is suddenly and illogically interrupted by shrill songs, very often only tenuously relevant to the plot itself. Cruel gags alternate with practical jokes, which are occasionally rather sophisticated. The mechanics of the stage remain visible and function as a play outside the play.

These tricks, which follow one another in rapid succession, do not allow the spectator a moment of respite. They spread an air of excitement such as children might experience when they visit a circus. They seldom fail to impress even the connoisseur, who recognizes them as important steps in the liberation of modern theater from the limitations of realistic stagecraft. Brecht's most exciting Alienation Effect, however, lies in the human sphere. He likes to present characters who are alienated from themselves and from one another. His figures often seem to move in a vacuum where the most unexpected must be expected. Man is shown as "an animal with a peculiar smell";[12] his words belie his feelings, his deeds belie his words. The dialogue proceeds erratically, the figures bluff

---

7 *SP*, p.xxxi. 8 *SCH*, pp. 19, 20. 9 S. H. Butcher, *Aristotle's Theory of Poetry and Fine Art* (London, 1895), pp. 87, 83. 10 Bertolt Brecht, *Stücke VI* (Frankfurt, 1957), p. 221; Willett, p. 179. 11 *SCH*, p. 19. 12 Bertolt Brecht, "Vom armen B. B.," *Hundert Gedichte* (Berlin, 1952), p. 59.

each other as well as the audience. In this world without human mercy, even the good is possible — as an Alienation Effect.

Although Brecht claimed to be "the Einstein of the new stage form" [13] (thereby comparing, by implication, his non-Aristotelian drama to Einstein's non-Euclidean geometry), he was far from being the originator of a new dramaturgy. One has only to remember the epic elements in Strindberg's dream and ghost plays where the balanced construction of the realistic stage is already willfully and consciously disrupted. Reaching back into his romantic heritage, the great Swedish innovator used quite a variety of Alienation Effects but did not choose to attach any "sociological" strings to them. Strindberg, in turn, was one of the moving forces of German expressionism, in the wake of which Brecht moved along during his formative, pre-Marxist, days.

Nor was Brecht's activism foreign to the writers of the expressionist generation, who rose up in arms against their fathers and charged them with the guilt of World War I and social injustice. They too countered the passive enjoyment of art with the active demand for social Utopia. "We are against music," wrote Ludwig Rubiner in his manifesto, *Man in the Middle*, of 1917, "we are against music,— and for man's awakening to community. . . . We are against novels,— and for instruction in living; we are against dramas,— and for instruction in doing deeds; we are against images,— and for examples." [14] With this pronouncement Brecht's later declaration of principles shares one decisive aspect: he too knew very well and defined clearly what he was against. A certain ambiguity prevailed, however, when he had to declare what he was for. Let us take, for example, the following sentences from the "Little Organum for the Theater," which he published in 1948:

The ancient and medieval theaters alienated their characters by using masks of people and animals, and the Asiatic theater still uses musical and pantomimic Alienation Effects. These effects undoubtedly prevented empathy; yet the technique rested on hypnotically suggestive foundations. . . . The social aims of the ancient effects were entirely different from ours. . . . The new effects have nothing bizarre about them; it is an unscientific vision which immediately stamps the alien as bizarre. [15]

By 1948 Brecht had learned a lot about the theater, especially the Eastern one; he was quite prepared to acknowledge the existence of Alienation Effects before and outside of his epic theater — and to declare them unacceptable. But what about the "scientific" newness of his own achievements? Peachum, in *The Threepenny Opera*, considers the organization of his army of beggars. During his monologue a large board comes down from the flies bearing the inscription, IT IS MORE BLESSED TO GIVE THAN TO RECEIVE, [16] while at the same time Peachum's real intentions, which are directed toward a personal profit, become more and more apparent. Later in the play Peachum is told by his daughter Polly that she has married Mackie the Knife; she sings a song which says nothing about her marriage but instead is quite candid about her loss of innocence. While she sings, she is steeped in a most incongruous golden light. An organ is lit up. Three lights come down on a bar, and a board is lowered which spells out the very news she herself

---

13 Mordecai Gorelik, "Brecht: 'I Am the Einstein of the New Stage Form,'" *Theatre Arts*, XLI (March, 1957): 72; Willett, p. 178. 14 Quoted from Albert Soergel, *Dichtung und Dichter der Zeit*, Neue Folge. *Im Banne des Expressionismus* (Leipzig, 1925), p. 370. 15 Translated by Beatrice Gottlieb, *Accent*, XI (1951): 26. 16 *The Modern Theatre*, Eric Bentley, ed., I (Garden City, 1955): 114.

is keeping from her parents. Since they know their offspring, they catch on immediately.[17]

In the opera's finale, Mackie the Knife is saved from the gallows by the appearance, on horseback, of the corrupt John Brown, sheriff of London, who brings a completely unwarranted pardon from the queen. Peachum moralizes: "Mounted messengers from the queen come far too seldom, and if you kick a man he kicks you back again. Therefore never be too ready to oppose injustice."[18] Sense makes nonsense, and nonsense sense. The opposite is always true. But you cannot even rely on this kind of truth, for truth is set spinning around its own axis and vanishes amidst the laughter which its dizzying revolutions have evoked.

Are not these Alienation Effects bizarre? No, says Brecht, they are not; they only seem so to eyes unaccustomed to the perspectives of dialectical materialism. Yet, one can easily counter Brecht's apodictic assertion with Eric Bentley's observation that "there was a small production of *Threepenny Opera* in Russia some thirty years ago! Despite the visit of the Berlin Ensemble in 1957, the Russians are still (1960) not doing any Brecht plays."[19] Could it be that Russian eyes, adjusted as they are to the vision of dialectical materialism, miss the superb fun spread by these Alienation Effects, and for this very reason remain impervious to the epic theater as a whole?

About dialectical materialism, or "the method of the new science of society," Brecht says in the "Little Organum":

This method, in order to show how society is susceptible of change, treats social conditions as though they were "on trial" and convinces us of all their contradictions. Before this method nothing exists unless it is changing and is thus in disharmony with itself. The same is also true of the feeling, opinions, and attitudes with which people express their current modes of living together.[20]

Brecht's claim to have put social conditions "on trial" is doubtless justified. He has done so with great aplomb in his *Galileo* (1937-39), where the Inquisition of Pope Urban VIII offered an easy target and at the same time an ample arsenal of characters and artistically convincing symbols.

The same method, it may be noted, has failed him dismally in *The Resistible Ascent of Arturo Ui*, a political cartoon parodying Hitler's career, which Brecht never released for the stage and which was performed only after his death. How was it possible that the same method, based on scientific insights, should lead to such divergent results? Had he not chosen the scientific approach as a safeguard against artistic debacle? The answer may lie in the observation that in *Galileo* not only the social conditions are "on trial," but the human condition of the hero as well. To be sure, Galileo, who succumbs to the Inquisition, publicly abjures his theories, and yet gains immortality by smuggling the manuscript of his *Discorsi* out of Italy, is a dubious hero. But the very ambiguity of his character, that is, his humanity, secures him the interest of the spectators. After all, he defeats the society against which he is pitted, not by bravery, but by cunning. Western audiences have grown tired of victors, unless they are at the same time defeated, and, as G. B. Shaw has demonstrated time and again, they succumb more readily to a display of intellectual versatility than to the exhibition of character. Charles Laughton, who collaborated with Brecht in translating the script, played Galileo and could be relied upon to act out fully, as Brecht had asked him to do, the determination of this

17 Ibid., pp. 137–8. 18 Ibid., p. 192. 19 *SP*, p. xxxvii. 20 *Accent*, XI (1951): 27.

man "to find the easy way and to employ his reason in low pursuits as well as high." [21]

Galileo shares his cunning with many of Brecht's other heroes — with the judge, Azdak, in *The Caucasian Chalk Circle*, for example, or with Mother Courage — and, in the final analysis, with Bertolt Brecht himself. Walter Jens has related an incident from Brecht's high-school days which foreshadows the Alienation Effects the writer was to use later on the stage. According to this story, Brecht and a classmate were about to fail a course. Both wrote highly unsatisfactory examinations. The classmate erased a few mistakes and complained. The teacher held the bluebook against the light, discovered the erasures, and had the student expelled from school. Brecht, on the other hand, added a few red marks, complained, and proved to the teacher that he, the instructor, had committed the worst error authority can commit by making a mistake himself. The teacher conceded "clerical errors," Brecht passed the course and was saved.[22] The friend had taken the teacher's authority for granted; he felt put on trial and acted accordingly. By trying to extricate himself from his predicament, he sealed the verdict the teacher was all too ready to pronounce. Brecht, on the other hand, reversed the position by putting authority on trial. He realized that the most vulnerable spot in authority's system was its feeling of invulnerability. There he attacked and succeeded.

The professor's "social condition" determined his thinking to such an extent that he unwittingly fell into the trap the smart student had set for him. This incident anticipates the thoughts of Brecht's Mother Courage, who reflects, while the soldiers lead her son to the execution: "I think they'll let us have him. Thank goodness, they are bribable. They're no wolves, they're human and after money. . . . Cor-

ruption is our only hope. As long as there is corruption, so long will there be mild judgments, and even the innocent can survive his trial. . . ." [23] Again, it is not the accused who is on trial here. It is the accusers who are accused. Quite plausibly Mother Courage expects their "social condition" to corrupt their thinking and the bribe to save her son. Yet she miscalculates and Swiss Cheese is shot; but it happens only because Mother Courage's love was still more corruptible than the justice of the judges, and her greed for money had dwarfed theirs. She forgot that she, too, was "on trial."

Brecht, however, never forgot. In 1934 he composed a pamphlet which was to be distributed illegally throughout Hitler's Germany. He called it "Five Difficulties Incurred while Writing the Truth," and prefaced it with the following sentences:

> He who wants today to fight ignorance and to write the truth, has to overcome at least five difficulties. He must have the *courage* to write the truth, although it is suppressed everywhere; the *smartness* to recognize it, although it is hidden everywhere; the *tricks of the trade* [he said "Kunst," which means "art"] to make it operative as a weapon; the *judgment* to select those in whose hands it will be effective; and the *cunning* to spread it among the chosen ones.[24]

Cunning is mentioned last, for it is, at least in Brecht's mind, the basic requirement to be expected from those who fight for truth.

But what, again, is this truth? In Hitler's Germany it could easily be defined as the exact opposite of everything the regime stood for. Outside of Nazi Germany and after the war, Brecht was ready to answer:

21 Ibid., p. 35. 22 Walter Jens, "Protokoll über Brecht: Ein Nekrolog," *Merkur*, X (1956): 994. 23 Bertolt Brecht, *Stücke VII* (Frankfurt, 1957), pp. 124–5; SP p. 290. 24 Bertolt Brecht, *Versuche 20–21* (Berlin, 1950), p. 87.

dialectical materialism. But what would happen if dialectical materialism itself were betrayed by those who professed to realize it in their politics? Bentley reports that "Stalin's pact with Hitler in 1939 was a baffling blow" to Brecht,[25] and I know of at least one poem in which Brecht turned the full force of his wit and anger against the East German authorities whom he had chosen as his masters after 1948. Among the papers in his estate, the following lines were discovered, written under the impact of the rioting on the borders of East and West Berlin, June 17, 1953:

THE SOLUTION

After the uprising on June 17th
The secretary of the Writers' Union
Had handbills distributed on Stalin Boulevard
On which it said that the populace
Had lost the confidence of the government
And could regain it only by doubling
Its output. In view of this would it be
Not simpler if government
Dissolved the populace and elected
Another people?[26]

The East German Writers' Union and the administration they served were just as much conditioned by their social status as Brecht's middle-class high-school teacher had been some forty years before. Needless to say, the official attitude Brecht adopted after the East Berlin uprising was one of loyalty to the Communist party. But his cunning may have reached further than this. It is at least thinkable that he constructed his brilliant and incisive theory of the epic theater in order to be protected not only as a private citizen, but also as a creative playwright — protected, that is, from those whose ranks he had joined. Having made cunning, as he understood it, the individual's supreme weapon in the struggle for existence, he would have been a fool and — what was worse in his eyes — a

dilettante, had he not secured himself and his work against his political friends as well as against his enemies. Unlike his Mother Courage, he proved clairvoyant: in spite of all official misgivings, the Soviet Union gave him the Stalin Peace Prize in 1954, and East Germany still seems to subsidize the Theater am Schiffbauerdamm.

In saying this, I do not intend to minimize the contribution which Brecht's non-Aristotelian theater has made to the development of the modern stage. Along with Strindberg and O'Neill, Pirandello and Antonin Artaud, Brecht belongs to those who have reconquered the reality of imagination for the contemporary drama. What I question is merely the relevance of his political thinking to his aesthetic theory. Being the most dynamic dramatist Germany had produced since the days of Grabbe and Büchner, he could hardly be satisfied with coming to rest in as closed a system as Marxism is, in spite of its dialectics. More likely, the Marxist superstructure of his theory may have served him as a last camouflage.

The trouble with Brecht is that he was so cunning that he succeeded in outwitting even the most cunning among his critics, right or left. He was a cryptic man and a champion in the art of leaving unwelcome questions open. When his work is at its best, it is just as inscrutable as he was. As a result, *The Caucasian Chalk Circle* (1943–45), his last major effort, has been hailed as both "the outstanding example of the technique of the 'epic' drama" [27] and a "Parable for the Theater," [28] which, at least on the surface, are somewhat contradictory

---

25 *SP*, p. xlix. 26 Marianne Kesting, *Bertolt Brecht in Selbstzeugnissen und Bilddokumenten* (Reinbek, 1959), p. 141. 27 Esslin, p. 311. 28 Bertolt Brecht, *Parables for the Theatre: Two Plays*, trans. Eric Bentley and Maja Apelman (New York, 1948), cover.

classifications.[29] Yet both descriptions are very much to the point.

The *Chalk Circle* is epic theater primarily because it consists of three loosely connected parts: the prologue, the story of Grusha the kitchen maid, and the story of Azdak the village recorder. The prologue is set in Soviet Russia and occurs, as Bentley points out, "at a date later than the year when Brecht started work on the play." [30] Russian peasants who return to a village destroyed by the Germans are engaged in a discussion bordering on a quarrel: one group claims the valley as a homestead, the other plans to irrigate it and to use it for vineyards and orchards. The latter group wins out. To celebrate the reconciliation, the play of the *Chalk Circle* proper is performed.

Its first part describes Grusha's rescue of the Governor's deserted child, her flight before the revolution, her marriage to a peasant who is supposedly dying, and finally the return of the Governor's wife and her claim for the child. The second part traces the career of Azdak from village recorder to judge, for he becomes the magistrate who tries the case of the child. Not only do the two actions cover roughly the same span of time — both begin with the revolution which set the Governor and his wife to flight and started Azdak on his career — but they also receive equal comment from the Story Teller, who takes the stage at the end of the prologue. A crossbreed between Greek chorus and personified Alienation Effect, the Story Teller also has the final words:

Take note what men of old concluded:
That what there is shall go to those who are
    good for it,
Thus: the children to the motherly, that they
    prosper
The carts to good drivers, that they are driven
    well

And the valley to the waterers, that it bring
    forth fruit.[31]

These words hark back to the prologue, and their moral adds the distinction of *Lehrstück* or didactic play to those of epic drama and parable.

But in order to arrive at this moral Brecht had to change radically the old story of the chalk circle. This story, incidentally, did not come to him from Chinese sources, as the prologue claims, but from *Der Kreidekreis*, written in 1925 by the expressionist playwright, Klabund. In Brecht's version it is not the physical mother who is discovered by the Solomonic judgment of the chalk circle. Instead Azdak awards the child to Grusha, his foster mother, who had saved him by sacrificing her personal happiness and risking her life for his rescue. In this scene the parabolic elements of the plot stand out in bold relief. Furthermore, it is a modern parable in that it is told not to exemplify a doctrine, but rather to reveal a paradox: Grusha's sacrifice is recognized as superior to the natural ties which bind the Governor's wife to her own child.

As if to stress the climactic character of this scene, Brecht constructed the two parts of the play so that the life histories of both Grusha and Azdak are crowned by it. The time sequences of both actions converge here and break the parallel structure of the epic drama. The courtroom scene stands all by itself in an atmosphere of timelessness, the air of the parable. All the conditioning forces — social distinctions, revolution, and war — recede to reveal the exemplary deeds of the maid and the model wisdom of the judge. Moreover, Azdak, who really is a cunning rogue very much after Brecht's

---

29 Brecht himself speaks occasionally of a "parabolic type of non-Aristotelian drama," e.g., in the notes to *The Round Heads and the Pointed Heads* (*Stücke VI*, p. 213).   30 *SP*, p. xlvii.   31 *SP*, p. 587.

own heart, is all but transported into immortality:

And after that evening Azdak disappeared and
    was not seen again.
The people of Grusinia did not forget him but
    long remembered
The period of his judging as a brief golden age
Almost an age of justice.[32]

Cleverly inserting the words "brief" and "almost," Brecht fortified his play against all critics who would charge him with "hero worship."

It depends entirely on the spectator's reaction to the prologue and his evaluation of it, whether he will consider the *Chalk Circle* to be a didactic play in the epic manner or a dramatic parable presented with all the persuasiveness of the modern imaginary theater. In the former case it is the valley that matters, and not the child; the future of the commonweal prevails over the individual's longing for his past; and the rights of motherhood, like the possession of a few plots of land, can be decided by arbitration. In the latter case it is Grusha's human virtue — to use a word which would have made Brecht cringe with distaste — which leads us to accept Azdak's judgment. Her victory is, after all, a victory of goodness and charm over the wickedness and frigidity of the real mother.

If we argue Grusha's case on the human level, however, we shall find it hard to accept the living child as symbol of a valley, which is an inanimate thing, no matter how much fruit it may produce after irrigation. Nor shall we be able to identify the full-blooded personality of the kitchen maid with the flat figures who populate the prologue. Grusha, who is humble and dignified, naïve and witty, as peasant woman often are — and Brecht has given her some of his most lyrical lines — hardly fits in with those Russian peasants who speak like editorials and act as the party expects them to act. In other words, although the prologue lives up to its ideological intentions and proclaims the Marxist moral of this epic drama, as a work of art it belongs among the worst Brecht has ever written.

The real question is, however, whether in this prologue Brecht's imagination was stifled by his desire to conform with the philosophy of the Communist party, or whether he actually wanted the prologue to be so poor a specimen of writing that it lost all power when it was actually presented on the stage. Performances in the West have omitted the prologue without doing harm to the artistic effectiveness of the play. Moreover, Brecht himself included in the prologue the highly ambiguous question: "You arrange the redistribution of vines and tractors, why not of songs?"[33] Did he want to say here that Russian literature, the officially sponsored "Social Realism," was in need of a revision?

The prologue itself pays lip service to the state, and even to Stalin, since it is set in Stalin's homeland, Georgia; but the drama, in its playfulness, defies the limitations of state-controlled art. Or was Brecht secretly poking fun at the very idea that someone would be so Philistine as to think that one could redistribute songs — and construct plays — like tractors? Did he wish to regain his independence and dignity as a writer simply by asking a silly question? If he did, then this line would indeed rank among the most cunning of his Alienation Effects. Tongue in cheek, he would have justified the prologue where he treats literature as one treats tractors, and he would have pointed to the play, where he produces literature in the only possible way —

32 Ibid., pp. 586, 587. 33 *SP*, p. 503.

namely, as literature. Then, the play would have succeeded as obviously as the prologue failed, and yet he would have done nothing more than pose a question.

In any case Brecht does not confine his question to the prologue; in the play of the *Chalk Circle*, Brecht continues to ask questions, but they become so infinitely more complex that it is difficult to find an answer at all. What becomes of Azdak? And, more important, can this judgment be upheld? The true mother should be the one who can pull the child out of the circle. However, the trial establishes Grusha as the mother, Grusha who, contrary to the traditional story, refuses to hurt the child. Although she has done more than her duty, and even her love, had required her to do, she is certainly not the true mother of the child. What is the truth behind this truth? Brecht has persuaded us to agree with Azdak's judgment, but our "Yes" is a stunned and puzzled one. It continues to affect and afflict us and invites us to return again and again to the play and to reopen the case. Doing this, we only follow Brecht's bidding.

The Good Woman of Setzuan ends altogether with a question:

In your opinion, then, what's to be done?
Change human nature or—the world? Well:
    which?
Believe in bigger, better gods or—none?
How can we mortals be both good and rich?
The right way out of the calamity
You must find for yourselves. Ponder, my
    friends,
How man with man may live in amity
And good men—women also—reach good ends.
There must, there must, be some end that
    would fit.
Ladies and gentlemen, help us look for it.[34]

A convinced Marxist may be able to answer the first set of Brecht's questions; the second set ("How man with man may live in amity . . .") is — undoubtedly on purpose

— phrased in a way so general that it remains tantalizingly open. This "open" ending of Brecht's play is, on the surface, nothing but the logical consequence of his aesthetic theory which was meant to "extort decision" from the spectators. One excellent way to do so is to force them to answer "Yes" or "No." But was Brecht so sure that they would give him the expected answer? The bourgeois audiences which, in the early thirties, exposed themselves willingly to the titillations of *The Threepenny Opera* were far from being converted to Brecht's dialectical materialism. Today it is downright impossible to imagine a West German braving the Berlin wall and crossing over into the Eastern sector for good, in response to the questions put to him by *The Good Woman* or any other Brecht play he has read or seen performed at home.

Was Brecht the playwright superior to Brecht the theoretician in that he granted his audiences complete freedom, the freedom to say "Yes" or "No"? It almost seems so, for his questions became more and more unanswerable the more his stature as a dramatist grew. To side with the progressive peasants in the prologue to the *Chalk Circle* demanded no important decision, especially when one heeded the party line. But it took all of Brecht's skill and inventiveness as a dramatist to make us side with Azdak and Grusha at the end of the parabolic part of the play, and even so we answered only with a very tentative "Yes." One could almost say that the later Brecht singled out the plays which he wanted to survive by basing them on questions that were difficult to answer, if they could be answered at all.

This is especially true of *Mother Courage* (1938–39). In the final scene dumb Kattrin sacrifices herself to save the children of the

---

34 *Parables for the Theatre*, p. 106, but omitted in *SP*.

city of Halle from a night attack. She stakes her life, just as Grusha risks hers to rescue the Governor's son. Moreover, Kattrin is killed, whereas Grusha is rewarded — Grusha keeps both her life and the child. Kattrin's death is bound to carry the audience along by way of the same process of empathy, or identification, against which Brecht's theory of the epic theater is directed. The cunning Brecht did what he could to brake the emotional force with which he had informed the climax of his best-known play. In the program notes to *Mother Courage*, he published a double picture, the right side showing Kattrin, sitting on the straw-thatched roof of a peasant hut, drumming and braving the fatal salvo; on the left side, however, he had juxtaposed a photo from a French newspaper, with the following caption:

> Raymonde Dien faces a French Military Court in Bordeaux. She has been accused of having thrown herself before a train carrying arms to the war in Vietnam. She declared: "I have stopped the train because there are already enough mothers who have lost their sons. I am prepared to repeat this action any day." [35]

This prime example of an extended Alienation Effect is, of course, a double falsification: ideologically, dumb Kattrin does not roll the drum because she is an antimilitarist, but because she cannot bear the thought of innocent children being slaughtered wholesale. Raymonde Dien acted as an agent, deliberately, perhaps on orders from headquarters; dumb Kattrin, on the other hand, acts on the spur of the moment, desperately, as a human being, mustering her last strength to break through a lifelong solitude. Raymonde Dien served as the model for a politically effective poster; dumb Kattrin performs a tragic act. And Raymonde Dien stayed alive, as the newspaper clipping of her trial proves, whereas dumb Kattrin paid for her pity with a sacrificial death.

Obviously stunned by the tragic impact he had produced, Bertolt Brecht declared rather lamely: "The spectators may identify themselves with dumb Kattrin in this scene; they may feel empathy with this human being and be happy to observe that such energies are extant in them — however, the process of empathy will not be complete here ("jedoch werden sie sich nicht durchaus eingefühlt haben"). [36] The playwright retires behind the dogmatist who assures him that his creative genius did not "completely" pierce the systematic cobweb of his theory. What else was this retraction but a security measure, not unlike the one by means of which Brecht's Galileo saved his own skin, abjuring his discoveries? Both Galileo and his author are men who, with a twinkle in their eyes, agree to the proposition that "if there are obstacles, the shortest line between two points may be the crooked line." [37]

Was Brecht so anxious to uphold his theory and be foolproof against the Inquisition of his day? Or was he, conversely, so sure of the tragic force emanating from Kattrin's death scene that he did not mind one more intellectual sleight of hand? Albrecht Schöne has called this scene "the self-alienation of Brecht's Alienation tendencies." It shows, he says, "the unconditional and presents compassion as a force beyond any dispute; it grows into a parable of human behavior which is no longer in any way subject to the criticism from the viewpoint of any following period." [38] One can put it much more simply: Kattrin's sacrificial death is unabashedly moral.

---

35 *Theaterarbeit* (Dresden, 1952), p. 273. 36 *Theaterarbeit*, p. 244. 37 *SP*, p. 398. 38 Albrecht Schöne, "Bertolt Brecht: Theatertheorie und dramatische Dichtung," *Euphorion*, LII (1958), 272–96.

Is the epic theater perhaps a "moral institution"? Brecht himself asked this question, quoting a speech young Schiller had delivered in 1784 before the Prince Elector's Academy in Mannheim and published later under the title, *Die Schaubühne als eine moralische Anstalt betrachtet*. Schiller, the popularizer of Kant and educator of the German middle classes, had always been a thorn in Brecht's side. His play, *St. Joan of the Stockyards* (1929–31) is, among other things, a vicious parody of Schiller's romantic *Maiden of Orleans*. And yet, although Schiller's drama appeared to him as the epitome of "culinary" stagecraft, he could not completely detach his epic theater from the ethics of Schiller's dramaturgy.

> We spoke [Brecht says], not in the name of morality but on behalf of the damaged. These are really two different things, because the damaged are often told, with moral authority, that they have to make do with their conditions. In the eyes of these moralists the people are there for the sake of morality, instead of the other way round. Be this as it may . . . you will understand from what I said to what extent and in what sense the epic theater is indeed a moral institution.[39]

Brecht is begging the question here, instead of facing Schiller's revolutionary idealism, he argues against his feeble nineteenth-century followers ("these moralists"), who watered down and obfuscated Schiller's principles and are forgotten today. Brecht's last sentence, the "open ending" of his statement, however, does not completely close the loophole by which morality could sneak even into his plays.

It is doubtful whether Brecht read any more of Schiller's essay than its title. Critics of the drama who did were able to establish more subtle connections. Ernst Bloch, for instance, speaks of the epic

theater as a "paradigmatic" rather than a "moral" institution.[40] The distinction is a rarefied one. If Brecht wanted the underprivileged and "damaged" to profit from his plays, then he was coming dangerously close to Schiller's precept that the stage is "to teach us to wield greater justice towards the miserable and to judge them with increased clemency. Only when we fathom the depth of their oppression are we allowed to adjudicate upon them." If the paradigms in Brecht's didactic plays are meant to establish a healthy balance between the society of the future and their rulers, then he could have found the idea of this kind of *Lehrstück* anticipated by Schiller:

> The stage could be used to correct the opinions of the nation about their administration and executives, provided that the chiefs and guardians of the state would grasp this opportunity. On the stage the legislature would talk to the subjects through alien symbols, would answer their complaints even before they were uttered, and would favorably prejudice their doubts without seeming to do so. Even tradesmen and inventors could and would be inspired by the stage if the poets would take the trouble to be patriots and the state would deign to hear them.

Here Schiller envisages the stage less as a moral institution than as a subtle propaganda machine working for the balance of the utopian state of the future. Brecht's Communist state, on the other hand, was far from being utopian. It hardly ever

---

39 "Ist das Theater etwa eine moralische Anstalt?" *SCH*, *pp.* 71, 72. 40 Ernst Bloch, *Das Prinzip Hoffnung*, I (Berlin, 1953): 441 ff. See also Marianne Kesting, *Das epische Theater* (Stuttgart, 1959), p. 57 ff. Kesting also refers to her paper, "Das Theater als eine marxistische Anstalt betrachtet," *Augenblick* (December, 1956), which was inaccessible to me.

listened to him. Therefore, he had to hide behind the more extreme demands of his theory, lest he be forced to change the text of his plays, as indeed he was in the case of his opera, *The Trial of Lucullus* (1951).

In the final analysis Schiller, too, persuaded his spectators to come to a decision. This decision, with which he concludes his essay, is "to be human." [41] Deeply convinced of man's inhumanity, Brecht harangued his audiences through his Alienation Effects, urging them to *become* human. It is this dynamic that distinguishes the epic theater from Schiller's drama. Inasmuch as this dynamic shows man to be "on trial" and "in the process" of becoming, Brecht's epic theater is a legitimate offspring of the expressionist revolution of the twenties and of European theatrical history in general. Since his aesthetic theory is a mechanism, both of offense and defense, it may well be recognized for what it is: the intellectual mimicry behind which a creative mind hid from outward persecution and inward doubts.

This creation at times leaves its "epicality" behind to grow into theater, great theater, pure and simple. Whether the greatness of these individual scenes will bestow lasting life upon them, only history can tell, and it is harder in Brecht's case than in many another to predict the outcome of time's selective processes. [42] Brecht himself threw in his lot with Marxism, as if he were banking on its ultimate victory. But so far it has been the free West which has welcomed this writer, discussed him, learned from him, and performed his plays. Paradoxically, Brecht's survival may depend on the survival of the West which he, by all ordinary standards, had tried so hard to prevent.

---

41 *Schillers sämtliche Werke*, X (Leipzig, n.d.): 46, 48, 49. **42** Otto Mann's verdict, "It is impossible to appreciate Brecht as a dramatic writer because he failed to follow the tradition and to present (dramatic) worlds" (*B. B.—Mass oder Mythos?* [Heidelberg, 1958], p. 110), attempts to eliminate the Brecht problem instead of solving it.

THE THREEPENNY OPERA

*A Play with Songs in Three Acts
based on John Gay's
The Beggar's Opera*

Bertolt Brecht

*English Version by
Eric Bentley and Desmond Vesey*

CHARACTERS

MACHEATH, *nicknamed Mackie the Knife*
JONATHAN JEREMIAH PEACHUM,
    proprietor of the firm "The Beggars' Friend"
CELIA PEACHUM, *his wife*
POLLY PEACHUM, *his daughter*
BROWN, *chief of police in London*
LUCY, *his daughter*
GINNY JENNY
SMITH
THE REVEREND KIMBALL
FILCH

*A ballad singer, the gang, beggars, whores,
constables*

PROLOGUE

Market Day in Soho

*Beggars are begging, thieves thieving, whores
whoring. A ballad singer sings a Moritat.*

THE MORITAT OF MACKIE THE KNIFE

And the shark he has his teeth and
There they are for all to see.
And Macheath he has his knife but
No one knows where it may be.

When the shark has had his dinner
There is blood upon his fins.
But Macheath he has his gloves on:
They say nothing of his sins.

All along the Thames Embankment
People fall down with a smack.
And it is not plague or cholera:
Word's around that Mac is back.

On a blue and balmy Sunday
Someone drops dead in the Strand.
And a man slips round the corner.
People say: Macheath's on hand.

And Schmul Meyer still is missing
Like many another rich young man.
And Macheath has got his money.
Try to prove *that* if you can!

(PEACHUM *with his wife and daughter stroll
across the stage from left to right.*)

Jenny Towler was discovered
With a jackknife in her breast.
And Macheath strolls down the dockside
Knows no more than all the rest.

Where is Alphonse Glite the coachman?
Was he stabbed or drowned or shot?
Maybe someone knows the answer.
As for Mackie, he does not.

One old man and seven children
Burnt to cinders in Soho.
In the crowd is Captain Mackie who
Is not asked and does not know.

And the widow not yet twenty
(Everybody calls her Miss)
Woke up and was violated.
What did Mackie pay for this?

(*There is a burst of laughter from the whores,
and a man steps out from among them and
walks quickly across the stage and exit.*)

GINNY JENNY: Look! That was Mackie the
    Knife!

ACT ONE

SCENE ONE   In order to combat the increasing
hardheartedness of men, Mr. J. Peachum, man
of business, has opened a shop where the
poorest of the poor may acquire an appearance that will touch the stoniest of hearts.

The Wardrobe Room of Jonathan Jeremiah Peachum's Establishment for Beggars

PEACHUM'S MORNING ANTHEM

Wake up, you old Image of Gawd!
Get on with your sinful backsliding!
Continue to perpetrate fraud!
Jehovah will do the providing!

Go barter your brother, you bear!
Sell your wife at an auction, you lout!
You think Our Lord God isn't there?
On Judgment Day you will find out.

PEACHUM (*to the audience*): Something new — that's what we *must* have. My business is too difficult. You see, my business is trying to arouse human pity. There are a few things that'll move people to pity, a few, but the trouble is, when they've been used several times, they no longer work. Human beings have the horrid capacity of being able to make themselves heartless at will. So it happens, for instance, that a man who sees another man on the street corner with only a stump for an arm will be so shocked the first time that he'll give him sixpence. But the second time it'll be only a threepenny bit. And if he sees him a third time, he'll hand him over cold-bloodedly to the police. It's the same with these spiritual weapons.

(*A large board is let down from the flies and on it is written: "It is more blessed to give than to receive."*)

What's the use of the finest and most stirring sayings painted on the most enticing boards if they get used up so quickly? There are four or five sayings in the Bible that really touch the heart. But when they're used up, one's daily bread's just gone. Take that one there: "Give and it shall be given unto you" — how threadbare it has become in the three weeks we've had it. Always something new must be offered. We can fall back on the Bible again, but how often can *that* be done?

(*There is a knock.* PEACHUM *opens the door, and a young man named* FILCH *enters.*)

FILCH: Peachum & Co.?

PEACHUM: Peachum.

FILCH: Then you're the owner of the firm called "The Beggars' Friend"? I was sent to you. Oh, those sayings! What an investment! I suppose you've got a whole library of such things? Well, that's something quite different! Fellows like us — we'd never get an idea like that, and not being properly educated, how could business ever flourish?

PEACHUM: Your name?

FILCH: Well, you see, Mr. Peachum, I've had bad luck ever since I was a boy. My mother was a drunkard, my father a gambler. From an early age I had to fend for myself. And without the loving hand of a mother to guide me I sank deeper and deeper into the morass of the great city. I never knew a father's care or the blessings of a contented home. So now you see me . . .

PEACHUM: So now I see you . . .

FILCH (*confused*): . . . see me . . . completely destitute, a prey to my own desires.

PEACHUM: Like a wreck on the high seas, and so on. Tell me, wreck, in which district do you recite this nursery rhyme?

FILCH: What do you mean, Mr. Peachum?

PEACHUM: Of course, you deliver this speech in public?

FILCH: Yes, you see, Mr. Peachum, there was a nasty little incident yesterday in Highland Street. I was standing quietly and miserably at the corner, hat in hand, not meaning any harm. . . .

PEACHUM (*turning over the pages of a notebook*): Highland Street. Yes. That's the one. You're the crawling blackleg that Honey and Sam caught yesterday. You had the impertinence to solicit passers-by in District 10. We let it go at a good beating, as we took it you didn't know where God lives. But if you let yourself be seen there again, we shall have to use the saw. Understand?

FILCH: Please, Mr. Peachum, please! What can

I *do* then, Mr. Peachum? The gentlemen really beat me black and blue, and then they gave me your business card. If I was to take off my coat, you'd think you was looking at a mackerel.

PEACHUM: My young friend, if you don't look like a flounder, my people were a sight too easy with you. This young sprout comes along and imagines that if he sticks out his paws he'll be all set for a juicy steak. What would you say if someone took the best trout out of your pond?

FILCH: But you see, Mr. Peachum — I haven't got a pond.

PEACHUM: Well, licenses are only granted to professionals. (*He points in a businesslike way to a large map of London.*) London is divided into fourteen districts. Everyone wishing to ply the begging-trade in any one of them has to have a license from Jonathan Jeremiah Peachum and Company. My God, anyone could come along — "a prey to his own desires"!

FILCH: Mr. Peachum. Only a few shillings stand between me and total ruin. I *must* be able to do something with two shillings in hand. . . .

PEACHUM: One pound.

FILCH: Mr. Peachum! (FILCH *points beseechingly at a poster which reads: "Shut not your ears to misery."*)

(PEACHUM *points to a curtain in front of a showcase, on which is written: "Give and it shall be given unto you."*)

FILCH: Ten shillings.

PEACHUM: And fifty per cent of the weekly takings. Including outfit, seventy per cent.

FILCH: And please, what does the outfit consist of?

PEACHUM: The firm decides that.

FILCH: Well, what district can I start on?

PEACHUM: Top half of Baker Street. That'll be a bit cheaper. It's only fifty per cent there, including outfit.

FILCH: Thank you. (*He pays.*)

PEACHUM: Your full name?

FILCH: Charles Filch.

PEACHUM: Correct. (*Shouts.*) Mrs. Peachum!

(MRS. PEACHUM *enters.*)

This is Filch. Number 314, Upper Baker Street. I'll enter it myself. Of course, you would want to start now, just before the Coronation — the chance of a lifetime to earn a little money. Outfit C for you. (*He draws back the linen curtain in front of a showcase in which are standing five wax models.*)

FILCH: What's that?

PEACHUM: These are five basic types of misery best adapted to touching the human heart. The sight of them induces that unnatural state of mind in which a man is actually willing to give money away.
Outfit A: Victim of the Progress of Modern Traffic. The Cheerful Cripple, always good-tempered — (*He demonstrates it.*) — always carefree, effect heightened by a mutilated arm.
Outfit B: Victim of the Art of War. The Troublesome Twitcher, annoys passers-by, his job is to arouse disgust — (*He demonstrates it.*) — modified by medals.
Outfit C: Victim of the Industrial Boom. The Pitiable Blind, or the High School of the Art of Begging. (PEACHUM *displays him, advancing unsteadily toward* FILCH. *At the moment when he bumps into* FILCH, *the latter screams with horror.* PEACHUM *stops instantly, gazes at him in amazement, and suddenly roars*) He feels pity! You'll never make a beggar — not in a lifetime. That sort of behavior is only fit for the passers-by! Then it's Outfit D! — Celia, you've been drinking again! And now you can't see out of your eyes. Number 136 has been complaining about his neck-rag. How often must I tell you a gentleman will not have filthy clothing next to his skin. Number 136 has paid for a brand-new costume. The stains — the only thing about it capable of awakening pity — were to be put on by

neatly ironing in paraffin wax! Never trouble to think! Always have to do everything oneself. (*to* FILCH) Undress and put this on, but keep it in good condition!

FILCH: And what happens to my things?

PEACHUM: Property of the firm. Outfit E: Young man who's seen better days, preferably one who "never thought he would come down to this."

FILCH: Oh, so you're using that too. Why can't *I* have the better days outfit?

PEACHUM: Because nobody believes in his own misery, my boy. If you've got the stomach-ache and say so, it only sounds disgusting. Anyway, it's not for you to ask questions. Just put these things on.

FILCH: Aren't they rather dirty?

(PEACHUM *gives him a piercing glance.*)

I'm sorry, Mr. Peachum, I'm sorry.

MRS. PEACHUM: Get a move on, sonny, I'm not going to hold your trousers till Christmas.

FILCH (*suddenly with great determination*): But I'm not going to take my shoes off! Not for anything. I'd rather chuck the whole thing. They were the only present I had from my poor mother, and never, never, however low I may have fallen . . .

MRS. PEACHUM: Don't talk rubbish. I know you've got dirty feet.

FILCH: Well, where do you expect me to wash my feet? In the middle of winter?

(MRS. PEACHUM *leads him behind a folding screen, then sits down left and begins ironing candle-grease into a suit.*)

PEACHUM: Where's your daughter?

MRS. PEACHUM: Polly? Upstairs.

PEACHUM: Was that man here again yesterday? The one who always comes when I'm out?

MRS. PEACHUM: Don't be so suspicious, Jonathan! There isn't a finer gentleman alive, and the Captain takes quite an interest in our Polly.

PEACHUM: Um.

MRS. PEACHUM: And if I can see an inch before my nose, Polly is fond of him too.

PEACHUM: There you go, Celia! Throwing your daughter around as if I were a millionaire! So she's going to marry! And do you think our miserable business would last another week if the filthy customers had only *our* legs to look at? A husband! He'd soon have us in his clutches. That he would. Do you think your daughter would be any better than you at keeping her mouth shut in bed?

MRS. PEACHUM: You've got a nice opinion of your daughter!

PEACHUM: The worst! The very worst! She is nothing but a mass of sensuality.

MRS. PEACHUM: Well, she certainly doesn't get that from you!

PEACHUM: Marry! My daughter should be to me what bread is to the starving. (*He thumbs through the Bible.*) That's actually written somewhere in the Bible. Marriage is a disgusting business anyhow. I'll soon beat the marriage out of her.

MRS. PEACHUM: Jonathan, you're just ignorant.

PEACHUM: Ignorant! What's his name, then — this *gentleman*?

MRS. PEACHUM: People just call him always "The Captain."

PEACHUM: So you haven't even asked him his name! Very nice!

MRS. PEACHUM: Well, we wouldn't be so ill-bred as to ask him for his birth certificate; him being such a gentleman, inviting us to the Octopus Hotel for a little hop.

PEACHUM: Where!

MRS. PEACHUM: To the Octopus. For a little hop.

PEACHUM: Captain? Octopus Hotel? I see —

MRS. PEACHUM: The gentleman never touched me and my daughter except with kid gloves on.

PEACHUM: Kid gloves!

MRS. PEACHUM: Now I come to think of it, he always has gloves on — white ones, white kid gloves.

PEACHUM: Ah! White kid gloves and a stick with an ivory handle and spats over his patent leather shoes and a nice polite manner and a scar . . .

MRS. PEACHUM: On his neck. How do you know all this about him?

(FILCH comes out.)

FILCH: Mr. Peachum, could you give me a few tips on what to do? I always like to have a system and not go at things haphazard.

MRS. PEACHUM: He wants a system!

PEACHUM: He can be an idiot. Come back this evening at six and you'll be given the necessaries. Now, get out!

FILCH: Thank you, Mr. Peachum, thank you very much. (Exit.)

PEACHUM: Fifty per cent! — And now I'll tell you who this gentleman with the kid gloves is — he's Mackie the Knife!

(He runs up the stairs into POLLY's bedroom.)

MRS. PEACHUM: Lord save us! Mackie the Knife! Jesus, Mary and Joseph! Polly! Where's Polly!

(PEACHUM comes slowly downstairs.)

PEACHUM: Polly? Polly hasn't been home. Her bed's not touched.

MRS. PEACHUM: Then she's been having supper with that wool merchant. I'm certain of it, Jonathan.

PEACHUM: For our sake, I hope it was the wool merchant.

(MR. and MRS. PEACHUM step in front of the curtain and sing. Song illumination: a golden light. The organ is lit up. Three lights come down on a bar from above, and on a board is written:)

THE I-FOR-ONE SONG

PEACHUM: I for one
Like to spend the night at home and in my
bed.
She prefers fun:
Does she think the Lord keeps busy pouring
manna on her head?

MRS. PEACHUM: Such is the moon over Soho
Such is that magic "Can you feel my heart
beating" spell
Oh, it's "Whither thou goest, I will go with
thee, Johnny"
And the new moon's shining on the
asphodel.

PEACHUM: I for one
Like to do what has a purpose and a goal.
They prefer fun:
After which of course they end up in the
hole.

BOTH: So where is their moon over Soho?
What's left of their confounded "Can you
feel my heart beating" spell?
Where now is their "Whither thou goest, I
will go with thee, Johnny!"
For the old moon's waning and you're shot
to hell!

SCENE TWO   Deep in the heart of Soho, Mackie the Knife celebrates his wedding with Polly Peachum, daughter of the king of the beggars.

An Empty Stable

MATTHEW (nicknamed "Money Matthew," carrying a lantern and pointing a revolver round the stable): Hi! Hands up, if anyone's there!

(MACHEATH enters and walks round by the front of the stage.)

MACHEATH: Well? Is anyone here?

MATTHEW: Not a soul. We can have our marriage here safe enough.

POLLY (enters in a wedding dress): But this is a stable!

MACHEATH: Sit down on the crib for a while, Polly. (*to the audience*) Today, in this stable, my marriage to Miss Polly Peachum will be celebrated; she has followed me for love, in order to share the rest of my life with me.

MATTHEW: A lot of people in London will be saying this is the riskiest thing you've ever done, luring Mr. Peachum's only child out of his own house.

MACHEATH: Who *is* Mr. Peachum?

MATTHEW: He himself would say he was the poorest man in London.

POLLY: But you're not thinking of having our marriage here? It's just a nasty, common stable. You can't invite the clergyman here. And besides, it isn't even ours. We really ought not to begin our new life with a burglary, Mac. This is the happiest day of our lives!

MACHEATH: Dearest child, everything shall be as you wish. Not a stone shall touch your little feet. The furnishings are on the way at this very moment.

MATTHEW: Here comes the furniture!

(*There is a sound of heavy wagons arriving. Half a dozen men enter, carrying furniture, carpets, crockery, etc., and soon the stable is transformed into an over-ornate living room.*)

MACHEATH: Junk!

(*The men place their presents down on the left, congratulate the bride, and report to the bridegroom.*)

JACOB (*nicknamed "Hook-finger Jacob"*): Here's luck! At 14 Ginger Street there were some people on the second floor. We had to smoke 'em out.

ROBERT (*nicknamed "Robert the Saw"*): Good luck! A copper in the Strand got in our way.

MACHEATH: Amateurs!

ED: We did what we could, but three people in the West End are goners. Good luck!

MACHEATH: Amateurs and bunglers!

JIMMY: An old gentleman got something he wasn't expecting. I don't think it's serious. Luck!

MACHEATH: My orders were: bloodshed to be avoided. It makes me quite sick when I think of it. *You'll* never make businessmen. Cannibals — but never businessmen!

WALTER (*nicknamed "Wally the Weeper"*): Good luck! Half an hour ago, madam, that harpsichord still belonged to the Duchess of Somerset!

POLLY: Whatever furniture is this?

MACHEATH: How do you like it, Polly?

POLLY (*crying*): All those poor people, just for a few bits of furniture!

MACHEATH: And what furniture! Junk! You're right to be angry. A rosewood harpsichord — and a Renaissance sofa. That's unforgivable. And where's a table?

WALTER: A table?

(*They lay planks across the feeding troughs.*)

POLLY: Oh, Mac, I'm so unhappy. Let's hope anyhow the clergyman won't come!

MATTHEW: But he will. *We* told him the way quite clearly.

WALTER (*pushes forward the improvised table*): A table!

MACHEATH (*seeing* POLLY *crying*): My wife is upset. And where are the other chairs? A harpsichord and no chairs! Never trouble to think. How often does it happen that I have a wedding? Shut your trap, Weeper! How often does it happen, I'm asking, that I leave anything to you? It makes my wife unhappy from the start.

ED: Dear Polly . . .

MACHEATH (*knocking his hat from his head*): "Dear Polly!" I'll knock your head into your guts with your "dear Polly," you sewer rat! Whoever heard the like — "dear Polly"! Maybe you've slept with her?

POLLY: But Mac . . .

ED: I swear that . . . !

WALTER: Madam, if there's anything more you'd like here, we'll go out again . . .

MACHEATH: A rosewood harpsichord and no chairs! (*Laughs.*) What do you say to that, as the bride?

POLLY: Well, it could be worse.

MACHEATH: Two chairs and a sofa, and the bridal pair sit on the ground.

POLLY: Yes, that's a fine thing.

MACHEATH (*sharply*): Saw the legs off the harpsichord! Come on! Come on!

(*Four of the men saw the legs off the harpsichord and sing:*)

Bill Lawgen and Mary Syer
They were spliced last Tuesday night by law!
Where the bride's gown came from he did not know
She'd no name for her man but So and So
And yet they got a license from the Registrar!
(A toast!)

WALTER: And so, all's well that ends well. We have another bench, madam.

MACHEATH: Might I now request you gentlemen to take off your rags and dress yourselves respectably? After all, this isn't the wedding of a nobody. And Polly, may I ask you to get busy with the grub hampers?

POLLY: Is that the wedding breakfast? Is it all stolen, Mac?

MACHEATH: Of course, of course.

POLLY: I'd like to know what you'd do if there was a knock at the door and the sheriff came in!

MACHEATH: Then I'd show you what your husband *can* do.

MATTHEW: Not a chance of it today. All the police are lining the streets. The Queen's coming to town for the Coronation on Friday.

POLLY: Two knives and fourteen forks! A knife for each chair!

MACHEATH: What a washout! That's the work of apprentices, not trained men. Haven't you any idea of style? You ought to be able to tell the difference between Chippendale and Louis Quatorze.

(*The rest of the gang now return, wearing smart evening dress, but their behavior, during the rest of the scene is unfortunately not in keeping with their attire.*)

WALTER: We wanted to bring the most valuable things. Look at that wood! The material is absolutely first-class.

MATTHEW: Sssst! Permit me, Captain . . .

MACHEATH: Come here, Polly.

(*The two of them pose for congratulations.*)

MATTHEW: Permit me, Captain, on behalf of all, on the happiest day of your life, the springtide of your career — its turning point, one might say — to offer you our heartiest congratulations and . . . so forth. It's horrible — this gassy talk. Well, anyway — (*Shakes* MACHEATH's *hand.*) — chin up, boys!

MACHEATH: Thank you. That was very nice of you, Matthew.

MATTHEW (*shaking* POLLY's *hand, after having patted* MACHEATH *affectionately on the back*): Ah, it's spoken from the heart! Well, keep your head up, old man, I mean — (*Grinning.*) — as far as your head's concerned never let it droop.

(*Roars of laughter from the men.* MACHEATH *suddenly catches hold of* MATTHEW *and gently jerks him to the floor.*)

MACHEATH: Hold your trap. Keep your dirty jokes for your Kitty: she's the right slut for them.

POLLY: Mac, don't be so common.

MATTHEW: I object to you calling Kitty a slut . . . (*Stands up with difficulty.*)

MACHEATH: Oh! You object, do you?

MATTHEW: And what's more, I never have dirty jokes for her. I respect Kitty far too much for that. Which maybe you can't understand, being made the way you are. And you ought to know about dirty jokes! You think Lucy hasn't told me the things you've said to her? I'm a kid-gloves gent compared to that.

(MACHEATH *gives him a look*.)

JACOB: Stop it. This is a wedding! (*They pull him back.*)

MACHEATH: A fine wedding, eh, Polly? To see these gutter-rats all round you on the day of your marriage? You never thought your husband would be let down by his friends like this. That'll teach you.

POLLY: I think it's nice.

ROBERT: Tripe! No one's letting you down. A little difference of opinion can happen any time. Your Kitty is as good as anyone else. Now come on with the wedding present, my boy.

ALL: Come on, get on with it!

MATTHEW (*offended*): There!

POLLY: Oh! A wedding present! How sweet of you, Mr. Money Matthew! Look, Mac, what a lovely nightdress!

MATTHEW: Another dirty joke, eh, Captain?

MACHEATH: All right, now. Didn't want to offend you on this festive occasion.

WALTER: Well, and what about this? Chippendale. (*He uncovers an immense Chippendale grandfather clock.*)

MACHEATH: Quatorze.

POLLY: It's wonderful. I'm so happy. I can't find words, your kindness is so fantastic. A shame we haven't a home for it, isn't it Mac?

MACHEATH: Think of it as a beginning. All beginnings are difficult. Many thanks, Walter. Now clear the stuff away — food.

JACOB (*while the others are clearing the table*): Of course, I've forgotten to bring anything. (*Emphatically to* POLLY) Believe me, young lady, I feel very embarrassed.

POLLY: Don't mention it, Mr. Hook-Finger Jacob.

JACOB: All the boys throw their presents around and I stand here with nothing. Put yourself in my place. But this always happens to me! I could tell you of some fixes I've been in! Boy! You wouldn't believe them! The other day I met Ginny Jenny and said to her, "Now look, you old cow," I said . . .

(*He suddenly sees* MACHEATH *standing behind him and walks away without a word.*)

MACHEATH (*leads* POLLY *to her seat*): This is the finest food you'll get anywhere today, Polly. Shall we start?

(*They all sit down to the wedding breakfast.*)

ED (*pointing to the service*): Lovely plates, Savoy Hotel.

JACOB: The egg mayonnaise is from Selfridge's. We had a jar of goose liver too. But on the way here Jimmy ate it out of spite. He said he had an empty belly.

WALTER: Respectable people don't say "belly."

JIMMY: And, Ed, don't gobble your eggs so, today of all days!

MACHEATH: Can't someone sing something? Something delightful?

MATTHEW (*choking with laughter*): Something delightful! That's a proper word! (*Under* MACHEATH'S *annihilating glance, he sits down, embarrassed.*)

MACHEATH (*knocking a dish out of someone's hand*): As a matter of fact, I didn't wish to start eating yet. Instead of this "On-with-the-food-and-into-the-trough" exhibition from you men, I'd have preferred something festive. Other people always do some such thing on a day like this.

JACOB: What sort of thing?

MACHEATH: Must I think of everything myself? I'm not asking for an opera here. But you might have arranged something more than eating and telling dirty jokes — well, a day like this just shows how far one can count on one's friends.

POLLY: The smoked salmon's wonderful, Mac.

ED: I'll bet you've never ate salmon like it. Mac has it every day. You're in the honey-pot all right. I always said Mac'll make a fine match for a girl with a feeling for higher things. I said so to Lucy yesterday.

POLLY: Lucy? Who is Lucy, Mac?

JACOB (embarrassed): Lucy? Well, you know, you mustn't take it so seriously.

(MATTHEW has stood up and is making furious gestures behind POLLY to silence JACOB.)

POLLY (sees him): Are you wanting something? The salt? What were you going to say, Mr. Jacob?

JACOB: Oh nothing. Nothing at all. I really wasn't going to say anything. I'll be getting my tongue burnt.

MACHEATH: What have you got in your hand, Jacob?

JACOB: A knife, Captain.

MACHEATH: And what have you got on your plate?

JACOB: A trout, Captain.

MACHEATH: I see. And with the knife, I believe, you are eating the trout. That is unheard of, Jacob. Have you ever seen such a thing, Polly? Eating fish with a knife! A person who does that is a pig, do you understand me, Jacob? Try to learn — You'll have a lot to do, Polly, before you can teach such oafs to behave like gentlemen. Do you even know what the word means: a gentleman?

WALTER: I know the difference from a woman!

POLLY: Oh, Mr. Walter!

MACHEATH: Well, don't you want to sing a song? Nothing to brighten up the day a bit? It's to be just another damn, sad, ordinary, dirty day like any other? And is anyone keeping watch at the door? Maybe you'd like me to do that? Perhaps I should stand guard at the door, today of all days, so you can stuff yourselves here at my expense?

WALTER (sullenly): What do you mean: at my expense?

JIMMY: Shut up, Wally. I'll go out. Who'd come here anyway? (Exit.)

JACOB: It'd be funny if all the wedding guests were copped today!

JIMMY (bursts in): Captain, the coppers!

WALTER: Tiger Brown!

MATTHEW: Garn, it's the Reverend Kimball.

(KIMBALL enters.)

ALL (shout): Good evening, Reverend Kimball!

KIMBALL: Well, well, well, so I've found you at last! In a little hut I find you; a small place, indeed, but your own.

MACHEATH: The Duke of Devonshire's.

POLLY: How do you do, your Reverence. I'm so happy you've come, on the happiest day of our lives . . .

MACHEATH: I request an anthem for the Reverend Kimball.

MATTHEW: How about "Bill Lawgen and Mary Syer"?

JACOB: That's right, "Bill Lawgen" should do.

KIMBALL: It would be pleasing to hear your voices raised in song, my men.

MATTHEW: Let's begin, gents.

(Three of the men stand up and sing, hesitating, flat and uncertain.)

WEDDING SONG FOR POORER PEOPLE

Bill Lawgen and Mary Syer
They were spliced last Tuesday night by law!
(I give you Bill and Mary, Gawd bless 'em!)
Where the bride's gown came from he did not know
She'd no name for her man but So and So
And yet they got a license from the Registrar!
(A toast!)

Do you know what your good wife does? No!
Will you let her go on doing it? No!
(I give you Bill and Mary, Gawd bless 'em!)
Billy Lawgen said to me: It's fine
So long as just one part of her is mine.
(The swine!)

MACHEATH: Is that all? Paltry!

MATTHEW (*choking again*): Paltry! Just the right word, gents. Paltry.

MACHEATH: Hold your trap!

MATTHEW: Well, I meant — no life, no swing, nothing!

POLLY: Gentlemen, if nobody will do anything, I myself will sing a little song as best I can, and in it I'm going to imitate a girl I once saw in a little bar in Soho. She was the washing-up skivvy, and I must tell you that everyone laughed at her, and then one day she spoke to the customers and told them the things I am going to sing to you now. So this is the little bar — you must imagine it being filthy dirty — and she stood behind it from morning to night. There's her slop pail and that's the cloth she used for drying the glasses. Where you are sitting, sat the men who laughed at her. You can laugh, too, so that everything is just as it was; but if you can't, then you needn't. (*She begins, pretending to wash glasses and muttering to herself.*) Now one of you must say — you for instance, Mr. Walter — (*Pointing at* WALTER) — "And when is your ship coming home, Jenny?"

WALTER: And when is your ship coming home, Jenny?

POLLY: And another says — you, perhaps: "Do you still wash up the glasses, Pirate Jenny."

MATTHEW: Do you still wash up the glasses, Pirate Jenny?

POLLY: Yes, and now I'll begin.

(*Song illumination: golden light. The organ is lit up. Three lights on a bar come from above, and on a board is written:*)

PIRATE JENNY

Gentlemen, today you see me washing up the glasses
And making up the beds and cleaning.
When you give me p'raps a penny, I will curtsey rather well.
When you see my tatty clothing and this tatty old hotel
P'raps you little guess with whom you're dealing.
One fine afternoon there will be shouting from the harbor.
Folk will ask: what's the reason for that shout?
They will see me smiling while I rinse the glasses
And will say: what has she to smile about?
    And a ship with eight sails and
    With fifty great cannon
    Sails into the quay.

They say: go and wipe your glasses, my girl
And their pennies are thrown to me.
And I thank them for the pennies and I do the beds up right
(Though nobody is going to sleep in them that night)
And they haven't the least idea who I may be.
One fine afternoon there will be roaring from the harbor.
Folk will ask: what's the reason for that roar?
They will see me standing just beside the window
And will say: now what's she sneering for?
    And the ship with eight sails and
    With fifty great cannon
    Will shoot up the town.

Gentlemen, I fear this puts an end to your laughter
For your walls, they will all cave in.
And this whole fair city will be razed to the ground.
Just one tatty old hotel will survive safe and sound.
Folk will ask what special person dwells therein.

And all night long round this hotel there will
be shouting.
Folk will ask: why was it this they'd spare?
Folk will see me leave the place the following
morning
And will say: so that's who was in there!
And the ship with eight sails and
With fifty great cannon
Will run flags up the mast.

And a hundred men will come ashore before
it's noon
And will go where it's dark and chill.
And every man they find, they will drag
along the street
And they'll clap him in chains and lay him
at my feet
And they'll ask: now which of these are we
to kill?
And when the clock strikes noon it will be
still down by the harbor.
When folk ask: now just who has got to
die?
You will hear me say at that point: All of
them!
And when their heads fall, I'll say:
Whoopee!
And the ship with eight sails and
With fifty great cannon
Will sail off with me.

MATTHEW: Very nice, comic, eh? How she does
it, the young lady!

MACHEATH: What d'you mean: *nice*? That's art,
not nice. You did it wonderfully, Polly. But
before such swine — pardon me, your
Reverence — there's no point, it's wasted.
(*In an undertone to* POLLY) Anyway, I don't
approve of you doing this play-acting, kindly
drop it in future.

(*Loud laughter at the table. The gang are making fun of the parson.*)

What have you got in your hand, your
Reverence?

JACOB: Two knives, Captain.

MACHEATH: And what have you got on your
plate, your Reverence?

KIMBALL: Smoked salmon, I think.

MACHEATH: And with the knife, I believe,
you're eating the salmon?

JACOB: Have you ever seen the like, eating fish
with a knife! A person who does that is
nothing more than a . . .

MACHEATH: Pig. Understand me, Jacob? That'll
teach you.

JIMMY (*bursting in*): Captain! The coppers! It's
the sheriff himself.

WALTER: Brown! Tiger Brown!

MACHEATH: Yes, Tiger Brown it is. It's Tiger
Brown, Sheriff of London and pillar of the
Old Bailey, who is about to enter Captain
Macheath's poor little abode. Now you'll
learn something!

(*The gang creep away.*)

JACOB: It's the gallows for us.

(BROWN *enters.*)

MACHEATH: Hello, Jacky!

BROWN: Hello, Mac! Now I haven't got much
time, I must leave in a minute. Do you *have*
to pick on somebody else's stable? *Another*
burglary.

MACHEATH: But Jacky, it's so convenient. I'm
delighted you could come to partake of old
Mac's wedding breakfast. May I introduce
my wife, Polly, née Peachum. Polly, this is
Tiger Brown. Eh, old man? (*Slaps him on
the back.*) And these are my friends, Jacky.
You've probably seen them all before.

BROWN (*in embarrassment*): I'm here in my
private capacity, Mac.

MACHEATH: So are they. (*He calls them. They
come, hands up.*) Hi, Jacob!

BROWN: That's Hook-Finger Jacob, he's a dirty
skunk.

MACHEATH: Here! Jimmy, Robert! Walter!

BROWN: Well, we'll forget it for today.

MACHEATH: Hi, Ed! Matthew!

BROWN: Sit down, gentlemen, sit down.

ALL: Thank you, sir.

BROWN: Happy to meet the charming wife of my old friend Mac.

POLLY: Don't mention it, sir.

MACHEATH: Sit yourself down, you old rascal, and start in on the whisky! Polly! Gentlemen! Today you see in your midst a man whom our sovereign's inscrutable wisdom has chosen to set high over his follow men, and who yet has remained through fair weather and foul my friend. You all know who I mean, and you, too, know who I mean, Brown. Ah, Jacky, do you remember when you were a soldier and I was a soldier and we served together in India? Jacky, old man, shall we sing them the "Song of the Heavy Cannon"? (*They sit side by side on the table.*)

(*Song illumination: a golden light. The organ is lit up. Three lights come down from above on a bar, and on a board is written:*)

THE SONG OF THE HEAVY CANNON

John was a soldier and so was James
And George became a sergeant in short order.
But the army is not interested in names:
They were soon marching north to the border.
What soldiers live on
Is heavy cannon
From the Cape to the Cutch Behar.
If it should rain one night
And they should chance to sight
Pallid or swarthy faces
Of uncongenial races
They'll maybe chop them up to make some beefsteak tartare.

Now John was rather cold at night
And James, he found the whisky "rather hot, sir."
But George said: "Everything's all right
For the army simply cannot go to pot, sir."
What soldiers live on
Is heavy cannon
From the Cape to Cutch Behar.
If it should rain one night
And they should chance to sight

Pallid or swarthy faces
Of uncongenial races
They'll maybe chop them up to make some beefsteak tartare.

John's gone west and James is dead
And George is missing and barmy.
Blood, however, is still blood-red:
They're recruiting again for the army.

(*As they all sit there, they march in time with their feet.*)

What soldiers live on
Is heavy cannon
From the Cape to Cutch Behar.
If it should rain one night
And they should chance to sight
Pallid or swarthy faces
Of uncongenial races
They'll maybe chop them up to make some beefsteak tartare.

MACHEATH: We were boyhood friends, and though the great tides of life have swept us far apart, although our professional interests are quite different — some might even say diametrically opposed — our friendship has survived it all. That'll teach you something. Castor and Pollux, Hector and Andromache, and so forth. Seldom have I, the simple hold-up man — well, you know what I mean — seldom have I undertaken the smallest job without giving my friend Brown a share of the proceeds (a considerable share, Brown) as a token and a proof of my unswerving loyalty to him. And seldom has the all-powerful Sheriff — take that knife out of your mouth, Jacob — organized a raid without previously giving a little tip-off to me, the friend of his youth. Well . . . and so on, and so on . . . it's all a matter of give and take. That'll teach you. (*He takes* BROWN *by the arm.*) Well, Jacky, I'm glad you've come. That's what I call real friendship. (*A pause while* BROWN *sorrowfully regards a carpet.*) Genuine Shiraz.

BROWN: From the Oriental Carpet Company.

MACHEATH: We get all our carpets there. Do you know, I had to have you here today,

Jacky. I hope you don't feel too uncomfortable, being in the position you are.

BROWN: You know, Mac, I can't refuse you anything. But I must be going. I've got so much on my mind. If the least thing should go wrong at the Coronation . . .

MACHEATH: Jacky, you know my father-in-law is a repulsive old swine. If he were to raise some sort of stink about me, are there any records in Scotland Yard that could be used against me?

BROWN: In Scotland Yard there is not the slightest thing against you, Mac.

MACHEATH: Of course not.

BROWN: I saw to that. Good night.

MACHEATH: Aren't you all going to stand up?

BROWN (to POLLY): All the best!

(Exit BROWN accompanied by MACHEATH.)

JACOB (who meanwhile with MATTHEW and WALTER has been conferring with POLLY): I must admit I couldn't repress certain trepidations when I heard Tiger Brown was coming!

MATTHEW: You know, miss, we have our contacts with the highest authorities.

WALTER: Yes. Mac always has an extra iron in the fire which the likes of us haven't a glimmering of! But we have our little irons in the fire too. Gentlemen, it's half past nine.

MATTHEW: And now — the high spot.

(All retire to the back, behind a hanging carpet which conceals something. MACHEATH enters.)

MACHEATH: What's up now?

MATTHEW: Another little surprise, Captain.

(Behind the carpet they sing "The Wedding Song for Poorer People," very softly and full of feeling. However, when they get to the end of the first verse, MATTHEW tears down the carpet and they sing on, bawling at the top of their voices and beating time on a bed which stands behind.)

MACHEATH: Thank you, friends, thank you.

WALTER: And now the unobtrusive departure.

(The gang exeunt.)

MACHEATH: And now sentiment must come into its own, for otherwise man becomes a mere slave to his work. Sit down, Polly.

(Music.)

Do you see the moon over Soho?

POLLY: I see it dearest. Can you feel my heart beating, beloved?

MACHEATH: I can feel it, beloved.

POLLY: Whither thou goest, I shall go with thee.

MACHEATH: And where thou stayest, there too shall I stay.

(Both sing:)

MACHEATH: And if there's no license or Registrar
Nor lovely flowers to make you a crown

POLLY: And if I don't know exactly who you are
Or where I got hold of this gown:

BOTH: The platter from which you are eating your bread
Don't you keep it long, throw it down
For love lasts forever (or not so long)
In many and many a town.

SCENE THREE For Peachum, who knows the hardness of the world, the loss of his daughter means nothing less than total ruin.

Peachum's Establishment for Beggars

Right, PEACHUM and MRS. PEACHUM. In the doorway stands POLLY, in hat and coat, a small suitcase in her hand.

MRS. PEACHUM: Married? First we load her fore and aft with dresses and hats and gloves and parasols, and when she's cost as much as a sailing ship to rig out, she flings herself in the gutter like a rotten tomato. Have you really gone and got married?

(Song illumination: golden light. The organ is lit up. Three lights come down on a bar, and on a board is written:)

IN A LITTLE SONG POLLY GIVES HER PARENTS A HINT OF HER MARRIAGE WITH THE GANGSTER MACHEATH

When I was a girl, and an innocent girl
(I was innocent once as were you)
I thought that perhaps I might interest some fellow
And so I must know just what to do.
And if he's a rich fellow
And if he's a nice fellow
And his collar is as white as snow
And if he knows how he should treat a real lady
Then I must tell him: No.
That way I can hold my head up high
And be a lady comme il faut.
Yes, the moon shines bright until it's day!
Yes, the boat is launched and duly sails away!
And that's just how far things go.
For one must not rush a fellow off his feet!
No, one must be cold and very slow.
For, hey presto, so much might happen!
The only word to use is: No.

The first man who came was a man from Kent
Who was all that a man should be.
The second, oh, he had three schooners in the harbor
And the third one was crazy for me.
And as they were rich men
And as they were nice men
And their collars were as white as snow
And as they knew how they should treat a real lady
I had to say to each one: No.
That way I could hold my head up high
And be a lady comme il faut.
Yes, the moon shone bright till it was day!
Yes, the boat was launched and duly sailed away!
And that's how far things could go.
For one must not rush a fellow off his feet!
No, I must be cold and very slow.
For, hey presto, so much might happen!
But not if I should whisper: No.

And yet one afternoon (and that day the sky was blue)
Came someone who did not ask.
And he hung his bowler hat upon the nail inside my bedroom
And applied himself to his task.
And as he was not rich
And as he was not nice
And even his Sunday collar was black as a crow
And as he didn't know how he should treat a real lady
I could not tell him: No.
This way I couldn't hold my head up high
Or be a lady comme il faut.
Oh, the moon shone bright the whole night long
But the boat was tied up good and strong
And it all had to be just so.
For a man must simply rush us off our feet
And one really needn't be so cold or slow.
For, hey presto, it had to happen:
I could not tell that someone No.

PEACHUM: So now she's become a crook's hussy! *Very* nice. That's lovely.

MRS. PEACHUM: If you're already so immoral as to marry at all, why must it be a horse thief and a footpad? That'll cost you dear some day! I should have seen it coming. Even as a child she had a head as swollen as the Queen of England.

PEACHUM: So she really got married.

MRS. PEACHUM: Yes. Yesterday afternoon at five o'clock.

PEACHUM: To a notorious criminal! Come to think of it, it shows great courage in the man. If I have to give away my daughter, the last support of my old age, my house will fall in and my last dog will desert me. Why, I couldn't give away the dirt under my fingernails without risking death from starvation. If the three of us can get through the winter on one log of wood, we may live to see next year. We *may*.

MRS. PEACHUM: What are you thinking of? This is our reward for everything, Jonathan.

I shall go mad. Everything is going round in my head. I can't stand any more. Oh! (*She faints.*) A glass of brandy!

PEACHUM: There! See what you've done to your mother. Quick! A crook's trollop, that's fine, that's charming. Strange how the old lady has taken it to heart.

(POLLY *returns with a bottle of brandy.*)

The last consolation left for your poor mother!

POLLY: Go on, you can give her two glasses. *My* mother can carry twice as much when she's not herself. That'll put her on her legs again. (*During the whole of this scene she has a radiantly happy expression on her face.*)

MRS. PEACHUM (*revives*): Oh! Now she's showing her wicked false sympathy and solicitude again!

(*Five men enter.*)

BEGGAR: I must complain most strongly. Because this place is a pigsty. Because this isn't a proper stump, but just a mess, and I won't waste my money on it.

PEACHUM: What do you want? It's as good as the others, only you don't keep it clean.

BEGGAR: All right — then why don't I earn as much as the others? No, you can't put that over on me. (*Hurls the stump away.*) I might as well cut off my real leg, if I wanted such junk.

PEACHUM: Well, what *do* you want? What can *I* do about it if people have hearts of granite. I can't make you five stumps! In ten minutes I can make such a wreck out of any man that a dog would howl if he saw him. What can I do if *people* won't howl? There, take another stump, if one's not enough for you. But look after your things.

BEGGAR: That'll have to do.

PEACHUM (*tries a false arm on another beggar*): Leather is no good, Celia. Rubber is more repulsive. (*to the third*) The bruise is going down, and it's your last. Now we can start

all over again. (*Examining the fourth*) Of course, natural scabs are never the same as artificial ones. (*to the fifth*) What's happened to you? You've been eating again. You'll have to be made an example of.

BEGGAR: Mr. Peachum, I really haven't eaten much, my fat's unnatural, I can't help it.

PEACHUM: Neither can I. You're dismissed. (*Turning his back to the second beggar.*) Between "giving people a shock" and "getting on their nerves" there's obviously a difference, my friend. I need artists. Today, only artists give people the right sort of shock. If you'd work properly, your public would be forced to appreciate you. But that never occurs to you. So naturally I cannot extend your engagement.

(*The beggars exeunt.*)

POLLY: Please consider him. Is he handsome? No. But he makes a living. He offers me an existence. He's a first-class burglar, a far-sighted and experienced street robber. I could tell you exactly what he's got saved up. A few more successful enterprises and we can retire to a little house in the country, just like that Mr. Shakespeare father admires so much.

PEACHUM: Well then, it's all quite simple. You're married. What do you do when you're married? Don't bother to think. You get a divorce. Eh? Is that so hard to arrange?

POLLY: I don't know what you mean.

MRS. PEACHUM: Divorce.

POLLY: But I love him, how can I think of divorce?

MRS. PEACHUM: Polly, aren't you ashamed of yourself?

POLLY: Mother, if you've ever been in love . . .

MRS. PEACHUM: Love! Those damned books you've been reading have turned your head. Polly, *everyone* does it!

POLLY: Then I shall be an exception.

MRS. PEACHUM: I'll beat your bottom, you exception!

POLLY: All mothers do that, but it's no use. Because love is greater than a beaten bottom!

MRS. PEACHUM: Polly, don't try my patience too far.

POLLY: I won't let you rob me of my love!

MRS. PEACHUM: Another word, and you'll get a box on the ears.

POLLY: Love is the greatest thing in the world!

MRS. PEACHUM: And that fellow has several women. When he's hanged, there'll be half a dozen of them reporting as widows, each probably with a brat in her arms. — Oh, Jonathan!

PEACHUM: Hanged! How did you come to think of hanging? It's a good idea! Go outside, Polly.

(*Exit* POLLY.)

You're right. The idea's worth forty pounds.

MRS. PEACHUM: I know what you mean. Tell the sheriff.

PEACHUM: Of course. Besides, this way we get him hanged free. . . . It'll be two birds with one stone. Only we've got to find out where he's hiding.

MRS. PEACHUM: I can tell you, my dear. He's with his whores.

PEACHUM: But they won't give him up.

MRS. PEACHUM: Leave it to me. Money rules the world. I'll go straight to Wapping and talk to the girls. If this fine gentleman meets a single one of them two hours from now, he's a goner.

POLLY (*who has been listening behind the door*): My dear Mama, you can save yourself the trouble. Before Mac would speak to such a woman, he'd give himself up to the police. And if he went to the police, the Sheriff would offer him a cocktail, and over a cigar they'd discuss a certain business in this street where things aren't quite as they should be either. For, dear Papa, the Sheriff was very merry at my wedding.

PEACHUM: What's the name of this Sheriff?

POLLY: His name is Brown. But you'd only know him as Tiger Brown. Because all who are afraid of him call him Tiger Brown. But my husband, you see, calls him Jacky. They were boyhood friends.

PEACHUM: I see, they're friends, are they? The Sheriff and the number one criminal. Then they're probably the only friends in this fine city.

POLLY (*rhapsodically*): Whenever they had a cocktail together, they'd stroke each other's cheek and say, "If you'll have another, I'll have another." And whenever one went out, the other's eyes grew moist and he'd say, "Whither thou goest, I will go too." There's nothing against Mac in Scotland Yard.

PEACHUM: I see. Between Tuesday evening and Thursday morning, Mr. Macheath — surely a much married gentleman — has enticed my daughter Polly Peachum from her parental home under the pretext of marriage. Before this week is over, this will be sufficient to bring him to the death he so richly deserves. "Mr. Macheath, you once had white kid gloves and a stick with an ivory handle and a scar on your neck and you frequented the Octopus Hotel. All that remains is your scar, the least valuable of your distinguishing marks, and henceforth you will frequent only prison cells, and soon you won't frequent anywhere . . ."

MRS. PEACHUM: Oh, Jonathan, you'll never succeed, for it's Mackie the Knife you're dealing with. They say he's the greatest criminal in London. He takes what he wants.

PEACHUM: Who is Mackie the Knife? Polly, get ready, we're going to the Sheriff of London. And *you're* going to Wapping.

MRS. PEACHUM: To his whores.

PEACHUM: For the wickedness of the world is so great you have to run your legs off to avoid having them stolen from under you.

POLLY: And I, Papa, will be very glad to shake Mr. Brown by the hand again.

(All three walk to the front of the stage and to song illumination sing the first finale. On the board is written:)

FIRST THREEPENNY-FINALE
ON THE UNCERTAINTY OF HUMAN
CIRCUMSTANCES

POLLY: There's a thing I want to try:
  Once in this my dark existence
  To reward a man's persistence.
  Do you think I aim too high?

PEACHUM *(with a Bible in his hands)*: The right
    to happiness is fundamental:
  Men live so little time and die alone.
  Nor is it altogether incidental
  That they want bread to eat and not a stone.
  The right to happiness is fundamental.
  And yet how great would be the innovation
  Should someone claim and get that right —
    hooray!
  The thought appeals to my imagination!
  But this old world of ours ain't built that
    way.

MRS. PEACHUM: How I wish I could supply
  Philanthropical assistance
  To relieve your dark existence
  But one must not aim so high.

PEACHUM: To be a good man — what a nice
    idea!
  And give the poor your money? That is fine!
  When all mankind is good, His Kingdom's
    near!
  Who would not like to bask in Light Divine?
  To be a good man — what a nice idea!
  But there's the little problem of subsistence:
  Supplies are scarce and human beings base.
  Who would not like a peaceable existence?
  But this old world is not that kind of place.

POLLY AND MRS. PEACHUM:

I fear he's right, $\begin{cases} \text{my} \\ \text{your} \end{cases}$ dear old dad:
  The world is poor and men are bad.

PEACHUM: Of course, he's right, your dear old
    dad:
  The world is poor and men are bad.
  An earthly paradise might be arranged
  If this old world of ours could but be changed

But that can never be arranged.
  Your brother might be fond of you
  But if the meat supply won't do
  He'd cut you down right where you stood.
  (We'd all be loyal if we could.)
  Your good wife might be fond of you
  But if your love for her won't do
  She'd cut you down right where you stood.
  (We'd all be grateful if we could.)
  Your children might be fond of you
  But if your pension would not do
  They'd cut you down right where you stood.
  (We'd all be human if we could.)

POLLY AND MRS. PEACHUM: We do not mind
    confessing
  The whole thing is depressing.
  The world is poor and men are bad
  And we have nothing more to add.

PEACHUM: There is of course no more to add.
  The world is poor and men are bad.
  We would be good, instead of base
  But this old world is not that kind of place.

ALL THREE: We take no comfort from your
    bunk
  For everything's a heap of junk.

PEACHUM: The world is poor and men are bad
  There is of course no more to add.

ALL THREE: We do not mind confessing
  The whole thing is depressing.
  We take no comfort from your bunk
  For everything's a heap of junk.

ACT TWO

SCENE ONE   Thursday afternoon. Mackie the Knife takes leave of his wife before fleeing across Highgate Moor to escape his father-in-law.

The Stable

POLLY *(enters)*: Mac! Mac! Don't be afraid, it's me.

MACHEATH *(lying on a bed)*: What's the matter? What are you looking like that for, Polly?

POLLY: I've just been to see Brown, and my father was there too, and they're plotting to catch you. My father threatened something terrible, and Brown stuck up for you at first; but he gave in later, and he thinks you ought to disappear for a while. Mac, you must pack quickly!

MACHEATH: What! Pack? Nonsense! Come here, Polly! We're going to do something quite different from packing.

POLLY: No, Mac, we can't now. I'm so frightened. They were talking about hanging all the time.

MACHEATH: I don't like it, Polly, when you're moody! There's nothing against *me* in Scotland Yard.

POLLY: No, perhaps there wasn't. But today there's a terrible lot. Listen, I've brought the list of charges with me. I don't know whether I shall get through it, it's endless: you've killed two shopkeepers, and committed more than thirty burglaries, twenty-three street robberies, arsons, attempted murders, forgeries, perjuries — and all in eighteen months. You're a terrible person, Mac. And in Winchester you seduced two sisters, both under the age of consent.

MACHEATH: They told me they were twenty-one. And what did Brown say?

(*He stands up slowly and walks to the right along the footlights, whistling.*)

POLLY: He caught me up in the corridor and said he couldn't do anything more for you. Oh, Mac! (*She throws her arms around his neck.*)

MACHEATH: Well then, if I *must* go, you'll have to take over the business.

POLLY: Don't talk of business now. I can't bear it! Mac, kiss your Polly again and swear that as far as she is concerned you'll never, never . . .

MACHEATH (*interrupts her and leads her to the table, where he pushes her down into a chair*): These are the account books. Listen carefully. This is a list of the staff. (*Reads.*)

Hook-Finger Jacob, a year and a half in business; let's see what he's brought in. One, two, three, four, five gold watches. Not much, but it's good skilled work. — Don't sit on my lap. I'm not in the mood now. And here's Walter — Wally the Weeper — an unreliable swine. Fences stuff on his own account. Three weeks grace for him, then the gallows. Simply report him to Brown.

POLLY (*sobbing*): Simply report him to Brown.

MACHEATH: Jimmy the Second, an impudent customer — profitable but impudent. Pinches sheets from under the finest female backsides in the land. Give him a rise.

POLLY: I'll give him a rise.

MACHEATH: Robert — call him Robert the Saw — a petty thief without a trace of genius. He won't end on the gallows, he'll never come to anything.

POLLY: Never come to anything.

MACHEATH: Otherwise carry on the same as before: get up at seven, wash, take one bath a day, and so forth.

POLLY: You're right, Mac, I shall just have to set my teeth and keep an eye on the business. What's yours is mine, isn't it, Mackie? But, Mac, what about your rooms? Shall I give them up? I'm horrified at the rent!

MACHEATH: No, I need them.

POLLY: But why? They only cost us money.

MACHEATH: You seem to think I'm never going to come back.

POLLY: What do you mean? You can take them again! Mac . . . Mac, I can't stand it any longer. I look at your lips and I don't hear what you're saying. Will you be true to me, Mac?

MACHEATH: Of course I'll be true to you. I'll repay like with like. Do you think I don't love you? It's just that I look further ahead.

POLLY: I'm so glad, Mac. You think of me when they're after you like bloodhounds . . .

(When he hears the word "bloodhounds," MACHEATH *stiffens, stands up, crosses to the right, takes off his coat and starts washing his hands.*)

MACHEATH (*hurriedly*): Send all the profits to Jack Poole's banking house in Manchester. Between ourselves, it's only a question of weeks before I switch to banking exclusively. It's safer as well as more profitable. In two weeks at the most the money must be out of this business. And then you'll go to Brown and hand the whole list of names to the police. In four weeks at the most, all this scum of the earth will be standing their trial at the Old Bailey.

POLLY: But Mac! How can you look them in the eye when you're going to double-cross them like this and have them as good as hanged? Can you still shake them by the hand?

MACHEATH: Who? Money Matthew, Hook-Finger Jacob, Robert the Saw, Wally the Weeper . . . those jailbirds?

(*Enter the gang.*)

Gentlemen, I'm very glad to see you.

POLLY: . . . gentlemen.

MATTHEW: Captain, I've got the plans for the Coronation here. There's a day of good hard work ahead of us. The Archbishop of Canterbury arrives in half an hour.

MACHEATH: When?

MATTHEW: Five-thirty. We must go at once, Captain.

MACHEATH: Yes, you must go at once.

ROBERT: What do you mean: *you*?

MACHEATH: As far as I'm concerned, I'm afraid I've got to take a short trip to the country.

ROBERT: What? Are they going to nab you?

MATTHEW: And just when the Coronation's coming off! A Coronation without you will be soup without a spoon.

MACHEATH: Shut your mouth. I'm handing over the management of the business to my wife for a short time. — Polly. (*He pushes her to the front and then retires to the back, where he watches her.*)

POLLY: Men, I think our Captain can go away without having to worry. We shall get along fine, eh?

MATTHEW: I've got nothing to say. But I don't know if a woman . . . at a time like this . . . I'm not saying anything against *you*, ma'am . . .

MACHEATH (*from the back*): What do you say to that, Polly?

POLLY: You've made a good start, you son of a bitch! (*Screaming*) Of course you're not saying anything against me, or these gentlemen here would long ago have had your trousers off and tanned your bottom. Isn't that so, gentlemen?

(*A short pause, then they all clap like mad.*)

JACOB: She's all right!

WALTER: Bravo! Our new captain knows the answers! Hurrah for Polly!

ALL: Hurrah for Polly!

MACHEATH: It's a shame I can't be in London for the Coronation. It'll be a gold mine. Every house empty during the day, and at night all the best people drunk. That reminds me, Matthew — you drink too much. Last week you made it obvious that it was you that set fire to the children's hospital at Greenwich. If this happens again, you're sacked. Who set fire to the children's hospital?

MATTHEW: I did.

MACHEATH (*to the others*): Who set it on fire?

THE FIVE OTHERS: You did, Captain.

MACHEATH: Who did?

MATTHEW (*sullenly*): You did. This way, the likes of me will never come up in the world.

MACHEATH (*with a gesture of hanging*): You'll come up all right, if you try to compete with me. Did you ever hear of an Oxford professor letting all his scientific mistakes be made by some assistant? Of course not: he takes the credit for them himself.

ROBERT: Ma'am, now you're in command while your husband's away . . . payday every Thursday, ma'am.

POLLY: Every Thursday, men!

(*Exit gang.*)

MACHEATH: And now, good-bye, my love. Keep fresh, and don't forget to make up every day, just as if I were there.

POLLY: And you, Mac, promise me you'll never look at another woman, and that you'll leave London at once. Believe me, your little Polly doesn't say this out of jealousy, but because it's important!

MACHEATH: But, Polly, why should *I* bother with second-hand goods? I love only you. When it's dark enough I shall start out, get my black stallion from . . . oh, some stable or other, and before you can see the moon from your window, I shall be far beyond Highgate Moor.

POLLY: Oh, Mac, don't tear my heart from my body. Stay with me and let us be happy.

MACHEATH: But I have to tear my own heart from my body, for I have to go and no one knows when I shall return.

POLLY: It lasted such a little while, Mac.

MACHEATH: And now it's over?

POLLY: Mac, last night I had a dream. I was looking out of the window and I heard laughter in the street, and when I looked up I saw our moon, and the moon was quite thin, like a penny that's all worn away. Don't forget me, Mac, in the strange cities.

MACHEATH: Of course I shall never forget you, Polly. Kiss me, Polly.

POLLY: Good-bye, Mac.

MACHEATH: Good-bye, Polly. (*As he exits*)
For love lasts forever (or not so long)
In ever so many a town.

POLLY (*alone*): And he never will come back again! (*She sings*)

Sweet while it lasted
And now it is over.
Tear out your heart
Say "Good-bye, good Polly!"
What use is your weeping
(Blessed Virgin, restore me)
When it's plain my mother
Knew all this before me!

(*The bells ring.*)

The Queen is now in London on her way.
Where shall we be on Coronation Day?

INTERLUDE

(MRS. PEACHUM *and* GINNY JENNY *step out in front of the curtain.*)

MRS. PEACHUM: So if you see Mackie the Knife in the next few days, run to the nearest copper and report him. You'll get ten shillings for it.

GINNY JENNY: But do you think we'll see him if the police are after him? When the hunt starts, he won't be wasting any time with us.

MRS. PEACHUM: Let me tell you this, Jenny: if all London were after him, Macheath is not the man to give up his old habits.

(*She sings:*)

THE BALLAD OF SEXUAL SUBMISSIVENESS

Now here's a man who fights old Satan's battle:
The butcher, he! All other men, mere cattle!
He is a shark with all the world to swim in!
What gets him down? What gets 'em all down? Women.
He may not want to, but he'll acquiesce
For such is sexual submissiveness.
    He does not heed the Bible nor the Statute Book.
    He says he is an egomaniac.
    If women look at him, he won't look back
    For girls can murder with a look.
    His fortitude by daylight is surprising

But when the night is falling, he is rising.

And many saw the tragic fall of many:
The great Macheath fell into Harlot Jenny.
Those who stood by might swear his sins were scarlet
But when they died, who buried them? Some harlot.
They may not want to, but they acquiesce
For such is sexual submissiveness.
    Some read the Bible; others take a Law Degree;
    Some join the Church and some attack the State;
    While some remove the celery from their plate
    And then devise a theory.
    By evening all are busy moralizing
    But when the night is falling, they are rising.

SCENE TWO   The Coronation bells have not yet rung out and Mackie the Knife is already among his whores at Wapping. The girls betray him. It is Thursday evening.

A Brothel in Wapping

An ordinary evening. The whores, mostly in their shifts, are quietly ironing, playing draughts, washing themselves: a middle-class idyll. JENNY *sits alone on one side.* HOOK-FINGER JACOB *is reading the newspaper without anyone paying the slightest attention to him. In fact, he is rather in the way.*

JACOB: He won't come today.

WHORE: Won't he?

JACOB: I don't think he'll *ever* come again.

WHORE: That would be a pity.

JACOB: Would it? If I know him, he's out of the city by this time. Up and away!

(*Enter* MACHEATH. *He hangs his hat on a nail and sits on the sofa behind the table.*)

MACHEATH: My coffee, please!

VIXEN (*repeats astounded*): "My coffee, please!"

JACOB (*horrified*): Why aren't you in Highgate?

MACHEATH: Today is Thursday. I cannot let such trifles disturb my habits. (*He throws his charge-sheet on the floor.*) Besides, it's raining.

GINNY JENNY (*reads the charge-sheet*): "In the name of the Queen, Captain Macheath is herewith charged with triple . . ."

JACOB (*snatching it from her*): Am I there too?

MACHEATH: Of course, the whole staff.

GINNY JENNY (*to another whore*): Look, here are the charges. (*Pause*) Mac, give me your hand. (*He holds out his hand as he drinks from a coffee cup in the other.*)

DOLLY: Yes, Jenny, read his hand.

(*She holds forward a paraffin lamp.*)

MACHEATH: A rich legacy?

GINNY JENNY: No, not a rich legacy.

BETTY: Why are you looking at him like that, Jenny? It's enough to give anyone the shivers.

MACHEATH: A long journey in the near future?

GINNY JENNY: No, not a long journey.

VIXEN: What do you see then?

MACHEATH: Only good news, please! No bad!

GINNY JENNY: Oh well! I see a narrow strip of darkness there and a little love. And then I see a large T, which means the treachery of a woman. Then I see . . .

MACHEATH: Stop. I'd like to have a few details about the narrow strip of darkness and the treachery: for example, the name of the treacherous woman.

GINNY JENNY: I can only see that it begins with J.

MACHEATH: Then it's wrong. It begins with P.

GINNY JENNY: Mac, when the Coronation bells ring out from Westminster, you'll have a bad time of it.

MACHEATH: Go on. (JACOB *laughs raucously.*)

What's the matter? (*He goes across to* JACOB, *and reads.*) Quite wrong, there were only three.

JACOB (*laughs*): That's just it.

MACHEATH: Nice underwear you have here.

WHORE: From the cradle to the coffin, underwear comes first.

OLD WHORE: I never use silk. The gentlemen immediately think you're ill.

(GINNY JENNY *edges stealthily out of the door.*)

SECOND WHORE (*to* GINNY JENNY): Where are you going, Jenny?

GINNY JENNY: You'll see. (*Exit.*)

MOLLY: But plain linens put them off.

OLD WHORE: I've had great success with plain linen.

VIXEN: That's because the gentlemen feel at home with it.

MACHEATH (*to* BETTY): Have you still got the black braid?

BETTY: Yes, still the black braid.

MACHEATH: And what sort of underwear do you have, my dear?

SECOND WHORE: Oh, I'm so ashamed, I can't bring 'em to my room, my aunt hates men. And in doorways, you know, you just can't have on underwear.

(JACOB *laughs.*)

MACHEATH: Finished?

JACOB: No, I'm just at the "rapes."

MACHEATH (*again sitting on the sofa*): But where's Jenny got to? Ladies, long before my star rose over this town . . .

VIXEN: Long before my star rose over this town . . .

MACHEATH: I lived in the poorest circumstances with one of you fair ladies. And though I am Mackie the Knife now, in my present happiness I shall never forget the companions of my darker days: above all Jenny, whom I loved best of all the girls. Listen!

(*As* MACHEATH *sings,* GINNY JENNY *stands outside the window right and beckons to* CONSTABLE SMITH. *Then* MRS. PEACHUM *joins her. All three stand under the street lamp and look into the house.*)

THE BALLAD OF THE FANCY MAN

MACHEATH: Once upon a time — who knows
    how long ago? —
We shared a home together, I and she.
My head and her abdomen turned the trick.
I protected her and she supported me.
(Some say it's different, but I say it's slick.)
And when a wooer came I crept out of our
    bed
And got myself a schnapps and showed
    myself well-bred.
When he shelled out, I said: Auf Wiedersehn
If any time you'd care to, come again!
For half a year we had no cause to roam
For that bordello was our home from home.

(*Enter* GINNY JENNY *through the door: behind her,* SMITH.)

GINNY JENNY: At that same time — it's rather
    long ago —
He took the bloom off our relationship.
For when the cash was short, he bawled me
    out.
One day he yelled: I'm going to pawn your
    slip!
(A slip is nice but one can do without.)
And then — you know how 'tis — I felt a
    certain pique.
I asked him more than once: how did he
    have the cheek?
Then he would pummel me, would my good
    pal
And I would end up in the hospital.
Life was all honey from the honeycomb
In that bordello which was home from home.

BOTH TOGETHER ALTERNATELY:

BOTH: And at that time — long, long, long,
    long ago —

HE: (To think of it just now gives me a lift)

SHE: By day alone could we two sport and play

HE: For night was usually her working shift. (The night is usual, but there's also the day.)

SHE: One day I felt beneath my heart a young Macheath.

HE: We then and there agreed: I should lie underneath.

SHE: An unborn child, you know, so often crushes.

HE: At that, *this* child was destined for the rushes.

BOTH: Though that bordello was our home from home.
In half a year we were constrained to roam.

(*Dance.* MACHEATH *picks up his swordstick: she hands him his hat; and he is still dancing when* SMITH *lays a hand on his shoulder.*)

MACHEATH: Has this rat hole still got only one exit?

(SMITH *attempts to handcuff* MACHEATH. MACHEATH *pushes against his chest, so that he stumbles over backward. Then* MACHEATH *jumps out of the window. But outside are* MRS. PEACHUM *and other policemen.*)

MACHEATH (*calmly and very politely*): Good evening, madam.

MRS. PEACHUM: My dear Mr. Macheath! My husband always says: "The greatest heroes in history have always tripped up over little obstacles."

MACHEATH: May I inquire how your husband is?

MRS. PEACHUM: Better — now. Well, you can take your leave of these ladies. Officers, take Mr. Macheath to his new lodgings. (*He is led off.* MRS. PEACHUM *speaks through the window.*) The gentleman will be living henceforth at the Old Bailey. If you should wish to visit him, ladies, you will always find him at home. I knew he'd be here with his whores! I will settle the bill. Farewell, ladies. (*Exit.*)

GINNY JENNY: Hey Jacob! Something's happened.

JACOB (*who, on account of his intensive reading, has noticed nothing*): Where's Mac?

GINNY JENNY: The coppers were here!

JACOB: No! And here was I quietly reading . . . boys, boys, boys! (*Exit.*)

SCENE THREE   Betrayed by the whores, Macheath is freed from prison through the love of another woman.

Prison in the Old Bailey. A Barred Cage

(*Enter* BROWN.)

BROWN: I hope my men don't catch him! Dear God, I hope he's beyond Highgate Moor thinking of his old friend Jacky! But he's thoughtless, like all men. If they should bring him in now, and he were to look at me with those faithful friendly eyes, I couldn't stand it. Thank God, there's a moon: once he's out in the country, he'll find his way all right. (*Noise outside.*) What's that? Oh God, they've got him.

MACHEATH (*tied with heavy ropes and guarded by six constables, enters proudly*): Well, my minions, here we are again! Back in our old home. (*He sees* BROWN, *who has retreated to the farthest corner of the cell.*)

BROWN (*after a long pause, under the fearful gaze of his former friend*): Mac, I didn't do it . . . I did everything I could . . . don't look at me like that, Mac . . . I can't bear it . . . Your silence is terrible! (*He shouts at a constable.*) Don't pull at that rope, you swine! Say something, Mac. Say something to your old friend Jacky! Lighten his darkness, I beseech you . . . (*He rests his head against the wall and weeps.*) He doesn't think me worth a word. (*Exit.*)

MACHEATH: That miserable Brown! That evil conscience incarnate! And a creature like that is made Sheriff of London! Lucky I didn't bawl him out. I'd intended doing something of the sort. But then I thought a good, piercing, punishing stare would send the shivers down his back. It worked. I looked at him and he wept bitterly. I got that trick from the Bible.

(*Re-enter* Smith *with handcuffs.*)

Well, Mr. Jailer, I suppose those are the heaviest you could find? With your permission, I should like a more comfortable pair.

(*He takes out his check book.*)

Smith: Certainly, Captain, we have them here at all prices. It depends what you want to pay. From one to ten guineas.

Macheath: How much do none cost?

Smith: Fifty.

Macheath (*writes out a check*): The devil of it is, all that business with Lucy will come out. And when Brown hears what I've done to his daughter behind his friendly back, he'll turn into a real tiger for the first time in his life.

Smith: You've made your bed: lie on it.

Macheath: I'll bet that trollop is waiting outside. I shall have a fine time from now till the execution.

So, gentlemen, is this what you'd call living?
Take no offence if Mackie disagrees.
While still a babe I heard with grave
    misgiving:
None but the well-to-do can take at ease.

(*Song illumination: golden light. The organ is illuminated. Three lights come down on a bar from above — and on the board is written:*)

The Secret of Gracious Living

Great praise is always lavished on great
    thinkers
Who think of books (but do not think of
    dinner)
In some old shack where even rats grow
    thinner —
I can't abide such solitary stinkers!
For Simple Living simply does not pay
And I'd be glad to hear the last of it.
From here to Rome no turtledove or tit
Would live on such a menu for one day.
Let 'em keep their freedom! Let 'em keep their
    fleas!
Only the well-to-do can take their ease.

Those brave adventurers whose quaint
    addiction
Is Truth and Freedom in and out of season
And risking their own necks for no good
    reason
(Materials for adventurous non-fiction):
See how they waste the wintry evenings
    napping
Then silently with wintry wife to bed
Their solemn thoughts three thousand years
    ahead
And both their ears agog for cheers and
    clapping!
Let 'em keep their bravery! I've a better
    wheeze:
None but the well-to-do can take their ease.

In spring I ask: could there be something to it?
Could not Macheath be great and solitary?
But then the year works round to January
And I reply: My boy, you'll live to rue it.
Poverty makes you sad as well as wise
And bravery mingles danger with the fame.
Poor, lonely, wise and brave — in heaven's
    name!
Good-bye to greatness! I return the prize
With this my repartee of repartees:
None but the well-to-do can take their ease.

(*Enter* Lucy.)

Lucy: You miserable wretch, you! How can you look me in the face after all that has happened between us?

Macheath: Lucy, have you no heart? When you see your own husband in this condition?

Lucy: My husband! You brute! So you think I know nothing about what you've been up to with Miss Peachum? I could scratch your eyes out!

Macheath: Lucy, seriously, you're not so silly as to be jealous of Polly?

Lucy: So you're not married to her, you beast?

Macheath: Married! That's a good one! I visit a certain house. I talk to her. Now and then I give her a sort of kiss, and the silly bitch runs around boasting that she's married to me. My darling Lucy, I'll do anything to reassure you; if you really do believe she and I are married — well and good. What more can a gentleman say? He cannot say more.

LUCY: Oh, Mac, I only want to become an honest woman.

MACHEATH: If you think you'll become an honest woman by being married to me — good. What more can a gentleman say?

(*Enter* POLLY.)

POLLY: Where's my husband? Oh, Mac, there you are. You needn't be ashamed of me. After all, I am your wife.

LUCY: Oh, you miserable fiend!

POLLY: Mackie in prison! Why didn't you escape across Highgate Moor? You told me you wouldn't go to those women any more. I knew what they'd do to you; but I didn't say anything; I believed you. Mac, I'll stick with you to the death. — Not a word, Mac, not a look. Oh, Mac, think how your Polly's suffering!

LUCY: Oh, the trollop!

POLLY: What's that, Mac? Who is that woman? Tell her who I am. Am I not your wife? Look at me, am I not your wife?

LUCY: You treacherous swine, have you got two wives, you monster?

POLLY: Say something, Mac. Am I not your wife? Haven't I done everything for you? When I entered the state of matrimony I was pure and innocent, you know that. Didn't you hand over the gang to me? And I did everything as we arranged, and I was to tell Jacob to . . .

MACHEATH: If you two would shut your traps for five minutes I could explain the whole thing.

LUCY: No, I will not shut my trap. I can't stand it, it's more than flesh and blood can stand.

POLLY: Yes, my love, it's clear that woman there . . .

LUCY: That woman!

POLLY: . . . that woman has a certain physical priority. At least to all outward appearances, my love. Such aggravation is enough to drive one mad.

LUCY: Aggravation! That's rich! What have you gone and picked up! This dirty slut! So that's your great conquest! That's your beauty of Soho!

(*Song illumination: a golden light. The organ is lit up. Three lights come down on a bar from above and on a board is written:*)

THE JEALOUSY DUET

LUCY: Come right out, Old Soho's beauty queen!
  Let me see those legs they call so pretty!
  I should delight to recite the praises
  Of the fairest figure in our city!
  You might, it is true, produce quite an effect on Mackie!

POLLY: Oh I might? Oh I might?

LUCY: If the whole idea were not so wacky!

POLLY: Is that right? Is that right?

LUCY: He has better things to do.

POLLY: Has he better things to do?

LUCY: Than to try his hand on you.

POLLY: Than to try his hand on me?

LUCY: Ha ha ha ha ha, it can't be fun
  To get mixed up with such a one!

POLLY: Very well, let's wait and see.

LUCY: Very well, let's wait and see.

TOGETHER: Polly⎫
  Lucy⎭ loves Mac
  I actually adore him.
  He loves me back:
  All other women bore him.
  A man will not dissever
  A bond that lasts forever
  To please some filthy creature!
  Ludicrous!

POLLY: Yes, they call me Soho's beauty queen!
  When they see these legs, they call them pretty!

LUCY: But do they?

POLLY: They all delight to recite the praises
Of the fairest figure in our city!

LUCY: Shit-pot!

POLLY: Shit-pot yourself!
I have, please observe, produced quite an
effect on Mackie!

LUCY: Oh you have? Oh you have?

POLLY: And it's you, my dear, who are so
wacky!

LUCY: So it's me? So it's me?

POLLY: Who, if either hand were free.

LUCY: Who, if either hand were free?

POLLY: Would not try that hand on me?

LUCY: Would not try that hand on you?

POLLY: Ha ha ha ha ha! But as for you
Who'd dip his spoon in such a stew?

LUCY: Very well, let's wait and see.

POLLY: Very well, let's wait and see.

TOGETHER: Lucy ⎱
           Polly ⎰ loves Mac

I actually adore him.
He loves her back:
All other women bore him.
A man will not dissever
A bond that lasts forever
To please some filthy creature!
Ludicrous!

MACHEATH: And now, dear Lucy, be calm.
This is just a trick of Polly's. She wants to
make trouble. They're going to hang me,
and she wants to be able to call herself my
widow. Really, Polly, this is not the right
moment.

POLLY: You have the heart to deny me?

MACHEATH: And you have the heart to chatter
about me being married to you? Why, Polly,
must you add to my misery? (*Shakes his
head reproachfully.*) Polly, Polly!

LUCY: Really, Miss Peachum, you're making a
show of yourself. Quite apart from the fact

that it's monstrous of you to excite a poor
gentleman in this plight!

POLLY: The simplest rules of decorum, my dear
madam, would teach you, I believe, that a
person should behave with somewhat more
restraint toward a gentleman in the presence
of his wife.

MACHEATH: Seriously, Polly, that's really carrying a joke too far.

LUCY: And if you, my good madam, want to
start a row in the prison here, I shall find
myself compelled to summon a warder to
show you the door. I should be sorry to
have to do it, Miss Peachum.

POLLY: Mrs.! Mrs.! Mrs. Macheath! Permit
me to tell you this — Miss! — these airs
don't suit you in the least! My duty compels me to remain with my husband.

LUCY: What do you say to that? What do you
say? She won't go! She stands there and
waits to be thrown out! Shall I speak more
plainly?

POLLY: You — shut your filthy mouth, you
slut, or I'll give you a smack in the chops,
dear Miss!

LUCY: I'll have you kicked out, Miss Insolence! It's no use mincing words with you.
You don't understand delicacy.

POLLY: You and your delicacy! I'm compromis-
ing my own dignity! And I'm too good for
that . . . I am! (*She weeps loudly.*)

LUCY: Well, look at my stomach, you trollop!
Aren't your eyes open yet?

POLLY: Oh! That! I suppose you're hoping to
make something out of it? You should never
have let yourself in for it, you fine lady!

MACHEATH: Polly!

POLLY (*sobbing*): This is really too much, Mac,
this shouldn't have happened. I just don't
know what I shall do!

(*Enter* MRS. PEACHUM.)

MRS. PEACHUM: I knew it. She's with her fancy
man. Come here this minute, you filthy trol-

lop. When your man's hanged, you can hang yourself with him. A fine way to behave to your poor old mother: she has to come and fetch you out of prison. So, he has two at a time — that Nero!

POLLY: Leave me alone, mama, you don't know . . .

MRS. PEACHUM: Come home this minute!

LUCY: Listen to that, your mama has to tell you how to behave.

MRS. PEACHUM: Quick march!

POLLY: Wait! I must just . . . I must just say something to him . . . really . . . it's very important.

MRS. PEACHUM (gives her a box on the ears): And that's important too — now — quick march.

POLLY: Oh! Mac! (She is dragged off by MRS. PEACHUM.)

MACHEATH: Lucy, you behaved wonderfully. Of course, I was sorry for her. That's why I couldn't treat the silly bitch as she deserved. You thought at first there was some truth in what she said? Am I right?

LUCY: Yes, I did think so, dearest.

MACHEATH: Had it been true, her mother would never have got me into this mess. A mother behaves like that only to a seducer, never to a son-in-law.

LUCY: It makes me so happy, when you speak like that from the heart. I love you so much, I'd almost rather see you hanged than in the arms of another girl. Isn't it extraordinary?

MACHEATH: Lucy, I'd like to owe my life to you.

LUCY: It's wonderful, the way you say that. Say it again!

MACHEATH: Lucy, I'd like to owe my life to you.

LUCY: Shall I escape with you, dearest?

MACHEATH: Well, it'll be difficult to hide if we escape together. But as soon as the search is

over, I'll have you fetched — by express post, too, as you can imagine!

LUCY: How can I help you?

MACHEATH: Bring me my hat and stick.

(LUCY exits and returns with his hat and stick and throws them into his cell.)

MACHEATH: Lucy, the fruit of our love which you carry beneath your heart will forever bind us together.

(Exit LUCY.)

(SMITH enters, goes into the cage and says to MACHEATH:)

SMITH: Give me that stick.

(After a short chase in which SMITH, armed with a chair and crowbar, drives MACHEATH before him, MACHEATH leaps over the bars. Constables pursue him.)

BROWN (off): Hello, Mac! Mac, please answer! It's Jacky. Mac, please be kind and answer, I can't bear it! (Enters.) Mackie! What's up? He's gone. Thank God! (He sits down on the bench.)

(Enter PEACHUM.)

PEACHUM (to SMITH): My name is Peachum. I have come to claim the forty pounds reward offered for the capture of the bandit Macheath. (He appears in front of the cage.) Hey! Is that Mr. Macheath there?

(BROWN remains silent.)

Ah! So the other gentleman has gone out for a little walk? I come here to visit a criminal and whom do I find but Mr. Brown! Tiger Brown in, and his friend Macheath out.

BROWN (groaning): Mr. Peachum, it's not my fault.

PEACHUM: Of course not, how could it be? You would never be so . . . as to get yourself into this situation . . . would you, Brown?

BROWN: Mr. Peachum, I am beside myself.

PEACHUM: I believe you. You must feel horrible, Brown.

BROWN: Yes, this feeling of helplessness is crushing. The boys do just what they like! It's terrible, terrible!

PEACHUM: Would you like to lie down a little? Just shut your eyes and behave as though nothing had happened. Imagine you're lying in a lovely green meadow with little white clouds overhead. The main thing is to get this nasty affair out of your mind. Everything that's happened, and above all what's still to come.

BROWN (*uneasily*): What do you mean?

PEACHUM: It's wonderful the way you're taking it. If I were in your position, I'd simply collapse and go to bed and drink hot tea. And I'd arrange to have a nice cool hand stroking my forehead.

BROWN: Damn you! I can't help it if a man escapes! The police can't do anything!

PEACHUM: Oh! So the police can't do anything. You don't think we shall have Mr. Macheath back here again?

(BROWN *shrugs his shoulders.*)

Then what's going to happen to you, Brown, will be a horrible injustice. Of course, people will say that the police shouldn't have let him escape. — No, I can't quite see that brilliant Coronation procession yet.

BROWN: What do you mean?

PEACHUM: I might remind you of an historic instance, which, although it aroused considerable excitement in its time, fourteen hundred years B.C., is unknown to the larger public of today. When the Egyptian king Rameses the Second died, the chief of police of Nineveh, or it may have been Cairo, was guilty of some petty injustice toward the lower classes. Even at that time the results were terrible. The coronation procession of the new queen, Semiramis, was, as the history books state, "a succession of catastrophes caused by the all too lively participation of the lower classes." The historians are far too squeamish to describe what Semiramis had done to her chief of police.

I only remember vaguely; but there was talk of snakes which she nourished at his bosom.

BROWN: Really?

PEACHUM: The Lord be with you, Brown. (*Exit.*)

BROWN: Now only an iron hand will do any good! Sergeant, a conference! Emergency!

(*Curtain.* MACHEATH *and* GINNY JENNY *step in front of the curtain and sing. Song illumination.*)

SECOND THREEPENNY-FINALE

MACHEATH: Now all you gentlemen who wish to lead us
Who teach us to desist from mortal sin
Your prior obligation is to feed us;
When we've had lunch, your preaching can begin.
All you who love your paunch and our propriety
Take note of this one thing (for it is late):
You may proclaim, good sirs, your fine philosophy
But till you feed us, right and wrong can wait!
Or is it only those who have the money
Can enter in the land of milk and honey?

VOICE OFF: What does a man live by?

MACHEATH: What does a man live by? By resolutely
Ill-treating, beating, cheating, eating some other bloke!
A man can only live by absolutely
Forgetting he's a man like other folk!

CHORUS OFF: So, gentlemen, do not be taken in:
Men live exclusively by mortal sin.

GINNY JENNY: All you who say what neckline is decreed us
And who decide when ogling is a sin
Your prior obligation is to feed us
When we've had lunch, your preaching can begin.
You who insist upon your pleasure and our shame
Take note of this one thing (for it is late):

Your fine philosophy, good sirs, you may
    proclaim
But till you feed us, right and wrong can
    wait!
Or is it only those who have the money
Can enter in the land of milk and honey?

VOICE OFF: What does a man live by?

GINNY JENNY: What does a man live by? By
    resolutely
Ill-treating, beating, cheating, eating some
    other bloke!
A man can only live by absolutely
Forgetting he's a man like other folk!

CHORUS OFF: So, gentlemen, do not be taken
    in:
Men live exclusively by mortal sin.

ACT THREE

SCENE ONE The same night Peachum prepares for action. By means of a demonstration
of misery he hopes to disorganize the Coronation procession.

The Wardrobe Room of Peachum's
Establishment

*The beggars are painting boards with such
inscriptions as "I gave my eye for my king,"
etc.*

PEACHUM: Gentlemen, at this very hour, in
    our eleven branches between Drury Lane
    and Wapping, there are one thousand four
    hundred and thirty-two men like you work-
    ing on such boards as these in order to be
    present at the Coronation of our Queen.

MRS. PEACHUM: Come on, come on! If you
    won't work, you can't beg. You hope to be
    a blind man, and you can't even write a
    proper K! That's supposed to be a child's
    handwriting, not an old man's!

(*Exit* PEACHUM.)

(*Roll of drums.*)

BEGGAR: There's a guard of honor lining up!
    Little do they dream that today, the grandest

day of their military lives, they've got to
    deal with us!

FILCH (*enters and announces*): Here comes a
    dozen benighted birds, Mrs. Peachum. They
    say they're to be given their money here.

(*Enter the whores.*)

GINNY JENNY: My dear madam . . .

MRS. PEACHUM: Well, well, well, you look as
    though you've all fallen off your perches!
    I suppose you've come for the money for
    your Macheath? You'll get nothing. Under-
    stand? Nothing.

GINNY JENNY: And what are we to understand
    by that, madam?

MRS. PEACHUM: Bursting into my room in the
    middle of the night! Coming to a respect-
    able house at three in the morning! You'd
    do better to sleep off the effects of business.
    You look like skim milk.

GINNY JENNY: So we're not to get our contrac-
    tual fee for having Mr. Macheath nabbed,
    madam?

MRS. PEACHUM: Quite correct. In fact, you'll
    get something you don't like, instead of your
    blood money.

GINNY JENNY: And why, madam?

MRS. PEACHUM: Because your wonderful Mr.
    Macheath has vanished again into thin air.
    That's why. Now get out of my decent
    house, ladies.

GINNY JENNY: That's the limit. Don't you try
    that on with us! I give you fair warning,
    not with us!

MRS. PEACHUM: Filch, the ladies want to be
    shown out.

(FILCH *approaches the girls.* GINNY JENNY
pushes him away.)

GINNY JENNY: I'd advise you to keep your dirty
    mouth shut . . . or!

(*Enter* PEACHUM.)

PEACHUM: What's the matter? I hope you
    haven't given them any money. Well, what's

the matter, ladies? Is Mr. Macheath in prison or is he not?

GINNY JENNY: Leave me in peace with your Mr. Macheath. You're not a patch on him. I had to send a gentleman away tonight because I wanted to cry on my pillow every time I thought how I had sold that real gentleman to you. Yes, ladies, and what do you think happened this morning? Not an hour ago, when I had just cried myself to sleep, I heard a whistle, and there in the street below stood the gentleman I'd been crying for, and he asked me to throw the key down to him: he wished to forget the wrong I had done him — in my arms. He's the last gentleman left in London, ladies. And if our colleague Suky Tawdry isn't with us now, it's because he went from me to her, to comfort her as well.

PEACHUM (to himself): Suky Tawdry . . .

GINNY JENNY: So now you know. You're dirt compared to him. You lowdown informers!

PEACHUM: Filch, run quickly to the nearest police station and say Mr. Macheath is staying with Miss Suky Tawdry.

(Exit FILCH.)

But ladies, why are we quarreling? Your money will be paid, of course. My dear Celia, wouldn't it be better if you went and made the ladies a nice cup of coffee, instead of insulting them?

MRS. PEACHUM: Suky Tawdry!

(She sings the third verse of the "Ballad of Sexual Submissiveness.")

Now here's a man who toward the gallow races.
The quicklime's brought that will rub out his traces.
He's dead the minute hangmen do their duty.
And what's his mind on now, this chap? Some beauty.
Here at the gallows' foot he'll acquiesce
For such is sexual submissiveness.
He's had it. He's been sold. He marches to his doom.

He's seen the money in a female's hand
And he begins to understand
That woman's orifice will be his tomb.
His self-reproaches are uncompromising
But, as the night is falling, he is rising.

(Exit MRS. PEACHUM.)

PEACHUM: Come on, come on! You'd all be rotting in the sewers of Wapping if I hadn't spent sleepless nights working out how to extract a few pence from your poverty. And I did work out something: that the rich of the earth indeed create misery, but they cannot bear to see it. They are weaklings and fools just like you. As long as they have enough to eat and can grease their floors with butter so that even the crumbs that fall from their tables grow fat, they can't look with indifference on a man collapsing from hunger — although, of course, it must be in front of *their* house that he collapses.

(Re-enter MRS. PEACHUM with a tray full of coffee cups.)

MRS. PEACHUM: You can come to the shop tomorrow and fetch your money: but *after* the Coronation.

GINNY JENNY: Mrs. Peachum, you leave me speechless.

PEACHUM: Fall in! We assemble in an hour outside Buckingham Palace. Quick march!

(The beggars fall in.)

FILCH (bursts in): The coppers! I never got as far as the station. The coppers are here already!

PEACHUM: Hide yourselves. (to MRS. PEACHUM) Get the orchestra ready! And when you hear me say "harmless," understand me, harmless . . .

MRS. PEACHUM: Harmless? I don't understand a thing.

PEACHUM: Of course you don't understand a thing. So when I say "harmless" . . .

(There is a knocking on the door.)

Thank God, that's the password, harmless, then play some sort of music. Now get out.

(*Exit* Mrs. Peachum. *The beggars, excepting a girl with the board* A victim of military despotism, *hide with their things behind the clothes racks on the right.*)

(*Enter* Brown *with constables.*)

Brown: And now, Mr. Beggars' Friend, we take action! Handcuff him, Smith. Ah, so those are a few of your charming notices. (*To the girl*) "A Victim of Military Despotism" — is that you, my dear?

Peachum: Good morning, Brown, good morning. Slept well?

Brown: Eh?

Peachum: Morning, Brown.

Brown: Is he speaking to me? Does he know any of you? I don't think I have the pleasure of your acquaintance.

Peachum: Haven't you? Morning, Brown.

Brown: Knock his hat off, Smith.

(Smith *does so.*)

Peachum: Listen, Brown, since your way leads *past* my house — I said *past*, Brown — I can now ask you to put a certain Macheath under lock and key.

Brown: The man is mad. Smith, stop laughing. Tell me, Smith, how is it possible that this notorious criminal is allowed at large in London?

Peachum: Because he's your friend, Brown.

Brown: Who?

Peachum: Mackie the Knife. Not me, I'm not a criminal. I'm just a poor man, Brown. You can't treat me badly. Listen, Brown. You are on the verge of the worst hour of your life. Would you like a cup of coffee? (*to the whores*) Girls, give the gentleman a drink, that's not the way to behave. We're all friends here. We all obey the law. The law is simply and solely made for the exploitation of those who do not understand it or of those who, for naked need, cannot obey it. And whoever would pick up the crumbs of this exploitation must strictly obey the law.

Brown: You think our judges are bribable?

Peachum: On the contrary, sir, on the contrary! Our judges are totally unbribable: no amount of money can bribe them to dispense justice.

(*A second roll of drums.*)

Departure of the troops to line the route! Departure of the poorest of the poor half an hour later!

Brown: Quite right, Mr. Peachum. Departure of the poorest of the poor in half an hour. They're departing for their winter quarters in prison. (*to the constables*) Well, boys, round 'em up. All the patriots you can find here. (*to the beggars*) Have you ever heard of Tiger Brown? Tonight, Mr. Peachum, I have found the solution and, I may add, I have saved a friend from death. I shall simply smoke out your whole nest. Then I shall lock you all up for — yes, what *for*? For street-begging! You seem to have warned me that you were going to bother me and the Queen with your beggars. These beggars I shall now arrest. That'll teach you something.

Peachum: All very fine — but what beggars?

Brown: These cripples here. Smith, we'll take the patriotic gentlemen with us right away.

Peachum: Brown, I can save you from overstepping your duty. Thank God you came to me! Of course you can arrest these few people, they are *harmless, harmless* . . .

(*Music starts and plays a few introductory bars of "The Song of the Futility of all Human Endeavor."*)

Brown: What's that?

Peachum: Music. They play as well as they can. "The Song of Futility." Don't you know it? That'll teach you something!

(*Song illumination: golden light. The organ is lit up. Three lights come down from above on a bar, and on a board is written:*)

The Song of the Futility of all Human
Endeavor

A man lives by his head.
That head will not suffice.
Just try it: you will find your head
Will scarce support two lice.
>   For the task assigned them
>   Men aren't smart enough or sly.
>   Any rogue can blind them
>   With a clever lie.

Go make yourself a plan
And be a shining light.
Then make yourself a second plan
For neither will come right.
>   For the situation
>   Men aren't bad enough or vile.
>   Human aspiration
>   Only makes me smile.

Go running after luck
But don't you run too fast:
We all are running after luck
And luck is running last.
>   For the real conditions
>   Men are more demanding than is meet.
>   Their ideal ambitions
>   Are one great big cheat.

PEACHUM: Your plan was ingenious, Brown, but impracticable. All you can arrest here are a few young people who arranged a small fancy-dress ball to celebrate the Coronation of their Queen. But when the really poor ones come — there's not a single one here now — you'll see they'll come in thousands. That's the trouble. You've forgotten the monstrous number of the poor. If they were to stand there in front of the Abbey, it wouldn't be a very cheerful sight. They don't look very nice. Do you know what erysipelas is, Brown? Well, think now of a hundred people with erysipelas on their faces. And then these mutilated creatures at the door of the Abbey? We would rather avoid that, Brown. You say the police will make short work of us poor people. But you don't believe it yourself. What will it look like if six hundred poor cripples have to be knocked down with your truncheons because

of the Coronation? It will look bad. Enough to make one sick. I feel ill, Brown, just to think of it. A chair, please.

BROWN (*to* SMITH): This is a threat. It's blackmail. We can't do anything to this man. In the interest of the public order we can't do anything to this man. Such a thing has never happened before!

PEACHUM: It has happened now, Brown. I'll tell you something: you can do what you like to the Queen of England, but just try and tread on the toes of the poorest man in London and we'll do you brown, Mr. Brown.

BROWN: Then I'm to arrest Mackie the Knife? Arrest him? You can talk! You've got to catch your man before you can arrest him.

PEACHUM: When you say that, I cannot contradict you. So I shall produce him for you. We'll see if there's any morality left! Jenny, where is Mr. Macheath staying?

GINNY JENNY: With Suky Tawdry, at 621 Oxford Street.

BROWN: Smith, go at once to 621 Oxford Street. Suky Tawdry's flat, arrest Macheath and bring him to the Old Bailey. In the meantime I must change into my full-dress uniform. On occasions like this, I have to wear full dress.

PEACHUM: Brown, if he's not hanged by six . . .

BROWN: Oh, Mackie, it didn't work. (*Exit* BROWN: *with constables.*)

PEACHUM (*calling after him*): That's taught you something, Brown.

(*A third roll of drums.*)

>   Drums — the third time! A fresh plan of campaign! New destination: the Old Bailey! Quick march!

(*Exeunt the beggars.*)

PEACHUM (*sings*): Since men are just no good
>   Pick up a piece of wood
>   And hit them on the head with it!
>   Then maybe they'll be good.

>   For the human function
>   They'll be good when they are dead.

So without compunction
Hit them on the head!

(*In front of the curtain appears* GINNY JENNY *with a hurdy-gurdy. She sings:*)

THE SONG OF SOLOMON

King Solomon was very wise
So what's his history?
He came to view this world with scorn
And curse the hour he was born
Declaring all is vanity.
King Solomon was very wise
But long before the day was out
The consequence was clear, alas!
And wisdom 'twas that brought him to this
  pass:
A man is better off without.

You saw Queen Cleopatra too
And what her talents were.
Oh, it was quite a life she led
Until her past caught up with her!
Two emperors joined her in bed:
Such goings-on in Babylon!
But long before the day was out
The consequence was clear, alas!
Her very beauty brought her to this pass:
A woman's better off without.

And Julius Caesar: he was brave.
His fame shall never cease.
He sat like God on an altarpiece
And then they tore him limb from limb
And Brutus helped to slaughter him.
Old Julius was very brave
But long before the day was out
The consequence was clear, alas!
His bravery 'twas that brought him to this
  pass:
A man is better off without.

You know the inquisitive Bertolt Brecht.
His songs — you loved them so.
But when too oft he asked where from
The riches of the rich did come
You made him pack his bag and go.
Oh how inquisitive was Brecht!
But long before the day was out

The consequence was clear, alas!
Inquisitiveness had brought him to this pass:
A man is better off without.

And here you see our friend Macheath.
His life is now at stake.
So long as he was rational
And took whate'er there was to take
His fame was international.
But then he got emotional
And though the day is not yet out
The consequence is clear, alas!
Emotion 'twas that brought him to this pass:
A man is better off without.

SCENE TWO   The battle for possession.

An Attic Bedroom in the Old Bailey

SMITH: Miss, Mrs. Polly Macheath would like
  to speak to you.

LUCY: Mrs. Macheath? Show her in.

(*Enter* POLLY.)

POLLY: Good morning, madam. Madam, good
  morning!

LUCY: What can I do for you?

POLLY: You recognize me again?

LUCY: Of course I recognize you.

POLLY: I've come to beg pardon for my behavior yesterday.

LUCY: Very interesting.

POLLY: I have no excuse at all for my behavior
  yesterday, except — my unhappiness.

LUCY: I see.

POLLY: You must forgive me. I was very upset
  yesterday by Mr. Macheath's behavior. He
  really shouldn't have placed us in such a
  position, don't you agree? You can tell him
  so, when you see him.

LUCY: I — I — don't see him.

POLLY: You *do* see him.

LUCY: I do *not* see him.

POLLY: I'm sorry.

LUCY: He is very fond of you.

POLLY: Oh no, he loves you, I know that all right.

LUCY: You're very kind.

POLLY: But a man always fears a woman who loves him too much. And the natural result is that he neglects that woman and avoids her. I saw at first glance that he was bound to you in some way which I naturally couldn't guess.

LUCY: Do you mean that, honestly?

POLLY: Certainly. Of course. Very honestly.

LUCY: Dear Miss Peachum, we have both loved him too much!

POLLY: Perhaps that was it. (*Pause.*) And now, I'll explain how it came about. Ten days ago I saw Mr. Macheath for the first time in the Octopus Hotel. My mother was there too. Later — that is, the day before yesterday — we were married. Yesterday I discovered the police wanted him for a great many crimes. And today I don't know what will happen. So you see, twelve days ago I wouldn't have dreamed I could ever fall for a man. (*Pause.*)

LUCY: I quite understand, Miss Peachum.

POLLY: Mrs. Macheath.

LUCY: Mrs. Macheath.

POLLY: And, indeed, during the last few hours I have been thinking a lot about this fellow. It's not so simple. For, you see, Miss Brown, I have every reason to envy you his behavior toward you the other day. When I had to leave — coerced, I must admit, by my mama — he showed not the slightest regret. But perhaps he hasn't got a heart, just a stone in its place. What do you think, Lucy?

LUCY: Dear Miss Peachum, I am not quite sure if the fault lies entirely with Mr. Macheath. Perhaps you should have kept to your own sort, Miss Peachum.

POLLY: Mrs. Macheath.

LUCY: Mrs. Macheath.

POLLY: You're quite right — or at least I ought to have kept everything, as my father says, "on a business basis."

LUCY: Of course.

POLLY (*weeps*): He is all that I have.

LUCY: My dear, this is a misfortune that can happen to the cleverest woman. But you are legally his wife, comfort yourself with that. Child, I can't bear to go on seeing you so depressed. May I offer you a little something?

POLLY: A little what?

LUCY: A little something to eat?

POLLY: Oh, yes, please! A little something to eat!

(*Exit* LUCY.)

(*To herself*) The silly little fool!

LUCY (*returning with coffee and cakes*): Now that'll be enough.

POLLY: You really give yourself too much trouble. (*Pause. She eats.*) A lovely picture you have of him. When did he bring it?

LUCY: What do you mean — bring it?

POLLY (*innocently*): I meant, when did he bring it up here.

LUCY: He didn't bring it.

POLLY: Didn't he give it to you right here in this room?

LUCY: He never was in this room.

POLLY: I see. But there would have been nothing in that. The paths of fate are already terribly complicated!

LUCY: Don't talk such tripe all the time. You came here to spy around!

POLLY: You know where he is, don't you?

LUCY: I? Don't *you* know?

POLLY: Tell me where he is this minute!

LUCY: I haven't the slightest idea.

POLLY: Then you don't know where he is? Word of honor?

LUCY: No, I don't. And you don't know either?

POLLY: No! This is monstrous! (POLLY *laughs and* LUCY *weeps.*) He has two responsibilities now and he's run out on both of us!

LUCY: I can't bear it any longer. Oh, Polly, it's so awful!

POLLY (*happily*): But I'm so glad that at the ending of this tragedy I've found a friend like you. Have some more? Another cake?

LUCY: Some more! Oh, Polly, don't be so kind to me. Really I don't deserve it! Oh, Polly, men aren't worth it!

POLLY: Of course men aren't worth it. But what can one do?

LUCY: I'll come clean. Will you be angry with me, Polly?

POLLY: What?

LUCY: It's not real.

POLLY: What isn't?

LUCY: This! (*She points to her stomach.*) I did it all for that crook!

POLLY (*laughs*): It was a trick. Wonderful! You are a little fool! Listen — you want Mackie? I'll give him to you. Take him when you find him.

(*There is a sound of voices and steps outside.*)

What's that?

LUCY (*at the window*): It's Mackie! They've caught him again.

POLLY (*collapses*): Then all is over!

(*Enter* MRS. PEACHUM.)

MRS. PEACHUM: Ah, Polly, so here you are. Change your dress. Your husband's going to be hanged. I've brought your widow's weeds.

(POLLY *starts to undress and puts on the widow's weeds.*)

You'll look lovely as a widow! Now cheer up a bit.

SCENE THREE   5 a.m. Friday. Mackie the Knife, who once more went back to his whores, has again been betrayed by them. He is now about to be hanged.

The Death Cell

The bells of the City are ringing. Constables bring MACHEATH, *handcuffed, into the cell.*

SMITH: In here with him. The bells have rung once already. (*to* MACHEATH) Try and behave like a man. I don't know how you manage to look so washed out. I should think you must be ashamed of yourself! (*to the other constables*) When the bells ring for the third time — that'll be at six o'clock — he must be already hanged. Get everything ready.

A CONSTABLE: Every street in Newgate has been jammed with people for the last quarter of an hour. It's impossible to get through.

SMITH: Extraordinary! How do they know already?

CONSTABLE: If it goes on like this, the whole of London will know in half an hour. Those who were going to the Coronation will all come here instead. The Queen will have to drive through empty streets.

SMITH: That's why we shall have to hurry. If we're through by six, people can be back on the Coronation route by seven. Get on with it.

MACHEATH: Hi, Smith! What's the time?

SMITH: Haven't you got eyes? Four minutes past five.

MACHEATH: Four minutes past five.

(*As* SMITH *shuts the door of the cell from the outside,* BROWN *enters.*)

BROWN (*questioning* SMITH, *with his back to the cell*): Is he there?

SMITH: You want to see him?

BROWN: No, no, no, for God's sake, manage it all yourself. (*Exit.*)

MACHEATH (*suddenly bursting into a soft and*

rapid torrent of speech): Listen, Smith, I won't say a thing about bribery, don't worry. I know all about that. If you let yourself be bribed, you'll at least have to get out of the country. You'd have to do that. And you'll also need money to live on for the rest of your life. A thousand pounds, will that do? Don't speak! In twenty minutes I'll let you know if you can have that thousand pounds by midday. I'm not mentioning anyone's feelings. Go outside and think it over carefully. Life is short and so is money. And I'm not sure I can raise any. But let anyone in here who wants to see me.

SMITH (*slowly*): You're talking nonsense, Mr. Macheath. (*He withdraws to the side of the stage.*)

MACHEATH (*sings, softly and very quickly*):

Hark to the voice that pleads for pity, hark!
Macheath lies here — beneath no hawthorn tree
Nor under elms but in a dungeon dark.
He was struck down by angry Fate's decree.
God grant you all may hear what he doth say!
Him thickest walls surround and chains entwine.
Do you not ask, my friends, where he hath strayed?
When he is dead, brew elderberry wine!
But while he still doth live, lend him your aid.
Or must his martyrdom endure for aye?

(MATTHEW *and* JACOB *appear in the passage.* SMITH *intercepts them on their way to* MACHEATH.)

SMITH: We-e-ll, my boys! You look like a gutted herring!

MATTHEW: Now the Captain's away, it's I who have to get the ladies pregnant — so, when they're arrested, they can plead "Not responsible for their actions." One needs the physique of a stallion for this job. Can I speak with the Captain?

(SMITH *lets them pass, then exit.*)

MACHEATH: Five twenty-five. You've taken your time.

JACOB: Well, after all . . .

MACHEATH: After all, after all, I'm going to be hanged, man! But I've no time to argue with you. Five twenty-eight. How much can you draw out of your private deposits immediately?

MATTHEW: At five o'clock in the morning?

JACOB: Is it really as bad as all that?

MACHEATH: Four hundred pounds? Can you manage that?

JACOB: Well, and what about us? That's all there is.

MACHEATH: Are you going to be hanged, or am I?

MATTHEW (*excitedly*): Did we sleep with Suky Tawdry instead of making ourselves scarce? Did we sleep with Suky Tawdry or did you?

MACHEATH: Shut your gob. I'll soon be sleeping somewhere else than with that trollop. Five thirty.

JACOB: I suppose we'll have to do it, Matthew.

SMITH (*enters*): Mr. Brown told me to ask what you'd like for — breakfast.

MACHEATH: Leave me alone! (*to* MATTHEW) Will you or won't you? (*to* SMITH) Asparagus.

MATTHEW: I'm certainly not going to be shouted at!

MACHEATH: I'm not shouting at you! It's only because . . . Now, Matthew, are you going to let me be hanged?

MATTHEW: Of course we won't let you be hanged. Whoever suggested that? But that's all. Four hundred pounds is all there is. One's allowed to say that, I suppose.

MACHEATH: Five thirty-eight.

JACOB: Hurry, Matthew, or it'll be too late.

MATTHEW: If we can only get through. The streets are jammed. This riff-raff!

MACHEATH: If you're not here by five minutes to six, you'll never see me again. (*Shouts.*) You'll never see me again . . . !

SMITH: They're off. Well, how goes it? (*He makes a gesture of paying out money.*)

MACHEATH: Four hundred.

(SMITH *walks away, shrugging his shoulders.*)

MACHEATH (*calling after him*): I must speak to Brown.

SMITH (*as the constable enters*): You've got the soap?

CONSTABLE: It's not the right sort.

SMITH: You'll be able to set the thing up in ten minutes.

CONSTABLE: But the trap isn't working yet.

SMITH: It *must* work, the bells have rung the second time.

CONSTABLE: This is a hell of a place!

MACHEATH (*sings*):

Alas, he's fallen from his high estate.
All his affairs have gone from bad to worse.
Oh ye who recognize nor God nor Fate
But place your bets upon your own fat purse
You'd better rescue him or, well-a-day,
He'll drag you all down to that dungeon grim.
Run then unto the Queen for your Macheath.
Tell her the pass he's come to. Say of him:
That man of sorrows, Queen, has fangs for teeth.
Or must his martyrdom endure for aye?

(*Enter* POLLY.)

SMITH: I can't let you in. Your number's sixteen. It's not your turn yet.

POLLY: What do you mean: my number's sixteen? I am his wife. I must speak to him.

SMITH: Then five minutes at the most.

POLLY: What do you mean, five minutes! That's ridiculous. Five minutes! You just can't say that. It's not as simple as all that.

This is good-bye forever. And there's such a lot that has to be said between man and wife . . . Where is he?

SMITH: Well, can't you see him?

POLLY: Oh yes. Thank you!

MACHEATH: Polly!

POLLY: Yes, Mackie, here I am.

MACHEATH: Yes, of course.

POLLY: How are you? Very done up? It's hard.

MACHEATH: Yes, and what will *you* do? What will become of you?

POLLY: Oh, our business is doing very well. That's the least of our troubles. Mackie, are you very nervous? Who *was* your father? There's so much you haven't told me. I don't understand it all: you were really always quite healthy.

MACHEATH: Polly, can't you help me out?

POLLY: Of course.

MACHEATH: With money, I mean. I talked to the warder here . . .

POLLY (*slowly*): The money has gone to Southampton.

MACHEATH: And you haven't any?

POLLY: No, I haven't any. But do you know, Mac, perhaps I could speak to someone . . . maybe the Queen herself! (*She breaks down.*) Oh, Mackie!

SMITH (*pulling* POLLY *away*): Got your thousand pounds?

POLLY: Good luck, Mac, take care of yourself! Never forget me! (*Exit.*)

(SMITH *and a constable bring on a table with a plate of asparagus on it.*)

SMITH: Is the asparagus tender?

CONSTABLE: It is. (*Exit.*)

(BROWN *enters and walks over to* SMITH.)

BROWN: What does he want, Smith? I'm glad you waited for me with the table. We'll take it with us, so he'll see what consideration we have for him. (*They both carry the table into the cell. Exit* SMITH. *Pause.*) Hello, Mac. Here's your asparagus. Won't you try a little?

MACHEATH: Don't trouble yourself, Mr. Brown, there are other people who will do me the last honors.

BROWN: But Mackie!

MACHEATH: I should like the account! Forgive me if, in the meanwhile, I eat. After all, this is my last meal. (*He eats.*)

BROWN: Good appetite! Oh, Mac, you wound me as with a red-hot iron!

MACHEATH: The account, sir, please! No sentimentality.

BROWN (*sighing, draws a little notebook out of a pocket*): I have brought it, Mac. Here is the account for the last six months.

MACHEATH (*scathingly*): I see. So you've only come to get your money out of me.

BROWN: Mac, you know that's not true . . . !

MACHEATH: All right, you shan't be the loser. What do I owe you? But please let me have a detailed statement. Life has made me mistrustful . . . And you're the one who ought to know why.

BROWN: Mac, when you speak like that, I can't think straight.

(*There is a loud banging behind.*)

SMITH (*off*): All right, that will hold.

MACHEATH: The account, Brown.

BROWN: Very well — if you insist, there are the rewards for the arrests you or your people made possible. You received from the Government in all . . .

MACHEATH: Three murderers at forty pounds each makes a hundred and twenty pounds. A quarter of that for you is thirty pounds, which we owe you.

BROWN: Yes — yes — but I really don't know,

Mac, at the last minute, as it were, if we can . . .

MACHEATH: Please cut out the slop. Thirty pounds. And the one in Dover eight pounds.

BROWN: But why only eight pounds, for there was . . .

MACHEATH: Do you believe me or do you not? So for the last half year there's thirty-eight pounds due to you.

BROWN (*sobbing loudly*): A life-time together . . . I knew your every thought . . .

BOTH: . . . by just looking in your eyes.

MACHEATH: Three years in India — Johnny and James were both on the scene — five years in London and this is all the thanks I get. (*He shows what he will look like when hanged.*)

Here hangs Macheath who ne'er a soul did wrong:
A former friend his former friend betrays.
And hanging by a rope a fathom long
His neck can tell him what his bottom weighs.

BROWN: Mac, if you're going to treat me like this . . . ! Who attacks my honor attacks me! (*He runs angrily out of the cage.*)

MACHEATH: Your honor?

BROWN: Yes, my honor! Smith, begin! Let the people in! (*to* MACHEATH) Excuse me, please.

SMITH (*entering hurriedly, to* MACHEATH): I can still get you away, but in one minute it'll be too late. Have you got the money?

MACHEATH: Yes, as soon as the boys get back.

SMITH: There's no sign of them. Well — that's off.

(*People are admitted:* PEACHUM, MRS. PEACHUM, POLLY, LUCY, *the whores, the* REVEREND KIMBALL, MATTHEW *and* JACOB.)

GINNY JENNY: They didn't want to let us in, but I told them: if you don't take your something heads out of my way, you'll get to know Ginny Jenny better than you like!

PEACHUM: I am his father-in-law. Pardon me, which of those present is Mr. Macheath?

MACHEATH (*presents himself*): Macheath.

PEACHUM (*walks past the cage*): Fate, Mr. Macheath, has decreed that you should become my son-in-law without my knowing you. The circumstances in which I meet you for the first time are very tragic. Mr. Macheath, you once had white kid gloves, a stick with an ivory handle, and a scar on your neck, and you frequented the Octopus Hotel. There remains the scar on your neck, which is probably the least valuable of your distinguishing marks, and now you only frequent jails, and very soon you won't frequent anywhere . . .

(POLLY *walks sobbing past the cage and stands right.*)

MACHEATH: What a pretty dress you're wearing.

(MATTHEW *and* JACOB *come past the cage and stand right.*)

MATTHEW: We couldn't get through because of the crowd. But we ran so fast I thought Jacob was going to have a stroke. If you don't believe us . . .

MACHEATH: What do the men say? Have they got good places?

MATTHEW: There, Captain, we knew you'd understand. Look, we don't get a Coronation every day. The men have to earn when they can. They ask to be remembered to you.

JACOB: Kindly.

MRS. PEACHUM (*walks past the cage and stands right*): Mr. Macheath, who would have thought of this when a week ago we had a little dance together at the Octopus Hotel?

MACHEATH: Yes, a little dance.

MRS. PEACHUM: But here on earth below Fate is cruel.

BROWN (*to the* REVEREND KIMBALL *at the back*): And with this man I stood at Azerbaijan, shoulder to shoulder, under withering fire!

GINNY JENNY (*comes to the cage*): Us Drury Lane girls are in a terrible fix. Not a soul's gone to the Coronation; they all want to see you. (*She stands right.*)

MACHEATH: To see me.

SMITH: Come on! Six o'clock. (*He lets him out of the cage.*)

MACHEATH: We will not keep the people waiting. Ladies and gentlemen, you see here the vanishing representative of a vanishing class. We bourgeois artisans, who work with honest jimmies on the cash boxes of small shopkeepers, are being swallowed up by large concerns backed by banks. What is a picklock to a bank share? What is the burgling of a bank to the founding of a bank? What is the murder of a man to the employment of a man? Fellow citizens, I herewith take my leave of you. I thank you all for coming. Some of you have been very close to me. That Jenny should have given me up astonishes me greatly. It is a clear proof that the world will always be the same. The concurrence of several unfortunate circumstances has brought about my fall. Good — I fall.

(*Song illumination: golden light. The organ is lit up. Three lights come down from above on a bar and on a board is written:*)

BALLAD IN WHICH MACHEATH BEGS PARDON OF ALL

All you who will live long and die in bed
Pray harden not your hearts against us others
And do not grin behind your beards, my brothers,
When you behold us hung till we are dead.
Nor do not curse because we came a cropper.
Be not, as was the Law to us, unkind:
Not every Christian has a lawful mind.
Your levity, my friends, is most improper.
O brother men, let us a lesson be
And pray to God that He may pardon me.

And now the stormwinds with the rain conspire
To wash the flesh we once did overnourish

And ravens gouge our eyes out with a flourish,
These eyes which see so much and more desire.
We were not always virtuous, alas,
That's why you'll see us hanging by the neck
For every greedy bird of prey to peck
As were we horses' offal on the grass.
So, brother men, let us a warning be
And pray to God that He may pardon me.

The wenches with their bosoms showing
To catch the eye of men with yearnings
The urchins just behind them going
In hopes to filch their sinful earnings
The outlaws, bandits, burglars, gunmen
All Christian souls that love a brawl
Abortionists and pimps and fun-men
I cry them mercy one and all.

Except the coppers — sons of bitches —
For every evening, every morning
Those lice came creeping from their niches
And frequently without a warning.
Police! My epidermis itches!
But for today I'll let that fall
Pretend I love the sons of bitches
And cry them mercy one and all.

O, I could smash their ugly faces
And crush them with an iron maul!
But one can't always hold the aces.
I cry them mercy one and all.

SMITH: If you please, Mr. Macheath.

MRS. PEACHUM: Polly and Lucy, stand by your
husband in his last hour.

MACHEATH: Ladies, whatever may have been
between us . . .

SMITH (*leads him off*): Come on!

PASSAGE TO THE GALLOWS

(*All exeunt through the doors left. These doors
are set in the wings. Then they re-enter from
the other side of the stage, all carrying hur-
ricane lamps. When* MACHEATH *is standing on
the gallows,* PEACHUM *speaks.*)

PEACHUM: So, gentlemen, to this point we have
come.

You all can see what Captain Mackie's
fate is.
Which proves that in the whole of Christendom
Nothing is granted any of us gratis.

But lest you jump to the conclusion
That we are parties to the deal, and in
collusion,
Macheath will *not* be hanged till he is dead.
We have devised another end instead.

You all will hear (yes, all; it's rather loud)
Mercy give Justice quite a dreadful hiding.
This is an opera, and we mean to do you
proud.
The Royal Messenger will make his entrance
— riding.

(*On the board is written:*)

THE ARRIVAL OF THE MOUNTED MESSENGER

THIRD THREEPENNY-FINALE

CHORUS: Hark, who comes?
The Royal Messenger riding comes!

(*Riding high,* BROWN *enters as the messenger.*)

BROWN (*recitative*): On the occasion of her
Coronation, our Gracious Queen commands
that one Captain Macheath shall at once be
released. (*All cheer.*) At the same time he is
raised to the permanent ranks of the
nobility. (*Cheers.*) The castle of Marmarel
and a pension of ten thousand pounds a
year are his as long as he shall live, while to
all happy couples here our great Queen
presents her very cordial congratulations.

MACHEATH: A rescue! A rescue! I was sure of
it. Where the need is greatest, there will
God's help be nearest.

POLLY: A rescue! A rescue! My dearest Mackie
has been rescued. I am so happy.

MRS. PEACHUM: So, now the whole thing has
a happy end! How calm and peaceful would
our life be always if a messenger came from
the king whenever we wanted.

PEACHUM: Therefore all remain standing where you are now and sing the chorale of the poorest of the poor, of whose difficult life you have shown us something today. In reality their end is generally bad. Mounted messengers from the Queen come far too seldom, and if you kick a man he kicks you back again. Therefore never be too eager to combat injustice.

(*All sing to the organ and walk forward.*)

Combat injustice but in moderation:
Such things will freeze to death if left alone.
Remember: this whole vale of tribulation
Is black as pitch and cold as any stone.

The Glass Menagerie

In one of John Murray Anderson's *New Faces* revues in the fifties, comedian Ronnie Graham swung in a hammock, did an imitation of the young Truman Capote (who had burst upon the literary scene with an evocative novel of Southern decadence called *Other Voices, Other Rooms*), and announced, "Ah'm not a unhealthy writer — Ah'm *sick*." It used to be fashionable to make fun of Tennessee Williams, too, who was so closely identified with sexual maladjustment in the drama that when he wrote about heterosexual, sane people in his comedy *Period of Adjustment* (1960) *Time* claimed he did it "with the sly delight of a cannibal devouring a cookie." Today it is clear that however uneven his work or odd his characters, Williams' career in the theatre has been nothing to laugh at. He is, it seems, certain to rank higher than Arthur Miller, William Inge, and many other promising writers of his generation. He has already written at least two of the masterpieces of the American theatre, *The Glass Menagerie* and *A Streetcar Named Desire*, and still may forge out of *Camino Real* or another play "that long delayed but always expected something that we live for," The Great American Play. He has won Pulitzer Prizes and New York Drama Critics' Circle Awards, though lately he has not won much acclaim. He says he "slept through the sixties" (and critic Kenneth Tynan assured him, "You didn't miss a thing"). Some hope that Williams will regain his earlier strength and will emerge with more great plays and the Nobel Prize. Hemingway won it for his style and his simple theory of "grace under pressure." Williams is a greater stylist and has a deeper, if narrower, sympathy: his is the romantic's for the lost cause, the poet's for the maimed, the outcast, the fragile, the lonely, "the people who are not meant to win." He combines compassion with his bleak view:

> There is a horror in things, a horror at the heart of the meaninglessness of existence. Some people cling to a certain philosophy that is handed down to them and which they accept. Life has a meaning if you're bucking for heaven. But if heaven is a fantasy, we are in this jungle with whatever we can work out for ourselves. It seems to me that the cards are stacked against us. The only victory is how we take it.

If Samuel Beckett could win the Nobel Prize with his "end-game" view of life, then Williams can.

Thomas Lanier Williams (born 1914) was only a boy when his father, a shoe salesman, was transferred from Mississippi to St. Louis in 1918, "forced to live in a congested neighborhood . . . about as cheerful as an Arctic winter." He and his sister Rose, particularly sensitive, were horrified at the cat fights in the alley beneath their window in a building the color of "dried blood and mustard." His sister created in her little room a "light and delicate" refuge from the harsh world and "collected a large assortment of little glass articles . . . mostly little glass animals." Years later this memory inspired *The Glass Menagerie* and he wrote:

> By poetic association they came to represent, in my memory, all the softest emotions that belong to recollection of things past. They stood for all the small and tender things that relieve the austere pattern of life and make it endurable to the sensitive. The areaway where the cats were torn to pieces was one thing — my sister's white curtains and tiny menagerie of glass were another. Somewhere between them was the world we lived in.

Into the play also went his sister Rose, her mental imbalance transformed into a physical deformity; Clark Mills, a friend who worked with him, became The Gentleman Caller; Williams himself was the dreamy, ambitious Tom; and his mother, a game but garrulous faded Southern belle, emerged as Amanda Wingfield, one of the greatest creations of the American drama and (as played by Laurette Taylor in the original Broadway production in 1945) totally unforgettable.

Since that epoch-making opening night, a long succession of plays and films has followed, some vast successes (for Mary McCarthy calls him rather harshly "a talent which is firmly rooted in the American pay-dirt as a stout and tenacious carrot") and some disappointing failures. (Two of these failures, *Camino Real* and *The Milk Train Doesn't Stop Here Any More*, he has perseveringly rewritten and offered again.) Recently *Small Craft Warnings* and other works not quite so well received have shown that his talent is far from exhausted and indeed may be undergoing still another "period of adjustment" preparatory to a culminating masterpiece. In the long list, however, so far there has not been a play as tender, as touching, and as certain to last as *The Glass Menagerie*. We present that, therefore, with production notes by the author for the play in which he managed to avoid all the sensationalism of homosexuality and nymphomania, drug addiction and alcoholism, castration and cannibalism that we find in some of his other works, while at the same time making a deeper and more lasting impression than he yet has done with any other play — indeed than most people have done so far in the American theatre.

The Author's Production Notes

Being a "memory play," *The Glass Menagerie* can be presented with unusual freedom of convention. Because of its considerably delicate or tenuous material, atmospheric touches and subtleties of direction play a particularly important part. Expressionism and all other unconventional techniques in drama have only one valid aim, and that is a closer approach to truth. When a play employs unconventional techniques, it is not, or certainly shouldn't be, trying to escape its responsibility of dealing with reality, or interpreting experience, but is actually or should be attempting to find a closer approach, a more penetrating and vivid expression of things as they are. The straight realistic play with its genuine frigidaire and authentic ice-cubes, its characters that speak exactly as its audience speaks, corresponds to the academic landscape and has the same virtue of a photographic likeness. Everyone should know nowadays the unimportance of the photographic in art: that truth, life, or reality is an organic thing which the poetic imagination can represent or suggest, in essence, only through transformation, through changing into other forms than those which were merely present in appearance.

These remarks are not meant as a preface only to this particular play. They have to do with a conception of a new, plastic theatre which must take the place of the exhausted theatre of realistic conventions if the theatre is to resume vitality as a part of our culture.

THE SCREEN DEVICE
There is *only one important difference between the original and acting version of the play* and that is the *omission* in the latter of the device which I tentatively included in my *original* script. This device was the use of a screen on which were projected magic-lantern slides bearing images or titles. I do not regret the omission of this device from the present Broadway production. The extraordinary power of Miss Taylor's performance made it suitable to have the utmost simplicity in the physical production. But I think it may be interesting to some readers to see how this device was conceived. So I am putting it into the published manuscript. These images and legends, projected from behind, were cast on a section of wall between the front-room and dining-room areas, which should be indistinguishable from the rest when not in use.

The purpose of this will probably be apparent. It is to give accent to certain values in each scene. Each scene contains a particular point (or several) which is structurally the most important. In an episodic play, such as this, the basic structure or narrative line may be obscured from the audience; the effect may seem fragmentary rather than architectural. This may not be the fault of the play so much as a lack of attention in the audience. The legend or image upon the screen will strengthen the effect of what is merely allusion in the writing and allow the primary point to be made more simply and lightly than if the entire responsibility were on the spoken lines. Aside from this structural value, I think the screen will have a definite emotional appeal, less definable but just as important. An imaginative producer or director may invent many other uses for this device than those indicated in the present script. In fact the possibilities of the device seem much larger to me than the instance of this play can possibly utilize.

The Music

Another extra-literary accent in this play is provided by the use of music. A single recurring tune, "The Glass Menagerie," is used to give emotional emphasis to suitable passages. This tune is like circus music, not when you are on the grounds or in the immediate vicinity of the parade, but when you are at some distance and very likely thinking of something else. It seems under those circumstances to continue almost interminably and it weaves in and out of your preoccupied consciousness; then it is the lightest, most delicate music in the world and perhaps the saddest. It expresses the surface vivacity of life with the underlying strain of immutable and inexpressible sorrow. When you look at a piece of delicately spun glass you think of two things: how beautiful it is and how easily it can be broken. Both of those ideas should be woven into the recurring tune, which dips in and out of the play as if it were carried on a wind that changes. It serves as a thread of connection and allusion between the narrator with his separate point in time and space and the subject of his story. Between each episode it returns as reference to the emotion, nostalgia, which is the first condition of the play. It is primarily Laura's music and therefore comes out most clearly when the play focuses upon her and the lovely fragility of glass which is her image.

The Lighting

The lighting in the play is not realistic. In keeping with the atmosphere of memory, the stage is dim. Shafts of light are focused on selected areas or actors, sometimes in contradistinction to what is the apparent center. For instance, in the quarrel scene between Tom and Amanda, in which Laura has no active part, the clearest pool of light is on her figure. This is also true of the supper scene, when her silent figure on the sofa should remain the visual center. The light upon Laura should be distinct from the others, having a peculiar pristine clarity such as light used in early religious portraits of female saints or madonnas. A certain correspondence to light in religious paintings, such as El Greco's, where the figures are radiant in atmosphere that is relatively dusky, could be effectively used throughout the play. (It will also permit a more effective use of the screen.) A free, imaginative use of light can be of enormous value in giving a mobile, plastic quality to plays of a more or less static nature.

THE GLASS MENAGERIE

Tennessee Williams

CHARACTERS

AMANDA WINGFIELD, *the mother*

A little woman of great but confused vitality clinging frantically to another time and place. Her characterization must be carefully created, not copied from type. She is not paranoiac, but her life is paranoia. There is much to admire in Amanda, and as much to love and pity as there is to laugh at. Certainly she has endurance and a kind of heroism, and though her foolishness makes her unwittingly cruel at times, there is tenderness in her slight person.

LAURA WINGFIELD, *her daughter*

Amanda, having failed to establish contact with reality, continues to live vitally in her illusions, but Laura's situation is even graver. A childhood illness has left her crippled, one leg slightly shorter than the other, and held in a brace. This defect need not be more than suggested on the stage. Stemming from this, Laura's separation increases till she is like a piece of her own glass collection, too exquisitely fragile to move from the shelf.

TOM WINGFIELD, *her son*

And the narrator of the play. A poet with a job in a warehouse. His nature is not remorseless, but to escape from a trap he has to act without pity.

JIM O'CONNOR, *the gentleman caller*

A nice, ordinary, young man.

SCENE   *An Alley in St. Louis.*

PART I   *Preparation for a Gentleman Caller*

PART II   *The Gentleman Calls*

TIME   *Now [c. 1944] and the Past.*

SCENE ONE

The Wingfield apartment is in the rear of the building, one of those vast hive-like conglom-erations of cellular living-units that flower as warty growths in overcrowded urban centers of lower middle-class population and are sympto-matic of the impulse of this largest and funda-mentally enslaved section of American society to avoid fluidity and differentiation and to exist and function as one interfused mass of autom-atism.

The apartment faces an alley and is entered by a fire escape, a structure whose name is a touch of accidental poetic truth, for all of these huge buildings are always burning with the slow and implacable fires of human desperation. The fire escape is included in the set — that is, the land-ing of it and steps descending from it.

The scene is memory and is therefore nonrealis-tic. Memory takes a lot of poetic license. It omits some details; others are exaggerated, according to the emotional value of the articles it touches, for memory is seated predominantly in the heart. The interior is therefore rather dim and poetic.

At the rise of the curtain, the audience is faced with the dark, grim rear wall of the Wingfield tenement. This building, which runs parallel to the footlights, is flanked on both sides by dark, narrow alleys which run into murky canyons of tangled clotheslines, garbage cans, and the sinister lattice-work of neighboring fire escapes. It is up and down these side alleys that exterior entrances and exits are made, during the play. At the end of TOM's *opening commentary, the dark tenement wall slowly reveals (by means of a transparency) the interior of the ground floor Wingfield apartment.*

Downstage is the living room, which also serves as a sleeping room for LAURA, *the sofa unfold-ing to make her bed. Upstage, center, and divided by a wide arch or second proscenium with transparent faded portieres (or second curtain), is the dining room. In an old-fashioned what-not in the living room are seen scores of transparent glass animals. A blown-up photo-graph of the father hangs on the wall of the living room, facing the audience, to the left of the archway. It is the face of a very handsome young man in a doughboy's First World War cap. He is gallantly smiling, ineluctably smiling, as if to say, "I will be smiling forever."*

The audience hears and sees the opening scene in the dining room through both the transparent fourth wall of the building and the transparent gauze portieres of the dining-room arch. It is during this revealing scene that the fourth wall slowly ascends, out of sight. This transparent exterior wall is not brought down again until the very end of the play, during TOM'S *final speech.*

The narrator is an undisguised convention of the play. He takes whatever license with dramatic convention is convenient to his purposes.

TOM *enters dressed as a merchant sailor from alley, stage left, and strolls across the front of the stage to the fire escape. There he stops and lights a cigarette. He addresses the audience.*

TOM: Yes, I have tricks in my pocket, I have things up my sleeve. But I am the opposite of a stage magician. He gives you illusion that has the appearance of truth. I give you truth in the pleasant disguise of illusion.

To begin with, I turn back time. I reverse it to that quaint period, the thirties, when the huge middle class of America was matriculating in a school for the blind. Their eyes had failed them, or they had failed their eyes, and so they were having their fingers pressed forcibly down on the fiery Braille alphabet of a dissolving economy.

In Spain there was revolution. Here there was only shouting and confusion.

In Spain there was Guernica. Here there were disturbances of labor, sometimes pretty violent, in otherwise peaceful cities such as Chicago, Cleveland, Saint Louis . . .

This is the social background of the play.

(*Music.*)

The play is memory.

Being a memory play, it is dimly lighted, it is sentimental, it is not realistic.

In memory everything seems to happen to music. That explains the fiddle in the wings.

I am the narrator of the play, and also a character in it.

The other characters are my mother, Amanda, my sister, Laura, and a gentleman caller who appears in the final scenes.

He is the most realistic character in the play, being an emissary from a world of reality that we were somehow set apart from.

But since I have a poet's weakness for symbols, I am using this character also as a symbol; he is the long delayed but always expected something that we live for.

There is a fifth character in the play who doesn't appear except in this larger-than-life-size photograph over the mantel.

This is our father who left us a long time ago.

He was a telephone man who fell in love with long distances; he gave up his job with the telephone company and skipped the light fantastic out of town . . .

The last we heard of him was a picture post-card from Mazatlan, on the Pacific coast of Mexico, containing a message of two words —

"Hello — Good-bye!" and no address.

I think the rest of the play will explain itself. . . .

(AMANDA'S *voice becomes audible through the portieres.*)

(LEGEND ON SCREEN: "OU SONT LES NEIGES"[1])

(*He divides the portieres and enters the upstage area.*)

(AMANDA *and* LAURA *are seated at a drop-leaf table. Eating is indicated by gestures without food or utensils.* AMANDA *faces the audience,* TOM *and* LAURA *are seated in profile. The interior has lit up softly and through the scrim we see* AMANDA *and* LAURA *seated at the table in the upstage area.*)

AMANDA (*calling*): Tom?

TOM: Yes, Mother.

---

1 "Where are the snows [of yesteryear]?" part of the refrain of François Villon's "Ballade of Dead Ladies."

AMANDA: We can't say grace until you come to the table!

TOM: Coming, Mother. (*He bows slightly and withdraws, reappearing a few moments later in his place at the table.*)

AMANDA (*to her son*): Honey, don't *push* with your *fingers*. If you have to push with something, the thing to push with is a crust of bread. And chew — chew! Animals have sections in their stomachs which enable them to digest food without mastication, but human beings are supposed to chew their food before they swallow it down. Eat food leisurely, son, and really enjoy it. A well-cooked meal has lots of delicate flavors that have to be held in the mouth for appreciation. So chew your food and give your salivary glands a chance to function!

(TOM *deliberately lays his imaginary fork down and pushes his chair back from the table.*)

TOM: I haven't enjoyed one bite of this dinner because of your constant directions on how to eat it. It's you that make me rush through meals with your hawk-like attention to every bite I take. Sickening — spoils my appetite — all this discussion of — animals' secretion — salivary glands — mastication!

AMANDA (*lightly*): Temperament like a Metropolitan star! (*He rises and crosses downstage.*) You're not excused from the table.

TOM: I'm getting a cigarette.

AMANDA: You smoke too much.

(LAURA *rises.*)

LAURA: I'll bring in the blanc mange.

(*He remains standing with his cigarette by the portieres during the following.*)

AMANDA (*rising*): No, sister, no, sister — you be the lady this time and I'll be the darky.

LAURA: I'm already up.

AMANDA: Resume your seat, little sister — I want you to stay fresh and pretty — for gentlemen callers!

LAURA: I'm not expecting any gentlemen callers.

AMANDA (*crossing out to kitchenette. Airily*): Sometimes they come when they are least expected! Why, I remember one Sunday afternoon in Blue Mountain — (*Enters kitchenette.*)

TOM: I know what's coming!

LAURA: Yes. But let her tell it.

TOM: Again?

LAURA: She loves to tell it.

(AMANDA *returns with bowl of dessert.*)

AMANDA: One Sunday afternoon in Blue Mountain — your mother received — *seventeen!* — gentlemen callers! Why, sometimes there weren't chairs enough to accommodate them all. We had to send the nigger over to bring in folding chairs from the parish house.

TOM (*remaining at portieres*): How did you entertain those gentlemen callers?

AMANDA: I understood the art of conversation!

TOM: I bet you could talk.

AMANDA: Girls in those days *knew* how to talk, I can tell you.

TOM: Yes?

(IMAGE: AMANDA AS A GIRL ON A PORCH, GREETING CALLERS)

AMANDA: They knew how to entertain their gentlemen callers. It wasn't enough for a girl to be possessed of a pretty face and a graceful figure — although I wasn't slighted in either respect. She also needed to have a nimble wit and a tongue to meet all occasions.

TOM: What did you talk about?

AMANDA: Things of importance going on in the world! Never anything coarse or common or vulgar. (*She addresses* TOM *as though he were seated in the vacant chair at the table although he remains by portieres. He plays this scene as though he held the book.*) My callers were gentlemen — all! Among my callers were some of the most prominent young planters of the Mississippi Delta — planters and sons of planters!

(TOM *motions for music and a spot of light on* AMANDA.)

(*Her eyes lift, her face glows, her voice becomes rich and elegiac.*)

(SCREEN LEGEND: "OU SONT LES NEIGES")

There was young Champ Laughlin who later became vice-president of the Delta Planters Bank.

Hadley Stevenson who was drowned in Moon Lake and left his widow one hundred and fifty thousand in Government bonds.

There were the Cutrere brothers, Wesley and Bates. Bates was one of my bright particular beaux! He got in a quarrel with that wild Wainwright boy. They shot it out on the floor of Moon Lake Casino. Bates was shot through the stomach. Died in the ambulance on his way to Memphis. His widow was also well-provided for, came into eight or ten thousand acres, that's all. She married him on the rebound — never loved her — carried my picture on him the night he died!

And there was that boy that every girl in the Delta had set her cap for! That beautiful, brilliant young Fitzhugh boy from Greene County!

TOM: What did he leave his widow?

AMANDA: He never married! Gracious, you talk as though all of my old admirers had turned up their toes to the daisies!

TOM: Isn't this the first you've mentioned that still survives?

AMANDA: That Fitzhugh boy went North and made a fortune — came to be known as the Wolf of Wall Street! He had the Midas touch, whatever he touched turned to gold!

And I could have been Mrs. Duncan J. Fitzhugh, mind you! But — I picked your father!

LAURA (*rising*): Mother, let me clear the table.

AMANDA: No, dear, you go in front and study your typewriter chart. Or practice your shorthand a little. Stay fresh and pretty! — It's almost time for our gentlemen callers to start arriving. (*She flounces girlishly toward the kitchenette.*) How many do you suppose we're going to entertain this afternoon?

(TOM *throws down the paper and jumps up with a groan.*)

LAURA (*alone in the dining room*): I don't believe we're going to receive any, Mother.

AMANDA (*reappearing, airily*): What? No one — not one? You must be joking! (LAURA *nervously echoes her laugh. She slips in a fugitive manner through the half-open portieres and draws them gently behind her. A shaft of very clear light is thrown on her face against the faded tapestry of the curtains. Music: "The Glass Menagerie" under faintly. Light.*) Not one gentleman caller? It can't be true! There must be a flood, there must have been a tornado!

LAURA: It isn't a flood, it's not a tornado, Mother. I'm just not popular like you were in Blue Mountain. . . .

(TOM *utters another groan.* LAURA *glances at him with a faint, apologetic smile. Her voice catching a little.*)

Mother's afraid I'm going to be an old maid.

(*The Scene Dims Out with "Glass Menagerie" Music.*)

SCENE TWO

"Laura, Haven't You Ever Liked Some Boy?"

On the dark stage the screen is lighted with the image of blue roses.

Gradually LAURA'*s figure becomes apparent and the screen goes out.*

The music subsides.

LAURA *is seated in the delicate ivory chair at the small clawfoot table.*

She wears a dress of soft violet material for a kimono — her hair tied back from her forehead with a ribbon.

She is washing and polishing her collection of glass.

AMANDA *appears on the fire-escape steps. At the sound of her ascent,* LAURA *catches her breath, thrusts the bowl of ornaments away and seats herself stiffly before the diagram of the typewriter keyboard as though it held her spellbound.*

Something has happened to AMANDA. *It is written in her face as she climbs to the landing: a look that is grim and hopeless and a little absurd.*

She has on one of those cheap or imitation velvety-looking cloth coats with imitation fur collar. Her hat is five or six years old, one of those dreadful cloche hats that were worn in the late twenties and she is clasping an enormous black patent-leather pocketbook with nickel clasps and initials. This is her full-dress outfit, the one she usually wears to the D.A.R.

Before entering she looks through the door.

She purses her lips, opens her eyes very wide, rolls them upward and shakes her head.

Then she slowly lets herself in the door. Seeing her mother's expression LAURA *touches her lips with a nervous gesture.*

LAURA: Hello, Mother, I was — (*She makes a nervous gesture toward the chart on the wall.* AMANDA *leans against the shut door and stares at* LAURA *with a martyred look.*)

AMANDA: Deception? Deception? (*She slowly removes her hat and gloves, continuing the sweet suffering stare. She lets the hat and gloves fall on the floor — a bit of acting.*)

LAURA (*shakily*): How was the D.A.R. meeting? (AMANDA *slowly opens her purse and removes a dainty white handkerchief which she shakes out delicately and delicately touches to her lips and nostrils.*) Didn't you go to the D.A.R. meeting, Mother?

AMANDA (*faintly, almost inaudibly*): — No — No. (*Then more forcibly*) I did not have the strength — to go to the D.A.R. In fact, I did not have the courage! I wanted to find a hole in the ground and hide myself in it forever!

(*She crosses slowly to the wall and removes the diagram of the typewriter keyboard. She holds it in front of her for a second, staring at it sweetly and sorrowfully — then bites her lips and tears it in two pieces.*)

LAURA (*faintly*): Why did you do that, Mother? (AMANDA *repeats the same procedure with the chart of the Gregg Alphabet.*) Why are you —

AMANDA: Why? Why? How old are you, Laura?

LAURA: Mother, you know my age.

AMANDA: I thought that you were an adult; it seems that I was mistaken. (*She crosses slowly to the sofa and sinks down and stares at* LAURA.)

LAURA: Please don't stare at me, Mother. (AMANDA *closes her eyes and lowers her head. Count ten.*)

AMANDA: What are we going to do, what is going to become of us, what is the future? (*Count ten.*)

LAURA: Has something happened, Mother? (AMANDA *draws a long breath and takes out the handkerchief again. Dabbing process.*) Mother, has — something happened?

AMANDA: I'll be all right in a minute, I'm just bewildered — (*Count five.*) — by life. . . .

LAURA: Mother, I wish you would tell me what's happened!

AMANDA: As you know, I was supposed to be inducted into my office at the D.A.R. this afternoon. (*Image: A swarm of typewriters*) But I stopped off at Rubicam's Business College to speak to your teachers about you having a cold and ask them what progress they thought you were making down there.

LAURA: Oh. . . .

AMANDA: I went to the typing instructor and introduced myself as your mother. She didn't know who you were. Wingfield, she said. We don't have any such student enrolled at the school!

I assured her she did, that you had been going to classes since early in January.

"I wonder," she said, "if you could be talking about that terribly shy little girl who dropped out of school after only a few days' attendance?"

"No," I said, "Laura, my daughter, has been going to school every day for the past six weeks!"

"Excuse me," she said. She took the attendance book out and there was your name, unmistakably printed, and all the dates you were absent until they decided that you had dropped out of school.

I still said, "No, there must have been some mistake! There must have been some mix-up in the records!"

And she said, "No — I remember her perfectly now. Her hands shook so that she couldn't hit the right keys! The first time we gave a speed-test, she broke down completely — was sick at the stomach and almost had to be carried into the wash-room! After that morning she never showed up any more. We phoned the house but never got any answer" — while I was working at Famous and Barr, I suppose, demonstrating those — Oh!

I felt so weak I could barely keep on my feet!

I had to sit down while they got me a glass of water!

Fifty dollars' tuition, all of our plans — my hopes and ambitions for you — just gone up the spout, just gone up the spout like that.

(LAURA *draws a long breath and gets awkwardly to her feet. She crosses to the victrola and winds it up.*)

What are you doing?

LAURA: Oh! (*She releases the handle and returns to her seat.*)

AMANDA: Laura, where have you been going when you've gone out pretending that you were going to business college?

LAURA: I've just been going out walking.

AMANDA: That's not true.

LAURA: It is. I just went walking.

AMANDA: Walking? Walking? In winter? Deliberately courting pneumonia in that light coat? Where did you walk to, Laura?

LAURA: All sorts of places — mostly in the park.

AMANDA: Even after you'd started catching that cold?

LAURA: It was the lesser of two evils, Mother. (*Image: Winter scene in park*) I couldn't go back up. I — threw up — on the floor!

AMANDA: From half past seven till after five every day you mean to tell me you walked around in the park, because you wanted to make me think that you were still going to Rubicam's Business College?

LAURA: It wasn't as bad as it sounds. I went inside places to get warmed up.

AMANDA: Inside where?

LAURA: I went in the art museum and the birdhouses at the Zoo. I visited the penguins every day! Sometimes I did without lunch and went to the movies. Lately I've been spending most of my afternoons in the Jewel-box, that big glass house where they raise the tropical flowers.

AMANDA: You did all this to deceive me, just for deception? (LAURA *looks down*) Why?

LAURA: Mother, when you're disappointed, you get that awful suffering look on your face, like the picture of Jesus' mother in the museum!

AMANDA: Hush!

LAURA: I couldn't face it.

(*Pause. A whisper of strings.*)

(LEGEND: "THE CRUST OF HUMILITY")

AMANDA (*hopelessly fingering the huge pocketbook*): So what are we going to do the rest of our lives? Stay home and watch the parades go by? Amuse ourselves with the glass menagerie, darling? Eternally play those worn-out phonograph records your father left as a painful reminder of him?

We won't have a business career — we've given that up because it gave us nervous indigestion! (*Laughs wearily*) What is there left but dependency all our lives? I know so well what becomes of unmarried women who aren't prepared to occupy a position. I've seen such pitiful cases in the South — barely tolerated spinsters living upon the grudging patronage of sister's husband or brother's wife! — stuck away in some little mouse-trap of a room — encouraged by one in-law to visit another — little birdlike women without any nest — eating the crust of humility all their life!

Is that the future that we've mapped out for ourselves?

I swear it's the only alternative I can think of!

It isn't a very pleasant alternative, is it?

Of course — some girls *do marry.*

(Laura *twists her hands nervously.*)

Haven't you ever liked some boy?

Laura: Yes. I liked one once. (*Rises*) I came across his picture a while ago.

Amanda (*with some interest*): He gave you his picture?

Laura: No, it's in the year-book.

Amanda (*disappointed*): Oh — a high-school boy.

(screen image: jim as high-school hero bearing a silver cup)

Laura: Yes. His name was Jim. (Laura *lifts the heavy annual from the claw-foot table.*) Here he is in *The Pirates of Penzance.*

Amanda (*absently*): The what?

Laura: The operetta the senior class put on. He had a wonderful voice and we sat across the aisle from each other Mondays, Wednesdays, and Fridays in the Aud. Here he is with the silver cup for debating! See his grin?

Amanda (*absently*): He must have had a jolly disposition.

Laura: He used to call me — Blue Roses.

(image: blue roses)

Amanda: Why did he call you such a name as that?

Laura: When I had that attack of pleurosis —

he asked me what was the matter when I came back. I said pleurosis — he thought I said Blue Roses! So that's what he always called me after that. Whenever he saw me, he'd holler, "Hello, Blue Roses!" I didn't care for the girl that he went out with. Emily Meisenbach. Emily was the best-dressed girl at Soldan.[2] She never struck me, though, as being sincere. . . . It says in the Personal Section — they're engaged. That's — six years ago! They must be married by now.

Amanda: Girls that aren't cut out for business careers usually wind up married to some nice man. (*Gets up with a spark of revival.*) Sister, that's what you'll do!

(Laura *utters a startled, doubtful laugh. She reaches quickly for a piece of glass.*)

Laura: But, Mother —

Amanda: Yes? (*Crossing to photograph.*)

Laura (*in a tone of frightened apology*): I'm — crippled!

(image: screen)

Amanda: Nonsense! Laura, I've told you never, never to use that word. Why, you're not crippled, you just have a little defect — hardly noticeable, even! When people have some slight disadvantage like that, they cultivate other things to make up for it — develop charm — and vivacity — and — charm! That's all you have to do! (*She turns to the photograph.*) One thing your father had *plenty of* — was *charm!*

(Tom *motions to the fiddle in the wings.*)

(*The Scene Fades Out with Music*)

Scene Three

(legend on screen: "after the fiasco —" Tom *speaks from the fire-escape landing.*)

Tom: After the fiasco at Rubicam's Business College, the idea of getting a gentleman cal-

---

2 A large, centrally-located St. Louis high school.

ler for Laura began to play a more and more important part in Mother's calculations.

It became an obsession. Like some archetype of the universal unconscious, the image of the gentleman caller haunted our small apartment. . . .

(IMAGE: YOUNG MAN AT DOOR WITH FLOWERS)

An evening at home rarely passed without some allusion to this image, this specter, this hope. . . .

Even when he wasn't mentioned, his presence hung in Mother's preoccupied look and in my sister's frightened, apologetic manner — hung like a sentence passed upon the Wingfields!

Mother was a woman of action as well as words.

She began to take logical steps in the planned direction.

Late that winter and in the early spring — realizing that extra money would be needed to properly feather the nest and plume the bird — she conducted a vigorous campaign on the telephone, roping in subscribers to one of those magazines for matrons called *The Homemaker's Companion*, the type of journal that features the serialized sublimations of ladies of letters who think in terms of delicate cuplike breasts, slim, tapering waists, rich, creamy thighs, eyes like woodsmoke in autumn, fingers that soothe and caress like strains of music, bodies as powerful as Etruscan sculpture.

(SCREEN IMAGE: GLAMOR MAGAZINE COVER)

(AMANDA *enters with phone on long extension cord. She is spotted in the dim stage.*)

AMANDA: Ida Scott? This is Amanda Wingfield!
We *missed* you at the D.A.R. last Monday!
I said to myself: She's probably suffering with that sinus condition! How is that sinus condition?
Horrors! Heaven have mercy! — You're a Christian martyr, yes, that's what you are, a Christian martyr!
Well, I just now happened to notice that your subscription to the *Companion's* about to expire! Yes, it expires with the next issue, honey! — just when that wonderful new

serial by Bessie Mae Hopper is getting off to such an exciting start. Oh, honey, it's something that you can't miss! You remember how *Gone With the Wind* took everybody by storm? You simply couldn't go out if you hadn't read it. All everybody *talked* was Scarlett O'Hara. Well, this is a book that critics already compare to *Gone With the Wind*. It's the *Gone With the Wind* of the post-World War generation! — What? — Burning? — Oh, honey, don't let them burn, go take a look in the oven and I'll hold the wire! Heavens — I think she's hung up!

Dim Out

(LEGEND ON SCREEN: "YOU THINK I'M IN LOVE WITH CONTINENTAL SHOEMAKERS?")

(*Before the stage is lighted, the violent voices of* TOM *and* AMANDA *are heard.*)

(*They are quarreling behind the portieres. In front of them stands* LAURA *with clenched hands and panicky expression.*)

(*A clear pool of light on her figure throughout this scene.*)

TOM: What in Christ's name am I —

AMANDA (*shrilly*): Don't you use that —

TOM: Supposed to do!

AMANDA: Expression! Not in my —

TOM: Ohhh!

AMANDA: Presence! Have you gone out of your senses?

TOM: I have, that's true, *driven* out!

AMANDA: What is the matter with you, you — big — big — *idiot*!

TOM: Look! — I've got *no thing*, no single thing —

AMANDA: Lower your voice!

TOM: In my life here that I can call my *own*! Everything is —

AMANDA: Stop that shouting!

Tom: Yesterday you confiscated my books! You had the nerve to —

Amanda: I took that horrible novel back to the library — yes! That hideous book by that insane Mr. Lawrence (Tom *laughs wildly*.) I cannot control the output of diseased minds or people who cater to them — (Tom *laughs still more wildly*.) but i won't allow such filth brought into my house! No, no, no, no, no!

Tom: House, house! Who pays rent on it, who makes a slave of himself to —

Amanda (*fairly screeching*): Don't you DARE to —

Tom: No, no, I musn't say things! *I've* got to just —

Amanda: Let me tell you —

Tom: I don't want to hear any more! (*He tears the portieres open. The upstage area is lit with a turgid smoky red glow.*)

(Amanda's *hair is in metal curlers and she wears a very old bathrobe, much too large for her slight figure, a relic of the faithless Mr. Wingfield.*)
(*An upright typewriter and a wild disarray of manuscripts is on the drop-leaf table. The quarrel was probably precipitated by* Amanda's *interruption of his creative labor. A chair lying overthrown on the floor.*)
(*Their gesticulating shadows are cast on the ceiling by the fiery glow.*)

Amanda: You *will* hear more, you —

Tom: No, I won't hear more, I'm going out!

Amanda: You come right back in —

Tom: Out, out, out! Because I'm —

Amanda: Come back here, Tom Wingfield! I'm not through talking to you!

Tom: Oh go —

Laura (*desperately*): — Tom!

Amanda: You're going to listen, and no more insolence from you! I'm at the end of my patience!

(*He comes back toward her.*)

Tom: What do you think I'm at? Aren't I supposed to have any patience to reach the end of, Mother? I know, I know. It seems unimportant to you, what I'm *doing* — what I *want* to do — having a little *difference* between them! You don't think that —

Amanda: I think you've been doing things that you're ashamed of. That's why you act like this. I don't believe that you go every night to the movies. Nobody goes to the movies night after night. Nobody in their right minds goes to the movies as often as you pretend to. People don't go to the movies at nearly midnight, and movies don't let out at two a.m. Come in stumbling. Muttering to yourself like a maniac! You get three hours' sleep and then go to work. Oh, I can picture the way you're doing down there. Moping, doping, because you're in no condition!

Tom (*wildly*): No, I'm in no condition!

Amanda: What right have you got to jeopardize your job? Jeopardize the security of us all? How do you think we'd manage if you were —

Tom: Listen! You think I'm crazy *about the warehouse*? (*He bends fiercely toward her slight figure.*) You think I'm in love with the Continental Shoemakers? You think I want to spend fifty-five *years* down there in that — celotex interior! with — fluorescent — tubes! Look! I'd rather somebody picked up a crowbar and battered out my brains — than go back mornings! I *go*! Every time you come in yelling that God damn "Rise and Shine!" "Rise and Shine!" I say to myself, "How *lucky dead* people are!" But I get up. I *go*! For sixty-five dollars a month I give up all that I dream of doing and being *ever*! And you say self — *self's* all I ever think of. Why, listen, if self is what I thought of, Mother, I'd be where he is — gone! (*Pointing to father's picture.*) As far as the system of transportation reaches! (*He starts past her. She grabs his arm.*) Don't grab at me, Mother!

Amanda: Where are you going?

TOM: I'm going to the *movies!*

AMANDA: I don't believe that lie!

TOM (*crouching toward her, overtowering her tiny figure. She backs away, gasping*): I'm going to opium dens! Yes, opium dens, dens of vice and criminals' hang-outs, Mother. I've joined the Hogan gang, I'm a hired assassin, I carry a tommy-gun in a violin case! I run a string of cat-houses in the Valley! They call me Killer, Killer Wingfield, I'm leading a double-life, a simple, honest warehouse worker by day, by night a dynamic *czar* of the *underworld, Mother.* I go to gambling casinos, I spin away fortunes on the roulette table! I wear a patch over one eye and a false moustache, sometimes I put on green whiskers. On those occasions they call me — *El Diablo!* Oh, I could tell you things to make you sleepless! My enemies plan to dynamite this place. They're going to blow us all sky-high some night! I'll be glad, very happy, and so will you! You'll go up, up on a broomstick, over Blue Mountain with seventeen gentlemen callers! You ugly — babbling old — *witch.* . . . (*He goes through a series of violent, clumsy movements, seizing his overcoat, lunging to the door, pulling it fiercely open. The women watch him, aghast. His arm catches in the sleeve of the coat as he struggles to pull it on. For a moment he is pinioned by the bulky garment. With an outraged groan he tears the coat off again, splitting the shoulder of it, and hurls it across the room. It strikes against the shelf of LAURA's glass collection, there is a tinkle of shattering glass. LAURA cries out as if wounded.*)

(MUSIC. LEGEND: "THE GLASS MENAGERIE")

LAURA (*shrilly*): My glass! — menagerie. . . . (*She covers her face and turns away.*)

(*But AMANDA is still stunned and stupefied by the "ugly witch" so that she barely notices this occurrence. Now she recovers her speech.*)

AMANDA (*in an awful voice*): I won't speak to you — until you apologize! (*She crosses through portieres and draws them together behind her. TOM is left with LAURA. LAURA*

clings weakly to the mantel with her face averted. TOM *stares at her stupidly for a moment. Then he crosses to shelf. Drops awkwardly on his knees to collect the fallen glass, glancing at* LAURA *as if he would speak but couldn't.*)

(*"The Glass Menagerie" steals in as the Scene Dims Out*)

SCENE FOUR

The interior is dark. Faint light in the alley.

A deep-voiced bell in a church is tolling the hour of five as the scene commences.

TOM *appears at the top of the alley. After each solemn boom of the bell in the tower, he shakes a little noise-maker or rattle as if to express the tiny spasm of man in contrast to the sustained power and dignity of the Almighty. This and the unsteadiness of his advance make it evident that he has been drinking.*

As he climbs the few steps to the fire-escape landing light steals up inside. LAURA *appears in nightdress, observing* TOM's *empty bed in the front room.*

TOM *fishes in his pockets for door key, removing a motley assortment of articles in the search, including a perfect shower of movie-ticket stubs and an empty bottle. At last he finds the key, but just as he is about to insert it, it slips from his fingers. He strikes a match and crouches below the door.*

TOM (*bitterly*): One crack — and it falls through! (LAURA *opens the door.*)

LAURA: Tom, Tom, what are you doing?

TOM: Looking for a door key.

LAURA: Where have you been all this time?

TOM: I have been to the movies.

LAURA: All this time at the movies?

TOM: There was a very long program. There was a Garbo picture and a Mickey Mouse and a travelogue and a newsreel and a preview of coming attractions. And there was an organ solo and a collection for the milk-fund — simultaneously — which ended up in a terrible fight between a fat lady and an usher!

LAURA (*innocently*): Did you have to stay through everything?

TOM: Of course! And, oh, I forgot! There was a big stage show! The headliner on this stage show was Malvolio the Magician. He performed wonderful tricks, many of them, such as pouring water back and forth between pitchers. First it turned to wine and then it turned to beer and then it turned to whiskey. I know it was whiskey it finally turned into because he needed somebody to come up out of the audience to help him, and I came up — both shows! It was Kentucky Straight Bourbon. A very generous fellow, he gave souvenirs. (*He pulls from his back pocket a shimmering rainbow-colored scarf.*) He gave me this. This is his magic scarf. You can have it, Laura. You wave it over a canary cage and you get a bowl of goldfish. You wave it over the gold-fish bowl and they fly away canaries. . . . But the wonderfullest trick of all was the coffin trick. We nailed him into a coffin and he got out of the coffin without removing one nail. (*He has come inside.*) There is a trick that would come in handy for me — get me out of this 2 by 4 situation! (*Flops onto bed and starts removing shoes.*)

LAURA: Tom — Shhh!

TOM: What're you shushing me for?

LAURA: You'll wake up Mother.

TOM: Goody, goody! Pay her back for all those "Rise an' Shines." (*Lies down, groaning.*) You know it don't take much intelligence to get yourself into a nailed-up coffin, Laura. But who in hell ever got himself out of one without removing one nail?

(*As if in answer, the father's grinning photograph lights up.*)

Scene Dims Out

(*Immediately following: The church bell is heard striking six. At the sixth stroke the alarm clock goes off in* AMANDA's *room, and after a few moments we hear her calling: "Rise and Shine! Rise and Shine! Laura, go tell your brother to rise and shine!"*)

TOM (*sitting up slowly*): I'll rise — but I won't shine.

(*The light increases.*)

AMANDA: Laura, tell your brother his coffee is ready.

(LAURA *slips into front room.*)

LAURA: Tom! — It's nearly seven. Don't make Mother nervous. (*He stares at her stupidly. Beseechingly*) Tom, speak to Mother this morning. Make up with her, apologize, speak to her!

TOM: She won't to me. It's her that started not speaking.

LAURA: If you just say you're sorry she'll start speaking.

TOM: Her not speaking — is that such a tragedy?

LAURA: Please — please!

AMANDA (*calling from kitchenette*): Laura, are you going to do what I asked you to do, or do I have to get dressed and go out myself?

LAURA: Going, going — soon as I get on my coat! (*She pulls on a shapeless felt hat with nervous, jerky movement, pleadingly glancing at* TOM. *Rushes awkwardly for coat. The coat is one of* AMANDA's, *inaccurately made-over, the sleeves too short for* LAURA.) Butter and what else?

AMANDA (*entering upstage*): Just butter. Tell them to charge it.

LAURA: Mother, they make such faces when I do that.

AMANDA: Sticks and stones can break our bones, but the expression on Mr. Garfinkel's face won't harm us! Tell your brother his coffee is getting cold.

LAURA (*at door*): Do what I asked you, will you, will you, Tom?

(*He looks sullenly away.*)

AMANDA: Laura, go now or just don't go at all!

LAURA (*rushing out*): Going — going! (*A second later she cries out. Tom springs up and crosses to door. AMANDA rushes anxiously in. Tom opens the door.*)

TOM: Laura?

LAURA: I'm all right. I slipped, but I'm all right.

AMANDA (*peering anxiously after her*): If anyone breaks a leg on those fire-escape steps, the landlord ought to be sued for every cent he possesses! (*She shuts door. Remembers she isn't speaking and returns to other room.*)

(*As Tom enters listlessly for his coffee, she turns her back to him and stands rigidly facing the window on the gloomy gray vault of the areaway. Its light on her face with its aged but childish features is cruelly sharp, satirical as a Daumier print.*)

(MUSIC UNDER: "AVE MARIA")

(*Tom glances sheepishly but sullenly at her averted figure and slumps at the table. The coffee is scalding hot; he sips it and gasps and spits it back in the cup. At his gasp, AMANDA catches her breath and half turns. Then catches herself and turns back to window.*)

(*Tom blows on his coffee, glancing sidewise at his mother. She clears her throat. Tom clears his. He starts to rise. Sinks back down again, scratches his head, clears his throat again. AMANDA coughs. Tom raises his cup in both hands to blow on it, his eyes staring over the rim of it at his mother for several moments. Then he slowly sets the cup down and awkwardly and hesitantly rises from the chair.*)

TOM (*hoarsely*): Mother. I — I apologize, Mother. (*AMANDA draws a quick, shuddering breath. Her face works grotesquely. She breaks into childlike tears.*) I'm sorry for what I said, for everything that I said, I didn't mean it.

AMANDA (*sobbingly*): My devotion has made me a witch and so I make myself hateful to my children!

TOM: *No*, you *don't*.

AMANDA: I worry so much, don't sleep, it makes me nervous!

TOM (*gently*): I understand that.

AMANDA: I've had to put up a solitary battle all these years. But you're my right-hand bower! Don't fall down, don't fail!

TOM (*gently*): I try, Mother.

AMANDA (*with great enthusiasm*): Try and you will SUCCEED! (*The notion makes her breathless.*) Why, you — you're just *full* of natural endowments! Both my children — they're *unusual* children! Don't you think I know it? I'm so — *proud!* Happy and — feel I've — so much to be thankful for but — Promise me one thing, Son!

TOM: What, Mother?

AMANDA: Promise, Son, you'll — never be a drunkard!

TOM (*turns to her grinning*): I will never be a drunkard, Mother.

AMANDA: That's what frightened me so, that you'd be drinking! Eat a bowl of Purina!

TOM: Just coffee, Mother.

AMANDA: Shredded wheat biscuit?

TOM: No. No, Mother, just coffee.

AMANDA: You can't put in a day's work on an empty stomach. You've got ten minutes — don't gulp! Drinking too-hot liquids makes cancer of the stomach. . . . Put cream in.

TOM: No, thank you.

AMANDA: To cool it.

TOM: No! No, thank you, I want it black.

AMANDA: I know, but it's not good for you. We have to do all that we can to build ourselves up. In these trying times we live in, all that we have to cling to is — each other. . . . That's why it's so important to — Tom, I — I sent out your sister so I could discuss something with you. If you hadn't spoken I would have spoken to you. (*Sits down.*)

TOM (*gently*): What is it, Mother, that you want to discuss?

AMANDA: *Laura!*

(TOM *puts his cup down slowly.*)

(LEGEND ON SCREEN: "LAURA")

(MUSIC: "THE GLASS MENAGERIE")

TOM: — Oh — Laura . . .

AMANDA (*touching his sleeve*): You know how Laura is. So quiet but — still water runs deep! She notices things and I think she — broods about them. (TOM *looks up*) A few days ago I came in and she was crying.

TOM: What about?

AMANDA: You.

TOM: Me?

AMANDA: She has an idea that you're not happy here.

TOM: What gave her that idea?

AMANDA: What gives her any idea? However, you do act strangely. I — I'm not criticizing, understand *that!* I know your ambitions do not lie in the warehouse, that like everybody in the whole wide world — you've had to — make sacrifices, but — Tom — Tom — life's not easy, it calls for — Spartan endurance! There's so many things in my heart that I cannot describe to you! I've never told you but I — *loved* your father. . . .

TOM (*gently*): I know that, Mother.

AMANDA: And you — when I see you taking after his ways! Staying out late — and — well, you *had* been drinking the night you were in that — terrifying condition! Laura says that you hate the apartment and that you go out nights to get away from it! Is that true, Tom?

TOM: No. You say there's so much in your heart that you can't describe to me. That's true of me, too. There's so much in my heart that I

can't describe to *you!* So let's respect each other's —

AMANDA: But, why — *why*, Tom — are you always so *restless?* Where do you *go* to, nights?

TOM: I — go to the movies.

AMANDA: Why do you go to the movies so much, Tom?

TOM: I go to the movies because — I like adventure. Adventure is something I don't have much of at work, so I go to the movies.

AMANDA: But, Tom, you go to the movies *entirely* too *much!*

TOM: I like a lot of adventure.

(AMANDA *looks baffled, then hurt. As the familiar inquisition resumes he becomes hard and impatient again.* AMANDA *slips back into her querulous attitude toward him.*)

(IMAGE ON SCREEN: SAILING VESSEL WITH JOLLY ROGER)

AMANDA: Most young men find adventure in their careers.

TOM: Then most young men are not employed in a warehouse.

AMANDA: The world is full of young men employed in warehouses and offices and factories.

TOM: Do all of them find adventure in their careers?

AMANDA: They do or they do without it! Not everybody has a craze for adventure.

TOM: Man is by instinct a lover, a hunter, a fighter, and none of those instincts are given much play at the warehouse!

AMANDA: Man is by instinct! Don't quote instinct to me! Instinct is something that people have got away from! It belongs to animals! Christian adults don't want it!

TOM: What do Christian adults want, then, Mother?

AMANDA: Superior things! Things of the mind

and the spirit! Only animals have to satisfy instincts! Surely your aims are somewhat higher than theirs! Than monkeys — pigs –

Tom: I reckon they're not.

Amanda: You're joking! However, that isn't what I wanted to discuss.

Tom (*rising*): I haven't much time.

Amanda (*pushing his shoulders*): Sit down.

Tom: You want me to punch in red at the warehouse, Mother?

Amanda: You have five minutes. I want to talk about Laura.

(LEGEND: "PLANS AND PROVISIONS")

Tom: All right! What about Laura?

Amanda: We have to be making some plans and provisions for her. She's older than you, two years, and nothing has happened. She just drifts along doing nothing. It frightens me terribly how she just drifts along.

Tom: I guess she's the type that people call home girls.

Amanda: There's no such type, and if there is, it's a pity! That is, unless the home is hers, with a husband!

Tom: What?

Amanda: Oh, I can see the handwriting on the wall as plain as I can see the nose in front of my face! It's terrifying!
  More and more you remind me of your father! He was out all hours without explanation! — Then *left! Good-bye!*
  And me with the bag to hold. I saw that letter you got from the Merchant Marine. I know what you're dreaming of. I'm not standing here blindfolded.
  Very well, then. Then *do* it!
  But not till there's somebody to take your place.

Tom: What do you mean?

Amanda: I mean that as soon as Laura has got somebody to take care of her, married, a home of her own, independent — why, then you'll be free to go wherever you please, on land, on sea, whichever way the wind blows you!
  But until that time you've got to look out for your sister. I don't say me because I'm old and don't matter! I say for your sister because she's young and dependent.
  I put her in business college — a dismal failure! Frightened her so it made her sick at the stomach.
  I took her over to the Young People's League at the church. Another fiasco. She spoke to nobody, nobody spoke to her. Now all she does is fool with those pieces of glass and play those worn-out records. What kind of a life is that for a girl to lead?

Tom: What can I do about it?

Amanda: Overcome selfishness!
  Self, self, self is all that you ever think of!

(Tom *springs up and crosses to get his coat. It is ugly and bulky. He pulls on a cap with ear-muffs.*)

  Where is your muffler? Put your wool muffler on!

(*He snatches it angrily from the closet and tosses it around his neck and pulls both ends tight.*)

  Tom! I haven't said what I had in mind to ask you.

Tom: I'm too late to —

Amanda (*catching his arm — very importunately. Then shyly*): Down at the warehouse, aren't there some — nice young men?

Tom: No!

Amanda: There *must* be — *some* . . .

Tom: Mother — (*Gesture.*)

Amanda: Find out one that's clean-living — doesn't drink and — ask him out for sister!

Tom: What?

Amanda: For *sister!* To *meet!* Get *acquainted!*

Tom (*stamping to door*): Oh, my go-osh!

Amanda: Will you? (*He opens door. Implor-*

ingly) Will you? (*He starts down*) Will you? Will you, dear?

TOM (*calling back*): YES!

(AMANDA *closes the door hesitantly and with a troubled but faintly hopeful expression.*)

(SCREEN IMAGE: GLAMOR MAGAZINE COVER)

(*Spot* AMANDA *at phone.*)

AMANDA: Ella Cartwright? This is Amanda Wingfield!

How are you, honey?

How is that kidney condition? (*Pause*) Horrors! (*Pause*)

You're a Christian martyr, yes, honey, that's what you are, a Christian martyr!

Well, I just now happened to notice in my little red book that your subscription to the *Companion* has just run out! I knew that you wouldn't want to miss out on the wonderful serial starting in this new issue. It's by Bessie Mae Hopper, the first thing she's written since *Honeymoon for Three*.

Wasn't that a strange and interesting story? Well, this one is even lovelier, I believe. It has a sophisticated, society background. It's all about the horsey set on Long Island!

(*Fade Out*)

SCENE FIVE

LEGEND ON SCREEN: "ANNUNCIATION." *Fade with music.*

It is early dusk of a spring evening. Supper has just been finished in the Wingfield apartment. AMANDA *and* LAURA *in light-colored dresses are removing dishes from the table, in the upstage area, which is shadowy, their movements formalized almost as a dance or ritual, their moving forms as pale and silent as moths.*

TOM, *in white shirt and trousers, rises from the table and crosses toward the fire-escape.*

AMANDA (*as he passes her*): Son, will you do me a favor?

TOM: What?

AMANDA: Comb your hair! You look so pretty when your hair is combed! (TOM *slouches on sofa with evening paper. Enormous caption "Franco Triumphs"*) There is only one respect in which I would like you to emulate your father.

TOM: What respect is that?

AMANDA: The care he always took of his appearance. He never allowed himself to look untidy. (*He throws down the paper and crosses to fire-escape.*) Where are you going?

TOM: I'm going out to smoke.

AMANDA: You smoke too much. A pack a day at fifteen cents a pack. How much would that amount to in a month? Thirty times fifteen is how much, Tom? Figure it out and you will be astounded at what you could save. Enough to give you a night-school course in accounting at Washington U! Just think what a wonderful thing that would be for you, Son!

(TOM *is unmoved by the thought.*)

TOM: I'd rather smoke. (*He steps out on landing, letting the screen door slam.*)

AMANDA (*sharply*): I know! That's the tragedy of it. . . . (*Alone, she turns to look at her husband's picture.*)

(DANCE MUSIC: "ALL THE WORLD IS WAITING FOR THE SUNRISE!")

TOM (*to the audience*): Across the alley from us was the Paradise Dance Hall. On evenings in spring the windows and doors were open and the music came outdoors. Sometimes the lights were turned out except for a large glass sphere that hung from the ceiling. It would turn slowly about and filter the dusk with delicate rainbow colors. Then the orchestra played a waltz or a tango, something that had a slow and sensuous rhythm. Couples would come outside, to the relative privacy of the alley. You could see them kissing behind ash-pits and telephone poles.

This was the compensation for lives that passed like mine, without any change or adventure.

Adventure and change were imminent in

this year. They were waiting around the corner for all these kids.

Suspended in the mist over Berchtesgaden, caught in the folds of Chamberlain's umbrella —

In Spain there was Guernica!

But here there was only hot swing music and liquor, dance halls, bars, and movies, and sex that hung in the gloom like a chandelier and flooded the world with brief, deceptive rainbows. . . .

All the world was waiting for bombardments!

(AMANDA *turns from the picture and comes outside.*)

AMANDA (*sighing*): A fire-escape landing's a poor excuse for a porch. (*She spreads a newspaper on a step and sits down, gracefully and demurely as if she were settling into a swing on a Mississippi verandah.*) What are you looking at?

TOM: The moon.

AMANDA: Is there a moon this evening?

TOM: It's rising over Garfinkel's Delicatessen.

AMANDA: So it is! A little silver slipper of a moon. Have you made a wish on it yet?

TOM: Um-hum.

AMANDA: What did you wish for?

TOM: That's a secret.

AMANDA: A secret, huh? Well, I won't tell mine either. I will be just as mysterious as you.

TOM: I bet I can guess what yours is.

AMANDA: Is my head so transparent?

TOM: You're not a sphinx.

AMANDA: No, I don't have secrets. I'll tell you what I wished for on the moon. Success and happiness for my precious children! I wish for that whenever there's a moon, and when there isn't a moon, I wish for it, too.

TOM: I thought perhaps you wished for a gentleman caller.

AMANDA: Why do you say that?

TOM: Don't you remember asking me to fetch one?

AMANDA: I remember suggesting that it would be nice for your sister if you brought home some nice young man from the warehouse. I think that I've made that suggestion more than once.

TOM: Yes, you have made it repeatedly.

AMANDA: Well?

TOM: We are going to have one.

AMANDA: *What?*

TOM: A gentleman caller!

(THE ANNUNCIATION IS CELEBRATED WITH MUSIC)

(AMANDA *rises.*)

(IMAGE ON SCREEN: CALLER WITH BOUQUET)

AMANDA: You mean you have asked some nice young man to come over?

TOM: Yep. I've asked him to dinner.

AMANDA: You really did?

TOM: I did!

AMANDA: You did, and did he — *accept?*

TOM: He did!

AMANDA: Well, well — well, well! That's — lovely!

TOM: I thought that you would be pleased.

AMANDA: It's definite, then?

TOM: Very definite.

AMANDA: Soon?

TOM: Very soon.

AMANDA: For heaven's sake, stop putting on and tell me some things, will you?

TOM: What things do you want me to tell you?

AMANDA: *Naturally* I would like to know when he's *coming!*

TOM: He's coming tomorrow.

AMANDA: *Tomorrow?*

Tom: Yep. Tomorrow.

Amanda: But, Tom!

Tom: Yes, Mother?

Amanda: Tomorrow gives me no time!

Tom: Time for what?

Amanda: Preparations! Why didn't you phone me at once, as soon as you asked him, the minute that he accepted? Then, don't you see, I could have been getting ready!

Tom: You don't have to make any fuss.

Amanda: Oh, Tom, Tom, Tom, of course I have to make a fuss! I want things nice, not sloppy! Not thrown together. I'll certainly have to do some fast thinking, won't I?

Tom: I don't see why you have to think at all.

Amanda: You just don't know. We can't have a gentleman caller in a pig-sty! All my wedding silver has to be polished, the mono-grammed table linen ought to be laundered! The windows have to be washed and fresh curtains put up. And how about clothes? We have to *wear* something, don't we?

Tom: Mother, this boy is no one to make a fuss over!

Amanda: Do you realize he's the first young man we've introduced to your sister?
It's terrible, dreadful, disgraceful that poor little sister has never received a single gentle-man caller! Tom, come inside! (*She opens the screen door.*)

Tom: What for?

Amanda: I want to ask you some things.

Tom: If you're going to make such a fuss, I'll call it off, I'll tell him not to come!

Amanda: You certainly won't do anything of the kind. Nothing offends people worse than broken engagements. It simply means I'll have to work like a Turk! We won't be bril-liant, but we will pass inspection. Come on inside (Tom *follows, groaning.*) Sit down.

Tom: Any particular place you would like me to sit?

Amanda: Thank heavens I've got that new sofa! I'm also making payments on a floor lamp I'll have sent out! And put the chintz covers on, they'll brighten things up! Of course I'd hoped to have these walls re-papered. . . . What is the young man's name?

Tom: His name is O'Connor.

Amanda: That, of course, means fish — to-morrow is Friday! I'll have that salmon loaf — with Durkee's dressing! What does he do? He works at the warehouse?

Tom: Of course! How else would I —

Amanda: Tom, he — doesn't drink?

Tom: Why do you ask me that?

Amanda: Your father *did!*

Tom: Don't get started on that!

Amanda: He *does* drink, then?

Tom: Not that I know of!

Amanda: Make sure, be certain! The last thing I want for my daughter's a boy who drinks!

Tom: Aren't you being a little bit premature? Mr. O'Connor has not yet appeared on the scene!

Amanda: But will tomorrow. To meet your sister, and what do I know about his charac-ter? Nothing! Old maids are better off than wives of drunkards!

Tom: Oh, my God!

Amanda: Be still!

Tom (*leaning forward to whisper*): Lots of fellows meet girls whom they don't marry!

Amanda: Oh, talk sensibly, Tom — and don't be sarcastic! (*She has gotten a hairbrush.*)

Tom: What are you doing?

Amanda: I'm brushing that cow-lick down!
What is this young man's position at the warehouse?

Tom (*submitting grimly to the brush and the interrogation*): This young man's position is that of a shipping clerk, Mother.

AMANDA: Sounds to me like a fairly responsible job, the sort of a job *you* would be in if you just had more *get-up*.

What is his salary? Have you any idea?

TOM: I would judge it to be approximately eighty-five dollars a month.

AMANDA: Well — not princely, but —

TOM: Twenty more than I make.

AMANDA: Yes, how well I know! But for a family man, eighty-five dollars a month is not much more than you can just get by on. . . .

TOM: Yes, but Mr. O'Connor is not a family man.

AMANDA: He might be, mightn't he? Some time in the future?

TOM: I see. Plans and provisions.

AMANDA: You are the only young man that I know of who ignores the fact that the future becomes the present, the present the past, and the past turns into everlasting regret if you don't plan for it!

TOM: I will think that over and see what I can make of it.

AMANDA: Don't be supercilious with your mother! Tell me some more about this — what do you call him?

TOM: James D. O'Connor. The D. is for Delaney.

AMANDA: Irish on *both* sides! *Gracious!* And doesn't drink?

TOM: Shall I call him up and ask him right this minute?

AMANDA: The only way to find out about those things is to make discreet inquiries at the proper moment. When I was a girl in Blue Mountain and it was suspected that a young man drank, the girl whose attentions he had been receiving, if any girl *was*, would sometimes speak to the minister of his church, or rather her father would if her father was living, and sort of feel him out on the young man's character. That is the way such things

are discreetly handled to keep a young woman from making a tragic mistake!

TOM: Then how did you happen to make a tragic mistake?

AMANDA: That innocent look of your father's had everyone fooled!

He *smiled* — the world was *enchanted!*

No girl can do worse than put herself at the mercy of a handsome appearance!

I hope that Mr. O'Connor is not too good-looking.

TOM: No, he's not too good-looking. He's covered with freckles and hasn't too much of a nose.

AMANDA: He's not right-down homely, though?

TOM: Not right-down homely. Just medium homely, I'd say.

AMANDA: Character's what to look for in a man.

TOM: That's what I've always said, Mother.

AMANDA: You've never said anything of the kind and I suspect you would never give it a thought.

TOM: Don't be so suspicious of me.

AMANDA: At least I hope he's the type that's up and coming.

TOM: I think he really goes in for self-improvement.

AMANDA: What reason have you to think so?

TOM: He goes to night school.

AMANDA (*beaming*): Splendid! What does he do, I mean study?

TOM: Radio engineering and public speaking!

AMANDA: Then he has visions of being advanced in the world!

Any young man who studies public speaking is aiming to have an executive job some day!

And radio engineering? A thing for the future!

Both of these facts are very illuminating. Those are the sort of things that a mother should know concerning any young man who comes to call on her daughter. Seriously or — not.

TOM: One little warning. He doesn't know about Laura. I didn't let on that we had dark ulterior motives. I just said, why don't you come and have dinner with us? He said okay and that was the whole conversation.

AMANDA: I bet it was! You're eloquent as an oyster.

However, he'll know about Laura when he gets here. When he sees how lovely and sweet and pretty she is, he'll thank his lucky stars he was asked to dinner.

TOM: Mother, you musn't expect too much of Laura.

AMANDA: What do you mean?

TOM: Laura seems all those things to you and me because she's ours and we love her. We don't even notice she's crippled any more.

AMANDA: Don't say crippled! You know that I never allow that word to be used!

TOM: But face facts, Mother. She is and — that's not all —

AMANDA: What do you mean "not all"?

TOM: Laura is very different from other girls.

AMANDA: I think the difference is all to her advantage.

TOM: Not quite all — in the eyes of others — strangers — she's terribly shy and lives in a world of her own and those things make her seem a little peculiar to people outside the house.

AMANDA: Don't say peculiar.

TOM: Face the facts. She is.

(THE DANCE-HALL MUSIC CHANGES TO A TANGO THAT HAS A MINOR AND SOMEWHAT OMINOUS TONE)

AMANDA: In what way is she peculiar — may I ask?

TOM (gently): She lives in a world of her own — a world of — little glass ornaments. Mother. . . . (Gets up. AMANDA remains hold-ing brush, looking at him, troubled.) She plays old phonograph records and — that's about all — (He glances at himself in the mirror and crosses to door.)

AMANDA (sharply): Where are you going?

TOM: I'm going to the movies. (Out screen door.)

AMANDA: Not to the movies, every night to the movies! (Follows quickly to screen door.) I don't believe you always go to the movies! (He is gone. AMANDA looks worriedly after him for a moment. Then vitality and optimism return and she turns from the door. Crossing to portieres.) Laura! Laura! (LAURA answers from kitchenette.)

LAURA: Yes, Mother.

AMANDA: Let those dishes go and come in front! (LAURA appears with dish towel. Gaily) Laura, come here and make a wish on the moon!

(SCREEN IMAGE: MOON)

LAURA (entering): Moon — moon?

AMANDA: A little silver slipper of a moon. Look over your left shoulder, Laura, and make a wish!

(LAURA looks faintly puzzled as if called out of sleep. AMANDA seizes her shoulders and turns her at an angle by the door.)

Now!
Now, darling, wish!

LAURA: What shall I wish for, Mother?

AMANDA (her voice trembling and her eyes suddenly filling with tears): Happiness! Good fortune!

(The violin rises and the stage dims out.)

(The Curtain Falls)

SCENE SIX

(IMAGE: HIGH SCHOOL HERO)

TOM: And so the following evening I brought Jim home to dinner. I had known Jim slightly in high school. In high school Jim was a hero. He had tremendous Irish good nature and vitality with the scrubbed and polished look of white chinaware. He seemed to move in a continual spotlight. He was a star in basketball, captain of the debating club, president of the senior class and the glee club, and he sang the male lead in the annual light operas. He was always running or bounding, never just walking. He seemed always at the point of defeating the law of gravity. He was shooting with such velocity through his adolescence that you would logically expect him to arrive at nothing short of the White House by the time he was thirty. But Jim apparently ran into more interference after his graduation from Soldan. His speed had definitely slowed. Six years after he left high school he was holding a job that wasn't much better than mine.

(IMAGE: CLERK)

He was the only one at the warehouse with whom I was on friendly terms. I was valuable to him as someone who could remember his former glory, who had seen him win basketball games and the silver cup in debating. He knew of my secret practice of retiring to a cabinet of the wash-room to work on poems when business was slack in the warehouse. He called me Shakespeare. And while the other boys in the warehouse regarded me with suspicious hostility, Jim took a humorous attitude toward me. Gradually his attitude affected the others, their hostility wore off and they also began to smile at me as people smile at an oddly fashioned dog who trots across their path at some distance.

I knew that Jim and Laura had known each other at Soldan, and I had heard Laura speak admiringly of his voice. I didn't know if Jim remembered her or not. In high school Laura had been as unobtrusive as Jim had been astonishing. If he did remember Laura, it was not as my sister, for when I asked him to dinner, he grinned and said, "You know, Shakespeare, I never thought of you as having folks!"

He was about to discover that I did. . . .

(LIGHT UP STAGE)

(LEGEND ON SCREEN: "THE ACCENT OF A COMING FOOT")

(*Friday evening. It is about five o'clock of a late spring evening which comes "scattering poems in the sky"*)

(*A delicate lemony light is in the Wingfield apartment*)

(AMANDA *has worked like a Turk in preparation for the gentleman caller. The results are astonishing. The new floor lamp with its rose-silk shade is in place, a colored paper lantern conceals the broken light fixture in the ceiling, new billowing white curtains are at the windows, chintz covers are on chairs and sofa, a pair of new sofa pillows make their initial appearance.*)

(*Open boxes and tissue paper are scattered on the floor.*)

(LAURA *stands in the middle with lifted arms while* AMANDA *crouches before her, adjusting the hem of the new dress, devout and ritualistic. The dress is colored and designed by memory. The arrangement of* LAURA'S *hair is changed; it is softer and more becoming. A fragile, unearthly prettiness has come out in* LAURA: *she is like a piece of translucent glass touched by light, given a momentary radiance, not actual, not lasting.*)

AMANDA (*impatiently*): Why are you trembling?

LAURA: Mother, you've made me so nervous!

AMANDA: How have I made you nervous?

LAURA: By all this fuss! You make it seem so important!

AMANDA: I don't understand you, Laura. You couldn't be satisfied with just sitting home, and yet whenever I try to arrange something for you, you seem to resist it.
(*She gets up.*)
Now take a look at yourself.
No, wait! Wait just a moment — I have an idea!

LAURA: What is it now?

(AMANDA *produces two powder puffs which she wraps in handkerchiefs and stuffs in* LAURA'S *bosom.*)

LAURA: Mother, what are you doing?

AMANDA: They call them "Gay Deceivers"!

LAURA: I won't wear them!

AMANDA: You will!

LAURA: Why should I?

AMANDA: Because, to be painfully honest, your chest is flat.

LAURA: You made it seem like we were setting a trap.

AMANDA: All pretty girls are a trap, a pretty trap, and men expect them to be.

(LEGEND: "A PRETTY TRAP")

Now look at yourself, young lady. This is the prettiest you will ever be!

I've got to fix myself now! You're going to be surprised by your mother's appearance! (*She crosses through portieres, humming gaily.*)

(LAURA *moves slowly to the long mirror and stares solemnly at herself.*)
(*A wind blows the white curtains inward in a slow, graceful motion and with a faint, sorrowful sighing.*)

AMANDA (*off stage*): It isn't dark enough yet. (*She turns slowly before the mirror with a troubled look.*)

(LEGEND ON SCREEN: "THIS IS MY SISTER: CELEBRATE HER WITH STRINGS!" MUSIC)

AMANDA (*laughing, off*): I'm going to show you something. I'm going to make a spectacular appearance!

LAURA: What is it, Mother?

AMANDA: Possess your soul in patience — you will see! Something I've resurrected from that old trunk! Styles haven't changed so terribly much after all. . . .

(*She parts the portieres.*)

Now just look at your mother!

(*She wears a girlish frock of yellowed voile with a blue silk sash. She carries a bunch of jonquils — the legend of her youth is nearly revived. Feverishly.*)

This is the dress in which I led the cotillion.

Won the cakewalk twice at Sunset Hill, wore one spring to the Governor's ball in Jackson!

See how I sashayed around the ballroom, Laura?

(*She raises her skirt and does a mincing step around the room.*)

I wore it on Sundays for my gentlemen callers! I had it on the day I met your father —

I had malaria fever all that spring. The change of climate from East Tennessee to the Delta — weakened resistance — I had a little temperature all the time — not enough to be serious — just enough to make me restless and giddy! — Invitations poured in — parties all over the Delta! — "Stay in bed," said Mother, "you have fever!" — but I just wouldn't — I took quinine but kept on going, going! — Evenings, dances! — Afternoons, long, long rides! Picnics — lovely! — So lovely, that country in May — All lacy with dogwood, literally flooded with jonquils! — That was the spring I had the craze for jonquils. Jonquils became an absolute obsession. Mother said, "Honey, there's no more room for jonquils." And still I kept on bringing in more jonquils. Whenever, wherever I saw them, I'd say, "Stop! Stop! I see jonquils!" I made the young men help me gather the jonquils! It was a joke, Amanda and her jonquils! Finally there were no more vases to hold them, every available space was filled with jonquils. No vases to hold them? All right, I'll hold them myself! And then I — (*She stops in front of the picture.* MUSIC) met your father!

Malaria fever and jonquils and then — this — boy. . . .

(*She switches on the rose-colored lamp.*)

I hope they get here before it starts to rain.

(*She crosses upstage and places the jonquils in bowl on table.*)

I gave your brother a little extra change so he and Mr. O'Connor could take the service car home.

LAURA (*with altered look*): What did you say his name was?

AMANDA: O'Connor.

LAURA: What is his first name?

AMANDA: I don't remember. Oh, yes, I do. It was — Jim!

(LAURA *sways slightly and catches hold of a chair.*)

(LEGEND ON SCREEN: "NOT JIM!")

LAURA (*faintly*): Not — Jim.

AMANDA: Yes, that was it, it was Jim! I've never known a Jim that wasn't nice!

(MUSIC: OMINOUS)

LAURA: Are you sure his name is Jim O'Connor?

AMANDA: Yes. Why?

LAURA: Is he the one that Tom used to know in high school?

AMANDA: He didn't say so. I think he just got to know him at the warehouse.

LAURA: There was a Jim O'Connor we both knew in high school — (*Then, with effort*) If that is the one that Tom is bringing to dinner — you'll have to excuse me, I won't come to the table.

AMANDA: What sort of nonsense is this?

LAURA: You asked me once if I'd ever liked a boy. Don't you remember I showed you this boy's picture?

AMANDA: You mean the boy you showed me in the year book?

LAURA: Yes, that boy.

AMANDA: Laura, Laura, were you in love with that boy?

LAURA: I don't know, Mother. All I know is I couldn't sit at the table if it was him!

AMANDA: It won't be him! It isn't the least bit likely. But whether it is or not, you will come to the table. You will not be excused.

LAURA: I'll have to be, Mother.

AMANDA: I don't intend to humor your silliness, Laura. I've had too much from you and your brother, both!

So just sit down and compose yourself till they come. Tom has forgotten his key so you'll have to let them in, when they arrive.

LAURA (*panicky*): Oh, Mother — *you* answer the door!

AMANDA (*lightly*): I'll be in the kitchen — busy!

LAURA: Oh, Mother, please answer the door, don't make me do it!

AMANDA (*crossing into kitchenette*): I've got to fix the dressing for the salmon. Fuss, fuss — silliness! — over a gentleman caller!

(*Door swings shut.* LAURA *is left alone.*)

(LEGEND: "TERROR!")

(*She utters a low moan and turns off the lamp — sits stiffly on the edge of the sofa, knotting her fingers together.*)

(LEGEND ON SCREEN: "THE OPENING OF A DOOR!")

(TOM *and* JIM *appear on the fire-escape steps and climb to landing. Hearing their approach,* LAURA *rises with a panicky gesture. She retreats to the portieres.*)

(*The doorbell.* LAURA *catches her breath and touches her throat. Low drums.*)

AMANDA (*calling*): Laura, sweetheart! The door!

(LAURA *stares at it without moving*)

JIM: I think we just beat the rain.

TOM: Uh-huh. (*He rings again, nervously.* JIM *whistles and fishes for a cigarette.*)

AMANDA (*very, very gaily*): Laura, that's your brother and Mr. O'Connor! Will you let them in, darling?

(LAURA *crosses toward kitchenette door.*)

LAURA (*breathlessly*): Mother — you go to the door!

(AMANDA *steps out of kitchenette and stares furiously at* LAURA. *She points imperiously at the door.*)

LAURA: Please, please!

AMANDA (*in a fierce whisper*): What is the matter with you, you silly thing?

LAURA (*desperately*): Please, you answer it, *please!*

AMANDA: I told you I wasn't going to humor you, Laura. Why have you chosen this moment to lose your mind?

LAURA: Please, please, please, you go!

AMANDA: You'll have to go to the door because I can't!

LAURA (*despairing*): I can't either!

AMANDA: *Why?*

LAURA: I'm *sick!*

AMANDA: I'm sick, too — of your nonsense! Why can't you and your brother be normal people? Fantastic whims and behavior!

(TOM *gives a long ring.*)

Preposterous goings on! Can you give me one reason — (*Calls out lyrically*) COMING! JUST ONE SECOND! — why you should be afraid to open a door? Now you answer it, Laura!

LAURA: Oh, oh, oh . . . (*She returns through the portieres. Darts to the victrola and winds it frantically and turns it on.*)

AMANDA: Laura Wingfield, you march right to that door!

LAURA: Yes — yes, Mother!

(*A faraway, scratchy rendition of "Dardanella" softens the air and gives her strength to move through it. She slips to the door and draws it cautiously open.*)

(TOM *enters with the caller,* JIM O'CONNOR.)

TOM: Laura, this is Jim. Jim, this is my sister, Laura.

JIM (*stepping inside*): I didn't know that Shakespeare had a sister!

LAURA (*retreating stiff and trembling from the door*): How — how do you do?

JIM (*heartily extending his hand*): Okay!

(LAURA *touches it hesitantly with hers.*)

JIM: Your hand's *cold*, Laura!

LAURA: Yes, well — I've been playing the victrola. . . .

JIM: Must have been playing classical music on it! You ought to play a little hot swing music to warm you up!

LAURA: Excuse me — I haven't finished playing the victrola. . . .

(*She turns awkwardly and hurries into the front room. She pauses a second by the victrola. Then catches her breath and darts through the portieres like a frightened deer.*)

JIM (*grinning*): What was the matter?

TOM: Oh — with Laura? Laura is — terribly shy.

JIM: Shy, huh? It's unusual to meet a shy girl nowadays. I don't believe you ever mentioned you had a sister.

TOM: Well, now you know. I have one. Here is the *Post Dispatch*. You want a piece of it?

JIM: Uh-huh.

TOM: What piece? The comics?

JIM: Sports! (*Glances at it.*) Ole Dizzy Dean is on his bad behavior.

TOM (*disinterest*): Yeah? (*Lights cigarette and crosses back to fire-escape door.*)

JIM: Where are *you* going?

TOM: I'm going out on the terrace.

JIM (*Goes after him*): You know, Shakespeare — I'm going to sell you a bill of goods!

TOM: What goods?

JIM: A course I'm taking.

TOM: Huh?

JIM: In public speaking! You and me, we're not the warehouse type.

TOM: Thanks — that's good news.

But what has public speaking got to do with it?

JIM: It fits you for — executive positions!

TOM: Awww.

JIM: I tell you it's done a helluva lot for me.

(IMAGE: EXECUTIVE AT DESK)

TOM: In what respect?

JIM: In every! Ask yourself what is the difference between you an' me and men in the office down front? Brains? — No! — Ability? No! Then what? Just one little thing —

TOM: What is that one little thing?

JIM: Primarily it amounts to — social poise! Being able to square up to people and hold your own on any social level!

AMANDA (off stage): Tom?

TOM: Yes, Mother?

AMANDA: Is that you and Mr. O'Connor?

TOM: Yes, Mother.

AMANDA: Well, you just make yourselves comfortable in there.

TOM: Yes, Mother.

AMANDA: Ask Mr. O'Connor if he would like to wash his hands.

JIM: Aw, no — no — thank you — I took care of that at the warehouse. Tom —

TOM: Yes?

JIM: Mr. Mendoza was speaking to me about you.

TOM: Favorably?

JIM: What do you think?

TOM: Well —

JIM: You're going to be out of a job if you don't wake up.

TOM: I am waking up —

JIM: You show no signs.

TOM: The signs are interior.

(IMAGE ON SCREEN: THE SAILING VESSEL WITH JOLLY ROGER AGAIN)

TOM: I'm planning to change. (He leans over the rail speaking with quiet exhilaration. The incandescent marquees and signs of the first-run movie houses light his face from across the alley. He looks like a voyager.) I'm right at the point of committing myself to a future that doesn't include the warehouse and Mr. Mendoza or even a night-school course in public speaking.

JIM: What are you gassing about?

TOM: I'm tired of the movies.

JIM: Movies!

TOM: Yes, movies! Look at them — (A wave toward the marvels of Grand Avenue.) All of those glamorous people — having adventures — hogging it all, gobbling the whole thing up! You know what happens? People go to the movies instead of moving! Hollywood characters are supposed to have all the adventures for everybody in America, while everybody in America sits in a dark room and watches them have them! Yes, until there's a war. That's when adventure becomes available to the masses! Everyone's dish, not only Gable's! Then the people in the dark room come out of the dark room to have some adventures themselves — Goody, goody! — It's our turn now, to go to the South Sea Island — to make a safari — to be exotic, far-off! — But I'm not patient. I don't want to wait till then. I'm tired of the movies and I am about to move!

JIM (incredulously): Move?

TOM: Yes.

JIM: When?

TOM: Soon!

JIM: Where? Where?

(THEME THREE MUSIC SEEMS TO ANSWER THE QUESTION, WHILE TOM THINKS IT OVER. HE SEARCHES AMONG HIS POCKETS)

TOM: I'm starting to boil inside. I know I seem dreamy, but inside — well, I'm boiling! —

Whenever I pick up a shoe, I shudder a little thinking how short life is and what I am doing! — Whatever that means, I know it doesn't mean shoes — except as something to wear on a traveler's feet! (*Finds paper.*) Look —

JIM: What?

TOM: I'm a member.

JIM (*reading*): The Union of Merchant Seamen.

TOM: I paid my dues this month, instead of the light bill.

JIM: You will regret it when they turn the lights off.

TOM: I won't be here.

JIM: How about your mother?

TOM: I'm like my father. The bastard son of a bastard! See how he grins? And he's been absent going on sixteen years!

JIM: You're just talking, you drip. How does your mother feel about it?

TOM: Shhh! — Here comes Mother! Mother is not acquainted with my plans!

AMANDA (*enters portieres*): Where are you all?

TOM: On the terrace, Mother.

(*They start inside. She advances to them. TOM is distinctly shocked at her appearance. Even JIM blinks a little. He is making his first contact with girlish Southern vivacity and in spite of the night-school course in public speaking is somewhat thrown off the beam by the unexpected outlay of social charm.*)

(*Certain responses are attempted by JIM but are swept aside by AMANDA's gay laughter and chatter. TOM is embarrassed but after the first shock JIM reacts very warmly, grins and chuckles, is altogether won over.*)

(IMAGE: AMANDA AS A GIRL)

AMANDA (*coyly smiling, shaking her girlish ringlets*): Well, well, well, so this is Mr. O'Connor. Introductions entirely unnecessary. I've heard so much about you from my boy. I finally said to him, Tom — good

gracious! — why don't you bring this paragon to supper? I'd like to meet this nice young man at the warehouse! — Instead of just hearing him sing your praises so much!

I don't know why my son is so stand-offish — that's not Southern behavior!

Let's sit down and — I think we could stand a little more air in here! Tom, leave the door open. I felt a nice fresh breeze a moment ago. Where has it it gone to?

Mmm, so warm already! And not quite summer, even. We're going to burn up when summer really gets started.

However, we're having — we're having a very light supper. I think light things are better fo' this time of year. The same as light clothes are. Light clothes an' light food are what warm weather calls fo'. You know our blood gets so thick during th' winter — it takes a while fo' us to *adjust* ou'selves! — when the season changes . . .

It's come so quick this year. I wasn't prepared. All of a sudden — heavens! Already summer! — I ran to the trunk an' pulled out this light dress — Terribly old! Historical almost! But feels so good — so good an' cool, y' know. . . .

TOM: Mother —

AMANDA: Yes, honey?

TOM: How about — supper?

AMANDA: Honey, you go ask Sister if supper is ready!
You know that Sister is in full charge of supper!
Tell her you hungry boys are waiting for it.
(*to* JIM)
Have you met Laura?

JIM: She —

AMANDA: Let you in? Oh, good, you've met already! It's rare for a girl as sweet an' pretty as Laura to be domestic! But Laura is, thank heavens, not only pretty but also very domestic. I'm not at all. I never was a bit. I never could make a thing but angel-food cake. Well, in the South we had so many servants. Gone, gone, gone. All vestige of gracious living! Gone completely! I wasn't prepared for what the future brought me. All of my gentlemen callers were sons of planters and so of course I assumed that I would be married to one and raise my family on a large piece of land with plenty of servants. But man proposes — and woman accepts the proposal! — To vary that old, old saying a little bit — I married no planter! I married a man who worked for the telephone company! — That gallantly smiling gentleman over there! (*Points to the picture.*) A telephone man who — fell in love with long-distance! — Now he travels and I don't even know where! — But what am I going on for about my — tribulations?

Tell me yours — I hope you don't have any! Tom?

Tom (*returning*): Yes, Mother?

Amanda: Is supper nearly ready?

Tom: It looks to me like supper is on the table.

Amanda: Let me look — (*She rises prettily and looks through portieres.*) Oh, lovely! — But where is Sister?

Tom: Laura is not feeling well and she says that she thinks she'd better not come to the table.

Amanda: What? — Nonsense! — Laura? Oh, Laura!

Laura (*off stage, faintly*): Yes, Mother.

Amanda: You really must come to the table. We won't be seated until you come to the table!

Come in, Mr. O'Connor. You sit over there, and I'll —

Laura? Laura Wingfield!

You're keeping us waiting, honey! We can't say grace until you come to the table!

(*The back door is pushed weakly open and* Laura *comes in. She is obviously quite faint, her lips trembling, her eyes wide and staring. She moves unsteadily toward the table.*)

(legend: "terror!")

(*Outside a summer storm is coming abruptly. The white curtains billow inward at the windows and there is a sorrowful murmur and deep blue dusk.*)

(Laura *suddenly stumbles — she catches at a chair with a faint moan.*)

Tom: Laura!

Amanda: Laura!

(*There is a clap of thunder.*)

(legend: "ah!")

(*Despairingly.*)

Why, Laura, you *are* sick, darling! Tom, help your sister into the living room, dear!

Sit in the living room, Laura — rest on the sofa.

Well!

(*To the gentleman caller.*)

Standing over the hot stove made her ill! — I told her that it was just too warm this evening, but —

(Tom *comes back in.* Laura *is on the sofa.*)

Is Laura all right now?

Tom: Yes.

Amanda: What *is* that? Rain? A nice cool rain has come up!

(*She gives the gentleman caller a frightened look.*)

I think we may — have grace — now. . . .

(Tom *looks at her stupidly.*)

Tom, honey — you say grace!

Tom: Oh . . .

"For these and all thy mercies —"

(*They bow their heads,* Amanda *stealing a nervous glance at* Jim. *In the living room* Laura, *stretched on the sofa, clenches her hand to her lips, to hold back a shuddering sob.*)

God's Holy Name be praised —

(*The Scene Dims Out*)

Scene Seven

A Souvenir.

Half an hour later. Dinner is just being finished in the upstage area which is concealed by the drawn portieres.

As the curtain rises LAURA *is still huddled upon the sofa, her feet drawn under her, her head resting on a pale blue pillow, her eyes wide and mysteriously watchful. The new floor lamp with it shade of rose-colored silk gives a soft, becoming light to her face, bringing out the fragile, unearthly prettiness which usually escapes attention. There is a steady murmur of rain, but it is slackening and stops soon after the scene begins; the air outside becomes pale and luminous as the moon breaks out.*

A moment after the curtain rises, the lights in both rooms flicker and go out.

JIM: Hey, there, Mr. Light Bulb!

(AMANDA *laughs nervously.*)

(LEGEND: "SUSPENSION OF A PUBLIC SERVICE")

AMANDA: Where was Moses when the lights went out? Ha-ha. Do you know the answer to that one, Mr. O'Connor?

JIM: No. Ma'am, what's the answer?

AMANDA: In the dark!

(JIM *laughs appreciatively.*)

   Everybody sit still. I'll light the candles. Isn't it lucky we have them on the table? Where's a match? Which of you gentlemen can provide a match?

JIM: Here.

AMANDA: Thank you, sir.

JIM: Not at all, Ma'am!

AMANDA: I guess the fuse has burnt out. Mr. O'Connor, can you tell a burnt-out fuse? I know I can't and Tom is a total loss when it comes to mechanics.

(SOUND: GETTING UP: VOICES RECEDE A LITTLE TO KITCHENETTE)

   Oh, be careful you don't bump into some-thing. We don't want our gentleman caller to break his neck. Now wouldn't that be a fine howdy-do?

JIM: Ha-ha!
   Where is the fuse-box?

AMANDA: Right here next to the stove. Can you see anything?

JIM: Just a minute.

AMANDA: Isn't electricity a mysterious thing?
   Wasn't it Benjamin Franklin who tied a key to a kite?
   We live in such a mysterious universe, don't we? Some people say that science clears up all the mysteries for us. In my opinion it only creates more!
   Have you found it yet?

JIM: No, Ma'am. All these fuses look okay to me.

AMANDA: Tom!

TOM: Yes, Mother?

AMANDA: That light bill I gave you several days ago. The one I told you we got the notices about?

(LEGEND: "HA!")

TOM: Oh — Yeah.

AMANDA: You didn't neglect to pay it by any chance?

TOM: Why, I —

AMANDA: Didn't! I might have known it!

JIM: Shakespeare probably wrote a poem on that light bill, Mrs. Wingfield.

AMANDA: I might have known better than to trust him with it! There's such a high price for negligence in this world!

JIM: Maybe the poem will win a ten-dollar prize.

AMANDA: We'll just have to spend the remainder of the evening in the nineteenth century, before Mr. Edison made the Mazda lamp!

JIM: Candlelight is my favorite kind of light.

AMANDA: That shows you're romantic! But that's no excuse for Tom..
    Well, we got through dinner. Very considerate of them to let us get through dinner before they plunged us into everlasting darkness, wasn't it, Mr. O'Connor?

JIM: Ha-ha!

AMANDA: Tom, as a penalty for your carelessness you can help me with the dishes.

JIM: Let me give you a hand.

AMANDA: Indeed you will not!

JIM: I ought to be good for something.

AMANDA: Good for something? (*Her tone is rhapsodic.*) You? Why, Mr. O'Connor, nobody, *nobody's* given me this much entertainment in years — as you have!

JIM: Aw, now, Mrs. Wingfield!

AMANDA: I'm not exaggerating, not one bit! But Sister is all by her lonesome. You go keep her company in the parlor!
    I'll give you this lovely old candelabrum that used to be on the altar at the Church of the Heavenly Rest. It was melted a little out of shape when the church burnt down. Lightning struck it one spring. Gypsy Jones was holding a revival at the time and he intimated that the church was destroyed because the Episcopalians gave card parties.

JIM: Ha-ha!

AMANDA: And how about you coaxing Sister to drink a little wine? I think it would be good for her! Can you carry both at once?

JIM: Sure. I'm Superman!

AMANDA: Now, Thomas, get into this apron!

(*The door of kitchenette swings closed on* AMANDA's *gay laughter; the flickering light approaches the portieres.*)
(LAURA *sits up nervously as he enters. Her* speech at first is low and breathless from the almost intolerable strain of being alone with a stranger.*)

(THE LEGEND: "I DON'T SUPPOSE YOU REMEMBER ME AT ALL!")

(*In her first speeches in this scene, before* JIM's *warmth overcomes her paralyzing shyness,* LAURA's *voice is thin and breathless as though she has just run up a steep flight of stairs.*)

(JIM's *attitude is gently humorous. In playing this scene it should be stressed that while the incident is apparently unimportant, it is to* LAURA *the climax of her secret life.*)

JIM: Hello, there, Laura.

LAURA (*faintly*): Hello. (*She clears her throat.*)

JIM: How are you feeling now? Better?

LAURA: Yes. Yes, thank you.

JIM: This is for you. A little dandelion wine. (*He extends it toward her with extravagant gallantry.*)

LAURA: Thank you.

JIM: Drink it — but don't get drunk!

(*He laughs heartily.* LAURA *takes the glass uncertainly; laughs shyly.*)
    Where shall I set the candles?

LAURA: Oh — oh, anywhere . . .

JIM: How about here on the floor? Any objections?

LAURA: No.

JIM: I'll spread a newspaper under to catch the drippings. I like to sit on the floor. Mind if I do?

LAURA: Oh, no.

JIM: Give me a pillow?

LAURA: What?

JIM: A pillow!

LAURA: Oh . . . (*Hands him one quickly.*)

JIM: How about you? Don't you like to sit on the floor?

LAURA: Oh — yes.

JIM: Why don't you, then?

LAURA: I — will.

JIM: Take a pillow! (LAURA *does. Sits on the other side of the candelabrum.* JIM *crosses his legs and smiles engagingly at her.*) I can't hardly see you sitting way over there.

LAURA: I can — see you.

JIM: I know, but that's not fair, I'm in the lime-light. (LAURA *moves her pillow closer.*) Good! Now I can see you! Comfortable?

LAURA: Yes.

JIM: So am I. Comfortable as a cow! Will you have some gum?

LAURA: No, thank you.

JIM: I think that I will indulge, with your permission. (*Musingly unwraps it and holds it up.*) Think of the fortune made by the guy that invented the first piece of chewing gum. Amazing, huh? The Wrigley Building is one of the sights of Chicago — I saw it summer before last when I went up to the Century of Progress. Did you take in the Century of Progress?

LAURA: No, I didn't.

JIM: Well, it was quite a wonderful exposition. What impressed me most was the Hall of Science. Gives you an idea of what the future will be in America, even more wonderful than the present time is! (*Pause. Smiling at her.*) Your brother tells me you're shy. Is that right, Laura?

LAURA: I — don't know.

JIM: I judge you to be an old-fashioned type of girl. Well, I think that a pretty good type to be. Hope you don't think I'm being too personal — do you?

LAURA (*hastily, out of embarrassment*): I believe I *will* take a piece of gum, if you — don't mind. (*Clearing her throat*) Mr. O'Connor, have you — kept up with your singing?

JIM: Singing? Me?

LAURA: Yes. I remember what a beautiful voice you had.

JIM: When did you hear me sing?

(VOICE OFF STAGE IN THE PAUSE)

VOICE (*off stage*)

O blow, ye winds, heigh-ho,
A-roving I will go!
 I'm off to my love
 With a boxing glove —
Ten thousand miles away!

JIM: You say you've heard me sing?

LAURA: Oh, yes! Yes, very often. . . . I — don't suppose — you remember me — at all?

JIM (*smiling doubtfully*): You know I have an idea I've seen you before. I had that idea as soon as you opened the door. It seemed almost like I was about to remember your name. But the name that I started to call you — wasn't a name! And so I stopped myself before I said it.

LAURA: Wasn't it — Blue Roses?

JIM (*Springs up. Grinning*): Blue Roses! — My gosh, yes — Blue Roses!
 That's what I had on my tongue when you opened the door!
 Isn't it funny what tricks your memory plays? I didn't connect you with high school somehow or other.
 But that's where it was; it was high school. I didn't even know you were Shakespeare's sister!
 Gosh, I'm sorry.

LAURA: I didn't expect you to. You — barely knew me!

JIM: But we did have a speaking acquaintance, huh?

LAURA: Yes, we — spoke to each other.

JIM: When did you recognize me?

LAURA: Oh, right away!

JIM: Soon as I came in the door?

LAURA: When I heard your name I thought it

was probably you. I knew that Tom used to know you a little in high school. So when you came in the door — Well, then I was — sure.

Jim: Why didn't you say something, then?

Laura (*breathlessly*): I didn't know what to say, I was — too surprised!

Jim: For goodness' sakes! You know, this sure is funny!

Laura: Yes! Yes, isn't it, though . . .

Jim: Didn't we have a class in something together?

Laura: Yes, we did.

Jim: What class was that?

Laura: It was — singing — Chorus!

Jim: Aw!

Laura: I sat across the aisle from you in the Aud.

Jim: Aw.

Laura: Mondays, Wednesdays, and Fridays.

Jim: Now I remember — you always came in late.

Laura: Yes, it was so hard for me, getting upstairs. I had that brace on my leg — it clumped so loud!

Jim: I never heard any clumping.

Laura (*wincing at the recollection*): To me it sounded like — thunder!

Jim: Well, well, well, I never even noticed.

Laura: And everybody was seated before I came in. I had to walk in front of all those people. My seat was in the back row. I had to go clumping all the way up the aisle with everyone watching!

Jim: You shouldn't have been self-conscious.

Laura: I know, but I was. It was always such a relief when the singing started.

Jim: Aw, yes, I've placed you now! I used to call you Blue Roses. How was it that I got started calling you that?

Laura: I was out of school a little while with pleurosis. When I came back you asked me what was the matter. I said I had pleurosis — you thought I said Blue Roses. That's what you always called me after that!

Jim: I hope you didn't mind.

Laura: Oh, no — I liked it. You see, I wasn't acquainted with many — people. . . .

Jim: As I remember you sort of stuck by yourself.

Laura: I — I — never have had much luck at — making friends.

Jim: I don't see why you wouldn't.

Laura: Well, I — started out badly.

Jim: You mean being —

Laura: Yes, it sort of — stood between me —

Jim: You shouldn't have let it!

Laura: I know, but it did, and —

Jim: You were shy with people!

Laura: I tried not to be but never could —

Jim: Overcome it?

Laura: No, I — I never could!

Jim: I guess being shy is something you have to work out of kind of gradually.

Laura (*sorrowfully*): Yes — I guess it —

Jim: Takes time!

Laura: Yes.

Jim: People are not so dreadful when you know them. That's what you have to remember! And everybody has problems, not just you, but practically everybody has got some problems.

You think of yourself as having the only problems, as being the only one who is disappointed. But just look around you and you will see lots of people as disappointed as you are. For instance, I hoped when I was going to high school that I would be further along at this time, six years later, than I am now — You remember that wonderful write-up I had in *The Torch*?

LAURA: Yes! (*She rises and crosses to table.*)

JIM: It said I was bound to succeed in anything I went into! (LAURA *returns with the annual.*) Holy Jeez! *The Torch!* (*He accepts it reverently. They smile across it with mutual wonder.* LAURA *crouches beside him and they begin to turn through it.* LAURA's *shyness is dissolving in his warmth.*)

LAURA: Here you are in *The Pirates of Penzance!*

JIM (*wistfully*): I sang the baritone lead in that operetta.

LAURA: (*raptly*): So — *beautifully!*

JIM (*protesting*): Aw —

LAURA: Yes, yes — beautifully — beautifully!

JIM: You heard me?

LAURA: All three times!

JIM: No!

LAURA: Yes!

JIM: All three performances?

LAURA (*looking down*): Yes.

JIM: Why?

LAURA: I — wanted to ask you to — autograph my program.

JIM: Why didn't you ask me to?

LAURA: You were always surrounded by your own friends so much that I never had a chance to.

JIM: You should have just —

LAURA: Well, I — thought you might think I was —

JIM: Thought I might think you was — what?

LAURA: Oh —

JIM (*with reflective relish*): I was beleaguered by females in those days.

LAURA: You were terribly popular!

JIM: Yeah —

LAURA: You had such a — friendly way —

JIM: I was spoiled in high school.

LAURA: Everybody — liked you!

JIM: Including you?

LAURA: I — yes, I — I did, too — (*She gently closes the book in her lap.*)

JIM: Well, well, well! — Give me that program, Laura. (*She hands it to him. He signs it with a flourish.*) There you are — better late than never!

LAURA: Oh, I — what a — surprise!

JIM: My signature isn't worth very much right now.
   But some day — maybe — it will increase in value!
   Being disappointed is one thing and being discouraged is something else. I am disappointed but I am not discouraged.
   I'm twenty-three years old.
   How old are you?

LAURA: I'll be twenty-four in June.

JIM: That's not old age!

LAURA: No, but —

JIM: You finished high school?

LAURA (*with difficulty*): I didn't go back.

JIM: You mean you dropped out?

LAURA: I made bad grades in my final examinations. (*She rises and replaces the book and the program. Her voice strained.*) How is — Emily Meisenbach getting along?

JIM: Oh, that kraut-head!

LAURA: Why do you call her that?

JIM: That's what she was.

LAURA: You're not still — going with her?

JIM: I never see her.

LAURA: It said in the Personal Section that you were — engaged!

JIM: I know, but I wasn't impressed by that — propaganda!

LAURA: It wasn't — the truth?

JIM: Only in Emily's optimistic opinion!

LAURA: Oh —

(LEGEND: "WHAT HAVE YOU DONE SINCE HIGH SCHOOL?")

(JIM *lights a cigarette and leans indolently back on his elbows, smiling at* LAURA *with a warmth and charm which lights her inwardly with altar candles. She remains by the table and turns in her hands a piece of glass to cover her tumult.*)

JIM (*after several reflective puffs on a cigarette*): What have you done since high school? (*She seems not to hear him.*) Huh? (LAURA *looks up.*) I said what have you done since high school, Laura?

LAURA: Nothing much.

JIM: You must have been doing something these six long years.

LAURA: Yes.

JIM: Well, then, such as what?

LAURA: I took a business course at business college —

JIM: How did that work out?

LAURA: Well, not very — well — I had to drop out, it gave me — indigestion —

(JIM *laughs gently.*)

JIM: What are you doing now?

LAURA: I don't do anything — much. Oh, please don't think I sit around doing nothing! My glass collection takes up a good deal of time. Glass is something you have to take good care of.

JIM: What did you say — about glass?

LAURA: Collection I said — I have one — (*She clears her throat and turns away again, acutely shy.*)

JIM (*abruptly*): You know what I judge to be the trouble with you?

   Inferiority complex! Know what that is? That's what they call it when someone low-rates himself!

   I understand it because I had it, too. Although my case was not so aggravated as yours seems to be. I had it until I took up public speaking, developed my voice, and learned that I had an aptitude for science. Before that time I never thought of myself as being outstanding in any way whatsoever!

   Now I've never made a regular study of it, but I have a friend who says I can analyze people better than doctors that make a profession of it. I don't claim that to be necessarily true, but I can sure guess a person's psychology. Laura! (*Takes out his gum.*) Excuse me, Laura, I always take it out when the flavor is gone. I'll use this scrap of paper to wrap it in. I know how it is to get it stuck on a shoe.

   Yep — that's what I judge to be your principal trouble. A lack of confidence in yourself as a person. You don't have the proper amount of faith in yourself. I'm basing that fact on a number of your remarks and also on certain observations I've made. For instance that clumping you thought was so awful in high school. You say that you even dreaded to walk into class. You see what you did? You dropped out of school, you gave up an education because of a clump, which as far as I know was practically nonexistent! A little physical defect is what you have. Hardly noticeable even! Magnified thousands of times by imagination!

   You know what my strong advice to you is? Think of yourself as *superior* in some way!

LAURA: In what way would I think?

JIM: Why, man alive, Laura! Just look about you a little. What do you see? A world full of common people! All of 'em born and all of 'em going to die!

   Which of them has one-tenth of your good points! Or mine! Or anyone else's, as far as that goes — Gosh!

   Everybody excels in some one thing. Some in many!

(*Unconsciously glances at himself in the mirror.*)

   All you've got to do is discover in *what*! Take me for instance.

(*He adjusts his tie at the mirror.*)

   My interest happens to lie in electrodynamics. I'm taking a course in radio engineering at night school, Laura, on top of a fairly responsible job at the warehouse. I'm taking that course and studying public speaking.

LAURA: Ohhhh.

JIM: Because I believe in the future of television!

(*Turning back to her.*)

I wish to be ready to go up right along with it. Therefore I'm planning to get in on the ground floor. In fact I've already made the right connections and all that remains is for the industry itself to get under way! Full steam —

(*His eyes are starry.*)

Knowledge — *Zzzzzp! Money — Zzzzzzp!* — *Power!*

That's the cycle democracy is built on!

(*His attitude is convincingly dynamic.* LAURA *stares at him, even her shyness eclipsed in her absolute wonder. He suddenly grins.*)

I guess you think I think a lot of myself!

LAURA: No — o-o-o, I —

JIM: Now how about you? Isn't there something you take more interest in than anything else?

LAURA: Well, I do — as I said — have my — glass collection —

(*A peal of girlish laughter from the kitchen.*)

JIM: I'm not right sure I know what you're talking about.
What kind of glass is it?

LAURA: Little articles of it, they're ornaments mostly!
Most of them are little animals made out of glass, the tiniest little animals in the world. Mother calls them a glass menagerie!
Here's an example of one, if you'd like to see it!
This one is one of the oldest. It's nearly thirteen.

(MUSIC: "THE GLASS MENAGERIE")

(*He stretches out his hand.*)

Oh, be careful — if you breathe, it breaks!

JIM: I'd better not take it. I'm pretty clumsy with things.

LAURA: Go on, I trust you with him!

(*Places it in his palm.*)

There now — you're holding him gently! Hold him over the light, he loves the light! You see how the light shines through him?

JIM: It sure does shine!

LAURA: I shouldn't be partial, but he is my favorite one.

JIM: What kind of a thing is this one supposed to be?

LAURA: Haven't you noticed the single horn on his forehead?

JIM: A unicorn, huh?

LAURA: Mmm-hmmm!

JIM: Unicorns, aren't they extinct in the modern world?

LAURA: I know!

JIM: Poor little fellow, he must feel sort of lonesome.

LAURA (*smiling*): Well, if he does he doesn't complain about it. He stays on a shelf with some horses that don't have horns and all of them seem to get along nicely together.

JIM: How do you know?

LAURA (*lightly*): I haven't heard any arguments among them.

JIM (*grinning*): No arguments, huh? Well, that's a pretty good sign! Where shall I set him?

LAURA: Put him on the table. They all like a change of scenery once in a while!

JIM (*stretching*): Well, well, well, well — Look how big my shadow is when I stretch!

LAURA: Oh, oh, yes — it stretches across the ceiling!

JIM (*Crossing the door*): I think it's stopped raining. (*Opens fire-escape door.*) Where does the music come from?

LAURA: From the Paradise Dance Hall across the alley.

JIM: How about cutting the rug a little, Miss Wingfield?

LAURA: Oh, I —

JIM: Or is your program filled up? Let me have a look at it (*Grasps imaginary cards.*) Why, every dance is taken! I'll just have to scratch some out. (WALTZ MUSIC: "LA GOLONDRINA") Ahhh, a waltz! (*He executes some sweeping turns by himself then holds his arms toward* LAURA.)

LAURA (*breathlessly*): I — can't dance!

JIM: There you go, that inferiority stuff!

LAURA: I've never danced in my life!

JIM: Come on, try!

LAURA: Oh, but I'd step on you!

JIM: I'm not made out of glass.

LAURA: How — how — how do we start?

JIM: Just leave it to me. You hold your arms out a little.

LAURA: Like this?

JIM: A little bit higher. Right. Now don't tighten up, that's the main thing about it — relax.

LAURA (*laughing breathlessly*): It's hard not to.

JIM: Okay.

LAURA: I'm afraid you can't budge me.

JIM: What do you bet I can't. (*He swings her into motion.*)

LAURA: Goodness, yes, you can!

JIM: Let yourself go, now, Laura, just let yourself go.

LAURA: I'm —

JIM: Come on!

LAURA: Trying!

JIM: Not so stiff — Easy does it!

LAURA: I know but I'm —

JIM: Loosen th' backbone! There now, that's a lot better.

LAURA: Am I?

JIM: Lots, lots better! (*He moves her about the room in a clumsy waltz.*)

LAURA: Oh, my!

JIM: Ha-ha!

LAURA: Oh, my goodness!

JIM: Ha-ha-ha! (*They suddenly bump into the table.* JIM *stops.*) What did we hit on?

LAURA: Table.

JIM: Did something fall off it? I think —

LAURA: Yes.

JIM: I hope it wasn't the little glass horse with the horn!

LAURA: Yes.

JIM: Aw, aw, aw. Is it broken?

LAURA: Now it is just like all the other horses.

JIM: It's lost its —

LAURA: Horn!
    It doesn't matter. Maybe it's a blessing in disguise.

JIM: You'll never forgive me. I bet that that was your favorite piece of glass.

LAURA: I don't have favorites much. It's no tragedy, Freckles. Glass breaks so easily. No matter how careful you are. The traffic jars the shelves and things fall off them.

JIM: Still I'm awfully sorry that I was the cause.

LAURA (*smiling*): I'll just imagine he had an operation.
    The horn was removed to make him feel less — freakish!

(*They both laugh.*)

    Now he will feel more at home with the other horses, the ones that don't have horns. . . .

JIM: Ha-ha, that's very funny! (*Suddenly serious.*) I'm glad to see that you have a sense of humor.

You know — you're — well — very different!

Surprisingly different from anyone else I know!

(*His voice becomes soft and hesitant with a genuine feeling.*)

Do you mind me telling you that?

(LAURA *is abashed beyond speech.*)

I mean it in a nice way. . . .

(LAURA *nods shyly, looking away.*)

You make me feel sort of — I don't know how to put it!

I'm usually pretty good at expressing things, but —

This is something that I don't know how to say!

(LAURA *touches her throat and clears it — turns the broken unicorn in her hands.*)

(*Even softer.*)

Has anyone ever told you that you were pretty?

(PAUSE: MUSIC)

(LAURA *looks up slowly, with wonder, and shakes her head.*)

Well, you are! In a very different way from anyone else.

And all the nicer because of the difference, too.

(*His voice becomes low and husky.* LAURA *turns away, nearly faint with the novelty of her emotions.*)

I wish that you were my sister. I'd teach you to have some confidence in yourself. The different people are not like other people, but being different is nothing to be ashamed of. Because other people are not such wonderful people. They're one hundred times one thousand. You're one times one! They walk all over the earth. You just stay here. They're common as — weeds, but — you — well, you're — *Blue Roses!*

(IMAGE ON SCREEN: BLUE ROSES)

(MUSIC CHANGES)

LAURA: But blue is wrong for — roses. . . .

JIM: It's right for you! — You're — pretty!

LAURA: In what respect am I pretty?

JIM: In all respects — believe me! Your eyes — your hair — are pretty! Your hands are pretty!

(*He catches hold of her hand.*)

You think I'm making this up because I'm invited to dinner and have to be nice. Oh, I could do that! I could put on an act for you, Laura, and say lots of things without being very sincere. But this time I am. I'm talking to you sincerely. I happened to notice you had this inferiority complex that keeps you from feeling comfortable with people. Somebody needs to build your confidence up and make you proud instead of shy and turning away and — blushing —

Somebody — ought to —

Ought to — *kiss you,* Laura!

(*His hand slips slowly up her arm to her shoulder.*)

(MUSIC SWELLS TUMULTUOUSLY)

(*He suddenly turns her about and kisses her on the lips.*)

(*When he releases her,* LAURA *sinks on the sofa with a bright, dazed look.*)

(JIM *backs away and fishes in his pocket for a cigarette.*)

(LEGEND ON SCREEN: "SOUVENIR ")

Stumble-john!

(*He lights the cigarette, avoiding her look.*)

(*There is a peal of girlish laughter from* AMANDA *in the kitchen.*)

(LAURA *slowly raises and opens her hand. It still contains the little broken glass animal. She looks at it with a tender, bewildered expression.*)

Stumble-john!

I shouldn't have done that — That was way off the beam. You don't smoke, do you?

(She looks up, smiling, not hearing the question.)

(He sits beside her a little gingerly. She looks at him speechlessly — waiting.)

(He coughs decorously and moves a little farther aside as he considers the situation and senses her feelings, dimly, with perturbation.) *(Gently.)*

Would you — care for a — mint?

(She doesn't seem to hear him but her look grows brighter even.)

Peppermint — Life-Saver?
My pocket's a regular drug store — wherever I go . . .

(He pops a mint in his mouth. Then gulps and decides to make a clean breast of it. He speaks slowly and gingerly.)

Laura, you know, if I had a sister like you, I'd do the same thing as Tom. I'd bring out fellows and — introduce her to them. The right type of boys of a type to — appreciate her.
Only — well — he made a mistake about me.
Maybe I've got no call to be saying this. That may not have been the idea in having me over. But what if it was?
There's nothing wrong about that. The only trouble is that in my case — I'm not in a situation to — do the right thing.
I can't take down your number and say I'll phone.
I can't call up next week and — ask for a date.
I thought I had better explain the situation in case you — misunderstood it and — hurt your feelings. . . . . .

(Pause.)

(Slowly, very slowly, LAURA's look changes, her eyes returning slowly from his to the ornament in her palm.)

(AMANDA utters another gay laugh in the kitchen.)

LAURA *(faintly)*: You — won't — call again?

JIM: No, Laura, I can't.

(He rises from the sofa.)

As I was just explaining, I've got strings on me.
Laura, I've — been going steady!
I go out all of the time with a girl named Betty. She's a home-girl like you, and Catholic, and Irish, and in a great many ways we — get along fine.
I met her last summer on a moonlight boat trip up the river to Alton, on the *Majestic*.
Well — right away from the start it was — love!

(LEGEND: LOVE!)

(LAURA sways slightly forward and grips the arm of the sofa. He fails to notice, now enrapt in his own comfortable being.)

Being in love has made a new man of me!

(Leaning stiffly forward, clutching the arm of the sofa, LAURA struggles visibly with her storm. But JIM is oblivious, she is a long way off.)

The power of love is really pretty tremendous!
Love is something that — changes the whole world, Laura!

(The storm abates a little and LAURA leans back. He notices her again.)

It happened that Betty's aunt took sick, she got a wire and had to go to Centralia. So Tom — when he asked me to dinner — I naturally just accepted the invitation, not knowing that you — that he — that I —

(He stops awkwardly.)

Huh — I'm a stumble-john!

(He flops back on the sofa.)

(The holy candles in the altar of LAURA's face have been snuffed out. There is a look of almost infinite desolation.)

(JIM glances at her uneasily.)

I wish that you would — say something. (*She bites her lip which was trembling and then bravely smiles. She opens her hand again on the broken glass ornament. Then she gently takes his hand and raises it level with her own. She carefully places the unicorn in the palm of his hand, then pushes his fingers closed upon it.*) What are you — doing that for? You want me to have him? — Laura? (*She nods.*) What for?

LAURA: A — souvenir . . .

(*She rises unsteadily and crouches beside the victrola to wind it up.*)

(LEGEND ON SCREEN: "THINGS HAVE A WAY OF TURNING OUT SO BADLY!")

(OR IMAGE: "GENTLEMAN CALLER WAVING GOODBYE! — GAILY")

(*At this moment* AMANDA *rushes brightly back in the front room. She bears a pitcher of fruit punch in an old-fashioned cut-glass pitcher and a plate of macaroons. The plate has a gold border and poppies painted on it.*)

AMANDA: Well, well, well! Isn't the air delightful after the shower? I've made you children a little liquid refreshment.

(*Turns gaily to the gentleman caller.*)

Jim, do you know that song about lemonade?

"Lemonade, lemonade
Made in the shade and stirred with a spade —
Good enough for any old maid!"

JIM (*uneasily*): Ha-ha! No — I never heard it.

AMANDA: Why, Laura! You look so serious!

JIM: We were having a serious conversation.

AMANDA: Good! Now you're better acquainted!

JIM (*uncertainly*): Ha-ha! Yes.

AMANDA: You modern young people are much more serious-minded than my generation. I was so gay as a girl!

JIM: You haven't changed, Mrs. Wingfield.

AMANDA: Tonight I'm rejuvenated! The gaiety of the occasion, Mr. O'Connor!

(*She tosses her head with a peal of laughter. Spills lemonade.*)

Oooo! I'm baptizing myself!

JIM: Here — let me —

AMANDA (*setting the pitcher down*): There now, I discovered we had some maraschino cherries. I dumped them in, juice and all!

JIM: You shouldn't have gone to that trouble, Mrs. Wingfield.

AMANDA: Trouble, trouble? Why, it was loads of fun!

Didn't you hear me cutting up in the kitchen? I bet your ears were burning! I told Tom how outdone with him I was for keeping you to himself so long a time! He should have brought you over much, much sooner! Well, now that you've found your way, I want you to be a very frequent caller! Not just occasional but all the time.

Oh, we're going to have a lot of gay times together! I see them coming!

Mmm, just breathe that air! So fresh, and the moon's so pretty!

I'll skip back out — I know where my place is when young folks are having a — serious conversation!

JIM: Oh, don't go out, Mrs. Wingfield. The fact of the matter is I've got to be going.

AMANDA: Going now? You're joking! Why, it's only the shank of the evening, Mr. O'Connor!

JIM: Well, you know how it is.

AMANDA: You mean you're a young workingman and have to keep workingmen's hours. We'll let you off early tonight. But only on the condition that next time you stay later.

What's the best night for you? Isn't Saturday night the best night for you workingmen?

JIM: I have a couple of time-clocks to punch, Mrs. Wingfield. One at morning, another one at night!

AMANDA: My, but you *are* ambitious! You work at night, too?

JIM: No, Ma'am, not work but — Betty! (*He crosses deliberately to pick up his hat. The band at the Paradise Dance Hall goes into a tender waltz.*)

AMANDA: Betty? Betty? Who's — Betty!

(*There is an ominous cracking sound in the sky.*)
JIM: Oh, just a girl. The girl I go steady with! (*He smiles charmingly. The sky falls.*)

(LEGEND: "THE SKY FALLS")

AMANDA (*a long-drawn exhalation*): Ohhhh . . . Is it a serious romance, Mr. O'Connor?

JIM: We're going to be married the second Sunday in June.

AMANDA: Ohhhh — how nice!
Tom didn't mention that you were engaged to be married.

JIM: The cat's not out of the bag at the warehouse yet.
You know how they are. They call you Romeo and stuff like that.

(*He stops at the oval mirror to put on his hat. He carefully shapes the brim and the crown to give a discreetly dashing effect.*)

It's been a wonderful evening, Mrs. Wingfield. I guess this is what they mean by Southern hospitality.

AMANDA: It really wasn't anything at all.

JIM: I hope it don't seem like I'm rushing off. But I promised Betty I'd pick her up at the Wabash depot, an' by the time I get my jalopy down there her train'll be in. Some women are pretty upset if you keep 'em waiting.
AMANDA: Yes, I know — The tyranny of women!
(*Extends her hand.*)
Good-bye, Mr. O'Connor.
I wish you luck — and happiness — and success! All three of them, and so does Laura! — Don't you, Laura?

LAURA: Yes!

JIM (*taking her hand*): Good-bye, Laura. I'm certainly going to treasure that souvenir. And don't you forget the good advice I gave you.

(*Raises his voice to a cheery shout.*)

So long, Shakespeare!
Thanks again, ladies — Good night!

(*He grins and ducks jauntily out.*)

(*Still bravely grimacing, AMANDA closes the door on the gentleman caller. Then she turns back to the room with a puzzled expression. She and LAURA don't dare to face each other. LAURA crouches beside the victrola to wind it.*)

AMANDA (*faintly*): Things have a way of turning out so badly.
I don't believe that I would play the victrola.
Well, well — well —
Our gentleman caller was engaged to be married!
Tom!

TOM (*from back*): Yes, Mother?

AMANDA: Come in here a minute. I want to tell you something awfully funny.

TOM (*enters with macaroon and a glass of the lemonade*): Has the gentleman caller gotten away already?

AMANDA: The gentleman caller has made an early departure.
What a wonderful joke you played on us!

TOM: How do you mean?

AMANDA: You didn't mention that he was engaged to be married.

TOM: Jim? Engaged?

AMANDA: That's what he just informed us.

TOM: I'll be jiggered! I didn't know about that.

AMANDA: That seems very peculiar.

TOM: What's peculiar about it?

AMANDA: Didn't you call him your best friend down at the warehouse?

TOM: He is, but how did I know?

AMANDA: It seems extremely peculiar that you wouldn't know your best friend was going to be married!

TOM: The warehouse is where I work, not where I know things about people!

AMANDA: You don't know things anywhere! You live in a dream; you manufacture illusions!

(*He crosses to door.*)

Where are you going?

TOM: I'm going to the movies.

AMANDA: That's right, now that you've had us make such fools of ourselves. The effort, the preparations, all the expense! the new floor lamp, the rug, the clothes for Laura! All for what? To entertain some other girl's fiancé!

Go to the movies, go! Don't think about us, a mother deserted, an unmarried sister who's crippled and has no job! Don't let anything interfere with your selfish pleasure!

Just go, go, go — to the movies!

TOM: All right, I will! The more you shout about my selfishness to me the quicker I'll go, and I won't go to the movies!

AMANDA: Go, then! Then go to the moon — you selfish dreamer!

(TOM *smashes his glass on the floor. He plunges out on the fire escape, slamming the door.* LAURA *screams — cut by door.*)

(*Dance-hall music up.* TOM *goes to the rail and grips it desperately, lifting his face in the chill white moonlight penetrating the narrow abyss of the alley.*)

(LEGEND ON SCREEN: "AND SO GOODBYE . . .")

(TOM's *closing speech is timed with the interior pantomime. The interior scene is played as though viewed through soundproof glass.* AMANDA *appears to be making a comforting speech to* LAURA *who is huddled upon the sofa. Now that we cannot hear the mother's speech, her silliness is gone and she has dignity and tragic beauty.* LAURA's *dark hair hides her face until at the end of the speech she lifts it to smile at her mother.* AMANDA's *gestures are slow and graceful, almost dancelike, as she comforts*

the daughter. At the end of her speech she glances a moment at the father's picture — then withdraws through the portieres. At close of TOM's *speech,* LAURA *blows out the candles, ending the play.*)

TOM: I didn't go to the moon, I went much further — for time is the longest distance between two places —

Not long after that I was fired for writing a poem on the lid of a shoe-box.

I left Saint Louis. I descended the steps of this fire escape for a last time and followed, from then on, in my father's footsteps, attempting to find in motion what was lost in space —

I traveled around a great deal. The cities swept about me like dead leaves, leaves that were brightly colored but torn away from the branches.

I would have stopped, but I was pursued by something.

It always came upon me unawares, taking me altogether by surprise. Perhaps it was a familiar bit of music. Perhaps it was only a piece of transparent glass —

Perhaps I am walking along a street at night, in some strange city, before I have found companions. I pass the lighted window of a shop where perfume is sold. The window is filled with pieces of colored glass, tiny transparent bottles in delicate colors, like bits of a shattered rainbow.

Then all at once my sister touches my shoulder. I turn around and look into her eyes . . .

Oh, Laura, Laura, I tried to leave you behind me, but I am more faithful than I intended to be!

I reach for a cigarette, I cross the street, I run into the movies or a bar, I buy a drink, I speak to the nearest stranger — anything that can blow your candles out!

(LAURA *bends over the candles.*)

— for nowadays the world is lit by lightning! Blow out your candles, Laura — and so goodbye. . . .

(*She blows the candles out.*)

(*The Scene Dissolves*)

Antigone

Jean Anouilh (born 1910) studied law, worked in an advertising agency, and briefly served as secretary to the actor Louis Jouvet (1887–1951). Jouvet encouraged the dramatist Jean Giraudoux (1882–1944) by convincing him that his novel of Franco-German rapprochment, *Seigfried et le Limousin*, would make a good play. Jouvet directed *Siegfried* (1928), and all but one of Giraudoux's other plays; it was *Siegfried* that encouraged Anouilh to turn to the stage. He wrote *Humulus le muet* and *Mandarine* (both 1929) and *Attila le magnifique* (1930, never published or staged) before he established himself as a melancholy and poetic romantic with *L'Hermine* (1932), the first of Anouilh's plays to be produced. With the production of *Le Bal des Voleurs* (1932, the English version is called *Thieves' Carnival*) he moved into the front ranks of modern playwrights. He confirmed his reputation with *pièces noires* ("black plays") and *pièces roses* ("pink plays"), and comedies both *brillantes* and *grinçantes*, glittering "surfaces [which] cast the spectator back into himself and into a genuine world — that of man's unenviable lot," to quote the conclusion to David I. Grossvogel's interesting chapter on Anouilh in *20th Century French Drama* (1961).*

In *La Sauvage* (written 1934, produced 1938) and *Le Voyageur sans bagages* (1936), two of his "black plays," Anouilh clearly established that he could "wear the tragic mask with ease," while in his "pink plays" the same themes of dire poverty, threatened innocence and the role of memory were more wittily and lightly handled in such plays as *Le Rendez-vous de Senlis* (1937) and *Léocadia* (1939). Among his "brilliant" plays were *L'Invitation au château* (1947, adapted by Fry as *Ring Round the Moon*), *Mademoiselle Colombe* (1951), and *La Répétition* (*The Rehearsal*, 1950). Among his bitter *pièces grinçantes* are *Ardèle, ou la Marguerite* (1948), *La Valse des toréadors* (*The Waltz of the Toreadors*, 1952), and *Pauvre Bitos* (*Poor Bitos*, 1956). History forms the background for two great theatrical successes: *L'Alouette* (1953, *The Lark*, about Joan of Arc), *Becket* (1959, about St. Thomas à Becket, Archbishop of Canterbury, and King Henry II), and *La Foire d'empoigne* (about Napoleon and King Louis XVIII, written

---

* This is the paperback text from Columbia University Press, who originally published the book as *The Self-Conscious Stage in Modern French Drama* (1958).

1959, produced 1962). Greek myth underlies such plays as *Eurydice* (1941), *Antigone* (1942), and *Médée* (1946), just as it does other successes of the modern French theatre like Jean-Paul Sartre's *Les Mouches* (*The Flies*, 1942, based on the Orestes myth, which Anouilh has also handled) and *The Infernal Machine* (an adaptation of *Oedipus Rex*), and Jean Giraudoux's *La Guerre de Troie n'aura pas lieu* (1935, adapted by Christopher Fry as *Tiger at the Gates*). In a theatre style stemming directly from Molière and Italian comedy (all the critics agree) but with a twentieth-century cynicism "which is to say *no* to existence" (as Henri Clouard and Robert Leggewie say in *French Writers of Today*, 1965), Anouilh has added wit to pessimism and poetry to despair, "more poetry of the theatre," wrote Stephen Spender, "than anything a contemporary poet has yet put in metrical lines upon a stage." When to the charm of plays like *Eurydice* (*Legend of Lovers*) or the modernity of *L'Hurluberlu* (1959) the theatrical savvy of André Barsacq (Anouilh's director until 1953) or the multi-faceted talents of the Pitoëff family (Georges, Ludmilla, and their son Sacha) or some other directors were added, the theatrical effect of an Anouilh play was overwhelming. Broadway audiences hailed his *Time Remembered* and *The Lark*, more select theatres around the world welcomed *Ardèle* and *Ring Round the Moon*, and millions enjoyed his discussion of "the honor of God" in the filmed version of *Becket* that starred Peter O'Toole and Richard Burton.

One of the most brilliant examples of Anouilh's unique combination of theatricality and thought is his version of the Antigone story, written exactly 2300 years after that of Sophocles. The reader will find many interesting points of similarity and difference between Aristotle and Anouilh. The modern version of the ancient story has been translated for *Mirrors for Man* by Alex Szogyi, Chairman of the Department of Modern Languages at Hunter College of The City University of New York. This is the first printed translation of the entire play. Professor Szogyi has also written a brief introduction especially for this volume.

Preface to Antigone
ALEX SZOGYI

Jean Anouilh's *Antigone* was first performed on February 4, 1944, during the Nazi occupation of Paris, at the Théâtre de l'Atelier. It has had numerous revivals ever since, both in France and abroad. The revival of *Antigone* at the Théâtre Hébertot was one of the greatest successes of that theatre season. *Antigone* was the first play I saw in France when I first came to live there in 1950. My own translation of the play was first performed some 19 years later. I never suspected that I would eventually translate the play. It had had a successful run on Broadway in an adaptation by Lewis Galantière, and no other translation was ever performed anywhere. I had never seen the production nor had I ever read the play in English. It came as a great surprise when a director at Hunter College asked me to translate for him the sections that had been left out. I refused to add to another translator's work, but agreed to do my own version, as close to the original as I thought I could come. The advantage of working for college theatre is that a non-professional director is so much more often adventurous. A commercial production on Broadway doesn't dare. The only thing I asked was that the text not be cut. It was played at Hunter College and then, a year later, at Trenton State College. It is amusing to me to note that the play has probably only been seen in its entirety in these two places. One day, perhaps, when translating is well organized and truly appreciated, plays will be translated integrally first and then adapted for specific purposes afterward. But theatre people will have to be daring and trusting for that to occur.

Plays are both events and literature. Corneille's *Le Cid* (1636), was the first triumph of a form which was to be codified as seventeenth century classical tragedy. Victor Hugo's *Hernani* (1830) ushered in the romantic period of French drama. Some plays remain documents. Others survive as vital theatre as well as literature. *Hernani* is now chiefly a date and the declaration of Victor Hugo's romantic manifesto. *Le Cid* lives again whenever an excellent actor such as Gérard Philippe makes its lyric poetry contagious and exciting.

Of all Anouilh's plays, *Antigone* seems easily destined for immortality. A quarter of a century has elapsed since it first symbolized France's oppression by Nazi Germany and it is perhaps not too early to assess the reasons why it remains valid.

For the French who first saw it, *Antigone* seemed a parable of the Vichy-dominated government. Creon was the soul of fascism and Antigone the nay-saying spirit of the French resistance movement, preferring death to dishonor. At any period, Antigone's revolt against nonconformity is a yea-saying to the forces of life pitted against the forces of oppression. It is the courageous act of the young forever intransigent to the despotism of the conforming old.

For the Greeks of Sophocles' time, the religious aspect of the play was paramount. Not to bury her brother would have seemed a sacrilege to a deeply religious person. A primitive shudder lurks behind the Greek Antigone. For the French, the forces of political realism are pitted against an uncompromising humanity. A moral imperative looms behind the French Antigone. For those of us who see the play in these years of our domestic unrest, the 1970's, the play seems doubly ironic: Creon comes off as the more sympathetic of the two characters (perhaps because Anouilh wished to mask his protest under the guise of a benevolent despot) and Antigone's intransigence seems the arrogant petulance of youth. Antigone refuses to accept any of the goods of life and drives her fiancé, Hémon, to despair and death. Creon proves to her that she doesn't even know which of her brothers she is burying. Her act loses all its logical validity by the end of the play and seems little more than a revolt against traditional taboos. Antigone is a confused girl with an inflexible death wish. She might have influenced Creon more had she lived to be the power behind the throne. We may even read the play now as an inverted parable: youth must revolt for what it believes but revolt for revolt's sake seems meaningless when it leads to needless destruction. Antigone's moral suicide is not religiously motivated. Too often in Anouilh's play, she seems a willful child in love with false realities because she cannot cope with mature relationships.

Anouilh cast his play into a parody of tragic form. We have some of the outward trappings of classical tragedy including the conventional arrival of the messenger at the end of the play to announce the terrible final details, but the development of the play is a linear pageant in which each of the characters of the myth materializes for a moment with Antigone. We are made to be present at a re-enacting of familiar events and there is never any doubt as to the depressing outcome of these events. However, as in Camus' *Stranger* (the most redeeming feature of mid-century French literature is its consistent passionate humanism), there is a deep love of life beneath all the apparent negativity. Antigone's relationship to her nurse is the crystallization of bourgeois love as the talks with the soldier represent the cruelty of bourgeois indifference. Antigone's love of the beauties of nature seems the primitive awe which is the highest manifestation of bourgeois aspiration heavenward. The sadness that the play projects is the knowledge of the existence of a system, an implacable force which corrupts and demeans all human beings inevitably. Anouilh's consistent message is that the world is not a very good place to be alive in, and his exalted heroines carry that message to an untimely demise. To make that message clear, he pits two forms of intransigence head on. And since tragedy is a free form, we are made to see that we are free to reach our own conclusions.

ANTIGONE

Jean Anouilh

Translated by Alex Szogyi

A neutral décor. Three identical doors. As the curtain rises, all the characters are on stage. They chatter away, knit, play cards. The PROLOGUE *leaves the group and comes forward.*

THE PROLOGUE: Well, then, here are the characters who will enact the story of Antigone for you. Antigone is the little thin one seated back there, not saying anything. She is looking straight ahead of her. She is thinking. She is thinking that she'll be Antigone in a little while, that she will loom up suddenly from out of the spare, swarthy, withdrawn young lady that nobody in the family took seriously to confront the world alone, alone against Creon, her uncle, who is King. She is thinking that she is going to die, that she is young and that she should have liked to live. But there is nothing to be done about it. She is Antigone and it is going to be necessary that she play her role to the hilt. . . . And, since the curtain has gone up, she senses that she is being separated with dizzying haste from her sister Ismene who is talking and laughing with a young man, separated from all of us right here calmly contemplating her, from all of us who do not have to die this night.

The young man to whom the blond, beautiful, happy Ismene, is speaking, is Hemon, Creon's son. He is Antigone's fiancé. Everything led one to believe he would choose Ismene: his love of dancing and games, his zest for life and success, his sensuality as well, for Ismene is far more beautiful than Antigone; but then one evening, one evening at a ball when he had danced only with

Ismene, an evening when Ismene had been absolutely dazzling in her new dress, he had suddenly crossed the room to find Antigone staring off into space, just as she is now, her arms clasping her knees, and he asked her to become his wife. No one ever understood why. Antigone raised her serious eyes toward him without astonishment and she said yes to him with a little sad smile . . . The orchestra started up a new number, Ismene was gaily laughing, in the midst of the other boys and now it was he who was going to be Antigone's husband. He didn't know that it was never meant that Antigone should have a husband on this earth, and that this princely honor earned him only the right to die.

This robust man with white hair, next to his page, is Creon. He is the King. He is wrinkled, he is tired. He plays at the difficult game of leading men. Long ago, in Oedipus' time, when he was only the most important personage at court, he liked music, beautiful bindings, long strolls among the little antique shops of Thebes. But Oedipus and his sons are dead. He has left his books, his objects. He has rolled up his sleeves and taken over their kingdom.

Sometimes, in the evening, when he is tired, he asks himself whether it isn't a fruitless task to lead men. If it isn't a sordid job better left to others more rough and ready. . . . But then, in the morning, precise problems are presented which must be resolved, and he gets up calmly, like a worker facing his day.

The old lady sitting knitting next to the nurse who brought up the children is Eurydice, Creon's wife. She will knit during the entire tragedy until her turn comes to get up and die. She is good, dignified and loving; but she is no help to him at all. Creon is alone with his little page who is too young to be any help to him at all.

That pale fellow dreaming over there in the back, leaning up against the wall, a solitary figure, is the Messenger. It is he who will come in a little while to announce the death of Hemon. That is why he has no desire to chat or to mix with the others. He already knows . . .

Finally, the three red-faced men who are playing cards, their helmets down over the back of their necks, are the guards. They're not bad fellows, they have wives, children and little troubles like everybody else. They smell of garlic, leather and red wine and they are completely devoid of imagination. They are police officers, quite innocent and satisfied with themselves and their sense of justice. For the moment, until a new ruler duly appointed orders them to arrest him in his turn, they are Creon's officers of the law.

And now that you know them all, they will be able to act out their story for you. It begins at the moment when the two sons of Oedipus, Eteocles and Polyneices, who were to reign over Thebes one year each in turn, fought and killed each other under the walls of the city. Eteocles the elder, at the end of his first year of power, refused to give up his place to his brother. Seven great foreign princes whom Polyneices had won over to his cause were vanquished in front of the seven doors to Thebes. Now the city is saved, the two fraternal enemies are dead and Creon, the King, has ordered that Eteocles, the good brother, be given imposing funeral rites, but that Polyneices, the good-for-nothing, the rebel, the gutter-snipe, shall remain unmourned and without a burial place, a prey to crows and jackals. Whoever dares to render him the last rites shall be pitilessly put to death.

(*While the* PROLOGUE *spoke the characters left one by one. The* PROLOGUE *disappears also.*)

(*The lighting has changed on stage. It is now a grey and pale dawn in a house which is sleeping.*)

(ANTIGONE *opens the door slightly and comes in on tip-toe, her shoes in hand. She remains for one instant immobile, listening. The nurse appears.*)

NURSE: Where have you been?

ANTIGONE: I've been taking a walk, nurse. It was beautiful. All grey. Now, you can't imagine, everything is already pink, yellow and green. Just like a post card. You must

get up earlier, nurse, if you wish to see a world without color.

(*She is about to go.*)

NURSE: I get up while it is still dark, I go to your room to see if you haven't thrown off your covers in your sleep and I don't find you in bed!

ANTIGONE: The garden was still sleeping. I surprised it, nurse. It didn't even know I was there. A garden which hasn't thought about men is so beautiful.

NURSE: You went out. I was at the back door, and you had left it open.

ANTIGONE: The fields were all wet and waiting. Everything was waiting. I made an enormous amount of noise all alone on the road and I was embarrassed because I knew very well that it was not I who was awaited. So, I took off my sandals and I slipped into the countryside without being seen . . .

NURSE: You'll have to wash your feet before you go back to bed.

ANTIGONE: I won't be going back to bed this morning.

NURSE: At four o'clock in the morning! It wasn't even four! I get up to see whether she wasn't uncovered. I find her bed cold and nobody in it.

ANTIGONE: Do you think that if one got up like that every morning it would be as beautiful every morning, nurse, to be the first girl outside?

NURSE: Nighttime! It was nighttime! And you want to make me believe that you were taking a walk, liar! Where did you go?

ANTIGONE (*with a strange smile*): It's true, it was still night. And I was all alone in the countryside thinking it was already morning. It's marvellous, nurse. I was the first one to believe in the day today.

NURSE: Play the fool! Go ahead and play the fool! I know what you're up to. I was a girl once, too, you know. And not easy to manage either, but hard headed just like you. Where did you go, you naughty girl?

ANTIGONE (*suddenly serious*): No. Not naughty.

NURSE: You had a rendez-vous, eh? Try and deny it.

ANTIGONE (*softly*): Yes, I had a rendez-vous.

NURSE: You're in love?

ANTIGONE (*strangely, after a silence*): Yes, nurse, yes, the poor fellow. I have a lover.

NURSE (*bursting*): Aha! A fine thing! You, the daughter of a King! You take the trouble, the trouble to mention them! They're all the same. But you weren't like the others, primping in front of the mirror, putting on lipstick, anything to be noticed. How many times did I say to myself: "My God, this little one, she's not coquettish enough! Always with the same dress on and poorly combed. The boys will only have eyes for Ismene with her curls and her ribbons and they'll dump *her* on my shoulders." Well, you know, you were like your sister, and, worse yet, hypocrite! Who is it? Some good-for-nothing, eh? A boy you can't bring home to your family and you say: "Here, he's the one I love, I want to marry him." That's it, eh, isn't it? Answer me, you big braggart!

ANTIGONE (*still with a trace of a smile*): Yes, nurse.

NURSE: And she says yes! God help us all! I got her when she was a little slip of a thing; I promised her poor mother that I'd make an honest girl of her, and now look! But that's not how it's going to be, my dear. I am only your nurse and you may treat me like an old fool, all right! But your Uncle, your Uncle Creon will hear about this. I promise you that!

ANTIGONE (*suddenly a little weary*): Yes, nurse, my Uncle Creon will find out. Leave me now.

NURSE: And you'll see what he'll say when he finds out that you get up in the middle of the night. And what about Hemon? Your fiancé! For she has a fiancé! She is engaged and at four o'clock in the morning she leaves her bed to go running off with someone. And her only answer is, "Leave me alone," and "don't say anything about it." You know what I ought to do? Beat you like when you were little.

ANTIGONE: Now, now, you shouldn't get all excited. You shouldn't be too mean to me this morning.

NURSE: Not get all excited! Not get all excited! I promised your mother. What would she say to me if she were here? "You old fool, yes, old fool, you couldn't keep my little girl pure for me. Always calling after her, playing watch dog, hovering around her with woolens so she doesn't catch cold, or tonics to build her up; but at four o'clock in the morning you are asleep, old fool, you are asleep. You who cannot shut your eyes, and you let her escape, you old fool and when you get there the bed is cold!" That's what your mother will say to me, up there, when I shall go up, and I'll be ashamed, deathly ashamed if I weren't already dead, and I'll only be able to lower my head and answer: "Madame Jocaste, it's true."

ANTIGONE: No, nurse. Don't cry any more. You look mother right in the face when you go to join her. And she'll say: "Good day, nounou, thanks for little Antigone. You took good care of her." She knows why I went out this morning.

NURSE: You don't have a lover?

ANTIGONE: No, nounou.

NURSE: Are you making fun of me, then? Don't you see I'm too old for that. You were my favorite, despite your bad ways. Your sister was sweeter, but I always thought it was you who loved me. If you loved me you would have told me the truth. Why was your bed cold when I came to tuck you in?

ANTIGONE: Don't cry any more, please, nounou. (*She embraces her.*) Well, my good little old red apple. You remember when I rubbed your cheeks and make them shine? My little old wrinkled red apple. Don't let your tears flow into all the little furrows, just for foolishness like this — for nothing. I'm pure, I have no other lover than my fiancé, Hemon. I swear to you. If you like, I can even swear to you that I shall have no other lover . . . Keep your tears; you may perhaps need them yet, nounou. When you cry like that,

I become a little girl again . . . and I must not be a little girl this morning.

(*Enter* ISMENE.)

ISMENE: You're up already? I was just in your room.

ANTIGONE: Yes, I'm up already.

NURSE: Now both of you! . . . Are you both going mad getting up before the servants? Do you think it's good to be up in the morning without eating, is that the thing for princesses to do? You're not even properly dressed. You see that you'll be the death of me yet.

ANTIGONE: Leave us, nurse. It's not cold, I assure you: It's already summer. Go and make us some coffee. (*She sits down, suddenly fatigued.*) I'd like a little coffee, please, nounou. It would do me good.

NURSE: My little dove! Her head is swimming from having had nothing to eat and here I stand like some idiot instead of giving her something warm. (*She goes out quickly.*)

ISMENE: Are you sick?

ANTIGONE: It's nothing. A little fatigue. (*She smiles.*) It's because I got up too early.

ISMENE: I couldn't sleep either.

ANTIGONE (*still smiling*): You must sleep. You'll be less beautiful tomorrow.

ISMENE: Don't make fun of me.

ANTIGONE: I'm not. It reassures me this morning that you're beautiful. When I was little, I was so unhappy, you remember? I got you all full of dirt, I put worms on your neck. Once, I tied you to a tree and I cut your hair, your beautiful hair . . . (*She caresses* ISMENE's *hair.*) How easy it must be not to think up mischief when you have such beautiful smooth hair, so beautifully arranged around your head!

ISMENE (*suddenly*): Why have you changed the subject?

ANTIGONE (*softly, without ceasing to caress her hair*): I haven't changed the subject . . .

ISMENE: You know, I've been thinking, Antigone.

ANTIGONE: Yes.

ISMENE: I've been thinking all night. You're crazy.

ANTIGONE: Yes.

ISMENE: We can't do it.

ANTIGONE (*after a silence, with her small voice*): Why?

ISMENE: They would have us put to death.

ANTIGONE: Of course they would. To each his own role. *He* must put us to death and *we* must go and bury our brother. That's how the roles have been distributed. What can we do about it?

ISMENE: I don't want to die.

ANTIGONE (*sweetly*): I, too, don't want to die.

ISMENE: Listen, I was thinking all night. I'm the older one. I think more than you do. You always give yourself up to the first thought to cross your mind, and so what if it's foolish. I'm more level-headed. I reflect.

ANTIGONE: There are times when one musn't reflect too much.

ISMENE: Yes, Antigone. It's horrible, of course, and I too have pity for my brother, but I think I understand our Uncle a little.

ANTIGONE: I don't wish to understand a little.

ISMENE: He is the King. He must set the example.

ANTIGONE: But I am not the King. And I don't have to set an example . . . The things that go on in that head of hers, little Antigone, such a dirty thing, such a stubborn girl, such a bad girl, you have to put her in a corner or down a hole. And that's all she deserves: All that was expected of her was not to disobey!

ISMENE: Now, come on! You're frowning, you're staring right into space and you're launched without listening to anybody.

Listen to me. I'm right more often than you are.

ANTIGONE: I don't want to be right.

ISMENE: At least try to understand.

ANTIGONE: Understand . . . That's the only word you have in your mouth, all of you, ever since I was a little girl. You had to understand that you can't touch the water, the beautiful cold and fleeting water because it gets the flagstones wet, can't touch the earth because that stains dresses. You had to understand that you musn't eat everything at once, nor give everything in your pockets to the beggar you encounter, nor run, with the wind until you fall to the ground, nor drink when you're warm nor bathe either too early or too late, but just exactly when you don't want to! Understand. Always understand. I don't want to understand. I will understand when I am old. (*She finishes softly.*) If I become old. Not now.

ISMENE: He's stronger than we are, Antigone. He's the king. And the whole city thinks as he does. There are thousands and thousands around us, swarming in all the streets of Thebes.

ANTIGONE: I'm not listening to you.

ISMENE: They will jeer at us. They'll seize us with their thousand arms, jeer at us with their thousand faces congealed into a single gaze. They will spit into our face. And in our open cart we'll have to move ahead surrounded by their hate, their zeal and their cruel laughter stalking us to our death. And there will be the guards with their imbecilic faces, looking congested over their stiff collars, their huge scrubbed hands, their cattle-like gaze — so that you think you can kep shouting forever, trying to make them understand, but they're like slaves and they will always do as they are told, scrupulously, without knowing whether it's for good or evil . . . Suffer? We'll have to suffer, feeling the pain mount, until it gets to the point when one can't bear it anymore; it will eventually have to stop, and yet it will con-

tinue and even increase, like a piercing scream . . . Oh I cannot, I cannot bear it . . .

ANTIGONE: How well you've thought everything out.

ISMENE: All night. Didn't you?

ANTIGONE: Yes, of course.

ISMENE: I'm not very brave, you know.

ANTIGONE (*softly*): Nor I. But what does it matter?

(*A silence.* ISMENE *asks suddenly.*)

ISMENE: Don't you have any desire to live?

ANTIGONE (*a murmur*): No desire to live . . . (*and softer yet, if that were possible*) Who got up first, in the morning, if only to feel the cold air on her skin? Who went to bed last, and only when she was so exhausted with fatigue, just to live a little more at night? Who cried when she was very young, thinking there were so many little animals, so many blades of grass in the meadow knowing you can't touch them all?

ISMENE (*with a sudden movement toward her*): My little sister . . .

ANTIGONE (*pulls back and cries out*): Oh no! Leave me alone! Don't caress me! Let's not whine together now. You've thought it all out, you say? You think that the entire city howling at you, the pain and the fear of death are enough?

ISMENE (*lowers her head*): Yes.

ANTIGONE: Take advantage of these pretexts.

ISMENE (*throwing herself at her*): Antigone! I beg of you! It's for men to believe in ideas and to die for them. You are a girl.

ANTIGONE (*her teeth clenched*): A girl, yes. Haven't I wept enough for being a girl!

ISMENE: Your happiness is right there ahead of you and you have only to take it. You are engaged, you're young, you're beautiful.

ANTIGONE (*hollow sound*): No, I am not beautiful.

ISMENE: Not beautiful as we are, but in another way. You know perfectly well that it's you that all the little boys stare at in the street; that it's you the girls look at when you pass by, suddenly mute without being able to take their eyes off you until you've turned the corner.

ANTIGONE (*with a barely perceptible smile*): Little boys, little girls . . .

ISMENE (*after a moment*): And Hemon, Antigone?

ANTIGONE (*inaccessible*): I shall speak to Hemon in a little while: Hemon will be a settled matter in a little while.

ISMENE: You're mad.

ANTIGONE (*smiles*): You always told me I was mad, in everything, ever since I can remember. Go back to bed, Ismene . . . It's daylight now, you see, and, anyway, I can't do anything about it. My dead brother is now surrounded by guards exactly as if he had succeeded in becoming king. Go back to bed. You're still pale with fatigue.

ISMENE: And you?

ANTIGONE: I have no desire for sleep . . . But I promise you I won't move from here until you return. Nurse will bring me something to eat. Go and sleep some more. The sun is just rising. Your eyes are heavy with sleep. Go . . .

ISMENE: You will let me convince you, won't you? You'll let me talk to you again?

ANTIGONE (*a little tired*): I will let you speak to me, yes. I will let you all speak to me. Now go and sleep, please, or you'll be less beautiful tomorrow. (*She watches her leave with a sad little smile, then suddenly weary, she falls into a chair.*) Poor Ismene! . . .

(NURSE *enters.*)

NURSE: There, a nice cup of coffee and some toast, for my pigeon. Eat up.

ANTIGONE: I'm not very hungry, nurse.

NURSE: I toasted them myself and buttered them the way you like them.

ANTIGONE: You're nice, nounou. I'll just drink a little.

NURSE: Where does it hurt?

ANTIGONE: Nowhere, nounou. But make me nice and warm just like when I was sick . . . Nounou stronger than the fever, nounou stronger than a nightmare, stronger than the mocking shadow of the wardrobe transformed hour by hour on the wall, stronger than the thousand insects of silence which nibble away at everything, somewhere in the night, stronger than the night itself with its mad hooting one cannot bear — nounou, stronger than death. Give me your hand just as you did when you remained at my bedside.

NURSE: What's the matter, my little dove?

ANTIGONE: Nothing, nounou. It's just that I am still a little too young for all of this. But only you must know that.

NURSE: What do you want me to do for you, my turtledove?

ANTIGONE: Nothing, nounou. Only hold your hand against my cheek, like this. (*She remains a moment, her eyes closed.*) Now, I'm not afraid any more. Neither of the big bad wolf, nor of the sandman, nor of the bogeyman who passes and takes all the children away . . . (*another silence, she continues in another tone.*) Nounou, you know, Dulcie, my dog . . .

NURSE: Yes.

ANTIGONE: Promise me you'll never scold her.

NURSE: An animal who dirties everything with her paws! She shouldn't be allowed inside the house.

ANTIGONE: Even if she dirties everything. Promise, nurse.

NURSE: Must I let her spoil everything without saying anything?

ANTIGONE: Yes, nounou.

NURSE: Oh! Now that would be a bit too much!

ANTIGONE: Please, nounou. You love Dulcie,

with her big long fat tail. And after all, you really like to brush things up. You would be very unhappy if everything always stayed clean. So please don't scold her.

NURSE: What if she pisses on my rugs?

ANTIGONE: Promise that you won't scold her all the same. I beg of you, say it, please, nounou . . .

NURSE: You're taking advantage with all your wheedling . . . All right. All right. I'll wipe up without saying anything about it. You're making a monkey out of me.

ANTIGONE: And then, promise me too that you'll speak to her, that you'll speak to her often.

NURSE (raising her shoulders): Me talking to animals!

ANTIGONE: But especially *not* as if you were talking to an animal. But to a real person, the way I do . . .

NURSE: Ah, no, not that! At my age, to play the idiot! But why should you want the whole house to talk to her as you do, to this animal?

ANTIGONE (softly): Were I, for one reason or another, unable to talk to her anymore . . .

NURSE (not understanding): Not talk to her any more, any more? Why?

ANTIGONE (turns her head away slightly and then adds, in a rough voice): But, if she were too sad, if she seemed all the same to be waiting too expectantly — her nose under the door like when I go out — perhaps it would be better to have her killed, nounou, without hurting her.

NURSE: Have her killed, my darling? Have your dog killed? But you're crazy this morning!

ANTIGONE: No, nounou.

(HEMON appears.)

There's Hemon. Leave us, nurse. And don't forget that you swore to me. (ANTIGONE runs to HEMON.) Hemon, forgive me for our quarrel last night and for everything. I was wrong. Please forgive me.

(The NURSE goes out.)

HEMON: You know very well I forgave you as soon as you slammed the door shut. Your perfume was still there and I had already forgiven you. (He holds her in his arms, he smiles, he looks at her.) Who did you steal this perfume from?

ANTIGONE: From Ismene.

HEMON: And the lipstick, the powder, the beautiful dress?

ANTIGONE: From Ismene, also.

HEMON: Why did you make yourself so beautiful?

ANTIGONE: I'll tell you. (She huddles a little closer to him.) Oh! my darling. How stupid I was. A whole evening spoiled. A beautiful evening.

HEMON: We'll have other evenings — Antigone.

ANTIGONE: Perhaps not.

HEMON: And other fights too. Happiness is full of quarrels.

ANTIGONE: Happiness, yes . . . Listen, Hemon.

HEMON: Yes.

ANTIGONE: Don't laugh at me this morning. Be serious.

HEMON: I am serious.

ANTIGONE: And hold me. Tighter than you ever have before. So that all your strength may be pressed into me.

HEMON: There. With all my strength.

ANTIGONE (in a breath): That's good. (They remain for a moment without a word, then she begins softly.) Listen, Hemon.

HEMON: Yes.

ANTIGONE: I wanted to tell you this morning . . . The little boy that we would have had together . . .

HEMON: Yes.

ANTIGONE: You know, I would have defended him against everything.

HEMON: Yes, Antigone.

ANTIGONE: Oh! I would have squeezed him so tight he would never have been afraid, I swear it, not of the oncoming night, nor of the shadows . . . Our little boy, Hemon! He would have had an insignificant mother, her hair badly combed — but better than all the real mothers in the world with their big bosoms and their big aprons. You believe that don't you?

HEMON: Yes, my love.

ANTIGONE: And you believe too, don't you, that I would have been a true wife?

HEMON (*holds her*): I have a true wife.

ANTIGONE (*cries out suddenly, huddling close to him*): Oh! you loved me, Hemon, you did love me, are you really sure you did love me, that evening?

HEMON (*cradles her gently*): Which evening?

ANTIGONE: Are you quite sure that at the ball when you came to me in my corner, you didn't go to the wrong girl? You're sure that you've never regretted it since, never thought, even deep down, not even once, that it was Ismene you should have asked for?

HEMON: Idiot!

ANTIGONE: You love me, don't you? Do you love me as a woman? Your arms enfolding me aren't lying to me, are they? Your great big hands placed on my back don't lie, nor your smell, nor your good warmth, nor all this great confidence I feel when I put my head on the hollow of your neck?

HEMON: Yes, Antigone, I love you as a woman.

ANTIGONE: I'm dark and thin. Ismene is rosy and golden as a fruit.

HEMON (*murmuring*): Antigone . . .

ANTIGONE: Oh! I'm blushing with shame. But this morning I must know. Tell me the truth, please. When you think I will belong to you, do you feel that a great empty space is being hollowed out of you . . .

HEMON: Yes, Antigone.

ANTIGONE (*breathy, after a time*): I feel that way. And I wanted you to know that I would have been very proud to have been your wife, your true wife, on whom you would have placed your hand in the evening, when you were sitting down, without giving it a thought, as upon something belonging to you. (*She has drawn away from him, she has taken another tone.*) There. Now, I am going to tell you just two things more. And when I have said them, you must leave without any question. Even if they seem to you to be extraordinary, even if they hurt you. Swear to me.

HEMON: What else have you to say to me?

ANTIGONE: Swear first that you'll leave without saying anything. Without ever looking back. If you love me, swear it.

HEMON (*after a moment*): I swear it.

ANTIGONE: Thank you. Now then. Yesterday first. You asked me before why I had worn one of Ismene's dresses, this perfume and this lipstick. I was stupid. I wasn't very sure that you really wanted me and I did all that in order to be a little more like other girls, to make you want me.

HEMON: So that was why?

ANTIGONE: Yes. And you laughed and we quarreled and my bad temper got the best of me. I ran away. (*She adds in a lower voice.*) But I had come to you last evening, so that you would make love to me, so that I might become your wife before. (*He draws back, he is about to speak, she cries out.*) You swore to me not to ask why. You swore to me, Hemon! (*She says in a lower voice, humbly.*) Please . . . (*And she adds, turning away, hard.*) Besides, I am going to tell you. I wanted to be your wife last night because that is how I love you, very strongly, and that — I'm going to hurt you, oh my darling, forgive me! — that never, never can I marry you. (*He remains stupefied, mute: she runs to the window, she cries out.*) Oh Hemon, you swore it! Go away, leave right away without saying anything. If you speak, if you take one step toward me, I'll throw myself out this window. I swear it, Hemon. I swear it to you on the head of the little boy that we have had together in a dream, the little boy that I shall never have. Now go, quickly. You will find out tomorrow. You will find out in a while. (*She ends with such despair that* HEMON *obeys and goes off.*) Please leave, Hemon. That's all you can still do for me, if you love me.

(*He has gone. She remains motionless, her back to the audience, then she shuts the window, comes and sits down on a little chair in the middle of the stage and says softly, as if strangely at peace.*) There. It's all over with Hemon, Antigone.

ISMENE (*she has entered, calling*): Antigone! . . . Ah, you're here!

ANTIGONE (*motionless*): Yes, I'm here. What do you want?

ISMENE: I can't sleep. I was afraid you might go out, and try to bury him even though it's daytime. Antigone, my little sister, we're all of us here close to you, Hemon, nounou, and I, and Dulcie, your dog . . . We love you and we are alive, and *we* need you. Polyneices is dead and he didn't love you. He was always a stranger to us, a bad brother. Forget him, Antigone, as he forgot us. Let his hard shadow wander eternally without a burial place, because that is Creon's law. Do not attempt what is above and beyond your strength. You're always game for everything, but you are so small, Antigone. Stay with us, don't go there tonight, please.

ANTIGONE (*she has risen, a strange little smile on her lips, she goes towards the door and from the threshold, softly, she says*): It's too late. This morning, when you met me, I was coming from there. (*She has gone out,* ISMENE *follows her shouting.*)

ISMENE: Antigone!

(*As soon as* ISMENE *has gone out,* CREON *enters by another door with his page.*)

CREON: A guard, you say? One of those guarding the body? Bring him in.

(*The guard enters. He is a brute. For the moment he is green with fear.*)

GUARD (*presents himself at attention*): Private Jonas of the Second Company.

CREON: What do you want?

GUARD: You see, chief. We drew lots to see who would come. I lost. Well, you see, chief. I came because they thought it would be better if only one explains, because all three of us couldn't leave our post. We're the three on guard duty around the body.

CREON: What do you have to tell me?

GUARD: There are three of us, chief. I'm not alone. The others are Durand and Corporal Boudousse.

CREON: Why didn't the Corporal come?

GUARD: That's right, chief. That's what I said right away, I did. It's the Corporal who has to go. When there are non-commissioned officers, they're responsible. But the others said no and they wanted to draw lots. Must I go and get the Corporal, chief?

CREON: No. You speak, since you're here.

GUARD: I've been in the service for seventeen years. I enlisted, I've got medals, two citations. I've got a good clean record, chief. I only obey my orders. My superiors always say: "With Jonas you rest easy!"

CREON: That's good. Speak up. What are you afraid of?

GUARD: Ordinarily, it should have been the Corporal. I'm up for Corporal, but I haven't got my stripes yet. I'm supposed to get 'em in June.

CREON: Will you speak up? If something has happened, all three of you are responsible. Stop trying to figure out who should have been here.

GUARD: Well, then, chief: the body . . . We did keep the watch! It was the two o'clock changing of the guard, the toughest one. You know, chief, it's the moment when night is about to end. Your eyes feel like lead, the back of your neck is stiff, and all these shadows moving about and the fog at sunrise . . . Oh! they chose their hour well! . . . There we were, we were all talking, we were warming our feet by beating the soles against each other's feet. We weren't sleeping, chief, all three of us will swear on that; we weren't sleeping! Besides, in that cold . . . Suddenly, I look at the body . . . we were two steps away, but I kept looking at him from time to time anyhow . . . That's how I am, chief, I'm meticulous. That's why my superiors always say: "You can trust Jonas..." (*A gesture from* CREON *stops him, he shouts suddenly.*) I saw him first, chief! The others will tell you I gave the alarm!

CREON: The alarm? Why?

GUARD: The body, chief. Somebody had covered it. Oh! not altogether. They didn't have the time with us next to them. Just a little bit of earth . . . But just enough all the same to hide it from the vultures.

CREON (*goes to him*): Are you sure it wasn't an animal who did it, scratching?

GUARD: No, chief. At first that's what we hoped, too. But the earth was thrown over him, according to the rites. It was somebody who knew what he was doing.

CREON: Who dared? Who was mad enough to defy my law? Did you find any footprints?

GUARD: Nothing, chief. Nothing but a print lighter than a bird's trail. After, on further examination, Guard Durand found a shovel, a little child's shovel, quite old and rusty. We thought it couldn't have been a child who had done it. The first sentry kept it anyhow for the investigation.

CREON (*muses a little*): A child . . . The broken opposition and already it's springing up and undermining all over the place. The friends of Polyneices with their gold blocked in Thebes, the leaders of the common mob stinking of garlic, suddenly allied with the princes, and the priests always trying to preach a little something in the midst of all this . . . A child! They must have thought that would be more touching. I could see

him, their child, with the face of a paid killer and the little shovel carefully wrapped up in a paper under his jacket. Unless they set a real child to do it with a few pat phrases. A priceless innocence in the hands of the party. A real palefaced little boy who will spit at my guns. His precious and very fresh blood on my hands, a double windfall. (*He goes to the man.*) Perhaps they have accomplices among my own guard. Listen here, you . . .

GUARD: Chief, we did everything we should! Durand sat down for a half hour because his feet hurt him, but, chief, *I* remained standing during the whole time. The first sentry will tell you.

CREON: With whom have you discussed this affair?

GUARD: With nobody, chief. We drew lots right away, and I came.

CREON: Listen well to me. Your guard duty is doubled. Send away the replacement guards. Here's the order. I only want *you* near the body. And not a word. You are guilty of negligence, you will be punished at any rate, but if the rumor is heard in the city that someone covered Polyneices' body, all three of you will die.

GUARD (*shouting*): We didn't talk, chief, I swear it! But I'm here and perhaps the others said something at the changing of the guard . . . (*He sweats buckets, he stammers.*) Chief, I've got two kids. One of them is a tiny baby. You'll be my witness for me that I was here, chief, before the court martial. *I* was here with you! I have a witness! If somebody talked, it's the others, it won't be me! *I* have a witness, I do!

CREON: Go quickly. If nobody finds out, you'll live. (*The guard goes out running.* CREON *remains silent a moment. Suddenly, he murmurs*) A child. (*He has taken the little page by the shoulder.*) Come, boy. Now we must go and recount all of this . . . And then the pretty task will begin. Would *you* be willing to die for me? Would you think to go there with your little shovel? (*The little boy looks at him. He goes out with him, caressing his head.*) Yes, of course, you would go right away . . . (*He is heard to be sighing as he goes out.*) A child . . . (*They have gone out. The Chorus enters.*)

CHORUS: There we are. Now the spring is wound tight. All it needs to do is to unwind itself. That's what is so convenient about tragedy, all it needs is a little push to get it going, a little something, a look for a second at a girl passing by in the street, the desire for honor one fine morning, on waking, just as one gets a yen to eat something, one question too many that you ask yourself one evening . . . That's all. Afterwards, all you have to do is let yourself go along with it. You're calm. It happens all by itself. It's been worked out very carefully, well oiled from the beginning of time. Death, deception, despair are all there, waiting right around the corner as well as the outbursts, the storms, and the silences; all the silences: the silence when the arm of the executioner is raised at the very end; the silence at the beginning, when the two lovers are nude facing each other for the first time, without daring to budge right away, in the darkened room; the silence when the cries of the crowd burst forth around the conqueror — it's like a film whose sound has stopped suddenly, all those open mouths from which nothing emerges, all that clamor which is nothing but an image, and the victor, already vanquished, alone in the midst of his silence . . .

Tragedy is clean. It's restful, it's certain. In the drama, with its traitors, its inveterate evil-doers, its persecuted innocents, its avengers, its bloodhounds, its glimmers of hope; it's becoming frightful to die, just as it does when there's an accident. One might perhaps have arrived in time with the police. In tragedy all is tranquil. First of all, you're among familiars. We're all innocent after all! It's not because there is one who kills and another who is killed. It's a question of a distribution of roles. And then, above all, tragedy is restful because we know that it's all hopeless, disgusting hope; you're caught, you're finally caught like a rat in a trap,

with all heaven above down on your back, and all you have to do is to cry out — not to moan or complain — but shout at the top of your lungs what you have to say, that you had never said, that you perhaps hadn't even found out yet. And it was all to no avail, just to be able to say it to yourself, to learn it for yourself. In the drama, one struggles because one hopes to get out of it. It's degrading. It's practical. In this realm, it's totally gratuitous. Tragedy is for kings. It is the ultimate!

(ANTIGONE *has entered, pushed by the guards.*)

GUARD (*who has recovered his self-assurance*): Come on, come on, none of your lip! You'll explain yourself in front of the chief. I'm only obeying orders. What you were doing there, I don't want to know. Everybody's got excuses, everybody's got some objection to make. If we listened to everybody, if we had to understand we'd really be in for it. Now come on! Hold her, you guys, and no nonsense! What she has to say to me, I don't want to know!

ANTIGONE: Tell them to let me alone with their filthy hands. They're hurting me.

GUARD: Their filthy hands? You might be polite, Miss . . . *I'm* polite.

ANTIGONE: Tell them to leave me alone. I am Oedipus' daughter, I'm Antigone. I will not try to escape.

GUARD: Oedipus' daughter, yes! The prostitutes you pick up during the evening watch also tell you to be careful, that they're the girl friend of the chief of police! (*They enjoy the situation.*)

ANTIGONE: I'll die but I won't have them touching me!

GUARD: What about the dead bodies, eh, and the earth, you weren't afraid to touch them? You say "their filthy hands" . . . Take a look at yours! (ANTIGONE *looks at her hands held by handcuffs with a small smile. They are full of earth.*) So you had your shovel taken away from you? You had to do it over again with your nails, a second time? Oh boy, what nerve. I turn my back for one second, I ask for a chew of tobacco and there she goes, in the time it takes to say thanks, and she is there, scratching like a little hyena. And in broad daylight! And did she kick up a commotion when I tried to catch her, the bitch! She would've jumped me if she could! She was shouting she had to finish . . . she's mad, yes she is!

SECOND GUARD: I arrested another crazy coot the other day. She was showing her ass to people.

GUARD: Say, Boudousse, are all three of us going to tie one on to celebrate this one!

SECOND GUARD: At Crazy Louie's! He's got the best vino.

THIRD GUARD: We've got a leave coming up Sunday. Suppose we brought the wives?

GUARD: No, let's keep it to ourselves . . . Women always cause trouble and the little brats have always got to piss. Say, Boudousse, a while back who'd have believed we'd be wanting to have such a good time!

SECOND GUARD: Maybe they'll give us a reward.

GUARD: They might if it's important enough.

THIRD GUARD: Flanchard, from the third platoon, when he got his hands on the go-between last month, he got double pay for the month.

SECOND GUARD: Hey! You know what I propose, if we get the double pay: instead of going to Crazy Louie's, we'll go to the Arab Palace.

GUARD: To drink? You crazy or something? The stuff costs twice the price at the Palace. It's O.K. if you want to get laid. Listen to me: I'll tell you what we'll do: first we'll go to Crazy Louie's, we get tanked up real good and then we go to the Arab's. Say, Boudousse, remember the big fat broad, from the Palace?

SECOND GUARD: Oh! boy, did you tie one on that day!

THIRD GUARD: What about our wives, if we get double pay, they're bound to get wind of it. If that happens, maybe we'll really be in a mess.

GUARD: We'll see about it then. Living it up is one thing. Now, if there's a celebration in the barracks yard like when they give out decorations, the women will come and the kids too. Then we'll all go off to Crazy Louie's.

SECOND GUARD: Yeah, but we'll have to call in the order ahead of time.

ANTIGONE (asking in a small voice): I'd like to sit down for a moment, please.

GUARD (after a moment's reflection): That's all right, let her sit down. But don't let her out of your sight, boys.

(CREON enters; the guard shouts immediately.)

GUARD: Attention!

CREON (has stopped, surprised): Let this girl go. What's going on here?

GUARD: It's the body guard, chief.

CREON: Guarding the body?

GUARD: We called in the change of the guard.

CREON: I told you to send them away! I told you to say nothing.

GUARD: We said nothing, chief. But when we arrested this one here, we thought we'd better come over. And this time we didn't choose up lots. We just preferred to come over all three of us.

CREON: Imbeciles! (to ANTIGONE) Where did they arrest you?

GUARD: Near the body, chief.

CREON: What were you doing near the body of your brother? You know that I had forbidden anyone to approach it.

GUARD: What was she doing, chief? That's why we've brought her. She was scratching the ground with her hands. She was covering up the body again.

CREON: Do you know what you're saying?

GUARD: Chief, you can ask the others. We dug up the body when I got back; but with the sun shining so hot, as it began to stink we went up a little higher, just to be out of the path of the wind. We told ourselves that in the middle of the day there was no risk. However we made up our minds, to be absolutely sure, that one of the three of us would keep his eye on him at all times. But at noon, in the dazzling sun, and with the odor getting stronger all the time, since the wind had fallen off, it was like being hit over the head. It was no use opening my eyes wide, the atmosphere was shaking like jelly, I couldn't see any more. I went over to my buddy to ask for a wad of tobacco to get over it . . . the time it takes to stick it in my cheek, chief, the time it takes to say thanks. I turn around: there she is scratching with her hands. In broad daylight! She must have known we couldn't miss seeing her. And when she saw that I was running toward her, do you think she stopped, that she tried to escape? No. Not her. She continued with all her might, as fast as she could as if she didn't see me coming. And when I got hold of her, she struggled like a little she-devil, she wanted to keep on going, she shouted to let go, that the body wasn't fully covered . . .

CREON (to ANTIGONE): Is this true?

ANTIGONE: Yes, it's true.

GUARD: They uncovered the body again, of course, and then we changed the guard, without mentioning anything, and we brought her to you, chief. Here.

CREON: And last night, the first time, was it you, as well?

ANTIGONE: Yes. It was with a little iron shovel which we used to build castles in the sand on the beach on vacations. It happened to be Polyneices' shovel. He had carved his name with a knife on the handle. That's why I left it near to him. But they took it. Then, the second time, I had to begin all over again with my hands.

GUARD: It might as well have been a little animal scratching. Even at the first glance, in the hot trembling air, my buddy said: "But no, it's an animal." "You think so," I said to him, "it's too smart for an animal. It's a girl."

CREON: Very well, I may be asking you for a report later. For the moment, leave me alone with her. Take these men next door, my boy. No one must know they are here until I return to see them.

GUARD: Must we put the handcuffs back on her, chief?

CREON: No.

(*The guards have gone out, preceded by the little page.* CREON *and* ANTIGONE *are alone facing each other.*)

CREON: Did you meet anyone on your way?

ANTIGONE: No, no one.

CREON: Are you quite sure?

ANTIGONE: Yes.

CREON: Then, listen to me: you will go back to your home, go to bed, say that you have not gone out since yesterday. Your nurse will corroborate what you say. I shall get rid of these three men.

ANTIGONE: Why? Since you know very well I'll just begin all over again. (*A silence. They look at one another.*)

CREON: Why did you try to bury your brother?

ANTIGONE: I had to.

CREON: I had forbidden it.

ANTIGONE (*softly*): I had to just the same. Those who are not buried wander eternally without ever finding repose. If my brother, when he was living, was exhausted from a long hunt, I would have taken off his shoes. I would have given him something to eat, I would have made his bed. . . . Today Polyneices has ended his hunt. He is returning to the house in which my father and my mother and Eteocles also await him. He has a right to rest.

CREON: He was a rebel and a traitor, you know that.

ANTIGONE: He was my brother.

CREON: You had heard the edict proclaimed at every crossroads, you had read the poster pasted up on the walls of the city?

ANTIGONE: Yes.

CREON: You know the fate promised to whoever should dare to give him last rites?

ANTIGONE: Yes, I knew.

CREON: You thought perhaps that being the daughter of Oedipus, the daughter of Oedipus' pride, was enough to put you above the law.

ATIGONE: No. I didn't believe that.

CREON: First and foremost the law is made for you, Antigone, first and foremost the law is made for the daughters of kings!

ANTIGONE: If I were a servant doing dishes, when I heard the edict read, I would have wiped the greasy water from my hands and I would have gone out in my apron and buried my brother.

CREON: That's not true. If you had been a servant, you would not have doubted that you would die and you would have remained home to weep for your brother. But you thought that you were of royal blood, my niece and the fiancé of my son, and that, come what may, I wouldn't dare put you to death.

ANTIGONE: You are mistaken. On the contrary, I was certain that you would have me put to death.

CREON (*looks at her and murmurs suddenly*): The pride of Oedipus. The stubborn pride of Oedipus. Yes, now that I have found him again in the depths of your eyes, I believe you. You must have thought that I would put you to death. To you that seemed to be quite a natural way for you to end up, you proud thing! Your father was the same way — I'm not talking about happiness, there was no question of it — human unhappiness was too small for him. In your family, simple humanity makes you uncomfortable. Nothing satisfies you but destiny and death. Killing your father and sleeping with your mother and finding out about it all afterward, greedily, detail for detail. Words which condemn you are such a heady brew, eh? And how you do drink them up greedily when your name is Oedipus or Antigone. And the easiest thing to do after that is still to put out your eyes and then go and beg with the children on the roads . . . Well, no. Times have changed for Thebes. Thebes now has a right to a prince without a past. Thank God my name is only Creon. I have my two feet on the ground, my two hands stuck into my pockets and, since I am king, with less ambition than your father, I have resolved to busy myself quite simply with making the order in this world a little less absurd, if that is possible. It is not even an adventure, it is an every-day occupation and like all occupations, it's not always amusing. But since I am here to do it, I am going to get it done. . . . And if tomorrow some dirty messenger descends from the mountains to tell me that he is not very sure of my birth, I will just tell him quite simply to go back where he came from and for such a little reason I will not run off to accuse my aunt and start checking dates and times. Kings have better things to do, my girl, than indulge in personal sentimentality. (*He has gone up to her; he takes her in his arms.*) Now, listen carefully to me. You are Antigone, you are Oedipus' daughter, good, but you are twenty years old and not long ago, all this would have been settled with some dry bread and a good slap. (*He looks at her smiling.*) Put you to death! Have you looked at yourself lately, you little sparrow! You're too thin. Rather fatten up a bit, to make a good sturdy boy for Hemon. Thebes needs that much more than your death, I assure you. Do as I tell you. You will return to your home immediately and keep quiet. I'll be responsible for the silence of the guards. Now, go! And don't devastate me like that with your eyes. You take me for a brute, I understand, and you must be thinking that

I am decidedly quite commonplace. But for all your bad character I love you all the same. Don't forget I was the one who gave you your first doll, not so long ago.

(ANTIGONE *doesn't answer. She is about to go. He stops her.*) Antigone! This is the door leading to your room. Where are you going by that one?

ANTIGONE (*has stopped, she answers him gently, without impudence*): You know very well . . .

(*A silence. They look at one another standing face to face.*)

CREON (*murmurs, as if to himself*): What kind of game are you playing.

ANTIGONE: I am not playing.

CREON: Don't you understand that if in a little while someone else besides these three brutes finds out what you have tried to do, that I shall have to put you to death? If you just keep quiet now, if you give up this folly, there's a chance I can save you, but in five minutes it will be too late. Do you understand that?

ANTIGONE: I must go and bury my brother. They have uncovered him.

CREON: You'd go and make this absurd gesture again? There is another guard standing by the body of Polyneices and, even if you succeed in covering him up again, he will uncover his body, you know that very well. What else can you accomplish but bloody your nails again and be caught?

ANTIGONE: Just that, I know. But that, at least, I can do. And one must do what one can.

CREON: Then *you* really believe in this orthodox burial? If one doesn't throw a bit of earth over the body accompanied with the Priest's formula, the shade of your brother will be condemned to wander about forever? You have heard the priests of Thebes recite this formula? You have seen these poor beaten drudges curtailing their gestures, swallowing their words, hurrying over this dead person to be able to take on another before the noon meal?

ANTIGONE: Yes, I've seen them.

CREON: Did you never think that if it were a person you loved truly, who was there, lying in this box, that you would suddenly start screaming? To tell them to be silent, to go away?

ANTIGONE: Yes, I thought of that.

CREON: And now you risk death because I have refused your brother this ridiculous passport, this mass produced stammering over his remains, this pantomime which you would be the first to be ashamed of and get sick from if it wasn't sincere. It's absurd!

ANTIGONE: Yes, it's absurd.

CREON: Then why do you make this gesture? For others, for those who believe in it? To set them against me?

ANTIGONE: No.

CREON: Neither for others nor for your brother? For whom then?

ANTIGONE: For no one. For myself.

CREON (*looks at her in silence*): So you really want to die? Already you look like a little trapped animal.

ANTIGONE: Don't let yourself be tender with me. Do as I do. Do what you have to do. But if you are a human being, do it quickly. That is all I ask of you. My courage won't last forever, that much is true.

CREON (*comes closer*): Antigone, I want to save you.

ANTIGONE: You are the king, everything is within your power, but that you cannot do.

CREON: You think not?

ANTIGONE: Neither to save me nor to contradict me.

CREON: Proud creature! Little Oedipus!

ANTIGONE: You can only put me to death.

CREON: And if I have you tortured?

ANTIGONE: Why? to make me weep, to ask to be forgiven, so that I'll swear to do everything you want and then start it all over again, when I'm not suffering any more?

CREON (*squeezing her arm*): Listen carefully to me. You've cast me as the villain, of course, and you're the heroine. But don't take too much advantage of it, little pest . . . If I were an ordinary brute of a tyrant, I would have had your tongue pulled out long ago, your limbs pulled apart and had you thrown into an abyss. But you see something in my eyes which hesitates, you see that I allow you to keep talking instead of calling my guards so you defy me, you attack as much as you can. What do you think you'll get out of it, you little fury?

ANTIGONE: Let go of me. You're hurting my arm.

CREON (*squeezing tighter*): Not really. I must remind you that I am the stronger. I need that.

ANTIGONE (*cries out a bit*): Ay!

CREON (*his eyes laughing*): That's perhaps what I should do, after all, quite simply twist your wrist, pull your hair as they do with all girls who play games. (*He keeps looking at her. He becomes serious again. He speaks quite close to her.*) I am your uncle, let that be understood, but we're not very nice to each other in our family. It must seem funny to you all the same, this king one can scoff at who listens to you, this old man who is all powerful and who I assure you has seen so many people killed, just as tender as you, and who stands here, taking all this trouble to try to prevent you from dying.

ANTIGONE (*after a time*): You're squeezing too hard now. It doesn't hurt any more. I have no more feeling in my arm.

CREON (*looks at her and lets her go with a little smile. He murmurs*): Yet God knows that I have other things to do today, and I'm going to take the time to save you all the same, little pest. (*He makes her sit down on a chair in the middle of the stage. He takes off his jacket, he walks towards her, heavy, powerful in his shirt sleeves.*) The day after a revolution, there is a great deal of work to

be done, I assure you. But urgent business can wait. I don't want you to die for a matter of politics. You're worth more than that. Because your Polyneices, this mourned shadow and this guarded decomposing body and all this pathos which inspires you, is just a matter of politics. I may not be a tender man, but I do have scruples; I like what is clean, proper and spotless. You think it doesn't disgust me as much as it does you, this meat rotting in the sun? In the evening, when the wind comes from the sea, one already smells it in the palace. It makes me nauseous. However, I will not even shut my window. It's disgusting, and I can tell you, it's stupid, monstrously stupid, but all of Thebes must smell it for some time. You can believe that I would have had your brother buried were it only for hygiene's sake! But to make those brutes I govern understand, the whole city must stink from the cadaver of Polyneices for a month.

ANTIGONE: You're disgusting.

CREON: Yes, my dear. My job calls for it. We can discuss whether or not one must or must not do it. But if one does it, it must be done this way.

ANTIGONE: Why are you doing it?

CREON: One morning, I awoke to find myself king of Thebes. And God knows there were other things in life I loved more than power . . .

ANTIGONE: Then you should have said no!

CREON: I could have. Only I felt suddenly like a worker who refused to do a piece of work. It didn't seem honest to me. So I said yes.

ANTIGONE: Well, so much the worse for you. I did not say "yes." What do your politics, your necessity, your poor little stories mean to me? I can still say "no" to all that I do not like and I am the only judge. And you, with your crown, with your guards, with your pomp because you have said "yes," all you can do is to put me to death.

CREON: Listen to me.

ANTIGONE: If I wish, *I* don't have to listen to

you. You have said "yes." I have nothing more to learn from you. Not you. There you sit drinking in my words. And if you don't call your guards, it is because you will listen to what I have to say.

CREON: You amuse me.

ANTIGONE: No. I frighten you. That's why you are trying to save me. It would be more convenient just the same to keep little Antigone alive and mute in the palace. You are too fastidious to make a good tyrant, that's all. But all the same you'll have me put to death in a little while, you know, and that's why you're afraid. A man who is afraid is ugly.

CREON (*in a dull, hollow voice*): Well, yes, I am afraid if you remain obstinate I will be obliged to have you killed. I wouldn't want to.

ANTIGONE: I'm not obliged to do what I don't want to do! Perhaps you couldn't have wished to refuse my brother a tomb either? Say it, you wouldn't have wanted to?

CREON: I have said just that.

ANTIGONE: But you did it all the same. And now, you are going to have me killed without wanting to. And that's what it means to be king!

CREON: That's it!

ANTIGONE: Poor Creon! My nails are broken, full of earth and your guards have given me black and blue marks on my arms, I am eaten up with panic, yet I am the queen.

CREON: Then have pity on me, live. The body of your brother which is rotting under my windows, is enough payment to restore order in Thebes. My son loves me. Don't force me to pay with you as well. I have paid enough.

ANTIGONE: No. You have said "yes." Now you'll never stop paying!

CREON (*shakes her suddenly, losing his temper*): But good God, you little idiot! Try to understand for a moment. *I've* tried hard to understand you. Someone must say yes. There must be someone to steer the ship of state. It's springing leaks. It's full of crimes, stupidity, misery . . . And its helm is tossing about. The crew no longer wants to obey; they only think of pillaging the hold and the officers are already constructing a comfortable little life raft for themselves, just for themselves, with the necessary provision of water just to get themselves out of there. The mast is cracking, and the wind is whistling and the sails are being torn apart and all these brutes will die together, because they are thinking only of their own skin, their precious skin and their petty little affairs. Do you think, then, that there is time to play at being delicate, to know whether to say "yes" or "no," to wonder whether you might have to pay too dearly one day and still be a man afterwards? You take your end of the helm, you hold up your head before a deluge of water, you yell out an order and you shoot into the crowd on the first person who makes a move. Into the crowd! The crowd has no name. It's like the wave which has just swept over the bridge in front of us; the wind which slaps you down, and those in the group that fall have no name. And neither do I; I, clutching on to the helm no longer have a name. It's only the ship which has a name and the storm. Do you understand that?

ANTIGONE (*shakes her head*): I do not want to understand. That's all right for you. I am not here to understand. I am here to say no to you and to die.

CREON: It's easy to say no!

ANTIGONE: Not always.

CREON: In order to say yes, you must sweat and roll up your sleeves, you have to grab hold of life with both your hands and get into it up to the elbows. It is easy to say no, even if you must die! All you have to do is to stand still and wait. To wait to live, to wait to be killed. It's too cowardly. It's an invention of men. Can you imagine a world in which the trees would have said no to the sap, where the animals would have said no to the hunting instinct or to love? Animals, they at least, are good and simple and tough. They go, pushing each other along, one after the other, courageously, on the same path. And if they fall, the others pass and as many as are lost, there will always be one of each species ready to make little ones again and to take up the same path with the same courage, exactly like those who passed before.

ANTIGONE: Some dream for a king, eh? It would be so simple to be a king if men were all animals.

(*A silence.* CREON *looks at her.*)

CREON: You detest me, don't you: (*She does not answer, he continues as if talking to himself.*) It's strange. I have often imagined this dialogue with a pale young man who had attempted to kill me and whom I couldn't draw anything out of afterwards but hate. But I didn't dream that it would be this way with you and for such a stupid reason . . . (*He has taken his head in his hands. One senses he is at the end of his tether.*) Listen to me for the last time. My role is the ungrateful one, but it is my role and I am going to have you killed. But, before, I want you to be sure of your own role. Do you know why you want to die, Antigone? Do you know for what sordid story you'll be signing away your bloody little name?

ANTIGONE: What story?

CREON: The story of Eteocles and Polyneices, your brothers. No, you think you know but you don't know. Nobody knows it in Thebes but me. And it seems to me that *you* too have the right to know it this morning. (*He dreams a moment, his head in his hands, leaning on his knees. He can be heard murmuring.*) It's not a very nice one, you shall see. (*And he begins in a hollow voice, without looking at* ANTIGONE.) What do you remember about your brothers in the beginning? Two playmates who scorned you, of course, who broke your dolls, eternally whispering secrets in each other's ears to enrage you?

ANTIGONE: They were grown up . . .

CREON: After, you must have admired them with their first cigarettes, their first long pants and then they began to go out at night, to smell like men, and they no longer had an eye for you.

ANTIGONE: I was a little girl . . .

CREON: And when they returned, you were aware that your mother cried, your father became angry, you heard the doors shut, and you heard derisive laughter in the corridors. And they passed in front of you, insolent and spineless, reeking of wine.

ANTIGONE: Once, I had hidden behind a doorway, it was morning, we had just arisen and they had just gotten back. Polyneices saw me, he was quite pale, his eyes were shining and he was so beautiful in his evening dress! He said to me: "So, there you are." And he gave me a big paper flower that he had brought back from his night out.

CREON: And you kept this flower, didn't you? And yesterday, before going off, you opened your drawer and you looked at it, for a long time, to give yourself courage?

ANTIGONE (*shudders*): Who told you that?

CREON: Poor Antigone, with her souvenir flower! Do you know who your brother was?

ANTIGONE: All I do know is that you would be speaking ill of him.

CREON: A little imbecilic roisterer, a tough little carnivorous animal without a soul, a little brute just good enough to drive faster than anybody else in his cars, to squander more money in the bars. Once when I was there, your father had just refused to make good a large sum that he had lost in gambling; he turned pale and raised his fists, shouting some disgusting word!

ANTIGONE: That's not true!

CREON: His brutish fist aimed right in your father's face! It was pitiful. Your father was seated at his table, his head in his hands. He was bleeding from the nose. He was crying. And Polyneices stood in a corner laughing unpleasantly, lighting up a cigarette.

ANTIGONE (*almost begging now*): It's not true!

CREON: Remember, you were twelve years old. You hadn't seen him in a long time. It's true isn't it?

ANTIGONE (in a hollow voice): Yes, it's true.

CREON: It was after this quarrel. Your father tried to keep him out of court. He had enlisted in the Argian army; the man hunt began against your father, against this old man who had not yet made up his mind to die, to let go of his kingdom. Assassination attempts came one after another and the killers we captured always ended up by admitting they had received the money from Polyneices. And not only from him. Because that is what I want you to know, the behind-the-scene facts of this drama in which you want so much to play a role in the kitchen where everything is cooked up. I had arranged for an imposing funeral in honor of Eteocles yesterday. Now Eteocles is a hero and a saint for Thebes. The people were all there. The school children donated their pennies out of their moneybox for a wreath; and the old men, moved by false sentiments, with their tremulous voices, exaggeratedly extolled the good brother, the faithful son of Oedipus, the loyal prince. I even made a speech. All the priests of Thebes turned out in full force with official expressions on their faces. And the military honors . . . we had to. You can well understand that after all I couldn't afford the luxury of having a traitor in both camps. Now I am going to tell you something, something that only I know, something terrible; Eteocles, this pillar of virtue wasn't worth any more than Polyneices. The good son had *also* tried to have his father assassinated, the loyal prince had *also* decided to sell Thebes to the highest bidder. Do you think that's strange? For that betrayal which has kept the body of Polyneices out there rotting in the sun: I have proof that Eteocles who now sleeps in his marble tomb, was also preparing to commit murder. It's just chance that Polyneices got there ahead of him. We are dealing with two arrant knaves, thick as thieves, who were deceiving each other while deceiving us and they slit each other's throats like the two gangsters they were to settle accounts.

Only, as it happened I had to make a hero out of one of them. So, I gave the order to search out their bodies. Very likely they had run each other through. They found them embracing for the first time in their lives, and then the charge of the Argian cavalry had passed over their bodies. They were cut to pieces, Antigone, unrecognizable. For my national funeral I had one of the bodies picked up, the least destroyed of the two, and I gave the order to let the other rot where it was, I don't even know which one it was. And I assure you it's all the same to me.

(There is a long silence, they do not move, nor do they look at one another, then ANTIGONE says gently.)

ANTIGONE: Why do you tell me this? (CREON gets up, puts on his jacket.)

CREON: Would it have been better to have let you die for this ridiculous cause?

ANTIGONE: Perhaps. I don't know. (There is another silence. CREON approaches her.)

CREON: What are you going to do now?

ANTIGONE (gets up like a somnambulist): I am going back up to my room.

CREON: Don't stay alone too long. Go and see Hemon this morning. Get married quickly.

ANTIGONE (in a breath): Yes.

CREON: Nothing else matters. And you were going to waste it! I understand you, at twenty I would have done as you did. That's why I drank in your words. I listened from the depths of time to a thin little pale Creon like you and who only thought of giving everything as you did. Marry quickly, Antigone, be happy. Life is not what you think it is. It is a fluid which young people let flow through their open fingers without realizing it. Close your hands. Close your hands quickly. Hold it. You'll see, life will become a simple hard thing that one nibbles at, seated in the sun. They will tell you the opposite because they need your strength and your zeal. Don't listen to them. Don't listen to me when I make my next speech in front of the tomb of Eteocles. It will not be truthful. Nothing is true but that which one leaves unsaid. You will learn too, too late: life is like a book one loves, it is a child playing at your feet, a tool one holds firmly in one's hand, a bench on which to rest in the evening in front of one's home. You will continue to hate me, but to discover this about life is the ridiculous consolation of old age: life is perhaps nothing but happiness!

ANTIGONE (*murmurs, a lost look on her face*): Happiness . . .

CREON (*a little ashamed suddenly*): A poor word, eh?

ANTIGONE (*gently*): What kind of happiness will be mine? What kind of happy woman shall she become, this little Antigone? What sinful things will she have to do, she too, day by day, in order to snatch with her teeth her little scrap of happiness? Tell me, to whom must she lie, smile on, sell herself to whom? While she averts her eyes, who must she allow to die?

CREON (*shrugging his shoulders*): Be quiet, you are mad!

ANTIGONE: No, I will not be quiet. I want to know how to go about it, I want to know how to be happy. Immediately, since one must choose immediately. You tell me how beautiful life is. I want to know how I must go about living.

CREON: You love Hemon?

ANTIGONE: Yes, I love Hemon. I love a young, hard Hemon; an exacting and faithful Hemon, like me. But if your form of life, your happiness must pass over him with its attrition, if Hemon can't go pale when I go pale, if he must no longer believe I am dead when I am five minutes late, if he can no longer feel alone in the world and detest me when I laugh without his knowing why, if he must become a stranger when he is close to me, if he too must learn how to say "yes," then I don't love Hemon any more!

CREON: You don't know what you are saying any more. Keep quiet.

ANTIGONE: Yes, I know what I am saying, but it is you who no longer understand me. I am speaking to you from too far away now, from a kingdom into which you can no longer enter with your wrinkles, your wisdom, your belly. (*she laughs.*) Ah, I am laughing, Creon! I am laughing because suddenly I see you at the age of fifteen! You had the same air of impotence and the same belief that you were all powerful. All that life has added are those little lines on your face and this fat around you.

CREON (*shakes her*): Will you ever keep quiet?

ANTIGONE: Why do you disgust me with your happiness! With your life which you must love no matter what. Like dogs who lick whatever they find. And a little good luck for every day if one is not too demanding. I want everything, right away, and altogether — or else I refuse! I don't wish to be modest and to content myself with a little piece if I have been a good girl. I want to be sure of everything today and may it be as beautiful as when I was little — or else I'll die.

CREON: Now begin, begin, like your father!

ANTIGONE: Like my father, yes! We are those who ask questions right up to the bitter end. Until there isn't the remotest little chance of living hope, the slightest chance of hope to strangle. We are those who latch on to it when we meet up with it, your hope, your dear hope, your filthy hope!

CREON: Shut up! If you could only see yourself shouting these words, how ugly you are.

ANTIGONE: Yes, I'm ugly! They're disgusting, aren't they, these outcries, these startling leaps, this gutter fight. Papa only became beautiful after, when he was quite sure, finally sure, that he had killed his father, that it was really his mother he had slept with. And that nothing, nothing more could save him. Then he suddenly calmed down, he had a kind of smile on his face, and he became beautiful. It was over. All he had to do was to shut his eyes to see no more! Oh! your faces, your poor stupidly optimistic faces! It is you who are ugly, even the best looking among you. You all have something ugly in the corner of your eye or your mouth. You said it a while back, Creon, in the kitchen. You all have the hands of cooks!

CREON (*pulverizing her arm*): I command you to keep quiet now, do you hear?

ANTIGONE: You order me, cook? You think you can order me to do something?

CREON: The antechamber is full of people. Do you want to ruin yourself? People will hear you.

ANTIGONE: Well then, open the doors. Then they'll really hear me!

CREON (*who tries to shut her mouth with force*): Will you ever shut up, for Heaven's sake?

ANTIGONE (*struggling*): Come quickly, cook! Call out your guards!

(*The door opens. Enter* ISMENE.)

ISMENE (*crying out*): Antigone!

ANTIGONE: What do you want, you too?

ISMENE: Antigone, pardon me! Antigone, you see, I've come, I'm brave. I'll go with you now.

ANTIGONE: Where will you go with me?

ISMENE: If you put her to death, you'll have to kill me along with her!

ANTIGONE: Oh, no! Not now. Not you! It must be me, alone. Don't imagine you can come and die with me now. It would be too easy.

ISMENE: I don't wish to live if you die . . . I don't want to live without you!

ANTIGONE: You have chosen life and I chose death. Leave me alone with your lamentations. You should have gone this morning, on all fours, in the dark. You should have gone and scratched the earth with your nails while they were nearby and be caught by them like a thief!

ISMENE: All right, I'll go tomorrow!

ANTIGONE: You hear, Creon? She too. Who knows what may happen if the others listen to me? What are you waiting for: silence me; what are you waiting for: call out your guards. Come, Creon, a little courage, it's only a bad moment to get over. Come, cook, since you must.

CREON: (*cries out suddenly*): Guards! (*The guards appear instantly.*) Take her away.

ANTIGONE (*gives out with a huge cry, relieved*): At last, Creon!

(*The guards jump on her and take her away. ISMENE goes out shouting after her.*)

ISMENE: Antigone! Antigone!

(CREON *has remained alone, the* CHORUS *enters and goes to him.*)

CHORUS: Are you mad, Creon? What have you done?

CREON (*who looks directly ahead of him*): She had to die.

CHORUS: Don't let Antigone die, Creon! We shall all have to bear the consequences for centuries.

CREON: She wanted to die. Not one among us was strong enough to make her go on living. I understand it now, Antigone was made to die. She herself didn't know it perhaps, but Polyneices was only a pretext. When she had to give up that pretext, she immediately formed another. What was important for her was to refuse and to die.

CHORUS: She is a child, Creon.

CREON: What do you want me to do? Condemn her to live?

HEMON (*enters shouting*): Father!

CREON (*runs to him, embraces him*): Forget her, Hemon, forget her, my child.

HEMON: You are mad, father, Let me go.

CREON (*holding him tighter*): I tried everything to save her, Hemon. I tried everything, I swear it to you. She doesn't love you. She could have lived. She preferred her madness and death.

HEMON (*shouts, trying to break away from his embrace*): But Father, they've taken her away!

CREON: She has spoken now. All Thebes knows what she did. I am obliged to put her to death.

HEMON (*pulls himself away*): Let me go!

(*A silence. They are face to face. They look at one another.*)

CHORUS (*approaches*): Can't you make something up, say that she is mad, shut her up?

CREON: They will say that it isn't true. That I am saving her because she was going to be the wife of my son. I cannot.

CHORUS: Can't you gain time, let her escape tomorrow?

CREON: The mob knows already, it is howling around the palace. I can't do anything.

HEMON: Father, the crowd is nothing! You are the master in Thebes.

CREON: I am the master before the law. Not after.

HEMON: Father, I am your son, you cannot let them take her from me!

CREON: Yes, Hemon. Yes, my son, I can. Courage. Antigone can live no more. Antigone has already left us all.

HEMON: Do you think I can live without her? Do you think I would accept your life? To face each day, from morning to night, without her! Your agitation, your chatter, your emptiness, without her.

CREON: You must accept it, Hemon. Everyone of us experiences it: that more or less sad, more or less distant day when he must finally accept being a man. For you, it is to-day . . . And as you stand before me, with these tears in the corners of your eyes and your heart hurting, you are my little boy, for the last time . . . When you have turned away, when you have crossed this threshold, it will be all over.

HEMON (*recoils a bit and says softly*): It is already over.

CREON: Don't judge me, Hemon. Don't judge me, not you, too.

HEMON (*looks at him and says suddenly*): This great force and this courage, this giant god that carried me off in his arms and saved me from monsters and shadows, was it you? This forbidden odor and this good evening bread, under the lamp light; when you showed me books in your study, was it you?

CREON (*humbly*): Yes, Hemon.

HEMON: Every evening, all this pride, all those books full of heroes, must it come to this? To be a man, as you say, and to be too happy to live?

CREON: Yes, Hemon.

HEMON (*shouts suddenly like a child, throwing himself into his arms*): Father, it's not true! It's not you, it's not today! We are not both of us at the foot of this wall at which we must only say yes. You are still powerful, you are, as when I was little, Oh! I beg of you, father, oh how I admire you, how I admire you still! I am too alone and the world is too empty if I can no longer admire you.

CREON (*detaches him from himself*): We are all alone, Hemon. The world is empty. And you have admired me too long. Look at me, that is what it means to become a man, to see the face of your father face to face one day.

HEMON (*looks at him, then recoils shouting*): Antigone! Antigone! Help!

(*He goes out running.*)

CHORUS (*going to* CREON): Creon, he went out like a madman.

CREON (*who looks into the distance, directly in front of him, immobile*): Yes, poor boy, he loves her.

CHORUS: Creon, you must do something.

CREON: I can no longer do anything.

CHORUS: He left, mortally wounded.

CREON (*in a hollow voice*): Yes, we are all mortally wounded.

(ANTIGONE *enters the room, pushed by the guards who stand with their backs up against the door, behind which one can hear the howling crowd.*)

GUARD: Chief, they're storming the palace.

ANTIGONE: Creon, I don't wish to see their faces any more, I don't wish to hear their shouting any more, I don't want to see anyone any more! You have my death now, that is enough! Arrange it so I don't have to see anybody any more until it's all over.

CREON (*goes out yelling to the guards*): The guards at the doors! The palace must be emptied! You: remain here with her.

(*The two other guards go out, followed by the* CHORUS. ANTIGONE *remains alone with the first guard.* ANTIGONE *looks at him.*)

ANTIGONE (*suddenly*): Well, is it you?

GUARD: Who me?

ANTIGONE: My last man's face.

GUARD: Guess so.

ANTIGONE: Let me look at you . . .

GUARD (*draws back embarrassed*): That's enough of that.

ANTIGONE: Was it you who arrested me a while back?

GUARD: Yes, it was me.

ANTIGONE: You hurt me. You didn't need to hurt me. Did I look like I wanted to escape?

GUARD: Enough of that! It was either you or me.

ANTIGONE: How old are you?

GUARD: Thirty-nine years old.

ANTIGONE: You have children?

GUARD: Yes, two.

ANTIGONE: You love them?

GUARD: That's none of your business.

(*He begins to pace up and down the room; for a moment, one hears only the sound of his footsteps.*)

ANTIGONE (*asking quite humbly*): Have you been a guard for a long time?

GUARD: After the war. I was a sergeant. I reenlisted.

ANTIGONE: Must you be a sergeant to be a guard?

GUARD: On principle, yes. Either a sergeant or having trained with a special squad. A sergeant loses his rank. I'll give you an example: I meet a recruit from the army, he doesn't have to salute me.

ANTIGONE: Oh yes?

GUARD: Yes. Only you see, he usually does. The recruit knows that the guard is a noncommissioned officer. It's a matter of pay: you have the ordinary pay of a guard, like those in the special squad, and for six months, as a bonus, you get a supplementary sergeant's pay. Only, as a guard, you have other advantages. Lodging, heat, benefits in the end. A married guard with two children gets to make more than a regular sergeant.

ANTIGONE: Oh yes?

GUARD: Yes. That's why sergeants and guards don't get along. You may have noticed that a sergeant makes believe he looks down on a guard. Their great problem is advancement. On the one hand, that's only fair. Advancement for guards is slower and harder than it is in the army. But don't forget that a brigadier in the guards is better than being a master sergeant.

ANTIGONE (*says to him suddenly*): Listen . . .

GUARD: Yes.

ANTIGONE: I'm going to die in a little while.

(*The guard doesn't answer. A silence. He paces up and down. A moment later, he starts again.*)

GUARD: On the other hand, you get more consideration as a guard than a sergeant does on active duty. The guard is a soldier, but he's almost a civil servant . . .

ANTIGONE: You think it hurts to die?

GUARD: I don't know. I heard them say you

won't soil the town with your blood; they're going to wall you up in a hole.

ANTIGONE: Alive?

GUARD: Well, yes, in the beginning.

(*A silence. The guard rolls a wad of tobacco.*)

ANTIGONE: Oh tomb! Oh nuptial bed! Oh my subterranean home . . . (*She is quite small in the midst of this large empty room. She seems a bit cold. She puts her arms around herself. She murmurs*) All alone . . .

GUARD (*who has finished wadding his tobacco*): In the caverns of Hades, at the doors to the city. In broad daylight. Now that's a strange fatigue duty for guards. First they were all for sending the army. But, at last news, it seems that it'll be the guards that make up the squad. They work the guards! Is it any wonder that guards are jealous of sergeants on active duty . . .

ANTIGONE (*murmurs, suddenly weary*): Two animals . . .

GUARD: What do you mean, two animals?

ANTIGONE: Even animals would huddle close to each other to keep warm. I am alone.

GUARD: If you need anything, that's different. I can call.

ANTIGONE: No. Only if you would give someone a letter when I'm dead.

GUARD: What do you mean, a letter?

ANTIGONE: A letter I shall write.

GUARD: Oh, no, not that! No fooling around! A letter! What a nerve! Me take such a big risk, for such a little thing!

ANTIGONE: I'll give you this ring if you accept.

GUARD: Is it gold?

ANTIGONE: Yes, it's gold.

GUARD: You know, if they search me, it's court-martial for me. What's it to you? (*He looks at the ring again.*) If you like, what I can do is I can write in my notebook what you want to say. Then I'll tear out the page. In my writing, it's not the same.

ANTIGONE (*her eyes closed, she murmurs with a poor fixed grin*): In your writing . . . (*She shudders a little.*) This is too ugly, if you don't want to, I . . . (*Quickly*) Yes. Keep the ring and write. But do it quickly . . . I'm afraid we don't have any more time . . . Write: "My darling . . ."

GUARD (*who had taken his notebook and sucks in his mouth*): Is it for your boy friend?

ANTIGONE: My darling, I wanted to die and you probably won't love me any more . . .

GUARD (*repeats slowly with his gross voice writing*): "My darling, I wanted to die and you probably won't love me any more . . ."

ANTIGONE: And Creon was right, it's terrible now, next to this man, I no longer know why I am dying. I am afraid . . .

GUARD (*who is working hard at the dictation*): "Creon was right, it's terrible . . ."

ANTIGONE: "Oh! Hemon, our little boy. Only now do I know how simple it was to live . . .

GUARD (*stops*): Hey, you're going too fast. How can I get all this down? I need a little time after all . . .

ANTIGONE: Where are you?

GUARD (*reading back what he has done*): "It's terrible now next to this man . . ."

ANTIGONE: I no longer know why I am dying.

GUARD (*writes, sucking in his mouth*): "I no longer know why I am dying . . ." One never knows why one dies.

ANTIGONE (*continues*): I'm afraid . . . (*She stops. She rises up suddenly.*) No. Erase all of that. It's better that nobody ever know. It's as if they were to see me naked and touch me after I am dead. Say only: "Forgive me."

GUARD: So, I take out the ending and I put in forgive me in its place?

ANTIGONE: Yes, Forgive me, my darling. Without little Antigone, you would all have been quite happy, I love you . . .

GUARD: "Without little Antigone, you would all have been quite happy, I love you . . ."

ANTIGONE: Yes, that's all.

GUARD: It's a strange letter.

ANTIGONE: Yes, it's a strange letter.

GUARD: What's the address?

(*At this moment the door opens. The other guards appear.* ANTIGONE *gets up. Looks at them, looks at the first guard who has risen behind her, he pockets the ring and arranges the notebook, with an important air . . . He sees* ANTIGONE'S *look. He yells to save face.*)

GUARD: O.K.! Now, no nonsense!

(ANTIGONE *gives a poor smile. She lowers her head. She goes off without a word toward the other guards. They all go out.*)

CHORUS (*enters suddenly*): There! It's over for Antigone. Now, Creon's turn approaches. They will all have to go through it.

MESSENGER (*bursts into the room, shouting*): Terrible news. They have just thrown Antigone into her abyss. They hadn't finished rolling the last blocks of stone in place when Creon and all those who surrounded her heard wailing coming from inside the tomb. Everyone kept quiet and listened, for it wasn't the voice of Antigone. It was a new voice which came from the depths of the abyss . . . everybody looked at Creon, and he was the first to guess it, he who always knows everything ahead of others, yelled suddenly like a madman: "Remove the stones!" The slaves threw themselves against the piled up blocks and Creon was among them, sweating, his hands bloodied. The stones finally gave way and the thinnest one slipped into the opening. Antigone was at the bottom of the tomb hanged with the cords of her own belt, red cords, green cords, blue cords which made her a kind of child's collar, and Hemon was on his knees holding her in his arms and moaning, his face hidden in her dress. They moved one more block and Creon was able finally to descend. His white hairs could be seen in the darkness, at the bottom of the abyss. He tried to raise Hemon, he begged him. But Hemon couldn't hear him. Then suddenly Hemon rose, his eyes black, and he never looked more like the boy he used to be; he looked at his father without saying anything, and, suddenly, he spit in his face and drew his sword. Creon jumped back. Then Hemon looked at him with the eyes of a child, heavy with scorn, and Creon couldn't avoid his gaze: it was as sharp as a knife blade. Hemon looked at this trembling old man at the other end of the cavern, and without a word, he plunged his sword into his own belly and lay down against Antigone, embracing her in a huge red pool of blood.

CREON (*entering with his page*): I lay them down one next to the other. They are cleansed now. Two lovers the morning after their first night. It's all over for *them.*

CHORUS: Not for you, Creon. You have something else to learn yet. Eurydice, the queen, your wife . . .

CREON: A good woman speaking always of her garden, her preserves, her knitting, her eternal knitting for the poor. It's curious how the poor have eternally needed knitting. One might say they only needed knitting . . .

CHORUS: The poor of Thebes will be cold this winter, Creon. When she learned of the death of her son, the queen put down her knitting needles, wisely, after having ended her line steadily as everything she does, a little more calmly than she generally does. And then she passed into her bed chamber, her chamber perfumed with lavender, with the little embroidered doilies and the plush frames, to cut her throat, Creon. She is lying in state now on one of the little old fashioned twin beds, in the same place where you saw her as a girl one evening, and with the same smile, scarcely a little sadder. And if it weren't for that large red stain on the pillow around her neck, you could believe she was sleeping.

CREON: She too. They're all sleeping. That is good. It's been a terrible day. (*A pause. He says in a hollow voice*) It must be good to sleep.

CHORUS: And now you are all alone, Creon.

CREON: All alone, yes. (*A silence. He places his hand on his page's shoulder*) Little one . . .

PAGE: Sir?

CREON: I will tell it to you. What the others don't know; there is a job to get done, you just can't cross your arms. They say that it's a filthy job, but if someone doesn't do it, who will?

PAGE: I don't know, Sir.

CREON: Of course, you don't know. You're fortunate! It would be best never to know. Are you anxious to grow up?

PAGE: Oh yes, Sir!

CREON: You're mad, little one. One must never grow up. (*The clock strikes in the distance. He murmurs*) Five o'clock! What do we have today at five o'clock?

PAGE: Court, Sir.

CREON: Well, if we must go to court, little one, we'll go to it. (*They go out,* CREON *leaning on the* PAGE.)

CHORUS (*coming forward*): And there it is. Without little Antigone, it's true, they would all have been quite content. But now, it's all over. They're content all the same. All those who had to die are dead. Those who believed one thing and then those who believed another — even those who believed in nothing and got caught in the middle without understanding anything. The dead are all alike, all quite stiff, quite useless, quite rotten, and those who still live will begin slowly to forget them and to mix up their names. It's all over with. Antigone is calmed now, we shall never know of what fever. Her duty has been returned to her. A great sad peace falls over Thebes and over an empty palace in which Creon begins to wait for death . . .

(*While he spoke, the guards have entered. They have installed themselves on a bench, their litre of red wine next to them, their helmets on the back of their necks, and they have begun a round of cards.*)

CHORUS: Only the guards remain. It's all the same to them; it's none of their affair. They continue playing cards . . .

(*The curtain falls rapidly as the guards play their trump cards.*)

END OF ANTIGONE

America Hurrah

About a decade ago Gerald Weales, writing of *American Drama Since World War II* (1962), looked back at an off-Broadway theatre of an earlier and more golden age:

> There was a time when the words off-Broadway theatre called up a picture of a dedicated group, held together by esthetic or ideational concerns, determined to change the state of the theatre or the state of the world. Today, the words suggest a producing unit with a much smaller investment than Broadway demands, with a small house to play in, with special Equity contracts, with a play that is likely to be as safe as it is experimental.

Today we are even farther from such dedicated off-Broadway groups of the past as the Provincetown Theatre and The Group Theatre and even Theatre Guild. "Off-Broadway" has come to mean, in many cases, slightly cheaper "Broadway-type" productions. A strike has recently obtained a pay raise for off-Broadway actors. Ticket prices reflect increased production costs and a strictly exploitive approach in many cases: even a tiny theatre may have three or four ticket prices, none of them cheap and some of them as much as ten dollars. Off-Broadway is enjoying hits comparable to Broadway — *Oh, Calcutta!* and *The Boys in the Band* are typical of the sexploitation successes — and these occasionally turn up after a while in Broadway theatres, having made it "off," using Broadway as "the road"!

But now there is a ferment and experimentation in a comparatively new movement which stands in the same relation to off-Broadway as off-Broadway used to stand to Broadway, before The Circle in the Square and such institutions became as much a part of the Establishment New York scene as Lincoln Center. This vital theatre, which has produced Sam Shepard (soon snapped up by Lincoln Center), Rochelle Owens (a product of the Judson Poets' Theatre in a Greenwich Village church which seems to stage everything but religious services), Murray Mednick (of Theatre Genesis of St. Mark's-in-the-Bouwerie church), and Jean-Claude van Itallie, is described thus by Robert J. Schroeder in his anthology of *The New Underground Theatre* (1968):

> The established American theatre often appears to think first of real estate and then of plays to perform in the buildings. Underground plays are presented in otherwise unused church lofts, coffee houses, cellars, empty

lofts and store buildings. It is not unusual to find a playwright, a director and an acting troupe moving almost like the medieval strolling players, from loft to loft, and from neighborhood to neighborhood, constantly harried by city zoning officials and permit-checkers.

As off-Broadway produced its hits and its discoveries (*The Threepenny Opera* and *The Fantasticks*, Edward Albee and Murray Schisgal), so this "off-off-Broadway"* theatre is making its mark and one hopes that it will have a more permanent effect than the off-Broadway reputations which have faded: good playwrights such as Jack Richardson, Jack Gelber, Arthur Kopit, and the rest whose time seems to have passed. The Caffe Cino (which launched the off-Broadway movement in 1958) is gone, victim of the "permit-checkers," but now Ellen Stewart's La Mama and Joseph Papp's Public Theatre are solidly established; the only danger is that success will make them think in off-Broadway or even Broadway terms. Already Lincoln Center threatens to be Public Theatre Uptown.

Joe Cino in the early sixties was a daring and dedicated impresario who introduced playwrights like Lanford Wilson (*The Madness of Lady Bright*, *This is the Rill Speaking*, etc.) to a faithful coffee-house crowd. When at the end of the sixties I wrote a summary of "the American drama since 1914" for Gassner and Quinn's *Reader's Encyclopedia of World Drama* and mentioned Joe Cino's contribution, my editor queried: "Who is Cino? No reference books seem ever to have heard of him." Joe was dead and so was his coffee-house, and Tom Eyen's dramatic obituary of Joe had not yet been written. But Joe's idea had spread to the Take 3 coffee-house (which presented *Ubu the King* in September 1960)** and was to inspire the lasting Café La Mama (Experimental Theatre Club) which, under the indomitable Ellen Stewart, has finally found a permanent home in New York and has set up branches in South America, Europe, and (for all I know) by now maybe Antarctica to do a *Snow Balls* by Paul Foster. The Judson Memorial Church has had an active experimental theatre (featuring Rev. Al Carmines) since 1961, St. Mark's-in-the-Bouwerie has had its Theatre Genesis since 1964, and at various times the scene has been active with The Hardware Poets Theatre, the Playwrights' Unit (Albee et al.), the NYU group that scored with *Dionysus in '69* and *Commune*, the theatre of the Westbeth artists' development, The Bridge, The Negro Theatre Ensemble, Tom Eyen in a cellar and Tom Eyen with *The Dirtiest Show in Town*. At various times off-off-Broadway audiences have seen plays as different as *The Great American Desert* and Ibsen revivals; *Mr. Jello* and *The Recruiting Officer*; musicals like *Little Mary Sunshine* and *Your Own Thing*; *The Octoroon* and *The Reckoning*. Writers have included LeRoi Jones and Frank O'Hara, Ken-

---

* This clumsy but accepted term was coined by critic Jerry Tallmer of *The Village Voice* in 1960.
** The program stated that the production was intended to represent "a return to the original idea of off-Broadway theatre, in which imagination is substituted for money, and plays can be presented in a way that would be impossible in the commercial theatre."

neth Koch and Douglas Turner Ward, Robert Whitman and Tom Sankey, Robert Lowell and William Alfred, Lonne Elder III and Ronald Tavel.

"Off-off-Broadway" has room for everything: for *Fortune and Men's Eyes* and *The Faggott*, for nudie shows and *You're a Good Man Charlie Brown*, *The Me Nobody Knows* and a host of playwrights nobody knows, shows that are free at The Old Reliable bar, for a few dollars at the Public Theatre or the Pocket Theatre, for more at the Cherry Lane or the Astor Playhouse, for a "contribution" in many a Bowery loft or unlikely hall or restaurant. Most of it consists of vanity production and boring junk. Yet every once in a while, there's a diamond in the dung, a new playwright of talent and an exciting cast. And if there's nothing new that's good or good that's new this week, then why not *Fuente ovejuna* or *Woyzeck* or a kooky *Macbeth* or a *Hedda Gabler* (with Hedda as a sweet kid, courtesy of the Aesthetic Realists) or (say) the *Shariputra-prakarana* in the nude with multi-media effects on a bill with *Dance of Death*?

A graduate of this lively scene, with plays produced by The Open Theatre (Joseph Chaikin's group "to explore and experiment"), Café La Mama, Caffe Cino, The Playwrights' Unit, The Actors' Studio, The Pocket Theatre, and elsewhere, is Jean-Claude van Itallie (born in Brussels 1936, Harvard class of 1958). In 1965 his *America Hurrah*, an attack on plastic people and aspects of The American Dream, premièred at La Mama, directed by Michael Kahn, designed by Robert Wilson, dolls by Tania Leontov, and starring Cheryl Kilgren, John Mintun, Fay Chaiken, and Heidi Zimmerli. Later as three one-act plays *America Hurrah* moved to the Pocket Theatre on Third Avenue and still later was seen in Europe, Minneapolis, and elsewhere. Joseph Chaikin's direction first gave form to "Interview" and Jacques Levy was ring-master for the circuses of "TV" and "Motel," with Ruth White mind blowing as the motelkeeper. In them, said Robert Brustein in a glowing review in the *New Republic* (3 December, 1966), van Itallie has

> discovered the deepest poetic function of the theatre which is not, like most American dramatists, to absorb the audience into the author's own personal problems under the pretext that they are universal, but rather to invent metaphors which can poignantly suggest a nation's nightmares and afflictions. These metaphors solve nothing, change nothing, transform nothing, but they do manage to relax frustration and assuage loneliness by showing that it is still possible for men to share a common humanity — even if this only means sharing a common revulsion against what is mean and detestable.

One thing that critic Brustein does not mention here is that in its way *America Hurrah* was more of an anti-LBJ political play than was *MacBird*.

Finally, when you have read a play, it is always interesting to compare your reactions with those of other critics. Here, for example, are some critical responses to *America Hurrah*, a view of America, from London critics:

These productions, in which the characters speak their thoughts, talk over and through each other, mime, strut, wear masks, open and shut their mouths with no sound emerging, whine, whimper and twitch, are based on the fallacy that confusion is best conveyed by something that is itself confused. . . . It seems to assume that *L'Assommoir* [*The Dram Shop*] would be a more powerful novel if Zola had written it when he was drunk. But whereas *Interview* is crushingly dull, there are many details in *TV* such as the distressed pop singer who is kept on the screen a few moments too long, which are very funny. The political satire is tamer than one had expected, and a sermon is accompanied by the most prolonged fit of vomiting I have known in a theatre.

The third play, *Motel,* is a different matter. It is an example of that exaggerated Puritanism, the *sæva indignatio* [savage indignation] of Swift, which it is easy to mistake for pornography. It is direct, concentrated, hard-centered, relentless and clear Grand Guignol [horror show] shaking hands with Savonarola [the Renaissance Carrie Nation], horrible and merciless. It is the sort of play that I should like to condemn for it is obsessed with evil to the point of madness, but I should be dishonest if I did not record that it is superbly, if foully, well done, that it has a shattering effect and that this effect — on a healthy mind — is cathartic not titillating. . . .

This is what the Puritan Fathers thought that fornicators were like. It is worlds away from the complacent charity of *La Dame aux camélias.* Far from being an incitement to vice, it is a vindication of the morality that the middle classes used to preach even if they did not practise it. But one such vindication is enough: for me at any rate. — *Harold Hobson.*

This is the theatre of puncture; van Itallie doesn't take an issue and hammer it over the head. His mind and his cast work together like quick-silver, jumping from nightmare to nightmare. . . . — *Helen Dawson.*

There has been a good deal of talk, and altogether too much written, about Antonin Artaud's *Theatre of Cruelty* and its efforts to shock the audience into a new awareness of itself or something. But how often is that restless spirit truly evoked?

. . .

On paper it may not sound a very original idea, but in the theatre, using huge dolls inhabited by the players, the impact is grotesquely impressive in a way that leaves the audience slightly stunned.

What does the sketch mean? Is it a metaphor of the grosser American way of life? Or just a rude comment on motels? That depends on the spectator. — *Eric Shorter.*

His strength in these three pieces lies in his treatment of his material rather than in its selection. The most imaginative and original of the three pieces, the last one, illustrates this most clearly; the point made is a simple one (that Americans have no respect for the amenities provided for them) and the treatment is uncommonly vivid. . . . extremely funny and sharply moral: and an extra quality is obtained by the use of vast dolls instead of actors to carry out these outrages, so giving a feeling of cold unemotionalism to the monstrous proceedings. — *B. A. Young.*

Jean-Claude van Itallie ranges over a great deal of national territory (though curiously, like [Jules] Feiffer in *Little Murders,* he ignores race hatred), but what he always holds in focus is the tension between public conformity and personal alienation. He shows the great bland superstructure of office life, political pronouncements, luxuriously serviced anonymity and sponsored television with its steady output of soothing cant and corpselike smiles: and he shows individuals (in their own way no less standardized) calling for help, deceiving their wives as news comes in from Vietnam, and finally tearing the emblems of their civilization apart.

. . . "All modern here, but . . . with a tang of home. . . . The toilet flushes of its own accord." A great theatrical image; and one that triumphantly survives the transatlantic crossing. — *Irving Wardle.*

Those who expect keen critical comment on the Great American Dream will be disappointed. The rewards of the evening, and the evening is finally very rewarding, are not to be found in the freshness of any comment Mr. van Itallie has to make. The satirical content of his plays is really no more than that in Pop Art, where a reproduction of Batman in a frame is held to be a sufficient comment on the place of Batman in our civilization. Where *America Hurrah* makes its claim to be seen is in the uses to which the author and his directors have put the stage. By the final play the nerve endings have been expertly singed. The mind, however, is unassailed.

. . . Mr. van Itallie, an ex-Harvard writer of Public Affairs programmes, has chosen such large and obvious targets — psychiatrists, advertising, Lucy Bird and television, naturally — that your ordinary, soft-spoken, buttoned down, all-American Dad, quietly dedicated to white-neighbours and the world-wide defect of Communism, can see the show and feel, comfortably, that only the hicks are being got at. The attack, indeed, is not specifically relevant to America. . . .

. . .

The last play, *Motel,* is a genuine inspiration. Visually and emotionally the play is superb: what it actually says is less clear. Like most of the *Theatre of Cruelty* it is very theatrical; but no one actually gets hurt. — *John Mortimer.*

There you have half a dozen London critics reacting to *America Hurrah,* and you can compare and contrast their views with those of American critics, whose opinions are more easily found, and your personal estimate of the work. Become a dramatic critic yourself, "the humble servant of genuine art," articulating precisely why you admire what you admire, and (as Robert Brustein writes in his provocative *Seasons of Discontent*):

The implacable enemy of pseudo art, waging war on all the conditions which produce it, including the writer's cynicism, the producer's greed, the actor's ambition, and the spectator's spiritual emptiness.

AMERICA HURRAH

Three One-Act Plays

Jean-Claude Van Itallie

INTERVIEW

A Fugue for Eight Actors

CHARACTERS

FIRST INTERVIEWER
FIRST APPLICANT
SECOND APPLICANT
THIRD APPLICANT
FOURTH APPLICANT
SECOND INTERVIEWER
THIRD INTERVIEWER
FOURTH INTERVIEWER

The set is white and impersonal.

Two subway stairs are at the back of the stage. On the sides there is one entrance for Applicants and another entrance for Interviewers.

The only furniture or props needed are eight grey blocks.

The actors, four men and four women, are dressed in black-and-white street clothes. During the employment agency section only, Interviewers wear translucent plastic masks.

There is an intermittent harpsichord accompaniment: dance variations (minuet, Virginia reel, twist) on a familiar American tune. But much of the music (singing, whistling, humming) is provided by the actors on stage. It is suggested, moreover, that as a company of actors and a director approach the play they find their own variations in rhythmic expression. The successful transition from one setting to the next depends on the actors' ability to play together as a company and to drop character instantaneously and completely in order to assume another character, or for a group effect.

(*The* FIRST INTERVIEWER *for an employment agency, a young woman, sits on stage as the* FIRST APPLICANT, *a Housepainter, enters.*)

FIRST INTERVIEWER (*standing*): How do you do?

FIRST APPLICANT (*sitting*): Thank you, I said, not knowing where to sit.

(*The characters will often include the audience in what they say, as if they were being interviewed by the audience.*)

FIRST INTERVIEWER (*pointedly*): Won't you sit down?

FIRST APPLICANT (*standing again quickly, afraid to displease*): I'm sorry.

FIRST INTERVIEWER (*busy with imaginary papers, pointing to a particular seat*): There. Name, please?

FIRST APPLICANT: Jack Smith.

FIRST INTERVIEWER: Jack what Smith?

FIRST APPLICANT: Beg pardon?

FIRST INTERVIEWER: Fill in the blank space, please. Jack blank space Smith.

FIRST APPLICANT: I don't have any.

FIRST INTERVIEWER: I asked you to sit down. (*Pointing.*) There.

FIRST APPLICANT (*sitting*): I'm sorry.

FIRST INTERVIEWER: Name, please?

FIRST APPLICANT: Jack Smith.

FIRST INTERVIEWER: You haven't told me your MIDDLE name.

FIRST APPLICANT: I haven't got one.

FIRST INTERVIEWER (*suspicious but writing it down*): No middle name.

(SECOND APPLICANT, *a woman, a Floorwasher, enters.*)

FIRST INTERVIEWER: How do you do?

SECOND APPLICANT (*sitting*): Thank you, I said, not knowing what.

FIRST INTERVIEWER: Won't you sit down?

SECOND APPLICANT (*standing*): I'm sorry.

FIRST APPLICANT: I am sitting.

FIRST INTERVIEWER (*pointing*): There. Name, please?

SECOND APPLICANT (*sitting*): Jane Smith.

FIRST APPLICANT: Jack Smith.

FIRST INTERVIEWER: What blank space Smith?

SECOND APPLICANT: Ellen.

FIRST APPLICANT: Haven't got one.

FIRST INTERVIEWER: What job are you applying for?

FIRST APPLICANT: Housepainter.

SECOND APPLICANT: Floorwasher.

FIRST INTERVIEWER: We haven't many vacancies in that. What experience have you had?

FIRST APPLICANT: A lot.

SECOND APPLICANT: Who needs experience for floorwashing?

FIRST INTERVIEWER: You will help me by making your answers clear.

FIRST APPLICANT: Eight years.

SECOND APPLICANT: Twenty years.

(THIRD APPLICANT, *a Banker, enters.*)

FIRST INTERVIEWER: How do you do?

SECOND APPLICANT: I'm good at it.

FIRST APPLICANT: Very well.

THIRD APPLICANT (*sitting*): Thank you, I said, as casually as I could.

FIRST INTERVIEWER: Won't you sit down?

THIRD APPLICANT (*standing again*): I'm sorry.

SECOND APPLICANT: I am sitting.

FIRST APPLICANT (*standing again*): I'm sorry.

FIRST INTERVIEWER (*pointing to a particular seat*): There. Name, please?

FIRST APPLICANT: Jack Smith.

SECOND APPLICANT: Jane Smith.

THIRD APPLICANT: Richard Smith.

FIRST INTERVIEWER: What EXACTLY Smith, please?

THIRD APPLICANT: Richard F.

SECOND APPLICANT: Jane Ellen.

FIRST APPLICANT: Jack None.

FIRST INTERVIEWER: What are you applying for?

FIRST APPLICANT: Housepainter.

SECOND APPLICANT: I need money.

THIRD APPLICANT: Bank president.

FIRST INTERVIEWER: How many years have you been in your present job?

THIRD APPLICANT: Three.

SECOND APPLICANT: Twenty.

FIRST APPLICANT: Eight.

(FOURTH APPLICANT, *a Lady's Maid, enters.*)

FIRST INTERVIEWER: How do you do?

FOURTH APPLICANT: I said thank you, not knowing where to sit.

THIRD APPLICANT: I'm fine.

SECOND APPLICANT: Do I have to tell you?

FIRST APPLICANT: Very well.

FIRST INTERVIEWER: Won't you sit down?

FOURTH APPLICANT: I'm sorry.

THIRD APPLICANT (*sitting again*): Thank you.

SECOND APPLICANT (*standing again*): I'm sorry.

FIRST APPLICANT (*sitting*): Thanks.

FIRST INTERVIEWER (*pointing to a particular seat*): There. Name, please?

(FOURTH APPLICANT *sits.*)

ALL APPLICANTS: Smith.

FIRST INTERVIEWER: What Smith?

FOURTH APPLICANT: Mary Victoria.

THIRD APPLICANT: Richard F.

SECOND APPLICANT: Jane Ellen.

FIRST APPLICANT: Jack None.

FIRST INTERVIEWER: How many years' experience have you had?

FOURTH APPLICANT: Eight years.

SECOND APPLICANT: Twenty years.

FIRST APPLICANT: Eight years.

THIRD APPLICANT: Three years four months and nine days not counting vacations and sick leave and the time both my daughters and my wife had the whooping cough.

FIRST INTERVIEWER: Just answer the questions, please.

FOURTH APPLICANT: Yes, sir.

THIRD APPLICANT: Sure.

SECOND APPLICANT: I'm sorry.

FIRST APPLICANT: That's what I'm doing.

(SECOND INTERVIEWER, *a young man, enters and goes to inspect Applicants. With the entrance of each Interviewer, the speed of the action accelerates.*)

SECOND INTERVIEWER: How do you do?

FIRST APPLICANT (*standing*): I'm sorry.

SECOND APPLICANT (*sitting*): Thank you.

THIRD APPLICANT (*standing*): I'm sorry.

FOURTH APPLICANT (*sitting*): Thank you.

SECOND INTERVIEWER: What's your name?

FIRST INTERVIEWER: Your middle name, please.

FIRST APPLICANT: Smith.

SECOND APPLICANT: Ellen.

THIRD APPLICANT: Smith, Richard F.

FOURTH APPLICANT: Mary Victoria Smith.

FIRST INTERVIEWER: What is your exact age?

SECOND INTERVIEWER: Have you any children?

FIRST APPLICANT: I'm thirty-two years old.

SECOND APPLICANT: One son.

THIRD APPLICANT: I have two daughters.

FOURTH APPLICANT: Do I have to tell you that?

FIRST INTERVIEWER: Are you married, single, or other?

SECOND INTERVIEWER: Have you ever earned more than that?

FIRST APPLICANT: No.

SECOND APPLICANT: Never.

THIRD APPLICANT: Married.

FOURTH APPLICANT: Single, NOW.

(THIRD INTERVIEWER, *a woman, enters.*)

THIRD INTERVIEWER: How do you do?

FIRST APPLICANT (*sitting*): Thank you.

SECOND APPLICANT (*standing*): I'm sorry.

THIRD APPLICANT (*sitting*): Thank you.

FOURTH APPLICANT (*standing*): I'm sorry.

(FOURTH INTERVIEWER, *a man, appears on the heels of* THIRD INTERVIEWER.)

FOURTH INTERVIEWER: How do you do?

FIRST APPLICANT (*standing*): I'm sorry.

SECOND APPLICANT (*sitting*): Thank you.

THIRD APPLICANT (*standing*): I'm sorry.

FOURTH APPLICANT (*sitting*): Thank you.

ALL INTERVIEWERS: What is your Social Security Number, please?

(*Applicants do the next four speeches simultaneously.*)

FIRST APPLICANT: 333 dash 6598 dash 5590765439 dash 003.

SECOND APPLICANT: 999 dash 5733 dash 699075432 dash 11.

THIRD APPLICANT (*sitting*): I'm sorry. I left it home. I can call if you let me use the phone.

FOURTH APPLICANT: I always get it confused with my Checking Account Number.

(INTERVIEWERS *do the next four speeches in a round.*)

FIRST INTERVIEWER: Will you be so kind as to tell me a little about yourself?

SECOND INTERVIEWER: Can you fill me in on something about your background please?

THIRD INTERVIEWER: It'd be a help to our employers if you'd give me a little for our files.

FOURTH INTERVIEWER: Now what would you say, say, to a prospective employer about yourself?

(APPLICANTS *address parts of the following four speeches, in particular, directly to the audience.*)

FIRST APPLICANT: I've been a Union member twenty years, I said to them, if that's the kind of thing you want to know. Good health, I said. Veteran of two wars. Three kids. Wife's dead. Wife's sister, she takes care of them. I don't know why I'm telling you this, I said smiling. (*Sits.*)

SECOND APPLICANT (*standing*): So what do you want to know, I told the guy. I've been washin' floors for twenty years. Nobody's ever complained. I don't loiter after hours, I said to him. Just because my boy's been in trouble is no reason, I said, no reason — I go right home, I said to him. Right home. (*Sits.*)

THIRD APPLICANT (*standing*): I said that I was a Republican and we could start right there. And then I said that I spend most of my free time watching television or playing in the garden of my four-bedroom house with our two lovely daughters, aged nine and eleven. I mentioned that my wife plays with us too, and that her name is Katherine, although, I said casually, her good friends call her Kitty. I wasn't at all nervous. (*Sits.*)

FOURTH APPLICANT (*standing*): Just because I'm here, sir, I told him, is no reason for you to patronize me. I've been a lady's maid, I said, in houses you would not be allowed into.

My father was a gentleman of leisure, AND what's more, I said, my references are unimpeachable.

FIRST INTERVIEWER: I see.

SECOND INTERVIEWER: All right.

THIRD INTERVIEWER: That's fine.

FOURTH INTERVIEWER: Of course.

(APPLICANTS *do the following four speeches simultaneously.*)

FIRST APPLICANT: Just you call anybody at the Union and ask them. They'll hand me a clean bill of health.

SECOND APPLICANT: I haven't been to jail if that's what you mean. Not me. I'm clean.

THIRD APPLICANT: My record is impeccable. There's not a stain on it.

FOURTH APPLICANT: My references would permit me to be a governess, that's what.

FIRST INTERVIEWER (*going to* FIRST APPLICANT *and inspecting under his arms*): When did you last have a job housepainting?

SECOND INTERVIEWER (*going to* SECOND APPLICANT *and inspecting her teeth*): Where was the last place you worked?

THIRD INTERVIEWER (*going to* THIRD APPLICANT *and inspecting him*): What was your last position in a bank?

FOURTH INTERVIEWER (*going to* FOURTH APPLICANT *and inspecting her*): Have you got your references with you?

(APPLICANTS *do the following four speeches simultaneously, with music under.*)

FIRST APPLICANT: I've already told you I worked right along till I quit.

SECOND APPLICANT: Howard Johnson's on Fifty-first Street all last month.

THIRD APPLICANT: First Greenfield International and Franklin Banking Corporation Banking and Stone Incorporated.

FOURTH APPLICANT: I've got a letter right here

in my bag. Mrs. Muggintwat only let me go because she died.

(INTERVIEWERS *do the next four speeches in a round.*)

FIRST INTERVIEWER (*stepping around and speaking to* SECOND APPLICANT): Nothing terminated your job at Howard Johnson's? No franks, say, missing at the end of the day, I suppose?

SECOND INTERVIEWER (*stepping around and speaking to* THIRD APPLICANT): It goes without saying, I suppose, that you could stand an FBI Security Test?

THIRD INTERVIEWER (*stepping around and speaking to* FOURTH APPLICANT): I suppose there are no records of minor thefts or, shall we say, borrowings from your late employer?

FOURTH INTERVIEWER (*stepping around and speaking to* FIRST APPLICANT): Nothing political in your Union dealings? Nothing Leftist, I suppose? Nothing Rightist either, I hope.

(APPLICANTS *and* INTERVIEWERS *line up for a square dance. Music under the following.*)

FIRST APPLICANT (*bowing to* FIRST INTERVIEWER): What's it to you, buddy?

SECOND APPLICANT (*bowing to* SECOND INTERVIEWER): Eleanor Roosevelt wasn't more honest.

THIRD APPLICANT (*bowing to* THIRD INTERVIEWER): My record is lily-white, sir!

FOURTH APPLICANT (*bowing to* FOURTH INTERVIEWER): Mrs. Thumbletwat used to take me to the bank and I'd watch her open her box!

(*Each* INTERVIEWER, *during his next speech, goes upstage to form another line.*)

FIRST INTERVIEWER: Good!

SECOND INTERVIEWER: Fine!

THIRD INTERVIEWER: Swell!

FOURTH INTERVIEWER: Fine!

(APPLICANTS *come downstage together; they do the next four speeches simultaneously and directly to the audience.*)

FIRST APPLICANT: I know my rights. As a veteran. AND a citizen. I know my rights. AND my cousin is very well-known in certain circles, if you get what I mean. In the back room of a certain candy store in the Italian district of this city my cousin is VERY well known, if you get what I mean. I know my rights. And I know my cousin.

SECOND APPLICANT (*putting on a pious act, looking up to heaven*): Holy Mary Mother of God, must I endure all the sinners of this earth? Must I go on a poor washerwoman in this City of Sin? Help me, oh my God, to leave this earthly crust, and damn your silly impudence, young man, if you think you can treat an old woman like this. You've got another thought coming, you have.

THIRD APPLICANT: I have an excellent notion to report you to the Junior Chamber of Commerce of this city of which I am the Secretary and was in line to be elected Vice President and still will be if you are able to find me gainful and respectable employ!

FOURTH APPLICANT: Miss Thumblebottom married into the Twiths and if you start insulting me, young man, you'll have to start in insulting the Twiths as well. A Twith isn't a nobody, you know, as good as a Thumbletwat AND they all call me their loving Mary, you know.

ALL INTERVIEWERS (*in a loud raucous voice*): Do you smoke?

(*Each* APPLICANT, *during his next speech, turns upstage.*)

FIRST APPLICANT: No thanks.

SECOND APPLICANT: Not now.

THIRD APPLICANT: No thanks.

FOURTH APPLICANT: Not now.

ALL INTERVIEWERS (*again in a harsh voice and bowing or curtsying*): Do you mind if I do?

FIRST APPLICANT: I don't care.

SECOND APPLICANT: Who cares?

THIRD APPLICANT: Course not.

FOURTH APPLICANT: Go ahead.

(INTERVIEWERS *form a little group off to them-selves.*)

FIRST INTERVIEWER: I tried to quit but couldn't manage.

SECOND INTERVIEWER: I'm a three-pack-a-day man, I guess.

THIRD INTERVIEWER: If I'm gonna go I'd rather go smoking.

FOURTH INTERVIEWER: I'm down to five a day.

(APPLICANTS *all start to sneeze.*)

FIRST APPLICANT: Excuse me, I'm gonna sneeze.

SECOND APPLICANT: Have you got a hanky?

THIRD APPLICANT: I have a cold coming on.

FOURTH APPLICANT: I thought I had some tissues in my bag.

(APPLICANTS *all sneeze.*)

FIRST INTERVIEWER: Gesundheit.

SECOND INTERVIEWER: God bless you.

THIRD INTERVIEWER: Gesundheit.

FOURTH INTERVIEWER: God bless you.

(APPLICANTS *all sneeze simultaneously.*)

FIRST INTERVIEWER: God bless you.

SECOND INTERVIEWER: Gesundheit.

THIRD INTERVIEWER: God bless you.

FOURTH INTERVIEWER: Gesundheit.

(APPLICANTS *return to their seats.*)

FIRST APPLICANT: Thanks, I said.

SECOND APPLICANT: I said thanks.

THIRD APPLICANT: Thank you, I said.

FOURTH APPLICANT: I said thank you.

(INTERVIEWERS *stand on their seats and say the following as if one person were speaking.*)

FIRST INTERVIEWER: Do you

SECOND INTERVIEWER: speak any

THIRD INTERVIEWER: foreign

FOURTH INTERVIEWER: languages?

FIRST INTERVIEWER: Have you

SECOND INTERVIEWER: got a

THIRD INTERVIEWER: college

FOURTH INTERVIEWER: education?

FIRST INTERVIEWER: Do you

SECOND INTERVIEWER: take

THIRD INTERVIEWER: shorthand?

FOURTH INTERVIEWER: Have you

FIRST INTERVIEWER: any

SECOND INTERVIEWER: special

THIRD INTERVIEWER: qualifications?

FIRST INTERVIEWER: Yes?

FIRST APPLICANT (*stepping up to* INTERVIEWERS): Sure, I can speak Italian, I said. My whole family is Italian so I oughta be able to, and I can match colors, like green to green, so that even your own mother couldn't tell the difference, begging your pardon, I said, I went through the eighth grade. (*Steps back.*)

SECOND INTERVIEWER: Next.

SECOND APPLICANT (*stepping up to* INTER-VIEWERS): My grandmother taught me some Gaelic, I told the guy. And my old man could rattle off in Yiddish when he had a load on. I never went to school at all excepting church school, but I can write my name good and clear. Also, I said, I can smell an Irishman or a Yid a hundred miles off. (*Steps back.*)

THIRD INTERVIEWER: Next.

THIRD APPLICANT (*stepping up to* INTER-VIEWERS): I've never had any need to take shorthand in my position, I said to him. I've a Z.A. in business administration from Philadelphia, and a Z.Z.A. from M.Y.U. night school. I mentioned that I speak a little Spanish, of course, and that I'm a whiz at model frigates and warships. (*Steps back.*)

FOURTH INTERVIEWER: Next.

FOURTH APPLICANT (*stepping up to* INTER-

VIEWERS): I can sew a straight seam, I said, hand or machine, and I have been exclusively a lady's maid although I CAN cook and will too if I have someone to assist me, I said. Unfortunately, aside from self-education, grammar school is as far as I have progressed. (*Steps back.*)

(*Each* INTERVIEWER, *during his next speech, bows or curtsies to the* APPLICANT *nearest him.*)

FIRST INTERVIEWER: Good.

SECOND INTERVIEWER: Fine.

THIRD INTERVIEWER: Very helpful.

FOURTH INTERVIEWER: Thank you.

(*Each* APPLICANT, *during his next speech, jumps on the back of the* INTERVIEWER *nearest him.*)

FOURTH APPLICANT: You're welcome, I'm sure.

THIRD APPLICANT: Anything you want to know.

SECOND APPLICANT: Just ask me.

FIRST APPLICANT: Fire away, fire away.

(*The next eight speeches are spoken simultaneously, with* APPLICANTS *on* INTERVIEWERS' *backs.*)

FIRST INTERVIEWER: Well unless there's anything special you want to tell me, I think —

SECOND INTERVIEWER: Is there anything more you think I should know about before you —

THIRD INTERVIEWER: I wonder if we've left anything out of this questionnaire or if you —

FOURTH INTERVIEWER: I suppose I've got all the information down here unless you can —

FIRST APPLICANT: I've got kids to support, you know, and I need a job real quick —

SECOND APPLICANT: Do you think you could try and get me something today because I —

THIRD APPLICANT: How soon do you suppose I can expect to hear from your agency? Do you —

FOURTH APPLICANT: I don't like to sound pressureful, but you know I'm currently on unemploy —

(*Each* APPLICANT, *during his next speech, jumps off* INTERVIEWER's *back.*)

FIRST APPLICANT: Beggin' your pardon.

SECOND APPLICANT: So sorry.

THIRD APPLICANT: Excuse me.

FOURTH APPLICANT: Go ahead.

(*Each* INTERVIEWER, *during his next speech, bows or curtsies and remains in that position.*)

FIRST INTERVIEWER: That's quite all right.

SECOND INTERVIEWER: I'm sorry.

THIRD INTERVIEWER: I'm sorry.

FOURTH INTERVIEWER: My fault.

(*Each* APPLICANT, *during his next speech, begins leap-frogging over* INTERVIEWERS' *backs.*)

FIRST APPLICANT: My fault.

SECOND APPLICANT: My fault.

THIRD APPLICANT: I'm sorry.

FOURTH APPLICANT: My fault.

(*Each* INTERVIEWER, *during his next speech, begins leap-frogging too.*)

FIRST INTERVIEWER: That's all right.

SECOND INTERVIEWER: My fault.

THIRD INTERVIEWER: I'm sorry.

FOURTH INTERVIEWER: Excuse me.

(*The leap-frogging continues as the preceding eight lines are repeated simultaneously. Then the* INTERVIEWERS *confer in a huddle and come out of it.*)

FIRST INTERVIEWER: Do you enjoy your work?

FIRST APPLICANT: Sure, I said, I'm proud. Why not? Sure I know I'm no Rembrandt, I said, but I'm proud of my work, I said to him.

SECOND APPLICANT: I told him it stinks. But what am I supposed to do, sit home and rot?

THIRD APPLICANT: Do I like my work, he asked

me. Well, I said, to gain time, do I like my work? Well, I said, I don't know.

FOURTH APPLICANT: I told him right straight out: for a sensible person, a lady's maid is the ONLY POSSIBLE way of life.

SECOND INTERVIEWER: Do you think you're irreplaceable?

ALL APPLICANTS: Oh, yes indeed.

ALL INTERVIEWERS: Irreplaceable?

ALL APPLICANTS: Yes, yes indeed.

THIRD INTERVIEWER: Do you like me?

FIRST APPLICANT: You're a nice man.

SECOND APPLICANT: Huh?

THIRD APPLICANT: Why do you ask?

FOURTH APPLICANT: It's not a question of LIKE.

FIRST INTERVIEWER: Well, we'll be in touch with you.

(*This is the beginning of leaving the agency. Soft music under.* APPLICANTS *and* INTERVIEWERS *push their seats into two masses of four boxes, one on each side of the stage.* APPLICANTS *leave first, joining hands to form a revolving door.*
All are now leaving the agency, not in any orderly fashion. INTERVIEWERS *start down one of the subway stairs at the back of the stage and* APPLICANTS *start down the other. The following speeches overlap and are heard indistinctly as crowd noise.*)

FOURTH INTERVIEWER: What sort of day will it be?

FIRST APPLICANT: I bet we'll have rain.

SECOND APPLICANT: Cloudy, clearing in the afternoon.

THIRD APPLICANT: Mild, I think, with some snow.

FOURTH APPLICANT: Precisely the same as yesterday.

SECOND APPLICANT: Can you get me one?

FIRST INTERVIEWER: See you tomorrow.

THIRD APPLICANT: When will I hear from you?

SECOND INTERVIEWER: We'll let you know.

FOURTH APPLICANT: Where's my umbrella?

THIRD INTERVIEWER: I'm going to a movie.

FIRST APPLICANT: So how about it?

FOURTH INTERVIEWER: Good night.

THIRD APPLICANT: Can you help me, Doctor, I asked.

(*When all of the actors are offstage, the* FOURTH INTERVIEWER *makes a siren sound and the following speeches continue from downstairs as a loud crowd noise for a few moments; they overlap so that the stage is empty only briefly.*)

FIRST INTERVIEWER: It'll take a lot of work on your part.

SECOND INTERVIEWER: I'll do what I can for you.

THIRD INTERVIEWER: Of course I'll do my best.

FIRST INTERVIEWER: God helps those who help themselves.

FIRST APPLICANT: I have sinned deeply, Father, I said.

FIRST INTERVIEWER: You certainly have. I hope you truly repent.

SECOND INTERVIEWER: In the name of the Father, etcetera, and the Holy Ghost.

THIRD INTERVIEWER: Jesus saves.

FOURTH APPLICANT: I said can you direct me to Fourteenth Street, please?

FIRST INTERVIEWER: Just walk down that way a bit and then turn left.

SECOND INTERVIEWER: Just walk down that way a bit and then turn right.

THIRD INTERVIEWER: Take a cab!

FOURTH APPLICANT: Do you hear a siren?

ALL INTERVIEWERS: What time is it?

FIRST APPLICANT: Half-past three.

SECOND APPLICANT: It must be about four.

THIRD APPLICANT: Half-past five.

FOURTH APPLICANT: My watch has stopped.

FIRST INTERVIEWER: Do you enjoy your work?

SECOND INTERVIEWER: Do you think you're irreplaceable?

THIRD INTERVIEWER: Do you like me?

(*The actor who played the* FOURTH INTERVIEWER *comes on stage while continuing to make the loud siren noise. The actress who played the* FOURTH APPLICANT *comes on stage and speaks directly to the audience.*)

FOURTH APPLICANT: Can you direct me to Fourteenth Street, please, I said. I seem to have lost my — I started to say, and then I was nearly run down.

(*The remaining actors return to the stage to play various people on Fourteenth Street: ladies shopping, a panhandler, a man in a sandwich board, a peddler of "franks and orange," a snooty German couple, a lecher, a pair of sighing lovers, and so on. The actors walk straight forward toward the audience and then walk backwards to the rear of the stage. Each time they approach the audience, they do so as a different character. The actor will need to find the essential vocal and physical mannerisms of each character, play them, and help them immediately to assume another character. The* FOURTH APPLICANT *continues to address the audience directly, to involve them in her hysteria, going up the aisle and back.*)

FOURTH APPLICANT: I haven't got my Social Security — I started to say, I saw someone right in front of me and I said, could you direct me please to Fourteenth Street, I have to get to Fourteenth Street, please, to get a bargain, I explained, although I could hardly remember what it was I wanted to buy. I read about it in the paper today, I said, only they weren't listening and I said to myself, my purpose for today is to get to — and I couldn't remember, I've set myself the task of — I've got to have — it's that I can save, I remembered, I can save if I can get that bargain at — and I couldn't remember where it was so I started to look for my wallet which I seem to have mislaid in my purse, and a man — please watch where you're

going, I shouted with my purse half-open, and I seemed to forget — Fourteenth Street, I remembered, and you'd think with all these numbered streets and avenues a person wouldn't get lost — you'd think a person would HELP a person, you'd think so. So I asked the most respectable looking man I could find, I asked him, please can you direct me to Fourteenth Street. He wouldn't answer. Just wouldn't. I'm lost, I said to myself. The paper said — the television said — they said, I couldn't remember what they said. I turned for help: "Jesus Saves" the sign said, and a man was carrying it, both sides of his body, staring straight ahead. "Jesus Saves" the sign said.

(*The passers-by jostle her more and more.*)

FOURTH APPLICANT: I couldn't remember where I was going. "Come and be saved" it said, so I asked the man with the sign, please, sir, won't you tell me how to, dear Lord, I thought, anywhere, please, sir, won't you tell me how to — can you direct me to Fourteenth Street, PLEASE!

(*The passers-by have covered the* FOURTH APPLICANT. *All actors mill about until they reach designated positions on the stage where they face the audience, a line of women and a line of men, students in a gym class. The* SECOND INTERVIEWER *has stayed coolly out of the crowd during this last; now he is the Gym Instructor.*)

GYM INSTRUCTOR: I took my last puff and strode resolutely into the room. Ready men, I asked brightly. And one and two and three and four and one and two and keep it up.

(*The* GYM INSTRUCTOR *is trying to help his students mold themselves into the kind of people seen in advertisements and the movies. As he counts to four the students puff out their chests, smile, and look perfectly charming. As he counts to four again, the students relax and look ordinary.*)

GYM INSTRUCTOR: You wanna look like the guys in the movies, don't you, I said to the fellahs. Keep it up then. You wanna radiate that kinda charm and confidence they have in the movies, don't you, I said to the girls.

Keep it up then, stick 'em out, that's what you got 'em for. Don't be ashamed. All of you, tuck in your butts, I said loudly. That's the ticket, I said, wishing to hell I had a cigarette. You're selling, selling all the time, that right, miss? Keep on selling, I said. And one and two and three and four and ever see that guy on TV, I said. What's his name, I asked them. What's his name? Aw, you know his name, I said, forgetting his name. Never mind, it'll come to you, I said. He comes in here too. See that, I said, grabbing a guy out of line and showing 'em his muscle. See that line, I said, making the guy feel good, know what that is? It's boyishness, I said. You come here, I said, throwing him back into the line, and it'll renew your youthfulness, I said, taking a deep breath. And one and two and three and four and smile, I said, smiling. Not so big, I said, smiling less. You look like creeps, I said, when you smile that big. When you smile, hold something back. Make like you're holding back something big, I said, a secret, I said. That's the ticket. And one and two and three and four and . . . (*Accelerating the rhythm to a double count.*) Anybody got a cigarette, I said suddenly, without thinking. I was just kidding, I said then, sheepishly. One and two and three and four, I said, wishing I had a cigarette. And one and two and three and four . . .

(*The rapid movements of the gym class become the vibrations of passengers on a moving subway train. The actors rush to the boxes stage left, continuing to vibrate. Two of the actors stand on the boxes and smile like subway advertisements while the others, directly in front of them, are pushed against each other on the crowded train. They make an appropriate soft subway noise, a kind of rhythmic hiss and, as the subway passengers, form their faces into frozen masks of indifference.*)

SECOND APPLICANT (*squeezing her way to an uncomfortable front seat and speaking half to herself*): God forgive me . . . you no-good chump, I said to him, I used to love you . . . not now. Not now . . . God forgive me . . . God forgive me for being old. Not now, I

said. I wouldn't wipe the smell off your uncle's bottom now, not for turnips, no. God forgive me . . . Remember how we used to ride the roller coaster out at Coney Island, you and me? Remember? Holding hands in the cold and I'd get so scared and you'd get so scared and we'd hug each other and buy another ticket . . . Remember? . . . Look now, I said. Look at me now! God forgive you for leaving me with nothing . . . God forgive you for being dead . . . God forgive me for being alive . . .

(*The actress who played the* THIRD INTERVIEWER *slips out of the subway as though it were her stop and sits on a box, stage right, as a* TELEPHONE OPERATOR. *The other actors form a telephone circuit by holding hands in two concentric circles around the boxes, stage left; they change the hissing sound of the subway into the whistling of telephone circuits.*)

TELEPHONE OPERATOR: Just one moment and I will connect you with Information.

(*The* TELEPHONE OPERATOR *alternates her official voice with her ordinary voice; she uses the latter when she talks to her friend Roberta, another operator whom she reaches by flipping a switch. When she is talking to Roberta, the whistling of the telephone circuit changes into a different rhythm and the arms of the actors, which are forming the circuit, move into a different position.*)

TELEPHONE OPERATOR: Just one moment and I will connect you with Information. Ow! Listen, Roberta, I said, I've got this terrible cramp. Hang up and dial again, please; we find nothing wrong with that number at all. You know what I ate, I said to her, you were there. Baked macaroni, Wednesday special, maple-nut fudge, I said. I'm sorry but the number you have reached is not — I can feel it gnawing at me at the bottom of my belly, I told her. Do you think it's serious, Roberta? Appendicitis? I asked. Thank you for giving us the area code but the number you have reached is not in this area. Roberta, I asked her, do you think I have cancer? One moment, please, I'm sorry the number you have reached — ow! Well, if it's lunch,

Roberta, I said to her, you know what they can do with it tomorrow. Ow! One moment, please, I said. Ow, I said, Roberta, I said, it really hurts.

(*The* TELEPHONE OPERATOR *falls off her seat in pain. The whistling of the telephone circuit becomes a siren. Three actors carry the* TELEPHONE OPERATOR *over to the boxes, stage left, which now serve as an operating table. Three actors imitate the* TELEPHONE OPERATOR'S *breathing pattern while four actors behind her make stylized sounds and movements as surgeons and nurses in the midst of an operation. The* TELEPHONE OPERATOR'S *breathing accelerates, then stops. After a moment the actors begin spreading over the stage and making the muted sounds of a cocktail party: music, laughter, talk. The actors find a position and remain there, playing various aspects of a party in slow motion and muted tones. They completely ignore the* FIRST INTERVIEWER *who, as a* GIRL AT THE PARTY, *goes from person to person as if she were in a garden of living statues.*)

GIRL AT THE PARTY (*rapidly and excitedly*): And then after the ambulance took off I went up in the elevator and into the party. Did you see the accident, I asked, and they said they did, and what did he look like, and I said he wore a brown coat and had straight brown hair. He stepped off the curb right in front of me. We had been walking up the same block, he a few feet ahead of me, this block right here, I said, but she wasn't listening. Hi, my name is Jill, I said to somebody sitting down and they looked at me and smiled so I said his arm was torn out of its socket and his face was on the pavement gasping but I didn't touch him and she smiled and walked away and I said after her, you aren't supposed to touch someone before — I WANTED to help, I said, but she wasn't listening. When a man came up and said was it someone you knew and I said yes, it was someone I knew slightly, someone I knew, yes, and he offered me a drink and I said no thanks, I didn't want one, and he said well how well did I know him, and I said I knew him well, yes, I knew him very well. You were coming together to the party,

he said. Yes, I said, excuse me. Hi, my name is Jill, did you hear a siren, and they said oh you're the one who saw it, was he killed? (*Becoming resigned to the fact that no one is listening.*) And I said yes I was, excuse me, and went back across the room but couldn't find another face to talk to until I deliberately bumped into somebody because I had to tell them one of us couldn't come because of the accident. It was Jill. Jill couldn't come. I'm awfully sorry, I said, because of the accident. She had straight brown hair, I said, and was wearing a brown coat, and two or three people looked at me strangely and moved off. I'm sorry, I said to a man, and I laughed, and moved off. I'm dead, I said to several people and started to push them over, I'm dead, thank you, I said, thank you, please, I said, I'm dead, until two or three of them got hold of my arms and hustled me out. I'm sorry, I said, I couldn't come because of the accident. I'm sorry. Excuse me.

(*The* GIRL AT THE PARTY *is lowered to the floor by two of the men and then all fall down except the actor who played the* FOURTH INTERVIEWER. *He remains seated as a* PSYCHIATRIST. *The* THIRD APPLICANT, *on the floor, props his head up on his elbow and speaks to the audience.*)

THIRD APPLICANT: Can you help me, Doctor, I asked him.

(*The* PSYCHIATRIST *crosses his legs and assumes a professional expression.*)

THIRD APPLICANT: Well, it started, well it started, I said, when I was sitting in front of the television set with my feet on the coffee table. Now I've sat there hundreds of times, thousands maybe, with a can of beer in my hand. I like to have a can of beer in my hand when I watch the beer ads. But now for no reason I can think of, the ad was making me sick. So I used the remote control to get to another channel, but each channel made me just as sick. The television was one thing and I was a person, and I was going to be sick. So I turned it off and had a panicky moment. I smelled the beer in my hand and as I vomited I looked around the living room for something to grab on to, something to look at, but there was just our new furniture. I tried to get a hold of myself. I tried to stare straight ahead above the television set, at a little spot on the wall I know. I've had little moments like that before, Doctor, I said, panicky little moments like that when the earth seems to slip out from under, and everything whirls around and you try to hold onto something, some object, some thought, but I couldn't think of anything. Later the panic went away, I told him, it went away, and I'm much better now. But I don't feel like doing anything anymore, except sit and stare at the wall. I've lost my job. Katherine thought I should come and see you. Can you help me, Doctor, I asked him.

PSYCHIATRIST:
Blah, blah, blah, blah, blah, blah, HOSTILE.
Blah, blah, blah, blah, blah, blah, PENIS.
Blah, blah, blah, blah, blah, blah, MOTHER.
(*Holding out his hand.*)
Blah, blah, blah, blah, blah, blah, MONEY.

(*The* THIRD APPLICANT *takes the* PSYCHIATRIST'S *hand and gets up, extending his left hand to the next actor. This begins a grand right and left with all the actors all over the stage.*)

ALL (*chanting as they do the grand right and left*):
Blah, blah, blah, blah, blah, blah, HOSTILE.
Blah, blah, blah, blah, blah, blah, PENIS.
Blah, blah, blah, blah, blah, blah, MOTHER.
Blah, blah, blah, blah, blah, blah, MONEY.
Blah, blah, blah, blah, blah, blah, HOSTILE.
Blah, blah, blah, blah, blah, blah, PENIS.
Blah, blah, blah, blah, blah, blah, MOTHER.
Blah, blah, blah, blah, blah, blah, MONEY.

(*Forming couples and locking hands with arms crossed, continuing to move, but in a smaller circle.*)

Blah, blah, blah, blah, blah, blah, blah.
Blah, blah, blah, blah, blah, blah, blah.

(*Now they slow down to the speed of a church procession. The women bow their heads, letting their hair fall forward over their faces. The "blah, blah, blah" continues, but much more slowly while some of the women accompany*

it with a descant of "Kyrie Eleison." After they have gone around in a circle once this way, the actor who played the FOURTH INTERVIEWER sits with his back to the audience as a Priest. The FIRST APPLICANT kneels next to him, facing the audience as if in a confessional booth. The other six actors are at the back of the stage in two lines, swaying slightly, heads down. The women are in front with their hair still over their faces.*)

FIRST APPLICANT (*crosses himself perfunctorily and starting to speak; his manner is not impassioned; it is clear that he comes regularly to repeat this always fruitless ritual*): Can you help me, Father, I said, as I usually do, and he said, as usual, nothing. I'm your friend, the housepainter, I said, the good housepainter. Remember me, Father? He continued, as usual, to say nothing. Almost the only color you get to paint these days, Father, I said, is white. Only white, Father, I said, not expecting any more from him than usual, but going on anyway. The color I really like to paint, Father, is red, I said. Pure brick red. Now there's a confession, Father. He said nothing. I'd like to take a trip to the country, Father, I said, and paint a barn door red, thinking that would get a rise out of him, but it didn't. God, I said then, deliberately taking the Lord's name in vain, the result of taking a three-inch brush and lightly kissing a coat of red paint on a barn door is something stunning and beautiful to behold. He still said nothing. Father, I said, springing it on him, Father, I'd like to join a monastery. My wife's sister, she could take care of the kids. Still nothing. Father, I said again, I'd like to join a monastery. Can you help me, Father? Nothing. Father, I said, I've tried lots of things in my life, I've gone in a lot of different directions, Father, and none of them seems any better than any other, Father, I said. Can you help me, Father, I said. But he said nothing as usual, and then, as usual, I went away.

(*The* FIRST APPLICANT *and the* FOURTH INTERVIEWER, *who haven't moved at all during the confession, move upstage to join the others as the music starts up violently in a rock beat.*

The actors do a rock version of the Virginia reel.)

SECOND INTERVIEWER (*loudly*): My

(*All bow to partners.*)

FOURTH APPLICANT (*loudly*): fault.

(*All dos-à-dos.*)

SECOND APPLICANT (*loudly*): Excuse

(*All circle around.*)

FOURTH INTERVIEWER (*loudly*): me.

(*All peel off.*)

FIRST INTERVIEWER (*loudly*): Can you

SECOND APPLICANT (*loudly*): help

FIRST APPLICANT: me?

FOURTH INTERVIEWER (*loudly*): Next.

(*All continue dancing, joining hands at the center to form a revolving door again. They repeat the preceding eight speeches. Then the SECOND INTERVIEWER speaks rapidly, as a SQUARE DANCE CALLER.*)

SQUARE DANCE CALLER: Step right up, ladies and gents, and shake the hand of the next governor of this state. Shake his hand and say hello. Tell your friends you shook the hand of the next governor of the state. Step right up and shake his hand. Ask him questions. Tell him problems. Say hello. Step right up, shake his hand, shake the hand, ladies and gents, of the next governor of the state. Tell your folks: I shook his hand. When he's famous you'll be proud. Step right up, ladies and gents, and shake his hand. Ask him questions. Tell him problems. Say hello. Step right up, ladies and gents. Don't be shy. Shake the hand of the next governor of this state.

(*The actors have formed a crowd, downstage right, facing the audience. They give the impression of being but a few of a great number of people, all trying to squeeze to the front to see and speak to the political candidate. The FOURTH INTERVIEWER, now a POLITICIAN, stands on a box, stage left, facing the audience. The SECOND INTERVIEWER stands by the crowd and keeps it in order.*)

POLITICIAN: Thank you very much, I said cheerfully, and good luck to you, I said, turning my smile to the next one.

(*The FIRST INTERVIEWER, panting as the GIRL AT THE PARTY, squeezes out of the crowd and rushes up to the POLITICIAN, who smiles at her benignly.*)

POLITICIAN: Our children ARE our most important asset, I agreed earnestly. Yes they are, I said solemnly. Children, I said, with a long pause, are our most important asset. I only wish I could, madame, I said earnestly, standing tall, but rats, I said regretfully, are a city matter.

(*The FIRST INTERVIEWER returns to the crowd while the THIRD INTERVIEWER, as the TELEPHONE OPERATOR, rushes up to the POLITICIAN. She appeals to him, making the same noise she made when her stomach hurt her.*)

POLITICIAN: Nobody knows more about red tape than I do, I said knowingly, and I wish you luck, I said, turning my smile to the next one.

(*The THIRD INTERVIEWER returns to the crowd and the FOURTH APPLICANT goes up to the POLITICIAN.*)

POLITICIAN: I certainly will, I said, with my eyes sparkling, taking a pencil out of my pocket. And what's your name, I said, looking at her sweetly and signing my name at the same time. That's a lovely name, I said.

(*The FOURTH APPLICANT returns to the crowd while the THIRD APPLICANT, as an OLDER MAN, shakes the POLITICIAN's hand.*)

POLITICIAN: Yes sir, I said, those were the days. And good luck to you, sir, I said respectfully but heartily, and look out for the curb, I said, turning my smile to the next one.

(*The THIRD APPLICANT returns to the crowd and the SECOND APPLICANT approaches the POLITICIAN.*)

POLITICIAN: Indeed yes, the air we breathe IS foul, I said indignantly. I agree with you entirely, I said wholeheartedly. And if my opponent wins it's going to get worse, I said with conviction. We'd all die within ten years, I said. And good luck to you, madame, I said politely, and turned my smile to the next one.

(*The* FIRST APPLICANT *approaches him, his cap in his hand.*)

POLITICIAN: Well, I said confidingly, getting a bill through the legislature is easier said than done, and answering violence, I said warningly, with violence, I said earnestly, is not the answer, and how do you do, I said, turning my smile to the next one.

(*Next, two* SIGHING LOVERS — *we saw them on Fourteenth Street — played by the* FIRST *and* SECOND INTERVIEWERS, *approach the* POLITICIAN.)

POLITICIAN: No, I said, I never said my opponent would kill us all. No, I said, I never said that. May the best man win, I said manfully.

(*Half-hearted cheers. The* FIRST *and* SECOND INTERVIEWERS *return to the crowd.*)

POLITICIANS: I do feel, I said without false modesty, that I'm better qualified in the field of foreign affairs than my opponents are, yes, I said, BUT, I said, with a pause for emphasis, foreign policy is the business of the President, not the Governor, therefore I will say nothing about the war, I said with finality.

(*The crowd makes a restive sound, then freezes.*)

POLITICIAN: Do you want us shaking hands, I asked the photographer, turning my profile to the left. Goodbye, I said cheerfully, and good luck to you too.

(*The crowd makes a louder protest, then freezes.*)

POLITICIAN: I'm sorry, I said seriously, but I'll have to study that question a good deal more before I can answer it.

(*The crowd makes an angry noise, then freezes.*)

POLITICIAN: Of course, I said frowning, we must all support the President, I said as I turned concernedly to the next one.

(*The crowd makes a very angry sound, then freezes.*)

POLITICIAN: I'm sorry about the war, I said. Nobody could be sorrier than I am, I said sorrowfully. But I'm afraid, I said gravely, that there are no easy answers. (*Smiles, pleased with himself.*) Good luck to you too, I said cheerfully, and turned my smile to the next one.

(*The* POLITICIAN *topples from his box, beginning his speech all over again. Simultaneously, all the other actors lurch about the stage, speaking again in character: the* SHOPPER ON FOURTEENTH STREET, *the* GYM INSTRUCTOR, *the* SUBWAY RIDER, *the* TELEPHONE OPERATOR, *the* GIRL AT THE PARTY, *the* ANALYSAND, *and the* HOUSEPAINTER. *Simultaneously, they all stop and freeze, continue again, freeze again, then continue with music under. The* SECOND INTERVIEWER, *acting as policeman, begins to line them up in a diagonal line, like marching dolls, one behind the other. As they are put into line they begin to move their mouths without sound, like fish in a tank. The music stops. When all are in line the* SECOND INTERVIEWER *joins them.*)

SECOND INTERVIEWER: My

FOURTH APPLICANT: fault.

SECOND APPLICANT: Excuse

FOURTH INTERVIEWER: me.

FIRST INTERVIEWER: Can you

SECOND APPLICANT: help

FIRST APPLICANT: me?

FOURTH INTERVIEWER: Next.

(*All continue marching in place, moving their mouths, and shouting their lines as the lights come slowly down.*)

SECOND INTERVIEWER: My

FOURTH APPLICANT: fault.

SECOND APPLICANT: Excuse

FOURTH INTERVIEWER: me.

FIRST INTERVIEWER: Can you

SECOND APPLICANT: help?

FIRST APPLICANT: me?

FOURTH INTERVIEWER: Next.

TV

The youth Narcissus mistook his own reflection in the water for another person . . . He was numb. He had adapted to his extension of himself and had become a closed system.

Marshall McLuhan

CAST

HAL
SUSAN
GEORGE
An Actress plays HELEN FARGIS, THE PRESIDENT'S WIFE, a UGP RESEARCHER, a MEMBER OF THE ROCK AND ROLL GROUP, a PEACE MARCHER, LILY HEAVEN, THE HEADACHE SUFFERER, a SINGER IN THE EVANGELIST CHOIR, and MOTHER in "My Favorite Teenager"
An Actor plays HARRY FARGIS, FIRST NEWS ANNOUNCER, STEVE, THE PRESIDENT, a UGP RESEARCHER, a MEMBER OF THE ROCK AND ROLL GROUP, WEATHER ANNOUNCER, HE in the Billion Dollar Movie, EVANGELIST, and FATHER in "My Favorite Teenager"
An Actor plays WONDERBOY, SECOND NEWS ANNOUNCER, THE MAN IN THE CIGARETTE COMMERCIAL, BILL, UGP ANNOUNCER, a MEMBER OF THE ROCK AND ROLL GROUP, ONE YOUNG MAN FROM NEW YORK CITY, LILY HEAVEN'S ANNOUNCER, RON CAMPBELL, JOHNNY HOLLAND, and a SINGER IN THE EVANGELIST CHOIR
An Actress plays THE WOMAN IN THE CIGARETTE COMMERCIAL, THE PRESIDENT'S OLDER DAUGHTER, a UGP RESEARCHER, a MEMBER OF THE ROCK AND ROLL GROUP, a PEACE MARCHER, FAMOUS TELEVISION PERSONALITY, CAROL, SHE in the Billion Dollar Movie, and a SINGER IN THE EVANGELIST CHOIR

An Actress plays SALLY, THE PRESIDENT'S YOUNGER DAUGHTER, THE SPANISH TEACHER, a UGP RESEARCHER, a MEMBER OF THE ROCK AND ROLL GROUP, ANNIE KAPPELHOFF, LADY ANNOUNCER, LUCI, a SINGER IN THE EVANGELIST CHOIR, and DAUGHTER in "My Favorite Teenager"

The set is white and impersonal. There are two doors on the stage right wall: one leads to the rest rooms, the other to the hall.
Downstage right is the control console in a television viewing room. It faces the audience. Above the console, also facing the audience, is a screen. Projected on it, from the rear, is the logo of a television station.
Downstage left is a water cooler, a closet for coats, and a telephone. Downstage right is a bulletin board. Upstage center is a table with a coffee maker on it.
HAL and SUSAN are seated at the console, SUSAN in the middle chair. They are both in their twenties. HAL is playing, as he often will, with his penknife: whittling pencils, paring his nails, or throwing it at the bulletin board. SUSAN is involved with the papers on the console, with sharpening pencils, and so forth.
At the back of the stage, on the left, are the five actors who will portray what will appear on television. For the moment they have no light on them and their backs are to the audience.
To indicate the correlation of the events and dialogue on television with those which occur in the viewing room, the play is printed in two columns.

HAL: So what do you say?

SUSAN: I don't know.

HAL: That doesn't get us very far, does it?

SUSAN: Well it's such a surprise, your asking. I was planning to work on my apartment.

HAL: I'll help you, after the movie.

SUSAN: That's too late. One thing I have to have is eight hours' sleep. I really have to have that.

(GEORGE *enters: he is older than* HAL *and* SUSAN, *and is in charge of the viewing room.*)

HAL: Hi, George.

SUSAN: Hello, George.

GEORGE (*to* SUSAN): Is that a new dress?

SUSAN (*nodding toward* HAL): He didn't even notice.

(GEORGE *puts his coat and jacket in the closet and puts on a cardigan sweater.*)

GEORGE: How many check marks have you made, Hal?

HAL: I don't know, George. I don't count.

SUSAN: I got it on Fourteenth Street. I love going into places like that because they're so cheap.

GEORGE: If you don't make at least a hundred check marks, they'll dock you. That's what the totals count column is for.

SUSAN (*looking at herself in a mirror*): Have I lost any weight?

GEORGE: Where would you lose it from?

HAL: George, how come they haven't asked us for a detailed report in nearly three weeks?

GEORGE: How should I know?

HAL: Think they're forgetting about us, George?

SUSAN: I was trying to tell in the Ladies, but the fluorescent light in there just burns your eyes.

HAL: I've never been to the Ladies. You think I'd like it?

GEORGE: This viewing room is the backbone of the rating system.

HAL: He said that to you LAST month, George. Things move fast.

GEORGE: Are you trying to make me nervous?

HAL: Maybe.

GEORGE: Well don't, because my stomach is not very good this morning.

SUSAN: I want to know seriously, and I mean seriously, do you think I've lost any weight?

GEORGE: Where from?

HAL: Why don't you let yourself go?

SUSAN: What do you mean?

HAL: Just let nature take its course.

SUSAN: What if nature wants you to be a big fat slob?

HAL: Then be a big fat slob.

SUSAN: Thanks.

HAL, SUSAN, *and* GEORGE *sit down and get ready for the day's work.* GEORGE *turns a dial on the console which turns on TV. Two of the People On Television turn around to play* HELEN *and* HARRY FARGIS.
All of the People On Television are dressed in shades of gray. They make no costume changes and use no real props. Their faces are made up with thin horizontal black lines to suggest the way they might appear to a viewer. They are playing television images. Their style of acting is cool, not pushy. As television characters, they have only a few facial masks, such as "cute," "charming," or "serious," which they use infallibly, like signals, in the course of each television segment.
After each television segment, the People involved in it will freeze where they are until it is time for them to become another character.
As the play progresses, the People On Television will use more and more of the stage. The

impressions should be that of a slow invasion of the viewing room. HAL, SUSAN, *and* GEORGE *will simply move around the People On Television when that becomes necessary. Ultimately, the control console itself will be taken over by television characters, so that the distinction between what is on television and what is occurring in the viewing room will be lost completely.*
The attention of the audience should be focused not on a parody of television, but on the relationship of the life that appears on television to the life that goes on in the viewing room.
All of the actors will need to be constantly aware of what is happening on all parts of the stage, in order to give and take the attention of the audience to and from each other, and also in order to demonstrate the influence of the style of certain television segments on the behavior of HAL, SUSAN, *and* GEORGE.)

HAL: Why try to look like somebody else?

(*Slide on screen: Wonderboy's face.*)

(HELEN *and* HARRY FARGIS *are at home.* HELEN *is baking cookies.*)

HELEN: Harry, what are you working on in the garage?

SUSAN: I'm trying to look like myself, thin. Very thin.

HAL (*offering him one*): Want a cigarette, George?

GEORGE: No, thanks.

HAL: Just one?

GEORGE: No.

SUSAN: Hal, why don't you try to help George instead of being so cruel?

HAL: I'm just offering him a cigarette.

GEORGE (*as* HAL *takes the cigarette away*): Give me one.

SUSAN: Hal, that's utter torture for George.

GEORGE: Give me one.

SUSAN: Don't, George. He's just playing cat and mouse.

HAL: That's right, George. Don't have one. I'm just playing cat and mouse.

(*Lights a cigarette.*)

GEORGE: Just give it to me, will you?

SUSAN: Try to control yourself for just another half hour, George.

HARRY: If I succeed in my experiments, nobody in the world will be hungry for love. Ever again.

HELEN: Hungry for love? Harry, you make me nervous.

HELEN: You really do.

HARRY: Men will put down their arms.

HELEN: You haven't been to work for a week now. You'll lose your job.

HARRY: You don't understand. This is more important.

HELEN: Oh, Harry. I don't understand you at all any more. I really don't.

(HARRY *goes back to the garage.* HELEN *mumbles to herself as she cleans up the kitchen.*)

HELEN: I don't know.

HELEN: I just don't know. He used to be so docile.

HELEN: And now I just don't know —

HARRY (*calling from garage*): Helen!

HELEN: Harry?

HARRY: Helen, my experiments.

HELEN: Harry, what?

HARRY: A terrible mistake.

HELEN: Harry, your voice —

GEORGE: No.

SUSAN: Why not?

GEORGE: Because I don't wanna control myself for just another half hour.

HAL: Whatever you want, George.

(*Hands a cigarette to* GEORGE.)

SUSAN: What was the point of that, Hal?

HAL: No point.

HARRY (*his voice getting lower and gruffer*): For the love of heaven, Helen, keep away from me.

HELEN: What happened?

HARRY: I can't restrain myself anymore. I'm coming through the garage door. (*Comes through the garage door, wearing a monster mask; his voice is now very deep and gruff.*) I'm irresistibly attracted to you, Helen, irresistibly.

HELEN: Eeeeeeeeeeeeeeeeeeeek!

HARRY (*stepping toward her*): Helen, I love you. (*Goes to embrace her.*)

HELEN: Harry, you're hideous. Eeeeek! Eeeeeeeeeeeeek! Eeeeeeeeeeeeek!

(*As* HELEN *screams,* WONDERBOY *is discovered, in mufti, doing his homework.*)

WONDERBOY: Two superquantums plus five uranium neutrons, and I've got the mini-sub fuel. Hooray. Boy, will my friends in the U.S. Navy be pleased. Hey, what's that? Better use my wonder-vision. Helen Fargis seems to be in trouble. Better change to Wonderboy. (*As if throwing open his shirt.*) And fly over there in a flash. (*Jumping as if flying.*) I guess I'm in the nick of time. (*With one super-powerful punch in the jaw he subdues* HARRY, *the monster.*)

HELEN: Oh, Wonderboy, what would have happened if you hadn't come? But what will happen to IT?

WONDERBOY: I'll fly him to a distant zoo where they'll take good care of him.

HELEN: Oh, Wonderboy, how can I ever repay you?

WONDERBOY: Are those home-baked cookies I smell?

SUSAN: The president of the company has an Eames chair.

GEORGE: How do you know that?

SUSAN: Jennifer showed it to me.

GEORGE: You asked to see it?

SUSAN: Don't worry George. He wasn't there. I just had this crazy wild impulse as I was passing his office. I wanted to see what it looked like. Isn't that wild?

HAL: Did you sit in it?

SUSAN: I didn't dare. What would I have said if he'd come in?

(GEORGE *goes to the rest room.*)

HAL: I love you, Mr. President of my great big company, and that's why I'm sitting in your nice warm leather arm chair.

SUSAN: You're perverted. I don't want to be a person working in a company who's never seen her president.

SUSAN (*to Hal, who has gotten up*): While you're up —

HAL: What?

SUSAN: You know. Get me a Coke. (*Titters at her own joke.*)

(HELEN *smiles at* WONDERBOY *through her tears; he puts his arm around her shoulders.*)

WONDERBOY: Tune in tomorrow, boys and girls, when I'll subdue a whole country full of monsters.

(*Slide: "Winners Eat Wondrex."*)

WONDERBOY: And in the meantime, remember: winners eat Wondrex. (*Smiles and jumps in the air, as if flying away.*)

(*Slide: little girls with shopping bags.*)

FIRST NEWS ANNOUNCER: Little girls with big shopping bags means back to school season is here again. Among the many shoppers in downtown New York were Darlene, nine, Lila, four, and Lucy Gladden, seven, of Lynbrook, Long Island.

(*Slide: the Vice President.*)

FIRST NEWS ANNOUNCER: In Washington, D.C., as he left John Foster Dulles Airport, as President Johnson's favorite.

(*Slide: second view of the Vice President.*)

FIRST NEWS ANNOUNCER: Representative, the Vice President said he was bursting with confidence.

(*Slide: first view of Vietnamese mourners.*)

SECOND NEWS ANNOUNCER: U.S. spokesmen in Saigon said families would be given adequate shelter and compensation. Our planes are under strict orders not to return to base with any bombs. The United States regrets that a friendly village was hit. The native toll was estimated at sixty.

(*Slide: second view of Vietnamese mourners.*)

(HAL *goes out through the hall door.* GEORGE *returns from the rest room.*)

GEORGE (*turning TV sound off*): Can I come over tonight?

SUSAN: Not tonight. (*Goes to bulletin board.*)

GEORGE (*following her*): Why not tonight?

SUSAN: Because I don't feel like it.

GEORGE: You have a date?

SUSAN: What business is that of yours? Don't think because —

GEORGE: Who with?

SUSAN: None of your business.

GEORGE: What about late, after you get back, like one o'clock?

SUSAN: That's too late. I need lots of sleep.

GEORGE: I'll call first.

SUSAN: You'd better.

(*Whenever* HAL, SUSAN, *and* GEORGE *have nothing else to do, they stare straight ahead, as if at a television screen.* GEORGE *and* SUSAN *do this now.*

HAL *comes back with two Cokes.* GEORGE *goes to the telephone and dials it.*)

GEORGE: Hello, dear. Yes, I'm here. Listen, I'm afraid I have to take the midnight to three shift.

(HAL *turns TV volume on.*)

GEORGE: I've got to. The night supervisor is out.

GEORGE: And I've already said I would.

SECOND NEWS ANNOUNCER: This was high, explained spokesmen, in answer to questions, because of the type of bomb dropped. These are known as Lazy Dogs. Each Lazy Dog bomb contains ten thousand slivers of razor-sharp steel.

(*Slide: third view of Vietnamese mourners.*)
(*Volume off.*)
(*Slide: a pack of Longford cigarettes superimposed on a lake.*)
(*Two People On Television do a silent commercial for Longford cigarettes: a man lights a woman's cigarette and she looks pleased.*)

(*Slide on the screen: "The Endless Frontier."*)

(SALLY *and* BILL *are two characters in the Western.*)

SALLY: Don't go, Bill.

BILL: I've got to.

SALLY: Oh, Bill.

(BILL *leaves.*)

GEORGE: Listen, let's talk about it over dinner, huh? I'll be out after you go to sleep and in before you wake up so what's the difference? Listen, let's talk about it over dinner, I said. Listen, I love you. Goodbye. (*Hangs up.*)

HAL (*watching TV intently but talking to GEORGE*): You have to take the midnight to three shift, George? That's really too bad.

HAL: Got a call while I was out?

GEORGE (*snapping TV volume off*): Do either of you want to take on some evening overtime this week?

SUSAN: Which?

GEORGE: Five to midnight Tuesday and Thursday.

HAL: Thursday.

SUSAN: Oh, all right, I'll take Tuesday.

HAL: Did you want Thursday?

SUSAN: I'd like to get the apartment finished.

HAL: Then give me Tuesday.

SUSAN: Not if you HAVE something on Thursday.

HAL: No sweat.

SUSAN: Oh, I know. It was that talk with that man.

(HAL *turns TV volume on.*)

GEORGE (*snapping TV volume off*): What talk with what man?

SUSAN: A man he has to talk to.

GEORGE: About a job?

HAL: I probably won't even see him.

GEORGE: What kind of job?

HAL: For the government. I tell you I probably won't see him.

SALLY: Oh, Bill.

(SALLY *fixes her hair in the mirror.*)

(SALLY *is surprised by* STEVE, *the villain, who has just been waiting for* BILL *to ride off.*)

SALLY: Steve!

STEVE: Bill's dead, Sally.

SALLY: I don't believe you.

(*Volume off.*)

(STEVE *tries to embrace* SALLY. *She slaps him hard as he approaches her. He tries it again. She slaps him again. He tries it a third time. She gets him a third time. Then he grabs and kisses her despite her terrible struggling.*)

(BILL, *his arm wounded, appears again. Seeing* STEVE *with* SALLY, *he draws and aims.*)

BILL: Sally, duck!

(*Volume off.*)

(SALLY *ducks.* BILL *shoots* STEVE, *then goes to* SALLY *to make sure she's all right.* STEVE, *however, is not badly wounded and he reaches for* BILL's *gun. The gun falls to the floor and they fight.* SALLY *tries to get into the fight but is pushed away.*)

GEORGE: If you quit, Hal, I'll need three weeks' notice. If you care about severance pay.

HAL (*turning TV volume on*): I haven't seen him yet, even.

GEORGE: Or about me.

HAL: I wasn't going to mention it.

SUSAN: I'm sorry. It was my fault.

GEORGE (*turning volume off*): Just don't spring anything on me. If you don't like the job, leave. But don't spring anything on me because I can't take it, you know that.

HAL: George, I'm NOT quitting.

SUSAN: He likes this job too much, George.

HAL: I love it more than my own life. I wouldn't leave it for all the world. Honest Injun, George. (*Turns volume on.*)

GEORGE: Can you imagine what I'd have to go through to train another person? Can you?

SUSAN: Listen, I just remembered a joke. There's this writing on the subway. "I love grills" it says on the wall. So somebody crosses out "grills" and writes in "girls." "I love girls" it says now. And then somebody else writes in, "What about us grills?" (*Laughs and laughs over this.*)

SUSAN: What about us grills? Isn't that fantastic.

HAL: What's the matter with you?

(BILL *is losing his fight with* STEVE *because of his wounded arm.* STEVE *is about to get the gun.*)

SALLY (*warningly*): Bill!

(*Volume off.*)

(*In the nick of time,* SALLY *shoots* STEVE *in the back with a rifle. As he falls he makes a mute appeal to her. He is dead now and she is appalled at what she's done.*)

SALLY (*embracing* BILL): Oh, Bill!

BILL: I love you, Sally.

SALLY (*touched*): Oh, Bill.

BILL: Let's move to another town.

SALLY (*delighted*): Oh Bill.

(BILL *and* SALLY *ride off together into the dusk.*)

(*Slide: the President and his family.*)

SECOND NEWS ANNOUNCER: The President is accompanied by his wife, Lady Bird Johnson, and by his two daughters, Lynda Bird Johnson and Luci Baines Johnson Nugent, who lives in nearby Austin with her husband Patrick Nugent, President Johnson's son-in-law.

(*Slide: second view of the President and his family.*)

(*The President appears at a podium reading a*

speech. He is indeed accompanied by his wife and daughters.)
(Slide: the President alone.)

SUSAN (*still laughing*): I think that's the funniest thing I ever heard.

HAL: Shhhh.

PRESIDENT: We will stamp out aggression wherever and whenever.

(SUSAN *continues laughing.*)

HAL: Shhhhh. Stop it.

SUSAN: I can't.

SUSAN: I can't stop. Get the water.

PRESIDENT: We will tighten our defenses and fight, to guarantee the peace of our children, our children's children, and their children.

(GEORGE *gets up to get some water.* HAL *wants to watch TV and can't hear it at all because of* SUSAN's *laughter.*)

PRESIDENT: That all men are not well-intentioned or well-informed or even basically good, is unfortunate.

HAL: This is easier. (*Slaps* SUSAN *very hard on the face.*)

SUSAN: Ow!

PRESIDENT: But these people will not be indulged.

(*Applause by the* PRESIDENT's *family. No sound in this play need be put on tape; all of it can be provided by the People On Television.*)

SUSAN: Just who do you think you are!

HAL: Are you finished?

SUSAN: I couldn't help it.

PRESIDENT: Those who are our friends will declare themselves publicly. The others, we will not tolerate.

(*Slide: second view of the President alone.*)

SUSAN: Sadist.

PRESIDENT: Belief in American success and victory is the cornerstone of our faith.

SUSAN: Why didn't anyone get water?

GEORGE: Don't look at me.

PRESIDENT: Whatever else may chance to happen on far-off shores, nothing, I repeat nothing, will be allowed to disturb the serenity of our cities and suburbs, and when we fight we fight for a safer and more comfortable America, now and in years to come. Thank you.

SUSAN: You don't slap people because they're sick.

(*Slide: third view of the President and his family.*)

HAL: Every day we go through the same thing. You laugh. We bring you water. You spill the water all over everybody, and half an hour later you stop.

SUSAN: Give me the water, George. I'm going to take a pill.

GEORGE: What makes you laugh like that?

(HAL *lowers the volume but does not turn it off.*)

SUSAN: I'm a hysteric. I mean I'm not constantly hysterical but sometimes I get that way. I react that way, through my body. You're a compulsive, Hal, a nasty little compulsive.

HAL (*turning volume off*): How do you know?

SUSAN: I've discussed it with my analyst. Hysterics react through their bodies. Compulsives react compulsively.

GEORGE: What does he say about me?

SUSAN: He doesn't.

GEORGE: Hmph.

HAL: How long have you been going now? Twenty-seven years?

SUSAN: A year, wise guy.

HAL: How long do you expect to be going?

SUSAN: It might take another two or three years.

GEORGE: I know people who have gone for ten or twelve years.

HAL: Don't you think that's a lot?

GEORGE: If you need it, you need it. It's a sickness like any other sickness. It's got to be looked after.

HAL: What did they do in the old days?

GEORGE (*turning volume up*): They stayed sick.

SECOND NEWS ANNOUNCER: The President and his family will now be cheered by the cadet corps.

(*The President and his family respond to cheers like mechanical dolls. Turning his back, the* SECOND NEWS ANNOUNCER *provides us with one hummed bar of "So Hello Lyndon."*)

(*A Spanish Teacher appears.*)

(*Slide: the Spanish Teacher's face.*)

(*Volume low.*)

SPANISH TEACHER: Buenos dias muchachos and muchachas. Hello, boys and girls. Muchachos. Boys. Muchachas. Girls. Aqui es la casa. Here is the house. Casa. House.

(*Volume off.*)

(*The* SPANISH TEACHER *finishes the lesson.*)
(*Efficient researchers walk back and forth across the stage, checking things, nodding at each other curtly, and so on.*)
(*Slide: the efficient researchers.*)

(*Volume up.*)

UGP ANNOUNCER: Who are they? They are a community of devotion.

(*Slide: "UGP" in very Germanic lettering.*)

UGP ANNOUNCER: Men and women whose lives are dedicated to the researching of more perfect products for you. Get the benefit of a community of devotion. Look for the letters UGP whenever you buy a car, radio, television set, or any of a thousand other products. Their tool: devotion. Their goal: perfection.

(*Slide: a civil rights demonstration.*)

SUSAN: My analyst has been going to HIS analyst for twenty-five years.

HAL: How do you know?

SUSAN: He told me.

FIRST NEWS ANNOUNCER: Three men were critically injured during a civil rights demonstration in Montgomery, Alabama today.

GEORGE: Can you feel the tranquilizer working?

SUSAN: A little bit. I think so.

(*Slide: the Vice President.*)

FIRST NEWS ANNOUNCER: This afternoon the Vice President arrived in Honolulu. As he stepped off the plane he told newsmen things are looking up.

GEORGE: Maybe I should have one too.

(*Slide: a map of China.*)

FIRST NEWS ANNOUNCER: The Defense Department today conceded that United States aircraft may have mistakenly flown over Chinese territory last month. It regrets the incident.

SUSAN (*turning volume off*): Are you upset?

(*Volume off.*)

GEORGE: I can feel my stomach.

(*Slide: a rock and roll group.*)

SUSAN (*reaching into her bag to give him a pill*): Here.

(*A rock and roll group is seen singing and playing.*)

GEORGE: I'd like some coffee.

HAL: I'd like some lunch.

SUSAN: Lunch! I'll get it.

(*Dashes into her coat and is almost out the door.*)

HAL: Hey.

SUSAN: Rare with onion and a danish. I know. So long, you guys.

HAL (*throwing his penknife into the bulletin board*): Think she's all right?

GEORGE: People wouldn't say this was a crazy office or anything like that.

HAL: Nope.

GEORGE: She's really a nice girl, isn't she?

HAL (*doing calisthenics*): Yup.

GEORGE: You like her, don't you?

HAL: Yup.

GEORGE: I mean you don't just think she's a good lay, do you?

HAL: What makes you think I lay her?

GEORGE: Well, don't you?

HAL: George, that's an old trick.

GEORGE: I'm just trying to find out if you really like her.

HAL: Why do you care?

GEORGE: I feel protective.

HAL: That's right. She's half your age, isn't she?

GEORGE: Not exactly half.

HAL: How old are you, George, exactly?

GEORGE: Forty-three.

HAL (*crossing to water cooler*): Humph.

GEORGE: What's that mean?

HAL: I was just wondering what it was like to be forty-three.

GEORGE: It stinks.

HAL: That's what I thought.

GEORGE: You'll be forty-three sooner than you think.

HAL: I'll never be forty-three.

GEORGE: Why not?

HAL: I don't intend to live that long.

GEORGE: You have something?

HAL: No. I just don't intend to live that long.

(*Returns to console and turns volume on.*)

GEORGE (*sits*): You're probably a socialist.

HAL: A socialist?

GEORGE: A socialist at twenty and a Republican at forty. Everybody goes through that cycle.

GEORGE: It's healthy.

HAL: Are you a Republican, George?

GEORGE: That's right.

HAL: You know I have a lot of friends who won't even speak to Republicans.

GEORGE: I'd rather not discuss politics.

(*The rock and roll group bows.*)
(*Slide: a group of peace marchers.*)
(*A group of peace marchers appears.*)

FIRST NEWS ANNOUNCER: A group of so-called peaceniks marched down the center mall of the capital today, singing:

(*The peace marchers sing "We Shall Over-come."*)

FIRST NEWS ANNOUNCER: One young man from New York City predicted:

ONE YOUNG MAN FROM NEW YORK CITY: The Washington Monument's going to burst into bloom and —

(*It is as if the sound were cut off on the word he was going to say, but we can read "Fuck" on his lips.*)

(*Slide:* ANNIE KAPPELHOFF.)

FIRST NEWS ANNOUNCER: A little girl, Annie Kappelhoff, had her own opinion:

ANNIE (*as if leading a cheer*): Burn yourselves, not your draft cards, burn yourselves, not your draft cards —

(*The sound is cut off on* ANNIE, *too, as she continues the same cheer.*)

FIRST NEWS ANNOUNCER: Later in the day Annie was the star of her own parade. She's head-cheerleader of Wilumet High School in Maryland. Today Annie cheered her team on to victory, thirty to nothing, over neighboring South Dearing. Annie is also an ardent supporter of the young American Nazi party, and hopes to become a model. And now, a message.

(*Slide: a jar of K-F soap-cream.*)

FAMOUS TV PERSONALITY: Are you one of those lucky women who has all the time in the world?

FAMOUS TV PERSONALITY: Or are you like most

HAL: Why not?

GEORGE: Because we probably don't see eye to eye.

HAL: So?

GEORGE: So I'd rather not discuss it. And my stomach's upset.

of us: busy, busy, busy all day long with home or job so that when evening comes you hardly have time to wash your face, much less transform yourself into the living doll he loves.

FAMOUS TV PERSONALITY: Well then, K-F is for you. More than a soap. More than a cream. It's a soap-cream. You apply it in less time than it takes to wash your face and it leaves your skin tingling with loveliness. Try it. And for an extra super thrill, use it in the shower.

(*Slide*: LILY HEAVEN.)

LILY HEAVEN'S ANNOUNCER: The Lily Heaven Show, ladies and gentlemen, starring that great star of stage, screen, and television: Lily Heaven.

(*Out through imaginary curtains comes* LILY HEAVEN, *very starlike. She greets her audience in her own inimitable way. She sings a line from a popular American love song.*)

(*There is a special knock on the viewing room door.*)

HAL: What's that?

GEORGE: Nothing.

(GEORGE *turns volume off.*)

HAL: What do you mean, nothing?

GEORGE (*calling*): One minute.

HAL (*getting panicky*): One minute until what?

(GEORGE *turns out the lights in the viewing room.*)

HAL: I knew it. What's going on?

GEORGE (*calling*): Okay.

HAL: Okay what? What? What?

SUSAN (*coming through the door with a cake with lighted candles on it*): Okay this, stupid.

HAL: Oh my God, you're crazy.

SUSAN and GEORGE: One, two, three. (*Singing.*)
Happy Birthday to you,
Happy Birthday to you,

(*Volume off.*)

(*Slide: a second view of Lily Heaven.*)

Happy Birthday dear Ha-al,
Happy Birthday to you.

(SUSAN *kisses* HAL *on the lips.*)

SUSAN: Happy Birthday. You had no idea, did
you?

HAL: No.

GEORGE: Happy Birthday.

HAL: Thanks a lot.

SUSAN: Make a wish and blow.

(HAL *blows on the candles but doesn't get them
all.*)

SUSAN: Well, almost.

(GEORGE *turns the viewing room lights on
again, and* SUSAN *gets two presents from the
closet.*)

SUSAN: People thought I was crazy walking
down the hall with this cake and this lunch
in a paper bag. And I was petrified one of
you would swing the door open while I was
waiting in the corridor and knock me down
and the cake and everything. I was almost
sure you'd guessed, Hal, when I put the
presents in my locker this morning.

HAL: I hadn't.

SUSAN: I love birthdays. I know it's childish
but I really do. Look at the card on George's.

HAL: It's cute.

SUSAN: Open it.

(HAL *opens the package. It's a tie.*)

HAL: Well thanks, George. I can use this.

(*Makes a mock noose of it around his neck.*)

GEORGE: You're welcome.

SUSAN (*looking at the label as if she hadn't
seen it before*): It's a good tie.

GEORGE: What'd you expect?

(GEORGE *is biting into an egg salad sandwich.*
HAL *starts to open the second present.*)

SUSAN (*stopping* HAL): Save mine for when we
eat the cake, so the birthday will last longer.

HAL: George, there's egg salad all over the dials.

GEORGE (*turning volume on*): Sorry.

SUSAN: Here's a napkin. I'll make some coffee.

GEORGE: Good.

(GEORGE *and* HAL *are mesmerized by* LILY HEAVEN. SUSAN *is paying no attention but is fussing with the coffee things and putting paper bags, as party hats, on* HAL *and* GEORGE.)

GEORGE: Give me another of those tranquilizers, please. The first one doesn't seem to have done a thing.

(HAL *turns the volume off.* SUSAN *has plugged in the hot plate and coffee maker. She also has some real coffee and a jar of dried cream, some sugar and sugar substitute in little bags stolen from a luncheonette, napkins and little wooden stick-stirrers.*)

HAL (*who has been opening his present*): Say, this is nice.

SUSAN: It's an art book.

HAL: I can see that.

GEORGE: Hal especially interested in art?

SUSAN: A person doesn't have to be especially interested in art to like it.

(LILY HEAVEN *finishes singing and bows.*)

LILY HEAVEN: So long, everybody.

LILY HEAVEN: This is Lily Heaven saying so long.

(*Applause from part of* LILY HEAVEN's *audience, played by the People On Television, who stand behind her.*)

LILY HEAVEN (*as if each sentence were her last*): Here's wishing you a good week before we meet again. From all of us here to all of you out there: so long. Thanks a lot and God bless you. This is Lily signing off. I only hope that you enjoyed watching us as much as we enjoyed being here. So long. It's been wonderful being with you. Really grand, and I hope you'll invite us into your living room again next week. I only wish we could go on but I'm afraid it's time to say so long, so from the actors and myself, from the staff here, I want to wish you all a very very good week. This is your Lily saying so long to you. So long. So long. So long. So long. Have a happy, and so long. Till next week. Bye. So long. Bye. So long.

(*Slide: a weather map.*)

WEATHER ANNOUNCER: And now, the weather.

(*Volume off.*)

HAL: It must have cost a lot, Susan. Here, George. (*Passes* GEORGE *a piece of cake.*)

SUSAN: Well, as a matter of fact, I got it on sale at Marboro.

HAL: If I had a place for it everything would be fine. Cake, Susan?

SUSAN (*to* GEORGE): Hal still doesn't have a place.

(*Slide: Miracle Headache Pills.*)
(*Still without volume, an advertisement for Miracle Headache Pills: a woman is seen before and after taking the pills.*)

GEORGE: What kind of place are you looking for?

HAL: I'd like to find an apartment with more than one small room for under a hundred dollars.

SUSAN: Do you want to live in the Village?

HAL: Makes no difference.

GEORGE: Don't live down there.

SUSAN: Why not?

GEORGE: It's too crowded.

SUSAN: It's not so crowded, and in the Village you can see a lot of wonderful faces.

GEORGE: Yes, well frankly I've been working for a living for twenty-one years and I resent having to support a lot of bums on relief.

SUSAN: That's not the Village. That's the Bowery.

(LADY ANNOUNCER *begins to speak, still without volume.*)

GEORGE: Let's not talk about it.

SUSAN: Why not?

(*Slide: First Federal Savings Bank.*)

GEORGE: I already told Hal that people with differing points of view shouldn't talk about politics. And I shouldn't be eating this cake either.

LADY ANNOUNCER: And now First Federal Savings and Kennel-Heart Dog Food present Luncheon With Carol, a program especially designed for the up-to-date woman. Our topic for today: I Quit. And here's Carol.

(*Snaps volume on.*)

(*Slide:* CAROL *and* RON CAMPBELL.)

CAROL: Hello, ladies. This is Carol. I have as my guest today Mr. Ron Campbell just back from an eighteen month tour of duty in Vietnam. Mr. Campbell was a member of the famed Green Berets. He is a holder of the Bronze Star and the South Vietnamese Order of Merit; he has been nominated for the U.S. Silver Star. A few weeks ago he was offered a field commission as captain. But instead of accepting, what did you do, Ron?

RON: I quit.

CAROL: That's right, you quit. Tell us why you quit, Ron, when you were obviously doing so well.

RON: I didn't like being there.

CAROL: You didn't?

RON: No.

CAROL (*cheerfully*): I see.

RON: We're committing mass murder.

CAROL (*interested*): Yes?

RON: We're trying to take over a people that don't want to be taken over by anybody.

CAROL: Now, Ron, American boys are out there dying so somebody must be doing something wrong somewhere.

RON: Whoever in Hanoi or Peking or Washington is sending men out to be killed, THEY'RE doing something wrong.

CAROL (*interested in his opinion, tolerant*): I see.

RON: You do? Well I was there for a year and a half and every day I saw things that would make you sick. Heads broken, babies smashed against walls —

CAROL (*deeply sympathetic*): I KNOW.

RON: You know?

CAROL: War is horrible.

RON: Listen —

CAROL: Thank you, Ron. We've been talking this afternoon, ladies, with Ron Campbell, war hero.

RON: Will you let me say something, please?

CAROL (*tolerating him, kindly*): And a fascinating talk it's been, Ron, but I'm afraid our time is up.

RON: One —

CAROL (*with her special smile for the ladies*): Ladies, see you all tomorrow.

SUSAN (*dreamily*): I think I'm floating further and further left.

GEORGE: You don't know a thing about it.

SUSAN: I was listening to Norman Thomas last night —

LADY ANNOUNCER: This program was brought to you by First Federal Savings and Kennel-Heart Dog Food. The opinions expressed on this program are not necessarily those of anyone connected with it. A dog in the home means a dog with a heart.

(*Slide: Kennel-Heart Dog Food.*)

LADY ANNOUNCER: Kennel-Heart. Bow-wow. Wow.

GEORGE: I'm going to the Men's Room.

(*Slide: "Billion Dollar Movie."*)

SUSAN: Poor George.

HAL: You still haven't told me about tonight.

SUSAN: Told you what about tonight?

(*A very English man and a very English woman appear in the movie.*)

HE: Sarah.

SHE: Yes, Richard.

HAL: Are we going to the movies or are we not going to the movies?

HE: Our old apartment.

SUSAN: I don't know. I can't make up my mind.

SHE: Yes, Richard. It's still here.

HAL: That's just fine.

HE: It seems very small to me.

SHE: It does to me, too.

SUSAN: I want to work on my apartment.

HAL: Okay.

HE: Do you think we can live in it again?

SHE: Not in the old way.

SUSAN: I should really get it done.

HE: In a better way.

HAL: You're right.

SHE: You've changed too, Richard, for the better.

HE: So have you, darling, for the better.

SUSAN: Suppose I let you know by the end of the afternoon?

HAL: Suppose we forget I ever suggested it.

SUSAN: Oh, all right, I'll go. Happy?

HAL: I'm so happy I could put a bullet through my brain.

SUSAN: Sugar?

HAL: You're like my grandmother.

SUSAN: How?

HAL: She asked me if I took sugar every day we lived together. It was very comforting.

HAL: Hal, she used to say to me, my grandmother, you're going to be a big man.

HAL: Everybody's going to love you. She used to sing that song to me: "Poppa's gonna buy you a dog named Rover, and if that dog don't bark, Poppa's gonna buy you a looking glass, and if that looking glass should break, you're still the sweetest little boy in town."

SUSAN: That's nice.

(GEORGE *enters and goes directly to telephone.*)

SHE: I've learned a lot.

HE: Maybe that's what war is for.

(*The People On Television hum "White Cliffs of Dover" under the following.*)

SHE: The brick wall in front of the window is gone.

HE: We'll rebuild for the future.

SHE: I hope there is never any more war. Ever, ever again.

HE: Amen.

(*Slides "The End."*)
(*The People On Television sing, meaningfully, the last line of "White Cliffs of Dover": "Tomorrow, just you wait and see."*)

(FIRST NEWS ANNOUNCER *appears.*)

(*Slide: baseball player.*)

FIRST NEWS ANNOUNCER: Baseball's Greg Pironelli, fifty-six, died today of a heart attack in St. Petersburg, Florida. He hit a total of four hundred and eighty home runs and had a lifetime batting average of three forty-one.

(*Slide: a baseball game.*)

FIRST NEWS ANNOUNCER: In 1963, the year he was elected to baseball's hall of fame in Cooperstown, New York, Pironelli suffered his first stroke. Pironelli owned a Florida-wide chain of laundries.

(*Slide: "Johnny Holland Show."*)

JOHNNY: We're back.

(*Slide: JOHNNY and LUCI.*)

JOHNNY: That's a very pretty dress you've got on, Luci.

LUCI: Thank you, Johnny.

GEORGE: Hello, darling? Listen, I've gotten out of it. Isn't that good news? The midnight shift.

JOHNNY: How does it feel living in Austin after all the excitement of the big wedding?

LUCI: It feels fine.

GEORGE: I'm looking forward to being home nice and comfy with you.

JOHNNY: Do you miss your father?

GEORGE: You know my stomach is killing me. Sure I will. Wait a minute.

LUCI: Oh sure, I miss him.

(GEORGE *takes out a pencil.*)

GEORGE: Toothpaste. Cauliflower. That's a good idea.

JOHNNY (*awkward pause*): I guess your heart belongs to Daddy, huh?

GEORGE: Large face cream. Why large? No, I don't care. I was just asking.

LUCI: That's right.

JOHNNY (*awkward pause*): Is your father hard to get along with?

GEORGE: Okay. Listen, I'm really looking forward to seeing you.

LUCI: Oh, no. When I want something I just march right in, cuddle up in his lap, and give him a great big kiss.

(*Slide: a second view of Johnny and Luci.*)

JOHNNY (*awkward pause*): So you'd say your father is affectionate?

LUCI: Very affectionate.

GEORGE: No, I haven't been drinking, and it's rotten of you to ask.

JOHNNY (*awkward pause*): Does he ever ask your advice about important matters?

GEORGE: Okay, okay. Bye. (*Hangs up telephone.*)

LUCI: Well, one day I told him what I thought, good and proper, about all those nervous nellies interfering with my Daddy's war.

(JOHNNY *does a double take of scandalized amusement to the audience.*)
(*Slide: Johnny doing double take.*)

JOHNNY: And what did he say?

LUCI: He laughed.

SUSAN: Have a little coffee, George.

GEORGE: No, thanks.

HAL: Oh, come on, George, have a little coffee.

GEORGE: A sip.

JOHNNY: It's lovely talking to you, Luci.

SUSAN: Sugar or superine?

GEORGE: Sugar.

LUCI: It's nice talking to you too, Johnny.

JOHNNY: We'll be back.

SUSAN: George.

(Slide: "Johnny Holland Show.")

GEORGE: Don't take care of me. I said sugar.

SUSAN: Whatever you want, George.

(An EVANGELIST appears with his choir, which is singing "Onward Christian Soldiers.")
(Slide: the EVANGELIST.)

EVANGELIST: If we could look through the ceiling of this wonderful new air-conditioned stadium we could see the stars. Nonetheless I have heard them in faraway countries, I have heard them criticize, criticize us and the leaders we know and love.

SUSAN: George, what are you eating now?

GEORGE: Chicken sandwich.

SUSAN: Give me a bite.

(HAL plays with his penknife. SUSAN eats another piece of cake. GEORGE eats his chicken sandwich.)

EVANGELIST: Why? Well I will tell you why. They criticize us because we are rich, as if money itself were evil. Money, the Bible says, is the root of evil, not evil itself. I have seen a roomful of men and women, powerful Hollywood celebrities at four o'clock A.M. in the morning, listening to me with tears streaming down their faces crying out to me that they had lost touch with God.

(GEORGE starts to cough.)

EVANGELIST: "In God We Trust" is on our coins, ladies and gentlemen —

(Slide: a second view of the EVANGELIST.)
(The Evangelist choir sings "Onward Christian Soldiers.")

SUSAN: What's the matter, George?

(GEORGE motions her away and continues to cough.)

HAL (turning volume off): Spit it out, George.

(Volume off.)

SUSAN: Hal, leave him alone.

HAL: George, spit it out. (Thumps GEORGE on the back.)

SUSAN: Hal! George, is it epilepsy?

HAL: It's something in his throat.

SUSAN: Try to tell us what it is, George.

HAL *and* GEORGE: Chicken!

HAL: He has a chicken bone stuck in his throat.

SUSAN: Oh my God. Well give him some water.

(GEORGE's *choking is getting worse.*)

HAL: Water will wash right by it. Let me look.

(*Holds* GEORGE's *head and looks into his mouth.*)

   Don't move, George. I want to take a look.

(*Looks in* GEORGE's *mouth.*)

   There it is.

SUSAN (*also looking*): Ugh, it's stuck in his throat. I'll get some water.

(HAL *and* SUSAN *let go of* GEORGE, *who falls to the floor.*)

HAL: Not water.

SUSAN: Why not?

HAL: Because water will wash right past the thing. It needs something to push it out.

SUSAN: Like what?

HAL: Like bread.

SUSAN: Bread? Bread will get stuck on the bone and he'll choke.

HAL: You're wrong.

SUSAN: I'm right.

HAL: Bread will push it right down.

SUSAN: Water will do that.

HAL: You're wrong.

SUSAN: It's you that's wrong and won't admit it.

HAL: I'm going to give him some bread.

SUSAN: I won't allow it.

HAL: YOU won't allow it?

SUSAN: It'll kill him.

HAL: He's choking right now and I'm going to give him some of this bread.

SUSAN: Give him water.

HAL: I said bread.

SUSAN (*starting to walk past* HAL): And I said water.

HAL (*grabbing her arm.*) Bread.

SUSAN: Water. Ow, you're hurting me.

(GEORGE *is having a very bad time.* HAL *and* SUSAN *turn to look at him, speaking softly.*)

SUSAN: Let's call the operator.

HAL: It would take too long.

SUSAN: And he wouldn't like anyone to see him.

HAL: Why not?

SUSAN: I don't know.

(*At this point* GEORGE *finally coughs the thing up, and his cough subsides into an animal pant.*)

SUSAN (*Going to him, patting him*): Poor George.

HAL: It's over.

SUSAN: No thanks to you.

HAL: Nor you.

SUSAN (*putting* GEORGE'S *head on her breast*): He might have choked. Poor George.

GEORGE (*pushing her away*): Fuck!

(GEORGE *lurches against the console on his way to the bathroom, accidentally turning on the volume.*)

EVANGELIST CHOIR (*still singing "Onward Christian Soldiers."*): "With the cross of Jesus —"

(*Slide:* MOTHER, FATHER, *and* DAUGHTER *in "My Favorite Teenager."*)

(HAL *changes channels from the* EVANGELIST'S *meeting to "My Favorite Teenager."*)

SUSAN (*sitting in her chair*): Poor George.

MOTHER: Why aren't you going?

DAUGHTER (*Sitting in* GEORGE'S *chair at the control console*): Because I told Harold Sternpepper he could take me.

MOTHER: Yes, and —

DAUGHTER: Well, Harold Sternpepper is a creep. Everybody knows that.

(*The remaining People On Television make the sound of canned laughter.*)

HAL (*sitting in his chair*): What movie are we going to?

MOTHER: So, why —

DAUGHTER: Oh, because I was mad at Gail.

(*Canned laughter.*)

SUSAN: I don't know.

MOTHER: What about Johnny Beaumont?

HAL: What about George?

SUSAN: What about him?

DAUGHTER: What about him?

HAL: Well, I guess it's none of my business.

MOTHER: Well, I guess it's none of my business.

FATHER: What's the matter?

GEORGE (*returning*): What's the matter?

(*Slide: second view of* MOTHER, FATHER, *and* DAUGHTER *in "My Favorite Teenager."*)

SUSAN: Nothing.

DAUGHTER: Nothing.

GEORGE: Going somewhere?

FATHER: Why aren't you dressed for the prom?

DAUGHTER: I'm not going to the prom.

SUSAN: We're going to the movies.

FATHER: Why not? Why isn't she going, Grace?

MOTHER: Don't ask me. I just live here.

(HAL *and* SUSAN *and* GEORGE *are slowing down because they are mesmerized by "My Favorite Teenager."*)

(*Canned laughter.*)

FATHER: Why doesn't anybody tell me anything around here?

GEORGE: What movie are you going to?

(*Canned laughter.*)

DAUGHTER (*getting up from* GEORGE'S *chair*): Oh, why don't you two leave me alone? I'm not going because nobody's taking me.

GEORGE: Mind if I come along?

FATHER (*sitting in* GEORGE'S *chair*): Nobody's taking my little girl to the junior prom? I'll take her myself.

SUSAN: Oh, George, you don't really want to.

DAUGHTER (*stifling a yelp of horror*): Oh no, Daddy, don't bother. I mean how would it look, I mean —

GEORGE: I'd be pleased as punch.

SUSAN: Hal, say something.

HAL (*to* GEORGE): You look bushed to me, George.

GEORGE: Who's bushed?

(GEORGE *sits in his chair.*)

(HAL, SUSAN, *and* GEORGE *are completely mesmerized by the TV show.*)

FATHER: I'd be pleased as punch.

DAUGHTER (*aside to* MOTHER): Help.

(*Canned laughter.*)

MOTHER (*to* FATHER): Now, dear, don't you think for your age —

(*Canned laughter.*)

FATHER: My age?

(*Canned laughter.*)

FATHER (*standing and doing a two-step*): I'd like to see anybody laugh at my two-step.

(*Canned laughter.*)

DAUGHTER (*In despair*): Oh, Daddy. Mother, DO something.

(*Canned laughter.*)

MOTHER (*putting her arm around* GEORGE's *shoulders*): I think it's a very nice idea. And maybe I'll go with Harold Sternpepper.

(*Canned laughter.*)

DAUGHTER (*loudly, sitting on* HAL's *knee*): Oh, Mother, oh, Daddy, oh no!

(*The canned laughter mounts. Music.*)
(*Slide: "My Favorite Teenager."*)

(*Now they all speak like situation-comedy characters.*)

HAL: What movie shall we go to?

GEORGE: Let's talk about it over dinner.

HAL: Who said anything about dinner?

(*All of the People On Television do canned laughter now. They are crowded around the control console.*)

SUSAN: Isn't anybody going to ask me what I want to do?

(*Canned laughter.*)

GEORGE: Sure, what do you want, Susan?

HAL: It's up to you.

(*Slide:* HAL, SUSAN, *and* GEORGE *with the same facial expressions they now have on the stage.*)

SUSAN: Well, have I got a surprise for you two. I'M going home to fix up my apartment and you two can have dinner TOGETHER.

(HAL, SUSAN, *and* GEORGE *join in the canned laughter. Then, lights off. Slide off. Curtain call: all are in the same position, silent, their faces frozen into laughing masks.*)

MOTEL

A Masque for Three Dolls

. . . after all our subtle colour and nervous rhythm, after the faint mixed tints of Conder, what more is possible? After us the Savage God.

W. B. Yeats

MOTEL-KEEPER
MAN
WOMAN
MOTEL-KEEPER'S VOICE

Lights come up on the MOTEL-KEEPER *doll. The intensity of the light will increase as the play continues.*
The MOTEL-KEEPER *doll is large, much larger than human size, but the impression of hugeness can come mainly from the fact that her head is at least three times larger than would be normal in proportion to her body. She is all gray. She has a large full skirt which reaches to the floor. She has squarish breasts. The hair curlers on her head suggest electronic receivers. The* MOTEL-KEEPER *doll has eyeglasses which are mirrors. It doesn't matter what these mirrors reflect at any given moment. The audience may occasionally catch a glimpse of itself, or be bothered by reflections of light in the mirrors. It doesn't matter; the sensory nerves of the audience are not to be spared.*
The motel room in which the MOTEL-KEEPER *doll stands is anonymously modern, except for certain "homey" touches. A neon light blinks outside the window. The colors in the room, like the colors in the clothes on the* MAN *and* WOMAN *dolls, are violent combinations of oranges, pinks, and reds against a reflective plastic background.*
The MOTEL-KEEPER'S VOICE, *which never stops, comes from a loudspeaker, or from several loudspeakers in the theatre. The* VOICE *will be, at first, mellow and husky and then, as the light grows harsher and brighter, the* VOICE *will grow harsher too, more set in its pattern, hard finally, and patronizing and petty.*
An actor on platform shoes works the MOTEL-KEEPER *doll from inside it. The actor can move*

only the doll's arms or its entire body. As the VOICE *begins, the arms move, and then the* MOTEL-KEEPER *doll fusses about the room in little circles.*

MOTEL-KEEPER'S VOICE: I am old. I am an old idea: the walls; that from which it springs forth. I enclose the nothing, making then a place in which it happens. I am the room: a Roman theatre where cheers break loose the lion; a railroad carriage in the forest at Compiègne, in 1918, and in 1941. I have been rooms of marble and rooms of cork, all letting forth an avalanche. Rooms of mud and rooms of silk. This room will be slashed too, as if by a scimitar, its contents spewed and yawned out. That is what happens. It is almost happening, in fact. I am this room.

(*As the* MOTEL-KEEPER'S VOICE *continues, the doors at the back of the room open and headlights shine into the eyes of the audience; passing in front of the headlights, in silhouette, we see two more huge dolls, the* MAN *and the* WOMAN.)

MOTEL-KEEPER'S VOICE: It's nice; not so fancy as some, but with all the conveniences. And a touch of home. The antimacassar comes from my mother's house in Boise. Boise, Idaho. Sits kind of nice, I think, on the Swedish swing. That's my own idea, you know. All modern, up-to-date, that's it — no motel on this route is more up-to-date. Or cleaner. Go look, then talk me a thing or two.

(*The* WOMAN *doll enters. Her shoulders are thrown way back, like a girl posing for a calendar. Her breasts are particularly large and perfect, wiggleable if possible. She has a cherry-lipstick smile, blond hair, and a garish patterned dress.*
Both the MAN *and the* WOMAN *dolls are the same size as the* MOTEL-KEEPER *doll, with heads at least three times larger than would be normal for their bodies. The* MAN *and the* WOMAN *dolls, however, are flesh-colored and have more mobility. The actors inside these dolls are also on platform shoes. There is absolutely no rapport between the* MOTEL-KEEPER *and the* MAN *and* WOMAN. *All of the* MOTEL-KEEPER'S *remarks*

are addressed generally. She is never directly
motivated by the actions of the MAN and
WOMAN *dolls.*
As the WOMAN *doll enters, she puts down her
purse and inspects the room. Then she takes
off her dress, revealing lace panties and bra.*)

MOTEL-KEEPER'S VOICE: All modern here but, as
I say, with the tang of home. Do you understand? When folks are fatigued, in a strange
place? Not that it's old-fashioned. No. Not
in the wrong way. There's a push-button
here for TV. The toilet flushes of its own
accord. All you've got to do is get off. Pardon
my mentioning it, but you'll have to go far
before you see a thing like that on this route.
Oh, it's quite a room. Yes. And reasonable.
Sign here. Pardon the pen leak. I can see
you're fatigued.

(*The* WOMAN *doll goes into the bathroom.*)

MOTEL-KEEPER'S VOICE: Any children? Well,
that's nice. Children don't appreciate travel.
And rooms don't appreciate children. As it
happens it's the last one I've got left. I'll just
flip my vacancy switch. Twelve dollars,
please. In advance that'll be. That way you
can go any time you want to go, you know,
get an early start. On a trip to see sights, are
you? That's nice. You must get your luggage
while I unlock the room. You can see the
light.

(*The* MAN *doll enters carrying a suitcase. He
has a cigar and a loud Florida shirt. He closes
the door, inspects the room, and takes off his
clothes, except for his loudly patterned shorts.*)

MOTEL-KEEPER'S VOICE: There now. What I say
doesn't matter. You can see. It speaks for
itself. The room speaks for itself. You can
see it's a perfect 1966 room. But a taste of
home. I've seen to that. A taste of home.
Comfy, cozy, nice, but a taste of newness.
That's what. You can see it. The best stop on
route Six Sixty-Six. Well, there might be
others like it, but this is the best stop. You've
arrived at the right place. This place. And a
hooked rug. I don't care what, but I've said
no room IS without a hooked rug.

(*Sound of the toilet flushing.*)

MOTEL-KEEPER'S VOICE: No complaints yet.
Never. Modern people like modern places.
Oh yes. I can tell. They tell me. And reasonable. Very very reasonable rates. No cheaper
rates on the route, not for this. You receive
what you pay for.

(*Sound of the toilet flushing again.*)

MOTEL-KEEPER'S VOICE: All that driving and
driving and driving. Fatigued. You must be.
I would be. Miles and miles and miles.

(*The* MAN *doll begins an inspection of the bed.
He pulls at the bedspread, testing its strength.*)

MOTEL-KEEPER'S VOICE: Fancy. Fancy your ending up right here. You didn't know and I
didn't know. But you did. End up right here.
Respectable and decent and homelike. Right
here.

(*The* WOMAN *doll comes back from the bathroom to get her negligee from her purse. She
returns to the bathroom.*)

MOTEL-KEEPER'S VOICE: All folks everywhere
sitting in the very palm of God. Waiting,
whither, whence.

(*The* MAN *doll pulls the bedspread, blankets,
and sheets off the bed, tearing them apart. He
jumps hard on the bed.*)

MOTEL-KEEPER'S VOICE: Any motel you might
have come to on Six Sixty-Six. Any motel.
On that vast network of roads. Whizzing by,
whizzing by. Trucks too. And cars from
everywhere. Full up with folks, all sitting in
the very palm of God. I can tell proper folks
when I get a look at them. All folks.

(*The* MAN *doll rummages through the suitcase,
throwing clothes about the room.*)

MOTEL-KEEPER'S VOICE: Country roads, state
roads, United States roads. It's a big world
and here you are. I noticed you got a license
plate. I've not been to there myself. I've not
been to anywhere myself, excepting town for
supplies, and Boise. Boise, Idaho.

(*Toilet articles and bathroom fixtures, including toilet paper and the toilet seat, are thrown
out of the bathroom. The* MAN *doll casually
tears pages out of the Bible.*)

MOTEL-KEEPER'S VOICE: The world arrives to me, you'd say. It's a small world. These plastic flowers here: "Made in Japan" on the label. You noticed? Got them from the catalogue. Cat-al-ogue. Every product in this room is ordered.

(*The* MAN *doll pulls down some of the curtains. Objects continue to be thrown from the bathroom.*)

MOTEL-KEEPER'S VOICE: Ordered from the catalogue. Excepting the antimacassars and the hooked rug. Made the hooked rug myself. Tang of home. No room is a room without. Course the bedspread, hand-hooked, hooked near here at town. Mrs. Harritt. Betsy Harritt gets materials through another catalogue. Cat-al-ogue.

(*The* WOMAN *doll comes out of the bathroom wearing her negligee over her panties and bra. When the* MAN *doll notices her, he stops his other activities and goes to her.*)

MOTEL-KEEPER'S VOICE: Myself, I know it from the catalogue: bottles, bras, breakfasts, re-frigerators, cast iron gates, plastic posies.

(*The* WOMAN *doll opens her negligee and the* MAN *doll pulls off her bra. The* MAN *and* WOMAN *dolls embrace. The* WOMAN *doll puts lipstick on her nipples.*)

MOTEL-KEEPER'S VOICE: paper subscriptions, Buick trucks, blankets, forks, clitterclack darning hooks, transistors and antimacassar, vinyl plastics,

(*The* MAN *doll turns on the TV. It glares viciously and plays loud rock and roll music.*)

MOTEL-KEEPER'S VOICE: crazy quilts, paper hair-pins, cats, catnip, club feet, canisters, bani-sters, holy books, tattooed toilet articles, tables, tea cozies,

(*The* MAN *doll writes simple obscene words on the wall. The* WOMAN *doll does the same with her lipstick.*)

MOTEL-KEEPER'S VOICE: pickles, bayberry candles, South Dakotan Kewpie Dolls, fiber-glass hair, polished milk, amiable grand-pappies, colts, Galsworthy books, cribs, cabinets, teeter-totters,

(*The* WOMAN *doll has turned to picture-making. She draws a crude cock and coyly adds pubic hair and drops of come.*)

MOTEL-KEEPER'S VOICE: and television sets. Oh I tell you it, I do. It's a wonder. Full with things, the world, full up. Shall I tell you my thought? Next year there's a shelter to be built by me, yes. Shelter motel. Everything to be placed under the ground. Signs up in every direction up and down Six Sixty-Six.

(*The* MAN *and* WOMAN *dolls twist.*)

MOTEL-KEEPER'S VOICE: Complete Security, Security While You Sleep Tight, Bury Your Troubles At This Motel, Homelike, Very Comfy, and Encased In Lead, Every Room Its Own Set, Fourteen Day Emergency Supplies $5.00 Extra,

(*The rock and roll music gets louder and louder. A civil-defense siren, one long wail, begins to build. The* MAN *and* WOMAN *dolls proceed methodically to greater and greater violence. They smash the TV screen and picture frames. They pull down the remaining curtains, smash the windows, throw bits of clothing and bedding around, and finally tear off the arms of the* MOTEL-KEEPER *doll.*)

MOTEL-KEEPER'S VOICE: Self-Contained Latrine Waters, Filters, Counters, Periscopes and Mechanical Doves, Hooked Rugs, Dearest Little Picture Frames for Loved Ones — Made in Japan — through the catalogue. Cat-a-logue. You can pick items and pro-ducts: cablecackles — so nice — cuticles, twice-twisted combs with corrugated calis-thenics, meatbeaters, fish-tackles, bug bombs, toasted terra-cotta'd Tanganyikan switch blades, ochre closets, ping-pong balls, didies, Capricorn and Cancer prognostics, crackers, total uppers, stick pins, basting tacks . . .

(*The* MOTEL-KEEPER'S VOICE *is drowned out by the other sounds — siren and music — which have built to a deafening pitch and come from* all parts of the theatre. The door opens again and headlights shine into the eyes of the audience. The actor inside the MOTEL-KEEPER doll has slipped out of it. The MAN and WOMAN doll tear off the head of the MOTEL-KEEPER doll, then throw her body aside. Then, one by one, the MAN and WOMAN dolls leave the motel room and walk down the aisle. Fans blow air through the debacle on stage onto the audience. After an instant more of excruciatingly loud noises: blackout and silence. It is preferable that the actors take no bow after this play.)

Meat Joy

It is odd to think that American theatre should have such a reputation for "realism" when, if you ask people to name some typically American plays, you hear mention of plays as far from "realism" as *Our Town* (1938) by Thornton Wilder, *Death of a Salesman* (1958) by Arthur Miller, *The Sand Box* (1959) and other plays by Edward Albee, and so on. If there is something very American about American drama it may be a kind of moralizing — what the German critic Hebbel described as "the orange in the dead pig's mouth." But it is hardly "realism." And most recently there has not been an emphasis on writers and their texts but on directors and actors and action on the stage.

A departure from oralizing and quite in harmony with the trend away from words has been the Happening, which Allan Kaprow claims to have invented. Of course he did not, for it has been around in one form or another as far back as recorded history goes, but Kaprow did help, in a very American way, to publicize it in a new form, or as a new fad. Recently, it has seemed that everyone who could rope off a street or borrow a loft or a "performing garage" was staging a Happening. The best ones I went to took place outdoors and involved everything from nudes playing the cello under water to lots of people just standing around (which made it difficult to distinguish the event from a political demonstration or the crowd gathered at the scene of an accident). Nowadays Happenings are chiefly indoors and spectator sport and are getting so mixed up with human be-ins, plays (like *Dionysus in '69* and *Commune*), rock and other pop events and pseudo-events, that few people are very clear about what they are or when one is watching/experiencing/participating in one.

New Yorkers in living memory have been treated to balloons going up, streets being tied up (with string), and all sorts of happenings (or Happenings). One presumes that this sort of thing has been going on all around the country and that the "in" (or "far-out") crowd in many places have been staging Happenings. If they have not, they ought to be.

My choice for the classic Happening is Carolee Schneemann's *Meat Joy*, the work of an artist who has a sharp eye for not seeing reality (or not seeing what other people see) and, being American, of course has some sort of "message" in it all, which gives us something to talk about. Don't be too concerned if you don't clearly see a message: it is not immoral to miss the "moral" of it.

I certainly do not wish to go on at length here about what it all means, especially since we will be presenting the Happening itself in outline (the scenario for action) and also some introductory or explanatory notes. Explaining it, in fact, is about the only error I can find that this talented and stimulating woman has made in connection with this work. If you are interested in its argument against "fragmentation, depersonalization, and, in general, inertness, non-sensuousness," you will appreciate the notes. If you like Action painter Jackson Pollock's paintings ("Jack the Dripper") as paint interestingly applied, you will want to action without the excuses.

Richard Schechner, then editor of *Tulane Drama Review*, once stole a technique from Brecht and contrasted ordinary plays with Happenings in two columns like this:

TRADITIONAL	NEW
plot	images/events
action	activity
resolution	open-end
roles	tasks
themes/thesis	no set meaning
stage distinct from auditorium	one area for all
script	scenario
flow	compartments
single focus	multi-focus
audience watches	audience often participates, sometimes does not exist
product	process

As with Brecht's comparison of "Aristotelian" and "Epic" theatre, a certain amount of cheating has been done to create these parallels or contrasts, but the effect is worth thinking about, as are the origins (the painter's aesthetic, graphic arts, technology, psychology, music, dance, Dada, Zen, ill-bred and political puppet theatre, Antonin Artaud and John Cage, etc.). From this chart and these notes and the text of *Meat Joy* one can learn many of the questions that ought to be asked about theatre in general. One should also be able to learn how to make one's own Happening happen. Try one with bandages or aluminum foil or unrecycleable garbage or some of the 200,000,000 used auto tires Americans discard each year. Try one with pasta. Try one in which chance determines what happens next and another in which not even the spectators are permitted to deviate even the slightest from the "script." Try one in which the audience does not know that a Happening is going on. Try one in which absolutely nothing happens. Use your imagination.

Notes

Meat Joy began to evolve from dream sensation images in journals stretching as far back as early 1960; by February of 1964 they constituted a more elaborated series of drawings and notes. I was becoming increasingly aware of the possibility of capturing certain interactions between physical, metabolic changes and their effect on dream content, as well as on my sensory orientation upon and after waking; in capturing their releasing of random memory fragments (as well-defined sound, light, weather, and environment kernels from the past) in the immediate present.

At this time I made a photographic study called *Eye Body*. It involved the use of my body as source of collage transformations — its juxtaposition/extension to constructions, kinetic light boxes and the constructed environment I had been making in my studio generally; ambiguities both spatial and tactile; change of flesh forms by paint, grease, water, oil, powder, crayon, transparent plastic, combined with forms of the glass, wood, motors which I had been using in my work. The intention of *Meat Joy*, like all these images, was the visual transformation of the naked body-as-environment.

Then I received an invitation from Jean-Jacques Lebel to make a Happening for his first "Festival of Free Expression" in Paris, to occur in May. There was no financial possibility then of managing the trip, but the images which were to become *Meat Joy* increased with the provocation of the unknown, highly charged city — Paris:

In February of 1964 I wrote to Lebel:

There are now several works moving in minds-eye towards the possibility of an extreme time/space change (that is, being in Europe), tentatively identified as *Meat Joy*, and *Divisions and Rubble;* . . . *Meat Joy* shifting now; relating to Artaud, McClure, and French Butcher Shops — carcass as paint (it dripped right through Soutine's floor) . . . flesh jubilation . . . extremes of this sense . . . it may involve quantities of dark fabric and paint drawn from performance area outward into audience to become inundation of all available space — action and viewing space interchanged, broken through. Smell, feel of meat . . . chickens, fish, sausages? I see several girls whose gestures develop from tactile, bodily relationship to individual men and a mass of meat slices. Specific sequence of collision and embrace . . . rising, falling counterpoints to bodies . . . very dark (very bright). Hand held lights spotting color cover movements. My Visual Dramas (Kinetic Theater . . . Concretions) can take substance from the materials I *find* to work with: this means that any particular space, any debris unique to Paris and any "found" performers (picked off the street!) would be potential structural elements for the piece. I've been working a great deal with the Judson dancers for love of their non-dance movement and their aggressive, expansive interest in changing the very physical traditions which have given their bodies extraordinary scope and strength, and my pieces for them impose space relations, provoke personal responses which will work inclusively with any chosen or found environment; so that I do not require or want any special predetermined "set-up." What I find will be what I need.

At this point I should make it clear that my traditions are non-literary, non-verbal — "Kinetic Theatre" is my particular development of the "Happening." It is probably precisely my lack of connections with traditional theatre which left me free to evolve a new theatrical form. I am a painter, which means that even though I may not be working with paint on canvas, my sensibility is shaped in visual worlds and these are strongly tactile, plastic, concretely dimensional. I can trace three basic formal conditions which led me from painting to theatre:

1.   The unlimited range of materials (in Kinetic Theatre) — objects, people, lights, sounds, etc.— all acting as an extension of the more gradually broadened range of materials which I had used in my collages, painting-constructions, light-boxes, kinetic constructions, etc.;

2.   The moving body in space (formal unit of Kinetic Theatre) as an extension of the eye-to-hand gesture that generates the paint-stroke;

3.   The fluid, actually present environment (of Kinetic Theatre) as a metaphorical extension of an environment relatively fixed in painting by visual selection of inner-eye imagery.

Meat Joy was the first Kinetic Theatre piece I did in which I used performers almost entirely without previous experience in theatre. First in Paris, then in London and New York, I did actually pick (as I had suggested to Lebel) potential performers from crowds in bars, restaurants, concert halls, and streets. In Paris it was difficult and amusing, since I spoke only a few words of French. (The subsequent rehearsals were exceedingly strange; communication usually depending on hand and body gestures, facial expression and a raft of freshly memorized French words strung together to — hopefully — indicate my essential ideas.) I looked for people whose presence I responded to: simplicity, intensity, a self-contained yet open quality. In common they had a natural sexual presence — unself-conscious and vital and "untrained" bodies which moved integrally,

rhythmically in commonplace actions. They might be shy or exuberant, plump or skinny — I found contrasting types, a spectrum of qualities.

The performers had to develop a rich and freely expressive responsiveness to one another. In choosing them I had always to sense that those who would provoke my conception of the piece would in turn be complementary to each other and that the affinity they might feel for one another would develop through the nature of our work together just as the relationship between any of the performers within the context of their instructions would freely transform and intensify the quality of those instructions. My sense of the total quality of the piece was clear from the beginning — in some very internalized way — but was never explicitly imposed, because the performers had to slowly discover and reveal all those detailed experiences which would realize my images. It was like a journey we embarked on together. Only I knew the destination, but they would discover it for themselves.

The performers approached the work, not by assuming characterization or predetermined attitudes, but with what was spontaneously available and expressive in their own personalities. To maintain this the actions had to feel good to them, yet carry them beyond their own expectations of what was likely or possible, remaining clearly unique in the context of our associations. The performers transformed as well as realized the imagery of the piece. At every stage it was a collage process.

Since all the movements of *Meat Joy* take shape by sequences of bodily contact between the performers, we had to establish trusting and pleasurable feelings among ourselves. It involved what Lee Baxandall (describing his performing experience in Water Light/Water Needle) called "putting ourselves in one another's hands." (Literally and figuratively this was true.) A certain amount of surfacing intellectual and psychological trash had to be cleared for performers to feel free. This would necessitate leading them into actions, physical movements which would in themselves answer questions of feeling and response and relationship — the experiences of the body would re-form/inform their mental stance. Early rehearsals began with wrestling sessions: all eight of us on a small mat going through "exercises" of pinching, poking, rolling, tumbling, and crawling. We did other exercises of catches and carries, jumps and falls in which one person assumed responsibility for the weight, direction, and reactions of another: men to men, women to women, as well as men to women. We disposed of conventions of reserve exploring these modes of contact while concentrating a responsive attentiveness on one another. We conscientiously recognized the relation of muscular response and emotional engagement — handling, feeling, carrying, learning each other's weight, muscular strength, type of gestures, and rhythms in action. While these exercises centered on the entire body, I also made exercises for the hands, working with objects in preparation for the materials of the work to come: we made fish and chicken shapes, stuffing plastic with paper; we juggled, threw, kneaded, tossed, and drew on each other. The primary focus for all actions was the immediate animate environment, our relation to the immediate present.

It was important to avoid literal explanations of motive or circumstance to the performers. All "motives" grew directly out of their *physical* engagement with each other and our materials. The performers were free to explore a metaphoric scope of vesture as their own embodiment of tactile-kinetic sensation. The areas of actions moved between dream and banality, rooted in our particular present. Presence rather than interpretation. I told the performers: "The focus is never on the self, but on the materials, gestures, and actions which we generate and which involve us. Sense that we become what we see, what we touch. A certain tenderness (or empathy) is pervasive — even to the most violent actions: cutting, chopping, throwing chickens, for instance. Our senses — tactile, visual, aural — should be completely identified with our immediate environment; either in action, or simply sitting and not moving."

Finally, after intensive work on action/reaction spans, use of material, placement, time duration, co-ordination of movements, cue systems, the performers understood the work as a process combining my need to "see" it and their ability to realize it — that the piece belonged to them to enjoy, rummage in, recast. If their actions were unpolished, crude, sometimes amused or bewildered, then that was what they experienced and projected and would be aware of, rather than some imposed attitude outside of what they actually felt and experienced. All mechanical, intellectual, predictable notions of movement and relationship were behind us, and at this point I would vary materials and instructions to sustain a certain tension; to create an off-balance quality to ensure responses which were totally engaged — that is, both spontaneous and accurate. Just *before* the performers were comfortable and secure about procedure I would change sequences and instructions to keep them diverse, complex, and surprising so as to provoke not only the kind but the quality of involvement I wanted.

In *Meat Joy* I needed a natural, uncontrolled flow between physical action and facial expression, and this had to be learned — to work with a natural, unset face; that they could laugh, grimace, screech, stare blankly, say ouch and even fart or belch.

My original intention was that we perform naked; I visualized the natural bodies in action — clear and present. The bikinis we wore were a reluctant compromise.

Certain parameters of the piece function unchangeably; others vary with each performance. Sequences, light, sound, material are developed in rehearsal and co-ordinated with one another during each performance. Attitude, gesture, relationships between performers and performers and objects are structured in rehearsal and left to freely evolve in each performance. The fish, chickens, and hot dogs were never used before actual performance. The Paint Attack which occurs at the conclusion of the piece we rehearsed as a projective exercise with brushes, dry sponges, working with ideas of contour, mass, color distribution, and energy impulse being directed by the action of arm and body movements, as in painting.

The idea of using particular popular songs throughout the main sections of the piece was clear to me in the very early stages of co-ordinating fleeting or insistent images and motions. *Meat Joy*, in its overall rhythmic structure and physical layout is circular in form — cut through by shafts of diagonal, vertical, horizontal movement and action; circular clusters of figures are a recurring element. And the rock-and-roll songs are not only circular in their very disk-spun nature but in their own thematic and rhythmic form. I planned on their regular three-minute durations and to break into the songs and between them with overlapped, faded, and dominating sequences of street sounds (which I intended to tape in Paris): a transposition of the current, permeating sound environment of the two cities — the sound ambiance that would persistently surround and move into my senses as I was making *Meat Joy*.

The popular songs I chose to use were mainly current American ones (with some

English, Italian heard in Europe) and whether rock 'n' roll, Mersey sound, or Detroit sound, they formed a motley and rather "funky" selection. Most are full of speed, propulsive rhythms, sexual energy — no wilting, nostalgic, slow vibrato for lost, glimpsed, idealized, future-promised "romance"; songs about "making It" — without sentimental hypocrisy or artificial misery. What the gray ones found shocking and objectionable in The Sound when it first appeared (and I remember the outrage and moral offensiveness older people felt) was its fervent, emotional intensity (often couched in "secret," metaphorical language or "nonsense" innuendo), explicit sexual vigor, and the movement this released in the new dances — crude, raw, energetic, "ungraceful"— which could involve the entire body — not just fancy footwork or a pattern of stylized leading and following — and which, further, might involve the entire culture.

The Rue de Seine sounds which intercut between each song are composed mostly of the cries and shouts of street vendors who were selling fish, chickens, sausages, vegetables, and flowers under my window — these cries dominate noises of street traffic — cars starting, stopping, honking, screeching — and often resemble bellowing cows, crying birds, humming animals. These noises are rich and strange; they induce a displacement of the sound continuity I have set up — enlarging, confounding the associative range of the songs.

I made a separate score for each aspect of the piece — one, for instance — in which the rock-and-roll Rue de Seine sounds and actions are related to lighting. Within certain areas of agreement the lighting technician and the sound technician were free to improvise, to vary and adapt their "scores" throughout the piece. They followed formal aspects of the piece, but were also responsive to subtle energy changes of both the performers and the audience. As with everyone else involved in the performance, they had to be very carefully attuned to the nature of the choices they were free to make; delicate balances in the over-all relations of the elements could be destroyed by wrong choices.

Each performer also had a "score" for make-up; there were certain colors, tones, and structural effects which I saw for each face. I worked out a make-up for each performer — almost painting the face, but without letting it become precisely like-a-painted-face; finally the performers were encouraged to adapt this further for themselves.

My lighting ideas are always difficult to realize, and I've had to have patient and imaginative lighting technicians to work with. I will know that I want "a muddy light in a pool over here which then turns to diffuse gold . . . in another area something blue and wet looking and a blast of green turning up over there." I make an elaborate painted light score, with diagrams of possible movement and duration, and then I find out what is actually possible. I've never wanted dramatic or "theatrical" lighting; the color focus must be integral to the work and must be on the performers themselves — that is, not so as to turn them green, but rather to have greenness come from them; not to dramatize a fixed space, but to provide a pacing of color in this particular environment. The lighting in *Meat Joy* was keyed to the larger rhythms of the piece in subtle washes, with concentrations of strong illumination for certain energy clusters, and so as to focus intensities.

There are four black-outs in *Meat Joy*, which I use to compact or shatter a sequence — to concentrate in the eye the sensory effect of actions and gestures usually aiming for a total sensory receptivity on the part of the audience; actions and gestures setting up an intensive demand on visual, aural, and kinetic response. The audience is assaulted with moving lights, colors, textures; shifting directions, lines of actions in space; units of small, contained gestures — any and all of which carry the essential character of the work, which contains them in this compressed time and space. To break this, then, is suddenly to insert a "blank" in which perception is halted, the imagery settling into the mind, fusing, spreading.

The figure described as Serving Maid functions in a way related to the function of the rock-and-roll sounds. She becomes an image of continuity — repeatedly moving in and out of the action to fulfill her banal tasks; her reappearance becomes as predictable or likely as the occurrence of another rock-and-roll song. It is as if this figure and the songs are some skin or envelope which enfold the action. The sound is conceived as almost a drone, with particular songs and particular sections of songs used for an intrusive, disruptive quality (ingathering aural sense, provoking connections of popular culture and breaking these connections in the context of the piece's action — often ironically, humorously, *i.e.:* "My Boy Lollipop," as the fish, chickens, and hot dogs are thrown onto the fallen performers; "Anyone Who Had A Heart," during the "undressing walk."). The Serving Maid moves flatfootedly, efficiently, endlessly from task to task — dealing with fantastic refuse, rubbish, props, and then introducing materials matter-of-factly which will unleash the most extraordinary excesses and indulgences on the part of the performers.

I wanted *Meat Joy* to follow the direction which its formative drawings and notes had indicated: to be excessive, indulgent, a flesh celebration with all sorts of materials as extensions of flesh (the fish, chickens, hot dogs, paper-strewn floor, wet paint, transparent plastic, brushes, ropes); a propulsion toward the ecstatic; an emotional range shifting precariously between tenderness, banality, wildness, precision, and abandon — with these qualities so juxtaposed as to be ambiguously mixed — simultaneously comic, disturbing, exhilarating.

These interior processes which have become visions — which have become enacted imagery — assume a receptivity, a viewing response which is also fluid, engaged, open, enlarging; an unlimited possibility for perceptual continuities and juxtapositions in the viewer. I wanted my audience to be an energy complement enclosing and corresponding to the energy stream of performance. I placed the audience as close as possible to the performance area, surrounding it like a skin. My over-all conception is that of a sensory arena. Performance allows me involvement with changing metaphors, including every possibility of sensory ambiguity: the transference of aural to tactile, taste to feel, gesture to taste, shape to gesture to action: an inundation and intensification of sensory information.

Audience reaction to all this can be violently antipathetic: the pleasures of the body in free, energetic motion, erotic physical contact, may be considered "disgusting" or "boring" or an "imposition" or confused with an outright sexual act. On the other hand, and as I hope, the audience may take the action into themselves because it is present, immanent, and "real." Or, they may even become involved with dream/wish material: they may wish that would happen to them some time (they always wanted to be slathered with paint, to roll in piles of papers), they wanted to do that too, they could have imagined all this themselves. (And some, I have even learned, actually find emotional levels set off in them which lead them to change or enlarge some aspect of their own lives.)

The creation of *Meat Joy* was one way my own energies could be cast against fragmentation, depersonalization, and, in general, inertness, non-sensuousness — both in the theatre and out. I'm pleased when audience response to *Meat Joy* is: "Yes! — life is really like that . . ." For me it is. I'm not interested in "fantasy."

Meat Joy is dedicated to James Tenney.

MEAT JOY

Scenario

Carolee Schneemann

CAST

CENTRAL MAN
CENTRAL WOMAN
TWO LATERAL MEN
TWO LATERAL WOMEN
INDEPENDENT WOMAN
INDEPENDENT MAN
SERVING MAID

THE SERVING MAID in black, with a huge starched white apron. She functions throughout as a stage-manager-in-the-open, wandering in and out of the performance area to care for practical details: gathering discarded clothing, spreading plastic sheeting, dumping the fish and chickens, distributing props. Performers call out to her when necessary. Her matter-of-fact actions are deceptive, since cues and co-ordinations of materials and sequences often depend on her.

THE CENTRAL MAN and CENTRAL WOMAN hold the major intensity and are the main energy source.

THE LATERAL MEN and LATERAL WOMEN perform as complements/doubles.

THE INDEPENDENT WOMAN sets up a private world on her mattress, at the perimeter of action; she joins the others during "men lighting women under plastic."

THE INDEPENDENT MAN joins the INDEPENDENT WOMAN from the audience. He arrives dressed in street clothes over bikini pants. All other men wear bikini pants under work clothes. The women wear bikini pants and bras covered with stringy, colored feathers. The CENTRAL WOMAN enters in blouse and skirt. INDEPENDENT WOMAN wears a kimono over a bikini covered with scrappy tiger fur.

SETTING

The audience is seated in a long, narrow horse-shoe curve, bisected by two narrow aisles. The curve moves right around the performing area. There are fewer seats than people to occupy them, and so part of the audience is seated on the floor as close to the performance area as possible. A separation of more than two feet between audience and performers creates a spatial energy lapse which I will wish to avoid in this work. The movements, colors, bodies, odors of the piece should overflow into the audience. The horseshoe curve faces a balcony or open tier; beneath the balcony the performers make most of their entrances and exits.

PROLOGUE

As the audience enters and is seated the tape of "Meat Joy Notes as Prologue" is begun. The tape combines an overlapping collage of my voice reading the written material formative to Meat Joy (the entire piece is described, as well as discarded, unrealizable imagery); my beginning French exercises (from a French dictionary and a picture book entitled Look and Learn); a ticking clock and noises of the street recorded from the window in my room in Paris, Rue de Seine.

At this time the performers carry in a long table, chairs, trays with make-up, cups, brandy, water, etc. The table is set facing the audience, close to the entrance-exit area. The performers wear old shirts and robes over their costumes; as they face the make-up table mirror, their backs are to the audience. The tape is twenty minutes long, and for its duration I move among the performers, who sit casually at the table, completing their make-up. We talk, sew last feathers on, smoke, and drink from cups. Before the conclusion of the tape the audience is restive, annoyed by the barrage of words from the amplified tape. The tape ends. We carry away the table. Lights out with exception of a small illumination above the balcony.

Lights and Sound	*Action*
Meat Joy Notes, French Lesson tape. Lights dim in hall; spot on table. 20 min.	SERVING MAID and stage hands cover entire floor with heavy plastic sheets. Performers assembled at long table. Make up, free movement, talk. Audience enters.
Small work light; work noises; blackout.	Make-up table cleared away. LATERAL MEN to balcony. LATERAL WOMEN lie down in audience area.
Rock-and-roll — Rue de Seine tape at full blast. "One for the Money," "Blue Suede Shoes." Narrow spot from balcony to floor below.	From the balcony LATERAL MEN drop huge plastic sheets to position. Five large paper scraps flutter down. Slow fall of paper to *inundation* making the central pyre below five feet high — momentum/cascade. (Huge hunks of paper, mostly shiny white, some gold, blue.)
Low-level light fans into center. "Tutti Frutti," Rue de Seine.	LATERAL MEN slide down rope from balcony; across floor to find their partners lying in audience area. They pull them out by their feet, lift and carry them to positions in front and to sides of center paper pile.
Soft spot follows.	CENTRAL MAN and WOMAN enter from under balcony, beginning of Undressing Walk — slow motion. She walks backward, always no more than a few paces separate them; they keep eyes on one another. The undressing is done as a slow series of exchange motions, one after the other but with a pause in between; only one hand is used at a time in a clear, sustained, slow reaching to the clothing of the other. If the action of undoing a button or pulling a shirt free takes more than a few moments that action is left uncompleted; the other takes his turn; the uncompleted action is returned to. (Example: it takes about six slow, pulling gestures to pull out the man's shirt. Four separate moves to get it over his head/or down his arms since only one motion at a time is allowed.) Each article of clothing taken off is dropped slowly, clearly. The woman simply steps out of her skirt, which the man loosens, and keeps walking. The man's pants require a sequence similar to that of blouse-over-the-woman's-head; the exchanges are halted; he raises blouse, pauses, keeps walking, raises it further; her arms follow, pause, raise, lift it away. Their facial expressions are concentrated on one another.
Lights up on sides (over "Body Packages").	Simultaneously the LATERAL MEN begin Body Package. The girls rest on their backs where they have been carried, their arms remain free as the men slowly, deliberately walk into the paper pyre, select a few large papers and bring them back, placing them on the torsos of the
Rue de Seine.	

Rue de Seine.

Rue de Seine, "From Me to You."

girls; they pile up a nice fat mound of paper and tuck it around their hips, some of it vertically up over their shoulders, where it also functions as padding for the "Body Rolls." When the Body Package is sufficient they call to the Serving Maid: "Rope!" She brings a length to each one, and they tie in the papers at the girls' waists.

In related rhythms, each man gets up and begins walking away, looking back; they break into long, circling runs as approaches/feints to their Body Package.

Dull amber-gold light.

The INDEPENDENT WOMAN walks in and out carrying her mattress, tea set, pillows, books, cakes, and oranges, and sets up her space to the right of pyre, beyond Body Package, at the edge of the audience — their feet nearly in her bed.

"Baby Love."

Rue de Seine.

LATERAL MEN after several feints at top speed skid in by Body Packages (like skidding into First base), gather girls in their arms and in unbroken motion begin Body Roll. Their actions are not precisely co-ordinated; each has a particular speed and direction to his rolls (one cutting space laterally, fast; the other short, slower rolls in eddying circles). If they roll into each other or the Undressing Walk which occurs simultaneously, or part of the audience, they stop, rest, shift directions of rolling.

"Where Did Our Love Go."

Rue de Seine.

When they wish, each man stops, raises his partner on her feet — papers flutter and spread; he adjusts the papers attentively; goes down and takes her on top of him and begins rolls again. Or he may rise onto his knees and lift her onto her knees: they stretch arms out slowly, and exchange slow pushes, bending back as far as the push propels them. They join and roll.

CENTRAL MAN and WOMAN, now undressed, have completed their series of circling walks. They exit.

Brief black-out.

Rue de Seine.

"That's the Way Boys Are."

CENTRAL WOMAN hides in center paper pile completely covered by papers. SERVING MAID with flashlight walks about gathering up discarded clothing. INDEPENDENT WOMAN continues to eat, pour tea, shift things about in her space. CENTRAL MAN into audience opposite pyre; he sits on the floor between chairs. LATERAL COUPLES lie where they were as lights went out, resting.

Diffuse gold light.

Brightening light.

LATERAL MEN carry women forward, close to pyre, the women acquiescent, relaxed. They place the women on their backs, tuck their legs up against their chests. The men then run to and from the central paper pyre, carrying armfuls of papers, which they drop and spread over the women. (They are careful not to expose the CENTRAL WOMAN.) They are brisk and conscientious — watchful of what they do.

Rue de Seine.

"Baby Love."

INDEPENDENT MAN comes from the audience; he walks slowly to the INDEPENDENT WOMAN and speaks with her, asking if he may join her on the mattress. They speak together. He carefully removes his jacket, tie, shoes, and pants, and settles onto the mattress. She offers him tea and cake. They read something, talk, and play a game of bouncing oranges on their stomachs and then exchanging them by bounces.

"From Me to You."

Rue de Seine.

When the LATERAL WOMEN are completely covered with papers, the LATERAL MEN rush to the central pyre, rummaging; they find the CENTRAL WOMAN's feet, which they seize and pull straight up into the air. She is raised on her hips beneath the paper, and immediately begins Leg Choreography — the legs moving as if dancing upright, walking, pedaling a bicycle, etc. The men quickly pack the loose papers down and around her hips to expose the legs; they run around the pile punching and hitting loose papers into the center. They return to their own partners, repeating these actions around them individually. They crouch down to watch the motions of the legs they have thus set off.

Flickering amber beam follows CENTRAL MAN.

CENTRAL MAN comes slowly, deliberately from audience, across floor to central pyre. He seizes moving legs of CENTRAL WOMAN and drags her out of the pyre, papers streaming behind her. He lifts her into an awkward hold, moving across the floor.

LATERAL MEN have slipped off their outer pants and jumped into the pile of papers; they lie flat on their backs, hips raised, buttocks touching women's buttocks. They scoop up and scatter papers over their heads and torsos until only their legs show: Leg Mixture.

"Anyone Who Had a Heart," Rue de Seine.

CENTRAL MAN, comes parallel to the paint table, suddenly drops CENTRAL WOMAN. Motionless. They look at each other, she raises her arms slightly and he grasps her hands and jerks her up in the air as high as he can, taking her weight against his chest. He shakes her as long and violently as possible until they fall over onto the paint table. He has fallen on his back, she on top of him.

Soft spot on paint table.

Motionless. Very slowly she slips off him, reaching under the table with one hand to pull out brushes, paint bowls (puts bowls on table at his side, keeping one in her hand, with brush); rising, moving toward his head. Begins Love-Paint-Exchange, as she moves around in back of the table slowly painting his face, chest, arms, sex, thighs, feet, legs.

"Wishin' and Hopin'."

Rue de Seine.

LATERAL MEN stand up out of leg and paper pile. They begin running jumps across floor and back into pile; then they leap over the women in the pile, alternating this with short bursts of running. The women, still with their legs in the air and on their backs, slowly swiveling, complicating the hurdle they present.

"My Guy."

Rue de Seine.

"That's the Way Boys Are."

As the CENTRAL WOMAN comes around the table, painting his legs, the CENTRAL MAN sits up, reaches for paint brush in her hand and takes it. He drops his legs over the side of the table and begins gently painting her face; slowly standing, painting her body. She takes up another brush and bowl and they start to exchange body-paintings, gathering speed across the floor where the LATERAL MEN still run. They drop brushes and bowls, mix wet paint on their bodies directly, surface against surface, twisting, turning, faster and faster. Exit.

Black-out.

LATERAL COUPLES exit in dark. SERVING MAID hands women plastic sheets; flashlights with cords attached are given to the men.
She brings plastic sheet to INDEPENDENT COUPLE and gathers up brushes, bowls, clothing as LATERAL WOMEN and CENTRAL WOMAN go into performance area where they cover themselves with a plastic sheet; they sit apart in a roughly triangular formation. The INDEPENDENT COUPLE cover themselves with a plastic sheet but remain sitting up.

Black-out.

The men release lights on ropes in wide arcs . . . very slow, large patterns of movement. The lights are colored red and green. They mutually watch the lights, coordinating directions and rhythms as they walk in slow wide arcs; faster light arcs: variations of vertical, horizontal, diagonal patterns; over heads of the audience, as high as possible, as low as possible, with sudden shifts of light shafts back toward center; the men come closer together — staccato light sequence as they pull ropes in closer. They fall quickly to the floor and fan out in Alarm Positions (starfish). Women begin slow, *angular* movements under plastic: angling elbows, knees, feet (all pointed parts) to shape plastic. INDEPENDENT COUPLE do variations of this together. Rustling in the dark; men scuttle across floor to spot fragments, details of moving form of women and INDEPENDENT COUPLE. Back and forth; abrupt. Movement subsiding as women turning under sheets slowly move into center of floor; men crawl on their stomachs . . . closing in, they flicker the lights off into the plastic . . . on . . . off . . . not moving. All these figures are now grouped closely together in a kind of heap. The INDEPENDENT COUPLE has rolled over into this heap. They lie still.

From their pile the performers call for "Rosette"— the Intractable Rosette (how to get four flesh bodies moving as one combined unit — as a water-lily, a carousel, a floating stone sculpture?). Men gather women into circular formation, back to back. This sequence of attempts to turn the women into sculptural shapes which can move as a unit is not pre-set. They all improvise. The women link arms or legs; the men may take ropes to tie their legs or arms together; they arrange them lying down, sitting up, spread-eagled, rolled in a ball, and they try to move them (star, wheel, flower, crystal) as if they were one solid structure. Each time the "unit" falls apart; they all shout instructions, suggestions, ideas, advice, complaints. And each time the women are set and the men begin to move them (synchronized) they roll apart, lose balance, fall over, get squashed, etc. The men may choose The Tree as the final arrangement; here the men stand the women up, raise their hands and fingers high over their heads, touching their hands together in the center. Each man stands close against the grouped women, encircling with his arms as many as he can. They all try to move as a free-wheeling circle, which is impossible. They fall over, yelping. They lie motionless.

SERVING MAID enters with dignity, carrying a huge tray of raw chickens, mackerel, strings of hot dogs. Slowly, extravagantly she strews fish, chickens and hot dogs over all the bodies. Wet fish, heavy chickens, bouncing hot dogs — bodies respond sporadically — twitching, pulling back, hands reaching, touching out of the pile, grunts and groans, giggles. Grasping one of the new objects they sit up to examine their situation. Individual instructions for fish and chickens are evolved: slips, flops, flips, jumps, throwing and catching, drawing, falling, running, standing still, patting, sucking, eating, stuffing, rubbing, slapping, exchanging, stroking. (Ex-

---

"Non Ho L'Eta."
Slow central lights.

Rue de Seine,
"Non Ho L'Eta."

Rue de Seine.

"Maybe I Know."

Rue de Seine.

"My Guy."

Rue de Seine.

Full light.
"Non Ho L'Eta."
Rue de Seine.

"My Boy Lollipop."
Rue de Seine.

"Where Did Our Love Go." Rue de Seine. "Baby Love." Rue de Seine.

ample: LATERAL WOMAN attacked by others; INDEPEN-
DENT WOMAN concentrates her activities on the periphery
of the group until someone pulls her in; INDEPENDENT
MAN with fish follows contours of woman's body with
it, while at the same time this same woman may be engaged with some one else or several others.) Tenderly,
then wildly. All are to be inundated finally with fish,
chickens, hot dogs. The smell of raw fish permeates the
entire room.

"Bread and Butter."
Rue de Seine.

"Anyone Who Had a
Heart."
Rue de Seine.
"That's the Way
Boys Are."

Rue de Seine.

Call goes out for "hats." Women again propped in a
circle, back to back. SERVING MAID brings plastic scarves
and hairpins. Each man makes a secure but wild hat for
a woman. Call goes out for "paint." SERVING MAID
scurries back in with large green and orange buckets full
of colored paints, brushes, sponges, which she distri-
butes among the men. Deliberately each man paints a
brilliant linear face on a woman; then each man thoughtfully paints a woman's body; they continue, faster and
faster, to cover them with paint — stroked, streaked,
thrown, hurled (three hundred years of painting techniques combined).

The women may smile contentedly, amusedly at first.
They watch the movement of the paint until finally they
are yelling, howling, twisting, turning; trying to rise

"I Only Want to Be
with You."

slipping and falling on the splattered plastic. Each man
grabs up a woman and carries/drags her out over the
littered floor as CENTRAL WOMAN hollers, "Enough,
enough!"

Black-out

Time: 60–80 minutes

The Paris Cast   *The New York Cast*

Carolee Schneemann	CENTRAL WOMAN	Carolee Schneemann
Daniel Pommereulle	CENTRAL MAN	James Tenney
Danielle Auffrey	LATERAL WOMAN	Dorothea Rockburne
Romain Denis	LATERAL MAN	Tom O'Donnell
Annina Nosei	LATERAL WOMAN	Irina Posner
Claude Richard	LATERAL MAN	Robert D. Cohen
Rita Renoir	INDEPENDENT WOMAN	Sandra Chew
Jacques Seiler	INDEPENDENT MAN	Stanley Gochenouer
Claudia Hutchins	SERVING MAID	Ann Wilson

May 1964 Centre Americain
Blvd Raspail
Festival de la Libre Expression I

November 1964
Judson Church

The Songs (Collaged with Paris Street Noises)

Blue Suede Shoes	Elvis Presley
Tutti Frutti	Elvis Presley
Anyone Who Had a Heart	Dionne Warwick
From Me to You	The Beatles
That's the Way Boys Are	Lesley Gore
Non Ho L'Eta	Gigliola Cinquetti
Riggazzi	Gigliola Cinquetti
My Boy Lollipop	Millie Small
Where Did Our Love Go	The Supremes
Baby Love	The Supremes
Bread and Butter	The Newbeats
I Only Want to Be with You	Dusty Springfield
Wishin' and Hopin'	Dusty Springfield
My Guy	Mary Wells

The Owl Answers

The American Negro (now called black) first appeared in American theatre as an "Ethiopian entertainer," featured in minstrel shows and "coon shows" throughout the eighteenth and nineteenth centuries. The twentieth century found him a headliner in vaudeville, where Bert Williams and "Bojangles" Robinson were great stars. However, as late as the 1920's he was just an object of amusement in Noble Sissle's *Chocolate Dandies*, in Harlem clubs that catered to socialites slumming "in diamonds and pearls," and in Broadway musicals with revealing titles like *Shuffle Along* and *Black Birds*. In the serious theatre, black actors had to struggle for recognition in plays written by whites, though some actors made histrionic history: Charles Gilpin in O'Neill's *Emperor Jones*, Frank Wilson in Paul Green's *In Abraham's Bosom*, Richard B. Harrison in Marc Connelly's *Green Pastures*, and Paul Robeson in such plays as Shakespeare's *Othello*. Canada Lee appeared in various classical roles and somewhat evened the score for the blackface of Al Jolson and Eddie Cantor by appearing in whiteface.

Early black playwrights still remain unknown to most people. Who speaks of William Wells Brown and his *The Escape; or, A Leap to Freedom* (1858), Angeline Gimke's *Rachel* (1916), Ridgely Thomas, Frank Wilson, Willis Richardson, Alain Locke, or the *plays* of Hall Johnson and Langston Hughes? Not until 1959, when Lorraine Hansberry's first play *A Raisin in the Sun* opened with a cast full of names that were to become famous in time — Ruby Dee, Sidney Poitier, Diana Sands, Claudia McNeill, Lonne Elder III, and Douglas Turner [Ward] were some of them — did a play written by a black about black life in America receive wide attention. Brooks Atkinson praised its "vigor and veracity," the New York Drama Critics' Circle Award was bestowed on Hansberry, the youngest (and the only black) playwright up to that time, the movie version won the Cannes Film Festival prize, and white America became aware of the problems depicted in the poem by Langston Hughes ("Father of the Harlem Renaissance") from which Hansberry took her title:

> What happens to a dream deferred?
> Does it dry up
> Like a raisin in the sun?

The black voice was always there, but perhaps it is typical that the whites date it from the first moment they paid it close attention.

Before presenting *The Owl Answers*, a black play by another and more recent American woman playwright, Adrienne Kennedy, a short article by Lorraine Hansberry will serve as an introduction.

Lorraine Hansberry was cruelly cut off by cancer at 34 while her awkward, didactic drama of *The Sign in Sidney Brustein's Window* was foundering on Broadway in 1965. She did not live to see her tragic life and inspiring writings (adapted by Robert Nemiroff as *To Be Young, Gifted and Black*) make a hit in New York and then enjoy a successful national tour. Perhaps her considerable personal charm caused her to be overrated. Emory Lewis proclaimed her "a major U.S. writer" and James Baldwin eulogized "Sweet Lorraine" in *Esquire*. She was decidedly not a major talent, but she did bring black problems (and black audiences) to the theatre. She inspired even better writers, and she challenged the "TV Tube" credo of America that "the present social order is here forever" and "Negroes do not exist." For too brief a time she did exist, gifted and black, and she helped to make Ralph Ellison's "invisible man" visible on the stage.

In "Bop," one of the Harlem stories in which Langston Hughes' character Simple speaks his mind, we find this exchange:

> "You bring race into everything," I said, "even music."
> "It is everything," said Simple.

Perhaps race isn't everything. But it is something, something important, and after Lorraine Hansberry it was the inspiration (as was her success) of a whole new generation of black playwrights. Today the theatre, in New York and Newark and New Orleans and elsewhere, is speaking to and for the large minority. Black drama is still not receiving the attention it deserves, especially in light of theatre's power to reach the masses and to be more immediate and more forceful than print. Historians are chronicling the slave trade and unearthing fascinating slave narratives, as well as writing of Frederick Douglass, W. E. B. DuBois and moderns like Malcolm X and Eldridge Cleaver. Julius Lester has collected *Black Folktales* for children (with some mention of white masters, "all of whom are portrayed as vicious or stupid," by the way) and Abraham Chapman has produced two anthologies of *Black Voices*. Nancy M. Tischler (*Black Masks: Negro Characters in Modern Southern Fiction*) and other scholars are turning out solid academic studies for university presses. More and more schools are offering Black Studies programs. Countee Cullen, James Weldon Johnson, and older writers are being brought to the attention of readers who imagined that Ralph Ellison, Richard Wright, and James Baldwin were the first black writers of all time. Here in America the balance is being redressed.

But sometimes it seems that there is more notice and encouragement of the dramatists of Black Africa (John Pepper Clark, James Ene Henshaw, Lewis Nkosi, among recent ones) than there is in America of American achievement. The historians of *The Free Southern Theatre* — a movement the Kirkus review called activity in "black backwaters" — say the play "was *not* the thing, communications and involvement were, as this small, fragmented troupe tried with all aesthetic earnestness to create a black theatre within the framework of black experience." Today there is an important as well as a vital black theatre. At its best it soars high above politics and propaganda and discusses race without rancor while not neglecting to inculcate a sense of pride and proportion in a minority which (as Christine X. Johnson wrote in *Muhammed's Children*, 1963) must "grow up in a belief that it is great to be born BLACK, and not a calamity, or a disgrace."

We have passed beyond both Ossie Davis' amusing views of what he calls "the Negro profession" and segregation as "ridiculous because it makes perfectly wonderful people, white and black, do ridiculous things," beyond, too, the blind fury of LeRoi Jones' "killing white people, killing the shit they've built." We have art that can help toward eradicating prejudice and command admiration, not simply exploit prejudice and shock, drama (as playwright Ed Bullins said) that is "not a higher form of white art in blackface," original, "something entirely different and new that encompasses the soul and spirit of black people, and that represents the whole experience of our being here in this oppressive land." Following Davis' *Purlie Victorious* (and the musical *Purlie*) and Loften Mitchell's *A Land Beyond the River* have been Charles Gordone's *No Place to be Somebody* and more incisive insights from Douglas Turner Ward (*Happy Ending, Day of Absence*), Lonne Elder III (*Ceremonies in Dark Old Men*), Ed Bullins (*Goin' a Buffalo, In New England Winter*), LeRoi Jones* (*Dutchman, The Slave, Slave Ship*, as well as his four *Revolutionary Plays*), and violent but also forceful works from William Wellington Mackey, Charles H. Fuller, Jr., Ben Caldwell, Marvin X, Salimu, Sonia Sanchez, and many others.

The word that comes to mind about Adrienne Kennedy is not "violence" but "power." She was born in Pittsburgh in 1931 and made her mark in the off-Broadway theatre with *Funnyhouse of a Negro*, which won the Obie (best off-Broadway play of the year). Her other works include *A Lesson in a Dead Language, A Rat's Mass, A Beast's Story*, and *The Owl Answers*, which premièred at Lucille Lortel's White Barn Theatre in Westport, Connecticut, at the end of the 1965 summer season. The cast, directed by Michael Kahn, then was:

---

* Mr. Jones is the Imamu Ameer Baraka of the Cultural Nationalist Movement.

She	Ellen Holly
Bastard's Black Mother	Lynn Hamilton
Goddam Father	Bill Moor
The White Bird	Ross Parkes
The Negro Man	Milton Irons
Shakespeare	Michael Warren Powell
Chaucer	Alex Giannini
William the Conqueror	Patrick Gorman

Before the play, some background from Lorraine Hansberry:

Me Tink Me Hear Sounds in de Night
LORRAINE HANSBERRY

I was visited some weeks ago by a young actress, a member of the cast of a quite successful Broadway show, who had herself won considerable praise from critics and audiences. I also knew her to be among the truly serious students of her profession: one of those devoted actors who spend so many self-imposed extra hours per week in dance, acting, and voice studios. She was twenty-four, deeply talented, profoundly dedicated to her work, possessed of a vigorous Broadway credit, and — a Negro.

So we spoke at length of her career. Had she, for instance, had offers of other work when the current show closed? "Well," she told me between two sighs, "there is a fall-coming show that I was called in to read for. It turned out to be an opportunity to play Young Negro Problem again." She explained discerningly that an American author, on the incomplete, if desperately welcome, rebound from stereotypes, had written a part for someone who was to make an entrance as a Social Question and exit as a Social Question. And that swiftly.

"How," she asked, "can anybody study for *that*? How can you find shading and character in the absence of shading and character?" As an actress she wanted to know how it was possible to interpret humanly that which was simply devoid of human definition. When would contemporary dramatists not be afraid to invest Negro characters with ordinary human complication, now that, to some degree, more overtly obnoxious traditions had started to fade?

Thinking of her excellent notices in the current show, I asked if what she had described had *really* been the only sign of future work. She laughed and replied, "Oh, no. I had a television call to read for a *traditional*. Not a maid; the *other* category, the 'native girl' bit. And, thought I, a job is a job. So I got the script, studied the lines, and went to the reading. And I read: *'Me sit on me hummock and me tink me hear sounds in de night and den . . .'* I finally just choked up on it, and closed the book and thanked the people for hearing me, and left. I just can't make that scene any more, my dear. Dis here native is tired of sittin on de hummock!"

When she departed I was left to reflect on the general situation of Negroes in the American theatre. The authors of the two plays we had discussed were not singularly stupid or untalented people; the question was larger and deeper than their mere inadequacy in dealing with certain kinds of characterization. They had been trapped creatively by an old, monumentally encompassing, and deeply entrenched legacy from history.

The sixteenth-century spirit of mercantile expansionism that swept Europe, and gave rise to colonial conquest and the European slave trade, was also father of a modern concept of racism. The concept made it possible to render the African a "commodity" in the minds of white men, and to alienate the conscience of the rising European humanism from identification with the victims of that conquest and slave trade. In order to accommodate programs of commerce and empire on a scale never before known in history, the Negro had to be placed arbitrarily outside the pale of recognizable humanity in the psychology of Europeans and, eventually, of white America. Neither his soul nor his body was to be allowed to evoke empathy. He was to be — and, indeed, *became*, in a created mentality of white men — some grotesque expression of the mirth of nature; a fancied static vestige of the primeval past; an eternal exotic who, unlike men, would not bleed when pricked nor revenge when wronged. Thus for three centuries in Europe and America alike, buffoonery or villainy was his only permissible role in the hall of entertainment or drama. And notwithstanding the few later exceptions in Europe (the most distinguished, of course, being the career of Ira Aldridge, an American-born Negro actor of the nineteenth century who toured Europe in Shakespearean companies and achieved considerable recognition), in America the sight or even the notion of a Negro gripped in the complex agonies of a Hamlet outraged a cultural legend as today it yet embarrasses it.

That is why, 140 years ago, local hoodlums descended on the African Repertory Theatre Company at Bleecker and Mercer Streets in New York City, and harassed its actors and audiences out of existence. And that is why Negroes are not integrated in our theatre today.

It is this old historical situation that confronts a theatre, some of whose dramatists are currently baffled by Negro character, and whose producers and their receptionists are reduced to rudeness or apologetic embarrassment as they face the miraculously stubborn and increasing battalion of dark, hopeful faces among the multitude of other hopeful faces in their famous outer offices.

Presumably talent, all talent, is good for the theatre as democracy is for a democratic nation. But to say so is to ignore that breathlessness and perplexed expression in the countenance of our theatre as it asks, over and over again, "What can *realistically* be done about integrating the Negro in the theatre, given the present racial climate in the United States?"

The question implies that to integrate Negro actors in most dramatic situations is to perpetuate a social lie and invalidate the responsibility of art. It also has a way of starting at the point where artistic questions *are* relevant. It rather sneakingly ignores a stupendous area where "art" has nothing to do with discrimination in the theatre. For instance, I have never had the experience of purchasing a ticket from a Negro in a Broadway box office; I cannot imagine it to be a matter of either art or qualification, since, I can testify from personal experience, short-temperedness is not limited to white people, and it is that trait, we have all come to assume, that is the prime qualification for those legendary posts. Nor have I ever purchased a box of mints, or received my program, from a Negro lobby vendor or usher. And, to proceed to more important areas, I have not, in my wanderings backstage, found my 10 per cent represented in the handling of flats, lights, or properties, or calling time to the actors. Only on the rarest of occasions have I spotted Negroes in the orchestra pits (I believe only at New York's City Center does that phenomenon occur with even minimal regularity); and never, of course, wielding the baton, despite the lingering legend of a certain people's acute "musicalbility." Similar observations may be made of the chorus lines in our musical comedies.

As for the situation among other echelons of the theatre — the actors, writers, and directors — I think only the first two deserve more concentrated thought than the categories already covered. Directors should be men or women who are sufficiently talented to have works of art put under their direction. I cannot believe that their height, diet, place of birth, or race will affect those talents. Naturally it is to be desired that a director have adequate cultural reference to his script, but intelligence dictates that we do not hesitate to appoint plays with Japanese settings to Americans, or American settings to decidedly English directors, and so on. When they are good directors they direct well; when they are

poor ones they direct poorly. I have never been able to tell by the quality of a mounting what kind of accent a director has; only whether or not he has done a professional and imaginative piece of work. It would, indeed, take an imaginative piece of argument to show how or why it should be different for Negro directors.

The question of the employment of Negro actors, however, does raise interesting questions, which, it may be argued, in a different sociological atmosphere would be only minor questions of production techniques. But at the moment a fascinating and revealing dichotomy exists within the theatre's most literate circles with regard to the use of Negro actors. People who are most bored and outraged by what they call Ibsenesque or Shavian "boxes" on the imagination of the contemporary theatre, who long for fancy and illusion to take utter command, who can deliver whole sermons on the Philistinism of breaking "real eggs" on stage, very often are, astonishingly enough, among the first to shout betrayal of "realistic" attitudes if one speaks of putting a Negro actor into a non-Negro role. It is most curious. Whoever said, for instance, that Queen Titania was white — or anything else? Or the incidental postman, policeman, clerk, or schoolmate in that contemporary play? Or *all* the people in that New York City crowd scene that is allegedly in Times Square. It takes rather more of a trick to imagine a good many urban American scenes without Negroes than with them.

But, above all, to defend a color barrier in the theatre is to ignore or argue against its essence, which has always been illusion. We do not get the blind to play the blind, or infants to play infants. Nor do we move Southern mansions or oceans on stage. It is not necessary. Our theatre must attain a sufficient degree of maturity and sophistication to put aside artificial barriers, to acknowledge that any truly qualified actor, Negro or white, who is made up properly, can do the job. I am speaking, of course, of roles that specify particular skin and hair coloring. When such matters are irrelevant rather than intrinsic, they should be viewed for what they are, and not be made the imagined basis for such barriers.

With regard to Negro writers, the theatre is yet saddled with the notion that their materials are necessarily parochial, and consequently without interest to the general theatregoing public. It is a difficult attitude to prove by looking back over the last six or seven years, when a vast total of *three* scripts by Negro writers was allowed to reach the Broadway stage for judgment by the *public*. It is interesting to note that of the three, two were quite first-rate efforts. The first found a steady and appreciative audience off Broadway when its Broadway run came to a close, and a subsequent motion-picture sale made a rather tidy sum for its investors. The second not only copped a prize, and earned over a million and a half at last count; it ran more than a year (an excellent record, in view of the disturbingly poor showings made by dramas these days), and got itself scheduled for national tour this season; it received production and translation throughout the world, and only its motion-picture production schedule prevented the American company from being sent abroad, as requested by our government, *to represent our national drama*. That is a peculiar kind of parochialism. And even the third show, a dreadful little piece, lasted several weeks too long, in my opinion, before it was buried. Viewed from any point of view, it is hardly a ratio that the rest of Broadway could duplicate.

The above should not be confused, as it often is, with the production of "Negro shows" by non-Negro writers, a somewhat different field. Such shows can be produced more easily, and they are in an area that requires the most revolutionary transition. In the theatre it is our dramatists and musical-comedy book writers who have the largest responsibility for presenting our world to us with ever-increasing penetration and illumination. Sad to say, they have, with only a few fine and notable exceptions, an exceedingly poor tradition to draw on with regard to Negroes because of the scale of the old alienation.

The Negro, as primarily presented in the past, has never existed on land or sea. It has seldom been a portrait of men, only a portrait of a concept, and that concept has been a romance and no other thing. By its very nature white supremacy longed for the contentment of the Negro with "his place"; one is always eager to believe that *somebody else* is exhilarated by "plenty of nuttin'." Since real-life Negroes — with their history of insurrection, "underground railways," mass enlistments in the Union army, petitions, delegations, organizations, press, and literature, and even music of protest — have failed to oblige, the white writer, in the main, has not failed to people *his* "Negro world" with Negroes who did not seem to know that slavery was intolerable, or that the subsequent and lingering oppression was a form of hell on earth. Thus in the make-believe domains of Porgy and Brutus Jones, only the foibles of *other Negroes* are assaulted; otherwise the heady passions of this particular happy breed are committed only to sex, liquor, and mysteriously motivated ultra-violence, usually over "dis or dat womans." A larger scale of dreams and anguish eluded their creators, and showed some otherwise great creative imaginations to be incapable of the recognition of the universal complexity of humankind.

This does not imply that malice has always been the intent. It would be as foolish to think that Mark Twain or Mrs. Stowe tried to defeat their own humanist protests as to suppose that Marc Connelly, in a different vein, ever dreamed that he was writing a racist document in *The Green Pastures*. Rather, it is a matter of a partially innocent cultural heritage that, out of its own needs, was eager to believe in the colossal charm, among other things, of "childlike" peoples. From that notion, presumably, came the tendency to find non-Negro dramatic and musical materials rendered "quaint" when performed by "all-colored casts." From such an astonishing idea we have been treasured with the likes of *Carmen Jones* in the past, and will undoubtedly be treated to something like *Honeychile Tosca* in the future before it is exhausted. It is also interesting to note, in view of the hoped-for transition, that these translations "to the Negro" have generally meant (aside from adding saxophones and red dresses) haphazardly assaulting the English language beyond recognition, as if the Negro people had not produced an idiom that has a real and specific character, which is not merely the random exclusion of verb endings.

That does not suggest a counterdesire to see Negroes talking (or behaving) just like "everybody else" because, by and large, Negroes do no such thing, as conscientious playwrights will swiftly discover. And neither does "everybody else." American speech is as varied as the wind, and few of our sophisticated writers would dream of putting the speech of Texans into the mouths of New Yorkers for any purpose save that of the broadest comedy. So there is nothing extraordinary in the expectation that Negro speech must eventually be presented with artistic respect for its true color, nuances, and variations as they exist for each class and generation.

Finally, I think that American writers have already begun to believe what I suspect has always been one of the secrets of fine art: that there are no simple men. Chinese peasants and Congolese soldiers make drastic revolutions in the world while the obtuse and myth-accepting go on reflecting on the "inscrutability and eternal placidity" of those people. I believe that when the blinders are dropped, it will be discovered that while an excessively poignant Porgy was being instilled in generations of Americans, his truer-life counterpart was ravaged by longings that were, and are, in no way alien to those of the rest of mankind, and that bear within them the stuff of truly great art. He is waiting yet for those of us who will but look more carefully into his eyes, and listen more intently to his soliloquies. We must not be intimidated by the residue of the past; the world is paying too large a price for the deception of those centuries; each hour that flies teaches that Porgy is as much inclined to hymns of sedition as to lullabies and love songs; he is profoundly complicated and interesting; everywhere he is making his own sounds in the night. I believe that it is within the cultural descendants of Twain and Whitman and Melville and O'Neill to listen and absorb them, along with the totality of the American landscape, and give back their findings in new art to the great and vigorous institution that is the American theatre.

THE OWL ANSWERS

Adrienne Kennedy

CHARACTERS

SHE who is CLARA PASSMORE who is the VIRGIN MARY who is the BASTARD who is the OWL
BASTARD'S BLACK MOTHER who is the REVEREND'S WIFE who is ANNE BOLEYN
GODDAM FATHER who is the RICHEST WHITE MAN IN THE TOWN who is the DEAD FATHER who is REVEREND PASSMORE
THE WHITE BIRD who is REVEREND PASSMORE'S CANARY who is GOD'S DOVE
THE NEGRO MAN
SHAKESPEARE
CHAUCER
WILLIAM THE CONQUEROR

The characters change slowly back and forth into and out of themselves, leaving some garment from their previous selves upon them always to remind us of the nature of SHE who is CLARA PASSMORE who is the VIRGIN MARY who is the BASTARD who is the OWL's world.

SCENE: *A New York subway is the Tower of London is a Harlem Hotel Room is St. Peter's.*

The scene is shaped like a subway car. The sounds are subway sounds and the main props of a subway are visible — poles, fans, lights. Two seats on the scene are like seats on the subway, the seat in which SHE WHO IS sits and

NEGRO MAN's *seat. The colors of the subway props are black.*

Seated is a plain, pallid, middle-aged Negro woman, wearing a cotton summer dress that is too long, a pair of white wedged sandals. Her hair is tightly curled and exceedingly well combed in the manner a great many prim Negro women wear their hair. SHE sits staring into space. SHE is CLARA PASSMORE *who is the* VIRGIN MARY *who is the* BASTARD *who is the* OWL. *Scene moves, lights flash, a sense of exploding imprisonment.*

SHE WHO IS *speaks in a soft voice as a Negro schoolteacher from Savannah would.* SHE WHO IS *carries white handkerchiefs,* SHE WHO IS *carries notebooks that throughout the play like the handkerchiefs fall.* SHE *will pick them up, glance frenziedly at a page from a notebook, be distracted, place the notebooks in a disorderly pile, drop them again, etc.*

The scene should lurch, lights flash, hand straps move, gates slam. When THEY come in and exit, THEY move in the manner of people on a train, too. There is the noise of the train, the sound of moving steel on the track.

The WHITE BIRD's wings should flutter loudly.

The gates, the High Altar, the ceiling, and the Dome are like St. Peter's; the walls are like the Tower of London.

The music which SHE WHO IS hears at the most violent times of her experience should be Haydn's Concerto for Horn in D (Third Movement).

Objects on the stage (beards, wigs, faces) should be used in the manner that people use everyday objects such as spoons or newspapers.

The Tower Gate should be black, yet slam like a subway door.

The gates slam. FOUR PEOPLE enter from dif-

ferent directions. THEY *are* SHAKESPEARE, WILLIAM THE CONQUEROR, CHAUCER, *and* ANNE BOLEYN, *but too they are strangers entering a subway on a summer night, too they are the guards in the Tower of London. Their lines throughout the play are not spoken specifically by one person but by all or part of them.*

THEY: Bastard. (THEY *start at a distance eventually crowding her. Their lines are spoken coldly.* SHE WHO IS *is only a prisoner to them.*) You are not his ancestor. Keep her locked there, guard. Bastard.

SHE: You must let me go down to the chapel to see him. He is my father.

THEY (*jeering*): Your father?

SHE: He is my father.

THEY: Keep her locked there, guard. (CHAUCER *locks the gates.*)

SHE: We came this morning. We were visiting the place of our ancestors, my father and I. We had a lovely morning, we rose in darkness, took a taxi past Hyde Park through the Marble Arch to Buckingham Palace, we had our morning tea at Lyons, then came out to the Tower. We were wandering about the gardens, my father leaning on my arm, speaking of you, William the Conqueror. My father loved you, William —

THEY (*interrupting*): If you are his ancestor why are you a Negro? Yes, why is it you are a Negro if you are his ancestor? Keep her locked there.

SHE: You must let me go down to the chapel to see him.

(THEY *stare coldly,* CHAUCER *and* SHAKESPEARE *exit, slamming the gate, scene moves, lights flash.* ANNE BOLEYN *and* WILLIAM THE CONQUEROR *remain staring at her.* CHAUCER *and* SHAKESPEARE *return carrying a stiff dead man in a black suit. The most noticeable thing about him is his hair — long, silky, white hair that hangs as they bring him through the gate and place him at her feet.*)

THEY: Here is your father.

THEY *then all exit through various gate entrances.* SHE *picks up the dead man, drags him to a dark, carved, highback chair on the right. At the same time a dark* NEGRO MAN, *with a dark suit and black glasses on, enters from the right gate and sits on the other subway seat. Flashing, movement, slamming of gate, fans twirl. The* NEGRO MAN *sits up very straight and proceeds to watch* SHE WHO IS. *Until he speaks to her, he watches her constantly with a wild, cold stare.*)

The DEAD FATHER *appears dead. He is dead. Yet as* SHE *watches, he moves and comes to life. Throughout the play when the characters change and come to life it must give the impression of logic yet be understood that the other state actually existed. When the* DEAD FATHER *was dead, he was dead; when he is the* REVEREND, *he is the* REVEREND. SHE WHO IS *always watches them as they change, for this is her mental state. The* DEAD FATHER *removes his hair, takes off his white face, from the chair he takes a white church robe and puts it on. Beneath his white hair is dark Negro hair. He is now* REVEREND PASSMORE. *After he dresses he looks about as if something is missing, seizes the gate, exits, and returns with a gold bird cage that hangs near the chair and a white battered Bible. Very matter-of-factly he sits down in the chair, stares for a moment at the cage, then opens the Bible, starting to read.* SHE *watches, highly distracted, until he falls asleep. Movement, flash, twirl.*)

ANNE BOLEYN *has remained behind during that time where she stands near a subway pole. She throws red rice at* SHE WHO IS *and the* DEAD FATHER *who is now* REVEREND PASSMORE. *They see her.* SHE *exits and returns with a great black gate (like the gate at Valladolid) and places the gate where the pole is. It is clear now that she has erected the gate but she cannot pass through it.* SHE WHO IS *runs to* ANNE BOLEYN.)

SHE: Anne, Anne Boleyn. (ANNE *throws rice at* SHE WHO IS CLARA PASSMORE *who is the* VIRGIN MARY *who is the* BASTARD *who is the* OWL.) Anne, you know so much of love, won't you help me? They took my father away and will not let me see him. They locked me in this tower and I can see them taking his body across to the chapel to be buried and see his white hair hanging down. Let me into the chapel. He is my blood father. I am almost white, am I not? Let me into St. Paul's Chapel. Let me please go down to St. Paul's Chapel. I am his daughter. (ANNE *appears to listen quite attentively, but her reply is to turn into the* BASTARD'S BLACK MOTHER. *She takes off part of her own long dress and puts on a rose-colored cheap lace dress, the kind of a dress a Southern Negro woman might wear to dress up in, and anything dark on her face.* SHE WHO IS's *reaction is to run back to her subway seat.* SHE *drops her notebooks. The* BASTARD'S BLACK MOTHER *opens her arms to* SHE WHO IS. SHE *returns to the gate.*) Anne. (*As if trying to bring back* ANNE BOLEYN.)

BASTARD'S BLACK MOTHER (*laughs and throws a white bridal bouquet at her*): Clara, I am not Anne. I am the Bastard's Black Mother, who cooked for somebody.

(*Still holding out her arms, she kneels by the gate, her kinky hair awry, eyes closed, she stares upward, praying. Suddenly she stops praying and pulls* SHE WHO IS *through the gate.*)

(*The* WHITE BIRD, *with very loud fluttering wings, flies down from St. Peter's Dome and goes into the cage.* REVEREND PASSMORE *gets up and closes the cage door.*)

SHE: Anne, it is I.

BASTARD'S BLACK MOTHER: Clara, you were conceived by your Goddam Father who was the Richest White Man in the Town and somebody that cooked for him. That's why you're an owl. (*Laughs.*) That's why when I see you, Mary, I cry. I cry when I see Marys, cry for their deaths.

(*The* WHITE BIRD *flies in the cage.* REVEREND *reads.*)
(*The* BASTARD'S BLACK MOTHER *stands at the gate, watches, then takes off rose lace dress and*

black face; *beneath her black face is a more pallid Negro face; pulls down her hair, longer dark hair, and puts on a white dress. From a fold in the dress she takes out a picture of Christ, then kneels and stares upward. She is the* REVEREND'S WIFE. *Scene moves, flashes.*)

REVEREND'S WIFE (*kneeling.* REVEREND *stands and watches her.* REVEREND'S WIFE *takes a vial from her gown and holds it up*): These are the fruits of my maidenhead, owl blood Clara who is the Bastard Clara Passmore to whom we gave our name, see the owl blood, that is why I cry when I see Marys, cry for their deaths, Owl Mary Passmore.

(SHE *gets up, exits from a side gate.* THEY *come in.* SHE WHO IS *goes to the* REVEREND *as if to implore him. He then changes into the* DEAD FATHER, *resuming his dirty white hair.* THEY *stand about.*)

SHE: Dear Father, my Goddam Father who was the Richest White Man in the Town, who is Dead Father — you know that England is the home of dear Chaucer, Dickens and dearest Shakespeare. Winters we spent here at the Tower, our chambers were in the Queen's House, summers we spent at Stratford with dearest Shakespeare. It was all so lovely. I spoke to Anne Boleyn, Dead Father. She knows so much of love and suffering and I believe she is going to try to help me. (*Takes a sheaf of papers from her notebooks; they fall to the floor.*) Communications, all communications to get you the proper burial, the one you deserve in St. Paul's Chapel. They are letting you rot, my Goddam Father who was the Richest Man in the Town — they are letting you rot in that town in Georgia. I haven't been able to see the King. I'll speak again to Anne Boleyn. She knows so much of love.

(*Shows the papers to the* DEAD FATHER *who sits with his hair hanging down, dead. She begins to unbutton her dress fitfully; naturally, since she is the black mother's bastard, her skin is black underneath. The* NEGRO MAN *continues to watch her.* SHE WHO IS *moves about, flash twirling,* REVEREND'S WIFE *prays.* SHE WHO IS *goes again to the* DEAD FATHER, *takes him by*

the hair, stares into his dead face. WHITE BIRD
flies inside the cage. REVEREND'S WIFE stops
praying, watches, smiles. Scene moves, fluttering of wings, lights flash.)

DEAD FATHER: If you are my ancestor why are
you a Negro, Bastard? What is a Negro doing
at the Tower of London staying at the
Queen's House? Clara, I am your Goddam
Father who was the Richest White Man in
the Town and you are a schoolteacher in
Savannah who spends her summers at
Teachers College. You are not my ancestor.
You are my bastard. Keep her locked there,
William.

(THEY stare at her like passengers on a subway,
standing, holding the hand straps.)

SHE: We were wandering about the garden, you
leaning on my arm, speaking of William the
Conqueror. We sat on the stone bench to
rest. When we stood up you stumbled and
fell onto the walk — dead. Dead. I called
the guard. Then I called the Warden and told
him my father had just died, that we had
been visiting London together, the place of
our ancestors and all the lovely English, and
my father just died. (She reaches out to
touch him.)

DEAD FATHER: You are not my ancestor.

SHE: They jeered. They brought me to this
tower and locked me up. I can see they're
afraid of me. From the tower I saw them
drag you across the court . . . your hair hanging down. They have taken off your shoes
and you are stiff. You are stiff. (Touches
him.) My dear father.

(Music: Haydn.)

DEAD FATHER: Daughter of somebody that
cooked for me. (Smiles.)

(He then ignores SHE WHO IS, changes into the
REVEREND, takes the Bible and starts to read.
The WHITE BIRD flies inside the cage. Wings
flutter. The REVEREND'S WIFE praying, lights a
candle. The REVEREND watches the BIRD, sits
down, watches the BIRD flutter, as though he
expects something from him . . . as an answer,
REVEREND'S WIFE lights another candle, then

puts on her black face, rose dress. Some of the
red rice has fallen near her, she says "Oww,"
and starts to peck at it like a bird. She then sits
up facing front on her knees, eyes wide open,
very still, "Oww," she repeats, "Ow." SHE
WHO IS wanders about, then comes to speak to
the BASTARD'S BLACK MOTHER who remains
seated like an owl.)

(End music.)

SHE: It was you the Bastard's Black Mother
who told me. I asked you where did Mr.
William Mattheson's family come from and
you, my Black Mother, said: I believe his
father came from England. England, I said.
England is the Brontës' home. Did you know
Black Bastard's Mother, who cooked for
somebody, in the Reverend's parlor — there
in a glass bookcase are books and England is
the home of Chaucer, Dickens, and Shakespeare. Black Mother who cooked for somebody Mr. William Mattheson died today. I
was at the College. The Reverend's Wife
called me, Clara who is the Bastard who is
the Virgin Mary who is the Owl. Clara, who
is the Bastard who is the Virgin Mary who is
the Owl, Clara she said the Reverend told me
to call and tell you Mr. William Mattheson
died today or it was yesterday he died yesterday. It was yesterday. The Reverend told me
to tell you it was yesterday he died and it is
today they're burying him. Clara who is the
Bastard, you mustn't come. Don't do anything foolish like come to the funeral, Mary.
You've always been such a fool about that
white man, Clara.

But I am coming, the Black Bastard's Mother. I am coming, my Goddam Father who was
the Richest White Man in Jacksonville,
Georgia. When I arrive in London, I'll go out
to Buckingham Palace, see the Thames at
dusk, and Big Ben. I'll go for lovely walks
through Hyde Park, and to innumerable
little tearooms with great bay windows and
white table cloths on little white tables and
order tea. I will go all over and it will be
June. Then I'll go out to the Tower to see
you, my father.

(BASTARD'S BLACK MOTHER has remained like

an owl. THEY *come on and stand as passengers on the subway speaking at random.*)

THEY: If you are his ancestor what are you doing on the subway at night looking for men? What are you doing looking for men to take to a hotel room in Harlem? Negro Men? Negro Men Clara Passmore?

(*In reply the* BASTARD'S BLACK MOTHER *laughs a bird laugh. The* WHITE BIRD *flies out of the cage.*)

SHE (*runs to the* BIRD): My dead father's bird: God's Dove. My father died today.

BIRD (*mocking*): My father died today God's Dove.

SHE: He was the Richest White Man in our Town. I was conceived by him and somebody that cooked for him.

BIRD: What are you doing in the Tower of London then?

(*The* REVEREND *becomes the* DEAD FATHER *who comes forward, takes the* BIRD, *puts him in the cage, shuts the door.*)

SHE: My father. (*He turns, stares at her, and comes toward her and dies; it is his death in the gardens.*) What were you saying of William, my father, you loved William so. (*She holds him in her arms. He opens his eyes.*)

DEAD FATHER (*waking*): Mary, at last you are coming to me.

(*Music: Haydn.*)

SHE: I am not Mary, I am Clara, your daughter, Reverend Passmore — I mean Dead Father.

(BIRD *flies in the cage.*)

DEAD FATHER: Yes, my Mary, you are coming into my world. You are filled with dreams of my world. I sense it all.

(*Silence except for the wild fluttering of the* BIRD's *wings.* NEGRO MAN *stares, lights flash, sound of steel on the track, movement.*)

NEGRO MAN: At last you are coming to me. (*Smiles.*)

DEAD FATHER: Mary, come in here for eternity. Are you confused? Yes, I can see you are confused.

(THEY *come on.*)

THEY: Are you confused?

(*One of them,* CHAUCER, *is now dressed as the* REVEREND. *He comes, falls down onto the empty high-backed chair, and sits staring into the Bible.*)

DEAD FATHER: So at last you are coming to me, Bastard.

(BASTARD'S BLACK MOTHER *exits from gate, returns, part owl with owl feathers upon her, dragging a great dark bed through the gate; the gate slams.*)

BASTARD'S BLACK MOTHER: Why be confused? The Owl was your beginning, Mary. (*Begins to build with the bed and feathers the High Altar; feathers fly.*)

SHE: He came to me in the outhouse, he came to me under the porch, in the garden, in the fig tree. He told me you are an owl, ow, oww, I am your beginning, ow. You belong here with us owls in the fig tree not to somebody that cooks for your Goddam Father, oww, and I ran to the outhouse in the night crying oww, Bastard they say the people in the town all say Bastard, but I, I belong to God and the owls, ow and I sat in the fig tree. My Goddam Father is the Richest White Man in the Town but I belong to the owls, till Reverend Passmore adopted me they all said Bastard . . . then my father was a reverend. He preached in the Holy Baptist Church on the top of the hill, on the top of the Holy Hill, and everybody in the town knew then my name was Mary. My father was the Baptist preacher and I was Mary. (THEY *enter, slamming, lights flash, stand about passengers, the* NEGRO MAN *stares.* SHE *sits in the subway seat.*)

I who am the ancestor of Shakespeare, Chaucer, and William the Conqueror, went to London the Queen Elizabeth, London they all said who ever heard of anybody going to London but I went. I stayed in my cabin the whole crossing, solitary. I was the only

Negro there. I read books on subjects like the History of London, the Life of Anne Boleyn, Mary Queen of Scots, and Sonnets. When I wasn't in the cabin I wrapped myself in a great sweater and sat over the dark desks in the writing room and wrote my father. I wrote him every day of my journey. (*Pause.*)

I met my father once when my mother took me to visit him and we had to go into the back door of his house. (*Talking to herself.* NEGRO MAN *stares.*)

I was married once briefly. On my wedding day the Reverend's Wife came to me and said when I see Marys I cry for their deaths, when I see brides, Clara, I cry for their deaths. But the past years I've spent teaching alone in Savannah. And alone I'm almost thirty-four, I who am the ancestor of somebody that cooked for somebody and William the Conqueror. (BASTARD'S BLACK MOTHER *looks more like an owl.* DEAD FATHER *dies again.* BASTARD'S BLACK MOTHER *bangs at the gate.* THEY *all laugh. The* NEGRO MAN *stands before* SHE WHO IS. SHE *screams at the* DEAD FATHER *and the* MOTHER.)

You must know how it is to be filled with yearning.

(THEY *laugh.* REVEREND *stares into the cage.* MOTHER *bangs at the gate.*)

NEGRO MAN (*touches her*): And what exactly do you yearn for?

SHE: You know.

NEGRO MAN: No, what is it?

SHE: I want what I think everyone wants.

NEGRO MAN: And what is that?

SHE: I don't know. Love or something, I guess.

NEGRO MAN: Out there Owl?

DEAD FATHER: In St. Paul's Chapel Owl?

THEY: Keep her locked there, guard.

BASTARD'S BLACK MOTHER: Is this love to come from out there?

SHE: I don't know what you mean.

DEAD FATHER: I know you don't.

THEY: We know you don't.

SHE: Call me Mary.

NEGRO MAN: Mary?

THEY: Keep her locked there.

DEAD FATHER: If you are Mary what are you doing in the Tower of London?

NEGRO MAN: Mary?

(*The* REVEREND *gets up, goes to the cage, in a silent gesture, takes the* WHITE BIRD *from the cage, holds the* BIRD *in his hand, gazes into its eyes, tugs at his beard; and gazes into the* BIRD'S *eyes. The* BASTARD'S BLACK MOTHER *reappears on the other side of the gate, owl feathers about her, bearing a vial, still wearing the long black hair of the* REVEREND'S WIFE.)

BASTARD'S BLACK MOTHER: When I see sweet Marys I cry for their deaths, Clara the Reverend took my maidenhead and I am not a Virgin any more and that is why you must be Mary always be Mary Clara. (*Goes on building the High Altar; the* BIRD *laughs.*)

SHE: Mama. (*The* BASTARD'S BLACK MOTHER *stops building, stares, then turns into* ANNE BOLEYN, *while* CLARA *stands, calling.*) Mama. (*Watches her change to* ANNE BOLEYN, *who goes on building.* THEY *watch.*)

BASTARD'S BLACK MOTHER: What are you doing on the subway if you are his ancestor?

SHE: I am Clara Passmore. I am not His ancestor. I ride, look for men to take to a Harlem Hotel Room, to love, dress them as my father, beg to take me.

THEY: Take you?

SHE: Yes, take me Clara Passmore.

THEY: Take you, Bastard?

SHE: There is a bed there.

(*The* WHITE BIRD *laughs like the* MOTHER.)

WILLIAM: And do they take you?

SHE: No, William.

WILLIAM: No?

SHE: Something happens.

WILLIAM: Happens?

CHAUCER: Happens?

SHE: Something strange always happens, Chaucer.

CHAUCER: Where?

SHE: In the hotel room. It's how I've passed my summer in New York, nights I come to the subway, look for men. It's how I've passed my summer. If they would only take me? But something strange happens.

ANNE: Take you, Mary? Why, Mary?

(ANNE BOLEYN *builds.* THEY *exit,* CLARA *dressed like the* VIRGIN *in a blue crepe shawl, wanders about, then goes to* ANNE.)

SHE: Anne, you must help me. They, my Black Mother and my Goddam Father and the Reverend and his wife, they and the teachers at the school where I teach, and Professor Johnson, the principal to whom I'm engaged, they all say London, who in the hell ever heard of anybody going to London. Of course I shouldn't go. They said I had lost my mind, read so much, buried myself in my books. They say I should stay and teach summer school to the kids up from Oglethorpe. But I went.
  All the way from Piccadilly Circus out there in the black taxi, my cold hands were colder than ever. Then it happened no sooner than I left the taxi and passed down a gray walk through a dark gate and into a garden where there were black ravens on the grass when I broke down. I broke down and started to cry, oh the Tower, winters in Queen's House, right in front of everybody. People came and stared. I was the only Negro there. The guard came and stared, the ravens flew and finally a man with a black hat on helped me out through the gate into the street. I am never going back, Anne. Anne, I am never going back. I will not go.

THEY: Keep her locked there, guard.

(*The* NEGRO MAN *comes toward her. She dresses him as God putting a crown upon his head. The* REVEREND *watches them. A light*

comes into the Tower as though a cell door has been opened.)

SHE: God, do you see it? Do you see? They are opening the cell door to let me go.

NEGRO MAN: See it, Mary?

SHE: They are opening the cell door to let me go down to St. Paul's Chapel where I am yearning to go. Do you see it?

NEGRO MAN: Love? Love Mary?

SHE: Love?

NEGRO MAN: Love in St. Paul's Chapel?

SHE: No, no, the love that exists between you and me. Do you see it?

NEGRO MAN: Love Mary? (*He takes her hand; with his other hand, he tries to undress her.*)

SHE: Love God.

NEGRO MAN: Love Mary?

SHE: Love God.

(THEY *bring the* DEAD FATHER *and leave him at her feet.*)

THEY (*simultaneously*): Bastard, you are not His ancestor, you are not God's ancestor.

NEGRO MAN: Love Mary?

SHE: Love God. Yes.

BASTARD'S BLACK MOTHER (*calls*): Clara. Clara. (*The* REVEREND *watching.*)

THEY: Open the door. Let her go, let her go, guards. Open the cell door.

(THEY *exit leaving the gates open.* NEGRO MAN *will not release* SHE WHO IS CLARA *who is the* BASTARD *who is the* VIRGIN MARY *who is the* OWL.)

SHE: Go away. (*The* REVEREND *goes back to his chair.*) Go away. (*The* NEGRO MAN *will not release her.*)

(*The* REVEREND'S WIFE *goes on building the High Altar with owl feathers, prays, builds, prays, stops, holds out her hand to* SHE WHO Is, *puts up candles, puts up owl feathers, laughs, puts more candles on the High Altar.*)

REVEREND'S WIFE (*calls*): Owl, come sit by me. (*The* REVEREND'S WIFE *does not look at* SHE WHO IS *but rather stares feverishly upward, her gestures possessing the fervent quality of Biblical images. Sitting on the High Altar she holds one of her hands over her shoulder as though she drew near the fingers of a deity; suddenly her hand reaches inside her gown and she pulls up a butcher knife.*) Clara. (*Staring upward, holding the knife.*)

SHE: Yes, the Reverend's Wife who came to me on my wedding day and said I cry for the death of brides. Yes?

REVEREND'S WIFE: I told the Reverend if he ever came near me again — (*She turns the butcher knife around.*) — does he not know I am Mary Christ's bride. What does he think does he think I am like your black mother who was the biggest whore in town. He must know I'm Mary, only Mary would marry the Reverend Passmore of the church on the top of the Holy Hill. (*Turns the knife around, staring at it.* SHE WHO IS *goes through the gate. The* REVEREND'S WIFE *tries to get her to sit on the High Altar. When she does not the* REVEREND'S WIFE *then drags the bed, which is the High Altar through the gate to the center of the scene, arranges it, then goes on building, owls and feathers, candles.*) We adopted you, took you from your bastard birth Owl. (*Goes on building.*)

(*The* NEGRO MAN *stands and waits for* CLARA.)

SHE: Home, God, we're home. Did you know we came from England, God? It's the Brontës' home too. Winters we spent here at the Tower. Our chambers were in the Queen's House. Summers we spent at Stratford. It was so lovely. God, do you remember the loveliness?

(NEGRO MAN *stares at her, green light begins coming,* WHITE BIRD *flies out, end of the lights, flashing, fans twirling, subway sounds.*)

BIRD: If you are the Virgin what are you doing with this Negro in a Harlem Hotel Room? Mary?

SHE: My name is Clara Passmore.

BIRD: Mary.

(WHITE BIRD *laughs like the* MOTHER. *The* REVEREND'S WIFE *lights candles.*)

NEGRO MAN: What is it?

SHE: Call me Mary, God.

NEGRO MAN: Mary?

SHE: God, do you remember the loveliness?

(*The* REVEREND'S WIFE *lights more candles and moves closer with the butcher knife, calling.*)

REVEREND'S WIFE: Clara.

(*The* BIRD *flies wildly, the* REVEREND *sits in the chair reading the white tattered Bible. For an instant he seems as though he might get up and come forward but he does not, instead he smiles and goes on reading the Bible.*)

NEGRO MAN: What is it? What is it? What is wrong? (*He tries to undress her. Underneath, her body is black. He throws off the crown she has placed on him.*) What is it? (*The* WHITE BIRD *flies toward them and about the green room.*) Are you sick?

SHE (*smiles*): No, God. (SHE *is in a trance.*) No, I am not sick. I only have a dream of love. A dream. Open the cell door and let me go down to St. Paul's Chapel. (*The blue crepe shawl is half about her.* SHE *shows the* NEGRO MAN *her notebooks from which a mass of papers fall.* SHE *crazily tries to gather them up.*)

Communications, God, communications, letters to my father. I am making it into my thesis. I write my father every day of the year.

God, I who am the Bastard who is the Virgin Mary who is the Owl, I came here this morning with my father. We were visiting England, the place of our ancestors, my father and I who am the Bastard who is the Virgin Mary who is the Owl. We had a lovely morning. We rose in darkness, took a taxi past Hyde Park, through the Marble Arch to Buckingham Palace. We had our morning tea at Lyons and then we came out to the Tower.

And I started to cry and a man with a black hat on helped me out of the gate to the street. I was the only Negro here.

They took him away and would not let me see him. They who are my Black Mother and my Goddam Father locked me in the fig tree and took his body away and his white hair hung down.

Now they my Black Mother and my Goddam Father who pretend to be Chaucer, Shakespeare, and Eliot, and all my beloved English, come to my cell and stare and I can see they despise me and I despise them.

They are dragging his body across the green, his white hair hanging down. They are taking off his shoes and he is stiff. I must get into the chapel to see him. I must. He is my blood father. God let me into his burial. (*Kneeling.*)

I call God and the Owl answers. (*Softer.*)

It haunts my Tower calling, its feathers are blowing against the cell wall, speckled in the garden on the fig tree, it comes feathered great hollow-eyed with yellow skin and yellow eyes, the flying bastard. From my Tower I keep calling and the only answer is the Owl God. (*Pause. Stands.*)

I am only yearning for our kingdom God.

(*The* WHITE BIRD *flies back into the cage,* REVEREND *reads, smiling, the* DEAD FATHER *lies on cell floor. The* MOTHER, *now part the* BLACK MOTHER *and part the* REVEREND'S WIFE *in a white dress, wild kinky hair, part feathered, comes closer to* CLARA.)

MOTHER: Owl in the fig tree, owl under the house, owl in outhouse. (*Calling cheerfully the way one would call a child, kissing* SHE WHO IS.) There is a way from owldom. (*Kissing her again.*) Clara who is the Bastard who is the Virgin who is the Owl.

SHE: My Black Mother who cooked for somebody who is the Reverend's Wife. Where is Anne Boleyn?

MOTHER: Owl in the fig tree do you know it? Do you? Do you know the way to St. Paul's Chapel, Clara? (*Takes her hand.*) I do. Kneel, Mary, by the gate and pray with me who is your black mother who is Christ's Bride. (*She holds up the butcher knife.*) Kneel by the High Altar and pray with me. (*They kneel; she smiles.*) Do you know it, Clara,

do you Clara Bastard? (*She kisses her.*) Clara, I know the way to St. Paul's Chapel. I know the way to St. Paul's Chapel, Clara.

(*Green light dims suddenly, fluttering of* WHITE BIRD's *wings, when the lights grow bright the* MOTHER *has killed herself with the butcher knife and all about is blood, flesh, and feathers, fluttering of* WHITE BIRD's *wings is loud.* SHE *and the* NEGRO MAN *stand amid blood, flesh and owl feathers, the* DEAD FATHER *stands, arises and sets fire to the High Altar with the candles.*)

(*Music: Haydn.*)

SHE (*the* NEGRO MAN *tries to kiss her, they are upon the burning High Altar, the* WHITE BIRD *flies out, laughs*): God, say you know I love you, Mary, yes, I love you. That love is the oldest, purest testament in my heart. Say, Mary, it was a testament imprinted on my soul long before the world began. I pray to you, Mary, God say Mary I pray to you. Darling, come to my kingdom. Mary, leave owldom — come to my kingdom. I am awaiting you.

(*The* NEGRO MAN *tries again to kiss her. The* WHITE BIRD *picks up the dead* MOTHER *and takes her to the top of St. Peter's Dome. They remain there watching. The* REVEREND *reads the Bible, smiling.*)

NEGRO MAN: What is wrong?

SHE: Wrong, God?

NEGRO MAN: God?

SHE: Wrong, God?

NEGRO MAN: God?

(*They are upon the burning High Altar. He tries to force her down, yet at the same time he is frightened by her. The* DEAD FATHER *who has been holding the candles, smiles, then falls dead again. The* NEGRO MAN *tries to undress* SHE WHO IS THE BASTARD, WHO IS. *When he touches her, she screams like an owl.*)

SHE: *Negro!* (*Music ends.*) Keep her locked there, guard. (*They struggle.*) I cry for the death of Marys. (*They struggle. She screeches.*) Negro! (*She tries to get out of the room but he will not let her go.*)

Let me go to St. Paul's Chapel. Let me go down to see my Goddam Father who was the Richest White Man in the Town. (*They struggle; he is frightened now.*) God, God call me, Mary. (*She screeches louder.*) God!! (*Suddenly she breaks away, finds her notebook, and from it withdraws the butcher knife still with blood and feathers upon it, and very quickly tries to attack him, holds the knife up, aiming it at him, but then dropping it just as suddenly as a gesture of wild weariness. He backs away from her. She screeches. He backs further. She falls* down onto the side of the burning bed. The NEGRO MAN *backs further out through the gate.* SHE, *fallen at the side of the Altar burning, her head bowed, both hands conceal her face, feathers fly, green lights are strong, Altar burning,* WHITE BIRD *laughs from the Dome.* SHE WHO IS CLARA *who is the* BASTARD *who is the* VIRGIN MARY *suddenly looks like an owl, and lifts her bowed head, stares into space and speaks.*) Ow . . . oww.

CURTAIN

Justice

The Moorish domination of Spain may have delayed for a while the development of the religious drama which in England gave rise to the mysteries, miracles, and moralities such as *Everyman*. However, in the Middle Ages Spain created a number of *autos sacramentales* (somewhat like the English mystery and morality plays) which led directly to Spain's greatest playwrights of the Renaissance, Calderón de la Barca (1600–1681), author of *La vida es sueño* (*Life is a Dream*) and Lope Félix de Vega Carpio (1562–1635), author of some 2200 long and short plays in Spain's "golden age", including *Fuente ovejuna* (*The Sheep Well*), which the Soviets have called the first proletarian drama because of its attitude toward the common people of Spain.

The Spanish classical drama and the modern Spanish genius evident in such plays as Garcia Lorca's *The House of Bernarda Alba* are more suitable for advanced students. Included here, however, is a piece of the lively drama of Spanish-speaking Americans, to show how the traditions of the old strolling players of Spain have continued today in new ways and how Lope's exciting theatre — "Give me four trestles, four boards, two actors, and a passion"— survives in new guise in the streets.

In 1580 the greatest of Spanish writers, Cervantes, in his *Don Quixote* described the strolling players of Spain whom the Knight of La Mancha encountered on the road:

> Don Quixote was about to make a reply, but was interrupted by the sight of a cart crossing the highway, filled with the most varied and weird assortment of persons and figures that could be imagined. He who drove the mules and served as carter was an ugly demon, and the vehicle was open to the heavens and had neither awning nor framework on which to stretch it. The first figure that Don Quixote beheld was that of Death himself, with a human countenance. Next came an angel with large and painted wings. At one side was an emperor with what appeared to be a gold crown on his head, and at Death's feet was the god Cupid, without a bandage over his eyes, but with his bow, his quiver, and his arrows. There was also a knight in full armor, except that he had no morion, or helmet, but instead wore a hat decked with vari-colored plumes.

The troupe is in costume for *The Parliament of Death* and has not bothered to change, for it is the season of Corpus Christi (when plays are given) and, under the management of Angulo el Malo (*fl.* 1580), are playing two villages rather close together: they are on the way to the second show of the day. Augustin de Rojas, who wrote many *loas* (monologues) and *comedias* (three-act plays, not necessarily comic) in the period, in 1603 was able to enumerate as many as eight different kinds of troupes:

> A *bululú* is a player who travels alone and afoot. He enters a village, goes to the curate, and tells him that he knows a *comedia* and a *loa* or two . . . he mounts upon a chest and begins to recite, remarking as he goes on: "Now the lady enters and says so-and-so," and continues his acting while the curate passes round the hat. . . . A *raque* consists of two men; they enact an *entremes* [interlude of comedy and music] or portions of an *auto* . . . they wear a beard of sheepskin, play a drum, and charge two *maravedis* . . . they contentedly sleep in their clothes, go barefoot, are always hungry, rid themselves of their fleas among the grain in summer, and do not feel them in winter on account of the cold. . . . A *gangarilla* [little company of three or four men and a boy to play women's parts] will borrow a woman's skirt and bonnet which they sometimes forget to return. They play an *auto*, two comic *entremeses*, and charge four *maravedis*. . . . A *cambeleo* [five men and a woman singer] has two *autos*, a *comedia*, and three or four *entremeses*, and a bundle of clothes that a spider could carry. . . .

And so it goes until we reach the full *compañía* and truly professional players:

> They take with them fifty *comedias*, more than 7000 pounds of luggage, sixteen persons who act, thirty who eat, one who takes money at the door (and God knows what he steals).

A far cry from the thrown-together stage with blanket backdrop of the strolling troupes of vagabonds, the performers at fairs and the Spanish equivalent of "penny gaffs" at gatherings of all sorts, and the *commedia dell'arte* troupes of Italy (which reached Spain in the early sixteenth century)! Even when there were many beautiful professional theatres in the big cities of Spain and a flourishing drama, small groups of independent actors brought the drama right into the streets and courtyards, not just the palaces but the patios, of the country. Maugham stated that "at no time and in no country" has the drama "flourished so luxuriantly as in Spain" in the period 1580–1680, some 30,000 plays having been performed.

Today the *autos* of old Spain have been replaced by the *actos* of Spanish-speaking Americans; the *juegos de escarnio* ("plays of mockery") banned centuries ago by the ancient kings of Castille and Leon have been succeeded by bitter dramatic skits exposing the plight of the *barrios*. These contemporary plays are written in the mixed English and Spanish dialect of the Chicanos (Mexican-Americans). As Luis Valdez explains in the *Tulane Drama Review*, XI (Summer, 1967), there is a vigorous *teatro campesino* in California, Texas, and other states where Mexican-Americans mix with the *Anglos* and try to get the rights guaranteed them by the treaty the

United States made with Mexico as far back as 1848 (Guadalupe-Hidalgo). The people as hero and the play as direct appeal to the people, both old Spanish traditions, are notable in the recent Chicano drama.

Recently *La Huelga* (the strike of grape-pickers in which Cesar Chavez emerged as a national figure) developed into *La Causa* (the civil rights movement of the Chicanos), and one of the most effective propaganda devices of the movment has been the *teatro campesino*. Like the "guerrilla theatre" of other activists in New York and elsewhere, the *teatro campesino* has taken grievances against the *gabacho* (white man) to the streets, to the people. Valdez' original farmers theatre in Delano, California, in 1965, designed to radicalize and educate the grape-pickers, inspired Guadalupe de Saavedra in Los Angeles in 1968 and now has its counterparts among radicals of *La Raza* ("The Race") around the country.

The *acto* called *Justice* by de Saavedra is a product of this revolutionary theatre, a simple scenario which in performance can be expanded like a *commedia dell' arte* outline and taken from place to place like one of the old Spanish street plays. This play can tell us much about the vitality and the direction of the modern theatre — and about its debt to the most ancient kinds of presentation, Lope's proletarian drama with the people as hero, *autos* both didactic and diverting, simple messages conveyed with symbolic characters and a few lines of dialogue, the power of drama (born of ritual) which only requires a few planks and a passion.

JUSTICE

Guadalupe de Saavedra

CHARACTERS

NARRATOR
OLD FARMER (*Honkie Sam*)
DOG
MADRE (*Mother*)
COMPADRE (*Friend*)
LITTLE GIRL
FIGURE IN BLACK
VILLAGERS

(*Narrator comes on stage.*)

NARRATOR: Quihoble, Raza.[1] Les voy a contar un cuento de mi pueblo. I am going to tell you a tale of my village. In the old days, there lived an old, pale, sickly excuse for a human being named Honkie Sam.

(HONKIE *makes his entrance from right. He wears a Texas hat and a sign round his neck: "Honkie Sam." He prances and struts about the stage.*)

Now, Honkie Sam had gotten his entire fortune by stealing and robbing from the pobre.

HONKIE: W-aaa-lll, you know how it is. Law of the jungle: And after all, I am the whitest dude in the universe, and you know that *White* is *all pure.*

NARRATOR: As always happens to those that are greedy, Sam has spread himself too thin. Sam stood in danger of losing all that he had. He couldn't sleep at nights. Y, sabes que,[2] he had developed ulcers. Now, the people of my village had over the years gotten a fill of Honkie Sam.

(SAM *continues pacing on the left of the stage. On the right side,* TWO VILLAGERS *appear and start talking to each other. They wear signs: "Madre" and "Compadre."*)

MADRE: Oye, compadre, el Honkie Sam nos trata como animales. Ayer[3] he demanded all of our corn.

COMPADRE: That's right. Sabes que, yesterday they took most of my plata.[4] There is hardly enough left for us to eat, y menos to have a small tragito de pulque now and then.[5] Que hacemos?[6] (*They drop to their knees.*)

MADRE *and* COMPADRE: Dios nuestro ten piedad de nosotros.[7]

NARRATOR (*as* VOICE OF GOD): My children, this is your God talking to you. Over. (*They pray.*) I have only one thing to say to you. Don't waste time! Organize! Over and out.

(MADRE *and* COMPADRE *look at the heavens amazed, then move off stage.*)

NARRATOR: Meanwhile, back at the ranch, Sam was in mortal fear. Honkie bought himself some dogs and trained them.

HONKIE (*snaps his fingers*): Here, boy. Here, boy.

(*The* DOG *enters. On his head is a police helmet and round his neck, a sign: "Dog." He licks his master's boots while wagging his tail, then lays himself down at his feet.*)

NARRATOR: The dogs had no mind of their own. They were conditioned to act by remote control.

HONKIE (*holds* DOG *by collar and snaps his fingers*): Go, boy, go!

DOG (*to audience*): Arf! Arf! *Kill! Kill! Kill! Kill!* Arf! Arf! Arf!

HONKIE: Down, boy, down. Sit, sit (*Pulls* DOG *to his side and watches over his property.*)

NARRATOR: Honkie sent his dogs to maim and brutalize the populace.

---

1 *Quihoble, Raza:* "Greetings, [people of my] race." 2 *Y, sabes que:* "And, you know . . ." 3 *Oye, compadre . . . Ayer:* "Listen, friend, Honkie Sam treats us like animals. Yesterday . . ." 4 *plata:* "silver," i.e., money. 5 *y menos . . . pulque:* much less to have a small drink of *pulque* [a drink made from fermented cactus juice.] 6 *Que hacemos?:* "What do we have?" 7 *Dios nuestro . . . nosotros:* "Oh God, have mercy on us."

(HONKIE *turns* DOG *loose.* DOG *heads toward backstage. Two sharp, screeching screams are heard.* DOG *returns to master's side.*)

The dogs became known as the *mad dogs.*

(*The* DOG *then makes mad faces and noises.*)

And the people of the village became more and more concerned, and they sent a delegation to Honkie Sam.

(*Enter* VILLAGERS, *with the* NARRATOR *joining in, marching in a single line, singing.*)

VILLAGERS (*in unison*):

De colores,
De colores,
Se pinta los campos en la primavera.[8]

(*The* VILLAGERS *stop in front of* HONKIE SAM. HONKIE *holds the* DOG *by the collar. The* DOG *growls. The* VILLAGERS *recoil, meekly hold their hands in front of them.*)

COMPADRE: Mister Sam, we came, señor, to beg you to please tell your pets to be more careful. They have begun to hurt our people. This we beg, please. (*Turns to other* VILLAGERS.) Is that not so?

HONKIE: W-aaa-l, now. Le's see, mah little brown brothers. Mah friends, come now, let us reason together. (*Takes out a pot of atole, dips fingers in, and feeds the* VILLAGERS.)[9] Here is one for you. And some for you. And Honkie would never forget you. Go now, mah chillun.

(VILLAGERS *march off stage, with the exception of the* NARRATOR, *who returns to his position.*)

NARRATOR: But Honkie was slick. He was lying and he knew it. Honkie did not call his dogs off, but instead unleashed them and gave them free rein.

HONKIE (*chuckling, turns* DOG *loose*): I'll teach them stupid idiots. Dirty Mexicans! (*Walks off stage.*)

(DOG *is roaming in the center of the stage. A* VILLAGE GIRL *starts to walk across the stage. The* DOG *attacks her and kills her, then runs off stage. A* VILLAGER *walks on stage, finds the* GIRL, *and calls out.*)

VILLAGER: ¡Auxilio![10] Help! Help! Help!

(*Other* VILLAGERS *enter and gather round the body.*)

SECOND VILLAGER: This is too much. I have had it.

THIRD VILLAGER: Sí, mano,[11] we must do something ourselves.

SECOND VILLAGER: I say that the guilty dog should die.

THIRD VILLAGER: Sí, sí, the dog must die.

(VILLAGERS *pick up the body. They chant and march off chanting "The dog must die!" The* DOG *enters and walks around. A hooded* FIGURE IN BLACK *enters and shoots the* DOG. *The* DOG *dies. The hooded* FIGURE IN BLACK *steps to stage left.*)

NARRATOR: That very night the mad Dog was killed by forces unknown.

HONKIE (*heard from off stage*): Here, boy. Where are you at? Here, boy.

(*He enters, sees the dead* DOG, *and kneels beside it, crying, sobbing, broken-hearted, and lost.*)

NARRATOR: And this continued. Every time that a dog attacked a person of the village, the carcass of the dog would be found in the gutter—dead, dead, dead.

(HONKIE'S *crying gets louder and louder.*)

And it came to pass that the dogs, stupid as they were, got the message and no longer attacked the village people.

DOG (*half-raising himself to a semi-sitting position*): Ujule,[12] we may be mad dogs, but

---

8 "With colors,/With colors,/The fields are painted in spring." 9 *Atole* (a viscous corn-meal paste) here symbolizes the leftovers of a meal. *Honkie* is giving the people poor food. 10 *Auxilio!*: "Help!" 11 *Sí, mano:* "Yes, brother . . ." *Mano* is a shortened form of *hermano.* 12 *Ujule:* "Of course."

we know when to quit. Brother dogs: hell, no, we won't go! (*Starts chanting, stops when* HONKIE *hits him on the head.* HONKIE *is still crying.*)

NARRATOR: The people of the village were proud of their accomplishments. They had met and learned the meaning of Justice.

FIGURE IN BLACK (*uncovers a sign that reads "Justice"*):

Yo soy la Justicia.
  Soy hijo de la verdad.
Tengo una mano de acero
  Para el que no quiera pagar.[13]

(*The people of the village come on stage.* JUSTICE *walks over to them. The* VILLAGERS *and* JUSTICE *embrace each other.*)

NARRATOR: Justice belongs to the people. In the final analysis, it is the people who administer it. (*Walks over and joins the group.*)

(*The group then points their fingers at* HONKIE SAM *and begins advancing toward him in slow motion, driving him off the stage while echoing slogans.*)

GROUP IN UNISON:
  ¡Viva la Justicia!

¡Viva la Verdad!
¡Viva la Causa!
¡Viva la Raza! [14]

(*After* HONKIE SAM *is driven off the stage, the group faces the audience and with clenched fists shouts:*)

¡Orale, raza, no se deje!
¡Organise, raza! [15]

(*One of the women begins to have labor pains. Everyone gathers round her. Someone calls [to audience]: "Is there a doctor in the house?" Another cries: "She's having a baby!" Then, another cries: "It's a boy! It's a boy!" Everyone forms a stage picture of the Nativity scene with the woman who just gave birth cradling a picture [as Mary held Jesus] of Che Guevara.*)

---

13 "I am Justice./I am the son of truth./I have a fist of steel/For him who will not pay."   14 "Long live Justice!/Long live Truth!/Long live the Cause!/Long live the People!"   15 "Listen, people don't be had!/Organize, people!" California's United Farm Workers with AFL/CIO affiliation formed El Teatro Campesino. Now they have broken from the union as El Centro Campesino Cultural.

Show and Tell

Now that you have read, analyzed, discussed and reconsidered some plays, you may be able to write your own. Of course playwriting is an art and being a great or even a competent dramatist takes talent, but remember *art* is related to *artifice* and everyone can have fun taking a crack at the craft of drama. Playwriting can be learned.

Begin gradually. Start with recording a conversation you might overhear in the subway, the bus, the cafeteria, the line at the movies, and so on. Get your raw material from eavesdropping, but remember that dialogue is pithier, more pointed than conversation. Trim it down, sharpen its points, make sure it has a beginning, a middle, and an end, and that it gets somewhere. In the subway you will often hear amusing exchanges:

"You look wonderful, Daisy. What's your secret?"
"Sshh! Don't tell—but I'm *having an affair!*"
"Really? Who's catering?"

Sometimes you just hear "one-liners":

"If my mother were alive today, she'd turn over in her grave."

or

"Imagine! Ten bucks he calls 'a nominal charge'. I call that nominal in name only!"

or

"Nostalgia is a thing of the past."

or

"Well one thing about being a hermit: you meet a better class of people."

But "one-liners" can't make a scene, unless you are very expert in stitching them together. Give your little scene a shape. Someone sits down beside a friend in the bus, for instance: there's your opening. Later she has to get off; it's her stop: there's your conclusion. It can be as simple as that. Just be sure something *happens* in your "slice of life": a character is revealed, an anecdote is told, a point is made.

Next you might try to write an additional scene for one of the plays in this collection. Continue *The Pot of Gold*, give Everyman another experience of worldly things failing him in his necessity, give Faustus another chance to show off his magic in another comic scene (or to converse in private with Cornelius and Valdes), supply any scene you think is missing from *Macbeth* (some critics think it incomplete as it stands, and it already seems to contain material by Thomas Middleton, so you might as well collaborate with Shakespeare, too). Your aim in eavesdropping and building on reality was to catch the peculiarities of colloquial speech. Your aim here, in this impressionist's trick of mimicking another dramatist, will be to make your additional scene appear to be all of a piece with the rest: to capture the style of Plautus (or Plautus' translator), Marlowe's "mighty line," Shakespeare's powerful and imaginative blank verse. Perhaps you might want to start with a more modern work. Can you write like O'Neill or with Synge's poetic prose? Give it a try. Even if you fail, the experiment will teach you something valuable about the style of the writer you are attempting to imitate.

Now try adapting other material, putting it into dramatic form. Begin by building a little playlet on some old joke you think is funny. Shaggy dog stories are often fun and you could adapt one in the episodic style of *Every-*

man. Be sure, when you write punchlines, that you write the lines so that the laugh comes at the end, where it will not be drowned by additional dialogue. The writer of comedy has to give people something to laugh at and make it possible for them to do so. Comic writers as well as comic actors find their timing is even more important than it is in tragic dialogue.

Then graduate to adapting a short story as a one-act play. Choose one with lots of dialogue and few characters, a single setting and continuous time (if possible). Remember that drama is not "just words," so leave room for significant gestures, pauses, and action. Be sparing with stage directions. Elaborate stage directions are often the mark of the amateur. Certainly avoid unplayable stage directions: describe what your audience should see and hear, not what you think about it. How could anyone act a direction like "they do not know the secret in the poet's heart" or "he enters as if he has an aunt who is sick in Passaic, New Jersey"? Also, don't get fancy in describing sets, etc. A designer would not be able to produce a set described as a "subway heaped in modern myth." You could try a story as easy as Poe's "The Tell-Tale Heart" (which would be a monologue) or one comprising several scenes, such as Hawthorne's "Young Goodman Brown." You might find all the dialogue you really need right in the story (as in Hemingway's "The Killers") or have to invent from scratch a scene only referred to, not shown, in the story (as in John Updike's "A & P"). Remember that a short story is not a play and that in adapting it for the stage (or a radio play, a teleplay or film) you'll have to fit it to the medium. Try to avoid using a narrator to link scenes if you can.

After working with materials that give you a headstart on plot, characterization, and even dialogue, you'll want to turn to short plays entirely of your own invention. An intermediate step might be a modernized adaptation of an older piece of material: a fable of Aesop transferred to a modern fraternity house (family/commune/summer camp) with the animals transformed into people (Mr. Fox and Henrietta in an office, for instance); a short story by Borges or Kafka or Boccaccio or Dostoevsky

translated to a contemporary setting in Atlanta or Dallas or Marin County or Martha's Vineyard. Or you could make your theme an old saying or proverb and invent a plot to illustrate it. Do it seriously or make fun of it, as Ionesco does in a playlet of which the moral is "Many a major makes a minor." What could you do with "She who hesitates is won" or "When you try to cultivate people, you may turn up some clods"? At last you'll write your own one-act play with a completely original story-line (protagonist, antagonist, clear-cut struggle and outcome) and characters more or less drawn from your friends and/or your reading. Take W. Somerset Maugham's advice: stick to the point like grim death. Be concrete, concise. Cut whenever you can. Have something to say and say it as forcefully and as economically as you can. Take a bit of advice from *Alice in Wonderland*: when you get to the end, stop. Show whenever you can, instead of telling, and don't let characters explain themselves in words when you can find actions that are suitable. Leave room between the lines for the other members of the dramatic team (actors, director, designer) to work in, but give them all the guidance they'll need to amplify the ideas in your dialogue.

At the beginning, use any of the many simple formulas: boy meets girl/boy loses girl/boy gets girl; someone returns unexpectedly (causing problems); two people converse/act unaware of the irony of what they are saying/doing; riddle is solved. Goethe tells us that Schiller took exception to the statement by the Italian scholar Gozzi that there are only thirty-six dramatic situations "but he was unable to find even so many as Gozzi." The meticulous Georges Polti devoted a book to analyzing them. He discussed supplication; deliverance; crime followed by vengeance and vengeance for kindred upon kindred; pursuit; disaster; falling prey to cruelty or misfortune; revolt; daring enterprise; abduction; enigma or riddle; obtaining; enmity or rivalry of kinsmen; murderous adultery; madness; fatal imprudence; involuntary crimes of love (including incest); slaying a kinsman unrecognized; self-sacrifice for an ideal, for kindred, for passion; necessity of sacrificing loved ones; rivalry of superior and inferior; adultery; crimes of love; discovery of dishonor of a loved one; true love not running smoothly; an enemy loved; ambition; conflict with God; mistaken jealousy; erroneous judgment; remorse; recovery of a lost one; loss of loved ones. That's it: all the possible plots and subplots under those headings and numerous subheadings. Under his "Twentieth Situation (Self Sacrificing for an Ideal. The Hero; the Ideal; the 'Creditor' or the Person or Thing Sacrificed)" Polti describes *Antigone* as XX A (3): *Life Sacrificed in Filial Piety*, which also describes *The Phoenician Women* by Aeschylus, and the *Antigones* of Euripides, Alamanni, Alfieri, etc. With his help, or with one of the many guides like Eric Heath's *Story Plotting Simplified* (1941), you ought not to have much trouble with plot. You may even be able to take your story from life, trimming it to a plot that is credible, not too heavy on coincidence, clear, gripping, and so on.

Make sure your plot has these elements:

conflict, characters in opposition or predicament;*
donné (situation at the start) followed by complication (due to forces inside or outside the characters);
one or more crises involving doubt and suspense;
the climax, or highest point of the action, with (as simultaneous as possible) the big peripety or change in direction (up for comedy, down for tragedy);
the *dénouement* and falling action;
the conclusion.

There are many other hints one could give, such as:

choose a title only after you have written the play and make it vivid (preferably with an action verb and a striking image) and memorable, whether it is straightforward, symbolic, or whatever;
keep props to a minimum but "plant" carefully those you will need;
once you reach the end of your play and

know precisely how it comes out, go back and prepare for the conclusion more carefully;
don't make the ends of lines too similar or actors will foul up their cues;
don't keep any people on stage you don't need and motivate just enough—not too much nor too little—all entrances and exits;
make your dialogue live by using colorful expressions, metaphors, similes, etc., but not too fancy and never inconsistent with the character who must speak it;
if characters must move on their lines—not all actors can speak and move at the same time—give them enough words to cover the actions, such as a speech that will get them to the door for an exit, etc.;
don't clutter the set with too much furniture or too many people;
have the characters use each other's names in dialogue to remind the audience who's who, when necessary, but not awkwardly;
have reasonable transitions not only from scene to scene but also from speech to speech;
don't make speeches, scenes, acts, *anything* all of the same length;
work for pace in every speech, scene, and act, and provide dialogue and action that are to be performed at varying speeds;
emphasize whatever is important, generally by repetition, repetition, repetition;
don't be afraid to be too obvious in making any point—it's easier to trim later than reinforce;
read the lines aloud to see if they are playable (take out awkward constructions, sentences that might be misinterpreted, obscure words, hard-to-pronounce bits, etc.) and walk through the action to see that you have left time for it (and that there will be no painful stage waits or extended passages of

---

* Josephina Niggli in *Pointers on Playwriting* (1945) says that in both *Doctor Faustus* and *Macbeth*, for instance, the conflict is simply: "Hero's ambition for personal success at any cost opposed by society's demand for payment."

silence), that characters can manage necessary costume changes, etc.;

after you have decided all that you need in the way of set and costumes, see if you can eliminate inessentials;

after you have finished the first draft of the play, see if you can cut one or more of the characters: a telephone can bring news more economically than a visitor, by taking the curtain up after tea has been served you may be able to "fire" a servant, and so on;

on the second revision of the play try to cut out all unnecessary verbiage;

go back and "plant" at the beginning (or near it) any explanatory details you find you have awkwardly dragged in near the end;

check over your exposition: do you have all you need? more than you need?;

revise the stage directions and speech tags to be sure everything is clear and say things like "GEORGINA *fusses with her hair*" instead of "GEORGINA *is terribly anxious over the imminent arrival of the man she wishes to impress*" or "JOHN *puts his cigar out in the yolk of a fried egg*" instead of "JOHN *is a slob!*";

make sure your typescript is in proper play form before submitting it to anyone important to read.

And so on. But the best way is to study competent practitioners to learn the tricks of the trade and develop whatever abilities you have by practice. If you are moved to write, skip the rest of this pep talk. Write a skit for your campus club. Write a pageant for your community organization. Write a children's play. Write. Remember, most people don't want to write, because it's a lonely and often thankless job, but would just like to *have* written, to have it all over, the book on the stands, the play on the boards, the scenario realized as a film, the fame and the cocktail parties and the sense of achievement and the money. Works are created not by those who want to have written but by those who want to write.

Writing may be a hobby or a habit or an obsession or a neurosis, but writers are those who write. If you didn't write today, today you are not a writer. Mediocre writers write because they can; good writers write because they have talent and try hard; great writers write because they have genius and they have to. Want to be a writer? Start writing.

You can write a play. It may be a simple dramatization of a fairy tale or a joke or it may be a passable college effort (these are usually one-acters, though longer plays are easier), a two-act commercial comedy, a five-act verse tragedy. God knows what. You may not be able to write a *good* play. Maybe you have no insight into human motivations, a tin ear for dialogue, no imagination, and better things to do than to sit at a typewriter when other people are out having fun. But you'll never know until you give it an honest try. (It doesn't have to be great. You'll be surprised at what pride you'll be able to take in a modest achievement, "a poor thing but mine own.") The thrill of seeing your work produced, by Broadway or the local Boy Scouts, of hearing actors saying your very own words, has made many a budding dramatist think it was worth it all.

These days, it seems, the only explanation of the television wasteland and the fact that movies are worse than ever (in general), that Broadway is a disaster area and community theatre hardly ever graced with an original, that off-Broadway (and experimental theatre in general) is practically the exclusive province of the inarticulate, self-indulgent, vain and deluded, monumentally boring, incompetent, must be this: what's being created now is largely junk but, on the other hand, many things being written, however unpromising, somehow do manage to get on, eventually, somewhere. So, if you have any talent at all we need you and even if you don't you can probably make some kind of a go of it, if you are determined enough.

Writing a play is not easy. Each really great new dramatist redefines drama. But you may find an instructor who can create a class full of like-minded dramatic aspirants, a congenial atmosphere for criticizing your own work and the work of others, and an urge in you to write which is helped along by his useful hints on technique. If so, great. Take a course. (Of course if you *really* can write plays, and want to, quit school today and become a professional playwright right away. If you *really* can write you may not need encouragement and direc-

tion, and you certainly don't need an academic degree.)

In any case, course or no course, why not use what you've learned about dramatic technique to show and tell some story? Why not write a play?

Putting on a Play

One of the very best ways to understand the drama is to have some part in presenting it. You can easily read plays and stage them in your head, listen to them on records, perhaps even see them on television, in the movies, or on stage. You might try to persuade your local drama groups, in college or in the community, to present one of the plays you are studying. You might be able to take some part in it — on stage, backstage, in the front of the house — yourself.

This book presents a number of plays you might choose. Write to the copyright holders or their agents for permission and royalty information. Note especially the new translations of classic works especially prepared for this collection of *Mirrors for Man*. Professor Szogyi's version of Jean Anouilh's *Antigone*, for instance, has already been presented by Trenton State College's Department of Speech and Theatre and your college or group might want to stage:

EVERYMAN (anon.) a Modern Version by L. R. N. Ashley. Apply to L. R. N. Ashley, in care of The Department of English, Brooklyn College (CUNY), Brooklyn, New York.

WOYZECK (Büchner) translated from the German by Walter Sorell. Apply to Rosica Colin, 4 Hereford Square, London, SW7, England.

THE LADY OF THE CAMELLIAS (Dumas *fils*) translated from the French by L. R. N. Ashley. Apply to L. R. N. Ashley, in care of The Department of English, Brooklyn College (CUNY), Brooklyn, New York.

UBU THE KING (Jarry) translated from the French by Margaret Ganz and L. R. N. Ashley. Apply to the translators, in care of The Department of English, Brooklyn College (CUNY), Brooklyn, New York.

ANTIGONE (Anouilh) translated from the French by Alex Szogyi. Apply to Creative Management Associates or in care of Hunter College (CUNY), New York, New York.

Other plays in the book are obtainable in acting editions, for example:

2 men/2 women; 1 (interior) set
THE GLASS MENAGERIE (Williams). Apply to Dramatists Play Service, 14 East 38th Street, New York, New York. Royalty for small groups: $50 for the first performance, $25 for each subsequent performance.

1 man/3 women; 1 (interior) set
RIDERS TO THE SEA (Synge). Apply to Walter H. Baker Inc., 100 Summer Street, Boston, Massachusetts. Royalty: $10.

Caution: Never announce a play for production until you have obtained permission in writing from the copyright holder(s) or agent(s). When applying for permission, state the nature of your group (college, etc.), the size of the auditorium where the play will be presented, admission charge(s) if any, number of performances planned.

Audio-Visual Aids to the Study of Drama

Every age has had its forms of popular entertainment. In ancient Greece the audience sat in huge amphitheatres and watched tragedies and satyr plays. In ancient Rome they had theatres in which they were closer to the actors on the stage and entertained largely with comedies. In the Middle Ages, when drama was reborn from the rituals of the church, people were educated and amused by liturgical drama and secular plays. In Shakespeare's day they flocked to the theatres on London's Bankside to stand in the pit (or sit in the galleries or even upon the stage itself) to watch gory tragedies and to listen to soaring poetry. In Restoration England and at the glittering court of Louis XIV, aristocratic audiences were captivated by wit combats and moved by tragedy in which very little action took place on the stage. In the eighteenth century the audience grew middle-class and sentimental; in the nineteenth, they became content with spectacle and, towards the end of the century, they enjoyed well-made problem plays. In the twentieth century audiences have welcomed both departures from realism (such as expressionism) and naturalistic plays with the common man as victim in melodrama and hero in tragedy, even the Theatre of the Absurd. And in the twentieth century, too, their horizons have been broadened and all concepts of entertainment and communication affected by the cinema, radio, and television.

In *Film: The Creative Process* (second edition, 1967), which Jay Leyda in the Preface hails as "the first useful, articulate, open, and stimulating American film book," John Howard Lawson presents us with a sound aesthetic of the film art and describes its development and achievements as a "unique narrative art form," our century's new way of telling stories in sight and sound. Radio drama and more recently teleplays have been added to the cinema so that now the stage has been supplemented by (and in many ways affected, even threatened by) new kinds of "theatre."

The "legitimate" stage of live actors will always retain its special magic, but today it is increasingly making use of "mixed media" and in order to understand it better we should compare and contrast it with film, radio, and television. Film can achieve effects that the "scenes, machines and dancing" of the Restoration stage and the spectacular theatre of the Victorian period could not, while radio drama puts the emphasis once again on the words and the "imaginary forces" of the listener, and television brings drama right into our livingrooms.

Those who learn to appreciate stage plays through an anthology such as this will perhaps go on to stage in their heads the classic film scripts now being published, the teleplays of Horton Foote, Rad Bradbury, Gore Vidal, Paddy Chayevsky and other writers for the home screen, and the best radio plays of an earlier time, from *Sorry, Wrong Number* to Orson Welles' frightening *War of the Worlds*. Each medium has its own rules, but a basic understanding of drama will assist one to appreciate it in any form.

For those who cannot attend, or stage their own, "legitimate" plays, the vast library of films that has been built up in this century can be of great use.

Take the appreciation of Shakespeare, for instance. Though Shakespeare's genius, and the theatre of his time, led him to concentrate on the power of language, his works have proved fodder for the film. At first the cameras merely recorded stage action. As early as 1908, D. W. Griffith, the first authentic genius of the cinema, made *The Taming of the Shrew*, wordless, of course. There was even a one-reel version of *King Lear* in 1909. The great stage actors made films: Sir Johnston Forbes Robertson played *Hamlet* for the camera in 1913 and in 1922 the Swedish actress Asta Nielsen essayed the role of the Gloomy Dane. As soon as sound arrived, Shakespeare really came into his own, though one of the early films, *The Taming of the Shrew* with Douglas Fairbanks and Mary Pickford (1929) bore the immortal credit: "Additional Dialogue by Sam Taylor." To help you visualize the Elizabethan stage, Laurence Olivier's *Henry V* (1944) is invaluable. To see his *Hamlet* or *Richard III* or *Othello* or one of the several exciting versions of *Romeo and Juliet* is to gain new insight into Shakespeare. Your reading of *Macbeth* could well be accompanied by seeing one of the film versions, which include: Sir Herbert Beerbohm Tree's (directed by Griffith) of 1916, Orson Welles' production of 1953, Maurice Evan's version (originally designed for television but shown in cinemas), or even "rewrites" of Shakespeare's play such as the modernized one which starred Paul Douglas (*Joe Macbeth*, 1955) or the Japanese Toho production (*Throne of Blood*, 1957).*

Greek theatre may make more sense to you if you can see William Butler Yeats' version of *Oedipus Rex* as produced by the Stratford (Canada) Festival Company and filmed by Oedipus Rex Productions (Toronto) for distribution by Motion Picture Distributors, Inc. You may not be able to see the German film of *Wozzeck*, but many film societies can get the Greta Garbo film version of *Camille*, made in 1936 by Metro-Goldwyn-Mayer. You can see either the old German version of Brecht's *Threepenny Opera* (with Lotte Lenya) or the Brandon Films version of 1960. Gay's *Beggar's Opera* was made into a lively color film in 1954 by British Lion Studios (distributed in America by Warner Brothers). Many film versions of plays depart considerably from the original—Shakespeare's *Tempest* was made into a science-fiction film in 1956 as *Forbidden Planet*, and Anthony Mann once announced plans to do *King Lear* as a Western — but others are quite faithful to the playwright's intentions.

For a long time Bernard Shaw refused to allow his works to be filmed. But then along came the Hungarian director Gabriel Pascal and talked him into it. With a phenomenally expensive production of Shaw's *Caesar and Cleopatra* (1946) and a classic film of *Pygmalion* (with Leslie Howard as Professor Higgins, 1938, released in America through MGM) Pascal made cinema history. Other Shaw plays adapted for the screen were: *How He Lied to Her Husband* (1931), *Arms and the Man* (1932), *Major Barbara* (1941), (Pascal directing), *Androcles and the Lion* (1952), *The Devil's Disciple* (1955), *St. Joan* (1957), *The Doctor's Dilemma* (1959), *The Millionairess* (1961), and, of course, *My Fair Lady* (1963), the musical version of *Pygmalion* starring Audrey Hepburn and Rex Harrison.

In reference books on the cinema you can find many other famous plays listed with their screen adaptations. Remember that sometimes the titles are changed. For example, Ossie Davis' *Purlie Victorious* was filmed by the Hammer organization in 1963 as *Gone are the Days*. Some playwrights have written also for the screen. When Tennessee Williams worked for MGM he did a script, one of many they didn't want, called *The Gentleman Caller*. It was first seen as a play, *The Glass Menagerie*, then filmed. Leslie Halliwell's *Filmgoer's Companion: From Nickelodeon to New Wave* (revised and expanded, 1967) is not very polite about Williams, calling him an "American playwright whose sleazy characters have proved popular screen fodder," but Williams' films include *Baby Doll* (from *27 Wagons Full of Cotton and Other One-Act Plays*, released by Warner Brothers in 1956), *Cat on a Hot Tin Roof* (1958), *The Fugitive Kind* (*Orpheus Descending*, 1960), *A Period of Adjustment* (*High Point over a Cavern*, 1963), *The Roman*

---

* *Cf. Beacon Lights of Literature* (4 vols.), edited by Marquis E. Shattuck, Rudolph W. Chamberlain, and Edwin B. Richards (1940).

Spring of Mrs. Stone (from the novel of the same title, 1962), *The Rose Tattoo* (1954), *A Streetcar Named Desire* (1951), *Suddenly Last Summer* (1960), *Summer and Smoke* (done by Paramount in 1935 and also 1961), *Sweet Bird of Youth* (1962), *The Night of the Iguana* (1964), even a bomb with Elizabeth Taylor and Richard Burton called *Boom* (still another version of *The Milk Train Doesn't Stop Here Any More*).

Another playwright whose work has been extensively filmed is Luigi Pirandello: *As You Desire Me* (1932), *Henry IV* (1948), *The Late Mathias Pascal* (1937), *This Love of Ours* (from *Come, Prima Meglio di Prima* by Universal Pictures in 1945 and as *Never Say Goodbye* by Universal International Pictures in 1956). Three of Pirandello's short stories (*The Fan*, *The Night Tuxedo*, *The Lap Dog*) were filmed as *Of Life and Love* (1958).

If you can manage to see the film of any play you are studying, whether through a "classic" or art film house, a film society, a college booking or a "late show" on television, you will find that it gives you a new perspective. It is particularly useful to help you to visualize costume pieces, but remember that the recent cinema is an art on its own and does adapt stage plays (when it does not use materials written directly for the screen). Ferdinand Zecca said: "I am rewriting Shakespeare—the wretched fellow has left out the most marvelous things." So he added close-ups, panoramas, crowd scenes, etc. *Henry V*, moving from the confines of The Globe to the full potential of the cinema screen, gives you some idea of the difference between the plays of Shakespeare as originally conceived and as adapted for the motion pictures.

You may find it difficult to accompany your study of stage plays with viewings of relevant films, though you might be able to persuade the Audio-Visual people in your department or your college library to help and there are many excellent books which you might consult, including: Allardyce Nicoll's *Film and Theater* (1936), Robert Richardson's *Literature and Film* (1969), and William Jinks' *The Celluloid Literature* (1971). Your instructor may find useful ideas in *The Motion Picture and the Teaching of English*, by Marion C. Sheridan et al. (1965); *Film: A Montage of Theories*, edited by Richard Dyer MacCann (1966); *Film Form* and *Film Sense*, both by Sergei Eisenstein (1949); Jacob Lewis' *Introduction to the Art of the Movies* (1960) and *The Rise of the American Film* (1939); Siegfried Kracauer's *From Caligari to Hitler* (1947) and *Theory of Film* (1960); and recent books on the exciting new cinema such as Sheldon Renan's *An Introduction to the American Underground Film* (1967) which demonstrate the affinities between "off-Broadway" theatre and film.

In his *Histoire comique des états de la lune et du soleil*, Cyrano de Bergerac (1619–1655) forecast the use of the phonograph to record speech. Today it is a fact. If you cannot see actors play the script for you on stage or on the screen, cinema or television, you can have them read it to you through the medium of spoken arts recordings. From your school or local library collection you might borrow recordings to listen to, play text in hand. Some of those available to help you in the study of the plays in *Mirrors for Man* are:

Antigone, in Greek, Folkways 9912; in English, McGill University (Canada) students, Folkways 9861.

L'Avare, *The Miser*, in French, Comédie Française, Period 1506.

Brecht on Brecht, Original Broadway Cast, Columbia 021-278, stereo 02S-203.

The Lady of the Camellias, Eva LaGallienne and Cast, Caedmon 1175.

The Cherry Orchard, Jessica Tandy and Minnesota Theatre Company, Caedmon TRS 314.

Sir Michael Redgrave Reads Chekhov, other plays, Spoken Arts SA 828.

Dr. Faustus, Frank Silvera and Cast, *Wellsprings of Drama*: Vol. IV, Caedmon TC 1033.

Richard Burton and Oxford Dramatic Society, Angel 36378.

Robert Culp and Cast, Library Editions 4005.

EVERYMAN, Burgess Meredith and Cast, *Wellsprings of Drama*: Vol. II, Caedmon TC 1031.

THE GLASS MENAGERIE, Montgomery Clift, Julie Harris, Jessica Tandy, David Wayne, Caedmon TRS-M-301.

MACBETH, Sir Alec Guinness, Pamela Brown, Old Vic Company, RCA Victor LM 6010.

Cambridge University Marlowe Society, Tony Church, Irene Worth, London A 4343, stereo 1316 S.

Anthony Quayle, Gwen Ffrangcon Davies, Stanley Holloway, and Cast, Caedmon SRS-M-231, stereo S-231.

excerpts from Caedmon SRS-M/S-231, Caedmon 1167.

The Living Shakespeare, Redgrave, Living Shakespeare, N8Y 8835.

Mercury Theatre, Orson Welles, Fay Bainter — condensed, Columbia Masterworks, C–33.

Dublin Gate Company, directed by Hilton Edwards — excerpts, Spoken Arts 782.

John Barrymore — excerpts, Audio Rarities LPA 2202.

selection, *Highlights from the Tragedies*: Vol. I, Argo DA–1.

selection, *Homage to Shakespeare*, Argo 2 NF–4.

selection, *Shakespeare: Soul of an Age*, Caedmon TC 1170.

selection, *Scenes from Shakespeare* (McMaster), Spoken Arts 766-7.

selection, *Shakespeare Scenes and Soliloquies for Actors*: Vol. I, Mícheál MacLiammóir and Hilton Edwards, Spoken Arts 836.

selection, [Dame] *Flora Robson in Macbeth*, Harvard Vocarium, HFS 1906–7.

selection (retelling), *Tales from Shakespeare by Charles and Mary Lamb*, Spoken Arts SA 976.

selection, *Scenes and Speeches from Shakespeare*, EMI CLP–1738.

selection, Book IV: *Shakespearean Dramatic Poetry*: Album No. 2, London Library of Recorded English.

selection, *One Man in His Time: Sir John Gielgud*, Philips ABL 3331.

selection, *Scenes from Shakespeare* (Paul Rogers), Spoken Arts 723.

THE MISER, Robert Symonds and Lincoln Center Repertory Theatre (1969), Caedmon TRS 338.

selections, *The Golden Treasury of French Drama*, Jean-Louis Barrault and Madeleine Renaud, Spoken Arts 715.

Nō, Noh: Two Major Dramas sung and performed in Japanese, Players of the Komparu and Kanze Schools of Noh, Tokyo, Caedmon TC 2019.

RIDERS TO THE SEA, *Riders to the Sea* and *In the Shadow of the Glen*, Radio Eireann Productions, Spoken Arts 743.

selection (Frank O'Connor), *The Irish Literary Tradition*, Folkways FL 9825.

THE SCHOOL FOR SCANDAL, Command Company, Command (S) 13002.

Sir John Gielgud, Sir Ralph Richardson, and Cast, Caedmon (S) 305.

Kirkland Acting Group, Library Editions 4014.

WOZZECK (the opera version by Alban Berg), Lear, Fischer-Dieskau, Wünderlich, Böhm Berlin German Opera (in German), Deutsche Grammophon Gesellschaft, 1889-2, 138991-2.

Dmitri Mitropoulos and New York Philharmonic (in German), Columbia SL–118.

selections, Leinsdorf and Boston Symphony (German), RCA Victor LM/LSC–7031.

selections, Dorati and London Symphony (German), Mercury 50278, 90278.

Comparing various readings of *Macbeth*, for instance, is an interesting exercise. Of course other plays are available by some of our authors (*The Critic* and *The Rivals* by Sheridan, *Tartuffe* and others by Molière, *Uncle Vanya* and *The Three Sisters* by Chekhov, *An Evening with George Bernard Shaw* and *Shaw's Don Juan in Hell*, etc.). Where a playwright in *Mirrors for Man* is not represented, as for example Wycherley, another play from the same period is often useful: Congreve's *Love for Love* or *The Way of the World*, for example. Library Editions (4002) offers a Robert Culp version of Ibsen's *Ghosts* in the absence of a recording of *The Wild Duck*, while several readings of *Hedda Gabler* are available (one on the Blanche Yurka record, *Dear Audience*). In addition, there are a number of lectures and other presentations on the general subject of theatre. These include:

Directing a Play (a lecture delivered by the late Sir Tyrone Guthrie at the West Side YMCA, New York), Folkways FL 9840.

Talking about Theatre (interviews by Walter Harris with Sir Noël Coward, Albert Finney, Peter Hall, Séan Kenny, Siobhan McKenna, Harold Pinter, Dame Sybil Thorndike, Kenneth Tynan, and Peter Ustinov), London 5717.

Styles in Shakespearean Acting 1890-1950 (a tape available from AETA, Michigan State University).

Echoes of Greece (a brilliant lecture on Greek theatre by Edith Hamilton, author of *The Greek Way*), Spoken Arts.

Edward Gordon Craig: Radio Talks (a series of lectures on three records by one of the great theatre designers), Discurio ECG 1-3, (order from Discurio, 9 Shepherd Street, Shepherd's Market, London W1, England).

The Art of Ruth Draper (five records made just before her death by one of the greatest monologuists, Spoken Arts 779, 793, 799, 800, 805 (all five as a set numbered RD 5).

New developments in television and recording tape and cassettes promise to make still more valuable and convenient aids available to the student. With educational films that may be rented from The Museum of Modern Art (21 West 53rd Street, New York, New York) and commercial companies — see the Appendix to Sheldon Renan's *An Introduction to the American Underground Film* for 8mm and 16mm distributors, the lists in William Jinks' *The Celluloid Literature* or other references for 16mm distributors of standard materials — the study of the drama and the theatre can be facilitated and enhanced by audio-visual aids. Basic references are: *Feature Films on 8. and 16. A Directory of Feature Films Available for Rental, Lease, and Sale in the U.S.*, compiled and edited by James L. Limbacher, 2nd ed. (New Haven: Reader's Press, 1968); *Index to 16mm Educational Films* by the National Information Center for Educational Media (Los Angeles: University of Southern California; New York: McGraw-Hill, 1967).

"My language is plain," asserted Brett Harte's character in the poem of Truthful James, but theatre people, like other professionals, often use technical and specialized terms which require some explanation. In my "Glossary of Theatrical Terms" in *How to Read a Play* (forthcoming in Simon & Schuster's "Papertexts" Series) I defined hundreds of theatrical terms and jargon and slang used in the stage, screen, radio, and television branches of theatre art, from words that have passed into common speech (*exit, close-up*) to those associated with the technical side of television production (*velocitator, waxing*), from ancient Greek terms (*epilogue, prolepsis*) to new meanings for common words (*dolly, strike*). For extensive definitions of terms that will be found in plays themselves, from stage directions (*upstage*) to the arcane abbreviations of production scripts in films and television (*F/X, OOV, VO, CU, VLS,* etc.), as well as such terms appearing in discussion and criticism (*business, comedy of intrigue, peripety, Theatre of Cruelty*), the student can consult *How to Read a Play.* Here we have room for only a brief list of terms that are likely to be useful in discussing the plays in *Mirrors for Man.*

Abstract set Decorative, indefinitely localized setting, from a complex, multi-purpose architectural *unit set* to an abstraction based on some romantic locale ("a wild, broken mountaintop").

Absurd, Theatre of the This type of drama, usually dated from Jarry's *Ubu Roi* and superbly studied in Martin Esslin's book *The Theatre of the Absurd,* is based on the assumption that life is illogical, meaningless, a tragic farce. As in Samuel Beckett's *Waiting for Godot,* "Nothing happens, nobody goes, it's awful." It is seen in the plays of The School of Paris (Beckett, Ionesco, Genet, Arrabal, and others), the work of Harold Pinter and what Kenneth Tynan calls

the Pinteretti, the television plays of Welshman Alun Owen, and in many other *avant-garde* modern works, though it is now mixing with symbolism and black comedy and losing its original character to some extent.

Act To perform as an actor, to pretend, to impersonate a character. Also, a major division of a play, determined either by its nature (climaxes in the action) or the circumstances of its performance (commercial interruptions on radio or television).

Acting The plays in *Mirrors for Man* should be read in the light of the acting styles predominant in the periods in which they were written: the grandiose chanting of Greek actors wearing masks with built-in megaphones and stalking in large outdoor theatres, the witty (and sometimes obscene) Roman actors, the religiously-motivated actors presenting the Morality of *Everyman,* the acting with *panache* (flair) common in the time of Molière, the romantic acting of the theatre of Dumas *fils,* the "epic" presentations of Brecht, and so on. Over the centuries actors have been both puppets and "personalities," have employed both elocution and psychology, have declaimed and improvised, have used many methods and The Method. Read the play in whatever style you think it was first acted in. Later you may wish to do a modern "production" of it in your head, for (to use one example) *The Beggar's Opera* can not only be revised as *The Threepenny Opera* but the eighteenth-century play can also be presented in modern style.

Ad lib Abbreviated Latin phrase now used to mean free improvisation of *lines* or *business,* to pad a part or fill a void, as when an actor *blows up* (forgets his lines), misses a *cue,* etc.

Aesthetic distance The spectator's psychic detachment from the work of art, allowing him to view with some objectivity the action of the play and to regard the horrors of *Macbeth*, for example, with "rapturous awe" but not a sense of personal danger. The best essay on the topic is Edward Bullogh's *A Modern Book of Aesthetics*.

Affective memory   One of the principal techniques discussed in Stanislavsky's *An Actor Prepares* shows the actor a Method for re-creating on stage the necessary emotions for his part by setting in advance gestures, etc., derived from memories of his own life experiences. Whereas in the Bio-Mechanics of Meyerhold's system the actor becomes a kind of puppet, in the Method (at least as commonly misunderstood) he becomes a kind of lay psychiatrist.

Alienation effect   The A-effect (or *Verfremdungseffect*) of Brecht's *Epic Theatre* creates a distance by the narrative nature of the presentation and the employment of various multi-media devices to interrupt the action, interpret it, and remind the spectator to look for instruction and courses of action, not entertainment and opportunities for *empathy*.

Allegory   As in *Everyman* and many later plays, characters embody abstractions and present parables that demand interpretation of their secondary levels of meaning.

Anagnorisis   The Greek "disclosure" of important information by sudden revelation or the "recognition" by a character of his own nature and of reality.

Antagonist and **protagonist**   See *Conflict*.

Anticlimax   Sometimes just as effective as its opposite (*climax*), this is a letdown in the intensity of the play. If unintentional, it is a fault.

Aside   The proximity of the audience in certain theatres made acceptable brief, direct remarks to the audience which other characters on stage were not supposed to hear. *The School for Scandal* and other plays use this device. In modern plays it is often intended to be awkward or funny. See also *direct address* and *soliloquy*.

Atmosphere   A loose term vaguely referring to the "quality" created by a scene, etc.

Auditorium   A Latin word for the place where

the people hear the play, whereas *theatre* stresses that the audience sees a play (*spectators*).

Back projection   Used to create a scenic background with slides or film, this device which employs a translucent screen, often used in the cinema (passing scenery as viewed from a supposedly moving car, etc.) is now sometimes used in the legitimate theatre in this age of *multimedia* productions. Yvan Goll's use of it was an early example.

Background   Scenic elements farthest from the viewer, whether a painted *drop*, a scenic *flat* of canvas or hardboard, a projected slide or film (see *back projection*), etc. Music is also said to create *background* and the term can also describe the social conditions which serve as the play's genesis or affect its audiences: *Everyman* has a religious background, *Mrs. Warren's Profession* a social background, etc. *The Glass Menagerie* at the beginning establishes an historical context or *background*.

Ballad opera   A popular drama generally of romantic plot with music, the recitative of Italian opera having given way to prose dialogue and the arias to songs, specially composed or (as in *The Beggar's Opera*) arranged from traditional airs or popular tunes.

Bathos   A sudden drop from the sublime to the ridiculous; if intentional, for comic effect.

Blocking   Movements of the actors decided by the director who once simply heard the play read by the actors (hence *rehearsal*) but in modern theatre also directs their movements, *business*, etc.

Burlesque   A parody or travesty (from the Italian *burla*, mockery), whence also *burletta* (skit with music). Also used of *vaudeville*, though some would reserve the term to describe such plays as *The Beggar's Opera*, which burlesques Italian opera.

Business   Silent acting and *gestures*, whether in the *stage directions* described by the playwright or settled by the director, which the reader must imagine being performed at all times by the actors, whether they are speaking or not. In *commedia dell'arte* the bare scenario was fleshed out by the *lazzi* and *burle* ("bits" and jokes) of the performers) as, in the modern theatre, we have the *schtick* (piece of business) or *routine*. In the part of the Porter in *Macbeth*, for instance, the original actor may well have added so much *business* to his part as to prompt the sort of criticism of irrelevant *improvisation* that Shakespeare excoriates in Hamlet's advice to the Players.

Catastrophe In *tragedy*, the downward turn (see *peripety*) of the hero's fortune.

Catharsis The meaning of this term (usually translated as "purgation") in Aristotle's *Poetics* is still debated, but many believe it signifies a purging of the emotions of awe and pity created at a performance which constitutes a moving and moral, emotional and aesthetic, experience.

Character A person in a play, or some of his distinguishing characteristics. An eccentric part based on *humor* (a word originally meaning "liquid" — as now in the *aqueous humor* of the eye — and referring to the theory that personality was affected by the balance or imbalance in the system of four liquids, corresponding to the four elements of fire, water, earth, and air which Galen described), hence a *character actor*, one who plays the *role*, often exaggerated, of a person so affected. Aristotle said a dramatic character ought to be either "consistent or consistently inconsistent." See *probability*. Actors speak of "getting into character," "creating a character," etc., referring to consistency in a part.

Chorus In early Greek drama singers and dancers commented on the *episodes* of action. Sophocles stabilized the group at 15. Later a *chorus* was a single narrator (as in *Doctor Faustus* or Shakespeare's *Henry V*), the *raisonneur* (explainer) in French plays, or a group (as in Eliot's *Murder in the Cathedral*). Tom serves as chorus in *The Glass Menagerie*. Chorus effects are created in *Epic Theatre* and many other kinds of plays.

Cliché Once vivid, now outworn metaphors or stereotyped characters, situations, etc., *clichés* are now as important to *melodrama*, *soap opera*, *Westerns* and other popular art forms as *conventions* in the drama, the slowest of all the major arts to abandon devices that work.

Climax From the Greek for "ladder," the *climax* is the highpoint of the action, reached by a series of steps after the *generating circumstance* sets the wheels in motion. Building *climaxes* in scenes and plays is one of the principal skills needed in *dramaturgy*. One must always identify the climax in a speech, a scene, a play.

Closet drama Some plays, as Molière said, are good only to put on the shelf of the library, unsuited for the stage. It is uncertain whether the sensational tragedies of Seneca were played or read aloud; it is certain that many poetic plays (written in the last century by Lord Tennyson and Stephen Phillips, for example) were written without attention to the demands of performance. The Romantic Poets wrote many such unplayable plays: Wordsworth *The Borderers* (1796), Byron *Manfred* (1817) Shelley *Prometheus Unbound* (1819), Keats *Otho the Great* (1820), etc. Modern poets in many cases cannot distinguish between what Ronald Peacock aptly calls "the poet of the theatre and the poet in the theatre."

Coincidence We demand more order in art than we find in life and more credibility in a dramatic story than in actual experience. Dramatic plots are usually carefully contrived, but *coincidence* (concurrent events, or the accidental and for the playwright's purpose convenient occurrence) must also be used to make some plots work— and some look like life. Some *coincidence* is acceptable and creates *verisimilitude* (life-like quality); too much, or too incredible, coincidence can destroy all credulity in an audience, though a skillful dramatist like Shakespeare can get away with coincidences (such as the plague in Mantua in *Romeo and Juliet*, the details of *The Murder of Gonzago* play in *Hamlet*) that a lesser man would shy away from or bungle.

Comedy from the Greek *comos* (revel, masquerade), *comedy* amusingly deals with human behavior rather than the seriousness of the human condition. *Comedy* reaches a happy ending after some entertaining crises arising out of character and situation. Contrast *farce*. Among many helpful writers on the subject are George Meredith and Henri Bergson.

Comedy, Greek Greek comedy dealt with people and problems less exalted than those found in *tragedy*, creating joy, even satirizing and reforming, finding its raw materials in everyday life and fantasy, politics and myth, buffoonery and burlesque. Old Comedy was succeeded (*c.* 400 B.C.) by Middle Comedy and (after 336

B.C.) New Comedy. Aristophanes (*c.* 450–*c.* 385 B.C.) was the satirical genius of Middle Comedy and of the leaders of the New Comedy (Diphilus, Philemon, and Menander) only a little of the work of the latter survives. The capering *satyr plays* of Old Comedy — we have a complete play of this type by Sophocles, and some others — were followed by Greek comedies that laid the foundations of the Roman comedies of Plautus (and much that was to follow) and some that, in their sensationalism and sentimentality, presaged *melodrama.*

Comedy, High   A vague term to describe comedy based on character as opposed to supposedly lesser forms, such as *farce.* In the works of Shakespeare, it reaches great heights and in modern times it has appeared in various odd combinations: mixed with the Absurd, for instance, in the works of Harold Pinter. Any play in which laughter is combined with thought is liable to be praised as *high comedy,* especially by those who deem *comedy* lower than *tragedy* and wish to give it a supporting adjective of approbation.

Comedy of Errors   Plautus firmly established the comic device of mistaken identities or misrepresentation resulting in *irony* and risible cross-purposes. Shakespeare copied him in *The Comedy of Errors* and surpassed him in *Twelfth Night.* A classic example is Oliver Goldsmith's *She Stoops to Conquer* but the device is as modern as tonight's television comedy.

Comedy of Humours   As mentioned above, the physician Galen and other ancients believed in the *humors* (or *humours,* in the older spelling) that influenced human health and behavior. Ben Jonson (1572?–1637) combined stereotyped characters (derived from Plautus and Terence) with the *humours* theory to create didactic but delightful masterpieces of comedy involving characters driven by a single dominant trait. Molière's *Miser* owes something to this theory of character and comedy.

Comedy of Intrigue   In the *comedy of intrigue* rather simplified characters are enmeshed in an ingenious series of scenes revolving around deception and machinations, as in Ben Jonson's *Volpone* or Molière's *Miser.*

Comedy of Manners   The *comedy of manners* is a refined, sophisticated, witty and trenchant comment on social behavior, involving caricatures and generalizations to some extent but which is fundamentally serious in its comments on society. Its plots are complex, its characters less so but endowed with great wit and speaking sparkling dialogue, often epigrammatic. Wilde's *Importance of Being Earnest* shows that the traditions of Wycherley's *Country Wife* still flourished centuries later.

Comedy, Roman   The only indigenous Roman drama, *Roman comedy* was at first bantering and later frankly lewd, going the Greeks (with their huge red-leather phalluses) one better (or worse), so that Terence (195?–159 B.C.), probably the best Roman dramatist, was unpopular and Plautus (*c.* 254–184 B.C.) pre-eminent largely because he strove for belly-laughs, established deathless character types, and was not ashamed of boisterous humor. Because his plays (with those of Terence) were studied in Tudor times by Latin scholars, Plautus had a profound effect on Elizabethan comedy and later on the English and French drama of the seventeenth century.

Comedy, Sentimental   The *laughing comedy* of Goldsmith and Sheridan was a reaction to the lachrymose and sentimental plays that followed the discovery of Colley Cibber, Sir Richard Steele, and others, that a crying binge could be combined with a happy ending, a fact that is still obvious in *soap opera, melodrama, tragicomedy,* and other *sentimental comedy* descendants that attempt to amuse, instruct, and give the emotions a workout.

Comic relief   A comic episode in an otherwise tragic piece offers a "change as good as a rest," an opportunity to release laughter without necessarily slackening tension. Thomas De Quincey's essay "On the Knocking at the Gate in *Macbeth*" is the classic discussion of *comic relief,* but the student who recognizes the parallels between the comic and tragic scenes in *Doctor Faustus* and other plays will be aware that the device is widely used.

Commedia dell'arte   An Italian phrase meaning "comedy of the guild," *commedia dell'arte* involved small groups of traveling players (such as described in our discussion above of classic Spanish drama of which the *Teatro campesino* is the inheritor) cast to type and fleshing out a *scenario* (plot outline) with *improvisation* and *ad libs.* The style and stereotypes influenced later drama from Shakespeare to harlequinades.

Commercial In the *legitimate theatre* (the stage) *commercial* is the adjective used to describe the financially viable, the play tailored to the public taste, certain of acceptance. A financial failure that the critics love is called a *succès d'estime,* but every playwright wants a *hit,* which involves commercial success. If the play is good, this can crown a revival or the newest departure of experimental theatre, a Broadway (London: West End) or off-Broadway (London: *fringe*) production. If plays are meant to be seen, it would seem that the first requirement is that they *run.*

Complication The "thickening" of the *plot.*

Confidant(e) A male (or female) character in whom some more important character confides, a fairly cheap sort of *exposition* through the use of a *foil.* But compare the effectiveness of *Hamlet's* Horatio or even *Antigone's* Ismene. The French name suggests the frequency of this device in French drama.

Conflict The essence of *drama* (action) is the *agon* (struggle) between the *protagonist* and the *antagonist.* (The third actor added to Greek drama gave us a *tritagonist,* but the word is infrequently used.) If the conflict is exciting the audience will grant the "willing suspension of disbelief" (Coleridge) and *empathize* with the "imitation of an action" (Aristotle) that constitutes the drama. The hero could, of course, confront not another person but circumstances, nature, or his own nature (the latter involving the necessity for some means of making interior struggle externally visible, such as *expressionism*). In Marlowe's *Doctor Faustus* some of the inner struggle is represented in the arguments between the Good and Bad Angels.

Convention Every art has its shorthand methods, its *conventions,* the "running together" of artist and audience on matters settled by tradition and common consent. The men who move scenery in the *nō* plays are dressed in black and, by *convention,* invisible to the audience. The *fourth wall* is, by convention, missing in the *box set* of the *proscenium theatre. Conventions* operate smoothly and are hardly noticed – until someone tries to hang a picture on the *fourth wall,* for

instance. There are also conventions of *gesture,* of *acting,* of lighting, etc.

Coup de théâtre See *theatricality.*

Cross To move on the set, as *"Crosses down left and exits."* In a working script sometimes simply *"X".*

Cruelty, Theatre of See Antonin Artaud's *Theatre and its Double* and the plays of Artaud and his colleague Roger Vitrac (1899–1952), with whom Artaud founded the Théâtre Alfred Jarry (1927). Elements of this movement to present on the stage sado-masochistic fantasies and unpleasant realities are to be found in plays as far apart as Seneca's and *Ubu the King,* Shakespeare's *Titus Andronicus* and Weiss' *Marat/Sade.*

Cue A signal for action. To actors, the last word(s) before their *line* or *speech,* printed in their *sides* (part).

Curtain raiser Usually not the person who raises the curtain (most often done today by a union member who pushes a button — only he can do it) but a brief *piece* (often humorous) preceding the *main attraction* (even if tragic), the stage's equivalent of the cinema's *short [subject]* or cartoon.

Curtain scene The final moments of a scene before the curtain falls, usually climactic.

Cyclorama The sky *drop* background, shortened to *cyc.*

Decorum Aristotle's *Poetics* stressed the dignity of tragedy presented in honor of a god, around the altar of Dionysus, as a religious as well as a civic event. It had to have "a certain magnitude" and to "express the universal," to have grandeur and seriousness and not depend upon the spectacular or the "monstrous," "for we must not demand of Tragedy any and every kind of pleasure, but only that which is proper to it." Thus began the emphasis on *decorum,* the proper, proportionate and ordered qualities. Later (in seventeenth-century France) this came to mean conformity to accepted social standards and tragedy written by hard and fast rules. Neoclassical tragedy (such as *heroic drama*) made a fetish of *decorum* and produced "chill and senseless imbecility."

Dénouement Greek plays specialized in a sudden reversal and *catastrophe*. Later French plays artificially tied up the knot of the *plot* and then united it (which is what *dénouement* means). It results in the *falling action*.

Deus ex machina The Romans used this term to describe the "god out of the machine" who was let down to solve the problems of Greek plays. The term now means a contrivance of *plot* to extricate characters from plot *complications*, an overly obvious *dénouement*. Aristotle says that "the unravelling of the plot, no less than the complication, must arise out of the plot itself."

Dialogue Technically, an exchange of words between two persons only, but used to describe all speech in drama. Originally the chorus, divided in half, answered *antistrophe* to *strophe*. Then one actor was added to converse with them, then two, then (with Sophocles) three, and *dialogue* as we know it now was created. The playwright's *dialogue* offers the basis on which all the other members of the dramatic team work to create the play. His choice of words is *diction*.

Diction *Diction* is used to describe the words the playwright chooses to express his ideas (and sometimes to describe the actor's delivery of them, the way the words are spoken). It should be equal to the aim of the play, create the *tone* as well as the action desired, and be neither "too familiar or too remote" (Dr. Samuel Johnson). It can help the playwrights as well as the actors to express themselves, and to present their attitudes.

Direct address A character speaks directly to the audience, not in *soliloquy*, as in the *parabasis* of Greek comedy, the chorus of *Doctor Faustus*, *asides*, etc.

Director The artistic organizer and interpreter of the script who conducts the rehearsals of the play, sets *blocking*, guides interpretations, etc. The British habit of calling him the *producer* is dying out, for in American theatre a *producer* is a business manager for a play (in television sometimes a series of plays) and gets the *backing* of *angels* (investors) for a production.

Disaster Greek for "evil stars" (bad luck, cruel fate), *disaster* is the calamity which befalls the hero of *tragedy*. (When the play itself meets with disaster it is called a *flop*, a *turkey*, or a *bomb*, though in Britain to "go like a bomb" confusingly means "a success.")

Dithyramb The hymn sung in unison around the altar of Dionysus in the festivals of ancient Greece that gave birth to Western drama. When *impersonation* was added by the *enthusiasts* (those inspired by the god to represent him), drama was born.

Domestic tragedy A play depicting bourgeois misfortunes or family difficulties, taking common people as its subjects. *The London Merchant* (1731) is in the tradition. As the middle class and the mercantile ethic dominated the audience, *domestic tragedy*, often based on real events, came to the fore, though earlier Aristotle had stressed that *tragedy* presents essentially "not what has happened, but what may happen," deals in universals more than in social conditions, and concerns "the spectacle of a virtuous man brought from prosperity to adversity" not by The System but by "some error or frailty" in an otherwise high and noble character. Still Aristotle's suggestions concerned only the best of the plays he had seen and there is no reason why Arthur Miller or some other dramatist cannot create "modern tragedy" that deals with the Willie Lomans (low men) of the world, important because they are representative if not grand. Woyzeck is fully grand enough to be tragic. But is he a victim of himself or of society?

Down stage, up stage, upstage Early theatres had raked stages for better visibility and greater effect from scenery painted in perspective. Stages are usually flat today, but *up stage* still means "away from the audience" and to go *down stage* is to approach the *footlights* (or the front of the stage, where footlights used to be). To *upstage* an actor is to try to outdo him or to be more "visible" than he. Remember that stage directions were first intended for acting scripts and *prompt copies* in the playhouse, so *down stage* and *up stage* (like *stage left* and *stage right*) are from the actor's point of view, not the audience's.

Drama The Greek word for a play stresses "action," though it excelled in presenting *character*, which Aristotle defined as action "which reveals a moral purpose, showing what kind of things a man chooses or avoids," and mere movement was not "action." Thus a *melodrama* might be full of excitement and have little real *drama* in it. In French use *drame* came to mean a serious play not properly a *tragedy*. Is *The Lady of the Camellias* a drama or a *drame*? A *tragedy*? How would you describe *Six Characters in Search of an Author*?

Dramaturg A German word for the reader and artistic director on the permanent staff of a theatre who examines plays for production and works with the playwright to revise or adapt the script for presentation.

Drop A painted backcloth, hung or *dropped* from a *batten* or pipe. It can be *flown* (raised) above the stage or *set*.

Dumb show A scene without words, often used in the Elizabethan theatre to present allegorical or symbolic characters in an action parallel to or interpreting the main action. The visions of the Seven Deadly Sins in *Doctor Faustus* and of the line of kings in *Macbeth* are *dumb shows* and the common English use is illustrated in the *mime* that precedes the words of the play within the play in *Hamlet*. *Dumb show* survives even in *Happenings*.

Empathy As sympathy is feeling for a character, *empathy* is feeling with him, what the Germans in their term (*Einfühlung*) suggest is getting inside the character (so that you will duck when something is thrown at his head, etc.) *Comedy* keeps us at a distance to judge (as does *Epic theatre*) while *tragedy* and especially *melodrama* wants to draw us into the make-believe and create "the willing suspension of disbelief" (Coleridge). Sometimes we can be brought to scream warnings to heroes on the screen with the naïveté (or absorption) that caused a sailor to jump onto the stage at Drury Lane to save Desdemona from death at the hands of Othello. The live theatre creates *empathy*, especially with the modern practice of darkening the *auditorium*, as no other dramatic presentation can and recent innovations in theatre attempt to increase it by bringing the actors among the audience, etc. At LeRoi Jones' *Slave Ship* you are *on* the ship. Grotowski's actors drip sweat on you. *Happenings* engulf you.

Entr'acte French term for the diversion (often musical) between acts (British: in the *intervals*) of a play.

Epic theatre The name given by Brecht to his Marxist *propaganda plays* which attempted with A-Effect (see *alienation effect*) to keep audiences aware they were viewing a play, not life (see *empathy*), and "to shake or enrage them" — so you see Brecht is not totally alien to emotion — "into revolutionary action against social injustice." He considered this a reaction against classical (Aristotelian) drama, though it is related to *problem plays*, the French *pièces à thèse* (plays with a thesis to propound). Look for devices of *epic theatre* in earlier plays too, such as *Everyman* and *Woyzeck*.

Epilogue See *prologue* and plays like *The Country Wife*.

Episodic structure "Of all plots and actions the episodic are the worst," wrote Aristotle. "I call a plot 'episodic' in which the episodes or acts succeed one another without probable or necessary sequence." Thus *Antigone* and other Greek plays (in which the *episode* was a feature) are not "the worst" and *Macbeth* transcends the structure of *history plays*. Plays created for the bare platform stage (Shakespeare's *Antony and Cleopatra* with several locales and more than 30 scenes) create scenery (and financial) problems for the modern theatre, lead to *unit sets*, *abstract sets*, revolving stages, etc., as the stage strives for the freedom of the film. Consider *Woyzeck* as a motion picture script, better suited to the cinema than, say, *Six Characters in Search of an Author*.

Establish *Establish* means to confirm for the audience. Macbeth's "Is this a dagger which I see before me . . .?" *establishes* his vision (hallucination). Shakespeare used poetry to *establish* lighting effects (night), scenery, etc., on his bare stage: "On your imaginary forces work." In *melodrama*, music is used to *establish* mood, for instance, but note that the music of the verse does this in all poetic plays, as the lyrical prose does in *Riders to the Sea*. Any play with words cannot be entirely without some "music" of its own. The background music of *The Glass Menagerie* is no more effective than the cadences and suggestiveness of Tennessee Williams' language.

Exit Latin: "He goes [off]." Plural: *exeunt*. *Exeunt omnes*: "They all go [off]." The opposite is *manet*: "He remains."

Exposition Latin for "laying it out," telling the

audience what they need to know of *plot* that they do not witness. Ibsen is probably the greatest master of subtly (or to least economically and acceptably) providing relevant background (for heredity and environment are always forces in his plays and The Past a leading character) through *dialogue*, etc. Lesser dramatists (or other fashions) rely on *prologues*, *choruses*, *confidants*, etc.

Expressionism Expressionist drama concerns itself with the inner reality and uses abstractions, *symbols*, etc., to probe through highly original means and to give an inner and spiritual fact an outer and palpable reality, as in the highly inventive plays of Strindberg. *Expressionism* was very popular in Germany after World War I, a major device in the works of O'Neill, and others. It tends to develop into *symbolism*, as indeed did the *naturalistic* plays of Ibsen and others. Look for it in plays from the earliest times, however, for it is inherent in all drama to some extent.

Extras The crowds, the spear-carriers, supernumeraries, generally non-speaking supporting characters that "swell a progress." The Victorian theatre, more lavish in spectacle than earlier theatres, had *walking ladies and gentlemen*, "bit players" or *extras* who walked on in big productions. Shakespeare in *Julius Caesar* and elsewhere made the crowd a character. Commercial considerations and concentration keep modern casts fairly small and *ensemble acting* has taken the sting out of being an *extra*.

Fable Aristotle thought that "the most important of all is the structure of the incidents," and thus "the incidents and the plot are the end of a tragedy; and the end is the chief thing of all." *Fable*, sometimes called "the soul of tragedy," is an English term for the *plot* of a play. The Greeks called it the *mythos*. It is interesting to look for the *fable* in an unusual presentation such as *Meat Joy* or *The Owl Answers*.

Farce The word is derived from the French for "stuffed" and the improbable *plot* of *farce* is crammed with violent and hilarious things, ludicrous misunderstandings, sometimes irrational and (if possible) always irresistible laughter. *Comedy* aims at a wise smile (George Meredith says), but *farce* works for the side-splitting guffaw. The classic French *farces* of Georges Feydeau (1862–1921) show how an

initially outrageously improbable situation can be developed according to a wild logic. The secret is speed: *farce* cannot stand up under meticulous and sober examination. Feydeau and other brilliant *farceurs* dazzle with footwork and keep the *dialogue* witty and brisk. Apparently great farces are harder to write than great *tragedies*; at least (although the public clamors for them in every age) they are fewer. *Farce* is also difficult to read, making great demands on the reader's ability to visualize the breathless action and the actors' mugging and timing.

Feed Theatre slang for "provide." "*Feed* me a line." "*Feed* me the *cue*." A *feed* line is the one the straightman delivers to elicit the *punch line* in a comedy. Look for them in *The Pot of Gold*.

Fill in On stage a performer may *fill in* for an absent colleague who cannot *appear* (or even who has missed his *cue*). A touring company may accept a *fill-in engagement* in their schedule. A *fill in light* on stage, in television, or cinema provides secondary illumination of areas left in shadow by the *key light* (main source). *Filler* in all media is padding, extra material (generally added for timing reasons). Look for it in less than perfect plays and performances. It is not the same as *ad libs*, but planned.

Flashback *Exposition* and other material associated with the past may be inserted in a *flashback*, which takes the audience into the past relative to the rest of the narrative. The stage is less congenial to this than cinema or television but some modern plays are as influenced by those media as by the traditional legitimate stage. Look for *flashback* in *The Glass Menagerie*.

Flat In scenery, canvas-and-wood constructions *lashed* together (with ropes) and (often) fixed to the stage with *stage screws*, forming a *set*. In television it can mean an image lacking in contrast, and in all media a bad actor (dead as the scenery) or a listless, toneless delivery, which is not colorful, not *high key*, of a line. Also used of a partially-realized character.

Flies The space over the *proscenium* stage from which scenery and lighting devices function. In arena staging (*theatre in the round*, or the "three-quarters" or some other variation) this equipment may be in sight over the stage. Some arty directors prefer to show it, though it distracts some audiences, especially when it works better than the actors do. In the American theatre the word *flies* is also used to describe the spaces on either side of the stage backstage, but these should be called the *wings*.

Follow To come after — "That's a hard banjo act to follow" was heard in vaudeville and revues — or to keep in a spotlight (*follow spots* are used). An artist's *following* is his faithful audience or fans (short for "fanatics") who may either urge him on or lock him into the tried and true, limiting his career. "The Drama's laws, the Drama's patrons give."

Foreshadowing The Greek *prolepsis*. Aristotle said that "with respect to the requirements of art, a probable impossibility is to be preferred to a thing improbable and yet possible" and stressed that ideally the recognitions should arise "from the incidents themselves, where the startling discovery is made by natural means." In *Antigone*, or in *The Wild Duck*, there is a sense of the inevitability as well as the credibility of the end and along the way the audience is given hints about the eventual outcome. The anticipation of coming events, created through *foreshadowing*, aids in presenting *exposition* and establishing *motivation*. Consider how this is done with Hedwig in *The Wild Duck* or even in *The School for Scandal*.

Form Simply defined as the total organization of structure, style, tone, and the rest; the whole result of the dramatist's method and approach to his desired effect. Everything that serves this is *functional*.

Fourth wall See *conventions*.

Front of the house The part of the theatre (*auditorium*, box office, etc.) in front of the *proscenium* arch. Hence *front of the house manager* (as opposed to *stage manager*, the man in charge backstage during performances).

Generating circumstance The event which precipitates the *rising action* of the play.

Gesture Bodily movement expresses emotion and conveys meaning. Actors used to learn *conventional* gestures to express "jealousy," "fear," "surprise," etc., and strike stock poses. Now they frequently "work out of themselves" (see

affective memory) and many do not trouble to learn their craft through *eurhythmics* (to acquire rhythm and grace) or *mime*. But acting is largely learned, and delivering speeches even in modern plays may demand breath control the average person simply does not have, while to play great tragic parts of old an actor must have vocal equipment and skills like a singer. And as voices and delivery must be learned, so *gesture* and grace (especially for stylized productions of plays like *The Country Wife*) must be acquired through study. Gestures must convey.

Greek theatre At the height of the Greek drama, plays were performed at great festivals in huge, open-air theatres seating as many as 16,000 people. It all began with Thespsis of Icaria on a cart, surrounded by his audience. In the *theatron* (seeing place) the central focus (there the altar of Dionysus) stood in the centre of a dancing place (*orchestra*) and the audience sat around on hillsides and, later, seats as in a football stadium. The early tent of hides (*skene*) was replaced by a permanent building with two jutting wings (*paraskena*) which served as a background and like the *tiring house* (dressing rooms) of the Elizabethan theatre. In front of it was a low stage (*proskenia*). From these words we get our words "scenery," "wings," "proscenium." A mechanical *mechane* lowered the gods from the top of the building (see *deus ex machina*). A platform on wheels (*ekkyklema*) enabled them to bring on dead bodies, etc., and prefigured our *wagon stages* of today. There is some debate about the use of scenery, but it seems that Sophocles had *periaktoi* (revolving prisms with painted scenes on the sides), capable of quick scene change.

Guignol Taking its name from a character in the popular Punch and Judy show, the *guignol* was first a French puppet play. Later a theatre called Théâtre du Grand Guignol was established in Paris which used real actors and elaborate devices to produce sensational and horrible effects: guillotining, burning at the stake, disembowelment, etc. *Grand Guignol* refers to this blood-and-gore quality of theatre and it has survived from the time of Shakespeare (who put Gloucester's eyes out in *King Lear* and brought Macbeth's head in on a pole, not to mention what happens to poor Lavinia in *Titus Andronicus*) until now, having recently been given a boost by horror films and *The Theatre of Cruelty*.

Hamartia Usually translated as "tragic flaw," this Greek word can mean a fault, a weakness, a vice (such as *hubris*: "overweening pride") or even a misstep, a mistake, an intellectual error. According to *The Poetics*, the tragic hero must have this flaw, though he is not a villain, indeed a man "better than in actual life." He must be "a man who is not eminently good and just" — for then his fall would be unbearable — "yet whose misfortune is brought about not by vice or depravity, but by some error or frailty." Examine the tragic flaws and *hamartias* of Creon and Antigone.

Happening When text becomes least important of all, when plays are defined as "the things anybody can see by looking" (Gertrude Stein), when *improvisation* is joined to preparation (or replaces it), when identities of actor and audience become confused and the spectator may be an *extra* or superfluous, then we are ready for *Happenings*, anti-theatre (or at last anti-realistic drama) "in which nontextual elaborations entirely occupy the key place ordinarily given to words" (Michael Benedikt). Allan Kaprow (who claims to have invented the *happening*) stresses its way of fuzzing the line between life and art. He also says that a *happening* "should be performed once only" and that "audiences should be eliminated entirely." If all happenings were like Kaprow's, this might well happen. Consider *Meat Joy*. Could you make a happening of another play in *Mirrors for Man*? How? Why would a *happening* not based on literary materials probably be better than one that was?

Heroic drama Sir William D'Avenant introduced this *genre* in 1656 with his spectacular *The Siege of Rhodes*, in the "scenes, machines and dancing" tradition of the court *masque*. The Restoration saw many bombastic, inflated plays featuring a noble hero struggling with (a) love and (b) honor, generally in an exotic setting amid Indian emperors and quick scene changes. The *plot* flip-flops *peripeties*, the end is happy after bloody trials (see *tragicomedy*) and verse is rhodomontade except in the "good bits" of Dryden's *The Conquest of Granada* and *Aurenge-zebe*. The Duke of Buckingham's *Rehearsal* (1672) is credited with having killed *heroic drama*, but anyone who has seen the DeMille (and the run of DeMille) supercolossal film epics knows it is only sick, not dead. We have omitted the type from *Mirrors for Man*.

History play *History plays* present various exciting episodes from the story of an historical (or even mythical) personage or from a chronicle (whence it is sometimes *chronicle plays*) in a loosely-knit, panoramic, romantic way. Shakespeare wrote many of these (as did Strindberg and other moderns) and coped with problems of *episodic structure* inherent in the form because of chronology or omissions. The "Living Newspaper" of the American Depression and the street plays of today, as well as documentary plays (such as Hochhuth's *Soldiers*), films and television documentaries or pseudodocumentaries, Westerns, etc., are related to this *genre*.

Imagery Imagery communicates and colors through concrete and particular figurative language or symbols, chiefly in rhetorical or poetic drama. "*Spurgeonism*" is image listing in the style of the author of the compendious *Shakespeare's Imagery* but serious criticism of drama sees in the interpretation of *imagery* and image patterns a key to the fullest understanding of plays. In the theatre, *imagery* may have an almost subliminal effect but the reader can analyze the details and examine the devices of this poetic tool in prose plays (of course) as well as those in verse. Look for the imagery in *The Wild Duck*, for instance.

Improvisation However much an actor "sets" in rehearsal, to some small extent at least every performance means "making it up as you go along" as well as giving the impression that that is what you are doing on stage. In modern theatre schools "theatre games" are often played and the actor learns to *improvise*. The *commedia dell'arte* and The Method and many other acting techniques require it. Joan Littlewood's Theatre Workshop at Stratford (the London Stratford, 1953–1964) added *improvised* details to scripts by Brendan Behan, Shelagh Delaney, and others. William Saroyan's *Sam, the Highest Jumper of them All* (1960) and numerous off- and off-off-Broadway plays since were "made up" by the actors. *Improvisation* lies at the heart not only of theatre-game groups like Mike Nichols and Elaine May, The Premise, The Establishment, Second City, etc., but of preparing to play a part in *The Cherry Orchard* or *The Pot of Gold*.

Induction An introductory scene, establishing characters and relationships and getting the play's *tone* set, the action underway, or the context clear. Consider the opening scene, with the witches, in *Macbeth*.

Interior monologue Equivalent to a *soliloquy*. The character speaks his mind to himself.

Interlude A development of the *Morality play*, so-called because it was presented between other entertainments or activities at a banquet.

Irony The *peripety* in *tragedy*, "by which the action veers round to its opposite, subject always to our rule of probability or necessity" (Aristotle), involves dramatic *irony*. Verbal *irony* is not just sarcasm but involves giving a speech (dramatic *irony* does this with an action) a meaning opposed to the apparent meaning; it "lets the audience in on something" a character in the play does not comprehend, or realize. Recall King Duncan's initial description of Macbeth's castle, which we know holds evil. *Antigone* and *The School for Scandal* contain *irony* in a high degree, but you can find it in Gregers Werle and the Gentleman Caller and in many other places.

Kabuki See *nō*.

Line A single sentence of *dialogue* is a *line*; a series of lines delivered together, a *speech*. Also, the *drops* are attached to their battens by three *lines* (ropes). "Line, please," is the way an actor requests prompting. There is a *story line* in a *plot*.

Liturgical drama Drama derived from the Mass or other medieval religious rites, such as the elaboration of the *trope*. Sometimes the term is used to cover the Spanish *autos sacramentales* and a wide range of other plays, from oriental plays derived from religious ritual to Western plays on religious topics such as Eliot's *Murder in the Cathedral* or Fry's *A Sleep of Prisoners*, Macleish's *J.B.*, etc., not properly so described.

Mask A short form of *masquerade*, the *masque* (court entertainment). Also, a disguise or face covering: the comic and tragic *masks* of Greek theatre (with megaphones built in), the *persona* (cloth masks) of Roman theatre, the caricature faces worn in *commedia dell'arte*, the *masks* of oriental drama, of modern *expressionist* drama, etc. Also, the act of concealing anything from the audience's view: the scenery could *mask* an entrance, etc.

Masque An entertainment originally confined to dancing and *tableaux* and later incorporating allegorical characters, songs, *dialogue*. Milton's *Comus* is perhaps the most famous. Ben Johnson's allegorical *masques* (featuring elaborate scenery by Inigo Jones) contained an *antimasque* in which low or grotesque characters burlesqued the main action. The dances that end seventeenth-century plays may recall the *masque*.

Matinée An early performance of a play, not in the morning (as the French name would suggest) but in the afternoon. A *matinée idol* is a dashing romantic actor calculated to appeal to those who frequent *matinées*, often housewives in town for shopping and the theatre.

Melodrama Originally drama with music (to heighten effect), by the nineteenth century *melodrama* was a separate *genre* of sentimental and sensational drama dealing with extreme (if insignificant) conflicts and featuring simplified, stereotyped characters (hero, villain, lady in distress), played with little subtlety and much *panache* (flair) for thrilling effect. *Melodrama* is fundamentally just drama overdone, so there are elements of it in many plays; and, as one man's "sentiment" is another man's "sentimentality," it is both deathless and deplored. Great *melodramas* include Thomas Kyd's *Spanish Tragedy* and such favorites of the Victorians as *East Lynne* and *The Bells*, *The Count of Monte Cristo* and *The Corsican Brothers*. Radio, television, and the cinema have much exploited *melodrama* because of the popular appeals of its *coups de théâtre*. Both *The Lady of the Camellias* and *Mrs. Warren's Profession* deal with a subject fraught with melodramatic potential.

Mime Silent acting, sometimes with imaginary *properties*. The French play *L'Enfant prodigue* is all *mime* and hence not dramatic literature, but *mime* may often enter plays you read. See *business*.

Mimesis A play, said Aristotle, is not an action but "an imitation of an action." The word *mimesis* means *imitation*, and ought to warn "living theatre" and actors "living the part" that drama is art, not life.

Miracle play A play based on a Biblical story. *Cycles* (related series) of these were produced, chiefly on *pageant* wagons, by the Guilds (trade unions) of the Middle Ages at York, Chester, Wakefield and elsewhere in England. On the Continent they were produced as late as the sixteenth century, often in *simultaneous* (multiple) *sets*. Their characters entered the later drama along with their pageantry.

Mise-en-scène The French for scenery, the *set* of the play. Occasionally called the *décor*, though that word is chiefly used to describe decoration or design.

Mood lighting Gordon Craig in *Toward a New Theatre* (1913) demonstrated that the colors and intensities of *key lights*, etc., can create *atmosphere* or mood: he showed flights of steps made into different dramatic *sets* by change of lighting. In New York there was recently a fad for *15-watt* (or "Jean Rosenthall") lighting, dimly evocative. The new trend seems to be "Peter Brook" glare, returning to the Victorian idea of as much light on the stage as possible (with *limelight* and *gaslight* before the Savoy used electricity for the first time in the early 1880's). The stage still can have murky sets, but film and television cameras need a certain amount of light, as anyone who has seen a "night scene" in a movie photographed in broad daylight will testify. In reading, imagine the lighting. The green light in the attic of *The Wild Duck* gives a suggestion of an underwater effect, carrying on the symbolism of the play which involves a wounded wild duck holding onto the underwater weeds. Watch in plays for simple lighting effects: the stage brightens to cheer up the audience, darkens for mystery, terrors, etc. Watch Shakespeare create "lighting effects" with poetry.

Morality Play A late medieval didactic sort of play with allegorical characters, such as Good Deeds and Everyman. In Spain the *genre* developed into *autos sacramentales*. See *allegory* and *miracle play*.

Motivation *Motivation* refers to the more or less logical (or psychological) explanations offered for the actions of the characters. Note, however (as Edgar Allan Poe pointed out) that the characters in Shakespeare's plays (for instance) are characters in Shakespeare's plays and *not* people: they should be judged in the light of that inescapable fact.

Musical intention of the text Sir John Gielgud's book on acting, *Stage Directions* (1963, paperback 1966), stresses this concept of plays seen in terms of beauty, grace, pattern, "exquisite cadenzas and variations," and "complete harmony of effect." Note the *musical intention* when reading dramatic literature aloud or playing it in your head.

Myth A *myth* through "a large, controlling image . . . gives philosophical meaning to the facts of everyday life" (Mark Schorer) and is "a language in which inner experience, feelings and thoughts are expressed as if they were sensory events of the outside world" (Eric Fromm). What is the *myth* common to the two versions of the Antigone story in *Mirrors for Man* and how do Sophocles and Anouilh differ in their handling of it?

Naturalism In reaction to *romanticism's* escapism, *naturalism* tends to face up to its concept of "reality" (stressing the seamy side but alleging that it makes no moral pronouncements, ethical judgments, or alterations in what it photographs) whether giving us a *slice of life* of the *Lower Depths* (in Maxim Gorki's play) or realistically following John Osborne's *kitchen-sink school* of modern British drama (see *Look Back in Anger*). Émile Zola was the master of the naturalist novel and his age saw the triumph of *naturalism* in the theatre, but by the time Stanislavsky (real name: Andreyev) had developed a *naturalistic* style of acting, *naturalism* had segued into *symbolism*, *expressionism*, and other attempts to get beneath the superficialities. *Naturalism's* basic "hands off" policy won't work (someone has to aim the camera, develop the film, etc., and selection, the basis of art, enters in) but it was a useful corrective to the worst excesses of *romanticism*. To think an artist can be "objective" is itself a romantic idea.

Neoclassicism This was an alleged return to classical traditions and principles (as interpreted after the Renaissance had recovered the past) which tried to imitate the ancients according to partially misconceived "rules" such as the *unities*, the advice of Aristotle and such having hardened into iron-clad regulations in the hands of Castelvetro, etc.

Nō This lyrical Japanese drama reached prominence in the fifteenth century (supposedly invented by Kwanami and his son Seami, but actually much older) and exists now as codified in the seventeenth century as a sophisticated and aristocratic entertainment. It is played on a slightly raised stage with the audience seated on two sides, the two main actors (the *shite* is the first, the *waki* the second) performing in highly ritualized style, accompanied by music (ten singers, four musicians), and presenting on one program five plays and three interspersed *kyogen* (farces) in seven hours. Its popular development is *kabuki* whose plays are so crowded with incident that a program consists of songs, dances, and scenes from various plays rarely seen in their entirety. In *nō*, actors wear masks; in *kabuki*, they are elaborately made up according to old *conventions*, by which, also, men impersonate women in the dramas. See *Japanese Theatre* by Faubion Bowers.

Obligatory scene "An obligatory scene is one which the audience (more or less clearly and consciously) foresees and desires, and the absence of which it may with reason resent" (William Archer). Archer took the term from *scène à faire*, a term devised by Francisque Sarcey, the French critic from whom Strindberg gained his conviction that one ought to face up to the *obligatory scene*, indeed concentrate on it.

Optique du théâtre The "theatre view," an acceptance (for instance) of the fact that the characters in *The Cherry Orchard* speak English for us or those in *Miss Julie* do not speak Swedish. Chapter 22 of Coleridge's *Biographia Literaria* discusses how the artist achieves "the willing suspension of disbelief" which prevents us from asking questions about some of the things shown on stage, for we know we are seeing *mimesis*, not reality. The term *optique du théâtre* was borrowed from the French actor François Réné Molé (1734–1802) by English critic George Henry Lewes (1817–1878). See also *empathy* and *alienation effect*.

Orchestra See *Greek theatre*. In the modern American theatre, the *orchestra* is the ground floor of seats, what the British (remembering the groundlings who stood in the Elizabethan theatre) still call the *pit*, or *stalls*.

Pantomime In America, synonymous with *mime*. In Britain, Yuletide tradition presents a topical revue more or less based on a fairy story (*Cinderella*) or a folk tale (*Dick Whittington and his Cat*) but up-dated with topical references. See also *dumb show*.

Paper To fill a theatre's empty seats with nonpaying customers (*paper the house*) by giving away free tickets (often to friends of the cast who form a claque). Sometimes in off-Broadway extended to cover distribution not only of *freebies* (free tickets) but discount tickets (*twofers* — half-price, two-for-one tickets).

Paradox An apparently inconsistent statement actually true. Much used by Shaw and Wilde, but also in *tragedy*. Somewhat related to *irony*.

Pastoral drama Renaissance Italy's sterilized and stylized "nymphs and shepherds" in idyllic shenanigans as criticized in Shakespeare's *As You Like It. The Beggar's Opera* was described as a "Newgate pastoral," Newgate being a prison.

Pathos Suffering, the plight that evokes sympathy and compassion, but not the "pity and terror" of tragedy's *catharsis*. Overdone, it leads to *sentimental comedy* and *melodrama* and can descend into *bathos*. See *The London Merchant*.

Peripety The Greek *peripeteia* ("reversal") in the *plot*, "by which the action veers round to its opposite," not "a virtuous man brought from prosperity to adversity" nor "a bad man passing from adversity to prosperity" but the *protagonist* (see *conflict*) betrayed by his *tragic flaw*. In *comedy* the reversal is from unhappy to happy.

Personæ The *masks* of the Roman theatre, hence the *dramatis personæ* = "the persons of the play," the characters represented.

Pit See *orchestra*.

Plot See *fable*. The climactic series of actions in a play; loosely, the story. There may be a *subplot* as well as the *main plot, parallel plots, double plots*, etc.

Poetic drama Employs meter, metaphor, and other devices of poetry. All drama tends toward the poetic in its symbols, *imagery*, etc. Compare *The House of Bernarda Alba* and *Riders to the Sea*, both in prose, with poetic plays in verse.

Poetic justice Thomas Rymer (1678) used this term to describe the rewarding of the good and the punishing of the bad (which Wilde cynically said was the definition of fiction). It is often applied in a pat and moralizing way, as in *The London Merchant*, when it is resented by modern audiences, who even have anti-heroes and villain-heros.

Poetics, The Throughout this glossary we have been quoting Aristotle's *Poetics* so often that the student must by now be aware of its hold on criticism. Gerald F. Else's *Aristotle's Poetics* helps to explain it.

Probability Logical likelihood in *character* or *plot*. But note that every play demands some *optique du théâtre* and has its own *donné* (assumptions, situation you are expected to accept as a starting point) and creates its own artistic world, therefore having an internal logic of its own. The rule seems to be the same on the stage as at the box office: what the traffic will bear, what you can get away with asking for.

Problem play The *problem play* attacks a social or moral problem (real, as in Ibsen or Shaw; theatrical, as in Sir Arthur Wing Pinero's *The Second Mrs. Tanqueray*) in dramatic form, often effectively but sometimes melodramatically or simplistically. Though the theatre is more congenial to emotion than ideas, ideas can be made dramatic. Molière's *Miser* tackles a dateless problem of mankind, as does *Everyman*, but does not offer a simple solution to it. The *thesis play*, on the other hand, not only has a question to discuss but an answer to give, advising on the solution to moral, ethical, political, or social problems, and it tackles questions that can be answered (marriage, for example, or some other perfectable human institutions) and not those that cannot (death). Is *The Wild Duck* a problem play? *Mrs. Warren's Profession? The School for Scandal?* See Ramsden Balmforth's study.

Progression The forward movement of *plot*.

Prolepsis See *foreshadowing*.

Prologue Introductory speech, often in verse. Compare *exposition* and *chorus*. In the Restoration and eighteenth century the *prologue* (sometimes not written by the playwright) could comment on matters outside the play. At the other end came the *epilogue*, often begging for applause.

Propaganda plays *Miracle* and *Morality plays* were religious propaganda. We have seen that Shaw said all art is propaganda. Brecht's *epic theatre* gives us a lecture and in modern Russia and China the drama has been pressed into the service of the State. All art "teaches delightfully" (Horace) but the question involves the balance between art for art's sake and the *plugging* of propaganda. Chekhov and Wilde may not take sides in their work. Compare them with dramatists who do — or attack the assertion that they do not.

Properties *Stage props* (chairs, etc.), *personal props* (a fan, etc.), some I like to call "inanimate actors" because in the plays of Ibsen and others they actually do a great deal of work: a pipe in *Ghosts* brings the dead Chamberlain Alving on stage in the person of his son Oswald; a portrait of General Gabler dominates the first act of *Hedda Gabler*, while the pistols he gave her are loaded with significance, as is the cherry orchard in Chekhov's play. The man who supervises *properties* is himself called *Props*, and his lists are called *prop sheets*. Union rules make a clock on the mantle the concern of the stagehands, a watch worn on an actor's wrist a costume *prop*, a watch left on a table something else: all very complicated.

Proscenium arch The center door of the old Greek *skene* (see *Greek theatre*) has grown and grown, from framing the *inner stage* of the Elizabethans and the *picture stage* in front of which Restoration actors moved to being the picture frame of the *box set's* little world. Now we have improvisatory stages which are *arenas,* *open, thrust*, etc., and some have no *proscenium arch* but just the old Greek *proskene* platform or cleared *orchestra* space. In the off-Broadway play *Commune* the whole theatre was a *set* and the audience perched wherever they liked on it or in it. If it is desired to narrow a fixed *proscenium arch*, an *inner proscenium* is provided.

Rake See *down stage*.

Reaction A *take* (silent response) to a *line* or situation. Actors respond to audience *reaction* and try to prompt and control it.

Realism Remember that the theatre is not real and that *realistic theatre* is something of a contradiction in terms. Is the dialogue of Ionesco more or less *realistic* than that of Ibsen, or Wilde, or Wycherley? In reaction to expansive *romanticism*, the nineteenth-century theatre tried *realism* — the history of the theatre is the chronicle of the pendulum swinging back and forth between *realism* and departures from it — to kill off *melodrama* and to put to good use the artificial machinery of the *well-made play*. Is *The Wild Duck* or *The Cherry Orchard* realistic? Is *Six Characters in Search of an Author* more or less *realistic* than *America Hurrah?* Under the lights of the stage the real looks false, so we can never have the real, just the *realistic*, and *expressionism* is just as avid in the pursuit of truth as *naturalism*.

Recognition scene See *anagorisis*. The discovery should ideally be concomitant with the *peripety*. This "must" of old *tragedy* is sometimes omitted with the lesser heroes of *Death of a Salesman* and similar plays.

Régisseur A French term for "stage manager" but in Russia and Germany it generally means "director" and in America is chiefly confined to ballet companies.

Repetition Groups are not as "quick on the uptake" as single people. Crowds do not grasp ideas as efficiently as individuals, and things slip by in performance so quickly that unless *repetition* is employed something that in a novel or poem might be pondered will be lost. (Someone always coughs on the important line.) Live theatre has many ways, however, of getting a point across and *dialogue* is but one of them: what it says may be repeated by the costumer, the lighting man, the actor. If you study a script you will see *repetition* (the word "honest" in *Othello*, for instance; "nothing" in *King Lear*; images of disease in *Hamlet*; images of clothing in *Macbeth*) unnoticed (consciously) in performance. In plays people repeat each other's names, for example, much more frequently than is done in ordinary conversation. But *dialogue* is not ordinary conversation, though one might strive to make it seem so.

Revenge play The Senecan play (see *closet drama*), violent and bloody, came to Elizabethan England through the translations of Jasper Heywood and spawned *melodramas* like *The Spanish Tragedy*, tragedies like *Hamlet* and *The Duchess of Malfi*, and many other plays based on the revenge motif (creating a nice conflict between traditional values and Christian morality). They are called *tragedies of blood* when as gory as *Titus Andronicus*.

Rhetoric Language (often elaborate, balanced, ranting, eloquent, artificial, hortatory, soaring) designed to arouse emotion, to impress and please by form. In *heroic drama*, it is rather stilted. It leads to *stentorian* (loud) acting. One could discuss the rhetoric of speeches in *The Lady of the Camellias*, where ordinary people speak in somewhat hifalutin (or eloquent) ways. Some parody of *rhetorical* devices is found in *Ubu the King*.

Ritual Drama often develops out of the ceremonies and rites of religion when *impersonation* is added. Some modern experimental theatre is making considerable use of *ritual*.

Romantic drama *Romanticism* was once defined as "the addition of strangeness to beauty" and *romantic drama* flees for aesthetic and escapist reasons into the world of the exotic, the remote, the idyllic and the ideal for its more or less expansive, panoramic, often extravagant plays. For those who go to the theatre to get away from "real life," *The Lady of the Camellias* or *Love Story* or Edmond Rostand's *Cyrano de Bergerac* are great opportunities to enter a world of other people's problems, noble sacrifices and pathetic tragedies, swashbuckling and intoxicating lyricism, etc. The *neo-romantic drama* is always ready whenever the public tires of *realism*.

Satire From "the stuffing of a roast," and confused with the *satyr plays* of the Greeks, *satire* "knocks the stuffing" out of pretensions, affectations, foibles and follies. Audiences like it, so long as it doesn't get "too close to home": they like to see the vices of others (or the follies) excoriated or entertainingly twitted. Real *satire* brings us to the *Theatre of Cruelty* and painful moments in the theatre seat, squirming. Like good poetry, satire is "a criticism of life," and most of us prefer to see the other fellow hauled over the coals.

Scene The *setting* or *background* of the action. Also, an *episode* or other subdivision of a play. The French classical drama (and some others) mark a new scene whenever a character enters or *exits*, a new act whenever the stage is empty (even for a moment). Modern plays use a different basis. *Behind the scenes* means *backstage*, out of the audience's view. See also *mise-en-scène*. Notice scene divisions in Dumas *fils*.

Scrim In scenery parlance, a gauze *drop* or cloth transparent when lit from behind, used for dissolve or transformation effects. Also, rope ends or loose tags of canvas in the jargon of *grips* and stagehands. From television some theatre people have taken *scrim* for the wire gauze used to diffuse a light.

Script What is written: the dramatist's words and/or all details of *dialogue*, action, effects, etc. — the basis of the production — so-called because originally handwritten. (Today most plays are produced from *typescripts*.) A *scenario* is a more or less bare *script*: an outline of the scenes.

Sentimentality A demand for a greater emotional response than is earned or justified — you see the subjective element's place here — which in the eighteenth century was popular because it played on the desire to be thought to have *sensibility* (the ability, refinement, sensitivity, to respond, if possible with tears, to "the distress rather than the faults of mankind" — Oliver Goldsmith).

Sight lines The lines of vision of the audience in the theatre: what they can see of the acting area. Badly-constructed *auditoriums* have many partial or obstructed views caused by the silly but *conventional* arrangement of boxes, etc. Very modern theatres are more *open*, but the fad of *theatre-in-the-round* (actually almost always "three-quarters round" or something like that) ensures that at any given time a quarter or a third of the audience cannot see the actor's face and the need to keep the actor turning toward all his audiences in turn contributes to dervish-like *blocking*.

Slapstick Low comedy (essentially visual) based on the *property* stick which old clowns used to use to beat each other on stage. Details that would be added in a production of *The Pot of Gold* are *slapstick* comedy.

Slice of life A narrowed, detailed, presumably objective description of a facet of human life. (French: *tranche de vie*.) See *naturalism*.

Soliloquy A long *aside* to the audience, representing by *convention* thoughts in the mind of the speaker. If the speech were directed to someone else on stage it would be a *monologue* or *tirade*. See *interior monologue*.

Special effects Scenic and dramatic effects achieved on the *set*, as opposed (in cinema and television) to *technical effects* created in the dark room, etc.

Spectacle One of the six elements of Aristotle's drama: the show, the visible part, the pageantry and panoply of plays.

Spotlights Strong lights that can *throw* beams on the *set*. They can be focused, tinted with gelatin filters, etc.

Stage directions Notes in the text *re* the movement, interpretation, setting, effects, and so on, which must be created in performance or imagined in reading. They should not be used by dramatists for editorial intrusions of the sort found in novels. But see Shaw. Early playwrights (many of whom were closely associated with the production of their own plays) used few *stage directions* or none, these being added by whoever held the *prompt copy* in rehearsals. Sir James M. Barrie (who wrote *Peter Pan* and *The Admirable Crichton*) did not compose the *stage directions* for his printed texts until he saw his plays staged: then he just described what he saw the actors doing. Amateur playwrights seem to distrust actors (or are aware that no one could figure out how to play the parts they write) and precede every speech with a *tag*: "sorrowfully," "excitedly," "with an air of one who has lost most of his confidence in the ability of the world to understand his complexity," etc.

Stage whisper A supposed whisper but (one hopes) loud enough to be heard throughout the *auditorium*. Formerly much used with *asides*. Modern actors, not trained much to *project* their voices (or unused to performing in large theatres) find *stage whispers* difficult and many have to be "wired for sound" to get their ordinary speeches to the back of the *house*.

Stanislavsky, Constantine Sergeevich (1865–1938) Russian advocate of psychological *realism* in acting, author of *An Actor Prepares, Building a Character, My Life in Art*. His "Method" has been much adapted (or misunderstood) by Lee Strasburg's Actor's Studio (New York) and other schools but is well interpreted in *The Stanislavski Method* (Sonia Moore, 1965) and even better in *Method — or Madness?* (Robert Lewis, 1958). His name and The Method come up in almost every modern discussion of theatre. He misunderstood *The Cherry Orchard* (in which he created the part of Lopakhin) but his emphasis on natural acting, psychological depth, and fitting the actor to the role and subordinating all to a unified production was very important in creating the modern theatre.

Stichomythia A quick exchange of "half lines" in question and answer, etc. The term shows its origin in the Greek drama.

Stock character Greek comedy established a number of *stock characters* which Northrup Frye in *The Anatomy of Criticism* lists under four rubrics: the *alazon* (imposter, hypocrite, or boaster — in Roman comedy the *miles gloriosus* or boasting soldier), the *eiron* (who deprecates himself and exposes the boaster), the *bomolochus* (buffoon who entertains with clowning or amuses with his manners or characteristic speech), and the *agroikos* (the butt of jokes, the straightman). Stock characters developed from the *commedia dell'arte*, the *pageant* plays, the *humor comedy*, etc.

Stock response The standard or predictable *reaction* of the uncritical audience.

Strike Remove, as a *set* or *property*. Also, to take (*strike*) a pose.

Subject The principal concern of a drama.

Surrealism Sprung from *romanticism*, connected with Tristan Tzara's *Dada* (an anti-rational art movement, 1916) and *expressionism's* concern with the inner things, *surrealism* goes far beyond ordinary logic to the logic of the subconscious, the stuff of dreams. It has brought many experiments to the modern theatre in the wake of Jarry, Goll, and others.

Suspense A "hang-up" of exciting uncertainty. In Greek drama (where some assert the myths were well-known to all the audience) *suspense* could lie as much in the "how" as the "what," but it should never culminate in a real surprise, only the fulfillment of the intelligent and sensi-

tive expectation. "The art of the theatre is the art of preparations" (Dumas *fils*).

Symbolism The Greek word *symballein* meant "to throw together," and *symbolism* uses one thing to stand for another (a flag for a country, a specific story to depict the whole fate of man) and connects one world of art with another of reality. Kenneth Burke defines a *symbol* as "the verbal parallel to a pattern of experience." Much used in *expressionism* but also to be found in *naturalistic* and *realistic* plays. Hamlet speaks of a desire "to take arms against a sea of troubles." A symbol may be as complex as the wild duck or the glass menagerie or the meat of *Meat Joy*, established by *convention* or created for the particular use.

Synopsis A brief, written outline of the main action or sequence of events in a *plot*. The outline of the story *line*, sometimes for production called a *treatment*.

Tempo The timing or pace of the action, reading of a *speech*, etc.

Théâtre de l'Inexprimé "Theatre of the Unspoken" (French) developed in the 1920's by Jean-Jacques Bernard as a reaction against the verbose French *romantic* fad and based on the belief that dialogue was much less important than action on stage which expressed the "inexpressible." It was a forerunner of the modern theatre in which words are less important than they used to be.

Theatre in the round Thespis on the cart again but considered a novel departure from the *proscenium* stage. The Elizabethan platform stage or recent *thrust* stage carried farther. In the twentieth century Max Reinhardt [Goldmann] (1873–1943) staged spectaculars: *Oedipus Rex* in Berlin's Zirkus Schumann and Hofmannstahl's *Jederman* in front of the cathedral of Salzburg, etc. The German *Bauhaus* movement also advocated getting drama out of the theatres (onto balconies, into parks, etc.). The Moscow Realist Theatre wrapped the audience around the play. Andre Villiers in Paris' *Théâtre en rond* and Margo Jones in Dallas' Arena Theater followed suit and both were hailed as innovators.

Théâtre Total A concept of theatre as essentially a director's medium, playing down the text. The chief exponent has been the French actor Jean-Louis Barrault (born 1910).

Theatricalism   Alexander Tairov in Russia and other directors reacted against *naturalism* in production (see *Stanislavsky*) and created *theatricalism*, characterized by extreme stylization in acting, design, and production. This in turn produced the *formalism* of Vsevold Meyerhold and others and (of course) a reaction: the revolutionary *propaganda plays* of Vladimir Mayakovsky (author of *The Bed Bug*) and others. A good example of action/reaction — the pendulum of taste — in the theatre.

Theatricality   The *coups de théâtre* (bold strokes in performance) that thrill the emotional may annoy the intellectual, who has always distinguished between *dramatic* (good) and *theatrical* (bad). But all good plays must work on stage and be "good theatre," and are designed to be seen by audiences, not autopsied by critics. Still, *stagey* remains a term of abuse.

Theme   The central idea informing the play. Because every significant detail of a play should contribute to the *theme*, we must be cautious about trying to sum it all up in a simple declarative sentence and remember that "what it is all about" is not "what it is" or "all about it."

Time   A play can be set in a specific time (say, 1841) or in The Present (in which case the period in which it was written must be determined and the question asked if that is significant or accidental). In some circles it is fashionable to produce old plays (say Shakespeare) in arbitrarily chosen *period* costumes, reflecting more of the director's desire to be thought original than to give the play the right *setting* and *tone*. In producing plays in your head as you read, it is best to follow the playwright's advice about time and place of the action.

Tirade   A long, *rhetorical soliloquy* or monologue in which a character analyzes his motives, anatomizes a situation, or otherwise holds up the "necessary business of the play." Fortunately, the *tirade* is chiefly confined to the French drama, whence the term comes.

Tone   The general effect or feeling of the play. See *atmosphere*. The *tone* can be comic, cynical, ironic, hilarious, bitter, pathetic, strident, etc.

The whole production must be built on a full understanding of the *tone* the director and his collaborators wish to establish.

Tragedy   This is one of the terms that is too big for any glossary entry. In defining terms above we have mentioned how in classical *tragedy* mythical heroes (and in modern *tragedy* representative "little men") are presented in a struggle (*agon*) between character and fate, self and circumstance, etc., generally ending in *catastrophe* because of the "solemnity of the remorseless working of things" (Alfred North Whitehead). The hero often comes to a recognition or *anagorisis* in which he sees how his tragic flaw has inexorably brought on his defeat and the *reversal* (*peripety*) of his fortunes. He accepts his punishment with a dignity that arouses our pity and fear, producing *catharsis* of our emotions. *Tragedy*, even when it does not involve noble persons, must concern itself with noble ideas and exalted emotions, great waste and great sorrow, and it strives for elevation in language and style. *Tragedy* is moral and speaks of order and justice, ending with "the order of the universe" reasserted after disruption. *The Poetics* stresses magnitude of subject, nobility of hero (though flawed), necessity for dignity and *decorum*, importance of the unities, the crucial *climax*, the emotional *catharsis*.

Tragedy's elements   *The Poetics* lists these as: Spectacle, Song, Diction, Plot, Character, and Thought.

Tragicomedy   A romantic combination of *tragedy* and *comedy* that enables a writer to offer all the excitement of danger and distress and the satisfaction of a happy ending: "port after stormy seas . . . doth greatly please." It mixes bits of other *genres* in a frank search for laughs and thrills. Though perhaps fundamentally rather superficial, *tragicomedy* was brought to a high level by Beaumont and Fletcher in the early seventeenth century, since which time many plays could bear the label if not the praise. Dryden in his *Essay of Dramatick Poesie* (1668) found it "absurd" because we have "here a course of mirth, there another of sadness and passion, and a third of honor and a duel: thus, in two hours and a half, we run through all the fits of Bedlam." But some will always prefer the *smorgasbord* buffet to the sit-down dinner and modern playwrights have found the form convenient not only because it is popular, with its mixture of the mirthful and the melancholy, the satisfying and the serious, but also because the modern temper tends to resist looking at things as black or white, tragic or comic, and likes to deal in greys. See *Modern Tragicomedy* by Karl S. Guthke and *Modernism in Modern Drama* by Joseph Wood Krutch, among others.

Tragic flaw   See *hamartia* and *tragedy*.

Tropes   "Interpolations" (into the Mass) whose sketchy *dialogue* (sung in *strophe* and *antistrophe* by the choir) led to the *liturgical drama* and all its later developments and replacements. The brief *Quem quaeritis?* trope can be said to be the earliest post-classical drama of significance.

Unities   Aristotle's suggestion that *tragedy* that is good "endeavours, as far as possible to confine itself to a single revolution of the sun, or but slightly to exceed this limit" eventually locked the *neoclassical* drama into a tight 24-hour *unity* of time. His statement that *unity* in *plot* was not merely "unity of the hero" but "one action, and that a whole, the structural unity of the parts being such that, if anyone of them is displaced or removed, the whole will be disjointed and disturbed" became the law of *unity* of action, which seems a little more defensible than *unity* of place and time, for *unity* of action gives coherence and concentration to the fairly economical art of the drama, while the other too often lend it artificiality it does not need, though

some playwrights (Sophocles and Ben Jonson among them) seem positively to thrive on what others find to be galling limitations.

Walk-on   A part without *lines*. See *extras*. A small part with a few *lines* is a *bit* or (if the player is a *star* or otherwise remarkable) a *cameo* ("a little gem"). It has been said that "there are no small parts, only small actors," but *bit players* often have egos as big as those of *headliners* and there is a lot of euphemism involved in discussing small parts. For the reader of dramatic literature, who gets to play all the parts, the small parts are important too. Indeed, the *walk-ons* are often among the hardest parts to visualize: the *bravura* little parts that *bit players* and *character* actors so often play with gusto are often difficult to "perform" in a reading. They deserve the reader's special attention. Especially he should be aware of the effect of actors who "stand around" and do not speak, parts often slighted in visualizing a play from the printed page. We might have included a play like *Marat/Sade* in *Mirrors for Man* were it not so difficult for readers to keep the whole stage in mind and all the small ensemble actors "moving" and *reacting* as the action proceeds.

Well-made play   The *pièce bien faite* of Eugène Scribe (1791–1861) featured rigorous and supposedly *realistic* cause and effect. It was raised from talent to genius by Ibsen. The careful construction (*well-made*) of Scribe and Victorien Sardou (1831–1908), plus Ibsen's social conscience, affected Shaw and others who wrote these "melodramas with the fisticuffs left out."

77509

PN
6112
A88

ASHLEY, LEONARD
MIRRORS FOR MAN.

DATE DUE

GAYLORD   PRINTED IN U.S.A.